THE BUSINESS OF
TOURISM

THE BUSINESS OF
TOURISM

Ninth Edition

J. Christopher Holloway
Claire Humphreys

PEARSON

Harlow, England • London • New York • Boston • San Francisco • Toronto • Sydney
Auckland • Singapore • Hong Kong • Tokyo • Seoul • Taipei • New Delhi
Cape Town • São Paulo • Mexico City • Madrid • Amsterdam • Munich • Paris • Milan

Pearson Education Limited
Edinburgh Gate
Harlow
Essex CM20 2JE
England

and Associated Companies throughout the world

Visit us on the World Wide Web at:
www.pearson.com/uk

First published 1983
Ninth edition published 2012

ISBN: 978-0-273-75514-2

British Library Cataloguing-in-Publication Data
A catalogue record for this book is available from the British Library

Library of Congress Cataloging-in-Publication Data
Holloway, J. Christopher.
   The business of tourism / J. Christopher Holloway, Claire Humphreys. -- 9th ed.
       p. cm.
   Includes index.
   ISBN 978-0-273-75514-2
   1. Tourism.   2. Tourism--Marketing.   I. Humphreys, Claire.   II. Title.
   G155.A1H647 2012
   910.68--dc23

                                                    2012004920

10 9 8 7 6 5 4 3
16 15 14

Typeset in 9.5/12pt Giovanni by 35
Printed and bound in Great Britain by Ashford Colour Press Ltd

Brief contents

Contents

Supporting resources

Visit **www.pearsoned.co.uk/holloway** to find valuable online resources

For instructors

- An instructor's manual containing teaching notes and guidance on case studies
- PowerPoint slides that can be downloaded and used for presentations
- Testbank of assessment questions

For more information please contact your local Pearson Education sales representative or visit **www.pearsoned.co.uk/holloway**

Preface to the ninth edition

Innovation, innovation, innovation . . . this text has stood the test of time by adapting and developing, in tune with the tourist industry, over the nearly 30 years since its first publication. In that time, the industry, and patterns of tourism, have been transformed. This has necessitated substantial rewrites of our text in shorter and shorter time spans – three years is now typical – and a need to walk a tightrope between presenting material that is enduring while ensuring that the contents do not date too swiftly; indeed, technological developments in the industry are now moving so rapidly that they can be outlined only broadly in a text of this nature, since any detailed applications are likely to be overtaken by innovation within a few months of publication.

The move to e-books is an inevitable feature of innovation in the academic field, but we have embraced this, since it is seen as complementary rather than competitive with hard copy. The ability to annotate text, to select readily from a variety of material relating to the different sectors in the industry, and to benefit from constant re-examination and reconsideration of the material is more easily carried out with hard copy, and evidence from the world of books points towards a preference for possession of hard copies – sales of many books are found to increase, as readers become familiar with a work and subsequently add it to their library in hard copy format.

Since the previous edition we have seen a continuation, even deterioration, in the global financial crisis, which will undoubtedly have a significant impact on tourist behaviour in the coming years, exemplified by late bookings, continued search for value for money and more careful selection of destinations and suppliers, necessitating flexibility and adaptation in the industry. Consequently, the focus of this book reaffirms the importance of technological impact, the striving for efficiency and cost-cutting, the management of change and crisis. Above all, the aim of the text is to ensure students continue to receive a good grounding in the basics of tourism management, along with a sound understanding of the complexities of tourist behaviour and the ever-changing and multidisciplinary nature of tourism.

We would like to thank the numerous contributors from the travel industry for their input in this new edition, and in particular our thanks go to Rob Davidson of the University of Greenwich for his continued contribution of the chapter on Business Tourism and associated case studies.

Chris Holloway
Claire Humphreys

Guided tour

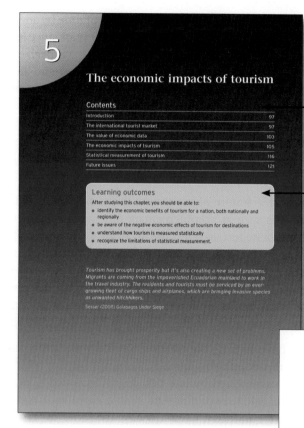

The chapter **Contents** will help you to map your journey through the chapter, highlighting important steps along the way.

The **Learning outcomes** enable you to focus on what you will gain from reading each chapter.

Boxed **Examples** help put the theory into practice by giving interesting perspectives from around the world.

EXAMPLE Public ownership of tourism attractions

The public sector can be involved in a number of ways in attracting tourists. In some cases, local or national government may have ownership of a building or destination (perhaps a national park for example) and will operate the facility as a tourist attraction in order to provide public access to the facility or to fund its upkeep and management.

In other cases, governments may provide grant funding to private-sector tourism businesses to support activities that are felt to be in keeping with government agendas. An example of this is the funding provided by the UK government to museums in order to encourage wider access to these cultural resources.

Port Arthur, Tasmania
Established as a prison settlement in the 1830s, this historic site – considered to be one of the best preserved convict settlements, and listed as a World Heritage site location – provides insight into an important aspect of Australian history (see Figure 8.3).

The site is managed on behalf of the people of Tasmania by a specially established authority which receives significant funding for its conservation work from the Tasmanian government. It also earns revenue from its tourism activities, including ticket sales, gift shop and restaurants. It attracts around 250 000 domestic and international visitors annually, with a further 50 000 attendees at the evening historic ghost tours (Port Arthur Historic Sites, 2011).

Figure 8.3 Port Arthur penal settlement
Photo by Claire Humphreys

While some countries provide key elements of the travel industry through national or local government, other countries may choose to allow the private sector to provide these facilities. For example BAA, the UK leading airport owner, is an example of a former public body (formerly the British Airports Authority, now a PLC), that exercises control over six UK airports. The privatization of airports has proved lucrative for BAA, but there is concern that the current pattern of ownership is not in the best interests of the consumer (or the airlines that use BAA airports).

Questions and discussion points stimulate further thought and debate and can be used when preparing for exams.

Tasks help you to put the concepts you have learned about to practical use.

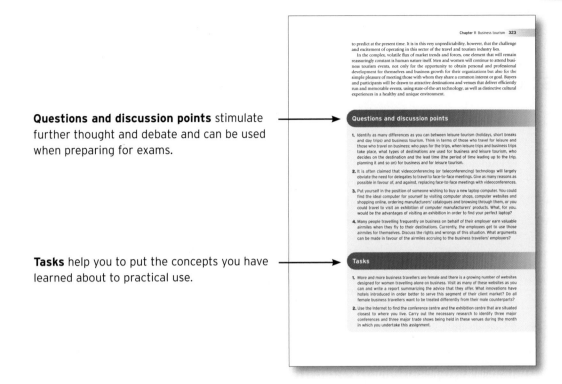

Visit the end of the book for ten in-depth, example-rich **Case studies**. They provide a range of material for seminars and private study by illuminating real applications and implications of the topics covered in the book.

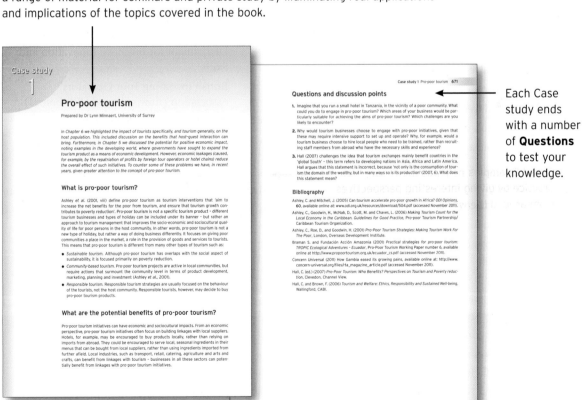

Each Case study ends with a number of **Questions** to test your knowledge.

List of abbreviations

AA	(1) American Airlines
	(2) Automobile Association
AAA	American Automobile Association
ABTA	Association of British Travel Agents
ABTAC	Association of British Travel Agents' Certificate
ABTOT	Association of Bonded Travel Organizers Trust
ACE	(1) Association of Conference Executives
	(2) Association of Cruise Experts
ACORN	A Classification of Residential Neighbourhoods
ACTE	Association of Corporate Travel Executives
ADS	approved destination status
AENA	Aeropuertos Espanoles y Navegacion Aerea
AFTA	Australian Federation of Travel Agents
AIC	Airbus Integrated Company
AIDA	Awareness, Interest, Desire, Action
AIEST	Alliance Internationale d'Experts Scientifiques de Tourisme
AIT	Air inclusive tour
AITO	Association of Independent Tour Operators
ALM	additive layer manufacturing
ALVA	Association of Leading Visitor Attractions
AONB	area of outstanding natural beauty
APD	Air Passenger Duty
APEX	Advance purchase excursion fare
APM	air passenger miles
ARDA	American Resort Development Association
ARTAC	Association of Retail Travel Agents' Consortia
ASEAN	Association of South East Asian Nations
ASM	available seat mile
ASTA	American Society of Travel Agents
ATC	air traffic control
ATOC	Association of Train Operating Companies
ATOL	Air Travel Organizer's Licence
ATP	Accredited Travel Professional
ATTF	Air Travel Trust Fund

AUC	Air Transport Users' Council
AVE	*Alta Velocidad Espagnola* (Spanish high-speed train)
B2B	business to business
B2C	business to consumer
BA	British Airways
BAA	British Airports Authority (organization that operates airports, now privatized, formerly publicly owned)
BABA	book a bed ahead
B&B	bed-and-breakfast accommodation
BACD	British Association of Conference Destinations (formerly British Association of Conference Towns, BACT)
BCG	Boston Consulting Group
BEA	British European Airways (later merged with BOAC to form British Airways)
BHA	British Hospitality Association
BH&HPA	British Holiday and Home Parks Association
BIS	Department for Business, Innovation and Skills
BITOA	British Incoming Tour Operators' Association (now renamed UKInbound)
BITS	Bureau International de Tourisme Sociale
BOAC	British Overseas Airways Corporation, later merged with BEA to form British Airways
BRADA	British Resorts and Destinations Association
BRIC	Brazil, Russia, India and China
BSR	Business for Social Responsibility
BTA	(1) British Tourist Authority (now VisitBritain)
	(2) British Travel Association
BW	British Waterways
CAA	Civil Aviation Authority
CAB	Civil Aeronautics Board (USA)
CASA	Civil Aviation Safety Authority
CBI	Confederation of British Industry
CECTA	Central European Countries Travel Association

CFRP	carbon fibre reinforced plastic
CI	Conservation International
CILT	Chartered Institute of Logistics and Transport
CIM	Chartered Institute of Marketing
CIMTIG	Chartered Institute of Marketing Travel Industry Group
CIT	Chartered Institute of Transport
CITES	Convention on International Trade in Endangered Species
CLIA	Cruise Lines International Association
CoPE	Certificate of Personal Effectiveness
CPD	continuous professional development
CPT	Confederation of Passenger Transport
CRC	Cooperative Research Centre
CRN	Countryside Recreation Network
CRS	computer reservations system
CSR	corporate social responsibility
CTAC	Creative Tourist Agents' Conference
CTC	certified travel counsellor
DCLG	Department for Communities and Local Government
DCMS	Department for Culture, Media and Sport
DDA	Disability Discrimination Act
DEFRA	Department for Environment, Food and Rural Affairs
DfT	Department for Transport
DMO	Destination Management Organization
DP UK	Destination Performance UK
DTCM	Department of Tourism and Commerce Marketing
DTI	Department of Trade and Industry
DVT	deep vein thrombosis
EADS	European Aeronautic Defence and Space Company
EC	European Commission
ECPAT	End Child Prostitution, Pornography and Trafficking
EIA	environmental impact assessment
ELFAA	European Low Fares Airlines Association
ERDF	European Regional Development Fund
ETB	English Tourist Board (later, the English Tourism Council)
ETC	(1) English Tourism Council (now integrated with VisitBritain) (2) European Travel Commission
EU	European Union
EWEA	European Wind Energy Association
EWEC	European Wind Energy Conference and Exhibition
FFP	frequent flyer programme
FHA	Family Holiday Association
FIT	fully inclusive tour
FOC	flag of convenience
FTO	Federation of Tour Operators
FTTSA	Fair Trade in Tourism South Africa
FTV	Fair Trade Volunteering
GBTA	Guild of Business Travel Agents
GDP	gross domestic product
GDS	global distribution system
GIP	Global Infrastructure Partners
GIT	group inclusive tour-basing fare
GNP	gross national product
GRT	gross registered tonnage
GWR	Great Western Railway
HCIMA	Hotel and Catering International Management Association (now Institute of Hospitality)
HSS	high-speed sea service
HUP	Hypersonic Upgrade Programme
IAAPA	International Association of Amusement Parks and Attractions
IAE	International Aero Engines
IAG	International Airlines Group
IATA	International Air Transport Association
IBTA	International Business Travel Association
ICAO	International Civil Aviation Organization
ICE	intercity express
IEFT	International Education Fairs of Turkey
IFAPA	International Foundation of Airline Passenger Associations
IFTO	International Federation of Tour Operators
IHEI	International Hotel Environment Initiative
IHG	Intercontinental Hotels Group
II	Interval International
IIT	independent inclusive tour
ILG	International Leisure Group
IMO	International Marine Organization
IPS	International Passenger Survey
IRTS	International Recommendations for Tourism Statistics

ISIC	International Standard Industrial Classification
ISP	Internet service provider (a company providing Internet access for commercial payment)
IT	(1) inclusive tour (2) information technology
ITM	Institute of Travel Management
ITS	International Tourist Services
ITT	Institute of Travel and Tourism
ITX	inclusive tour-basing excursion fare
IUCN	International Union for the Conservation of Nature
IWM	Imperial War Museum
IYE	International Year of Ecotourism
LAC	Limits of Acceptable Change
LCA	Leading Cruise Agents
LCLF	low-cost low-fare
LDC	lesser-developed countries
LGBT	lesbian, gay, bisexual and transgender
LMS	London, Midland and Scottish
LNER	London and North Eastern Railway
LOCOG	London Organizing Committee of the Olympic and Paralympic Games
LTU	Lufttransport-Unternehmen
MIA	Meetings Industry Association
MICE	meetings incentives conferences and events
MMC	Monopolies and Mergers Commission (now Competition Commission)
MOMA	Museum of Modern Art, New York
MTOW	maximum take-off weight
NAITA	National Association of Independent Travel Agents (later Advantage, now part of Triton)
NATS	National Air Traffic Service
NBC	National Bus Company
NEAP	Nature and Ecotourism Accreditation Programme
NGO	non-governmental organization
NHS	National Health Service
NITB	Northern Ireland Tourist Board
NPTA	National Passenger Traffic Association
NQAS	National Quality Assurance Schemes
NRS	National Readership Survey
NTB	(1) National Tourist Board (2) former National Training Board of ABTA
NTO	National Tourist Organization

NVQ	National Vocational Qualifications
ODA	Olympic Delivery Authority
OECD	Organisation for Economic Co-operation and Development
OITS	International Organization of Social Tourism
ONS	Office for National Statistics
OTE	Organization for Timeshare in Europe
PATA	Pacific Area Travel Association
P&O	Peninsular and Oriental Steam Navigation Company
PCO	Professional Conference Organizer
PNR	passenger name record
PPP	public–private partnership
PSA	Passenger Shipping Association
PSR	passenger–space ratio
PTA	Polytechnic Touring Association
QAA	Quality Assurance Agency
QC	quota count
RAC	Royal Automobile Club
RCI	(1) Resort Condominiums International (2) Royal Caribbean International
RDAs	Regional Development Agencies
RFF	Reseau Ferré de France (French equivalent of Britain's Network Rail, responsible for operating the national rail track)
RFID	radio frequency identification
RTB	Regional Tourist Board
RV	recreational vehicle
SARS	severe acute respiratory syndrome
SAS	Scandinavian Airlines System
SATH	Society for Accessible Travel and Hospitality
SAVE	Support Abandoned Villages and their Environments
SDR	Special Drawing Rights
SME	small- to medium-sized enterprise
SMERF	social, military, educational, religious and fraternal
SNCF	Societé Nationale des Chemins de Fer
SOLAS	Safety of Life at Sea, International Convention for the
SPR	size to passenger ratio
SR	Southern Railway
SSSI	Site of Special Scientific Interest
STB	Scottish Tourist Board (now VisitScotland)
STOL	short take-off and landing

SUV	sports utility vehicle	UFI	Union des Foires Internationales
TAC	Travel Agents' Council	UGC	user-generated content
TALC	Tourist Area Life Cycle	UKTS	United Kingdom Tourism Survey
TCF	Travel Compensation Fun	UN	United Nations
TCN	Tourism Society Consultants' Network	UNEP	United Nations Environment Programme
TDAP	Tourism Development Action Plan	UNESCO	United Nations Educational, Scientific and Cultural Organization
TEFL	Teaching English as a Foreign Language		
TEN-T	Trans-European Network for Transport	UNWTO	United Nations World Tourism Organization
TGV	Train à Grande Vitesse		
TIC	Tourist Information Centre	VAQAS	Visitor Attraction Quality Assurance Schemes
TIER	Tourism Industry Emergency Response Group	VAT	value added tax
		VFR	visiting friends and relatives
TIM	Tourism Income Multiplier	VLJ	very light jet
TIP	tourist information point	VTOL	vertical take-off and landing
TMC	travel management companies	WAM-V	Wave Adaptive Modular Vessel
TMP	The Mersey Partnership	WCS	Wildlife Conservation Society
TOC	Tour Operators' Council	WHO	World Health Organization
TOP	Thomson Open-line Programme (Thomson Holidays' computer reservations system)	WIG	wing-in-ground
		WISE	wing-in-surface effect
TOSG	Tour Operators' Study Group (now Federation of Tour Operators, FTO)	WPC	wave-piercing catamaran
		WTB	Wales Tourist Board
TRIPS	Tourism Resource Information Processing System	WTO	World Tourism Organization (now UNWTO)
TSA	Tourism Satellite Account	WTTC	World Travel and Tourism Council
TTA	Travel Trust Association	WWF	World Wide Fund for Nature
TTC	Travel Training Company	WWW	World Wide Web
TUI	Touristik Union International	YHA	Youth Hostels Association
UATP	Universal Air Travel Plan		

Acknowledgements

We are grateful to the following for permission to reproduce copyright material:

Figures
Figure 1.1 from UNWTO – WTO Methodological Supplement to World Trade Statistics 1978 ©UNWTO, 9284401012; Figure 1.2 adapted from The framework of tourism: Towards a definition of tourism, tourist, and the tourist industry, *Annals of Tourism Research*, 6, 390–407 (Leiper, N. 1979), with permission from Elsevier; Figure 4.1 from *Motivation and Personality*, Pearson Education, Inc (Maslow, A. 1987); Figure 4.6 from The concept of the tourist area life-cycle of evolution: implications for management of resources, *Canadian Geographer*, 24 (1), 5–12 (Butler, R. 1980); Case Study 6, figure 2 from Imperial War Museum; Case Study 7, figure 1 from 'Like' image, www.facebook.com.

Screenshots
Screenshot Figure 20.4 from Visit Dublin phone application, Image courtesy of Fáilte Ireland

Tables
Table 4.1 from *Tourism: principles, practices, philosophies*, Wiley, New York (McIntosh, R. W., Goeldner, C. R. and Ritchie, J. R. B. 1995); Table 4.3 adapted from Harrison, E. and Rose, D., The European Socio-economic Classification (ESeC), Draft User Guide (University of Essex, February 2006); Table 6.1 from Doxey, G. V. (1975), Travel and Tourism Research Association, 'A causation theory of visitor-resident irritants: methodology and research inferences', Proceedings of the Travel Research Association Sixth Annual Conference, San Diego; Table 6.2 from *Hosts and Guests: The Anthropology of Tourism*, 2 ed (Smith, V. 1989) Reprinted with permission of the University of Pennsylvania Press; Table 7.1 adapted from *Tourism Planning: An integrated and sustainable development*, Van Nostrand Reinhold (Inskip, E. 1991); Table 9.2 adapted from Euromonitor; Table 10.5 adapted from ALVA, http://www.alva.org.uk/visitor_statistics/; Table 13.1 adapted from Airline Business, May 2011, Flightglobal; Table 18.1 adapted from UNWTO Tourism Highlights, 2011, http://mkt.unwto.org/sites/all/files/docpdf/unwtohighlights11enlr_1.pdf; Case Study 5, table 1 from Rob Shaw, OAG: World Crisis Analysis White Paper, 2011 (www.oagaviation.com/WorldCrisisAnalysis). Copyright Rob Shaw, OAG Aviation.

Text
Box on page 23 adapted from *English Travel Writing: from Pilgrimages to Postcolonial Explorations*, Palgrave USA (Korte, B.); Example on page 642 adapted from Travel Compensation Fund, 'Annual report', www.tcf.org.au, TCF (2010); Case Study 1, page 666 from Minnaert, L., School of Hospitality and Tourism Management, University of Surrey, http://www.surrey.ac.uk/; Case Study 5, page 690 from Buncle, T., 2011, Yellow Railroad, http://www.yellowrailroad.com, Tom Buncle is Managing Director of Yellow Railroad, an international destination consultancy that specialises in advising countries, regions and cities how to improve their competitiveness as tourism destinations. His particular areas of expertise are: destination branding, marketing strategy, sustainable tourism development and crisis recovery; Case Study 9, page 721 from Robbins, D. & Bragg, L., 2011, School of Tourism, Bournemouth University; Case Study 10, page 730 from Shipway, R. & Henderson, H., 2011, School of Tourism, Bournemouth University.

Photographs

Alamy Images: Barry Lewis 44, Iain Masterton 366; Jon Cassidy: 684, 686; Chris Holloway: 30, 52, 55, 137, 157, 209, 212, 216, 221, 234, 257, 264, 265, 270, 274, 279l, 279r, 330, 347, 352, 423, 430, 446, 470, 479, 485, 499, 508, 547, 548, 586, 619, 651, 722; Claire Humphreys: 13, 18, 41, 73, 133, 159, 165, 166, 170, 187, 206, 207, 210, 217, 222, 227, 242, 256, 261, 262, 280, 281, 336, 346, 349, 358, 360, 397, 409, 425, 430b, 455, 468, 474, 483, 491, 503, 509, 511, 615, 627, 652, 655; Imperial War Museum: 704; Pro Sky 678; Queen Elizabeth II Conference Centre.

Cover images: *Front:* Getty Images

In some instances we have been unable to trace the owners of copyright material, and we would appreciate any information that would enable us to do so.

Part 1

Defining and analysing tourism and its impacts

1

An introduction to tourism

Contents

Learning outcomes

After studying this chapter, you should be able to:

- recognize why tourism is an important area of study
- define what is meant by tourism - both conceptually and technically - and distinguish it from travel, leisure and recreation
- identify the composition and major characteristics of tourism products
- outline the various forms of tourist destination and their appeal
- explain why destinations are subject to changing fortunes.

Every native of every place is a potential tourist, and every tourist is a native of somewhere.

Kincaid (1988) *A Small Place*, 18

Why study tourism?

Tourism is a global industry, with almost a billion international trips taken annually, and it is forecast that this will expand to 1.6 billion by 2020. This book will introduce you to this vast and fascinating industry. Through its various chapters, you will first learn about the factors that have led up to making this the world's fastest-growing business, then examine what that business entails. You will look at the nature of tourism, its appeal, its phenomenal growth over the past half century, the resulting impact on both developed and developing societies and, above all, its steady process of **institutionalization** – that is to say, the manner in which tourism has become commercialized and organized since its inception, but more especially over the past half-century. It will also be about travel, but only those forms of travel specifically undertaken within the framework of a defined tourism journey.

The tourism business deals with the organization of journeys away from home and the way in which tourists are welcomed and catered for in the destination countries. Those who plan to work in this industry will be responsible for ensuring that the outcome of such journeys, whether domestic or international in scope, is the maximizing of satisfaction in the tourist experience.

Formal study of tourism is a relatively recent development, the result of which has been that the tourism business has sometimes lacked the degree of professionalism we have come to expect of other industries. Indeed, in many destination countries it remains the case that much of the industry is in the hands of amateurs – sometimes inspired amateurs, whose warmth and enthusiasm is enough to ensure that their visitors are adequately satisfied, but amateurs nonetheless. However, a warm climate, friendly natives and a few iconic attractions are no longer enough in themselves to guarantee a successful tourism industry – least of all within the principal destination countries of the developed world, which now find themselves in an increasingly competitive environment in the battle to attract global tourists.

In itself, this unwillingness to develop a more professional approach to delivering the tourism product and building careers in the industry is a surprise, given that, for many developing nations, tourism was, even in the early twentieth century, if not the key industry, then certainly among the leading industries in their economies. This attitude is still more surprising in the developed world, given the early importance of international and domestic tourism in countries such as the USA, Spain, France, Switzerland and the UK.

It was the expansion of tourism in the 1960s and 1970s that finally led to the recognition that the study of tourism was something to be taken seriously. Up to that point, the educational focus had been on training for what were perceived to be low-level craft skills that could be learned principally by working alongside experienced employees, to watch how they did the job and emulate them. This would be typical of the way in which hotel and catering workers, travel agents, tour operator resort representatives, visitor attractions employees and airline ground handling staff would be expected to learn their jobs. Not surprisingly, in many cases this merely helped to perpetuate outdated modes of work, not to say errors in practice. In due course, those who performed best in these skills would be promoted to management roles – once again with no formal training – and expected to pick up their management skills as they went along. Gradually, it became recognized that this was not the ideal way to amass all knowledge and skills, and that a more formal process of learning, based on a theoretical body of knowledge and its practical application, would lead to improved professionalism in the industry. From basic-level craft skills, academic courses emerged in the 1970s, 1980s and 1990s at diploma, degree and, ultimately, postgraduate levels to train and educate the workers and managers of the future, as well as equip them with the necessary knowledge and skills to cope at all levels with the rapid changes that were to occur in the tourism industry in the closing years of the last century.

Recognition of the need for formal training is one thing. Determining the body of knowledge that should be appropriate for someone planning to spend a lifetime career in the industry is something else. Tourism is a complex, multidisciplinary subject, requiring knowledge of not only business and management but also such diverse disciplines as law, town and country planning, geography, sociology and anthropology. There is as yet no common agreement among academics, or between academics and practitioners, as to what should form the **core curriculum** of a tourism programme (although attempts at this have been made as we can see in the example below) and, in many countries, practitioners still make clear their preference for courses delivering practical skills over more academic content. The difficulty the tourism industry faces is that trainers will deliver only the knowledge required by employees who will be taking up work in a specific tourism sector, while a career in that industry today is likely to require frequent transfers between the different sectors – and, initially, an overview of how each of these operates. Any formal programme of tourism education must take these needs into account and prepare students for a life in the industry as a whole. Due to the multidisciplinary nature of tourism, however, courses offered in this subject in colleges and universities around the world differ substantially in content, some choosing to deliver what is essentially a business and management programme tuned to the specific needs of the industry, others focusing on issues such as sustainable tourism or public-sector planning for tourism, where the input may be built around urban and regional planning programmes. Still others may choose to deliver courses where the focus is on understanding tourists, drawing on the disciplines of psychology, sociology and anthropology. A well-rounded student of tourism is going to require some knowledge of all of these disciplines, and it is to be hoped that, given time, common agreement can be reached globally between academics and across the industry on what best mix of these disciplines would form the ideal curriculum for a career in tourism.

EXAMPLE **UK Quality Assurance Agency – benchmark for tourism programmes**

The QAA introduced benchmark statements to clarify academic expectations and standards related to degree qualifications. Initially developed in 2000, the tourism benchmark statements were reviewed and updated in 2008 to reflect developments in the industry.

The current UK QAA benchmark for tourism proposes that an honours graduate in tourism should be able to:

- demonstrate an understanding of the concepts and characteristics of tourism as an area of academic and applied study, including being able to:
  - understand and appreciate the potential contributions of disciplines that help to explain the nature and development of tourism
  - explain and challenge theories and concepts which are used to understand tourism
  - explain and challenge the definitions, nature and operations of tourism
  - demonstrate an understanding of the domestic and international nature and dimensions of tourism
  - utilize a range of source material in investigating tourism
  - demonstrate an awareness of the dynamic nature of tourism in modern societies
  - understand the intercultural dimensions of tourism
- demonstrate an understanding of the nature and characteristics of tourists and, in particular:
  - be able to explain the patterns and characteristics of tourism demand and the influences on such demand
  - have an understanding of the ways in which tourists behave at destinations
  - understand the cultural significance of tourism for tourists and societies

- demonstrate an understanding of the products, structure of and interactions in the tourism industry, including being able to:
  - demonstrate an understanding of the structure, operation and organization of the public, private and not-for-profit sectors and their activities
  - evaluate the factors that influence the development of organizations operating in tourism
  - analyse relations between consumers of tourism and the providers of tourism services
- demonstrate an understanding of the relationships between tourism and the communities and environments in which it takes place, in particular:
  - being able to evaluate the contribution and impacts of tourism in social, economic, environmental, political, cultural and other terms
  - have an understanding of, and being able to evaluate, the approaches to managing the development of tourism through concepts of policy and planning
  - appreciating the ethical issues associated with the operation and development of tourism
  - have an understanding of the issues and principles of sustainability and social responsibility in the context of tourism.

Source: QAA, 2008

Defining tourism

A good starting point for any textbook that sets out to examine the tourism business is to try to define what is meant by the terms 'tourist' and 'tourism' before going on to look at the many different forms that tourism can take. While an understanding of the term's meaning is essential, in fact the task of defining it is very difficult. It is relatively easy to agree on technical definitions of particular categories of 'tourism' or 'tourist', but the wider concept is ill defined.

We can go on to say that, self-evidently, the tourist is one who engages in tourism. Tourism involves the movement of a person or persons away from their normal place of residence: a process that usually incurs some expenditure, although this is not *necessarily* the case. Someone cycling or hiking in the countryside on a camping weekend in which they carry their own food may make no economic contribution to the area in which they travel, but can nonetheless be counted as a tourist. Many other examples could be cited in which expenditure by the tourist is minimal. We can say, then, that tourism usually, but not invariably, incurs some expenditure of income and that, further, money spent has been earned within the area of normal residency, rather than at the destination.

The term 'tourism' is further refined as the movement of people away from their *normal* place of residence. Here we find our first problem. Should shoppers travelling short distances of several kilometres be considered tourists? Is it the *purpose* or the *distance* that is the determining factor? Just how far must people travel before they can be counted as tourists for the purpose of official records? What about that growing band of people travelling regularly between their first and second homes, sometimes spending equal time at each?

Clearly, any definition must be specific. In the USA, in 1973, the National Resources Review Commission established that a domestic tourist would be 'one who travels at least 50 miles (one way)'. That was confirmed by the US Census Bureau, which defined tourism 11 years later as a round trip of at least 100 miles. However, the Canadian government defines it as a journey of at least 25 miles from the boundaries of the tourist's home community, while the English Tourism Council proposed a measure of not less than

20 miles and three hours' journey time away from home for a visit to constitute a leisure trip, so consistency has by no means yet been achieved.

Early attempts at defining tourism

One of the first attempts at defining tourism was that of Professors Hunziker and Krapf of Berne University in 1942. They held that tourism should be defined as 'the sum of the phenomena and relationships arising from the travel and stay of non-residents, in so far as they do not lead to permanent residence and are not connected to any earning activity'. This definition helps to distinguish tourism from migration, but it makes the assumption that both *travel* and *stay* are necessary for tourism, thus precluding day tours. It would also appear to exclude business travel, which is connected with 'earning activity', even if that income is not earned in the destination country. Moreover, distinguishing between business and leisure tourism is, in many cases, extremely difficult as most business trips will combine elements of leisure activity.

Earlier still, in 1937, the League of Nations had recommended adopting the definition of a 'tourist' as one who travels for a period of at least 24 hours in a country other than that in which he or she usually resides. This was held to include persons travelling for pleasure, domestic reasons or health, those travelling to meetings or otherwise on business and those visiting a country on a cruise vessel (even if for less than 24 hours). The principal weakness in this definition is that it ignores the movements of domestic tourists.

Later, the United Nations' Conference on International Travel and Tourism, held in 1963, considered recommendations put forward by the International Union of Official Travel Organizations (later the United Nations World Tourism Organization) and agreed to use the term 'visitor' to describe 'any person visiting a country other than that in which he has his usual place of residence, for any reason other than following an occupation remunerated from within the country visited' (Unstats.un.org/unsd/publication/SeriesF/SeriesF_80e.pdf – accessed February 2012). This definition was to cover two classes of visitor:

1. tourists, who were classified as temporary visitors staying at least 24 hours, whose purpose could be categorized as leisure (whether for recreation, health, sport, holiday, study or religion) or business, family, mission or meeting
2. excursionists, who were classed as temporary visitors staying less than 24 hours, including cruise travellers but excluding travellers in transit.

Towards an agreed definition

Once again, these definitions fail to take into account the domestic tourist. The inclusion of the word 'study' above is an interesting one as it is often excluded in later definitions, as are longer courses of education.

A working party for the proposed Institute of Tourism in the UK (which later became the Tourism Society) attempted to clarify the issue and reported, in 1976:

> Tourism is the temporary short-term movement of people to destinations outside the places where they normally live and work, and activities during their stay at these destinations; it includes movement for all purposes, as well as day visits or excursions.

This broader definition was reformulated slightly, without losing any of its simplicity, at the International Conference on Leisure-Recreation-Tourism, organized by the International Association of Scientific Experts in Tourism (AIEST) and the Tourism Society in Cardiff, Wales, in 1981:

> Tourism may be defined in terms of particular activities selected by choice and undertaken outside the home environment. Tourism may or may not involve overnight stay away from home.

Finally, the following definition devised by the then World Tourism Organization (WTO) was endorsed by the UN's Statistical Commission in 1993 following an International Government Conference held in Ottawa, Canada, in 1991:

> Tourism comprises the activities of persons travelling to and staying in places outside their usual environment for not more than one consecutive year for leisure, business or other purposes.

These definitions have been quoted here at length because they reveal how broadly the concept of tourism must be defined in order to embrace all forms of the phenomenon and how exceptions can be found for even the most narrowly focused definitions. Indeed, the final definition could be criticized on the grounds that, unless the activities are more clearly specified, it could be applied equally to someone involved in burglary! With this definition, we are offered guidance on neither the activities undertaken nor the distance to be travelled. In fact, with the growth of timeshare and second home owners, who in some cases spend considerable periods of time away from their main homes, it could be argued that a tourist is no longer necessarily 'outside the home environment'. It is also increasingly recognized that defining tourists in terms of the distances they have travelled from their homes is unhelpful, as locals can be viewed as 'tourists' within their own territory if they are engaged in tourist-type activities, and certainly their economic contribution to the tourism industry in the area is as important as that of the more traditionally defined tourist.

Figure 1.1 illustrates the guidelines produced by the United Nations World Tourism Organization (UNWTO) (then, the WTO) to classify travellers for statistical purposes. Some loopholes in the definitions remain, however. Even attempts to classify tourists as those travelling for purposes unconnected with employment can be misleading if one looks at the social consequences of tourism. Ruth Pape (1964) has drawn attention to the case of nurses in the USA who, after qualifying, gravitate to California for their first jobs as employment is easy to find and they can thus enjoy the benefits of the sunshine and leisure pursuits for which the state is famous. They may spend a year or more in this job before moving on, but the point is that they have been motivated to come to that area not because of the work itself, but because of the area's tourist attractions. Frequently, too, students of tourism, after completing their course, return to work in the areas in which they undertook work placements during their studies, having found the location (and, often, the job) sufficiently attractive to merit spending more time there. People increasingly buy homes in areas where they can enjoy walking, skiing or other leisure activities, so that tourism is literally on their doorsteps, yet this growing group of 'resident tourists' is not taken into consideration for statistical purposes. Indeed, the division between work and leisure is further blurred today by the development of e-mail and websites that offer immediate access from wherever a worker happens to be spending time. This has led many to buy second homes in the countryside, where work may be engaged in between bouts of leisure and relaxation. Internet cafés and laptop computers allow workers to keep in touch with their business while away from home, further blurring the distinction between travel for work and travel for leisure. Many examples could also be given of young people working their way around the world (the contemporary equivalent of the Grand Tour?) or workers seeking summer jobs in seaside resorts.

Finally, we must consider the case of pensioners who choose to retire abroad in order to benefit from the lower costs of living in other countries. Many Northern Europeans move to Mediterranean countries after retirement, while Americans similarly seek warmth, and gravitate to Mexico; they may still retain their homes in their country of origin, but spend a large part of the year abroad. Canadians, and Americans living in northern states, are known as 'snowbirds' because of their migrant behaviour, coming down in their mobile homes and caravans to the sunshine states of the US south west during the winter months to escape the harsh winters of the north. Once again, the motivation for all of

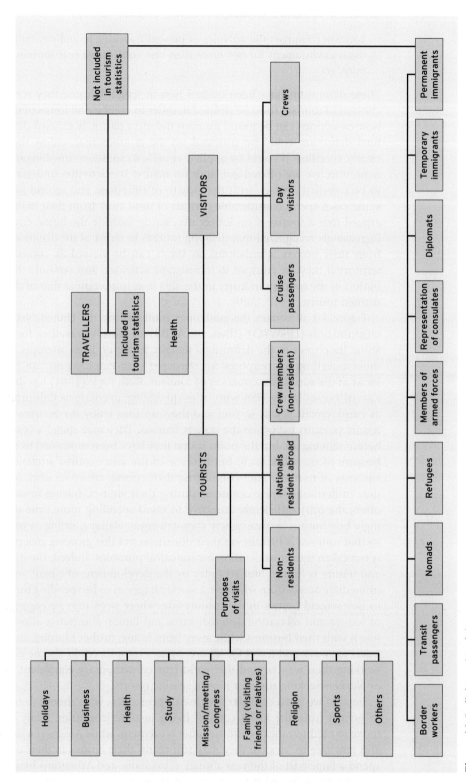

Figure 1.1 Defining a tourist
Courtesy of the UN World Tourism Organization

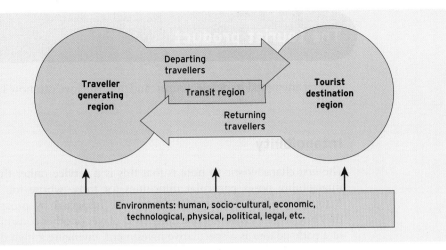

Figure 1.2 The tourism system
Source: adapted from Leiper, 1979

these people is not simply to lower their costs of living but also to enjoy an improved climate and the facilities that attract tourists to the same destinations.

Up to this point, definitions have been discussed in terms of their academic importance and for the purposes of statistical measurement. We need to recognize that the terms are used much more loosely within the industry itself, with a distinction being made between travel and tourism. If we think of **tourism as a system** (Leiper, 1979) (see Figure 1.2) embracing a generating region (where the market for tourism develops), a destination region or regions (places and areas visited by the tourist) and a transit zone (where some form of transport is used to move the tourist from, and back to, the generating region and between any destinations visited), it is becoming common practice among practitioners to refer to the second of these as comprising the *tourism industry*, with the other two referred to as the *travel industry*.

Conceptually, defining tourism precisely is a near-impossible task. To produce a technical definition for statistical purposes is less problematic. As long as it is clear what the data comprise, and one compares like with like, whether inter-regionally or internationally, we can leave the conceptual discussion to the academics.

 Statistical definitions

The Australian Bureau of Statistics proposes that 'Tourism comprises the activities of visitors', where 'A visitor is defined as any person taking a trip to a main destination outside his/her usual environment, for less than a year, for any main purpose (business, leisure or other personal purpose) other than to be employed by a resident entity in the country or place visited'.

The European Union (EU) requires that its member states collect data on tourism. To aid this, it has determined that the UNWTO definition of tourism should guide data collection. The UK Office of National Statistics (ONS) works within this framework, determining that tourism is defined as 'a movement of people to places outside their usual place of residence, pleasure being the usual motivation.' The ONS (ONS, 2010, 4) considers anyone making a trip as a visitor who is 'a traveller taking a trip to a main destination outside his/her usual environment, for less than a year, for any main purpose (business, leisure or other personal purpose) other than to be employed by a resident entity in the country or place visited'.

Source: ABS: http://www.abs.gov.au/AUSSTATS/abs@.nsf/Latestproducts/5249.0Glossary12010-11?opendocument&tabname=Notes&prodno=5249.0&issue=2010-11&num=&view=

The tourist product

Having attempted to define 'tourist' and 'tourism', we can now look at the tourist product itself.

Intangibility

The first characteristic to note is that this is a **service** rather than a tangible good. This intangibility poses particular difficulties for those whose job it is to market tourism. A tourist product cannot, for example, be inspected by prospective purchasers before they buy, as can a washing machine, DVD player or other consumer durable. The purchase of a package tour is a speculative investment, involving a high degree of trust on the part of the purchaser, the more so as a holiday is often the most expensive purchase made each year (although, with increasing affluence, many consumers are now able to purchase two or more such holidays annually). The necessary element of trust is heightened by the development of sales via the World Wide Web (WWW) and the introduction of ticketless booking for much air travel.

It has often been said that 'selling holidays is like selling dreams'. When tourists buy a package tour abroad, they are buying more than a simple collection of services, such as an airline seat, hotel room, three meals a day and the opportunity to sit on a sunny beach; they are also buying the temporary use of a strange environment, incorporating what may be, for them, novel geographical features – old world towns, tropical landscapes – plus the culture and heritage of the region and other intangible benefits, such as service, atmosphere and hospitality. The planning and anticipation of the holiday may be as much a part of its enjoyment as is the trip itself. Then, recalling the experience later and reviewing videos or photos are further extensions of the experience. These are all part of the product, which is, therefore, a psychological as well as a physical experience.

Heterogeneity

The challenge for the marketer of tourism is to match the dream to the reality. The difficulty of achieving this is that tourism is not a homogeneous but a **heterogeneous** product – that is, it tends to vary in standard and quality over time and under different circumstances, unlike, say, a television set. A package tour or even a flight on an aircraft cannot be consistently uniform: a bumpy flight, or a long technical flight delay, can change an enjoyable experience into a nightmare, while a holiday at the seaside can be ruined by a prolonged rainy spell.

Because a tour comprises a compendium of different products, an added difficulty in maintaining standards is that each element of the product should be broadly similar in quality. A good room and fine service at a hotel may be spoilt by poor food or the flight may mar an otherwise enjoyable hotel stay. An element of chance is always present in the purchase of any service and, where the purchase must *precede* the actual consumption of the product, as with tourism, the risk for the consumer is increased.

The introduction of **dynamic packaging**, which is rapidly changing the traditional package tour, is beginning to complicate this. Dynamic packaging is the process by which travel agents, or other retailers of travel, themselves put together flights, accommodation and other elements of travel and sell the resulting package of components to consumers. Of course, tourists can today put their own packages together through Internet suppliers, but if they choose to do so, uncertainty about the uniformity of the product is heightened. Even when packages are tailor-made by the travel agent or other retailer in a similar manner, the lack of a single tour operator or supplier to oversee the final package threatens to undermine the concept of a 'standard quality' product.

Inseparability

One of the factors influencing the heterogeneity of the product is that often people are involved in the delivery of the service and this human involvement may not be consistent in behaviour or demeanour. The interaction between the service provider – a waiter in a restaurant, for instance, or the holiday representative at a resort – and the customer can be influenced by the moods and emotions of each. But this highlights another characteristic of tourism, that it cannot be brought to the consumer. Rather, the consumer must be brought to the product and be present for the delivery of the service. This **inseparability** also means that the tourism product cannot be 'manufactured' at a place and time convenient to the supplier. For example, if the holidaymaker has been sold a guided tour then both the tour guide and the tourist need to be present at an agreed time and place for the transaction to take place.

Perishability

A fourth characteristic of tourism is its inability to be stockpiled for future use. If the hotel room is not sold for a particular night then that 'product' is lost forever – no one would buy a hotel room for use last month! Similarly, the unsold aircraft seat cannot be stored for later sale, as is the case with tangible products, but is lost forever once the plane is airborne; hence the great efforts that must be made by those in the industry to fill empty seats. This has implications for the industry and, as we will discuss in Chapter 18, tour operators work hard to ensure they maximize sales, perhaps offering last minutes discounted deals, to ensure that they earn money from these products before they are lost.

In the short term, at least, the supply of this product is fixed; the number of hotel bedrooms available at a particular destination cannot be varied to meet the changing demands of holidaymakers during the season, for example by last-minute discounting or other techniques. If market demand changes, as it does frequently in the business of tourism, the supply will take time to adapt. A hotel is built to last for many years, and must remain profitable throughout that period. These are all problems unique to tourism and call for considerable marketing ingenuity on the part of those in the business.

The nature of tourism

Now that we have made an attempt to define the concept of tourism, let us look at this topic systematically. It is useful to examine the characteristics of a tour in terms of the following five broad categories – motivation for the trip, the characteristics of the trip, the mode of organization, the composition of the tour and the characteristics of the tourist.

The motivation for a trip

Motivation identifies, first, the purpose of a visit. Purposes themselves fall into three distinct categories:

- holidays (including visits to friends and relatives, known as VFR travel)
- business (including meetings, conferences, etc.)
- other (including study, religious pilgrimages, sport, health, etc.).

It is important to be aware of the underlying purpose behind the tourist's travels, because each of these categories will reveal a different set of characteristics. Let us consider, for example, how business travel differs from leisure travel. The business traveller will have little discretion in choice of destination or the timing of the trip. In general, destinations will bear little similarity to the destinations of the leisure traveller, as enjoyment of the attractions and facilities do not form part of the purpose of the trip (even if those that exist may be enjoyed as an adjunct to it). Business trips frequently have to be arranged at short notice and for specific and brief periods of time – often only a day, even where substantial journey time is involved. For these reasons, business travellers need the convenience of frequent, regular transport, efficient service and good facilities (in terms of accommodation and catering) at the destination. Because their company will usually be paying for all the travel arrangements, business travellers will be less concerned about the cost of travel than they would if they were paying for it themselves. Higher prices are not likely to deter travel, nor will lower prices encourage more frequent travel. We can say, therefore, that business travel is relatively **price inelastic**. Holiday travel, however, is highly price elastic – lower prices for holidays to a particular destination will tend to lead to an increase in the total number of travellers, as tourists find the holiday more affordable, while others may be encouraged by the lower prices to switch their planned destination. Leisure travellers will be prepared to delay their travel or will book well in advance of their travel dates if this means that they can substantially reduce their costs.

While these generalities continue to hold, we must also recognize the fact that growing disposable income among the populations of the developed world is having the effect of reducing price elasticity for many holidaymakers as upmarket winter sports holidays, cruises, special interest and long-haul travel attract a greater percentage of the mass market travellers (especially the growing numbers taking second and third holidays every year). For these travellers, service is becoming more important than price. At the same time, narrowing profits in the business world, and restrictions placed on corporate travel budgets, are driving up elasticity among business travellers. In the latter case, the growth of the low-cost air carriers has made discounted air travel so attractive by comparison with fares on the established carriers (particularly first and business class) that low-cost airlines now claim a large proportion of their passengers are people travelling on business.

Beyond price, we must also identify other reasons for a specific type of holiday or resort being chosen. Different people will look for different qualities in the same destination. A particular ski resort, for example, may be selected because of its excellent slopes and sporting facilities, its healthy mountain air or the social life it offers to skiers and non-skiers alike (see Figure 1.3). The variety of motivations influencing demand for holidays is extensive and these are discussed in more detail in Chapter 4.

The characteristics of a trip

These define what kind of visit is made and to where. First, one can differentiate between **domestic** tourism and **international** tourism. The former refers to travel taken exclusively within the national boundaries of the traveller's home country. The decision to take one's holidays within the borders of one's own country is an important one economically as it will reduce the outflow of money from that country and have an impact on the balance of payments. Many governments therefore encourage residents to holiday in their own countries in order to aid the economy. Recession in the early part of the twenty-first century saw the growth of 'staycations' a new term describing the growing number of holidays taken in areas local to home.

Next, what kind of destination is being chosen? Will travel be to a seaside resort, mountain resort, country town, health spa or major city? Is it to be a single-centre visit, a multi-centre one (involving a stopover at two or more places) or a longitudinal tour that will involve extensive travel with brief overnight stays along the route? If a cruise is to be taken,

Figure 1.3 The Alpinglow Inn is popular with skiers as it is conveniently located adjacent to ski lifts

Photo by Claire Humphreys

statisticians have to decide whether or not to count this as international travel if the vessel visits foreign ports and, if so, whether to count each country visited as a separate visit to a foreign country or include only the main port visited. Does a one-night stopover in Miami before boarding a cruise vessel bound for the Caribbean count as a separate visit to the USA for the European or Asian visitor?

Next, what length of time is being spent on the trip? A visit that does not involve an overnight stay is known, as we saw earlier, as an excursion, frequently referred to as a 'day trip'. The expenditure of day trippers is generally less than that of overnight visitors and statistical data on these forms of tourism are often collected separately. A visitor who stops at least one night at a destination is termed a 'tourist', but can, of course, make day trips to other destinations which could even involve an international trip. For instance, a visitor staying in Rhodes may take a trip for the day by boat to the Turkish mainland; another in Corfu can go on an excursion to the nearby coastal resorts of Albania. For the purposes of Turkey's and Albania's records, that visitor will be recorded as an excursionist. Domestic American tourists travelling through New England often make a brief visit to the Canadian side of the Niagara Falls, hence are excursionists as far as the Canadian tourism authorities are concerned.

Finally, in order to maintain accurate records, some maximum length of time must be established beyond which the visitor can no longer be looked on as a tourist. There are different approaches here – some using a low figure of three months, others six months and, in some cases, a full year is viewed as the maximum period.

Modes of tour organization

This further refines the form that the travel takes. A tour may be **independent** or **packaged**. A package tour, for which the official term is 'inclusive tour' (IT), is an arrangement in which transport and accommodation are purchased by the tourist at an all-inclusive price.

The price of individual elements of the tour cannot normally be determined by the purchaser. The tour operator putting together the package will buy transport and accommodation in advance, generally at a lower price because each of the products is being bought in bulk, and the tours are then sold individually to holidaymakers, either directly or through travel agents. Agents and operators can also package independent inclusive tours by taking advantage of special net fares and building the package around the specific needs of the client. This is explained more fully in Chapter 18.

As explained earlier in this chapter, 'dynamic package' is the term used to describe holidays that are put together as tailor-made programmes, whether by the operator, the retailer or even by the holidaymakers themselves. This form of holiday package is rapidly changing the standard inclusive tour, although it is not thought that this will lead to the demise of the traditional package. Rather, operators are adjusting their products to make them more flexible by means of tailor-made alterations to duration and other arrangements.

The composition of the tour

This consists of the elements comprising the visit. All tourism involves travel away from one's usual place of residence, as we have seen, and, in the case of 'tourists' – as opposed to 'excursionists' – it will include accommodation. So, we must here identify the form of travel – air, sea, road or rail – that is to be used. If air transport is involved, will this be by charter aircraft or scheduled flight? If there is to be an overnight stay, will this be in a hotel, guesthouse, campsite or self-catering accommodation? How will the passenger travel between airport and hotel – by coach, taxi or airport limousine? A package tour will normally comprise transport and accommodation, often with transfers to and from the accommodation included, but, in some cases, additional services will be provided in the programme, such as car hire at the destination, excursions by coach or theatre entertainment. The inclusion of some form of comprehensive insurance is now demanded by most companies and is sold automatically with the tour, unless individual tourists can confirm that they are covered by alternative travel insurance.

The characteristics of the tourist

Analysis of tourism must include analysis of the tourist. We have already distinguished between the holidaymaker and the business traveller. We can also identify the tourist in terms of nationality, social class, sex, age and lifestyle. What life stage are they in? What type of personality do they have?

Such information is valuable not only for the purpose of record-keeping; it will also help to shed light on the reasons why people travel, why they select certain destinations and how patterns of travel differ between different groups of people. Research is now focusing much more intently on personality and lifestyle as characteristics which determine the choice of holidays, rather than looking simply at social class and occupation. The more that is known about such details, the more effectively can those in the industry produce the products that will meet the needs of their customers, and develop the appropriate strategies to bring those products to their attention.

The tourist destination

We can now examine the tourist destination itself. The nature of destinations will be explored in Chapter 9, but at this point in the book an initial understanding of what attracts tourists to different destinations will be helpful. A **destination** can be a particular resort or town, a region within a country, the whole of a country or even a larger area of the globe. For example, a package tour may embrace visits to three separate countries in Latin America that have quite distinct attractions – say, an initial visit to Peru to see the cultural life of the Peruvian Indians and the ruins at Macchu Pichu, followed by a flight to Buenos Aires, Argentina, for a typical capital city experience of shopping and nightlife, returning home via Cancún, Mexico, where a few days of recuperation are enjoyed at a beach resort.

This 'pick and mix' approach to the varieties of destination and their relative attractions is becoming increasingly common, with the earlier concept of being expected to choose between a beach holiday, cultural holiday, short-break city tour or some other uniform package arrangement no longer holding true. Cruise companies have come to recognize this and now commonly market fortnight combination holidays, consisting of several days of cruising, preceded or followed by a few days at a beach resort close to the port of embarkation.

In the case of cruises, for many tourists the 'destination' is the ship itself, and its actual ports of call may be secondary to the experience of life on board. Indeed, it is by no means unusual for regular cruise passengers to fail to disembark at ports of call, preferring to enjoy the company of the cruise staff and entertainment on board while the ship is in port.

In other examples, the destination and accommodation are inseparable – as is the case of a resort hotel that provides a range of leisure facilities on site. In such cases, it may be the tourist's objective to visit the hotel purely and simply because of the facilities that hotel provides and the entire stay will be enjoyed without venturing beyond the precincts of the hotel grounds. This is a characteristic that is commonly found among certain long-established resort hotels in the USA, but an example more familiar to UK holidaymakers would be the Sandals all-inclusive resorts in the Caribbean.

EXAMPLE A resort destination

Club Med operates premium all-inclusive resorts around the globe, providing an extensive range of facilities to keep holidaymakers entertained. To take one example - and this is representative of many of their resorts - we can look at the Cargèse resort on the island of Corsica. Located on the west coast, it is immediately adjacent to a beach suited to swimming and other watersports. To encourage holidaymakers onto the water the resort offers a sailing academy and provides catamarans, windsurfing and kayaking facilities.

For tourists preferring dry land the tennis academy may be more suited to their desires. Alternatively a chance to play badminton, basketball, volleyball, mini-football or participate in fitness classes may be preferred. The less active holidaymaker may choose to relax by the pool, or enjoy the concerts and shows. For those who wish to venture outside of the resort, full and half day excursions are offered. These might include visits to local World Heritage Sites.

Although it has been operating for more than half a century, Club Med launched its current approach in 2005, reinvigorating its appeal to markets demanding upmarket all-inclusive resorts. This has proved popular, and the company provided holidays for more than a million tourists in 2010.

All destinations share certain characteristics. Their success in attracting tourists will depend on the quality of three essential benefits that are offered: **attractions**, **amenities** (or facilities) and **accessibility** (or ease with which they can travel to the destination). At this point we will do no more than outline the variety of destinations attractive to tourists, before considering their attractions, amenities and accessibility.

Varieties of destinations

Destinations are of two kinds – either 'natural' or 'constructed'. Most are 'managed' to some extent, whether they are natural or constructed. National parks, for example, are left in their natural state of beauty as far as possible, but nevertheless have to be managed, in terms of the provision of access, parking facilities, accommodation (such as caravan and campsites), litter bins and so on.

Broadly, we can categorize destinations by delineating them according to geographical features, under the following three headings.

- *Seaside tourism*. This will include seaside resorts, natural beaches, boating holidays along coasts, coastal footpaths and so on.
- *Rural tourism*. This will include the most common category of lakes and mountains, but also countryside touring, 'agritourism' such as farm holidays, visits to vineyards, gardens, visits and stays at villages or rural retreats, river and canal holidays, wildlife parks and national parks.
- *Urban tourism*. This will include visits to cities and towns.

Health resorts, including spas (which are important to the tourist industries of many countries), may be based in rural, seaside or urban areas. Adventure holidays and active holidays, such as winter sports, are commonly associated with rural sites, but if one thinks of the appeal of towns such as St Moritz in Switzerland, Aspen in Colorado or Jackson Hole, Wyoming, in the USA, which developed primarily to attract winter sports enthusiasts, it must be recognized that pigeonholing all forms of tourism as being one or other of only these three types of destination is inappropriate.

All destinations can suffer from overuse and, for the most popular, this is a growing problem. The difficulties created by too great a demand and the need for careful management of city centres, beaches and natural countryside are subjects that are discussed in Chapters 6 and 7.

Attractions, amenities and accessibility

All destinations require adequate attractions, amenities and accessibility if they are to appeal to large numbers of tourists. In this section, we will look at these issues.

The more attractions a destination can offer, the easier it becomes to market that destination to the tourist. Listing and analysing attractions is no easy matter, especially when one recognizes that what appeals to one tourist may actually deter another.

Many of the attractions of a destination depend on its physical features: the beauty of mountains, the fresh air of a seaside resort and the qualities of a particular beach, the historical architecture, shopping and entertainment opportunities and 'atmosphere' of a great city. To these can be added numerous purpose-built attractions to increase the pulling power of the destination. For example, Blackpool maintains its lead among the seaside resorts in the UK by investing in indoor entertainments, a conference centre and other features that appeal to a cross-section of tourists. Key cities and capitals build new museums, art galleries or exhibition centres while former stately homes or castles are transformed by development into focal points for visits by tourists and day trippers alike.

Sometimes, the constructed attraction becomes a destination in its own right, as is the case with theme parks such as the Disney complexes in Anaheim (California), Orlando (Florida), near Paris, France, and in the Far East. Similarly, the success of many spa towns on the Continent rests on their ability to combine constructed attractions such as casinos with the assumed medical benefits of the natural springs, while the popular ski resorts must provide adequate ski runs, ski lifts and après-ski entertainment to complement their combinations of suitable weather and mountain slopes.

The operation of managed visitor attractions is dealt with in Chapters 10 and 16. At this point, therefore, it is sufficient to highlight certain distinctions between attractions.

First, attractions may be either *site* or *event* attractions. Site attractions are permanent by nature, while event attractions are temporary and often mounted in order to increase the number of tourists to a particular destination. Some events have a short timescale, such as an air display by the famed Red Arrows' close formation flyers, as part of a one-day event; others may last for many days (the Edinburgh Festival, for example) or even months (for instance, the Floriade Garden Festival in Holland). Some events occur at regular intervals – yearly, biennially (the outdoor sculpture exhibition at Quenington in the Cotswolds, England, is such an event), four-yearly (the Olympic Games) or even less frequently (the Oberammergau Passion Play in Germany and the Floriade Festival mentioned above occur only once every ten years), while other festivals are organized on an *ad hoc* basis and may, indeed, be one-off events. A destination that may otherwise have little to commend it to the tourist can, in this way, succeed in drawing tourists by mounting a unique exhibition, while a site destination can extend its season by mounting an off-season event, such as a festival of arts.

Second, destinations and their attractions can be either *nodal* or *linear* in character. A nodal destination is one in which the attractions of the area are closely grouped geo-graphically. Seaside resorts and cities are examples of typical nodal attractions, making them ideal for packaging by tour operators. This has led to the concept of 'honey pot' tourism development, in which planners concentrate the development of tourism in a specific locality. Whistler in Canada is an example of a purpose-built nodal tourism resort, built largely to satisfy the growing needs of winter sports enthusiasts. With its extensive range of accommodation, attractions and amenities, it now draws high-spend tourists throughout the year from all over the world. Linear tourism, however, defines an attraction spread over a wide geographical area, without any specific focus. Examples include the Shenandoah Valley region in the USA, the Highlands of Scotland or the so-called 'romantische Strasse' (romantic trail) through central Germany – all ideal for touring holidays, rather than just 'stay put' holidays. Motels or bed-and-breakfast accommodation spring up in such areas to serve the needs of the transient tourist, who may spend only one or two nights at a particular destination. Cruising is another form of linear tourism, currently enjoying growing popularity as it enables tourists to see a multitude of different sites conveniently and with minimal disruption.

It is important to remember that much of the attraction of a destination is intangible and greatly depends on its image, as perceived by the potential tourist. India may be seen by one group of travellers as exotic and appealing, while others will reject it as a destination because of its poverty or its unfamiliar culture. Images of a destination, whether favourable or unfavourable, tend to be built up over a long period of time and, once established, are difficult to change. The UK, for instance, is still seen by many as a fog-engulfed, rain-battered island with friendly but rather reserved inhabitants, an image reinforced in old Hollywood films and still frequently stereotyped in foreign media. Overcoming such stereotyping is an important task for a country's national tourist board.

Amenities are those essential services that cater to the needs of the tourist. These include accommodation and food, evening entertainment such as theatres, discotheques and bars, local transport, and the necessary infrastructure to support tourism – roads, public utility services and parking facilities. Naturally, such amenities will vary according to the nature of the destination itself: it would clearly be inappropriate to provide an extensive infra-structure in an area of great scenic beauty, such as a national park, and those planning to visit such a destination will recognize that the availability of hotels and restaurants must inevitably be limited. Such sites are likely to attract the camper and those seeking only limited amenities – indeed, this will be part of the attraction for them.

It should also be recognized that, on occasion, the amenity itself may be the attraction, as was discussed earlier in the case of a resort hotel offering a comprehensive range of *in situ* attractions. Similarly, a destination such as France, which is famed for its regional foods, will encourage tourists whose motive in travelling may be largely to enjoy their meals. In this case, the amenity is itself an attraction.

Finally, a destination must be accessible if it is to facilitate visits from tourists. While the more intrepid travellers may be willing to put themselves to great inconvenience in order to see some of the more exotic places in the world, most tourists will not be attracted to a destination unless it is relatively easy to reach. This means, in the case of international travel, having a good airport nearby, regular and convenient air transport to the region at an affordable price and good local connections to the destination itself (or, at very least, good car hire facilities). Cruise ships will be attracted by well-presented deep water ports with moorings available at reasonable cost to the shipping line and situated within easy reach of the attractions in the area. Cities such as Helsinki, Stockholm and Tallinn have the great advantage of providing deep water moorings close to the very heart of the capital, allowing passengers to disembark and walk into the centre of the city. Warnemünde is a popular port for cruise visitors to visit Germany as Berlin is a comfortable day's excursion by fast motorway from the coast, whereas Vilnius, capital of Lithuania, cannot attract cruise ships precisely because it is situated too far inland for the excursion market. Other travellers will be drawn by good access roads or rail services and coach links. Access is also important in getting around the locality at a destination. This may be achieved through local public transport, or providing facilities targeting visitors (see Figure 1.4).

On the other hand, if access becomes too easy, this may result in too great a demand and resultant congestion, making the destination less attractive to the tourist. The building of motorways in the UK opened up the Lake District and the West Country to millions of motorists, many of whom now find themselves within a two-hour drive of their destination. This has led to severe congestion due to the large numbers of weekend day trippers and summer holidaymakers during the peak tourist months.

It should be noted that the *perception* of accessibility on the part of the traveller is often as important as a destination's *actual* accessibility. In particular, the introduction of low-cost airlines operating from the UK to less familiar destinations on the Continent has led many people in the UK to perceive Mediterranean destinations as being more accessible than Cornwall or the Scottish Highlands in terms of both cost and travelling time. Such perceptions will undoubtedly affect decision-making when tourists are formulating their travel plans.

Figure 1.4 Tourists are pushed along the seafront (or Boardwalk) in Atlantic City, New Jersey. The Boardwalk is 4 miles long and these carts provide tourists with an exercise-free way of moving between the hotels, restaurants and casinos which dominate the seafront

Photo by Claire Humphreys

Summary

The chapter has highlighted the problem of defining tourism, but much of this difficulty can be appreciated in recognizing that this industry has many subsectors. This provides the student planning their career in tourism with many opportunities, whether they wish to work in travel operations, retail travel, the numerous transport sectors, the accommodation sector, marketing destinations or the many other areas we have not listed here. It is also important that the impacts of tourism are recognized; for tourism to remain sustainable, planning and management are vital activities.

Questions and discussion points

1. Why are characteristics such as social class, sex, age and lifestyle influential factors in holiday choice?

2. In the chapter we highlighted that tourism can be heterogeneous. What can the manager of a tourist attraction do to reduce inconsistencies in the delivery of their tourism product?

3. Why it important to have a suitable range of amenities if tourists are to be attracted to a destination?

Tasks

1. Staycations became popular at the end of the last decade. Explore the attractions in your area and write a list of the places you would visit and the things you would do if you had a one week staycation. Reflect on your motivations for choosing the items on your list - would they differ for your parents or grandparents?

2. For a country of your choice identify a rural, urban and seaside location popular with tourists. Write a report which compares and contrasts the different attractions available at each location to keep the holidaymaker entertained.

Bibliography

Hunziker, W. and Krapf, K. (1942) *Grundriss der Allgemeinen Fremdenverkehrslehre*. Zurich, Polygraphischer Verlag.

Kincaid, Jamaica (1988) *A Small Place*, New York, Farrar, Straus Giroux.

Leiper, N. (1979) The framework of tourism: Towards a definition of tourism, tourist, and the tourist industry, *Annals of Tourism Research*, **6** (2), 390–407.

ONS (2010) *Measuring Tourism Locally. Guidance Note 1: Definitions of Tourism*, London, Office for National Statistics.

Pape, R. (1964) Touristry: a type of occupational mobility, *Social Problems*, **11** (4), 327–336.

QAA (2008) *Hospitality, Leisure, Sport and Tourism*, Mansfield, Linney Direct.

UNSD/OECD (2010) *International Recommendations for Tourism Statistics 2008*, New York, United Nations.

2

The development and growth of tourism up to the mid-twentieth century

Contents

Learning outcomes

After studying this chapter, you should be able to:

- explain the historical changes that have affected the growth and development of the tourism industry from its earliest days
- understand the relationship between technological innovation and tourism development
- explain why particular forms of travel and destinations were chosen by the early tourists
- identify and distinguish between enabling conditions and motivating factors affecting tourism demand.

Horizons had been opened up under the Romans to such an extent that many individuals, not just soldiers or state officials, could make long journeys to all parts of the empire. In the words of Aristeides, every man could go where he wished.

Adams and Laurence (2001) *Travel and Geography in the Roman Empire*, 5

Introduction: the early years

A study of the history of tourism is a worthwhile occupation for any student of the tourism business, not only as a matter of academic interest but also because there are lessons to be learned that are as applicable today as in the past. One thing we learn from history is that the business of tourism, from its earliest days some 3000 years ago, shares many of the characteristics of the business as we know it today. Many of the facilities and amenities demanded by modern tourists were provided – albeit in a more basic form – all the way back then: not just accommodation and transport but also catering services, guides and souvenir shops.

The earliest forms of travel can be traced at least as far back as the Babylonian and Egyptian empires, some three millennia BC, but these originated for business purposes rather than leisure. People travelled largely out of obligation, for reasons of government administration, trade or military purposes. However, there is also evidence of significant movements of religious tourists to the sites of sacred festivals, from very early on. Leisure travel took a little longer to develop. It is traceable to as far back as c. 1500 BC, when the Egyptians began to travel to visit their pyramids, partly for reasons of religion but largely out of curiosity or for pleasure (Casson, 1994). Most travel, however, entailed very little pleasure and was viewed as a stressful necessity by travellers. Indeed, the origin of the word 'travel' is to be found in its earlier form of *travail* – literally, a painful and laborious effort.

Even earlier than this, around 1900 BC, we have evidence of travel literature – the classic *Epic of Gilgamesh*, an ancient Mesopotamian poem, written on clay tablets which still exist today. In this poem, the eponymous hero king is obliged to travel as both a challenge and an educational experience – perhaps the first example of what became known much later as the Grand Tour (Leed, 1991).

While some limited travel along the coasts and rivers of those ancient empires must have occurred even earlier than these dates, travel was greatly facilitated when shipwrights first designed vessels capable of travelling safely and relatively comfortably over open water some time after 3000 BC (Casson, 1994). These would primarily have been used to carry freight, but would also have been capable of carrying a limited number of passengers. One of the earliest recorded journeys for the purposes of tourism was that of Queen Hatshepsut, from Egypt to the land of Punt (now Somalia) in around 1480 BC (Goeldner and Ritchie, 2009). In landlocked areas, transport was, at the time, limited to donkey riding pending the introduction – probably by the Sumerians at first – of solid-wheeled wagons drawn by oxen or onagers (a type of wild ass), also from around 3000 BC.

In the first millennium BC, the world was to change dramatically, as new empires grew, fought and died. Most forms of transport around this time (such as the chariot) were first developed for military purposes, but this soon led to the use of horse-drawn wagons to convey goods and people. Horse riding also appeared, at first, in military guise, as warriors from Asia swept down from the Steppes. From about 500 BC, however, it was adopted by the Western nations, first in the form of cavalry, but, later, as a more peaceful form of transport.

A museum of 'historic antiquities' was opened to the public in the sixth century BC in Babylon, while, as we have noted, the Egyptians held many religious festivals, attracting not only the devout but also many coming to see the famous buildings and works of art in the cities. To provide for these throngs during the festivals, services of all kinds sprang up: street vendors of food and drink, guides, hawkers of souvenirs, touts and prostitutes. Some early tourists took to vandalizing buildings with graffiti to record their visit – Egyptian graffiti dating back to 2000 BC have been found.

From about the same date, and notably from the third century BC, Greek tourists travelled to visit the sites of healing gods. Because the independent city states of ancient Greece had no central authority to order the construction of roads, most of these tourists travelled by water and, as most freight also travelled in this fashion, the seaports prospered. The Greeks, too, enjoyed their religious festivals, which, in time, became increasingly orientated towards the pursuit of pleasure and, in particular, sport. Already by the fifth century BC Athens had become an important destination for travellers visiting major sights such as the Parthenon and so inns – often adjuncts of the temples – were established in major towns and seaports to provide for the travellers' needs. Innkeepers of this period were known to be difficult and unfriendly and the facilities they provided very basic: a pallet to sleep on, but no heating, no windows and no toilet facilities. Courtesans 'trained in the art of music, dance, conversation and making love' were the principal entertainment offered.

Early guides and guidebooks

Around 500 BC, some travellers took to recording their observations. Aristides, for example, made reference to the appalling conditions of the highways in Asia Minor in his *Sacred Discourses*. We have the writings of Herodotus, however, who lived between c. 484 and 424 BC, to thank for much of what we know of travel around this period. A noted historian and early traveller who can be accurately described as one of the world's first significant travel writers, he recorded extensively, and with some cynicism, the tall stories recounted to him by the travel guides of the day. It appears that these guides varied greatly in the quality and accuracy of the information they provided. The role of guides was divided between those whose task was to shepherd the tourists around the sites (the *periegetai*) and others who were to provide information for their charges (the *exegetai*). Liberties with the truth included the story that the great pyramids at Giza extended downwards into the Earth to the same extent as their height and the perfection of the dazzling white marble used in the greatest statues was such that viewers risked damaging their eyesight unless they averted their gaze. The philosopher Plutarch wrote to complain, a century before the birth of Christ, that guides insisted on talking too much about the inscriptions and epitaphs found at the sites, choosing to ignore the entreaties of the visitors to cut this short.

Guidebooks, too, made their appearance as early as the fourth century BC, covering destinations such as Athens, Sparta and Troy. Pausanias, a Greek travel writer, produced a noted 'Description of Greece' between AD 160 and 180 that, in its critical evaluation of facilities and destinations, acted as a model for later writers. Advertisements, in the form of signs directing visitors to wayside inns, are also known to have existed from this period.

It was under the Roman Empire, however, that international travel first became important. With no foreign borders between England and Syria, and with the seas safe from piracy owing to the Roman patrols, conditions favouring travel had at last arrived. Roman coinage was acceptable everywhere and Latin was the common language of the day. Romans travelled to Sicily, Greece, Rhodes, Troy, Egypt and, from the third century AD, the Holy Land. The Romans, too, introduced their guidebooks (*itineraria*), listing hostels with symbols to identify quality in a manner reminiscent of the present-day Michelin guides. The Roman poet Horace published an anti-travel ode following his travel experiences from Rome to Brindisi in 38–37 BC.

EXAMPLE   ## Travel writing through the ages

Travelogues, and accounts of travel, have taken on different styles and purposes over the centuries. Whilst travel writing may take the form of letters, diaries and journals composed during the trip, so travelogues often refer to the accounts composed retrospectively. Regardless of the form, the reading of travel literature has long held great attraction. 'Between the eighteenth and early twentieth centuries, accounts of travel were among the texts most commonly read' (p.2). Earliest accounts of journeys largely consisted of information and description of the places visited. The very writing of the 'story' was often seen to give meaning to the trip. The documenting of peacetime travel has existed for thousands of years, with the Greeks and Romans producing geographical and travel texts. By the late middle ages, many travelled (vagrants, royalty, missionaries, students) and many accounts of the journeys of merchants, missionaries and pilgrims existed. Travel writing in the sixteenth century consolidated into accounts of exploration and discovery of 'foreign places with fabulous races' (p.29), with a concern that earlier travel guides were prone to inaccuracies and lies. There was a shift from the heroic adventure to the scientist, writing to explain their world. Coupled with this was the growth in detail of atlases which attempted to provide greater levels of precision and accuracy. William Dampier's accounts of his journeys, a mix of scientific endeavours and privateer adventures (New Voyage around the World, 1697), were hugely popular reading when first published.

By the eighteenth century, the Grand Tour was widely practised by elite society, and widely discussed and recounted in literature. Renowned intellectuals (such as Samuel Johnson, John Milton, James Boswell, Henry Fielding, Horace Walpole, William Wordsworth and Lord Byron) travelled extensively to enhance their education and social skills, writing guidance on what could be gained from such travels. Works often included detail on everyday customs, to provide insights to others of the different cultures that could be expected to be experienced whilst travelling.

However, as greater levels of travel occurred, on well-trodden paths, following the routes of existing texts, so there was criticism from authors that such travel could offer little new in terms of literary insights. By the middle of the eighteenth century, travel writing therefore offered greater subjective accounts of journeys, incorporating the emotive experiences of the author whilst the end of the century reported a growing interest in the aesthetic landscape. Criticisms of the impacts of tourism were also appearing; Wordsworth's 'Guide to the Lakes' (1835) and Ruskin's 'Of Modern Landscapes' (1856) both decried the loss of the landscape to the invasion of tourists.

The nineteenth century saw the introduction of travel guides (such as those by Baedeker and Murray), whilst many Victorian travellers were documenting travel experiences, offering new perspectives on travel. Charles Dickens (American Notes, 1842), Anthony Trollope (North America, 1862) and Robert Louis Stevenson (An Inland Voyage, 1878) all provide accounts of their travels during this period.

Traditionally, travelogues were aimed at a male audience and male authors dominated the literary world. However, women were travelling at this time, with their husbands, as explorers, missionaries or just for pleasure. Often justification for travel was needed and their writing may have helped, in part, to have provided this. The form often took the shape of journals, diaries and letters.

Whilst critics of travel writing have proposed that the age of travel (rather than tourism) is over, therefore travel writing is dead, the modern day adventurers still write to tell their epic tales. Some may reflect the travels in the context of the changing political world whilst other embed their travels in wider discussions of human mobility. Importantly, in all its forms and styles travel literature today is still a popular read.

Source: adapted from Korte (2000) *English Travel Writing. From Pilgrimages to Postcolonial Explorations*

It is interesting to note, too, the growth of travel bureaucracy from the earliest stages of travel. Reference to passport-type documents can be traced to at least as far back as 1500 BC and there are biblical references to 'letters' allowing passage for travellers relating to the period around 450 BC (Lloyd, 2003). Later, exit permits were required to leave by many seaports and a charge was made for this service. The Roman *tractorium* is an early example of a passport-type document, issued during the reign of Augustus Caesar. Souvenirs acquired abroad were subject to an import duty and a customs declaration had to be completed.

The Roman Empire, too, suffered its share of 'cowboy operators', both at home and abroad. Among the souvenirs offered to Roman travellers were forgeries of Greek statues, especially works bearing the signature of Greece's most famous sculptor, Praxiteles. Popular souvenirs of the day included engraved glass vials, while professional stonecutters offered their services to inscribe graffiti on tourist sites. Roman writers of the day complained that Athens was becoming a 'city of shysters', bent on swindling the foreign tourist.

Domestic tourism flourished within the Roman Empire's heartland. Second homes were built by the wealthy within easy travelling distance of Rome – they were occupied particularly during the springtime social season. The most fashionable resorts were to be found around the Bay of Naples, and there is evidence of early market segmentation for these destinations. Naples itself attracted the retired and intellectuals, Cumae became a high-fashion resort, while Puteoli attracted the more staid tourist and Baiae, which was both a spa town and a seaside resort, attracted the downmarket tourist, becoming noted for its rowdiness, drunkenness and all-night singing. As the Roman philosopher Seneca put it, 'Why must I look at drunks staggering along the shore, or noisy boating parties?' (Casson, 1974, 32).

The distribution of administrators and the military during the days of the Roman Empire led to Romans making trips abroad to visit friends and relatives, establishing a precedent for the VFR movements of the present day. The rapid improvement in communications resulting from the Roman conquests aided the growth of travel. First-class roads, coupled with staging inns (precursors of the modern motels), led to comparatively safe, fast and convenient travel that was unsurpassed until modern times. There is even relatively recently found evidence that leisure cruises were taken by super-rich Romans: a 150-foot cruise ship, designed to provide luxurious travel along the coastal waters of the Mediterranean, was discovered by divers off the Sicilian coast in 2000. The ship was fitted with bedroom suites and even passenger lounges for social interaction.

Travel in the Middle Ages

Following the collapse of the Roman Empire and the onset of the so-called Dark Ages (fifth to eleventh century AD), travel became more dangerous, difficult and considerably less attractive – more synonymous with the concept of *travail*. The result was that most pleasure travel was undertaken close to home, although this does not mean that international travel was unknown. Adventurers sought fame and fortune through travel, merchants travelled extensively to seek new trade opportunities, strolling players and minstrels made their living by performing as they travelled (the most famous of these must be Blondel, a native of Picardy and friend of King Richard I, the Lionheart, whom he is reputed to have accompanied during the latter's crusade to the Holy Land). However, all these forms of travel would be identified either as business travel or travel from a sense of obligation or duty. In order for people to travel for pleasure, the conditions that favour travel must be in place.

Holidays played an important role in the life of the public. The word 'holiday' has its origin in the old English *haligdaeg*, or 'holy day' and, as we saw in the last chapter, from earliest times, religion provided the framework within which leisure time was spent. For most people, this implied a break from work rather than movement from one place to another. The village 'wakes' of the Middle Ages, held on the eve of patronal festivals, provide an example of such 'religious relaxation'. Such public holidays were, in fact, quite numerous – far more so than today; up until as recently as 1830, there were as many as

33 saints' days in the UK holiday calendar, which dispels the myth of peasants being engaged almost constantly in hard manual labour. For the pious, intent on fulfilling a religious duty, pilgrimages would be undertaken to places of worship, notably including Canterbury, York, Durham and, by the thirteenth century, Walsingham Priory in Norfolk. Chaucer's tales of one pilgrimage to Canterbury provide evidence that there was a pleasurable side to this travel, too.

Religious travel was not limited to the home country at this time. Once political stability was achieved on the Continent and in England following the Norman invasion in 1066, pilgrimages to important sacred sites abroad became increasingly commonplace. Among the most notable were Santiago de Compostela (where the ever-increasing flow of pilgrim tourists led to the creation of relatively sophisticated travel facilities along the pilgrim route by the fifteenth century), Rome and the Holy Land itself. Visits to the latter countries were generally routed via Venice, which itself became a wealthy and important stopover point and a trading centre for the pilgrims. In twelfth-century Rome, a marketing-orientated pope of the day encouraged the sale of badges bearing images of Saints Peter and Paul, iconic souvenirs of their visit (Fisher, 2004).

The focus on Western travellers has tended to mean that the development of travel elsewhere in the world has been ignored. Religious travel, to Mecca, birthplace of Mohammed, became important in the Middle East following the death of its founder in 632 and the rise of Islam. Yet Arab travel was by no means restricted to religious journeys.

Among many travellers, the name of Ibn Battuta (1165–1240) (Dunn, 1986) stands out. A spiritual philosopher, he undertook journeys comparable to those of Marco Polo, travelling over 70 000 miles in 25 years, visiting Russia, India, Manchuria and China, as well as nearer countries in North Africa and the Middle East. His travelogue, the *Rihla* (its full title may be translated as 'A Gift to the Observers concerning the Curiosities of the Cities and the Marvels encountered in Travels') examined not only the social and cultural history of Islam but also the politics, immigration and gender relations within the countries he visited.

Developments in road transport in the seventeenth to early nineteenth centuries

Before the sixteenth century, those who sought to travel had three modes for doing so: they could walk (many who were too poor to afford any other form of transport walked, regardless of the distance involved), ride a horse or be carried, either on a litter (carried by servants – an option restricted largely to the aristocracy) or on a carrier's wagon. This horse-drawn vehicle was slow and appallingly uncomfortable, as it had no springs. The roads of the time were poorly surfaced, potholed and, in winter, deeply rutted by the wagon wheels that churned the road into a sea of mud, making the journey an endurance test for passengers.

Toll roads were in evidence as early as 1267, but tollgates on turnpike roads became common from around 1663, adding to the cost of long-distance journeys. Any journey was also unsafe. Footpads and highwaymen abounded on the major routes, posing an ever-present threat to wayfarers. Apart from royalty and the court circle, who were always well guarded, only a handful of wealthy citizens, such as those with 'country seats' (second homes in the country) travelled for pleasure until well into the eighteenth century.

The development of the sprung coach was a huge advance for those who were obliged to travel. The construction of these coaches, in which the body of the coach was 'sprung' by being suspended from primitive leather straps, encouraged travel by offering a greater measure of comfort. The later introduction of metal, leaf-spring suspension further improved comfort. The invention in its most primitive form is traced to the Hungarian town of Kocs in the fifteenth century (from which the word 'coach' originates).

By the mid-1600s coaches were operating regularly in Britain, with records of a daily service operating between London and Oxford. The concept of the stagecoach, for which teams of horses would be used and changed at regular points along the route, greatly aided mobility. These appeared in England as early as the seventeenth century and were in use widely throughout Continental Europe by the middle of the eighteenth century (Austria, for example, introduced its first services in 1749). In the eighteenth century, the introduction of turnpike roads, which provided improved surfaces, for which tolls would be charged, enabled stagecoaches carrying between eight and 14 passengers to cover upwards of 40 miles a day during the summer. However, this still meant that a journey from London to Bath would take some three days, while the 400 miles to Edinburgh took fully 10 days.

Stagecoaches greatly aided the development of the North American colonies, with a service between Boston and New York introduced in 1772, and other routes serving Providence (Rhode Island), Philadelphia and Baltimore. However, mail coaches, which were to provide additional passenger accommodation, were not to make an appearance until the 1780s in Europe and the USA.

For those who could afford private transport, a wide variety of coaches came into service in the eighteenth and nineteenth centuries, including phaetons, landaus, barouches, broughams and cartouches.

Travel of some distance requires accommodation. At this time, such accommodation was basic. Inns sprang up to serve the needs of overnight guests and provide fresh horses, while lodgings or 'chambers' were available for rent to visitors when they arrived at their destinations.

Around 1815, the introduction of tarmacadam revolutionized the road systems of Europe and North America. For the first time, a hard surface less subject to pitting and ruts enabled rapid increases to be made in the average speed of coach services. Charabancs (public coaches drawn by teams of horses, with rows of transverse seats facing forwards) have been identified as far back as 1832. The name (which was derived from the French *char à bancs*, seated carriage) was later applied to the first motor coaches used for leisure travel in the early twentieth century. By the 1820s, the horse-drawn omnibus was a common sight in London and Paris, greatly improving local city transport. Mail coaches were now covering the distance between London and Bath in $12\frac{1}{2}$ hours, and the London to Brighton run was reduced to a little over five hours.

The Grand Tour

From the early seventeenth century, a new form of tourism developed as a direct outcome of the freedom and quest for learning heralded by the Renaissance. Under the reign of Elizabeth I, young men seeking positions at court were encouraged to travel to the Continent to finish their education. This practice was soon adopted by others high in the social circle and it eventually became customary for the education of a gentleman to be completed by a 'Grand Tour' (a term in use as early as 1670) of the major cultural centres of Europe, accompanied by a tutor and often lasting three years or more. Travel for reasons of education was affected by the fact that, under Elizabeth I, a special licence had to be obtained from the Crown in order to travel abroad, though universities had the privilege of granting licences themselves for the purpose of scholarship. The publication in 1749 of a guidebook by Dr Thomas Nugent entitled *The Grand Tour* gave a further boost to this educational travelling and some of the more intrepid ventured as far afield as Egypt. While ostensibly educational, as with the spas, the appeal soon became social and so pleasure-seeking young men of leisure travelled predominantly to France and Italy to enjoy the rival cultures and social life of cities such as Paris, Venice and Florence. By the end of the eighteenth century, the custom had become institutionalized for the gentry. The Grand Tour was by no means restricted to the British; Northern Europeans held a fascination with southern European countries and visits to cities in Italy in particular provided opportunities to develop their cultural knowledge of antiquity, architecture, music and arts. Such travels also provided opportunities to develop useful political and social contacts.

As a result, European towns and cities were opened up to the tourist (it was not until the close of the eighteenth century that the countryside, lakes and mountains held an appeal). Aix-en-Provence, Montpellier and Avignon became notable bases, especially for those using the Provence region as a staging post for travel to Italy. When pleasure travel followed in the nineteenth century, eventually to displace educational tours as the motive for Continental visits, this was to lead to the development of the Riviera as a principal destination for British tourists, aided by the introduction of regular steamboat services across the Channel from 1821 onwards. However, the Napoleonic wars early in the nineteenth century inhibited travel within Europe for some 30 years. By the time of Napoleon's defeat, the British had taken a greater interest in touring their own country.

EXAMPLE The rise of Nice as a popular tourist destination

Nice was seen initially as an unpleasant stopover point for those undertaking the Grand Tour. It was poor, had few facilities for the visitor and the roads along the Mediterranean coast were appalling. It was convenient geographically, however, and so, gradually, the number of English visitors grew.

By the end of the eighteenth century, a small colony of English invalids would winter in the town. The reputation of the town soon spread. Between 1860 and 1914, Nice was one of the fastest-growing European cities and entertainments proliferated, including shooting and roller skating.

Gradually, adjacent villages along the Côte d'Azur began to benefit from the prosperity of Nice. Not only the English, but wealthy Russians, too, were choosing to spend their winters in a more temperate climate. By the early twentieth century, however, newer resorts, such as Antibes and Cannes, had begun to entice visitors away from the town and its importance as a tourist base declined.

Authorization to travel

Travel outside the boundaries of one's country had often been subject to restrictions, as we have seen from constraints imposed by the state under the Roman Empire and even earlier authorities. In fact, at various times, some states have even imposed limitations on travel between towns and regions within their own territory. In eighteenth-century France, for example, internal passports were needed to travel between towns, while, prior to the War of Independence in America (1776–1781), similar internal passports were required to move between states.

The first use of the term 'passport' in law in Britain is thought to have occurred in 1548 (Lloyd, 2003). Such passports hark back directly to the medieval *testimoniale* – a letter from an ecclesiastical superior given to a pilgrim to avoid the latter's possible arrest on charges of vagrancy. Later, papers of authority to travel were more widely issued by the state, particularly during periods of warfare with neighbouring European countries.

Prior to the eighteenth century, few people travelled any great distance and those who did so were generally involved with affairs of state. Monarchs were suspicious of alliances with foreign states and vetted such travel carefully, issuing letters of authority to members of court, ostensibly to facilitate travel but equally to ensure that they were familiar with the movements of their subjects. In Britain, it was the prerogative of the monarch to control any movements of their subjects overseas and so, throughout the sixteenth and seventeenth centuries, applications had to be made for a 'licence to pass beyond the seas'. Such 'licences' became more frequent in the eighteenth and nineteenth centuries, but were prohibitively expensive for all but the wealthy as, in 1830, a British passport had cost £2/7/6 (or around £2.37 in today's decimal currency, equivalent to around £166 today), then a high weekly level of pay. Demand was to cut this figure to just 2/- (or 10 pence) by 1858 – still equivalent to a day's pay for many.

Nevertheless, from the late eighteenth century on, demand for travel was growing, to a point where it became impossible to issue passports in the traditional way. In Britain, it had been the practice for the Foreign Secretary to issue all passports, based on his personal knowledge of the applicant, but, by the mid-nineteenth century, this was clearly no longer practical.

The Alien Bill (1792) – introduced in Britain at a time when the government was becoming concerned about who was coming to Britain (in the lead-up to war with France) – required foreigners entering Britain to be in possession of passports from 1793 onwards and to register on arrival – the first modern form of immigration control. This restriction was not lifted until 1826. Curiously, however, around this period, countries such as France and Belgium appeared willing to issue passports to non-citizens, including Britons. Lloyd (2003) recounts the story of the poet Robert Browning eloping with Elizabeth Barrett Browning in 1846 travelling on a French passport.

By the mid-nineteenth century, many European countries began to abandon most passport requirements other than in times of war. This paralleled policy in the USA, which made no requirement for passports except during the Civil War (following the War of Independence, individual states, as well as the Department of Foreign Affairs, had been permitted to issue passports for foreign travel). Regulations were introduced in 1846 in the UK for the movement of merchants and diplomats, but those travelling purely for leisure were no longer obliged to carry formal documentation (although immigration controls were reintroduced in Britain by the Aliens Act of 1905).

Once a nation deems travel documents no longer necessary for its citizens, it becomes difficult to reimpose such a requirement. When Belgium sought to oblige visitors to present passports for inspection in 1882, there was widespread indignation in the British press. World War I was to change all this. New passports, accompanied by a photograph of the bearer, were widely introduced and the League of Nations standardized their design in 1921. Britain made passports compulsory in 1916, although by 1924 Belgium was again allowing Britons to travel on no passport excursions to the Continent.

Other political hindrances to travel

Many essentially political factors affect the movement of tourists between countries. A critical one is the political relationship between the generating and destination countries. All through history, the European nations have been at war with one another and clearly the desire to travel in the territories of a recent or former enemy will be limited, just as willingness to visit those of former allies will be enhanced. At times of tension, border controls will inhibit travel and some nationalities may be excluded, while, at the very least, visas or other documentary requirements may be imposed on less friendly nations. It has also been common, particularly in recent history, for countries to refuse entry to visitors who have travelled to or through a nation with which the destination country is in conflict or which it does not recognize (a number of Middle East countries refuse entry to visitors with an Israeli stamp in their passport, for example).

Decisions concerning the value of a currency relative to others, even where economically motivated, are nonetheless political. Such decisions directly affect the buying power of tourists travelling abroad and will either discourage travel or switch travellers to destinations where exchange rates are more favourable. Of course, the use of common currencies in different countries facilitates travel. As we have seen, under the Roman Empire the universal acceptance of Roman coinage greatly encouraged travel, by contrast with the vast range of currencies to be found, even within individual countries, in the Middle Ages. Fynes Moryson, an academic who travelled extensively on the Continent, was to write in 1589 that he found over 20 different coinages in Germany, five in the Low Countries and as many as eight in Switzerland. Moneychangers cheated visitors as a matter of course and were sometimes difficult to find. The adoption of the euro as a common currency in 17 of the 27 countries within the EU – the first such common currency since the days of the Roman Empire – has been a motivating factor in generating inter-European tourism. It also has its downside, however, as we shall see in the next chapter.

Further political hindrance occurs in the form of taxation, which has affected travel from the very earliest periods of tourism history. The opportunity to enhance a nation's coffers at the expense of the foreign tourist was also widely recognized in the Middle Ages. Indeed, the first spa tax is known to have been introduced in Bad Pyrmont, Saxony, as early as 1413. History also reveals how tourists react to high taxation, switching to other destinations where costs are lower, so measures to tax tourists are always subject to economic sensitivity.

The development of the spas

Spas were already well established during the time of the Roman Empire, but their popularity, based on the supposed medical benefits of the waters, had lapsed in subsequent centuries. They were never entirely out of favour, however. The sick continued to visit Bath throughout the Middle Ages. Renewed interest in the therapeutic qualities of mineral waters can be traced to the influence of the Renaissance in Britain and other European centres.

In 1562, Dr William Turner published a book drawing attention to the curative powers of the waters at Bath and on the Continent. Bath itself, along with the spa at Buxton, had been showing a return to popularity among those 'seeking the cure' and the effect of Dr Turner's book was to establish the credibility of the resorts' claims.

In 1626, Elizabeth Farrow drew attention to the qualities of the mineral springs at Chalybeate in Scarborough, which became the first of a number of new spa resorts. In the same year, Dr Edmund Deane wrote his *Spadacrene Anglica*, which praised what he claimed were 'the strongest sulphur springs in Great Britain' at Harrogate. This rapidly led to the popularity of the town as a spa resort – a role it continues to enjoy today.

Soon, an astonishing number of other spa resorts sprang up, sometimes in unlikely places. Streatham in south London, for instance, became briefly fashionable following the discovery of mineral springs there in 1659. Between 1560 and 1815, at one time or another as many as 175 different spas were operating in England, although only three of these – at Bath, Buxton and Hotwells in Bristol – actually incorporated thermal springs in their cures. By 1815, seven of the spas had purpose-built theatres to provide entertainment.

Figure 2.1 The Continental spa: the casino at Spa, Belgium
Photo by Chris Holloway

'Taking the cure' rapidly developed social status and the resorts changed in character as pleasure rather than health became the motivation for visits. Bath in particular became a major centre for social life for high society during the eighteenth and early nineteenth centuries, aided by visits from the monarchs of the day. Under the guidance of Beau Nash at the beginning of the eighteenth century, it soon became a centre of high fashion, deliberately setting out to create a select and exclusive image. The commercial possibilities opened up by the concentration of these wealthy visitors were not overlooked and facilities to entertain or otherwise cater for these visitors proliferated, changing the spas into what we would today term holiday resorts rather than watering places. The building of the Pump Rooms as a focal point within Bath was a key development, leading to the town's success as a resort, while Harrogate, similarly, benefited from the construction of its own Pump Room in 1841–1842.

Eventually, in the early nineteenth century, the common tendency of resorts to go 'downmarket' in the course of their lifecycle led to a changing clientele, with the landed gentry being replaced by wealthy merchants and the professional class. By the end of the eighteenth century, the heyday of the English spas was over, although they were to have a far longer lifecycle on the Continent (see Figure 2.1).

The popularity of the spas on the Continent may be ascribed to the belief in their efficacy by the general public, supported by members of the medical profession, to the extent that public funding was, and still is in some cases, provided by the state for those needing treatment. The town of Spa in Belgium gave its name to the concept of a centre for the treatment of illness through taking, or bathing in, the mineral waters (or later, by the application to the body of mud or other substances with perceived healing qualities). Spas rapidly became popular in Germany (town names with the appendage 'Bad' or 'Baden' all owe their origins to their spas), Italy (resorts with the title of 'terme' also originated as spas) and middle European countries such as Hungary and Czechoslovakia.

The spa town of Baden-Baden

Located in the foothills of the Black Forest in Germany, this town has a history as a popular spa location stretching back to the Roman days, although it fell out of favour throughout the Middle Ages. The early nineteenth century saw its revival, with visits by Queen Victoria, Kaiser Wilhelm I, Napoleon III, Berlioz, Brahms and Dostoyevsky enhancing its reputation as a sophisticated playground for the rich and famous (Frommer's, 2010). The town became a popular meeting place for celebrities, visiting to enjoy the benefits of the hot springs as well as the casino, races and luxury hotels. Today it offers thermal baths (with 800 000 litres of hot curative waters rising daily from 12 thermal springs), wellness and beauty therapies and medical facilities for health checks and rehabilitation; yet it is also the casino (Germany's oldest and largest), events, arts and shopping which bring tourists in their numbers.

There are interesting parallels between the decline of the English spas and of the English seaside resorts 150 or so years later. The spa towns were seen as attractive places in which to live and residents gradually supplanted visitors. Those residents tended to be older and their demands for more passive and traditional entertainment, with a preference for entertaining at home rather than seeking commercial entertainment, hastened the spas' economic decline. However, it was the rise of the seaside resorts that did much to undermine the success of the inland spas, just as later it would be the rise of the Mediterranean resorts which would lead to the decline of the UK and other more northerly seaside resorts.

The rise of the seaside resort

Until the Renaissance, bathing in the sea found little favour in Britain. Although not entirely unknown before then, such bathing as did occur was undertaken unclothed and this behaviour conflicted with the mores of the day. Only when the sea became associated with certain health benefits did bathing gain popularity.

The association of sea water with health did not find acceptance until the early years of the eighteenth century and, initially, the objective was to drink it rather than bathe in it. It is perhaps to be expected that health theorists would eventually recognize that the minerals to be found in spa waters were also present in abundance in sea water.

By the early eighteenth century, small fishing resorts around the English coast were beginning to attract visitors seeking 'the cure', both by drinking sea water and by immersing themselves in it. Not surprisingly, Scarborough, as the only traditional spa bordering the sea, was one of the first to exploit this facility for the medical benefits it was believed to offer, and both this town and Brighton were attracting regular visitors by the 1730s. However, it was Dr Richard Russell's noted medical treatise 'A dissertation on the use of sea water in the diseases of the glands, particularly the scurvy, jaundice, king's evil, leprosy, and the glandular consumption', published in 1752 (two years earlier in Latin), which is credited with popularizing the custom of sea bathing more widely. Soon Blackpool, Southend and other English seaside resorts were wooing bathers to their shores (see Figure 2.2). Blackpool, in fact, had attracted some categories of sea bather well before its growth as a resort. Workers in the area are known to have travelled there by cart in order to wash off the accumulation of dirt resulting from their jobs. The heyday of these 'Padjamers', as they were known, was in the century between 1750 and 1850.

Figure 2.2 An English beach scene in 1810, painted by English caricaturist James Gillray

The growing popularity of taking the cure, which resulted from the wealth generated by the expansion of trade and industry in the UK at the time, meant that the inland spas could no longer cater satisfactorily for the influx of visitors they were attracting. By contrast, the new seaside resorts offered almost boundless opportunity for expansion. Moral doubts about exposing one's body in the sea were overcome by the invention of the bathing machine and the resorts prospered.

EXAMPLE   **The use of bathing machines**

For elite society, bathing costumes were not considered 'proper' attire so attempts were made to ensure that the bather could change clothes and enter the sea with privacy. These machines were mostly wooden carts with walls and a roof, which were then wheeled from the beach into the water, allowing the bather to descend a few steps into the sea (Jennings and Gayle, 2007). It is known that these existed at beaches across the UK, and, perhaps through the influence of UK tourists, spread to resorts in France, Germany, Australia and the USA.

These contraptions were generally pulled into and from the water by human or horse power, although a machine, running on railway tracks and pulled by a static steam engine, operated in Folkstone, England. Its inventor, Walter Fagg, included nine changing rooms, showers and a toilet into the design. The machines remained in use into the early twentieth century (Spurrier, 2008).

As attitudes to mixed-sex bathing shifted so the need for such contraptions declined. Many machines initially became static changing rooms on the shorefront, and eventually fell out of use.

Undoubtedly, the demand for seaside cures could have been even greater in the early years if fast, cheap transport had been developed to cater for this need. In the mid-eighteenth century, however, it still took two days to travel from London to Brighton and the cost was well beyond the reach of the average worker, at the equivalent of six weeks' pay. Accommodation provision, too, grew only slowly, outpaced by demand, but all this was to change in the early nineteenth century.

First, the introduction of steamboat services reduced the cost and time of travel from London to the resorts near the Thames Estuary. In 1815, a service began operating between London and Gravesend and, five years later, to Margate. The popularity of these services was such that other pleasure boat services were quickly introduced to more distant resorts (the first commercial service between Scotland and Ireland was established in 1819). This development required the construction of piers to provide landing stages for the vessels. The functional purpose of the seaside pier was soon overtaken by its attraction as a social meeting point and a place to take the sea air.

It was the introduction of steamboat services also linking the UK and Continental Europe, however, that posed the first threat to Britain's seaside resorts. Brighton established a ferry link with Dieppe as early as 1761 and later this was followed by links between Dieppe and the towns of Shoreham and Newhaven. It has been estimated that by the 1820s some 150 000 visitors a year were travelling from the UK to mainland Europe, many for the purposes of visiting coastal resorts.

At first, from about 1780 onwards, travel was concentrated along the Riviera, between the mouth of the Var and the Gulf of Spezia. The Italian resorts benefited from direct steamer services from London and Liverpool to Genoa. Before the advent of the railways, stagecoaches or hired carriages took three weeks to travel from London to Rome, but direct steamboats to Italy were to reduce this by half. Soon, French resorts were attracting UK visitors along the north coast between Boulogne and Cherbourg. The UK visitors insisted on facilities that met their particular needs, including churches of their favourite denominations and British shops, chemists, physicians and newspapers. The more successful French resorts quickly provided these. From 1880 onwards, the Train Bleu offered wealthy UK visitors elegant sleeping accommodation from Paris to the Riviera, popularizing not only summer but also winter holidays to escape the cold of the British climate.

Seaside resorts were also finding favour with the nobility and wealthy of other countries by this time. Aristocratic Russians travelled to the Crimea, the Baltic and the South of France for their holidays, while wealthy Americans on the Eastern seaboard frequented the first resorts developed along the New Jersey, New York and New England coastlines, with the most wealthy of them building second homes in the nineteenth century along the Rhode Island shores.

Conditions favouring the expansion of travel in the nineteenth century

From this brief history of travel from earliest times to the nineteenth century, we can see that a number of factors have been at work in encouraging travel. We can divide these into two categories: factors that make travel possible (*enabling* factors) and those that persuade people to travel (*motivating* factors).

Historical perspective of enabling factors

In order for travel to be possible at all, people must have adequate time and money to undertake it. Throughout most of history, however, and until very recently, both of these have been the prerogative of a very few members of society. Leisure time for the masses was very limited. Workers laboured from morning to night, six days a week, and were encouraged to treat Sundays (and the not infrequent Saints' days) as days of rest and worship. Pay was barely adequate to sustain a family and buy the basic necessities of life. The idea of paid holidays was not even considered until the twentieth century.

Equally important, the development of pleasure travel depends on the provision of suitable travel facilities. The growth of travel and transport are interdependent: travellers require transport that is priced within their budget and is fast, safe, comfortable and convenient. As we have seen, none of these criteria was being met until the latter half of the eighteenth century, but, from the early nineteenth century onwards, rapid improvements in technology led to transport that was both fast and moderately priced.

The development of transport during the nineteenth century will be examined in greater detail shortly. Suffice it to say here that good transport must be complemented by adequate accommodation at the traveller's destination. The traditional places to stay for travellers in the Middle Ages were the monasteries, but these were dissolved in Britain during the reign of Henry VIII and the resulting hiatus acted as a further deterrent to travel for everyone apart from those planning to stay with friends or relatives. The gradual improvement in lodgings that accompanied the introduction of the mail coaches and stagecoaches went some way to correcting this shortage. The general inadequacy of facilities away from the major centres of population, though, meant that towns such as London, Exeter and York, with their abundant social life and entertainment as a magnet, were to become the first centres to attract large numbers of visitors for leisure purposes.

Other constraints awaited those prepared to ignore these drawbacks to travel. In cities, public health standards were low, so travellers risked disease – a risk compounded in the case of foreign travel. Exchange facilities for foreign travel were unreliable, rates of exchange were inconsistent and travellers risked being cheated, so they tended to carry large amounts of money with them, making them prey to highwaymen. Foreign currencies were, in any event, chaotic, as noted earlier. As we have also seen, travel documents of some kind were generally necessary, too, and, at times, not easy to come by. Political suspicion frequently meant long delays in obtaining permission to travel.

Historical perspective of motivating factors

Removing these constraints encourages growth in travel. The real motivation for travel must be intrinsic, however – the desire to travel for its own sake, to get away from one's everyday surroundings and become acquainted with other places, cultures and people. It was the rapid urbanization of the population in the UK that provided the impetus for travel in the nineteenth century.

The industrial revolution had led to massive migration of the population away from the villages and countryside and into the industrial cities, where work was plentiful and better paid. This migration was to have two important side-effects on the workers themselves. First, workers became conscious of the beauty and attractions of their former rural surroundings for the first time. Cities were dark, polluted and treeless. Formerly, workers had little appreciation of their environment – living in the midst of the natural beauty of the countryside, they accepted it without question. Now, they longed to escape from the cities in what little free time they had – a characteristic still evident among twenty-first-century city-dwellers, too. Second, the type of work available in the cities was both physically and psychologically stressful. The comparatively leisurely pace of life in the countryside was replaced by monotonous factory work, so any escape from its routine and pace was welcome.

The expansion of the UK economy that took place as a result of the increased productivity created by the industrial revolution led to growth in real purchasing power for every worker, while worldwide demand for British goods created a huge business travel market. Increased wealth stimulated rapid growth in the population at this time, too.

In short, the UK at the beginning of the nineteenth century stood poised on the threshold of a considerable escalation in the demand for travel. The introduction of modern transport systems at this point in history was to translate this demand into reality.

The age of steam

Two technological developments in the early part of the nineteenth century were to have a profound effect on transport and the growth in travel generally. These were driven by the arrival of steam power; the first of these was the advent of the railway, the second the development of steamships.

The railways

The first passenger railway was built in England, between Stockton and Darlington, in 1825. It was to herald a major programme of railway construction throughout the world and a huge shift in the ability to travel. We have noted the problems of travelling by road that existed up to that point and, although travel by canal had become possible by 1760, it was too slow a mode to attract travellers as it was used essentially for the carriage of freight. As a means of transport for all purposes, canals were to suffer a rapid decline after 1825, when railways made travel at 13 mph possible for the first time – which was also at least three miles an hour faster than the fastest mail coaches.

Invicta, the first steam-driven passenger train (based on the design of Stephenson's *Rocket*), made the first passenger journey between Whitstable Bay and Canterbury on 3 May, 1830, carrying day trippers. In the decade that followed the construction of a rail link between Liverpool and Manchester in the same year, trunk routes sprang up between the major centres of population and industry in the UK, on mainland Europe and throughout the world. In the USA, for example, passenger services on the east coast were being built from the 1820s and, by 1869, a transcontinental link was in place. One of the last great rail routes – the Trans-Siberian – opened in 1903, connecting Moscow with Vladivostok and Port Arthur (now Lüshun).

In the UK, after their initial function to serve the needs of commerce, new routes emerged linking these centres to popular coastal resorts such as Brighton, for the first time bringing these within reach of the mass of those travelling for pleasure. On the whole, however, the railway companies appeared to be slow to recognize the opportunities for travel for pleasure offered by the development of rail services, concentrating instead on providing for the needs of business travellers. Certainly, in the 1840s, the growth of regular passenger traffic was enough to occupy them: between 1842 and 1847, the annual number of passengers travelling by train rose from 23 million to 51 million.

Competition between the railway companies was initially based on service rather than price, although from the earliest days of the railways a new market developed for short day trips. Before long, however, entrepreneurs began to stimulate rail travel by organizing excursions for the public at special fares. In some cases, these took place on regular train services, but, in others, special trains were chartered in order to take travellers to their destinations, setting a precedent for the charter services by air that were to become so significant a feature of tour operating a century later. As an indication of the speed with which these opportunities were put in place, within 12 days of the rail line to Scarborough being opened in 1845, an excursion train from Wakefield was laid on to carry 1000 passengers to the seaside.

EXAMPLE **Tours by rail**

Thomas Cook, contrary to popular opinion, was not, in fact, the first entrepreneur to organize tours for the public. Sir Rowland Hill, who became chairman of the Brighton Railway Company, is sometimes credited with this innovation (others have suggested that the first package tour can, in fact, be traced to a group of tourists taken from Wadebridge to Bodmin to witness a public hanging!) and there were certainly excursion trains in operation by 1840. All the same, Cook was to have by far the greatest impact on the early travel industry. In 1841, as secretary of the South Midland Temperance Association, he organized an excursion for his members from Leicester to Loughborough, at a fare of 1 shilling (the equivalent of 5 pence) return. The success of this venture – 570 took part – encouraged him to arrange similar excursions using chartered trains and, by 1845, he was organizing these trips on a fully commercial basis.

The result of these and similar ventures by other entrepreneurs led to a substantial number of pleasure-bound travellers to the seaside. In 1844, it is recorded that almost 15 000 passengers travelled from London to Brighton on the three Easter holidays alone, while hundreds of thousands travelled to other resorts to escape the smoke and grime of the cities. The enormous growth in this type of traffic can be appreciated when it is revealed that, by 1862, Brighton received 132 000 visitors on Easter Monday alone.

Supported by a more sympathetic attitude to pleasure travel by public authorities such as the Board of Trade, the railway companies themselves were actively promoting these excursions by the 1850s, while at the same time introducing a range of discounted fares for day trips, weekend trips and longer journeys. By 1855, Cook had extended his field of operations to mainland Europe, organizing the first 'inclusive tours' to the Paris Exhibition of that year. This followed the success of his excursions to the Great Exhibition in London in 1851, which in all had welcomed a total of 3 million visitors.

Cook was a man of vision in the world of travel. The success of his operations was due to the care he took in organizing his programmes to minimize problems. He had close contacts with hotels, shipping companies and railways throughout the world, ensuring that he obtained the best possible service as well as cheap prices for the services he provided. By escorting his clients throughout their journeys abroad, he took the worry out of travel for the first-time traveller. He also made the administration of travel easier by introducing the hotel voucher in 1867, which allowed tourists to prepay for their hotel accommodation and produce evidence to the hotels that this had been done. In 1874, he also introduced the 'circular note', the precursor to today's traveller's cheque – a promissory note that could be exchanged abroad for local currency. This greatly helped to overcome the problems arising from the many different coinages in use in Europe. The latter was not a totally new concept – a certain Robert Herries set up the London Banking Exchange Company in 1772 in order to issue similar documents – but it was Cook (and, later, in North America, American Express, which introduced the first traveller's cheque in 1891) who popularized these ideas, making travel far more tolerable for the Victorian traveller.

The coincidental invention of photography in the mid-nineteenth century further stimulated overseas travel for reasons of prestige. For the first time, visitors abroad could be photographed against a background of the great historical sites of Europe, to the envy of their friends.

The expansion of the railways was accompanied by a simultaneous decline in the stagecoaches. Some survived by providing feeder services to the nearest railway stations, but overall road traffic shrank and, with it, the demand for the staging inns. These offered very different services from those expected of a hotel and, while the concept of the 'modern hotel' can be traced back as far as 1764, it was the railways, from around 1840 onwards, that were to drive the development of hotels as we know them today. Inns situated in resorts were quick to adapt to meet the needs of the new railway travellers, but the supply of accommodation in centres served by the railways was totally inadequate to meeting the burgeoning demand of this new market.

A period of hotel construction began, in which the railway companies themselves were leaders, establishing the great railway terminus hotels that came to play such a significant role in the hotel industry over the next 100 years. The high capital investment called for by this development led to the formation of the first hotel chains and corporations.

Social changes in the Victorian era all encouraged travel. The new-found interest in sea bathing meant that the expanding rail network favoured the developing resorts, accelerating their growth. At the same time, Victorian society placed great emphasis on the role of the family as a social unit, leading to the type of family holidays for which the seaside was so well suited. The foundations of traditional seaside entertainment were soon laid – military bands, minstrels and pierrots, Punch and Judy shows, barrel organs, donkey rides, music-hall and variety shows, and the seaside pier – all became essential components (BBC, 2010).

Resorts began to develop different social images, partly as a result of their geographical location: those nearer London or other major centres of population developed a substantial market of day trippers, while others deliberately aimed for a more exclusive clientele. These latter generally tended to be situated further afield, but, in some cases, their exclusivity arose from the desire of prominent residents to resist the encroachment of the railways for as long as possible. Bournemouth, for example, held out against the extension of the railway from Poole until 1870. Some areas of early promise as holiday resorts were quickly destroyed by the growth of industry – Swansea and Hartlepool, for example, and Southampton, where beaches gave way to the development of docks.

Health continued to play a role in the choice of holiday destinations, but the emphasis gradually switched from the benefits of sea bathing to those of sea air. Climate became a feature of the resorts' promotion. Sunshine hours were emphasized or the bracing qualities of the Scarborough air, while the pines at Bournemouth were reputed to help those suffering from lung complaints. Seaside resorts on the Continent also gained in popularity and began to develop their own social images – Scheveningen near The Hague, Ostend, Biarritz and Deauville offering the same magic for UK holidaymakers as the Mediterranean resorts were to provide a century later. Some overseas resorts flourished as a result of a reaction to middle-class morality in Victorian England – Monte Carlo, with its notorious gambling casino, being a case in point.

The desire to escape from one's everyday environment was as symptomatic of nineteenth-century life as it was to become in the middle of the twentieth century. Of course, destinations on the Continent were to attract only the relatively well off and the railways produced services to cater for these high-spend tourists. Trains such as the Train Bleu, which entered service between Paris and the Côte d'Azur and Rome in 1883, and the Orient Express of the same year, operating from Paris to the Black Sea, provided unsurpassed levels of luxury for rail travellers on the Continent.

Long-distance rail services became possible with the introduction of sleeping cars, invented in the USA by George Pullman and Ben Field in 1865 and introduced into Europe by the French Wagons-Lits company in 1869. These luxury carriages were first introduced into the UK on the London to Glasgow route in 1873 and were operating on the London to Brighton run by 1881. The first restaurant car arrived in 1879, on the London to Leeds route.

Other forms of holidaymaking – opened up by the advent of the railways on the Continent – arose from the impact of the Romantic Movement of mid-Victorian England. Even limited rail charters were introduced for travel to Germany, Italy, the French Riviera and Spain. The Rhine and the French Riviera in particular benefited from their new-found romantic appeal, while the invigorating mountain air of Switzerland, combining the promise of better health with opportunities for strenuous outdoor activities, was already drawing tourists from the UK by the 1840s. Mountaineering became a popular pastime for the British in the 1860s and was later spurred on by the introduction in Switzerland of skiing.

The use of skis as a sport is credited to a certain Bjorland Blom, Sheriff of Telemark in Norway, in the 1660s. By the beginning of the 1890s, visitors had transported the sport to Switzerland, while Mathias Zdardsky, similarly, brought skis to his native Austria in 1890. Sir Henry Lunn, the British travel entrepreneur, is credited with the commercialization of winter ski holidays in Switzerland, having organized packages to Chamonix before the end of the nineteenth century.

The railways made their own contributions to these developments, but, above all, they encouraged the desire to travel by removing the hazards of foreign travel that had formerly existed for travellers journeying by road.

The influence of rail travel on early tourism in North America

Just as tourism was growing within Europe during the nineteenth century, parallel patterns of tourism were developing across the Atlantic, too. At first, in the early part of the century, a few seaside resorts grew up to cater for tourists from the major North American conurbations within the original 13 states. Fashionable resorts developed at Newport, Rhode Island, Cape May and Atlantic City in New Jersey and along the Massachusetts coast, while more popular resorts closer to New York City, such as those on the coast of New Jersey and Long Island, catered to the needs of the masses, who could reach these on day trips. Spa resorts were also developing at this time, with Saratoga Springs in upstate New York becoming particularly popular. Others, in resorts such as French Lick, Indiana, White Sulphur Springs in West Virginia (popular with early US presidents), Hot Springs, Arkansas, and Glenwood Springs, Colorado, prospered and they still owe some economic dependence to their attraction as tourist resorts today.

The Americans were quick to adopt the newly invented steam railways, with the Baltimore and Ohio Railroad formed as early as 1830. The Pacific Railroad Act (1862) gave the green light to a cross-continental rail service, completed in 1869, that served both business and leisure needs. Interest in rugged landscapes, especially mountain tourism, ran parallel with this development in Europe, with travellers visiting the mountainous regions of eastern USA by the 1820s. The less adventurous visited the mountain ranges across New England. The Catskill Mountains, in upstate New York, were popular, an especial draw being the accommodation at the Mountain House, which flourished from 1824 until the 1930s (an early example of accommodation and destination being inseparable).

A short time later, Niagara Falls became the travellers' target, soon to be popularized by improved accessibility, with the development of paved roads and railways. Canadian tourism, meanwhile, was developing to cater to the needs of expanding populations in and around Toronto and Montreal, with visits to the St Lawrence Seaway, Niagara Falls and the Maine coast soon becoming popular. The absence of any border formalities between Canada and the USA, and the common language (at least for the large part of Canada), facilitated the movement of tourists between the countries, giving holidaymakers the comforting sense of reassurance with the familiar while 'travelling abroad' – a characteristic that continues to enhance travel in North America to this day.

Steamships

Just as the technological developments of the early nineteenth century led to the development of railways on land, so steam was also harnessed at sea, to drive new generations of ships. Here, necessity was the mother of invention. Increasing trade worldwide, especially with North America, required the UK to develop faster, more reliable forms of communication by sea with the rest of the world. Although, as we have seen, ferry services were operating as early as 1761 between Brighton and Dieppe, the first regular commercial cross-Channel steamship service was introduced in 1821, on the Dover – Calais route. The railway companies were quick to recognize the importance of their links with these cross-Channel ferry operators and, by 1862, they had gained the right to own and operate steamships themselves. Soon after, control over the ferry companies was in the hands of the railways, which rapidly expanded cross-Channel services.

EXAMPLE **Boat trains from the UK**

The railway companies recognized the benefits in operating boat trains, services which linked with steam-ship departures. By the mid-nineteenth century, railway companies were permitted to operate passenger steamers and so expanded their operations. In 1848, the Chester and Holyhead Railway introduced ferry services between Holyhead and Kingstown (now Dun Laoghaire) whilst London & South Western Railway established a route to the Channel Islands and Le Havre. Following on their success, South Eastern Railway gained permission in 1853 to run a Folkestone to Boulogne service. The UK railways also engaged in joint operations with their European counterparts, to coordinate services and routes (for example the London Brighton & South Coast Railway worked with Chemin de Fer de L'Ouest of France using the Newhaven to Dieppe route).

Source: Naughton, 2010

Deep sea services were introduced on routes to North America and the Far East, with the paddle-wheel steamer *Savannah* being the first to operate across the Atlantic, sailing between Savannah and Liverpool in 1819 and using steam as an auxiliary to sails. The Peninsular and Oriental Steam Navigation Company (later P&O) is credited with the first regular long-distance steamship service, beginning operations to India and the Far East in 1838. This company was soon followed by the Cunard Steamship Company, which, with a lucrative mail contract, began regular services to the North American continent in 1840. The UK, by being the first to establish regular deep sea services of this kind, came to dominate the world's shipping in the second half of the century, although it was soon to be challenged by other leading industrial nations on the popular North American route. This prestigious and highly profitable route prospered not only from mail contracts but also from the huge demand from passengers and freight as trade with the North American continent expanded. Later, the passenger trade would be boosted by the flow of emigrants from Europe (especially Ireland) and a smaller but significant number of American visitors to Europe. Thomas Cook played his part in stimulating the package tour market to North America, taking the first group of tourists in 1866. In 1872, he went on to organize the first round-the-world tour, taking 12 clients for 220 days at a cost of some £200 – more than the average annual salary at the time.

The Suez Canal, opened in 1869, stimulated demand for P&O's services to India and beyond, as Britain's Empire looked eastwards. The global growth of shipping led, in the latter part of the century, to the formation of shipping conferences, which developed cartel-like agreements on fares and conditions applicable to the carriage of traffic. The aim of these agreements was to ensure year-round profitability in an unstable and seasonal market, but the result was to stifle competition on the basis of price and eventually led to excess profits that were to be enjoyed by the shipping companies until the advent of airline competition in the mid-twentieth century.

Other late nineteenth-century developments

As the Victorian era drew to a close, other social changes came into play. Continued enthusiasm for the healthy outdoor life coincided with the invention of the first modern bicycle in 1866 (derived from the earlier and far more clumsy velocipede of 1818). A London Bicycle Club was established in 1875 and, three years later, the formation of a national Cyclists' Touring Club did much to promote the enjoyment of cycling holidays. This movement not only paved the way for later interest in outdoor activities on holiday but also may well have stimulated the appeal of the suntan as a status symbol of health and wealth, in marked contrast to the earlier association in Victorian minds of a fair complexion with gentility and breeding. The bicycle offered, for the first time, the opportunity for mobile rather than centred holidays and gave a foretaste of the popularity of motoring holidays in the early years of the following century.

Political stability in the final years of the nineteenth century and opening years of the twentieth also allowed the expansion of travel. Significantly, no conflicts occurred on the European Continent between 1871 and 1914 – one of the longest stretches of peacetime in history – and a Europe at peace was becoming an attractive place to visit, both for Europeans and tourists from further afield, such as the USA.

As tourism grew in the later years of the century, so the organizers of travel became established institutions. Thomas Cook and Sir Henry Lunn (who founded Cooperative Educational Tours in 1893, and whose name was retained until very recently in the company Lunn Poly, now renamed Thomson by its TUI owner) are two of the best-known names of the period, but many other well-known companies also became established at this time. Dean and Dawson appeared in 1871, Frames Tours in 1881 and the Polytechnic Touring Association (PTA) (which was to become the second half of the Lunn Poly brand) in 1888. In the USA, American Express (founded by, among others, Henry Wells and William Fargo of Wells Fargo fame) initiated money orders and travellers' cheques, although the company did not become involved in making holiday arrangements until early in the twentieth century.

EXAMPLE The Polytechnic Touring Association (PTA) and Henry Lunn - Lunn Poly

The Polytechnic of Central London (now the University of Westminster), founded by Quintin Hogg, established a touring association, to manage the travel arrangements for its members, some of whom were students. The origins of the touring association were reported to be 1888, with group visits to the Paris Exhibition in 1889 and the Chicago World Fair in 1893 also organized. However, there is some evidence that *ad hoc* trips to Switzerland, France and Wales were reported in the Polytechnic magazines as early as 1885. The trips were often educational, with physical activities such as hiking included in the programme. By the second decade of the twentieth century, over 16 000 people were participating in continental trips. So significant were their activities that Thomas Cook, the travel organizer, wrote to the government's education department to complain that this educational organization was competing unfairly with his own travel activities, as these tours were being offered to the wider public rather than just members of the Polytechnic.

So significant was the scale of this business that chalets were purchased, initially near Lucerne, then elsewhere in Europe, as a base for the holidaymakers. Following this, a steamship (the Ceylon) was purchased for cruises of the Norwegian fjords, with Polytechnic employees acting as guides.

The success of the PTA lay in offering cheaper travel and expanding the range of tours offered. They were also innovative; by the start of World War II they were offering a range of special-interest tours and all-inclusive 'master tickets', ensuring that travellers could participate in all the local excursions at no extra cost. In 1899, Henry Lunn proposed that the Polytechnic work with his own fledgling company on the winter travel programme. By the 1960s, the PTA business was merged with that of Henry Lunn to form the travel business Lunn Poly. This was later purchased by Thomson Holidays (now a part of the TUI group).

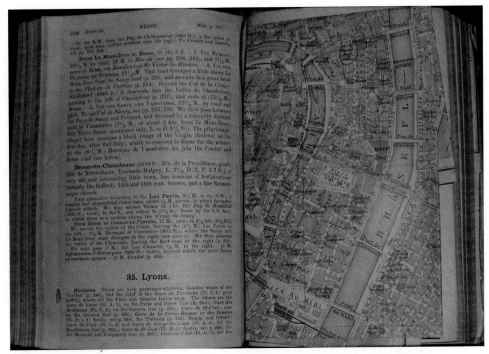

Figure 2.3 This excerpt, from Baedeker's 1914 guide to Southern France, shows the transport information for Lyon, along with a city plan. This century-old guide book varies little from modern day equivalents, providing information on things to see and places to stay

Photo by Claire Humphreys

Mention has already been made of the impact of photography on nineteenth-century travel. As the century drew to a close, the vogue for photography was accompanied by the cult of the guidebook. No UK tourist venturing abroad would neglect to take a guidebook, and a huge variety of these soon became available on the market. Many were superficial and inaccurate, but the most popular and enduring published were those of John Murray, whose 'Handbooks' appeared from 1837 onwards, and Karl Baedeker, who introduced his first guidebook (to the Rhine) in 1839. By the end of the century, Baedeker had become firmly established as the leading publisher of guidebooks in Europe (see Figure 2.3).

The years 1900-1950 and the origins of mass tourism

In the opening years of the twentieth century, travel continued to expand, encouraged by the gradually increasing wealth, curiosity (inspired, to some extent, by the introduction in the UK of compulsory education under the Education Act 1870), outgoing attitudes of the post-Victorian population and steady improvement in transport. Travellers were much safer from disease and physical attack, mainland Europe was relatively stable politically and documentation for UK travellers uncomplicated as, since 1860, passports had generally not been required for travel to any European country. The popularity of the French Riviera resorts as places for wealthier UK visitors to spend the winter is evidenced by the fact that, immediately before World War I (1914–1918), some 50 000 UK tourists are estimated to have been wintering on the coast.

Disastrous though it was, the Great War proved to be only a brief hiatus in the expansion of travel, although it led to the widespread introduction of passports for nationals of many countries. The prosperity that soon returned to Europe in the 1920s, coupled with large-scale migration, meant unsurpassed demand for travel across the Atlantic, as well as within Europe. The first-hand experience of foreign countries by combatants during the war aroused, for the first time, a sense of curiosity about foreign travel generally among the less well-off sectors of the community. These sectors were also influenced by the new forms of mass communication that developed after the war – the cinema, radio and, ultimately, television, all of which educated the population and encouraged an interest in seeing more of the world.

Forms of travel also began to change radically after the war. The railways went into a period of steady decline following the introduction of the motor car. Motorized public road transport and improved roads led to the era of the charabanc – at first, adapted from army surplus lorries and equipped with benches to provide a rudimentary form of coach. These vehicles achieved immense popularity in the 1920s for outings to the seaside, but their poor safety record soon resulted in licensing regulations being brought in to govern road transport. For those who could afford superior public transportation, more luxurious coaches also made an appearance. The coach company Motorways offered Pullman coaches – generally accommodating 15 people in comfortable armchairs with tables, buffet bars and toilets. These coaches operated in many parts of Europe and North Africa, were used on safaris in East and Central Africa and even provided a twice weekly service between London and Nice, taking a relaxing five to six days to make the trip.

It was the freedom of independent travel offered by the private motor car, however, that contributed most to the decline of the railways' monopoly on holiday transport. The extensive use of the motor car for holidaying has its origins in the USA, where, in 1908, Henry Ford introduced his popular Model T at a price that brought the motor car within reach of the masses. By the 1920s, private motoring was a popular pastime for the middle classes in the USA and, soon, camping and caravanning followed. Caravans (or trailers in American terminology) arrived by the 1930s, with '100 000 trailers on the road' by 1937 (Löfgren, 1999, 61). Equally, by the 1930s private motoring had arrived on a large scale in the UK and the threat to domestic rail services was clear, although Continental European rail services survived and prospered until challenged by the coming of the airlines.

In an effort to stem the decline, domestic rail services in the UK were first rationalized in 1923 into four major companies – the London, Midland and Scottish Railway (LMS), London and North Eastern Railway (LNER), Great Western Railway (GWR) and Southern Railway (SR) – and later nationalized following World War II, remaining under public control until again privatized in the mid-1990s.

While long voyages by sea were popular as means of leisure travel, the concept of cruising caught on only slowly. Among early examples of ship voyages treated essentially as a cruise, the Matson Line services between the US West Coast and Hawaii were to open up those islands to tourism. The Royal Hawaiian Hotel – built to accommodate visitors in the 1920s to those then exotic islands – was one of the first to offer what we today know as 'all-inclusive' holidays, although hotels along the French Riviera and in Switzerland were to follow suit. Hawaii was to remain an upmarket destination until mass package tours arrived with air services in the 1950s.

The era of the Great Depression

The 1930s are generally thought of as a period when the economic collapse in the Western world was similarly accompanied by the collapse of the international tourist market. While it is true that travel was severely curtailed, the Depression hit Europe rather later than the USA and, in the early 1930s, there remained a substantial market for those with sufficient wealth to travel. In the UK, however, government-imposed limits on foreign exchange for travel abroad proved a severe constraint.

The ever-resilient travel industry reacted with typical enterprise. The formation of the Creative Tourist Agents' Conference (CTAC) in the early 1930s brought together the leading travel agents (who were by this time also tour operators), including Thomas Cook, Dean and Dawson, Hickie Borman Grant, Frames, Sir Henry Lunn, Pickfords, Wayfarers' Touring Agency, the Workers' Travel Association and the PTA. These formed what amounted to a cartel to hold down and fix prices for foreign excursions. The PTA was instrumental in persuading the Continental railways to discount their fares for bulk purchases – a move the railways had always resisted in the past. Soon, special rail charters were being organized to Germany, Italy, the Riviera and Spain and, by 1938, the PTA was operating its own regular train charters to Switzerland – then one of the most popular destinations on the Continent. This agency also packaged one of the first air charters, approaching Imperial Airways (which was in financial difficulties) in the opening years of the decade to charter a Heracles to carry 24 passengers from Croydon airport to Paris and to Basle in Switzerland (Studd, 1950). By 1932, the company was carrying nearly 1000 passengers by air to the Continent, mainly then as a means of avoiding foreign currency payments to rail and bus companies abroad, and the following year it organized a 14-day air cruise to seven European capitals. Doubtless these air charters would have been continued, but the partial recovery of Imperial Airways' financial situation led the carrier to withdraw charter privileges, ending these first entrepreneurial modern package tours and making the point that tour operators of the future would have to avoid dependence on suppliers over whom they had no control – a lesson the first large-scale operators were quick to learn.

Cruising remained a popular holiday for those who could afford it. The formation of the Soviet Union after World War I had led the country to build up a strong fleet of cruise vessels. These carried some 5000 tourists from the UK to Russia in 1932, curious to learn about the country and its new political system. By 1938, it has been claimed that as many as a million holidaymakers were cruising on 139 cruise ships (Studd, 1950).

The growth of the airline industry

The arrival of the airline industry signalled the beginning of the end – not only for long-distance rail services but also, more decisively, for the great steamship companies. UK shipping lines had been under increasing threat from foreign competition throughout the 1920s, with French, German and US liners challenging UK supremacy on the North Atlantic routes particularly.

The first commercial air routes were initiated – by Air Transport & Travel, the forerunner of British Airways (BA) – as early as 1919, from Hounslow airport, London, to Paris. In the same year, a regular service was introduced in Germany between Berlin, Leipzig and Weimar. The infant air services were expensive (nearly £16 for the London–Paris service, equivalent to several weeks' average earnings) and uncertain (passengers were warned that forced landings and delays could occur). Consequently, initial growth in air services was limited to short-haul flights, over land. It was to be many years before air services achieved the reliability and low price that would make them competitive with world shipping routes.

In America, Pan American Airways was formed in 1927, introducing transatlantic air services in the 1930s, initially using flying boats (long-haul services were delayed due to the inability to fly higher than 4000 feet). In addition to its expense, however, the aircraft proved unreliable and uncomfortable by modern standards, so long-distance journeys necessitated frequent stopovers.

In the early years, commercial aviation was more important for its mail-carrying potential than for the carriage of passengers. Only with the technological breakthroughs in aircraft design achieved during and after World War II did air services prove a viable alternative to shipping for intercontinental travel. As for air package holidays, although the PTA reintroduced limited air charters in 1947, the holiday market would have to wait until the 1950s before this form of transport came into its own. The important sector of air travel is discussed in detail in Chapter 13.

The arrival of the holiday camp

Among the major tourism developments of the 1930s, the creation of the holiday camp deserves a special mention. Aimed at the growing low-income market for holidays, the camps set new standards of comfort, offering 24-hour entertainment at an all-inclusive price. They were efficiently operated, with the added benefit of childminding services – a huge bonus for young couples on holiday with their children. This was in marked contrast to the lack of planned activities and the often surly service offered by the traditional seaside boarding houses of the day.

The origin of these camps goes back to early experiments by organizations in the UK such as the Co-operative Holidays Association, Workers' Travel Association and Holiday Fellowship (although some summer camps for boys, such as those offered by the Young Man's Holiday Camp run by Joseph Cunningham on the Isle of Man, have been dated to as early as 1887). In the USA, summer camps for children were already a strong institution by the early twentieth century. The popularity and widespread acceptance of holiday camps by the adult public, however, have commonly been ascribed to the efforts and promotional flair of Billy (later Sir Billy) Butlin. Supposedly, Butlin, who built his first camp at Skegness in 1936, met a group of disconsolate holidaymakers huddled in a bus shelter to avoid the rain on a wet summer afternoon (although it is thought he was also influenced by a visit to Trusville Holiday Village in Mablethorpe, Lincolnshire, which had been opened and operated successfully by Albert Henshaw since 1924). Butlin determined to build a camp with all-weather facilities, for an all-in price. The instant success of the concept led to a spate of similar camps being built by Butlin (see Figure 2.4) and other entrepreneurs such as Harry Warner and Fred Pontin in the pre-war and early post-war years. On the Continent, pre-war Germany had introduced the concept of the highly organized and often militaristic health and recreation camp that enabled many to enjoy holidays who would otherwise have been unable to afford them.

In France, the 'villages de vacance' arose from similar political and social influences. The success of this concept of all-in entertainment was later to be copied by hotels

Figure 2.4 The holiday camp era – Butlin's camp at Skegness
© Barry Lewis/Alamy

(we noted earlier that the all-inclusive hotel with its own leisure complex had originated in the USA even earlier – for example, Grossingers resort hotel in the Catskills flourished as a popular all-inclusive destination in its own right, targeting principally the New York Jewish market).

Interest in outdoor holidays and healthy recreation was also stimulated by the Youth Hostels Association (YHA) in 1929 (the French equivalent opened in the same year), which provided budget accommodation for young people away from home.

The popular movement to the seaside

In spite of the rising appeal of holidays abroad for those who could afford them, mass tourism between the wars and in the early post-World War II era remained largely domestic. This period saw the seaside holiday become firmly established as the traditional annual holiday destination for the mass of the UK public. Suntans were, for the first time, seen as a status symbol, allied to health and time for leisure (see Figure 2.5). Blackpool, Scarborough, Southend and Brighton consolidated their positions as leading resorts, while numerous newer resorts – Bournemouth, Broadstairs, Clacton, Skegness, Colwyn Bay – grew rapidly in terms of both visitors and residential population. Until the Great Depression of the 1930s, hotels and guesthouses proliferated in these resorts. The tradition of the family holiday, taken annually over two weeks in the summer, became firmly established in the UK at this time.

The growing threat of competition from the European mainland was already apparent, for those who chose to take note of it. From the 1920s onwards, the Mediterranean Riviera had begun to attract a summer, as well as a winter, market from the UK, while the resorts of northern France were seen as cheaper and began to offer competition for the popular south coast resorts of Brighton, Hove, Folkestone and Eastbourne. These nearby French resorts, however, were seen primarily as places for short summer holidays rather than the longer winter stays that had been popular with a wealthy UK clientele in the nineteenth century.

Figure 2.5 A traditional mid-twentieth-century beach holiday

Photo reproduced by courtesy of Miriam Humphreys

The growth of public-sector involvement

It was in this period that the UK experienced the first stirrings of government interest in the tourism business. The UK was well behind other European countries in this respect. Switzerland, for example, had long recognized the importance of its inbound tourism and was actively involved in both promoting tourism overseas and gathering statistics on its visitors.

The British Travel and Holidays Association was established by the government in 1929, but, with the theme 'travel for peace', its role was seen as essentially promotional and its impact on the industry was relatively light, until a change in status some 40 years later. By the outbreak of World War II in 1939, the UK government had at least recognized the potential contribution tourism could make to the country's balance of payments. Equally, it had recognized the importance of holidays to the health and efficiency of the nation's workforce. The French government had already introduced holidays with pay in 1936 and the publication of the Amulree Report in 1938 led to the first Holidays with Pay Act for the UK in the same year. This encouraged voluntary agreements on paid holidays and generated the idea of a two-week paid holiday for all workers. Although this ambition was not fulfilled until several years after the end of World War II, by the outbreak of war some 11 million of the 19 million workforce were entitled to paid holidays – a key factor in generating mass travel.

Summary

In this chapter, we have seen how social changes have led to a shift in the desires and motivations for holidays, influencing the growth of both domestic and international travel. We have also examined the technological changes, especially within the transport sector, which have enabled travel to take place, as well as to expand, as we moved into the twentieth century. Finally, the development of touristic areas, such as spas, seaside resorts and holiday camps, has been described. In Chapter 3 we will see how contemporary mass tourism developed with further advances in technology and, above all, improved standards of living throughout the developed world.

Questions and discussion points

1. Identify the motivating and the enabling factors that encouraged the growth in participation on a Grand Tour.

2. Consider the period before the twenty-first century. How has the speed of travel changed? How has this affected travel behaviour?

3. Explain how the development of the railways changed leisure travel.

Tasks

1. The quote at the beginning of the chapter suggests that under the Romans 'every man could travel where he wished'. Discuss the factors that made travel possible to a wider market, highlighting the factors that may have restricted travel for the masses.

2. There are many classic travelogues written pre-twenty-first century. Examine some of these texts to allow you to discuss how guidebooks and travel writing may have influenced whether and how people travelled at the time of their publication. Comment on whether you think travel literature can have the same effect today.

Bibliography

Adams, C. and Laurence, R. (eds) (2001) *Travel and Geography in the Roman Empire*, London, Routledge.

BBC (2010) *The Victorian Seaside*, London, BBC.

Casson, L. (1974) *Travel in the Ancient World*, London, George Allen and Unwin; (1994) Baltimore, MD, Johns Hopkins University Press.

Dunn, R. E. (1986) *The Adventures of Ibn Battuta, a Muslim Traveler of the 14th Century*, Berkeley CA, University of California Press.

Fisher, N. (2004) Footbinding protest badge, *The Times*, 4 August.

Frommer's (2010) *Baden-Baden travel guide*, available online at: http://www.frommers.com/destinations/baden-baden/ (accessed November 2011).

Goeldner, C. R. and Ritchie, J. R. B. (2009) *Tourism: Principles, Practices, Philosophies*, 11th edn, Hoboken NJ, John Wiley.

Jennings, G. and Gayle, J. (2007) *Water-Based Tourism, Sport, Leisure, and Recreation Experiences*, Boston MA, Butterworth-Heinemann.

Korte, B. (2000) *English Travel Writing. From Pilgrimages to Postcolonial Explorations*, Basingstoke, Palgrave.

Leed, E. J. (1991) *The Mind of the Traveller: From Gilgamesh to Global Tourism*, New York, Basic Books.

Lloyd, M. (2003) *The Passport: the History of Man's Most Travelled Document*, Stroud, Sutton Publishing.

Löfgren, O. (1999) *On Holiday: A History of Vacationing*, Berkeley CA, University of California Press.

Naughton, A. (2010) *Railway Shipping Services*, Transport Britain, available online at: http://www.railwaybritain.co.uk/railway%20shipping%20services.html (accessed November 2011).

Spurrier, N. (2008) The lost technology of bathing – [engineering heritage], *Engineering & Technology*, **3**, 94–95.

Studd, R. G. (1950) *The Holiday Story*, London, Percival Marshall.

Further reading

Brodie, A., Sargent, A. and Winterby, G. (2005) *Seaside Holidays in the Past*, Northampton, English Heritage.

Burke, T. (1942) *Travel in England: From pilgrim and packhorse to light car and plane*, London, Batsford.

Feifer, M. (1985) *Going Places: The ways of the tourist from Imperial Rome to the present day*, London, Macmillan.

Hern, A. (1967) *The Seaside Holiday: The history of the English seaside resort*, London, Cresset Press.

Inglis, F. (2000) *The delicious history of the holiday*, London, Routledge,

Perrottet, T. (2003) *Route 66 AD: Pagan holiday on the trail of ancient Roman tourists*, London, Random House.

Pimlott, J. A. R. (1947) *The Englishman's Holiday: A social history*, Brighton, Harvester Press.

Swinglehurst, E. (1982) *Cook's Tours: The story of popular travel*, London, Blandford Press.

Ward, C. and Hardy, D. (1986) *Goodnight Campers! The history of the British holiday camp*, London, Mansell Publishing.

Website

Seaside History (the history of the British seaside holiday): **www.seasidehistory.co.uk**

3

The era of popular tourism: 1950 to the twenty-first century

Contents

Learning outcomes

After studying this chapter, you should be able to:

- describe the factors giving rise to mass tourism after 1950
- explain the origins and development of the package holiday
- understand the significance of rapid change in political, social and economic circumstances giving rise to the current uncertainties facing the tourism industry.

In the post-war period it has been the sun, not the sea, which is presumed to produce health and sexual attractiveness. The ideal body has come to be viewed as tanned. This viewpoint has been diffused downwards through the social classes with the result that many package holidays present this as one of the main reasons for going on holiday.

Urry (2002) *The Tourist Gaze*, 2nd edn, 35

Tourism since World War II

In the aftermath of World War II, the long and deprived years led to an increased desire to travel to foreign destinations, although the ability to do so was limited for many – restricted by both political barriers and inadequate finance. In the UK, as in other lands in Europe, there were also strict limits on the availability of foreign currency – a major barrier to cross-border travel. Nevertheless, the war had given rise to a curiosity among many British travellers to witness the sites of battles such as those fought on the Normandy beaches and at St Nazaire, while North Americans and Japanese alike felt similarly drawn to sites of conflict in the Pacific, such as Iwo Jima and Guadalcanal – although it was to take some 40 years or more before interest in these historic military battle sites was to approach the level of those of World War I. Interest was also limited to the sites on the western front in Europe – the horrors of warfare on the eastern front were such that neither side showed much inclination to visit the former battlefields, many of which were, in any case, banned to visitors until after the fall of the Soviet government. The extensive theatre of war had introduced the many combatants not only to new countries but also to new continents, generating new friendships and an interest in diverse cultures. Another outcome of the war, which was radically to change the travel business, was the advance in aircraft technology that was soon to lead to a viable commercial aviation industry for the first time. With the ending of the war in 1945, the first commercial transatlantic flight took place between New York and Bournemouth, calling at Boston, Gander and Shannon. That flight, operated by American Overseas Airlines using a Douglas DC4, served to point the way ahead, although the cost and the time involved – a result of the frequent stops required – ensured that long-haul flights would not become popular until the advent of the jet age.

The surplus of aircraft in the immediate post-war years, a benevolent political attitude towards the growth of private-sector airlines and the appearance on the scene of air travel entrepreneurs such as Harold Bamberg (of Eagle Airways) and Freddie Laker (of Laker Airways) aided the rapid expansion of air travel after the war. More significantly for the potential market, however, aircraft had become more comfortable, safer, faster and, in spite of relatively high prices in the early 1950s, steadily cheaper by comparison with other forms of transport. The war had seen many new airports built in Europe to serve the military and these were later adapted for civilian use. This was to prove particularly valuable in opening up islands in the Mediterranean that were formerly inaccessible or time-consuming to reach by sea.

Commercial jet services began with the ill-fated Comet aircraft in the early 1950s (withdrawn from service after crashes resulting from metal fatigue), but advances in piston engine technology were already beginning to impact on price. With the introduction of the commercially successful Boeing 707 jet in 1958, the age of air travel for the masses had arrived, significantly reducing the demand for sea travel.

The number of passengers crossing the Atlantic by air exceeded those by sea for the first time in 1957 and, although the liners continued to operate across the Atlantic for a further decade, their increasingly uncompetitive costs, high fares (saddled by conference agreements on routes across the Atlantic and Pacific that banned discounting) and the length of the journey time resulted in declining load factors (the ratio of the amount carried in relation to full capacity) from one year to the next. The new jets, with average speeds of 800–1000 kph, compared with older propeller-driven aircraft travelling at a mere 400 kph, meant that an air traveller could reach a far more distant destination within a given time (the key New York to London route fell from 18 hours in 1949 to just seven hours in 1969) than had been possible before. This was particularly valuable for business journeys where time was crucial.

The early 1970s saw the arrival of the first supersonic passenger aircraft, the Anglo-French Concorde. Never truly a commercial success (the governments wrote off the huge development costs), it nevertheless proved popular with business travellers and the wealthy. Travelling from London or Paris to New York in three and a half hours, it allowed businesspeople for the first time to complete their business on the other side of the Atlantic and return home without incurring a hotel stopover. The limited range and carrying capacity (just over 100 passengers) of the aircraft, and restrictions regarding sonic booms over land, acted as severe constraints on operable routes. The fatal crash near Paris of a chartered Concorde in 2000 sealed the aircraft's fate. Following modifications the aircraft were returned to a scheduled service in November 2001, but the low passenger numbers (a result particularly of the 9/11 attacks that year) led to its withdrawal from service in 2003. It is thought unlikely that any further commercial supersonic aircraft development will take place within the next 20 years (although the possibility of private supersonic jets arriving rather sooner than this is discussed in Chapter 13).

The development of the package tour

Inclusive tours by coach soon regained their former appeal after the war. The Italian Riviera was popular at first – French resorts proving too expensive – and resorts such as Rimini became affordable for the North European middle market. The inclusive tour by air – or 'package tour' as it has become known – was soon to follow.

Cheap packages by air depend on the ability of tour operators to charter aircraft for their clientele and buy hotel beds in bulk, driving down costs and allowing prices to be cut. Initially, the UK government's transport policy had restricted air charters to the movement of troops, but as official policy became more lenient, the private operators sought to develop new forms of charter traffic. Package holidays were the outcome, as the smaller air carriers and entrepreneurs learned to cooperate.

In the late 1950s, the larger airlines began to purchase the new jets, allowing smaller companies to buy the stock of second-hand propeller-driven aircraft coming on to the market, which were then put into service for charter operations. For the first time, holiday tourists could be transported to Mediterranean destinations faster than, and almost as cheaply as, trains and coaches. These new charter services soon proved highly profitable. Meanwhile, across the Atlantic, the first stirrings of an air package holiday industry emerged as regional operators began chartering aircraft from so-called 'supplemental' carriers on routes between major cities in the USA and Canada and the Caribbean Islands.

Although there are instances of charter flights as early as the 1920s (Thomas Cook, for example, had organized an escorted charter, believed to be the first, to take fans from New York to Chicago in 1927 to see the Dempsey–Tunney heavyweight title fight) and the National Union of Students is known to have been organizing charter flights for its members as early as 1949, Vladimir Raitz is generally credited with founding the mass inclusive tour business as we know it today using air charters. In 1950, under the Horizon Holidays banner, he organized an experimental package holiday trip using a charter flight to Corsica. By chartering the aircraft and filling every seat instead of committing himself to a block of seats on scheduled air services, he was able to reduce significantly the unit cost of his air transport and, hence, the overall price to his customers. He carried only 300 passengers in the first year, but repeated the experiment the following year and was soon operating profitably. Other budding tour operators, both in the UK and on the Continent, were soon copying his ideas (Club Méditerranée being among the best-known of the early entrepreneurs) and, by the early 1960s, the package holiday to the Mediterranean had become an established product for the mass holiday market.

The Spanish coastline and the Balearic Islands were the first to benefit from the new influx of mass tourism from the UK, Germany and the Scandinavian countries, often transported by the Douglas DC-3 aircraft. First, the Costa del Sol, then other coasts along the

Figure 3.1 The mass market beach holiday – Grömitz is a popular German resort in Mecklenburg Bay, North Germany

Photo by Chris Holloway

eastern seaboard, the islands of Majorca, Ibiza and, finally by the 1970s, the Canaries became, in turn, the destinations of choice for millions.

By 1960, Spain was already welcoming 6 million tourists every year and this was to grow to 30 million by 1975. Italy, Greece and other Mediterranean coastal regions all benefited from the 'rush to the sun'. Greece in particular, although slower to develop than Spain, provided a cheaper alternative as prices in the latter country rose. Only 50 000 visited in 1951, but a decade later this had grown to 500 000 and, by 1981, Greece was vying with Spain, welcoming 5 500 000.

The Nordic countries were also soon setting up their own package holiday arrangements to the Mediterranean and began to compete with the UK and their southern counterparts for accommodation along the Mediterranean coast. In Denmark, Pastor Eilif Krogager conducted a group of package tourists by coach to Spain in 1950, using the name of his village, Tjaereborg, as the company name. In 1962, Tjaereborg Travel moved into the air charter market with the formation of Sterling Airways, which soon became Western Europe's largest privately owned charter airline of the period.

The influence of currency restrictions

In the UK, post-war difficulties in the economy forced the government to impose ever tighter controls on foreign exchange. For a brief interval in 1947, a travel ban was imposed, during which no foreign currency allowance was made. Although the ban was lifted in early 1948, severe currency restrictions remained into the late 1960s, at which point the foreign currency (V-form) allowance for travel abroad was limited to £50 per person (for business travellers, additional funds, under T-form regulations, were granted). There was, however, a silver lining to this particular cloud: it encouraged people to take package holidays rather than travel independently. As air transport costs were payable in sterling and as only the foreign currency element of the tour – the *net* costs of accommodation and transfers – had to be paid out of the allowance, the benefits of dealing with an operator became clear. The limits were relaxed from 1970 onwards and, with further liberalization of air transport regulations and longer paid holidays, which encouraged a growing number of tourists to take a second holiday abroad each year, a new winter holiday market emerged in the 1970s. With a more even spread of package holidays throughout the year, operators found that they were able to reduce their unit costs still further, so package holiday prices continued to fall, boosting off-season demand. The UK was not alone within Europe in imposing currency restrictions during these early post-war years. Indeed, exchange controls were not totally abolished in France until as recently as 1990.

The influence of transport developments

A further technological breakthrough in air transport occurred in 1970, when the first wide-bodied jets (Boeing 747s), capable of carrying over 400 passengers, appeared in service. The unit cost per seat fell sharply and the result was an increased supply of seats at potentially cheaper fares. This innovation meant that, once again, the aviation industry had to unload cheaply a number of obsolescent, although completely air-worthy, smaller aircraft and these were quickly pressed into service for charter operations.

The innovation coincided with a steady increase in demand by North American visitors to Europe for basic tours of the UK and the Continent, hitting as many 'high spots' as possible in a 10- to 14-day visit. This gave rise to the concept of the 'milk run' – a popular route that would embrace the top attractions in one or more countries in a limited time-scale for the first-time visitor (see Figure 3.2). The availability of cheaper air transport enabled visitors to take short 'taster' tours around Western Europe, visiting the key cities, which provided an introduction to long-haul travel for millions of Americans.

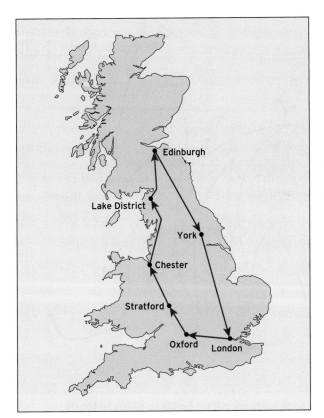

Figure 3.2 The linear tour – an example of the 'milk run' around Britain

The movement to the sun

By the 1960s, it was clear that the future of mass market leisure travel was to be a north–south movement, from the cool and variable climates of North America and northern Europe, where the mass of relatively well-off people lived, to the sunshine and warmth of the temperate to tropical lands in the southern part of the northern hemisphere (see Figure 3.3). These southern countries were also, for the most part, less well developed economically and so offered low-cost opportunities for the formation of a tourism industry. The new breed of tourism entrepreneurs involved with packaging tours recognized this trend very early on. Major hotel chains, too, were quick to seize the opportunities for growth in these countries and those such as Sheraton and Hyatt in the USA quickly expanded into Mexico and the Caribbean, as well as into Florida and Hawaii – the states offering the most attractive climates for tourism development. Hawaii in particular proved popular as an 'overseas' destination, following its incorporation into the USA (from 100 000 visitors in 1955, the flow of tourists increased to 2 million in 1970 and 6.5 million by 1990).

In Europe, UK and German tour operators such as Thomson and TUI developed bulk inclusive tours to the Mediterranean and North Africa and, due to increasing volume, were able to charter jumbo jets for the first time, bringing prices still lower. As transport costs fell, operators were also able to attract a mass market for long-haul travel on chartered jumbo jets. Florida – boosted particularly by the attractions of the Walt Disney World Resort and Miami Beach – has become almost as popular a destination for Europeans as the major Mediterranean destinations.

By the end of the twentieth century, the expert packaging of these tours had been extended to include many other types of destinations. Initially, tours to cultural and heritage sites (see Figure 3.4), city breaks to major cities like London, Paris, Rome, Brussels and Amsterdam and river cruises on the Rhine or Danube were being efficiently packaged and

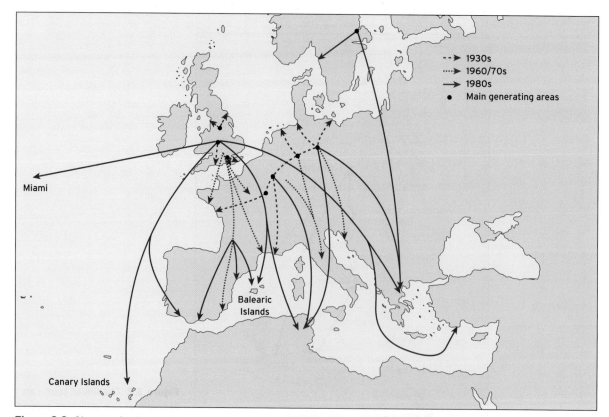

Figure 3.3 Changes in destination trends for mass market holidays, 1930s to 1980s

Figure 3.4 Cultural tourism – visitors to Playa Major, Salamanca, Spain
Photo by Chris Holloway

sold to the northern European market. The result was that, by the end of the 1960s, some 2.5 million Britons were taking packaged holidays abroad each year. By the end of the 1980s, this had grown to over 11 million, with over 70% of the UK population having been abroad on holiday at least once in their lives.

Whilst travellers from many European countries also rely heavily on package travel, this varies by nation. In 2009, consumer spending per household on package travel stood at US$324 for Western Europe whilst the level for Eastern Europe was US$171. Even within Western Europe the levels of spending varied significantly (see Table 3.1). These variations are likely to reflect both the attitudes to independent travel and the dominance of international travel. In the UK, whilst the effects of the turbulent economic climate led to a fall in spending on package holidays, they still made up over 40% of total retail sales on travel (Euromonitor, 2010).

Table 3.1 Consumer expenditure on package holidays

Country	Expenditure (€ per household)
Austria	748
Belgium	677.4
Finland	516.3
France	47.2
Germany	137.9
Greece	486.5
Italy	103.5
Netherlands	557.4
Portugal	152.3
Spain	646.2

Source: Euromonitor, 2010

Identikit destinations

One important result of the growth of the mass tourism market was that those responsible for marketing tourist destinations recognized that they had to satisfy tourists sharing broadly similar aspirations, regardless of their country of origin. The destinations accepted that, apart from geographical location, there was little to differentiate one resort from another and consumers' needs were centred on good climate and beaches, reasonable standards of food and accommodation, good opportunities for entertainment and shopping and low prices.

Often consumers themselves cared little which country they were in, as long as these criteria were fulfilled. The larger the mass market, the less distinctive destinations are likely to be, especially if they are small and have only recently been developed. One can find newly built 'marina'-type resorts with yachting basins, hotel/apartment/villa accommodation, similar restaurants, cafés and shops, as well as golf, tennis, water sports, folk singers and barbecue nights in any one of a dozen countries around the Mediterranean, Caribbean, North Africa and the South Pacific. Vernacular architecture has given way to the standard monobloc development typical of all beach resorts from Miami Beach to Australia's Gold Coast, by way of Benidorm and the faceless resorts of Romania and Bulgaria (including the optimistically named 'Golden Sands' and 'Sunny Beach').

This is also true even where business travellers attending conferences abroad are concerned. A convention centre, for example, is today likely to be a multipurpose venue containing facilities for conferences and committee/lecture rooms and including modern single or twin-bedded hotel rooms with private facilities, restaurants with banqueting rooms, bars, exhibition space, a leisure centre with pool, indoor and outdoor sports facilities and good scheduled transport links. The location may be Birmingham, Barcelona or Brisbane, but, once inside their hotel or conference centre, delegates may not even notice where they are. Indeed, one can find ubiquitous furniture of identical design (such as faux Regency chairs spray-painted in gold) in conference centres and hotels throughout the world.

The term **identikit destination** is used to define and identify this form of resort. Each place has emerged following comprehensive market research among various generating markets to find products with guaranteed mass demand. They may be contrasted with the piecemeal development of resorts two or three generations ago, the attractions at which may have been developed with very different aims and markets in mind. This is not to say that all identikit destinations are chasing identical markets. Many may be 'downmarket' in their attractiveness – that is, they may offer cheap tourism to a large number of people with the image of great popularity – while others may offer a more upmarket, but nonetheless uniform, image, offering the perception of higher quality and, thus, more expensive services to fewer visitors. In the former category we may think of Benidorm, Magaluf, Benitses in the Mediterranean, Miami Beach in Florida or Seefeld in Austria, while in the latter category we may think of Tahiti, Fiji, Malindi in Kenya or Barbados. Many identikit destinations have been developed through the activities of multinational tour companies, such as the all-inclusive resorts run by Sandals in the Caribbean, France's Club Méditerranée, Germany's Robinson Club or the USA's Sheraton Hotel chain. Within their establishments, the mass tourist will find a comforting degree of uniformity. Mass tourism has therefore demanded, and been supplied with, products designed specifically for its needs, as revealed through the process of market research. Such products are *user-orientated* as opposed to *resource-orientated* (based on the resources available at a destination).

Many of these identikit destinations, however, are now finding themselves at a disadvantage as the world tourism market becomes more sophisticated. Research by the former English Tourism Council revealed that one of the weaknesses of many English seaside resorts has been their failure to project a unique image. Those that have succeeded

– notably Blackpool and a handful of other major or minor resorts – have done so through a combination of significant investment and differentiation from other, often similar, resorts. Those resorts unable to make the investment needed to change their image are faced with the prospect of decline or have to appeal to newer, generally lower-spend markets. The later years of the last century found several of the formerly popular Mediterranean resorts attracting new tourists from the central European countries to replace the gradual decline in numbers of Western European visitors. One saving grace for those identikit destinations that developed around the core of an established town has been the ability to retain and improve the original 'old town', which is now promoted as a tourist attraction in its own right.

Private motoring and holidays

After a slow post-war recovery, the standard of living rose steadily in the 1950s and after. Many people could contemplate buying their first car, even if it were second-hand. For the first time, the holiday masses had the freedom to take to the roads with their families in their own private cars and, in the UK, the popular routes between London and the resorts on the south coast were, in those pre-motorway days, soon clogged with weekend traffic.

The flexibility that the car offered could not be matched by public transport services and both bus and rail lost the holiday traveller. In 1950, some two out of every three holiday-makers took the train for their holidays in the UK; this fell to one in seven by 1970. In this period, private car ownership in the UK rose from 2 million to over 11 million vehicles and, by the end of the 1980s, it had risen to some 20 million. Government data reveal that the proportion of UK households with access to a car increased from 52% in 1971 to 75% by 2007 (DfT, 2011).

This trend led, in turn, to a growth in camping and caravanning holidays. Ownership of private caravans stood at nearly 800 000 by the end of the 1980s (excluding static caravans in parks), while holidaymakers in the UK made more than 4.75 million trips with a towed caravan in 2009. In addition to this, almost 8 million UK trips used static caravan accommodation (Enjoy England, 2010). This form of tourism has been a cause for some concern, however, as the benefits to a region of private caravan tourism are considerably less than most other forms of tourism (owners can bring most of their own food with them and accommodation spend is limited only to caravan park fees). Also, caravans tend to clog the holiday routes in summer. Both mobile and static caravans on site are perceived as something of an eyesore, too.

EXAMPLE **Packaging the camping holiday**

The 1950s saw increased interest in camping holidays as they provided an affordable option for many holiday-makers. However, by the 1980s the availability of cheap hotel and self-catering accommodation through package holidays reduced interest in this form of travel. Significantly, though, the market that had grown used to the freedoms of camping was ideally served with the introduction of packaged camping holidays, which arranged sea crossings where necessary, as well as providing tent, beds, stoves and kitchenware and, in some cases, private toilet facilities. The camping product further developed through the introduction of mobile homes (static caravans), chalets and lodges at holiday parks.

Interestingly, recent years have seen a turn-round for this product, as luxury, glamorous camping (or 'glamping') has experienced an increase in demand. Camping at festivals, hiring pods, yurts (complete with four-poster beds, wood-burning stoves and roll-top baths) or luxury tents have helped to inspire this growth.

The campsites have also improved their offering, with child-friendly sites offering play areas, family bathrooms and more varied entertainment (The Times, 2007).

Companies such as Canvas Holidays and Vacansoleil, both established in the 1960s, are still operating today, having updated their product to meet the changing demands of the customer. This has included providing greater levels of luxury and additional facilities within the accommodation. Other players in the market include Keycamp and Eurocamp, as well as Haven and Park Resorts.

Research into the market in 2009 highlighted the fact that 20% of UK adults had taken a camping or caravanning holiday in the previous three years, the core market being families. Interestingly, it seems that tent camping appeals to the younger generation (perhaps the influence of music festivals) whilst static caravans are predominantly used by the older generation (Mintel, 2009).

The switch to private transport led to new forms of accommodation that catered for this form of travel. The UK saw the development of its first motels, modelled on the American pattern, which are the contemporary version of the staging inn for coach passengers. Furthermore, the construction of a new network of motorways and other road improvements made the journeys to more distant resorts manageable for those in centres of population and, in some cases, changed both the nature of the market served and the image of the resort itself.

The ever resourceful tour operators met the private car threat to package holidays by devising more flexible packages, such as fly–drive holidays, with the provision of a hire car at the airport on arrival. Hotels, too, spurred on by the need to fill their rooms off-peak, devised their own programmes of short-stay holidays, tailored to the needs of the private motorist.

Another effect was that the demand for car rental *abroad* rose sharply, too, as the overseas holidaymaker was emboldened to move away from the hotel ghettos, so car rental businesses in popular areas profited accordingly.

The shipping business in the post-war period

By contrast with other elements of the travel business, passenger shipping companies, hit by rising costs and competition from the airlines, were struggling to survive. Forced to abandon their traditional liner routes by the 1960s, some attempted to adapt their vessels for cruising. In this, they were far from successful as vessels purpose-built for long-distance, fast, deep sea voyages are not ideally suited to cruising, either economically or from the standpoint of customer demand. Many were incapable of anchoring alongside docks in the shallower waters of popular cruise destinations such as the Caribbean islands.

Companies that failed to embark on a programme of new construction, either due to lack of resources or foresight, soon ceased trading. Others, such as the Cunard Line, were taken over by conglomerates outside the travel or transport industries. American cruise lines, beset by high labour costs and strong unions, virtually ceased to exist.

Many new purpose-built cruise liners, however, of Greek, Norwegian and, later, Russian registry, soon appeared on the market to fill the gaps left by the declining maritime powers. These vessels, despite their registry, were based primarily in Caribbean or Mediterranean waters.

UK shipping was not entirely devoid of innovations at this time. Cunard initiated the fly–cruise concept in the 1960s, with vessels based at Gibraltar and Naples and passengers flying out to join their cruise in chartered aircraft.

The rapid escalation of fuel and other costs during the 1970s threatened the whole future of deep sea shipping, but, although declared dead by the pundits, this sector refused to lie down. Gradual stabilization of oil prices and control of labour costs (largely by recruiting from developing countries) enabled the cruise business to stage a comeback in the 1980s and 1990s, led by entrepreneurial shipping lines like Carnival Cruise Line, the American operator that set out to put the fun back into cruising. More informality, to appeal to more youthful family markets, helped to turn the business round, so that, by the end of the twentieth century, cruising had again become a major growth sector. Carnival absorbed many of the traditional carriers, including UK companies Cunard and P&O, and had the financial backing necessary to make substantial investment in new vessels. This is discussed in greater detail in Chapter 14.

By contrast with the cruise business, ferry services achieved quite exceptional levels of growth between the 1950s and the end of the century. This largely resulted from the increased demand from private motorists to take their cars abroad, influencing particularly routes between Scandinavian countries and Germany, and between the UK and Continental Europe. This growth in demand was also better spread across the seasons, enabling vessels to remain in service throughout the year with respectable load factors (although freight demand substantially boosted weak passenger revenue in the winter period). Regular sailings, with fast turnarounds in port, encouraged bookings, and costs were kept down by offering much more restricted levels of service than would be expected on long-distance routes. Hovercraft and jetfoil services were introduced across the Channel, although their success was limited by technical problems and being unable to sail in severe weather. Reliable, fast ferry services were further enhanced with the advent of the catamarans in the 1990s.

The growing importance of business travel

The growth in world trade in these decades saw a steady expansion in business travel, individually and in the conference and incentive travel fields, although recession in the latter part of the century caused cutbacks in business travel as sharp as those in leisure travel. As economic power has shifted between countries, so emerging nations have provided new patterns of tourism generation. In the 1970s, Japan and the oil-rich nations of the Middle East led the growth, while in the 1980s, countries such as Korea and Malaysia expanded both inbound and outbound business tourism dramatically. The acceptance of eight Eastern European nations (together with Malta and Cyprus) into the EU in May 2004 led to new growth areas in the movement of tourists during the first decade of the century, plus the rise of a new, free-spending elite within the Russian community and adjacent countries has resulted in those nationalities being among the fastest-growing sector in international tourism, albeit from a low base. Meanwhile, uncertainty in the Western world – particularly the fall and slow recovery of the stock market since the events of September 2001, followed more recently by economic recession – has continued to limit the recovery of business and leisure travel well into the twenty-first century.

Nevertheless, business travel of all kinds remains of immense importance to the tourism industry, not least because the per capita revenue from the business traveller greatly exceeds that of the leisure traveller. Motivational factors involving business travel are discussed in the next chapter and the nature of business travel is explored more fully in Chapter 11, but it should be stressed here that business travel often complements leisure travel, spreading the effects of tourism more evenly in the economy. A major factor is that business travellers are not generally travelling to areas that are favoured by leisure travellers (other than in the very particular case of the incentive travel market). Businesspeople have to go to locations where they are to conduct business, which generally means city centres, and often those cities have little to attract the leisure tourist. Travel also takes place all year round, with little peaking, and the demand for hotels occurs between Mondays and Fridays, encouraging the more attractively situated hotels to target the leisure market on weekends. Occasionally, spouses will travel to accompany the business traveller, so their leisure needs will have to be taken into consideration, too. In some cases the business traveller will elect to stay at the destination after business has been concluded – these tourists are termed *extenders*. It is therefore often difficult to distinguish between business and leisure tourism.

Although business travel is less price elastic than leisure travel, as was noted earlier, efforts to cut costs in the world of business today are ensuring business travellers no longer spend as freely as they did formerly. Fewer business travellers now travel first class or business class on airlines than before (many are making use of the new budget airlines to minimize costs), less expensive hotels are booked and there is even a trend to travel on weekends to reduce prices. Companies are buying many more tourism products, particularly air tickets, through the Internet, where they can shop around for the cheapest tickets. These changes are not seen as short-term trends and, in future, any distinction between the two major tourist markets is likely to become less apparent.

Conferences and exhibitions

Conferences and formal meetings have become very important to the tourism industry, both nationally and internationally, with continued growth between the 1960s and the end of the century. The UK conference market alone is responsible for the organization of some 700 000 individual conferences each year, the very large majority lasting just one or two days.

Exhibitions account for another form of business travel. Major international exhibitions can be traced to at least as far back as the Great Exhibition, held at Crystal Palace in London in 1851, and world fairs have become common events in major cities around the globe as a means of attracting visitors and publicizing a nation's culture and products. Many national events are now organized on an annual basis, some requiring little more than a field and marquees or other temporary structures – the Royal Bath & West agricultural show being one example of a major outdoor attraction, held annually in the UK's West Country. As such events have grown and become more professionally organized, so have they, too, become an important element in the business of tourism.

The all-inclusive holiday

Mention has already been made of the trend for *all-inclusive* holidays. As the term indicates, such a holiday includes everything – food, alcoholic drinks, water sports and other entertainment at the hotel. The attractions of this form of tourism are obvious – it is often seen by tourists as offering better value, because they can pay up front for the holiday, know what their budget will be well in advance and be unconcerned about changes in the value of foreign currency or the need to take large sums of money abroad. For more timid foreign travellers or those who are concerned about being badgered by local souvenir sellers and 'beach salesmen', there is the added reassurance that they do not even have to leave the hotel complex to enjoy their holidays.

Critics argue that the growth of all-inclusive holidays has implications for the local economy, as local bars, shopkeepers and others no longer stand to benefit from visitors to the same extent as before. At the same time, greater profits can leak back overseas when the all-inclusive holiday sites are foreign-owned. Whilst there are many concerns regarding the impacts of this form of tourism, operators themselves argue that, by keeping tourists in 'ghettos', they are in fact helping to reduce the negative impact of tourism on both the local population and environment.

In its modern form, this type of tourism originated in the Caribbean, and upmarket tour operators such as Sandals have promoted these programmes very successfully to the US and European markets. The concept later moved downmarket, however, and became popular in the more traditional European resorts, such as those of the Balearic Islands. Further expansion is seen as a direct threat to the livelihoods of many in the traditional coastal resorts.

Mass market tourism in its maturity

Mass market tourism to southern European resorts can be said to have entered a period of maturity by the 1980s. Although still showing steady growth, expansion was not on the scale found between the 1950s and 1970s. Short-haul travel was changing geographically, with tourists seeking new resorts and experiences. Portugal, having an Atlantic rather than a Mediterranean coast, wisely kept an upmarket image for its developments in the Algarve, while the Canaries, being within the crucial four hours' flying time from northern European airports, were the closest destinations to offer guaranteed warm winter sunshine and prospered from their year-round appeal. Other rather more exotic destinations attracted the upmarket winter holidaymaker. Tunisia, Morocco, Egypt and Israel pitched for the medium-haul beach markets. As prices rose in the traditional resorts, tourists moved on to cheaper, and less developed, destinations still close at hand. Turkey – seen as cheap and mildly exotic – boomed in the 1980s, proving an attractive alternative to Greece. The then Yugoslavian Adriatic Coast provided charming architecture and cultural attractions in its seaside resorts, although good sandy beaches were missing. Malta had always had an appeal with the more conservative British tourist, but Crete and Cyprus began to attract larger numbers. Spain woke up to the despoliation of its resorts and made efforts to upgrade them, especially on the island of Majorca and in popular coastal towns such as Torremolinos.

EXAMPLE The changing face of Benidorm

What was once a small fishing village on the east coast of Spain has become synonymous with the mass-market package holiday. It has been said that Benidorm was the creator of the biggest industry in Spain (Mallet, 2008) and Zaragoza Otis, mayor of Benidorm from 1950-1967, was vital in seeing the potential to be gained from tourism. He encouraged a change in both legislation and attitudes that stimulated demand. The town's rapid growth in the 1970s and 1980s led to the construction of many high-rise hotels, a concrete skyline of over 300 sky-scrapers, far removed from the Spanish pensiones and olive groves that existed in the 1950s (see Figure 3.5). So successful was this approach that it became a model for many of the Spanish Costas (Keeley, 2008).

Figure 3.5 Benidorm skyline in 1986
Photo reproduced by courtesy of Miriam Humphreys

However, by the 1990s, the town was showing the hallmarks of the worst aspects of mass tourism – unslightly buildings and on-going construction, polluted beaches and sea water, a despoilt natural environment, and home to the ubiquitous British lager-lout (Rice, 1991). Consequently, it was becoming seen as a tacky rather than exotic holiday destination (Davison, 1989). Furthermore, as demand by Northern Europeans switched, often to the cheap fly-drive resorts of the USA, so Benidorm had to work hard to ensure that tourists kept visiting. In the 1990s, the town employed a PR company in the UK to work on its image problems (Rice, 1991). Restrictions on development, construction controls, infrastructure development and beach and street cleaning all followed, to help enhance the overall experience for the visitor.

Yet, even though there has been a shift in attitude to mass-tourism package holidays, Benidorm is still a popular domestic and international holiday destination, with more than 6 million visitors arriving annually.

By the end of the century, it was becoming clear that seaside tourism was moving in a new direction. Visitors were no longer willing simply to lie on a beach; they sought activities and adventure. For the young, this meant action, from sports to bungee jumping and discos. Taking over popular resorts on Ibiza and in Greece, they encouraged the family holiday market to move on. For the older tourist, it meant more excursions inland to cultural sites and attractive villages.

The long-haul market was changing, too. Attempts to sell some long-haul destinations as if they were merely extensions of the Mediterranean sunshine holidays failed to take into account the misunderstandings that could occur between hosts and guests, first in the Gambia, then in the Dominican Republic. Cruising, dormant for so long, suddenly found a new lease of life. Long-haul beach holidays in Kenya and Thailand, marketed at costs competitive with those in Europe, attracted Western tourists.

The American and Northern European markets were joined by a rising flow of tourists from other parts of the world. The Asian market has become a leading source of business for the travel industry – in the West as well as throughout Australasia. The flow of Japanese tourists to Australia is particularly noteworthy. Travel times to Australia are shorter than those to Europe and, equally importantly, because the travel is largely within the same longitude, there is no time change or jet lag to face. With typically only eight days of holiday, avoidance of jet lag becomes an attractive bonus for the Japanese market and makes Australia doubly attractive. Absence of jet lag is also helping to accelerate tourism to South Africa from the European nations, although uncertainty over crime and the country's political future remains.

Destinations in the Pacific began to attract Europeans in significant numbers, just as they have long attracted the Japanese and Australian markets. A large proportion of these visitors, however, were using the Pacific islands as stopover points for a night or two rather than a holiday base. The impact of technology can be seen when, for the first time, aircraft became capable of flying direct between the west coast of the USA and Australia with the introduction of the Boeing 747-400SP aircraft. Tahiti, slightly off the direct route between these continents and long established as an attractive stopover point but expensive for longer holidays, immediately suffered a sharp decline in visitors as the airlines concentrated their promotion efforts on direct non-stop services between Los Angeles and Sydney or Auckland.

The influence of information technology

The development of technology that can manage the reservation information held by tour operators, airlines and hotels has had a significant influence on the operations of such companies. Computer systems that can hold and process large amounts of data have become a key business tool for many tourism companies.

The 1970s saw the introduction of computer reservation systems (CRS) by airlines. Such systems provided them with the capability of tracking seat pricing and availability on their ever-expanding routes and schedules. By the 1980s, those systems were being installed in travel agencies, too, as the airlines realized that the agents could enter the data for the bookings, thus making them more productive for the airline. The most prominent CRSs (now known as global distribution systems (GDSs) used within the airline distribution systems) are Amadeus, Sabre, Galileo and Worldspan (the latter two merging in 2007), while regional systems also exist (such as Axess, based in Japan, and Abacus, which serves the Asia Pacific region). Often, however, the regional GDSs have links with the 'big four' GDSs. The 1990s saw the introduction and rapid growth of the Internet, allowing business to customer (B2C) systems to be developed alongside business to business (B2B) systems provided by GDS. This was coupled with the development of mass produced personal computers.

The affordability of computers and the penetration of the Internet, including the availability of broadband access, have ensured that more customers than ever before can now search for information about holiday destinations, compare travel companies (and user reviews) as well as reserve travel products online. The growth of online booking was partially fuelled by the budget airlines offering cheaper rates for online reservations, but was also encouraged by customers seeing this method of booking their travel as more convenient. The numbers of people booking their travel online has often been suggested as a threat to travel agents, but, while in some countries the high street travel agents may have declined, online travel agencies are prospering.

Furthermore, experienced travellers are prepared to book separate elements of their travel online, either direct with providers or through an intermediary, often using price comparison websites to explore the range of products open to them. Coupled with the expectation that they can book their travel online, many customers also expect short response times. They expect to have an accurate picture of the availability of their chosen product and that they will receive almost immediate confirmation of their booking, usually via e-mail. E-mail correspondence – to address questions either prior to or post booking – must therefore be dealt with quickly, usually within hours, as customers are rarely prepared to wait days for a response.

The introduction of the Internet has also led to adaptations being made to business practices. As the budget airlines encouraged booking online, customers became more comfortable with the idea of making their own reservations, which significantly impacted on the chain of distribution. Some scheduled airlines saw opportunities to sell seats direct to the customer, in the process becoming less reliant on travel agents (and, consequently, reducing levels of commission payments). More recently, travel agents have fought back, trying to make themselves indispensable to customers by offering a specialized service, creating holidays from separately selected elements, rather than offering standard packages. This is known as dynamic packaging and is discussed in more detail in Chapter 19. A further development has been the introduction of online travel intermediaries, who act as a convenient outlet for last-minute sales.

Database and Web technology has now developed to a point where companies can tailor the information they provide to customers, adjusting the Web page content according to the customer profile (determined overtly or covertly through methods such as tracking sites visited or prior bookings). Such adaptability can enhance sales by more closely matching customer needs to relevant product offers. This can also help to develop customer loyalty to particular websites.

Search engines can be an important factor for both travel companies and holiday destinations. While there are several search engines that people use to track down information, customers rarely move beyond the first few pages of results. Therefore, achieving a high ranking for key search terms can be important in ensuring that customers reach their website.

Destinations use advanced technology that allows them to offer customers detailed information about the locality, as well as providing an accommodation reservation system. Such destination management systems can help to provide a coherent link between the many small companies operating at a destination, as well as feeding information to other websites, thus further extending the marketing reach for the destination.

Back office systems have also been enhanced by the affordability of computer systems, allowing travel businesses to develop databases of customer records, which are used to enhance their marketing activities, as well as financial accounts systems and sales records. The convenience of storing customer details and sales data means that business decisions can be made that are based on analysis of this information – especially useful if there are plans to invest in activities such as new marketing campaigns.

Finally, we need to consider the impact of both wi-fi and mobile technology. Wi-fi technology has allowed many travel businesses to provide customers with convenient access to the Internet. In the past, businesses such as hotels would have charged customers to use Internet systems as they had to invest in installing network cables throughout the building. The minimal costs of installing wi-fi systems, however, as well as the wider availability of wi-fi zones in coffee shops, airports and other areas, has led to customers expecting access to the Internet as standard (and often for minimal or no charge).

Mobile technology is also increasing access to the Internet, as more phones are WAP-enabled and as the cost of accessing websites is seen to be more affordable. This allows customers to access the Web while on the move. This has required travel companies and destinations to provide mobile-compatible versions of their web pages. Furthermore, the development of text messaging now allows travel companies to send booking confirmations or travel updates to a customer's mobile phone. The growth in ownership of smartphones has led to the development of 'apps', small programs which allow phone users to easily perform specific activities, such as accessing information and consumer reviews, making reservations, receiving traffic updates and many other such activities. This area of technology holds perhaps the greatest potential for changing the way travel companies interact with their customers.

Summary

In this chapter we have seen how the destinations visited have changed in the post-war period, with the attraction of the sun, sea and sand leading to a movement towards the Mediterranean seaside resorts of Europe. The development of these destinations, and the difficulties faced in trying to differentiate themselves in an increasingly competitive marketplace has also been highlighted. The introduction of the all-inclusive product, growth in private car ownership and the maturity of mass-market tourism have also been discussed in terms of their influence on popular tourist destinations.

Questions and discussion points

1. Compare and contrast how the increasing level of private car ownership may affect both traditional summer holidays and short-break vacations.

2. Explain how all-inclusive resorts can be a beneficial form of development for the host population. Identify the key concerns of such an approach.

3. Summarize how the business travel sector has changed over the past 50 years and, by thinking about the many influences on supply and demand, predict how it might change over the next decade.

Tasks

1. Investigate the many different mobile phone 'apps' currently available which are related to travel. Using examples of different apps, write a report which discusses how these phone tools may influence:

   (a) How tourists will gather information about destinations and attractions

   (b) How tourists book a holiday

   (c) How tourists travel around at destinations.

2. Pick one of the Spanish Costas to investigate. Discuss how the destination has had to adapt as demands from tourists have changed over the past 50 years.

Bibliography

Davison, J. (1989) Strife begins at 40 for the Jaded Package: Spanish Package Holidays, *The Sunday Times*, 3 September.

DfT (2011) *National Travel Survey: 2010*, available online at: http://assets.dft.gov.uk/statistics/releases/national-travel-survey-2010/nts2010-01.pdf (accessed November 2011).

Enjoy England (2010) *United Kingdom Tourism Survey – UK 2009 Results*, available online at: http://www.visitengland.org/Images/UK%20-%202008%20vs%202009%20Annual%20data_tcm30-19924.pdf (accessed November 2011).

Euromonitor (2010) *Travel Retail – United Kingdom*, UK, Euromonitor, July.

Keeley, G. (2008) The Man who built Benidorm bows out aged 85, *The Guardian*, 2 April.

Mallet, V. (2008) Outside Edge: Sex, Drink and Benidorm's Heritage, *Financial Times*, 28 November.

Mintel (2009) *Camping and Caravanning – UK*, Mintel, May.

Rice, A. (1991) Benidorm Concentrates on Improving the Environment, *The Observer*, 25 August.

The Times (2007) *Why We're all Happy Campers*, Times online, available at: http://www.thetimes.co.uk/tto/travel/holidays/camping-holidays/article1738214.ece (accessed November 2011).

Urry, J. (2002) *The Tourist Gaze*, 2nd edn, London, Sage.

Further reading

Barton, S. (2005) *Working-class Holidays and Popular Tourism: 1840–1970*, Manchester, Manchester University Press.

Bray, R. and Raitz, V. (2001) *Flight to the Sun: The Story of the Holiday Revolution*, London, Continuum.

Grant, G. (1996) *Waikiki Yesteryear*, Honolulu, Mutual Publishing.

Inglis, F. (2000) *The Delicious History of the Holiday*, London, Routledge.

Löfgren, O. (1999) *On Holiday: A History of Vacationing*, Berkeley, CA, University of California Press.

Lukas, S. (2008) *Theme Park*, London, Reaktion Books.

Segreto, L., Manera, C. and Pohl, M. (2009) *Europe at the Seaside: the Economic History of Mass Tourism in the Mediterranean*, New York, Berghan Books.

4

The demand for tourism

Contents

Learning outcomes

After studying this chapter, you should be able to:

- distinguish between motivating and enabling factors
- understand the nature of the psychological and sociological demands for tourism
- recognize how the product influences consumer demand
- be aware of some common theories of consumer behaviour, such as decision-making and risk avoidance
- be aware of the factors influencing demand and how demand is changing in the twenty-first century.

Last year the number of visits abroad by the Chinese reached 47m, 5m more than the number of foreign visitors to China. The Chinese also made 1.6 billion trips at home – a staggering total, but not much more than one each. According to WTTC forecasts, Chinese demand for travel and tourism will quadruple in value in the next ten years. At present China ranks a distant second, behind the United States, in terms of demand, but by 2018 it will have closed much of the gap.

The Economist (2008) A new itinerary – travel and tourism

Introduction

An understanding of why people buy the holidays or business trips they do, how they go about selecting their holidays, why one company is given preference over another and why tourists choose to travel when they do is vital to those who work in the tourism industry. Since the 1970s this field has garnered significant research interest by academics from across the globe, with a variety of themes and models being offered. From the early work, the most frequently cited research ideas are perhaps those of Dann (1977), Crompton (1979) and Iso-Ahola (1982). More recently, the refinement of Pearce's travel career ladder (Pearce and Lee, 2005) has been of significant interest.

Motivation and purpose are closely related and, earlier in this book, the principal purposes for which tourists travel were identified. These were classified into three broad categories: business travel, leisure travel and miscellaneous travel, which would include, amongst other things, travel for one's health and religious travel. However, simply labelling tourists in this way only helps us to understand their *general* motivations for travelling – it tells us little about their specific motivation or the needs and wants that underpin it, and how those needs and wants are met and satisfied. It is the purpose of this chapter to explain the terms and the complex interrelationship between factors that go to shape the choices of trips made by tourists of all kinds.

The tourist's needs and wants

If we ask prospective tourists why they want to travel to a particular destination, they will offer a variety of reasons, such as 'It's somewhere that I've always wanted to visit' or 'Some friends recommended it very highly' or 'It's always good weather at that time of the year and the beaches are wonderful. We've been going there regularly for the past few years'. Interesting as these views may be, they actually throw very little light on the real motivations of the tourists concerned because they have not helped to identify their *needs* and *wants*.

People often talk about their 'needing' a holiday, just as they might say they need a new carpet, a new dress or a better lawnmower. Are they, in fact, expressing a need or a want? 'Need' suggests that the products we are asking for are necessities for our daily life, but this is clearly seldom the case with these products. We are merely expressing a desire for more goods and services, a symptom of the consumer-orientated society in which we live.

Occasionally, a holiday (or at least a break from routine) can become a genuine need, as is the case with those in highly stressful occupations where a breakdown can occur if there is no relief from that stress. Families and individuals suffering from severe deprivation may also need a holiday, as is shown by the work of charitable organizations such as the Family Holiday Association (discussed in Chapter 17).

Let us start by examining what it is we mean by a need. People have certain physiological needs, and satisfying these is essential to survival: they need to eat, drink, sleep, keep warm and reproduce – all needs that are also essential to the survival of the human race. Beyond those needs, we also have psychological needs that are important for our wellbeing, such as the need to love and be loved, for friendship and to value ourselves as human beings and have others value and respect us. Many people believe that we also have inherently within us the need to master our environment and understand the nature of the society in which we live. Abraham Maslow conveniently grouped these needs into a hierarchy (see Figure 4.1), suggesting that the more fundamental needs have to be satisfied before we seek to satisfy the higher-level ones.

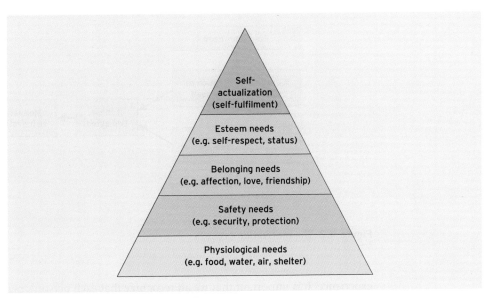

Figure 4.1 Maslow's hierarchy of needs

The difficulty with exploring these needs is that many people may actually be quite unaware of their needs or how to go about satisfying them. Others will be reluctant to reveal their real needs. For example, few people would be willing openly to admit that they travel to a particular destination to impress their neighbours, although their desire for status within the neighbourhood may well be a factor in their choice of holiday and destination.

Some of our needs are **innate** – that is, they are based on factors inherited by us at birth. These include biological and instinctive needs such as eating and drinking. However, we also inherit genetic traits from our parents that are reflected in certain needs and wants. Other needs and wants arise out of the environment in which we are raised and are therefore **learned** or socially engineered. The early death of parents or their lack of overt affection being shown towards us may cause us to have stronger needs for bonding and friendship with others, for example. As we come to know more about genomes, following the discovery of the human genetic code, DNA, early in the twenty-first century, so we are coming to appreciate that our genetic differences are, in fact, very slight, indicating that most of our needs and wants are conditioned by our environment.

Travel may be one of several means of satisfying a need and, although needs are felt by us, we do not necessarily express them and we may not recognize how travel actually satisfies our particular needs. Consequently, if we re-examine the answers given earlier to questions asking why we travel, it may be that, in the case where respondents are confirming the desire to return to the same destination year after year, they are actually expressing the desire to satisfy a need for safety and security, by returning to the tried and tested. The means by which this is achieved – namely, a holiday in a resort well known to them – reflects the respondents' 'want' rather than their need.

The process of translating a need into the motivation to visit a specific destination or undertake a specific activity is quite complex and can best be demonstrated by means of a diagram (see Figure 4.2).

Potential consumers must not only recognize that they have a need, but also understand how a particular product will satisfy it. Every consumer is different and what one consumer sees as the ideal solution to the need another will reject. A holiday in Benidorm that Mr A thinks will be something akin to paradise would be for Mr B an endurance test; he might prefer a walk in the Pennines for a week, which Mr A would find a tortuous

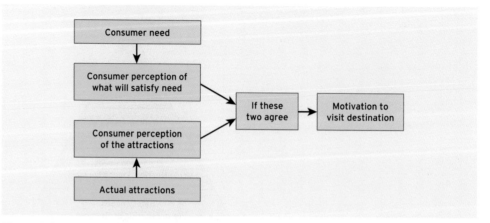

Figure 4.2 The motivation process

experience. It is important that we all recognize that each person's perception of a holiday, like any other product, is affected by experiences and attitudes. Only if the perception of the need and the attraction match will a consumer be motivated to buy the product. The job of the skilled travel agent is to subtly question clients in order to learn about their individual interests and desires and find the products to match them. Those selling more expensive holidays may need to convince their clients that the experience on offer is worth paying the difference over and above what they had expected for an ordinary holiday.

Travel motivation

We have established that motivation arises out of the felt wants or needs of the individual. For some people the motivation to travel is aimed at achieving a broad objective, such as getting away from the routine and stress of the workplace in order to enjoy different surroundings and a healthy environment. Alternatively, the tourist may decide to take a holiday in the Swiss Alps, to take walks in fresh mountain air and enjoy varied scenery, good food and total relaxation. Marketing professionals sometimes refer to these two forms of motivation as **'push'** factors and **'pull'** factors – that is, the tourist is being pushed into a holiday by the need to get away from their everyday environment, but other factors may be at work to pull, or encourage, them to travel to a specific destination. For this reason, marketing staff realize that they will have to undertake their promotion at two distinct levels, persuading the consumer of the need to take a holiday and also showing those consumers that the particular holiday or destination the organization is promoting will best satisfy that need.

Push factors

Perhaps one of the earliest academics to write about push and pull factors in relation to tourism was Graham Dann (1977). His work, in relation to Barbados, noted that greater interest had been shown in research towards the pull factors, with push factors being given minimal attention, despite the assertion that choice of destination is 'consequent on [a tourist's] prior need to travel' (186). He suggested that push factors predispose the tourist to want to travel (for reasons such as escape and nostalgia). Ryan (1991) also explored the push factors which encouraged travel to occur, categorising these into 11 themes:

- the motivation to escape from perceived mundane environments
- relaxation and recuperation
- the opportunity to play, providing adults with an opportunity to regress into the care-free state of childhood
- strengthening of family bonds and the opportunity to spend time with other family members
- gaining status and prestige amongst one's peers (both at home and while on holiday)
- social integration with hosts and other guests
- romance and sexual opportunity
- the opportunity for educational development and broadening of the mind
- self-fulfilment and self-discovery which may potentially be life-changing
- wish fulfilment and the achievement of long-desired goals
- shopping.

While shopping may seem a somewhat banal reason, it is a popular and commonly expressed reason for travel and has led to increased tourism numbers for destinations such as New York, Dubai and several border towns such as Calais in France. Importantly, these motivations, independently or in combination, stimulate individuals to travel. It is then down to the pull factors to determine which destination or resort is chosen to meet their desires.

Pull factors

We have recognized that tourists may have many different motives for wanting to take a holiday. These motives may be fulfilled by a variety of destinations; therefore, distinguishing between one location and an alternative may be achieved by considering the pull factors for each. Richardson and Fluker suggest that these 'pull consumers towards a particular destination' (2004, 67). Pull factors many include:

- range of attractions, including the natural environment, cultural resources and a welcoming host population
- availability and quality of amenities
- special events
- infrastructure and accessibility
- suitable weather conditions
- positive image as a safe, entertaining, interesting place to visit.

The pull factors can help the tourist choose the destination which best meets their motivations. However, it may be that some pull factors may stimulate motivation to travel – for example, the hosting of the 2012 Olympics in London may stimulate domestic tourists to visit the capital in order to witness this sporting occasion, whereas without the event a visit to London may never have been considered.

While on the subject of the Olympics as a pull factor, research (Preuss, 2005) acknowledged that hosting this mega event may actually deter tourists from visiting, perhaps concerned that costs and congestion would spoil the holiday experience. The industry is hinting that this may be the case for London 2012 (BBC, 2011).

Categories of tourist motivation

If we look at the varied forms of leisure tourism that have become a part of our lives in the past few years, we will quickly see that certain types of holiday have become popular because they best meet common, and basic, needs. The 'sun, sea and sand' holiday that caters to the mass market is essentially a passive form of leisure entailing nothing more stressful than a relaxing time on the beach, enjoyment of the perceived healthy benefits of sunshine and saltwater bathing, good food and reasonably priced alcohol (another relaxant). The tendency among certain groups of tourists abroad to drink too much and misbehave generally is, again, a reflection of need, even if the result is one that we have come to deplore because of its impact on others. Such tourists seek to escape from the constraints of their usual environment and enjoy an opportunity to 'let their hair down', perhaps in a more tolerant environment than they would find in their own home country.

Those travelling on their own might also seek opportunities to meet other people or even find romance (thus meeting the need to belong and other social needs).

In the case of families, parents can simultaneously satisfy their own needs while also providing a healthy and enjoyable time for their children on the beach. Parents may also be given the chance to get away and be on their own while their children are being cared for by skilled childminders.

McIntosh *et al.* (1995) summarized these different tourism motivations into four categories: physical, cultural, interpersonal and status and prestige (Table 4.1). Fulfilling these motivations can be achieved through a range of activities. For example, the tourists viewing Leonardo's painting La Gioconda (also known as the Mona Lisa) may feel that the experience fulfils some of their cultural, status and prestige motivations (see Figure 4.3).

What is provided, therefore, is a **bundle of benefits**, and the more a particular package holiday, or a particular destination, can be shown to provide the range of benefits sought, the more attractive that holiday will appear to the tourist compared with other holidays on offer. The bundle will be made up of benefits that are designed to cater to both general and specific needs and wants.

Today, there is a growing demand for holidays that offer more strenuous activities than are to be found in the traditional 'three S' holidays, such as trekking, mountaineering or yachting. These appeal to those whose basic needs for relaxation have already been satisfied (they may have desk-bound jobs that involve mental, rather than physical, strain) and they are now seeking something more challenging. Strenuous activities provide opportunities for people to test their physical abilities and, while this may involve no more than a search for health by other means, there may also be a search for competence – another need identified by Maslow. Because such holidays are purchased by like-minded people, often in small groups, they can also help to meet other ego and social needs.

The growing confidence and physical fitness of many tourists (and not just the young!) have put 'extreme sports' on the agenda of many holiday companies. Formerly limited to

Table 4.1 Tourism motivators

Physical motivators	Cultural motivators
• Refreshing the body • Reducing mental stress • Improve physical health • Exercising • Having fun and enjoyment	• Curiosity about foreign lands and people • Developing historical or cultural interests • Attending cultural events • Exploring local music, folklore, lifestyles, art etc.
Interpersonal motivators	Status and prestige motivators
• Maintaining and enhancing relationships with friends and family • Making new friends • Escaping own routine environment (including escape from one's own family)	• Gaining status and recognition from others • Pursuing one's own hobbies • Continuing education and self-development

Source: McIntosh *et al.*, 1995

Figure 4.3 Tourist curious to see Leonardo da Vinci's painting La Gioconda (also known as Mona Lisa) may feel this experience fulfils some of their cultural motivations

Photo by Claire Humphreys

winter sports such as skiing and snowboarding and summer white water rafting, adventure holidays now embrace off-piste skiing, snowboarding, windsurfing, BMX biking, paragliding, heliskiing, kitesurfing, kitebuggying, landboarding and base jumping (leaping off tall buildings with parachutes – seldom available as a legal activity!) – the range of activities increasing each year.

EXAMPLE **Bootcamp holidays**

The desire to get fit has led to the growth of many holiday 'bootcamps'. These vacations provide health food regimes with organized physical activities and, in the case of many luxury bootcamps, massages and treatments to ease the aches and pains. While this may not seem like a holiday, demand has been increasing in recent years.

To serve more specialist markets, there are also training holidays for cyclists, triathletes and marathon runners. One such company is Embrace Sports, who regularly organize triathlon training holidays. A typical week-long holiday would include:

- daily run (5-10 miles), swim, or cycle ride (40-70 miles)
- open water swimming technique session
- strengthening and conditioning exercise class
- aquathon time trials
- running track sessions.

While such an intense exercise schedule would not suit everybody, part of the appeal for those who do take part is the opportunity to meet other people with a shared interest in triathlons.

It must also be recognized that many tourists are constantly seeking novelty and different experiences. However satisfied they might be with one holiday, they will be unlikely to return to the same destination. Instead, they will be forever seeking something more challenging, more exciting, more remote. This is, in part, an explanation for the growing demand for long-haul holidays. For other people, such increasingly exotic tourist trips satisfy the search for status.

The need for self-actualization can be met in a number of ways. At its simplest, the desire to 'commune with nature' is common to many tourists and can be achieved through scenic trips by coach, fly–drive packages in which routes are identified and stopping-off points recommended for their scenic beauty, cycling tours or hiking holidays. Each of these forms of holiday will find its own market in terms of the degree of rural authenticity sought, but all, to some extent, meet the needs of the market as a whole.

Alternatively, the quest for knowledge can be met by tours such as those offered to cultural centres in Europe, often accompanied by experts in a particular field. Self-actualization can be aided through packages offering painting or other artistic 'do-it-yourself' holidays. Some tourists seek more meaningful experiences through contact with foreign residents, where they can come to understand the local cultures. This process can be facilitated through careful packaging of programmes arranged by organizers, who build up suitable contacts among local residents at the destination. Local guides, too, can act as 'culture brokers', overcoming language barriers or helping to explain local culture to inquisitive tourists, while at the same time reassuring more nervous travellers.

As people come to travel more and as they become more sophisticated or better educated, so their higher-level needs will predominate in their motivation to go on a particular holiday. Companies in the business of tourism must always recognize this and take it into account when planning new programmes or new attractions for tourists.

The motivations of business travellers

Those travelling on business often have different criteria that need to be considered. They are, in general, less price-sensitive and more concerned with status than leisure travellers. They are motivated principally by the need to complete their travel and business dealings as efficiently and effectively as possible within a given timeframe – this reflects their companies' motivation for their trip. They will, however, also have personal agendas that they take into account. Through the eyes of their companies, then, they will be giving consideration to issues such as speed of transport and how convenient it is for getting them to their destinations, the punctuality and reliability of the carriers and the frequency of flights so that they can leave at a time to suit their appointments and return as soon as their business has been completed. Decisions about their travel are often made at very short notice, so arrangements may have to be made at any time. They need the flexibility to be able to change their reservations at minimal notice and are prepared to pay a premium for this privilege. The arrival of the low-cost airlines, however, has persuaded many to stick with a booking as large savings can be achieved in this way, even for a flight within Europe.

Travel needs to be arranged on weekdays rather than weekends – most businesspeople like to spend their weekends with their families. Above all, businesspeople will require that those they deal with – agents, carriers, travel managers – have substantial, in-depth knowledge of travel products. It is known that many business travellers will undertake their own searches online for information, frequently competing with their own travel managers for data on prices and flights, in the belief that their own research ability is superior to that of the travel experts.

Personal motivation enters the scene when the business traveller is taking a spouse or partner with them and when leisure activities are to be included as an adjunct to the business trip. A businessperson may also be interested in travelling with a specific carrier in order to take advantage of frequent flyer schemes that allow them to take a leisure trip with the airline when they have accumulated sufficient miles. This may entail travelling on what is neither the cheapest nor the most direct route.

Factors such as these can cause friction between travellers and their companies as the decision regarding whether or not to travel, how and when, may not rest with the travellers themselves, but rather with senior members of their companies, who may be more concerned with ensuring that the company receives value for money than comfort or status.

It was believed that when videoconferencing facilities were introduced a few years ago, this would herald the decline of business travel. In fact, the reverse has occurred – traditional meetings continue, while conferences and trade shows are continuing to expand.

Facilitators

Up to now, we have dealt with the factors that motivate tourists to take holidays. In order to take a holiday, however, the tourist requires both time and money. These factors do not motivate in themselves, but they make it possible for prospective tourists to indulge in their desires. For this reason, they are known as **facilitators**.

Facilitators play a major role in relation to the specific objectives of the tourist. Cost is a major factor in facilitating the purchase of travel, but, equally, an increase in disposable income offers the tourist the opportunity to enjoy a wider choice of destinations. Better accessibility of the destination, or more favourable exchange rates against the local currency, easier entry without political barriers and friendly locals speaking the language of the tourist all act as facilitators, as well as motivating the choice of a particular destination over others.

A growing characteristic within wealthier countries in this new century is the presence of 'cash rich, time poor' consumers who are prepared to sacrifice money to save time. The implications of this phenomenon are significant for the industry. Those who can offer the easiest and fastest communication opportunities, prices and booking facilities, coupled with reliability and good service, can gain access to a wealthy, rapidly expanding market. Whether this race will be won by the direct selling organizations using websites and call centres or retailers using new sales techniques (such as experienced travel counsellors prepared to call on customers at times convenient to them and in their own homes, including evenings and weekends) remains to be seen.

Segmenting the tourism market

So far in this chapter we have looked at the individual factors that give rise to our various needs and wants. In the tourism industry, those responsible for marketing destinations or holidays will be concerned with both individual and aggregate, or total, demand for a holiday or destination. For this purpose, it is convenient to categorize and segment demand according to four distinct sets of variables – namely, geographic, demographic, psychographic and behavioural. These categories are examined in more detail in a companion book to this text (Holloway, 2004), but will be briefly summarized here.

Geographic variables

These are determined according to the areas in which consumers live. These can be broadly defined by continent (North America, South America, Asia, Africa, for example), country (such as the UK, France, Japan, Australia) or according to region, either broadly (for instance, Nordic, Mediterranean, Baltic States, US mid-western States) or more narrowly (say, the Tyrol, Alsace–Lorraine, North Rhine–Westphalia, UK Home Counties). It is appropriate to divide areas in this way only where it is clear that the resident populations' buying or behaviour patterns reflect commonalities and differ from those of other areas in ways that are significant to the industry.

The most obvious point to make here is that chosen travel destinations will be the outcome of factors such as distance, convenience and how much it costs to reach the destination. For example, Europeans will find it more convenient, and probably cheaper, to holiday in the Mediterranean, North Americans in the Caribbean, Australians in Pacific islands such as Fiji and Bali. Differing climates in the generating countries will also result in other variations in the kinds of travel demand.

Demographic variables

Segmentation is frequently based on characteristics such as age, gender, family composition, stage in lifecycle, income, occupation, education and ethnic origin. The type of holiday chosen is likely to differ greatly between 20–30-year-olds and 50–60-year-olds, to take one example. Changing patterns will also interest marketers – declining populations, increasing numbers of elderly consumers, greater numbers of individuals living alone and taking holidays alone or increases in disposable income among some age groups – all these factors will affect the ways in which holidays are marketed.

Significant factors influencing demand in the UK market in recent years have been the rise in wealth among older sectors of the public, as their parents – the first generation to have become property owners on a major scale – died, leaving significant inheritances to their offspring. This, and the general rise in living standards, fuelled demand for second homes both in the UK and abroad, changing leisure patterns and encouraging the growth of low-cost airlines to service the market's needs.

Demographic distinctions are among the most easily researched variables and, consequently, provide readily available data. Market differentiation by occupation is one of the commonest ways in which consumers are categorized – not least because it offers the prospect of a ready indication of relative disposable incomes. Occupation also remains a principal criterion for identifying social class.

EXAMPLE | **Contesting the stereotypes**

In 2010, the New Zealand government published the results of research into the domestic tourism segments, reporting the activities enjoyed when on holiday. The stereotype that Kiwis are looking for thrills and non-stop adrenalin-packed fun was blown apart. The results actually revealed that what domestic tourists do most is eat, shop – and very little else. The most popular activity was dining (29%), followed by shopping (22%) and nothing (13%). Following this were activities such as walking (9%), fishing (4%) and golf (1%), with visiting museums and galleries an option for 3% of domestic holidaymakers (Sunday Star-Times, 2010).

As well as refuting the stereotype, the research also provided more detailed segmentation data, separating the market by gender, age, lifecycle, ethnic group, educational level, occupation, income and region of residence (Ministry of Economic Development, 2010).

Table 4.2 Social grade classification system based on occupation

Classes	Designation
A	Higher managerial, administrative and professional
B	Intermediate managerial, administrative and professional
C1	Supervisory, clerical and junior managerial, administrative and professional
C2	Skilled manual workers
D	Semi-skilled and unskilled manual workers
E	State pensioners, casual and lowest grade workers, unemployed with state benefits only

The best-known socio-economic segmentation in the UK was introduced after World War II and is still widely used in market research exercises, including those conducted under the aegis of the National Readership Surveys (NRS). Using this tool, the consumer market is broken down into six categories on the basis of the occupation of the head of household (see Table 4.2).

The ABC1 grouping – still in common use in the media – has been of key interest to the travel industry, which has identified this segment as major travellers, having both leisure and the funds to purchase high-end holidays. However, this attempt to distinguish between market segments on the grounds of social class arising from occupation is open to criticism – indeed, patterns of purchasing or behaviour are now less clearly determined by social class. The belief that touristic motivations can be ascribed largely to occupation, given the changes taking place in twenty-first-century society, can be misleading. Furthermore, while the proportion of those travelling on holiday each year is, as one would expect, far higher among the higher income brackets than among the lower, in an era where plumbers and electricians may earn up to twice as much as university lecturers, segmentation by occupation clearly has flaws.

Various attempts have been made in recent years to overcome this stigmatic characterization by occupation. A new system of social classification was introduced in the UK in 2001 which then informed efforts to progress a European socio-economic classification system (see Table 4.3).

Table 4.3 European socio-economic classification system

Classes	Designation
1	Large employers, higher grade professional, administrative and managerial occupations
2	Lower grade professional, administrative and managerial occupations and higher grade technician and supervisory occupations
3	Intermediate occupations
4	Small employer and self-employed occupations (excluding agriculture, etc.)
5	Self-employed occupations (agriculture, etc.)
6	Lower supervisory and lower technician occupations
7	Lower services, sales and clerical occupations
8	Lower technical occupations
9	Routine occupations
10	Never worked and long-term unemployed

Source: adapted from Harrison, E. and Rose, D., The European Socio-economic Classification (ESeC), Draft User Guide (University of Essex, February 2006: available at http://www.iser.essex.ac.uk/archives/esec/user-guide)

Despite the concerns regarding the use of occupation as a segmentation method, categorizing demand for a company's products by social class can be of some value in helping to determine advertising spend and the media to be employed. Similarly, breaking down demand by age group is also helpful – even vital if the aim is, say, to develop holidays that particularly appeal to young people.

Market research in recent years has been transformed by the efforts of researchers to bring together both geography and demography, through a process of pinpoint **geodemographic** analysis. This is based on combining census data and postcodes to reveal that fine-tuning by region can produce a picture of spend and behaviour that will be common to a large proportion of the population of that region. Among the best known of such systems is ACORN (A Classification of Residential Neighbourhoods), operated by CACI Limited, which takes into account such factors as age, income, lifestyle and family structure. However, even with the sophistication and refinement of this approach, this will not be sufficient to explain all of the variations in choice between different tourist products, and for this we must look to consumer psychographics for further enlightenment.

Psychographic variables

This approach to segmenting the market focuses on characteristics related to lifestyle, attitudes and personality (Reid and Bojanic, 2010). Beyond simple demographic distinctions, as buyers, we are heavily influenced by those immediately surrounding us (our so-called **peer groups**), as well as those we most admire and wish to emulate (our **reference groups**). In the former case, while we may develop choices favoured by our parents and teachers in early life, as we become more independent, we prefer to emulate the behaviour of our immediate friends, fellow students, colleagues at work or others with whom we come into regular close contact. In the latter case, the influence of celebrities is becoming paramount, as the holiday choices and behaviour of pop idols, cinema and TV 'personalities' and those in the media and modelling worlds come increasingly to influence buying patterns, particularly those of younger consumers.

In short, the ways in which significant others live and spend their leisure hours exerts a strong influence on holiday consumerism among all classes of client. Some niche cruise companies have marketed themselves for many years on the basis that their passengers will mingle with celebrities and public figures, and the Caribbean island of Mustique successfully promoted itself as an exclusive hideaway for the rich, largely because Princess Margaret had been a frequent visitor. The choice of a private island in the Seychelles as the honeymoon destination of Prince William and his bride, the popular and newly created Duke and Duchess of Cambridge, in 2011 will undoubtedly have an influence on travel demand to that destination over the next few years.

As members of society, we tend to follow the norms and values reflected in that society. We all like to feel that we are making our own decisions about products, but do not always realize how other people's tastes influence our own and what pressures there are on us to conform. When we claim that we are buying to 'please ourselves', what exactly is this 'self' that we are pleasing? We are, in fact, composed of many 'selves'. There is the self that we see ourselves as, often highly subjectively; the ideal self, how we would like to be; there is the self as we believe others see us; and the self as we are actually seen by others. Yet, none of these can be construed as our real self – if, indeed, a real self can be said to exist outside of the way we interact with others. Readers will be aware that they put on different 'fronts' and act out different roles according to the company in which they find themselves, whether family, best friend, lover, employer. Do any of these relationships truly reflect our real self?

The importance attached to this theory of self, from the perspective of this text, is the way in which it affects those things that we buy and with which we surround ourselves.

This means that, in the case of holidays, we will not always buy the kind of holiday we think we would most enjoy or even the one we feel we could best afford, but, instead, we might buy the holiday we feel will give us status with our friends and neighbours or reflect the kind of holiday we feel that 'persons in our position' should take. Advertisers will frequently use this knowledge to promote a destination as being suited to a particular kind of tourist and will perhaps go further, using as a model in their advertisements some well-known TV personality or film star who reflects the 'typical tourist at the destination', with whom we can then mentally associate ourselves.

In the same way, status becomes an important feature of business travel as such travellers are aware that they are representing their companies to business associates and must therefore create a favourable impression. As their companies usually accept this view and pay their bills, this is one of the reasons business travel generates more income per capita than does leisure travel.

Behavioural variables

This allows us to segment markets according to their usage of the products. This is a much simpler concept, and facts about consumer purchasing can be ascertained quite readily through market research. The frequency with which we purchase a product, the quantities we buy, where we choose to buy (from a travel agent or direct, using company websites, for example) and the sources from which we obtain information about products are of great interest to marketers, who, armed with this knowledge, will be able to shape their strategies more effectively in order to influence purchases. A key element in this is to know which benefits a consumer is looking for when they purchase a product. The motives for buying a lakes and mountains holiday, for example, can vary substantially. Some may be seeking solitude and scenic beauty, perhaps to recover from stress or to enjoy a painting or photography holiday; some will seek the social interaction of small hiking groups or evening chats in the bar of their hotel with like-minded guests; others will be looking for more active pastimes, such as waterskiing or mountaineering. Only when the organization arranging the holiday knows which elements of the product appeal to their customers can a sale effectively take place.

EXAMPLE Segmentation by booking characteristics

While for some looking forward to their holiday is part of the excitement, other travellers often decide to wait until the last minute to make their reservations. This last-minute market is not new but continues to attract attention from suppliers. In March 2010, a new online travel agency, bookinglate.com, was launched in the UK. Its owner, John McLean, justified the move, believing that 'there was a gap in the market for a retailer offering late bookings due to the increasing demand from holidaymakers holding out for the best deal' (Travel Weekly, 2011).

Another booking characteristic which attracts a small segment is that of the 'mystery hotel' product. Customers are provided with outline details of the product (perhaps the general location, travel dates and quality rating) but are only advised of the actual hotel after the booking has been confirmed. Such an approach allows hotel companies to list their excess stock, without directly affecting their direct retail rates. To service this market, online travel company Expedia announced the launch of their 'secret saver hotels' programme in November 2010 (Expedia, 2010).

Consumer processes

If all consumers responded in the same way to given stimuli, the lives of marketing managers would become much easier. Unfortunately, it has to be recognized that, while research continues to shed more light on our complex behaviour, the triggers that lead to it are still poorly understood. We can make some generalizations, however, based on research to date that can assist our understanding of consumer processes and, in particular, those of decision-making. Marketing theorists have developed a number of models to explain these processes. Perhaps the best-known, as well as the simplest, model is known as AIDA (see Figure 4.4).

This model recognizes that marketing aims to move the consumer from a stage of unawareness – of either the product (such as a specific destination or resort) or the particular brand (such as an individual package tour company or a hotel) – through a number of stages, to a point where the consumer is persuaded to buy a particular product and brand. The first step in this process is to move the consumer from unawareness to awareness. This entails an understanding of the way in which the consumer learns about new products.

Anyone thinking about how they came to learn about a particular destination they have visited quickly recognizes how difficult it is to pinpoint all the influences – many of which they may not even be consciously aware of. Every day, consumers are faced with hundreds of new pieces of knowledge, including information about new products. If we are to retain any of this information, the first task of marketing is to ensure that we perceive it – that is, become conscious of it.

Perception is an important part of the learning process. It involves the selection and interpretation of the information that is presented to us. As we cannot possibly absorb all the messages with which we are faced each day, many are consciously or unconsciously 'screened out' from our memories. If we are favourably predisposed towards a particular product or message, there is clearly a greater likelihood that we will absorb information about it. So, for example, if your best friend has just returned from a holiday in the Cayman Islands and has enthusiastically talked to you about the trip, that may stimulate your interest. If you then spot a feature on the Cayman Islands on television, that may further arouse your interest, even if, up to the point when your friend mentioned the place, you had never even heard of it. If what you see in the television programme reinforces the image of the destination that you gained from your friend, you might be encouraged to seek further information on the destination, perhaps by searching the Web or contacting the tourist office representing the destination. At any point in this process, you might be put off by what you find – for instance, if you perceive the destination as being too far away, too expensive or too inaccessible for the length of time you are contemplating going

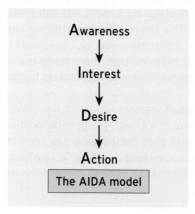

Figure 4.4 The AIDA model

away, you may search no further. If, however, the search process leads you to form a positive image of the destination, you may start mentally comparing it with others towards which you are favourably disposed.

The process of making choices involves constant comparison, weighing up one destination against others, estimating the benefits and the drawbacks of each as a potential holiday destination. As this process goes on, three things are happening – linked to image, attitude and risk.

Image

First, we develop an **image** of the destination in question. Here, it is important to realize that the image may be a totally inaccurate one, if the information sources we use are uninformed or deliberately seek to distort the information they provide. We may then find that we become confused about the image itself. For example, in the early 1990s, the UK media were full of exaggerated reports of muggings of tourists in the Miami area, while the destination itself continued to try to disseminate a positive image and the tour operators' brochures concentrated on selling the positive benefits of Miami with little reference to any potential dangers faced by tourists.

Images are built around the unique attributes that a destination can claim. The more these help to distinguish it from other similar destinations, the greater the attraction for the tourist. Those destinations that offer truly unique products, such as the Grand Canyon in the USA, the Great Wall of China or the pyramids in Egypt, have an inbuilt advantage, although, in time, the attraction of such destinations may be such that it becomes necessary to 'de-market' the site to avoid it becoming overly popular. In the early 1990s, the Egyptian Tourist Office also faced the problem of negative publicity, associated with attacks made on tourists by Islamic fundamentalists soon after the country experienced a large influx of Western tourists, many of whom failed to conform to the norms of behaviour expected in an Islamic country. A major objective of tourist offices in developing countries is that of generating a long-term positive image of the destination in their advertising, to give it a competitive edge over its competitors.

EXAMPLE ## Stereotyping destination images

Destination branding is a key component in encouraging visitors to consider a destination for their holiday. Standing out from the competition requires a distinctiveness and appeal which matches the desires and needs of the market. But creating an image which will appeal to different markets is often a hard task to achieve.

VisitBritain recognized these different needs and introduced two separate strategies – 'Classic Britain' (with beefeaters and black cabs) for the first time visitor and 'Dynamic Britain' for the repeat visitor looking for something more unexpected and inspirational (Roberts, 2009). Developing a successful brand image can be difficult, however. In 2006, Tourism Australia launched a short-lived and controversial campaign using the line 'So, where the bloody hell are you?' Industry representatives commented that this portrayed Australians as 'yobbos, while sophisticated, multicultural Australia is being ignored' (Alexander, 2006). However, the reality may be that many tourists develop their image of a destination from TV, films, even major sporting events. For Australia, the influence has come from the global distribution of TV shows such as Steve Irwin's *The Crocodile Hunter*, the soap opera *Neighbours*, and the Paul Hogan *Crocodile Dundee* films. Perception of the destination was further shaped by images shown throughout the 2000 Sydney Olympics.

Thus, the destination image is created from a variety of sources of information, making it necessary to promote the destination in a way which appeals to the customer's expectations – giving the customer what they know, rather than contradicting their beliefs (Alexander, 2006).

By contrast with those destinations offering unique attractions, many traditional seaside resorts, both in the UK and increasingly elsewhere, suffer from having very little to distinguish them from their competitors. The concept of the **identikit destination** as the popular choice for tourists is becoming outdated and simply offering good beaches, pleasant hotels and well-cooked food in an attractive climate is no longer enough in itself. In some way, an image must be developed by the tourist office to distance the resort from others. Then, for example, if changes in exchange rates or inflation rates work against the destination, it may still be seen as having sufficient 'added value' to attract and retain a loyal market.

Attitude

Second, we develop an **attitude** towards the destination. Several theorists suggest that an individual's lifestyle in general can best be measured by looking at their activities (or attitudes), interests and opinions – the so-called **A–I–O model**.

Attitude is a mix of our emotional feelings about the destination and our rational evaluation of its merits, both of which together will determine whether or not we consider it a possible venue for a holiday. It should be stressed at this point, however, that, while we may have a negative image of the destination, we may still retain a positive attitude towards going there because we have an interest in seeing some of its attractions or learning about its culture. This was often the case with travel to the Communist Bloc countries before the collapse of their political systems at the end of the 1980s, and, similarly, notwithstanding the increasing strains in the early twenty-first century on relationships between Western nations and countries with large Islamic populations, interest in their tourist sites and cultures remains high.

Risk

Third, there is the issue of **risk** to consider when planning to take a trip. All holidays involve some element of risk, whether in the form of illness, bad weather, being unable to get what we want if we delay booking, being uncertain about the product until we see it at first hand, and whether it represents value for money. We ask ourselves what risks we would run if we went there, if there is a high likelihood of their occurrence, if the risks are avoidable and how significant the consequences would be.

Some tourists, of course, relish a degree of risk, as this gives an edge of excitement to the holiday, so the presence of risk is not in itself a barrier to tourism. Others, however, are risk averse and will studiously avoid risk wherever possible. Clearly, the significance of the risk will be a key factor. So, there will be much less concern about the risk of poor weather than there will be about the risk of crime. The risk averse will book early, may choose to return to the same resort and hotel they have visited in the past, knowing its reliability; book a package tour, rather than travel independently.

The American Hilton and Holiday Inn chain hotels have been eminently successful throughout the world by offering some certainty about standards in countries where Americans could feel at risk regarding 'foreign' food, poor plumbing or other perceived inadequacies of a tour that are preventable if there is good forward planning. Travel businesses such as cruise lines, which offer a product with a reassuring lack of risk, can – and do – make this an important theme in their promotional campaigns.

Risk is also a factor in the methods chosen by customers to book their holidays. There is evidence that much of the continuing reluctance shown by some tourists to seek information and make bookings through Internet providers can be attributed, in part, to the lack of face-to-face contact with a trusted – and, hopefully, expert – travel agent and, in part, to the suspicion that information received through the Internet will be biased in favour of the information provider.

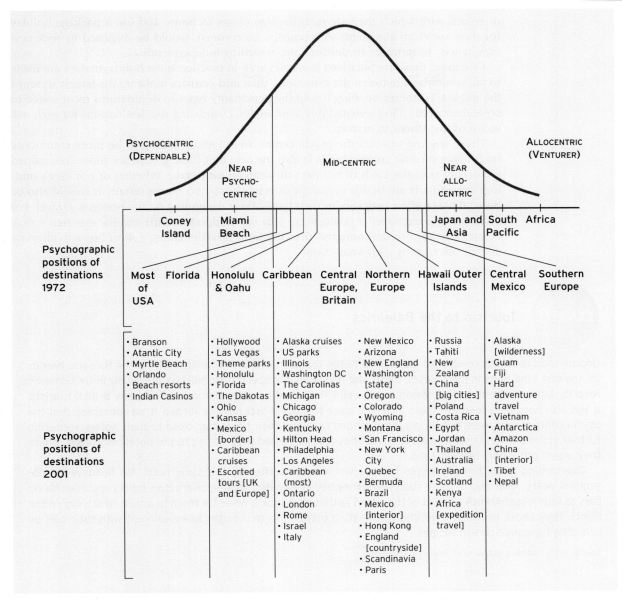

Figure 4.5 Tourist typology and travel destination choice – Plog's Allocentric and Psychocentric scale

Risk and tourist typologies

The extent to which risk is a product of personality is an issue that has been addressed by a number of tourism researchers, most notably Stanley Plog (1972). Essentially, Plog attempted to determine the relationship between introvert and extrovert personalities and holiday choice, and his theories have been widely published in tourism texts (see Figure 4.5).

Plog's theory attempted to classify the population of the USA by distinguishing between those judged to be **allocentrics** – those seeking variety, self-confident, outgoing and experimental – and **psychocentrics** – those who tend to be more concerned with themselves and the small problems of life. The latter are often anxious and inclined to seek security. The theory would suggest that psychocentrics would be more inclined to return to resorts with which they are familiar, stay closer to home and use a package holiday for their travel arrangements. Allocentrics, by contrast, would be disposed to seek new experiences, in more exotic destinations, travelling independently.

Of course, these are polarized examples and, in practice, most holidaymakers are likely to fall somewhere between the extremes – thus **mid-centrics** make up the largest sector of the market. Furthermore, Plog linked the personality types to destinations most suited to serve their needs. Plog revisited this work in 2001, updating the destinations for each risk sector of the American market.

Those tending towards the psychocentric were found by Plog to be more commonly from lower-income groups, but it is also the case that these groups are more constrained financially as to the kinds of holidays they can afford to take. Whether or not Plog's findings are similarly applicable to European markets is by no means certain. It should also be noted that travellers may vary in their level of risk depending on the reason for travel. For instance, a young traveller taking a gap year trip to develop skills and life experience may be prepared to consider more risk than the same traveller taking a short break to alleviate distress after sitting their final exams.

EXAMPLE   Tourism to the Balearics

Unpublished research conducted during the 1980s found that British tourists visiting the Balearic Islands for the first time were, in many cases, those who had tended to spend their holidays previously in UK domestic resorts. Although by that date Majorca was well established as a popular venue for many British tourists, it was also becoming seen by others as a safe place to enjoy a first holiday abroad. It was observed that the psychocentrics who were holidaying there tended to spend their time at or close to their hotels, venturing further afield only on organized excursions. They also restricted their eating to the hotel restaurant, where they would order only familiar food.

Overcoming initial timidity, these tourists would return, often to the same hotel, for holidays in subsequent years. After two or three such visits, they became bolder, seeking alternative hotels and even hiring cars to tour lesser-known regions of the island (although it took a while for them to adjust to driving on the right). They chose to widen their choice of eating places, too, and began to experiment with their diet by selecting typically Spanish recipes.

Source: Chris Holloway, unpublished research, 1981-1983

Plog recognized that personalities change over time and, given time, the psychocentric may become allocentric in their choice of holiday destination and activity as they gain experience of travel. It has long been accepted that many tourists actually seek novelty from a base of security and familiarity. This enables the psychocentric to enjoy more exotic forms of tourism. This can be achieved by, for instance, such tourists travelling through unfamiliar territories by coach in their own 'environmental bubble'. The provision of a familiar background to come home to after touring, such as is offered to Americans at Hilton Hotels or Holiday Inns (referred to earlier in this chapter), is a clear means of reassuring the nervous while in unfamiliar territory.

It is a point worth stressing that extreme pyschocentrics (or, indeed, those unable to travel due to ill-health reasons) may benefit from experiences of virtual travel. Increasingly sophisticated computers can replicate the experience of travel to exotic locations with none of the risk or difficulties associated with such travel. Already, armchair travellers can benefit from second-hand travel abroad by means of the now numerous holiday programmes and travelogues available via the television screen, a popular form of escapism.

Making the decision

The process of sorting through the various holidays on offer and determining which is the best for you is inevitably complex, and individual personality traits will determine how the eventual decision is made. Some people undertake a process of **extensive problem solving**, in which information is sought about a wide range of products, each of which is evaluated and compared with similar products.

Other consumers will not have the patience to explore a wide variety of choices, so will deliberately restrict their options, with the aim of **satisficing** (a balance between satisfying and sacrificing) rather than trying to guarantee that they buy the best possible product. This is known as **limited problem solving** and has the benefit of saving time.

Many consumers engage in **routinized response behaviour**, in which choices change relatively little over time. This is a common pattern among brand-loyal consumers, for example. Also some holidaymakers who have been content with a particular company or destination in the past may opt for the same experience again.

Finally, some consumers will buy on **impulse**. While this is more typical of products costing little, it is by no means unknown among holiday purchasers and is, in fact, a pattern of behaviour that is becoming increasingly prevalent – to the dismay of the operators, who then have less scope for forward planning and reduced opportunities to gain from investing deposits in the short term. Impulse purchasing is a valuable trait, though, where 'distressed stock' needs to be cleared at short notice and can be stimulated by late availability offers in particular.

Fashion and taste

Many tourism enterprises – and, above all, destinations – suffer from the effects of changing consumer tastes as fashion changes and 'opinion leaders' find new activities to pursue, new resorts to champion. It is difficult to define exactly what it is that causes a particular resort to lose its popularity with the public, although, clearly, if the resources it offers are allowed to deteriorate, the market will soon drift away to seek better value for money elsewhere.

Sometimes, however, it is no more than shifts in fashion that cause numbers of tourists to fall off. This is most likely to be the case where the site was deemed a fashionable attraction in the first place. This happened, for example, to Bath after its outstanding success as a resort in the eighteenth century, and the celebrity culture of the late twentieth and early twenty-first centuries has reinforced this trend. Resorts in the Mediterranean, such as St Tropez (fashionable from the 1960s and 1970s onwards after film star Brigitte Bardot chose to reside there) and the Costa Smeralda in Sardinia (developed by the Aga Khan and attracting a number of well-known Hollywood stars) became popular venues for the star-struck. Similarly, increasing wealth in this century, compounded by the availability of relatively cheap flights, have tended to mean that the celebrity resorts are further afield. In the Caribbean, Barbados – in particular, the Sandy Lane Hotel – attracts many celebrities and others who seek to bask in their light. Travel journalists make a point in their articles of identifying celebrities who have been spotted holidaying at certain resorts, further boosting demand.

It remains the case, however, that all products, including tourism, will experience a lifecycle of growth, maturity, saturation and eventual decline if no action is taken to arrest

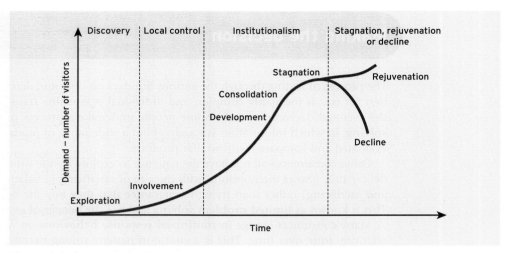

Figure 4.6 Tourist Area Life Cycle

it Generally, this will entail some form of innovation or other investment helping to revitalize the product. This change in demand over time was charted by Richard Butler (1980), in his research into the Tourist Area Life Cycle (TALC).

The Tourist Area Life Cycle (TALC)

The TALC (sometimes known as the Resort Lifecycle) (Figure 4.6) drew on academic research related to the product lifecycle, which recognized that demand changed over time as fashions and new competitors provided greater opportunities for customers to alter their purchase patterns. Butler (1980) created a classic model which visually depicted the changes that occur in demand over time and, whilst there has since been a range of criticisms regarding its validity, it has been widely used in research to help understand the cycle of destination development.

Each stage of the lifecycle reflects different characteristics of demand and supply.

- *Exploration.* At this stage there are few tourists visiting and interaction with the local population is likely to be high. The visitors who do arrive are likely to be from the 'allocentric' end of the typology scale and are likely to make use of local infrastructure as few dedicated tourist facilities will exist.

- *Involvement.* A small increase in annual visitor numbers will have occurred and, as a consequence, some tourism resources, such as guest houses and restaurants, will have been developed. These are likely to be owned by local entrepreneurs, who will consider some limited promotion of the destination. A tourist season may start to emerge and the local government may be encouraged to provide supporting infrastructure.

- *Development.* A significant number of tourists arrive annually and external organizations (such as global tour operators and international hotel chains) will begin to be established at the destination. The destination is likely to be attracting the mid-centric tourists.

- *Consolidation.* The number of tourists visiting each year is still growing but now at a slower rate. International chains and franchises are present, which may reduce the power of the local population to control the style and nature of tourism development. Tourists are likely to have limited contact with the local population.

- *Stagnation*. At this stage, visitor numbers are no longer increasing, being maintained by repeat visits from its psychocentric client base. Major efforts in marketing are necessary to maintain demand as the destination may fall out of fashion. Social and environmental problems may be occurring and tourist resources may be rather dilapidated.

- *Decline*. Without new investment the destination is likely to experience a decline in visitor numbers and tourist facilities may close, unable to maintain economic viability.

- *Rejuvenation (lifecycle extension)*. To avoid decline, it is necessary to reinvigorate the destination, often though investment. This may be provided by local government, desiring to maintain jobs and the social wellbeing of the local community. New facilities may be constructed to attract new markets or to encourage existing markets to revisit or stay longer.

There has been some criticism of this model as an effective predictor of development. Critics point out that the 'tourist area' may not be a neatly bounded region, and development (and decline) of resources such as attractions, accommodation and the natural environment may happen at different speeds and times. As facilities age, their fashionableness and perceived quality may also be affected; thus, investment is required continually, not just when nearing the decline phase. It is also important to note that not all sectors can manage the same capacity of visitors – for instance, the capacity of transport arriving at an island may be lower than the potential accommodation provision – so pent-up demand may ensure a longer lifecycle than would perhaps otherwise be expected. Finally, it should be noted that demand does not come from one homogeneous market, as business tourism, VFR and leisure tourism all compete for space and use of resources at the destination.

Demand is also influenced by external factors. This may include events such as economic recession or terrorist activity. It may also be influenced by changes in consumer behaviour. Fashion, of course, is one element critical to this process. In recent years, however, there has also been a swing towards improving health and wellbeing, affecting the types of holiday and activities chosen. As a direct consequence, most large hotel chains now incorporate a health centre as an element in their facilities.

Physical fitness already plays a larger role in our lives than in the past and is directly responsible for the growth in activity holidays. Tour operators have learned to cater for this changing demand pattern. Greater concern about what we eat has led to better-quality food, better preparation, better hygiene and cuisine that caters for increasingly segmented tastes, from veganism and vegetarianism to low glycemic index, high protein and fat-free diets. Similarly, the growing interest in personal development and creativity and the desire to lead a full, rich life promises well for those planning special interest and activity holidays of all kinds, especially the arts.

Awareness of how to be healthier, of course, includes greater concern about the danger of developing skin cancer as a result of exposure to the sun. In Australia, where love of the sun is inbuilt in the culture, the number of new cases of skin cancer diagnosed each year ran into the hundreds of thousands, of which around 1000 proved fatal. As a result, the authorities there launched a nationwide, and highly effective, campaign to reduce cancer by encouraging sunlovers to cover up and use sunscreen. As the depletion of the ozone layer heightens risk, so tourists will be forced to reconsider the attraction of the beach holiday – at least, in the form in which it has been offered up to the present. The fashionableness of suntans may well disappear. This was, after all, a twentieth-century phenomenon; up until the early part of that century, tans were disparaged by the middle classes as they were indicative of those who worked outside – that is, 'the labouring classes'. Despite the widespread media coverage of skin cancer, however, it is proving difficult to change long-standing attitudes. This is an issue that will be dealt with in depth in Chapter 6.

Factors influencing changes in tourist demand

It is fitting to complete this chapter by recognizing that patterns of demand in tourism are affected by two distinct sets of factors. First, we have factors that cannot be predetermined or forecast but which influence changes, sometimes with very little advance warning. The second set of factors includes cultural, social and technological changes developing in society, many of which can be forecast and for which there is time to adapt tourism products to meet new needs and expectations.

In the first category, we must include changes influenced by economic or political circumstances, climate and natural or artificial disasters. Economic influences will be examined more thoroughly in the following chapter, but here it is salutary to look at just some of the factors that have impacted on demand for foreign tourism so severely in recent years.

Undoubtedly, the outbreak of war has been the single greatest threat to foreign travel for the past half century. Millions of tourists visited the former Yugoslavia every year during the 1980s, but this market virtually disappeared in the 1990s when civil wars broke out. The Vietnam War and its aftermath killed off much tourism to South-East Asia in the 1960s and 1970s. War in the Middle East curtailed travel there, with long-term significant impact on leisure travel to Iraq. Further upheavals in the Middle East in Tunisia, Libya, Egypt, Syria and Bahrain at the end of the first decade of the twenty-first century have substantially discouraged both popular and cultural tourism to the area. Civil war and ethnic strife have similarly inhibited the development of tourism in many African countries.

Recently, it has also been the threat of terrorist attacks, actual or perceived, that has inhibited global travel – both Western fear of travel to Muslim countries and a general fear of travel to cities threatened by Islamic extremists. Terrorism has been a factor with which the tourism industry has had to cope for at least the past 25 years, with some attacks directly targeting tourists and others indirectly influencing either tourism demand or supply.

EXAMPLE   **Bomb blasts impact on Majorca tourism**

A series of bomb attacks hit the Spanish island in the peak holiday season in 2009 – the first bomb killed two Spanish policemen, with subsequent attacks a week later causing further concern. Whilst the attacks did not directly target tourism, many holidaymakers were indirectly affected.

Holiday plans were thrown into chaos in the immediate aftermath as flights to the island were cancelled or diverted as the airport closed. Cruise ships were also affected by the closure of the seaport. Despite the attacks, and the immediate inconvenience, few tour operators cancelled their provision.

Tourism is vital to the Balearic Islands, which earn 80% of their gross domestic product (GDP) from the industry, and receive more than 10 milion tourists annually (Times of Oman, 2009). For an island already experiencing decline due to the recession, strong euro and competition from destinations such as Cyprus and Turkey, terrorism provided a further challenge to their image.

The escalation in the number of attacks, together with the near-certainty of officials that further attacks would take place, especially in the USA and UK, has led to long-term uncertainty about growth prospects for global travel. Political unrest invariably destabilizes the desire to travel, although it has to be said that the populace of some countries, such as the USA, are far more averse to risk-taking in travel abroad than are others, such as the UK and Germany.

No less serious for global travel has been the threat posed by the rising impact of disease on a worldwide scale. The emergence of more virulent and vaccine-resistant forms of malaria in Africa and Asia has discouraged tourists from visiting those areas. Countries in Asia suffered the extra blow of a serious outbreak of severe acute respiratory syndrome (SARS) early in 2003, which led to the cancellation of many flights and tourist movements. Indeed, travel to China virtually ceased, apart from its adjacent neighbours, for a period of some six months. During this time, the UK was also severely hit by outbreaks of disease. First, there was the discovery of BSE in UK herds, which, although with only limited ability to cross the species to humans, scared away many potential visitors. Subsequently, there was an outbreak of foot and mouth disease, which, while far less dangerous to human beings, received massive negative publicity in the form of scare stories in the foreign press (to some extent, the result of inept and draconian control measures in the UK that were perceived as actively discouraging tourists from visiting rural areas). More recently, the swine flu pandemic – caused by a new strain of the H1N1 virus – believed to emanate from Mexico and spread by travellers who had visited the region – created a global concern that deaths would be on the scale of the Spanish Flu epidemic of 1918/19. While the World Health Organization (WHO) did report 18 000 known deaths from the disease, this was far lower than the initial expectations, and subsequent research suggests it was no more severe than seasonal strains of flu (Randall, 2010).

EXAMPLE **An unwanted holiday memento**

In 2010, singer and X-Factor judge Cheryl Cole became a high-profile victim of malaria, after contracting the illness whilst on holiday in Tanzania. Despite taking anti-malaria tablets while travelling she nevertheless contracted the disease, leading to hospitalization for several days. It is believed that more than 2000 people return to the UK each year infected, with about 10% of this number dying from the disease (Porter, 2010).

Finally, one must include the issue of climate change, which is contributing to natural disasters affecting tourist destinations globally. Areas already prone to heavy rainfall or hurricanes have witnessed conditions that have been catastrophic for locals and tourists alike, crowned by the disasters of the tsunami in the Far East at the end of 2004 and the impact of Hurricane Katrina on New Orleans and the US Gulf Coast in 2005. More recently, volcanic eruptions in Iceland led to the global cancellation of flights in parts of the northern hemisphere, with aircraft grounded for weeks, and a resultant huge economic impact on international tourism.

Some low-lying countries, especially islands in the Pacific, are already having to come to terms with the fact that their nascent tourism industries are doomed by rising sea levels, with the costs of safeguarding their coastlines too great to be practicable. Other developing countries, such as the Maldives, which have invested heavily in tourism in response to the boom in long-haul travel and the demand for active water-based adventure holidays, face the threats posed by global warming with trepidation.

The future pattern of tourist demand

Few of these events were predictable in advance. The lesson for the industry has been that, wherever possible, companies must be prepared for rapidly changing circumstances, often at very short notice. They need to build up an organization and products that are flexible and adaptable so that they can cope with change. The lessons for governments have been that the tourism industry is often vital to the economy and recovery should be supported with public funds if small firms are to remain viable.

In terms of demand for foreign travel, undoubtedly such events compound fears of foreign travel generally, and those most averse to risk-taking – our psychocentrics – are likely to choose to spend their holidays nearer to home or at the very least in countries viewed as being safer. Such a trend may even be welcomed by environmentalists, eager to see a fall in the demand for long-haul air travel, but this is to ignore the economic consequences for the destination countries concerned, several of which have no ready alternative means of generating foreign income and investment.

Social and lifestyle changes

Social change is easier to predict, as are long-term trends in travel patterns. All too often, however, the industry has been slow to respond to these indicators. We know, for example, that only one family in four in the UK now conforms to the stereotypical pattern of two parents and two children, and increasing numbers of people are living alone or bringing up children as single parents, yet such 'untypical' families are often not welcomed by operators as their pricing structures weigh unfairly against such tourists. Similarly, with increasing life expectancy, the rise in divorce and fall in marriage rates, there are now some 7 million single-person households in the UK, yet high additional charges for single tourists in package tours remain the norm and the demand for single accommodation is often difficult to meet.

Other notable changes in UK society include an increase in spending power of working women and the earlier maturation of children, leading to a demand for more adult holidays. Children now exert much more influence in the making of travel decisions and are tending to travel more with friends than in the traditional family group.

Perhaps most notable has been the impact of a growing market of senior citizens who are active, have high levels of spending power and are looking for new experiences in their travels (for those who dismiss the senior market as unadventurous, it's worth bearing in mind that Dennis Tito, the world's first space tourist, was over 60 when he took his space flight in 2001). The over-50s today account for one-third of all the disposable income in the UK. While the total population of the UK is expected to fall in the medium term, it is estimated that there will be a 31% increase in the over-55s by 2020, with many of them taking early retirement to spend the inheritances arising from the sale of their parents' properties on long-haul and cruise holidays.

Predictions about longevity have suggested that people born today will live longer than earlier generations, but it is clear that lifespan is affected by where you live for much of your life. It is also clear than gender is significant, with women living longer than men – in Russia the difference is more than a decade (Table 4.4). The UK received more than 5 million seniors (over 55s) in 2009, nearly one-fifth of all visitors – an increase from the one-eighth that this segment contributed in 1993.

Another fast-growing market is the lesbian, gay, bisexual and transgender (LGBT), now commonly referred to as the 'pink market'. Members of this group in the UK typically take one domestic and two foreign holidays each year. They earn more – and spend more – than the average traveller. They particularly enjoy travelling to destinations where their sexual orientation is unquestioned, such as Montreal, Bangkok and the Sydney Mardi Gras festival. This market has already been successfully tapped in the USA, where travel propen-

Table 4.4 Life expectancy at birth (for persons born 2005–2010)

	Men	Women
South Africa	50	53
Russian Federation	60	73
India	62	65
Brazil	69	76
China	71	75
Czech Republic	73	80
Denmark	76	81
USA	77	81
Germany	77	82
UK	77	82
France	78	85
Israel	79	83
Japan	79	86
Australia	79	84
Iceland	80	83

Source: United Nations Statistical Division, 2011

sity is high: 91% take annual holidays (54% overseas) compared with a national average of only 64% (9% overseas).

EXAMPLE **Pink mountain tourism**

The Himalayan kingdom of Nepal has, in recent years, experienced significant political instability. At the height of the unrest, few tourists visited but by 2010 about 500 000 visitors had returned to this newly established republic. Now, efforts to recover the tourism economy have seen significant promotional efforts, aimed at attracting up to a million visitors a year.

With gay and lesbian rights enshrined in law, the destination now welcomes this market. Opportunities being promoted to gay visitors include wedding and honeymoon celebrations at the Mount Everest base camp.

This market is seen as lucrative – estimated to be worth $100 billion globally – and the goal for Nepal is to attract 200 000 gay tourists annually. Travel agencies dedicated to this market have already been established to meet the potential demand.

Source: Buncombe, 2011

Travellers of all kinds are now both sophisticated and demanding, often being more familiar with world travel destinations and attractions than those selling the products. This produces a new kind of challenge to the industry to provide a professional level of service that it is still a long way from achieving.

There are many other clear social trends in the industry in the opening years of the twenty-first century for which suppliers and agents must learn to cater. Greater choice in consumer purchasing of all kinds is leading to demand for more flexible packages of differing durations. Many will require tailor-made approaches to packaging and companies are establishing divisions specifically for this purpose. This has led to the phenomenon of **dynamic packaging**, where agents and operators put together individual elements of the package, usually by searching websites. This process, however, is labour-intensive and requires great product knowledge. This is explained in greater detail in Chapter 19.

Earlier, reference was made to the way in which the mass demand for passive beach holidays has given way to demand for more active holidays of all kinds, even from those in the upper age brackets. Special interest holidays now cater for the widening range of hobbies of a leisure-orientated society. Adventure holidays, both domestic and foreign, are now packaged by operators to appeal to a range of markets.

In the latter years of the last century, tour operators attempted to gain market share by cutting prices and making budget offers that often fell below the quality levels anticipated by consumers. Selling on price rather than quality became the keynote for the industry. Consumers were encouraged to buy on price and seek out the cheapest. Inevitably, the rising numbers of complaints forced companies to reconsider value for money and quality assurance, although deep discounting remains the bugbear of the industry, for both traditional package tours and the cruise market.

In the format of package tours, we find demand moving in two distinct directions. On the one hand, self-catering has become increasingly popular, partly as a cost-saving exercise but equally as a means of overcoming the constraints imposed by package holidays in general and the accommodation sector in particular. Set meals at set times gave way to 'eat what you please, where you please, when you please'. In reply, the package tour industry provided the product to meet this need: the French gîte holidays became popular and across Southern Europe self-catering villas and apartments flourished, while in the UK demand moved from resort hotels and guesthouses to self-catering flats. Hundreds of thousands of Britons invested in timeshare properties in order to own their own 'place in the sun' or increasingly found their own accommodation abroad, while the operators provided 'seat only' packages on charter aircraft to cater for their transport needs.

The other side of the coin is reflected in the growth in demand for all-inclusive holidays, which we looked at earlier in this chapter. This particular type of holiday is likely to experience continuing demand, both for short- and long-haul destinations.

The market for short-break holidays of between one and three nights has also expanded rapidly, becoming frequently an addition to the principal holiday. The UK tourism industry has benefited as many of these breaks are taken within the UK, helping to make up for the decline in traditional two-week summer holidays at the seaside. The choice of short-break destinations abroad has also widened, with the traditional destinations of Paris, Amsterdam, Brussels, Barcelona and Rome being joined by Budapest, Prague, Krac ów, Reykjavik, Carcassonne, Graz, Kaunas, Trieste and even New York.

Long-haul traffic has enjoyed a steady rise as disposable incomes were matched by ever-reducing air fares, especially across the Atlantic. Holidays to the USA boomed, especially to Florida. Many Britons now own second homes there, not only along the coast but also within easy driving distance of Orlando, where the popular Disney World theme park attracts millions eager to rent self-catering accommodation during their stay. Once again, this market is threatened by substantial rises in ticket prices (some BA long-haul flights were carrying fuel surcharges in excess of £200 per passenger as this text went to press), although in general the market is far more price-inelastic than that for budget carriers.

Second home ownership

Perhaps the most significant development has been the increase in second home ownership. Accurate statistics on this trend are difficult to find (doubtless in part because many residents are unwilling to keep the tax authorities advised of their owning homes abroad), but the most recent government figures claim some 177 000 English households owned homes abroad in 2004, while some 229 000 residents owned second homes within the UK. Other sources, however, put levels of UK property ownership abroad far higher, with some estimates suggesting that as many as 500 000 Britons own properties in France alone. This has fuelled the growth of the low-cost airlines from and to regional airports on the Continent. These figures do not include the large number of British citizens who no longer count the UK as their principal place of residence. Around 1 in 12 Britons – some 5.5 million – live abroad, and 385 000 British residents left the UK in the 12 months to July 2007 (more than half of whom were native Britons). A decision to live abroad does not indicate a willingness to cut off all connections with the mother country, so these changes in country of residence in themselves generate subsequent high levels of tourism mobility in both directions.

Second home ownership has also been driven by greater media attention. TV programmes – such as *A Place in the Sun* and *Wanted Down Under*, both of which help UK residents to find homes in overseas locations – encourage the idea of living abroad, either permanently or as a frequent visitor. So popular has this become that consumer trade shows have been established to further assist those thinking of living abroad.

Summary

All this is not to say that the traditional sun, sea and sand holiday is in terminal decline, but those still loyal to this form of holiday are seeking more activities. Notably, this includes increased demand for cultural visits inland from the popular resorts of Spain and Greece. Nor are these traditional holidaymakers content merely to seek out the familiar beaches of the Mediterranean – many are now travelling as far afield as Pattaya Beach and Phuket in Thailand, Goa in India and Mombasa in Kenya to enjoy their beaches in more exotic surroundings.

The traditional 'law of tourism harmony' – every aspect of the tour being of broadly similar standard and quality – has given way to a 'pick and mix' approach, in which savings may be effected in one area in order to indulge oneself in another. Tourists may decide, for example, to choose cheap B&B accommodation while eating out at expensive restaurants; others are booking cheap flights on low-cost airlines and luxury hotels at their destinations, on the grounds that the flight lasts a mere couple of hours, while they intend to stay several days in the hotel, so standards there are more important. By contrast, the term 'Hilton Hippies' has been used to describe those who may want to engage in rough activities such as mountain-biking by day, but look for luxury in their overnight accommodation.

In most developed countries, those in work have been forecast to enjoy increased disposable incomes and a higher propensity to travel abroad, although such forecasts are now challenged by the severe global recession affecting tourist-generating countries. Recovery is expected to take five or more years, and meanwhile this is likely to increase the demand for domestic holidays at the expanse of foreign travel, and to increase demand for budget travel to the detriment of more free-spending holidays. At the same time, there will continue to be a relatively high number of unemployed in the population, most of whom will be unable to take holidays of any kind. In the past, those with spouses who have not wished to travel abroad have tended not to do so themselves, but lifestyle changes could mean that an increasing number of happily married couples will choose to holiday separately, each 'doing their own thing'.

Those charged with the task of marketing to tourists must be fully familiar with these and other patterns of tourist behaviour and any trends that might suggest these are changing. Some such changes will be generated by tourists themselves, others will come about as a result of changes taking place in the business environment and in society as a whole. What must be recognized is that the pace of change in the world of tourism is constantly accelerating, requiring entrepreneurs to react faster than they have needed to do in the past. Of equal importance is the requirement for the industry to recognize that protection of the environment and the indigenous populations in the destination countries must also be taken into account. Companies will also have to ensure that any new initiatives do not depart from the obligation to ensure products are sustainable.

Questions and discussion points

1. Maslow's Hierarchy of Needs is a well-known model related to motivation. Discuss whether this is helpful as an approach to understanding tourism motivation.

2. The 'Senior' or 'Grey' market is said to be growing. However, serving this market may require some adaptations to the product. Identify the changes which may need to be made if this market is to be served by tourist attractions and tour operators.

3. How might the motivations of business travellers differ from those of leisure travellers? How can a hotel attempt to meet the needs of both segments?

Tasks

1. Investigate the annual tourist arrivals numbers for a country of your choice. Try to ensure you have at least 50 years of arrivals data. Plot these data on a chart to examine the lifecycle of demand. Write a report which examines this lifecycle in comparison to the theory developed by Richard Butler. What does the lifecycle suggest about the development of the destination?

2. Interview three different tourists. Ask them about their motives for travelling and why they chose the destinations they visited. Compare and contrast the responses. What does this tell us about tourist typologies?

Bibliography

Alexander, H. (2006) So who the bloody hell are we?, *The Sydney Morning Herald*, 30 March.

BBC (2011) *London Olympics Tourism Warning*, available online at: http://www.bbc.co.uk/news/uk-15610343 (accessed November 2011).

Brousse, C. (2009) *ESeC: the European Union's Socio-economic Classification project*, INSEE – Courrier des statistiques, English series no. 15.

Buncombe, A. (2011) Himalayan kingdom throws open its doors to gay tourists, *The Independent*, 10 January.

Butler, R. (1980) The concept of the tourist area life-cycle of evolution: implications for management of resources, *Canadian Geographer*, **24** (1), 5–12.

Crompton, J. L. (1979) Motivations for pleasure vacation, *Annals of Tourism Research*, **6** (4), 408–424.

Dann, G. M. S. (1977) Anomie, Ego-enhancement and Tourism, *Annals of Tourism Research*, **4**, 184–194.

Expedia (2010) *Expedia.co.uk launches new opaque booking service for hoteliers with 'Expedia Secret Saver Hotels'*, available online at: http://press.expedia.co.uk/innovation/secret-saver-52 (accessed November 2011).

Holloway, J. C. (2004) *Marketing for Tourism*, 4th edn, Harlow, Prentice Hall.

Iso-Ahola, S. E. (1982) Toward a social psychological theory of tourism motivation: a rejoinder, *Annals of Tourism Research*, **9**, 256–261.

Maslow, A. (1954) *Motivation and Personality*, New York, Harper, p. 31.

McIntosh, R. W., Goeldner, C. R. and Ritchie, J. R. B. (1995) *Tourism: principles, practices, philosophies*, New York, Wiley.

Ministry of Economic Development (2010) *Domestic Tourism Segmentation Research*, available online at: http://www.tourismresearch.govt.nz/Data--Analysis/Research-projects-reports-and-studies/Research-Reports/Domestic-Tourism-Segmentation-Research (accessed November 2011).

Pearce, P. L. and Lee, U.-I. (2005) Developing the travel career approach to tourist motivation, *Journal of Travel Research*, **43** (3), 226–237.

Plog, S. (1972) *Why destination areas rise and fall in popularity*, unpublished paper presented to the Southern Chapter of the Travel Research Association, Los Angeles.

Porter, M. (2010) Malaria myths and mistakes; Cheryl Cole is one of the lucky ones – malaria kills half a billion people worldwide every year, *The Times*, 13 July.

Preuss, H. (2005) The economic impact of visitors at major multi-sport events, *European Sport Management Quarterly*, **5** (3), 283–303.

Randall, T. (2010) *Swine Flu Found No More Severe Than Seasonal Virus*, available online at: www.bloomberg.com/news/2010-09-07/swine-flu-in-children-is-no-more-severe-than-seasonal-virus-study-finds.html (accessed November 2011).

Reid, R. D. and Bojanic, D. C. (2010) *Hospitality Marketing Management*, 5th edn, Hoboken, NJ, Wiley.

Richardson, J. I. and Fluker, M. (2004) *Understanding and Managing Tourism*, French's Forest, Pearson Hospitality Press.

Roberts, J. (2009) Travel marketing: shaping the destination, *Marketing Week*, 24 September.

Ryan, C. (1991) *Recreational Tourism: A social science perspective*, London, Routledge.

Sunday Star-Times (2010) We're Ho-Hum on holidays, *Sunday Star-Times – Fairfax New Zealand*, 6 June.

The Economist (2008) A new itinerary – travel and tourism, *The Economist*, 17 May.

Times of Oman (2009) Spain's tourism sector shaken by ETA attack in Majorca, *Times of Oman*, 2 August.

Travel Weekly (2011) *Bookinglate.com launches for bargain hunters*, available online at: http://www.travelweekly.co.uk/Articles/2011/03/10/36444/bookinglate.com-launches-for-bargain-hunters.html (accessed November 2011).

United Nations Statistical Division (2011) *Social Indicators: Life Expectancy*, available online at: http://unstats.un.org/unsd/demographic/products/socind/health.htm#tech (accessed November 2011).

Further reading

Cohen, E. (1974) Who is a tourist? A conceptual classification, *Social research*, **39** (1), 164–182.

Krippendorf, J. (1984) *The Holiday Makers: Understanding the impact of leisure and travel*, Oxford, Heinemann.

Ross, G. (1994) *The Psychology of Tourism*, Elsternwick, Hospitality Press Pty Ltd.

Ryan, C. (2003) *Recreational Tourism: demands and Impacts*, Clevedon, Channel View Publications.

5

The economic impacts of tourism

Contents

Learning outcomes

After studying this chapter, you should be able to:

- identify the economic benefits of tourism for a nation, both nationally and regionally
- be aware of the negative economic effects of tourism for destinations
- understand how tourism is measured statistically
- recognize the limitations of statistical measurement.

Tourism has brought prosperity but it's also creating a new set of problems. Migrants are coming from the impoverished Ecuadorian mainland to work in the travel industry. The residents and tourists must be serviced by an ever-growing fleet of cargo ships and airplanes, which are bringing invasive species as unwanted hitchhikers.

Sesser (2008) Galapagos Under Siege

Introduction

As highlighted in the quote above, the experience of the Galapagos Islands, off the coast of Ecuador, is that tourism can bring both economic benefits and costs. Globally, tourism as an economic activity is important for the many countries that try to obtain a share of this estimated $6 trillion industry (WTTC, 2011a). While it can bring in wealth and economic benefits, there are also consequences for those nations and their regions. Therefore it is important to understand the economic impacts of tourism.

This is a complex topic that can only be touched on in this text. Those who wish to examine the subject in depth are referred to texts designed for this purpose, such as Bull (1995), Tribe (2005) and Vanhove (2005). The aim of this chapter, therefore, is primarily to explore the economic impacts of tourism resulting from national and international tourist flows and the ways in which this is measured and recorded. In later chapters, the economics of the firm, the industry and its various sectors will be examined. First, however, we will look at the movement of tourists internationally and some of the economic factors influencing those flows.

The international tourist market

Tourism is probably the single most important industry in the world. According to the World Travel and Tourism Council (WTTC, 2011b), the global tourism industry would account for 2.8% of global gross domestic product (GDP) in 2011, while the broader impacts (including the indirect effects on the economy as a result of tourism) would mean that it could be expected to account for 9.1% of global GDP. Furthermore, it was estimated that the total contribution of the travel and tourism industry worldwide would provide 258.5 million jobs, representing 8.8% of total employment. According to the most recent estimate by the United Nations World Tourism Organization (UNWTO), 880 million international trips were taken in 2009. Whilst this was a decline on previous years, perhaps attributable to the turbulent economic climate at that time, this still led to worldwide tourism receipts for 2009 of US$852 billion (see Table 5.1).

The rapid increase in international travel during the early post-war years – exceeding 10% per annum from 1950 to 1960 – could not be permanently sustained, of course, as it reflected the pent-up demand that had built up in the war years and the slow economic recovery after the war. It is worth noting, however, that, apart from the odd hiccup, from 1970 to the 1990s annual growth ran above 4%, even in the early 1990s when there was a global recession. Although 2009 saw a decline in international arrivals, average growth since 2000 has been 3% (UNWTO, 2010) and early estimates for 2010 suggested that arrivals would exceed 930 million. The good news for the tourism industry, therefore, is that, despite the decline in 2009, the long-term trend is forecast to be an upward one.

Domestic tourism

It is important to note that the data above relate to international travel and the figures do not include the vast number of people taking trips within their own countries. Often, in fact, much higher levels of domestic tourism take place. Here, Americans lead the field, with over 1.4 billion domestic trips in 2010, compared to 64 million international outbound trips. India and China both have fast-growing markets for domestic tourism, with 741 million and 1.2 billion domestic trips, respectively (Euromonitor, 2011). For many

Table 5.1 A profile of international tourist arrivals and receipts, 1950–2007

Year	Arrivals (m)	Receipts (US $bn)
1950	25.3	2.1
1960	69.3	6.9
1970	165.8	17.9
1980	278.2	106.5
1990	445.8	272.9
1995	544.9	410.8
2000	685.5	476.4
2001	683.8	464.4
2002	702.8	482.3
2003	689.8	524.2
2004	764.4	633.0
2005	803.4	676.5
2006	847.3	742.0
2007	901.1	857.4
2008	918.8	940.6
2009 (P)	880.1	852.0

Note: Excludes international fares. (P) = provisional
Source: UNWTO, 2010

Table 5.2 A comparison of domestic trips with international tourist arrivals (2010)

Country	Domestic trips (m)	International arrivals (m)	Ratio of domestic trips to international arrivals
USA	1429.3	59.0	24.4
China	1229.6	54.2	22.7
India	741.0	5.7	129.5
Brazil	310.6	5.3	58.6
Japan	292.8	8.6	34.0
France	208.2	77.5	2.7
UK	135.7	29.3	4.6
Italy	81.6	45.4	1.8
Australia	66.4	5.8	11.5
Austria	11.9	21.5	0.6

Source: based on Euromonitor, 2011

countries, the number of domestic trips far exceeds the level of arrivals from international tourists (see Table 5.2). It is important to consider, however, that the spending of international tourists may be higher than that of domestic tourists.

Trends in international travel

As controls over the freedom of movement of populations in many countries are lifted, many are seeking the opportunity to travel outside their own borders for the first time, not least residents of China, now the fourth biggest generator of overseas tourist expenditure.

Table 5.3 Leading tourism-generating countries, 2009 (based on provisional tourism expenditure)

Position	Country	Expenditure (US$ billion)
1	Germany	81.2
2	USA	73.2
3	UK	50.3
4	China	43.7
5	France	38.5
6	Italy	27.9
7	Japan	25.1
8	Canada	24.2
9	Russian Federation	20.8
10	Netherlands	20.7

Source: UNWTO, 2010

The UNWTO therefore continues to take an optimistic view of the long term, estimating that international tourism trips will reach 1.6 billion by 2020 (UNWTO, 2010), with the mature regions of Europe and the Americas experiencing slower growth than Asia, the Middle East and Africa.

International tourism is generated, for the most part, within the nations of Europe, North America and China – the result of low prices, frequent flights and large, relatively wealthy populations (see Table 5.3). It is interesting to note that the top ten generating countries are responsible for almost half the total expenditure on foreign travel, whilst expenditure by the top four countries accounts for well over a quarter of all tourism spending globally.

As the Chinese gain greater freedom of movement, travel has become an aspiration for many urban professionals with the financial means to participate in leisure travel. Although China is a significant tourism-generating country in terms of expenditure, many of the international journeys made are regional. The two special administrative regions of Macau and Hong Kong remain primary destinations, with South Korea, Japan, Malaysia and Singapore also proving popular for this market. Historically, Japan has also been growing strongly as a tourism-generating country, with government encouragement and changes in attitudes to work and loyalty to their firms influencing the Japanese to travel abroad in greater numbers and for longer periods of time. However, a stagnating economy and the recent tragic earthquake and tsunami may lead to shifts in travel patterns for this population.

Looking at the flow of international tourism over the long term, one can conclude that the tourism business is surprisingly resilient. Whatever short-term problems emerge – acts of terrorism, medical emergencies such as SARS, avian flu and the swine flu pandemic in 2009, the 2004 Asian tsunami, flooding in places such as New Orleans following Hurricane Katrina in 2005 and Queensland's Gold Coast in 2011, Iceland's volcano eruption and subsequent ash cloud in 2010 and the earthquakes in Christchurch, New Zealand and Japan in 2011 – tourists eventually return in ever greater numbers.

Tourist destinations

While Western Europe continues to dominate, fluctuations in exchange rates and the turbulent financial climate impacted on visitor arrivals – the past few years have seen a growth in popularity for Eastern Europe, although countries such as Poland and the Czech Republic posted declines in visitor numbers between 2007 and 2009 (UNWTO, 2010).

Table 5.4 Leading tourism-receiving countries, 2009 (based on provisional international tourist arrivals in millions) and their tourism receipts

Position	Country	Arrivals (millions)	Receipts (US$ billion)	Receipt per arrival (US$)
1	France	74.2	49.4	665.74
2	USA	54.9	93.9	1711.19
3	Spain	52.2	53.2	1018.11
4	China	50.9	39.7	779.85
5	Italy	43.2	40.2	930.85
6	UK	28.0	30.0	1071.52
7	Turkey	25.5	21.3	833.14
8	Germany	24.2	34.7	1432.84
9	Malaysia	23.6	15.8	667.00
10	Mexico	21.5	11.3	525.54

Source: UNWTO, 2010

Early signs of recovery were seen in the visitor arrival numbers for 2010, with emerging economies experiencing stronger growth (8%) compared to advanced economies (5%) (UNWTO, 2011a).

Simply looking at receipts, though, will not give a sound picture of the value of tourism to an economy. It is important to consider how many tourists make up the total receipts (see Table 5.4). The countries with the highest receipts per arrival are generally those where prices are highest and include countries such as Sweden and Japan. In economic terms, the financial value of tourism to a country may be more important than the number of tourists it receives. It is vital, therefore, that the average spends of tourists from different countries are assessed, which may be influenced by the average length of time tourists from a particular country stay in a country and their average daily spend.

Propensity to travel

It is also important to take account of factors likely to lead to the growth or decline of tourism from each country. Residents of countries where GDP is high are perhaps more likely to be able to afford to take holidays, often international, each year. The potential for growth is high for those living in Eastern Europe, whose income, for the most part, is rising strongly since the fall of communism. The entry of several of these countries into the EU in 2004 has already boosted tourism in both directions within Europe.

The BRIC countries (Brazil, Russia, India and China) are all expected to experience a rise in the middle-income classes and, with a correlation between affluence and international and domestic travel patterns (WTTC, 2011), these markets hold significant potential for growth. China particularly is expected to dominate and with a population of more than one billion, a small percentage increase in outbound travel can correlate to millions of additional trips.

In spite of the high revenues generated from Americans travelling abroad, only a small minority of the population actually possesses a passport. Most American tourists tend to travel to adjacent countries that, until recently, did not require them to carry passports. Also, because of the size and diversity of their own landscape, many are content to take holidays within their own country.

So the *propensity* to take holidays abroad is another important characteristic to take into account. The propensity to take foreign holidays varies considerably within Europe, too. It is high among the Scandinavians – no doubt this is due in part to the long winters and lack of sunshine – while only a quarter of Italians share this desire for foreign travel. Traditionally, Italians are surprisingly unadventurous in their travelling, with nearly half of those travelling on holiday being content to return to the same resort, and even the same hotel, every year for a decade. The French, too, prefer to travel within their own country, often to second homes in the countryside, rather than venture abroad. Although Britons have a reputation for travelling abroad, a third of the population takes no holidays at all during the year (but not necessarily the same third every year).

We should also recognize that, while tourism expenditure in aggregate will be highest for wealthy countries having large populations, the high levels of disposable income among the populations of smaller nations with a significant proportion of wealthy residents, such as Switzerland or Luxembourg, will tend to lead to higher levels of participation in international tourism. Where international borders are close to places of residence – as is the case with Switzerland and Luxembourg – this will significantly increase the propensity to travel abroad.

To help understand the travel habits of particular nations, it is possible to calculate the **travel propensity** – that is, the percentage of the population taking trips. This can be considered in two dimensions – the **net travel propensity** and the **gross travel propensity**.

Net travel propensity reflects the percentage of the population that has travelled for at least one trip (though many will have taken more). As some of the population will not have taken a trip at all, the net travel propensity will be less than 100%. Research into the Swiss travel market has identified a net travel propensity of 88% of the population taking at least one trip in 2007 (Laesser and Bieger, 2008), although the levels for most countries are likely to be much lower than this (Table 5.5).

Table 5.5 Net travel propensity of selected European countries (2006)

Country	Percentage of the population taking a trip (of four nights or longer)
Austria	62.1
Belgium	45.1
Czech Republic	51.6
Denmark	64.4
Estonia	22.7
Germany	80.7
Greece	43.8
Finland	57.3
France	61.5
Italy	49.1
Latvia	18.3
Lithuania	26.3
Luxembourg	49.7
Netherlands	68.0
Norway	74.4
Poland	32.7
Portugal	27.3
Spain	44.6
UK	60.8

Source: Eurostat, 2008

Gross travel propensity reflects the total number of trips taken in relation to the total population. In areas, such as Western Europe, where the local population may take several trips, the gross travel propensity may exceed 100% (as those who have been on multiple trips counterbalance those who have not travelled at all).

EXAMPLE   **UK gross travel propensity**

The gross travel propensity of the British to take a holiday - that is, the ratio of trips taken in relation to the total population - is high (see Table 5.6). The total number of trips is 174.56 million and, for a population of 62.3 million, this provides a gross travel propensity of 280%. The propensity for international travel is lower at 89.2%.

Table 5.6 Trips taken by the UK population, 2006

Population (million)	Domestic trips (million)	International trips (million)
62.3	119.0	55.56

Sources: ONS, 2011a, b; VisitEngland et al., 2011

Other factors affecting the economic value of tourism

While there are many factors that motivate people to travel abroad, a major one is likely to be the relative cost compared with their income. Since greater demand levels can lead to lower prices, with transport and accommodation costs falling for each additional person booked, there is a direct relationship between cost, price and demand (see Figure 5.1). This helps to explain the vicious price wars in the travel industry, designed to capture market share and increase numbers, which have been so much a feature of competition in the travel industry over the past 20 years.

The continued popularity of the no-frills airlines has seen an increase in the number of routes being offered, opening up low-cost travel to places in Eastern Europe as well as islands such as Malta. This trend is likely to continue, unless sharply curtailed by rising fuel prices or the imposition of fuel taxes to offset pollution.

Other factors to take into account include attitudes to the use of leisure time. In the USA, some 30% of the workforce takes less than half the holiday time to which they are entitled – and this is in a country where the average paid holiday is still only two to three weeks compared with the four to five weeks now standard throughout Europe. The Japanese, as can be seen in Table 5.7, seldom take their full entitlement. Despite an entitlement of at least 36 days, they typically take just over half of this. Even in the UK, roughly a fifth of the working population fails to take its full entitlement (Expedia, 2010).

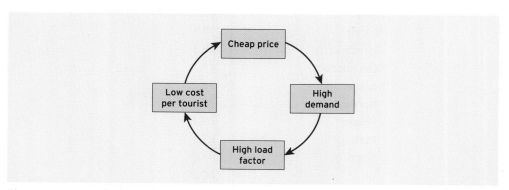

Figure 5.1 Relationship between cost, price and demand

Table 5.7 Total number of days of holiday entitlement

Country	Total days (statutory minimum and public holidays)	% of holiday taken
France	40	92
Japan	36	55
UK	36	91
Italy	31	82
New Zealand	31	90
Germany	30	93
Australia	28	83
USA	25*	82
Canada	19	90

* USA – there is no mandatory minimum but typically 15 days holiday is provided plus 10 public holidays.

Sources: Mercer, 2009; Expedia, 2010

The value of economic data

Gathering data on tourists is a vital task for the government of a country, generating vital information for its own national tourist office and the providers of tourism services. Governments need to know the contribution that tourism makes to the economy in terms of income, employment, investment and the balance of payments. Concern about regional development requires that these statistics be sufficiently refined to allow them to be broken down by region. Governments will also wish to compare their tourism performance with that of other countries, as well as to establish how well they are doing in attracting tourists to the country over a period of time.

Tourism organizations, whether in the public or the private sector, need such data to enable them to forecast what will happen in the future. This means identifying trends in the market, patterns of growth and changing demand for destinations, facilities or types of holiday.

On the basis of this knowledge, future planning can be undertaken. The public sector will make recommendations and decisions regarding the **infrastructure** and **superstructure** needed to support growth. Infrastructure will include, for example, the building of new airports and seaport terminals or the expansion of existing ones, the provision of new or improved roads to growing destinations and the improvement of other services, such as public utilities, including water and electricity, which will be needed to cope with the expected expansion of tourism. Some of these plans may take many years to implement. For example, the discussions surrounding the building of a fifth terminal at London's Heathrow airport took place over more than a decade, far longer than the time taken to actually construct the terminal itself.

Superstructure comprises the tourist amenities needed – hotels, restaurants, shops and other services that tourists take for granted when they visit. It cannot necessarily be assumed that these services will be provided by developers in the private sector. If a new destination is being developed, there will be a degree of risk involved while the destination becomes established, so developers may be reluctant to invest in projects such as hotels until there is proven demand at the destination. Governments or local authorities can themselves undertake the construction of hotels, as often occurs in developing countries, or they can encourage hotel construction by underwriting costs or providing subsidies of some kind until the destination becomes established. Similarly, private companies can use the statistics that demonstrate growth or market change, extending or adapting their products to meet the changing needs of the marketplace.

To show how this information can be used, let us take the example of a destination such as London, which attracts a high volume of overseas visitors. The flow of those visitors will be affected by a great many different factors. For example, if tourists can purchase more pounds sterling for their own currency, or air fares to the destination have fallen, or a major event, such as an international sports event – the Olympics – is being organized, all these factors will encourage tourists to visit the city.

Negative factors also have an effect. Terrorist activity in the capital (as in July 2005) affected decisions to come to the UK, while other global events – war in Iraq and SARS in 2003, avian flu in 2004/05, the swine flu pandemic in 2009 – all influence travel plans. US tourists are particularly sensitive to the threat of terrorism and will revert to holidaying at home if they sense that the risk of foreign travel is increasing. Negative first impressions, such as air pollution in the city, extensive littering, a decaying and overcrowded public transport system, even large numbers of homeless people on the streets, can all affect tourism adversely, tourists deciding to go elsewhere or recommending to their friends that they do so.

EXAMPLE | ## The influence of exchange rates – a UK example

Recessions may hit countries to different extents, so that, in one year, the forecast might be for a reduced number of tourists from the USA, but a growth in the number from Japan.

In the third quarter of 2000, the pound fell sharply against the dollar, while remaining relatively strong against European currencies. This encouraged Americans to travel to the UK and the British to visit the Continent, while tourists from countries such as Germany and France were dissuaded from coming to the UK and, similarly, fewer Britons visited the USA. In 2004/05, however, the dollar weakened against both sterling and the euro, increasing travel from the UK and the Continent to the USA (and, incidentally, further heightening the demand for second homes in Florida for the British). In 2007/08, the dollar again weakened against the pound (at times reaching a rate of US$2 for £1). However, 2008 also saw sterling weaken by about 20% against the euro, making Europe a more expensive proposition for UK travellers, and, by the autumn of that year, against a background of threatening recession, sterling was falling fast against both the dollar and the euro. Turkey and Croatia in particular benefited from the expensive cost of purchasing euros.

This uncertainty about currency movements makes forward planning difficult, adding another element of risk to product pricing, although this can be offset to some extent by the forward purchasing of foreign currencies. If the UK does eventually join the euro, one benefit will be that it will help to stabilize their travel business with Europe. It will also allow British travellers to share with their counterparts in other EU countries the benefits of using a single currency across several countries, leading to a substantial saving on foreign exchange when calculating the costs of a holiday abroad. Such savings are less likely to be welcomed by those in the industry who provide foreign exchange facilities, however!

Companies and tourist offices will have to take all of these factors into account when drawing up their promotional campaigns – and may need to consider employing staff with the appropriate language skills to deal with any new incoming markets. On the basis of the forecasts made, organizations must decide where they will advertise, to whom and with what theme.

International tourism depends on more than merely the economic behaviour of tourists, however. As we noted in the previous chapter, it is also influenced by motivators arising from the tourists' efforts to meet their psychological or sociological needs.

The economic impacts of tourism

As with other industries, tourism affects the economy of those areas – whether regions, countries or continents – where it takes place. These are known as tourist **destinations**, or **receiving areas**, and many become dependent on an inflow of tourism to sustain their economy. This is especially true of developing countries, some of which are largely or almost totally dependent on tourism.

The areas from which the tourists come to visit these destinations are known as **generating areas** and, of course, as the tourists are taking their money with them to spend in other places, this represents a net loss of revenue for the generating area and a gain for the receiving area. We can say that incoming tourist spend is an **export**, while outgoing tourist spend is an **import** (as the tourist is buying services from overseas).

EXAMPLE Tourism exports and imports

Priscilla is an American tourist who travels from New York to Sydney. While there, she spends money on accommodation, food and attending a concert at the Opera House. Her total spend is AUS$400.

Therefore, this American tourist has bought in these services from Australia, counting as an IMPORT on the US balance of payments. The Australian economy has benefited from selling these services to this foreign tourist and thus the transaction is considered an EXPORT on the Australian Balance of Payments (Figure 5.2).

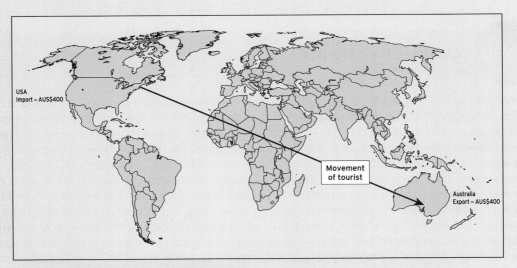

Figure 5.2 An American tourist in Australia

The flow of tourists between generating and receiving areas can be measured in four distinct ways. We must examine the effect on **income**, **employment**, the area's **balance of payments** and **investment and development**. Let us look at each of these in turn.

Income

Income is earned from selling goods and services to tourists. Whilst some of this income will pay interest and rent, in a labour-intensive industry such as tourism, the greatest proportion of this earned income is likely to be spent on paying wages and salaries for those working in jobs either directly serving the needs of tourists or benefiting indirectly from the tourists' expenditure. Income will be greater in those areas that generate large numbers of tourists, where visitors tend to stay for longer periods, where the destination attracts an upmarket or more free-spending clientele and where there are many opportunities to spend.

It is essential to recognize that, while income may be greatest where levels of pay are high and there is relatively little unemployment in the area, tourism may in fact be of greater importance in those areas where there are few other opportunities for employment. Thus, 'tourism is one of the major export sectors of poor countries and the leading source of foreign exchange in 46 of the 49 least developed countries' (Bolwell and Weinz, 2008, 1).

Of course, tourism is also a major income generator in the Western world. In the UK, to take one example, tourism is of prime importance in areas where there is little manufacturing industry, such as in the Scottish Highlands, western Wales and Cornwall. While tourism jobs are often seen as low-paid and seasonal, many are neither seasonal nor temporary. As to low-paid jobs, one must take into account that, without tourism, many workers would have no source of income at all.

Income is also generated from interest, rent and profits of tourism businesses. These could include, for example, the interest paid on loans to an airline in order to buy aircraft or rent paid to a landowner for a car park or campsite near the sea. We must also count taxation on tourism activities, such as sales tax (for example, value-added tax – VAT), room taxes on hotel bills, duty and taxation on petrol used by tourists and other direct forms of taxation that countries may choose to levy on tourists to raise additional public income. Austria, Belgium, Hungary, the Netherlands and Spain all impose some form of tourist tax. Equally, most countries levy a departure tax on all passengers travelling by air, while in the USA airline taxes are levied on both departing and arriving travellers.

EXAMPLE **Cities tax their tourists**

The economic recession of 2008/09 saw many governments struggle to fund key public services and capital projects. To help provide funds for the restoration of the Colosseum in Rome, the local government announced the introduction of a tourist bed tax. This was highly controversial, leading to a call for street marches and protests. However, the Deputy Mayor Mauro Cutrufo argued that 'For the first time millions of visitors to Rome will leave behind a contribution to city services, which are for their use as well' (ANSA, 2010).

Several other cities, such as Paris and New York, already operate similar schemes. The Scottish city of Edinburgh has recently received encouragement from local trade union leaders to implement a bed-tax, to help fund council services. The proposed charge, likely to be in region of £1, would be added to hotel room bills and the proceeds would be used to fund the local festivals (Blackley, 2011). While local government support for this is currently limited, there is support from VisitScotland, the national tourist board, to look at ways to raise additional funds though a voluntary scheme to gather donations from visitors when they pay their bills in restaurants and hotels.

Table 5.8 Total contribution of travel and tourism to GDP, 2010

Country	Percentage
Macau	87.2
Aruba	74.7
Antigua and Barbuda	74.1
Maldives	68.1
Anguilla	57.4
British Virgin Islands	57.2
Seychelles	55.1
Barbados	46.6
St Lucia	45.7
Cape Verde	40.2

Source: WTTC, 2011b

The sum of all incomes in a country is called the **national income** and the importance of tourism to a country's economy can be measured by looking at the proportion of national income that is created by tourism. Some regions of the world, particularly island states, are heavily dependent on the income from tourism (see Table 5.8). Some might see this as an unhealthy overdependence on one rather volatile industry.

Attempts at measuring the impact of tourism are always difficult because it is not easy to distinguish the spend by tourists from the spend by others, in restaurants or shops, for example. In resorts, even such businesses as laundromats – which we would not normally associate with the tourism industry – might be highly dependent on the tourist spend where, for instance, a large number of visitors are camping, caravanning or in self-catering facilities.

Furthermore, tourism's contribution to the income of an area is enhanced by a phenomenon known as the **tourism income multiplier (TIM)**. This arises because money spent by tourists in the area will be re-spent by recipients, augmenting the total.

Tourism multiplier

The multiplier is the factor by which tourist spend is increased in this process of re-spending. This is easiest to demonstrate by way of the following fictitious example.

EXAMPLE | **The tourism income multiplier**

A number of tourists visit Green Paradise Island, spending £1000 in hotels and other facilities there. This amount is received as income by the hoteliers and owners of the facilities, who, after paying their taxes and saving some of the income, spend the rest. Some of what they spend goes on buying items imported into the area, but the rest goes to shopkeepers, suppliers and other producers inside the area. These people, in turn, pay their taxes, save some money and spend the rest.

From the £1000 of tourist spend, let us assume that the average rate of taxation is 20% and that people are saving on average 10% of their gross income, so are left to spend 70% on goods and services (for this example, this would be £700). Let us further assume that, of this £700, the tourist has spent £200 on goods and services imported from other areas, while the remaining £500 is spent on locally produced goods and services, which is money that is retained within the local community. The original £1000 spent by the

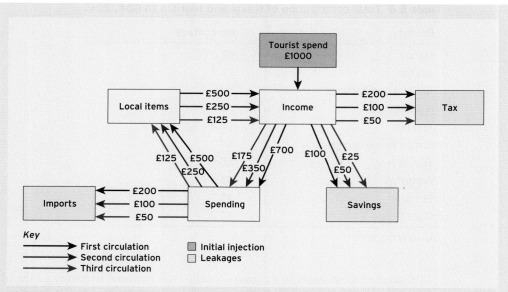

Figure 5.3 The multiplier effect of the circulation of income

tourists will then circulate in the local community as shown in Figure 5.3, in the category 'First circulation', the arrows shown in black.

Of the £500 spent within the community, some will go to tourism businesses, that, in turn, will make payments to their local suppliers for such items as food. The shopkeepers or restaurateurs then pay their employees, who, in turn, shop in other shops locally, although some of what they purchase will have been brought into the region from outside.

This second circulation (the arrows shown in red) highlights the further spend by the recipients, including taxation (again at 20%), savings (10%) and leakages due to the purchase of imports.

Once again, the income received by employees and local businesses will circulate through the economy (third circulation, the arrows shown in blue) and so the cycle goes on, with a declining level of expenditure at each level of circulation.

The money spent directly by tourists is considered to be the **direct income** received by a destination. This spend goes to tourism businesses, which provide tourists with the goods and services they require for their holiday (for example, accommodation, meals, guided tours). These tourism businesses will then spend some of this earned income obtaining goods and services from their suppliers, which allows them to fulfil their obligations to the tourists. For example, a tourism business providing guided tours may have to pay entry fees to an attraction or the salary for a guide. This secondary spend of income is termed **indirect income**. At this stage, some spend – such as residents spending their pay on food in a local supermarket or a visit to the cinema – may occur. Such spend is known as **induced income**, available as a result of direct or indirect tourist expenditure.

EXAMPLE   The effect of leakages on the tourism income multiplier

Each time the money is circulated in this way, some will be lost to the area. For example, taxes paid are transmitted outside the area, some savings, similarly, may be removed from the area and some of the spend has gone on paying for goods imported into the area from other regions of the country or even from abroad.

Expenditures that mean money is lost to other areas are known as **leakages** from the system. Leakages in this sense can therefore be regional or national, the latter being a loss of revenue to the country as a whole.

So far, how much income has been created? From Figure 5.3, we can calculate this by considering the money entering the field marked 'income'; it is £1000 + £500 + £250 + £125 +... A progression is developing and, by adding up all the figures (until the circulations become so small that the additional income is negligible) or by using the appropriate mathematical formula, we will find that the total sum is £2000. The original injection of £1000 by tourists visiting the area has multiplied by a factor of 2 to produce an income of £2000.

It is possible to forecast the value of the multiplier if one knows the proportion of leakages in the local economy. The formula for this is:

$$\text{multiplier} = \frac{1}{\text{proportion of leakages}}$$

In the example provided in Figure 5.3, tax was 20/100ths of the original income, savings were 10/100ths of income and imports were 20/100ths of income. Total leakages, therefore, amounted to 50/100ths, or half (0.5) of the original income. The multiplier can be found by applying the formula:

$$\text{multiplier} = \frac{1}{0.5 \text{ (half of original income)}} = 2.0$$

The portion of leakage is 0.5 so the multiplier is 2. Hence the initial tourist spend of £1000 has led to an increase in income of £2000.

Leakages

So, in an economy with a high proportion of leakages – caused by factors such as high tax rates (although we must remember that the government may choose to reinvest this tax money in the local economy, so much of it may not be lost for all time) or where many of the goods demanded by consumers are imported – the tourism income multiplier may be quite low and then the economy will not benefit greatly from tourism. Local hotels may also be foreign-owned, so profits achieved are then transmitted to the hotel chain's head office and lost to the area. This might be true of other tourist facilities in the area, and even local ground-handling agents or coach operators may be owned by companies based elsewhere, leading to further losses in the multiplier effect.

If, alternatively, many firms are in the hands of locals and leakages of these kinds are minimized, the multiplier effect may be quite high and then tourism will contribute far more than the amount originally spent by the tourists themselves.

The principal reasons for leakages include:

- cost of imported goods, especially food and drink
- foreign exchange costs of imports for the development of tourist facilities
- remittance of profits abroad
- remittance of pay to expatriates
- management fees or royalties for franchises
- payments to overseas carriers and travel companies
- costs of overseas promotion
- additional expenditure on imports resulting from the earnings of those benefiting from tourism.

EXAMPLE **National tourism income multiplier**

Many studies have been undertaken of the tourism income multiplier in different areas, ranging from individual resorts, such as Eastbourne and Edinburgh in the UK, to entire countries, such as Barbados and Fiji (see examples in Figure 5.4). In most cases, the multiplier has varied between 1 and 2.5 (estimates have put it at about 1.7 for the UK as a whole and around 1.2–1.5 for individual towns and regions in the UK), although, in the case of some destinations in the developing world that depend heavily on outside investment and must import much of the food and other commodities demanded by tourists, the figure may be well below 1. The figure for Barbados, for instance, has been estimated at 0.60. Leakages in Western developed nations are generally estimated at around 10% of tourism income, while in developing economies with strong tourism dependency, such as Fiji, the Cook Islands, Mauritius and the Virgin Islands, estimates suggest that imports consume between 36 and 56% of gross tourism receipts.

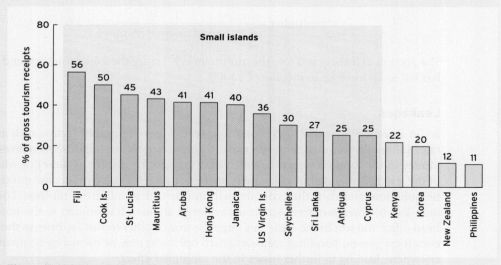

Figure 5.4 Leakage of foreign exchange earnings in 16 countries
Courtesy of UN World Tourism Organization

Employment

The WTTC anticipates that employment in tourism will rise from 258.6 million jobs in 2011, accounting for 8.8% of total employment, to more than 323.8 million jobs by 2021 (WTTC, 2011b). The industry's importance to many economies as a generator of employment is therefore clear. Several of the leading tourist destinations in the world are developing countries and, in some tourism-dependent economies such as the Caribbean, as many as 25% of all jobs are associated with the industry.

Jobs are created in travel agencies, tour operators and other intermediaries who supply tourist services in both the generating and destination areas. Transport companies such as airlines also employ staff to serve tourists in both areas, but the bulk of employment is in the destination country. The jobs range from hotel managers to deckchair attendants, from excursion-booking clerks to cleaners employed in the stately homes that are open to the public or maintenance staff who keep the rides going at leisure centres or theme parks in the resort.

Many of these jobs are seasonal or part time, so tourism's contribution to full-time employment is considerably less than the total employment figures may suggest. While this is a criticism of the industry in economic terms – and one that has resulted in large sums of money being spent in an effort to lengthen the tourist season in many resorts – it is important to realize that these jobs are often being created in areas where there is little alternative employment. It is also worth making the point that many of the jobs attract those who wish to work seasonally, such as students seeking jobs as resort representatives during the summer or householders who wish to open their house for summer periods only as bed-and-breakfast establishments.

For countries that are major receiving destinations or enjoy a strong domestic demand for tourism, employment figures will be far higher. On balance, tourism as a form of employment is economically beneficial, although efforts must be made to create more full-time jobs in the industry. The extent to which tourism benefits employment can be seen when it is appreciated that, given the figure quoted earlier, roughly 1 job in 12 in the world is directly ascribed to tourism. Tourism is considered by many to be the largest industry in the world and it is believed to be growing the fastest.

Just as tourism is globally important, so it is important for regions within an economy. The multiplier that affects income in a region affects employment in the same way. If tourists stay at a destination, jobs are directly created by the tourism industry there. Those workers and their families resident in the neighbourhood must also buy goods and services locally, their families require education and need medical care. This, in turn, gives rise to jobs in shops, schools and hospitals to serve their needs. The value of the employment multiplier is likely to be broadly similar to that of the tourism income multiplier, assuming that jobs with average rates of pay are created.

Recent developments in technology, however, are threatening labour opportunities in tourism. For example, computer reservation systems (CRS) are rapidly replacing manual reservation systems and, as a result, many booking clerk jobs in large companies such as airlines, tour operators and hotel chains are disappearing. Similarly, the trend towards online bookings via the Internet threatens jobs in travel agencies and suppliers. Call centres are replacing branch shops and, increasingly, these are set up abroad, in countries with low levels of pay, such as India. Fortunately for the future of the industry, the tourist often seeks a high level of personal service at the destination – the nature of the tourist experience thus ensuring that technology cannot replace many jobs (although, as discussed in Chapter 18, even the key job of resort representative has been sharply curtailed in recent years). The success of tourism in a country, however, will, in part, be dependent on an adequate supply of skilled labour with the right motivation towards employment in the industry and appropriate training.

Tourism employment in China

Tourism has been recognized as being important for the Chinese economy. Increasing affluence has allowed the local population to travel, moving the country to 4th place in the table for international tourist expenditure whilst domestic tourism is also significant with more than a billion trips being taken annually. Coupled with this is a growing inbound market which saw more than 54 million arrivals in 2010.

As a consequence of this increased demand for tourism, the tourism industry in China is expected to recruit more than a million new employees over the next decade. However, recent research examining the views of the Chinese population highlighted concerns regarding attitudes towards careers in the tourism industry. Similarly perhaps to other destinations, there was apprehension that the jobs would be low-skilled, low-paid, seasonal and the work would be repetitive. Interestingly, the existing industry was said to be lacking in expertise, particularly in management, leading to a poor reputation and low social status for workers such as tour guides.

One key conclusion of the research was that while tourism was an interesting industry to enter when young, providing an opportunity for independence, few saw this as a long-term profession. This may well prove problematic for the industry in the future.

Source: Jiang and Tribe, 2009

Balance of payments

In a national context, tourism may have a major influence on a country's balance of payments. International tourists are buying tourist services in another country and those payments are noted in a country's accounts as 'invisibles'. A British resident going on holiday to Portugal will be making an invisible payment to that country, which is a debit on the UK's balance of payments account and a credit to Portugal's balance of payments. Similarly, the money spent by an American visitor to the UK is credited to the UK's balance of payments, becoming an invisible receipt for the UK, while it is debited as a payment against the American balance of payments. It is important to remember at this point that, as mentioned earlier, the outflow of British money in the form of spending abroad by British residents counts as an *import*, while the inflow of foreign holidaymakers' money spent in the UK counts as an *export*.

The total value of receipts minus the total payments made during the year represents a country's **balance of payments on the tourism account**. This is part of the country's entire invisible balance, which will include other services such as banking, insurance and transport. This latter item is, of course, also important for tourism. If an American visitor to the UK decides to travel on a UK airline, then a contribution is made to the UK's invisible receipts, while the fare of a Briton going on holiday to Portugal flying with TAP Airlines is credited to Portugal and represents a debit on the UK balance of payments account. Of course, with the demise of national airlines and the growth of global integration, it may no longer be the case that the leading airlines will in the future be so clearly identified with their country of origin and, if the majority shareholding is abroad, ultimately the profits, if not the earnings, will find their way to other countries in the form of leakages.

Some countries, particularly developing countries, cannot afford to have a negative balance of payments as this is a drain on their financial resources and, in such a case, they may be forced to impose restrictions either on the movement of their own residents or the amount of money that they may take abroad with them. Some countries may suffer severe deficiencies in their tourism balance of payments, which can sometimes be offset by manufacturing exports. Germany and Japan have in the past been examples of countries heavily in deficit on the tourism balance of payments, but which have nevertheless enjoyed a surplus overall through the sale of goods overseas. With both countries now finding it increasingly difficult to compete against low-pay economies in the industrial sector, they are now seeking to boost their own inbound tourism to compensate for this net outflow on the tourism account. By contrast, Spain and Italy both enjoy a strong surplus on their tourism balance of payments as they are popular receiving countries with fewer residents going abroad for their own holidays.

EXAMPLE Tourism balance of payments for the UK

Throughout the 1970s, the UK enjoyed a surplus on its tourism balance of payments, reaching a peak during 1977, the year of the Queen's Silver Jubilee. Since then, however, spending by British tourists travelling abroad has increased faster than receipts the country has gained from overseas tourists, with the result that, as we have seen, there has been a net, and steadily increasing, deficit since 1986.

For a country such as the UK, which has experienced a steady decline in terms of trade (amount of our goods sold abroad, compared with the amounts of goods that we import), it is important to try to redress the balance by a better showing on our invisible exports. The government has attempted to resolve this deficit by encouraging more visitors to come to the UK via the marketing efforts of the national tourist boards, or more Britons to take domestic holidays.

The recession which occurred at the end of the first decade of the twenty-first century did encourage more Britons to consider domestic holidays, aiding the balance of payments (as can be seen in Figure 5.5). However, despite this improvement, the negative balance is still substantial.

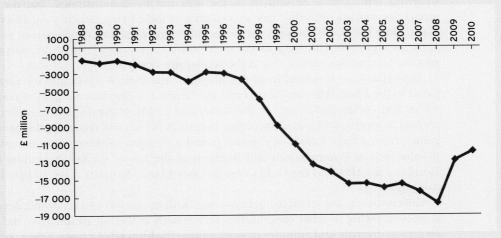

Figure 5.5 UK balance of payments on travel

Investment and development

One factor helping to determine the success or otherwise of tourism in a region is the level of investment, whether private or public, in the industry. Unfortunately, tourism – indeed, leisure generally – has historically been seen by private investors as high-risk investments. Banks are reluctant to lend money for tourism projects and developers are not very willing to take investment risks. This often means that tourism cannot take off until the public sector is prepared to 'kick-start' the economy – that is, invest risk capital in order to encourage the development of tourism. This might take the form of grants or low-interest loans to private developers or, in some more centrally operated economies, it may mean that government itself builds and runs facilities such as hotels for tourists.

EXAMPLE   **Government investment demanded to boost tourism in Victoria**

The state government of Victoria, Australia is being urged to invest in the local tourism infrastructure in order to boost the local and regional economies. Suggested investment projects include:

- establishing a car-ferry service between Phillip Island (renowned for its Penguin wildlife) and the mainland
- constructing an interpretative centre for the Great Ocean Road coastal highway
- upgrading rail and highway links.

The new infrastructure would create jobs both in the construction process and in the operation, improvements and expansion of the tourism industry. The justification for making this investment lies with the increase in arrivals from China and India, reportedly up 18% and 10% respectively. In addition, the improvements made through government investments are expected to encourage confidence in the region, creating inward investment from the private sector.

Sources: Gray, 2010; Rayner, 2011

Investment is something of a chicken and egg situation. There may be an unwillingness to invest until a flow of tourists to the area can be demonstrated, but the area will attract few tourists until they can see evidence of there being sufficient facilities to attract them. Once tourism is shown to be successful, however, private developers or government agencies are often willing to invest even further in the area – in short, success breeds success. Economists refer to this as the **accelerator concept**.

Areas that have benefited from this phenomenon include Spain and the Mexican East Coast in the 1960s, Hawaii, Tunisia and the Languedoc-Roussillon region of France in the 1970s and Turkey and Greece in the 1980s and 1990s. Naturally, the attraction of these regions to tourists will also attract other industries, which will recognize the benefits to be gained from a large inflow of consumers and a pleasant working environment for staff. Resorts such as Bournemouth and Brighton in the UK or the fast-expanding resorts of Florida in the USA and the Gold Coast in Queensland, Australia, have all benefited from this phenomenon.

Unfortunately, the relationship between growth in tourism and economic development is uneven, owing to other complicating factors such as the rate of inflation, the ability of an area to diversify and attitudes to work among the local labour force. Often, key workers are brought in from outside the area in cases where the local labour force is either unwilling or unable to adapt to the needs of the tourism industry. This may lead to leakages as pay is repatriated, thus reducing the economic benefit to the area. Consequently, the risk for such investment remains high, as it does in many other areas of the economy.

Balancing economic diversification with overdependence on tourism

For some countries or even regions, such as rural areas or declining industrial areas, tourism may offer an opportunity to diversify the economy, increasing the variety of empowerment opportunities available for the local population. In addition to this, any downturn in one particular sector may be offset by an increase or stability in other sectors.

An example of this is the city of Bradford in the UK, which sought to encourage tourism to the city when it suffered a decline in the textile and engineering industries – the traditional mainstays of its economy. An initiative by the local government in the mid-1980s saw the introduction of initiatives and funding to encourage tourism to the city. By the turn of the millennium, the number of hotel bednights sold annually in the city had quadrupled, to over 370 000 (Hope and Klemm, 2001).

In some rural areas, tourism is being amalgamated with farming businesses to provide additional income as well as new products for an area. Farm tourism, or **agritourism** (discussed at greater length in Chapter 9), is just one form of rural tourism that can help to bring income and jobs to remote areas.

Such a reliance on attracting visitors must be placed in context, however. While tourism has been used as a catalyst for expanding economies, perhaps in less developed countries or regions, a concern raised is that overreliance on this one sector can bring difficulties. A significant downturn in tourist demand, perhaps through no fault of the destination, will reduce tourist numbers, leaving the destination economically vulnerable. For destinations where tourism is an important component of the economy, attracting tourists from many different source regions as well as different market segments may help to spread the risk. This will not guard against problems experienced in the local destination area, however.

EXAMPLE   Hawaii tourism hit by the Japanese earthquake

The earthquake and subsequent tsunami which devastated the north-east coast of Japan in March 2011 has had far reaching impacts on the island state of Hawaii. The ocean wave hit the islands with a surge of just over 1 metre, causing an estimated $30 million of damage to property, piers and road infrastructure.

More significant in the longer term may be the impact of this natural disaster on its economy. The island is heavily reliant on tourism and particularly Japanese tourists, who make up 18% of the total international visitors they receive. Furthermore, the Japanese tourists are seen to be high-spenders – estimates suggest they spend over $100 a day more than Americans who visit the islands.

The extent of the decline and the time to rebound is an unknown. The Kobe earthquake in 1995 saw an initial decline of 12%, but demand returned within a year. However, the damaging effects of the tsunami and resulting problems with nuclear plants have left the Hawaiian tourism industry with concerns that the impact on demand will be longer lasting.

Although tourism is valuable to many economies, often, as noted, acting as a catalyst for attracting inward investment, the pressures it places on the economy should also be acknowledged and it should not be relied on to the exclusion of other opportunities.

Inflationary pressures

While tourism can bring money into a tourism destination, creating job opportunities and wealth, the demand for resources (including land and labour) can push the cost of those resources higher as that very demand creates an imbalance in terms of supply. As prices of those resources rise, it can create an inflationary effect – employees seek higher levels of pay in order to be able to afford the higher costs of accessing land or property, food and entertainment and so on. Ultimately, some of the local population may be unable to afford the increased costs and become excluded from accessing their own community's resources.

EXAMPLE   Is tourism to blame for inflation in Argentina?

Following devaluation of the peso in 2002, Argentina experienced growth in international tourist numbers as the depressed value of the local currency helped to make Argentina a more affordable destination than previously. By 2006, visitor numbers had increased by more than 120%. This increase in demand was beneficial for the country as it provided employment, brought in foreign currency and encouraged inward investment. It was estimated that more than $3.61 billion was spent by foreign tourists in 2005, amounting to 7% of GDP.

Alongside this apparent success, however, was a concern – inflation. The increased demand led to price rises for products such as hotel rooms. Furthermore, the pressure on supply meant that there was a scarcity of rooms and prices went up – both of which effectively crowded out the domestic market. Furthermore, tourism businesses themselves were having to deal with the higher levels of pay demanded by their employees, as inflationary pressure eroded the purchasing power of their pesos.

Inflation rates of 15–18% in 2008/09 continued to impact on the industry, and the financial crisis, unfavourable exchange rates and the H1N1 pandemic affected inbound visitor numbers. This was compounded by devaluation of currencies in neighbouring Brazil and Chile, leading to a 10% decline in inbound and domestic tourism. Forecasts suggest that the high inflation rates will continue to restrict travel as the sector remains expensive relative to its international competitors.

Sources: Casey, 2006; Euromonitor, 2010

The opportunity cost of tourism

Further to the key economic impact discussed above, it is necessary also to consider that, by developing tourism, many resources (such as land, labour and capital investment) are used to support the industry, thus making them unavailable for other industries. This is termed the **opportunity cost**.

Crompton proposes that 'Opportunity costs are the benefits that would be forthcoming if the public resources committed to a tourism project were (1) redirected to other public services or (2) retained by the taxpayer' (2006, 75). This principle acknowledges the lost opportunities as a result of using such resources for tourism development and those costs should be set against the benefits received.

A further area of opportunity cost to be considered is that of taxation. When governments tax residents, in order to be able to invest in tourism projects, they reduce the spending capability of the local population, which can impact on the multiplier effect of induced or indirect expenditure. Thus, any positive effect of the tourism project may need to be set against the negative impact on residents' spending.

Statistical measurement of tourism

Gathering data on tourism is a vital task for the government of a country. Governments need to know the contribution that tourism makes to the economy in terms of income, employment, balance of payments and investment. Sufficiently detailed figures must be available in order to know how they have affected regional as well as national economies. Governments will wish to examine trends over time, not only within the country, but also in comparison with the performance of other, competing countries. National tourist offices will employ this information to forecast growth, plan for tourism in their areas and as a guide for their promotional campaigns.

Information must be both **quantitative** and **qualitative** in nature – that is, data should be provided about not only the numbers and composition of tourists but also their nature and purpose. For example, national statistics on tourism should include:

- the number of international visitors (arrivals) as well as the number of domestic tourists
- how these are distributed over the months of the year
- the countries generating the international tourists and the regions generating the domestic tourists
- the growth, year on year, of those tourists
- their spend – in absolute terms and how they distribute it between accommodation, transport, shopping, catering and so on
- their mode of travel – that is, what form of transport they use, whether they are travelling independently or on an inclusive tour
- the duration of their visit
- the types of accommodation they use
- the purposes of their visit – whether leisure, business or visiting friends and relatives (VFR)
- demographic profiles – age, group composition, social class
- psychographic profiles – personality, lifestyle, interests and activities
- what these tourists seek and the extent to which they are satisfied with what they find.

This is a great deal of information and relates to both inbound and domestic tourism. Data must also be gathered for outbound tourism – residents travelling abroad. Thus, the task of collecting tourism data is daunting, but it is vital that governments undertake it and ensure, as far as is possible, that the data collected are based on commonly defined criteria, so that meaningful comparisons can be made between countries.

If the collection of data allows the nation to know what trends are developing over time, what patterns of growth are taking place and how tastes and preferences are changing over time, this information will enable governments to determine where to site roads and airports, where to make provision for expansion in local government plans and in what countries to increase or decrease the spend on advertising (as well as how to redirect the themes of advertisements when it is found that new types of tourists are being reached).

The private sector will benefit from this information, too, when deciding whether or not and where to invest in hotels or tourist attractions and the forms those facilities should take. Furthermore, the industry requires an understanding of the propensity to take holidays – that is, the proportion of the population choosing to take a holiday each year and, in particular, a holiday abroad or more than one holiday a year – and how that propensity is affected by a growth in disposable income.

Public-sector planners must be aware of the multiplier effect, which will call for sophisticated research techniques if the figures produced are to be accurate.

We will examine the two most commonly used measurements of tourism – international and national surveys.

International surveys

Statistics of intra-European and transatlantic tourist flows were collected even before World War II. The systematic collection of tourism data on a global scale, however, can be dated back to the early post-war years. The methods of measurement used have been gradually refined and improved in recent years, particularly in those developed countries that have seen tourism expand rapidly.

EXAMPLE   **The UK International Passenger Survey (IPS)**

In the UK, information on travel into and out of the country is obtained in a variety of ways. Until the early 1960s, most basic data on incoming tourism were obtained from Home Office immigration statistics, but, as the purpose of gathering such data was to control immigration rather than to measure tourism, the data had major weaknesses, including a failure to distinguish the purpose of travel – obviously a key statistic when surveying tourists. The government, therefore, decided to introduce a regular survey of visitors entering and leaving the country.

The International Passenger Survey (IPS) has enabled data to be collected on tourists since 1964. It is undertaken by the Office of National Statistics for the Department for Culture, Media and Sport and the national tourist boards, and over a quarter of a million international travellers are interviewed annually. Records are made of the number of visitors, purpose of their visit, geographical region visited, their expenditure, mode of travel, transport used and duration of stay. The information is based on their country of residence, so, for example, the large number of British visitors living in America and travelling to visit friends and relatives in the UK each year would be counted as American visitors. This information is published quarterly and compounded annually in the government's *Business Monitor* series (MQ6, *Overseas Travel and Tourism*).

The IPS is a random sample of all visitors travelling into or out of the UK via the major seaports and airports and the Channel Tunnel, stratified by port of arrival or departure, time of day and mode of transport used.

Global tourism statistics – covering traffic flows, expenditure and trends over time – are collated annually by the UNWTO and the Organization for Economic Cooperation and Development (OECD). The figures are published in the UNWTO's *World Tourism Statistics Annual Report* and *Compendium of Tourism Statistics* and in the OECD's annual *Tourism Policy and International Tourism*. These statistics are not always strictly comparable, however, as data-gathering methods vary and differences in the definitions of terms remain.

Other surveys are undertaken to provide additional data on the volume of tourists and their expenditure, although reductions in resources have led to cutbacks in the collection of data by the public-sector bodies, so supplementary information is now largely collected by private organizations. For example, IPK International undertakes more than half a million interviews each year, asking populations of more than 50 countries about their travel behaviour. The results of these interviews are published in the *World Travel Monitor* and *European Travel Monitor*. They also provide businesses with extracts of data, on request, ensuring that they can access the most relevant data for their needs. It should be mentioned that full reports as well as data extracts are often quite expensive to purchase.

National surveys

It is important for both national and regional governments to have data on domestic tourism. With this in mind, many governments invest in surveys that can provide details of the travel habits of residents. The EU has encouraged its member states to extend their statistical data collection related to the tourism market and industry.

Occupancy surveys for accommodation in Spain

Following an EU directive requiring the collection of tourism data, the Spanish Institute of Statistics introduced the Hotel Occupancy Survey in 1996, gathered through a sample of 6000 hotels by means of a questionnaire. This survey examines the number of overnight stays and levels of occupancy of hotel establishments as well as details related to guest nationality and length of stay.

In addition, other forms of accommodation are also surveyed in order to understand more about this sector of the industry. They include:

● the Tourist Accommodation Occupancy Survey, which covers tourist apartments

● the Campsite Occupancy Survey, which provides data on tourist stays at campsites

● the Rural Tourist Accommodation Occupancy Survey, which covers establishments registered as rural tourist accommodation.

The data are reported on both a national and regional basis.

These surveys complement the expenditure, national and inbound surveys (FRONTUR and EGATUR) also undertaken by the Ministry of Industry, Tourism and Trade.

Source: Instituto Nacional de Estadíctica, Hotel Occupancy Survey, available online at: **http://www.ine.es/en/inebmenu/mnu_hosteleria_en.htm** (accessed November 2011)

In the UK, as in other countries in Europe, surveys are regularly carried out on tourism flows within the country. The most important of these is the 'United Kingdom Tourism Survey' (UKTS) on behalf of VisitBritain, VisitScotland, VisitWales and the Northern Ireland Tourist Board. This survey was originally carried out using monthly telephone interviews, but, since 2005, over 2000 adults are now questioned face-to-face on a weekly basis. Information is collected on the volume and value of all trips involving at least one overnight stay, including the purpose of the trip, accommodation and transport used, activities engaged in, the method of booking and demographic details of respondents.

National tourist boards often provide the funding for surveys that provide data on tourism in their area. For example, in the UK, the national tourist boards collect information on hotel occupancy in each of their own regions.

Techniques and problems regarding measurement of tourism

From the descriptions of the methods for gathering tourist statistics outlined above, it can be seen that most research employs quantitative methods in order to provide descriptive information about issues such as when and where tourists travel, where they come from, how long they stay and how much they spend. In some cases, this information is available in considerable levels of detail. For instance, expenditure can be broken down into sectors (shopping, food, accommodation) and data on visits can be identified by tourism region within the country. Although the data collected are not above criticism, by and large there is a sufficient body of information on which to base decisions.

The demand for qualitative research

Research dealing with why people travel is far more limited, however. This situation is beginning to change, though, as organizations become more concerned with understanding the behaviour of tourists – how they choose their destinations, what they do when they arrive and why, what satisfies them, their purchasing patterns (preferences to book directly rather than through an agent or to book early rather than close to departure time).

None of these factors is easily addressed by the use of structured questionnaires – a more qualitative approach to research is needed. This can involve lengthy interviews in the home or in panels, or focus groups, where consumers talk about their behaviour under the guidance of a skilled interviewer. Some information is best obtained by observation rather than questioning – for example, watching how customers visiting a travel agency choose their brochures from the racks.

All these types of research are expensive, and time-consuming to administer. What is more, unlike quantitative methods, they cannot be subjected to tests of statistical probability in order to 'prove' the accuracy of the findings, no matter how carefully and scientifically the information is collected. Many organizations are therefore reluctant to commission research involving qualitative methods, although a growing number of research experts now recognize that they may produce richer and more complete data than the more common survey. After all, the information provided by the use of question-naires will only be as accurate as the honesty of the answers, but it is particularly difficult to know if respondents are answering questionnaires honestly or giving sufficient thought to the questions. This problem is compounded where mailed questionnaires are used.

Some criticisms of quantitative methods

Asking questions of passengers arriving at a destination is, in reality, a survey of their intentions rather than an accurate picture of what those passengers actually end up doing while in the country. Equally, surveys carried out on departing travellers require good levels of recall, so some answers will be, at best, guesswork, especially where the aim is to assess the expenditure that the tourist has incurred.

The categories or definitions used may vary by survey. For instance, the travel survey for Finnish residents limits the sample to adults aged between 15 and 74, which may effec-tively ignore the unique travel habits of the increasingly significant senior citizen (or grey) market. Age is not the only definitional difficulty. One of the issues of comparing data for different countries as reported by the UNWTO is that some countries may count inter-national tourists by country of residence, while other countries use nationality (determined either by passport or based on immigration forms completed on arrival).

Even if common definitions are used, direct comparisons may be misleading. For example, an international journey may require an American resident to make a trip of several hundred kilometres or cross a stretch of water, which will usually mean forward planning, while a resident of Continental Europe may live within a couple of kilometres of an international border and think nothing of crossing it regularly to go shopping or for a meal out. In some cases, it is even difficult to think of border crossings as international. The Schengen Agreement, for example, eradicated border controls between several of the EU countries, with the result that monitoring visitors has become much harder. Another issue is that some countries still use hotel records to estimate the number of visitors – a system known to be notoriously inaccurate because visitors travelling from one hotel to another are counted twice, while those staying with friends and relatives will be omitted entirely from the count.

While some international standards for methods of data collection and definitions of terms have become widely accepted, particularly among the developed countries, small variations continue to make genuine comparison difficult, not only between countries but also within a country over a period of time. Above all, if specific types of tourist activity are being examined, as part of a larger sample of general tourists, limits of confidence may fall sharply. Some survey data in the past have produced results that are accurate only to within 20% either way, owing to the small number of respondents in the particular category being examined.

Accurate measures of tourist expenditure are equally difficult to make. Shopping surveys have problems distinguishing between residents and tourists, and tourists frequently under- or overestimate their expenditure. Above all, much of the real tourist expenditure is not recorded at all, especially in developing countries, because it is not taken into account. This includes secondary spend by recipients of tourist monies and even direct spend by tourists in shops and other outlets. In countries where cash, rather than credit cards, is still the normal means of payment and bargaining common for even the smallest of items, calculating spending patterns reliably is particularly difficult.

Tourism satellite accounts (TSAs)

In an effort to provide more accurate assessment, the UNWTO has introduced the concept of the **tourism satellite account (TSA)**. This technique attempts to include all such indirect expenditures and their resultant contribution to GDP and employment. The technique was approved as an international standard by the United Nations Statistical Commission in 2000. It created a set of standardized procedures that aim to ensure that all countries are operating similar systems and, thus, the resulting data are comparable across nations. By 2010 it was reported that 60 countries had produced, or were developing systems to produce, tourism satellite accounts (UNWTO, 2011b).

The creation of a TSA provides information regarding the economic importance of tourism for a national economy, as well as providing details of both the employment created by tourism and the tax revenues earned as a direct result of tourism activity. Such information can assist with planning tourism resources and may encourage greater awareness of the tourism industry and further investment in the industry.

The implementation of TSAs, however, is fraught with difficulties. It is not only expensive and time-consuming to employ, but accepts all tourism expenditure as beneficial, disregarding the question of sustainability. Neither can the results revealed in one country or region necessarily be transposed to another as each situation is unique and there is no magic formula that will allow estimates of statistical measures to be obtained without full-scale research within the area.

EXAMPLE   The value of tourism in the Falkland Islands

In 2009, the Falkland Islands presented their tourism satellite accounts, confirming the value of tourism to these remote islands in the South Atlantic. The accounts reveal that tourists spent £6.6 million in 2008/09, accounting for 5% of the Islands GDP. Tourism indirectly contributes to several sectors of the economy, including transport, catering and retail.

Developing the TSA was seen to be important at it 'provides a tool for both the tourism industry and government to measure growth and properly plan for the future, and it will have policy implications for employment, education, infrastructure and transport' (Brock, 2009).

Future issues

The economic downturn which hit many economies across the globe has helped to reveal the resilience of the tourism industry. Although international travel saw a decline in 2009 to 880 million trips, there was an immediate rebound in 2010, with an estimated 935 million trips having taken place. During this short downturn, domestic tourism continued to provide significant contribution to many economies. As was highlighted in this chapter, the propensity to travel is often high for developed nations, whose populations still desire holidays even when economies are in recession.

Whilst the economic impact of tourism is of significant interest to local and regional governments – the efforts to standardize the TSA system providing evidence that accurate information identifying the importance of this industry to the wider economy is highly prized – increased interest in the social and environmental impacts is now being seen. Arguments about the need for sustainability are helping to address the 'grow at all cost' attitude toward tourism development.

The emerging markets of China and India in particular will provide interesting opportunities for the tourism industry. With such large populations, the travel propensity does not need to be high for markets to be significant. For example, if just 1% of the Chinese population decided to take an international trip this would account for more than 13 million trips, whilst if the international travel propensity of the Indian population reached that of the UK (approximately 115%) this would more than double the existing levels of international tourism. With the potential to serve such large markets, the industry is likely to adapt its provision to meet the demands of these markets.

The collection and dissemination of data related to the economic impacts of tourism has been greatly assisted by computerization. Both the UNWTO and the WTTC provide online access to parts of their databases, with many reports and statistics available at no charge. This can assist those involved with the planning and development of tourism – informing decisions about new markets, making comparisons between countries and understanding more about tourism in their home countries.

Questions and discussion points

1. What factors can cause leakages, which can impact on the value of the economic multiplier? How might these leakages be reduced?

2. Some taxes levied by governments are specifically targeted at tourists. These include arrival and departure taxes, and hotel 'bed' taxes. Discuss whether such taxes are likely to dissuade tourists from visiting a destination.

3. Americans were estimated to have made 38 844 301 international trips in 2009, in addition to 1 898 800 000 domestic trips that same year. The population was estimated as 305 529 000. Using these data, calculate the gross travel propensity for both international and domestic travel. How might this information be useful for a travel agency based in the USA?

Tasks

1. Visit the website for the WTTC and locate the country reports available through their economic research pages (**http://www.wttc.org/eng/Tourism_Research/Economic_Research/**). Select two countries to compare and contrast. For each country, review their Impact Research Report to comment on inbound and domestic tourism expenditure, the

contribution of travel and tourism to both GDP and employment and the relative rankings to world average. What do the two reports tell us about tourism in each country? Why do the two countries differ?

2. Interview two students who are studying tourism. Ask them for their views on working in the tourism industry. Particularly focus on their views on pay, hours and their long-term career aspirations. What do these views suggest about the nature of employment in the tourism industry?

Bibliography

ANSA (2010) Rome to tax visitors in the New Year, *ASEAN*, 24 December.

Blackley, M. (2011) Union calls for tourist tax to help fund city services, *Edinburgh Evening News*, 15 February.

Bolwell, D. and Weinz, W. (2008) *Reducing poverty through tourism*, Geneva, International Labour Office.

Brock, J. (2009) Satellite Account is a Falklands' First, *South Atlantic Islands News Team (SAINT)*, 22 October.

Bull, A. (1995) *The Economics of Travel and Tourism*, 2nd edn, Melbourne, Longman.

Casey, M. (2006) Argentina finds new inflation culprit in tourism sector, *Dow Jones International News*, 8 February.

Crompton, J. L. (2006) Economic impact studies: instruments for political shenanigans, *Journal of Travel Research*, **45** (1), 67–82.

Euromonitor (2010) *Travel and tourism – Argentina*, London, Euromonitor.

Euromonitor (2011) *Travel and tourism statistics*, London, Euromonitor.

Eurostat (2008) *Tourism Statistics*, Luxembourg, European Communities.

Expedia (2010) *Vacation Deprivation survey*, available online at: http://press.expedia.co.uk/travel-trends/vacation-deprivation-57 (accessed November 2011).

Gray, D. (2010) Appeal for big tourism investment, *The Age*, 21 May.

Hope, C. A. and Klemm, M. S. (2001) Tourism in difficult areas revisited: the case of Bradford, *Tourism Management*, **22** (6), 629–635.

Jiang, B. and Tribe, J. (2009) Tourism jobs – short lived professions: student attitudes towards tourism careers in China, *Journal of Hospitality, Leisure, Sports and Tourism Education*, **8** (1), 4–19.

Laesser, C. and Bieger, T. (2008) *Travel Market Switzerland 2007: Technical Report and Results*, St Gallen, IDT.

Mercer (2009) *Employer statutory and public holiday entitlements – global comparisons*, available online at: http://uk.mercer.com/press-releases/1360620 (accessed November 2011).

ONS (2011a) *Annual mid-year population estimates 2010*, London, Office for National Statistics.

ONS (2011b) *Travel Trends 2010*, London, Office for National Statistics.

Rayner, M. (2011) More four- and five-star accommodation could help attract tourists, *The Ballarat Courier*, 8 February.

Sesser, S. (2008) Galapagos under siege, *Wall Street Journal*, January.

Tribe, J. (2005) *The Economics of Leisure and Tourism*, 3rd edn, Oxford, Butterworth-Heinemann.

UNWTO (2010) *Tourism Highlights*, Madrid, UNWTO.

UNWTO (2011a) *World Tourism Barometer*, Madrid, WTO, 9 (1), February.

UNWTO (2011b) *Basic concepts of the tourism satellite account (TSA)*, available online at: www.unwto.org/statistics/tsa/project/concepts.pdf (accessed November 2011).

Vanhove, N. (2005) *The Economics of Tourism Destinations*, Oxford, Elsevier.

VisitEngland *et al.* (2011) *The UK Tourist: Statistics 2010*, London, VisitEngland, VisitScotland, Visit Wales, Northern Ireland Tourist Board.

WTTC (2011) *Viewpoint – Autumn*, London, World Travel and Tourism Council: http://www.wttc.org/research/economic-impact-research/regional-reports/bric/.

WTTC (2011a) *WTTC downgrades global T&T growth estimates for 2011 & 2012; maintains long-term confidence*, available online at: http://www.wttc.org/news-media/news-archive/2011/wttc-downgrades-global-tt-growth-estimates-2011-2012-maintains-l/ (accessed November 2011).

WTTC (2011b) *Economic Impact Data and Forecasts*, available online from: www.wttc.org (accessed November 2011).

Further reading

Lennon, J. (ed.) (2003) *Tourism Statistics: International perspectives and current issues*, London, Continuum.

Stabler, M. J., Papatheodorou, A. and Sinclair, M. T. (2010) *The Economics of Tourism*, 2nd edn. Abingdon, Routledge.

UNWTO, *World Tourism Barometer* (monthly) available online at: http://www.unwto.org/facts/menu.html.

UNWTO, *Tourism Satellite Accounts*, available online at: http://www.unwto.org/statistics/tsa/project/concepts.pdf.

Websites

Organization for Economic Co-operation and Development (OECD): **www.oecd.org**

UN World Tourism Organization (UNWTO): **www.unwto.org**

World Travel and Tourism Council: **www.wttc.org**

6

The socio-cultural impacts of tourism

Contents

Learning outcomes

After studying this chapter, you should be able to:

- understand the various ways in which tourism can impact on the populations of both destination and generating countries
- identify and evaluate different approaches to finding solutions to problems caused by these impacts
- understand the concept, and importance, of sustainable tourism in a socio-cultural context
- recognize the need for adequate planning and cooperation between the private and public sectors as means of overcoming problems.

With the emergence of tourism the admirable virtue of hospitality has turned into a trade and a source of profit. But in the big travel business it is obviously the needs of tourists and their promoters that count. What local people feel, think and want is less important. How else can one explain the fact that there is very little information about what they think of it all.

Krippendorf (1984) *The Holidaymakers*, 44

Introduction

Since Krippendorf reported the lack of concern for the views of the host population, attitudes have shifted somewhat, although it is perhaps fair to say that the power of the tourism business is still a dominant factor. Up to this point, it has been generally accepted that tourism is, for the most part and with relatively few exceptions, beneficial to both generating and destination countries. Environmentalists, however, are less sure that this is the case and many are arguing for a decline – or, at very least, a stabilization – in the volume of global travel as an essential measure to save the planet. In this chapter, we will look at a different and, in many ways, darker side of the tourism business – its impact (other than in purely economic terms) on those who participate in tourism and the residents of countries subject to tourist flows. This will mean looking at socio-cultural issues affecting both the hosts and the tourists.

As we saw in the previous chapter, tourism can be a potent force for economic good, creating employment and wealth. Equally, it can be argued that tourism provides a basis for widening our understanding of other societies, developing and maintaining links, reducing tensions and even avoiding conflicts. Indeed, in the first half of the twentieth century, tourism was seen, and actively promoted by the authorities in many countries, as a force for good.

While the interplay between tourists and their hosts was seen initially as a means of stabilizing relations between nations, it readily became apparent that foreign visitors with a curiosity about other cultures could, through their enthusiasm, ensure the survival of those very cultural attractions that might otherwise have withered away for lack of support. This book contains numerous examples of the ways in which incoming tourism has benefited the culture and traditions of a particular country or region. In the UK, for example, many great buildings – particularly those serving the needs of eighteenth- and nineteenth-century industry – would have been lost had it not been possible to convert those same factories, mills and warehouses into living and working museums for tourists. With the increasing secularization of Western societies, arguably it is also tourists who will eventually ensure that our great cathedrals survive as the costs of maintaining these buildings for dwindling numbers of worshippers can no longer be borne by the ecclesiastical authorities alone. Similarly, whole inner-city and dockland areas have been restored and developed to make them attractive as tourist sites. Even a city such as London would be a poorer place without tourists. Around 40% of London's West End theatre tickets are bought by tourists and undoubtedly the variety of theatres available to Londoners owes much to patronage by visitors (this is also true of New York and other great cultural cities). Tourists' use of other public facilities can help fund their provision, thus enabling residents to enjoy a better and cheaper service than would otherwise be possible. In rural areas and small seaside resorts, too, many heritage attractions, such as local museums, art galleries and provincial theatres, would be forced to close without tourist support. Country crafts, pubs, even the restoration of traditional pastimes (such as morris dancing in England), all owe their survival, in part, to the interest in them shown by tourists.

The rapid growth of tourism during the twentieth century produced problems, however, as well as opportunities on a vast scale for both developed and developing countries. Authorities in these countries came to realize that unrestrained and unplanned tourist development could easily aggravate problems to the point where tourists would no longer wish to visit the destination – and residents would no longer wish to receive them. This is, therefore, not just an environmental issue: a point can be reached where residents feel

Table 6.1 Irridex model of stress relative to tourism development

Stages	Characteristics	Symptoms
Stage 1	Euphoria	Visitors welcomed, little formal development
Stage 2	Apathy	Visitors taken for granted, contacts become commercial
Stage 3	Irritation	Locals concerned about tourism, efforts made to improve infrastructure
Stage 4	Antagonism	Open hostility from locals, attempts to limit damage and tourism flows

Source: Doxey, 1975

swamped by the sheer numbers of tourists at peak periods of the year, resulting in disenchantment and, eventually, alienation, with the risk of growing numbers of altercations taking place between residents and visitors.

The breakdown in host–guest relationships can be largely ascribed to the volume of visitors. Doxey (1975) developed an Irritation Index (or 'Irridex') model of the relationship between the growth of tourism and community stress (see Table 6.1). In the early stages of tourism development, the locals are euphoric, pleased to see investment and improved job prospects for local people. The comparatively small numbers and the fact that most tourists will belong to the 'explorer' category and accept the norms and values of the hosts mean that tourists are welcomed and even cultivated as 'friends'. As locals become used to the benefits they receive from tourism and aware of the problems that tourism generates as it grows, so they come to accept it and their meetings with tourists become more commonplace and commercial. Further growth leads to a general feeling among locals that tourists are an irritant rather than a benefit, as they note how tourism is changing their community and their cultural norms. In the final stages, locals show open antagonism towards the steady stream of visitors, many of whom will have the attitude that locals are there to meet the tourists' needs, and will not attempt to adapt to local norms.

Naturally, this is a simplified model of the fairly complex relationships that actually develop between tourists and locals. Other factors that must be taken into account are:

- the length of time tourists stay in the community (those staying longer will fit in better and be seen as making a more effective contribution to the local economy)
- the cultural gap between locals and tourists (domestic tourists, sharing the values of the locals, will be less resented than those who have no understanding)
- the dominance of tourism as an industry (in areas where tourism is the main industry then residents may be more tolerant of visitor demands as they are more reliant on the success of this sector)
- the ratio of tourists to locals (where the ratio is high then hosts may feel overwhelmed).

Examples abound of the antagonism engendered between locals and tourists, even within the UK. An attitude change among locals can be detected by changes in the vocabulary of tourism. For example, in some parts of England, derogatory terms such as 'grockles' or 'emmets' are in use and locals may carry bumper stickers on their cars that read, 'I'm not a tourist, I live here'. An example of open hostility was seen in the city of Bath, where hoses were turned on open-top tour buses in which guides use megaphones to provide a commentary.

The socio-cultural effects of tourism

It is clear that the host population is influenced by their engagement with tourism. The host destination can experience many cultural and social impacts as a result of the influx of large numbers of people, often sharing different value systems and away from the constraints of their own environment.

The socio-cultural impact of mass tourism is most noticeable in less developed countries, but is by no means restricted to them as tourism has contributed to an increase in crime and other social problems in such diverse centres as New York and London, Hawaii and Miami, Florence and Corfu.

Any influx of tourists, however few, will make some impact on a region, but the extent of that impact is dependent not just on numbers but also on the kinds of tourists the region attracts. Those who generally go on mass tourism package holidays are less likely to adapt to the local cultures and will seek amenities and standards found in their home countries, while independent travellers or backpackers will adapt more readily to an alien environment. This has been exemplified in a model devised by Valene Smith (see Table 6.2).

According to Smith's model, explorers – tourists whose main interest is to meet and understand people from different cultures and backgrounds – will fully accept and acclimatize to the foreign culture. Such travellers generally travel independently and blend in as much as possible. As increasingly remote areas of the world are 'packaged' for wealthy tourists, however, and as ever larger numbers of tourists travel further afield to find relaxation or adventure, they bring with them their own value systems, often expecting or demanding the lifestyle and facilities to which they are accustomed in their own countries.

Criminal activities

At its simplest and most direct, the flow of comparatively wealthy tourists to a region may attract petty criminals, as evidenced by increases in thefts or muggings – a problem that has become serious in some areas of the Mediterranean, Florida, Latin America, the Caribbean and Russia. For example, as tourism expands in Central and Eastern Europe, taxi drivers in those countries have been found to overcharge gullible tourists, in some

Table 6.2 Levels of adaptation of tourists to local norms

Types of tourists	Numbers of tourists	Adaptation to local norms
Explorer	Very limited	Adapts fully
Elite	Rarely seen	Adapts fully
Off-beat	Uncommon, but seen	Adapts well
Unusual	Occasional	Adapts somewhat
Incipient mass	Steady flow	Seeks Western amenities
Mass	Continuous influx	Expects Western amenities
Charter	Massive arrivals	Demands Western amenities

Source: Smith, 1992

cases by manipulating their meters. Tourists may also be seen as easy prey when making purchases in shops or from street vendors. This has become a noted problem in London, where street vendors have overcharged tourists for items such as ice-cream. A familiar anecdote in Continental European nations is that the pricing policy of shop goods in resort regions falls into three bands: the cheapest price is available to locals, a slightly higher price is demanded from visitors with sound knowledge of the local language and the highest price is applied to visitors with little or no knowledge of the language.

EXAMPLE **Holiday scams**

Research in 2009 revealed that 10% of British holidaymakers have been the victim of a con or a scam while on holiday. The types of scams include taxi drivers charging higher prices by taking indirect routes and shopkeepers increasing prices for holidaymakers. The problem is rife across European tourist resorts, but the research identified Tenerife (7% of all visitors), Turkey (4%) and Paris (4%) as conman hotspots.

The research also revealed that the scale of holiday cons was being underestimated because only one in ten holidaymakers actually reported the crime to police. The impact of these crimes is not just financial; it can upset victims and ruin a holiday.

Source: Fentiman, 2009

Where gambling is a cornerstone of tourism growth, prostitution and organized crime often follow. Indeed, concerns about the proposed unlimited expansion of Las Vegas-style mega-casinos in UK cities led to the government abandoning plans for their introduction. Certain countries that have more relaxed laws on sexual behaviour than those in the West attract tourists who are in search of sexual encounters, with their governments often turning a blind eye to crimes such as organized child abuse. In some countries – for example, Germany and Japan – tour operators specialize in organizing sex package tours to destinations such as the Philippines and Thailand. This public promotion of commercial sex, especially where it involves sex with minors, has come under increasing criticism in the Western world from organizations such as End Child Prostitution, Pornography and Trafficking (ECPAT) and Tourism Concern. The UK, along with other members of the G8 countries, has passed legislation to enable paedophiles to be prosecuted in their home countries for offences committed abroad.

Crime is also an influential factor on the levels of demand. In areas where crime is perceived to be high, tourists are often deterred from visiting. For some developing countries seeking to develop a tourism industry it is vital to ensure that they project an image of security and safety for tourists, something which may be difficult to achieve when political instability and poverty are rife. In the summer of 2010 the soccer World Cup was hosted in South Africa. Prior to this event taking place, significant press coverage focused on the need for visiting spectators to consider their own safety during their visit, citing statistics to suggest the country has the highest homicide rate in the world. The South African Tourist board worked tirelessly to refute this image, highlighting the many events hosted previously without incident. During the event, security was increased and the event passed largely without incident.

EXAMPLE **Ghana introduces tourist police**

Ghana Police service created a unit dedicated to the security and safety of tourists, in recognition of the growing importance of tourism in the country. The 'Tourism Police' will station officers at locations frequented by visitors, such as airports, hotels, attractions, beaches and market places. The key role of these officers is to handle claims and complaints from tourists and to investigate tourist-related crimes. The tourist police would also be involved in ensuring that tourism enterprises hold the required permits, health certificates and insurances.

The Deputy Superintendent of Police confirmed that the introduction of this specialist unit was necessary because security issues were tied to a destination's image, meaning that it was necessary to ensure that the country has a positive image for safety if the rapid growth of tourism was to be sustained. The introduction of the Tourism Police was supported, in principle, by the Ghana Tourist Board.

Source: Jun, 2010

Demonstration effect

There are a number of less direct, and perhaps less visible, effects on tourist localities, including the phenomenon known as 'relative deprivation'. The comparative wealth of tourists may be resented or envied by the locals, particularly where the influx is seen by the latter as a form of neo-colonialism, as in the Caribbean or some African countries. Locals can experience dissatisfaction with their own standards of living or way of life and seek to emulate those of the tourists. This is known as the *demonstration effect*. In some cases, the effect of this is superficial, as in the adoption of the tourists' dress or fashions, but in others the desire to emulate the tourists can threaten deep-seated traditions in the community, as well as leading to aspirations that are impossible to achieve. The perceived parade of affluence (with tourists flaunting cameras, mp3 players, mobile phones, jewellery and other valuables) can create discontent amongst the host population. The witnessing of these symbols of wealth can create aspirations within the indigenous people.

It is not just the demonstration of material goods, but also social behaviours which can be influential. Tourists away from their home environment may feel more sexually liberated and as a consequence seek out 'holiday romances' or sexual encounters. Similarly, levels of alcohol consumption may be higher when on vacation, as local wines and spirits are tasted. Viewed by the local population, this may give a misconception that tourists are often alcohol-fuelled and promiscuous. This may influence the hosts, especially the younger members of the population, who may feel these are acceptable norms of behaviour.

In some cases, however, tourism can also have a positive influence if it encourages the local population to adjust their actions to enhance their own or their own society's wellbeing. It has also been argued that viewing the freedom of tourists has also encouraged change, especially in some regions where women, who may have traditionally been restricted to the home, may seek opportunities to establish their own career, and to travel independently.

The demonstration effect concept has also highlighted the fact that in some cases it is the tourist whose behaviour is adjusted. Examples are noted in the clothes worn – such as sarongs, salwar-kameez (tunic length shirts and trousers worn commonly in India), stetson hats – or tourists return home and try to seek out the variety of cuisines experienced during their travels.

Changes in employment

Tourism can bring a greater range of job opportunities, which may be coupled with higher levels of pay, when compared to workers from agricultural and rural communities. Therefore migration to touristic areas such as beach resorts and cities, often by younger sectors of the population, can leave areas bereft of a balanced workforce. Agricultural regions that experience this out-migration must then rely on the elderly population to sustain their activities. The migrants, freed from the restrictions of their families and home environments, may abandon their traditional values, this in turn leading to breakdowns in traditional family structures and support systems.

Tourism often demands that its employees, especially those in the hospitality industry, work unsocial hours. This may include working on religious days and holidays. This can impact on family life as work demands mean that celebrations may have to be deferred. Also impacting on family life are the work opportunities that tourism offers for women. This may take the traditional homemaker into the workplace and requires a restructuring in the roles played within the family.

The impact of second home ownership

The phenomenon of second homes abroad is due in large part to the increase in travel, which has led to greater awareness of, and desire for, residences in attractive resorts on the European Continent, and around the Mediterranean in particular. One survey (drawing on statistics provided by the office of the Deputy Prime Minister) revealed that 229 186 English households owned second homes outside of the UK in 2004, while other sources have put the figure even higher, suggesting that the total for UK second home ownership in France alone may be as high as half a million. Where expatriates are willing to learn the language and blend in with the culture, little conflict emerges, but where large groups of British (or other nationals) buy homes within a small region and begin to seek products and forms of entertainment with which they are familiar in their own country, this can transform the indigenous culture and undermine traditional lifestyles. Many of these homes are bought with the intention of renting, largely to nationals of the same country as the owners, which reinforces both the cultural gap and transitional nature of the inter-actions between locals and tourists.

Of course, the problems arising from second home ownership are not restricted to homes purchased abroad. In the UK, there has been resentment between locals and 'incomers' from other parts of the country, which is compounded where regional rivalries already exist. This has happened where second homes have been purchased in attractive areas of Wales by English incomers as it has driven up house prices and owners may intend to rent out their properties only to tourists. Where these homes are occupied infrequently, this leads to resentment by shopkeepers and others who fail to benefit. If it is not an all year round destination, this can soon result in an apparently 'dead' village in the off-season where a high percentage of the homes are owned by outsiders. In some regions, such as South Hams, Devon, prices have been driven up to a point where houses can no longer be purchased by locals. In the popular coastal resort of Salcombe, 45% of homes are said to be owned by outsiders – the highest percentage in the country after Central London.

Exploiting local culture

Sometimes, locals are exploited as 'tourist objects'. In picturesque localities such as villages, local residents can be annoyed by coachloads of tourists descending on the village to peer through their windows or swamp local bars and pubs in order to 'get a flavour' of the local life.

Exploitation of this kind can result in both sides seeing any contact in purely commercial terms. In Kenya's Masai Mara region, the Masai tribespeople extract payment for photographs, either of themselves or of a 'real' (but purpose-built) village. Charging for photographs has become the norm in many parts of the world. In exchange, feeling themselves exploited, tourists feel that it becomes acceptable to steal the towels from their hotel, so the host–guest relationship has changed to one of supplier and customer.

EXAMPLE **Exploiting the Padaung**

A more extreme example of human exploitation is to be found in Thailand, where, on the border with Myanmar (Burma), refugee Padaung tribeswomen have been forced into 'human zoos' as objects of curiosity for tourists. These refugees are known as 'long-neck' or 'giraffe' women due to the brass rings worn around their necks and, although overseas tour operators have refused to deal with this trade, during the high season, around 150 tourists daily pay local operators to visit their camps.

While outcries in the world's press have helped to release some of these women from virtual slavery, in other cases Thailand has rejected their applications for exit visas under the UNHCR resettlement scheme because of their economic value to the villages and, at the same time, the refugees are not given opportunities to take up Thai citizenship. They are paid £24 a month (if wearing rings), but receive payment only during the high season, having to depend on food aid at other times. Another encampment is planned at Sattahip, near the popular resort of Pattaya Beach, to expand on this form of tourism.

Source: Tourism in Focus, 2008, 6

In these situations, the role of the courier or representative as a 'culture broker' becomes vital. These members of the industry enjoy local knowledge (and are often from the local community), help to avoid misunderstandings, interpret the local culture for visitors and explain what is appropriate and inappropriate behaviour for the guests. Interpretation plays an important role in sustainable tourism and the guide as interpreter of local customs provides one of the most effective means of communication.

Breaking cultural taboos can produce a backlash; for example, Alassio banned bikinis in the streets, and in the Alto Adige region of the Italian Dolomites in 1993 a local movement erupted spontaneously to prevent the spread of topless bathing in the lakes, although other residents expressed their concern that the publicity accorded this might dissuade some tourists from visiting the area! In Greece, what has become known as the 'Shirley Valentine factor' (after the title of the film dealing with the issue of British women escaping a humdrum life at home to find romance in Greece) has led to a reaction from women in Corfu and Crete, who resent the attention Greek men pay to foreign females and feel that Greek women are now undervalued. It is also true to say, however, that some Greek women have welcomed the increasing liberation from male dominance that tourism has brought.

EXAMPLE **Ignorance of local cultural tradition**

Following the crash of a Pakistani Airlines plane over Nepal in 1992, it was reported that UK Embassy officials were appalled by the public display of the bodies for relatives of the English victims, which they described as a 'grotesque peepshow'. In Nepal, however, viewing the remains of the dead is an important part of the act of grieving, so the Nepalese were merely extending this courtesy to the foreign mourners.

A lack of understanding of local cultural traditions is common where those traditions appear to be contrary to what we view as tasteful and appropriate. British tourists in Tokyo may be surprised to see signs outside some nightspots declaring 'Japanese only here', reflecting a nineteenth-century imperialist tradition that has long died out in the Western world.

The controversy of the photograph

Photography itself is a sensitive issue for many. Tourists from the West expect to be permitted to take what may often be intrusive photographs at will, yet seldom feel it necessary to seek permission from their subjects. In some less developed countries it is viewed as offensive to take any pictures of people, while in others care must be exercised to avoid taking photographs of landscapes that include military or quasi-military installations. Some British planespotters were arrested, prosecuted and jailed for just such an activity at a Greek airport and released only after the intercession of the UK government – planespotting is an unknown, not to say eccentric, activity in Greece. Similarly, birdwatchers have been arrested in some countries when using binoculars close to militarily sensitive areas.

Staged authenticity

Given the constraints of time and place, tourists demand instant culture – an opportunity to sample, even if superficially, the 'foreignness' of the destination. This gives rise to what Dean MacCannell (1989) has referred to as **staged authenticity**, in which a search by tourists for authentic experiences of another culture leads to locals of that culture either providing those experiences or staging them to appear as realistic as possible. In this way, culture is in danger of becoming commercialized and trivialized, as when 'authentic' folk dances are staged for the package tourists as a form of cabaret in hotels or traditional tribal dances are arranged, often in an artificially shortened form, as performances for groups of tourists (see Figure 6.1). Such trivialization is not unknown in the UK, with pastiche 'mediaeval banquets', town criers and ceremonies reminiscent of earlier times. One proposal

Figure 6.1 Entertainers in Bali stage a display of traditional dances for tourists
Photo by Claire Humphreys

was made that the traditional ceremony of Changing the Guard should be mounted more frequently each day, in order to give tourists more opportunities to view it. Similarly, a suggestion was made (and considered seriously by the authorities) that Stonehenge be replicated in fibreglass near the actual site, to give the tourist an 'authentic' experience of seeing the stones more closely than is now possible.

Tourists will seek out local restaurants not frequented by other tourists in order to enjoy the 'authentic' cuisine and environment of the locals, but the very fact of their discovering such restaurants makes them tourist attractions and, ultimately, the 'tourist traps' that tourists are looking to avoid. Meantime, the locals move on to find somewhere else to eat.

The downgrading of the traditional hospitality towards tourists in Hawaii is exemplified by the artificial welcome to which they are subjected on their arrival at the islands. Traditionally, welcoming natives would place a lei of flowers around the neck of each tourist, but, over time, the cost of this courtesy and the huge volume of tourists has led to the lei being replaced by a plastic garland, reinforcing the impression of a commercial transaction, which this has now become.

EXAMPLE **Staging authenticity: the pastiche building**

One notable example of staging authenticity is to be found in the current construction of an entire pastiche French village - Domaine Haut-Gardegan. The village is being built by ski resort developer Intrawest, close to St Emilion. It will resemble classical early French mountain villages, but the only authentic buildings in the new village will be a ruined castle and stables, with a twelfth-century church on the outskirts.

A twist to staging authentic buildings is to first destroy them, then reconstruct them somewhere else. The home of former Beatle Ringo Starr at 9 Madryn Street, Toxteth, Liverpool is under threat to make way for redevelopment, but proposals have been made to reconstruct some or all of the building, brick by brick, within the new Museum of Liverpool. Beatles enthusiasts, meanwhile, are fighting to retain the original building *in situ*.

The authenticity of souvenirs

Tourists seek local artefacts as souvenirs or investments. In cases where genuine works are purchased, this can lead to the loss of cultural treasures from the country. Many countries now impose strict bans on exports of such items for this reason. Tourists, however, are often satisfied with purchasing what they believe to be authentic examples of local art, which has led to the mass production of poorly crafted works (sometimes referred to as **airport art**), such as are common among African nations and the Pacific islands. An effect of this is that it encourages the freezing of art styles in pseudo-traditional forms, as in the case of the apparently 'mediaeval' painted wooden religious statuary produced in Oberammergau and other villages in southern Germany. In turn, artists and craftspeople are subtly encouraged to change their traditional styles, making their works in the colours that are found to be most attractive to the tourists or reducing the sizes of their works to make them more readily transportable.

It is perhaps too easy to take a purist stance in criticizing these developments. One must also point to the evident benefits that tourism has brought to the cultures of many tourist destinations. Indeed, in many cases it has helped to regenerate an awareness and pride in local culture and traditions. But for the advent of tourism, many of those traditions would have died out long ago. It is facile to ascribe cultural decline directly to the impact of tourism – it is as likely to be the result of mass communication and technological development.

Maintaining local traditions

As Western (and specifically American) culture is the dominant influence around the world, it will inevitably undermine other cultures, particularly those of the developing world. It is equally clear, however, that tourism from the Western nations travelling to such nations has led to a revival of interest in tribal customs in those countries. It is not just in developing countries that this is the case – the revival of morris dancing in English communities is a direct result of the impact of tourism. Traditional local cuisines in the UK, too, have been regenerated, with the support of the national tourist boards with 'taste of England', 'taste of Wales' and 'taste of Scotland' schemes – a concept regenerated in promotions undertaken by VisitBritain since 2004, emphasizing once again the originality and quality of regional dishes in the UK. Dying local arts and crafts have been revived through cottage industries in rural areas that have benefited economically from the impact of tourism.

The hosts' impacts on tourists

While a considerable amount of research has now been undertaken into the effects of tourists on locals, rather less is available to tell us how locals, in turn, influence the tourists. What we do know, as mentioned earlier, is that we can ascribe our widening acceptance of foreign food, drink and fashions in the UK to the influence, in part, of overseas travel. The quality of foreign food, service, transport and hotel facilities has encouraged us to become more demanding in the provision of these things in the UK.

Early research (Gullahorn and Gullahorn, 1963) proposed that tourists go through three stages when adapting to the local culture of their holiday environment. In the first stage, the tourists are excited by the environment and the novelty of the situation; later, a second stage is reached in which the tourists become disillusioned with and more critical of the environment as they become accustomed to the situation. Finally, in what may be a slow process, they learn to adapt to the new setting and, in doing so, may experience 're-entry crisis', where it becomes difficult to adapt again to their home environment when they return.

Other studies have examined the extent to which pre-travel attitudes affect adaptability and whether travel broadens understanding or reinforces stereotypes (see, for example, Sutton 1967). The evidence suggests that a self-fulfilling prophecy is at work here – that, if we travel in the expectation of positive experiences, we will experience them. Much more work is needed, however, to explore the relationship between the tourist and the host from the tourist's perspective.

Host-guest interaction

There can be a problem regarding interactions between hosts and tourists in that any relationships which develop are usually fleeting and superficial, often conducted for commercial ends. A report by UNESCO (1976) identified four characteristics of host–guest relations in tourism:

- relationships are transitory and superficial
- they are undertaken under constraints of time and space, with visitors compacting sights into as limited amount of time as possible
- there is a lack of spontaneity in relationships – meetings tend to be prearranged to fit tour schedules, and involve mainly financial transactions

● relationships are unequal and unbalanced, due to disparities in the wealth and status of the participants.

Most tourists visiting a new country for the first time, who may be spending no more than a week there and do not expect to return, will be eager to condense their experiences, which tends to make the interactions brief and superficial. Add to this an initial fear of contact with locals, and tourists' comparative isolation – hotels often being dispersed, away from centres of local activity – and opportunities for any meaningful relationship become very limited. Few relationships are spontaneous; contact is generally with locals who work within the tourism industry or else it is mediated by couriers. Language may form an impenetrable barrier to genuine local contact and this limitation can lead to mutual misunderstandings. The relationship is further unbalanced by the status of the visitors, not only in terms of wealth but the fact that the tourists are on holiday while the locals are likely to be at work, often being paid to serve the needs of the tourists.

Changing languages

One impact of the increased scale of international tourism has been seen in the ability of the tourist and the host to communicate. Historically, the slower pace of travel may have allowed the visitor to learn at least a few words of the language in preparation for their experiences. However, today mass tourism, with couriers and reps available to help the tourist who does not speak the local language, means that few tourists would be deterred from visiting a destination because of language barriers.

The arrival of tourists at a destination has often encouraged the local population to learn the languages of their key markets, most commonly English, German and Spanish. Being able to converse with the tourist provides opportunities to sell their souvenirs, understand demands for food and drink, manage any complaints and attract the visitor to their business. To attract international tourists and enhance the visitor experience, local attractions like museums would then provide interpretation information, such as signs and guide in several languages.

This is not to say that developing language skills is a one-way affair. Tourists who regularly visit the same country may well seek to improve their knowledge of the local language in order to enhance their interaction with the local population. Phrase books (often printed, but now also widely available via mobile phone applications) have helped to enhance the interaction between hosts and guests.

Cultural transgressions

Although not exclusively a British problem, other patterns of behaviour among a small but significant minority of Britons while abroad have made such tourists unwelcome in several leading resorts on the Continent. Freed from the normal constraints of their everyday surroundings, many young tourists have been attracted to resorts promising unlimited cheap alcohol, 24-hour entertainment and readily available sex, either with fellow tourists or locals. Some of the less responsible tour operators have promoted these resorts to niche markets of youngsters, driving away the family market. This, in turn, has fuelled the growth of bars and discos offering popular music of the day, while resort reps for the operators organize bar crawls, earning high commissions from favoured bars.

The popularity of the resorts quickly led to their becoming overwhelmed by ill-behaved visitors, soon commonly referred to as 'lager louts'. Bar and street brawls, open drunkenness and impolite behaviour quickly led to conflicts with locals, not infrequently resulting in visitors being hospitalized. One after another, resorts such as Benitses and Kavos on

Corfu, Ibiza in the Balearics and Faliraki on Rhodes found their more traditional markets drying up. Efforts to change the image of the destinations were often taken too late. As local authorities intervened, imposing curfews, licensing bar crawls by groups, employing undercover police and even attempting to quarantine noisy groups within zones, the revellers simply moved on to other resorts, threatening their decline in turn.

This approach to tourism is not easily resolved, although the tour operators responsible for some of the worst excesses have sobered up as a consequence of the bad media publicity they received and modified their packages and promotions. The problem for the destinations – of how to regain public trust and to reposition their product – is less easily resolved.

Impacts on religious observances

Where cultural differences are tied to religion, conflicts may become greater. Some Islamic countries in the Middle East, such as the United Arab Emirates (UAE), have actively pursued policies to attract Western tourists, but expect them to respect local mores. Dubai, one of the Emirates States, is among those that initially turned a blind eye towards inappropriate beachwear or consumption of alcohol by visitors, but flagrant breaches of behaviour reduced levels of tolerance and led to a tightening up of control, notably in the case of two British tourists accused in 2008 of having sex on the beach and insulting the policeman who sought to arrest them.

As mentioned earlier, tourism can have an impact on the time available to worship and celebrate religious festivals. Furthermore, many religious and sacred buildings are popular attractions for tourists (see Figure 6.2), and managing the demands of visitors with the requirements of worshippers can prove difficult. The visitor may wish to observe, and

Figure 6.2 Tourists visit Sheikh Zahed Mosque, Abu Dhabi, UAE
Photo by Chris Holloway

often photograph, the building as well as the congregation, which can be distracting. However, banning tourists from such spaces is often impossible and the funding they provide through entry fees often assists the maintenance and upkeep.

The exploitation of indigenous populations

Perhaps the most serious accusation that can be made against tourism is the manner in which both members of the industry and destination authorities alike have exploited indigenous populations in their desire to develop tourism in ways that would maximize their own interests. There are countless examples of such exploitation, involving child labour, sexual exploitation and the wholesale removal of locals from their tribal lands to permit the development of tourism. There are several recent examples, too. The Masai tribespeople have been removed from their Ngorongoro crater hunting lands in Tanzania in order to allow tourists free movement to photograph wildlife. Botswana has evicted Gana and Gwi bushmen from their land in the central Kalahari game reserve to open the area to tourism. International opprobrium followed the removal and forced labour of Burmese people to enhance tourist projects in Myanmar.

Tourism Concern and other groups such as Tourism Watch in Germany have been particularly active in recent years in drawing attention to the exploitation of porters engaged in trekking and mountaineering tours in several countries. Publicity about their plight led to the formation of an International Porter Protection Group to oversee conditions on Mount Kilimanjaro, Tanzania (where porters were frequently obliged to carry loads of up to 60 kg for low pay, dressed in inadequate protective clothing: around 20 guides and porters die in their jobs each year), in the Himalayas and on the Inca Trail in Peru, where official guidelines are designed to ensure that packs do not exceed 20 kg and are weighed by government officials.

Sexual exploitation, especially of minors, has also been a cause of considerable concern in several developing countries, and pressure groups such as ECPAT and the World Council of Churches have encouraged the implementation of legislation to protect minors and prosecute offenders within their own countries for offences committed abroad. The UK reacted in 1997 with the passing of the Sex Offenders Act (UK), including a section that, for the first time, allowed such prosecutions to take place, although the difficulty of gathering evidence in developing countries has hindered the implementation of the Act.

Managing the social impacts of tourism

Sustainable tourism – in terms of the social impacts of tourism on indigenous populations – needs to be managed in two ways. First, it is important that good relations are established between locals and guests, so that guests are welcomed to the region or country and social interactions benefit both parties.

There are different approaches to ensuring this and the choice is essentially between two diametrically opposed management methods. Responsible officials can attempt to integrate guests into the local community and control the overall number of visitors so that the local population does not become swamped by tourists. This is really only practical where demand for the destination is limited to comparatively small numbers and the market attracted shows empathy for, and sensitivity towards, local culture. Thus, specialist tourism will allow for this solution to be adopted, but mass tourism will not.

Alternatively, officials can aim to concentrate the visitors in particular districts (sometimes referred to as tourist 'ghettos', often some distance away from residential neighbourhoods) so that any damage is limited to the few locals who will have contact with those guests, usually in the form of commercial transactions. In this way, most locals and visitors will not come into direct contact with one another, though this may also reduce the economic benefit of tourism to the local community. One solution of this kind is the integrated resort complex offering all-inclusive packages. Such resorts are becoming increasingly common at long-haul destinations – examples being found in Cancún, Mexico, Nusa Dua in Bali, Indonesia, Puerto Plata in the Dominican Republic and the Langkawi development in Malaysia. All-inclusive resorts can also be operated sustainably if locals are employed in skilled as well as less-skilled jobs at the site and much of what is consumed at the resort is produced in the surrounding area.

Government policies to attract large numbers of tourists have given way to policies designed to attract particular tourist markets. While this has, in most cases, meant trying to attract wealthy, high-spend visitors, it has sometimes led to a move to encourage visits by those who will have the least impact on local populations – that is, those who will integrate well and accept local customs rather than seek to impose their own standards on locals. Some have gone further, however. The local authority at Alassio, Italy, took rather extreme action in 1994 in an effort to discourage day trippers and sacopelisti (sleeping baggers) who slept on the beaches and brought little income into the town. It asked the railways to provide fewer trains to the resort on weekends. Tourists were also to be accosted and asked to show that they were carrying at least 50 000 lira as spending money. Such approaches are isolated, however, and, for the most part, destination authorities have recognized that their obligation is to grow tourism, while ensuring that, as far as possible, whatever impact tourists have on local populations should be beneficial to the locals.

Bringing economic benefits to locals

One other issue is the need to ensure that locals are involved in all stages of the development of tourism at a destination. This means that the onus is on developers and authorities to consult with locals at all levels during the process of development, encourage their participation and ensure that indigenous populations benefit economically from incoming tourism, by the provision of employment at all levels and ownership of facilities. All these activities, however, require a measure of sophistication among the local population, the provision of essential education and training, as well as assistance in raising finance for investment in local tourist businesses. The solution cannot be achieved merely by putting businesses into the hands of local residents. To illustrate this, the example can be given of a tour operating company in Arnhem Land, Australia, that was originally managed by foreign nationals, but was eventually handed over to local Aboriginal administration. While the new Aboriginal owners were fully capable of handling the operational aspects of the programme, they had little knowledge of, and no contacts with, the overseas markets they existed to serve and, in consequence, found it difficult to attract new business. Other, more recent, schemes, however, have been handled more successfully. One simple example is the innovation of employing local Bedouin tribesmen to act as escorts for groups of trekkers across the Sinai Peninsula. Similarly, a sustainable village project in Gomorszolos, Hungary, involves tours of small groups (a maximum of 12 people) staying in locally owned hotels, using local guides, and with local conservation projects being undertaken that are partly funded by the income generated by the tours.

EXAMPLE Blue Lagoon Cruises

Blue Lagoon Cruises operates in the Yasawa Islands northwest of Fiji. The company makes direct and indirect contributions of some £165 000 annually to the islands, whether visited or not. Locals are employed and care is taken to minimize the impact of tourists on the islands during visits.

This cruise operation includes calling at some of the more northerly, seldom visited islands, such as Rabi and Kioa, where locals have notable basketry skills and the economy can be boosted by craft sales. Funds earned are channelled into community halls, water tanks and the construction of sea walls against erosion.

The impacts of travel on tourists' health

An impact is a two-way process and we have examined many of the positive and negative effects of tourism in this chapter. It is notable how the lifestyles of many tourists have changed as a result of their experiences of travelling abroad. They often have more adventurous tastes in food, consume more wine at the expense of beers and hard spirits, and have a wider appreciation of foreign cultural activities, even a greater willingness to master the elements of a foreign language (a real breakthrough for the British!). These are just some of the things that tourists bring back with them to enrich their lives in their home countries. Unfortunately, other things they bring back with them can be less welcome.

Skin cancer

Severe sunburn is among the commonest of the ailments afflicting tourists from the generating countries – the result of a desire to maximize exposure to the sun during the brief period spent abroad on holiday. While sunburn is by no means uncommon among tourists visiting the seaside in northern communities, the increased intensity of the sun's rays nearer the equator has resulted in many tourists experiencing the pain and nausea that accompany a bad case of sunburn. But this may be just one impact of spending time in the sun.

The propensity to develop skin cancer has increased as the world's protective ozone layer has been reduced by atmospheric pollution. It is estimated that 80% of all skin melanomas affect fair-skinned people, and those who have experienced sunburn, especially in childhood, are at higher risk. Interestingly, the recent growth in use of tanning beds to gain and maintain a tan has also influenced statistics on skin cancer.

Although the danger has been recognized for some years and governments have mounted campaigns to draw attention to the problem, many tourists either remain ignorant of it or choose to ignore it in their desire to cultivate an attractive tan. In Australia, for example, the 'slip, slap, slop' campaign (slip on a T-shirt, slap on a hat, slop on suncream) has been far more effective in educating a country of sunlovers, resulting in a sharp decline in the number of all forms of skin cancer in that country.

Attitudes towards getting a suntan are expected to change only gradually over the next few years, with many tourists still choosing to visit seaside resorts for their perceived health and relaxation benefits. The media, with the support of health experts, are encouraging tourists to change their behaviour patterns while at the seaside, by applying high-factor suncreams or, better still, sunblocks, while sunbathing, reapplying these frequently if entering the water to swim, ensuring young children are well covered and generally reducing outdoor activities when the sun is at its most intense. Seaside resorts are coming to recognize that, if they are to survive, they must construct more indoor facilities and offer their visitors better protection from the sun (such as parasols, now commonly found on Caribbean beaches) while on the beach.

Dietary illnesses

Exposure to contaminated food results in other common holiday ailments, ranging from simple upset stomachs to hepatitis and dysentery. The incidence of these kinds of illnesses is increasing as holidaymakers become more adventurous, visiting areas of the world where poor hygiene and inadequate supervision are widespread and taking more risks when sampling the local food.

Infectious diseases

Tropical diseases are, similarly, becoming more commonplace, with malaria leading the field – several deaths occur each year among British tourists, many of whom disregard even the most basic recommended precautions. Some forms of malaria are becoming highly resistant to standard prescription drugs, although recent research offers hope of a vaccine within a generation.

Outbreaks of SARS have also severely impacted on recent tourist movements, especially to popular Asian countries, while the global spread of HIV/AIDS, especially but by no means restricted to African and Asian destinations, coupled with lax sexual mores among many travellers, compound the health threats for tourists.

The solution to most of these problems lies in better education, of both hosts and guests, with the onus being on the travel industry to get the message across to their customers through brochures, websites and on-the-spot resort representatives.

EXAMPLE   **The spread of swine flu**

In the spring of 2009, a new virus, H1N1 (or swine flu as it was known), spread from Mexico to many countries across the globe. Possibly between 45 and 90 million people caught swine flu in 2009, and the disease is estimated to have resulted in more than 17 000 deaths in 200 countries, though many of those who died were suffering from pre-existing conditions.

The spread of the disease was initially attributed to tourists returning home from Mexican holidays. But the problem became more complex as government officials complained that carriers of the virus were visiting tourist regions and further spreading the disease among the local population. For example, Indonesian authorities accused Australians of bringing the virus to Bali, and introduced the use of body temperature scanners at airports to identify potential carriers; similar border checks occurred between Nepal and India.

In the immediate aftermath of the outbreak, occupancy rates in Mexican hotels fell, perhaps not surprisingly, from 90% to a level around 20% as visitors cancelled their travel plans, airlines cancelled flights and cruise ships diverted to other ports of call. The impact on the Mexican population was significant. Many lost jobs as the H1N1 swine flu (coupled with the global financial crisis) led to 1.1 million fewer tourists visiting Mexico in 2009.

Politico-cultural impacts

Where significant economic benefits are likely to follow from influxes of tourists, tourism can be a force for good politically. This is exemplified by the 2008 Olympics, held in the Republic of China, where the government felt obliged, during the period in which the Games were in progress, to relax – if only marginally and temporarily – some of its authoritarian controls and display a more democratic face to the world. It is almost inevitable that large numbers of tourists visiting a country over extended periods of time will eventually influence the political culture of that country, often for the good.

Controversy inevitably surrounds the question of whether or not tourists should be encouraged to visit more extreme regimes – Myanmar (Burma) being a case in point. The argument favouring visits is that interactions between hosts and guests, however closely controlled, will be of some benefit to locals, culturally as well as economically, while the contrary view is taken by those who believe that tourist revenues flowing into authoritarian coffers benefit and reinforce the regime.

A presently more critical political issue confronting the global tourism industry, however, is the growth in terrorism, which threatens to undermine both travel and understanding between nations. Attacks directed against Westerners, especially in Islamic countries, can lead to a dramatic reduction in the flow of tourists to those countries, some of whose economies (Egypt and Bali, for example) are heavily dependent on tourism. Local civil wars in some popular areas of the globe inhibit tourism. Kathmandu in Nepal, for example, saw a sharp decline in tourist arrivals following the rise of Maoist revolutionaries in the country, but, with a more stable government in place following the deposition of the monarch, tourists are beginning to flow to the area again.

The UK foreign office frequently has been accused of ambivalence in the guidance given to tourists, while the industry itself – and travel insurance companies – are obliged to follow their governments' directives in determining whether or not holidays should be withdrawn following attacks. The authorities in the leading generating countries are seldom consistent in tackling these issues and tourists themselves tend to vary in their reactions. American tourists, for instance, show greater reluctance to travel to countries where there is a perceived threat, however remote, while European travellers appear more resilient. Indeed, following the events of September 11th 2001, Americans have been slow to travel abroad again, even to relatively safe countries, slowing the global expansion of tourism considerably.

Legislation and guidance protecting the tourist destination

Awareness of the need for planning is the first step in attempting to control the worst effects of mass tourism. However, in the early stages of such awareness, authorities failed to make the distinction between cultural and environmental impacts, with concern for sustainability initially concentrating largely on environmental issues. The origins of sustainable tourism legislation to cover both cultural and environmental impacts will therefore be examined at this point, while specifically environmental issues will be examined in the next chapter.

Broad awareness of the problems that tourism creates can be traced back to at least the 1960s, but it was another 20 years before they began to be addressed, with legislation introduced to dampen their impact. Influential voices made themselves heard, calling for a new tourism, variously described as 'sustainable tourism', 'ecotourism', 'green tourism', 'soft tourism' and, eventually, 'responsible tourism'. Proponents of sustainability have argued that **responsible tourism** should be defined as underpinning a properly thought out management strategy, with collaboration between the private and public sectors to prevent irreparable damage to the environment before it is too late.

One of the early expressions of concern was manifested when the United Nations World Tourism Organization (UNWTO) and the United Nations Environment Programme (UNEP) issued a joint declaration in 1982 calling for the rational management of tourism to protect, enhance and improve the environment. In the following year, they suggested employing zoning strategies to concentrate tourists in those regions that could best absorb them and disperse them where environments were viewed as being too fragile to sustain mass tourism.

It is important to recognize that not all tourists are seeking the same forms of tourism, just as the terms used above to describe the new tourism are not necessarily synonymous. Ecotourism in its early days was described by the environmentalist Hector Ceballos-Lascurain as, 'that tourism that involves traveling to relatively undisturbed natural areas with the specific object of studying, admiring and enjoying the scenery and its wild plants and animals, as well as any existing cultural aspects (both past and present) found in these areas' (1987, 13).

It is appropriate to argue that all forms of tourism should be 'sustainable' and not destroy the destination to which the tourist is attracted. Perhaps a better definition is that offered by the International Ecotourism Society itself: 'Ecotourism is responsible travel to natural areas that conserves the environment and improves the well-being of local people' (TIES, 2010). This definition makes it clear that such tourism includes responsibility to both the environment and the indigenous populations.

Tourism must be environmentally compatible, as the World Travel and Tourism Council (WTTC) proposed in its ten-point guidelines (see Figure 6.3). It will be noted that only two of the ten points refer specifically to issues that can be defined as socio-cultural.

1. Identify and minimize product and operational environmental problems, paying particular attention to new projects.
2. Pay due regard to environmental concerns in design, planning, construction and implementation.
3. Be sensitive to conservation of environmentally protected or threatened areas, species or scenic aesthetics, achieving landscape enhancement where possible.
4. Practise energy conservation, reduce and recycle waste, practise freshwater management and control sewage disposal.
5. Control and diminish air emissions and pollutants.
6. Monitor, control and reduce noise levels.
7. Control, reduce and eliminate environmentally unfriendly products, such as asbestos, CFCs, pesticides and toxic, corrosive, infectious, explosive or flammable material.
8. Respect and support historic or religious objects and sites.
9. Exercise due regard for the interests of local populations, including their history, traditions and culture and future development.
10. Consider environmental issues as a key factor in the overall development of travel and tourism destinations.

Figure 6.3 Guidelines for sustainable tourism
Courtesy of the World Travel and Tourism Council

By comparison, the following ten-point set of principles established by Tourism Concern (Eber, 1992) appears to achieve a more equal balance between socio-cultural and environmental elements:

1. using resources sustainably
2. reducing overconsumption and waste
3. maintaining diversity
4. integrating tourism into planning
5. supporting local economies
6. involving local economies
7. consulting stakeholders and the public
8. training staff
9. marketing tourism responsibly
10. undertaking research.

The issue of sustainability was boosted by the concern expressed by the United Nations General Assembly in the mid-1980s, which established a commission to look in depth at the planet's people and resources and make recommendations on ways to achieve long-term sustainable development. The Brundtland Commission presented its report *Our Common Future* in 1987, adopting the definition of sustainable development as, 'Development that meets the needs of the present without compromising the ability of future generations to meet their own needs' (un-documents.net/wced-ocf.htm – accessed February 2012).

The influence of this report soon led to the UN organizing a major international conference on the topic. The Conference on Environment and Development (the so-called Earth Summit) was held at Rio de Janeiro in 1992. Although tourism neither appeared as an issue in the original Brundtland Report, nor was included in the agenda of the Rio meeting, the industry's planning and development have been heavily influenced by the recommendations emerging from these two sources, most notably by the conference's Agenda 21 – a guide for local government action to reconcile development and sustainability regarding the environment.

The year 1992 was a momentous one for sustainability. The hospitality industry launched its International Hotel Environment Initiative (IHEI), designed to reduce the impact of staying visitors on the environment, while, in the same year, the UK-based pressure group Tourism Concern set out its own guidelines (listed above) and began actively to lobby the private sector to take more account of the need for sustainable planning. This volunteer-aided organization has been a leader in drawing the UK industry's attention to the issue of sustainability. It was first perceived as an irrelevant and esoteric subject, but is now taken more seriously by those responsible for planning and marketing.

By the start of the twenty-first century, the concept had become familiar, both within the industry and among the travelling public. The UNEP introduced its Initiative for Sustainable Tourism, which was aimed at tour operators and adopted, in 2000. This was followed by a UN declaration to designate 2002 as the International Year of Ecotourism (IYE). A World Summit on Sustainable Development was held in Johannesburg, also in 2002, and, for the first time, it took into account the importance of sustainability in the tourism industry. A world ecotourism summit held in Quebec in the same year, however, appears to have had relatively little impact. Nonetheless, 2002 proved to be the year when the industry in the UK began to take an active interest. As a direct result of the Johannesburg summit, the UK Foreign Office introduced a Sustainable Tourism Initiative, to which over 40 companies (including the leading tour operators) subscribed. The result was the formation of the Travel Foundation, which is strongly supported by both commercial and environmental organizations and industry bodies, such as the Association of British

Travel Agents (ABTA), Association of Independent Tour Operators (AITO) and the Federation of Tour Operators (FTO). The Foundation's stated aims are to change the practice of tourism to ensure that it makes a greater contribution to the welfare of the environment and populations of tourist destinations.

Other organizations with links to industry, such as the UNWTO and the WTTC, have added their support for the principles of sustainable development, which aim to minimize damage to the environment, wildlife and local indigenous populations. These organizations have particularly recommended the use of local building materials for tourist sites, recycling of waste and water and recruitment of locals for jobs within tourism. Together with the Earth Council, the two bodies also published a report (and subsequent progress updates), *Agenda 21 for the Travel and Tourism Industry: Towards Environmentally Sustainable Development*, encouraging the industry to take the lead in preserving the environment in the areas they develop.

EXAMPLE   The Travel Foundation

Two of the Travel Foundation's early activities to support sustainable tourism both centred on socio-cultural issues.

In Cyprus, tour operators were encouraged to develop small group tours to the interior of the island, to comparatively unspoilt villages, allowing the villagers to benefit both commercially and socially from interaction with tourists. The organization supported tours by Support Abandoned Villages and their Environments (SAVE) that were designed to encourage exploration away from the coastal resorts. Aiming to show visitors a true picture of Cypriot rural life, the tours have encouraged shops and other tourist facilities to open and labour forces to seek jobs in their villages rather than migrating to the coast.

In The Gambia, traders found it difficult to sell direct to customers, who resented being hassled on the beaches to buy what were often viewed as inferior products. The Foundation helped local traders to sell their products direct to tourists by overseeing quality control and compiling a directory of local businesses that met the improved standards. In 2002, The Gambia introduced a tax on all visitors arriving at Banjul Airport to raise revenue for tourism advertising and environmental improvements.

While joint action of this kind is invaluable, many businesses – particularly the smaller, independent companies, which were quick to recognize the value of selling the concept of sustainable tourism to their sophisticated markets – introduced their own policies to support sustainability. The AITO has shown great enthusiasm for its members to embrace responsible tourism, offering a series of guidelines, including:

- protection of the environment – flora, fauna, landscapes
- respect for local cultures – traditions, religions and the built heritage
- economic and social benefits for local communities
- conservation of natural resources, from the office to the destination
- minimizing pollution caused by noise, waste disposal and congestion.

The organization now awards from one to five gold stars to member companies in recognition of their efforts to ensure that tours are planned and operated responsibly. Initially a three-star award was the maximum possible but, since 2008, this has been expanded to recognize those organizations who go beyond this level.

One specialist long-haul operator and member of AITO that has had notable success in this field has been Journey Latin America, which has been awarded five stars by AITO.

EXAMPLE | **Journey Latin America**

In the Andes, Journey Latin America has worked with reputable local agents to protect porters and the environment on the Inca Trail. They operate using local guides, hotels and operators, encouraging their local suppliers to work towards responsible tourism.

In 2003, the company ran a clean-up campaign in the Cordillera Blanca, Northern Peru (where, as yet, there is little legislation to protect the environment). The company has stated its intention to help protect the integrity of indigenous populations, particularly those in the Amazon basin where adventure holidays are offered. They have also cooperated with Climate Care to offset the effect of carbon dioxide emissions in the flights that transport their staff travelling on business. They also work to raise awareness of responsible tourism amongst their travellers, including offering the opportunity to offset the impact of their flights.

Summary

In this chapter we have considered the effects that tourism can have on the host population. The changes that occur may offer positive opportunities to improve the quality of life for the residents and can provide opportunities for self-development and social interaction. It can encourage the local population to value cultural traditions and develop pride in their local area. There are, however, problems caused by an influx of tourists, which can be exacerbated by greater difference between the cultures of the host and the guest.

Importantly it is not just the host who experiences social impacts – tourists themselves can be victims of criminal activity or ill-health as an outcome of their travels. On the positive side, tourists can benefit from the interaction between host and guest, as they develop greater understanding of different cultures and places.

As recognition of the socio-cultural impact of tourism grows, it seems that both governments and the tourism industry itself are looking for new ways to protect indigenous cultures and unique destinations.

Questions and discussion points

1. The chapter suggests that tourist ghettos (concentration of tourists into a particular district) can act as a tool for managing the impact of tourism; it can certainly help to contain the spread of environmental damage caused by tourism, but how does this approach benefit the host population? How might the host population benefit from a more integrated approach to tourism development?

2. How important is authenticity in the following cases:
   (a) watching a hula show at a hotel in Waikiki, Hawaii
   (b) buying souvenirs from Masai tribespeople when visiting their village in East Africa
   (c) museum exhibits at the former concentration camp in Auschwitz.

3. Why might tourists be likely victims of petty crime or holiday scams? What are the likely effects on a destination where crime against tourists is widespread?

Tasks

1. The United Nations World Tourism Organization has implemented a campaign to protect children from exploitation in the travel industry (**www.unwto.org/protectchildren**). Investigate this initiative and write a report which identifies the different ways in which children may be negatively affected by the tourism industry. Discuss the many activities and campaigns which are being implemented by the tourism industry to protect this vulnerable group.

2. Write a short essay which highlights the many positive benefits that tourism can bring to a host population. Use examples to support your points. Suggest changes which can be made by the tourism industry to ensure that these positive benefits can be maximized.

Bibliography

Brundtland Commission (1987) *The Brundtland Report: World Commission on Environment and Development: Our common future*, Oxford, OUP.

Ceballos-Lascurain, H. (1987) The future of ecotourism, *Mexico Journal*, January, 13–14.

Doxey, G. V. (1975) A causation theory of visitor-resident irritants: Methodology and research inferences. *The Impact of Tourism: Travel Research Association Sixth Annual Conference Proceedings*, San Diego, CA, Travel Research Association, 57–72.

Eber, S. (1992) *Beyond the Green Horizon: Principles of sustainable tourism*, London, Tourism Concern/WWF.

Fentiman, P. (2009) Travellers warned to beware tourist cons, *Press Association National Newswire*, 24 August.

Gullahorn, J. E. and Gullahorn, J. T. (1963) An extension of the U-curve hypothesis, *Journal of Social Sciences*, **19** (3), 33–47.

Jun, X. (2010) Ghana launches tourism police, *Xinhua News Agency*, 2 March.

Krippendorf, J. (1987) *The Holidaymakers: Understanding the Impact of Leisure and Travel*, Oxford, Butterworth Heinemann.

MacCannell, D. (1989) *The Tourist: A New Theory of the Leisure Class*, 2nd edn, New York, Schocken Books.

Smith, V. (1992) *Hosts and Guests*, Oxford, Blackwell.

Sutton, W. A. (1967) Travel and understanding: notes on the social structure of touring, *International Journal of Comparative Sociology*, **8** (2), 218–223.

TIES (2010) *What is Ecotourism?*, available online at: http://www.ecotourism.org/site/c.orLQKXPCLmF/b.4835303/k.BEB9/What_is_Ecotourism__The_International_Ecotourism_Society.htm (accessed November 2011).

Tourism in Focus (2008) Padaung refugees trapped by tourism, *In Focus*, Spring, London, Tourism Concern.

UNESCO (1976) The effects of tourism on socio-cultural values, *Annals of Tourism Research*, 4, 74–105.

Further reading

MacCannell, D. (1989) *The Tourist: A New Theory of the Leisure Class*, 2nd edn, New York, Schocken Books.

Wall, G. and Mathieson, A. (2006) *Tourism: Change, Impacts and Opportunities*, Harlow, Pearson.

Websites

International Porter Protection Group (IPPG): **www.ippg.net**

The Travel Foundation: **www.thetravelfoundation.org.uk**

UN WTO Protection of Children in Tourism campaign: **www.unwto.org/protectchildren**

7

The environmental impacts of tourism

Contents

Learning outcomes

After studying this chapter, you should be able to:

- understand the various ways in which tourism can impact on the environment
- identify and evaluate different approaches to finding solutions to the problems caused by these impacts
- understand the importance of sustainable tourism as it relates to the environment
- recognize how appropriate planning and cooperation between the private and public sectors can help to ensure sustainability.

Unlike many of the trends that shaped the travel industry at the onset of 2009, such as a slumping economy and the coming of age of mobile travel, the genesis of green consumer products comes from a proliferation of personal values that revolve around contributing to a general good, rather than around financial gain or the convenience of better technology.

Rheem (2009) *Going green: the business impact of environmental awareness on travel*, 4

Introduction

In this chapter, we explore tourism's impacts on the environment and consider the growing awareness of the needs to be more sustainable. While the obvious focus will be on how tourism affects the environment at popular tourist destinations, we need to be aware at the same time that the rise in global tourism has environmental impacts that go far beyond those destinations alone. In fact, it is no exaggeration to say that tourism is a major contributor to the despoliation of the environment, notably as a result of transport's contribution to pollution, whether by air, sea or on land.

As tourism expands, so new destinations are put at risk; and twenty-first-century tourists are tending to seek out ever more remote areas of the globe.

EXAMPLE Antarctica

The Antarctic continent has become a regular target for mass tourism today, with cruise ships that can carry up to 600 passengers visiting the peninsula on a regular basis and passenger-carrying ice-breakers calling as far south as Scott's and Shackleton's bases. Annual figures for visitors to Antarctica were a mere 4800 in 1991, rose to 15 325 in 2001, reaching a peak in 2007 of over 47 000. The following seasons saw levels fall to around 35 000 annually and are expected to fall still further as regulations banning the use in the area of some fuel types will primarily affect the large passenger vessels (O'Reilly, 2010).

Package tourists can now enjoy visits to this least-explored continent that, in addition to penguin watching, can include anything from travel by snowmobile to 'adventure flights' to the South Pole itself.

The popularity of the huge penguin colonies (perhaps partly attributable to the film 'March of the Penguins') has meant that some of the colonies are receiving as many as three visits every day, impacting on the birds' behaviour and breeding patterns. One unexpected result of this influx has been the large number of birds contracting diseases found in chickens, thought to be the result of food carelessly discarded by visiting tourists.

There has also been a number of issues with the vessels themselves. In 2007, the MS NordKapp was involved in a minor accident whilst later that year 150 passengers and crew were airlifted from the MV Explorer before it sank in the Antarctic ocean after hitting an iceberg. In 2009, the Ocean Nova ran aground off the coast of Antarctica, with 65 passengers being evacuated for their own safety. The biggest concern is that some vessels were not built to withstand the environmental conditions, making them vulnerable in this inhospitable environment. Managing these issues is complex. The region is without recognized territorial sovereignty and as a consequence regulating tourism has to be achieved through collective agreement. Members of the International Association of Antarctic Tour Operators have adopted a voluntary code of practice to minimize the impacts of visitors, including limiting the numbers of passengers at any one site to 100, and restricting how close they may approach the penguin colonies. Guidelines to reduce the likelihood of the introduction of non-native species have also been produced. The difficulty, however, is in policing the many different policies and rulings.

In other ecologically sensitive regions, such as the Galapagos Islands, Costa Rica and Belize, the development of tourism is also controlled and efforts are made to ensure that all visitors respect the natural environment. The pressures of demand are difficult to resist, however, when the economic benefits to less-developed countries are significant. While in 1974 the authorities set an original target of 12 000 visits to the Galapagos (later revised to 40 000), visitors now number more than 100 000 (Epler, 2007), and the ceiling has been to all intents and purposes abolished. The burgeoning tourism industry has attracted residents, mostly from mainland Equador, leading to an increase in population levels from 5000 in the 1960s to more than 40 000 in 2010 (Barraclough, 2010).

The environmental effects of tourism

Transport pollution

Large-scale tourist movement requires the use of mass transportation, particularly by air, and, while aircraft are now twice as fuel-efficient as they were three decades ago, air travel has quadrupled in that time. In 1970, airline passengers travelled some 350 billion air passenger miles (APMs; this figure, of course, includes all forms of passengers, not merely tourists); by 2000, APMs had increased to 1500 billion and forecasts are for this to double by 2015 and triple by 2050 (given the rapid expansion of the low-cost carriers, these figures may prove conservative). Whilst the recent economic uncertainty may have some impact on these forecasts, the long-term increase in the number of flights over the next two decades is beyond doubt.

Apart from emissions of nitrous oxides (unfortunately, the introduction of quieter, more fuel-efficient and cleaner jet engines has the side-effect of increasing those emissions), these aircraft currently pump some 600 million tons of carbon dioxide into the upper atmosphere each year. According to the Intergovernmental Panel on Climate Change, this accounts for at least 3.5% of all greenhouse gases. Again, this will rise to 15% by 2050, on present estimates.

One EU study in 2004 claimed that air travel was responsible for 9% of all global warming whilst a 2007 article (Gossling and Peeters, 2007) asserted that for European residents air travel accounted for less than 20% of trips but almost 80% of the greenhouse gases released by tourism-related transport. In the UK alone, according to a Government Aviation White Paper in 2003, the number of people flying into and out of the UK would rise from 180 million to over 500 million in 2030, while an environmental audit committee estimated that aviation would have become responsible for two-thirds of all the UK's greenhouse gas emissions by 2050. These figures also do not take into account the costs of congestion, leading to stacking over airports and the resultant fuel waste – a problem that is likely to grow as air corridors become more crowded. The rapid expansion of the low-cost airlines, operating on short-haul routes, accounts for a sizeable increase in pollution figures, given that one-fifth of a short-haul aircraft's fuel load is burnt in take-off and landing.

Yet, in spite of the clear threat to world health, aviation fuel remains largely untaxed. Fuel taxation was ruled out at the 1944 Chicago Convention in order to boost the post-war airline industry and even VAT has not yet been applied to airline tickets, in spite of protests from the environmentalists. Aviation is specifically exempted from the Kyoto Protocol on climate change.

There are growing calls for a carbon tax on fuel, which it is thought would help lead to airlines converting from high-carbon kerosene to low-carbon liquid methane and, ultimately, the development of carbon-free liquid hydrogen fuels – a move likely to be hastened by the volatility in world oil prices. Any such tax, however, to be truly effective, would have to be applied globally and would encounter strong resistance from the airlines and authorities in countries such as the USA that are heavily dependent on low-price air travel. Alternatively, carbon trading agreements could be extended to airlines, requiring them to either reduce emissions or purchase expensive permits (fees for which would have to be recovered through higher ticket prices). Regionally, taxes have been mooted (in the UK, a government Green Paper, 'The future of aviation' (2000) accepted the principle that polluters should pay and the Royal Commission on Environmental Pollution proposed a green tax on air tickets in 2002), but not implemented. Existing aviation taxes, such as Air Passenger Duty (APD), have been significantly increased in recent years, although such approaches appear to offer airlines little incentive to reduce emissions or invest in new technology.

Interestingly, the growth of high-speed rail routes across Europe in recent years has led more business travellers to switch from air to train travel, as companies begin to monitor (and offset) their carbon impact.

EXAMPLE Offsetting the carbon dioxide damage

In 2008, Californian based airline Virgin America announced a partnership with Carbonfund.org to allow travellers the opportunity to offset the impact of their flight at the time of booking. Using independently verified projects, the airline offered its customers the opportunity to pay others to cut emissions on their behalf, for example payments would fund projects such as installing wind turbines in developing countries.

The growing number of airlines (more than 30 by 2010) offering offset schemes, with inconsistencies in the prices being charged, encouraged the United Nations to introduce a standard to calculate how much passengers should pay to offset their air travel and, while this approach focused only on carbon and not other emissions impacting on the environment, today this calculator does take into account aircraft types, route information and passenger load factors. In 2009, Virgin America became the first domestic airline in the USA to allow passengers to offset their impact whilst in-flight, using the seatback entertainment system. Despite increasing the convenience for passengers to offset the impact of their journey there has generally been low uptake of these initiatives.

Other forms of tourism transport make their own contributions to pollution. Up to 300 passenger ships now ply world cruise routes, carrying in excess of 15 million passengers each year. The US-based Ocean Conservancy estimates that, apart from the daily fuel burn, each ship generates some 30 000 gallons of sewage and 7 tons of rubbish each day – not all of it properly disposed of. Indeed, several leading cruise companies have been prosecuted in recent years for pollution of the seas and rigging instruments to deceive inspections. Waterborne vessels of all kinds, whether on the high seas or on inland rivers, lakes and canals, by cleaning out their tanks or dumping waste overboard, significantly contribute to water pollution, which, in turn, impacts on aquatic wildlife. Even without such illicit dumping, the sheer number of cruise vessels plying popular waterways such as the Caribbean poses a threat through leakages and congestion at key ports. Bermuda is one of several islands now imposing restrictions on the number of cruise ship visits permitted each year.

EXAMPLE Alaskan cruises

Alaskans, once overjoyed at the arrival of tourist ships, have become angered by the rapidly increasing numbers of cruise ships visiting the state, fearing contamination of their waters. Also, the large number of vessels being routed to the area to engage in whale-watching is having the effect of driving these mammals away from the Alaskan shores. The state's Department of Environmental Conservation now levies a charge on all cruise vessels to pay for the clean-up of pollution.

In 2010, Friends of the Earth published their cruise ship report card, which evaluated cruise lines in regard to their treatment of sewage, air pollution, water quality compliance and the provison of consumer information on environmental policies. Of particular interest in this case is the assessment of the extent to which ships violated water pollution standards designed to protect the Alaskan coast. Both Regent SevenSea Cruises and Carnival Cruises achieved an 'A' rating, whilst Princess Cruises scored only a 'D+' grade (FoE, 2010).

Inland waterways are, if anything, even more fragile and endangered than coastal waters as a result of excessive use by waterborne leisure transport, whether private or public. Apart from the danger of pollution caused by fuel or oil leaks in rivers, lakes and canals, unless strict speed limits are enforced, riverbanks may be damaged or undermined by the wash from passing boats, causing soil erosion and endangering wildlife. The popularity of the Norfolk Broads in the UK among boaters has led to overuse of these waterways during the past 50 years, with resultant damage to banks.

Finally, account must also be taken of the impact of the many millions of motorists using private and hire cars for their holidays and short breaks. While congestion is the more visible problem arising from the expansion in the numbers of vehicles at popular tourism destinations, pollution resulting from the concentration of exhaust gases in both city and rural tourist destinations can seriously affect the health of tourists and residents alike. The uncontrolled expansion of private vehicles in key tourist cities such as Bangkok can so adversely affect the visitor experience that it threatens to discourage visitors from either travelling there or staying in the city.

EXAMPLE   Venice

Venice, with its network of canals, receives up to 20 million visitors every year (Kington, 2009). Most are transported by water during their stay and gondola trips are an expensive but popular form of excursion.

The city is slowly sinking, and its paved areas are subject to frequent flooding. As public transport on the canals is largely motorized, the wash from these vessels is contributing to undermining the foundations of many historic buildings. The Italian government has given Venice the power to limit motorized transport, introduce speed limits and tolls on tourist boats and establish 'blue zones' where transport is limited to gondolas and rowing boats.

It is estimated that 70% of the tourists are daytrippers, arriving by bus, car, train and increasingly, cruise ship. More than 700 000 passengers disembark from the 500 ships docked annually, to spend the day visiting St Marks, before they depart again that night.

A significant proportion of the petrol purchased all over the world is for leisure purposes, whether for touring or day trips, and, in some regions, the exhaust fumes from these vehicles, when added to those from local traffic, can damage the clean air that is the prime attraction for tourists. This is particularly true of mountainous destinations, where not only touristic appeal but also even plant and animal life can be adversely affected.

EXAMPLE   Mountain resorts

Some popular mountain resorts, such as Zermatt in Switzerland, have banned non-residential private vehicles from the town, requiring tourists to use park and ride services or rack-and-pinion railways into the resort. The latter provide a picturesque additional attraction to visitors staying there.

The popularity of off-roading with sports utility vehicles (SUVs) is also damaging to the environment in sensitive areas of the world. This sport is popular among American tourists, and some wilderness areas are now under threat, particularly in Utah. Moab, southeast of

Salt Lake City, has attracted significant numbers of such vehicles, as have sand dunes in several parts of the world, where these vehicles can destroy sparse scrubland and erode the landscape.

Noise pollution by transport

All motorized forms of road, sea and air transport can intrude on the calm of a resort by raising noise levels, whether in rural surroundings or in residential areas, and this, too, must be considered a form of pollution.

Aircraft taking off and landing at busy airports severely disturb local residents and tourists alike. Authorities have long recognized the problem of air traffic noise and action has been taken to reduce it. For example, aircraft are grouped under three classes, known as chapters, according to the noise levels they emit. Under government regulations, especially in the USA, the more recently introduced Chapter 3 aircraft, such as the Airbus, are 85% less noisy than were Chapter 1 aircraft and are, consequently, allowed greater freedom to operate. The problem is compounded for night flights, where restrictions are often in force to reduce the problem. Noise limits were first set at Heathrow in 1959 and were applied to Gatwick in 1968 and Stansted in 1993. Although night flights are not banned (except for the noisiest types of aircraft), restrictions are imposed on the number of night departures and arrivals (Butcher, 2010). Noise at airports is an issue for many countries; in India, all airports are still obliged to accept jumbo aircraft throughout the night. Noise-related issues at Zurich airport have also led to heated debates between the Swiss and German governments, as flights into and out of this Swiss airport often follow routes over German territory.

Noise from waterborne vessels is most notable along coasts and in tranquil rural areas where boats using their motors can disturb the peace of the night when travelling along rivers and canals. New waterborne vehicles such as jet bikes and water bikes, often used offshore at popular beach resorts, are particularly noisy, and this (coupled with possible danger to life) has been a factor in attempts to reduce their use offshore at popular Mediterranean resorts.

Pollution at tourist destinations

The physical pollution of popular destinations poses a growing threat for global tourism. Perhaps the most widespread example is seen in coastal resorts, where beach and offshore water contamination is visible and, in some cases, can be life-threatening to bathers. In this respect, the UK's coastal resorts have in the past fared badly by comparison with their European neighbours, although recent years have witnessed marked improvements, following clean-up drives within the EU. Nevertheless, some bathing areas in the UK remain seriously contaminated by raw sewage or other pollutants.

Beaches in the UK are monitored in several ways. Key certification is in the hands of the environmental charity 'Keep Britain Tidy', awarding blue flags to beaches and bathing water satisfying certain minimal criteria, including water purity and freedom from litter and other pollutants on the beaches themselves. More criteria are applied to beaches qualifying as resorts rather than rural, but both require the beaches to meet at least the mandatory standards of bathing water applied in the EU. The Blue Flag campaign operates in some 40 countries in Europe, South Africa and the Caribbean. In 2010, more than 3450 beaches and marinas had achieved this award, 123 of which were in the UK.

Historically, several UK beaches failed to meet the increasingly stringent minimum standards required for Blue Flag status, so a lower standard (known as seaside awards) was set by the Department for Environment, Food and Rural Affairs (DEFRA), awarding yellow flags. In 2003, 332 beaches in the UK were awarded yellow and blue flag status (compared with only 92 in 1992, the first year of monitoring), while 105 achieved European Blue Flag standard. By 2005, however, 98% of beaches were passing the more stringent tests, with just 13 of the 562 failing. Nevertheless, a handful of UK tourist beaches, including such popular resorts as Blackpool, have consistently over the years failed to meet minimum standards. Perhaps it is as well that only some 7% of those spending time on beaches in the UK actually have any intention of bathing!

Construction of touristic infrastructure

Environmental 'pollution' is as much aesthetic as physical. An area of scenic beauty attracts greater numbers of tourists, so more and more of the natural landscape is lost to development, the countryside retreating before the growth of hotels and other amenities that spring up to cater for the tourists' needs. The eventual result is that the site is no longer seen as 'scenic' and the tourists move on to find somewhere more tranquil as well as beautiful. Similarly, without careful control, stately homes that try to meet the needs of visitors provide an ever-expanding range of facilities, such as larger car parks, cafés, shops, directional signposts and toilet facilities, all of which detract from the appeal of the main attraction. Extreme examples of despoliation of the scenery by signposting are readily found in the USA where, with fewer controls than are exercised in the UK, both countryside and towns can be destroyed by directional signs and advertising hoardings (however, some might argue that, at night, the forest of illuminated signs in towns such as Reno and Las Vegas is very much part of the attraction of the resort). There are fears that a relaxation of regulations in the UK could lead to a similar explosion of countryside signage.

Another aesthetic form of visual pollution is illustrated by the frequent insensitivity in the design of tourist buildings. Lack of planning control is often to blame, as developers prefer to build cheaply, resulting in high-rise concrete hotels lacking character and out of keeping with the surrounding architecture.

Many of the UK's towns are also losing their local character, as builders have chosen to build in ubiquitous (but cheap) London brick rather than the materials available locally (although planning authorities have adopted stricter measures in recent years to control this practice). In seaside resorts around the world, too, the concrete skyscraper hotel has become the norm. From Waikiki in Hawaii to Benidorm in Spain, tourists are confronted with a conformity of architecture that owes nothing to the culture or traditions of the country in which it is found.

Some far-seeing authorities have recognized the potential for this kind of damage and brought in controls to limit it. In some cases, this has led to an insistence that hotels be built using local materials or conform to the vernacular architecture – that is, styles indigenous to the region. Others require that buildings do not exceed a certain height. For example, Tunisia requires that new hotel developments in tourist resorts should be no higher than the normal height of the palm trees that will surround them. Mauritius has imposed constraints on both the architectural style and the materials employed in hotel building. While some critics have questioned the rather 'staged' results, with thatched cottages vaguely resembling African kraals, no-one doubts the appeal these accommodation units have for tourists. Such legislation clearly must apply to all buildings, not just those for tourism.

EXAMPLE **Lanzarote**

On Lanzarote, in the Canary Islands, all housing, apartments and hotels are required to conform to rigorous building regulations imposed by the Department of Tourism on the island. These control not only the style of the buildings but also the colours in which doors and windows may be painted – only white, blue or green paintwork is permitted.

Sometimes, planning controls have the effect of restricting innovation in architecture, leaving developers to play it safe by falling back on pastiche or bland designs, attractive only to the most conservative visitor. The attempt to protect local building styles and materials can sometimes have unexpected results, as in Ireland. The traditional corrugated iron roofs have now become such a familiar feature of the landscape that this has been designated a vernacular building material.

Sometimes, the problem of scale can relate to buildings far smaller than hotels, but it is no less significant. During the early 1990s, two historic properties were under threat owing to plans to either build or expand visitors' centres adjacent to the site. The Haworth Parsonage, once the home of the Brontë sisters on the Yorkshire Moors, was threatened with a massive expansion of the visitors' centre, which would have greatly exceeded the size of the original house. The project resulted in an outcry from the public and a rethinking of the plans. Similarly, trustees of the birthplace of Sir Edward Elgar, in the Malvern Hills, submitted plans for a new visitors' centre adjacent to, and much larger than, the composer's original cottage. This, too, led to a public outcry in the media. In this case, though, construction went ahead, with a visitor centre resembling, according to one architectural critic, a Tesco supermarket. The problem of providing sufficient room to accommodate all the visitors – some 10 000 a year – at such a small site is a common one and there is no easy – or at least cheap – solution. One plan proposed at Haworth was to conceal the new visitor centre underground, which, although an ideal solution, proved to be too costly for the available funds.

Visual pollution

Other common forms of visual pollution by tourists include littering, particularly in areas around picnic sites, and graffiti on buildings. It is a curious fact that even those tourists who come from large cities, where they are so used to seeing litter that they become unconscious of it, immediately become sensitive to litter at a tourist destination.

Resorts that have made the effort to improve their image in recent years tend to start by undertaking a drive against both rubbish in the streets and graffiti on buildings. An important point here is that litter bins should be not only readily available but also attractively designed. Unfortunately, at some sites, both in the UK and elsewhere, the fear of terrorist bombs or vandalism has caused rubbish bins to be sealed or removed, making rubbish disposal more difficult for tourists.

In environmentally sensitive areas of the world, such as wilderness regions, littering becomes a critical issue because these areas are too far from any public services that could resolve the problem, so the onus is on tourists themselves to safeguard the environment by taking their rubbish with them. This is a very real issue in the Himalayas, now that trekking has become so popular in the region. Many trekkers and organized trekking parties are failing to carry out their litter or dig latrines to hide human waste, with the result that some valleys have become littered with unsightly rubbish, much of which fails to decompose at the high altitudes there. Environmentalists and enlightened tour operators are encouraging visitors to ensure that their rubbish is either burned or carried out (although local villagers often make use of tins, bags or bottles left behind) and human waste is buried. The authorities are being encouraged to build more permanent composting toilets in frequented areas, using the twin vault principle – each vault being used in alternate years to allow waste to decompose. Nutrients from composted waste can then be used to encourage rapid growth of willow trees, providing a much-needed source of timber for local villagers.

Graffiti has become a common problem in the Western world, with thoughtless tourists desecrating ancient monuments with spray-painted, scratched and even chiselled messages. This, of course, is no new development: the Romans were chiselling their names on Greek monuments 2000 years ago. The sheer scale of modern tourism, however, has forced authorities to take action. In extreme cases, this had led to denial of access, as in the case of Stonehenge, where visitors are no longer permitted to walk among the stones themselves, but must be content to view them from a distance.

Erosion causes visual pollution too

The island of Sir Bani Yas, off the coast of Abu Dhabi, United Arab Emirates (UAE), has been developed under the direction of the resident sheikh from what was essentially a large sand bar into a green paradise, importing water at great expense from the mainland to irrigate the millions of trees which have been planted there, and populating the resultant forested areas with a selection of exotic African animals, which are allowed to roam freely. However, the island's shoreline is relatively flat and subject to erosion, necessitating the construction of artificial barriers to retain the long stretches of sandy beach which provide a further important attraction for

Figure 7.1 Protective artificial barrier at Sir Bani Yas, UAE
Photo by Chris Holloway

visitors. To reduce the visual pollution of these barriers, they have been cleverly designed to resemble large boulders, which over time will retain marine growths and appear natural (see Figure 7.1); a highly successful solution to what could have posed a major problem.

Noise pollution at destinations

Noise pollution is a common problem relating to contemporary life and not merely in towns. At the Treetops Hotel in Kenya's Masai Mara National Park, animals visiting the adjacent waterhole at night are driven from the site by the careless loud talk or laughter of a minority of the visitors waiting to see them. In the seaside resorts of the Mediterranean, building construction in fast-developing resorts can be both visibly and audibly offensive, especially during hours of darkness. The peace of the night is also frequently destroyed by late-night music clubs and bars catering to younger tourists. In some such resorts, the authorities have perceived the danger of negative publicity driving away the family market and authorized the police to undertake night patrols to combat excessive noise. One such example is Magaluf in Majorca, where police act against pubs or nightclubs registering noise levels higher than 65 decibels.

Goa tries to manage noise pollution

In an attempt to reduce the impact of noise pollution on the local population a committee in North Goa implemented an information campaign to encourage the beachfront bars and shack-owners to turn down the music. The polite persuasion is supported by regulation which limits noise between 10 pm and 6 am. The committee members, comprising government officials and local citizens, have been supplied with noise monitors, as have the local police, to patrol the area and crack down on the polluters.

However, there have been critics of this policy, who argue that cultural traditions for celebrations such as weddings include late-night music. These critics may have indirectly benefited from a lack of political will to implement this policy, as the police have failed to effectively prosecute many offenders.

An opportunity has also emerged from this attempt to reduce the impact of late-night entertainment with the introduction of 'headphone parties'. The revellers are provided with their own set of earphones on entry and can listen to a variety of music channels without disturbing the neighbourhood.

Problems of congestion and erosion

Perhaps the most self-evident problem created by mass tourism is that of congestion. In the previous chapter, we considered some of the social implications of overcrowding for tourists and, in this chapter, we will be equally concerned with the effects of overcrowding, in particular on the natural environment. Awareness that the number of tourists in an area was finite led to consideration of carrying capacities; the number of people an area can hold before the impacts caused are beyond recovery. Extensive academic research has explored the concept of overcrowding, especially within recreational settings, and, as a consequence, planning frameworks take into consideration the concept of the Limits of Acceptable Change (LAC). Stankey *et al.* (1985) in their introduction to the approach commented that the LAC is a reformulation of the carrying capacity concept, emphasizing the conditions desired in an area rather than the total use an area can tolerate. Whilst there has been much criticism highlighting difficulties with the implementation of such an approach, its conceptual ideas have underpinned much of the protection that has occurred since (McCool and Lime, 2001).

Carrying capacity

Congestion is a complex problem because it exists at both a psychological and a physical level. The latter is more easily measured – in terms of the capacity of an area to absorb tourists. Car parks, streets, beaches, ski slopes, cathedrals and similar features all have a finite limit to the numbers of tourists that they can accommodate at any given time. Theoretically, this is also true of entire regions and countries, although attempts to define the tourist capacity of a city or country have seldom been attempted. Most national tourist offices continue to develop policies aimed at creating an ever-expanding influx of tourists year-on-year without considering the ability of the areas to absorb those numbers, although some efforts may be made to divert these influxes to off-peak periods or to less crowded areas of the country. At the urban level, a few cities under extreme pressure, such as Florence and Venice, have taken more positive action.

Individual buildings attracting very high numbers of tourists have problems, requiring firm measures to manage and limit access. This can, of course, lead to disappointment for tourists. In recent years, crowds visiting the Uffizi Gallery and Galleria dell'Accademia (the site of Michelangelo's David) in Florence during peak holiday periods have become so great that the local authorities have had to take the unusual step of temporarily closing the buildings. Indeed, both Florence and Venice face exceptionally heavy demand from international tourists, the latter welcoming some 20 million tourists each year, with 1.5 million seeking admission to the Doge's Palace and St Mark's Square alone, while on some days as many as 40 000 tourists have visited the Baptistry of San Giovanni and the adjoining Duomo in Florence. Such crowds produce high levels of condensation, which affect the thirteenth- and fourteenth-century mosaics. The authorities have responded by reducing coaches to the city from 500 to 150 a day, charging them high fees for the privilege and spot-checking arterial roads out of the city to enforce compliance. Numbers admitted to the Baptistry were reduced to 150 at a time and, for the first time, charges were applied for entry. In 2005, Italy's new culture minister proposed a big increase in prices charged at the most popular sites in Italy, in the hope that tourists could be diverted to lesser-known museums and attractions, but tourists and officials felt that the suggestion would be impractical.

Another tourist site suffering from extreme popularity is the Taj Mahal in India. This building alone attracts some 2 million visitors a year and up to 6000 each day. Since 1995, a price differential was introduced, with higher entry charges for foreign visitors, and the Indian government periodically has attempted to impose further price increases (although these were reduced after tour operators complained). Such unique sites are highly price inelastic, however, so only a rationing system is likely to limit demand.

It is also necessary to understand the psychological capacity of a site – that is, the degree of congestion that tourists will tolerate before it starts to lose its appeal. Quantifying this is far more difficult than physical congestion as individual perceptions of capacity will differ, not only according to the nature of the site itself but also the market attracted to it. Expectations of a remote island paradise will mean that a beach in, say, Fiji will be judged overcrowded much more quickly than, say, a beach in the UK at Bournemouth, while in a resort such as Blackpool a much higher level of crowding may be tolerated, even welcomed, as part of the 'fun experience'.

One attempt to measure the psychological capacity of a beach was carried out at Brittas Bay in Ireland in the early 1970s. Aerial photographs were taken of the number of tourists on the beach on a crowded Sunday afternoon and a questionnaire was circulated to those on the beach to receive their views about the congestion that day. It was found that most visitors would accept around 1000 people per hectare (10 square metres per person) without feeling that the beach was overcrowded.

EXAMPLE   Koh Phi Phi Ley, Thailand

Koh Phi Phi Ley (Maya Bay) was, until the turn of the millennium, a rather isolated beach and natural beauty spot, one of the Phi Phi Island group near Phuket (see Figure 7.2). That is until 2000, when a popular film – *The Beach*, starring Leonardo di Caprio – romanticized for millions of young filmgoers the idea of 'lotus-eating' holidays in faraway places, resulting in hordes of backpackers descending on the area to search out the exact location of the film. The subsequent despoliation of the idyll was condemned by tourist officials in the country, although the resulting development of the nearby Ao Ton Sai resort on Koh Phi Phi Don has benefited locals economically. A five-fold increase in tourist fees was implemented in order to control visitor numbers to the site. The Phi Phi Island group were badly affected by the 2004 tsunami and authorities are keen to re-establish the area as a popular venue for tourism.

Figure 7.2 Koh Phi Phi in 1992
Photo by Claire Humphreys

In so-called *wilderness* areas, of course, the psychological capacity of the region may be very low, while areas sensitive to environmental damage may suffer physically even where there are comparatively few visitors. In the USA, Yellowstone and the Everglades National Parks are both physically under severe threat from tourism. Psychologically, too, they are so remote that any mass tourism will greatly reduce their attractiveness. In the UK, from

Table 7.1 Visitor capacity of selected sites

Site/activity	Visitors per day/hectare
Forest park	15
Suburban nature park	15-70
High-density picnicking	300-600
Low-density picnicking	60-200
Golf	10-15
Fishing/sailing	5-30
Speedboating	5-10
Waterskiing	5-15
Skiing	100 (per hectare of trails)
Nature trail hiking	40 (per kilometre)
Nature trail horseriding	25-80 (per kilometre)

Source: Inskip, 1991

the psychological viewpoint of the hiker, sites such as the Derbyshire Peak District should not support more than a handful of tourists per square kilometre, although the mass influx to its major centres, such as Dovedale on an August Bank Holiday, fails to act as a deterrent for the majority of day trippers. Indeed, it has been demonstrated in the case of Cannock Chase, the beauty spot near Birmingham, that this area draws tourists from the Midlands as much for its role as a social meeting place as for its scenic beauty.

The behaviour of tourists at wilderness sites will be another factor in deciding their psychological capacity. Many visitors to an isolated area will tend to stay close to their cars, so hikers who are prepared to walk a mile or so away from the car park will readily find the solitude they seek. This is obviously a key for tourism planners, as, by discouraging or forbidding car parking and access by vehicle to the more remote areas, they can then effectively restrict these areas to those seeking solitude.

Some authorities have tried to set standards for particular types of tourist activity as a guide to planners. Table 7.1 is based on one attempt, by the UNWTO (then, WTO), to lay down guidelines in terms of visitors per day per hectare.

The *ecological* capacity to absorb tourists must also be taken into account. While too many tourists in a built-up area such as the narrow shopping lanes of York or Brighton can detract from tourism, the physical wear and tear on the environment is limited – at least, in the short term. Too many tourists in a rural or otherwise fragile environment, however, can destroy the balance of nature. This can be seen in the increase in tourists visiting African safari parks, where the number of vehicles hunting for the 'big five' at any one time can resemble a car rally in some areas of the parks.

EXAMPLE   Macchu Pichu

The long lost Inca city of Macchu Pichu, now a UNESCO World Heritage site, was rediscovered only in 1911. It is now the country's major tourist attraction, with 85% of all visitors to Peru planning a visit there.

Public access was enhanced with the building of a railhead nearby and helicopter flights bring others from Cuzco. As a result, over 400 000 now visit the site annually and UNESCO has placed it on the danger list, recommending that daily admission should be limited to 2000 during the high season and 800 in the off season to avoid irreparable damage. The Peruvian government countered with a proposal to limit the number to 2500 daily and increased entry prices by 50%. In 2000, it also announced plans to build a cable car to replace the buses transferring tourists from the railhead to the top of the mountain, but a public outcry from UNESCO and the environmental lobby forced a retraction of the plan (although the cable car would have eliminated growing concern about the environmental damage caused by buses climbing the present steep access road).

Initially, the site could only be reached via the Inca Trail, a hazardous narrow footpath that appeared to place a natural ceiling on visitor numbers, but the growth in trekking has matched that of visits via public transport. Just 7000 trekkers arrived by trail in 1988, but, a decade later, this had risen to 66 000.

The Peruvian government was forced to impose new controls to reduce erosion of the path. Walkers unaccompanied by guides or porters were banned in 2001, entry charges to the site itself were tripled and limits were introduced on the number of tour operators organizing the guided treks. No more than 500 trekkers daily (including porters) are now permitted to use the trail. The fees paid, however, go to central government and are not used to protect or restore the site.

Another Inca city has been discovered at Cerro Victoria and the government hopes that this can be developed to take some of the pressure off Macchu Pichu.

Erosion

Some sites are particularly fragile. Many sand dunes have been destroyed or seriously eroded in the USA by the use of beach buggies and, as we noted earlier with respect to other sensitive ecological systems, by four-wheel drive vehicles. In the UK, similar problems are thrown up by motorcycle rallying, which can easily uproot the few clumps of dune grass on which an ecosystem depends. The UNEP has reported that three-quarters of all the sand dunes along the Mediterranean coastline between Spain and Sicily have disappeared as a direct result of the growth of tourism.

EXAMPLE   **The Great Barrier Reef**

The Great Barrier Reef off the coast of Queensland, Australia, is a World Heritage site, generating some AUS$1.5 billion per annum from tourism, but its 1450 miles of fragile coral reefs can be easily damaged by divers or snorkelers. Even touching or standing on live coral can be sufficient to kill it, yet some visitors go so far as to break off pieces for souvenirs. Coral can also be damaged by boats anchoring. Compounded by the effects of global warming, this is contributing to the death of large tracts of the Reef.

In an effort to reduce its destruction, in 2004 the Australian government banned commercial fishing from 44 000 square miles of the Reef. Companies that thrive by running boat trips for tourists to visit the Reef are now aware of the threat to their livelihood and are taking on the responsibility to educate their passengers. During the boat trips, tourists are given information on the fragility of the site and how it can be preserved by careful use.

In April 2010, a Chinese-registered oil tanker, Shen Neng 1, ran aground when taking a short-cut through the Great Barrier Reef National Park. Extensive efforts were made to manage the impact of the oil spill, protecting this environmental asset, the key element of Queensland's tourism product.

An idea of the effect of erosion can be gained from the experiences of the 14 UK National Parks, which receive over 100 million visitors annually. The pressure on the land can be immense. Table 7.2 records the number of visitors per square kilometre. Remember, however, that those using a park do not spread evenly over its area but often are attracted

Table 7.2 Visitors to National Parks in the UK

National Park	Visitor days per km²
Brecon Beacons	3 199
Broads	23 607
Cairngorms	663
Dartmoor	3 463
Exmoor	2 882
Lake District	6 632
Loch Lomond and the Trossachs	2 145
New Forest	23 684
Northumberland	2 304
North York Moors	6 276
Peak District	7 029*
Pembrokeshire Coast	21 739
Snowdonia	4 779
South Downs	24 015
Yorkshire Dales	7 123

* Data based on visitor numbers rather than visitor days.

(Visitor days takes into account that visitors may stay in the National Park for several days and therefore one person coming for a day = one visitor day, one person coming for a week = seven visitor days)

Sources: Association of National Parks Authorities

to key locations, often termed *honeypots*, as visitors swarm in large numbers to these places. A result is that in some areas footpaths are overused, leading to soil becoming compacted and grass and plants dying. Under some circumstances, the soil becomes loosened and is then lost through wind erosion. A report by the Lake District National Parks Authority (n.d.) revealed that a path from Birkside to Helvellyn had suffered such extensive erosion that the scar on the landscape was almost 8 metres wide and 300 metres long. To recover this path, a mechanical digger was dismantled, flown in parts up the mountainside and rebuilt. It was then used to move and reseed the soil to ensure a hard-wearing walking surface is created alongside a drainage ditch, thus providing a low-maintenance, natural path.

This followed similar efforts, made in the early 1990s, to counteract the erosion of footpaths. Across the moors near Haworth, some 25 000 visitors had turned parts of the Brontë Way into a quagmire, making it necessary to set flagstones into the track. Other running repairs have had to be made to long-distance footpaths such as those on the Pennine Way and Cleveland Way. Such artificial landscaping, of course, creates a very different visual landscape from the wild moorland it replaces, but it is a solution that is being used more widely as such footpaths have to deal with greater numbers of visitors each year.

Climbers, too, also damage the parks. With the increased interest in activity holidays, climbing is becoming a very popular pastime. Some 250 000 people climb Mam Tor in Derbyshire every year, for example, and this has so affected the mountain that the summit had to be restored with an importation of 300 tons of rock and soil.

To protect fragile environments, there are often restrictions and regulations introduced. Conflicts between different users, such as walkers, mountain bikers, horse riders and off-road vehicles, can occur and regulations may be needed to ensure that the needs of different groups are met. The impacts from these groups can also differ and thus a variety of protective activities may be needed. There is, however, an inevitable trade-off between protection and economic wellbeing, as is demonstrated by the imposition of controls in the English Lake District.

Lake District National Park

In 2005, the National Park Authority in the Lake District introduced a 10 miles per hour speed limit around Windermere Lake, aiming to reduce noise pollution and erosion and enhance the sense of peace for which the district is renowned.

Initially the decision had a severe impact on the economy of the region. The tourist information centre received 12 000 fewer enquiries in the first six months of the year, boat registrations and launches fell sharply and the waterskiers, jetskiers and powerboat drivers who are traditionally high spenders withdrew, leaving local firms to face business losses that are believed to be costing the local economy over £7 million annually. The local tourist board chairman accused the National Park Authority of 'ignoring its duty to foster the economic and social wellbeing of local communities'.

Five years later, there has been some reflection on the impact of this restriction. It was clear that the hardest hit were the powerboat and waterskiing businesses, who needed to diversify their activities to cater for more sailing and cruising. They continue to argue that there are other lakes in the area which offer tranquility so this popular and busy tourist location should have mixed use by allowing higher speeds in some parts of the lake.

Contrasting this is the view of those fishing these waters, which is overwhelmingly positive. The more tranquil atmosphere has led to an increasing number of anglers using the area. The cruise companies offering lake tours were only marginally affected by the ban, requiring minor modifications in their timetable to ensure that they could stay under the speed limit.

Concern has been noted that the loss of the waterskiing market has meant that the younger market segments have disappeared. Debates continue over the ban, but there is also now a concern that removing the speed limit would require business to readjust again to changing circumstances. Compromise may be that the regulation could be amended to allow special annual speedboat events to be held on Windermere, but this is yet to be supported by the National Park Authority.

Source: Edited from Boydon, 2010

Erosion of constructed sites by tourists

Although constructed sites are generally less fragile than natural ones, these too can be affected by erosion in the long term – externally by weather, internally by wear and tear from multiple visitors. Sites exposed to the elements may have to have access restricted, especially if they become so dilapidated that they pose a danger to visitors, as is the case with some historic castles.

The Acropolis in Athens has had to be partially closed to tourists to avoid wear and tear on the floors of the ancient buildings, while the wooden floors and staircases of popular attractions such as Shakespeare's birthplace in Stratford-upon-Avon or Beaulieu Palace in Hampshire also suffer from the countless footsteps to which they are subjected each year. Stratford, with a population of only 23 000, receives over 3.8 million visitors every year, a substantial proportion of whom will want to visit Shakespeare's birthplace or Anne Hathaway's cottage. The high numbers led major attractions to construct artificial walkways above the level of the floor to preserve the original flooring. Nearly a million people visit Bath's Pump Rooms and the Roman Baths complex each year and inevitably there are fears for the original stone flooring of the Baths. It may put the problem into context when it is revealed that Roman visitors, wearing hob-nailed boots, did even more damage to the original flooring than do contemporary visitors, though they were far fewer in number.

The danger of tourism to flora and fauna

Wildlife can be an important attraction for some tourist destinations. As we mentioned earlier, the Great Barrier Reef is popular for snorkelers and scuba-divers keen to view the fish and the coral, whilst destinations across Africa attract safari tourists intent on viewing the big game. However, tourism can cause many problems, harming the very wildlife the tourists have come to see.

Firstly, we need to recognize that the construction of tourist infrastructure, such as hotels, bars, restaurants and visitor centres, can reduce the land available to the wildlife. Fencing around developments can influence traditional grazing or migration patterns and can draw key resources, such as water, away from rivers and watering holes. There are also issues with the management of waste products; for instance, some wild animals may become scavengers if food remnants are left in accessible places. Animals may also scavenge through rubbish and be harmed by trying to consume plastic packaging, camera batteries and other such detritus. The construction process itself needs to be carefully managed to ensure that the noise does not scare away the wildlife and that it does not harm nesting grounds.

Even where tourism infrastructure is not adjacent to the wildlife, many tourists will still journey to view amazing flora and fauna. As mentioned at the beginning of the chapter, transport can cause pollution, impacting on the environment, but we also need to recognize that frequent visits by tourists can impact on the breeding patterns of wildlife as well as their patterns for foraging for food and their natural defence responses to humans. Without careful management, these can lead to a decline in the population size. This has affected loggerhead turtles in Greece and Turkey, and in the Caribbean, which are distracted from laying their eggs by the bright lights of tourist resorts or the use of search-lights to observe their coming ashore to lay eggs on the beach.

EXAMPLE   Saving the turtle

Widespread media publicity regarding the threat to the turtles' survival has resulted in much greater general awareness of the problem, and both operators and tourists have become more responsible when paying visits to egg-laying sites. The Travel Foundation, a charity financially supported by tour operators, made a financial award to Tobago, which has allowed beaches to be patrolled.

Tourists are now made aware of sustainability issues in a video shown at the airport on their arrival, and both hotel staff and guests are informed about the need to protect nesting turtles. Tourists have restricted access to egg-laying turtles, although small groups are permitted to observe them from a suitable distance. The Foundation has also provided funding for demarcation buoys to be positioned near reefs in Tobago (and in Cancún, Mexico) to protect the turtles from anchor damage by tourist boats.

At Philip Island, near Melbourne in Australia, 500 000 people a year come to sit and watch the evening 'penguin parade' of fairy penguins coming ashore to their nests. This event has become highly commercialized and the large crowds are proving hard to control, even though ropes are in place to prevent people getting too close to the penguins. Flash photography is forbidden and wardens caution the audiences against noise or even standing up, all of which disturb and alarm the penguins. In practice, however, the public frequently ignore these strictures.

Figure 7.3 Feeding the dolphins in Monkey Mia, Australia

Photo by Claire Humphreys

Animal behaviour can change as a result of prolonged exposure to tourists. In some countries, food lures are used to attract wildlife to a particular locality. For example, in Samburu National Park, Kenya, goats are slaughtered and hung up for crocodiles or leopards. This modifies hunting behaviour and may encourage dependency on being fed by humans. In some wildlife parks, hyenas are known to watch for assemblies of four-wheel drive vehicles in order to take the prey from cheetahs' hunts. 'Bearjams' are created in Yellowstone National Park, USA, as bears trade photo opportunities for offerings of food. The dolphins at Monkey Mia have long been a popular tourist attraction, with coach tours scheduling their arrival with feeding times (see Figure 7.3). In this case, the Western Australian Department of Conservation and Environment claim that dolphin-tourism can be sustained by supervision of the human–dolphin interaction, control of feeding and habitat protection.

EXAMPLE   Sustainable tourism in Botswana

An excellent example of sustainable tourism at a wildlife park is demonstrated at Xigera Camp, in Botswana's Okavango Delta. A sandpit between the river and camp is raked clean each night and, the following morning, the guide provides a short talk for the tourists, identifying the prints of nocturnal animals that have visited the site to drink.

Guests to the area are catered for at the 'chief's camp', situated on land leased by a specialist UK tour operator from tribal authorities and employing well-paid locals, some of whom provide trips by mokoro (dugout canoe) through the delta. Furnishing is luxurious but ethnic and food is sophisticated yet locally grown.

Tourists who choose to engage with nature by visiting wilderness areas, camping in forests and hiking across mountains will still have an impact on the environment. Campfires can draw on local wood and leave scorch marks on the landscape. Whilst each individual fire may seem to have only a small effect, when large numbers of tourists visit the overall impact can be unsustainable. Uneducated tourists may inadvertently cause wildfires, leading to vast tracts of land, some wildlife and occasionally homes being lost.

EXAMPLE Protecting Annapurna from the trekkers

Nepal has been renowned for its trekking opportunities for decades and many backpackers head to the Everest region. Yet it is estimated that about half of trekkers head to the western area of the country to walk in the Annapurna region (see Figure 7.4), with more than 60 000 visiting annually (Ministry of Tourism and Civil Aviation, 2010).

The region now faces many environmental problems exacerbated by this inundation of people. The Annapurna Conservation Area project was established in 1986 with the goal of encouraging more sustainable tourism. To fund conservation efforts, a fee is charged to enter the area, and checkpoints throughout the trekking area monitor this by ensuring that walkers hold the required permits.

One of its key projects was to minimize the use of firewood, in order to reduce forest depletion. The soaring number of visitors, whose fuel wood consumption is twice that of the local people, has exerted immense pressure on forest resources. Local businesses such as lodges were encouraged to convert to kerosene or fuel-efficient wood stoves, whilst tourists were informed about the variety of ways that they could reduce their impact – suggestions including avoiding showers if wood is to be burnt for hot water, avoid choosing foods which require lengthy cooking times, and eating at times when many others are ordering food so that batch cooking is possible. Another major issue the area faces is waste management. It has been estimated that a group of trekkers would create approximately 1 kg per person of non-biodegradable/non-burnable waste during the course of a 10-day trek. The ideal solution is to require that this rubbish is ported out of the region, but all too often this is left at mountain lodges, and builds up on the edge of villages as no waste-removal system exists.

Figure 7.4 Trekkers walking in Annapurna, Nepal
Photo by Claire Humphreys

Even souvenir hunting can affect the ecological balance of a region. The removal of plants has long given cause for concern (the Swiss were expressing anxiety about the tourists' habit of picking gentians and other alpine flowers even before the start of the mass tourism movement) and, in Arizona, visitors taking home cacti are affecting the ecology of the desert. Similarly, the removal, either as souvenirs or for commercial sale by tourist enterprises, of coral and rare shells from regions in the Pacific is also a cause for concern.

The desire to bring back souvenirs of animals seen abroad poses another form of threat to endangered species. The Convention on International Trade in Endangered Species (CITES) imposes worldwide restrictions on the importation of certain animals and animal products from countries visited by tourists. Around 34 000 endangered species have been identified and the importation of many of these or their by-products is banned, including ivory, sea turtle products, spotted cat furs, coral, reptile skins and seashells, as well as certain rare plants. Concern is also expressed about the ill-treatment of animals that are kept in captivity for the amusement of tourists. While performing bears have largely been removed from the streets of some Eastern European countries following EU pressure, they are still a common sight in China. Even within the EU, one can still find chimpanzees and monkeys exploited for tourist photographs in countries such as Spain, and, of course, bullfighting remains not only legal but also a popular tourist attraction in that country and the South of France. A number of action groups in the UK have been set up to protect and free these animals.

Other environmental consequences of mass tourism

Many popular tourist towns have narrow roads, leading not only to problems of severe traffic congestion but also potential damage to buildings, as coaches try to navigate through these streets. Increasingly, cars and particularly coaches are restricted in terms of access to the centres of such towns, with park and ride schemes or other strategies employed to reduce traffic. Impeding coaches from picking up and setting down passengers in the centre of towns such as Bath, Cambridge or Oxford, however, can make it very difficult for coach companies to operate as many are on short stopover visits as part of a day trip.

Many developing countries face similar problems of congestion and erosion as the popularity of long-haul travel expands. Goa in India was hailed by many operators as an 'unspoilt paradise', but its wide appeal since the 1990s has caused environmental lobbyists such as Tourism Concern to draw attention to the dangers the region faces. Water shortages in the area are aggravated by tourists' consumption (one 5-star hotel uses as much water as five villages and locals face water shortages while swimming pools are filled) and sand dunes have been flattened. Apart from the environmental impacts, there are also social costs. The private beaches mean access by the locals is denied and 'Westernization' of the local carnival dilutes the traditional identity and culture of the region. The problems of Goa have been well publicized in recent years, but this has had little effect on reducing the numbers of visitors or ensuring that tourism in the area is sustainable.

Sometimes, well-meaning attempts by tourist officials to 'improve' an attraction can have the opposite effect. Historic rock carvings over 3000 years old in Scandinavia were painted to make them stand out for visitors. When the paint eventually flakes off, a process that has speeded up with the effect of acid rain, it takes part of the rock surface with it.

Any development of tourism will inevitably require the sacrifice of some natural landscape to make way for tourist facilities. An extreme example of this is to be found in the demand for golf courses. It has been estimated that there are some 30 000 golf courses in the world, with a further 500 being built each year. Many of these are constructed in areas where water shortages would normally discourage their construction, such as in Dubai, Tunisia and the Egyptian desert, but the popularity of golf tourism drives their development. Golf as a holiday activity, especially among Japanese tourists, has led to a huge increase in demand for courses in the Pacific region. For example, the island of Oahu in Hawaii, which had already constructed 27 courses by 1985, received a further 30 applications after the Hawaii legislature agreed to allow them to be built on agricultural land. Apart from the loss of natural scenery, golf courses also require huge amounts of fresh water, which, in some areas of low rainfall, imposes a severe burden on local resources.

EXAMPLE **Sustaining golf in the desert**

Las Vegas is renowned as a casino destination. Visitors also head to the desert city for weddings, as a base for their visits to the Grand Canyon and to play golf; but the many golf courses require copious amounts of water, a precious resource.

In 2005 the local water authority (SNWA) established a scheme to encourage local residents and golf courses to remove turf and allow the land to return to desert scrub. As an incentive, $1.50 per square foot was paid in this 'cash for grass' scheme. The cash received helps cover the cost of remodelling the landscape and ultimately reduces the annual water bill for each course. By May 2009, it was estimated that 795 acres of turf have been removed, with savings in water usage of 1.9 billion gallons.

Source: Figueroa, 2009

The environmental impacts of winter sports tourism

One fragile ecosystem in Europe is under particular threat: the Alps. Because the system is spread across no fewer than seven countries, collaboration to prevent the worst of the environmental effects of tourism is made more difficult. The Alps receive over 50 million international visitors a year and some 7 million passenger vehicles cross them each year, as they lie at the heart of Europe. To accommodate the huge increase in winter sports tourism that has occurred since World War II, some 41 000 ski runs have been built, capable of handling 1.5 million skiers an hour.

The region suffers in a number of ways. The proliferation of ski-lifts, chalets and concrete villages above 6000 feet and the substantial deforestation required to make way for pistes have led to soil erosion, while the high volumes of traffic crossing the Alps contribute to the acid rain caused largely otherwise by factory emissions. Those emissions are having a serious impact on the remaining forests, 60% of which have now been affected. Artificial snowmaking machines have smothered alpine plants, reducing the vegetation, while wildlife has also declined as the animals' territories have been reduced. A new danger is posed by the introduction of roller skiing on grass and four-wheel-drive car racing in summer.

The potential damage, both ecological and economic, to the region is now so great that an organization, Alp Action, has been set up, with the support of the Aga Khan, to help preserve the Alps as a single ecosystem. It has to be added, however, that not all authorities welcome further control in this fashion. Some Swiss cantons have expressed concern at the potential slowdown in the economic development of their region that results from this conservation movement.

Some local authorities have taken steps to control overuse. At Lech and Zuers in Austria, skiers are counted by computer through turnstiles that give them access to the pistes. Once 14 000 – the deemed capacity – have been admitted, tourists are diverted to other sites. Lillehammer in Norway, site of the 1994 Winter Olympic Games, took account of the problems already occurring in the Alps when designing its new facilities. Apart from efforts to minimize tree clearance, the authorities also took steps to avoid visual pollution in an area where comparatively few buildings exist. Ski jump runs were moulded into the mountainside to ensure that they did not project above the tree line and similar efforts were made to conceal bobsleigh and luge runs in the forests. The speed-skating stadium was built 20 yards away from the water's edge to protect waterfowl and leak-proof cooling systems were embedded underground in concrete containers. Private cars were excluded from the town during the period of the Olympic Games.

Not only sports activities threaten snowscapes. Glaciers, the ecosystems of which are invariably fragile, attract large numbers of sightseers when located in accessible regions. At the Columbia Icefield in Banff National Park, Canada, giant snowmobiles are employed to bring tourists onto the glacier. The inevitable consequence will be damage to the surface of the site, unless strict control is exercised over the numbers of trips organized.

Positive environmental impacts of tourism

Whilst there has been much discussion throughout this chapter of the negative effects of tourism on the environment, tourism can also play a role in protecting the environment. Conservation and regeneration of historic buildings has been achieved in cases where they have successfully become tourist attractions, financial support coming from entry fees and donations. Beck and Bryan (1971, xxi) reported that 'many historic houses, villages, old churches and so on could not be kept in a proper state of repair without tourist money'. Entry fees can also help fund museums, galleries and other cultural and heritage resources, providing protection for future generations. There are also many cases where historic buildings have been converted for use as tourist facilities, such as hotels, restaurants and tourist attractions like craft centres and working museums.

EXAMPLE   **Tourism helps to restore Old Havana**

The crumbling buildings of Old Havana have been restored through an initiative which has relied on tourism revenue to fund restoration. The plan, which includes providing housing and services for the local public, restores old hotels, restaurants and buildings to attract tourists, and then uses the revenue gained from the resulting tourism to fund further restoration.

Despite poor living conditions in the area, few local residents want to leave. The district's charm – and the opportunity to make money from the thousands of tourists strolling its streets – are powerful attractions. And as tourism has expanded, so further redevelopment of the historical facades and buildings is achieved. Between 1994 and 2004, nearly 300 buildings were restored.

There are limitations to the project; it is estimated that the scale of the regeneration far exceeds the financial resources earned via tourism and poor quality of touristic experience has been cited as reason for low levels of repeat visitors. Still there have been some successes, which otherwise may not have been possible.

Source: Williams, 2007

Conservation of the natural environment can also be encouraged through tourism. Big game in Africa has been protected though a range of initiatives, such as safaris, which provide the local population with an income, through tourism. There has also been extensive debate regarding hunting tourism as a means of wildlife protection – the justification being that wealthy foreigners will pay significant sums to licensed operators to be allowed to stalk and shoot prey. Advocates argue that, properly managed, it can keep rising animal populations in check, while the high fees providing livelihoods for these tourist businesses generate funding for conservation and breeding programmes and can even benefit the hunted creature by providing a reason to conserve it (Rowe, 2009).

Conservation of landscapes, through the creation of national parks, has been discussed throughout this chapter, and the funding provided by tourist spending has become an important element in the continued maintenance of these regions. Importantly, tourism programmes designed to protect the environment can also provide education and awareness of sustainability among the local population.

Public-sector planning for control and conservation

We have now seen many examples of the environmental impact of tourism and a few illustrations of how the problems might be managed. Some argue that it is not enough for individual authorities to tackle the situation – it should be tackled on a global scale. Unfortunately, few governments so far have appeared willing to do so on this scale. International designation of an attraction as a World Heritage site by UNESCO undoubtedly helps, but Stonehenge (see Figure 7.5) – arguably the UK greatest heritage attraction – is so designated, yet the site has been called a 'national disgrace' by the Public Accounts Committee of the House of Commons, financial support from the Millennium Fund was refused and arguments continue about how best the site should be developed and protected. Estimated costs for burying the main road in a tunnel have doubled to around £470 million since the proposal was first made and possible alternative solutions have all been abandoned in the face of financial constraints. As a result, the site is threatened with being withdrawn from UNESCO's listing.

In Chapter 6, we looked at some of the moves that have been made since the early 1980s across the globe to embrace tourism sustainability. For the most part, the conferences and resulting papers have focused on making recommendations, leaving the question of mandatory control in the hands of national governments. Nonetheless, 150 countries signed up to the Agenda 21 proposals arising from the Rio Summit in 1992 and the EU has taken an active role in recent years in attempting to control the worst effects of environmental pollution, the Blue Flag scheme being typical of this. Costa Rica can be cited as an

Figure 7.5 Visitors to Stonehenge, Wiltshire
Photo by Claire Humphreys

outstanding example of a sustainability-aware developing country with a rapidly growing tourism market, issuing Certificates for Sustainable Tourism to tourist companies organizing holidays in the country.

The creation of national parks to preserve sites of scenic beauty is by no means of recent origin. As early as 1872, the USA established its first National Park at Yellowstone, while Europe's Abisco National Park in Sweden dates from 1909. The intention behind the creation of these parks was to ensure that visitors did not destroy the landscapes that they had come to see. Sustainability may be a word of recent origin in tourism, but the concept is much older. The World Conservation Union (IUCN) now recognizes more than 68 000 protected areas worldwide, covering an area of 5.7 million square miles, nearly 10% of the globe. As sustainability becomes a more important issue each year, the volume swells.

EXAMPLE   Gabon

After an approach by American ecologist and explorer Mike Fay to the Gabon President in 2002, that country's authorities announced at the Rio conference the planned creation of 13 new national parks, with the aim of becoming Africa's leading destination for eco-travel.

The new parks extend to over 11 000 square miles, around 11% of the country's land mass. The country has outstanding potential for ecotourism as it hosts marine, island, coral-reef, coastal, lagoon, swamp and rainforest environments (Laurance et al., 2006). Support for these parks has come from organizations such as the Wildlife Conservation Society (WCS), World Wide Fund for Nature (WWF), Conservation International (CI), ECOFAC, and the Smithsonian Institution.

One difficulty in establishing these parks is related to the relocation of the indigenous population. Resettling thousands of people onto new, equally fertile and prosperous, land is an expensive and slow process (Dowie, 2009). The balance between environmental protection and enhancing economic benefits and social wellbeing is always difficult to achieve.

Of course, most countries and local authorities are generally well-intentioned, but they can also inadvertently become partners in despoliation when putting commercial advantage before aesthetic considerations. Spain, for example, experienced a sudden boom in tourism during the 1960s, but went on to allow massive overdevelopment along its east coast and in the Balearic and Canary Islands, which nearly destroyed its success.

Failure to maintain the quality of the environment in other directions can also lead to a massive loss of tourist business, as the popular Spanish resort of Salou found, following a drinking water scare in 1989. The widespread fall-off in Western European visitors to Spain in the 1980s and 1990s (mitigated to some extent by a rise in Eastern European and Russian visitors), however, caused a reversal of policy and much greater control being exercised over speculative tourism development. A good example of this can be found in the Balearics.

Parliament passed legislation in 1991 to nominate large tracts of land in Majorca, Ibiza and Formentera as zones restricted from further development. In Majorca, only 4- and 5-star hotels were permitted to be constructed, with a minimum of 120 square metres of land per bed, in an effort to drive tourism upmarket. In order for planning permission to be granted for the construction of new hotels, developers have been required to purchase and knock down an existing and deteriorating hotel of inferior status. Badly run-down resorts such as Magaluf were given an injection of capital to widen pavements, introduce traffic-free zones, plant trees and shrubs and install new litter bins and graffiti-free seating.

In all, Spain spent over £300 million in a five-year period (ending in the early 1990s) on improving facilities for tourists along its coasts.

In 2003, the Balearics took a further step in sustainability, by introducing an eco-tax that was designed to fund sustainable improvements to tourism in the islands. Unfortunately, insufficient thought went into its implementation. Hotels were expected to collect this from guests themselves, but the resultant discontent led to the tax being scrapped by the new local government that was elected a year later.

Interestingly, the financial pressures experiences at the end of the 'noughties' led many local governments to revisit the issue of tourist taxation, ostensibly to provide funds to manage pressure caused by tourists. From January 2011, hotel taxes were introduced in Rome by the Italian state government – €3 for 4- and 5-star hotels and €2 for other hotels – to provide funds for improvement of services and infrastructure offered to the tourist (Cohen, 2010).

Other countries notable for their failure to provide adequate controls as their tourism industry boomed (and failure to learn the lessons from Spain's experience) include both Greece and Turkey. Among developing countries, Goa in India and the Dominican Republic in the Caribbean were both unprepared for the scale of the mass tourism generated by tour operators in the 1990s and failed to control their development adequately.

Spain's experience is a cautionary one, and the degree to which it has been successful in turning around its fortunes is notable. In general, however, the evidence suggests that, once a resort has gone downmarket, it can be very hard to bring back higher quality tourists. Simply constructing new high-price hotels will not lead to success in attracting a new market.

EXAMPLE Governmental control on entry

Some countries have taken the view that, where tourism does not already have a strong hold, it is best to control entry to reduce the danger of environmental and cultural despoliation occurring.

The Government of Bhutan only began to open its borders to tourism in the 1970s, but to ensure it protected its traditions and environment, a policy limited the number of foreign visitors to just 15 000 per year. They introduced high charges to reduce demand (at the time of writing, these are $250 per day, with reductions in the off season), but provided food, internal transport and lodging within these amounts. In 2010, Prime Minister Jigme Thinley announced plans to expand entry permits to allow 100 000 tourists by 2012, an almost threefold increase on current day levels. This plan has included allocating land across the country specifically to be used for the development of tourist resorts.

Mustang, the kingdom on the border with China, which was absorbed into Nepal in 1951, was closed to all tourists until 1992. The Nepalese government initially introduced a limit of just 1000 foreign tourists to the region each year, charging $700 for a 10-day permit, of which only about 10% goes back to the region. However, government statistics reported more than 1600 trekkers visited this region in 2009 (Ministry of Tourism and Civil Aviation, 2010).

At the local level, some form of public control is also essential to ensure that each new building is well designed and all existing buildings of quality are carefully preserved and restored. Heritage is also a sustainability issue, one that goes beyond the interests of tourism alone. It underpins the very fabric of a society and, in nations with a wealth of heritage buildings, each building lost through failure to protect it or enforce its restoration becomes an irreparable loss to the culture of those nations. Europe owes much of its tourism demand to the attractiveness of its traditional heritage and landscape, and destinations, whether rural, urban or seaside, that fail to concern themselves with the sustainability of their attractions cannot expect to retain their tourists.

EXAMPLE   **Environmental protection in the UK**

In the UK, sensitivity to the impact of tourism on the environment dates back at least as far as the nineteenth century. Concern over possible despoliation of the Lake District, then growing in popularity, led to the formation of a Defence Society in 1883 to protect the region from commercial exploitation. The National Trust was created in 1894 to safeguard places of 'historic interest and natural beauty' and promptly bought four and a half acres of coastal cliff-top in Cardigan Bay.

The National Parks and Access to the Countryside Act 1949 led to the formation of ten national parks in England and Wales, each administered by a National Park Authority. The Norfolk Broads achieved the equivalent national park status under the Norfolk and Suffolk Broads Act of 1988. The New Forest on the Hampshire/Dorset borders was raised to national park status in 2004 and the South Downs area followed recently (see Figure 7.6) – the latter being formed from two existing Areas of Outstanding Natural Beauty.

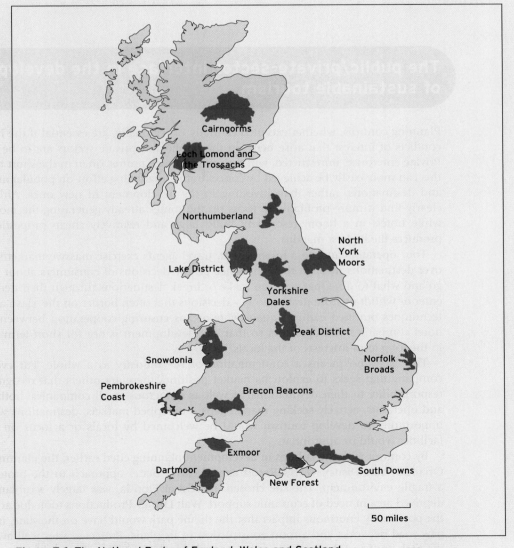

Figure 7.6 The National Parks of England, Wales and Scotland

Scotland created its first two designated national parks - Loch Lomond and the Trossachs, then the Cairngorms - in 2002 and 2003, respectively.

The National Parks Act also led to the designation of 37 areas (nearly 8% of the area of England and Wales) as Areas of Outstanding Natural Beauty, meriting protection against exploitation. The first of these, the Quantock Hills in Somerset, was so designated in 1957, while the last - the Tamar Valley in England's West Country - was designated as such in 1995. Since then, there have been numerous moves to protect features of historical or architectural interest or areas of scenic beauty from overdevelopment, whether from tourism or other commercial interests. Notable among these are some 150 designated nature reserves and a large number of Sites of Special Scientific Interest (SSSI), which contain rare flora or fauna. An EU Wildlife and Habitats Directive gives stronger protection to some of the most notable SSSIs, which were decreed special areas of conservation in 2000. The UK government recognizes the threat to these sensitive areas caused by growth in tourism and leisure generally and is attempting to control it, although the countryside remains under threat from the need for more land for the construction of roads, private housing, expansion of airports and similar developments.

The public/private-sector interface in the development of sustainable tourism

Planning controls, whether executed centrally or regionally, are essential if the inevitable conflicts of interest that arise between the public and private sectors are to be avoided. Private enterprise, unrestricted, will seek to maximize profits, often in the short term, and this can more easily be achieved by concentrating marketing effort on popular attractions and destinations, rather than investing in the development of new ones. Airlines will clearly find it more profitable to focus on the routes already generating the most traffic, while hotels in a boom resort will build large and relatively cheap properties if this produces the highest margins.

Tour operators and, to a lesser extent, travel agents exercise massive marketing power over destinations through their influence on the decisions of consumers about where to go and what to do. Operators can make or break destinations through their decisions to enter or withdraw from destinations – decisions that often border on the 'slash and burn' techniques outlined earlier. *Sustainability* means ensuring cooperation between carriers, hotel companies and operators so that any development is not for short-term gain but in the long-term interests of the locals.

This is by no means a condemnation of the industry as a whole. For every large company that seeks to exploit its market position, there are others that recognize their responsibility to their destinations, as well as numerous small companies, both airlines and operators, actively seeking market gaps – untapped markets, destinations where the opportunity to develop tourism would be welcomed by locals or a focus on superior facilities would be appropriate.

By contrast with the failures in development planning cited earlier, the planning of the Orlando Walt Disney World Resort site reveals a better approach to the protection of a fragile environment. The site chosen, in central Florida, was largely scrubland and a deprived area in need of economic support. Walt Disney Productions took due account of the potentially enormous impact that the theme park would have on the state, including new road networks and airport construction in its plans. Protected sites well away from the park itself and the emerging town were clearly designated and, arguably, the site itself stands as a model of good development. By contrast, the impact that development further south has had on the Everglades National Park, where the wetlands have been significantly affected by engineering to provide water for coastal expansion, including meeting the needs of tourists, has been far less positive.

 EXAMPLE **Tourism development in Dubai**

The coastline of the UAE in the Middle East can be cited as evidence of development planning for tourism. Dubai in particular has implemented plans to develop tourism as a strategy to reduce their dependency on oil. The 1980s saw efforts to expand tourism as a catalyst for attracting foreign investment, this focusing on business tourism, leading to a growth in tourist arrivals from 422 000 in 1985 to 1.6 million a decade later.

This success led to the creation of the Department of Tourism and Commerce Marketing (DTCM) as the 'principal authority for the planning, supervision and development of the tourism sector in the emirate' (DTCM, 2011). Alongside their marketing activities, DTCM works to maintain quality through its licensing role of the accommodation and travel trade sectors as well as through providing skills training to staff of local tourism enterprises.

Policies to remove or reduce restrictions on traditional dress, alcohol consumption and visa requirements all helped to expand visitor appeal further and by 2005 international arrivals were reported to have exceeded the 6 million mark.

Development of the '7-star' Burj-Al Arab hotel and the construction of artificial islands offshore have provided iconic landmarks to create a reputation as an innovative tourism destination (Sharpley, 2008). Importantly, tourism was cited in the Strategic Development Plan 2015 as a key sector to ensure future economic development.

The low-cost airlines have been widely criticized for the air pollution they generate, but, on the plus side, by exploiting opportunities at small regional airports and working in cooperation with specialist tour operators, they have brought prosperity to many regions that previously had only limited access to tourists. Clermont-Ferrand in France, Graz in Austria and Trieste in Italy all have reason to be grateful for their services in making these cities and regions more accessible to tourists. The budget airlines have also been responsible for generating substantial local employment for air crew and ground staff when concentrated at airports such as Stansted and Luton. Of course, the influx of travellers at these regional airports has often pressured local infrastructure, thus creating additional demands on the natural environment.

The travel industry is continuing to take sustainability more seriously, with greater cooperation evidenced between the public and private sectors. Other notable examples include the Australian Nature and Ecotourism Accreditation Programme (NEAP) and Cooperative Research Centre (CRC) for Sustainable Tourism, South Africa's Fair Trade in Tourism (FTTSA) and the developing Sustainable Tourism Stewardship Council launched in Latin America in 2003 to explore opportunities for certification within the industry.

The World Travel and Tourism Council (WTTC) has worked with the industry since 1994 to develop the Green Globe awards for sustainability (albeit initially with limited success) and promote guidelines for travellers, disseminated in the form of leaflets. The WTTC has also taken on responsibility for the Tourism for Tomorrow awards, initiated by BA, which gain widespread publicity for sustainable tourism enterprises. Finally, in the UK the formation of the Travel Foundation, referred to in the previous chapter, signals cooperation between the public and private sectors, including some of the largest companies in the industry, reflecting for the first time a real commitment by the industry to the idea of sustainability.

EXAMPLE **Green Globe**

This organization, a member of the UNWTO and part-owned by the WTTC, was established in 1992 and now operates internationally to provide certification of sustainability. It also provides training, education and marketing to encourage travel and tourism businesses to consider the environmental impact of their operations. By 1998, membership had reached 500 organizations in 100 countries.

Using internationally accepted criteria, Green Globe, via its certification bodies, assesses the environmental management strategies of those organizations seeking accreditation. This has included airports, hotels, tourist attractions, transport providers and conference venues. More recently, it has also branded tools which help to calculate carbon emissions and offset requirements.

Source: http://www.greenglobe.com

American-owned companies operating globally have been notable for their commitment to sustainability, reflecting a strong environmental movement in that country. Walt Disney Enterprises, to take one example, recycles oils, paints and cleaning materials used on its sites. The Intercontinental Hotels chain undertook a worldwide environmental audit at the beginning of the 1990s, which led to a policy of recycling waste and introducing cruelty free (not tested on animals) toiletries in guests' rooms.

Other examples include German airline Lufthansa, which introduced snacks at departure gates to avoid wastage resulting from serving in-flight meals (as well as being sustainable, this reduces fuel consumption on flights and is highly cost-effective!). The UK company Center Parcs planned its resorts as car-free zones, offering visitors the use of bicycles during their stay.

The accommodation sector has led the way in introducing sustainable approaches, though initially through their desire to save on costs. The now well-established policy of reducing laundry bills by limiting the frequency of washing towels has extended to other cost-saving tactics that offer sustainable benefits. For example, some hotels in Hawaii have installed flow regulators on showers and taps to control water wastage. Even small businesses in the accommodation sector have taken initiatives. Bloomfield House, a bed-and-breakfast establishment in Bath, England, introduced a 10% discount to guests arriving by public transport and similar discounts are offered by the Primrose Valley Hotel in St Ives, Cornwall.

The concept of the environmental audit is gaining acceptance among tourism companies, BA being one notable example of a firm having adopted it. While the publication of environmental reports, as an element of the annual report, has become a widespread policy among other industries in recent years, the travel industry is only gradually coming to terms with this innovation.

Summary

The many different negative impacts of tourism are now well reported, leading to awareness both by tourists and businesses alike. Efforts to reduce the damage caused by tourism have led to many environmental programmes being introduced, although these are often on a local scale. Importantly, some positive impacts of tourism on the environment do exist, and this has helped to ensure that buildings and landscapes are protected and maintained.

There is still scepticism among many commentators as to the extent to which sustainable activities can be viewed as a genuine response to the threat to our environment rather than a public relations exercise designed to win public favour. Many businesses chose to cut back on their sustainable investment when faced with difficult trading conditions in the post-2001 era and there is little doubt that a number will continue to pay no more than lip-service to the concept unless it can be shown to be in their financial interest to do so, based on demand from their customers. Whilst some tourists are believed to actively consider sustainability issues when considering their travel plans, there is still doubt about the majority of the travelling public's willingness to pay more for their holidays if they are designed to be more sustainable.

Nonetheless, what will have started out for many companies as no more than a marketing ploy may later turn to a genuine commitment to improve the environment as lobbying by environmental interests takes effect and public awareness of the issues spreads.

Questions and discussion topics

1. Several airlines now offer their passengers the opportunity to offset the carbon emissions of their journey by paying a fee to a project which seeks either to reduce carbon emissions from other activities (such as building wind-powered generators in developing countries) or through planting trees, which can help to offset the effect of the pollution in the atmosphere. Currently these initiatives are only taken up by a minority of travellers. Discuss whether such initiatives are likely to become mainstream.

2. Several local governments have introduced policies to reduce the level of visual pollution caused by tourism. Discuss the benefits of introducing such a policy.

3. Do you think attitudes towards sustainability and tourism have changed over the past ten years? What are the reasons for your view?

Tasks

1. Using carbon emissions calculators available online, compare the different results for a return flight from London to New York. Discuss the different costs provided to offset this journey and summarize the many different projects available to offset the carbon emissions.

2. Investigate the negative impacts of tourism on flora and fauna and write a short magazine article which attempts to persuade tourists that they need to consider these impacts when they take holidays,

Bibliography

Barraclough, C. (2010) Eco-trends in the Galapagos, *Americas*, **62**, 54–55.

Boydon, I. (2010) Windermere speed limit still divides opinion five years on, *Westmorland Gazette*, 8 April.

Beck, B. and Bryan, F. (1971) This other Eden: a study of tourism in Britain, cited in Wall, G. and Mathieson, A. (2006) *Tourism: change impacts and opportunities*, Harlow, Pearson.

Butcher, L. (2010) *Aviation: night flights*, House of Commons, available online at: http://www.parliament.uk/briefingpapers/commons/SN01252.

Cohen, A. (2010) Rome to levy hotel tax on Jan. 1, *Business Travel News*, available online at: http://www.businesstravelnews.com/Business-Travel/Travel-News-UK/Articles/Rome-To-Levy-Hotel-Tax-On-Jan--1, 23 November (accessed November 2011).

Dowie, M. (2009) *Conservation Refugees: the Hundred-Year Conflict Between Global Conservation and Native Peoples*, Cambridge, MA, MIT Press.

DTCM (2011) *About the DTCM*, available online at: http://www.dubaitourism.ae/AboutDTCM/DTCMProfile/tabid/118/language/en-US/Default.aspx.

Epler, B. (2007) *Tourism, the economy, population growth and conservation in the Galapagos*, Ecuador, Charles Darwin Foundation.

Figueroa, M. (2009) Golf: Other regions taking proactive stance to cut water use at golf courses, *North County Times*, San Diego, 18 May, available online at: http://www.nctimes.com/sports/golf/article_a70716b1-f80f-519e-9853-1683911bc6b9.html (accessed November 2011).

FoE (2010) *Cruise Ship Environmental Report Card*, available online at: www.foe.org/cruisereportcard (accessed November 2011).

Gossling, S. and Peeters, P. (2007) 'It does not harm the environment!' An analysis of the industry discourse on tourism, air travel and the environment, *Journal of Sustainable Tourism*, **15** (4), 402–417.

Inskip, E. (1991) *Tourism Planning: An integrated and sustainable development*, New York, van Nostrand Reinhold.

Kington, T. (2009) Who can now stop the slow death of Venice?, *The Observer*, 1 March.

Lake District National Parks Authority (n.d.) *Path erosion and management*, available online at: http://www.fixthefells.co.uk/path_erosion_factsheet.pdf (accessed November 2011).

Laurance, W. F., Alonso, A., Lee, M. and Campbell, P. (2006) Challenges for forest conservation in Gabon, Central Africa, *Futures*, **38** (4), 454–470.

McCool, S. F. and Lime, D. W. (2001) Tourism carrying capacity: tempting fantasy or useful reality?, *Journal of Sustainable Tourism*, **9** (5), 372–388.

Ministry of Tourism and Civil Aviation (2010) *Nepal Tourism Statistics 2009 (Annual Statistical Report)*, Kathmandu, Government of Nepal.

O'Reilly, L. (2010) New regulations for Antarctic tourism, *Travel and Tourism News*, 1 May.

Rheem, C. (2009) *Going Green: The business impact of environmental awareness of travel*, Sherman CT, PhoCusWright, February.

Rowe, M. (2009) Cruel to be kind?, *Geographical Magazine*, 1 February.

Sharpley, R. (2008) Planning for tourism: the case of Dubai, *Tourism and Hospitality Planning and Development*, **5** (1) 13–30.

Stankey, G. H., Cole, D. N., Lucas, R. C., Petersen, M. E. and Frissell, S. S. (1985) *The Limits of Acceptable Change (LAC) System for Wilderness Planning*, Ogden, UT, United States Department of Agriculture, General Technical Report INT-176.

Williams, M. (2007) Havana revival not a facade: Restored area's tourism funds aid to people, *Atlanta Journal-Constitution*, 4 March.

Further reading

Ballantyne, R., Packer, J. and Hughes, K. (2009) Tourists' support for conservation messages and sustainable management practices in wildlife tourism experiences, *Tourism Management*, **30** (5), 658–664.

UN Environment Program (2010) *Environmental impacts of tourism*, available online at: http://www.unep.fr/scp/tourism/sustain/impacts/environmental/ (accessed November 2011).

Wall, G. and Mathieson, A. (2006) *Tourism: Change Impacts and Opportunities*, Harlow, Pearson.

Websites

Blue Flag: **www.blueflag.org.uk**

Green Globe 21: **www.greenglobe.com**

Keep Britain Tidy Campaign: **www.keepbritaintidy.org**

Rainforest Alliance: **www.rainforest-alliance.org**

Responsible Tourism Partnership: **www.responsibletourismpartnership.org**

Tourism Concern: **www.tourismconcern.org.uk**

UNEP Tourism and Environment Programme: **www.unep.fr/scp/tourism**

Part 2

The travel and tourism product

8

The structure and organization of the travel and tourism industry

Contents

Learning outcomes

After studying this chapter, you should be able to:

- identify the integral and associated sectors of the travel and tourism industry
- explain the chain of distribution and how this applies within the industry
- understand the relationships between each industry sector
- be aware of the extent of integration within the industry and the reasons for this
- identify the factors leading to change within the industry and predict likely directions it may take in the future.

Before the days of the Internet when the GDS [Global Distribution Systems] had power over airlines and their distribution processes, they could – and did – charge a lot. Since the coming of the Internet and with it airline websites offering direct booking, the balance of power has shifted away from the GDSs and towards the carriers.

Slaughter (2011) The annual war between airlines and GDSs: isn't it time it stopped?

Introduction

This acknowledgement that there has been a shift in the distribution methods used by the tourism industry has been widely recognized and debated; but the shape of the future is not yet clear. Although initial opinion suggested that the Internet would lead to the death of the high-street travel agent, this prophecy proved too simplistic.

The tourist product is a complex amalgam of different services, each of which must be brought together and presented to customers by the various sectors of the industry. The demand for tourism is first created, then satisfied by the concentrated marketing efforts of a wide variety of organizers who provide tourist products and services. These together form the world's largest and fastest-growing industry. Because some of these services are crucial to the generation and satisfaction of tourists' needs, while others play only a peripheral or supportive role, defining what is meant by a 'tourism industry' is fraught with difficulties.

Several services, such as catering and transport, obviously serve the needs of consumers other than tourists, too. Other services, such as banks, retail shops and taxis – or launderettes in a resort where a significant number of tourists are in self-catering facilities – may only serve tourists' needs incidentally along with local residents' needs, although at peak periods of the year the former may provide the bulk of their income. Inevitably, what one decides to include in a definition of the tourism industry must be, to some extent, arbitrary. Figure 8.1, however, provides a framework for analysis based on those sectors commonly seen as forming the core of the industry.

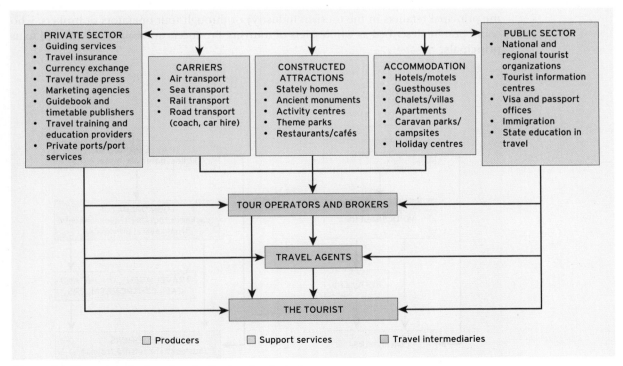

Figure 8.1 The network of sectors in the tourism industry

The chain of distribution for tourism

Figure 8.1 is also an illustration of the **chain of distribution** in the travel and tourism business. This phrase is used to describe the system by which a product or service is distributed from its manufacturing/creative source to the eventual consumers. The alternative term, **marketing channel**, can also be used to describe this system. Traditionally, products are distributed through the involvement of a number of intermediaries who link producers or manufacturers with consumers. These intermediaries are either wholesalers (who buy in large quantities from suppliers and sell in smaller quantities to others further down the chain), or retailers (who form the final link in the chain and sell individual products or a bundled set of products – such as package holidays – to the consumer). The structure of the chain of distribution is shown in Figure 8.2.

Producers, of course, are not obliged to sell their products through intermediaries. They may instead choose to sell direct to consumers or retailers, thus avoiding some or all of the intermediaries. Wholesalers, in turn, sometimes sell products direct to the consumer, avoiding the retailer.

Producers

The core tourism product consists essentially of transport, accommodation and attractions, whether constructed or natural. The producers, or 'manufacturers', of these services include air, waterborne, road and rail carriers, hotels or other forms of tourist accommodation and the various forms of constructed facilities designed to attract the leisure and business tourist, such as stately homes or heritage sites, amusement parks, conference and exhibition venues and other purpose-built activity centres such as ski resorts. These services can be sold to the tourist in a number of ways – either direct, through travel agents (still the principal retailers in the tourism industry) or through tour operators or brokers, who could best be described as wholesalers of tourism. Producers are sometimes referred to as **principals**.

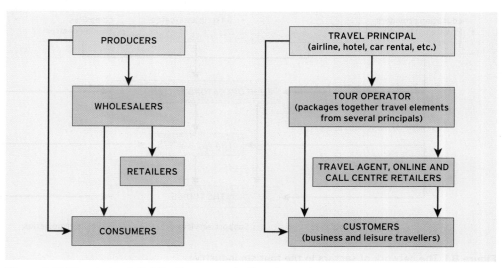

Figure 8.2 The chain of distribution or marketing channel

Wholesalers

Tour operators can be viewed as wholesalers because they buy a range of different tourist products (such as airline seats, hotel rooms or coach transfer facilities) in bulk, then bundle or 'package' these for subsequent sale to travel agents or to the tourist direct.

By buying a mixture of individual products and services and presenting them as a single product – the package holiday – they are seen by some theorists as *producers* of a *new* product rather than *wholesalers* of an *existing* product. This is a debatable point, but in the authors' view they are best viewed as intermediaries, in the sense that their fundamental role is to bulk purchase products, organize them into bundles and sell those bundles off individually (this is discussed in more detail in Chapter 18). The current pattern of trading – in which both tour operators and agents are moving towards dynamic packaging, which involves bundling products to meet a consumer's needs at the point of sale (or 'unbundling the package tour' as some operators express it) – is muddying the distinction between the roles of operators and agents.

EXAMPLE **Expedia negotiates with hotels to offer preferential rates**

Online travel company Expedia makes available 'on a stand-alone and package basis, travel products and services provided by numerous airlines, lodging properties, car rental companies, destination service providers, cruise lines and other travel product and service companies' (Expedia, 2010).

If we particularly focus on their sale of accommodation, this wholesaler earns revenue by using two approaches. The first, and by far the smaller of the two approaches in terms of earnings, is that of commission (known as the agency model). For each hotel room sold on a commission basis Expedia invoices the hotel – typically, commission rates are around 10% of the room rate.

The second approach, the merchant model, often earns much higher percentage returns and reflects the wholesale role taken on by Expedia. The merchant model operates using a pre-negotiated agreement for Expedia to sell a set number of rooms, provided to them at a net-rate lower than the hotel standard. Expedia can then mark up the rooms and sell to customers at levels the market will stand. The mark-up becomes the earnings for Expedia and can be as high as 40% of room rates. Expedia carries some of the risk related to the sale of the room and becomes the merchant, dealing with the customer directly in terms of ticketing, customer services and other matters. Expedia claims that, as the merchant, they 'generally negotiate supply allocation and pricing with suppliers [enabling] a higher level of net revenue per transaction as compared to that provided through the agency model' (Expedia, 2010). Furthermore, by working with other travel industry producers, Expedia can package travel components together for the customer, increasing the total value of the sale and, in turn, their own earnings.

Brokers – who bulk buy tourist products and sell in smaller quantities – are most frequently found in the distribution system within the air transport sector, although others involve themselves in the bulk purchase of hotel rooms or certain other services. As with tour operators, by purchasing aircraft seats in bulk, they are able to negotiate much lower prices, which can be sold on to tour operators or travel agents either individually or in quantity at net prices, allowing the other intermediaries to determine their own profit level and the selling price for the seats.

One of the commonest forms of brokering in the travel industry is found in the role of the **consolidator**. These are specialists working in airline brokerage who bulk purchase unsold charter aircraft seats to sell through intermediaries, thereby helping airlines to clear unsold 'stock'.

Retailers

Although retailing through the Internet is now becoming a significant threat to them, travel agents remain an important outlet for selling most travel products within the distribution chain, selling packages and travel services according to client demand. They carry no stock, simply acting as an intermediary between the consumer and the supplier and their main role is to provide a convenient network of sales outlets for the travelling public.

Traditionally, agents did not charge for their services as they were remunerated in the form of a commission on each sale they negotiated. One of the most significant changes in distribution patterns in recent years, however, has been the tendency for producers to either reduce commission payments or, in some cases, scrap them altogether, often forcing agents to charge their clients for their services. Airlines were among the first principals to withdraw commissionable sales, mainly in the belief that they could reach the consumer more cheaply by direct contact via the Internet, rather than depending on agents who, for the most part, retain no particular loyalty to any one supplier. This means that many agents are now obliged to add a fee when selling most airline tickets.

Some other transport companies and tour operators are beginning to follow suit, although the large operators are unlikely, at least for the foreseeable future, to adopt such a policy. There appears to be a global trend in travel retailing for agents to buy many of their principals' products at market price and add a service fee, but this presupposes there is an adequate level of agency sales expertise and product knowledge that adds value to the process when a customer books through an agent. In fact, the pressure on margins seldom allows retail agencies to provide the salaries and conditions that would enable them to recruit sales staff of the quality and skills needed to make this possible. This is discussed in more detail in Chapter 19.

Ancillary providers

Apart from these core services – of producers, wholesalers and retailers – a wide variety of ancillary and support services interact within the distribution system. For convenience, these can be divided into public-sector organizations (those funded, controlled or organized through central or local governments) and those that are privately owned.

The former include national tourism organizations, such as tourist offices, publicly owned airports or seaports, passport and visa documentation and other ancillary services like public education and training institutions offering courses in tourism.

The private sector includes privately owned airports and seaports, services offered by freelance guides, travel insurance and financial services (including foreign exchange and credit card facilities), travel trade newspapers and journals, printers of travel literature and publishers of guides and timetables, as well as a number of specialist marketing services, such as travel consultants, advertising agents and brochure design agencies. In addition, there are private visa agencies that will collect customers' documentation, check it and procure any necessary visas for a fee. This is becoming a more typical pattern for visa procurement as few embassies are willing to mail documents to clients and submission in person is often inconvenient, expensive and time-consuming. Most tour operators now use these intermediaries, too, as they have a good rapport with the embassies and consulates they use frequently and provide a dependable service.

The distinction between public and private bodies is not always straightforward. Some national and regional tourism organizations (the USA and the city of Berlin are two examples) are run as private consortia, having been delegated the role by the public sector. Others, while nominally public, would collapse without the financial support they receive from the private sector.

Public ownership of tourism attractions

The public sector can be involved in a number of ways in attracting tourists. In some cases, local or national government may have ownership of a building or destination (perhaps a national park for example) and will operate the facility as a tourist attraction in order to provide public access to the facility or to fund its upkeep and management.

In other cases, governments may provide grant funding to private-sector tourism businesses to support activities that are felt to be in keeping with government agendas. An example of this is the funding provided by the UK government to museums in order to encourage wider access to these cultural resources.

Port Arthur, Tasmania

Established as a prison settlement in the 1830s, this historic site – considered to be one of the best preserved convict settlements, and listed as a World Heritage site location – provides insight into an important aspect of Australian history (see Figure 8.3).

The site is managed on behalf of the people of Tasmania by a specially established authority which receives significant funding for its conservation work from the Tasmanian government. It also earns revenue from its tourism activities, including ticket sales, gift shop and restaurants. It attracts around 250 000 domestic and international visitors annually, with a further 50 000 attendees at the evening historic ghost tours (Port Arthur Historic Sites, 2011).

Figure 8.3 Port Arthur penal settlement
Photo by Claire Humphreys

While some countries provide key elements of the travel industry through national or local government, other countries may choose to allow the private sector to provide these facilities. For example BAA, the UK leading airport owner, is an example of a former public body (formerly the British Airports Authority, now a PLC), that exercises control over six UK airports. The privatization of airports has proved lucrative for BAA, but there is concern that the current pattern of ownership is not in the best interests of the consumer (or the airlines that use BAA airports).

Are there changes ahead for BAA?

Control of BAA passed into the hands of Spanish construction company Ferrovial in the summer of 2006 when it acquired over 80% of BAA's shares. BAA currently operates six UK airports, having sold Gatwick airport in 2009, for £1.5 billion. The airports operated are:

- Heathrow
- Stansted
- Glasgow
- Edinburgh
- Aberdeen
- Southampton.

This dominance of both the London and Scotland airport sectors has brought BAA to the attention of the Competition Commission.

Following an initial review early in 2008, the Competition Commission announced that its initial thoughts tended towards the view that 'common ownership of the BAA airports is a feature of the market that adversely affects competition between airports' (Competition Commission, 2008). It therefore concluded that – despite the sale of Gatwick airport – BAA must sell Stansted and either Edinburgh or Glasgow airports.

For the most part, the tourism industry depends for its success on a close working relationship between the private and public sectors. Many tourist attractions, such as heritage sites, are publicly owned, either by the state or local authorities, while public authorities are also frequently responsible for the promotion and distribution of information about tourism (through, for instance, their tourist information centres). This interdependence between private and public sectors, which is an important element in the dynamics of the industry, will be explored in subsequent chapters.

Common interest organizations

A feature of the tourism industry is the extent of the association, voluntary or otherwise, that has taken place between businesses and/or public-sector bodies that share similar interests or complement one another's interests in some way. Such associations can take a number of forms, but typically fall into one of three categories:

- *sectoral organizations* based on the interests of a particular sector of industry (or link in the chain of distribution)
- *destination organizations* concerned with a specific tourist destination, whether country, region or resort
- *tourism organizations* based on a concern with travel or tourism activity as a whole.

Each of these can in turn be subdivided according to whether they are trade or professional bodies. The latter are normally composed of individuals whose common interest is likely to be based on objectives that include establishing educational or training qualifications for the industry or the sector, devising codes of conduct to guide members' behaviour and limiting or controlling entry to the industry or sector. Membership of such bodies is often associated with a personal drive to enhance status and prestige.

Trade bodies, by contrast, are groupings of independent firms, the common purpose of which will include such aims as the opportunity to exchange views, cooperation (especially in the functions of marketing), representation and negotiation with other organizations and the provision of identifiable services to their members. In some circumstances, the trade bodies may also take on activities more generally associated with professional bodies, such as restricting entry to the industry or sector and providing or recognizing appropriate qualifications.

EXAMPLE **Professional bodies – the Tourism Society**

Operating in the UK for more than 30 years, the Tourism Society has over 1000 members, who are employed in the public, private and voluntary sectors of the tourism industry. The aim of the society is 'driving up standards of professionalism' (Tourism Society, 2011).

To work towards this aim, the Society holds a variety of conferences that help to develop the knowledge of its members and, in the past, they have provided communication and presentation skills workshops. Further, these conferences provide networking opportunities, which can open business opportunities for its members. In recent years, the Society has also worked to attract student members as they commence their careers in the tourism industry.

EXAMPLE **Trade bodies – Treasure Houses of England**

Many sectoral organizations come together in order to benefit from opportunities to bulk buy at discount prices from their suppliers or sell themselves more effectively and at lower cost. Websites that offer a range of products rather than a single one, for example, will be more effective in reaching the public.

Treasure Houses of England is one such example in the attractions sector of the industry. Composed of ten of the leading stately homes, palaces and castles in the UK, the consortium has its own website (**www.treasurehouses.co.uk**), produces a joint brochure and offers discounts at partner properties.

The structure of such bodies may vary considerably. In some cases – particularly in the larger organizations – there will be a paid administrative staff, while, in the case of smaller bodies (such as local marketing consortia), there may be no full-time staff and administration will often be carried out by volunteer staff seconded from member companies. A key characteristic of trade bodies, however, is that their membership is made up of autonomous companies or other organizations subscribing to the common purpose of the body concerned.

Sectoral organizations

Probably the most numerous organizations are those that reflect sectoral interests. As we saw in Figure 8.1, there is a wide range of sectors making up the tourism industry and each of these can be expected to have at least one common interest association. Professional bodies catering for sectoral interests include the Chartered Institute of Logistics and Transport (CILT) and the Institute of Hospitality (formerly the Hotel, Catering and International Management Association). The Chartered Institute of Marketing (CIM) has a section devoted to travel industry members, known as the Chartered Institute of Marketing Travel Industry Group (CIMTIG), while tourism consultants have their own professional body the Tourism Society Consultants' Network (TCN).

Some bodies provide their own training for the industry (such as the CILT), while others rely on training organizations set up separately for this purpose (the UK-based TTC Training, for example). The UK has a sector skills council representing the hospitality, leisure, travel and tourism industries – People 1st – the role of which is to develop occupational standards for training and support qualification bodies to provide a streamlined and appropriate range of qualifications for the industry.

Sectoral trade bodies may be regional, national or international in scope. Some international bodies retain significant influence over the activities of their members. An example is the International Air Transport Association (IATA), which continues in its role of negotiating with international airlines worldwide even though some of its erstwhile power has diminished under the impetus to liberalize this sector of the industry. The International Federation of Tour Operators (IFTO) draws its members from European national tour operating bodies, including the British Federation of Tour Operators (FTO) – an influential consultative body made up of 12 leading UK operators.

Apart from the FTO, other examples of UK national bodies include the Association of British Travel Agents (ABTA), which represents both tour operators and travel agents, the Meetings Industry Association (MIA) and UKinbound, representing organizations that make ground handling arrangements for incoming visitors to the UK. Similar bodies are to be found in all countries with a developed tourism industry. The American Society of Travel Agents (ASTA), for example, fulfils a similar role in the USA to that of ABTA in the UK, but also draws on members from other sectors of industry, as well as overseas members, due to the importance and influence of the USA as a tourist-generating country.

EXAMPLE **British Destinations**

Formed through a merger between the British Resorts and Destinations Association (BRADA) and Destination Performance UK (DP UK), this is a trade association for local government-funded tourism, private sector tourism partnerships and public/private destination management organizations. The common link between members is an interest in hosting visitors, and an enthusiasm to improve destinations and enhance the benefits which can be gained by attracting tourists to the area. The activities undertaken by British Destinations include lobbying, research and the promotion of best-practice within the industry.

Regional bodies will comprise groups such as local hoteliers or tourist attractions. These will often act as pressure groups in their relations with local tourist authorities, but also provide arenas for discussion on issues of mutual interest to members.

Destination organizations

A destination organization is one that draws its membership from both public- and private-sector tourism bodies that share a common interest in the development or marketing of a specific tourist destination. That destination may be a resort, state or region, a country or even an area of the globe. Membership of such bodies is open to firms or public-sector organizations rather than individuals. These bodies generally share two common objectives:

● to foster cooperation and coordination between the various bodies that provide, or are responsible for, the facilities or amenities making up the tourism product

● to act cooperatively to promote the destination to the travel trade and tourists.

Consequently, they are trade, rather than professional, bodies. Examples range from such globally important regional marketing bodies as the Pacific Area Travel Association (PATA) and the European Travel Commission (ETC), to local marketing consortia made up of groups of hotels or tourist attractions within a particular region or resort.

An example of a marketing consortium is the Central European Countries Travel Association (CECTA) – its members comprising public-sector (including national tourist organizations) and private-sector tourism interests (including airlines, care hire companies, attractions, tour operators and travel agents) – which represents combined interests in Germany, Austria, Hungary, the Czech Republic, Slovakia and Poland. This consortium was formed in 1999 in order to market this large European region more effectively, stress its geographically central, rather than Eastern European, roots and take advantage of opportunities for growth following the advent of four of these nations into the EU. At the other end of the scale, the Bournemouth Hotels and Restaurants Association, the Devon Association of Tourist Attractions and the Association of Bath and District Leisure Enterprises are all typical examples in England of localized groupings within a single country.

EXAMPLE **Tourism Whitsundays**

The Whitsundays region comprises 74 islands in the heart of the Great Barrier Reef, off the east coast of Australia. Attracting almost $^3/_4$ million tourists annually, this popular destination is supported and promoted by the regional tourism organization, Tourism Whitsundays.

The responsibilities and activities of the organization are wide-ranging and include:

- destination marketing – both domestically and internationally though attending expos, providing familiarization tours and developing advertising campaigns
- liaison with local industry to develop the tourism infrastructure, ensuring the quality, capacity and experience for visitors are maintained
- developing the region as a business tourism destination through the Whitsundays Convention Bureau
- providing a visitor information and booking centre.

Tourism Whitsundays is a not-for-profit organization funded by the state tourist board (Tourism Queensland), the regional council and through membership. Members of the organization must adhere to a code of conduct and are encouraged to partner with other members to support the industry and develop new opportunities. With more than 250 members, drawn from a variety of sectors – transport, accommodation, tour providers, catering, media and, importantly, community clubs and groups – this organization works with many who benefit directly and indirectly from tourism. To accommodate this diversity, different types of membership level are offered, with benefits and support differing accordingly.

Type of membership	Business type	Cost per annum (2010)
Non-tourism business	Non-tourism business with indirect tourism benefit	$540
Entry level tourism	Small to medium business with direct benefit from tourism	$1080
Domestic tourism	Australian market focus – tourism business wishing to have active involvement in national marketing	$1860
Introductory international tourism	One year only – introduction to international marketing – 'a toe in the water'	$2160
International tourism	Australian and international market focus – tourism business with involvement in national and international markets	$3840
Gold tourism	Large tourism business, active marketers and industry leaders	$12 000
Platinum tourism	Very large tourism business, active marketers, industry leaders and champions for the region	$30 000
Friends of Tourism Whitsundays	Individuals who support Tourism Whitsundays' efforts	$74
Associate	For not-for-profit community organizations	free of charge
Out of region	Tourism businesses outside of the Tourism Whitsundays region	$174

Source: Tourism Whitsundays, 2011

Tourism organizations

The activities of some bodies transcend sectoral boundaries within the industry. These organizations may have as their aim the compilation of national or international statistics on tourism or the furtherance of research into the tourism phenomenon.

The United Nations World Tourism Organization (UNWTO) plays a dominant role in collecting and collating statistical information on international tourism. This organization represents public-sector tourism bodies from most countries in the world. Also, the publication of its data enables comparisons of the flow and growth of tourism on a global scale.

Similarly, the Organisation for Economic Co-operation and Development (OECD) also has a tourism committee composed of tourism officials drawn from its member countries and provides regular reports comprising comparative data on tourism developments to and within these countries. Other privately sponsored bodies have been set up to produce supporting statistics, such as the World Travel and Tourism Council (WTTC), the members of which are drawn from over 30 leading airlines and tourist organizations. This body also regularly commissions and publishes research data.

Within countries, bodies are set up to bring together public and private tourism interests as a means of influencing legislation, encouraging political action or sometimes to overcome crises affecting the industry. In the UK, the Tourism Industry Emergency Response Group (TIER) was established to develop crisis plans and manage crisis response for the UK tourism industry and comprises representatives of VisitBritain, ABTA, UKinbound, British Hospitality Association, BA and the Association of Leading Visitor Attractions. Wider aims are designed to be achieved by the Tourism Alliance.

EXAMPLE **The Tourism Alliance**

In 2001, the travel industry in the UK was severely affected by foot-and-mouth disease in cattle, which restricted travel to the countryside and inhibited visitors from abroad, especially North America. Travel organizations recognized that they needed a common mouthpiece to lobby government and handle future problems affecting the industry, feeling that the existing bodies were inadequate for this purpose. Thus, the Tourism Alliance was formed, bringing together a mix of public and private organizations, including ABTA, the Association of Leading Visitor Attractions, the British Hospitality Association, British Incoming Tour Operators' Association (BITOA, now UKinbound), the Association of Recognized English Language Services, the British Beer and Pub Association, the British Holiday and Home Parks Association, together with the Local Government Association and national and regional tourist boards (excluding Wales and Scotland, which have their own tourism forums). The organization has come to form a strong pressure group and debating forum.

Many countries with a strongly developed tourism industry establish professional bodies composed of individual members drawn from several or all sectors of the industry. The purpose of these bodies is to promote the cause of the tourism industry generally, while simultaneously encouraging the spread of knowledge and understanding of the industry among members. For example, in the UK there are two professional bodies devoted to the tourism industry generally, although they tend to draw their membership from different sectors of industry. The Institute of Travel and Tourism (ITT) originated as an institute designed to serve the needs of travel agents and tour operators and still draws its membership largely from these sectors, while the Tourism Society, discussed earlier in this chapter, is a more recently formed professional body that attracts members particularly from the public sector, tourist attractions and the incoming tourism industry.

Integration in the tourism industry

A notable feature of the industry over recent years has been the steady process of integration that has taken place between sectors of the tourism industry. If we refer to our earlier model of the chain of distribution (Figure 8.2), we can identify this integration as being either **horizontal** or **vertical** in character. Horizontal integration is that taking place at any one level in the chain, while vertical integration describes the process of linking together organizations at different levels of the chain (some writers also refer to **diagonal integration** – a term used to describe links between complementary businesses within each level in the chain).

Horizontal integration

Horizontal integration can take several forms. One is the integration of two companies offering similar (and in some cases, potentially competing) products. Two hotels at the same seaside resort may merge, for example, or two airlines operating on similar routes may unite. Alternatively, an airline operating, for instance, between New York and Tokyo might advantageously take over another operating from Tokyo to Seoul, in order to provide an integrated and coordinated service, the better to compete with a direct service New York–Seoul. Such **mergers** may result from the takeover of one company by another or simply from a voluntary agreement between the two to merge and obtain the benefits, identified above, of a much larger organization. **Voluntary unions** can also be established, however, that allow the companies concerned to maintain their autonomy and separate identities while still obtaining the benefits of an integrated organization. This is the case with a **consortium** – an affiliation of independent companies working together to achieve a common aim or benefit. One example of this affiliation is the marketing consortium, which allows independent companies to gain economies of scale in, for example, mass advertising or the publication of a joint brochure. The Best Western consortium, for instance, among other activities, produces a brochure listing all their member hotels. Alternatively, a consortium may have as its prime benefit the ability to purchase supplies at bulk prices for its members – a feature of groupings of independent travel agents such as the Advantage consortium, which, in this way, can negotiate higher commission levels from tour operators and other principals.

A second form of integration occurs between companies offering complementary rather than competing products. An example would be the linking of an airline with a hotel chain. As both of these are *principals,* they are at the same stage of the chain of distribution and thus their integration is horizontal. Close links between the accommodation and transport sectors may develop as they are interdependent for their customers. Without hotel bedrooms available at their destinations, airline passengers may be unwilling to book seats, and vice versa. Recognition of this dual need has led many airlines to buy into or form their own hotel divisions, especially in regions of high tourist demand where bed shortages are common. This trend was common in the early years of the jumbo jet, when airlines woke up to the consequences of operating aircraft with 350 or more passengers aboard, each requiring accommodation over which the airline had little or no control. This led to the integration of several major airlines and hotel chains. Rising competition between airlines, which led to huge losses and massive investment in new aircraft, however, obliged many airlines to sell their hotel investments to raise capital in order to survive. Since those days, the more common form of this relationship has been to have closely linked computer reservations systems (CRSs), which allow the airlines a measure of control over hotel bedrooms without having to make a major capital investment in the accommodation sector. The growth of dynamic packaging in the early 2000s reinforced the need for airlines to have access to accommodation, many developing their own websites to include hotel accommodation at prices competitive with specialist hotel websites.

Airlines are increasingly seeking to benefit from liaisons that do not involve competition on the same routes. **Interlining agreements** allow airlines to benefit from connections globally. These are commercial agreements between airlines to provide travel routes for passengers that require the use of multiple airlines. For example, a flight from Germany to the Cook Islands (in the Pacific) may use flights operated by both Lufthansa and Air New Zealand. Such agreements have been extended to code-sharing, which allows an airline to allocate its own flight number to a service operated by another airline. Close links have also been developed through the global airline alliances that have formed in recent years, such as Star Alliance and One World. Combined, these links can mean that, for example, transatlantic routes can provide 'feeder' opportunities into the US network of domestic routes, allowing foreign airlines to compete with US airlines to carry passengers between two US domestic airports. Such agreements also overcome the problems faced if these airlines were to try to merge – a move often seen as anti-competitive and likely to be challenged by monopolies commissions, which favour open competition.

The changing nature of tourist demand may also cause companies to diversify their interests horizontally. In the previous century, shipping companies woke up far too late to the realization that the future of long-haul travel lay in the air and, by the time they began investing in airlines, the sums involved were too great for the loss-making shipping companies to absorb.

At the retailing level, integration is also common, but, because the traditional development of travel agencies has led in many cases to regional strengths, integration has tended to be regionally based, leading to the development of so-called 'miniples' – agencies with a significant number of branches within one region of the country only, which may well, within that region, outperform the multiple agents (more details of this are provided in Chapter 19). The massive growth in the number of branches of the big multiples has tapered off and has even been reversing in the opening years of the new century. Initially, this had led to some large travel companies taking over a miniple as a means of building or strengthening its profile in a particular region, but, as competition increased and the profits of large companies were squeezed, the process has been reversing and miniples are regaining their autonomy.

Tour operating has also experienced growth through integration in the past decade – first that between large companies in the UK and later internationally (see Chapter 18 for more details). Two of the UK's leading companies – Thomas Cook and Thomson Holidays – are now both in German hands (the latter, part of world leader TUI). While integration in the principal travel sectors is likely to continue, it is unlikely to be as frenetic as it has been in recent years, given the instability of the industry and that most companies are keen to see a return to stable profits rather than chasing expansion. Some major ventures, such as expansion by European companies into North America, have in fact been reversed as the companies have consolidated their positions.

Vertical integration

As noted, vertical integration is said to take place when an organization at one level in the chain of distribution unites with one at another level. This integration can be **forward** (or downward in the direction of the chain), such as in the case where a tour operator buys its own chain of travel agents or it can be **backward** (or upward, against the direction of the chain), such as in the case where a tour operator buys its own airline.

The merger of two Canadian tour operators

In the latter part of 2009, Sunwing Travel group merged with Signature Vacations (part of the TUI group) to form Canada's second largest tour operator, behind Transat. The global economic downturn had made this period a difficult time for the tourism industry and the merger sought to provide TUI with the opportunity to gain profitability in a competitive marketplace.

Sunwing, a privately owned business, provides package holidays and operates its own airline business. TUI – via First Choice Canada, its operating division – committed Signature Vacations, Selloffvacations (a retail operation) and $101 million, in return for a 49% stake in the amalgamated entity. At the time of the merger, Sunwing was estimated to have an 18% market share, while Signature held 12%.

In April 2010, Sunwing airlines became the exclusive carrier for Signature holidays, and, although merging computer systems was time-consuming for the two organizations, gains in operations efficiences have led to forecasts that this organization will be one of the fastest growing companies in Canada.

 Libra Holidays Group

In 2004, tour operator Libra Holidays bought Helios Airways, a largely scheduled airline, in a move to expand its Cyprus tour operating programme. Formerly, the company had held a stake in Excel Airways, reducing this investment in order to invest in its own carrier.

Backward integration in the form of a takeover (such as in the example above) is fairly uncommon. More frequently in the past, operators have set up their own airlines internally. Forward integration is more typical as organizations are more likely to have the necessary capital to buy businesses further down the chain of distribution as they require less capital investment than those above them in the chain. For example, even the largest independent travel agency chain might hesitate before embarking on an expansion to form its own airline. Even so, in rare cases, examples exist where even the smaller companies have successfully done so. Bath Travel, a miniple in England's south west, actually purchased its own aircraft to operate a limited programme of tours under the brand name Palmair, which it has successfully operated for a number of years. Strong brand loyalty in the region has undoubtedly helped to account for the success of this high-risk venture. It is true to say, however, that, generally speaking, the higher a company is in the chain of distribution, the greater the investment that will be required.

As with horizontal integration, organizations can achieve significant economies of scale by expanding vertically. Whereas total profits in individual sectors may be slight, a reasonable profit overall across the sectors may still be achieved by an integrated business that controls all levels in the chain. Even in a year of intense competition, tour operating companies owning their own airlines and retail sales outlets (neither of which may be committed to the exclusive sale of the operator's products) may still remain profitable.

As with the linking of complementary services in horizontal integration, many companies are concerned about ensuring the continuation of their supplies. A tour operator depending on a continuous supply of aircraft seats and hotel beds, and facing international competition for such supplies, can best ensure adequate and regular supplies by directly controlling them – that is, by integrating backwards, into the airline and hotel businesses.

EXAMPLE **Integration at WA Shearings**

An interesting example, combining vertical and horizontal integration, is that of leading UK coach operator Shearings, which merged with competitor Wallace Arnold.

For some years, Shearings has been putting into practice an ambitious programme to own its hotels. The company employs its fleet substantially in its role as tour operator, running coach tours, and secures two benefits from its hotel ownership: control over the quality and availability of accommodation at any time of the year and an opportunity to maximize profits on its hotel *and* tour operating businesses.

In addition to the 50 hotels it owns, as a result of its earlier merger with Wallace Arnold the company also has amongst its assets eight Wallace Arnold Travel agencies.

It is noticeable that the dominant partners in such mergers generally revert to the use of their own brand names after an appropriate interval; the original merger between the two coach companies led to the organization being rebranded WA Shearings, but later the WA element in the name quietly disappeared.

Large multinational corporations are well equipped financially to diversify their interests into new products when they see opportunities arise. Many of the leading European tour operators have integrated airlines. These vertical links between airlines and tour operators are further examined in Chapter 18.

The benefits of integration

All business is highly competitive and the tourism industry is no exception to this rule. Such competition, often encouraged by government policy, has been evident within the tourism industry, especially since the development of the mass market in travel that began in the 1960s. Following policies of deregulation, particularly those in the transport sector affecting air, rail and coach companies, competition became steadily fiercer throughout the latter part of the twentieth century and the early years of the new century. Competition forces companies to seek ways of becoming more efficient in order to cut costs. Integration makes this possible.

The benefits of scale

Horizontal integration enables companies to benefit from economies of scale by producing and selling more of a product. This reduces the unit cost of each product as the fixed costs incurred are spread over a larger number of units, whether these are hotel bedrooms, aircraft seats or package tours. Equally, buyers of these products, such as tour operators, can obtain lower net prices if they buy in larger quantities, just as airlines can negotiate lower prices if they order more aircraft from the manufacturers.

The savings achieved through both these economies of scale can be passed on to clients in the form of lower prices, making the product more attractive to the consumer. Vertical integration offers economies of scale through the integration of executive and administrative functions, as well as increasing leverage on the market through advertising and promotion.

The benefits of a changed distribution system

The World Wide Web is undermining some of the former purposes of integration by offering an alternative method of distribution and reducing the necessity of depending on so many links in the chain. Today, hoteliers need no longer depend on granting an allocation of beds to a local ground handler, who would then sell them on to a tour operator, who in turn would make them available to customers via a travel agent. Beds can be sold direct via a website and in any number of foreign languages to meet the world market's needs. In so doing, distribution prices can be held down to a level where they may well undercut those possibly using traditional distribution techniques.

The benefits of size

Large companies offer benefits to both suppliers and tourists. Suppliers, knowing the reputations of the major companies in the field, are anxious to do business with them, in the belief that such firms are less likely to collapse in the face of competition than the small ones (a belief that is not always well founded, as shown by the collapse of the International Leisure Group (ILG) – the UK's second-largest operator, at the beginning of the 1990s). The tour operator's operational risks are minimized because suppliers, faced with an overbooking situation, will be less likely to turn away clients from the tour operator who brings them so much business. Similarly, hotels uniting into larger groups will be able to negotiate better deals through their own suppliers for the bulk purchase of such items as food and drink, while larger airlines will bring greater bargaining strength to the negotiating table in their dealings with foreign governments for landing rights or new routes.

Most companies, if asked to identify their organizational goals, would cite market expansion as a major objective. Growth in a competitive environment is a means of survival and history testifies to the fact that few companies survive by standing still. Integration is a means of growth, enabling a company to increase its market share and simultaneously reduce the level of competition it faces by forcing less efficient companies out of business.

Greater sales generally mean more revenue, so, potentially, there will be more funds to reinvest in the company to assist with the costs of expansion. This in turn enables the company to employ or expand its specialist personnel. Nowhere is this truer than in those companies whose individual branches are quite small. A small chain of travel agents, for instance, or of hotels, may for the first time be able to employ specialist sales or marketing staff or recruit its own training staff or financial advisers.

Higher levels of revenue also release more money for the marketing effort – a programme of national advertising in the mass media may become a real possibility for the first time. For example, in the UK it has traditionally been common for the multiple travel agents (such as Thomas Cook or First Choice) to undertake a post-Christmas TV advertising campaign, the success of which has enabled these dominant market leaders to extend their share of the travel market further at the expense of the independents.

In addition to these broad benefits offered by integration generally, there are other advantages specific to horizontal or vertical integration, which we will now examine in turn.

Integration leads to control

Several of the leading operators have, in recent years, sought to own and operate their own hotels in key resorts abroad to ensure both the availability of rooms and some control over their price. Integration here can be achieved either by direct purchase or setting up joint venture companies with partners in the hotel industry or other sectors of the industry. Such integration can offer the added advantage of improved control over the quality of the product. This is frequently difficult to achieve otherwise in the case of some international hotels, and it is no easy matter to ensure that standards are uniform, consistent and of the required quality to suit the market. Although operators do own hotels, this has, up to now, been on a limited scale only, with many preferring to exercise control through a franchising scheme or branding, which allows control of standards while management remains in the hands of the hotel company.

Joint venture

Amadeus and Sabre, two industry giants in the global travel distribution sector, established a joint venture to provide improved payment systems for businesses operating in the tourism industry. Moneydirect, launched in 2007, provides secure, automated payment processing, clearing and reconciliation for travel suppliers such as hotels, tour operators, cruise lines and transport companies.

Whilst the origins of Moneydirect date back to 1991 in Australasia, the global expansion via this joint venture meant that anti-trust approval from the European Commission (EC) was necessary. The business now operates in the USA, UK, Canada, France, Germany and Italy.

Equally, the production sector will attempt to exercise control over the retailing of its products. Airlines, shipping services and hotels are all multimillion pound investments, yet, curiously, in the recent past they had to rely to a considerable extent on a fragmented, independent and frequently inexpert retail sector to sell their products. Travel agents carry no stock and therefore have little brand loyalty to a particular travel company. It was a logical step for principals to try to influence distribution by buying into retail agencies. Many domestic US airlines' shops compete with agents for the sale of flight tickets, although those shops are being cut back as the airlines encourage sales through their websites, or those of online distributors like Expedia and Opodo. BA also sought to enter the retail sector and established 17 retail shops in the UK. Despite efforts to reduce operating costs, however, management forecast long-term losses and announced the closure of all its shops by the end of 2006. The leading UK tour operators have their own retail agency chains and engage in the practice of **directional selling**, in which counter staff are expected to give priority to the sale of the parent company's products. This is discussed in more detail in Chapter 18.

Once again, this forward integration is becoming unnecessary with the growth of the World Wide Web. For *principals*, distribution can be achieved directly to the customer rather than through retailing or wholesaling divisions further down the ladder. The no frills carriers have depended least on the chain of distribution. Thus, easyJet has never used retail agents and Ryanair has now abandoned them. Both depend to such an extent on the Web that they even penalize any direct bookings taken via telephone from their clients with a higher charge.

Within the EU, vertical integration has drawn far less criticism from bodies such as the Competition Commission than has horizontal integration. In the UK, the Monopolies and Mergers Commission (MMC), as it then was, investigated the growing control of travel agency chains by tour operators and ruled that the links between operators and agents must be spelled out clearly at the point of sale (the travel agent). There are, however, some curious anomalies regarding the Commission's ruling, which exempts certain large operators and has failed to rule on sales via the Internet. Tourism organizations seeking to grow their operations may seek to expand across several sectors of the industry, both domestically and overseas, providing that this will not open them up to investigation by the monopolies bodies.

Vertical integration clearly poses a threat to independents in the retail sector. Airlines or tour operators opening their own retail outlets are likely to attract the market away from the independents by means of competitive pricing or other marketing tactics. Many independents have combated this threat by forming consortia, which allows them to negotiate better returns from their principals. This may in time lead to the creation of 'own brand' labels for tour operating (already tested on a limited scale), if this is judged the best means of competing with the multiples.

Conglomerates and international integration

No discussion about the changing structure of ownership within the tourism industry would be complete without an examination of the growing role of the conglomerates. These are organizations whose interests extend across a variety of different industries in order to spread the risks incurred by operating within a specific industry such as tourism. Although tourism has the reputation of being a highly volatile industry, the long-term growth prospects for leisure generally have attracted many businesses from outside the industry itself. Breweries, for example, have expanded into hotels and holiday centres. In Europe, conglomeration is well established in numerous countries. Germany, to take one example, invested heavily in travel and tourism businesses through its department stores and leading banks, although recently these have been divesting their interests as the global recession hit the German economy.

The travel industry is experiencing rapid internationalization in ownership. This is a process that has been hastened within Europe by the harmonization of member countries. Travel businesses have, as a result, been actively expanding their interests in each other's countries. While it is tempting to offer some examples of the current spate in such expansion, the pace of change is now so fast that any examples are likely to date very quickly. Readers are encouraged to keep in touch with the trade press in order to update their knowledge of this process. Suffice it to say that, increasingly, travel companies must look beyond their own national borders to understand the nature of the competition they face.

Summary

Throughout this chapter we have discussed changes to the way the tourism product is distributed to the customer. The discussion relating to both horizontal and vertical integration highlights that control over the chain of distribution is important to the success of many producers, as they seek to reach customers in a profitable manner. The Internet is providing new opportunities for distribution, which is correspondingly impacting on the structure of the industry.

We are also seeing increased liaison between the public and private sectors as both seek to maximize the benefits from their spending in areas such as marketing and promotion. Greater awareness of the impacts of tourism has perhaps also contributed to encouraging cooperation and partnerships which seek to ensure wider benefits and long-term sustainability. Reductions in government grants and funding experienced in many developed tourism destinations have also meant that the public sector is dealing with ever tighter budgets, often leading to restructuring and a more commercially oriented approach to their activities.

Questions and discussion points

1. Why are some tourist attractions owned by the state and funded by government grants?

2. Several professional bodies, such as the Tourism Society, Meeting Professionals International (MPI) and the Chartered Institute of Logistics and Transport (CILT) now offer discounted membership to students studying related subjects. How might a student benefit from joining their professional body? How does the organization benefit from encouraging students to join?

3. Why might different producers, such as attractions and hotels, work together to promote, market and manage their destination?

Tasks

1. Investigate a destination organization of your choice. Write a report which explains the goal of the organization and list the many different activities undertaken by the organization. Identify how the organization funds its activities and operation and discuss the implications of this.

2. Explain the difference between horizontal and vertical integration. Provide examples of both forms of integration. Discuss whether the expansion of the Internet will influence whether these two types of integration will continue to occur.

Bibliography

Competition Commission (2008) *BAA airports market investigation*, Competition Commission News Release 12/08, 22 April, available online at: http://www.competition-commission.org.uk/press_rel/2008/apr/pdf/12-08.pdf (accessed November 2011).

Expedia (2010) *United States Security and Exchange Commission Form 10-K*, available online at: http://www.expediainc.com/secfiling.cfm?filingID=1193125-10-28438, February 11 (accessed November 2011).

Port Arthur Historic Sites (2011) *Media Kit 2011*, available online at: http://www.portarthur.org.au/file.aspx?id=2266? (accessed November 2011).

Slaughter, S. (2011) The annual war between airlines and GDSs: isn't it time it stopped?, *Air and Business Travel News*, 5 May.

Tourism Society (2011) *About the Tourism Society*, available online at: http://www.tourismsociety.org/about (accessed November 2011).

Tourism Whitsundays (2011) *Partnership Prospectus*, available online at: http://www.tourismwhitsundays.com.au/Portals/0/Assets/Documents/Partnership/Partnership%20Prospectus%202011-12.pdf (accessed November 2011).

Websites

Best Western (consortia information): **www.whybestwestern.com**

OECD Tourism Department: **www.oecd.org**

Tourism Society: **www.tourismsociety.org**

UNWTO: **www.unwto.org**

9

Tourist destinations

Contents

Learning outcomes

After studying this chapter, you should be able to:

- understand the complexity of the destination as a tourism product
- recognize the importance of the image and the brand in destination marketing
- distinguish between different categories of destination
- understand the appeal of each form of destination
- explain why destinations are subject to changing fortunes.

A tourism destination is one of the key concepts of institutionalized tourism, but researchers and practitioners still disagree on how it should be defined. When building a destination-wide brand, constructing local geographies, or promoting cooperation among entrepreneurs within a region, we must understand the nature of tourism destinations.

Saraniemi and Kylänen (2011) Problematizing the concept of tourism destination: an analysis of different theoretical approaches, 133

Introduction: what defines a destination?

At the beginning of this book, we briefly outlined what is meant by a tourist destination. This chapter is devoted to expanding on that definition, so that we can learn to understand the appeal that different types of destination have for tourists.

As we start to think about destinations, it is useful to briefly come back to a concept we introduced in Chapter 4, that of the Tourist Area Lifecycle (TALC), which described how destinations rise and fall in popularity over time. This concept recognizes that, along with changes in demand, at each stage of destination development there are changes in the nature and levels of industry involvement (in the supply of attractions and amenities) as well as changes in government investment and support through the introduction of national and regional tourism organizations. Thus supply influences the characteristics of a destination at any point in time.

Describing all the characteristics that go to make up a destination is one of the more difficult tasks in the study of tourism. It would be easy to say that the desire to visit a particular destination is the underlying reason for all tourism, but in some instances this is far from the case. The destination may be only one element in the appeal of the trip – and sometimes a very minor one. When Concorde was flying, many tourists made it their lifetime ambition to travel on the world's only supersonic aircraft. Where it was flying *to* was of only minor interest to those enthusiasts. Equally, impressive cruise liners such as the *Queen Mary 2* may represent the actual destination for devotees of cruising and the ship's ports of call may be of only passing interest (some enthusiasts of cruising do not even disembark at ports of call en route). Anniversaries are often enjoyed on the Orient Express – the nostalgic rail journey offered by this distinguished train being the prime purpose for the trip – and the attraction of the long rail journey across Russia from Moscow to Vladivostok owes little to the brief stops that the train makes during its epic journey. Sometimes the ambition to drive along a historic route, such as the silk route across Asia, or iconic routes like Route 66 across the USA, outweighs the places visited during the drive. Consequently, we should recognize that, very often, the *transport* selected by tourists can be as important as the destination to which they are travelling, making it not merely a means to an end, but an end in itself.

In other examples, a key *tourist attraction* has become the destination. This is true of many theme parks. Orlando in Florida did not exist as a tourist destination a half century ago, before Walt Disney Productions decided to make it the site of its second development, just as the location of Alton Towers in Northamptonshire in the UK had little to interest the visitor before the construction of this major theme park. Certain hotels, such as Raffles in Singapore, have become famous in their own right as destinations, not because of where they are, but *what* they are.

In discussing destinations, we must always bear in mind two important considerations:

- the physical and psychological elements of destinations
- the image and promotion of a destination.

Physical and psychological elements of destinations

The image of a destination relates to a number of physical attributes – attractions and amenities, buildings, landscapes and so on – together with perceptions allied to the destination, which include less tangible attributes, such as the hospitality of the local population, atmosphere generated by being there, sense of awe, alienation, *Gemütlichkeit* or other emotions stimulated by the place. The sense of awe one experiences standing on the rim of the Grand Canyon in Arizona can be contrasted with the sense of foreboding experienced when passing through Glencoe in Scotland, the sombre location of the massacre of the MacDonalds by the Campbells in 1692. Visiting the World War II concentration camp at Auschwitz–Birkenau in Poland, now a major tourist destination, generates feelings of shock and revulsion, but underlines the fact that our choice of destination is not dependent on seeking only pleasure or entertainment. At the other end of the scale, different emotions are engendered in a visit to the formal gardens at the Japanese Royal Palace in Tokyo, the Kirstenbosch Botanic Gardens near Cape Town in South Africa, the picturesque English charm of villages such as Castle Combe in Wiltshire or the flower-bedecked balconies of houses in rural Germany, Austria and Switzerland. All of these destinations could be, and often are, marketed to horticultural enthusiasts and all offer a psychologically satisfying visual appeal to the viewer.

The image and promotion of a destination

Destinations have very different appeals to different markets. Some people love crowds, others love isolation and find crowded beaches unbearable. Holidays in the mountains, for some, will awaken thoughts of majestic landscapes with few visitors apart from the occasional hiker, such as might be found in Tierra del Fuego National Park in Argentina. Others may immediately think of expensive resorts like Gstaad in Switzerland or Courchevel in France, with their busy ski-slopes and lively social life in the bars and restaurants. It is fortunate that the appeals of destinations are so varied, allowing opportunities for tourism to be developed in almost any country and to almost any region, providing that they are aimed at the appropriate markets.

Destinations depend on their **image** for their success in attracting tourists, even if that image is frozen in time and no longer represents a true picture of the place. Most well-known tourist countries and destinations such as cities and beach resorts rely on the stereotypes that have been built up over the years and, as long as they remain positive, promotional bodies will seek to support such images in their advertising. Thus, the prevailing image of London for the foreigner is of guardsmen riding on horseback through the city, past Big Ben and the Houses of Parliament; Paris, on the other hand, remains forever the city of lovers, with couples embracing on the banks of the Seine with the Eiffel Tower or Notre Dame in the background. It matters little that these images are stale icons bearing little resemblance to real life in these modern cities. The power of an image is the branding iron that drives tourism and to jettison it in favour of a more modern, but less graphic, image is a far more difficult – and risky – task for marketing than keeping the original.

EXAMPLE   **Developing the image of South Africa**

Hosting the soccer World Cup in 2010 provided a significant opportunity for the brand development of South Africa. With US$5 billion invested in stadium and infrastructure and a further $100 million spend on a marketing campaign promoting the country across the globe, the economic returns were clearly important. However, of greater long-term significance was the potential to improve the nation brand.

While football dominated TV coverage, diverse tourism attractions were also publicized to a global audience – including the country's unique gastronomy, quality wines, entertainment in theatres and local taverns, and the more traditional attractions such as safaris. This provided interesting opportunities for South Africa Tourism to encourage international markets to consider South Africa as both a leisure and business tourism destination. Post-event research revealed that 'around 89 per cent of tourists said they would consider visiting South Africa again, while 96 per cent said they would recommend the country to friends and relatives'

(Bezuidenhout, 2010). Image enhancement also had an impact on the local population, as hosting this major event brought an increased feel-good factor (Zinn, 2010).

The marketing campaign included extensive use of social media. South Africa Tourism encouraged fans to give a 'Shout Out' on Facebook – where good wishes and congratulatory messages could be uploaded. Tweeting reached a record high of 3283 per second at the launch of the World Cup (normal levels were around 750 per second) with several celebrities posting comments, pictures and videos of their positive experiences of the event and the country. While such endorsements may provide only short-term benefits, these provided landmark opportunities for South Africa Tourism to enhance the destination image.

With tourism contributing 7.7% of GDP in 2010, tourism minister Marthinus van Schalkwyk asserted that the enhanced image developed as a result of hosting the World Cup would undoubtedly help South Africa as it sought to double the number of foreign tourists visiting the country to 15 million a year by 2020 (Roelf, 2011).

Aware of the importance of image in selling destinations, many countries have embarked on a process of **image creation**, with advertisements incorporating quickly communicated slogans and/or readily identifiable logos, often alongside the image of their iconic attraction, as a means of conveying the destination's properties to intending tourists. Slogans are generally emotive as much as informative. Recent examples include 'Malaysia – Truly Asia', 'Egypt – where it all began', New Zealand's '100% Pure' and 'Incredible India'. Others specifically focus on stimulating action – the USA encourages visitors to 'Discover America', Spain went with 'I need Spain' and New Zealand sought to enhance its 100% pure campaign in the UK market with a digital campaign that suggested 'it's about time'. Image creation is important in stimulating appeal for a destination.

EXAMPLE   There's nothing like Australia

Having experienced significant controversy with their earlier marketing campaign 'So where the bloody hell are you?' Tourism Australia later launched a new campaign, which ensured much greater involvement of both the tourism trade and the general public. Backed by research which revealed that Australians are keen to be included in the promotion of their country, the focus was to 'involve Australians because they are the experts on what makes Australia unlike anywhere else. It also harnesses the power of word-of-mouth endorsement' (Tourism Australia, 2010).

The first stage of the campaign was to involve the public in uploading images to a website (nothing likeaustralia.com), with explanations which started with the phrase 'There's nothing like . . .'. These images were then geotagged with their location to build a map of the many experiences available to visitors.

The campaign was launched in April 2010; Australians rose to the challenge and nearly 30 000 images were uploaded to the site in the first month. Tourism Australia used some of the best entries to form the basis of the print and video resources created to support the campaign. It has also been supported with the development of a smartphone application which encourages users to 'explore Australia through the eyes of locals' (Tourism Australia, 2011) and share their favourite images via Facebook and Twitter.

This campaign has thus created a database of unique images which help to show the multifaceted nature of the destination, as well inspiring a sense that the local population are keen to show off their country to visitors.

Destination promotion is of limited benefit, unless it is accompanied by other supporting factors. It is important here to stress the role played by transport companies in this. Budget airlines, for example, have expanded tourism to both existing and newly popular destinations by offering cheap fares and, in many cases, developing new provincial hubs. Many of these are sited in areas of which tourists had only limited knowledge previously. Among destinations to have benefited from the European no frills airlines in recent years are Turkey, Malta and the Baltic states of Estonia and Lithuania.

Categorizing destinations

It is convenient to divide destinations into five distinct groupings:

- The **centred** destination is the most frequent – a traditional form of holiday arrangement in which the tourist travels to the destination, where they expect to spend the majority of their time, with perhaps occasional excursions to visit nearby attractions. The classic seaside holiday, winter sports resort or short city break represent the most common types in this grouping.

- Destinations that form a **base** from where the surrounding region can be explored. Some of the UK's seaside resorts have successfully reformulated their marketing strategy to sell themselves as bases for exploring the nearby countryside. Urban locations have also established themselves as the regional tourism base. For example, the city of Cambridge, in the East Anglian region of the UK, has sought to develop its role as a base for exploring the surrounding areas, rather than attracting more visitors to the city itself.

- **Multicentre** holidays, where two or more destinations are of equal importance in the itinerary. A good example of such a holiday would be that of a tourist with an interest in exploring the new central European countries of the Baltic buying a package comprising stays in the three capitals of Tallinn, Riga and Vilnius.

- **Touring** destinations, which will be part of a linear itinerary, including stops at a number of points. A Caribbean cruise, for instance, will call at several ports en route, while a tour of the American Midwest or Far West or a rail journey across Canada will make stopovers a key element in the itinerary.

- **Transit** destinations, which merely provide an overnight stop en route to the final destination. Such stopovers may or may not be pre-planned, but occur at convenient points, particularly for drivers contemplating long journeys by car. Typical examples are tourists driving by car from the UK, Scandinavia or Northern Germany to a Mediterranean destination who identify useful points at which to stop en route when they become tired. Such a destination may offer touristic opportunities also, but not necessarily – the principal aim is to break the journey. Location – in terms of driving distances from key generating markets – is therefore a key factor in developing stopover traffic, but an equally important consideration is the availability of suitable overnight accommodation.

The categorizations above have segmented destinations by their use as a base or a transit location. It is also possible to categorize destinations by their physical or geographic characteristics. Each type of location, such as coastal, urban, rural, island or spa, will then encourage different forms of tourism to be developed.

Coastal tourism

When we think of coastal destinations, most of us conjure up an image of a typical **seaside resort** – this being the destination with most popular appeal along any coastline. The attractiveness of a seaside resort is often based on a combination of sun, sand and sea

Figure 9.1 Sun loungers, sea and sand, Le Touessrok Hotel, Mauritius
Photo by Claire Humphreys

(termed the 3 S's), which still appeals to the largest segment of the tourist market, either as a form of passive recreation – lying in a deckchair or on the sand and watching the sea (see Figure 9.1) – or as a location for more active pastimes, including water sports and beach games.

This form of tourism remains popular. In 2008, nearly one quarter of domestic holidays in the UK involved going to the beach (see Table 9.1) while in Australia more than a quarter of generation X (born approximately 1964–1977) and Y (born approximately 1978–1994) domestic tourists visit the beach – with levels declining to 19% for the senior market (Tourism Research Australia, 2008). Coastal resorts remain popular for international tourists, though cultural and sporting attractions rather than the beach itself may be part of the draw for these destinations. Spain experienced a 10% decline in the number of foreign visitors in 2009, as sun, sea and sand package holidays lost some of their appeal in favour of music festivals, gastronomy and heritage attractions (Johnson, 2011).

Many seaside resorts in the UK have moved on from their nineteenth-century image and now cater to a variety of different markets seeking very different benefits. The concept

Table 9.1 Type of holiday taken for last UK holiday in 2008 (%)

Beach/resort	23.1
City break	18.8
Lakes and mountains	8.9
Spas/health spas	0.6

Source: Mintel, 2009a

of a seaside resort can now embrace everything from the traditional workers' paradise to the village centred on a harbour catering to the yachting fraternity, or a cultural town with art galleries, museums and concert halls.

In the UK, it is the traditional resort that has suffered the sharpest decline, due to changing patterns in tourist demand. Above all, this is because these destinations have been slowest to invest in new facilities or renovate their heritage buildings. Many one-time popular resorts, such as Clacton, Cleethorpes, Llandudno, Skegness and Southport, have remained to a considerable extent frozen in time, with their sweet shops selling candy floss and rock, their amusement arcades and funfairs, donkey rides and fish and chip shops (see Figure 9.2). The market for these resorts has dwindled as older, loyal, regular visitors have died and their children choose to holiday overseas instead.

A handful of resorts accepted the challenge and invested. Blackpool remains popular simply due to its investment in funfair rides, nightlife amenities and its famous Illuminations – a light display. Modest investments by towns such as Scarborough have enabled the towns to survive, if not prosper, while some have striven to change their image by focusing on a single attraction. Bexhill-on-Sea, for example, benefits from the de la Warr Pavilion – perhaps the greatest example of mid-twentieth-century architecture in the country – that was narrowly saved from destruction and now, restored to its former glory, acts as a focus for contemporary art exhibitions. Brighton, with its pebbled beaches, has built on its proximity to London and its cultural facilities to remain an important short-break destination. It has also developed a major new marina to attract yacht owners, while also expanding other non-leisure industries. Margate, trading on its links with the painter J. M. W. Turner, has constructed a modern art gallery (see the Example) as part of regeneration plans designed to attract a new, more cultured market.

Figure 9.2 Donkey rides available on the Beach at Bridlington, North-East England
Photo by Claire Humphreys

EXAMPLE   Margate, Kent

This Southeast England resort grew in Victorian times and remained popular during the twentieth century, due to its famous Dreamland Amusement Park, first established in 1920, attracting the C2DE markets. These markets dried up with the growth of overseas holidays after World War II, however, and Dreamland closed.

Efforts have been made to revive the resort in this century, with the opening of a new contemporary art gallery which commemorates the importance of this area for the paintings of J. M. W. Turner (1775–1851). The eighteenth-century old town is being restored and streets pedestrianized, in the hope of emulating the success of other resorts like St Ives, Whitstable and Broadstairs, which boast attractive old town centres.

When Dreamland closed, all of the rides, except the listed Scenic Railway rollercoaster, were removed. In 2011, the local council sought a compulsory purchase order on the park, and it has plans to reopen Dreamland as a historic theme park, with vintage cafés and gardens (Medway Messenger, 2011).

While no one initiative can lead to regeneration, the variety of complementary initiatives being undertaken in Margate does give rise to hope that this historic seaside resort may experience a tourist revival.

A few genteel resorts, such as Eastbourne, Worthing and Deal, have largely resigned themselves to the role of retirement resort, while some larger resorts have diversified sufficiently to be no longer entirely dependent on tourism. Bournemouth, for example, while retaining its tourist market through new investment in attractions and the restoration of its Victorian heritage buildings, is also large enough to have attracted industry (particularly banking and financial services) and education (with its language schools and university) and these now boost its economy. The town is also close to the dense population centres of the south east.

EXAMPLE   Bournemouth invested in the surfing market

In an attempt to diversify the tourism markets attracted to the town, Bournemouth council invested £3m in constructing an artificial offshore reef, designed to create great surfing waves.

Sadly this has been plagued by controversy since it opened in November 2009, with early reports suggesting the quality of the waves created was poor, making it almost impossible to ride. In 2011, routine checks highlighted problems with the construction and positioning of the under-water sandbags, leading to the closure of the reef on safety grounds (Daily Telegraph, 2011).

Despite this, £100 million of infrastructure investment, improving accommodation stock, transport and entertainment facilities, has helped to improve the image of the destination, which has been particularly successful in attracting the business tourism sector.

The major beneficiaries of changing tourist tastes have been the myriad small fishing ports and seaside villages in the UK, which have largely retained their character and resisted the temptation to expand due to strict planning controls. The scenic beauty of the many resorts in Devon and Cornwall (and notably those based around an estuary, such as Salcombe or Falmouth), for example, have made them highly desirable for second home owners and the self-catering market. Shops and restaurants have moved upmarket and some resorts in the South West, such as Padstow, have been able to build a successful tourist market based largely on the quality of their seafood restaurants. Where there is a strong

Figure 9.3 The popular tourist resort of St Ives, Cornwall
Photo by Chris Holloway

cultural tradition, such as the colony of artists in St Ives (see Figure 9.3), this has led to a focus on the arts, attracting many galleries, including a notable extension of London's Tate Gallery, which attracts over 200 000 visitors a year – three times the number envisaged when it was constructed. Those with the best marina facilities appeal to the wealthiest members of the yachting fraternity, ensuring that the markets attracted to such destinations remain high-spend. Being essentially rural as well as on the coast, such resorts provide a good base for exploring the surrounding countryside. The extent to which demand will inevitably continue to outstrip supply in destinations like these will ensure their long-term success, providing they can resist the temptation to expand to the point where they are no longer small, quaint resorts.

Many former UK tourist resorts, however, cannot expect to regain their lost markets, given the significant movement of popular seaside tourism, over the past five decades, away from the colder, Northern European beaches towards those of the Mediterranean as prices of flights fell and the tourists could be assured of sunshine and warm water – something that was never guaranteed for beach holidays in Northern Europe.

Similarly, the lower fares have enabled Americans to fly to their warmer beaches in Florida or California or even further afield to Mexico, the Bahamas and the Caribbean, abandoning the traditional northern beaches of resorts such as Atlantic City and Wildwood, New Jersey or the Long Island beaches of New York State.

Atlantic City fought back by renovating its beachfront, introducing a decked promenade, and developing mega-casinos to attract the high-spend gamblers. This has restored the fortunes of the beachfront itself, but done little in terms of creating investment behind the foreshore (see Figure 9.4). Miami has successfully rebuilt its market, however, by investing massively in the restoration of its art deco hotels and apartments along Miami Beach, resulting in a regeneration of tourism that has boosted the town economically.

The USA benefits from the exceptional climate and sandy beaches along many of its coasts and, in consequence, has many long-established resorts. Florida and Hawaii, in particular, are noted internationally for the quality of their seaside resorts, although their best beaches are by no means the best-known ones. Research by Florida University's Laboratory for Coastal Research has regularly reported the best US beaches (based on

Figure 9.4 Beachfront promenade – Atlantic City
Photo by Claire Humphreys

50 criteria). However it should be noted that once a beach has been awarded the coveted number one position it is removed from the rankings. Estimates suggested that a top ranking can bring a 15–20% boost in visitor rankings. The 2011 top five were:

- Siesta Beach in Sarasota, Florida
- Coronado Beach in San Diego, California
- Kahanamoku Beach in Waikiki, Oahu, Hawaii
- Main Beach in East Hampton, New York
- Cape Hatteras in the Outer Banks of North Carolina

Coastlines

Apart from beaches and resorts themselves, coastlines have an obvious attraction for tourists, whether seen from the land – via coastal footpaths, cycleways or roadways (notable examples of the latter include the Pacific Coast Highway in California, Great Ocean Road in Victoria, Australia and the Amalfi Drive on Italy's west coast) – or from the sea (coastal excursions are still popular with tourists, even where no landing is included). England's longest coastal footpath – from Minehead to Poole in the South West – can take up to eight weeks to complete, tempting walkers who may not usually be attracted to the seaside to return time and again in order to undertake the walk in sections. In summer, excursion boats sail from Bristol and the Somerset and Devon coasts, circling, and in some cases landing on, the islands of Steep Holm, Flat Holm and Lundy. More ambitious visits are made by small cruise ships to islands in Arctic waters around Spitzbergen and Iceland, where conditions often do not favour landing, yet the bird and other wildlife along these coasts, coupled with the geological formations of the shoreline, still merit observation from seaborne craft of all sizes. Some islands in the Pacific and Caribbean offer little beyond coral atolls or inhospitable beaches, but, even here, cruise ships have organized calls to allow passengers to bathe, snorkel or simply enjoy the unique experience of being on a 'desert island'.

The new seaside tourism

The fall in long-haul air fares has meant that European sun, sea and sand tourism has now extended to distant destinations such as Phuket and Pattaya Beach in Thailand, as well as medium-haul resorts like Sharm el-Sheikh in Egypt and Monastir in Tunis. Both of the two latter resorts offer the opportunity to combine cultural visits with a traditional beach holiday. The monastery of St Catherine and the landscape around Mount Sinai have become major attractions in Egypt, while the Roman amphitheatre at el Djem and the opportunity to explore the fringes of the Sahara Desert have great appeal to tourists visiting the many resorts of the Tunisian coastline.

EXAMPLE A crisis-hit seaside resort

The sea was free of holidaymakers in the coastal resort of Sharm el-Sheikh in December 2010. Following a series of shark attacks, which mauled several swimmers and killed a German woman, the local authorities closed the beaches and attempted to track down the sharks.

Many reasons for the unusual spate of attacks have been proposed, with some experts blaming tourists for throwing food into the water to lure fish in order to get a better close-up view (Sherwood and Meikle, 2010). The shark attacks led to a short-term ban on snorkelling and diving, both popular activities which draw many tourists to this Egyptian resort. 'Beach tourism is believed to contribute about 66 per cent of Egypt's total income from tourism, which is expected to reach $12.3 billion in 2011' (Egyptian Gazette, 2011).

Whilst debates over the impact of the shark attacks on tourism numbers raged, another event was to hit the town. Political unrest that pushed the long-standing President Mubarak out of power and into house arrest in Sharm el-Sheikh led to a halving in the number of tourists visiting Egypt, as many foreign embassies advised against travel to the country.

In recent years, the Middle East has mounted strong campaigns to attract the North European markets to its seaside resorts, and Arabian Gulf developments such as Hurghada, el Aqaba and the aforementioned Sharm el-Sheikh have been successful in penetrating those markets, largely through the medium of package tours. Since the turn of the century, however, new destinations have risen to prominence within the Arabian Gulf, and particularly the United Arab Emirates (UAE).

Dubai in the UAE has been at the forefront of this development. Recognizing that supplies of oil – its major resource – are finite, the state has determined that its future lies in attracting international tourists, and it is investing massively with this in view. Notably, this has involved the construction of a new shoreline, together with offshore artificial islands, offering opportunities for the sale of exclusive second homes alongside luxury hotel accommodation. Its combination of sun, sea and sand with outstanding shopping opportunities and planned museums and art galleries is already seducing many tourists away from their traditional European holiday resorts, although July and August temperatures of 40 and 50°C in the Gulf may deter visitors in the peak summer periods.

Dubai is building the world's largest airport in anticipation of receiving up to 15 million tourists annually by 2015 – a huge increase on the present figure of 6 million. The new airport is also intended to act as a key hub for long-haul flights between Europe, the Far East and Australasia. To reach these figures, however, Dubai is now seeking to attract lower-income markets, offering opportunities for other Gulf states, such as Abu Dhabi (UAE), Qatar and Oman, to focus on wealthier holidaymakers by offering not only traditional seaside pursuits but also cultural visits to historic sites and adventure holidays using

Figure 9.5 4-wheel drive excursion in the Arabian Desert, Sharjah, UAE
Photo by Chris Holloway

four-wheel drive vehicles in the nearby desert (see Figure 9.5). Such packages are proving attractive to the new adventure-seeking middle-income tourists from Europe.

The future of the seaside

A question mark hangs over the long-term future of seaside resorts, in the face of the growing threat posed by **climate change**. Even in the relatively short term, sea levels are expected to rise 2–3 metres as a result of global warming. This would be enough to destroy popular resorts in countries like the Maldives and many of the low-lying islands and atolls of the Pacific. Research on the rapid escalation in the speed of ice melting in Antarctica is even more worrying, suggesting rises in sea level over the present century exceeding even these figures – enough to destroy virtually all established resorts. Should such a catastrophe occur, holidays to these areas would be the least of our problems, but already such projections are threatening long-term investment in tourist facilities in such locations.

EXAMPLE　A disappearing coastline

The Maldives is portrayed in tourism brochures as a beach paradise – with white sands, palm trees and crystal blue seas. This unspoilt image has helped to make tourism a key industry for the state, accounting for more than a quarter of GDP, and in 2009 it welcomed visitors numbers in excess of 655 000. The market is dominated by Europe but in recent years the numbers arriving from China have increased significantly.

However, a perilous fate awaits these shores. Although there are more than 1000 islands – or atolls – the largest is only about 2 miles long and the highest point on the islands is about 1.5 metres above sea level. Global warming forecasts predict that the sea will rise above this level and these paradise islands will disappear. There are efforts to protect the islands against the impacts of severe climate change, including working towards being carbon neutral, but one interesting initiative is to purchase land in India, Sri Lanka or Australia where the population of 390 000 could be relocated.

Other islands likely to suffer a similar fate, if climate change forecasts are to be believed, include the Seychelles in the Indian Ocean and the Marshall Islands, in the Pacific Ocean.

In the shorter term, consideration must be given to the impact of the sun on our holiday habits and the growing fear of skin cancer as research reveals the damage caused to the skin by more of the sun's rays penetrating a weakened ozone layer. Although many European and American tourists still tend to ignore the warnings being issued by scientists and the medical profession, the escalating figures for skin cancer among residents of the Northern hemisphere must inevitably start to influence demand for traditional seaside holidays. The challenge for the sunshine resorts will be to adjust both their facilities and their marketing to ensure that tourism can continue to survive without depending on the appeal of sun, sea and sand. One alternative is to provide facilities similar to those found at the beach but constructed indoors. The Ocean Dome at Miyazaki in Japan was the world's largest indoor beach; complete with plastic palm trees, artificial breeze, a surf machine and opening roof, it initially proved immensely popular with Japanese visitors as an alternative to the traditional beach holiday. Unfortunately, however, the huge capital investment in this high-tech project proved too great to allow the company to break even and it went out of business in 2001.

The development of the indoor 'tropical' pools at the Center Parcs sites in Northern Europe, while less ambitious in scope, have proved highly profitable. In countries where the appeal of outdoor pools is restricted by poor weather, such domes offer an attractive alternative for swimming and recreation alike.

Artificial beaches

In recent years, Dubai enjoyed great success with the development of artificial islands as tourist attractions. The Palm Jumeirah, a series of man-made islands in the shape of a palm, was to provide tourist accommodation and attractions as well as luxury apartments for local residents. However, the recession in 2008 coincided with reports that the artificial islands were sinking back into the sea. The subsequent investigations and court cases have led to the completion of the project being postponed.

Inspired by the opportunity to develop additional coastline, nearby Qatar has embarked on a programme to build its own artificial island – the Pearl-Qatar at Doha, the capital. Some residents have already moved onto the islands and restaurants and luxury shops are starting to be developed.

There are also plans in Russia for the construction of a 350-hectare artificial island in the shape of Russia. This island – to be known as Federation Island, near Sochi on the Black Sea coast – is due for completion in 2014. (Whether such constructions are prudent in the light of rising sea levels is entirely open to question.)

Urban tourism

Another category of destination is the **town** or **city**. While seaside tourism has struggled to maintain its historic attraction for visitors in many parts of the world, urban tourism has prospered in recent years. This has been fuelled by a growing interest in cultural activities such as visits to theatres, museums and art galleries, as well as in historical – and modern – architecture and the appeal of shopping as a leisure activity.

Most countries have a plentiful stock of towns and cities of both architectural and historic importance. Capital cities have long held a particular draw for tourists (see Table 9.2), and the low fares on no frills airlines have attracted new markets not only to major cities but also to smaller provincial towns throughout Europe, expanding the short city break holiday market of one to three nights. Formerly popular cities such as Amsterdam, London, Rome, Vienna and Paris have been joined by Dublin, Prague, Budapest and

Table 9.2 The top ten city destinations (by arrival numbers)

Rank	City	Tourist arrivals (2009)	Rank in 2008	Rank in 2006
1	London	14 059 000	1	1
2	Bangkok	9 986 000	3	2
3	Singapore	9 683 000	4	4
4	Kuala Lumpur	9 400 000	5	–
5	Antalya	8 868 000	7	–
6	New York City	8 479 000	2	6
7	Dubai	7 783 000	8	7
8	Paris	7 750 000	6	3
9	Istanbul	7 543 000	10	–
10	Hong Kong	7 011 000	9	5

Source: Euromonitor, 2011, 2010, 2007

Bucharest, for example. Barcelona continues to be a leading city for short-break holidays as it has all the benefits required by the short-stay visitor – good shops and restaurants, outstanding architecture (notably by Antoni Gaudí), quality hotels, fine museums and substantial investment in the local infrastructure. It also benefits from competitive prices compared with similar cities elsewhere in Europe. However, Barcelona, along with Rome and Seoul, has now been edged out of the top ten, replaced by two Turkish cities and the capital city of Malaysia. Interestingly, Beijing, host for the summer Olympic Games in 2008, received fewer tourists during its Olympic year (3.36 million) than in 2006 (3.59 million) and since (receiving 3.44 million in 2009).

Low transatlantic prices have made cities such as New York and Boston popular as short-break destinations for Europeans, especially for shopping trips (particularly – as we have seen more recently – when the value of the dollar is low against the pound and euro). Even Reykjavik, capital of Iceland, has become a popular short-break destination for Europeans for the past decade, in spite of its relatively high cost of living. Its attractions include its lively nightlife and the unusualness of its surrounding landscape, as well as the possibility of visiting a hot geyser nearby.

The UK is fortunate in that most incoming visitors have as their motivation the desire to see the country's heritage, much of which is found in the urban areas. Apart from London and its myriad attractions, architecturally, historically and culturally, all the leading destinations in the UK are dependent on their heritage to attract the overseas tourist. The university towns of Oxford and Cambridge, the Shakespeare connection with Stratford-upon-Avon, Windsor with its royal castle, the cities of Bath, York, Edinburgh and Chester, all feature on the standard coach tours sold to the package tour market abroad. Apart from their beauty, all these cities benefit from having a very clear image in the public eye and strong associations, making them easy to market as products composed of a complex of benefits.

While large cities such as Paris, New York and London have the capacity to absorb substantial numbers of tourists, smaller, very popular cities like Oxford and Cambridge in England, Bruges in Belgium and Sirmione on Lake Garda, Italy, suffer from severe congestion in summer, as thousands of foreign tourists visit by coach and car during the peak months, creating major problems of tourist management for the local authority. Marketing of these destinations has to focus on tight planning and control, coupled with efforts to extend the holiday season, so that tourists can be managed more easily. In Oxford and Cambridge, traffic pressures have become so intense that compulsory park and ride has become the norm. Both Sirmione and Bruges have ample parking facilities for cars and coaches on the outskirts of town, but these require visitors by car to either use bus transfers or walk some considerable distance to the heart of the city.

The urgent need for urban renewal in decaying cities coupled with rising interest in industrial heritage has led many governments to invest public funds in restoring previously dilapidated buildings as tourist attractions. Former warehouses, woollen mills in the north of England and other important centres of industry during the eighteenth and nineteenth centuries have been converted into museums or other buildings to attract tourists and the leisure market. In some cases, this has extended to entire areas of a city. An example is the jewellery quarter in Birmingham (now firmly on the tourist trail), where tourism has become an economic saviour, attracting residents back into the city centre. Other notable successes include the cities of Bradford and Glasgow, both of which suffered severe decline in the 1980s. They nevertheless contain some fine examples of Victorian and other architecture, which has become fashionable again after a long period of being out of favour. Bradford benefits from its location close to the Yorkshire Moors, and Haworth, home of the Brontës, now promotes itself as a base from which to tour, coupled with good shopping and entertainment.

As with all destinations, urban centres with an established reputation and image attract tourists more readily than those towns having no such clear image. Cities such as London, Paris, Rome, Venice and Amsterdam all have immediately recognizable, clearly differentiated images (although it is interesting to note that, in the 1990s, the London Tourist Board expressed concern that Japanese tourists were diverting to Paris rather than London, the explanation given being that, among Japanese visitors, female tourists are in the majority and they perceived Paris as being gentler and more feminine than London).

Cityscapes are an important element in the appeal to tourists, not least because they have a clearly defined centre, well-established shopping and entertainment districts, attractive enclaves and parkland. English towns are noted for their many parks and floral displays; Milan for cutting-edge clothes and furnishing shops; Stockholm has its Gamla Stan, or Old Town, for historical appeal as well as an attractive waterfront. Some cities, however, suffer from a lack of such a clearly defined centre to provide the focus for a visit. Los Angeles, Moscow and Tokyo have this disadvantage, which reduces their appeal to the independent traveller. This said, the primary appeal of Los Angeles for the international market is Hollywood, while the Kremlin provides a focal point for visits to Moscow, as does the Royal Palace for Tokyo.

City waterfronts

Stockholm is far from alone in benefiting from its waterfront location. Cities that had formerly been important seaports and had suffered from the decline in shipping in recent years were slow at first to exploit the value of their waterfront sites for leisure purposes. Today, many cities have transformed what was formerly a decaying port into an area of recreation for residents and visitors alike. An outstandingly successful example is the Inner Harbour at Baltimore, USA, which, through a combination of private and public investment, was one of the first to become a magnet for tourists due to the wide variety of attractions it introduced along the restored harbourfront. In Australia, Sydney's Darling Harbour has similarly benefited from renewal as a leisure and marine site, as has the Victoria and Alfred waterfront in Cape Town, South Africa. In the UK, more than a dozen waterfronts have been renovated, while retaining the many attractive warehouses and other features of their former port status. London's former Docklands, the Albert Dock area of Liverpool (the site of the Tate Gallery's first provincial art gallery) and docklands at Southampton, Bristol, Salford, Manchester, Swansea, Cardiff, Portsmouth (see Figure 9.6), Plymouth, Newcastle, Gloucester, Glasgow and Dundee have all been developed to attract tourists as well as commercial activity. Other cities around the world that have landscaped their water frontages to attract tourists are Boston, San Francisco, Fremantle (the port for Perth, Western Australia) and Toronto.

Figure 9.6 The Spinnaker Tower at the newly developed waterfront in Portsmouth, Hampshire

Photo by Chris Holloway

Rivers and canals flowing through city centres can, likewise, add appeal when land-scaped attractively. Major capitals, including Rome, London and Paris, have long traded on the appeal of their rivers, but, more recently, disused waterways have also been resurrected to appeal to tourists. A notable example is Birmingham's network of city centre canals, which have become a focal point for locals and visitors alike, with their outdoor canal-side cafés and pubs and narrowboat tours. Similarly, Bruges in Belgium successfully restored its canal network to make it a major feature of one of Europe's most attractive mediaeval cities.

Cities benefiting from a waterfront, but far from the coast, have the added option of creating an urban beach. This is what a growing number of cities have chosen to do, following the lead of Paris, which was the first inland city to create its own 'Paris Plage' in 2002 (see the example below). The idea was soon copied by other cities, including Berlin's Bundespressestrand, Amsterdam, Rome, Brussels, Vienna and London. Both Birmingham and Bristol have also tried this on a limited scale.

EXAMPLE   **The lure of the beach**

The feel of sand between the toes can be evocative of glorious summer holidays; and it is felt to be so important that the Paris government creates an urban beach annually alongside the Seine river. By closing the main thoroughfares and providing 2000 tonnes of sand, 3000 palm trees, deckchairs and a pool it attracts Parisians and tourists, who enjoy opportunities to relax, play beach volleyball, listen to open-air concerts, even enjoy an ice-cream (see Figure 9.7).

Figure 9.7 Paris Plage
Photo by Claire Humphreys

First introduced in 2002, the Paris Plage covers more than 2 kilometres and operates for a month from mid-July. Although the original intention was to benefit city residents, tourists soon found this to be another key attraction of the city and, each year, the beach regularly attracts 3 million visitors, helping to justify the $2.5 million it costs to run.

European Capitals of Culture

The EU boosts tourism to certain cities each year that can claim a strong cultural basis by awarding them the title **European Capital of Culture**. It has been offered to two cities each year since 2007 – exceptionally, three in 2010 – with each member country selected in turn for the honour. This award ensures that the chosen towns make substantial investments in infrastructure and superstructure in anticipation of the resulting increased tourist flows during the year of the award and for many years following. In 2008, Liverpool in England (along with Stavanger in Norway) was awarded the title. A diversity of interesting events led to success for the city, with visitor numbers increasing from 63 million to 75 million in 2008 (day visitors increasing 20% and staying visitors up by 6%) and the value of tourism to Liverpool's economy rising by 25% (Northwest RDA, 2010). Prior to Liverpool's designation in 2008, the UK last received the award in 1990, when Glasgow gained the title. The city enjoyed a substantial boost in tourism as a result of the designation and it was estimated that the award brought in some £2.5 billion in extra investment, a significant rise in hotel rooms and an increase in the number of tourism-related jobs to some 55 000. Above all, it changed the perception of Glasgow as a dirty, economically depressed city for all time.

The past capitals of culture are shown in Table 9.3 and nominees for 2013 to 2019 are shown in Table 9.4 although, while the countries have been identified, the specific towns or cities have not yet been selected beyond 2015.

Efforts to emulate the concept in the Americas, supported by the Organization of American States, have been frustrated by the financial basis for awards, in which regions are expected to put up funds in advance. UNESCO also sponsors the title of Arab Cultural

Table 9.3 European Capitals of Culture, 1985–2012

Year and city	Year and city
1985 Athens	2000 Avignon, Bergen, Bologna, Brussels, Helsinki, Krakow, Reykjavik, Prague, Santiago de Compostela
1986 Florence	
1987 Amsterdam	2001 Porto and Rotterdam
1988 Berlin	2002 Bruges and Salamanca
1989 Paris	2003 Graz
1990 Glasgow	2004 Genoa and Lille
1991 Dublin	2005 Cork
1992 Madrid	2006 Patras
1993 Antwerp	2007 Luxembourg and Sibiu
1994 Lisbon	2008 Liverpool and Stavanger
1995 Luxembourg	2009 Linz, Austria and Vilnius, Lithuania
1996 Copenhagen	2010 Essen, Germany, Pecs, Hungary and Istanbul, Turkey
1997 Thessaloniki	2011 Turku, Finland and Tallinn, Estonia
1998 Stockholm	2012 Guimarães, Portugal and Maribor, Slovenia
1999 Weimar	

Table 9.4 Nominees for European Capitals of Culture, 2013-2019

Year	Place
2013	Marseille, France and Kosice, Slovakia
2014	Umeå, Sweden and Riga, Latvia
2015	Mons, Belgium and Plzeň, Czech Republic
2016	Spain and Poland
2017	Denmark and Cyprus
2018	Netherlands and Malta
2019	Italy and Bulgaria

Capital, with Doha, Qatar enjoying this status in 2010. Whilst Sirte, Libya was nominated for 2011, the political unrest between the Gaddafi government and rebel forces effectively ruled out any cultural promotion. To date, neither the American nor the Arab Capital of Culture awards appear to develop the publicity or economic benefits so far achieved by the title European Capital of Culture. American and Arab Capitals of Culture are listed in Table 9.5.

Medical tourism

An increasingly important form of tourism, centred almost exclusively on urban areas, is that undertaken for medical reasons. While health tourism has a long history and is linked to spa tourism, about which more will be found towards the end of this chapter, the term **medical tourism** is now being used to refer to tourists who travel to another country specifically to consult specialists or undergo medical treatment. It has been estimated that the medical tourism industry is worth US$80 billion annually and rising at 20–30% annually (Picard, 2010).

Table 9.5 American and Arab Capitals of Culture

Year	American Capitals of Culture	Arab Capitals of Culture
2011	Quito, Equador	Sirte, Libya
2010	Santo Domingo, Dominican Republic	Doha, Qatar
2009	Asunción, Paraguay	Jerusalem, Palestine
2008	Brasilia, Brazil	Damascus, Syria
2007	Cuzco, Peru	Algiers, Algeria
2006	Cordoba, Argentina	Muscat, Oman
2005	Guadalajara, Mexico	Khatoum, Sudan
2004	Santiago, Chile	Sana'a, Yemen
2003	Panama City, Panama and Curitiba, Brazil	Rabat, Morocco
2002	Maceió, Brazil	Amman, Jordan
2001	Iquique, Chile	Kuwait City, Kuwait
2000	Mérida, Mexico	Riyadh, Saudi Arabia
1999	–	Beirut, Lebanon
1998	–	Sharjah, UAE
1997	–	Tunis, Tunisia
1996	–	Cairo, Egypt

British patients have sometimes been referred by the National Health Service for treatment in other EU countries, but others are seeking medical attention privately and often further afield. Private hospitals in Eastern Europe are now openly targeting patients in the UK who could not afford private treatment in their own country, but could be persuaded to pay the lower fees charged abroad. It has to be acknowledged that British patients are being driven not only by cost but also by NHS waiting lists and fear of MRSA, *C. Difficile* and other increasingly common diseases found in hospitals. One survey has suggested that 2.65 million UK residents have travelled – or plan to travel – abroad for medical treatment, with almost half travelling for dental treatments, just under one-third for cosmetic surgery and the remainder travelling for other treatment such as orthopaedic surgery and infertility therapy (Wall, 2010).

Similarly, large numbers of Austrians now travel abroad for treatment, particularly to Sopron in Hungary for dental treatment, and some towns on the Austro-Hungarian border now have economies based largely on dentistry. Many Danes travel to Szczecin in Poland for dental treatment, while the Finns visit Tallinn for eye tests and dental work.

Americans are responsible for some of the fastest growth in medical tourism. From just 150 000 tourists in 2004, numbers grew to three-quarters of a million travelling abroad for treatment in 2007 with a forecast that by 2012 this figure could be as high as 1.6 million (Deloitte, 2009). One interesting area of growth in this field for the USA is that of domestic medical tourism. As healthcare cost can vary widely across states, those who are uninsured, or some companies funding their employee's healthcare, are encouraged to seek out discount treatment in locations with spare capacity.

Good medical treatment delivered promptly, cheaply and efficiently is appealing in cases where lengthy waiting lists for operations exist, such as for hip replacements. Over 50 countries actively promote medical tourism and, whilst accurate figures are difficult to obtain because few countries separate data related to treatment of foreign nationals generally from those who have specifically travelled for medical tourism, one estimate suggested that 19 million medical tourists went abroad for treatment in 2005 (Jeffery, 2006) at a total cost of some £10.5 billion (a figure that some have estimated as having risen five-fold by 2008).

IVF treatment is promoted in medical centres in Kiev, Ukraine, cosmetic surgery in Venezuela, Brazil, Argentina and the UAE, while Budapest in Hungary and Cyprus promote dental treatment for visitors. Thailand, which, like Singapore, has a good record of Western medical training, offers private healthcare to medical tourists in Bangkok, Chiang Mai and Phuket, while South Africa attracts tourists for specialist cosmetic surgery. India has perhaps gone furthest, even taking a stand at the World Travel Market in London to promote its medical tourism. It offers specialist treatment at reasonable prices for dentistry, cosmetic surgery and alternative medicine such as Ayurveda. Organizations are now setting up package tours around such treatment, with accommodation at 4-star hotels included. Some forecasts put the total numbers travelling abroad for medical treatment at over 40 million by 2010.

There is some evidence that the medical traffic is not all one-way. Many wealthy visitors – reports place the number as high as 100 000 annually – are coming to the UK for medical treatment, some of them exploiting inadequate checks on NHS eligibility in order to receive treatment while on holiday in the UK. Exact figures on the numbers involved are hard to verify, but the government has taken steps to plug this loophole.

Rural tourism

The **countryside** offers a very different holiday experience from seaside and urban tourism. The widespread appeal of the countryside is of relatively recent origin, appreciation of nature dating back in the UK only as far as the nineteenth century, and even more recently in the case of other European countries. Initially limited to people in the higher socio-economic groups, led by those in aristocratic circles who enjoyed a 'seat in the country', its extension to the merchant, and later, labouring, classes emerged only as congestion and pollution made life unbearable in the big cities and escape to the countryside a necessity for health and tranquillity. Early appreciation of scenery, however, was somewhat artificial. Travellers to the countryside were accustomed to base their expectations of the landscape on memories of the highly imaginative and frequently hyperbolic paintings by popular artists of the Romantic Movement. In some cases, they even went so far as to observe the scenery by use of a 'Claude' glass – an elegantly framed mirror named after the eminent French landscape painter Claude Lorraine. Observers were encouraged to use these mirrors by standing with their backs to a scene and viewing its framed reflection.

Developing countries, even those with little appeal for the traditional tourist seeking attractive cities or beach resorts, are gaining from the increasing demand by more adventure-minded tourists for holidays 'off the beaten track'. In recent years, travellers have discovered such diverse rural gems as the Cameron Highlands in Malaysia, the northern hills of Thailand around Chiang Mai and the tropical heartland of Costa Rica, as well as unusual and attractive landscapes in more developed countries, such as the Cape York Peninsula in Australia and Canada's North West Territories. The popularity of rural beauty has led to regions such as Tuscany in Italy and the Ardèche in France becoming popular as second home locations for Northern Europeans.

The association of a particular rural area with literary or media connections can provide a powerful draw for tourism and regional tourist authorities have not been slow to take advantage of this. In England's West Country, Doone Country – set around the village of Oare and based on the North Devon setting of R. D. Blackmore's *Lorna Doone* – led the way for many other regions to promote their links with literature. It is possible to visit Catherine Cookson Country (the South Tyneside setting of many of her books) and the Tarka Trail in Devon, mythical home of Tarka the Otter, for example. Celebrities' places of birth or residence often serve to promote the image of an area (see Figure 9.8) and these

Figure 9.8 Beethoven's birthplace, Bonn, Germany

Photo by Chris Holloway

places are frequently available for tourist visits. For example, the home of the children's author Beatrix Potter in Ambleside, Cumbria, is now a National Trust property and has been open to the public for more than 60 years. The nearby village of Hawkshead also has a Beatrix Potter gallery – with information about her later life as well as an exhibition of her paintings – providing further encouragement for tourists to visit this rural area of the Lake District. In some cases, the links with historical or famous figures has led to annual festivals being held based on the celebrity's area of expertise, such as a literature festival. A Dylan Thomas Trail has been created in Wales that emphasizes the use of the Celtic Trail cycle route. Several sites in England have also promoted the association of their district with the mythical King Arthur, most notably the area around Tintagel in Cornwall.

Lakes and mountains

One of the principal draws of rural tourism is lakes and mountains – preferably a combination of the two. Areas offering both have been attracting visitors from the very beginnings of tourism. The Alps and Dolomites in central Europe – stretching through France, Switzerland, Germany and Italy – were catering to British and other holidaymakers as early as the nineteenth century, both for mountaineering and more leisurely pastimes such as walking. The attractiveness of the landscape in each of these countries is certainly heightened by the abundance of nearby lakes.

With a growing focus on activity holidays, mountaineering and high mountain trekking are gaining in popularity and may well help to offset any decline in winter sports resulting from inadequate snowfalls due to global warming. On a more modest scale, England's Lake District, with its combination of mountains and lakes, has special protection as a national park and ranks as one of the most popular tourist destinations in the UK.

The combination attracts distinct markets, with leisure visitors of all ages enjoying the scenery, either passively or on hikes, and younger, more active visitors mountaineering in summer, as well as participating in winter sports at other times, where circumstances

Figure 9.9 Ski Area – Val D'Isère
Photo by Claire Humphreys

allow. Demand for winter sports holidays is now putting huge pressures on the Alps, however, which have a fragile environment, easily damaged by overuse. Global warming is apparently affecting Alpine and other mountainous regions, with the snow line receding further up the mountainsides, leaving resorts at lower altitudes without snow for much of the season. This is causing Alpine regions to reinvest to focus their winter sports at higher altitudes. Snow lifts, gondolas and cable cars are under construction, with France alone investing more than 1 billion euros over a three-year period to retain their winter tourism markets (see Figure 9.9). Resorts at lower levels, however, will have to focus on generating warm weather, and other, activities in lieu of winter sports.

EXAMPLE Skiing in the Caucasus

The ski holiday market is, perhaps self-evidently, intensely seasonal, but is often associated with a high visitor-spend. The opportunity to bring income into mountain regions through this key industry has led the Russian and French presidents to sign an agreement to help develop a ski area in the Russian Caucasus. The area around Mount Elbrus – about 200 miles from the resort city of Sochi, which is set to host the 2014 Olympic Winter Games – already has established ski areas, but the existing development is limited.

The agreement expects to see France provide US$1.2 billion in investment, mostly in ski-lift equipment, whilst the Russian government will invest US$0.6 billion in upgrading local infrastructure.

The project is not without controversy. The initial proposal is to develop five mountain resorts, although environmentalists protest that the masterplan indicates that the development will encroach on strictly protected areas and a UNESCO World Heritage Site. Furthermore, the region has been unstable politically with extreme violence and corruption blighting the area (AFP, 2011).

Whether these ski resorts will attract significant numbers of international visitors remains to be seen. However, this may provide an appeal for the growing Russian ski market, meaning they avoid the need for visas and dealing with language barriers that travel to Western European resorts brings. Only time will tell as to whether this area can become a successful international ski venue.

The high cost of European ski resorts is making long-haul ski holidays more popular with Europeans. US resorts such as Aspen and Vail have long been popular, but other less familiar and more reasonably priced resorts such as Steamboat Springs in Colorado have been discovered by the European markets. Packages from the UK have also been launched to still more distant resorts such as Rusutsu and Niseko on Hokkaido Island, Japan, where snow is plentiful and skiing affordable. These two resorts are proving popular with the nearer markets of Canada and Australia, too.

The challenge of climbing major peaks in mountain ranges has moved on from the Alps to more adventurous locations like the Rockies, Andes and Himalayas. For those who do not want to climb, trekking to base camps along trails below the peaks has proved a challenge that is sought after by fit tourists of all ages. Specialist tour companies now organize both climbing and trekking expeditions even to Everest, forcing the Nepalese government to impose high charges for climbing rights in an effort to control numbers. Even though packages can cost in excess of £20 000, this seems to have little effect on stemming demand. For the less adventurous, simple rambling holidays are enjoyed by countless independent travellers to beauty spots all over the world and are also packaged for the inclusive tourist.

The scenic countryside

Although the climate in the UK and Ireland has proved a deterrent to those seeking to enjoy seaside holidays, it accounts for much of the demand for rural tourism. A temperate climate with frequent precipitation provides us with the richness of green fields and abundant woodlands that, coupled with rolling hills and stretches of water, make up the idyll that is the quintessential rural scenery of the British Isles. In spite of its small land mass, the countryside is incredibly diverse, from the meadows and tightly hedged fields in the south and west of England to the drystone walls and bleak moors of the north, from the flatlands and waterways of East Anglia and Lincolnshire to the lakes and mountains of Cumbria, from the wild beauty of the Welsh mountains and the Highlands and Islands of Scotland to the gentle Irish landscape surrounding the lakes of Killarney and the barren historic coastline of the adjacent Dingle Peninsula.

As modern living forces more and more of us to live in built-up areas, so the attraction of the countryside grows, many of us taking a day trip on the weekend or spending longer touring or perhaps holidaying on a farm. Rural tourism attracts international tourists, too, with a growing number of Continental visitors coming to tour the UK by car. In turn, many Britons take their cars to France or Germany to take touring holidays. The attraction of contrasts is important here: the Dutch, Danes and Swedes, who have flat scenery and waterways, find the undulating hills and mountains of their European neighbours very appealing.

To protect the vulnerable countryside from development and cater for the demand for rural recreation, the UK has created a network of national parks in England and Wales (as discussed in Chapter 7). Following the passing of the National Parks and Access to the Countryside Act (1949), the Peak District National Park was the first to be created, in 1952, soon followed by nine others. The Norfolk and Suffolk Broads were given similar protected status in 1988 and the New Forest in 2006. There are currently 15 areas (including three in Wales and two in Scotland) with national park status or equivalent, the latest to join being the South Downs National Park in Sussex, which already receives more than 39 million visitors a year. The Cairngorms National Park became the largest in the UK when it was designated in 2003, totalling 1466 square miles, although the exclusion of the highland area of Perthshire adjoining the site was controversial.

Trail tourism

Hiking or rambling has become a popular pastime, and the UK is fortunate to possess many country footpaths with public rights of way that the Ramblers' Association is anxious to protect as pressures on the countryside grow. In the UK, the Countryside and Rights of Way Act (2000), commonly known as the Right to Roam Act, opened up large areas of the country, giving ramblers the statutory right to ramble on 'access land' in England and Wales in 2005, extended in 2006 to beaches and coastlines. Natural England, the new national countryside agency, intends to open 2000 miles of coastline to walkers over time. The Land Reform (Scotland) Act 2003 offers similar rights in the North. The National Parks and Access to the Countryside Act also created a network of long-distance footpaths that are enjoying growing popularity with hikers (see the Example).

EXAMPLE **National trails**

The first national trail to be opened was the Pennine Way, in 1965. There are now 15 trails in England and Wales (see Figure 9.10).

- Pennine Way (268 miles)
- Cleveland Way (110 miles)
- Cotswold Way (102 miles)
- Glyndŵr's Way (135 miles)
- Hadrians Wall Path (84 miles)
- North Downs Way (153 miles)
- Offa's Dyke Path (177 miles)
- Peddars Way and Norfolk Coastal Path (93 miles)
- Pembrokeshire Coastal Path (186 miles)
- The Ridgeway (87 miles)
- South Downs Way (100 miles)
- South West Coastal Path (630 miles)
- Thames Path (184 miles)
- Yorkshire Wolds Way (79 miles)
- Pennine Bridleway (130 miles) – still under development

By far the longest, and perhaps among the most popular, is the South West Coast Path, which extends between the seaside resort of Minehead in Somerset and Poole Harbour in Dorset. It is estimated to take a 56 day walk to complete. In 2010, a European grant of £2.1 million was provided to focus on improving the visitor experience – to increase the estimated £222 million the trail already brings to the local economy.

An ambitious plan to develop a trail to embrace six countries in Europe was completed in 2007. The North Sea Trail covers around 3000 miles, running from the north of Scotland, through to Scarborough in England, then extending across to the Continent via the Netherlands, Germany, Denmark and Sweden towards the Arctic regions of Norway. The goal is to extend the trail to 7000 miles of coastal path, drawing on the shared history and culture of the communities that line the North Sea (Rowe, 2011). It is planned to develop cultural and trading links between the regions as well as to improve the economies of the areas adjacent to the trail. Tourism industries are being encouraged to provide supporting facilities and attractions which will help to enhance the experience of the walkers.

Trails are also popular in the USA, where wilderness areas give maximum scope for challenging, long-distance footpaths, as well as a plethora of shorter trails in urban areas.

Cycling, too, has experienced a regeneration of interest, as we will see in Chapter 15. This is a sport that is largely dependent on rural scenery (preferably flat land, although more active cyclists will also opt for hill touring or mountain bike holidays). Both independent and package tour cyclists are attracted to such holidays and operators offer inclusive tours by bike to a growing number of countries. Denmark and the Netherlands, in particular, offer ideal countryside for cycling, Denmark having woodland trails for cyclists that run alongside certain stretches of coastline, offering attractive glimpses of open sea through the trees. Most of these forms of tourism are also encouraged as examples of environmentally friendly tourism.

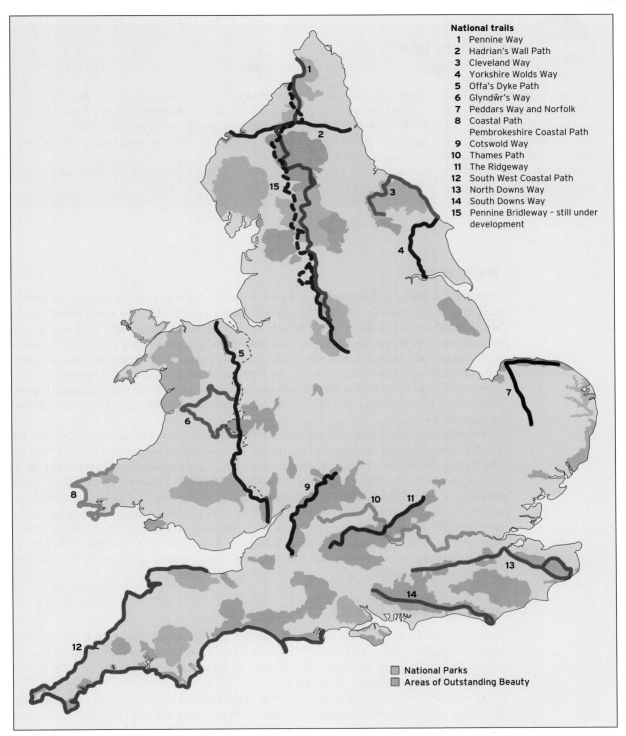

National trails
1. Pennine Way
2. Hadrian's Wall Path
3. Cleveland Way
4. Yorkshire Wolds Way
5. Offa's Dyke Path
6. Glyndŵr's Way
7. Peddars Way and Norfolk Coastal Path Pembrokeshire Coastal Path
9. Cotswold Way
10. Thames Path
11. The Ridgeway
12. South West Coastal Path
13. North Downs Way
14. South Downs Way
15. Pennine Bridleway – still under development

National Parks
Areas of Outstanding Beauty

Figure 9.10 National trails of England and Wales

EXAMPLE Trails in the USA

The USA is best known for its wilderness trails, often taking weeks to complete, such as the Appalachian Trail. The variety of such trails available can be exemplified by Maine, which, in addition to many rural trails (and the completion point of the Appalachian Trail), also offers a Garden and Landscape Trail, visiting more than 50 gardens and arboreta, a Maritime and Heritage Trail, visiting 30 different sites, and a Maine Art Museum Trail, taking in seven different museums.

In 2000, a new 4900-mile trail was opened between Delaware on the East Coast and Point Reyes in California, taking in a total of 13 states and 14 national parks.

Waterscapes

Demand for leisure and recreation using boats has always been popular among the British, and the rural waterways of the UK provide ideal opportunities for water-based tourist activities. The Norfolk and Suffolk Broads are a paradise for both yacht and motor boat enthusiasts. The Netherlands, France and Ireland are just three other European countries with canals and waterways and they attract growing numbers of tourists seeking the pleasure of 'messing about in boats', while the countless lakes of Finland and Sweden are also growing in popularity during the short Nordic summer, particularly with domestic tourists and second home owners. The appeal of water-dependent holidays will be fully explored in Chapter 14.

Sites that include major waterfalls are attractive to international tourists. Those that are readily accessible, such as Niagara Falls on the Canadian/USA border and Victoria Falls on the Zambia/Zimbabwe border, enjoy considerable popularity and have been built up as key destinations by their countries' tourism authorities. Zambian guides have more recently been escorting intrepid adventure tourists to the Devil's Pool at Victoria Falls, in which, at low water, it is possible (if slightly risky) to bathe on the very edge of the 360-foot drop – an experience promoted as 'swimming on the edge of the world'. More inaccessible falls – including the world's highest, Angel Falls in Venezuela – do not yet attract the numbers of tourists that could be anticipated at such unique scenic attractions if adequate transport and other infrastructure were in place.

Woodlands and forests

Areas of woodland and dense foliage provide yet another appeal for tourism. In the USA, the New England states of Vermont, New Hampshire and Maine and the Canadian eastern provinces attract large numbers of domestic and international tourists to witness the famous 'fall foliage' colours in the autumn.

More exotic foliage is available to tourists in the form of jungle and, in South America, the Amazon has become a popular supplementary tour for those travelling to Ecuador and Peru. Pristine jungle still exists in West Africa, which to date has been little exploited. Although small group tours are organized to see the gorillas in Rwanda and the Congo, tourism is limited by political instability in these areas of the world. Smaller but more accessible jungles still exist in developed countries, notably El Yunque Rainforest in Puerto Rico and rainforest in the Cape York area of Northern Queensland, Australia. Countries such as Borneo and Papua New Guinea also offer great potential for exploration of dense tropical forest, if political and potential health problems can be overcome.

EXAMPLE Walking the rainforest

The Amazon rainforest has a great appeal for some adventurous tourists and in recent years facilities have been developed to provide new ways of experiencing the forest. In Peru, the Inkaterra Reserva Amazonica has constructed a walkway, 30 metres above ground (see Figure 9.11), which allows the visitor to walk among the rainforest canopy – providing greater opportunity to have a close-up view of birds, monkeys and the other flora and fauna that make the rainforest unique.

Figure 9.11 Inkaterra Rainforest Walk
Photo by Claire Humphreys

In the UK, there are over 50 historic forests, as well as many further areas of woodland that attract day trippers or walking tourists. Burnham Beeches, near London, is noted for the superb foliage of its beech trees, while forests such as the New Forest (a royal forest and also a national park with a memorial commemorating the spot where King William Rufus met his death in a hunting accident) and Sherwood Forest (associated with Robin Hood) have close links with history, myth and literature.

Apart from its national parks, the UK has also introduced the concept of national forest parks – the Royal Forest of Dean becoming England's first national forest park in 1938. In the 1990s, the government announced the formation of a new National Forest, covering some 200 square miles, in the English Midlands. Some limited protection, at least in theory, is also afforded by designating sites as Areas of Outstanding Natural Beauty (AONB) or Sites of Special Scientific Interest (SSSI). There are 48 AONBs in England, Wales and Northern Ireland, and the North Pennines (covering 2000 square kilometres), in recognition of its world-class geological heritage, became the first European Geopark in 2003. This designation by UNESCO is expected to lead to greater interest in nature-based tourism and better protection for the environment. Scotland has another 40 sites paralleling the AONBs that are known as Natural Scenic Areas.

Agrotourism

Rural tourism, as we have seen, has long been popular with independent travellers and its importance to the economy of the countryside has been widely recognized in recent years. The concept of agrotourism (or agritourism) was developed in Italy and, from there, spread rapidly throughout the Mediterranean and beyond. Its aim is to develop sustainable tourism in agricultural areas of the countryside, and it has become an important feature of rural tourism planning following the success of the development of gîte holidays in France. French government grants were awarded in the post-war years to help convert decaying farm buildings into rural cottages for tourist accommodation, and the gîte holiday became popular, particularly with independent British tourists. The Portuguese quintas, or rural estates, also attracted a strong following among tourists eager to experience something a little different from the standard forms of holiday accommodation.

EXAMPLE Agritourism or agrotourism?

The terminology around this sector is yet to be firmly defined. Terms such as agritourism and agrotourism are often used interchangeably. Other terms, such as rural tourism and farm tourism, are also used to often denote similar activities. We can look at the some of the definitions brought together by Phillip *et al.* (2010) to recognize the overlap:

● *agritourism* – 'rural enterprises which incorporate both a working farm environment and a commercial tourism component'
● *agrotourism* – 'tourist activities of small-scale, family or co-operative in origin, being developed in rural areas by people employed in agriculture'
● *farm tourism* – 'rural tourism conducted on working farms where the working environment forms part of the product from the perspective of the consumer'.

What does seem to be clear is whether you consider the term 'agritourism', 'agrotourism' or 'farm tourism', all appear to be a subset of the wider rural tourism industry.

There is now a programme of strong financial support from the EU, with grants that are allowing rural tourism provision to become increasingly luxurious. Recent developments also take account of the interest in adventure sports, many of which are best enjoyed in rural communities, and outdoor sports such as ballooning, horse riding and mountain biking are also now catered for.

Spain, Portugal, Cyprus, Greece and Italy have all invested heavily in agrotourism. Notable developments include those in the Epirus province in north-western Greece and at Sierra Aracena, a province of Seville, in Spain.

EXAMPLE Agritourism in California

A recent survey of farmers in California highlighted the value of attracting tourism. In 2007 it was conservatively estimated by the US Department for Agriculture that California farms earned $35 million from their touristic activities. A recent survey suggested that just under a third of farms offering agritourism opportunities earned $50 000+ from these activities in 2008.

Agritourism is seen as an opportunity to diversify business operations and boost profit, and, given that many small farms are often family-run businesses, it is also seen as an opportunity to provide employment for family members (Rilla *et al.*, 2011). Research has also highlighted other motivations, such as wanting to educate visitors and the opportunity to interact with the general public as well as the local community.

The activities available to tourists are varied, including corn mazes, pumpkin patches, sales of farm process, 'pick-your-own' events, cookery classes, farm tours, weddings, conferences and festivals.

One aspect which has inhibited development of agritourism in California has been existing regulation which restricted agricultural land from being used for other commercial activities. However, improved guidance has allowed agritourism to be a recognized secondary activity for farms, making it easier to obtain the necessary permits.

The UK has also actively promoted its farming and rural holidays, which have become increasingly important to farmers as a source of revenue due to traditional revenues drying up. Tourist boards and local authorities have helped the private sector to develop new ideas in rural tourism. One example is that of the West Midlands region, which piloted short breaks involving culinary trails – a cider trail in Herefordshire and a pork pie trail at Melton Mowbray, famous for its pies – designed to link farmers, food producers and the tourism industry under the banner 'farms, food and peaceful surroundings'. The Department for Environment, Food and Rural Affairs (DEFRA) reports that around half of the UK's farmers – mainly those in the South of England – have initiated some form of tourism enterprise, bringing in extra income averaging £5000 per annum. Activities range from B&Bs to holiday cottages and equestrian centres.

The UK government recognizes that rural tourism, which is already worth £7.3 billion, has major opportunities for growth, both in areas directly and indirectly linked to tourism (Penrose, 2011). The crafts industry is a notable example of this, with potters, glassmakers, woodworkers, basketweavers and countless other craftspeople opening up outlets in the country to make and sell their wares. The Countryside Agency reported in 2004 that some 300 000 people in the UK now earned their living from rural crafts, earning in excess of £1 billion, and the agency anticipated that crafts were likely to eclipse farming within 15 years.

Finally, mention should be made of summer camps for children – long popular in North America and likely to be adopted in the UK on a larger scale in the future. Over 6 million children attend summer camps each year in the USA, bringing prosperity to the areas in which they are sited (notably New England), and UK authorities have reckoned that up to 600 000 children would be attracted to similar facilities in the UK. These would not necessarily have to be sited within areas of highest tourist appeal, helping to spread the benefits of rural tourism and avoiding congestion at popular destinations.

 EXAMPLE | **Summer camps in the UK**

Summer camps originated in the USA but are now prevalent across Europe and are, in some cases, subsidised by local or national government. These camps are often themed, many focusing on adventure and sporting activities.

Having been operating in UK for over 50 years, PGL is perhaps one of the best known providers of summer camps – so much so that their company name was rumoured to mean 'Parents Get Lost'*. They operate camps across the UK, France and Spain for children aged between 7 and 17. As well as summer camps for children they now offer family activity holidays and schools outdoor education courses.

A major competitor for PGL is Camp Beaumont. Established in 1980, they offer residential camps across the UK (and in the French Alps) catering for 8000 children annually. They provide both multi-activity and specialist themed camps, offering children opportunities to experience activities such as surfing, scuba-diving, horse-riding, tennis and even cheerleading. They also provide less active camps encouraging children to set up a radio station, or learn the arts of cookery, stagecraft or even being a spy.

Although most residential camps last a week, there is also growing provision for day-camps to bring excitement to the long summer holiday. Key UK providers include Super Camps (67 venues), King's Camps (40 venues) and Barracudas (24 venues).

The cost of participating in residential and day camps can be high, but there is research evidence showing that attendance at camps does help to boost confidence in children, and participation in extra-curricular activities can enhance academic performance (Irish Independent, 2011).

* PGL is actually the initials of the company founder - Peter Gordon Lawrence.

Wilderness areas

As open countryside becomes rarer in the developed countries, measures are introduced to protect what remains, especially where this has been largely untouched until recent years. We have seen how the UK established its national parks, but this country was merely following the lead set by the USA (see Figure 9.12), which designated the world's first national park at Yellowstone in 1872. This huge park, containing the famed Old Faithful geyser, covers an area of some 2.25 million acres on the borders between Wyoming, Montana and Idaho.

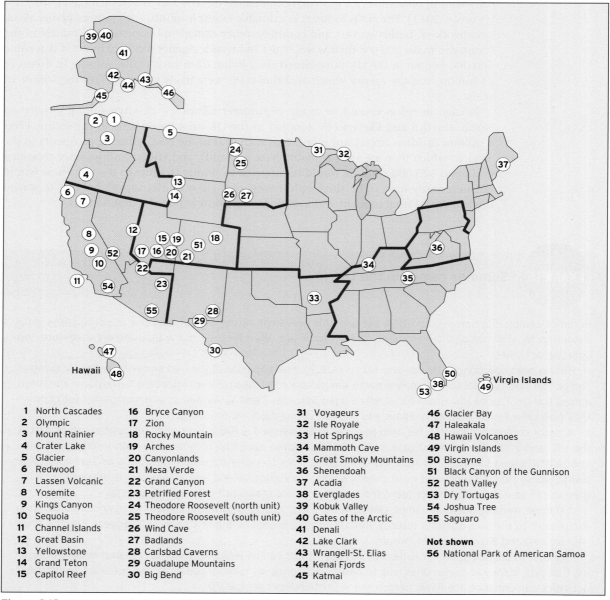

1	North Cascades	16	Bryce Canyon	31	Voyageurs	46	Glacier Bay
2	Olympic	17	Zion	32	Isle Royale	47	Haleakala
3	Mount Rainier	18	Rocky Mountain	33	Hot Springs	48	Hawaii Volcanoes
4	Crater Lake	19	Arches	34	Mammoth Cave	49	Virgin Islands
5	Glacier	20	Canyonlands	35	Great Smoky Mountains	50	Biscayne
6	Redwood	21	Mesa Verde	36	Shenendoah	51	Black Canyon of the Gunnison
7	Lassen Volcanic	22	Grand Canyon	37	Acadia	52	Death Valley
8	Yosemite	23	Petrified Forest	38	Everglades	53	Dry Tortugas
9	Kings Canyon	24	Theodore Roosevelt (north unit)	39	Kobuk Valley	54	Joshua Tree
10	Sequoia	25	Theodore Roosevelt (south unit)	40	Gates of the Arctic	55	Saguaro
11	Channel Islands	26	Wind Cave	41	Denali		
12	Great Basin	27	Badlands	42	Lake Clark	**Not shown**	
13	Yellowstone	28	Carlsbad Caverns	43	Wrangell-St. Elias	56	National Park of American Samoa
14	Grand Teton	29	Guadalupe Mountains	44	Kenai Fjords		
15	Capitol Reef	30	Big Bend	45	Katmai		

Figure 9.12 National Parks in the USA and territories

Since then, numerous national parks have been created in the USA and elsewhere throughout the world. The largest is North East Greenland National Park, covering an area of 373 300 square miles, but new parks are still being developed – for example, the formation of 13 new parks, covering 11 294 square miles, created out of virgin forest in Gabon, which is described in Chapter 7. This country currently has only a very small tourism industry, but hopes to attract a larger flow of tourists to replace the logging industry, which, in time, would threaten the destruction of the forest – the country's prime resource. Even these parks, representing 11% of the country, are tiny when compared to the total protected territory in Africa, amounting to some 850 000 square miles. The future may lie in better cooperation between countries with contiguous borders, to enable still larger parks to be created.

Many wilderness areas contain spectacular scenery, drawing huge tourist crowds in their peak seasons who have to be monitored and managed. Examples include the Grand Canyon, Bryce and Zion Canyons and Monument Valley, where the appeal of solitude and communing with nature – the original concept of the USA's national parks – is soon lost in midsummer due to the sheer numbers of visitors.

Another way to designate land masses is the safari park, most commonly found in South and East Africa. The Sabi Sabi Game Reserve in South Africa was the world's first designated wildlife park, but, as other African nations started to become aware of the threat to their wildlife resources and the appeal wild animals hold for tourists, the number of parks quickly expanded and rangers were introduced to reduce poaching.

Island tourism

One form of destination lies somewhere between the rural and coastal in terms of its attractiveness and, because of its growing appeal, deserves a section of its own here.

Initially, offshore islands, easily accessible by boat or aircraft from the mainland, proved a draw. Helgoland, north of Germany, for example, was a popular destination for German tourists between the two World Wars (before it was saturation bombed by the Allies in World War II; it is now undergoing redevelopment to encourage the return of domestic and foreign tourists) and islands such as the Danish Bornholm and the Swedish Gotland attracted first the domestic tourist and then, more recently, international cruise passengers sailing around the Baltic.

In the Atlantic, the Canaries and Madeira have, of course, attracted tourists for many years, but, more recently, operators have developed tours to more remote destinations such as the Azores and Cape Verde Islands. Often, their appeal is due to their isolation. They are predominantly rural in character and planning controls are often rigidly exercised to ensure that they remain unspoiled.

More recently, relatively inaccessible islands have become the challenge – especially those without air connections – the most isolated being sought out by specialist travellers. Examples include Pitcairn, St Helena, Tristan da Cunha, Easter Island and the Marquesas.

Lesser-known but less remote islands are also growing in appeal. Australia is a base for exploring many island paradises and they are now being actively promoted, to a greater or lesser extent, by the tourism authorities. Islands with which we are likely to become more familiar include Norfolk Island, Whitsunday Island, King Island, Flinders Island, Three Hummock Island and Cato Island. Still less exploited, the formerly off-limits Lakshadweep Islands have recently received permits from the Indian government for visits by cruise ships from Goa and are likely to be popular with those who have 'been everywhere and seen everything'.

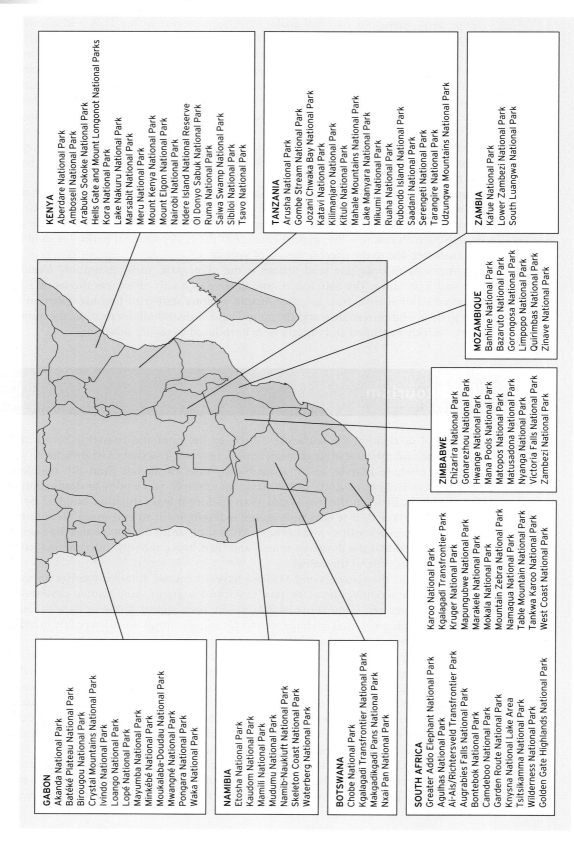

KENYA
Aberdare National Park
Amboseli National Park
Arabuko Sokoke National Park
Hells Gate and Mount Longonot National Parks
Kora National Park
Lake Nakuru National Park
Marsabit National Park
Meru National Park
Mount Kenya National Park
Mount Elgon National Park
Nairobi National Park
Ndere Island National Reserve
Ol Donyo Sabuk National Park
Ruma National Park
Saiwa Swamp National Park
Sibiloi National Park
Tsavo National Park

TANZANIA
Arusha National Park
Gombe Stream National Park
Jozani Chwaka Bay National Park
Katavi National Park
Kilimanjaro National Park
Kitulo National Park
Mahale Mountains National Park
Lake Manyara National Park
Mikumi National Park
Ruaha National Park
Rubondo Island National Park
Saadani National Park
Serengeti National Park
Tarangire National Park
Udzungwa Mountains National Park

ZAMBIA
Kafue National Park
Lower Zambezi National Park
South Luangwa National Park

MOZAMBIQUE
Banhine National Park
Bazaruto National Park
Gorongosa National Park
Limpopo National Park
Quirimbas National Park
Zinave National Park

ZIMBABWE
Chizarira National Park
Gonarezhou National Park
Hwange National Park
Mana Pools National Park
Matopos National Park
Matusadona National Park
Nyanga National Park
Victoria Falls National Park
Zambezi National Park

GABON
Akanda National Park
Batéké Plateau National Park
Birougou National Park
Crystal Mountains National Park
Ivindo National Park
Loango National Park
Lopé National Park
Mayumba National Park
Minkébé National Park
Moukalaba-Doudou National Park
Mwangné National Park
Pongara National Park
Waka National Park

NAMIBIA
Etosha National Park
Kaudom National Park
Mamili National Park
Mudumu National Park
Namib-Naukluft National Park
Skeleton Coast National Park
Waterberg National Park

BOTSWANA
Chobe National Park
Kgalagadi Transfrontier National Park
Makgadikgadi Pans National Park
Nxai Pan National Park

SOUTH AFRICA
Greater Addo Elephant National Park
Agulhas National Park
Ai-Ais/Richtersveld Transfrontier Park
Augrabies Falls National Park
Bontebok National Park
Camdeboo National Park
Garden Route National Park
Knysna National Lake Area
Tsitsikamma National Park
Wilderness National Park
Golden Gate Highlands National Park
Karoo National Park
Kgalagadi Transfrontier Park
Kruger National Park
Mapungubwe National Park
Marakele National Park
Mokala National Park
Mountain Zebra National Park
Namaqua National Park
Table Mountain National Park
Tankwa Karoo National Park
West Coast National Park

Figure 9.13 Major wildlife parks in South and East Africa

EXAMPLE Developing island tourism in the Mediterranean

The desire of many well-travelled tourists to seek out remote and less visited destinations has led to a rise in the appeal of islands. Many of them are underdeveloped, but can be located quite close to heavily populated regions. The Mediterranean offers one example of such islands.

While the French islands referred to below are well known, at least to domestic tourists, there are many other islands in this part of the world that are little visited, either because they have been seen as having little to attract tourists or access has been restricted by the authorities in order to protect the environment.

The Tuscan Archipelago, off the coast of Italy, is an example of the latter. The seven islands that make up the Archipelago are managed by the Tuscan Archipelago Parks Commission. Several of the islands are uninhabited and include a state-protected nature reserve and bird sanctuary. The islands have been off limits to all apart from researchers, but the Commission has now agreed to permit up to 1000 tourists each year to join guided visits to three of the islands: Pianosa, Giannutri and Montecristo. It is the last of these that is expected to attract the largest number of curious tourists, due to the famous book by Alexandre Dumas, *The Count of Monte Cristo*. Such an interest alone will not be enough to gain entry, however. Charges are set at €50 a head and, as tourists planning a visit are required to undertake an environmental-protection training session, few are choosing to make the effort to obtain the necessary permits (Hooper, 2010).

Although there are many areas with extensively developed islands in the Mediterranean which attract large numbers of international tourists, there are some which have enjoyed long-term popularity with domestic tourists, while others are relatively untouched. France, while boasting well-established beach resorts along its coasts, has also been able to build successfully on the appeal of its many offshore islands and, by carefully controlling development (in one case, by the creation of a national park), has enabled them to retain their natural landscape and seascape charm. On the west coast, the Île de Ré, Île d'Yeu and Belle-Île (near Quiberon) attract wealthy French visitors, as do the French islands off the Mediterranean coast, such as those near Hyères, the Île de Porquerolles, Île de Port-Cros and Île du Levant. By ensuring that supply never meets demand, these islands can select their markets on the basis of price alone. Other islands in the Mediterranean, such as the Italian islands of Ischia and Capri, have long drawn tourists in their thousands, but others, far less well known, have tourism potential for more environmentally sensitive visitors.

Spa tourism

One important element of health tourism is treatment at spas. The term 'spa' is said to have originated from the town of that name in Belgium, although some claim that 'Sanitas Per Aqua' – health through water – is the true derivation of the term, which has been applied equally to resorts that provide healthy air (often mountain or seaside resorts) and others offering so-called 'healing' waters.

Although the original spa in Belgium and others like it at Vichy and Aix-les-Bains in France or Wildbad and Baden Baden in Germany have developed into urban areas, often becoming popular destinations in their own right (Bath, Cheltenham, Harrogate, Scarborough and Buxton being good examples in the UK), most spas are still small enough to be considered rural destinations. They form an important element in international

Figure 9.14 Aquadome Hotel and Spa, Längenfeld, Austrian Tyrol
Photo by Chris Holloway

tourism – one too readily overlooked by students of tourism in the UK, a country where spas have fallen out of favour to some extent.

Back in the seventeenth century, Britain itself could boast more than 250 active spas. Some were surprisingly urban. Streatham Vale, for example, now a London suburb, was popular for its natural springs as early as 1659. By the twentieth century, though, their appeal had declined to a point where the final ten spa facilities, then under the control of hospitals, were taken over on the formation of the National Health Service in 1948, but had their financial support withdrawn in 1976. The last publicly funded spa, Bath, closed in 1978. Following massive investment and prolonged delays, however, it was re-opened in 2007 and has enjoyed considerable commercial success. Droitwich Spa has also lingered on, providing medical treatment in a private hospital with a small indoor brine bath.

On the Continent, though, spa tourism (and its study as a subject in tourism courses) remains popular, with an estimated 1200 active spas, and the industry makes a valuable economic contribution to the GDP of several countries (see Figure 9.14). In Germany, Hungary and the Czech and Slovak Republics, thermal treatment – in mud or mineral water baths – still plays an important role in healthcare. Italy's spas are also significant, with a large concentration around the Euganean Hills, south of Padua, notably at Albano Terme and Battaglia Terme, with some 200 hotels in the area being dedicated to the accommodation of spa visitors. North of Vicenza in the Dolomites, the spa town of Recoaro Terme has been noted since the eighteenth century for its mountain spring waters.

Asia is currently one of the most popular regions for spa tourism, with Thailand reported to have received 4 million international visitors arriving for spa holidays in 2009, and China and Indonesia, respectively, receiving 3.3 million and 2.5 million spa holidaymakers (Chitakasem, 2011),

Typical treatments at all these resorts include mud baths, hydrotherapy, saunas, mineral baths, steam baths and beauty treatments. The popularity of spas in other areas of the globe is also well established. An estimated 160 million visits were made to US spas in 2008 (Nichols, 2009), while in Japan, onsen (hot springs) such as Ikaho and Shirahone thrive on tourism (although scandals in the early 2000s, in which it was revealed that tap water was in some cases being provided in place of traditional water sources, severely undermined public confidence).

In the past, European spa treatments were often supported by the state health services, but escalating costs led to cutbacks. In 1996, for example, Germany reduced the amount of time state-funded health claimants were permitted to stay and reimbursement was limited essentially to treatment at domestic spas. Nevertheless, some 15 million Europeans daily continue to immerse themselves in thermal waters, in the belief that 'the cure' will alleviate their ailments, and the spas of Europe reap the benefits of this belief.

In the UK, which once attracted many domestic tourists to its spa towns, medical experts became more sceptical about the health benefits of spas in the twentieth century. Recent evidence concerning those with osteoarthritis and osteoporosis, and a growing interest in alternative medicine generally, is causing some medical experts to re-evaluate their former views, which is encouraging some former spas to reopen. National Lottery funding has been made available at Buxton, Malvern, Leamington Spa, Harrogate, Tunbridge Wells and Bath. Others may choose to follow suit if demand is evident, although not all funding will necessarily go towards recreating the medical facilities these famous spas once boasted.

Research by Mintel (2009b) estimated that almost a third of UK adults have experienced some sort of health and wellness activity while on holiday, in the UK and/or overseas, with the majority being spa/spa hotel visits. Treatment may include massage, manicures and pedicures – with a far lower number electing for medical treatment. A number of tour operators in the UK are featuring spa treatment abroad in their promotions, and over 300 000 British tourists continue to travel abroad specifically for treatment each year. The response to this demand is being met by the growth of purpose-built facilities supplied within the accommodation sector.

The successful destination

Three important points should be highlighted in relation to tourist destinations. First, the chances of their long-term success will be significantly enhanced if the benefits they offer are **unique**. There is only *one* Oberammergau Passion Play, there is only one Eiffel Tower, Grand Canyon or Big Ben, and these attractions can provide the focus for a destination's marketing campaign. Because of the singular properties of 'heritage' tourism, these types of destination retain their appeal even if their prices may become less competitive with those of other destinations, providing the increase is not exorbitant by comparison.

It is true to say, however, that the majority of the mass tourism movement is directed at sun, sea and sand destinations, which the Mediterranean and Caribbean countries provide so effectively. Such destinations are seldom unique and their customers do not require them to be so. They will be satisfied as long as the amenities are appropriate, the resort remains accessible and prices are competitive. Indeed, the similarities in attractions and amenities, as well as the way these destinations are marketed, gives rise to the concept of the **identikit destination**, which results from the evidence produced by market research studies designed to find common denominators for the various international markets in order to develop a product with guaranteed mass demand. Such destinations have been developed through the activities of multinational tourism organizations. In the development of such destinations, the emphasis changes from an attempt to distinguish the product to one that concentrates on maintaining or improving its image by offering good standards that reflect value for money and ensuring that the destination remains competitive with other similar destinations.

The second point to stress is that the **more benefits** a destination can offer, the greater will be the attraction of the destination. Multiple attractions provide added value, so the concentration within a specific geographical area of a number of different products appealing to different markets (such as the City of Boston, Massachusetts, with the seaside attractions of Cape Cod and the rural appeal of New England fall foliage on its doorstep) will improve its chances of success.

Third, it should be clear that no destination can rely on its past successes to continue to attract tourists. Most depend at least to some extent on visitors returning, so will need to update and augment their range of attractions continually to encourage repeat visits. This means there is a need for innovation and constant investment. Destinations, like all products that depend on consumer demand, have lifecycles – that is, they experience periods of growth, expansion and, eventually, decline (we discussed the destination lifecycle in Chapter 4). If we examine the history of any well-known resort, we can see the truth of this. Along the French Riviera, Nice, Cannes, Antibes, Juan les Pins and St Tropez have all in turn enjoyed their periods of being fashionable seaside resorts, but, ultimately, their visitors moved on to still more fashionable resorts, often to be replaced by less fashion-conscious, less free-spending tourists. A decline into decay can only be arrested through redevelopment and innovation. In some cases, resorts have been allowed to run down to an extent where the cost of renovation may be beyond the scope of the local authority and decay becomes inevitable.

EXAMPLE The case of Acapulco

Acapulco, on the Mexican Pacific coast and close to the US border, has been a hugely popular resort since the 1950s. Lack of investment in recent years, however, has allowed it to decline, to a point where the Mexican government recognized that a major scheme to upgrade the town was needed.

In spite of attracting some 6 million tourists every year, its beaches had become badly contaminated, with untreated effluent entering the water, and a population explosion in the surrounding suburbs had led to overcrowding and water shortages – water supplies being prioritized to serve the needs of the seafront hotel swimming pools. The fear was that the upper end of the market would be driven away and concern was also being expressed over rising crime rates resulting from turf wars between drug cartels in the district and the growth of child sex tourism.

Although the government announced its intention to invest 440 million pesos (some £21 million) in improvements, notably to improving sanitation services, on-going drug-related violence has discouraged international tourists, particularly college students on vacation. Until 2006, an average of 25 000 US spring-break visitors chose this Pacific coast resort each year, but in 2010, there were fewer than 6000 spring breakers (The Commercial Appeal – Memphis, 2011).

Design of the built and natural environment

More recently, attention has focused on the importance of the **public realm** in satisfying tourists once they have been attracted to a destination. The public realm may be commonly defined as the features of a destination that represent the environment in which the tourist stays and moves around, to include public amenities such as parks, squares, gardens, public toilets, litter collection, paved areas, street furniture, car parking and similar features of the built environment that are so important in creating the experience that tourists have and the image that they retain and later communicate to other potential travellers. These features complement the buildings – public and otherwise – that make up the physical characteristics of the tourist product.

Issues such as the size and scale of new buildings must be taken into consideration and, away from principal urban centres, buildings should be on a human scale that is not threatening to passers-by, but retains their interest. Most visitors to a town will explore it on foot, so good street-level design is vital. Use of local materials, whether in modernist or more traditional buildings, is important to create a sense of place. Local building materials are often more expensive to use than, say, concrete, but the additional costs are justified in the long run and may even bring in additional revenue from tourists anxious to see them in their own right. In the UK, examples may be found in the use of Bath stone in Bath, Cotswold stone in the Cotswolds, black-and-white half-timbering in the border country, thatch in the West Country and slate in the Lake District or Wales. Even for such mundane features as public toilets, the use of local and natural building materials can greatly enhance the end result; indeed, today it is sometimes insisted on by local authority planning departments. The benefit of using such materials is that they help to reinforce the characteristics of the brand image that the destination and tourist board is trying to create.

No building can be divorced from its setting and, just as thought must go into the design of the building itself, so the site itself must be landscaped attractively to maximize its appeal to visitors. Part of the attraction of an English village is the way in which the houses lie in the landscape, blending as if they were made for the setting. Where a development is on a slope, it becomes even more important to ensure that the buildings blend with the background. If the buildings are to be exposed to view – for example, a group of self-catering chalets high in the Alps – great care has to be taken to integrate them into the landscape. Buildings should not stand out on the skyline, but, if it is essential that they do, then their lines should be broken up with the use of trees and shrubs. On sloping sites, buildings can be 'stepped' or terraced up the hillside to keep their scale in harmony with the environment. Similarly, with waterside developments, buildings should be sited well clear of the waterfront itself, to allow for walkways along the banks that will attract both residents and visitors and ensure that those using the waterway are not intimidated by tall buildings.

The appeal of water is evident in the conversion for leisure use of so many redundant harbours and waterways in the UK. Here, the local authorities must determine whether the site is best retained as a dockland environment or themed as urban parkland. Enlightened authorities have come to recognize that the retention of traditional bollards, cranes and other paraphernalia of a dockside will provide a unique setting, making it even more attractive to visitors, together with the addition of a modest number of trees or shrubs.

Street furniture

Street furniture is something that we all take for granted, yet it plays an important part in reflecting the national landscape, too. One has only to think of the classic red telephone kiosks and letterboxes in the UK or the nineteenth-century 'pissoirs' (now sadly disappearing) and the traditional green boulevard chairs and tables still to be found on the streets of Paris to realize that such items play a part in formulating our picture of townscapes. In the UK, a great deal of attention has been paid in recent years to the design of public seating and litter bins, but any item of street furniture, from letterboxes to telephone kiosks, from litter bins to bus shelters, from public toilets to refreshment stalls, from lamp posts to railings, needs to be carefully designed to be in harmony with the surroundings and reflect the image of the area in which it is sited. Increasingly, these sites must be designed to resist vandalism and, where possible, graffiti, too.

Local authorities must first determine whether to adopt a classic or modern design for their setting. Heritage sites such as York or Chester are more likely to opt for a traditional and classic design to blend with the architecture of the area. Unfortunately, this has led to the development of a ubiquitous design in cast iron with gold motifs, frequently bearing the crest of the city, that, while tasteful and elegant, does little to distinguish the city's streets from countless others in the same country. These designs are better, however, than some of the products they replace, such as the plastic litter bin (all too often cracked or misshapen), in a choice of battleship grey or garish yellow. Litter bins in particular need to be big enough to accommodate the huge amounts of litter created today by takeaway shops and the council must have a policy of emptying these frequently, otherwise the benefits of good design will be lost as rubbish piles up around the base of the bin.

Cities on the European Continent, particularly those the centres of which were substantially rebuilt after the war or that wish to promote a modern, dynamic image, often adopt more modern designs. These can work equally well in the appropriate setting. Their cost may be substantially higher than more modest designs, but they not only improve the image of the city but also last much longer without repair or replacement.

Providing seating in towns and cities is a problem for the planners, as it tends to attract vagrants. The use of simple-to-maintain materials that will provide a brief respite for residents and tourists, but not encourage longer stays, can be the answer to the problem. Individual seats, rather than benches, also reduce their use by vagrants for sleeping.

Public amenities

Public toilets

Public toilets for tourists are often treated as a peripheral issue by planners, but their inadequacies are often picked on by tourist bodies such as UKinbound. Many tourist sites suffer from an inadequate supply of toilets, while others have had their toilets locked or shut down due to shortages of money for maintenance and supervision. Even Bath, one of the UK's principal tourist towns, has seen a sharp drop recently in the number of conveniences remaining open for tourists. While the UK is not unique in facing this problem, it is interesting to note that, in Japan, architectural competitions are promoted for public toilets, while the Chinese encourage architects to design toilets with the needs of American tourists in mind. The interest generated by the construction of the 'superloo' at Westbourne Grove in London, designed by architect Piers Gough in 1993 with an attached flower shop, reveals just how important good toilet design can be for tourism. This particular example not only won design awards but also was featured in English Heritage's advertisements in 1997. It should come as no surprise, therefore, that over 80 public toilets around the UK are actually listed buildings.

Car parks

Car parks are a particular problem for designers as they occupy large areas of land and are often visually intrusive. In the countryside, efforts are now made to ensure that they appear as natural as possible. For example, logs can be used to separate the bays, and the planting of substantial shrubs can help to conceal the cars themselves. Good, but not intrusive, lighting is important too, and the surface can be gravel rather than tarmac. In some small parking areas, it may be possible to use honeycomb concrete blocks that allow grass to grow through them, rendering the concrete surface almost invisible.

Car parks must, of course, be situated well away from any high-grade heritage sites, which may mean that there will need to be special provision for the disabled. In cities, the urban setting will mean more man-made materials can be used in the car parks' construction, but this no longer means high-rise concrete. Designs have become more fanciful, including, in one case, a mock mediaeval fortification. Car parks on open land have proved successful when they have been attractively furnished with decorative modern lamps and plenty of trees to break up the land mass. Given the high prices motorists are now resigned to paying for parking, underground car parks are often economically viable and, of course, have the least impact on the surrounding environment. In Salzburg, Austria – where public parking is at a premium – the local authority went so far as to blast a cavernous car park out of the adjacent cliff faces, underground parking being impractical.

Utility cables

Telephone and public utility lines can mar the appearance of even the most beautiful town or village. Fortunately, in the UK, local authorities have generally taken an enlightened view, hiding these unattractive necessities, but a visit to Spain or Greece will soon illustrate how much visual pollution is caused when overhead wires march along streets, linking into houses. Although the cost of burying wires is much higher, in the long run it is worth the investment if the site is much more attractive to visitors. The positioning of electricity pylons across the landscape in some of the most scenic parts of the UK – and the more recent intrusion of wind-powered electricity generators and mobile phone antennae – has also been strongly criticized by defenders of the traditional countryside.

EXAMPLE **Removing the pylons of power**

On winning the right to host the 2012 Olympic Games, one of the first tasks facing the Olympic Delivery Authority – responsible for constructing the infrastructure at the Olympic site – was to bury ten kilometres of power lines underground. The pylons spanning the site were considered an eyesore and burying the cables provided an improved public space across the park.

The power-cable debate has affected two other tourist regions in the UK. Campaigns have been launched to keep pylons away from the Cheddar Valley in Somerset, England as well as the Wallace Monument in Stirling, Scotland. In the latter case, support from local government ministers has been forthcoming, although this may not be enough to force change on the power companies who own the cabling.

Pedestrianization

Many towns popular with tourists have pedestrianized some of their principal thorough-fares. The result can greatly enhance the atmosphere of a street and encourage visitors to come shopping. Some of the UK's most attractive town centres, such as those of York, Brighton, Bath and Chester, and many Continental towns, feature narrow pedestrian walkways that have never been wide enough to support motor vehicles. In such towns, the narrowness of the lanes is their very attraction. Even in towns where such lanes do not exist, virtually all now have areas restricted to pedestrian use. In London, for instance, Covent Garden was redesigned on this basis after the fruit and vegetable market moved away.

Pedestrianizing will not in itself be enough to make the area a focal point for shoppers, however. The shops themselves must be appropriate for the setting and the street must be enhanced by well-designed street furniture, tree planting and the display of flowers or shrubs in tubs or other containers. When this is done tastefully, the end result can transform a street. The flipside, however, is that it will also attract much larger numbers of pedestrians, which can lead to congestion and a litter problem that the council must be prepared to tackle.

Horticultural displays

As mentioned above, the use of hanging baskets, floral beds in the centre of main access roads, extensive tree planting along the pavements and similar horticultural displays can make a pretty village outstanding and even an unattractive town bearable. Some of the UK's towns have made such a feature of their floral displays that they have become famous internationally. Bath's hanging basket displays are a highly attractive feature for summer visitors, while the massed floral beds that line the seafronts of towns such as Eastbourne and Worthing draw many older visitors to these resorts year after year. As many flowers bloom in spring, they can be used to attract visitors before the traditional peak summer season. Aberdeen is noted for its display of formal rose beds along its main roads, and on the Continent the sight of flower-bedecked chalets in Switzerland and Austria is indelibly associated with these countries' villages and highlighted in all tourist brochures.

The cost of transforming a town in this way is considerable, but, as a way to attract tourists, at the very least, councils need to consider investing funds to make the main approach roads more attractive – both those carrying car traffic to the centre and those providing the principal access for pedestrians to the centre from bus or train terminals. First impressions count for a lot when it comes to attracting tourists.

Art and tourism

There is a growing recognition today that art has a role to play in the tourism industry, not just through museums, galleries and arts events organized to attract the tourist, but in the everyday surroundings in which visitors find themselves. Ostensibly, 'street art' is designed to heighten the visual appeal of a town for its residents, but, once again, such embellishment will add to the attraction of the destination for the visitors, too. If the work displayed is by artists of international reputation, this will widen the appeal of the destination to international visitors. Sculptures by Henry Moore in Yorkshire or at the Serpentine in London, for example, attract dedicated groups of overseas and domestic visitors. Cities in the USA enforce local regulations requiring a small percentage of the total cost of any new development to be spent on public art at the site and the prestigious offices of major corporations will also judge it appropriate to enhance their forecourts with sculptures by leading artists of the day. In London, prominent British artists such as Eduardo Paolozzi were recruited to design the wall tiles during the renovation of the Central London Underground railway stations.

Towns can reinforce their images by the imaginative use of sculpture or art. In Germany, for example, Hamelin has its sculpture of the Pied Piper, while Bremen has greatly enhanced its pedestrian streets with scenes from Grimms' fairy tales. Brussels is famous for the Manneken Pis, the tiny bronze statue of a small boy urinating, copies of which are sold as tourist souvenirs, and photos of him feature on many postcards. Copenhagen's major draw is its Little Mermaid statue, based on the Hans Christian Andersen fairy tale. More recently, the city of Berlin brought back into the town centre a statue of Frederick the Great that had been considered politically unacceptable in East Berlin before the fall of the Wall.

The UK is becoming more aware of the importance of art and the way in which it can serve the interests of the tourist industry. Notable features include two water fountain sculptures by William Pye, 'Slipstream' and 'Jetstream', commissioned by BAA at Gatwick Airport and a 130-foot long sculpture, 'Train' by David Mach, which is a monument to the record-breaking steam locomotive 'Mallard'. Comprised of 185 000 bricks, it was unveiled in Darlington in 1997 (to considerable local criticism but widespread national publicity). Also, two sculptures, initially rebuffed by those in the locations where they were erected, achieved considerable publicity and, later, support from the local population when their benefits to tourism became clear. Artist Maggi Hambling's 12-foot high scallop shell memorial to composer Benjamin Britten on the beach near Aldeburgh, Suffolk, was initially vilified, too, as were Antony Gormley's series of Iron Men sculptures in his 'Another Place' setting on Crosby Beach, Merseyside. In the latter case, locals lobbied later, with the media, to defend the sculptures when the council proposed their removal, following their temporary display on the beach, and the council retracted. Both these artists' works have since become iconic symbols for the resorts in question.

Lighting

External street lighting can play an important role in enhancing a town, both with respect to the design of the lights themselves and to the effect they can create at night. Again, a choice must be made between traditional and modern lamps. Some towns have reinforced their quaintness by choosing authentic gas lighting, which has great popular appeal for tourists. In Norwegian villages in the weeks leading up to Christmas, the shopping streets are illuminated with real flares, giving visitors an impression of warmth and cosiness at a time when the long periods of darkness could otherwise lower the spirits of residents and visitors.

Floodlighting major attractions – a recognized practice for the great monuments in leading cities – has become much more widespread and its use can encourage tourists out on to the streets at night, thus extending the 'tourist day'. For example, the medieval town of Carcassonne in France operates son et lumière displays to narrate its history. European funding has also supported a joint initiative between Rouen and Amiens in France and Rochester and Canterbury in England that allows these cities to provide a series of free music and light events for visitors and the local population to enjoy.

White lights are normally recommended, the use of coloured lights – apart from settings where a fairground atmosphere is appropriate, such as at the Blackpool illuminations – being best avoided. For example, many observers feel the use of coloured lights to floodlight Niagara Falls turned a great spectacle into an example of downmarket kitsch. Limited use of coloured lighting can be helpful, though, in highlighting horticultural displays at night. Care must be taken not to over-light. Strong lights are particularly inappropriate in a village setting, for example.

EXAMPLE **Turn off the lights!**

The effects of lighting on the turtle population has been well documented – with concerns that, firstly, brightly lit beaches dissuade female turtles from laying their eggs and, secondly, any hatching turtles can be disoriented by the lights and fail to quickly find the safety of the water's edge. Campaigners across the globe are trying to protect the turtles by encouraging beachfront hotels and bars to reduce the amount of lighting they use at night.

One advantage of turning off the lights is the opportunity to attract the 'dark-sky' tourism market. Destinations which have environments with little or no light pollution make great places to view the stars and planets in the night sky. One example is 'Dark Sky Scotland', an initiative, led by the Royal Observatory Edinburgh, which includes providing training workshops for tourism businesses, so they can help ensure visitors have a greater appreciation of the night sky.

From Scotland in the north we move to the south of the UK – the Channel Island of Sark has become the first 'dark-sky' island in the world. The island has made efforts to reduce any light pollution, although as there are no street-lights and cars are banned, the island was already a dark place at night. The island is expecting to benefit from the increased interest in astronomy, and this designation should help to attract visitors outside of the popular summer months.

Figure 9.15 Keeping visitors safe, South Carolina, USA

Photo by Claire Humphreys

Finally, mention might be due here of holding firework displays to highlight key events, such as national holidays or other days of commemoration. Independence Day, 4 July, in the USA, Bastille Day, 14 July, in France, and Guy Fawkes Day, 5 November, in the UK, are all days where fireworks commonly round off the day's events.

Signposting

All visitors look for signposts, so they become the most visible of all forms of street furniture. These may be directional or informative (see Figure 9.15) (and Chapter 16 discusses the different ways they help the visitor).

Signs must be easily visible and legible, especially from a distance in the case of signs for vehicle drivers – generally, standards for road signs are set by local authorities or government departments of transport. Signs may also be subject to local government regulations, limiting their size and placement on safety or visual pollution grounds.

EXAMPLE **Tourist signs in the UK**

Following a long period where signposting was arbitrary and often banned from main roads in the UK, the Department for Transport introduced white-on-brown signs in 1986. There are 35 different pictographs representing every conceivable variety of tourist attraction. Regulations on the use of these and other signs are complex and quite restrictive. The use of white-on-brown signs, for example, is dependent on the numbers visiting the site (for example, historic houses must attract a minimum of 5000 visitors a year to warrant approval for the erection of a directional road sign). This, of course, introduces a catch-22 situation, where already well-established attractions are favoured over newly developed ones.

Politics and the need to cater for foreign visitors can often affect the layout and language of signs. In countries such as Belgium, in parts of Canada and in Wales, for example, bilingualism is the law, so every place name or instruction must be given in two languages. In the Baltic States, although there are many Russian speakers, the continuing resentment towards their former masters means that if any foreign language is to be used on signs, it is English. In China, Japan and Thailand, where many foreigners will drive cars but not understand the local scripts, signs in the large towns all have to be duplicated in English.

The media and their influence on tourist destinations

One means by which destinations can regenerate their tourism economy or, in some cases, grow one where earlier it had scarcely existed is through the impact of programmes in the media, whether film, television or radio. The growing interplay between the media and tourism deserves special mention, given the extent to which the tourism industry is now exploiting for its own ends consumer interest in sites associated with 'celebrities'.

A noteworthy aspect of postmodern culture is the fascination that fame, however transient, holds for many people, as witnessed by the appeal of reality shows on television which guarantee minor celebrities instant fame. Tourist destinations have not been slow to exploit opportunities for publicity in the media, especially cinema and television, either by promoting the sites associated with these celebrities or offering inducements to film within their territory. In many cases, governments have colluded with local authorities and the private sector by directly subsidizing the media's production costs, well aware that the publicity engendered by global distribution of a film or television programme will generate tourists' interest. In the UK, the National Trust now actively solicits film companies for its sites, following the success of their heritage buildings when used as settings for costume dramas. Lyme Park, near Stockport, the setting for the popular BBC film of Jane Austen's *Pride and Prejudice*, experienced a 178% increase in visitors following the drama's showing on UK TV. A report by the UK Film Council (2007) estimated that some 3 million visitors were influenced to visit the UK by images seen in films or on TV, such an effect boosting tourism revenue by around £1.8 billion each year.

EXAMPLE The case of Borat

In 2007, the film satire *Borat: Cultural Learnings of America for Make Benefit Glorious Nation of Kazakhstan* appeared on global screens. Ruthlessly pillorying the Kazakh nation, the comic actor Sacha Baron Cohen, in his role as Borat, became an overnight sensation, receiving equal measures of admiration and vilification for his depiction of life in the former Soviet satellite country.

To the surprise of many, the film actually succeeded in putting Kazakhstan on the map for the first time, stimulating travel enquiries. In the weeks following the opening of the film in the UK, there was an increase of 300% in searches for hotels in the country, while the Kazakh Embassy was receiving around 100 calls a week asking for information about tourist visas. Unknown to most of those who saw this movie, filming was actually done in the Romanian village of Glod, rather than Kazakhstan itself.

Tourist information offices all over the world are producing 'film maps' or 'movie maps' listing sites that appear in popular films. New York City has *Sex and the City* and *Seinfeld* tours, among numerous others, while Katz's Delicatessen, in the same city – site of the famous 'orgasm' scene in *When Harry met Sally* – has become a popular port of call for visitors from all over the world. In the UK, the enormous popularity of the book and film *The da Vinci Code* (the book alone sold over 50 million copies) enabled a popular 'trail' of sites associated with the film to be promoted by VisitBritain under the title 'Seek the truth', including Lincoln Cathedral (which quickly introduced a charge for visitors to see the actual locations used in the film), Rosslyn Chapel, Burghley House, Lincolnshire (standing in for the Chateau de Villette in Versailles) and Belvoir Castle, Leicestershire (Castel Gandolfo). The enormous popularity of the *Harry Potter* films, equally, has expanded travel to settings associated with the films in England – once again helped by a promotional trail entitled 'Discover the magic of Britain', which includes Gloucester Cathedral, Goathland Station (Hogsmeade) and Alnwick Castle (Hogwarts School of Witchcraft), which experienced a 230% increase in visitors following the film, generating £9 million extra revenue for the area (Visit Britain, 2011). In 2008, VisitBritain launched a 'Comedy England' campaign, designed to attract visitors to sites famous for comedy in film or television. The six-month campaign included reference to Torquay, setting for *Fawlty Towers*, Turville, site of *The Vicar of Dibley*, and Thetford, Norfolk, where *Dad's Army* was filmed.

Other parts of the world have also been quick to cash in on film and television settings as potential sources of revenue. The film *The Italian Job* has a cult following, to the extent that bespoke tours to the locations in Turin where it was filmed are now organized. A recent new version of the film boosted interest once more. In Australia, *Rogue* – a horror film in which day trippers in the Northern Territory are picked off one by one by a giant crocodile – was followed by another, *Wolf Creek* – in which backpackers (presumably the survivors) are again picked off in turn by a psychotic. Far from discouraging tourists, these two films led to a 10% increase in backpackers to the area, helped by a supporting promotion from Tourism Top End (the board for the Northern Territory).

The popularity of domestic TV series helps to boost domestic tourism. Visitors to the North East of England still flock to the sites on the Yorkshire Moors where the television series *Last of the Summer Wine* and *Heartbeat* were filmed, with Sid's Café in Holmfirth – used in the former production – a popular venue with visitors. Turville in Bucks, the setting for the popular TV series *The Vicar of Dibley*, quickly became a featured destination on the tourist trail. More recently, the numerous Bollywood films now shot in the UK are helping to encourage visitors from the Indian subcontinent. *Nammanna*, for example, filmed in 2007, led to a substantial number of visitors from India to Lake Windermere.

The popularity of certain cult films guarantees a steady audience of aficionados to the locations where the films were shot. The enduring appeal of the 1945 film *Brief Encounter*, shot at Carnforth railway station in Lancashire, entices many tourists, particularly Japanese, to the now restored station with its replica of the famous refreshment room, which is open to the public for the sale of food and drink. This is a classic example of staged authenticity, being a reconstruction of the film set, which itself was modelled on the original. Such lack of true authenticity, however, fails to deter visitors. The long-standing popularity of the film *The Railway Children* (1970, remade as a BBC TV film in 2000), which featured the Keighley and Worth Valley Steam Railway in West Yorkshire, led to the company promoting its *Railway Children* connections through leaflets, advertising and special events. More recently, the popularity in Germany of the Rosamund Pilcher novels, set in Cornwall, created a market for package tours to that area, especially the coastal resort of St Ives – a demand boosted by a German television series based on the books. In France, Provence tourist authorities have established a 'Marcel Pagnol route' to popularize the locations at which the French film *Manon des Sources* was filmed.

The power of Hollywood means that tourists, both domestic and foreign, flock to the locations of scenes in movies filmed in the USA. To cite recent examples of areas that formerly drew few tourists and now, as a result of popular films, attract many: the general store in Juliette, Georgia, which was the setting for the Whistlestop Café in *Fried Green Tomatoes* has now become a tourist attraction in its own right, and North Carolina, especially the area around Asheville, has been blessed by being the setting for numerous films in recent years, including *Cold Mountain*, *The Last of the Mohicans*, *Forrest Gump* and *Hannibal*. The state has actively promoted these settings in its marketing campaigns. The US tourism authorities ran a TV promotion in the UK during the winter of 2004/05, and again in 2007/08, with the strapline 'You've seen the films, now visit the sets', backed by scenes from famous films such as *Thelma and Louise*.

Entire regions and countries can be similarly boosted by media exposure. Notable in recent years has been the New Zealand government's exploitation of the *Lord of the Rings* cycle, with advertising directing tourists to film locations such as Matamata (Tolkien's Plains of Gorgoroth), Tongariro National Park and Nelson (the fact that Tolkien actually based Gorgoroth on the Ribble Valley area in England is conveniently overlooked!). Tunisia, where *Star Wars*, *Raiders of the Lost Ark* and *The English Patient* were filmed, has actively solicited film work and its tourism authority helped to develop an *English Patient* route for tourists. This phenomenon is not limited to Western settings and audiences. Bae Yong Joon, now known to fans as Prince Yong and the hero of the South Korean TV drama *Winter Sonata*, which has a huge following in Japan, made the country an acceptable destination for Japanese mass tourism, with a 10% increase in visitors in 2003. Packages that included visits to locations in the star's films sold well.

This is just a handful of examples to demonstrate the power of the media in influencing tourism – a factor that is, for the most part, fully taken into account and built on by tourist information authorities today in their efforts to promote 'cultural tourism'. There are concerns, however, when these films are made in remote beauty spots that subsequently attract large numbers of tourists. Khao Phingkan in Thailand was the setting for the James Bond film *The Man with the Golden Gun*. This ideal setting was rapidly destroyed by unplanned development of tourism. As we have seen earlier, a similar fate befell Maya Bay on Phi Phi Ley Island, following the popularity of *The Beach*, which starred Leonardo di Caprio (arguably, as much damage is done by the film crew at these locations as by subsequent tourism).

Destinations of the future

What is clear is that consumers of tomorrow's holidays will be less content with the mundane: the search is on for more adventurous, original forms of holiday to exotic destinations. The search for 'something different' is already beginning to undermine traditional identikit destinations and hotels, which will need to position themselves more clearly and adapt their products to appeal to niche markets. Consumers have control over the transmission of information, too, with websites devoted to exchanging information about destinations and accommodation and making recommendations. Others are devoted to complaints about specific accommodation, resorts or carriers.

This drive for the novel, however, is likely to be tempered by cost. Budget airlines have helped to make some destinations both more affordable and more accessible – stimulating demand for short breaks to urban areas as well as longer holidays spent exploring the surrounding region.

There have been predictions that underwater leisure cities will be built on the seabeds adjoining our coasts, where a controlled climate will make the annual exodus to the sun no longer necessary. Some of these predictions take us into the realms of science fiction, yet, we are already on the fringe of developing a space-tourism product so exploiting the untapped resources of the ocean for tourism may well be the next frontier to be explored. Some tour operators are already offering trips in a mini-submarine to the Amundsen Plain, 4400 metres below the sea at the North Pole, which are hailed as 'the ultimate adventure challenge'.

As we mentioned above, space as a destination is very close, with Japanese and American companies planning to build and launch hotels in space once the vehicles are available to get the tourists there. In 2004, SpaceShipOne won the US$10 million Ansari X prize, offered to encourage the development of space transport capable of taking people into space. To win the prize, the aircraft had to fly to the edge of space twice in a two-week period. Since this success, many companies have entered the market with plans to offer both edge-of-space flights and zero gravity flights. While announced timescales of 2015–2025 might be greeted with scepticism, the current acceleration in space exploration makes such developments feasible. It is no longer a question of if, but when.

Summary

It is clear that tourists are attracted by a variety of destinations, some which offer unique appeal whilst others are popular because they can provide a 'familiar' feel. Although tourists may claim to desire more than the traditional beach holidays, seaside destinations – especially in warm-water environments – still attract large numbers of tourists.

Destinations may help to develop their appeal by developing innovative attractions, or linking their marketing activities and place-branding to other fashionable products (such as films, books, events or celebrities). What is vital, however, is ensuring that the physical design of the destination – its landscape, amenities and infrastructure – appeals to the tourist which will then encourage them to visit.

Questions and discussion points

1. How do the characteristics of the tourism industry differ in rural tourism destinations when compared to urban tourism destinations?

2. The wedding of Prince William and Kate Middleton, in May 2011, brought an estimated 8000 journalists, photographers and media crew to London. More than 100 outside broadcast teams from across the globe provided TV coverage throughout the week leading up to the marriage and, at its peak, TV coverage was predicted to reach 2 billion people. London basked in unseasonable warm, sunny days and many iconic buildings such as Buckingham Palace and the Houses of Parliament featured in many of the images published. To what extent do you think this event will bring tourism to London in both the short term and the longer term? What types of tourist may be attracted because they viewed the press coverage of this event?

3. Water features prominently in most types of destination, with tourists often prepared to pay a premium to have a sea or lake view. Why might it have such as appeal?

Tasks

1. In Table 9.1 we list the top ten city destinations in the world. Produce a presentation which identifies the key reasons why tourists are attracted to these cities. Also identify any reported problems which may deter tourists from visiting in the future.

2. Choose an urban destination and produce a portfolio of ten images which highlights the design of the public realm. For each image provide a brief statement evaluating whether it is an example of the public realm enhancing or damaging the tourist experience.

Bibliography

AFP (2011) France to help develop Russia's Caucasus ski project, *Agence France Presse*, 18 June.

Bezuidenhout, N. (2010) Positive spin-offs from World Cup for country, *Cape Argus News*, 7 December.

Chitakasem, P. (2011) Spa tourism is big business in Asia Pacific, *Euromonitor*, 11 January.

The Commercial Appeal – Memphis (2011) Acapulco still popular despite deadly drug war – Though international tourism has taken a hit, *Associated Press*, 30 January.

Daily Telegraph (2011) Wipe out for Bournemouth's surf city plans as artificial reef splits, *Daily Telegraph*, 18 April.

Deloitte (2009) *Medical Tourism: update and implications*, available online at: http://www.deloitte.com/assets/Dcom-UnitedStates/Local%20Assets/Documents/us_chs_MedicalTourism_111209_web.pdf (accessed November 2011).

Egyptian Gazette (2011) 9 Sharm areas declared shark-free, *Egyptia Gazette*, 8 January.

Euromonitor (2007) *Top 150 City Destinations: London Leads the Way*, available online at: http:blog.euromonitor.com/2007/10/top-150-city-destinations-london-leads-the-way.html (accessed November 2011).

Euromonitor (2010) *Euromonitor International's Top City Destination Ranking*, available online at: http://blog.euromonitor.com/2010/01/euromonitor-internationals-top-city-destination-ranking.html (accessed November 2011).

Euromonitor (2011) *Euromonitor International's top city destinations ranking*, available online at: http://blog.euromonitor.com/2011/01/euromonitor-internationals-top-city-destinations-ranking.html (accessed November 2011).

Hooper, J. (2010) Dumas's Montecristo island opens to tourists, *The Guardian*, 2 August.

Irish Independent (2011) The upside of family downtime, *Irish Independent*, 20 June.

Jeffrey, F. (2006) Put it on the plastic, *Travel Weekly*, 9 June.

Johnson, M. (2011) Food, festivals and history to replace sun, sea and sand, London, *Financial Times*, 17 June.

Medway Messenger (2011) Dreamland regeneration action, Margate, *Medway Messenger*, 6 May.

Mintel (2009a) *Domestic Tourism – UK*, London, Mintel, December.

Mintel (2009b) *Health and Wellness Holidays – UK*, London, Mintel, October.

Nichols, M. (2009) U.S. spas seem recession-proof, says industry group, New York, *Reuters*, 6 July.

Northwest RDA (2010) *Press Release – New Independent Data Confirms Liverpool's Capital of Culture Success*, Warrington, Northwest Regional Development Agency, 11 January.

Penrose, J. M. P. (2011) *Government Tourism Policy*, London, DCMS, March.

Picard, A. (2010) Medical tourism: It's time for some tough debate, *The Globe and Mail-Canada*, 2 December.

Phillip, S., Hunter, C. and Blackstock, K. (2010) A typology for defining agritourism, *Tourism Management*, **31** (6), 754–758.

Rilla, E., Hardesty, S. D., Getz, C. and George, H. (2011) California agritourism operations and their economic potential are growing, *California Agriculture*, **65** (2), 57–65.

Roelf, W. (2011) S. Africa aims for 15 mln foreign tourists/yr by 2020, *Reuters News*, 20 April.

Rowe, M. (2011) This coast's so wild they build lighthouses on wheels, *The Independent*, 19 June.

Saraniemi, S. and Kylänen, M. (2011) Problematizing the concept of tourism destination: an analysis of different theoretical approaches, *Journal of Travel Research*, **50** (2), 133–143.

Sherwood, H. and Meikle, J. (2010) Sharm el-Sheikh tourist killed in new shark attack, *The Guardian*, 6 December.

Tourism Australia (2010) *There's nothing like Australia campaign brochure*, available online at: http://www.tourism.australia.com/en-au/documents/Corporate%20-%20Marketing/TNL_Campaign_Brochure.pdf (accessed November 2011).

Tourism Australia (2011) *Smartphone App*, authors personal research.

Tourism Research Australia (2008) *Through the looking glass: The future of domestic tourism in Australia*, Belconnen, TRA, February.

UK Film Council (2007) *Stately attractions: how film and television programmes promote tourism in the UK*, London, Olsberg/SPI.

Visit Britain (2011) *Films continue to draw visitors to Britain*, Press Release, 18 March.

Wall, E. (2010) Medical tourism costs under the microscope, *The Telegraph*, 13 August.

Zinn, E. (2010) Boost to our image of ourselves, *Pretoria News*, 16 July.

Websites

International Dark-Sky Association: **www.darksky.org**

Tourism Australia: **www.nothinglikeaustralia.com**

Travel Foundation: **www.thetravelfoundation.org.uk**

10

Tourist attractions

Contents

Learning outcomes

After studying this chapter, you should be able to:

- distinguish between a destination and an attraction and define each
- understand what it is that attracts tourists and which attractions appeal to each market
- appreciate the problem for attractions of changing tastes and fashions and propose solutions to overcome this
- recognize the potential for new attractions and how these can be developed.

Niagara Falls is very nice. I'm glad I saw it, because from now on if I am asked whether I have seen Niagara Falls I can say yes, and be telling the truth for once.

Steinbeck (1962) *Travels with Charley*, 66

Introduction: defining the attraction

As Steinbeck recognized, there are some attractions which claim iconic status, requiring all travellers to see them at least once in their lives. Often these attractions form part of a virtual list to be 'ticked off' as the tourist moves around the world in search of new experiences. Other such examples will include a visit to the Eiffel Tower when in France, or the Taj Mahal when in India. These tourist attractions may form part of the core reason for visiting the destination.

But what exactly do we mean by a **tourist attraction**? Trying to define it is no easy matter, but to understand the sector and how it operates we have to start with a definition. After all, it is generally the attraction that prompts the tourist to travel in the first place, but the concept of an 'attraction' is a very broad one, encompassing a great many different sights – and sites.

Defining tourist attractions

Sometimes we use the term synonymously with 'destination', the attraction in this case being the **benefits** inherent in the destination rather than any purpose-built facility specifically designed to appeal to tourists. The medieval town centre of Dinant, Southern Germany's Black Forest and Luquillo Beach in Puerto Rico are all 'attractions', but do not exist either primarily or necessarily to serve tourists' needs. Similarly, a trip to the seaside may be taken principally for the opportunity to enjoy a swim in the sea at a good beach in warm weather, while another trip may consist of a drive through the countryside to take in the scenery. For both trips, the attraction is the **destination** (in the first case, nodal, and, in the second case, linear), but in neither case is the attraction purpose-built to serve the interests of tourism, even if it may have been modified to do so. For example, the beach may have been cleaned up, deckchairs and windbreaks provided for hire and the appeal of the drive will be heightened if look-out points or picnic areas are provided by the local authority at which tourists are invited to stop off and enjoy their packed lunches. Equally, old buildings in town centres were not built with the purpose of bringing in tourists, but, over time, many have become architectural or historical sites that have tourist appeal.

All three of these 'destinations' – seaside resort, countryside and town – serve the needs of the local residents as well as tourists and, indeed, many residents may have chosen to live in that particular part of the world because of its attractiveness. German speakers have a useful term for this, *Freizeitswert*, implying the possession of enhanced leisure opportunities resulting from one's place of residence, a term which could usefully be incorporated into the English language.

There are other attractions, however, that *have* been constructed for the prime purpose of appealing to tourists, such as the Kröller-Müller Museum in the countryside near Otterloo in the Netherlands and, on a much larger scale, the Disney theme parks.

So, we must accept that no clear definition exists for the term. It is easiest just to accept that any site which appeals to people sufficiently to encourage them to travel there in order to visit it should be judged a 'tourist attraction'. It is helpful, however, to make some effort to categorize such attractions.

Swarbrooke (2002), who has considered a number of attempts at definition, splits attractions into four categories (modified here):

- features within the natural environment
- purpose-built structures and sites designed for purposes other than attracting visitors
- purpose-built structures and sites designed to attract visitors
- special events.

Similarly, Leask (2008) distinguishes between built and natural attractions, while also highlighting that distinctions could be drawn by ownership (public, private, voluntary or charity sector), intended markets (local, regional, national or international) and by entry policy (free or paid admission). Weaver and Lawton (2002) make further distinctions between attractions, suggesting that they are 'mainly natural or mainly cultural' (130), adding that both can be identified as either 'site'-based or 'event'-based.

For simplicity's sake, we can conclude that attractions may be defined as natural or constructed (whether or not purpose-built for tourism) and, if not constructed, they may still be to a greater or lesser extent 'managed' to suit the purpose of tourism or, more rarely, left entirely in their natural state.

Some sites attract tourists because of events that occur there or have occurred there in the past. In either case, they will then be known as event attractions, and these can be either temporary or permanent. Temporary events may be one-offs, at different sites on each occasion they occur (such as garden festivals in Europe that are arranged at intervals in different cities), while others (such as the Rio de Janeiro Carnival or New Orleans' Mardi Gras) are held at regular intervals at the same place. Some events are of very short duration – one day or even a matter of hours in the case of a concert.

Events, too, are also either artificial (constructed) or natural. The Changing of the Guard, for example, is a ceremony that attracts many overseas tourists visiting London, while the spring high tides that create the famous Severn Bore along the River Severn on the Wales–England border, the annual migration of wildebeest across the Serengeti Park in East Africa and the regular eruptions of Old Faithful, the geyser in Yellowstone National Park in the USA, are all examples of natural events that attract tourists.

Thus we can summarize this into four types of attraction:

1. natural sites;
2. natural events;
3. constructed sites; and
4. constructed events (see Table 10.1).

Many sites owe their continuing attraction to some event in the past. Liverpool is an example of somewhere that has become a place of pilgrimage for many visitors, due, in this case, to its links with The Beatles in the 1960s – a connection strongly promoted during 2008, when the city became a European Capital of Culture. Also, both John Lennon's home at 251 Menlove Avenue, Woolton, and Sir Paul McCartney's home at 20 Forthlin Road have been bought by the National Trust and are open to the public. Gettysburg in the USA, created a national military park in 1895, attracts millions of domestic tourists as it was the key battlefield site of the US Civil War in 1863, while Lourdes in France, a place of religious pilgrimage, owes its appeal entirely to events occurring in 1858, when a 14-year-old called Bernadette Soubirous was said to have experienced apparitions of the Virgin Mary.

One useful listing of different attractions was undertaken by the former English Tourism Council. While not totally comprehensive (its final category is something of a catch-all,

Table 10.1 Examples of different types of attraction

	Site	Event
Natural	Trekking through the Pantenal, Wetlands, Brazil	Travelling to see the Aurora Borealis (Northern Lights)
Constructed	Visiting Notre Dame Cathedral, Paris	Macy's Thanksgiving Day Parade, New York

while 'leisure attractions' might encompass anything from swimming pools and gymnasia to theme parks like the Walt Disney World Resorts), it does give us some direction for analysis of this sector of the industry:

- historic properties
- museums and art galleries
- wildlife parks
- gardens
- country parks
- workplaces
- steam railways
- leisure attractions
- other attractions.

In all, there are well over 6000 such attractions in the UK for which entrance figures are maintained, a quarter of these being historic properties and a similar number, museums. The Association of Leading Visitor Attractions (ALVA) reported that their top 150 visitor attractions (which include the British Museum, Westminster Abbey and Stonehenge) attracted almost 83 million visits in 2010 (ALVA, 2011). In addition to attractions with monitored visitor numbers, we must add the numerous buildings open to the public for which no attendance records are kept. There are, for instance, nearly 3000 Grade I listed churches in England alone and 15 000 churches altogether in the UK – VisitBritain estimates that these receive more than 13 million visits a year.

The total number of attractions continues to increase every year, boosted by the granting of heritage and lottery funding (the Millennium Fund at the turn of the century having accelerated the process). A few of these have proved almost instant successes. For example, Our Dynamic Earth in Edinburgh estimated, and budgeted for, 430 000 visitors a year, but actually received 500 000 in 1999, its opening year of operation. However, its annual numbers later dwindled to 200 000, and it received a financial bailout from the Scottish Government in 2008. Since then, it has introduced popular new exhibitions to increase numbers, but it is thought unlikely ever to achieve the estimated 400 000 visitors it originally budgeted for. Dynamic Earth is not unusual in failing to reach visitor targets – many other attractions have been hopelessly over-optimistic about their attendance figures and have either struggled to survive or collapsed – the notorious Millennium Dome perhaps being the outstanding example, running up debts in excess of £1 billion despite drawing the largest audiences in the country during the millennium year itself (it is noteworthy that, since being sold off to private enterprise, as the O_2 Arena it has now become one of the leading entertainment venues in the world). The National Centre for Popular Music in Sheffield, opened in 1999, was effectively bankrupt within seven months; estimating 400 000 visitors a year, it achieved only a quarter of that figure. The performance of the Earth Centre in Doncaster was even poorer. Forecasting 500 000 visitors when it opened in 1999, it attracted only 80 000 and collapsed financially in 2004. The following year, a 100 000 square feet community arts centre was proposed for West Bromwich, to be entitled 'The Public'. Funded by the Arts Council and the European Regional Development Fund (ERDF), its forecast was once again ambitious; expecting over half a million visitors each year, it actually received about one fifth of this number in its opening year.

While it would seem that many large-scale attractions are overambitious in their visitor expectations, most UK attractions do not anticipate hosting anything approaching these figures. Over 90% are geared to receiving fewer than 200 000 visitors annually and some of the smallest admit fewer than 10 000. These are not necessarily to be thought of as failing, however, if sponsored funding is available or costs are kept low and business plans carefully managed.

EXAMPLE   This museum won't give you the needle!

The Forge Mill Needle Museum, in the town Redditch, England, provides exhibits related to needles. This humble sewing implement may not seem to be the most exciting of themes to attract the tourist, but this museum tells the fascinating and sometimes gruesome story of needle-making in Victorian times. Models and recreated scenes provide a vivid illustration of how needles were once made and how Redditch came to dominate the industry by producing 90% of the world's needles.

The museum, opened in 1983 by the Queen, contains working machinery, images of the local needle industry, ornate needle cases, as well as extensive collections of needles made by local companies, some dating back almost 100 years.

Funding is by Redditch Borough Council and the museum has a small dedicated band of volunteers who, together with the staff, help to provide the tours, workshops for schools, special events and many other activities on offer. This brings around 20 000 visitors annually – highlighting that even the smallest of household items has the potential to become a successful attraction.

Table 10.2 identifies the top attractions in Europe. Note that many of the popular attractions are located in capital cities. The table also highlights the popularity of different types of attraction – with historic buildings and museums combined accounting for more than a third of all visits across Europe, while theme parks account for 10% of visits. If we look at the top three attractions in each country we can see that many could be considered world-renowned attractions, and this list includes many iconic structures – the importance of icons is discussed in the next section of this chapter.

It is important to recognize that many destinations owe their appeal to the fact that they offer a cluster of attractions within the immediate locality. Urban destinations are far less dependent on climate than are rural or coastal sites, and the UK (as in other temperate cities in Northern Europe, North America and Southern Australia) is fortunate in being able to attract year-round visitors to its cities' theatres, galleries and other indoor entertainments. The attraction of the seaside is also heightened, however – particularly in the UK, with its uncertain climate – by its being able to offer, either in the resort itself or within a short drive, a number of sites that are not weather-dependent, such as museums, amusement arcades, retail shopping malls, theatres and industrial heritage sites. In the UK, the need for a focal point, even in seaside resorts, had already been widely recognized by the nineteenth century – the great era for the construction of piers.

The focal point or icon

Contemporary tourism marketing implicitly or explicitly recognizes the importance of the focal point – or a synthesis of focal points – at a site, which acts as a magnet, attracting tourists. The focal point may be a historic building, such as a castle or monument, or it may be another type of construction owing its success to its architectural features, such as a tower, bridge or pier.

A supreme focal point is one that becomes a cultural icon, and the more popular tourist destinations are those blessed with such an attraction (see Figure 10.1). The fame of a cultural icon often extends far beyond the region itself, with the result that the images of the icon and destination are inseparable in the minds of prospective visitors. The power of such images has led to some locations setting out deliberately to create a cultural icon with which their region will be associated in the public mind – not always successfully. A few examples of the most successful will reveal the significance of the icon in tourism promotion (Table 10.3).

Table 10.2 Number of visits to tourism attractions in Europe (2009)

Country	Art galleries ('000)	Casinos ('000)	Circuses ('000)	Historic buildings/ sites ('000)	Museums ('000)	National parks/areas of natural beauty ('000)	Theatres ('000)	Theme/ amusement parks ('000)	Zoos/ aquariums ('000)	Other tourist attractions ('000)	Tourist attractions ('000)	Top 3 attractions
Austria	4 592.40	2 413.00	39	5 552.10	6 963.50	2 785.60	5 973.50	4 779.50	4 531.60	5 425.60	43 055.00	Schloß Schönbrunn/ Schauräume. Schönbrunner Tiergarten, Festung Hohensalzburg
Belgium	–	–	177.8	–	5 810.90	4 157.30	–	13 541.20	2 193.90	1 573.30	27 454.30	Antwerp Zoo, Walibi Belgium, Plopsaland
Bulgaria	1955.20	20.4	40.2	7 772.00	6 342.00	2 635.00	2 097.00	4.3	1 098.50	80.2	22 044.80	Varna Sea Garden, Vitosha Natural Park, Old Town of Sozopol
Croatia	770.9	436	20	1 805.90	1 589.10	2 119.40	1 396.10	–	611.4	1 486.10	10 235.00	Plitvice Lakes, Krka River, Pula Colosseum
Czech Republic	1 373.00	14.9	386.9	11 086.50	8 336.80	5 170.80	4 422.10	877.1	1 783.00	3 001.90	36 453.00	Prague Castle, Prague Zoo, Jewish Museum, Prague
Denmark	480	1 400.00	10.3	990	11 300.00	680	2 510.00	10 500.00	1 470.00	4 100.00	33 440.30	Tivoli, Dyrehavsbakken, Legoland
Finland	148	330.9	–	2 950.00	5 045.70	1 870.00	2 828.40	6 320.00	2 040.20	9 110.00	30 643.20	Linnanmäki Amusement Park, Suomenlinna Sea Fortress, Särkänniemi Amusement Park
France	25 670.70	64 450.10	12 920.50	29 115.50	42 900.00	8 855.90	7 677.00	60 000.00	17 414.20	82 058.30	351 062.20	Disneyland Paris, Musée du Louvre, Tour Eiffel
Germany	22 575.40	5 641.30	5 517.80	37 104.50	101 601.90	46 321.80	18 499.70	22 289.70	48 796.20	12 278.40	320 626.70	Cologne Cathedral, Europa-Park Rust, Reichstag, Berlin
Greece	321.2	3 293.70	276	5 970.50	2 813.50	2 999.00	1 460.60	3 699.00	495.7	341	21 670.20	Allou Fun Park, The Acropolis Museum, The Acropolis of Athens
Hungary	5 217.30	24	306.8	16 045.10	6 640.50	1 418.00	4 493.90	1 321.60	3 025.80	1 353.60	39 846.50	Széchenyi Thermal Bath, Parliament, Matthias Church

Country											Top attractions
Ireland	960.8	287.4	5 272.00	-	1759.90	611.7	821.7	685	1095.80	2 471.90	13 966.00	Guinness Storehouse, The National Gallery of Ireland, Cliffs of Moher Visitor Centre
Italy	6 801.30	1762.00	8 603.60	2 645.20	33 997.00	27 021.00	20 231.00	11 571.00	4 132.30	-	116 764.40	Anfiteatro Flavio, Musei Vaticani, Gardaland
Netherlands	-	6 189.00	50.7	349	25 765.00	2 012.00	18 778.00	13 584.00	11 045.00	-	77 772.70	De Efteling (Kaatsheuvel), Canal trips (Amsterdam), Diergaarde Blijdorp
Poland	3 990.00	1678.20	15 330.80	97.5	21 235.00	23 075.60	7 298.00	5 224.00	3 362.90	4 201.00	85 493.00	Sanctuary on Jasna Gora in Czestochowa, Tatrzanski National Park, Wolinski National Park
Portugal	116.2	380.7	2 990.00	93.8	325.8	408.9	246.1	509	664	2182.00	7 916.50	Shrine of Fatima, Caves do vinho do Porto, Oceanário de Lisboa
Romania	1 033.80	1640.50	1792.40	241.3	1072.40	1600.00	750	3.2	233.1	2 675.50	11 042.20	Parliament's House, Moldavian Monasteries, Sibiu
Russia	13 190.00	349	36 822.00	8 102.00	28 711.00	19 210.00	31100.00	5 721.00	9 622.00	14 997.00	167 824.00	Petergof (St Peterburg), Peter & Paul Fortress, Isaakievskiy Sobor (St Peterburg)
Slovenia	919.2	4 515.30	753.2	-	1449.60	854.2	797.7	89.9	233.4	36.1	9 648.60	Postojnska Jama, Blejski grad, Lj Grad
Spain	12 469.00	2 953.50	121 232.50	1112.50	15 052.50	10 682.50	11 035.00	13 163.20	10 562.50	7 256.20	205 518.90	Ciudad de las Artes y las Ciencias, Port Aventura, Alhambra
Sweden	1450.00	1212.20	12 112.00	-	16 380.00	-	3 122.00	7 123.00	4 412.00	12 887.00	58 698.20	Liseberg, Folkets Park Malmö, Kulturhuset
Switzerland	2 236.00	4 801.40	1452.00	-	4 498.00	4 866.00	-	2 278.00	5 296.00	1101.00	26 528.40	Zurich Zoo, Basle Zoo, Jungfraujoch
UK	2 942.30	16 117.90	38 465.10	2 473.40	74 257.50	127 770.40	21182.20	29 512.30	15 655.00	44 836.80	373 212.90	Blackpool Pleasure Beach, Xscape Milton Keynes, National Gallery

Source: Euromonitor, 2011

Figure 10.1 Christ the Redeemer, Corcovado mountain, Rio de Janeiro
Photo by Claire Humphreys

Table 10.3 International tourist icons

Location	Icons
London	Big Ben and the Houses of Parliament, Buckingham Palace
Paris	Eiffel Tower, Notre Dame
New York	Empire State Building, Statue of Liberty
San Francisco	Golden Gate Bridge
Sydney	Sydney Harbour Bridge, Opera House
Kuala Lumpur	Petronas Towers
Copenhagen	Little Mermaid statue
Bilbao	Guggenheim Museum

With the possible exception of the last in this list, none of these buildings was created with the deliberate intention of attracting tourists, yet, over time, their appeal has widened to a point where tourism flourishes because they exist. In the case of more recent projects (and no doubt boosted by the success of Bilbao, which, prior to the construction of the Guggenheim, had little to attract tourists), developers and architects have designed either with one eye on the potential for tourism or specifically with tourism in mind.

It is a postmodern irony that 80% of visitors to the Guggenheim do not enter the building – its attraction for many is not the artistic contents, but the building itself. Frank Gehry's innovative museum has influenced the design of countless more recent constructions straining for recognition as cultural icons within their communities, including the Kunsthaus in Graz, Austria, and the new Imperial War Museum in Manchester. Recruiting an architectural practice of international standing such as Foster and Partners (responsible, inter alia, for the renovated Reichstag in Berlin – see Figure 10.2 – the Millennium

Figure 10.2 The renovated Reichstag building in Berlin, designed by Foster Partners in 1999, has become an iconic symbol for the German capital

Photo by Chris Holloway

Footbridge in London and the Sage Concert Hall in Gateshead) is now seen as the first step in establishing a landmark building.

High towers used to be the icon-to-desire for tourist destinations. Today, it is more likely to be big wheels. Since the Prater fairground in Vienna built its 65-metre Riesenrad (big wheel) in 1897, engineers have sought to find ways to build still bigger ones. The London Eye – a 135-metre big wheel providing aerial views over the city – has proved both culturally and commercially successful, having rapidly become an integral component of Central London's cityscape. Following its success, other cities are striving to compete: Singapore has built a 165-metre big wheel, known as the Singapore Flyer, while the Chinese city of Nanchang erected the second highest observation wheel at 160 metres.

EXAMPLE **The Southern Star, Melbourne**

The Southern Star observation wheel was opened in December 2008, and was forecast to attract 1.5 million tourists to the Melbourne Docklands area. Yet barely two months later it was closed following concerns over structural defects. So problematic were these defects that a decision was eventually taken to dismantle the construction and erect a new wheel, using a different design. This new observation wheel is expected to be 120 metres in height and provide views across the central area of Melbourne.

It then took until 2011 to commence the rebuilding, and while the main spokes have been attached to the wheel hub, an official reopening date has not yet been predicted. Despite its short life, the closure of the wheel led to a noticeable drop in visitors to the area and its reconstruction is predicted to give people a reason for visiting the area again (Whitson, 2011). The benefits of the attraction are believed to be so great for the local area that this AUS$100 million attraction is eagerly awaited.

Table 10.4 UNESCO World Heritage sites in the UK

• Blaenavon Industrial Landscape	• Frontiers of the Roman Empire	• Saltaire
• Blenheim Palace	• Giant's Causeway and Causeway Coast	• St Kilda
• Canterbury Cathedral, St Augustine's Abbey, and St Martin's Church	• Heart of Neolithic Orkney	• Stonehenge, Avebury and Associated Sites
• Castles and Town Walls of King Edward in Gwynedd	• Ironbridge Gorge	• Studley Royal Park including the Ruins of Fountains Abbey
• City of Bath	• Liverpool – Maritime Mercantile City	• Tower of London
• Cornwall and West Devon Mining Landscape	• Maritime Greenwich	• Westminster Palace, Westminster Abbey and Saint Margaret's Church
• Derwent Valley Mills	• New Lanark	• Gough and Inaccessible Islands
• Dorset and East Devon Coast	• Old and New Towns of Edinburgh	• Henderson Island
• Durham Castle and Cathedral	• Pontcysyllte Aqueduct and Canal	• Historic Town of St George and Related Fortifications, Bermuda
	• Royal Botanic Gardens, Kew	

Note: The UK listing also includes the historic town of St George and related fortifications in Bermuda, as well as Henderson, Gough and Inaccessible Islands in the Pacific, which are dependent territories

It is worth stressing that, while cultural icons are crucial in attracting first-time visitors, all important tourist cities need to replenish and complement their stock of tourist attractions from time to time to encourage repeat business. The appeal of cities such as London and Paris is that they can attract so many visitors back again and again because of the wealth of attractions they offer – smaller, less well-known museums and newly constructed attractions alike.

The truly outstanding sites of architectural, cultural or historic importance around the world are recognized as UNESCO World Heritage sites. In 2011, 936 such sites were listed in 154 countries. They include 725 cultural sites, 183 natural sites and 28 of mixed composition. The UK, with 28 sites, has almost 3% of the total – for a small country, a favourable share as Table 10.4 reveals – although Italy, with 47 sites has over 5%. China has 41 sites and the USA, 21.

As we have highlighted there are many different types of attraction so for simplicity we will group the discussion under some common themes:

● historic buildings and heritage

● museums and galleries

● parks and gardens

● other forms of attractions

● events.

Historic buildings and heritage

Probably what most of us think of first, when considering the appeal of an urban location to tourists, are its historical and architectural features. Often they are subsumed into a general 'feel' of the destination, rather than there being an appreciation of any individual building – the sense that the town is old and beautiful, its buildings having mellowed over time and their architecture quintessentially representative of the region or nation and its people. Thus, old cobbled streets lined with protected shopfronts, gabled roofs and ornamental features, such as those to be found in towns like York in the UK, Tours in France, Rothenburg ob der Tauber in Germany, Aarhus in Denmark and Bruges in Belgium, all convey an overall impression of attractiveness and warmth, inviting us to shop there and enjoy the local food and lodgings (over 2500 hotels in the UK enjoy listed status, being of historic or architectural interest). These features are the supreme attraction of the 'old' countries of Europe, to which American, Arab and Japanese tourists alike are drawn when they first visit the country (and, where the UK is concerned, one should not underestimate the influence of Charles Dickens, whose nineteenth-century novels have had enormous impact in establishing the landscape and townscape images for which the country is known universally). In spite of an earlier disdain for older properties, the damage wrought by two world wars and the often poor quality of architectural construction in their aftermath, most nations in Europe have retained major elements of their old city centres, even, in some cases (as in Warsaw and Dresden), building entire replicas of the pre-war city centre in an attempt to regain their original character and heighten their appeal to visitors and residents alike.

EXAMPLE Protecting historic buildings in the UK

To retain and protect their heritage buildings the UK introduced a policy of listing historic buildings since 1950 (although the French had, in fact, introduced a similar, but less effective, policy at least 100 years earlier). Today, the nation boasts over 500 000 buildings listed as being of special historic or architectural interest.

In England and Wales, truly outstanding buildings fall into the Grade I category – of 'exceptional interest' – and make up about 2% of the total. A further 4% fall into the second category of Grade II* – of 'special interest'. Most others are listed as Grade II (in Scotland and Northern Ireland, similar buildings are categorized as A, B or C).

Today, all buildings in reasonable repair dating from before 1700 and most between 1700 and 1840 are listed, with strict controls over any cosmetic or structural changes to their exteriors. Among these, a handful (together with some of those scheduled as ancient monuments, but not necessarily all Grade I-listed buildings) stand out as icons, having sufficient power to draw visitors from all over the world. Castles and cathedrals, palaces and historic manor houses have such power, as do key sites of archaeological interest protected under the Ancient Monuments and Archaeological Areas Act (1979). The Tower of London alone receives over 2.4 million visitors annually, attracted not just by the building itself but also by the Crown jewels, which are on permanent display there.

At the other end of the scale, 'listed buildings' can include post-war prefabricated houses, garden sheds, army camps, pigsties, lamp-posts, even toilet blocks. The National Trust, with the aid of Heritage Lottery Funding, has even saved some of the last survivors of the back-to-back slums built in Birmingham between 1802 and 1831, some of which have been renovated and are now being rented out as visitor accommodation. The importance of all of these structures as key ingredients of our national heritage has been recognized by successive UK governments.

Apart from key sites, many other important buildings are open to visitors. There are believed to be well over 6000 historic houses, commonly referred to as 'stately homes', of which over 800 are open to the public. Some are under the care of the National Trust (National Trust for Scotland in Scotland), while others are in private hands. The Historic

Houses Association comprises around 1500 owners of private houses, of whom some 300 regularly open their houses to the public for at least 28 days a year (the minimum required to reduce inheritance tax). Some will only open by appointment and to small escorted groups, due to limitations of space. The particular value of all of these properties is their location, generally in the heart of the countryside, so they become a major support for rural tourism and the coach tour industry.

In Continental Europe, historic buildings play an equally important role in tourism for many countries. Notable among these are the châteaux of the Loire in France, Bavarian castles such as Neuschwanstein in Germany and medieval cities such as Florence and Venice in Italy. In Spain and Portugal, former stately homes – known, respectively, as paradores and pousadas and operated by the state – have been converted into luxury hotels, attracting upmarket touring visitors.

Although the history of the new world is shorter, funding is more readily available and early buildings that have survived are treasured. Americans take great pride in their prominent historic buildings, such as Monticello in Virginia – home of Thomas Jefferson, third president of the USA – while the town of Williamsburg in the same state has been preserved as a living museum of the colonial period. Buildings from the Spanish colonial period are also well preserved, including the missions of San Luis Rey in California, dating from 1789, and what is believed to be the nation's oldest house in St Augustine, Florida.

Seaside piers

The idea of a pier is a particularly British phenomenon. Very few are to be found in other countries, yet at one time the UK boasted more than 100. These soon proved to be attractions in their own right at many of the UK's most popular seaside resorts.

The first pier was constructed at Weymouth in 1812, soon followed by that at Ryde, Isle of Wight, in 1813. Their heyday, however, occurred between the mid-1800s and early 1900s, with 78 constructed between 1860 and 1910. They were first constructed to serve as walkways to reach the numerous paddle steamers moored offshore to provide excursions for holidaymakers, but were soon used for 'promenading' – a popular Victorian pastime. Margate Pier, built in 1853, was the first pier built purely for pleasure.

Piers have now become nostalgic accoutrements to seaside holidays at Victorian resorts and those that remain (some 55 in the UK in varying states of preservation) are currently enjoying something of a revival, with the formation of a National Piers Society to further public interest in their regeneration. Sadly it was too late to save the dilapidated West Pier in Brighton – a Grade I-listed pier – as it collapsed during a storm while efforts were still being made to raise funds for its restoration. Hastings Pier (see Figure 10.3), also on the south coast, was closed in 2006 over fears that the structure was unsafe. Plans to renovate the structure were sought, but this was interrupted when the main building was severely damaged by fire in October 2010.

Archaeological sites

Archaeology is the study of human antiquities, usually through excavation, and is generally thought to be concerned with pre- or early history, although much recent research is concerned with industrial archaeology – that relating to study of the industrial relics of the eighteenth and later centuries.

Areas where early civilizations arose, such as the countries of the Middle East, are rich in archaeological sites. Egypt, in particular, attracts visitors from around the world to sites such as the Pyramids at Giza, the burial sites at the Valley of the Kings and the temples at Luxor.

Figure 10.3 Hastings Pier before fire destroyed the main pavilion in 2010

Photo by Claire Humphreys

The UK is also rich in early historical sites, such as those at Chysauster prehistoric village in Cornwall, the Roman remains at Fishbourne in Sussex, with some of the richest mosaic flooring in the country, and the Skara Brae Neolithic site in the Orkney Islands. Myth and history are closely interwoven in our heritage and the legend of King Arthur, which locates his castle of Camelot at Tintagel, and the association of this mythical king with the archaeological digs at Cadbury Camp in Wiltshire, exercise a fascination for young tourists in particular.

In the early 1990s, the world's largest collection of paleolithic art, embracing hundreds of ice age drawings of animals, was discovered in a remote area of northern Portugal. A fierce battle then developed between those seeking to dam the area as a reservoir and others wanting to conserve the site for tourism. The latter won the day and the Côa Valley Archaeological Park was opened to the public in 1996.

Battlefields

Historic battlefield sites are also important tourist attractions, not least because many are situated in rural areas and encourage tourism to what otherwise may be unappealing countryside. A growing enthusiasm for knowledge of military encounters on the fields of battle has been encouraged by the popularity of historical documentaries on television, bringing awareness of these sites to a wider audience. In fact, many battlefield sites in the past have offered little for the tourist to see, the authorities feeling that the events taking place at the sites are best left to the visitors' imaginations. As a result, they have remained relatively undisturbed, but this also means that they are often under threat from development and may be compromised by the need for access roads. Local authorities are now making greater efforts to provide interpretation at these sites, using audio-visual displays and, in some cases, organizing associated events, such as staging mock battles at these sites on the anniversaries of the original engagements.

Battle re-enactment

Each year volunteers come to the town of Battle to re-enact the 1066 battle of Hastings. The event takes place at Battle Abbey, site of the original conflict, which operates a popular tourist attraction housing film and interactive displays which depict the story of the conquest of King Harold by William the Conqueror (see Figure 10.4).

More than 400 enthusiasts participate in the re-enactment and some 6000 visitors attend over the two-day event. English Heritage, managers of the sites, suggest that these tourists 'do not give the same attention to the property as visitors who choose to come at another time of the year, who buy the guidebook and make a more considered visit [but] those who come in October for the re-enactment leave the property excited and enthused by what they have seen, with the desire to learn more and with a positive image of heritage and history' (Burns, 2010).

Figure 10.4 Information board detailing the William the Conqueror trail located at Battle Abbey

Photo by Claire Humphreys

On the Continent, the sites of major battles – from the field of Waterloo to World War I and, increasingly, World War II – are attracting tourists in large numbers, as do the war graves. The museum at Ypres – the site of one of the major battles of World War I – received over 200 000 visitors in 2003, half of them British. Between 2010 and 2012, work to expand the museum to meet demand has been undertaken. Similarly, the USA preserves and commemorates its battle sites from both the War of Independence and the Civil War. A number of specialist tour operators focus on battle sites in their tour programmes, the best-known in the UK being Holts and Bartletts Battlefield Journeys. These companies have a high level of repeat business from amateur military strategists.

Industrial heritage

The UK became the seat of the industrial revolution in the eighteenth century and, over the past half century, interest has been awakened in the many redundant buildings and obsolete machinery dating back to this period. The fact that so many of the early factories and warehouses were also architectural gems has given impetus to the drive to preserve and restore them for tourism. Ironbridge – where the industrial revolution is claimed to have originated in 1709 – is now a UNESCO World Heritage site and has enjoyed the benefit of substantial tourism investment.

Other European countries as well as the USA and Australia have also recognized the tourism potential of such redundant buildings. Lowell, in Massachusetts, where a number of early mills survived intact, received massive federal government funding to be restored as an urban heritage park and, since the conversion of the buildings into museums, offices and shops, it has enjoyed considerable commercial success as an out-of-the-ordinary tourist destination.

The variety of industrial sites is astonishing. Early mining works in the UK, such as the coal and slate mines of South Wales or the copper mines of Cornwall, have been converted into tourist attractions, as have former docks and manufacturing buildings. Derelict textile mills in the north of England, driven out of existence by the importation of cheap textiles from developing countries following World War II, have taken on new life as museums or, in other cases, been converted into attractive new homes. The Big Pit Mining Museum at Blaenavon in South Wales and the Llechwedd Slate Caverns near Blaenau Ffestiniog in North Wales have both made important contributions to the local economy of the regions, with tourism helping to replace the former dependence on mining.

Other countries have emulated the UK in recognizing that their recent industrial heritage can play a part in attracting tourists. Countries with shorter histories, such as the USA and Australia, are fervent protectors of their earliest sites, both indigenous and of European origin. Former mining sites provide plenty of interest for tourists, not just in terms of their history but also sometimes for the opportunity they present for the tourists to do a spot of mining themselves. Bodie, California, was the site of early gold mining, and is now protected as Bodie State Historic Park. Tip Top, Arizona, was a silver mining area and is now attracting tourists, as is Macetown, New Zealand, an early gold mining area. Tourists in Australia are invited to pan for gold at former industrial sites (one of the authors struck lucky and still treasures the minute gold nugget he found!). Kolmanskop in Namibia, an abandoned diamond-mining town, is aiming to attract tourists to see not only its industrial heritage but also the lunar landscape that surrounds the site.

EXAMPLE   National Mine Park, Fuxin City, China

One of Asia's largest open-pit coal mines is now operating as a tourist attraction. Opened in 2009, the National Mine Park exhibits tools used in the blasting, drilling and mining process. There are also displays explaining the history, the need for mining and the environmental management pressures of modern industrial development.

The coal mine commenced operation in 1953 and produced over 200 million tonnes of coal. However, it was mined out in 2005, leaving the park area covering 28 square kilometres and, at its deepest, 175 metres below surface level. Converting this to a tourist attraction cost $58 million, but tourists can now travel to the bottom of the pit to see the different geological layers of the earth while learning more about the life of a miner.

Modern industrial tourism

As we can see in the example above, interest in industrial heritage has now widened to include the desire to observe *modern* industry, too. A number of companies have recognized the possibility of achieving good public relations by opening their doors to visitors, enabling them to visit a workshop or museum of some kind, and in some cases even permit a glimpse of work in progress at the factory.

American businesses were the first to recognize the public relations value of this sort of operation, and car companies in particular were soon arranging visits to manufacturing plants where prospective purchasers could watch cars being built. Today, this practice is widespread in the USA and is particularly beneficial in the sense that most automobile plants are not sited in areas that would normally attract tourists. Those that have been opened to the public include General Motors' Chevrolet Corvette factory in Bowling Green, Kentucky (it is one of the state's major tourist attractions), the Toyota assembly plant in Georgetown, also in Kentucky, GM's Saturn plant at Spring Hill, Tennessee, the Nissan plant in the same state at Smyrna, BMW's Zentrum visitor centre at its plant in Spartanburg, South Carolina, and the Ford Rouge factory near Detroit, Michigan – the traditional home of car manufacture. Some visits to these plants are booked months in advance, such is their popularity. German-based car plants have also developed their own themed attractions, with Opel Live at Rüsselsheim and Volkswagen's Autostadt in Wolfsburg. It is also possible to tour the Ferrari factory in Maranello, Italy, although you have to be a Ferrari owner to be allowed entry – so this could be a rather expensive attraction to visit.

Quite apart from creating good public relations, there are sound commercial reasons for doing this. Watching the production processes of, for example, modern china and glass will stimulate an interest in purchasing it and people can be encouraged to do so from a factory shop. At Cadbury's, the confectioners located in Bourneville, England, chocolates have been made by hand and are sold to the public individually by members of staff in traditional costumes. Other museums based on publicizing internationally popular products include Guinness in Ireland, Swarovski Crystal in Austria and Hershey Chocolate, Kelloggs and Coca-Cola in the USA.

China is probably the supreme example of a country where factory visits have been launched to encourage visitors to spend in their shops. What is often a minimal tour of the 'factory' itself is followed by an extended visit to the shop, fuelled by liquid refreshments to encourage visitors to purchase. In other countries where high-value goods are for sale (for example, in precious gem shops in Namibia or South Africa), coffee or wine is served to visitors and they are encouraged to take their time in the shop while perusing the products to encourage sales.

In 1980, the Sellafield nuclear fuel plant in England was opened to visitors to help counteract much negative publicity about nuclear energy that had appeared in the media. This quickly became a major, and quite unexpected, draw for tourists in the area; since then, other nuclear processing plants have also opened their doors to give guided tours.

Producers of alcoholic drinks have long tapped tourist markets. Wine producers in both the new and old world provide visitors with tours of the cellars and tastings, sherry producers in Spain welcome visitors to their bodegas and, similarly, more than 40 Scotch whisky distilleries allow visits by members of the public.

EXAMPLE   **Heritage Open Days**

English Heritage annually organizes a weekend of open days, which allows access to buildings not usually open to the public. The buildings often provide tours, talks and other events, many of which usually focus on the architecture and local culture. In 2010, around a million visitors took advantage of the free entry to explore a variety of unusual properties open to the public - including factories, offices, private homes, windmills, town halls and government buildings.

Established in 1994, the Heritage Open Days are part of a European initiative to provide access to historical venues; Doors Open Days in Scotland and Wales offer similar opportunities.

Many craftspeople depend on tourists visiting their studios in order to sell their products and, as these studios are frequently set in the countryside, they stimulate tourism to the area. For this reason, public funding is sometimes made available to help companies willing to open to the public, Langham Glass in the UK being an example.

The attraction of modern structures

In the earlier discussion of people's search for a cultural icon, it will be readily apparent that modern buildings are becoming almost as important as historic ones in their ability to attract tourists. Commercial offices, private houses, bridges, monuments and memorials, towers and many other constructions that represent a fusion of artistic creativity and high technology are all becoming important, when sufficiently spectacular.

Figure 10.5 The Burj al-Arab, Dubai, UAE
Photo by Chris Holloway

The more recently proliferating Holocaust museums and memorials in Europe and North America were not specifically designed with the intention of boosting tourism, but the outstanding quality and originality of their designs (and the widespread media publicity that followed their construction) are ensuring that they become popular places to visit. Often, the appeal of these new constructions is the 'wow' factor – the adrenalin rush that accompanies viewing many new spectacles, such as the towering 'seven star' Burj al-Arab Hotel in Dubai (see Figure 10.5).

Tourists have been – and still are – fascinated by the sight of tall towers or other buildings, the Eiffel Tower being an outstanding example and, as we have seen, an immediately recognizable icon of Paris. Many destinations still strive to impress their visitors by building the tallest, most impressive towers in the world, with the result that towers of all descriptions are rising ever higher, although few provide access for tourists to visit the summit.

As was the case with the Guggenheim in Bilbao, the significance of modern architecture's appeal is that many of the great buildings are constructed on sites that are not traditionally visited by tourists. The following ten buildings have been cited as 'worth a visit from the international tourist' (Binney, 2004):

● Museum of Fantasy, Bernried, Germany
● Bao Canal Village, China
● concert hall at León, Spain
● Bodegas Ysios, Rioja, Spain (designed by leading architect Antonio Calatrava)
● Parliamentary Library at New Delhi, India
● UFA Cinema, Dresden, Germany
● 'Aluminium Forest' Visitor Centre, Utrecht
● Tango Ecological Housing, Malmö, Sweden
● Art Museum, Milwaukee, USA (also by Calatrava)
● Modern Art Museum, Forth Worth, USA.

These are hardly mainstream tourist destinations, but several could be described as actively striving to build their tourism markets, and they are using contemporary architecture as one weapon in their arsenal to achieve this.

The fickleness of public taste in modern buildings is problematic, both in terms of whether or not such buildings deserve to be listed and/or protected and whether they are seen by tourists as worthwhile visiting. The numerous Art Deco period buildings in Miami Beach present us with a good example of this fickleness. For years they were spurned by the public and threatened with the prospect of being replaced by more modern hotels. Their value was not recognized until the 1990s, when there was a systematic campaign to restore them to their former glory.

The bridge is another type of structure that has always found favour with tourists. Indeed, American enthusiasts actually purchased and transported the former London Bridge, re-erecting it on Lake Havasu in Arizona. Tower Bridge in London, the Pont du Gard in France, the Golden Gate in San Francisco and the Sydney Harbour Bridge are all well-established tourist attractions in their own right.

Advances in engineering are making the construction of modern bridges ever more awe-inspiring. The opening in 2004 of the world's highest bridge, the Millau Viaduct bridge across the Tarn Valley (another Foster design), is attracting many sightseers to the Massif Central region of France, quite apart from the 10 000–25 000 motorists who need to drive across it each day. The tallest of the bridge's seven piers is 343 metres – taller than the Eiffel Tower – while vehicles cross at a height of 270 metres. Again, local residents, who at first complained about it, are now relishing the inflow of tourists that the bridge has generated.

Museums and art galleries

Both museums and art galleries are visited by huge numbers of tourists each year. In the UK alone, 67.8 million people visited museums and art galleries in 2010/11 (DCMS, 2011). Many are established primarily to serve the needs of the local inhabitants – at least initially – but others have quickly gained international reputations. Examples of the latter include the British Museum in London, the Ashmolean Museum in Oxford, the Louvre in Paris, the Smithsonian Museum in Washington DC and the Museum of Modern Art (MoMA) in New York. To these can now be added a number of exciting buildings in the Middle East designed by prominent architects, and either recently opened or currently under construction (see Figure 10.6). The significance of these for tourism is that they can act as a catalyst for visiting a destination and, in some cases, become the major reason for a visit to the destination, especially in cases where there are outstanding exhibitions.

Museums have a very long history and, in the UK, date back to at least the seventeenth century, when some private collectors opened their exhibitions for a fee. John Tradescant's Cabinet of Curiosities provided the foundation for the Ashmolean Museum at Oxford University in 1683. The equally famous Fitzwilliam Museum's art collection at Cambridge did not follow until 1816.

There are six main categories of museum in the UK:

- *National museums* usually funded directly by the Department for Culture, Media and Sport (DCMS) – these include such famous museums as the British Museum, National Gallery, Tate Britain and Tate Modern art galleries, Victoria and Albert Museum, Imperial War Museum and Royal Armouries, Leeds. Certain national museums are funded by the Ministry of Defence, such as the RAF Museum in Hendon and the National Army Museum, both in London.

- *Independent (charitable trust) museums* financed by turnover – the National Motor Museum at Beaulieu being an example.

Figure 10.6 The Doha Museum of Islamic Art, Qatar (architect I. M. Pei)
Photo by Chris Holloway

- *Independent non-charity museums* such as Flambards Museum in Helston, Cornwall. University collections are funded in a variety of ways, drawing on contributions from both public and private sources.
- *Regional museums* funded publicly or by a mix of public and private funding. The DCMS also funds museums such as the Geffrye and Horniman Museums in London and the Museum of Science and Industry in Manchester.
- *Local authority museums* such as the Cotswold Countryside Museum in Gloucester and the Georgian House and Red Lodge Museums owned by Bristol City Council.
- *Small, private museums* these depend entirely on private funding.

Museums have experienced two boom periods in recent history. The first of these was during the period between 1970 and the mid-1980s, when many of them were able to take advantage of government grants, coupled with charitable status, which meant that they avoided paying tax; and, later, especially in the lead up to the millennium celebrations, through Millennium Commission funding or Lottery grants. In the initial stage, a large number of redundant buildings, ideal for converting into museums, became available. The nostalgia boom and a generally positive view towards urban renewal and heritage all encouraged new museums to open. In the second stage, though, funding tended to favour larger projects.

The problem for those who manage museums is that the initial capital investment is not the only financial consideration. Many collections are donated or gifts of money are made in order to establish a museum, but steadily rising operating costs are seldom met by increases in revenue and, after the first two or three years, during which time the museum has novelty value, attendance figures slump. As new museums are opened, so the available market to visit them is more thinly spread. Museums have also been badly hit in recent years by the consequences of the Education Reform Act, which has made the financing of educational visits – a key sector for many museums – more difficult.

Many museum curators argue in favour of subsidies, on the grounds that their museums help to bring tourists to an area and, once there, they can be encouraged to spend. Certainly, clusters of museums and other complementary attractions, such as shops, do give rise to greater numbers of tourists. The Castlefield site in Manchester is a good example of a 'critical mass' of attractions sited close together, making it an attractive day out. Conference and exhibition halls have long been underwritten by local authorities on just these grounds, but they are much more constrained financially than in the past and, in some cases, have been forced to reduce the support they formerly provided to the museums in their territory. This has led to winter closures in some cases, or more restricted times of opening.

Museums have become increasingly self-sufficient, and their curatorial role is now less significant than their marketing one. The national museums in London were briefly obliged to introduce charges – or at the very least they 'suggested contributions' – in the 1990s, resulting in a very sharp drop in attendance. Those that did not introduce charges benefited. Those that did decide to charge, however, were able to invest in refurbishment, which, with government subsidies alone, would not have been possible. Since the obligation to charge has been removed, the galleries have experienced an upsurge in attendance and it is notable that seven of the top ten most visited attractions in the UK are museums or art galleries (see Table 10.5).

As a result of the reduction or withdrawal of public funding, museums have been obliged to become increasingly commercial in their approach. Buildings are redesigned to ensure that all visitors exit via the shop, and investigations are made into what sells or fails to sell, and into price-sensitivity. Galleries are hired for private functions, sponsorship is sought to finance exhibitions, sometimes even whole galleries (such as the Annenberg and Hutong Galleries at the British Museum). Catering also has become an important money-raiser, with increasing emphasis placed on the location and design of cafés and restaurants. All principal museums in the UK are now expected to engage in fund-raising, both publicly and through their memberships and friends' associations.

Museums not sited close to major centres of population or with poor accessibility generally find it difficult to attract tourists in large numbers. One notable exception, to which several references have been made already, is the Guggenheim in Bilbao, which rapidly became an authentic cultural icon soon after its construction.

EXAMPLE   The Guggenheim museums and their value to tourism

The Guggenheim museums have had particular success in attracting tourists, partly for their contents, but more notably for their architectural merit.

The construction of the Guggenheim in Bilbao was a deliberate move on the part of the local authorities to promote the city as an attractive place to visit. The proposed museum received very strong public-sector support and significant financial aid from the Guggenheim Foundation, which had the foresight to contract an outstanding architect, Frank Gehry, to design the unconventional building.

The result is that tourists beat a path to its door. There were over 1.3 million visitors in its first year, even though Bilbao had never been a traditional tourist destination and had, at least at that point, little else to attract tourists. Bilbao now enjoys success as a strong short-break destination and the museum has achieved more than 10 million visits in its first decade of operation.

There are currently Guggenheim museums in New York, Bilbao, Venice, Berlin and Las Vegas, and Frank Gehry has been retained to complete a sixth in Abu Dhabi. This is designed to put the UAE firmly on the cultural tourist map and will form part of a group of four world-class museums to be clustered on Saadiyat Island. Completion of the new Guggenheim is anticipated for 2013.

Table 10.5 ALVA attractions with over 1 million admissions in 2010

Attraction	Total visits
British Museum	5 842 138
Tate Modern	5 061 172
National Gallery	4 954 914
Natural History Museum	4 647 613
Science Museum (South Kensington)	2 751 902
V&A (South Kensington)	2 629 065
National Maritime Museum	2 419 802
Tower of London (HRP)	2 414 541 (c)
St Paul's Cathedral	1 892 467 (pt c)
National Portrait Gallery	1 819 442
Tate Britain	1 665 291
British Library	1 454 612
Westminster Abbey	1 394 427 (pt c)
National Galleries of Scotland (Edinburgh sites)	1 281 465 (pt c)
Old Royal Naval College Greenwich	1 274 957
Edinburgh Castle (Historic Scotland)	1 210 248 (pt c)
Chester Zoo	1 154 285 (c)
Royal Botanic Gardens, Kew	1 141 973 (c)
Kelvingrove Art Gallery & Museum (Glasgow)	1 070 521
Imperial War Museum (London)	1 069 358
Roman Baths & Pump Room, Bath	1 054 621 (c)
Canterbury Cathedral	1 033 463 (pt c)
Merseyside Maritime Museum	1 027 475
ZSL London Zoo	1 011 257 (c)
Stonehenge (EH)	1 009 973 (c)
Eden Project	1 000 511 (c)

Key: (c) charge for entry; (pt c) charge for entry to some areas or exhibitions.
Source: ALVA, 2011

To attract new audiences and bring back previous visitors, many museums are moving away from the concept of 'objects in glass cases' in favour of better interpretation and more active participation by the visitors. New techniques include guides dressed in period costume, audio-visual displays, self-guided trails using recordings, reconstructions of the past and interactive programmes that provide opportunities for hands-on experience.

In the kitchen of the oldest house in Toronto, to take one example, the guide demonstrates the making of soap, provides souvenirs of the finished product to the visitors and reveals that the soap can be eaten, too! Some museums are fully interactive, such as Explore at Bristol Museum, which is designed to explain science to those who do not know too much about it by giving them the opportunity to become involved in practical experiments. At the Big Pit Mining Museum in Blaenavon – a former colliery transformed into a mining museum in 1980 and now a World Heritage site – former miners act as guides, providing vividly illustrated tours that draw on their own former experiences in the mines. In a similar vein, former inmates interned on Robben Island under South African apartheid laws now address visitors to the island museum and show them the cell where Nelson Mandela was interned (see Figure 10.7).

Figure 10.7 A former political prisoner addresses visitors to the prison where Nelson Mandela was incarcerated on Robben Island, South Africa

Photo by Chris Holloway

An example of a 'living history' museum can be found at Llancaiach Fawr Manor, a sixteenth-century fortified house in the South Wales valleys. Here, actor/interpreters (more correctly referred to in mainland Europe as 'animateurs'), dressed in costumes of the period, act as 'below stairs' staff, guiding visitors around the site, using the language and speech patterns of the time and authentically recreating the year 1645.

Many museums, for example, are the former homes of famous people and the trustees have a curatorial and research role in safeguarding and investigating documents of its famous owner, as well as encouraging tourist trade for commercial reasons. A good example of this is Graceland, the former home of Elvis Presley in Memphis, Tennessee. Long after the star's death, it continues to attract huge crowds of fans who come to see his house, his former possessions and his grave – especially in the year 2005, the seventieth anniversary of his birth. Graceland has become one of the major tourist attractions in the USA and is listed in the National Register of Historic Places. With over 700 000 visitors annually, it is now second only to the White House itself in terms of the number of visitors it receives each year.

Parks and gardens

Gardens and arboreta

According to the National Botanic Garden of Wales, there are some 1846 botanic gardens in 148 countries around the world, which admit more than 150 million visitors every year.

Key sites, such as Kirstenbosch Botanic Gardens near Cape Town, South Africa, attract visitors from all over the world. The cultivation of gardens has an enthusiastic following in the UK, a fact not lost on those organizing visits; both private and public gardens, and arboreta, which are essentially museums for living trees and shrubs, are popular. The Royal Botanic Gardens at Kew attracted 1.4 million visitors in 2010.

Many gardens popular with visitors are in the care of the National Trust, generally as adjuncts to stately homes. In some cases (as is the case with Stourhead in Wiltshire), the gardens may prove a stronger draw than the houses themselves and, in others, only the gardens are open to the public. Great landscape architects of the eighteenth century, such as Capability Brown and Humphrey Repton, built splendid parks to complement great manor houses and, as recently as the twentieth century, famous gardens were still being constructed. The great garden designer Gertrude Jekyll is a notable example of this, her work often complementing that of the popular architect of great houses of the early part of the twentieth century, Sir Edwin Lutyens.

Apart from the gardens at Kew (a World Heritage site) and the Westonbirt Arboretum (see the Example), other popular attractions include Kew's offshoot, a 500-acre site at Wakehurst Place, Haywards Heath (one of the National Trust's most popular attractions), the grounds of Hampton Court and the famous Wisley Gardens. The proximity of all these to London helps to ensure their success with day trippers.

EXAMPLE Westonbirt Arboretum

Westonbirt, in Gloucestershire, is one of the most important arboreta in the UK. English Heritage have designated it a Grade I-listed landscape in its Register of Parks and Gardens of Special Historical Interest.

Managed by the Forestry Commission, because it is on the fringe of the Cotswolds it is easily accessible by tourists. It receives more than 350 000 visitors a year – partly due to the pattern of regular events mounted year round at the Arboretum. In addition to summer concerts, it stages an annual Festival of Wood (in which dead trees are turned into sculptures), open-air plays, and, between June and September, a Festival of the Garden, featuring pieces of installation art that are then sold to raise money for Tree Aid, a charity planting trees in Africa. On midwinter evenings it offers an illuminated trail, the trees emblazoned tastefully with white lights, which attracts many tourists who might otherwise never visit the site.

Westonbirt is actively supported through a 'friends association', which has over 25 000 members. The group has raised £2.5 million to help fund education, research and support for projects which preserve the forest.

Another highly successful attraction in the UK is the Eden Project in Cornwall, which received 1 285 000 visitors between April and September in its first year. Early research has indicated that 92% of all visitors stayed in holiday accommodation nearby when they visited and so the Cornish economy has been forecast to have benefited by some £1.8 billion over the site's first decade of operation, between 2001 and 2011. Its appeal is boosted by its proximity to another garden attraction, the Lost Gardens of Heligan, making it a popular coach trip for garden enthusiasts taking a short-break holiday.

Public and private sectors are now uniting to further this interest in all things horticultural. In Wales, a joint marketing initiative brought together seven leading gardens under the promotional theme Premier Gardens Wales. The bicentenary year of the Royal Horticultural Society, 2004, was declared the Year of Gardening in the UK, leading to the promotion of 200 prominent gardens around the country. Smaller private gardens are also regularly opened to the public throughout the summer each year under the National Gardens Scheme, to benefit charity. While primarily aiming to attract locals, in practice enthusiasts will travel considerable distances to visit some of these gardens and must certainly be counted among day tripper figures for these regions. Indeed, a number of visitors will even have travelled from abroad to visit these gardens.

Garden festivals (strictly speaking, these are event attractions) are also popular in Germany, France and the Netherlands. A national garden festival is held in Germany every two years and, in the Netherlands, every ten years. France, too, benefits significantly from garden tourism. The formal gardens attached to the châteaux in the Loire valley and Monet's garden at Giverny have become major international tourist attractions, the latter especially so since its restoration. North America also has its share of notable garden attractions. Perhaps the most famous are the Butchart Gardens on Victoria Island, British Columbia in Canada, but popular and much-visited botanic gardens in the USA include the Denver Botanic Gardens in Colorado and Longwood Gardens, a 1000-acre site founded by the du Pont family at Kennett Square, Pennsylvania, which attracts over 900 000 visitors a year.

Wildlife parks

Wildlife is a growing attraction for tourists and the tourism industry has responded to this interest in wildlife in different ways. At one time, the most common way for tourists to see wild animals was in the many zoos that exist in most countries around the world – and, as we can see in Table 10.2, four zoos make it into the list of top European attractions. The keeping of collections of animals goes back at least 2000 years, but the present-day concept of a zoo dates back only to the eighteenth century. In the UK, although zoos are known to predate the turn of the nineteenth century, the founding of the Zoological Society in London by Sir Stamford Raffles at the beginning of that century led to the interest that Victorian England took in caged animals.

Today, there are some 900 established zoos around the world, but attitudes to zoos have changed. People in Western countries have come to consider it cruel to keep animals in captivity. Nevertheless, zoos still enjoy high attendance figures, although not reaching the peaks of 30 years ago, and their administrators are adapting to this change. They now stress their curatorial role, preserving rare species of wildlife, rather than displaying animals for the purpose of entertainment. There was a fear at the end of the 1980s, as attendances fell, that London's famous zoo in Regent's Park might be forced to close. Although that fear receded with a massive private investment of capital, this sharpened awareness of zoos as a whole in the UK, renewing interest in visiting them and encouraged the construction of better facilities to keep the animals in more natural settings so they are now less constrained.

With the growth of long-haul travel, more tourists are taking advantage of the opportunity to see these animals in the wild, usually in safari parks. The best-known of these are situated in South and East Africa, as we saw in Figure 9.13 in the previous chapter. Some of these big game parks have become world famous, including Kenya's Masai Mara, Tsavo, Amboseli and Samburu Parks, Tanzania's Serengeti National Park and South Africa's Kruger National Park. The attraction of these parks lies in the opportunity to see big game, such as lions, elephants, leopards, buffalo and rhino – the so-called 'big five' (although poaching is rapidly diminishing numbers of the last of these). All of these parks feature in tour operators' long-haul programmes, although political uncertainty in many African countries and the lack of investment in some has hindered the expansion of tourism to the safari parks in recent years. This has, however, benefited some lesser-known parks in countries such as Botswana.

With the decline in zoo attendance, efforts have been made to introduce the atmosphere of the safari park in the UK, notably at the Marquess of Bath's property at Longleat in Wiltshire. Running costs for such projects are high as they need to provide maximum security to protect visitors. Another safari park at Windsor was attracting close to a million visitors a year, but still proved a financial failure, closing in 1992.

EXAMPLE Seeking the rare animal

Many adventure travellers, having visited the leading wildlife parks around the world, set out to seek the unusual, rare animals in some of the most remote places of the world. An example is the Iriomote Wildcat, of which fewer than 100 are thought to survive. They live on Iriomote Island, Japan – a 35-minute ferry ride from Ishigaki Island. The island's population is just 2325, but tourist numbers have been increasing dramatically over the past five years, with more than 405 000 visiting in 2007. Needless to say, with these numbers, opportunities for seeing the wildcat are as remote as the island, and some even doubt its continued existence (Onishi, 2008).

Another form of wildlife park is the wildfowl reserve. Birdwatching is a popular pastime in the UK, and the Wildfowl Trust at Slimbridge in Gloucestershire has been a model for other sites around the country as birds can be viewed in their natural setting.

Birdwatching also attracts the specialist long-haul market, with tour operators such as Naturetrek and Birdquest among a number offering specialist holidays for the study of bird life, frequently accompanied by well-known ornithology experts who will lecture to clients *en route*. The appearance of rare birds attracts the enthusiasts; thousands visit the Lizard in Cornwall every year in the hope of seeing the rare choughs, while it has been estimated that 290 000 annually visit osprey viewing sites in the UK, bringing around £3.5 million to the local economies.

Other attractions, for which tourism is a secondary consideration in some cases, include falconry centres and animal sanctuaries. Sanctuaries, of course, exist to protect and tend to wounded animals, but most are open to visitors, who make a useful contribution, through their admission fees, to the running costs of the project. In the Persian Gulf, the popularity of falconry, and the presentation of birds of prey at bird centres, attracts both domestic and foreign visitors (see Figure 10.8).

Finally, reference should be made in this section to the popularity of aquariums (now more commonly known as sealife centres). The popular revulsion to keeping animals in cages has not yet generally extended to fish (and, although there are movements to close down entertainments incorporating captive seawater mammals such as porpoises and dolphins, they remain popular in the USA).

On the Continent, the Sea Life Centre in Paris and Nausicaa, le Centre Nationale de la Mer, in Boulogne are two popular recent additions in this area. Many such centres have also been constructed in the USA, that at Monterey in California being particularly notable for both the size of the tanks (one of which includes a full-scale kelp forest) and the fact that there is a unique pen with direct access to the Pacific Ocean, allowing sea otters to swim in to and out of the setting at will.

Theme and amusement parks

Until now we have been discussing parks which draw on the natural environment to create the attraction. However, we must also consider parks which draw on a constructed environment to provide the entertainment. Purpose-built leisure parks are, not surprisingly, major attractions for tourists, and they receive the greatest number of visitors of all tourist attractions. It is estimated that total attendance of the top 25 theme parks worldwide was in excess of 189 million visits in 2010 (TEA, 2010).

The appetite for such parks to entertain the public seems never-ending and, in Europe, they have a very long history. Bakken, in Klampenborg near Copenhagen, lays claim to being the oldest amusement park in the world, having opened in 1583. London's Vauxhall

Figure 10.8 Birds of prey on show at the Bird Centre, Doha, Qatar
Photo by Chris Holloway

Gardens opened in 1661, followed in the eighteenth century by Ranelagh Gardens and the Tivoli Gardens in Paris. By the nineteenth century, entertainment parks were firmly established, with the Tivoli Gardens in Copenhagen, which first opened in 1843, soon becoming one of the world's leading centres of entertainment. This park continues to attract over 4 million visitors annually. Blackpool Pleasure Beach – the UK's first seaside entertainment centre – opened in 1896 and is still one of the most visited tourist attractions in the country, with nearly 6 million visitors.

The world's biggest amusement park became established at around the same time at Coney Island, in Brooklyn, New York City. The world's first roller coaster was built there in 1884 and, by 1895, an indoor amusement park, Sea Lion Park, had been added. Eventually, three separate parks – Luna Park, Steeplechase Park and Dreamland – opened on this seaside site between 1897 and 1904, with up to 250 000 visitors a day. A succession of fires destroyed two of the parks, but Luna Park remained popular until its decline after the Wall Street Crash in 1929, after which it struggled to survive, finally closing in 1944. Plans have been put forward to regenerate the area with a $1 billion investment, after its steady decline in the 1950s and 1960s. Australia emulated the success of Coney Island in its early years with its own Luna Park in Melbourne in 1912, followed by a second in Sydney in 1935.

The 1920s were the heyday of these amusement parks. The Great Depression caused attendances to decline until a new generation of theme parks arrived in the 1950s. Although de Efteling was opened in Europe as early as 1951 with a fairy tales theme, and Bellewaerde Park followed in 1954, it was Walt Disney Enterprises that popularized the concept of the theme park with its development at Anaheim, California in 1955, and it reinvigorated the market. It was followed by a number of Disney developments around Orlando in Florida, the first of which opened in 1971, and these now attract tourists from all over the world.

Today's amusement parks can be classified, according to size, into three distinct categories:

- local parks, catering largely to the day tripper market
- flagship attractions, such as the Tivoli or Prater in Vienna, which draw on national markets and attract a significant number of foreign visitors, too
- icon, or destination, parks, such as those of the Disney empire, which have become destinations in their own right and attract a worldwide market.

The USA alone boasts over 750 leisure parks, but the large Disney parks account for by far the greatest number of visitors. They attracted 120 million people in 2010 (The Magic Kingdom at Orlando alone attracted almost 17 million) and the 11 other Disney parks are listed among the top 25 world attractions. The second-largest US operator, Six Flags, caters for nearly 24 million people. Disney dominates in the USA, and has since developed further sites near Tokyo and Paris and in Hong Kong. More recently, Disney has partnered the Chinese Government to develop a new theme park in Shanghai, and talks are rumoured to be taking place to construct a park in India.

The clustering and scale of several attractions in one region of Florida, around Orlando, has given the European tourism industry the scope to develop package holidays focused on this region and, as a result, this destination has become one of the most popular in the world for long-haul package holidays. Visitors tend to spend several days visiting the parks, allowing a huge bed stock, approaching 100 000 rooms, to be constructed.

As we can see in Table 10.6, the Disney empire, with over 120 million visitors to its parks each year, has no direct competition. Its nearest global competitor, Merlin Entertainments Group, attracted 41 million in 2010, but is expanding rapidly, with ambitious plans to create five new attractions each year.

Table 10.6 Major theme park companies

Park owners	Total attendance (millions)	Examples of their parks
Walt Disney Attractions	120.6	Walt Disney World Resort, Florida; Disneyland, California; Disneyland Europe; Hong Kong Disneyland
Merlin Entertainments	41.0	Madame Tussauds; Legoland; Gardaland, Italy; Earth Explore, Belgium; Heide Park, Germany
Universal Studios	26.3	Universal Orlando Resort; Universal Studios Hollywood; Universal Studios Japan
Parques Reunidos	25.8	Warner Bros. Park, Madrid; Bobbejaanland, Belgium; Mirabilandia, Italy; Bonbonland, Denmark; Kennywood, USA
Six Flags	24.3	Six Flags: over Texas, Arlington; Magic Mountain, San Francisco; Discovery Kingdom, Los Angeles; Great America, Chicago; New England, Springfield
Cedar Fair Entertainment	22.8	Cedar Point, Ohio; Knott's Berry Farm, California; Canada's Wonderland, Ontario; Kings Dominion, Virginia; Dorney Park, Pennsylvania
Seaworld Parks	22.4	SeaWorld Orlando; Busch Gardens Tampa; Busch Gardens Williamsburg; Sesame Place, Pennsylvania
OCT Parks China	19.3	Splendid China; Windows on the World; OCT East Resort; Happy Valley Beijing; Happy Valley Shanghai; Happy Valley Shenzhen

Sources: TEA, 2010; C. J. Humphreys

The Walt Disney Company may also soon be challenged by another competitor, however, in the shape of Dubailand, scheduled to be completed by 2016. Originally, this was expected to be the world's largest theme park, but the 2008 recession led to this project being scaled down. Now, through an alliance with Six Flags, their first project outside of America, the area is expected to include a variety of family attractions as well as sports stadiums, golf courses, shopping malls and residential accommodation. Several attractions are already open and in 2011 a new ecotourism attraction, Desert Ranch, was announced as part of the next phase of development.

In Europe, theme parks tend to be smaller and have lower levels of investment in both development and marketing than do the Disney parks, and hence do not attempt to compete directly with them, instead drawing on mainly national markets.

The distinction between a **theme park** and an **amusement park** is not always a clear one, although the former is rather loosely based on some theme, whether geographical, historical or some other such concept. European theme park operators are searching constantly for new themes that will draw the crowds. Germany, which has long enjoyed a love affair with America's Wild West (largely through the popular Western novels of Karl May), opened a new park, Silver Lake City, near Berlin in 2004, based on the images projected by Hollywood films over the past century.

Before the development of such theming concepts, the predominant aim of the leisure park was to entertain by means of the traditional funfair, with stalls, helter-skelters, candy floss and other trappings that have been familiar for many decades. Later, parks began vying with one another to devise new rides and challenge younger visitors by incorporating ever more frightening 'white-knuckle' experiences in their major centrepieces. With the introduction of the new theme parks, while amusement rides remained an important element, the theme (such as associating the park with popular cartoon or TV characters as in Parc Asterix and Sesame Place) heightens the attraction for many. Building on the popularity of film and TV characters among younger visitors is important for a market that is composed chiefly of family groups.

EXAMPLE **Technological advances for theme parks**

Using technology to enhance the visitor experience has long been an important part of the theme park owner's armour. But the pace of technological development means that things once considered exotic and magical can quickly become routine.

Perhaps at the forefront of the technology armour is augmented reality – the use of digital technology to add information to everyday objects. Disney has incorporated this into its Haunted Mansion ride in Orlando. The system records an image of the visitor and projects this onto a screen which simulates a mirror, digitally adding ghosts and ghouls to interact with the image. This can involve the ghosts swapping people's heads or embellishing faces with beards. Thus the visitors become an integral part of the ride experience.

Mention should also be made of the success Lego has had in developing its own form of theme park in Europe. The global appeal of this children's building brick toy has enabled the company to expand the brand to its Legoland parks, first in its country of origin, at Billund in Denmark, and, later, to England, at Windsor, Günzburg in Germany, Carlsbad in California and, in 2008, Chicago, Illinois. The sheer scale of these developments is on a level with the major theme parks and in terms of visitor numbers they count among the more important tourism attractions in their countries.

On a much smaller scale, there are innumerable other model village type attractions scattered around the UK, usually based in popular tourist destinations to appeal to visitors as impulse visits. These form just one group of small attractions that tourists enjoy but generally receive little attention from academics or support from public-sector bodies. Other such forms of tourist entertainment include amusement arcades, model railways, waxworks (including the increasingly popular dungeon settings) and similar small commercial exhibitions. They may be indoor or outdoor attractions and, together, they make up the largest proportion of the attractions business. It would therefore be wrong to ignore their importance within the organizational structure of the industry, even though, individually, their income may be only a tiny fraction of that of the major amusement parks. Like all the smallest museums, their very existence is tenuous, often depending on the commitment of owner–managers and their families and a voluntary labour force.

Other attractions

The scope for providing new attractions to feed the insatiable appetites of tourists is never-ending and it would be quite impossible to cover the subject fully in a single chapter. Sometimes attractions are unique to a destination, but share some common features with those in other areas or countries, thus offering scope for creating joint marketing schemes or twinning. An example of this is the Walled Towns Friendship Circle, established as a marketing association in 1992 by a group of European towns that benefit from one characteristic tourist attraction: an encircling fortification wall. Others depend on a unique feature of the district, coupled with an imaginative initiative in marketing it. For example, after the discovery of Cleopatra's sunken city adjacent to Alexandria Harbour, packages were organized to the site to allow tourists to dive and explore the ruins.

Diving, in fact, has immense appeal as an activity undertaken when on holiday. This is in line with the growth in activity holidays generally and some of the more extreme activities associated with it include ice-diving, iceberg wall dives, mine diving (exploring flooded mineshafts) and wreck diving. Examples of the latter include:

- Truk Lagoon, Micronesia, where over 60 shipwrecks from the 1944 Japanese fleet, including the Fujikawa Maru, a 7000-ton freighter, offer ideal opportunities for underwater exploring
- Bikini Atoll, in the Marshall Islands, which has over 40 World War II wrecks to explore
- Pensacola, Florida, where the *USS Oriskany* was deliberately sunk 23 metres off the coast to provide the largest artificial reef in the world
- Vanuatu, in the Pacific, where lies the *SS President Coolidge*, a former liner and troopship.

If all that underwater activity is too extreme, a more relaxing opportunity is provided in the form of undersea scootering, with Bob (breathing observation bubble) trips available to see fish close up, in a number of resorts, including Tenerife, in the Canary Islands, St Thomas, in the US Virgin Islands, and Cancún, Mexico. No diving experience is necessary!

Transport-related attractions

Early forms of transport are another focus for tourists. In some cases, the equipment can be restored and brought back into service for pleasure trips, such as the many steam railways either in private hands or managed by trusts in the UK. Many of these railways run through very scenic countryside, especially those in Wales. The continuing role of classic modes of transport as tourist attractions will be examined more thoroughly in Chapters 14 and 15.

Transport museums are popular attractions in many countries. There are eight significant museums of transport and numerous smaller ones in the UK alone, encompassing a mix of aircraft, maritime vessels and public and private road transport.

Historic ships provide unique attractions for local museums. Some of the earliest are the Viking ships which have been found in Scandinavia, and some splendid museums have been created to display them, notably that at Roskilde in Denmark.

The only seventeenth-century warship to survive is the Swedish *Vasa*, which capsized and sank in Stockholm harbour soon after its launch in 1628. Raised in almost perfect condition, it is now a major museum attraction in Stockholm. Still in Scandinavia, Oslo in Norway provides the setting for the *Fram* – the vessel in which Roald Amundsen sailed in 1910, on his way to becoming the first person to reach the South Pole. Similarly, Captain Scott's vessel, the research ship *Discovery*, has now returned to Dundee, where it was built in 1901, and serves as a museum.

In the UK, the oldest surviving vessel built in Bristol's former shipping yards, the tug *Mayflower*, is still in working order and a key attraction on the floating harbour, offering regular trips for visitors in summer. Bristol is also the setting for Isambard Kingdom Brunel's *SS Great Britain* – the first iron-hulled screw-driven vessel, launched in 1843. Brought back from the Falklands as a rusting wreck in 1970, it is now being extensively restored with the aid of the Heritage Lottery fund. Together with the city's famous suspension bridge, also by Brunel, this early ship has helped to create a new identity for the city.

The sheer size and scale of more recent passenger vessels militates against their preservation. Perhaps the best-known of all twentieth-century ships, the *RMS Queen Mary*, was saved from the breaker's yard and is almost the only modern passenger ship to have been preserved, though sadly much of its original interior has been removed. It now serves as a dry-dock hotel near Long Beach, California, but the huge cost of its preservation has resulted over the years in big losses for its developers. Its sister ship, the *Queen Elizabeth 2*, completed its maritime career in 2008 and now awaits restoration as a floating hotel in Dubai.

The UK itself, formerly a leading maritime nation, has, sadly, no examples of its great passenger vessels of the last two centuries on display apart from the *SS Great Britain*, although there are numerous examples of fighting vessels from that and earlier centuries that have been preserved and are open to the public. *HMS Belfast*, a World War II cruiser, is moored near Tower Bridge in London and attracts some 200 000 visitors each year. Portsmouth is particularly lucky to have three great examples of historical maritime vessels, including Nelson's flagship, *HMS Victory*, the nineteenth-century *HMS Warrior* and the Tudor warship *Mary Rose*, raised from the sea in 1982 and still undergoing conservation (see Figures 10.9a and b). The combination of three vessels of historic value located close together in the same city acts as a powerful magnet for day trippers and helps to account for the large number of visitors who come to see them.

There are many vintage car museums throughout the UK, although Beaulieu is probably the best known of these. Vintage aircraft are preserved at Yeovilton, among other sites, while elsewhere museums have been devoted to early carriages, bicycles and canal boats. Where artefacts are too large to house indoors, the costs of preservation are very high, adding to the difficulties faced by museums that wish to focus on such attractions. This was a factor in the collapse of the Exeter Maritime Museum in 1996.

In general, the attractions we have been examining in this chapter up to this point have been permanent sites, available to visitors at any time of the year. We will now turn to examine attractions of a more temporary nature, either arranged specifically to encourage tourism or sufficiently attractive to encourage tourists as well as locals to visit the site.

Figure 10.9a *HMS Victory* and the band of the Royal Marines, Portsmouth

Photo by Chris Holloway

Figure 10.9b *HMS Warrior*, Portsmouth Harbour

Photo by Chris Holloway

Events

Tourists will also visit a place in order to participate in, or observe, an event. In some cases, the events occur regularly and with some frequency (for example, the Changing of the Guard in London). In others, the events are intermittent, perhaps annually or even less frequently (such as arts festivals; the Venice Bienniale for example, held every two years, the four-yearly Olympic Games or the Floriade flower festival, which takes place in or near a different Dutch city every decade, and in 2012 was held at Venlo). In still other cases, there may be *ad hoc* arrangements to take advantage of a particular occasion. Such arrangements can last for as little as a few hours (a Christmas pageant or street festival, say) or many months (events associated with the cities of culture award or those organized around a historic anniversary, such as Maritime Britain, commemorating the bicentennial anniversary of the Battle of Trafalgar in 1805).

Anniversaries are a crucial catalyst, whether the anniversary is of a past event, as in Trafalgar, or the birth or death of famous figures from the past. Tourism authorities will invariably look towards the 50th, 60th anniversaries or beyond and plan suitable events up to five years in advance. The 60th anniversary of the ending of World War II in 2005 is a case in point and it was exploited to the full both commercially and politically. The UK government announced an additional state holiday to mark the Queen's Diamond Jubilee in 2012.

If a centenary or even greater anniversary is involved, and the individual concerned was internationally famous, this provides an excuse for holding a major festival in their home town or country to attract foreign tourists. The 250th anniversary of Mozart's death in 2006, for example, offered scope for a worldwide celebration, not least in his home town of Salzburg.

Kaliningrad, Russia

The Russian enclave of Kaliningrad provided a curious opportunity for joint festivities in 2005 when the Germans celebrated the 750th anniversary of the founding of 'their' town, Konigsberg (the former name for the town), while the Russians celebrated the 60th anniversary of its fall to the Soviet army. Political compromise allowed the two countries to mark the occasion separately with renovation work. The Germans paid for the renovation of the cathedral, while the Russians built a new Orthodox church and opened a space gallery to celebrate the number of cosmonauts who grew up in the area.

Events will draw people to an area that otherwise may have little to attract them. They may be mounted to increase the number of visitors to a destination or help spread tourism demand to the shoulder seasons. One interesting example of this is the costume events mounted by the Sealed Knot Society in England, a voluntary body with an interest in English history of the Civil War period. This organization, *inter alia*, recreates battle scenes on the original sites, drawing very large audiences. The event may still influence the decision to visit long after it has finished. For example, costumes used in the carnival parades in Rio are made available for visitors to try, offering an experience of the event year-round (see Figure 10.10).

There is, of course, a direct relationship between the degree of attractiveness of the event and the distances visitors are willing to travel to visit it. Some events, such as finals for sports competitions, will have global appeal, while the appearance of top pop singers and bands at stadiums holding many thousands of fans will be marketed internationally as a package to include travel and hotel accommodation.

The variety of events held around the world is enormous. Even sites as inhospitable as the Arctic in winter can attract visitors with appropriate events. In Kemi and Rovaniemi, Finland (both close to the Arctic Circle), an annual Snow Show includes art installations created by leading sculptors, as well as snowmobile and husky riding. Visitors can stay at

Figure 10.10 Tourists in Rio can dress up in costumes designed for the Carnival – even if they are in the city long after the event is over
Photo by Claire Humphreys

Figure 10.11 More than 100 wooden houses line the streets to create the Winter Village in Reims, France. Street entertainers and a visit to the 'Chalet de Pere Noel' all serve to attract visitors

Photo by Claire Humphreys

the Snow Castle, an ice hotel. The staging of events in winter to bring in the off-season market is increasingly apparent. Throughout Europe, Christmas markets, a concept that originated in Germany and is still immensely popular there, have spread, to a point where numerous similar markets are now organized in towns and cities across the UK and northern Europe (see Figure 10.11).

This section has dealt with events aimed essentially at leisure travellers, but, of course, it must be remembered that events such as trade exhibitions and conferences are equally important for business travellers. This aspect of business travel is discussed in detail in Chapter 11, but it is worth mentioning here that many fairs, such as international expos – major but infrequent events – attract both business and leisure visitors. Often used as showcases to promote a country or its products, many of these are open to both trade and the general public and, if the appeal is strong enough, the destination can benefit from the fact that the markets it attracts are often high-spend international tourists willing to pay high gate fees, as well as inflated hotel prices for the duration of the fair. The success of many popular events can be jeopardized by greed, however, and overcharging by hotels, though widespread at events such as the Olympic Games, can both discourage some visitors and effect long-term damage on the reputation of the destination.

Arts festivals

Arts festivals have a long history in many countries, arising out of cultural and traditional festivals that often have local associations. In the UK alone, well over 500 arts festivals are held every year, lasting from two days to several weeks, and they attract some 3 million people, spending over £1 billion. More than half of these have been founded since 1980 and over 60% are professionally managed. Most depend on sponsorship and financial support from the local authority. The leading events in the UK, in terms of revenue achieved, include the Edinburgh Festival and Fringe Festival and the BBC Promenade Concerts.

Major exhibitions draw an international audience of mass tourists. In 1993, 1.1 million visitors attended the Barnes Foundation's exhibition 'A Century of Impressionism' held at the Musée d'Orsay in Paris, while a later showing of the Barnes Foundation's collection in Germany drew such crowds that the museum exhibiting the collection stayed open all night (a practice that later led to longer opening hours in Germany – Berlin has 'Die lange Nacht der Museen' twice a year, when all museums are open until at least midnight). The UK's Royal Academy has followed suit, on occasions opening for a full 24-hour period, thereby dramatically increasing their admission numbers. Blockbuster exhibitions, such as the Venice Biennale, frequently have as much to do with raising the social profile of the institution or city, and encouraging the public to perceive it as a leader in its field, as in directly raising revenue through entry tickets.

Several music festivals in Europe have achieved international recognition and visitors make significant contributions to the economies of the cities where they are held. In addition to these, there are countless smaller festivals in the countries concerned, each of which makes an important contribution to local revenues because of tourists' visits to them. While the largest festivals tend to run during the high season, many smaller events are held outside the peak summer periods, especially in places that are subject to heavy congestion at such times.

EXAMPLE   **The draw of Glastonbury Festival**

The first festival was held in 1970, with 1500 people in attendance. Held at Worthy Farm in Somerset, it has since grown to become a world-renowned music and performing arts event.

Covering an area of 900 acres, and with a perimeter almost 9 miles in length and with over 60 performance venues, the festival caters to the needs of a diverse audience. The Pyramid Stage attracts top name bands (U2 and Coldplay headlined in 2011) and can accommodate an audience of almost 100 000. Smaller stages, such as the Other Stage and John Peel Tent can also cater for audiences in the thousands.

	Licensed attendance	Glastonbury ticket price	Relative price (based on average earnings)
2009	135 000	£175	£175
2008	134 000	£155	£154
2007	135 000	£145 inc programme	£150
2006	No festival	-	-
2005	153 000	£125 inc programme	£140
2004	150 000	£112 inc programme	£130
2003	150 000	£105 inc programme	£127
2002	140 000	£97 inc programme	£122
1995	80 000	£65 (programme £5)	£110
1990	70 000	£38 (programme £3)	£80.70
1985	40 000	£16 (programme £0.90)	£51.40
1981	18 000	£8	£35.10
1979	12 000	£5	£29.90
1978	Informal event	-	-
1971	12 000	Free	-
1970	1500	£1 (inc free milk from the farm)	£20.90

It is now so popular that the tickets for the 2011 festival sold out in four hours. To reduce the likelihood that tickets are purchased by touts hoping to make a quick profit, all attendees are required to complete a photo registration process, which provides a unique reference number required when purchasing tickets.

On the back of Glastonbury's popularity, hundreds of different music festivals – with themes including jazz, classical, folk, opera, early music, indie and rock – are operating annually across the UK, with Bestival, Latitude, V festival, Hop Farm and Port Eliot all drawing large crowds. However, the rapid growth of provision of festivals has seen some struggle to attract enough festival-goers, or meet police security requirements, and as a consequence many have been cancelled. To put this into context, the efestivals guide (**www.efestivals.co.uk**) listed over 900 festivals taking place in the UK during 2011 but identified 40 which were cancelled for various reasons during the year.

Apart from music and the fine arts, crafts, drama, dance, literature and poetry festivals are popular. Some commemorate historical occasions and may be highlighted with parades, pageants and *son et lumière* events. Most provide an opportunity for hosts and guests to meet and get to know one another. As well as meeting a wide variety of tourists' needs, they also fulfil an essential requirement of contemporary tourism – that of sustainable development.

Other influential factors attracting visitors

We have concentrated on sites and events which attract tourists to destinations. But there are many other factors which motivate visitors to take a trip to a domestic or international destination. There are too many influences to examine them all in this chapter but we will pay particular attention to some key areas including:

- cultural tourism
- religious tourism
- shopping
- gastronomy tourism
- sports tourism
- dark tourism.

Cultural tourism

Cultural tourism – however it is defined – is one of the fastest-growing areas of tourism. In its widest definition it encompasses both 'high' and 'low' culture. The so-called 'fine arts' in all their forms – paintings and sculpture, decorative arts, architecture, classical forms of music, theatre and literature – are matched by 'popular culture' attractions, including sport and popular music, along with traditional forms of entertainment such as folk dancing, gastronomy and handicrafts. In postmodern societies, the former divisions between 'high' and 'low' culture have become increasingly artificial and certainly now have little relevance to the study of tourism as the industry has become adept at packaging and popularizing culture in *all* its forms.

France, noted for its dominance in the fine art field, has packaged art trails covering places Cézanne lived and frequented at Aix-en-Provence, Monet's garden at Giverny and areas associated with Gauguin, Manet, Renoir, Dégas, Pissarro and Sisley. Longer tours, too, such as the 'circuit Pissarro–Cézanne' and 'circuit Toulouse-Lautrec', have proved popular with cultural tourists.

Where a place is popularly identified with an author or artist, tourist interest follows automatically, but where such a link is less well established, it can still be built on. The poet Dylan Thomas' disparaging comments about the town and people of Laugharne have not stopped a steady flow of 25 000 visitors annually to the Boathouse where he lived between 1949 and 1953, despite the locals' preference for playing down this link. By contrast, the towns of Rochester and Broadstairs in Kent have both traded on their links with the Victorian author Charles Dickens.

A discussion of all the different forms of cultural attraction, ranging from 'high' to 'low' culture, would require a level of detail too extensive to be examined here, so you are directed to the many publications that focus on this sector to increase your knowledge of them and the issues arising from each.

Religious tourism

Travel for religious purposes tends to be grouped among the 'miscellaneous' forms of tourism, falling outside the central purposes of leisure or business. It would be unfair to dismiss it lightly, however, as it represents a most important feature in the worldwide movement of tourists. The UNWTO estimates that there are around 300 million visits each year to key religious sites, with Our Lady of Guadalupe, in Mexico, the most visited shrine. All told, religious tourism is thought to contribute around £18 billion annually to these destinations. Religious tourism may take a variety of forms including:

- pilgrimages
- missionary travel
- faith-based holidays
- retreats
- religious tourist attractions.

Millions who follow the faith of Islam make the obligatory once-in-a-lifetime pilgrimage to Mecca, the birthplace of Mohammed in Saudi Arabia. If taken at the time of Ramadan, this is known as the Great Pilgrimage, or Hadj. At other times, Umrah, or the Lesser Pilgrimage, attracts tourists for 11 months of the year. Some 2 million Muslims visit Mecca and Medina every year, of whom around 25 000 are from the UK; a further 100 000 British travel for the Umrah. While these trips are seen as an obligation arising out of the Islamic faith rather than a pleasure trip, they nevertheless bring substantial financial and commercial benefits to the country that caters to these tourists' needs. In Tongi, Bangladesh, the three-day Bishwa Ijtema gathering for blessings drew more than 3 million Muslim visitors from 80 countries in 2007.

Hindus are drawn to Amritsar and Varanasi in India, Buddhists to Shikoku in Japan, while Mount Kailas in China draws both Buddhists and Hindus to its peak to shed sins. Other multifaith sites include Jerusalem, which draws Christians, Jews and Muslims alike, due to its historical importance to all three religions. The political upheavals in that region, however, have discouraged the large numbers who would have been expected in earlier years. Bethlehem in particular, the claimed birthplace of Christ, being on the Palestinian side of the border, has suffered enormously from the slump in tourism to the region.

Prominent religious destinations for Christian pilgrims include the Vatican, St Katherine's monastery (often linked with visits to Petra in Jordan for package tours), Assisi and Lourdes (which has one of the highest concentrations of hotels in Europe). The second most visited Christian site is thought currently to be the remains of Padre Pio of Pietrelcina in Italy, with around 7 million visiting his shrine at San Giovannia Rotondo each year. Indeed, religious visits have become so important in Italy that monasteries in that country are applying to either sell off their buildings to developers or take in high-paying guests as the numbers of monks and nuns decline.

The pilgrim and day tripper

The Norfolk village of Walsingham celebrated its 950th anniversary as a pilgrimage destination in 2011. History reports that a series of visions of the Virgin Mary in 1061 led to an influx of Christian pilgrims. By the thirteenth century, the village was dominated by ecclesiastical buildings along with accommodation and catering facilities to serve the needs of the visitors. The twentieth century saw a revival of pilgrimages and some 300 000 visitors are believed to travel to the village annually.

One means of accessing this village is via the Wells and Walsingham miniature railway. This is the longest 10 1/4 inch narrow gauge railway in the world and steams the 4 miles from the coastal holiday resort of Wells. The timetable is designed to allow tourists to travel to Walsingham and spend a few hours exploring the village and its attractions, returning to the coast later in the day. More than 25 000 visitors journey on this steam train annually.

There is little current research data which distinguishes between leisure day trippers and the pilgrims but research completed in the 1990s revealed that around 13 000 guided tours were provided annually by the tourist office, with souvenir shops reporting that three-quarters of their merchandise had religious associations. This suggests that whilst a small number of visitors may arrive at the village purely because it is the terminus for an exciting trip on a stream railway, much of its appeal is linked to religious tourism.

Many observers believe that popular culture gives expression to emotions formerly reserved for faith; so we see secular mass tourists visit the graves of their idols or sites with which they are associated or met their death.

Specialist operators exist to provide services for religious tourism. Tours are often accompanied by spiritual leaders and, in one sense, can be defined as educational tourism, but in other instances (such as pilgrimages to Lourdes, to seek intercession for a cure), the motive comes closer to that of health tourism.

It is open to debate as to which category the religious theme parks that are now appearing belong in. One example is the Holy Land Experience, located close to Universal's theme park resort in Orlando. First introduced in the USA, the appeal of these parks is now spreading and there are plans to construct a Christian theme park in Mallorca. Part educational, part missionary, part entertainment and quasi-history, these parks appear to be finding a new market for the curious and the committed alike.

Shopping

Shopping plays an important role in tourism. While retailing is not normally considered a sector of the industry, tourist purchases make up a considerable part of the revenue of many shops and in resorts shops may be entirely or very largely dependent on the tourist trade. Shops selling postcards, souvenirs or local crafts are often geared specifically to the needs of visitors, and out of season may close down due to lack of demand.

Cross-border tourism is fuelled by shopping expeditions and, where large discrepancies in prices are noted on each side of the border, authorities often impose limits on purchases that can be transported back into the home country. For several years, the German and Austrian governments were concerned about cross-border shopping into Poland, the Czech and Slovak Republics and Hungary. Now that these countries have joined the EU, the concern has shifted, the governments in those countries now being concerned about shopping expeditions into the Ukraine and Russian Federation (although an obligation to obtain visas for entry into the Russian Federation acts as a hindrance). The EU's limit on importation of goods from non-EU countries, long limited to £145, increased to £340 in

2009, with a further increase to £390 in 2010. When there is a weak dollar, however, goods bought in the USA are still cheap, even after paying duty. With virtually no limit on the transfer of goods between EU countries, shopping expeditions from England to Calais across the Channel, from Helsinki to Tallinn across the Baltic and from Germany into Poland across the Oder are a major factor in the growth of tourism between these countries.

Tourist cities like London, Paris, Rome and New York owe much of their popularity to the quality of their shops, and large department stores such as Saks Fifth Avenue and Bloomingdales in New York, Kaufhaus des Westens (KaDeWe) in Berlin (claiming to be the largest store in the world) and Harrods in London are heavily dependent on visitors spending their money with them and, of course, expenditure on shopping is an important feature in the tourism balance of payments.

EXAMPLE   The Chinese shop in Paris

Parisien shops have come to rely more heavily on the spend of tourists, with popular department stores drawing in large numbers of shoppers. One example, Printemps, estimates that 40% of their sales are to international customers. One-third of this total is believed to be to Chinese visitors – with an average spend of $1660 each. Across France it is estimated that Chinese tourists spent $890 million in 2010.

Many of the Chinese visitors are in Paris as the culmination of a two or three week coach tour of Europe, which avoids the problematic – and often expensive – requirements of obtaining an individual travel visa.

To attact these shoppers many of the 'grand magasins' advertise extensively in China, while in their outlets Chinese speaking staff store maps in Chinese, and acceptance of Chinese credit cards also helps to encourage visitors through the door and to spend.

Source: edited from Erlanger, 2011

The downside in small towns popular with tourists is that shops with products appealing to tourists can squeeze out those serving the more basic needs of their residents, simply because they can best afford spiralling rates and rents.

Increasingly, shopping is being combined with other forms of leisure in the development of shopping malls, which have become virtual mini-towns in their own right, attracting huge numbers of visitors prepared to pass several hours enjoying themselves in an environment that encourages people to spend. China contains some of the world's largest shopping malls (the South China Mall in Dongguan, said to be the world's largest, is over 7.1 million square feet in area, while the Golden Resources Mall in Beijing, at 6 million square feet, offers a landscape embracing theme parks, bridges, giant windmills, pyramids, artificial rivers and a copy of Paris' Arc de Triomphe). Those in the West are almost as impressive; for instance, the Mall of America, built in 1992 at Bloomington, Minneapolis, claims to be the second most visited site in the USA, with some 40 million visitors a year. At 4.2 million square feet and offering 400 shops, 45 restaurants, 14 cinemas, a seven-acre amusement park and a miniature golf course, the site provides everything that the leisure shopper could hope for. It attracts a global market and, most notably, brings in shoppers from both European and Asian cities. The enormous West Edmonton Mall in Canada, covering an area of 48 city blocks in downtown Edmonton, vies with this mall to draw consumers from all over the world, boasting more than 800 shops, 110 eating establishments and seven themed attractions. There are on-site hotels and events are mounted throughout the year.

Bluewater in Kent, Meadowhall in Sheffield and the Merry Hill Centre near Birmingham are examples in the UK of malls that serve large urban areas, attracting shoppers away from the town centres. Because of the range of leisure facilities they also offer, they attract large numbers of 'tourist shoppers' who travel considerable distances to enjoy a mix of shopping with a day out to the country. The Bicester Village shopping centre near Oxford, where a range of top brand clothing outlets offer their products at discounted prices, is said to be the second most popular venue in the UK, after London, for Chinese tourists.

Souvenirs

No study of tourist shopping would be complete without a look at the role of souvenirs – essential items for most visitors. The collection of souvenirs as mementos of one's visit has a long history. Certainly, both Greek and Roman tourists were noted for their collections of memorabilia from their journeys and, later, during the period of the Grand Tours, prestigious souvenirs collected by aristocratic travellers would invariably include Italian landscape paintings and archaeological 'finds'. Historians have commented on how souvenirs were collected from the earliest days of travel in North America, when 'items cut from local rock or wood, beaded moccasins, baskets and . . . miniature canoes' featured prominently (Löfgren, 1999, 86).

Today, we can divide souvenirs into two groups; mementos picked up by tourists (often of little value in themselves but representative of the sites visited) and those bought commercially from shops or local traders. The former will include items such as pebbles and shells collected on the beach, pressed flowers or leaves from jungles and parks, lava from volcanic eruptions or small shards of broken pottery that abound in places such as the area surrounding former Chinese emperors' tombs. For the most part, the collection of these items is harmless, although removing plants, flowers or seeds from parks and gardens is not an act to be encouraged – indeed, it is banned in areas where plants are under threat. Edelweiss in Switzerland and cacti in Arizona, for example, have been protected by laws in this way. Similar laws prevent the collection of rare stones or fossilized trees such as those found in the Petrified Forest in Arizona. It was not uncommon in earlier centuries for travellers to chisel off small chunks of stone from monuments such as Roman amphitheatres and the Egyptian Sphinx or, at very least, to deface them with graffiti. In our more enlightened times, however, this practice is frowned on and diminishing.

Commercial souvenirs are not only essential items of shopping for many tourists but also for some, such as the Japanese, gifts are culturally obligatory; thus tourists buy mementos for themselves and for friends and relatives. This is one explanation for the relatively high spend of Japanese tourists abroad.

EXAMPLE   ## A memory of the big day

The royal wedding between Prince William and Catherine Middleton brought many visitors to London, and many returned home with souvenirs to remember the occasion. The variety of souvenirs is almost limitless, with the traditional tea towels and plates now in competition with commemorative coins, fridge magnets and, perhaps a little weirdly, a knit your own royal wedding – a book providing stitch-by-stitch guide to recreating the event in wool (Carne, 2011).

Souvenirs from the 2011 royal wedding are expected to earn retailers more than £100 million, but few will have value as collectables. Perhaps one of the more unusual souvenirs, with the potential to have value, was created by Chinese firm Guandong Enterprise, which produced mugs with a portrait of Kate with Prince Harry – brother to Prince William.

Some commercial souvenirs are bestowed on visitors without charge, such as the leis, garlands of flowers placed around the necks of visitors arriving in Hawaii (although mass tourism has resulted in the original flowers being largely superseded by plastic versions today). Visitors to China are often given small souvenirs of their visit, both while travelling within the country and when visiting sites such as the Great Wall in China.

The transmogrification of cheap baubles into indigenous craft items purchased by tourists as souvenirs is characteristic of recent tourism, exemplified by such items as straw donkeys and flamenco dolls from Spain, brass Eiffel Towers from Paris, straw hats from the Caribbean Islands or Bali and bamboo models of cormorant fishers from China. While widely derided, these mementos still have a place in many tourists' homes, and in the minds and emotions of their purchasers they retain an association with the places from where they originated. The name 'airport art' is frequently used for such debased crafts, which are often on sale to tourists at airports, but the popularity of these items cannot be denied. They do also make a valuable contribution to the economies of the countries where they are purchased.

Finally, the significance of postcards as essential purchases while abroad should be noted. Since the advent of photography, the desire to send pictures of destinations visited home to family, friends and neighbours has become a well-established ritual, the motives for which have frequently been questioned. Whether for social contact, out of a sense of obligation to those less fortunate, to demonstrate one-upmanship or simply to inform, the drive to send cards is universal and, particularly among the developing countries, they are cherished by those receiving them, being pinned up on the walls of homes, offices and bars, signifying to others possession of a wide circle of well-travelled friends. Although modern technology now allows us to send by e-mail or phone digital snaps taken on a mobile phone, there is something reassuring about the continuing popularity of the old-fashioned postcard; in the UK, 135 million postcards are still sent each year. The permanence of a postcard is also part of its attraction and a consequence has been the introduction of phone applications which allow travellers to submit their images and text, which are then printed in postcard format and posted to the recipient.

Gastronomic tourism

VisitBritain's research has shown that half of all visitors to the UK cite food and drink as being important to their holiday experience. Of course, eating and drinking have always been part of the enjoyment of a holiday, enhancing it where the food and drink in question are exceptional and/or exotic, as is often the case on holidays abroad. The extent to which Britons have become more adventurous in their eating and drinking habits in their own country can be directly attributed to their experiences as tourists abroad. There are instances, however, where the food and drink become the principal purpose of the trip, whether a short break or longer holiday. The reputation of French food and drink, to take one example, has led to this becoming a key attraction for many tourists of that country (although price escalation in French restaurants in recent years threatens to undermine this). The importance of good – or at least reliable – cuisine abroad anywhere is often a priority concern, not least as a measure of health and safety.

Countries with well-established reputations for their food or drink have ensured that these attractions are promoted prominently in their tourism campaigns, whether informally or in the form of package tours. Enhanced awareness of good food has led to more flexibility in packages, allowing tourists to 'eat around', either in partner hotels or associated restaurants.

Stimulated by programmes on television, a much greater interest is taken today in preparing attractive and healthy meals. A number of leading chefs, particularly those having made their names on TV, have established cookery courses and these attract gastronomy tourists from afar. Examples include:

The pressure of success

El Bulli, a remote beachside restaurant in Cala Montjoi, some two hours north of Barcelona, has closed. Yet this is not for lack of business – an estimated 2 million people attempt to make a reservation in a typical season. This Michelin starred restaurant is host to world-renowned chef Ferran Adrià and, following the announcement that 2011 would be its last season, only 8000 were able to make the difficult journey to experience this revolutionary cuisine experience – with a style often referred to as molecular gastronomy.

So why has it closed? Suggestion is that success is due to the creativity and inventiveness of the chef and time is needed to allow new creative ideas to flourish. The restaurateur claimed 'in order to save El Bulli, he would have to close it to the public' (Mcinerney, 2010). This is perhaps a common problem for many unique tourist attractions, where the demand of the public puts pressure on scarce resources, and restricting access provides the opportunity for recovery.

- Carla Tomasi, in Umbria and Sicily in Italy
- Alain Ducasse, a three Michelin star chef, in Paris, France
- Ferran Adrià, in Seville, Spain
- Rosemary Barron in Santorini, Greece
- Darina Allen in Cork, Ireland
- Rick Stein's Padstow Seafood School, England.

There is also a growing association between food and tourism within the UK; the days when sticks of rock and fish and chips were the best-known food products, and the quality of food served in hotels and restaurants was actually a disincentive to visit the country, are long gone. Michelin starred restaurants, gastropubs, farmers' markets, even English wines, are now gaining a reputation among overseas visitors. Regional tourism bodies, in response, have not been slow to adopt food as an attraction in its own right. At various points in the recent history of tourism, authorities have promoted 'Taste of England/ Wales/Scotland' campaigns, culminating in an 'Enjoy England, Taste England' promotion by VisitBritain that prominently features famous British chefs. Similarly, today, no museum or heritage attraction of any size is without its restaurant and shop, many of the latter selling food products grown or manufactured locally, such as Pontefract cakes, Kendal mint cake and local ice-creams.

The UK is just one of a number of countries now promoting food festivals as key events in the tourism calendar. There are food festivals in Ludlow, Nantwich and Abergavenny in the UK, while, in regions noted for particular food or drink products, events are mounted to celebrate their harvest – or simply to provide an excuse to widen their products' appeal. Examples include:

- Great British cheese festival, Cardiff, Wales
- Feria du Riz, Arles, France, celebrating rice dishes
- Galway Oyster Festival, Ireland
- I'Primi d'Italia, Foligno, Italy, celebrating first courses
- Truffle Festival, Alba, Italy
- Shrimp Festival, Honfleur, France
- Onion Festival, Weimar, Germany
- Chestnut Festival, Mourjou en Chataigneraie, France
- Baltic Herring Festival, Helsinki, Finland.

These are just a few examples of the autumn food festivals held in Europe, and it will be seen that the medium gives scope for an almost endless variety of activities centred on food and drink in some shape or form.

Sports tourism

The relationship between tourism and sports activities is now so well established that sports tourism is recognized as a field of study in its own right, and there are several books devoted to the subject (Higham, 2005; Weed and Bull, 2009).

At its most successful, sports tourism will draw the greatest number of tourists to any one site on the planet. Tickets to the Olympic Games, for example, are in such high demand that sports enthusiasts are attracted from all over the world. Similarly, football's World Cup, with matches staged throughout the world, also draws huge crowds. World-class events in golf and tennis witness demand for tickets well beyond the available supply. The economic benefits of these events to the destinations where they are staged can be enormous.

Of course, sports activities are not limited to events where tourists are merely passive observers. On the contrary, they also seek to participate – in rounds of golf on famous courses such as St Andrews, in improving their tennis with the professionals at coaching schools in Florida and in competitive games around the world.

The Olympics effect

The enormous investment required to mount Olympics events in a country has drawn a lot of media criticism, particularly in the UK, as host of the 2012 Games in London. Few believe the £9 billion cost to be justified and certainly not in the expectation of making a profit from the event. Montreal, which mounted the Games in 1976, still had an outstanding debt of £1.2 billion to be paid off by 2008, while Barcelona, where the Games were held in 1992, invested £6.5 billion in mounting the events; the cost to Athens in 2004, estimated by the government not to exceed €4.5 billion, may actually have amounted to as much as €13 billion, one estimate suggesting that the event cost Greece 6% of the country's GNP in that year. Atlanta did a little better; it spent only $2 billion in 1996 and claimed a profit equivalent to £525 million, but much of the infrastructure needed was already in place before the city won the Games. In 2000, Sydney overspent its £1 billion budget by £300 million, which was underwritten by the country's taxpayers.

EXAMPLE **London 2012**

The cost for the London 2012 Olympics has been extensively discussed, with the media constantly questioning cost overruns and whether such spending can be justified in times of recession and government cutbacks.

Since 2007, an agreed budget of £9.3 billion appears to have been an accurate assessment of the cost to establish the necessary infrastructure and venues. This has been funded by the public purse (£6 billion, of which £1.7 billion had already been earmarked for the regeneration of East London, even if the Olympics hadn't been held); the National Lottery (£2.1 billion); and the Greater London Authority and London Development Agency (£1.2 billion).

Additionally, the cost of operating the events for the Olympic and Paralympic Games, together with the opening and closing ceremonies, has been estimated at £2 billion, funded through the sale of tickets, broadcasting rights, merchandise and sponsorship.

To counter debate over the cost of the games, there has been extensive reporting of the potential of the event to leave a legacy both for the local area and the wider regional economy (Government Olympic Executive, 2011). The desire for legacy specifically focused on the opportunity:

- to encourage sports participation among the population
- to encourage economic growth
- to encourage community cohesion and engagement in society
- to encourage the regeneration of East London through the redevelopment of the Games site after the event.

Whether these legacies are achieved in the long term remains to be seen, but in the short term the high demand for tickets suggests that domestic and international visitor numbers and their spending in London, and the many regions hosting events such as sailing, mountain biking and football, will have helped to justify in part the investment made.

In terms of boosting tourism, certainly the events attracted large numbers of visitors to the cities at the time, but even this did not necessarily benefit the cities outside of the venues themselves. The European Tour Operators' Association claims that the Games attract only sports enthusiasts who do not spend money on leisure outside of the venues, and both Los Angeles and Sydney actually experienced downturns in the numbers of people visiting their other regular attractions during the period that the Games were taking place. Even the belief that long-term tourism is boosted has been questioned. After 1992, Barcelona was shown to have slower growth in visitor numbers than either Prague or Dublin (all becoming popular short-break destinations), while, in the aftermath of the Sydney event, New Zealand attracted more visitors than Australia (possibly accounted for by the popularity of *Lord of the Rings*, however). Seoul and Sydney both experienced a drop in tourist numbers in the year following the Games. In short, these events will certainly help to put a destination on the map, but may not necessarily ensure significantly large increases in the numbers of visitors thereafter than would be anticipated without the Games. Rather than measuring the impact of tourism as a justification, countries might be better advised to concentrate on the benefits achieved by reconstruction of impoverished areas. Athens in particular benefited from a vastly improved transport infrastructure. In both Athens and Sydney, however, the specially built venues have been severely under-utilized since the events were held there, and there must be concern that the same might happen to London after 2012. Nevertheless, the UK put great efforts into assuring the maximum success in driving tourism, both inbound and domestic, in 2012 and VisitLondon has estimated that the Olympics will have generated £2 billion in the period 2009–16.

Dark tourism

The beauty of tourism is that the number of products that can be devised to interest tourists is virtually unlimited. One reads regularly in the press of new ideas that have been promoted, of new – and frequently bizarre – reasons tourists advance for visiting a site. Perhaps our ideas of what it is appropriate to see have changed a little since the nineteenth century, when in England people would travel considerable distances to watch public hangings and, in the USA, Coney Island's amusement park displayed 300 dwarfs in 'Midget City' and publicly electrocuted Topsy, a performing elephant, as a tourist attraction.

Although such things would not be sanctioned today, there remains, nonetheless, a fascination – at times bordering on the macabre – with observing scenes such as those exploiting sudden and violent death. Rojek (1993) identifies these as 'black-spots' as he describes the flood of people who came to Scotland to see the scene of the Pan American Airlines crash at Lockerbie in 1988. Similarly, following the earthquake that rocked the city of San Francisco at the end of 1989, visitors to the city were asking to be accommodated in hotels that 'overlooked the collapsed freeway', while Gray Line offered Hurricane

Katrina tours in New Orleans following the disastrous flooding of the city. Ground Zero, the site of the 9/11 attack on New York's Twin Towers in 2001, is now firmly on the tourist circuit.

The terms **thanatourism** (Seaton, 1996) or, more commonly, **dark tourism** (Lennon and Foley, 2000) have been used to describe such tourists' fascination with death and the macabre. Motives for this may be thought questionable, although travel to 'dark' sites cannot necessarily be ascribed to gratuitous pleasure – visits to World War II concentration camps are popular, for instance (Auschwitz-Birkenau attracts more than 500 000 visitors every year), but these, especially by Israeli parties, can often take the form of a pilgrimage, while for others the visit is tied in with an historical interest. Places associated with the deaths of major celebrities, however, do attract more than their fair share of curious observers. Jim Morrison's tomb at Père-Lachaise cemetery in Paris is said to be the most-visited grave in the cemetery, while those of Oscar Wilde, Edith Piaf, Marcel Proust and other representatives of 'high culture' draw far fewer visitors. The outbuilding in Seattle where Kurt Cobain, of the band Nirvana, committed suicide in 1994 was torn down, but the site is still visited by hundreds of admirers, just as hundreds still seek out the underground road tunnel in Paris where Diana, Princess of Wales, met her death in a car crash.

Whatever the merits or otherwise of dark tourism, the quest for the bizarre features ever more prominently in the list of tourists' motivations. Sometimes this is a reflection of the desire for ever more dangerous activities, particularly among younger tourists. A press listing of the most dangerous streets in the world led to a flurry of interest in visiting those at Snake Alley, Taipei, Khao San Road, Bangkok, Tverskaya Ulitsa, Moscow, and King's Cross, Sydney, while a book appeared in 2006 directing potential tourists to the worst places in the world to visit (Cohen, 2006). *The Sunday Times* (Byrne, 1997) coined the term 'terror tourism' to describe the growing trend for tourists to plan visits to countries beset by political disturbances or even civil wars. Following the initial end to hostilities in Afghanistan and Iraq, specialist tour operators were quick to arrange visits to those countries for the more adventurous – or foolhardy – in spite of government warnings of the potential dangers, and difficulties faced by those booking in obtaining travel insurance. The problem for the industry is to judge whether such tourist attractions are educationally valuable or merely satisfy the prurient interests of the spectators. Indeed, the very term 'visitor attraction' when applied to sites such as these raises questions. Are visitors expecting to be entertained or does this desire arise from some deeper psychosis in modern society?

EXAMPLE   ## Viewing an unusual battlefield location

The Mekong Delta, in the south of Vietnam, attracts many tourists interested in exploring the varied landscapes and attractions. One attraction receiving nearly a million visitors annually is the Cu Chi tunnels.

The tunnels were constructed by the Viet Cong, to support guerrilla activities during the Vietnam war. Underground rooms, linked by an extensive tunnel network, provided space to store ammunition, medical supplies, food and many of the fighting force. More than 100 miles of tunnel were constructed, although much of this is no longer accessible.

Entry points to many of the tunnels were little more than 18 inches wide, and the tunnels themselves were less than a metre high. Yet to make this resource accessible to tourists, many of whom are much larger than their Asian counterparts, a significant amount of widening to the tunnels and entrances has been undertaken.

Above ground, the attraction also offers a rifle range, allowing visitors the opportunity to shoot an AK-47 assault rifle. This has led to some reports suggesting the attraction is rather too much like a theme park; yet clearly the money paid to experience this unique place is important to the local economy and provides funding for the renovation and protection of this important piece of Vietnamese history (Nguyen, 2011).

Whether prurient or otherwise, there is no doubt that countries with a dark history are not slow to cash in on its evident commercial value. In recent years, the world has seen the following:

● A museum of forensic medicine has opened in Bangkok, Thailand, displaying weapons used in murders, deformed babies and the hanged corpse of the serial child-killer and cannibal Si-Oui.

● A Lithuanian entrepreneur, Viliumas Malinauskas, has created a Stalin World theme park by preserving 65 bronze and granite statues of former Soviet leaders at Gruto Park, south west of Vilnius. Opened in 2001, the site includes reconstructed Gulag buildings, watchtowers and barbed wire fencing, with loudspeakers relaying marching music and Stalin's speeches. Plans to construct a railway between the theme park and the capital, along which visitors would be transported in cattle wagons, monitored by machine-gun-carrying guards in the observation towers, were greeted with outrage by Lithuanians who had suffered under the Soviet regime. Nevertheless, 200 000 visitors were admitted to the site in its first year.

● The Cambodian Government has turned Pol Pot's Khmer Rouge complex of huts and bunkers at Anlong Veng into a tourist resort.

● Visitors to Rwanda can tour genocide sites where a million Tutsis were massacred in 1994. The war crimes tribunals in Kigali were also open to tourists, who could also visit the bunker hideouts of the Rwandan Patriotic Front Army.

The UK has not been slow to trade on the attraction of dark tourism sites, either. Among World War II sites currently open to tourists or being groomed as future sites, one can include the Eden Prisoner-of-War Camp at Malton, North Yorkshire, where some 30 World War II huts house displays commemorating events during the war; air raid shelters in Stockport; the former secret bunker at Kelvedon Hatch in Essex (which receives 60 000 visitors a year); Hack Green nuclear bunker near Nantwich; and the bunker built during the 1950s near St Andrews, Scotland, to house the regional government in the event of a nuclear war. Also, National Park rangers regularly lead guided walks to the sites of 60 crashed World War II planes in the Peak District. In Belfast, tours are operated to former Northern Ireland troublespots, including the Falls Road, Shankill Road and the Peace Wall.

Certainly visits to sites of this nature can be illuminating and instructive, if not entertaining in the traditional sense of the word. Some sites, however, have been heavily restored – perhaps over-restored (as at the Auschwitz–Birkenau death camp, where the original gate and ovens have been replaced with replicas). The extent to which interpretation at such sites is objective is also always open to question, depending as it does on the political colour and viewpoint of the day and those presenting the data. At another death camp, in Buchenwald, Bauhaus university students were recently recruited to design souvenirs and memorabilia to be sold at the site to raise money for its preservation. The intentions were doubtless good, but many critics described the move as 'disrespectful'.

The scope for innovative tourism

Dark tourism is not always macabre, but it can be bizarre and, in addition to the somewhat gruesome examples given above, others are of genuine educational interest or are designed to entertain. Here are some of the more curious tourist attractions currently on offer, whether banal, bizarre or both.

● Take a self-guided tour of Adelaide's West Terrace cemetery, which reveals the stories behind the famous and the everyday citizens buried there.

- Corpses displayed as tourist attractions. Perfectly preserved bodies retrieved from bogs in Denmark are on display in museums at Silkeborg and Moesgaard. Exhibiting corpses in this manner, however, raises serious ethical questions.

- Deep Ocean Expeditions operates three-seat submersibles to descend 4000 metres to the ocean floor off Newfoundland to see the Titanic, at a cost in excess of £20 000.

- China has opened the site of a hitherto secret armaments factory to allow tourists to practise on the firing range with rocket launchers and anti-aircraft guns. The tour is particularly popular with Americans and Japanese.

- The world's first dung museum opened at Machaba safari camp in Botswana. Necklaces of dried polished dung can be bought in the shop. In Sweden, moose droppings are sold as souvenirs to tourists visiting Lapland and have been given as gifts to conference delegates. The reactions of the delegates to these gifts were not recorded.

- Lignite pits near Hamburg attract tourists because of their resemblance to the lunar landscape.

- Two-hour guided tours are available around the municipal rubbish dump at Fresh Kills, Staten Island, New York. Visits to urban sewers have also proved popular in some cities.

- Special tours and cruises are arranged for visitors to approach active or recently active volcanoes. These include sites in Ecuador, Sicily, Crete, Nicaragua, Iceland and the Azores.

- In New York City tours are offered to the Bowery, formerly the district for down-and-outs, and to East Harlem and the Bronx. In the latter tours, the former negative connotations associated with the areas have given way to an exploration of the districts' musical roots.

- Walking tours across the arches of Sydney Harbour Bridge have proved immensely popular. A jumpsuit and safety cable are obligatory accompaniments. So successful have these tours been that they have been emulated on bridges in Brisbane and Auckland. In the USA, the Purple People Bridge between Cincinnati, Ohio, and Newport, Kentucky – the longest pedestrian bridge in the USA, across the Ohio River – offers the more adventurous an opportunity to don harnesses and climb on to the upper trestles of the bridge, from where they walk out on to a glass floor above the river.

- Two-hour guided tours are on offer in Berlin's red light district, with off-duty prostitutes acting as tour guides. They will answer clients' questions on all aspects of the city, including their own activities.

- At Bovington Camp in Dorset, the Army's medical team puts on realistic displays of amputations for visitors.

- In Palermo, Sicily, tourists can be taken on tours to sites associated with the local Mafia, including a visit to a former Godfather's torture chamber.

- Many domestic tourists in the Philippines are attracted to the annual rite of Catholic fanaticism at San Pedro Cutud, where volunteers undergo crucifixion.

- Omanis visit Salalah, on the southern tip of Oman, between June and September each year because of the unusual rainfall in the monsoon season – this is the only area of the Arabian Gulf so affected. Perhaps the only example of rain *attracting* tourists?

- A Museum of Broken Relationships has opened in Berlin, where artefacts associated with break-ups are on display, including an axe used to smash an ex-girlfriend's furniture.

- On a lighter note, in June each year, the Festa do São João in Oporto, Portugal, encourages participants to hit each other over the head with plastic hammers. Overseas tourists are now making enquiries about joining in the fun.

Hoteliers are noted entrepreneurs, and many have introduced special events to attract out-of-season tourists or fill rooms during the recession. 'Murder weekends' have been popular, while one hotel offered heavy discounts to people whose surname was Smith. Perhaps the prize for originality should be awarded to the group of hotels situated near the M25, London's notoriously crowded orbital motorway. These developed a series of 'M25 theme nights', with a 'motorway madness' banquet.

Other hotels attract tourists because of the bizarre form of their accommodation. In the USA, tourists can stay at a former research laboratory; while the world's first underwater hotel, Jules' Undersea Lodge at John Pennecamp Coral Reef State Park in Key Largo, Florida, accommodates swimmers only, as guests need to make a 21-foot dive to access the entrance! They can also bed down in railway cabooses at the Featherbed Railroad Company in Nice, California, spend a night in the cell block at the Jailhouse Inn in Preston, Minnesota, or sleep underground in the Honeycombs at the Inn at Honey Run, Millersburg, Ohio. Lower Saxony in Germany offers Hay Hotels, where sleeping bags in hay are provided for visitors. The hotels are said to be popular with cycling tourists and others have been opened in Poland, Denmark, Italy and the Czech Republic.

EXAMPLE A topsy-turvy world

In 2010, Gettorf Zoo, in Germany, constructed a wooden house to attract tourists. The unusual thing about this house is that the building - and all the interior fixtures and fittings, including the furniture - is upside down.

This is by no means the first attempt to attract tourists by offering a different perspective on the world. Upside down houses have previously been opened to tourists in Trassenheide, Germany, Symbark, Poland, and Antalya, Turkey. There are also amusement parks built into upturned venues; for example, the House of Katmandu in Mallorca and Wonderworks in Florida.

While this may be an interesting novelty, it remains to be seen whether this uniqueness is significant enough to attract large numbers of tourists in the long term.

Summary

Throughout this chapter we have discussed the many different attractions which can encourage tourists to visit both popular tourist destinations and less usual places – effectively marketed, bizarre sites and events can draw tourists from quite a distance. Although there are too many different types of attraction to discuss them all in detail in such a text, we have highlighted the fact that some attractions, including heritage buildings, natural landscapes and events, form the basis of much of the appeal of many locations.

The attractiveness of a destination may be influenced by a variety of factors, some of which may be outside of the control of destination managers; for instance, popularity caused by being the setting for a film or book, the infamy caused by a tragic event or sudden rise in success as a gastronomic restaurant is awarded a treasured Michelin star. Alternatively, demand may wane if there is a lack of investment in new attractions, a requirement if repeat visitors are to be encouraged. That is not to say that all destinations may lose their appeal without investment. Some attractions are considered to be a 'must-see' and therefore will always draw tourists, providing other factors such as access and the amenities to support a visit are in place.

Questions and discussion points

1. Do you think being a UNESCO World Heritage Site is important in attracting all types of visitor to a historic location? What factors may influence whether the visitor will come to the site more than once?

2. As we highlighted in the chapter, there are many battlefield sites which are popular locations for tourists to visit. Is it right to use the sites where people have lost their lives as a tourist attraction? What factors may help to make this a more acceptable decision?

3. Why does the Disney theme park empire receive so many more visitors than any of its nearest rivals? How might its competitors try to grow their share of the market?

Tasks

1. Visit a tourist attraction and identify the variety of ways in which technology is being used to enhance the experience of the visitor. Prepare a presentation of this information, using audio and visual materials to support your findings.

2. Working in groups, develop some innovative ideas for a new tourist attraction to be opened in your town or city. Select your best idea and write a report explaining why you think this attraction is best suited to being developed at this destination. Provide a summary of the characteristics of the tourists who are likely to visit. Would this attraction charge an entry fee?

Bibliography

ALVA (2011) *Visit made in 2010 to visitor attractions in membership with ALVA*, available online at: http://www.alva.org.uk/visitor_statistics/ (accessed November 2011).

Binney, M. (2004) A guide to wonders of the modern world worth visiting, *The Times*, 10 May.

Burns, E. (2010) Re-enacting history, *Conservation Bulletin*, issue 64, English Heritage, Summer.

Byrne, C. (1997) Terror tourists queue up for trips to war zones, *The Sunday Times*, 16 March.

Carne, L. (2011) Good taste has no boundaries – There's more souvenirs than you can shake a sceptre at, *The Courier-Mail*, Queensland, 29 April.

Cohen, M. (2006) *No Holiday: 80 places you don't want to visit*, New York, The Disinformation Company.

DCMS (2011) *Museum and gallery monthly visitor figures*, available online at: http://www.culture.gov.uk/what_we_do/research_and_statistics/3375.aspx (accessed November 2011).

Erlanger, S. (2011) The Chinese tour Europe, but shop in Paris, *New York Times*, 25 September.

Government Olympic Executive (2011) *London 2012 Olympic and Paralympic Games Annual Report*, London, DCMS, February.

Higham, J. (2005) *Sports Tourism Destinations: Issues, opportunities and analysis*, Oxford, Elsevier.

Leask, A. (2008) The nature and role of visitor attractions, in Fyall, A., Garrod, B., Leask, A. and Wanhill, S., *Managing Visitor Attractions: New Directions*, Oxford, Butterworth-Heinemann, 3–15.

Lennon, J. and Foley, M. (2000) *Dark Tourism: The Attraction of Death and Disaster*, London, Continuum.

Löfgren, O. (1999) *On Holiday: A history of vacationing*, Berkeley, CA, University of California Press.

Mcinerney, J. (2010) It Was Delicious While It Lasted, *Vanity Fair*, **52** (10), 170.

Nguyen, Q. T. (2011) Heritage tourism and sacred boundaries, HCMC, *Saigon Times Weekly*, 29 January.

Onishi, N. (2008) Rare wildcat barely surviving on Japanese island, *New York Times*, 5 February.

Rojek, C. (1993) *Ways of Escape: Modern transformation in leisure and travel*, Basingstoke, Macmillan.

Seaton (1996) Guided by the dark: from thanatopsis to thanatourism, *International Journal of Heritage Studies*, **2** (4), 234–244.

Steinbeck, J. (1962) *Travels with Charley*, New York, Viking Penguin.

Swarbrooke, J. (2002) *The Development and Management of Visitor Attractions*, 2nd edn, Oxford, Butterworth-Heinemann.

TEA (2010) *Global Attractions attendance report*, Burbank, CA, Themed Entertainment Association.

Weaver, D. and Lawton, L. (2002) *Tourism Management*, 2nd edn, Milton, John Wiley.

Weed, M. and Bull, C. (2009) *Sports Tourism: Participants, policy and providers*, 2nd edn, Oxford, Elsevier/Butterworth-Heinemann.

Whitson, R. (2011) Observation wheel at a turning point, *Melbourne Herald-Sun*, 11 January.

Further reading

Anthony, R. and Henry, J. (2005) *The Lonely Planet Guide to Experimental Travel*, London, Lonely Planet Publications.

Hughes, H. and Duchaine, J. (2011) *Frommer's 500 Places to See Before They Disappear*, 2nd edn, Hoboken, NJ, Wiley Publishing.

Jencks, C. (2005) *The Iconic Building: The power of enigma*, London, Frances Lincoln.

Lukas, S. (2008) *Theme Park*, London, Reaktion Books.

UK Film Council (2007) *How Film and Television Programmes Promote Tourism in the UK*, London, UK Film Council.

Websites

Dark Tourism Forum: **www.dark-tourism.org.uk**

European Travel Commission consumer site: **www.visiteurope.com**

Hinterland Travel (tours to Iraq, Afghanistan, etc.): **www.hinterlandtravel.com**

Historic Houses Association: **www.hha.org.uk**

Regaldive: **www.regaldive.co.uk**

VisitBritain, unusual attractions: **www.visitbritain.com/en/Things-to-do/Secret-Britain**

Business tourism

Prepared by Rob Davidson

Contents

Learning outcomes

After studying this chapter, you should be able to:

- understand the principal sectors of the business tourism industry and distinguish between them

- explain the objectives of the different types of meetings that may be organized, the various venues in which they take place and the roles of meeting planners

- define incentive travel, compare it with other forms of workplace rewards and demonstrate awareness of the challenges of organizing successful incentive travel programmes

- distinguish between trade fairs and exhibitions and understand the roles of those companies that supply services to this sector of business tourism

- understand the principal motivations behind individual business travel and appreciate the factors that companies take into account regarding the features of the business trips made by their employees

- understand the main trends that are having an impact on business tourism in the early twenty-first century.

No grand idea was ever born in a conference, but a lot of foolish ideas have died there.

F. Scott Fitzgerald (1945), *The Crack-up*, 123

Introduction

Travelling for the purpose of carrying out trade and engaging in commerce was one of the earliest types of tourist activity undertaken by enterprising members of ancient civilizations. Even at times in history when those undertaking any form of travel had to contend with the ever-present dangers of attack from bandits, pirates and highwaymen, as well as the severe discomfort of slowly progressing along poorly constructed roads or across perilous seas, the business motive was strong enough to drive intrepid merchants and other entrepreneurs to leave their native lands in search of distant markets in which to buy or sell goods and products not found locally.

Today, business tourism – principally, travel for commercial, professional and work-related purposes – represents the major non-leisure form of tourism and business tourists are widely recognized as the highest-spending category of travellers. This chapter examines the different characteristics of the various categories of business tourism and the trends affecting this sector of the industry.

Modern-day business tourism takes four principal forms:

- travel for the purpose of attending conferences and other types of meetings
- incentive travel
- travel to attend an exhibition or trade fair
- individual business travel.

In the vast majority of cases, each category of business tourism is in some way connected to the traveller's professional life or to their role in the buying and selling process that underpins much of modern commercial life.

Meetings

Travelling in order to attend a meeting of some kind is one of the most widespread forms of business tourism. Meetings take many forms and vary enormously in size and purpose, but the meetings that stimulate business tourism are primarily those organized with an objective linked to the attendees' professional activity.

This is most evident when the meeting's attendees all belong to the same profession or trade and are all members of the same professional or trade association. Many of the highest-profile meetings belong to this **association** category of meetings. They can attract many thousands of attendees (or **participants** or **delegates**, as they are also known) and their economic impacts on the destinations in which they are held can be considerable. For example, the conference of the European Society of Cardiology, the members of which are medical professionals specializing in cardiovascular diseases, now regularly attracts over 20 000 delegates. These five-day events provide the delegates from all over Europe and beyond with an invaluable opportunity to meet together and exchange ideas and information on new challenges and new techniques related to the field of cardiovascular medicine. It is clear that the collective spending of the delegates on items such as transport, accommodation and catering brings extensive economic benefits to the businesses operating in the cities in which this event takes place. The cities in which the conference has been held in recent years are shown in Table 11.1.

Not all meetings are of this magnitude, however. The vast majority are held with colleagues who work for the same company, and these are known as **corporate** meetings.

Table 11.1 Locations of the European Society of Cardiologists' conferences, 2000–2010

Year and location	Number of active participants
2010 Stockholm, Sweden	22 044
2009 Barcelona, Spain	25 056
2008 Munich, Germany	23 605
2007 Vienna, Austria	23 091
2006 Barcelona, Spain	25 501
2005 Stockholm, Sweden	18 242
2004 Munich, Germany	19 049
2003 Vienna, Austria	19 574
2002 Berlin, Germany	19 342
2001 Stockholm, Sweden	16 025
2000 Amsterdam, The Netherlands	17 112

Companies, large and small, have a number of reasons for organizing meetings of their staff, but all are linked to the companies' need to operate effectively in the field of business. For example, many corporate meetings are held for the purpose of training staff in the skills and techniques that they need in order to perform well in the workplace – selling skills, customer relations skills, information technology skills and so on, depending on the nature of the company's business. Other types of corporate meetings may be arranged with the objective of giving managers the opportunity to discuss the company's future strategies – for marketing, expansion, crisis management and so on.

Most such meetings are comparatively small (ranging from a handful of employees to several dozen), so these can be held in the type of small seminar rooms offered for hire by hotels. Indeed, a visit to most 4-star and 5-star hotels will provide information on exactly which corporate events are being held there that day, as such meetings are usually prominently listed in the reception area, for the benefit of the delegates attending them.

All types of companies organize meetings for their staff, but some sectors tend to have more meetings than others. The finance (banking and insurance), medical and pharmaceutical, automotive and engineering sectors are the principal markets, in most countries, for the meetings industry.

While association and corporate meetings comprise the lion's share of this particular form of business tourism, they are not the only elements. **Governments and political organizations** at all levels (local, regional and national as well as international legislative bodies, such as the European Commission – EC) also need to hold regular meetings to discuss strategies, choose candidates and announce new initiatives.

Among the most visible of these meetings are the annual conferences of political parties that are held in most countries. In the UK, for example, the 127th annual conference of the Conservative Party was held in Birmingham in 2010. It attracted around 14 000 attendees, including Conservative Members of Parliament and Members of the European Parliament, councillors and policy advisers, as well as approximately 2000 representatives from the press and other media, business groups, charitable organizations, think tanks and campaigning organizations.

The other types of organizations that frequently hold meetings are neatly encapsulated in the American acronym **SMERF**, which stands for social, military, educational, religious and fraternal. The SMERF sector of demand for meetings is a useful catch-all category, covering most types of meeting that are not held by professional/trade associations, companies or government organizations.

- *Social meetings.* This segment includes all groups meeting primarily for social interaction, such as collectors, hobbyists, special interest groups and non-military reunions. An example of such a meeting would be the 2011 National Barbie® Doll Collectors Convention held in Fort Lauderdale, Florida, at the Harbor Beach Marriott Resort & Spa, from 27–30 July. The convention brought together over 1000 collectors of all ages and backgrounds for four days of presentations, competitions and fashion shows, all based on the famous Barbie Doll merchandise.

- *Military meetings.* This segment largely comprises the reunions of people who served in the armed forces during periods of conflict. The intensity – and often the tragedy – that can characterize such conflicts means that those who lived through them often find comfort in reuniting with their fellow fighters at regular intervals to discuss their wartime experiences and commemorate their comrades who did not survive the hostilities. Many such meetings bring together veteran servicemen and women, such as the reunion of 150 former British and Dutch servicemen who fought in operation Market Garden – an attempt by the Allies to take control of several bridges in the German-occupied Netherlands in September 1944. The four-day event was held under the auspices of the Market Garden Veterans' Association, and took place in The Prince of Wales Hotel, Southport, UK, in June 2011.

- *Educational meetings.* Those who attend such events are generally teachers, lecturers and academic researchers who meet in order to share their research in their particular subject area, as well as new challenges and other developments affecting the teaching of their specialist subject. A typical example of an educational meeting would be the annual conference of ATLAS (**www.atlas-euro.org**), an international association of lecturers specializing in the teaching of travel and tourism.

- *Religious meetings.* Some of the largest gatherings organized in the world's major cities are for the purpose of bringing together, for one or more days, people who share the same faith. At such events, worship and prayer are often combined with debates and workshops during which topical issues relating to the attendees' particular religion are discussed. The six annual Bible-preaching conventions run by the Christian community based in Katoomba, New South Wales, Australia, are examples of religious meetings.

- *Fraternal meetings.* This segment includes primarily meetings of sororities, fraternities and other fraternal organizations. The attendees at fraternal meetings are often people who went to school or university together and wish to reunite from time to time, to relive the memories of their student days. University alumni reunions are a typical example of a fraternal meeting.

Association meetings and corporate meetings compared

While government and SMERF meetings display a wide and often colourful variety of themes, the vast majority of meetings fall into either the association or corporate segments, but they differ considerably from each other in a number of important respects. Consequently, it is important to understand the distinguishing characteristics of these two segments and be able to compare them accurately. Table 11.2 highlights some of the most important contrasts between the association and the corporate segments of the meetings sector of business tourism.

The meetings industry

As recently as 20 years ago, the expression 'meetings industry' was hardly ever used, in the sense of an umbrella term describing all of those businesses existing wholly or partly in order to provide the wide range of facilities and services that are required to make meetings possible and ensure that they are run professionally and effectively. Now, the use of this

Table 11.2 Association and business conferences contrasted

Association conferences	Corporate conferences
Delegate numbers can be in the hundreds – even thousands	Delegate numbers tend to be fewer – usually under 100 and often a few dozen
The decision process for choosing the destination can be long and complex, often involving a committee	The decision process for choosing the destination is shorter and simpler – it is often made by one person
Spending per delegate per day can be moderate, as the delegates are usually paying out of their own pockets	Spending per delegate per day can be higher, as the delegates' companies are usually paying
These can last for several days, or even a week in the case of large international association conferences	These are generally shorter and often last for only one day
For associations, conferences represent an opportunity to make a profit, which can in turn be used to pay for the associations' running expenses	For companies, conferences represent a cost that must be financed out of the profits made elsewhere by the companies
Many association events are held in large, purpose-built conference centres	Many corporate events are held in the seminar rooms of hotels
The lead-time for an association conference can be several years	The lead-time for a corporate conference is usually much shorter than for an association conference
Association conferences are rarely cancelled as the by-laws of the association usually state that an annual conference must be held	Corporate conferences can be cancelled more easily, particularly in times of financial hardship for the company
Delegates' partners are usually welcome to attend association conferences, so parallel partners' programmes of events are often planned for them	Delegates' partners are rarely encouraged to attend

term is widespread and the meetings industry is firmly established as an expanding and vitally important profession in its own right. The principal elements of the meetings industry will now be reviewed.

Venues

All meetings require some form of venue in which the attendees can gather for the duration of the event. Derived from the Latin verb *venire* (to come), the word venue is used to denote the building in which delegates come together in order to attend the event. In its most basic form, a venue comprises four walls, a roof and a collection of chairs for the delegates' comfort, but the variety of venues is almost as great as the variety of meetings held within them.

Conference centres

Their city centre locations, sheer vastness and often iconic designs mean that these buildings are certainly the most visible indication that any city is active in hosting large meetings. Many conference centres, such as the harbour-front Hong Kong Conference and Exhibition Centre, have become important symbols of the cities in which they are located. These venues are most often used for meetings requiring large open spaces and are built on a scale that enables them to accommodate hundreds or even thousands of delegates. In addition, they generally offer space for the types of exhibitions that are often run in parallel with large conferences, as well as the high-quality audio-visual and other technical facilities that are essential to the success of such large-scale events.

In their construction, conference centres are either of the purpose-built or converted types. Most are purpose-built – that is, they were originally and solely planned to be venues for conferences (see Figure 11.1). Many of the most interesting and charming conference centres, however, particularly in Europe, were converted into meeting venues from their original, different, function (see Figure 11.2). Prisons, hospitals and factories are just a few of the types of buildings that have been converted into conference centres to

Figure 11.1 A purpose-built conference centre: the Queen Elizabeth II Conference Centre, London

Photo: courtesy Queen Elizabeth II Conference Centre

serve the meetings industry. For example, the Mediterranean Conference Centre in Valletta, Malta, was originally constructed as a military hospital, but was converted into an outstanding conference venue in 1990.

Their immense capacity makes conference centres, purpose-built or converted, particularly suitable for large meetings of associations. Because, as mentioned, attendees at international association conferences can number in their thousands, conference centres are usually the only type of venue capable of holding meetings on this scale, particularly when, as is often the case with medical events for example, space is required in which to situate a parallel exhibition of products relating to the theme of the conference.

Figure 11.2 A converted venue: le Palais Beaumont Pau, France

Photo: Historic Conference Centres of Europe, www.hcce.com, and Le Palais Beaumont Pau, www.paucc.com

Hotels

Long before the first conference centres were built, meetings were regularly taking place in rooms designed for the purpose in inns and hotels, and to this day they remain the preferred type of venue for most of the world's meetings.

Whether hotels are situated in city centres, suburban locations, airports or rural areas, most depend to a significant extent on the income they earn from renting out their meetings rooms and the conference-related spending on catering and (for residential events) accommodation. Many hotel chains have branded their meetings facilities to ensure that customers using them are assured consistent standards of facilities and quality, wherever in the world a particular hotel may be located.

EXAMPLE **Hilton Hotels**

Hilton Hotels' Hilton Meetings brand is designed to provide personalized meeting services that enable clients to hold successful and hassle-free meetings for groups of 50 guests or fewer. Hilton Meetings was created in 2000 at Hilton hotels in Britain and Ireland and gradually expanded globally, finally being introduced to the majority of Hilton hotels in North America in 2008.

Hilton business clients can choose between a formal boardroom setting and flexible multipurpose room for their small meetings. These well-designed layouts are complemented by guaranteed standards of Hilton Meetings service and amenities that aim to minimize the environmental impact while offering time-saving technology and consistent personalized service.

Hilton Meetings guests have access to fresh and contemporary meeting spaces with high-quality furnishings, local artwork to help stimulate creativity and advanced technology to keep guests plugged in. All rooms include a 3M™ Digital Easel that instantly records flipchart content electronically into a variety of formats for Mac and PC computers and enables collaboration with participants in multiple locations via a shared meeting application. Radio-controlled clocks, keeping accurate local time, help keep guests on time, while high-speed Internet connectivity keeps guests connected.

Tables are designed with built-in table-top power and data points for easy connections and chairs offer extra comfort with their padded armrests and lumbar support. Meeting rooms also contain a refrigerator and safe that can hold at least four laptops, have doors that lock for added security and outside-in spyhole viewers to minimize disruption.

Dedicated meetings specialists are assigned to each Hilton Meetings room to assist with individual service needs. A 'Service Connect System' button links guests directly with their meeting specialist. Each meeting planner receives a welcome kit containing specific details about their event, the hotel and the meeting space and a welcome wallet holding lunch and break menus. Hilton also serves meeting participants food and beverage items specifically selected to help boost their energy and keep their minds sharp (such as peach smoothies or mini shish kebabs with lemon yogurt sauce) along with complimentary tea and coffee served all day.

Hilton's e-Events online group booking tool, Guest List Manager and Personalized Group Web Page features allow event planners to easily book their group event or meeting and promote their event to attendees.

The Hilton Meetings products reinforce Hilton's commitment to environmental sustainability. The hotelier has reduced the use of chrome in meeting room furniture and fixtures and is using sleek hard surfaces for tables to eliminate the need for linens and the chemicals used for cleaning them. To further support the brand's efforts to increase local sourcing, artwork featured in rooms is acquired from local artists.

Hilton Meetings is also fully supported by new online event management and meeting planning tools, which helps to reduce paper waste. In-room signage provides guests with tips on how to be an environmentally sensitive meeting participant, such as turning off the lights before leaving the room and recycling paper when it is an option. Also, rooms include eco-friendly meeting materials made from recycled paper and biodegradable ink. These materials are placed on self-service stands to eliminate full place settings of notepads and pens, which often create unnecessary waste. To further attempt to reduce waste, notepads contain lines on both sides of each page.

With the notable exception of the 'convention hotels' found in US cities such as Las Vegas, which offer meetings facilities capable of hosting conferences of several thousand attendees, most meeting spaces located in hotels are designed for smaller events of several dozen or several hundred attendees. Indeed, many hotel boardrooms are exclusive venues for fewer than 20 attendees. The average size of seminar rooms and other meeting facilities offered by hotel venues makes them eminently suitable for corporate events such as staff training sessions or senior management strategy meetings.

Academic venues

In many countries, universities and other educational institutions are active suppliers of meetings facilities, particularly during student holiday periods and weekends. With their lecture theatres, classrooms, audio-visual facilities and catering services, such venues offer everything that is required to host meetings, large and small. When such meetings are hosted outside the teaching period, student accommodation may also be used by those attending residential events.

In several countries, universities have created their own marketing consortia to promote themselves as meetings venues. For example, Venuemasters (**www.venuemasters.co.uk**) is a consortium that promotes the facilities available for hire to meeting planners at over 85 academic venues in the UK and the Republic of Ireland. Venuemasters' members are venues that are either owned by an educational establishment or have as their core business the provision of further, higher or professional education. The consortium offers a venue-finding service for organizations and companies in search of meeting rooms and, if needed, accommodation for their events.

While rarely offering the standards of luxury found in 5-star hotels, academic venues have the advantage of being able to offer their facilities at fairly competitive rates. For that reason, they are often used as the location for meetings where attendees are paying out of their own pockets and costs have to be kept at a moderate level. Certain association events as well as some types of SMERF meetings are therefore natural clients of the academic venue sector of the meetings industry.

Unusual venues

This category includes the meetings facilities offered by a wide range of properties such as museums, stately homes, castles, theatres and theme parks as well as other tourist attractions such as zoos and aquariums. For most of these, the provision of meeting facilities is an activity that is secondary to the property's principal function, but, nevertheless, an important source of revenue. For example, many sporting venues, such as football stadiums and horseracing tracks, supplement the income they earn from such events by hosting meetings when the facilities are not being used for their original and principal purpose. The world-famous Stade de France in Paris is a typical example of an unusual venue of this type, advertising itself as a meeting venue for events of up to 5000 attendees.

The main motivation for holding a meeting in an unusual venue is to make the event memorable and attractive to attendees. The organization holding the meeting can also benefit from the reflected glory of the great prestige associated with certain unusual venues. For example, any meeting held in the Victoria and Albert Museum in London will automatically benefit from the considerable cachet associated with such a venerable institution.

Other suppliers

It is clear that, in order to run a successful meeting, much more is required than simply a suitable venue. A wide range of facilities and services is necessary for the smooth running of any such event.

Attendees need to be fed and refreshed at regular intervals during the meeting, so the provision of food and beverages is vital, whether for a simple coffee break or lunch or the type of sumptuous gala that is often held on the final evening of a grand conference.

On such occasions, the decoration of the tables and the dining room can be as important as the quality of the food and wines, particularly for prestigious events.

As well as professional catering, most meetings make extensive use of audio-visual resources to make their events look and sound as good as possible. This is one of the ways in which the production of meetings has changed most in the past few decades. The days of conference speakers making use of a flipchart or overhead projector to communicate with their audiences are long gone. In the twenty-first century, information and communications technology has revolutionized the meetings industry, as it has so many other sectors. Multiple screens, PowerPoint presentations and surround sound quality are now widespread, turning many large-scale conferences, such as those of political parties, into veritable 'shows', characterized by high-quality sound and near television production standards.

In an increasingly globalized world, the provision of interpreting services is of growing importance as meetings may well be attended by delegates who speak a variety of different languages. Conference interpreters are the people whose considerable skills make multilingual meetings possible and conference centres are generally designed to include interpreters' booths, where professional interpreters can listen to, translate and relay the conference speakers' words simultaneously and accurately – no easy feat.

Meeting planners

It is already evident from the above that the planning of meetings today can be a highly complex task. The destination and the venue must be chosen, the attendees' travel and, if necessary, visa requirements must be taken care of and their accommodation arranged, plus topics and speakers for the event must be selected. Some conferences, such as those of associations, must be marketed to prospective attendees and registration payments processed. At the actual event, someone must organize appropriate security measures, particularly if VIP attendees or speakers are involved, and someone must liaise with and manage the providers of audio-visual and catering services.

These tasks – and many more – are the responsibility of the **meeting planner**. In recent years, the role of the meeting planner has increasingly been recognized as a profession in its own right, and its importance in the meetings industry cannot be overestimated. Many now bear the job title 'professional conference organizer' or PCO, although a range of other titles exists, such as events planner, conference coordinator and meetings executive. Many meeting planners are employed by a single organization – usually an association or a company – organizing, on a full-time basis, all of the meetings, seminars and conferences that their organization needs.

Others, often called **independent meeting planners**, are self-employed, offering their services to a variety of associations and companies on a consultancy basis, charging a fee for the meetings that they organize on behalf of their clients. This arrangement can be particularly beneficial to smaller organizations that do not hold sufficient events on a year-to-year basis to justify having such a person on their payroll as a full-time, permanent member of staff.

What we have termed the 'meetings industry', therefore, comprises those men and women who earn their living from the provision of facilities and services for the successful running of meetings, large and small. Managing and marketing venues, supplying catering, interpreting and audio-visual services for meetings and taking responsibility for the coordination and planning of the actual meetings event – these are the principal functions of those who make successful events possible.

It is worth noting, however, that, while some individuals and companies operate entirely and solely within the meetings industry, for many others, this sector of business tourism represents only a part of their activities. For example, many venues, in addition to providing space for meetings, also hire out their facilities for events such as concerts, weddings and graduation ceremonies. In many organizations, the planning of meetings is only *part* of the job the person who undertakes the task, does – a part that may not even be reflected in their job title, as in the case of a training manager or human resources executive who also organizes events from time to time. Many airlines and hotels, for example, are hardly aware of the role that they play in supplying vital services to the meetings industry by transporting and accommodating attendees and speakers.

Incentive travel

One particular type of meeting is usually regarded as being sufficiently distinct from all the others to justify it being given its own separate category. **Incentive travel** is the name given to the travel, usually in groups, of employees who have been awarded a luxury trip, entirely paid for by their company, as a prize for high achievement at work. The practice of using incentive travel to motivate employees to work harder was originally started by American companies in the 1950s, and employers in the USA are still the major generators of this sector of business tourism. Since then, however, the use of incentive travel has spread throughout the industrialized world and is now widely recognized as being one of the most effective management tools for encouraging employees to be more productive and make a greater contribution to their employers' profitability.

Most incentive trips are won by individuals (or teams) who have sold, within a given period, the most units of whatever it is their companies make, whether this is tractors, insurance policies, pharmaceutical products or any other type of manufactured goods or services. For this reason, most of those who travel on incentive trips are members of their companies' salesforces.

Put simply, a company using incentive travel as a reward will announce a **competition** to their salesforce, informing them that their individual or team sales figures during a particular period (often 12 months) will be recorded for the purpose of determining who sold the most during that time. The prize for being one of the most successful salespeople during that period is the incentive trip, typically of three to five days' duration, which will be described in detail and in the most enticing terms, in order to encourage the sales staff to do their utmost in order to win the trip.

It would be no exaggeration to say that incentive travel is one of the most luxurious, highest-spending and therefore lucrative forms of tourism that exists. In order to motivate employees to work harder to achieve greater results in the workplace, the travel prize they are competing for must be an extremely attractive one. This is particularly the case when those competing to win the prize are managers who travel often, on business and for leisure, and are therefore not easily impressed by yet another flight and another hotel in a foreign destination. Exotic destinations, luxury accommodation and a dazzling variety of exciting and exclusive activities are classic features of incentive travel.

Incentive travel winners – those who get to go on these magnificent trips – must be given the impression that they are privileged and greatly valued by their employers, which is why incentive trips must delight and indulge those who are fortunate enough to receive this form of reward for their performance at work. The key word here is 'work' for, although incentive travel participants may look and behave like leisure tourists – dressing casually, relaxing, sightseeing and enjoying sporting and/or leisure activities – the motive underlying their trip is most definitely connected to the participant's working life, which is why this form of travel is firmly categorized within the business tourism sector.

Nevertheless, there are clearly alternative ways to motivate staff to work harder and reward them when they achieve outstanding results. The tool most commonly used by companies to 'incentivize' their employees is not incentive travel but *money* – usually cash bonuses for those who reach specific targets in their work. Gradually, however, more and more employers are beginning to realize that the use of incentive travel as a reward offers them a number of advantages that simply awarding staff the cash equivalent does not.

The advantages of incentive travel and cash

Advantages of incentive travel over cash

- Employees spend time with each other, at leisure. This informal networking offers them the opportunity of getting to know each other better, which in turn can help create a stronger team spirit when they return to work, having shared a number of enjoyable and memorable experiences together.

- For the few days of the trip, the company has an opportunity to inculcate 'company values' into some of its most productive employees. Pep talks are a common feature of incentive trips – motivational speeches praising the incentive travel winners for their hard work and extolling the qualities of the company they work for. This is one of the management techniques employed by companies to reduce staff turnover and, in particular, retain those employees who make the most valuable contribution to their company's profitability.

- Incentive travel is more effective than money at encouraging non-winners to try harder to win the next competition run by their company. The incentive travel winners' absence from work and their subsequent return, full of stories of what they have seen and done on their trip, make this a highly visible prize, as opposed to money, which is far less likely to be discussed with colleagues. Non-winners can be motivated to work harder to win next time when they hear their colleagues recount their incentive trip experiences.

- As incentive trips offer those who participate in them the opportunity to relax and/or engage in physical pursuits, it means that they tend to return to work refreshed and rested, and this boost to their wellbeing can be beneficial to their performance in the workplace. At the same time, it is undeniable that the use of cash awards offers its own advantages, when compared with sending high-achieving staff on incentive trips.

Advantages of cash over incentive trips

- Low risk. Cash awards are attractive by the very nature of their simplicity. Money is always welcomed by the recipient, but the participant's response to an incentive trip is less predictable. Poor weather, the wrong choice of incentive destination or disappointing accommodation are among the factors that can turn what should be an enjoyable, motivating reward into its opposite.

- No loss of productivity. When some of the company's highest-performing members of staff are absent from work for several days, enjoying an incentive trip, the impact on the company's profitability can be considerable. With cash awards, the winners continue to work and there is no negative impact on the company's sales figures.

- Flexibility. The employee in receipt of a cash bonus for meeting a demanding sales target, for example, can spend the money on whatever he or she wishes or needs. This could be, of course, a holiday or short break, in which case the tourism industry benefits from the spending of this award, but it could equally be spent on home improvements, repairs to the family car or simply invested in a savings account.

- Finally, in an era when attention is increasingly being focused on employees' work–life balance – the balance between the time they spend working and the time they spend with friends and family – it is widely recognized that awarding an incentive trip, however luxurious, as a prize for high achievement at work does mean that the participants are automatically obliged to spend additional time away from home in order to take part in the trip. This may not always be welcomed by employees, particularly those who already find themselves spending evenings away from their friends and families, travelling on company business. Cash bonuses, therefore, can be a more motivating prize for such employees.

The incentive travel industry

In our review of the principal elements of the meetings industry, it was seen that a number of specialist suppliers are required in order to make the effective functioning of meetings possible – venues, audio-visual companies, interpreters and so on. By way of contrast, the incentive travel sector of business tourism largely makes use of the same services, facilities and resources that are used by leisure tourists – airlines and other forms of transport, hotel accommodation, tourist attractions, guides, shops, cultural and sports events and so on. Of course, the incentive travel sector does tend to make most use of that end of the tourism market spectrum characterized by 4- and 5-star hotels, exclusive restaurants and privileged, private access to tourist attractions and prestigious events.

The one type of specialist agency required in order to facilitate the functioning of the incentive travel industry is the **incentive travel house**. This is the term commonly used for an agency that designs incentive programmes for its clients – companies using this technique to motivate their staff. Agency staff are professionals who oversee the entire operation, from designing the rules of the competition for employees and the selection of winners, through the choice of the destination and activities for the incentive trip to the planning of the detailed logistics for the trip, including all transport, accommodation and catering arrangements.

While some companies entrust the planning of their staff incentive programmes to high-street generalist travel agencies, they are in a small, declining minority. Most companies understand that the planning and execution of incentive trips is so extremely technical and demanding in terms of the high expectations of the winners, that this process is best placed in the hands of specialist incentive travel houses.

One of the many pressures that those employed by incentive travel houses must contend with is the necessity of creating the essential 'wow' factor for every trip they organize. It is often claimed that 'wow' is the most important word in the entire lexicon of the incentive travel sector of business tourism as any trip that fails to surprise, delight and inspire the participants in this way can fairly be said to have failed in its objectives.

Supplying that 'wow' factor, as all incentive travel professionals understand, is not simply a case of spending vast amounts of the client's money on extravagant entertainments for its winning employees. Great creativity and imagination are the essential qualities required by anyone wishing to work in this aspect of the incentive travel industry. A vivid, but not particularly unique, example of these qualities at work in the design of an incentive travel programme is the group of incentive winners on a trip to Finnish Lapland, who were given fishing rods and instructed on how to cut a round hole in the Arctic ice so that they could spend the day fishing as the native Lapps do. The cost of this simple activity was minimal, but the impact on the group was outstanding. It fired them with enthusiasm and enchantment – as all good incentive trips should.

Exhibitions and trade fairs

Some of the largest flows of business tourists are to be found when many thousands of people gather in a destination for one or more days to attend an exhibition. As the subject of this chapter is business tourism, the types of exhibition under consideration here are not of a cultural nature, such as exhibitions of paintings or sculptures found in art galleries and museums, but events where the exhibitors hire stands (or, in American English, booths) to present their companies' goods or services to those visiting the exhibition.

Although the word 'exhibition' is often used generically, it is common to distinguish between exhibitions, which attract the general public, and trade fairs (known as trade shows in the USA), which are mainly attended by business visitors. Thus, the Union des Foires Internationales (UFI), now known as the Global Association of the Exhibition Industry, gives the following definitions:

> Exhibitions are market events of a specific duration, held at intervals, at which a large number of companies present a representative product range of one or more industry sectors and sell it or provide information about it for the purposes of sales promotion. Exhibitions predominantly attract the general public.
>
> Trade fairs are market events of a specific duration, held at intervals, at which a large number of companies present the main product range of one or more industry sectors and mainly sell it on the basis of samples. Trade fairs predominantly attract trade and business visitors.
>
> UFI, 2011.

Those who travel in order to attend exhibitions are generally members of the public seeking to buy, or find information about, goods or services that they need for their own personal consumption. An example of this type of event could be the National Wedding Show, held in two UK venues each year: the Earls Court exhibition centre in London and the National Exhibition Centre in Birmingham. Between them, these two shows attract over 60 000 visitors – primarily future brides, grooms, bridesmaids and brides' mothers. Over 1100 exhibitors display the goods and services they supply for those getting married, including wedding dresses, flowers and honeymoon holidays. There is also a series of workshops on themes such as public speaking (for after-dinner speeches) and make-up and hair-styling for weddings.

Similarly, the organization IEFT (International Education Fairs of Turkey) runs an annual series of exhibitions that bring together education providers with Turkish students and their families, to promote study options available around the globe. Over 150 educational institutions from more than 25 different countries exhibited during the 2010 IEFT exhibitions, held in hotels in Istanbul, Ankara, Izmir, Adana, Konya, Eskisehir and North Cyprus. Almost 20 000 prospective students attended these events.

Those who visit trade fairs are people who are in search of goods and services that are vital to the effective functioning of their businesses. For example, Exposibram (**www.exposibram.org.br**) is the largest trade fair in Brazil for the mining industry. It takes place annually over a four-day period, and in 2011 was held in the city of Belo Horizonte, in the mining state of Minas Gerais. Exposibram attracted 43 000 visitors and 390 exhibitors from 27 countries. The exhibitors were companies and organizations specializing in mining equipment and technologies, mining consulting services, mining engineering services, mining software, research and development services, mining maintenance and environmental technologies. During the four days of the trade fair, a mining industry conference – the Brazilian Mining Congress – was held in parallel. Both events were held in the Expominas venue, which covers an area of 71 000 square metres.

An industry much more familiar to most people is the cinema sector of entertainment, which also has its own trade shows throughout the world. One such event is CineEurope, held at the Amsterdam RAI venue (**www.cinemaexpo.com**). Those who travel to this event, from all over Europe and beyond, are mainly proprietors and managers of cinemas in search of information on, and the opportunity to purchase, the latest equipment and services required by their businesses, such as seating, staff uniforms, food and beverage kiosks, amplifiers and projection equipment.

Having made this distinction between exhibitions and trade fairs, it is certainly not the case that *all* events fall neatly into one or the other category. It is possible for the same event to be both an exhibition *and* a trade show. For example, an event primarily aimed at those running businesses in the construction industry may also be open to members of the general public who are interested in DIY as both categories of visitors to such an event will be keen to see the vast range of building materials and tools on show. It is common in such cases to have certain days that are reserved for trade visitors only and others where the general public may also attend.

It is clear that each one of all the hundreds of thousands of goods and services that we use in our personal and professional lives are bought and sold at their own exhibitions and trade shows, in destinations all over the world. From everyday objects such as shoes, books and mobile telephones, through much more expensive items such as cars, boats and holiday homes, to services such as educational courses, investment products and ski holidays, they all have their specific events, sometimes regional, sometimes national and sometimes international, to which potential customers can travel, in order to obtain information, negotiate and even possibly make a purchase.

Regarding patterns of travel to such events, it is often claimed that travel to exhibitions follows a different pattern from travel to trade shows. As most visitors to exhibitions are members of the public – people travelling with friends and/or family members – they tend on the whole to be making day trips to such events. For example, a family may go to a local exhibition centre to visit a ski show with a view to buying new ski equipment or booking a ski holiday. For the family, this is a pleasant day out, the journey often made by car – much like a trip to their local shopping centre.

EXAMPLE   IAAPA Attractions Expo 2011

The International Association of Amusement Parks and Attractions (IAAPA – **www.iaapa.org**) is the largest international trade association for permanently situated amusement facilities worldwide, and is dedicated to the preservation and prosperity of the amusement industry. The types of facilities operated by IAAPA members include amusement parks, theme parks, waterparks, family entertainment centres, zoos, aquariums, museums, science centres, resorts and casinos. Each year the IAAPA hosts three trade shows worldwide, focused on the amusement park and attractions industry: IAAPA Attractions Expo, Asian Attractions Expo and Euro Attractions Show. Each is the premier attractions industry trade show in its region.

According to the IAAPA's own News Release:

- 25 000 people from 100 countries were expected to attend IAAPA Attractions Expo 2011 from 15-18 November in the Orange County Convention Center, Orlando, Florida.
- Owners, executives, managers and young professionals from nearly 6500 attractions, including theme and amusement parks, waterparks, family entertainment centres, zoos, aquariums, museums, science centres, resorts and casinos, would participate in the show.
- More than 1100 exhibitors were expected to showcase innovative products and services for the attractions industry, including theme park rides, show and event production services, food and beverage products and services, consultancy services, design services, ticketing systems and services, information technology system and more than 90 additional product categories.
- The IAAPA Attractions Expo 2011 would include over 100 education sessions and unique daily networking opportunities.

By way of contrast, many trade shows are of such a highly specialized nature that they attract business visitors from other regions and, indeed, other countries – even continents. Such visitors, because of the distances they have travelled, tend to stay longer at their destination, creating valuable business for hotels and restaurants, as well as for the transport companies.

Not only do travel patterns for exhibitions and trade shows differ, but this sector of business tourism may also be distinguished from the other sectors covered in this chapter in the sense that both exhibitions *and* trade shows stimulate the travel of not one but two groups of people: the exhibitors and the visitors. So, whether the visitors are families on day trips or business owners who have travelled internationally to attend the event, the exhibitors inevitably remain in the destination for the duration of the trade fair or exhibition, bringing business to the local hospitality industry. At large events, the numbers of exhibitors can be substantial. For instance, the number of exhibiting personnel at the World Travel Market in London (**www.wtmlondon.com**) was over 16 000 in 2010, making it extremely challenging for anyone to find a vacant hotel room in the city during the four days in November when the event took place.

The exhibition and trade fair industry

The successful planning, marketing, hosting and execution of exhibitions and trade shows calls for the concerted efforts and expertise of a wide range of specialist professionals.

Exhibition halls and exhibition centres rent out their facilities to provide the basic shelter and security that are necessary when hosting these events. They also have to provide all necessary utilities such as electricity, water, gas and communication connections (telephone, ISDN, the Internet), as well as a clear signage system. Infrastructures, such as restaurants, parking areas (usually one for exhibitors and another for visitors), toilets and entrance areas, are other integral parts of these venues. Moreover, as conferences and seminars are often held as well as fairs and exhibitions, appropriate meeting room facilities are also included at these venues.

As exhibition halls and exhibition centres are often vast buildings, requiring many hectares of space, they are frequently situated in areas where land is cheaper, well away from city centres. Frequently, they are to be found between the city's centre and its airport, where there is ample space for parking and easy access for visitors arriving by air. Venues may be either owned by the local municipality, as is generally the case in countries such as Germany, Italy and France, for example; or privately owned and rented out with a view to making a profitable return for their owners.

While large venues such as the Geneva Palexpo are the places where by far the most exhibition and trade shows are held, it is important to remember that many smaller events may be held in hotels or other buildings such as arenas, concert halls or conference centres. Some events, due to the nature of the goods being exhibited, are, in fact, more suited to outdoor venues. For example, agricultural shows, where livestock and farm machinery are on show, or aviation trade shows, such as the annual Cannes AirShow (**www.cannesairshow.com**) held at Cannes Mandelieu International Airport on the French Riviera, are generally held in the open air.

EXAMPLE   ## Bologna Exhibition Centre (BolognaFiere)

Located in the northern Italian city of Bologna, the Bologna Exhibition Centre extends over 375 000 square metres of covered and outdoors areas. Its total services area is 36 000 square metres. Its 18 halls are completely wired, air-conditioned and equipped with IT systems, and multiple events can be held simultaneously in the exhibition centre, thanks to its five separate entrances.

Flexibility and mobility indoors are ensured by a network of moving walkways and by a parking system with 14 500 covered parking spaces that can be reserved in advance.

Bologna Exhibition Centre is unique in Europe, in having its own motorway tollbooth, part of a plan - along with a dynamic third lane - that aims to reduce congestion by providing entrance directly to the Centre, thereby avoiding the ring road around Bologna. There is also a heliport located on the roof of Halls 16-18. In addition, a dedicated 'BolognaFiere' railway station handles special trains for exhibitions with the highest attendance.

On average, the Bologna Exhibition Centre hosts 27 exhibitions each year. During 2011, an above-average year in terms of event numbers, exhibitions held included:

MARCA - by BolognaFiere	Private label conference and exhibition	19/01/2011-20/01/2011
So Fresh - MARCA - by BolognaFiere	Conference and exhibition devoted to fresh foods	19/01/2011-20/01/2011
Arte Fiera - Art First	International exhibition of contemporary art	28/01/2011-31/01/2011
Fishing Show	Sports fishing show	11/02/2011-14/02/2011

Eudishow e Divex	19th international exhibition of underwater diving and equipment and spearfishing	11/02/2011–14/02/2011
ForumClub ForumPiscine	Expo and International Congress for Fitness, Wellness & Aquatic Clubs – Pool & Spa Expo and International Congress	24/02/2011–26/02/2011
Cosmoprof Worldwide Bologna	Heralded as the world's most important international event in the perfumery, cosmetics, hairstyle, beauty, nails and spa sector	18/03/2011–21/03/2011
Cosmopack – inside Cosmoprof	International exhibition of packaging	18/03/2011–21/03/2011
Bologna Children's Book Fair		28/03/2011–31/03/2011
Pasta Trend	The first major exhibition dedicated to the world of pasta	02/04/2011–05/04/2011
Lineapelle	International exhibition of leather, accessories/ components, synthetics/fabrics and models for footwear, leather goods, clothing and upholstery	06/04/2011–08/04/2011
Il Mondo Creativo Primavera	Exhibition of hobby and craft	08/04/2011–10/04/2011
Ambiente Lavoro	Exhibition of quality and safety in working places	03/05/2011–05/05/2011
Zoomark International	International exhibition of products and accessories for pets	12/05/2011–15/05/2011
Cosmofarma Exhibition	International exhibition of health, wellness and beauty products and services sold in pharmacies	13/05/2011–15/05/2011
Autopromotec	24th International biennial exhibition of automotive equipment and aftermarket products	25/05/2011–29/05/2011
Smau Business Bologna	Information & communication technology for small and medium-sized companies and public entities	08/06/2011–09/06/2011
R2B – Research to Business		08/06/2011–09/06/2011
Sana	International exhibition of natural products	08/09/2011–11/09/2011
Cersaie	International exhibition of ceramic tile and bathroom furnishings	20/09/2011–24/09/2011
Saie	International building exhibition	05/10/2011–08/10/2011
Saienergia	Renewable energy sources and low-energy technologies for sustainable building	05/10/2011–08/10/2011
Saie Precast Technologies	Living systems, equipment and machinery for the precast	05/10/2011–08/10/2011
Simac	International exhibition of machines and technologies for footwear and leather goods industries	18/10/2011–20/10/2011
Tanning – Tech	International exhibition of machines and technologies for the tanning industry	18/10/2011–20/10/2011
Model Game	Model making exhibition	19/11/2011–20/11/2011
Big Buyer	Exhibition conference of the office/home/school stationery products for Italian and foreign big buyers	23/11/2011–25/11/2011
Movint – Expologistica	International industrial and mechanical handling exhibition – exhibition of integrated means, systems and services for logistics and transport	27/10/2011–29/10/2011
Motor Show Bologna	International automobile exhibition	03/12/2011–11/12/2011

Exhibition and trade fair organizers

The organizers of these events are the people and organizations who create the exhibition or trade show, rent the venue, then market the event to prospective exhibitors and visitors. They earn a living from identifying opportunities for new exhibitions or trade shows and running these events, usually on a regular basis, for profit. A considerable amount of research must be carried out by them initially, to determine whether or not a particular theme for an exhibition or trade show is viable – in other words, are there sufficient numbers of exhibitors who are prepared to pay to have stands at an event dedicated to their industry? In turn, potential exhibitors will only agree to buy space at an event if they are satisfied that sufficient potential buyers will visit it, making their investment worthwhile. Therefore, one of the key tasks of organizers is to market it widely to potential visitors. The mark of a successful exhibition or trade show is when most exhibitors are satisfied with the numbers of visitors coming to their stands and most visitors are satisfied with the variety and range of products on display and, further, both groups consider it worthwhile returning to the event at a future date.

As stated earlier, visitors and exhibitors attend these events not only to buy and sell but also for the opportunity to attend educational sessions and networking events during the exhibition or trade show. It is another responsibility of the organizers to ensure that an interesting and topical series of seminars is programmed during the event and that there are adequate opportunities for attendees to mix and mingle informally – for example, at opening receptions or after-hours cocktail parties.

Stand/booth contractors

Most exhibitors rely on specialist contractors to design and build their stands. In recent years, this task has become an increasingly creative and technical one as stand design has become more imaginative and elaborate, using new materials and new technology to make exhibition stands ever more eye-catching and attractive to visitors.

High visibility is essential at such events where every exhibitor is vying with all the others to entice visitors to approach their stand and engage with those who are there to sell or provide information on their companies' products. Colour, layout, lighting and prominent display of the company's logo all have a part to play in making a stand attractive and welcoming to visitors. Contractors may also be used to construct the stand before the event and dismantle it at the end.

Individual business travel

The final sector of the business tourism industry that was identified earlier is that of individual business travel, which may also be termed **corporate** travel. This sector comprises the trips of all men and women whose work obliges them to travel, either regularly or on an occasional basis. These employees are often known by the somewhat tongue-in-cheek title of 'road warriors', due to the time that they spend 'on the road' carrying out company business.

In the modern world, most organizations require some of their employees to travel from time to time in order to conduct some aspects of the company's business. Often, the objective of such trips is to find new customers, in which case a sales or marketing manager may be required to travel in order to present the company's products or services to prospective clients and negotiate prices with them.

As companies expand internationally, with branches in more than one country – and more and more often, as a result of globalization, in more than one continent – staff find themselves travelling to meet their colleagues in other branches and work with them for a few days to solve a problem or share their expertise. This type of transient movement of staff between different branches of a company is another driver of individual business travel.

Some people, whether they are company employees or self-employed, find themselves travelling regularly on business due to the nature of the job they do. For example, most investigative journalists, whether for the print media, radio or television, could not work effectively without frequently travelling in order to carry out their enquiries. Similarly, those who have highly specialized skills, such as hostage negotiators or opera singers, often find themselves travelling to where their skills are needed at any particular time.

Given, therefore, the number of reasons that exist for employees travelling on company business, it should come as no surprise that individual business travel is a major expense for many firms. Indeed, spending on business travel is second only to spending on staff pay. For this reason, most companies put into place a number of measures to control and limit their employees' spending on transport and accommodation while travelling on company business.

The main technique used for this purpose is the company's **travel policy**. It is rare these days for any company or organization (except, perhaps, for the smallest) *not* to have a written travel policy giving staff clear guidance on how they can – and, more crucially, cannot – spend their employer's money on individual business travel. Most such policies will state, for example, which class of air travel the employee is entitled to use when flying somewhere on behalf of the company. Typically, this will depend on a variety of factors, such as the length of the journey to be undertaken (short-, medium- or long-haul) and the employee's level of seniority within their company (junior, middle or senior management). Similar constrictions may be included in the travel policy for other elements of business trips, such as the class of hotel that may be used or the class of vehicle that may be hired. In this way, companies and organizations attempt to avoid the type of anarchic free-for-all that could arise if no controls were in place.

Many companies find it worthwhile employing a **business travel manager** to monitor the travel of employees and ensure that they comply with the travel policy. Business travel managers may also have the responsibility of negotiating with suppliers such as airlines, hotels and car hire companies on behalf of their employer. Large companies, in particular, are in a powerful negotiating position by virtue of the sheer volume of travel their employees undertake each year. So, while members of the general public using hotels only once or twice a year have very little leverage in terms of negotiating rates for overnight accommodation, a company with a salesforce of 50 people, spending between them several thousand nights per year in hotel rooms, is advantageously positioned to bargain with a hotel chain that has properties in the cities visited regularly by its salespeople.

A common task of the business travel manager, therefore, is to negotiate with a limited number of airlines, hotel chains and car hire companies, guaranteeing them a certain volume of business annually in return for preferential rates for the company's employees. When such agreements exist, the employees are generally instructed (in the travel policy) to use those suppliers rather than others with whom the employer has not negotiated preferential rates.

Nevertheless, although companies are constantly seeking the best value for money from travel companies and accommodation providers, it would be a mistake to believe that they always look for the very cheapest fares and hotel rates for their staff who are travelling on business. There are three main reasons for employers wanting to avoid cutting their business travel costs to the bare minimum:

- staff comfort
- staff safety
- staff loyalty and morale.

Staff comfort

Travelling in comfort can be an important consideration when it is vital that staff arrive at their destination fully refreshed and immediately ready to do the job that they have been sent to do.

Managers taking a long-haul overnight flight may save their company a considerable sum of money by travelling in economy class, but the probability that they will be able to sleep well and work at their seat – on their laptops, for example – is much less than if they were travelling in business class, with more personal space, more legroom and less likelihood of being kept awake all night by the crying baby from hell in the seat behind them. If they have not been able to rest and relax, they will hardly be in a fit state to attend an important business meeting in order to make a presentation or negotiate on behalf of their company. They may even need a day to recover from the flight, which means that an extra night in a hotel must be paid for, as well as meals and other expenses. Most importantly, a whole day's work may effectively be lost after both the outward and return journey, due to the business traveller's loss of sleep.

When all of these considerations are taken into account, the economy class ticket may seem less of a bargain than it appeared to be at the time of booking.

Staff safety

Employers have a legal duty of responsibility to do everything within reason to ensure the safety of those travelling on company business.

It is often claimed that business travellers face an even greater range of dangers than those travelling for leisure purposes. They are much more vulnerable, due to the fact that they are likely to be travelling alone, they make more attractive targets for criminals as they may be carrying information in their laptops that could be commercially valuable if it fell into certain hands and, in some countries, businesspeople may be targeted by kidnappers, who understand that their employers will be prepared to pay a substantial ransom for their safe return. Women travelling on business often feel the presence of these and other dangers more acutely than men and a great number of self-help organizations and websites (such as **www.womentraveltips.com**) exist to give advice on how to stay safe when travelling on business.

The safety of business travellers must therefore be of paramount concern to their employers. Accordingly, when a company's employee has to arrange to stay overnight in another city, in order to meet a client, for example, the company will usually authorize the booking of a room in a city centre hotel, although it may be much cheaper to book a room in a more distant, suburban hotel. This reduces the business traveller's need to travel around by taxi or public transport in an unfamiliar situation, thereby decreasing risk.

Staff loyalty and morale

Although many claim to enjoy it, individual business travel can be extremely trying at times. It temporarily separates people from their friends and families and can be a source of stress and frustration, in the same way that travel for leisure purposes can. Jet lag, gruelling security measures at airports and loss of opportunities for exercise are just a few of the common complaints of frequent business travellers. If, on top of these privations, business travellers also feel that their companies are cutting travel and accommodation costs to the bare minimum, they are hardly likely to feel positive about the firm they work for.

Resentful and unmotivated members of staff tend to feel very little loyalty to their employers. So, most companies, keen to retain their most valuable members of staff, will avoid adopting a penny-pinching approach to travel expenses and will resign themselves to paying for the occasional in-room movie or mini-bar item enjoyed by their intrepid road warriors.

The individual business travel industry

Most of the facilities and services used by individual business travellers are also used by leisure travellers. What they need from these suppliers have been discussed in detail elsewhere in this book, so, here, a few of the specific needs of business travellers will be considered and contrasted with the requirements of those travelling on holiday or for other leisure purposes.

Transport

A glance at the type of full-page advertisement paid for by airlines targeting business travellers, or at those who book their trips, shows that a major priority for those travelling on company business is punctuality. The expression 'time is money' certainly applies to the countless hours spent each year by business travellers waiting at airports or railway stations for delayed or cancelled flights or trains. Notwithstanding their personal stress levels and frustration, well-paid executives in this situation are (even in the age of wireless communications and laptops) generally far less productive than they would be if they were at their desks working. Punctuality and reliability of service are therefore much sought-after qualities for the individual business travel market.

Frequency of services is also a feature that is taken into account by business travellers choosing which carrier to use. Many individual business trips have to be flexibly timed, due to the uncertainty that can exist over when the work will be completed and the traveller is able to make the trip back home. Negotiations, for example, can run into unforeseen complications that delay the return trip or, conversely, they can go faster than expected, leaving the business traveller free to return to base earlier than planned. In either case, a frequent transport service allows for the flexibility that is required by the traveller faced with an unanticipated change of schedule (the ability to make last-minute changes to their itineraries is often given by business travellers as a further reason for avoiding the very cheapest fares, as these rarely offer the advantage of this type of flexibility).

An onboard environment conducive to work is key. As mentioned earlier as a justification for the use of business class seats, the ability to work while on the move is a pre-occupation of many business travellers – and their employers. Even before the ubiquitous laptop became an indispensable item in the carry-on luggage of anyone between the age of 17 and 70, those travelling on business tended to work for at least part of their journey – briefing themselves to prepare for their meeting, catching up on work-related reading, working through company accounts and so on. A tranquil environment, good lighting and, on trains, wi-fi connectivity and power sources for laptop computers and mobile telephones are examples of the types of facilities much sought after by those who wish to remain as productive as possible while travelling on business.

Accommodation

As with transport, accommodation that offers guests the ability to continue to work productively is at a premium for the business traveller. While leisure guests may be attracted to hotels that promise to be a 'home away from home', business guests tend to seek facilities that turn a hotel into an 'office away from the office', with Internet connections and the possibility of having documents faxed, photocopied and even (in some hotel business centres) translated. Lounges in business-orientated hotels are just as likely to be used for one-to-one business meetings as for drinks between leisure guests. There are also a number of other hotel services that are particularly appreciated by the business market, such as early check-in/late check-out, laundry services and the serving of meals in hotel bedrooms.

Business travel agencies

All but the very smallest companies and organizations tend to use some form of intermediary to book their business travel services. Some may use their high street travel agency, if their business travel needs are fairly simple and low-volume, but most medium- and large-scale companies make use of specialist business travel agencies – or travel management companies (TMCs) as they have come to call themselves – to make their travel arrangements, including the booking of transport and accommodation, providing advice on visa and vaccination issues and even, in some cases, issuing guidance on business etiquette for the destinations concerned.

In order to keep control of spending on business travel, most companies opt to employ a single TMC, usually chosen following a competitive tendering process and remunerated on a management fee basis. Some TMCs are small- to medium-sized businesses, but others, such as American Express Business Travel and Carlson Wagonlit, are vast companies with a global presence.

To a large extent, the recent evolution of business travel agencies mirrors that of the retail travel agencies discussed in Chapter 19 and the article given in the Example analyses some of the challenges facing these intermediaries in the age of information technology.

The business travel market in China: huge potential for professional travel management?

In a 2010 White Paper, AirPlus International (**www.airplus.com**), published background information and key data on travel management in China. The document was written in cooperation with the Association of Corporate Travel Executives (ACTE – **www.acte.org**). This extract from the white paper provides insights into the Chinese business travel market and makes predictions for the future of business travel management in China.

Rapid economic growth – what does this mean for travel management?

The Chinese economy is growing rapidly, and with it the Chinese business travel market, which is currently the world's third largest. Experts predict business travel expenditure of USD 62 billion in 2010, and forecasts for the next ten years assume a figure of USD 277 billion for 2020. China would then progress from being the third- to the second-largest international business travel market, and would cooperate even more frequently with providers in the Western business travel industry. At present, however, there are still enormous differences in international and Chinese business travel standards in many areas, which often make it difficult for travel managers to handle cooperation, particularly in international companies with branches in China. The recipes for success that have proved their worth in business travel management in Europe or the USA cannot simply be adapted to the Chinese market. Economic activities in this region are subject to different mechanisms, not least among them the framework conditions imposed by massive growth. Only 10% of Chinese companies work according to Western standards, with suitable travel guidelines or analytical tools. Employees in China who travel with company credit cards and use them for payment represent only 13% of all Chinese business travellers. According to Volker Huber, Senior Vice President Global Distribution AirPlus International, there is another figure that shows how important it is to have standardised travel management tools: air travel accounts for 85% of all business trips within China. He points out that if the costs of this air travel are not correctly controlled and analysed, companies may be faced with unmanageable and exorbitant expenses.

Cost control has not yet become established

Few Chinese companies have an awareness of costs and their permanent analysis, or the willingness to let their staff handle travel more independently. Chinese travel managers obviously have much less time to perform their tasks than their international colleagues. Some 90% of Chinese business travel managers complain of time pressure, almost one third more than international travel managers (63%). 'But', concludes Huber, 'we expect this to change as the Chinese economy continues to grow over the next few years. We therefore urgently advise companies that operate in this market to give thought to effective travel management and to develop corresponding programmes'.

Trends in business tourism

The rest of this chapter looks at some of the most important trends that will present opportunities and challenges to the global business tourism industry in the years ahead. Many of those trends are already emerging and others may be anticipated because of changes in the wider market environment.

The market for business tourism services and facilities is an extremely dynamic one – one that is highly sensitive to changes in the political, economic and social environment. This sector is also affected by the accelerating rate of innovation in information and communications technology. On the one hand, it offers significant opportunities for the development of more attractive business tourism products, but, on the other, it may also create certain threats to the long-term prosperity of this sector.

Economic trends

Emerging markets

The rise of new business tourism destinations in many developing economies of the world is a major – and on-going – phenomenon in this sector. As recently as 60 years ago, North American cities and European capitals had a practical monopoly over the hosting of international association meetings, for example. They were virtually the only places equipped with the infrastructure required to host these large-scale events. The decades since then, however, have seen a burgeoning of destinations entering all sectors of the business tourism market: Australasia, South East Asia, South America and, more recently, Central and Eastern European countries and cities in the Middle East have entered the market as vibrant new destinations for the hosting of meetings, trade shows and incentive trips.

At the same time, developing economies create additional demand for business tourism events as their new businesses add to the need for corporate events, and members of the expanding professional classes increasingly have the means to travel to conferences and exhibitions in other countries.

This phenomenon is particularly seen in China and India, two of the world's fastest-growing economies, and countries widely believed to be major sources of international business tourism consumption in the years to come. These two countries represent the two economies that are set to generate the greatest expansion in outbound business travel for the short and medium term. Citizens of these countries are already travelling to other destinations in their own regions, on business, but they will extend their scope to Europe and other long-haul destinations in rapidly increasing numbers in the years ahead. In China, growing levels of personal disposable income, Chinese companies' investment overseas and a fast-increasing number of international air connections with cities in major destinations are factors that will ensure the rapid growth of Chinese outbound corporate meetings and incentive trips and Chinese delegates at international association meetings and exhibitions in the near future.

Growing corporate cost-consciousness

As competition between business tourism venues and destinations intensifies, buyers have become aware that they are purchasing services in a 'buyers' market'. Much of the corporate market in particular has lost no time in reaping the benefits of this situation and meeting planners have quickly learned how to negotiate to their best advantage. With no sign of imminent change in the relationship between supply and demand, corporate buyers are set to become even more cost-conscious in the years ahead.

Almost every survey of demand for business tourism events suggests that corporate buyers expect the number of events they organize to increase in the immediate and short-term future, but there is no corresponding indication that their budgets are going to increase at a proportional rate. On the contrary, most surveys reveal a general reduction of per-delegate expenses as the central issue for many companies becomes that of ensuring better overall value and a higher return on their investment. Therefore, all business tourism destinations, and the venues within them, must constantly look for ways to manage their tariffs and demonstrate their cost-effectiveness. Quality, but at an attractive price, will be a dominant requirement for the foreseeable future, as the majority of businesses now recognize the strengths of their considerable purchasing power.

Technology trends

Information and communications technology (ICT) has already transformed many aspects of the business tourism sector and there is no doubt that further advances in ICT will continue to have a profound impact on how such events are planned, promoted and experienced in years to come.

Young people now entering employment in this sector will never understand the extent to which the Internet alone has revolutionized the planning, marketing and execution of events such as conferences and exhibitions. It is rare indeed, nowadays, to find a major conference or exhibition without its own website, where potential participants can read, in advance, full details of the event, register to attend and plan their schedule for the event itself. Developments such as PowerPoint and hand-held devices that allow the audience to respond in real time to conference presentations have enhanced delegates' experience, while radio frequency identification (RFID) promises to make the tracking and identification of exhibition visitors more efficient. The rate of wi-fi deployment in conference and exhibition venues and in large hotels is expanding fast and is expected by almost all people travelling on business, as a means of keeping in touch with their colleagues and families, and continuing to work while 'on the road'. The social media, such as YouTube, Twitter, Facebook and Linkedin, are increasingly being used by business tourism destinations and venues as a way of reaching out to potential customers in this market; for example, many conference centres post short videos on YouTube, featuring testimonials from satisfied meetings planners who have used their venue.

Social trends

More female business tourists

Changes in the profile of the global working population have, in turn, had a very significant effect on the profile of participants in business tourism events. The most prominent of these is the on-going increase in the proportion of women in professional employment. Women's share of professional jobs continued to increase in the first few years of the twenty-first century in the vast majority of countries, and this trend shows every sign of continuing. Women are already well represented in a number of professions, such as healthcare and finance, that are expanding rapidly in most countries. Women are also making inroads into traditionally male-dominated professions. For example, in some countries, the women's share of the ICT sector is already significant.

This continuing trend means that there are more women travelling on business, for all work-related purposes, including participation in conferences and exhibitions. The growing presence of female delegates at such events has had a number of impacts on business tourism services, from how conference and exhibition venues are designed (more toilet facilities for women), to the food served during breaks (lighter and generally healthier).

Another indication of the femininization of the market is the increase in popularity of spas as incentive travel products – and not only for women. Partly through the influence of female participants, the spa has become an amenity that a growing number of delegates expect in hotels and resorts.

More older business tourists

The European and North American working population is ageing significantly and will continue to do so for the foreseeable future, adding to the proportion of those in employment who are in the older age categories. Increasingly, people in their 60s and 70s are remaining in employment, either through choice (they find fulfilment through their work) or through necessity (they cannot afford to retire).

With a significant proportion of workers in the older age groups working in managerial and professional positions, it is highly likely that they will continue to travel on business and to business events, for a number of reasons.

- Because they can! As members of the baby boom generation start to enter their 60s, it is clear that they are considerably healthier, fitter and more socially involved than those of the previous generation were at that age. Travelling to business events and fully taking part in them presents them with none of the physical challenges that their parents would have faced in their 60s.

- Older workers understand that networking is particularly important to them as the type of upper-level management positions they are often seeking are not likely to be advertised. Attending conferences of their professional associations provides them with a valuable opportunity to network.

- There is a positive relationship between older workers staying in the workforce and their need for on-going training opportunities. Particularly with so many older workers continuing to work in the fast-evolving 'knowledge industries', constant in-service training events are vital to them for keeping their skills up to date. This means that they will be increasingly present at corporate meetings that have a training objective.

- A growing number of retired people are choosing to continue being members of their professional associations – in many cases, for the mental stimulation that profession-based meetings provide, as well as for the opportunity to maintain contact with colleagues.

The challenge of attracting 'Generations X and Y'

Over the next few years, associations will face growing difficulties in attracting attendees to their events. This is partly due to the prevalent phenomenon of people being **time poor** – that is, a growing number of association members have extensive demands on their limited time. It appears, however, that the new and upcoming generation of association members – 'Generation X' (those born between 1964 and 1977) and Generation Y (born between 1978 and 1994) – may also take some convincing that there is value in attending conferences. Generation Xers, unlike their parents, do not so readily see the value of face-to-face events. As they have grown up with electronic media as a primary communication tool, face-to-face events are less attractive to them (this is even more the case with Generation Yers). If this contention proves to be accurate, it presents serious meeting attendance issues for associations, as these two generations, between them, account for a combined demographic of 120 million people in the USA alone.

What can be done to reach this vast and growing section of the workforce and interest them in attending meetings, incentives, conferences and events (MICE)? Understanding their profile, developing strategies and targeting each group with appropriate messages is the key to motivating Generations X and Y to join associations and attend their conferences. Both groups have a sophisticated understanding of technology and expect it to be well utilized; the Web wins over traditional media as a primary source of information; they often select personal fulfilment over monetary rewards, seeking a casual work environment, telecommuting options and time off to enjoy life.

As time moves on, the behaviour and preferences of Generations X and Y will come to shape corporate and association life. Therefore, time spent now in understanding their needs and convincing them of the rewards of attending face-to-face events will reap rewards in the future.

Corporate social responsibility (CSR)

The field of corporate social responsibility (CSR) has grown exponentially in the last decade as companies increasingly seek to engage with their stakeholders and deal with potentially contentious issues proactively. Now, more companies than ever are engaged in integrating CSR into all aspects of their business, encouraged by a growing body of evidence that CSR has a positive impact on businesses' economic performance.

The US-based organization Business for Social Responsibility (BSR) defines corporate social responsibility as 'achieving commercial success in ways that honour ethical values and respect people, communities, and the natural environment' (http://bsr.org/reports/BSR_AW_Intangibles-CSR.pdf). This organization also says that CSR means addressing the legal, ethical, commercial and other expectations that society has for business and making decisions that fairly balance the claims of all key stakeholders.

The business tourism industry itself is beginning to show increasing awareness of the need to demonstrate its CSR, and this will intensify in future years. As the drive for greater transparency grows, all industries and organizations, public as well as private, will be increasingly obliged to demonstrate their ethical, environmental and social credentials. All stakeholders in the business tourism industry, from airlines, hotels and venues to intermediaries and the delegates themselves, will need to examine their own commitment to CSR. This will mean that business tourism stakeholders will increasingly be obliged to demonstrate their concern for the natural environment as well as the host communities that live and work in the destinations where events take place. This is particularly the case when the standard of living of the host community is markedly below that of the business travellers themselves. The apparent luxury and extravagance that characterize certain events can stand out in very stark contrast to the abjectly poor and chronically disadvantaged conditions in which some of the local inhabitants live. For that reason, it is encouraging that a number of conference and incentive travel organizers have begun taking steps to invest in projects which have a positive impact on the communities residing in the destinations where their events are held. Conference delegates raising money for a local charity or incentive travel participants spending a day making environmental improvements to their destination are typical examples of this growing trend.

In the years ahead, more business tourism stakeholders will become aware of the benefits to themselves, and to host communities, of investing time and money in giving something back to underprivileged people living in some of the destinations where their events take place.

Summary

This chapter has reviewed the elements and characteristics of the business tourism sector, as well as some of the key trends and challenges that the sector is already dealing with and will continue to face in the future. There can be no doubt that the market environment for business tourism will continue to evolve and mutate in ways that are perhaps impossible to predict at the present time. It is in this very unpredictability, however, that the challenge and excitement of operating in this sector of the travel and tourism industry lies.

In the complex, volatile flux of market trends and forces, one element that will remain reassuringly constant is human nature itself. Men and women will continue to attend business tourism events, not only for the opportunity to obtain personal and professional development for themselves and business growth for their organizations but also for the simple pleasure of meeting those with whom they share a common interest or goal. Buyers and participants will be drawn to attractive destinations and venues that deliver efficiently run and memorable events, using state-of-the-art technology, as well as distinctive cultural experiences in a healthy and unique environment.

Questions and discussion points

1. Identify as many differences as you can between leisure tourism (holidays, short breaks and day trips) and business tourism. Think in terms of those who travel for leisure and those who travel on business; who pays for the trips, when leisure trips and business trips take place, what types of destinations are used for business and leisure tourism, who decides on the destination and the lead time (the period of time leading up to the trip, planning it and so on) for business and for leisure tourism.

2. It is often claimed that videoconferencing (or teleconferencing) technology will largely obviate the need for delegates to travel to face-to-face meetings. Give as many reasons as possible in favour of, and against, replacing face-to-face meetings with videoconferences.

3. Put yourself in the position of someone wishing to buy a new laptop computer. You could find the ideal computer for yourself by visiting computer shops, computer websites and shopping online, ordering manufacturers' catalogues and browsing through them, or you could travel to visit an exhibition of computer manufacturers' products. What, for you, would be the advantages of visiting an exhibition in order to find your perfect laptop?

4. Many people travelling frequently on business on behalf of their employer earn valuable airmiles when they fly to their destinations. Currently, the employees get to use those airmiles for themselves. Discuss the rights and wrongs of this situation. What arguments can be made in favour of the airmiles accruing to the business travellers' employers?

Tasks

1. More and more business travellers are female and there is a growing number of websites designed for women travelling alone on business. Visit as many of these websites as you can and write a report summarizing the advice that they offer. What innovations have hotels introduced in order better to serve this segment of their client market? Do all female business travellers want to be treated differently from their male counterparts?

2. Use the Internet to find the conference centre and the exhibition centre that are situated closest to where you live. Carry out the necessary research to identify three major conferences and three major trade shows being held in these venues during the month in which you undertake this assignment.

Bibliography

Fitzgerald, F. S. (1945) *The Crack-up*, New York, New Directions Books.

UFI (2011) *Definitions and types of fairs and exhibitions*, available online at: http://www.ufi.org/Public/Default.aspx?Clef_SITESMAPS=152#1.2 (accessed November 2011).

Websites

Hilton Meetings: **www.hilton.co.uk/meetings**

Venuemasters: **www.venuemasters.co.uk**

Women's travel tips: **www.womentraveltips.com**

The hospitality sector: accommodation and catering services

Contents

Learning outcomes

After studying this chapter, you should be able to:

- explain the structure and nature of the hospitality sector, distinguishing between the various categories of tourist accommodation and catering services

- describe how accommodation is classified and be aware of the problems involved in classification

- understand the nature of demand for accommodation and catering and how the sector has responded to changing patterns of demand over time

- understand the relationship between the hospitality sector and other sectors of the tourism industry.

The hospitable instinct is not wholly altruistic. There is pride and egoism mixed up with it.

Beerbohm (1921) Hosts and Guests, 131

Introduction

As Beerbohm recognizes, humans can find reward and pleasure in offering hospitality to others, whether they are guests staying in the home, or aiding the weary business traveller staying in yet another hotel. The hospitality sector is an important part of the tourism industry and can play a major role in the experience of the visitor. In this chapter, we will be principally concerned with examining the commercial accommodation and catering sector. It must not be forgotten, however, that this sector represents just one element of the hospitality business and is often in competition with large non-commercial hospitality suppliers that are no less important to tourism. The visiting friends and relations (VFR) market is substantial and, in addition, there is a wide variety of other forms of accommodation used by tourists, including the tourists' own camping and caravanning equipment, privately owned boats and – of increasing significance for tourism in the twenty-first century – second homes, whether in the home country or abroad. There is also a growing market for home exchanges and the swapping of timeshare accommodation, a market that the industry has facilitated through the establishment of timeshare exchange companies.

It is, in fact, difficult to distinguish between the strictly commercial and non-commercial aspects of the hospitality business. Youth hostels and YMCAs, for example, are not necessarily attempting to make a profit, but merely to cover their operating costs, while it is increasingly common, as noted earlier, to find educational institutions such as universities and schools hiring out their student accommodation to tourists outside the academic terms, in order to make some contribution to the running costs of the institutions. One result of this has been a marked increase in the quality of student accommodation, with en suite bathrooms now the norm in new buildings.

Other forms of tourism that, by their nature, embrace accommodation would include privately hired yachts or bookings on a cruise ship. Operators in some countries provide coaches that include sleeping berths, while in others packages are available using specially chartered trains that serve as the travellers' hotel throughout the trip. Independent travellers can also book sleeping accommodation on rail services and overnight ferry routes. To what extent should all these services be counted as elements of the commercial accommodation available to tourists?

Certainly, any study of tourism must take account of these overnight alternatives and the expansion or contraction in demand for sleeping arrangements that compete with the traditional accommodation sector. The rapid rise in cruise holidays over the past few years, to take one instance, will have affected demand for more traditional forms of holiday in which travel and somewhere to stay are the norm.

Tourists staying in private accommodation away from their homes, whether with friends and relatives or in second homes owned by themselves or their friends, are nevertheless still engaging in tourism and will almost certainly be contributing to tourist spend in the region, as they will tend to use local commercial transport, restaurants and entertainment. Their spend must therefore be included in tourism statistics for the region.

Apart from the economic benefits of such tourists at the destination, there are frequently commercial transactions in the home country associated with their trips. Tour operators and budget airlines sell flights to airports near second homes (indeed, the expanding ownership of second homes among Britons in France, Italy and Spain has been a big contributing factor to the strength of the budget carriers) and many tourists will hire cars during the period of their stay, for which, in some cases, payment will be made through agents in the home country before departure.

Airlines, recognizing that home exchanges can also represent a healthy source of flight revenue, have developed and commercialized the home exchange business by establishing directories to assist people in arranging exchanges. Some national or regional tourist offices also keep directories of homeowners who are prepared to make exchanges, and others maintain lists of local householders willing to invite guests from overseas into their homes for a meal (a particular feature of US hospitality). More recently, commercial brokers have been set up to facilitate home exchanges around the world, for a modest fee (in the UK, **www.homelink.org.uk** and **www.homexchangevacation.com**; in the USA, **www.homeexchange.com**, for example).

The structure of the accommodation sector

The accommodation sector comprises widely differing forms of sleeping and hospitality facilities that can be conveniently categorized as either serviced (in which amenities such as room cleaning and catering are included) or self-catering. These are not watertight categories as some forms of accommodation, such as holiday camps or educational institutions, may offer serviced, self-service or self-catering facilities, but they help in drawing distinctions between the characteristics of the two categories. Figure 12.1 provides an at-a-glance guide to the range of accommodation that tourists might occupy.

Hotels are the most significant and widely recognized form of overnight accommodation for tourists. They also form one of the key elements of most package holidays. What constitutes a hotel and distinguishes it from other forms of accommodation, however, is not always clear. VisitEngland has provided definitions for the many different categories of accommodation that it rates as part of its quality assurance scheme (see Table 12.1). We can see from this that there are several subcategories of hotel, all of which are separately distinguished from that of budget hotels.

The corporate chains

A feature of the industry is that, as mass tourism has developed, so have the large chains and corporations in the accommodation sector. The hotel and motel business has reached

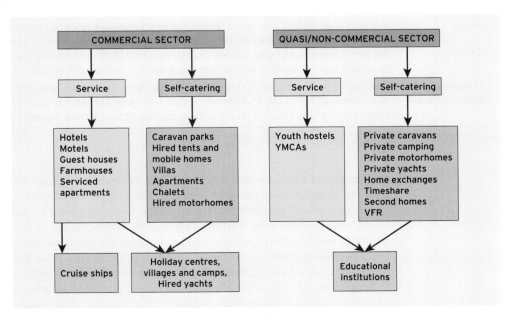

Figure 12.1 The structure of tourist accommodation

Table 12.1 Accommodation definitions established for the National Quality Assessment Scheme for England

Category of accommodation	Definition
Hotel	A hotel must have a minimum of 5 bedrooms, be licensed and offer dinner. Also all bedrooms must be en suite or have a private bathroom. Subcategories include Country House Hotel, Small Hotel, Town House Hotel and Metro Hotel (which may not offer dinner but is located within walking distance of other restaurants).
Budget hotel	Budget Hotels are always part of a large 'branded' hotel group offering clean and comfortable en suite facilities, 24-hour reservations and a consistent level of facilities.
Guest accommodation	These properties are likely to be smaller than hotels with perhaps more of a family home feel and approach, and a less structured service.
Self-catering	All accommodation with its own kitchen and bathroom facilities. Most take bookings by the week, generally from a Friday or Saturday, but short breaks are increasingly common.
Serviced apartment	Often found in big cities, these offer hotel services such as maid service and concierge in addition to a self-contained unit with a kitchen.
Parks	This includes parks which cater for Touring Caravans and/or Tents and may or may not include Individual Caravans (defined below), some of which may be available for hire. Subcategories include Holiday Park, Touring Park, Camping Park or a combination of these.
Holiday village	This usually comprises a variety of types of accommodation with the majority provided in custom-built rooms (e.g. Chalet, Hotel rooms) on a large complex. A range of facilities and activities are also available which may or may not be included in the tariff.
Hostel	Accommodation often in shared rooms with bunk beds although family rooms may be available. Hostels normally welcome individuals, families and groups, many of whom are staying on a short-term basis. Subcategories may include backpacker hostels, activity accommodation and bunkhouse.
University/ campus	As the name suggests, this scheme applies to educational establishments. In general, campus accommodation is on a college or university site, with some aspects of communal living space.
Individual caravans	This includes caravan holiday homes situated on farms, caravan parks, etc. which are let by the owner as self-catering accommodation.
Hire craft and hotel boat	This scheme covers narrowboats, cruisers and hotel boats in small and large fleets across England's waterways. Hotel boats are generally narrowboats that are worked by a crew, allowing guests to relax and only help if they want to.
Chalets	A chalet is a building normally constructed in timber, part brick or UPVC and used as holiday accommodation on a seasonal basis rather than as a permanent residence. These properties are often restricted in size and will usually be situated on a chalet park with similar properties. Chalets require individual planning consent and are permanent structures.
Alternative accommodation	Alternative accommodation refers to self-catering-based accommodation which is perhaps more unusual, for example: wigwams & camping pods; nomadic structures (e.g. tipis, yurts, safari tents, ready erected tents); railway carriages; treehouses; Romany caravans.

Source: VisitEngland, 2011

a stage of maturity in which a few major companies have come to dominate, if not the markets, then certainly the distribution chain. The policy of these groups is to create an international and uniform marketing image for each brand to assist sales around the world. One benefit of this uniformity is that, as new destinations develop, the existence of trusted brands can help give the consumer confidence to visit a perhaps untested location. For this reason, some governments in developing nations provided financial support to the major chains looking to develop hotels in their key cities and tourist areas.

Economies of scale have allowed the largest chains to increase their spend on international marketing, advertising and sales promotion in partnership with other sectors of the industry, such as transport companies and tour operators, while cutting costs and, in the case of the budget brands, reducing prices to consumers to well below those available through more traditional outlets. This expansion has also been aided by franchising, whereby hotels and motels are operated by individual franchisees paying royalties to the parent company for the privilege of operating under a brand name. This form of expansion has been used with great success around the world by companies such as Holiday Inns, while the Friendly Hotel group holds European franchises for such well-established brand names as Quality Hotels, Comfort Hotels and Sleep Inns. To expand rapidly, the chains have taken not just to franchising but also to entering into management contracts and joint ventures, with actual ownership of the properties declining.

 EXAMPLE   **Franchising the brand**

The business module of Intercontinental Hotel Group (IHG) uses three types of operational approach: franchised (by far the most significant sector of their business), managed and owned. Each type of approach requires different levels of resource – summarized in Table 12.2.

Table 12.2 IHG hotels

	Franchised (3783 hotels)	Managed (639 hotels)	Owned (15 hotels)
Ownership	Third party	Third party	IHG
Marketing	IHG	IHG	IHG
Staff	Employed by third party	IHG usually supplies general manager (and occasional other senior managers)	Employed by IHG
Level of capital investment by IHG	None	Low/none	High
Income earned for IHG	Fee – % of room revenue	Fee – % of total hotel revenue plus % of profit	All revenues and profits

Source: IHG, 2010

As we can see, franchising requires little capital investment and no human resource management. As a consequence, it provides an effective way to grow the brand quickly and with limited financial risk. Of course, establishing the brand and developing the franchise guidelines to ensure that consistency and quality are maintained is a key responsibility of the franchisor, in this case IHG.

Notable leading hotel chains (see, for example, Figure 12.2), often niche marketing with several brands, include the following.

- *InterContinental Hotels Group.* In 2011, IHG owned, managed or franchised over 4400 individual properties, spread over 100 countries. The largest hotel company in the world by number of rooms (more than 652 000), it franchises the great majority of its properties – some 3700. Once an offshoot of Bass Breweries, the hotel group is now independent, and in recent years has been active in adding properties to its portfolio. It now offers a range of branded products, including top of the range InterContinental and Crowne Plaza Hotels, Indigo, mid-scale Holiday Inn brands and, coming in a little above budget prices, the Express by Holiday Inn/Holiday Inn Express chain. It has also bought into the corporate hospitality market for extended stays, owning, franchising or operating the US brands Staybridge Suites by Holiday Inn and Candlewood Suites. As

Figure 12.2 The Kempinski Hotel, Geneva, Switzerland – this franchise chain operates 67 five star hotels in Europe, the Middle East, Africa and Asia, with a further 10 under development at the time of writing

Photo by Chris Holloway

we discussed in the example, the company's business model is currently to focus on franchising and managing brands, rather than owning hotel properties outright (IHG, 2010).

- *Hilton Worldwide.* Originally established by Conrad Hilton in 1919, this company now operates 3750 hotels, in 84 countries, comprising a mix of owned, leased, joint venture, managed, timeshare and franchised operations, with over 2000 operating under franchise. Hilton USA, bought by US investment company Blackstone in 2007, has now amalgamated once again with the Hilton Group UK, reunifying the brand after many years of separate ownership. Major brands include Hilton, Conrad, Doubletree, Embassy Suites, Hampton Inn, Hilton Garden Inn, Home2 Suites by Hilton, Homeward Suites and The Waldorf Astoria Collection. The company also owns the Hilton Grand Vacations timeshare brand. The company has almost 1000 new hotels in the pipeline, providing opportunities to further expand their global reach.

- *Marriott International.* This company operates around 3400 units, mainly under the Marriott label, with a range of franchised lower-priced brands such as Fairfield Inn. Apart from the Marriott label, they include Courtyard, SpringHill Suites and Renaissance hotels. To serve the luxury segment, they operate Bulgari Hotels and Resorts, Ritz Carlton and JW Marriott, while the extended stay market is served by Residence Inn, Execustay and Towneplace Suites. Three brands are extended to serve the timeshare market: Marriott vacation club, Grand residences and Ritz-Carlton Destination Club. Marriott launched a range of boutique hotels with Ian Schrager under the Edition brand, and in 2011 announced the expansion of the Autograph Collection – a portfolio of unusual upscale properties – into the European market, with hotels in Spain, Italy and Portugal among the first to be rebranded.

- *Starwood Hotels and Resorts.* This company operates around 1000 hotel properties, mainly managed (463), some owned (62) and a number franchised (502). Major brands include Sheraton Hotels and Resorts, Westin Hotels and Resorts, le Meridien, St Regis, Luxury Collection, W Hotels, Four Points by Sheraton, Aloft and Element. Eighty new hotels were scheduled for opening in 2011 with more than 100 due to open in 2012/13, highlighting the expansion plans for this organization. Starwood is the leading international chain for 4/5-star properties in China and in 2011 one new hotel was scheduled for opening every two weeks.

- *Accor.* The first non-US-operated hotel chain in this list, this French company has expanded substantially in the past few years and operates around 4200 units in 90 countries, with a variety of brands ranging from luxury to budget. Brands include Sofitel, Novotel, Mercure, Ibis and Formule 1. In North America, the brand operates under the Sofitel and Novotel brands alongside budget brands Motel 6 and Studio 6 (extended stay hotels). In a recent decision, the Sofitel brand has now been subdivided into three formats: Sofitel Luxury Hotels, Sofitel Legend (historic properties) and So by Sofitel (Boutique hotels aimed at the younger market). Current Sofitel units not fitting any of these categories adequately are being rebranded as Pullman Hotels. A new budget brand, All Seasons, was introduced in 2007, and Accor announced in 2011 that this was to be integrated into the Ibis brand (along with the former Etap brand). Accor owns or leases 55% of its hotels, while 22% are managed and 23% are franchised (Accor, 2011) and plans for expansion include the opening of more than 235 000 new rooms in the four years to 2015.

- *Louvre Hotels.* This group, formed through an amalgamation with Envergure and Golden Tulip, now manages more than 1000 hotels across 40 countries, although 90% of these are located in Europe. Its brands include the 2-star Campanile Hotels along with Kyriad Prestige, Kyriad, Première Classe, Tulip Inn, Golden Tulip and Royal Tulip.

Further afield, other notable chains include the Mandarin group, concentrated in the Pacific Rim area, while Indian-owned Oberoi Hotels have expanded into Egypt, the Far East and Australia.

As these chains market their products more aggressively, advertise extensively, work closely with large tour-operating organizations globally and, in addition to their own websites, provide an effective distribution network linked to the airline CRSs, they tend to have a more visible presence in the industry than their market share would suggest. In total bed terms, their stock is small compared with the multitude of independently owned facilities, but these, until recently, have had less ready access to both the market and other sectors of the industry. With the growth of commercial websites, smaller hotels now have greater opportunities to reach their customers directly, even if not on the scale of the large corporations. Some independents have seen the value of coming together as members of a consortium in order to compete more effectively with the large chains.

Consortia

Independent hotels around the world have frequently banded together to form loosely knit consortia. While this allows the group to obtain some of the economies of scale achieved by the large chains, such as benefits of mass purchasing, more critically it reinforces their marketing strength, enabling them to improve distribution through a united website and the websites of other leading suppliers. Many of the larger consortia, such as Best Western Hotels and Inter Hotels, operate on a global scale; others operate on a national scale, as does Classic Britain, the third largest hotel marketing consortium in the UK in 2009.

Similarly, some smaller, privately owned hotels have united within a themed consortium in order to market themselves more effectively at home and abroad. This is a highly appropriate strategy when developing a niche approach. For example, Small Luxury Hotels of the World, with over 500 hotels in 70 countries, focuses on building an image of hotels that are of a high standard but personal, while Grand Heritage Hotels – an American-owned consortium that is now drawing members from high-grade European hotels – emphasizes luxury and status. Other specialist consortia operating in the UK include Pride of Britain Hotels, Scotland's Personal Hotels and Great Inns of Britain.

 EXAMPLE **French consortium reaches the half-century**

Relais & Chateaux was established in 1954 by the owners of eight high-quality hotels located between Paris and the French Riviera who joined forces to promote their venues. Expansion in France led the way and the association had been operating for almost 20 years before they expanded outside of the country – first to Spain and Belgium and then, in 1975, beyond the frontiers of Europe. Now, half a century after the establishment of this consortium, there are 500 Relais & Chateaux properties operating in 60 countries.

Although Relais & Chateaux is keen to expand the number of properties in their association, the need to maintain quality standards and the unique ideals means that many who apply are not accepted; in 2011, only 36 of the 100 assessed were given membership, perhaps the most famous being the Bedford Post, owned and run by actor Richards Gere.

Once a hotel is given membership, it is required to pay an admission fee (in excess of €10 000) and annual membership fees of a similar amount. Audits using a mystery shopper approach occur approximately every three years, to ensure quality standards are being maintained. In return for this cost and effort, the hotel benefits from being associated with a strong brand, extensive marketing, brochure production and generation of bookings using web and smartphone technology.

Consumer loyalty

To encourage repeat business from their guests, most of the major hotel chains operate loyalty schemes. Similar in operation to the frequent flyer schemes offered by airlines, guests earn points based on the number of nights stayed and the overall hotel spend. These can then be redeemed for free nights' accommodation and room upgrades. Frequent guests will often be provided with an upgraded status, offering additional benefits such as late room check-outs and points bonuses. These programmes generally operate across-brand; for example, Marriott Rewards members earn points for their stays in Marriott, Courtyard or Ritz-Carlton hotels. Some examples are:

- Intercontinental: Priority Club Rewards
- Hilton Worldwide: Hilton HHonors
- Marriot International: Marriott Rewards
- Starwood: Starwood Preferred Guest
- Accor: A | Club
- Louvre Hotels: Flavours (linked to the Golden Tulip brands).

The hotel loyalty schemes often work in partnership with airlines. Frequent flyers may elect to have their points added not to the hotel scheme but to an affiliated airline loyalty programme, and the hotel chains often have agreements with several airline partners to make this possible.

The extent to which such programmes are effective in encouraging loyalty has often been debated, but it is helpful to realize that by encouraging their guests to be members the hotel chain can discover customer travel habits and preferences (Marriott Rewards members are even asked about their preference of pillow) and can undertake direct marketing accordingly.

Hotel development

As with other sectors of the tourism industry, there is a growing belief that a handful of mega-chains will in time come to dominate the global tourism market, with independents focusing on niche market opportunities.

A recent development has been the trend to initiate **brand extensions** across products – an example of which we have seen with the move by Bulgari into the hotel sector. The Versace brand has also moved into hospitality, with the opening in Australia of the Palazzo Versace. Several other fashion houses are developing plans to form partnerships with hotel chains that will bear the fashion brand's name, including Armani, Missoni and Moschino, which plan to focus on accommodation in or near prestigious shopping locations. Other examples of brand-stretching include *Maxim*, a men's magazine, which has opened a Las Vegas hotel and casino, while leading catering brands have also moved into accommodation, with McDonald's launching a chain of Golden Arch Hotels and the Hard Rock Café developing the Hard Rock Hotel brand.

Budget hotels

It is in the budget sector of the hotel industry that growth has been strongest in recent years, with a 50% growth in the five years to 2007 and forecasts that this market will treble by 2027. Responding to this demand, the large chains have been concentrating on creating or developing their own budget-priced properties – a field formerly left largely to independent organizations or leisure conglomerates.

In the UK, well-established companies such as Granada or catering subsidiaries of the big brewers were leaders in the development of what is now termed 'limited service' hotels, to distinguish them from the type of accommodation sought by the backpacker market. Brands new to the UK, such as Days Inn and Sleep Inn, are joining more familiar brands to capture a share of this fast-growing market, especially in city centre properties, which attract growing numbers of short break tourists. The two leading chains, Travelodge and Premier Inn, have a strong hold on the market, however, and are developing strategies to ensure they stay in front.

● *Travelodge*. Bought by Dubai Investment Capital in 2006 (and thus, in effect, a state-owned company), Travelodge is one of the leading budget brands, with over 400 hotels in the UK in 2011 and 28 000 bedrooms. They also operate 11 properties in Ireland and three in Spain. A number are in the pipeline and it has expectations of continuing this growth over coming years, with some 70 000 rooms by 2020, by which date it will control 10% of the UK market. By 2008, the company already possessed around 30 coastal properties in the UK and has announced its intention to build a further 55 new hotels in similar locations. The limited service approach means that rooms do not have telephones, irons or hairdryers, helping to keep overheads to a minimum.

● *Premier Inn*. In 2004, the brewers Whitbread acquired the Premier Lodge and Scottish & Newcastle Hotel brands, merging these into their Travel Inn brand and renaming the group Premier Travel Inn, later simplified to the present brand name. The company operated almost 600 hotels and 43 000 rooms in 2011, with plans to add another 4000 rooms by 2013. They also operate 1000 rooms internationally, with the bulk of this in properties operating in Dubai.

Recent trends are pointing towards a splintering of the budget hotel sector, with luxury budget accommodation at one end of the range, with brands such as City Inn and Big Sleep, while new super-budget brands, such as Yotel, Base 2 Stay, Tune Hotels and easy-Hotel, are emerging at the other.

EXAMPLE   The low-cost model comes to hotels

The budget hotel sector has a new player. Tune Hotels, part of a group which owns the AirAsia airline, has drawn on the low-cost airline model to provide limited-service accommodation with a yield-management booking system which encourages guests to make their reservations early to obtain the lowest prices.

Tune Hotels currently operates ten hotels – seven in Malaysia, two in Indonesia and one in the heart of London. Rapid expansion is planned through a franchise agreement with Red Planet hotels, which is expected to add 1000 hotel rooms to their portfolio. There are also reported plans for expansion into the Australian market, with properties in Melbourne, Darwin, the Gold Coast and Perth being developed.

In keeping with the low-cost model, customers wanting access to any extra services such as a television, refrigerator or towels will be charged a hire fee. In the London property, room prices are differentiated based on whether or not the guest requires a window.

In mainland Europe, Accor Hotels has exploited the deficiency in this sector by introducing the super-budget chains Formule 1 and Etap, while others on the Continent have popularized low-budget brands such as B&B Hotels, Mister Bed and Fimotel. These very low-priced hotels have managed to reduce costs by developing a unitary design and automating many of the services provided; reception desks are only manned for short periods of the day and, at other times, entry is by the insertion of credit cards into a machine on the external wall. Similarly, breakfasts are self-service and highly automated.

The introduction of this style of hotel into the UK has not been simple. Land costs push up prices in the UK, while restricted furnishings and services appear too basic for the UK market. For example, carpet soon replaced the linoleum that French hotel guests had seemed more willing to accept (undoubtedly, differing climates are a contributing factor to this choice).

The character property

The competition between luxury hotels has led to new forms of market segmentation, based on product differentiation. Country house or townhouse hotels place emphasis on giving a personal service. Boutique and designer hotels, especially those taking advantage of the fashion for cutting-edge design, have attracted widespread publicity (a glance in any bookshop at the range of books devoted to cutting-edge hotel design and 'hip' hotels will confirm this) and this has been given additional impetus by their tendency to attract celebrities and celebrity-hunters. Hotels in this category in London include The Halkin, Blakes, Great Eastern Metropolitan, One Aldwych, St Martin's Lane, the Sanderson and the Trafalgar Hilton, while in the USA there are the Hudson, Mercer, Morgans and Royalton Hotels in New York, the Avalon in Los Angeles and the Delano in Miami.

Ian Schrager was responsible for the ultra-chic Morgans Hotel in New York, but now believes that art, rather than designer, hotels signify the way forward. The Hotel Vittoria in Florence (one of the Una Hotel chain) has staked a claim to being the most fashionable in the world, with mural portraits on each door and surrealistic decor. The Gramercy Park has original paintings by cutting-edge artist Jean-Michael Basquiat, and the Winston Hotel Amsterdam has walls lined with original modern art, while the Künstlerheim Luise, Berlin, goes one better – offering rooms that, in decor, resemble paintings by van Gogh, Magritte or Edward Hopper.

An interesting development is the effort now being made to 'brand stretch', linking well-known branded products with accommodation. As we saw earlier, the Bulgari brand is already employed, marketed by Marriott; Versace has also moved into the field and Baccarat has announced its intention to build hotel resorts in Dubai and Shanghai. The Italian designer brand Missoni, in collaboration with the Rezidor hotel group, launched their first hotel in Edinburgh and followed this with an opening in Kuwait, with further hotels planned for Oman, Turkey and Brazil. The continuing appeal of high-status products for a celebrity-hungry market should ensure the success of this approach.

Other hotels have opted to go for the wow factor, either in relation to their architecture or sheer size. For example, the hotel Puerto America in Madrid, operated by Silken Hotels since 2005, has chosen to have each floor designed by a different famous architect. Size alone had little appeal in the past, as those mega-hotels in the former Soviet Union proved only too clearly, but if sold as luxury resorts in their own right, virtual cities within a city, they find a market as readily as the giant cruise ships carrying over 2000 passengers have done. Las Vegas boasts ten such mega-hotels with over 3000 rooms.

EXAMPLE   The biggest hotel in the world

Hotels around the world seek to set themselves apart from their competition by promoting their unique characteristics – some may choose to offer exquisite service, others may opt for unusually decorated rooms, or strive to be the greenest.

The construction of some hotels can provide a claim to fame. The biggest hotel, based on total number of rooms, is the Izmailovo Hotel Complex – a 3-star hotel in Moscow, with four towers, each 30 storeys high. The hotel can accommodation over 10 000 guests at any one time – although fortunately they are rarely likely to have that number all checking in on the same day!

Competing with this for size are the hotels of Las Vegas. The Venetian & Palazzo has 7000 rooms and suites spread across its three towers, whilst another five hotels in the city have over 4000 rooms each. The Las Vegas Convention and Visitors Authority (2010) claim the city has almost 150 000 hotel and motel rooms, with occupancy rates of around 80%, allowing the city to accommodate the 37 million visitors they receive annually.

The Burj al-Arab Hotel in Dubai (see Figure 10.5 on p. 265) is famed not only as the tallest hotel in the world, but also for its self-claimed classification of 7-star status, defining ultra luxury. Within Europe, the Gran Hotel Bali, in Benidorm, at 186 metres and 43 stories high, is the tallest in Spain and offers its own unique appeal. Central atriums with glass lifts, spectacular indoor and outdoor gardens or other eye-catching features all help to reinforce the hotel experience as being something more than just a room and a bed.

The Conrad chain, like many upmarket hotel operators, targets the corporate market, offering all-suite hotels as a principal feature in their luxury product, while hotels that have been converted from buildings formerly used for other purposes have deliberately retained their original character and have therefore appealed strongly to a business market of frequent users jaded by standardization and uniformity.

A good example of the latter is the small chain known as the Hotel du Vin & Bistro (part of the Malmaison Group), which purchases redundant properties in city centres, such as former warehouses and industrial buildings, redeveloping them as lodgings while retaining their original character. Emphasizing their catering strengths, they have succeeded in simultaneously creating some highly praised restaurants. On the European Continent, similar aims are shared by Malmaison's Continental hotels and Germany's Sorat chain, Spain's Melia Boutique and Derby Hotels.

Figure 12.3 The Inkaterra Reserva Amazonica Hotel, Peru

Photo by Claire Humphreys

Individual hotels have also succeeded in establishing unique personalities that attract niche markets. Examples in the UK include the Lace Market in Nottingham and the Scotsman in Edinburgh, housed in the former premises of *The Scotsman* newspaper. Such developments reveal alternative ways forward for hotel design – the days of the faceless and monolithic concrete block, favoured in the development of new resorts in the Mediterranean and elsewhere in order to permit rapid construction and cheap operation, are ending as the sophisticated travel market seeks better service and more character in its lodgings. This can be seen, for example, in the luxury lodges provided at the Inkaterra Reserva Amazonica Hotel, which offers the guest their own private plunge pool, complete with mesh roof to keep out the Amazon wildlife (for example, see Figure 12.3).

Hotels that can offer attributes unique to the country visited are always popular with tourists. The paradores in Spain or the pousadas of Portugal, national chains of state-operated inns located in historic properties, are proving highly successful despite their premium prices. Similarly, traditional haciendas in Mexico and the ryokans of Japan, which offer an authentic flavour of the country's culture, greatly appeal to the independent travel market. In the UK, individual character properties owned by the National Trust, the Landmark Trust and similar organizations are in great demand. One of the National Trust's most popular properties is Peel Bothy – a tiny former shepherd's home at Steel Rigg, Northumberland, offering only very basic facilities, but seen as full of character.

Hotels of character appeal as strongly to leisure travellers as they do to business travellers. In recent years, the country cottage style of accommodation has been popular and has been dutifully incorporated into specialist groupings by the tour operators. An association between these properties and a former owner who happens to be well known enhances their appeal. Among cottages available for rent in the UK are those formerly owned by the poet Shelley, as well as writers R. L. Stevenson, D. H. Lawrence and Thomas Hardy, for example. The rise in popularity of cottage accommodation may have been triggered by the interest in French gîtes that developed in the 1980s.

At the other end of the scale, the Mansions and Manors brand consists of around 200 manor house owners who will offer bed-and-breakfast accommodation on a selective basis to the 'right kind of clients', but have no wish to commercialize their product or advertise directly to the public. This group of houses is therefore marketed directly through tour operators overseas. In the USA, the consortium Historic Hotels of America, established with the support of the US National Trust for Historic Preservations, recruits only hotels at least 50 years old. Among its members are the 1773 Red Lion Inn at Stockbridge, Massachusetts, and a former Carmelite convent in Puerto Rico, which dates from 1651.

Classifying and grading accommodation

Categorizing accommodation units of differing types and standards is no simple matter. As we saw in Table 12.1, there are many different types of accommodation, each providing a variety of facilities and services to suit their market. The process of classification, either for the purpose of legislation or for the systematic examination of business activity, has been attempted on several occasions in the UK in the past (for example, under the Standard Industrial Classification System). These attempts were mainly designed to distinguish hotels and other residential establishments from sundry catering activities, however. Statistics seldom distinguish, for example, between guests staying at hotels and motels.

Within the small independent sector, the problem is even greater. There is a broad spectrum of private accommodation that ranges from the private hotel, through boarding house and guesthouse accommodation to bed-and-breakfast establishments, and in the UK under law there is no clear distinction between the private hotel and the boarding house. The only distinction between these two and the guesthouse is that the latter will not have more than four bedrooms or more than eight guests. This distinction is important for legislative purposes, but need not concern us further here.

Tourists, however, are interested not only in what different types of hotel offer in the way of facilities but also in the *quality* of the accommodation and catering they are being offered. To clarify these features, we need to distinguish between three terms: categorization, classification and grading. Although these terms are often used interchangeably, the following are their widely accepted definitions:

- *Categorization* refers to the separation of accommodation into types – that is, distinguishing between hotels, motels, boarding houses, guesthouses and so on.
- *Classification* distinguishes different examples of accommodation on the basis of certain physical features, such as the number of rooms with private bath or shower and so on.
- *Grading* identifies accommodation according to certain verifiable objective features of the service offered, such as the number of courses served at meals, whether or not 24-hour service is provided and so on.

Readers will note, however, that none of these terms refers to assessments of quality, which call for subjective evaluation and are therefore far more difficult – and more costly – to validate, especially when standards, particularly in catering, can change so rapidly over time.

Provision was made under the Development of Tourism Act 1969 for the compulsory classification and grading of hotel accommodation in the UK, but this was widely resisted by the industry itself, and the British Tourist Authority (BTA) made no attempt to impose it at the time, instead relying on a system of voluntary registration first introduced in 1975. The separate National Tourist Boards of England, Scotland and Wales were left to devise their own individual schemes. However, the three boards, in 1987, agreed a common scheme that graded hotels into six categories – 'listed', for the most basic property, or from one to five crowns, depending on the facilities offered. The system remained a voluntary one.

Two years later, the boards agreed a unified system of grading quality, additionally designating accommodation 'Approved', 'Commended', 'Highly Commended' or 'Deluxe', in ascending order of quality. This was planned to take into account such subjective issues as hospitality, service, food and decor.

We should note that the private sector had devised its own schemes for grading hotels – some national, some international in scope – and these were often more widely recognized by members of the public than were the public-sector designations. Of the private-sector schemes, the best known in the UK were those offered by the two motoring associations, the AA and RAC, both of which provided a star rating. In addition to these schemes, there were a number of guides on the market that provided subjective assessments of catering in hotels and other establishments, the best-known being the *Michelin Guide*, *Egon Ronay's Guide* and *The Good Food Guide*.

Over the years, further attempts were made in the UK to introduce legislation for a common grading scheme for hotels. Agreement was reached between the three national tourist boards and the motoring organizations to adopt a common classification scheme for bed-and-breakfast establishments from the year 2000 and further negotiations led to an agreement on a common star rating (one to five stars) that was introduced gradually over an 18-month period, beginning in 2006.

As far as common systems across Europe are concerned, the harmonization process within the EU gave an additional boost to these initiatives. There are complications, for example, in the fact that some countries impose higher rates of sales tax on their 5-star properties, making it unattractive for hotels in those nations to give their properties the higher rating even if standards are comparable with a 5-star property elsewhere. Research completed by the European Consumer Centres' Network examined the hotel ratings system across EU member states, as a prelude to considering whether standardization is possible. Their findings are summarized in Table 12.3. Clearly there are many differences between these approaches, and it is likely to be difficult for one system to be able to judge the variety of accommodation which exists across the Continent, so harmonization of these systems is unlikely to be agreed in the short term.

In the meantime, tour operators have devised their own systems for assessing properties used for package tours abroad, to meet the needs of their own clients, leading to additional confusion among the travelling public. Thomson Holidays, for example, uses its 'T-rating', based in part on its own customers' assessments of accommodation.

Table 12.3 highlights that many of the rating systems focus on judging accommodation based on the range of facilities rather than the quality of the service or the quality of the facilities. Within the sector, concern is focusing on the provision of adequate training and achievement of professional service standards. The long hours, poor salaries at lower levels and generally unattractive conditions of work within the hospitality sector, coupled with an unusually high staff turnover rate, even by the standards of the tourism business, have made it difficult to raise standards of professional service to acceptable levels. Employers and associations are concerned to ensure that 'hospitality assured' standards, as laid down by the European Foundation for Quality Management's Business Excellence model and based on a worldwide model of best practice, can be applied within their own establishments.

Table 12.3 Accommodation grading schemes in Europe

Country	Mandatory or voluntary system	Accommodation categories	Classification criteria
Austria	Voluntary	Hotels, guesthouses, pensions, B&B, apartments	Quality of service, external appearance, hotel entertainment (bars, leisure facilities) and additional facilities (parking, gardens), guest satisfaction
Belgium	Compulsory	Hotel, guest room, open recreation terrain, holiday accommodation, motel	Rooms (size, furnishings and facilities), building (rooms and technical facilities, such as elevators, phones) and services (luggage storage, room service)
Bulgaria	Compulsory	Hotels, motels, holiday settlements, family hotels, boarding houses, bungalow and campsites, separate rooms, country houses, houses	Geographic location (sea, mountain, town, etc.), activity (spa, business, etc), building construction, furnishing and staff skills
Cyprus	Compulsory	Hotels, hotel apartments, tourist villages, tourist villas, camping sites, traditional houses, tourist apartments	Size of rooms (and public areas), facilities offered (car park, room service, swimming pool, etc.), staffing levels
Czech Republic	Voluntary	Hotels, motels, pension campsites, chalets, walkers' dormitories, botels	Size of rooms, bathroom equipment, facilities, catering
Denmark	Compulsory	Hotels and hostels	Technical facilities and other facilities (radio, TV)
Estonia	Compulsory	Hotels, motels, guest houses, hostels, holiday villages and camps, holiday homes, visitor apartment, B&B	Ventilation, en suite facilities, size of beds
Finland	No hotel classification system exists		
France	Voluntary	Tourist hotels, hostels, guestrooms	Room size, lobby size, telephones, staff skills
Germany	Voluntary	Hotels, guest houses, taverns, inns, pensions	Two separate schemes cover these categories of accommodation
Greece	Compulsory	Hotels, motels, furnished apartments, mixed-type hotels, camping facilities, rooms to let	Size of bedroom, facilities and services, number of rooms, public spaces near to accommodation
Hungary	Compulsory	Hotels, convalescence hotels, wellness hotels, flophouses, apartment hotels, motels, camping, holiday resorts, tourist hotels, youth hostels	Size and equipment of bedrooms, number and equipment of bathrooms, number of restaurants, lift, reception services
Iceland	Voluntary	Hotels, hotel apartments, motels, rooming house/hostel, summerhouses, B&B	Reception and breakfast provision, night security
Ireland	Compulsory	Hotels, guesthouses, holiday hostels, youth hostels, holiday camps, caravan and camping sites, holiday cottages, holiday apartments	Size of bedrooms and public areas, provision of facilities and services (catering, porterage, etc.)
Italy	Compulsory	Hotel establishments, non-hotel establishments (B&B, youth hostels), open-air establishments (tourist villages, camping)	Room size, bathroom provision, employee numbers, catering, facilities (TV, telephone, parking, baggage store)

Table 12.3 *continued*

Country	Mandatory or voluntary system	Accommodation categories	Classification criteria
Latvia	Voluntary	Hotels, guest houses, campsites, youth hostels	Building and bedroom size, facilities and services provided
Lithuania	Compulsory	Hotels, guesthouses	Size of bedrooms and dining room, availability of rooms for people with a disability
Luxembourg	Voluntary	Hotels and hotel apartments	Bedrooms, bathrooms, washrooms in public spaces, services, cleanliness
Malta	Compulsory	Hotels, aparthotels, tourist villages, guesthouses, hostels, B&B	Room size, cleaning, furniture, room facilities (TV, safe, minibar), catering, reception services
The Netherlands	Compulsory	Hotels, camping, bungalow parks	Bedrooms, service quality, room functionality
Norway	Voluntary	Hotels, apartments, cabins, hostels, motels	Room size, facilities (bathrooms), catering, services provided
Poland	Compulsory	Hotels, motels, pension/guest house, camping, houses for tourists, youth hostels, bivouac	Environment outside the building, technical equipment
Portugal	Compulsory	Hotels, hotel apartments, inns, touristic villages, touristic apartments, resorts, holiday villas, rural tourism, camping and caravans	Premises, furniture, services (cleaning, catering, check-in/out), local environment
Romania	Compulsory	Hotels, hotel apartments, motels, hostels, villas, chalets, bungalows, holiday villages, camping, apartments for rent, ships, guesthouses, agrotourism	Building condition, reception services, technical facilities (elevator, air-conditioner), room size, room facilities (safe, minibar), leisure and business facilities
Slovakia	Compulsory	Hotels, botels, guest houses, apartment house, tourist hostel, holiday village, campground, campsite, private accommodation	Entrance area, catering, room fixtures and furnishings, communal spaces
Slovenia	Compulsory	Hotels, motels, pensions, inns, camps, apartments, holiday flat, holiday houses, private rooms, farmhouse, accommodation, marinas	Bedroom size, equipment and furnishings, cleaning frequency, accepting credit card payment
Spain	Compulsory	Camping, hostels, hotels, hotel apartments, private rooms, cruises, garni hotels, shelters, spas, holiday resorts, guest houses, motels, botels, rotels, boarding houses, rural houses	Room size, number of bedrooms, facilities and services, number of employees
Sweden	Voluntary	Hotels and hotel garni	Maintenance of public areas, technical facilities, guest rooms (sound proofing, furnishing, bathrooms, TV, telephone)

Source: ECC-Net, 2009

The nature of demand for accommodation facilities

The hotel product is made up of five characteristics:

- location
- mix of facilities (which will include bedrooms, restaurants, other public rooms, functions rooms and leisure facilities)
- image
- services it provides (including such indefinable features as the level of formality, personal attention, speed and efficiency of its staff)
- prices charged.

The location of a hotel will invariably be the first consideration when a tourist is selecting a hotel. Location implies both the destination (resort for the holidaymaker, convenient stopover point for the traveller, city for the business traveller) and the location within that destination. Thus, businesspeople will want to be accommodated in a city centre hotel close to the company they are visiting, while the seaside holidaymaker will seek a hotel as close as possible to the beach and transit travellers will want to be accommodated at a hotel convenient for the airport or a motel close to major roads.

In economic terms, a trade-off will occur between location and price. The leisure traveller will look for the hotel closest to the beach that still fits the budget, while the transit traveller may well opt for a more distant hotel that is prepared to offer a free transfer to the airport. Location is, of course, fixed for all time. Thus, if the site itself loses its attraction for visitors, the hotel will suffer an equivalent decline in its fortunes. In recent years, the media have given attention to the idea of 'pop-up hotels', which can be quickly and cheaply constructed in areas where temporary demand, perhaps stimulated by a short-term event such as a music festival, needs to be serviced (Thorpe, 2009). Despite advantages of reduced time and cost in construction, the extent to which this will influence supply is yet to be seen.

The fact that high fixed costs are incurred in both building and operating hotels compounds the risks of running them. City centre sites are extremely expensive to purchase and operate, so the room prices have to be high. The market may resist such prices, but is nevertheless reluctant to be based at any distance from the centres of activity, even when good transport is available. This has been evidenced by the problems facing incoming tour operators accommodating American visitors on budget tours to central London at prices that are competitive with other city centres. The reluctance of many overseas tour operators to accept accommodation on the outskirts of the city for their clients has, in the past, led to loss of business in favour of other European capital cities.

Again, the demand for hotels centrally located in capital cities, leading to high capacity and profits, has caused those in the hotel business to maximize profits by upgrading their accommodation and appealing to business clients, rather than catering for leisure tourists demanding budget accommodation. Special services were introduced to attract niche customers. The London Hilton, for instance, was among several that introduced a women only floor, in deference to the increasing numbers of women travelling alone on business. This included a private check-in facility, increased security cameras and double locks on bedroom doors.

Meanwhile, the French Accor Group was among the first to identify the market gap for low-priced accommodation in big cities as the established hotel chains went upmarket and, as we have seen, launched its Formule 1 and Etap brands to tap into these markets. The two large budget chains in the UK have also invested heavily in London, with several sites in the city. Major cities also have frequent high-profile events, such as conferences and exhibitions; at such times, the demand for hotel rooms is reflected in every hotel boosting its prices, so that the basic price advertised by the budget chains may, in practice, be seldom available.

EXAMPLE   Hotel development in London

As host of the Olympics in 2012, London experienced a boom in hotel development. Local authorities were encouraged to relax planning rules as part of the desire to expand and improve the capital's bedstock. Between 2010 and 2013 almost 15 000 new rooms were expected to be developed, with three classifications dominating – over 8000 rooms of 5-star and 4-star rating were due to come onstream, and a further 3000 budget rooms were forecast to be built (Visit London, 2010).

The increased supply is much needed. Demand for centrally located rooms is so great that hotels can maintain high prices – 2009 saw average room rates of £156.91 (O'Brien, 2011).

Hotels will seek to maximize their revenue by offering a wide range of different tariffs to the various market segments they serve. By way of example, one city hotel provides, apart from the normal rack rate (published room rate), at least nine other rates, including special concessions for corporate bookings, conference rates, air crew, weekender traffic and tour bookings. In the climate of recession experienced by hotels in recent years, it has also been possible for clients to negotiate substantial discounts if they book late in the day. Hotel managers, recognizing that any sale is better than none, allow the desk clerks to come to an agreement regarding any realistic offer, which may be as much as 50% lower than rack rate.

Hotel companies may be further constrained by the need to meet building regulations that apply to the location where they are building. Increasingly, concern about the environment and widespread recognition of the damage done to the architectural styles of resorts swamped by high-rise hotel buildings have led local authorities to impose stringent planning and other regulations on new buildings. This may mean using local (often more expensive) materials in place of concrete, using a vernacular style in the design of the building, limiting the height to four or five floors (some tropical destinations restrict hotel buildings to the height of the local palm trees) or restricting the total size of the building to ensure that it is in keeping with surrounding buildings.

Some characteristics of the hotel product

The demand for hotel bedrooms comes from a widely distributed market, nationally and internationally, whereas the market for other facilities that hotels offer will often be highly localized. In addition to providing food and drink for their own residents, hotels will be marketing these services (and sometimes additional services such as a leisure club with swimming pool) to other tourists or members of the local population. Clearly, hotels have to cater to at least two quite different market segments, which calls for different approaches to advertising, promotion and distribution.

Seasonality and periodicity

Another characteristic of the hotel product is that demand is seldom uniform throughout the year or even throughout the week. Tourist hotels suffer from seasonality, involving high levels of demand during summer peaks and little or no demand during the winter troughs, while hotels catering chiefly to businesspeople may find that demand drops during the summer. Care has to be exercised in pricing leisure market hotels; while a differential is expected between peak and low seasons, if it is too extreme, competitive destinations will attract visitors away or they will simply not come.

Business hotels also suffer from periodicity, with demand centred on Monday to Thursday nights, while there is little demand for Friday to Sunday nights. The lack of flexibility in room supply, coupled with the 'perishable' nature of the product (if rooms are unsold there is no opportunity to 'store' them and sell them later), mean that greater efforts must be made to unload unsold accommodation by attracting off-peak customers to hotels in holiday destinations and leisure and family markets to business hotels at weekends. This also means that the atmosphere of these hotels will be very different depending on when customers stay there. Even the most upmarket hotels well located in big cities are often loath to lose the prospect of high room occupancy at weekends and will feel obliged to take reservations for groups from some operators, but, at the same time, will do their utmost to avoid disruption to their regular business clients. This can result in groups being forced to check into and depart from hotels by back entrances. This, and other forms of distinctive handling, such as the allocation of separate dining areas in restaurants, can result in their being made to feel like second-class citizens, if not managed properly.

Even with creative marketing and high discounting, many tourist hotels in highly seasonal resorts will find their occupancy levels falling alarmingly in the winter. They must then face the decision as to whether it is better to stay open in the winter in the hope that they will attract enough customers to make some contribution to overheads, or to close completely for several months of the year. The problem with the latter course of action is that a number of hotel costs, such as rates, depreciation and salaries for management staff, will continue whether or not the hotel remains open. Temporary closure may also result in difficulties in recruiting good staff, if jobs are known to be only seasonal.

In recent years, more hotels, especially the larger chain hotels, have opted to remain open and offer enhanced packages for those willing to travel out-of-season. The increase in second holidays and out-of-season short breaks in the UK have helped to make more hotels viable all year round, although room occupancy remains low out of season in many of the more traditional resorts.

Yield management becomes the criterion in this situation – the aim being to maximize revenue for the hotel, depending on the circumstances it faces and based on supply and demand at any given time. The hotel sector is also heavily dependent on the extent to which the public sector is willing to invest in order to make the resort attractive out of season. Popular tourist destinations such as Bournemouth, through a process of continuous investment and a deliberate attempt to attract the conference and non-seasonal markets, have been able to draw in high numbers of winter tourists, making it economic for many more hotels to remain open all year round. This, in turn, stimulates further business as local attractions and events are also encouraged to stay open throughout the year.

Atmosphere and attractions

While we have talked chiefly in terms of the physical characteristics of the hotel, the psychological factors that attract visitors are no less important. Service, 'atmosphere', even the other guests with whom the customer will come into contact – all play a role when the choice of hotel is made. Only about a quarter of British holidaymakers choose to stay at hotels or guesthouses when holidaying in the UK, compared with some 47% who do so when abroad. The difference is accounted for by the large VFR market in the UK, while demand for camping, caravanning and self-catering holidays and the rising ownership of second homes provide alternative opportunities, both at home and abroad.

According to an overseas visitor survey carried out in the UK, 46% of overseas visitors stay in hotels at some point when visiting the UK, accounting for 24% of all nights spent in accommodation (VisitBritain, 2010), although the pattern varies, and many will choose a variety of different forms of accommodation during their holiday. Some 40% of visitors stayed in free accommodation provided by friends and relatives.

Factors such as class, age and lifestyle all have a bearing on the choice of sleeping accommodation, as they offer the guest a variety of attractions; some guests may be in search of a quiet night's sleep, while others seek out a likely bar for late night entertainment. In particular, the nature of, and consequent demand for, large hotels will be quite different from that for the small guesthouse or bed-and-breakfast unit. A large hotel may well provide attractions of its own, distinct from the location in which it is situated. Indeed, in some cases the hotel may be a more significant influence on choice than the destination. This is often true of large hotel/leisure complexes providing a range of inhouse entertainment, as is the case with a number of North American and, increasingly, European hotels.

Similarly, some hotels are so closely linked with the destinations which they serve that the combination of stay at hotel/destination becomes the established pattern. This is seen in Canada, where the resort of Lake Louise and the Chateau Lake Louise Hotel are inextricably linked. This type of hotel and resort combination is rarer in the UK, although Gleneagles Hotel in Perthshire, Scotland, with its golfing links, provides one such example. It is, however, increasingly a characteristic of package holiday hotels, and has been taken a stage further with the growth of the all-inclusive package holiday, in which all food, drink and entertainment are included in the price. The Sandals Hotel chain, based in the Bahamas and Caribbean, was a major initiator of this development.

The provision of a good range of attractions, as well as a drinks licence, can help to offset the disadvantages that result from the unavoidable impersonality of large hotels. As the chains gain more of a hold on the total pool of hotel beds, an increase in the average number of rooms in each hotel tends to follow as larger hotels benefit from economies of scale. Hotels with more than 100 rooms remain the exception, however, and smaller properties emphasize the personal nature of their service as a feature in their marketing.

Unique designs

Refurbishment of the larger, less attractive hotels is seldom a viable option, the alternative being to pull them down and construct new ones more in keeping with popular taste. In Majorca, the local authorities introduced legislation requiring unattractive mid-twentieth-century hotels to be demolished before new, higher-quality buildings could be constructed. This led to the removal of many 1960s concrete eyesores in ageing resorts like Magaluf, in favour of hotels with greater character.

In countries where change and novelty are features of market demand, hotel companies now 'theme' their properties to distinguish them from others, either in the style of their architecture or interior decoration. This, as was pointed out earlier in the chapter, is now becoming a common approach in expensive hotels around the world. Flamboyant architecture, often reminiscent of gothic fortresses, is springing up in the most unlikely places, such as Sun City in Southern Africa. There, a purpose-built resort complex has been designed to provide a simulacrum of 'African culture'; while in the Bahamas is to be found the extravagant Royal Towers of Atlantis on Paradise Island, where 'exotic' describes both the architecture and the prices.

Chain hotels provide in their budget for regular changes of decor to update their properties, while older hotels emphasize their traditional values and style. With the current boom in nostalgia, hotels that can retain the style of yesteryear, while nevertheless offering up-to-date features, such as modern bathrooms with good plumbing, can find a ready market for their product. A good example here is the restored Raffles Hotel in Singapore, which, after extensive refurbishment, has successfully blended modern comforts with the traditional architecture of the colonial era.

Increasingly, holidaymakers search for something different and unusual in the places they stay as part of their experience of travel. Specialist operators and independent hoteliers are catering to this need. Long-haul travellers can book into an authentic and traditional native long house in Skrang, Sarawak, while tourists to Canada are offered the choice of staying in a North American Indian tepee in Manitoba or an Inuit igloo in the Hudson Bay area.

EXAMPLE **Pipe dreams**

Das Park Hotel operates two 'hotels', offering guests a comfortable night's sleep in, what is best described as a chic but spartan room - inside a large concrete drainpipe. With facilities offering little more than a double bed, a place to store luggage, a lamp and an electrical socket to charge a phone, this is certainly not designed for the luxury market. To avoid the feeling of claustrophobia, each pipe has a small window cut into its side.

These drainpipe rooms are located in a public park which provides the supporting facilities, such as toilets and showers, while the wider area provides the guest with amenities like bars and cafes. The cost of a night's stay in this unique location? Whatever the guest feels they can afford and is prepared to pay to support the continuation of the project.

Das Park Hotel has been operating since 2006 and currently offers two locations - in the German town of Bottrop-Ebel and the Austrian town of Ottensheim - opening for the summer months, with reservations taken online; once confirmed, the guest receives by e-mail a code to unlock the door.

If drainpipes don't appeal, why not try ice hotels? Their number has expanded in line with popular demand and their appeal has helped to generate a winter tourism market in some most unusual locations, triggered by the construction of the world famous ice hotel at Jukkasjävi in Swedish Lapland. Others can be found in Chena Hot Springs, near Fairbanks in Alaska, at Kangerlussuaq in Greenland, in Canada near Quebec City (where a nightclub accommodating 400 is a feature), in Norway and in Switzerland, which boasts several, including those at Gstaad, Zermatt, Engelberg and Davos. All of these have to be freshly reconstructed after winter thaws each year and are generally open only between January and April, but they have proved a popular way to attract out-of-season tourists. For those seeking a similar experience in greater comfort, a heated glass igloo in Finland provides one alternative.

Other original approaches to accommodation include lighthouses along the Croatian coast, a windmill in Majorca, a police station in Lynton, Devon, a cider press in Abbeville, France, a signal box in County Kerry, Ireland, and converted pigsties in Garstang, Lancashire (The Piggeries) and Monteriggioni in Italy.

The impulse to do something different and sleep in something unique appears to be growing – the more far-fetched, the better. Treehouses have been constructed at several sites in the UK and the Orne District in France. The proprietor of the Dog Bark Inn at Cottonwood, Idaho, promotes his accommodation as the world's biggest beagle, and the sleeping accommodation is constructed within a giant carved sculpture of a dog. Another current fashion is underwater hotels. A modest and rather basic prototype, the Utter Inn on Lake Mälaren at Västerås in Sweden, appears to have started the trend, with others following at the Bahamas island of Eleuthera and in Key Largo, Florida. The Poseidon Mystery Island Hotel, expected to open in late 2012 in Fiji, will have 20 undersea rooms and a restaurant. Undersea dining is also in vogue in the Maldives and at Eilat, Israel, and more are planned in Dubai and other countries in the Middle East seeking to expand tourism.

These are all attempts at offering more than simply a room to sleep in. Today, adventurous tourists, whether travelling for business or pleasure, seek a package of physical and emotional experiences that together make up the total trip experience, and hoteliers are seeking to satisfy that need.

In some instances, tourists require no more than basic, but clean and comfortable, overnight accommodation. This is particularly true of adventure tourists such as trekkers and other backpackers, and a variety of simple accommodation is now being devised to meet this market's criteria. Micro-lodges provide one solution. To take one example, camping 'pods', accommodating up to four people, are available in some remote regions of the UK. These provide little more than a simple shelter and are without beds, backpackers being expected to lay their bedrolls on the hard foam floors.

Categories of accommodation

In this chapter we have, until now, focused much of our attention on hotels, highlighting the many chains that are involved in providing this form of accommodation. This is a competitive sector, and there is constant pressure to adapt to changing trends and demands from the marketplace. However, hotels have not only to innovate in order to compete with each other; they also face competition from other categories of accommodation, which we will now explore.

EXAMPLE   **The British holiday hotel**

The traditional British domestic holiday based on a one or two week stay in a small seaside hotel is an experience that is today all but dead. Many of these types of establishment have been forced out of business through an inability to respond to modern tourists' needs, the neglected buildings impacting on the overall image of the resort (see Figure 12.4). This has come about largely due to the appeal of holidays abroad, with packages being no more expensive than those in the UK, and budget flights costing less than domestic transport to the destination.

Overseas resorts have provided much better value for money and, of course, guaranteed sunshine. As a result of their experiences in hotels abroad, British holidaymakers now demand similar facilities in their home country, including improved

Figure 12.4 Run-down hotel located in the coastal resort of Hastings, England

Photo by Claire Humphreys

standards of cuisine, choice of entertainment and en suite accommodation. To survive, hotel proprietors have had to invest to meet these expectations.

The trend for domestic holidays to be of shorter duration posed both a threat and an opportunity. While short breaks help to extend the season, they also raise room costs, which cannot easily be recovered by higher prices, particularly during periods when the market is price-sensitive.

The once popular fully inclusive holiday, comprising three meals a day, taken at fixed times of the day in the hotel, no longer meets the requirements of modern tourists, who may wish to tour the surrounding area by car during the day and will therefore want to eat irregularly or even forgo a midday meal.

The B&B

The increasing desire of many tourists, particularly overseas visitors to the UK, to 'meet the people' and enjoy a more intimate relationship with the culture of the country they are visiting has benefited the smallest forms of accommodation unit, such as the guesthouse or bed-and-breakfast establishment (B&B). These are generally family run, catering to business tourists in the towns and leisure tourists in country towns, rural areas and the seaside.

B&Bs in particular provide a very valuable service to the industry, in that they can offer the informality and friendliness sought by many tourists (many B&Bs have no more than three bedrooms), cater for the impulse demand that results from holidaymakers touring by car or bicycle and conveniently expand the supply of beds during peak periods of the year in areas that are highly seasonal and where hotels would not be viable.

There are estimated to be about 11 500 B&Bs in the UK, of which more than one-third have been certified using the tourist boards' grading systems. Most have six or fewer guests as this obviates payment of business rates and neither a fire certificate nor public liability insurance is required in order to operate.

This form of accommodation was virtually unknown in North America until relatively recently, but has boomed since the 1980s as the Americans and Canadians brought back with them the experiences they had gained in Europe. In general, however, these North American properties have moved upmarket, providing much more luxurious accommodation and facilities than would normally be found in their European equivalents (for example, see Figure 12.5).

A derivation of the B&B – home stays – offer a budget alternative that provides opportunities for international tourists to meet and interact more closely with locals in their own homes. Much more time is spent with the hosts, who may organize visits to local attractions or help their visitors to learn the host language. Examples include a stay with a Maori family in New Zealand (**www.amhnz.com**), a home stay in Santiago, Chile, which combines Spanish language lessons at a nearby college (**www.cactuslanguage.com**) or the government-regulated home stays available in a Casa Particular in Cuba (**www.casaparticular.info**). Prices for stays in private homes often work out cheaper than those for a standard B&B.

Figure 12.5 An upmarket B&B at Boothbay Harbor, Maine, USA
Photo by Chris Holloway

Farmhouse holiday accommodation

Farmhouse holidays have also enjoyed considerable success in recent years, both in the UK and on the Continent. European countries with strong agricultural traditions, such as the UK and Denmark, have catered for tourists in farmhouse accommodation for many years and, as farmers have found it harder to pay their way by farming alone, owing to the reduction in agricultural subsidies within the EU, they have turned increasingly to tourism as a means of boosting revenue, particularly in the low season. A study of farm tourism carried out in 1991 revealed that, at that time, 15% of all farms in England (and 24% in the West Country) had some form of tourism project on their land.

The trend towards healthier lifestyles and the appeal of natural food and the outdoor life have also helped to make farm tourism popular. Within rural areas, tourist boards have provided assistance and training for farmers interested in expanding their accommodation for tourism. Both Ireland and Denmark have been notably successful in packaging modestly priced farm holidays for the international market, in association with tour operators and the ferry companies. In the case of Denmark, this has been a logical development as it attracts tourists to what is generally recognized as an otherwise expensive country for holidays if based on hotel accommodation.

 Farm tourism

Tourism has long been recognized as an important opportunity for some agricultural areas. In 1983, the UN Economic Commission for Europe examined opportunities of integrating farming and tourism to aid the development of rural areas. In addition to this, the decline in farm profits, both in Europe and the USA, encouraged owners to expand their tourism activities.

Farm Stay UK

This consortium, established in 1983, currently has 1200 members who provide quality-rated visitor accommodation on farms. The goal is to increase the occupancy rates and income earned from tourism through improving and coordinating marketing activities promoting the concept of farm tourism.

The consortium provides support for the farmers, including offering workshops and training programmes to help encourage business diversification and business development. They also maintain a database for their members' facilities, making it convenient for the public to find suitable farm accommodation.

Ranch tourism

Farm stays in the USA are also popular, although these are often promoted as ranch holidays. These are offered in several states, but notably in Arizona, Colorado and Texas. They are often working ranches which provide activities such as riding lessons, cattle herding, roping lessons and rodeos.

The accommodation may be in the form of bunkhouse cabins, although some ranches (often termed 'Dude Ranches') have invested in facilities to move upmarket, charging $250 or more a day for the experience.

Camping and caravanning

The market for camping and caravanning holidays in the UK is substantial – around one in every five holidays in the UK is taken in caravans. Bourne Leisure, the leading firm in the leisure park business, attracts about 4 million holidaymakers a year to its 50 holiday parks, hotels and resorts in the UK, operating under the Haven, Butlins and Warner brands. While many holidays are, of course, taken in private touring caravans (of which there are around 498 000 in Britain), motor home holidays are also becoming ever more

Figure 12.6 Caravan park at Perranporth, Cornwall

Photo by Claire Humphreys

popular, with 112 000 privately owned vehicles in the UK. Static caravan and mobile home sites (see Figure 12.6) number 335 000, located in over 4000 UK holiday parks (of which almost half are star rated).

Holiday parks entered the tourist boards' grading schemes in 1987 with the introduction of agreed codes of practice for operators, and a trade body, the British Holiday and Home Parks Association (BH&HPA), has been formed to represent the interests of operators.

EXAMPLE | **Glamorous camping attracts a luxury market**

Fuelled by the fashionable and the famous camping at music festivals, and a recession which saw many choose to cut back on their holiday spending – or at least not to be seen spending excessively on luxury holidays – so glamping was born. By 2010, camping and caravanning trips in England made up 13% of all domestic tourism trips and spending was estimated to be in the region of £1.6 billion (VisitEngland, 2010).

Glamping accommodation bears little resemblance to the tents that most campers experience. Although the wall of the tent may be canvas, most accommodations have floorboards, a wood-burning stove to provide heat, dining tables, sofas, and other home comforts including, literally, the kitchen sink. Bathrooms with hot showers and flush toilets are expected and some will even have a bath.

Glamping accommodation comes in many forms, from Romany caravans, tepees and wigwams to yurts, geodesic domes and treehouses. This is also no longer about domestic tourism, as destinations across the globe offer glamping opportunities to the international traveller.

Holiday centres

Although the Americans were running summer camps for children some years earlier, adult holiday camps as we know them today were very much a British innovation. They were introduced on a major scale in the 1930s and 1940s by three noted entrepreneurs – Billy Butlin, Fred Pontin and Harry Warner. Their aim was to provide all-in entertainment at a low price in chalet-style accommodation that would be largely unaffected by inclement weather.

The Butlin–Pontin–Warner style of holiday camp became enormously successful in the years prior to World War II and the early post-war era, but none is now family owned. Pontins still operates five sites in the UK and Butlins and Warners are now part of Bourne Leisure, retaining their focus on family entertainment. Warner Holidays, however, has changed direction markedly and is now marketed to adults only. Haven's appeal is to three different markets, described as 'lively, all-action', 'leisurely' and 'relaxing'.

For the most part, the balance of the market is split between large numbers of independent companies, each operating a small number of sites. Some of these operate under franchise agreements to improve their marketing. Hoseasons, to take one example, is a leading holiday site franchisor and operates around 330 franchise sites. The market for holiday centres remains highly seasonal, falling almost entirely between May and September. It had been customary for centres to close during the winter months, but improved marketing, including mini-breaks and themed events, has helped to extend sales into the 'shoulder' months of spring and autumn. As a percentage of the total accommodation used in domestic tourism, though, the figure for holiday centres remains relatively small.

Holiday centres have been affected as much as any other accommodation facilities by changes in public taste. Before the war, they attracted a largely lower middle-class clientele, but in the post-war period their market became significantly more working-class and the canteen-style catering service and entertainment provided reflected the needs of this market segment. Bookings were made invariably from Saturday to Saturday and most clients booked direct with the companies. Each company had a quite distinct image for its clientele, who were strongly brand-loyal and booked regularly with their particular favourite.

More recently, these camps have attempted to move upmarket – a process heralded by a change in nomenclature from camps to holiday centres, villages or parks. The former predominantly working-class orientation has been modified to cater for wider social tastes. Large chalet blocks have given way to smaller units with self-catering facilities. A choice of catering styles has been introduced, ranging from fully serviced through self-service to self-catering – the latter enjoying the greatest rates of growth.

Butlins in particular has invested huge sums of money in redeveloping its remaining three centres to give them a more upmarket image. Additionally, the company has recently moved into the hotel business, constructing its first hotel adjacent to its Bognor Regis centre. Guests enjoy superior accommodation, but must then purchase passes in order to enter the Butlins resort. These traditional centres now face strong competition from the new wave of holiday villages.

The new holiday villages

Holiday villages offer a new concept in resort marketing. In their present form, they owe their development to a Dutch innovator who opened the first of a chain of Center Parcs in The Netherlands in 1967, rapidly expanding into Belgium, France and the UK. These offered a very different holiday experience from that of traditional holiday centres, based on the recognition that North European resorts could not compete with sunnier climes and so facilities would have to take account of the inclement weather. This meant more indoor entertainment was provided as well as fully enclosed swimming pools.

Center Parcs first launched in the UK in 1987 and these upmarket holiday villages have now grown to four: Sherwood Forest in Nottinghamshire, Longleat Forest in Wiltshire, Elveden Forest in Suffolk and Oasis Whinfell Forest in Cumbria. A fifth, on the Duke of Bedford's estate near Woburn, delayed following planning appeals, is due to open in 2013.

Offering a wide choice of all-weather facilities – most notably vast indoor pools with domed glass roofs and settings designed to resemble a tropical beach – the villages had an extraordinary measure of success in their early years, with an average 96% occupancy all year round. Ownership is now split between those on the Continent and those in the UK. Another company with seven properties in The Netherlands, Gran Dorado, offers a similar product to that of Center Parcs.

Billy Butlin's early attempts to introduce his holiday camp concept to the Continent were unsuccessful, but more upmarket holiday villages have been highly successful. The market leader is Club Méditerranée, which is French-owned and has a worldwide spread of holiday villages, from France to Tahiti. The success of this organization, which in 1950 was among the first to enter the package holiday business, has been attributed to its unique approach to its clients, who are referred to as *gentils membres*. It had been the practice for beads to be used instead of hard currency to purchase drinks on site, which heightened the feeling for the holidaymakers of being divorced from the commercial world while on holiday. Sadly, however, Club Méditerranée experienced a decline in profits after failing to keep pace with holiday centre developments at the end of the 1990s and has been forced into an expensive programme of renovation to restore its position in the market, with many of the old tactics giving way to a more commercial approach. It now has 75 villages operating in 40 counties, having refocused its activity on high-end global tourism all-inclusive holidays.

Second home and timeshare ownership

Second homes

Some words are also appropriate here about the growth of second home ownership and the effect that this is having on the tourism industry. Owning a second home in the country or by the sea is not a new phenomenon. Since the age of the Grand Tour, the British aristocracy and, later, wealthy merchants invariably had a country seat to retreat to at weekends and through the summer to escape the heat and dirt of the big cities. Similarly, wealthy Parisians owned a second property readily accessible from the French capital. Americans have been buying homes along the north-eastern shores of the USA since the nineteenth century, culminating in the ostentatious residences built as summer homes for the very wealthy along the shores of Newport, Rhode Island, in the 1890s (The Breakers at Newport being the most famous of these). Later, holiday homes were built on the West Coast and in Florida. Today, many wealthy Americans have two holiday homes: a summer home along the Cape and a winter home in Florida. In Europe, Nordic residents have a long tradition of owning second homes by the sea, even if many are of very simple cottage construction. Löfgren (1999) claims that there were 500 000 such homes in Sweden by the 1970s, owned by a population totalling only some 8 million. A high proportion of these were built for Stockholm residents along the popular west coast of the country, some six hours' drive away. He estimated that 25% of Swedes and a similar number of other Nordic residents owned second homes by the close of the twentieth century, in comparison with 16% of the French and just 4% of Americans.

These early second homes, however, were almost invariably constructed as summer homes for the owners and their friends. What has marked the big change in more recent times has been the commercialization of the second homes market (for example, see Figure 12.7). Owners now buy to let, frequently renting out their property when not for their own use through commercial rental agencies who manage the properties for a commission. The holiday homes rental market has soared in recent years as owners moved into property as a principal investment when the share market collapsed.

British residents were rather later in getting into property, but have more than made up for their tardiness in a frenzy of buying since the 1990s. At first this was confined mainly to the UK, but, as prices soared and restrictions began to be imposed on property construction in the more popular areas of the countryside such as the Lake District, South Devon and the Cotswolds, Britons began to turn to cheaper accommodation in Italy, France, Spain (especially the Canary and Balearic Islands) and Greece. More recently, homes in Florida and the newly admitted countries of the EU, especially Malta, Cyprus and Slovenia, have been in demand. Historically, investment in second homes has been fuelled by both

Figure 12.7 Second homes at Gallinas Point, in the popular resort of St Ives, Cornwall, are largely rented out as self-catering apartments
Photo by Chris Holloway

an increase in disposable income among the better-off sections of British society and the fall in air transport prices. In the post 9/11 world, transatlantic fares dropped to an all-time low, while the growth of no frills airlines to smaller regional airports on the Continent has attracted investors to Romania, Bulgaria and Turkey (the last still intent on entering the EU eventually).

EXAMPLE Buy-to-let hotel rooms

The concept of buy to let moved on to the hotel sector, with guest rooms available for purchase on 99-year leases in commercial hotels. In one such transaction for a London property, investors were permitted to spend up to 52 nights per year in their room, at a nominal charge, while on bookings for the rest of the year owners would receive 45–50% of all the rental income. But is this just too good to be true? Organized as a partnership between Guestinvest and Alias Hotels, the company collapsed in 2008 and many of the hotel properties were sold off to fund creditors.

While several buy-to-let hotel schemes are still in operation, the recent downturn in both property values and travel has impacted on this sector significantly.

The exact number of second homes owned by British residents abroad is hard to establish and estimates vary wildly. A study by Saga Holidays in 2005 estimated that 324 000 second homes were owned in the UK, with another 178 000 abroad and that these figures would rise to 405 000 and 249 000, respectively, by 2015 (Lewis, 2005). By contrast, research by Grant Thornton (Judge, 2006) suggested a figure of 300 000 people owning second homes abroad, rising to 2 million by 2025. The Department for Communities and Local Government (DCLG) reported that there were 314 000 households with second homes in the UK and a further 389 000 households with second homes abroad (DCLG,

2010). A certain amount of under-reporting is perhaps inevitable, given the understandable desire to avoid releasing information on property ownership to the tax authorities. Certainly the number is sufficiently large to account for a fall in standard package holiday bookings, as owners (and renters) switch to the Internet to buy their no-frills flights.

What is of no less interest is the distribution of these second homes. France and Spain dominate for Britons with second homes abroad, with 22% each, The rest of Europe accounts for 29% with the rest of the world making up the remaining 27% (DCLG, 2010). In the UK, at least half – and some estimates suggest as much as three-quarters – of the housing stock in popular tourist locations consists of second homes. In Leysdown-on-Sea, on the Isle of Sheppey, second homes account for 65% of properties, while in the Cornish towns of Rock, Padstow and Trebetherick up to half of homes are second homes. Other areas of high second home ownership are Central London, the Lake District and Cumbria.

Timeshare

Where an outright purchase is beyond people's means, the concept of timeshare properties offers an alternative means of enjoying a holiday in one's second home, whether in the UK or abroad. Statistics on timeshare ownership are notoriously inaccurate and out of date, although an American Resort Development Association report (ARDA, 2004) estimated that, in 2002, around 6.7 million timeshares were owned around the world in 5425 locations. Nearly half of all owners are Americans. In UK, the Timeshare Consumers Association estimated that there were 405 000 owners in 2001, of which about a quarter owned properties in the UK. At that point, it was estimated that there were 131 timeshare resorts in the UK. Most of those owned abroad are in Spain (especially the Canaries) and Portugal. European ownership has triggered substantial demand for budget air tickets, undermining the traditional accommodation sector. Indeed, there are hotels in the UK that have responded to the challenge by converting some or all of their accommodation into timeshare ownership.

Timeshare is a scheme whereby an apartment or villa is sold to several co-owners, each of whom purchases the right to use the accommodation for a given period of the year, which may range from one week to several weeks. The initial cost of the accommodation will vary not only according to the length of time for which it is purchased but also depending on the period of the year chosen, so that a week in July or August, for example, may be three or four times the cost of the same accommodation in winter.

The scheme is reported to have been initiated at a ski resort in the French Alps in 1965, although at least one organization, the Ring Hotel chain in Switzerland, was developing along similar lines some years before this. By the early 1970s, timeshare had been introduced in the USA and the concept had also arrived in UK by the mid-1970s. Since then, it has enjoyed enormous success, boosted by schemes allowing owners to exchange their properties for others around the world during their period of ownership. A number of timeshare exchange organizations have been established, of which the largest and best-known are Resort Condominiums International (RCI), with 3 million members registered worldwide in 2004, and Interval International (II). These companies keep a register of owners and, for a fee, will facilitate home exchanges around the world and organize flights.

Unfortunately, the extensive development of timeshare properties led to high-pressure sales techniques being used by less reputable organizations, using street touts to approach tourists visiting resorts abroad. This led to some poor publicity for the scheme in the press. The Timeshare Developers' Association was formed to give the industry credibility and draw up a code of conduct for members. Since 1991, the Timeshare Council has overseen the regulation of timeshare within the UK. The Office of Fair Trading keeps a watching brief on development within the UK, while the Organization for Timeshare in Europe (OTE) has developed a code of conduct for its members, oversees quality and offers a free conciliation service for consumers dealing with members.

Timeshare is not without its problems. It has been found to be difficult to resell such properties due to the amount of new properties coming on to the market and, in some cases, management and maintenance fees have been high. There can be a problem in getting widely dispersed owners together to make decisions on the management of the property.

The poor image was marginally improved in the late 1980s when major hotel chains, such as Marriott, with its Vacation Club International brand, Walt Disney and Hyatt all entered the market; but with declining revenues, Marriott announced in 2011 that it was to divest itself of this segment of its operations (Lewis, 2011). Although hotel ownership expanded the product by introducing spas and other activities along with the basic timeshare holidays, this has not perhaps been enough to maintain interest in ownership.

Educational accommodation

The significance of the educational accommodation sector must also be recognized. Universities and other institutions of higher education seeking to increase contributions to their revenue through the rental of student accommodation during the academic holidays have marketed their accommodation to tour operators and others for budget holidays. Often situated in greenfield sites near major tourist destinations, such as Stirling or York, the universities have experienced considerable success in this venture and have further expanded their involvement with the leisure market by providing other facilities, such as activity centres and public rooms for themed holidays.

The standards of university accommodation have greatly improved in recent years to meet the expectations of students themselves as their standards at home have risen. En suite facilities are now the norm, bringing the standards up to the levels that budget holidaymakers have come to expect, and making them comparable to those of other accommodation for budget conferences and business meetings. This is proving to be a profitable source of revenue for the institutions during the academic holidays.

EXAMPLE **Cambridge colleges are key accommodation providers**

This East Anglian city has long been popular with tourists, but the limited supply of accommodation has led to high room rates. In 2008, the total number of rooms available year-round was 3529 (see Table 12.4)

Out of term-time the colleges add significantly to this provision, with almost 7000 rooms being provided, mostly to groups and conference delegates. One example of this is the most recent college to be built, Robinson College, which was opened in 1981. Integral to the design of the college were 170 en suite bedrooms, a theatre-style meeting space and breakout rooms, specifically in order for income to be earned from the conference and leisure tourism markets.

Table 12.4 Number of bedrooms available to tourists in Cambridge

Accommodation category	Rooms (2008)
B&Bs	201
Guest Houses	239
Hotels	1348
Self Catering	68
Caravan/Campsite	60
Youth Hostel	26
Colleges	6984
Total	**8926**

Source: VisitCambridge, 2009

The distribution of accommodation

Large hotel chains have in the past enjoyed advantages in gaining access to their markets through their links with the airline sector. This close relationship dates back to the early 1970s when airlines, introducing their new jumbo jets, hastily set about establishing connections with hotels to accommodate their increasing passenger numbers. As a result, hotel chains gained access to the airlines' global distribution systems (GDS), the computerized reservations networks that were a key factor in selling rooms to the international market.

While this link remains important, the development of the Internet has changed the nature of distribution, making the large hotel groups far more independent in their interface with customers. Apart from hotel representation on airline-owned (or formerly owned) websites such as Opodo and Orbitz, online agencies such as Expedia and Travelocity, which offer a range of travel products, feature hotels prominently and have become a powerful force in the distribution chain. Websites devoted to accommodation only are also springing up as alternatives to sites affiliated to carriers or other principals and intermediaries, with rooms at highly competitive prices. The larger hotel groups are increasingly relying on their own websites to reach their customers in an effort to cut costs by avoiding payment of commission to intermediaries.

EXAMPLE Booking hotels online

Hotels.com, part of the Expedia group, has grown to become one of the largest online hotel providers globally. The database, searchable via the Internet, offers access to 135 000 hotels, from large chain hotels to small, independently owned properties.

To encourage customers to use their system, hotels.com has developed a mobile app, allowing smartphone users to book conveniently. Having invested in this technology, the company experienced a 500% increase in bookings via mobile Internet. To further encourage loyalty among their customers, hotels.com operates a rewards scheme, which offers one free night's accommodation once the customer has stayed 10 nights – with the value of the free night being determined by the prices of the paid nights.

The efforts to gain and keep customers (hotels.com estimates that over 5 million customers come to their website monthly) helps to justify to hotel owners that a listing on the hotels.com database has the potential to bring in bookings.

For those hotels trying to offload rooms at the last minute, the company has a sister brand, hotwire.com, which focuses on the traveller who is looking for a heavily discounted rate for late booking. Whilst this brand has a much smaller audience, it provides an important service for hotels which are trying to offload unsold rooms in order to increase occupancy rates and make a contribution to the hotel's fixed costs.

Large hotels depend on group as well as individual business, so they must maintain contact with tour operators, conference organizers and others who bulk buy hotel bedrooms. The tourist boards can play a part in helping such negotiations by organizing workshops abroad to which the buyers of accommodation and other facilities will be invited.

All large hotel chains, and many smaller hotel companies, now have their own computer systems to cope with back-of-office and management information as well as providing access to their reservations system worldwide. Some chains maintain their own offices in key generating countries (and, of course, each hotel will recommend business and take reservations for others in the chain), while independent hotels reach the overseas markets through membership of marketing consortia. The former role of hotel representative agencies has dwindled as online booking agencies took over their role, and the few that survive, such as Utell International, are now substantially electronic agencies. Even the smallest hoteliers today operate interactive CRSs via the Internet, although their prospects of reaching customers are enhanced when this is done in association with other accommodation units.

Some will think of travel agents as being the obvious distributive outlets, but few agents, apart from those dealing regularly with business travellers, are keen to handle hotel bookings as distinct from comprehensive travel services, and, increasingly, travellers are prepared to search the World Wide Web themselves for their cheap airline seats and hotel rooms. Domestic bookings are traditionally made direct with hotels and, for reservations abroad, agents are unwilling to get involved unless they hold agreements with the hotels on the payment of commission. Some hotels will pay a standard 10%, while others allow only a lesser rate or restrict commissions to room sales outside peak periods. Many agents are also unwilling to deal with overseas hotels without making a charge for the service. Where hotels package their product in the form of short breaks or longer holidays, however, they may be sold, like any other package, through an agent. Here, the agent is clear about the commission accruing, but may still be reluctant to stock brochures describing the product due to the limited rack space. The growth of dynamic packaging – essentially, tailor-made programmes put together by an intermediary such as an operator or agent by a search of websites – may provide agents with scope to retain their customers' loyalty as they can show that they are offering expertise beyond what travellers can find for themselves. This is discussed in more detail in Chapter 19.

Traditionally, clients for UK holiday centres have also booked direct, but the centres are now more supportive of sales through travel agents. Leading companies such as Butlins now receive a substantial percentage of their sales in this way.

Finally, mention should be made of the sale of accommodation through public-sector tourism outlets. This is commonly found on the Continent; the Dutch tourist offices (VVVs) provide a reservation service for tourists and have done so for many years, to take one example. Today tourist information centres (TICs) in the UK also offer a booking service as one reflection of their increasingly commercial role. The 'Book a bed ahead' (BABA) system allows visitors to book either hotel or farmhouse accommodation through local TICs, for which a fee is charged and the TIC receives a commission from the principal. Increasingly, such bookings can be undertaken using a local computer reservations system, which improves the service that the TICs provide.

Environmental issues

All sectors of the tourism industry are becoming sensitized to the issue of ecotourism – that is, ecologically sound tourism that can be sustained as tourist numbers continue to grow. Hotels are in a position to take a lead on this issue. They are also frequently the recipients of complaints by the ecotourism lobby as a result of their practices. For example, hotels in Goa, in India, have been strongly criticized because of their profligate use of water for showers, swimming pools and so on in a region where the local inhabitants suffer from water shortages due to drought.

Where there are shortages of water, as there are, for example, in the Channel Islands in the UK, many hotels encourage their guests to use water sparingly – taking a shower rather than a bath, ensuring taps are turned off and taking other measures that reduce waste. Hotel proprietors elsewhere have recognized that there is unnecessary wastage; for instance, many guests would prefer not to have their towels and sheets replaced daily, and savings can be effected by offering guests the choice of having fresh linen (which they may indicate by leaving towels on the floor in the morning) or reusing their linen (indicated by hanging towels up).

One example of an eco-friendly approach in the industry was the launch of the International Hotels Environment Initiative, referred to in Chapter 6, which set out to monitor the environmental performance of the participating hotels and offer practical advice, especially to small independent hoteliers, on how they can manage their hotels in a more environmentally sensitive manner. This included encouraging them to reuse linen, use energy efficiently, take into consideration methods of rubbish disposal and even to consider replacing throwaway shampoo containers with shampoo dispensers in the bathroom. Such measures can provide substantial savings on costs for the hotels themselves, as well as helping to improve the environment as a whole and ensuring that, as far as possible, tourism in hotels is environmentally sustainable. This initiative has now been incorporated into the International Tourism Partnership, to encourage the wider tourism industry to consider the practical ways in which they can work towards greater sustainability.

EXAMPLE   Hotels go green

Hotel companies are working towards greater levels of waste reduction, as pressure to be more sustainable – and more cost-efficient – grows. Belgium-based Rezidor Hotel Group has encouraged many of its hotels to seek accreditation for its environmental management activities, including recognition from the Green Tourism Business Scheme, the Nordic Swan Eco-label and the Green Key. This is exemplified by the Radisson SAS Hotel in Edinburgh, which has worked on reducing carbon emissions through electricity savings, waste recycling and local purchasing

Another major chain, Marriott International, has been working with its supply chain to reduce its carbon footprint. This has been achieved though changing the everyday products they use; for example, purchasing toilet paper made from recycled materials. Marriott has also introduced sustainable room keys, replacing the 24 million plastic cards they use annually worldwide with a more environmentally friendly version.

Source: Gale, 2009

Catering

Distinguishing tourism catering

Catering, often seen along with hotels as distinct from other elements of the tourism product, is nevertheless a vital ingredient of the tourism experience, and, as we saw earlier in the discussion of gastronomy tourism in Chapter 10, it sometimes provides the prime motivation for a journey.

A day trip to a famous restaurant or a drive to visit a popular inn at the weekend are both familiar forms of excursion that must be included in statistics estimating tourists' expenditure. Similarly, longer holidays to France are often taken primarily or solely because of that country's strong tradition of outstanding food and drink.

One reason for the distinction between tourism and catering is that the latter is provided to both tourists and non-tourists alike (see, for example, Figure 12.8) and, as these two markets are seldom differentiated for statistical purposes, the exact contribution made

Figure 12.8 A traditional catering outlet serving the visitor and local alike

Photo by Claire Humphreys

by the hospitality sector to tourism is difficult to gauge. This is even truer of catering than accommodation as most guests staying at a hotel will be tourists, while many choosing to dine in a hotel restaurant or other eatery may well be locals simply enjoying a meal out. So while it may be difficult to make the distinction, we should be aware that our interest here will not be on institutional catering, which is generally non-tourism orientated (although even here we cannot be categorical, given that many people travelling on business to visit another office will eat in that office's staff restaurant), but it does largely discount all catering in schools and other places of education, factories and so on.

Catering consists of food and beverages, and tourism catering takes place in a range of facilities, to include hotels and motels, campsites and caravan parks, holiday camps and centres, restaurants, cafés, snack bars, pubs, nightclubs and even takeaway food shops. It will form an important element in many tourism-orientated facilities, including hotels, airports and catering outlets situated in popular tourist destinations like city centres and seaside resorts. In the latter, takeaways may provide a significant percentage of all food consumed by visitors, especially in the more downmarket resorts serving the needs of day trippers. The beauty of catering as a product is the variety of forms that it can take, ranging from a Michelin-starred restaurant to a humble takeaway, each offering a different experience and catering to very different markets.

EXAMPLE Record breaking catering

Visitors to the London 2012 Olympics have expected a record to be broken in the athletics, cycling, swimming or in one of the many other sports taking place. But a record was broken before the opening ceremony even took place.

Fast food giant McDonald's, a key sponsor of the Olympics since 1976, announced that one of its restaurants at the Olympic Park – there are four in all – is the biggest they have ever opened. This two-storey outlet can accommodate 1500 diners, and was forecast to serve 1.75 million meals during the 29 days of the Olympics and Paralympics.

Source: Ormsby, 2011

The meal experience

The **meal experience** can be said to comprise four elements:

● food and drink
● service
● decor, furnishing and fittings
● atmosphere.

By juggling these four elements, caterers can direct their efforts to reach a wide variety of niche markets, depending on the type of food served, its quality, level of service provided, the furnishings and price charged. A decision will be made as to whether the aim is to move customers through the eating place as quickly as possible, as in the case of many cafés in tourist destinations or hotels catering to tour operators' customers, or allow them to relax over a leisurely meal, as when dining in top-class restaurants – and commonly in many low-budget mainland European eating places; in Austria, racks with newspapers are often provided in city cafés, while in the UK newspapers, and perhaps now more commonly Wi Fi access, are provided. Such facilities are designed to encourage customers to linger over coffee or a meal.

Eating out in resorts popular with tourists has always been relatively price-sensitive, but excessive charges are not unusual, as we have seen in the case of Venice; and not only on the Continent – a recent report in the press drew attention to a charge of £9 for a bottle of mineral water in a central London restaurant! In line with rises in disposable income among tourists, the tendency has been to spend a greater proportion of one's holiday money on food and beverages. Just as, at one end of the price range, fast food and drink outlets like Starbucks, Costa, Burger King and the ubiquitous Irish pubs now proliferating all over Europe have benefited from this trend, so, at the other end of the market, have the higher-priced eating outlets moved to accommodate an increasing demand among tourists for exceptional meals, even if more budget accommodation is occupied.

Tourists today are seeking new experiences when they eat out. No longer satisfied with full-board or half-board deals that lock them into eating in their hotel, they seek different meal experiences each day. Some tourist hotels have tried to accommodate this need by allowing their guests to eat at other hotels in the area with which they have links; but the appeal of small, comfortable restaurants where they can eat well-cooked authentic local food is luring many tourists away from the all-inclusive package.

EXAMPLE Hungry for the familiar

Just as chain hotels offer guests a sense of security by knowing what to expect in terms of the product and service before they enter the premises, so the large catering chains provide a similar experience. Walk into a McDonald's the world over and the experience will largely be the same – with perhaps the menu offering a slightly different choice to cater for local tastes. This familiarity reassures and draws in the traveller.

As with hotels, many famous catering brands have expanded by offering franchise opportunities, notably including such names as McDonald's, Pizza Hut, Subway and Costa Coffee. These outlets are frequently present at transport hubs such as railway stations, catering for the needs of the travelling public.

Figure 12.9 This display kitchen lets the customer watch their food being prepared and freshly cooked. Le Touessrok, Mauritius

Photo by Claire Humphreys

As profits on food and beverage expenditure will often exceed those on the rooms, hotels are keen to do what they can to ensure their customers eat on the premises. Thus, hotels cater for their customers in restaurants, cafés, bars and through room service, and in larger hotels a range of different restaurants is provided, which might include ethnic food, a themed setting (such as a seafood restaurant), separate dining places to cater for business and leisure customers, group dining rooms for tour groups and one or more fast food outlets. In the Venetian Macao Resort Hotel, as one notable example, customers are faced with the choice of no fewer than 30 restaurants. Because of a commonly held view that the food in hotel restaurants is inferior to those found in nearby restaurants (a view not entirely without justification, especially in budget hotels where contract caterers may be delivering frozen food for microwave reheating), hotels are now making a greater effort to improve their food and service (see Figure 12.9), as well as offering greater choice to their customers.

EXAMPLE   **Are they eating in the hotel?**

Some years ago, the CEO of a large chain of corporate hotels in the USA visited a number of the properties incognito, to judge the extent to which customers were using the dining facilities. Addressing the concierges, elevator staff and receptionists, he asked each if they could recommend a good place to eat in the neighbourhood. He received lots of recommendations, but none suggested the hotel! The need to promote its own products was subsequently stressed to staff in the hotel's training programmes.

The problem of providing value for money is increased where group catering in hotels is concerned. Functions are widely catered for in hotels of all sizes from weddings to conferences, and the need to serve large groups quickly with a meal of an acceptable quality and still give good service is a challenge. This is frequently best met, in the case of large group meetings, by offering buffet rather than table service.

The widespread desire of people to experiment with new taste sensations is leading to much more adventurous dining out, and higher-priced restaurants are rising to the challenge. Heston Blumenthal, who has introduced highly unconventional food at his now world-famous restaurant The Fat Duck in Bray, Berkshire, has become renowned for such delicacies as snail porridge and mousse poached in liquid nitrogen. Sometimes, however, it is the bizarre that strikes a chord with customers, as exemplified by 'dining in the dark' – an idea initiated in 1999 by a restaurateur at Die Blinde Kuh in Zürich. His patrons, having selected their meals, are invited to eat in completely darkened rooms, served by blind waiters. The experience of such a key sense being removed allows diners to concentrate purely on the aroma of their food and its taste, which is said to enhance the experience. The restaurant has proved immensely popular and is fully booked at weekends for several months in advance. A Parisian restaurant, Dans le Noir, soon followed suit, but blindfolded its patrons; this proved so successful that a second was opened in London in 2005. Similar novelty meal experiences will undoubtedly follow.

Some restaurant chains have adopted a more conservative approach, but, by offering a unique dining experience, have shown that they can be hugely successful – one thinks of the Wagamama chain. Another successful innovation has been introduced at a restaurant in Israel, where e-menus have been provided on tables, enabling diners to order their meals from touch screens on the computers. This idea has also been adopted by uWink, a restaurant in Los Angeles, California, that allows each order to be customized to meet US demand. This not only cuts down on labour (much of the normal waiter service is dispensed with), but has actually boosted sales, particularly important for a busy restaurant where speed of service is a key ingredient.

In the UK, pubs have taken on a new lease of life as they have had to meet the challenges posed by drink driving laws and restrictions on smoking indoors (as well as threats that the EU will impose bans on outside heaters due to environmental considerations). Liberalization of the licensing laws, permitting alcohol to be served for more extended periods of the day, was one of the few rays of sunshine in an otherwise difficult period for this sector of the industry. This has helped to boost sales in pubs and inns catering particularly to stopover travellers, enabling the industry to compete more equally with its European neighbours. Many pubs have also now chosen to focus on food at the expense of beverages, with a large growth in the number of gastropubs, offering high-quality food. The evidence is that the hospitality industry can rise to the challenge of changing circumstances, with the result being greater flexibility and choice in eating out. While the quality and service of food in hotels still has a long way to go in the UK, the food and beverage sector generally is fast losing its reputation among international tourist markets for deplorable food and service.

Future developments in the hospitality sector

The recent history of the hospitality industry is dominated by the need for constant innovation to ward off competition by best meeting changing consumer demand for novelty and improved facilities. This pattern will surely continue, with markets broadly split between large chain hotels offering the wow factor, character properties marketed on the basis of architecture and history, fashion hotels, such as art hotels, filling niche markets and a rapidly growing budget sector selling not just on price but also on brand and image. The more extreme the design of the hotel, the less dependent it is on its location and, in a growing number of cases, the appeal will be the experience offered by the hotel rather than the location.

The growth of Internet-based review sites – one of the largest being TripAdvisor – means that hotels are now able to easily monitor the feedback their property is receiving from customers. As other travellers rely more heavily on this electronic word-of-mouth recommendation, so hotels must become more aware of the impact that negative experience can have on demand. TripAdvisor has over 40 million reviews from hotel guests, which include ratings of the service and facilities as well as comments on the stay, and hotels can respond on TripAdvisor to any of the reviews posted, though few hotels today are sufficiently aware of the power of social media to make use of these opportunities. Adversely, recent reports in the press have drawn attention to certain hotels paying guests, or upgrading them, for favourable comments – in some cases even posting their own reviews. As with all technology, websites can be open to misuse, making decisions more difficult for clients.

The challenge for the catering industry over the next few years, particularly at the budget end of the business, will be to control costs at a time when food prices are rocketing throughout the world. Good service and quality can, to some extent, compensate if it can be shown that the customer is receiving value for money. While fast food chains will continue to provide an important proportion of tourist meals, notably for younger travellers, there is evidence among older, better-off travellers that quality of food and service is more important than price and that, if restaurants deliver value for money to tourists, in attractive settings, they can thrive.

Questions and discussion points

1. What factors might influence whether a tourist chooses to stay in a chain hotel rather than a locally owned independent hotel of the same rating?

2. We discussed in this chapter the concept of 'glamping' – glamorous camping – which has grown in popularity over the past five years. Do you think this popularity can be sustained in the long term?

3. What factors influence whether hotel guests choose an all-inclusive catering package, whether they choose room-only accommodation, or something between these two extremes?

Tasks

1. In groups choose two hotels, one which should have more than 50 bedrooms and one which has fewer than 20 bedrooms. Interview the manager of each hotel to find out what are the key problems facing the hotel today. Compare and contrast the findings from these two interviews and present them to your colleagues.

2. Investigate the different loyalty schemes offered by hotel chains to identify the benefits of being a member. What is the value of the rewards in relation to the necessary spend? Do you think these membership schemes encourage repeat business?

Bibliography

Accor (2011) *Accor in Brief*, available online at: http://www.accor.com/fileadmin/user_upload/ Contenus_Accor/Commun/pdf/EN/accor_in_brief.pdf (accessed November 2011).

ARDA (2004) *Second homes and social trends*, Washington, DC, American Resort Development Association.

Beerbohm, M. (1921) Hosts and Guests, *And Even Now*, New York, Dutton, 127–146.

DCLG (2010) *Location of second homes, 2009–10*, English Housing Survey, available online at: http://www.communities.gov.uk/documents/housing/xls/1939640.xls (accessed November 2011).

ECC-Net (2009) *Classification of hotel establishments within the EU*, available online at: http:// ec.europa.eu/consumers/ecc/docs/hotel_establishment_classification_EU_en.pdf.

Gale, D. (2009) Green Around The Globe, *Hotels magazine*, 1 January.

IHG (2010) *Annual Report and Financial Statement 2010*, Buckinghamshire, Intercontinental Hotels Group.

Judge, E. (2006) Britons claim a place in the sun, *The Times*, 18 November.

Las Vegas Convention and Visitors Authority (2010) *Las Vegas Frequently asked questions*, Las Vegas Convention and Visitors Authority – Research Department, 11 March.

Lewis, A. (2011) Dumping timeshares, *The Wall Street Journal*, 20 February.

Lewis, P. (2005) Second homes, *Saga Magazine*, November.

Löfgren, O. (1999) *On Holiday: A history of vacationing*, Berkeley, CA, University of California Press.

O'Brien, T. (2011) Markets – Occupiers – Room Service – London's alive but needs more beds, *Property Week*, 18 March.

Ormsby, A. (2011) McDonald's super-size Olympics plan upsets health groups, *Reuters*, 21 July.

Thorpe, A. (2009) Pop-up hotels set to provide cheap temporary rooms, *The Observer*, 22 November.

VisitBritain (2010) *Overseas Visitors to Britain: Understanding Trends, Attitudes and Characteristics*, London, VisitBritain.

VisitCambridge (2009) *Surveys, Accommodation Stock & Visitor Figures 2008*, available online at: http://www.cambridge.gov.uk/public/docs/Tourism%20surveys%20and%20visitor%20 information.pdf (accessed November 2011).

VisitEngland (2010) The UK Tourist Statistics 2010, available online at: http://www.visiteng-land.org/Images/UK%20Tourist%202010%20FV_tcm30-28703.pdf (accessed November 2011).

VisitEngland (2011) *National Quality Assessment Scheme*, available online at: www.qualityin-tourism.com (accessed November 2011).

Visit London (2010) *London hotel development monitor*, London, Visit London and TRI Hospitality Consulting.

Websites

Dasparkhotel, Ottensheim: **www.dasparkhotel.net**

Gran Hotel Bali, Benidorm: **www.grupobali.com**

Module pop-up hotels: **www.m-hotel.org**

Organization for Timeshare in Europe: **www.ote-info.com**

Tripadvisor: **www.tripadvisor.com**

Underwater hotel: **www.poseidonresorts.com**

13

Tourist transport by air

Contents

Learning outcomes

After studying this chapter, you should be able to:

- understand the role that airlines and airports play in meeting the needs of tourism
- explain how air transport is organized and distinguish between different categories of airline operation
- understand the reasons for air regulation and the systems of regulation in force, both in the UK and internationally
- be aware of the dynamic nature of the airline business and the changes that have taken place in recent years
- analyse the reasons for success and failure of airlines' policies.

Heathrow is becoming a secondary hub ... Compare Heathrow's two runways to Europe's other major airports. Amsterdam Schiphol has five runways and Paris four. Frankfurt will soon open its fourth runway and Madrid is taking on a new strategic role as a major European hub with four runways and lots of room to grow. With the BA-Iberia merger, Madrid will gain the most from the UK's decision to stagnate Heathrow.

Giovanni Bisignani, Chief Executive Officer, IATA (A.B., 2011)

Introduction

Tourism is the outcome of people travelling, and the development of transport infrastructure is a key factor in its growth. The provision of adequate, safe, comfortable, fast and convenient public transport is a prerequisite for tourism. A tourist destination's accessibility is the outcome of, above all else, two factors: price (in absolute terms, as well as in comparison with competing destinations) and time (the actual or perceived time taken to travel between points of origin and destination).

Air travel (with a strong contribution from the no frills airlines in particular) has, over the past four decades, made short-, medium- and long-haul destinations accessible on both these counts, to an extent not previously imaginable. In doing so, it has substantially contributed to the phenomenon of mass market international tourism, with all the economic and social benefits and drawbacks that that has entailed. In the UK, consumer spending on air travel was £12.26 billion in 2010, and research suggests that it provides 141 000 direct jobs, with a further 93 000 jobs indirectly dependent on the industry (Oxera, 2009). That industry's growing carbon footprint, however, is giving increasing cause for concern.

Public transport, while an integral sector of the tourism industry, must also provide services that are not solely dependent on tourist demand. Road, rail and air services all owe their origins to government mail contracts, and the carriage of freight, whether separate from or together with passengers, makes a significant (and sometimes crucial) contribution to a carrier's revenue. It should also be recognized that many carriers provide a commercial or social service that owes little to the demands of tourists. Road and rail carriers, for example, provide essential commuter services for workers travelling between their places of residence and work. These carriers (and sometimes airlines, as in remoter districts of Scotland, and the mid-West in the USA) provide an essential social and economic transport network linking outlying rural areas with centres of industry and commerce, thus ensuring a communications lifeline for residents. The extent to which carriers can or should be commercially orientated while simultaneously being required to provide a network of unprofitable social routes is a constantly recurring issue in government transport policy.

Most forms of transport are highly **capital-intensive**. The cost of building and maintaining airports and regularly re-equipping airlines with new aircraft that have the latest technical advances requires massive investments of capital. Such levels of investment are available only to the largest corporations and, in some cases, subsidies from the public sector may be necessary for political or social reasons, such as those outlined above. At the same time, transport offers great opportunities for economies of scale, whereby unit prices can be dramatically reduced. For example, an airline operating out of a particular airport will have invested a huge amount of money upfront and will have to do so whether that airline operates flights four times a day or once a week. If those overheads can be distributed over a greater number of flights, however, the cost of an individual seat on a flight will fall.

Caution is advised, however, when considering economies of scale. There comes a point where an organization's further growth can result in diseconomies of scale, wiping out any former benefits gained as a result of size. The difficulties now faced by larger traditional airlines attempting to compete with the leaner, more efficient budget airlines point up exactly this dilemma. Major airlines, for reasons of prestige, have in the past tended to opt for expensively furnished high-rent city centre offices, imposing added burdens on overheads; today, they have generally opted to move out to airport locations. It is the subsidized airlines of the developing nations that retain their high-rent offices in city centres.

The airline business

In Chapter 3, we explored the way in which the development of air transport in the second half of the twentieth century contributed to the growth of tourism, whether for business or pleasure. Here we will explore the airline business of today in more detail.

Travel by air has become safe, comfortable, rapid and, above all, cheap, for two reasons. The first is the enormous progress in aviation **technology** that has occurred during this period, especially following the development of the jet airliner after World War II. The first commercial jet (the De Havilland Comet, operated by BOAC) came into service on the London–Johannesburg route in 1952. Problems with metal fatigue resulted in the early withdrawal from service of this aircraft, but the introduction of the hugely successful Boeing 707 – in service first with Pan American Airways in 1958 – and later the first jumbo jet, the Boeing 747, which went into service in 1970, led to rapid falls in seat cost per passenger kilometre (a common measure of revenue yield). The costs fell in both absolute terms and relative to costs of other forms of transport, particularly passenger shipping, which up to the mid-1950s had dominated the long-haul travel business.

Both engine and aircraft design have since been continuously refined and improved. The wings, fuselage and engines have been designed to reduce drag, and the engines have also become more efficient and less fuel-hungry. Increases in carrying capacity for passengers and freight have steadily reduced average seat costs, with jumbo jets accommodating up to 500 passengers.

The next phase in this development arrived in 2008, when the Airbus 'superjumbo' A380 – a double-decker aircraft seating between 550 and 800 passengers – entered service (initially with Singapore Airlines, see Figure 13.1), promising further economies of scale. Prices to passengers can only fall, however, if a high proportion of all those seats are filled. In the past, sudden jumps in capacity posed problems for airlines on some routes until seat demand caught up with supply.

Figure 13.1 The Airbus A380, in service with Singapore Airlines
© Iain Masterton/Alamy

Operating the A380

The Airbus A380 has been described as the 'new generation in flying' (Chance, 2010). The design of this vast jetliner required airports to strengthen runways and build new stands to accommodate the double-deck design and increased wingspan.

Seen as one solution to the increasingly congested skies, the Airbus A380 provided not just greater passenger capacity from one take-off slot, but improved environmental credentials; it produces less CO_2 per passenger than any other aircraft currently in service by major airlines. The design process also focused on reducing noise emissions, important in meeting airport regulations on night-time landings.

The operational costs per passenger are expected to be lower, but this is dependent on having demand to match; this may impact on the routes, and the airlines that will be prepared to invest in the A380. By July 2011, Singapore Airlines and Emirates were the primary users, although Lufthansa, Air France and Qantas have all ordered around a dozen of these aircraft each.

Of course, the introduction of these huge new aircraft poses other problems, too. They need reinforced runways, space to accommodate the wider wingspan when on airport stands, and new methods of ground handling had to be devised. There is the requirement to load and unload up to 1600 passengers for one aircraft within a limited space of time, too, which is challenging and requires extensively redesigned terminals. There are precedents, in the loading and unloading of cruise ships, which are now being designed to take up to 5000 passengers, all of whom have to be disgorged in a short space of time for excursions at ports of call.

The motivation behind the development of such large aircraft is not simply efficiency – it also helps to overcome problems caused by growing congestion at airports throughout the world. This is becoming critical at leading hub airports, where there are already acute shortages of take-off and landing slots.

The supersonic Concorde was perhaps the only aircraft the design of which ran counter to this drive for economies of scale. Introduced into service in 1976, Concorde carried 100 passengers at speeds in excess of 1400 miles per hour. Quite apart from the technical problems that have to be overcome when designing an aircraft for supersonic flight, speeds above Mach 1 substantially increase fuel burn, so most current airliners fly at around Mach 0.85, just subsonic. On some key global routes, however, speed is more important than cost and business travellers, celebrities and other wealthy air travellers were prepared to pay highly for the privilege of cutting their travelling time. In spite of this, the high cost of operation, restriction in the numbers that could be carried, its comparatively short range and the excessive noise it made limited Concorde's use largely to routes over oceans rather than land. The initial high development costs were written off by the UK and French governments and services were limited to flights between New York (and, initially, Washington) and London or Paris. The crash of a chartered Concorde in France in 2000 led to the grounding of all these aircraft and, despite modifications allowing a relaunch of this plane in 2001, it was removed from regular service in 2003 – the termination of any form of supersonic travel for the foreseeable future.

Replacing the large commercial supersonic aircraft will be a new breed of small executive jets currently under development. One such aircraft, the Cessna Citation X, is already in service and capable of reaching Mach 0.92, very close to the speed of sound. For the present, the industry is putting its faith in demand for just-subsonic aircraft satisfying the executive market for the next few years.

EXAMPLE A star attraction

Concorde became an iconic plane and, despite never being likely to cover the development costs, it has a place in aviation history. Once it was announced that the plane would be withdrawn from regular service the opportunity to fly on the final flights was widely sought. Ticket prices were reportedly in the region of $8000 as enthusiasts sought to experience supersonic travel while the chance existed.

Since then, the remaining 18 planes have mostly been located at air museums in the UK and North America – although Charles de Gaulle Airport in Paris and Heathrow Airport in London each retain one of these pieces of aviation history. Unfortunately, at Heathrow conflicting opinions between BA and BAA (owner of the airport) has resulted in the plane being moved from display and located on BA land away from the main passenger areas.

Since being grounded, these planes have proved popular attractions at their air museum homes. When it was announced that the plane on display at Filton Aerodrome in Bristol, UK, was to be taken out of public display indefinitely, tickets to see this attraction rocketed.

Periodically, crises have occurred in world oil supplies, resulting in escalating fuel costs. This had a huge impact on aircraft costs from 1973 to 1974 and, again, following the Gulf War in 1991, the 9/11 crisis in 2001, the subsequent war in Iraq and its aftermath. Although in the past these crises have proved to be generally of short duration, the on-going Middle East crisis and the rapid escalation in the cost of oil since 2007 further threatens to make aviation fuel far costlier over the next few years.

Some carriers will hedge by buying 20–65% of their fuel forward, helping to mitigate the worst impacts of escalating prices; for example, at the beginning of 2011 both United and Southwest had hedged around 63% of their fuel needs. Hedging will usually allow an airline the option to buy fuel at a set price in the future, and this option will only be taken if the price of fuel is higher than the agreed price. However, hedging is expensive as the risk is passed to the insurer who charges a premium for this peace of mind. An alternative hedging approach is one taken by Delta Airlines, which hedged fuel costs within a range of $75–90 a barrel in 2011. This meant that if the price of oil rose, the maximum they would pay was $90, although if the price fell then they would still have to pay a minimum of $75 per barrel. The gamble of hedging can be seen by looking at the prices of oil in 2008: it started the year at $90 a barrel and finished the year at $40, having surpassed $140 dollars during the summer period. Although hedging can bring stability to the balance sheet, the cost of this risk-reduction may not be justified, and some airlines, for example US Airways, have not hedged fuel needs in recent years.

EXAMPLE Are attitudes to fuel hedging shifting?

Nok Air, an Asian budget airline, part-owned by Thai Airways, has adamantly refused to get involved in fuel hedging, suggesting it is akin to gambling and likely to lose the business money.

More recently Emirates, who claim to be the world's largest airline (based on international passenger kilometres flown) announced that it has reduced its reliance of hedging, accepting that volatility in oil prices has meant they are spending less time trying to manage the risk.

Emirates' reticence is understandable. In 2007-08 the company saved $242 million (Kohlman, 2011) through hedging, but the following year had to write off almost twice that amount, having been locked into prices higher than those on the open market.

Of greater concern, however, is the realization that oil supplies are not infinite. Demand is growing sharply and will outstrip supplies within 20–40 years, even after allowing for new finds. Moreover, oil prices are unstable and can fluctuate rapidly. Prices are expected to remain high in the future, given the demand from new economic powerhouses such as China and India and the world political climate. Consequently, the aircraft industry is searching in the short term for new ways to improve fuel economy, but, in the longer term, it will be imperative to discover new means of powering aircraft, unless the industry is willing to embrace a sharp drop in the overall number of flights operated.

Many experts believe that the jet engine has now reached a stage of evolutionary sophistication that will make it increasingly difficult to produce further economies, so cost-cutting exercises have replaced technological innovation as a means of reducing prices to the public. To achieve weight reductions, some airlines have reduced the number of beverages carried, withdrawn seat phones, replaced divisions between classes with curtains and even withdrawn or reduced the number of pages in their in-flight magazines.

 EXAMPLE **Losing weight can save money**

Airlines are now making strenuous efforts to reduce the weight of the onboard equipment and catering. Investigation has considered the use of lighter seats, carrying less water for the washroom taps, and swapping the pilot's flight manuals for electronic versions accessible on tablets similar in style to iPads. This final initative could provide a weight reduction of 3 kilos per pilot, and an estimated saving of over $400 000 a year (Mathews, 2010).

In a move which has duel benefits for the environment, Singapore Airlines has trialled the introduction of an electronic version of its in-flight magazines, removing the printing costs of production as well as reducing the fuel burn for transporting these documents.

To save fuel, airlines have been shutting off an engine during taxiing, cleaning aircraft exteriors more frequently to reduce drag and removing dropped coins from the cabins. Gaining a confirmed landing time is also important because it can avoid the expense of circling at the destination airport. Finally, in a move also used by ships, cruising at a slower speed is now used to reduce fuel burn.

Airlines are obliged to carry some reserves of fuel for emergencies, but on certain routes they will also carry excess fuel in order to avoid refuelling at airports where fuel costs are high. Airlines facing low profits from competition have to weigh up the advantages of introducing the latest fuel-efficient aircraft against the high capital costs of buying them – a problem that will be discussed later in this chapter.

The search for more economy goes on all the same, however. There are promising developments in recent research that suggest the problems of carrying liquefied hydrogen rather than kerosene as fuel have been largely overcome. This would provide three times the energy per unit and allow aircraft to increase their range substantially. And, although engine technology may have peaked, advances are still being made in lightweight construction materials by aircraft manufacturers: techniques like ALM (additive layer manufacturing), in which powdered plastic and metal are melted together, are expected to lead to fuselages and wings up to 65% lighter than present materials. The European Aeronautic Defence and Space Company (EADS) has estimated that a weight reduction of just 1 kilo can save $3000 in fuel costs each year, amounting to a saving of $90 000 over the 30-year lifespan of the average aircraft (West, 2011). Multiplying this by the weight of the aircraft frame gives some indication of the massive cost saving potential of lightweight materials.

During the 1980s, the technological focus changed to the development of quieter aircraft and aircraft capable of taking off from, and landing on, shorter runways. The emphasis on quieter engines originated in the USA, where controls on noise pollution have forced airlines to re-equip their fleets or fit expensive modifications to existing aircraft. In turn, the airlines press their governments to relax controls over night flying as it would enable them to operate around the clock, easing congestion and increasing their productivity. The UK government – at one time reluctant to permit more than a token increase in night flying, especially from the London airports – is now under pressure to allow more flexibility, to reduce congestion.

Short take-off and landing (STOL) aircraft built by companies such as Fokker, Short and Saab for commuter services, seating 30–50 passengers, and slightly larger aircraft built for regional services, typically carrying 70–110 passengers, such as BAe Systems' RJX, Fairchild Dornier's 728 and 928JET and the Bombardier and Embraer CRJ and ERJ families, have all helped to revolutionize business travel, allowing airports to be sited much closer to city centres.

EXAMPLE   London City Airport

London City Airport, situated in the Docklands area, is an example of such a development that has been partly dependent on STOL technology for its success. The airport was initially hampered by the lack of good connections to central London and a short-sighted marketing decision to promote the airport exclusively as a business airport, with the expectation that passengers would arrive by taxi. The weakness of this strategy quickly became evident and public transport connections were encouraged. The airport now operates profitably and surface connections have improved with the construction and opening of a Docklands Light Railway station within the grounds, providing connections with the London Underground service. The result is that services and routes have now expanded substantially. Over 67 000 flights took off from this airport in 2010, transporting 2 750 000 passengers around Europe.

Its focus on the business traveller has not been lost, however. With a journey time of 25 minutes from the centre of London to the airport, and with short check-in times - 15 minutes for passengers with no hold luggage - BA chose the airport for its London–New York, business class only flights.

Another factor in the development of mass travel by air was the enterprise and creativity demonstrated by both air transport management and other entrepreneurs in the tourism industry. At a time of strictly regulated prices, the introduction of net inclusive tour-basing fares for tour operators, variable pricing techniques, such as advance purchase excursion (APEX) tickets and standby fares, helped to stimulate demand and fill aircraft seats. Later, innovative carriers introduced frequent flyer programmes (FFP), in which passengers are given additional free miles based on the mileage they accumulate with a carrier or one of its partners.

The budget airlines

By far the most important development in recent years has been the growth of **low-cost no frills airlines**. Prompted by the deregulation of the airline industry in the USA, many small regional carriers came into being to fight for a share of the potentially lucrative domestic airline market. Many, such as People's Express, faded quickly, but others, such as Southwest Airlines (formed as the first low-cost airline in 1971) maximized new opportunities and went from strength to strength – Southwest is now the largest domestic carrier in the world (in terms of the number of passengers carried), with over 106 million passengers (IATA, 2011).

With the liberalization of air transport in the EU a few years later, an explosion of no frills carriers emerged, led by Ryanair, which, under Michael O'Leary, sought initially to challenge the hold over the Irish market held by Aer Lingus, later undercutting fares and developing new routes to regional airports throughout Europe. The entrepreneur Stelios Haji-Ioannou followed with the launch of easyJet.

These and other small carriers, together with rising seat-only sales on the charter carriers' aircraft, were soon impacting on the profitability of major airlines, forcing them to develop their own low-cost offshoots, initially with mixed success. Both BA's and KLM's early attempts to compete via their budget brands Go and Buzz met with failure and they were absorbed into the easyJet and Ryanair empires, respectively.

Inevitably, the leading 'heritage' or full-service airlines must decide whether to take the budget airlines on at their own game or distance themselves from this sector of the market by premium pricing. The budget airlines are here to stay and represent a growing proportion of the overall market for passenger services by air. At the time of writing, there were around 40 low-cost airlines operating in Europe, carrying over 100 million passengers annually to more than 400 destinations – coincidentally, transforming the economies of many of those places.

Budget carriers have also thrived in other parts of the world. In the USA, to take one example, more than a dozen budget airlines were trading profitably up to the point where fuel prices began to spiral. Apart from Southwest, they include Frontier Airlines, Spirit Airlines (the first ultra-low-cost airline in the USA), WestJet Airlines, AirTran Airways and Jetblue Airways (in which Lufthansa made a 19% investment in 2006). These budget brands serve a wide network of routes throughout North America, including some routes into the Caribbean and Latin America, and carry many millions of passengers (see Table 13.1). Some of the established North American carriers made efforts to compete by forming their own budget brands, but with only limited success – Delta's Song was absorbed into the main carrier in 2006, and the activities of United's Ted were reincorporated into the operations of the parent company in 2009.

Table 13.1 Revenue passenger numbers* for North American low-cost carriers

Airline	Passenger numbers in 2010 (millions)
Southwest	88.2
AirTran	24.7
JetBlue	24.3
WestJet	15.2
Frontier	9.6

* Airlines can measure their passenger numbers by counting those who have been **enplaned** (which would include infants, those travelling on free flights gained through frequent flyer schemes, etc.) or by counting **revenue passengers** (those who have paid a commercial fare for their travel). The difference between these can be substantial. For example Southwest enplaned 106 million passengers in 2010 but flew only 88.2 million revenue passengers.

Source: Flightglobal, 2011

EXAMPLE   All you can fly tickets

In both 2009 and 2010, JetBlue offered unlimited travel tickets for one set fee – $699 in 2010. This 'all you can jet' pass allowed the holder travel on all JetBlue routes for 30 days. The pass operated between September and October, traditionally a quiet time for the airline, and this helped to fill seats.

Passengers were required to book their travel online and penalties for not flying on reserved seats were quite severe – a $100 fine and complete withdrawal of the pass. The airline did, however, allow cancellations up to three days before departure with no penalty. JetBlue only issued a limited number of these passes, and all sold out.

Social media discussions of this pass provided extensive – and mostly positive – coverage of the company's routes while press coverage of the charity auction of the last remaining pass for 2010 further enhanced awareness of the company. JetBlue clearly benefited from offering these passes.

Specialist niche carriers emerged to attract the top end of the market, creaming passengers from the business and first class seats of the established carriers. On transatlantic services, ill-fated American operators MaxJet and Eos and UK operator Silverjet introduced all-business class configurations, with fares aimed at undercutting the lead carriers. With smaller fleets than the budget carriers, however, these premium services do not benefit from the economies of scale available to the lead carriers. MaxJet went into receivership in 2007, followed by Eos and Silverjet the following year.

Low-cost medium- and long-haul airlines have now started to emerge; adapting the traditional business model which would rely on fast turnaround times allowing planes to cover multiple routes daily. Early into this market were Zoom – operating primarily on transatlantic routes – and Oasis, which served London and Vancouver from their base in Hong Kong. Both ceased trading in 2008. This has not deterred the industry though, and AirAsia X (the long-haul arm of budget airline AirAsia) has received praise for its operations serving longer routes using a low fare approach whereby customers pay for in-flight entertainment, food and even blankets.

The global recession at the end of the first decade of the twenty-first century has changed the travel behaviour of premium class passengers, with discounted tickets now being expected as part of the corporate agreements for business travel; and at the top end, passengers who would have considered first class passage now giving greater consideration to the use of private charters to meet their travel needs. This has significantly changed the trading landscape for both the low-cost carriers and the full-service airlines.

The organization of air transport

It is convenient to think of the civil aviation business as being composed of a number of elements, namely:

- equipment manufacturers
- airports
- air navigation and traffic control services
- airlines.

As was mentioned earlier, each of these is not dependent only on tourists for its livelihood. Apart from non-tourist civilian passengers, they also serve the needs of the military, as well as those of freight and mail clientele, but the tourist market is important for each of these elements so they must be included as components of the tourism industry.

Equipment manufacturers

Equipment manufacturers are made up of companies manufacturing commercial airframes and engines. The demand for airframes (fuselages and wings) can be conveniently divided between those for large jet aircraft – typically carrying between 130 and 500 passengers, which provide the bulk of passenger services throughout the world – and those for smaller aircraft – seating as few as 18 passengers, which are employed chiefly on business routes or provide feeder services from rural airports. Separately classified are those companies manufacturing private jets, such as the Learjet, typically seating just four to nine passengers. This last category also has a role to play in business tourism, as these jets are extensively employed in air taxi services, discussed later in this chapter.

The world demand for airframes is dominated by just two manufacturers, each of which has a roughly equal share of the market: the US-owned Boeing Aircraft Company (which swallowed what was then the second-largest airframe manufacturer, McDonnell Douglas, in 1997) and Airbus Integrated Company (AIC), the consortium responsible for building the European Airbus, 80% of which is built in mainland Europe and 20% (the wings) by BAe Systems in the UK. Airbus is now owned in part (51%) by Sogeade (representing Lagardère and Sogepa, the French state holding company), together with German-owned Daimler and SEPI (the Spanish state holding company), with the remaining 49% held by institutional investors and employees.

The first challenge to the duopoly of these giant manufacturers (since the demise of McDonnell Douglas) appeared in 2008 when Canadian-owned Bombardier announced its intention to build a competitive aircraft for the short-haul market, currently due in 2013, to be known as the C-Series. Bombardier is working in collaboration with COMAC, a corporation established by the Chinese government to reduce dependency on Airbus/ Boeing aircraft (COMAC's own competitive C919 is due onstream around 2014). They are also working currently on short- and medium-range aircraft, but expectations are that developing a long-haul, transcontinental jetliner will eventually be on their agenda. Finally, the Russian aircraft manufacturer, United Aircraft Company, is also expecting to have a competitive short-haul aircraft, the Irkut MS-21, in the sky by 2014.

A handful of small companies build airframes, generally for smaller aircraft operating largely on regional routes. The two most important of these are Bombardier and Embraer of Brazil. Several others have failed in recent years, including Fairchild, Dornier, de Havilland, Fokker, Shorts and Saab, while BAe ceased manufacturing regional jets in 2001. There are other potential challengers for the lucrative global markets in the shape of the Russians, who are marketing the Antonov 85-passenger 148 jet, and Sukhoi, who are part-nering Boeing to develop the Superjet 100. Both are specifically designed for short-haul routes. China and Japan are also threatening to compete with the lead manufacturers in the longer term.

Aircraft engines are manufactured quite separately, and three companies dominate this market: GE Aircraft Engines (USA), Pratt & Whitney (USA) and Rolls-Royce (UK). Due to the intense competition for contracts to supply engines to new airliners as they come onstream, these manufacturers, and other smaller companies, often cooperate in engine design and construction. One consortium set up for this purpose is International Aero Engines (IAE), comprising Pratt & Whitney, Rolls-Royce, MTU Aero Engines of Germany and Aero Engines Corporation of Japan. General Electric and Snecma (of France) co-operate under the banner of CFM International Aero Engines and Europrop Interna-tional comprises Rolls-Royce, Snecma, MTU Aeroengines and ITP (Industria de Turbo Propulsores). Pratt & Whitney and GE Aircraft Engines have worked together in the USA on the production of aero engines for the A380 superjumbo, in competition with Rolls-Royce.

As with airframes, we can see that this market, too, is effectively controlled by an oligopoly and the cost of aircraft development and production is now so high that international cooperation between the leading companies has become inevitable.

A single Airbus A340 costs $150–240 million, before discounts; an A380 around $300 million. From this, one can clearly see the importance of this industry to the coun-tries where they are built and, particularly, the regions in which aircraft frames and engines are constructed. Indeed, aviation represents some 10% of the US economy, with a million employees. The economic health of Seattle, headquarters of Boeing, is substantially depen-dent on the aviation industry. Toulouse in France and towns such as Broughton (North Wales, where Airbus A380 wings are built), Derby and Filton, near Bristol, are key centres of aircraft manufacture, and the economy of these cities and towns depends to a large extent on demand for new aircraft. Such demand is subject to global political and eco-nomic changes, however, so is extremely volatile.

Nevertheless, the potential long-term economic benefits of aircraft manufacture are such that other fast-developing low-cost countries are keen to enter the field, often with the backing of Western aircraft companies. The world's fourth-largest airframe manufacturer, Embraer, for example, is partly owned by a consortium of European aircraft manufacturers.

One further point to note is that aircraft, wherever they are manufactured in the world, are priced in US dollars, so currency shifts between the dollar and the euro are critical. Airbus costs are mainly in euros, so a hardening of this currency against the dollar – as occurred in 2007/08 – is detrimental to Airbus profitability, making it harder to sell aircraft on the world market, while Boeing's task is made easier. Cheaper dollars, however, would make it attractive for Airbus to buy more parts from US sources.

EXAMPLE   **The demand for commercial aircraft**

Despite the market downturn of recent years, the demand for commercial aircraft from Canadian-based Bombardier is looking positive. As an emerging competitor to the duopoly of Airbus and Boeing, it is now gaining orders for commercial planes on a scale to justify the investment in research and development (see Table 13.2).

Table 13.2 Demand for commercial aircraft

	Bombardier	Airbus	Boeing
New orders in 2010 (2009)	93 (88)	574 (271)	530 (142)
Deliveries in 2010 (2009)	97 (121)	510 (498)	462 (481)

These data do not take into account orders for small jets for executive hire or private use. Bombardier delivered over 100 business aircraft in 2010.

It is important to be aware that the number of new aircraft being ordered by airlines fluctuates wildly based on market conditions. For example, Boeing received orders for over 1000 aircraft in the three years between 2005 and 2007, but accepted orders for less than 300 planes in the two years prior to that. The low levels at the early part of the decade may be attributed, in part, to the restructuring which took place in the airline industry following events of 9/11. Later on, a greater number of jetliners were ordered as the airlines needed to replace ageing fleets with more fuel-efficient craft.

The introduction of the new A380 superjumbo in 2008 represents a significant gamble for the aircraft industry as to whether the future success of airlines will depend on high-frequency, low-volume routes or low-frequency, high-volume routes. This aircraft normally accommodates up to 550 passengers, although a single-class version, carrying up to 850 passengers, may be marketed for high-density routes like short domestic flights in Japan, where existing Boeing 747s are already operating with 569 seats.

Airbus Industrie is convinced that there is a market for these giant aircraft because the decreasing availability of take-off and landing slots at major airports and the growth of international air traffic favour large jets. It believes that around 35–40 city pairs have reached saturation point and expansion can only be achieved by increasing the passenger capacity of each aircraft.

To take one example, it is estimated that the advent of the A380 would allow London Heathrow to handle an additional 10 million passengers each year. In early 2008, the company upped its forecasted demand for superjumbos such as the A380 to 1700, then worth some £260 billion, and, by early 2008, it had taken firm orders amounting to 192. Airbus estimated its original breakeven point as being 250 aircraft, since adjusted to 370, but independent aviation experts have variously estimated it to be at between 420 and 515 aircraft, with escalating costs and disadvantageous exchange rates possibly driving this number up still further.

The manufacturer was hit by several serious delays due to technical problems in wiring up the aircraft, with repercussions on future orders. Only Singapore Airlines was able to get the aircraft into service by 2008, while major orders from carriers such as Emirates were delayed, although they now have more than a dozen operating in their fleet.

Boeing, on the other hand, is convinced that future demand is for fewer trunk routes and more point-to-point services, which require small- to medium-sized jets. Its own forecast is for fewer than 500 superjumbos and it claims that only some 15 routes could support such giants. If proved correct, it will be touch and go whether Airbus can ever recoup the huge investment needed to build these aircraft. Boeing has cancelled proposals to build a competing superjumbo aircraft, the so-called Sonic Cruiser (there have been a number of possible 'rethinks' about this strategy as Boeing would be severely disadvantaged if the superjumbo were to prove a success). It is also known to have considered the feasibility of building a blended-wing delta-shaped aircraft with an 800-seat capacity that would require a fuel load less than three-quarters that of a traditional jumbo and be far quieter in operation.

In the meantime, its strategy is to develop the new 787 Dreamliner – a 200–300-seat passenger aircraft with a range of 7600 miles at an estimated cost of $160 million – as a replacement for the current generation of 757 and 767 aircraft. It claims this will be 20% more fuel-efficient than the current 767 and, based on present industry estimates, it is also likely to be more fuel-efficient than the superjumbo, at 2.6 litres per passenger per 100 km, compared with estimates of 2.9 litres in the A380. This is largely due to lightweight materials used in the fuselage, which will be constructed of carbon fibre-reinforced plastic (CFRP), rather than aluminium, while the A380's fuselage is composed of a mix of CFRP and GLARE – a similarly lightweight laminate of aluminium and glass-fibre-reinforced glue.

The Boeing 787 Dreamliner was expected to be in service by the end of 2011 following several delays in construction, and Boeing is predicting sales of 3100 aircraft (with some 2000 757/767 aircraft then expected to be withdrawn from service over the next 20 years). It proved to be one of the fastest-selling aircraft of all time, with 817 orders placed by the beginning of 2008. However, enthusiasm has faded since then as extensive cancellations have meant that only 30 additional craft were ordered by the end of 2010. While waiting for delivery to come onstream, Boeing will concentrate on extending sales of its 747-400ER (extended range) jumbo and the smaller, reliable and cost-efficient 737-900 'workhorse' for the cheaper end of the industry.

EXAMPLE **Cancelling orders**

In March 2011, Etihad Airways cancelled its order for four 787 Dreamliners, following the announcement by Boeing that delivery would be delayed – the seventh delay to be announced. Etihad's current expansion plans meant that they did not want to wait, instead ordering three 777s to enhance their fleet.

An earlier cancellation for this aircraft had been received from AirBerlin, who decided to reduce their order from 25 Dreamliners to just 15. For AirBerlin the decision was taken to meet their strategic shift towards serving medium- rather than long-haul routes.

It is clear that the airlines and the aircraft manufacturers are heavily reliant on the operational activities of each other when the time-delay between design, construction and delivery of aircraft is many years.

Boeing currently produces the 777-200LR with a range of 10 847 miles. This provides airlines with by far the longest-range aircraft in the world, theoretically capable of non-stop flights between London and Australia (although the popular route to Sydney would be questionable, being against the prevailing winds). The longest commercial flight in the world at present is the New York to Singapore route – an $18^1/_2$-hour flight using Airbus 340-500s and covering a distance of nearly 10 000 miles. Whether or not passengers would be willing to travel even further than this without a stopover is open to question.

A second proposal was announced in 2005, to construct a new version of the 747-400, to be called the 747-8. This is to carry 467 passengers with a range of 14 800 km (similar to the Airbus A380) and the company sees this as filling a gap (in passenger capacity) between the 777 and A380.

Not to be outdone, and to the chagrin of Boeing, Airbus has plans to compete with the Dreamliner, too. Its A350 is designed in three models: the A350-800 will accommodate 270 passengers in a three-class configuration, while the longer-range A350-900 will carry 314 passengers. The A350-1000 will have capacity for 350 passengers and a range of 15 500 km. The design of this aircraft is believed to embrace materials that are fully composite in construction – that is, up to 70% of components are to be built of reinforced or hardened plastics. This will substantially cut weight and, therefore, reduce the amount of fuel burned. If problems similar to those facing the current generation of new aircraft are encountered, however, it is predicted that the A350-900 will appear in 2013, with the other two models following in 2016 and 2017.

After the advent of deregulation in the USA and Europe, as noted earlier, there was a demand for smaller aircraft to provide feeder services from rural (so-called 'spoke') airports into hub airports, where people would then catch their long-haul or intercontinental flights. This demand was met by small aircraft, either twin turboprops or, seating 50 or more, pure jets. Since then, passengers have demonstrated a preference for direct flights between regional airports, even if at slightly higher fares, with a resultant increase in the passenger-carrying capacity of aircraft and the demise of several manufacturers of smaller aircraft.

Airports

Airport ownership varies from country to country. Sometimes they are state-owned (often by local authorities), but elsewhere they may be in private ownership or else ownership will be split between the public and private sectors. In many German airports, for example, local and state governments share responsibility for running the airport, while in Milan, control is exercised by a combination of regional and local government and private enterprise. In Spain, all 47 airports (and some outside the country) are operated by the government-owned Aeropuertos Españoles y Navegacion Aerea (AENA) – the world's largest airport operator, which also runs all air traffic control in the country. In Portugal, Sweden, Finland and the Czech Republic, all airports have majority share ownership in the hands of the government. ACI Europe (2010) report that 78% of European airports are publically owned – although these airports handle only 52% of European passenger traffic, highlighting that private investors are chiefly operating at larger airports. Figure 13.2 shows airport ownership by sector for a number of European countries.

In the UK, it has been the practice in recent years for local authorities to divest themselves of their local airport ownership and return it to the private sector. Newcastle, Bristol, Leeds-Bradford and Exeter Airports have all been recently privatized, but Manchester Airport Group is a holding company comprising ten local authorities and operates not only Manchester Airport itself but also Bournemouth, Humberside and East Midlands Airports. A number of other local authorities retain a minority investment in Birmingham Airport. The significance of state ownership is that overheads and direct costs are more easily concealed, enhancing the airport's performance figures – on paper, at least.

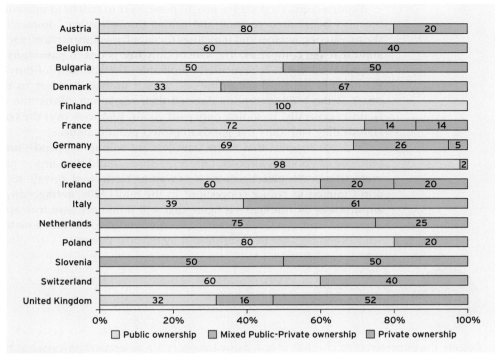

Figure 13.2 Ownership of airports by sector (%)

Source: ACI Europe, 2010

Under private ownership, however, it is easier to raise money to expand or develop new ventures.

Of the privatized airports, six in the UK – including two in the London area (Heathrow and Stansted) – are owned and operated by BAA – a private company formed by the denationalization of the former state-run British Airports Authority, under the terms of the Airports Bill (1985). BAA also owns and operates some airports overseas. In 2007, BAA was bought by ADI International, led by Spanish company Ferrovial, and these airports have been responsible for six of the world's fastest-growing long-haul routes since the turn of the century (closely followed by Singapore), with the key London–New York routes attracting 2 518 000 to J F Kennedy Airport and over a million to Newark, NJ in 2010.

Many of the airlines using these four airports would like to see BAA broken up to improve services, provide more competition and hold prices down – a move that now has the support of the Competition Commission. Its report, in early 2009, recommended the hiving off of three airports. Following this, Gatwick was sold to Global Infrastructure Partners (GIP) and the sale of Stansted and Edinburgh is expected to follow.

Airports are experiencing geometric growth, with some 4.6 billion passengers worldwide in 2010, according to the Airports Council International. Within the UK alone, some 210 million passengers passed through airports that year and even conservative forecasts expect this to increase to at least 470 million by 2030 (more extreme forecasts offer a figure of 500 million by 2021). The UK's leading airport – London's Heathrow, which handled a total of 65 million passengers in 2010 – remains the busiest international airport in the world. Atlanta, Beijing and Chicago Airports have greater throughputs when domestic passengers are taken into account, however – Atlanta handled some 89 million in 2010. Passenger numbers travelling through Beijing Airport are escalating rapidly, with an increase of 13% seen between 2009 and 2010 alone.

Airports require a good balance of passengers to freight to maximize their profitability, but also boost their revenue and profits through other commercial activities, such as shops, catering services and franchises for supplementary services, such as foreign exchange and car rental companies. The sale of duty-free goods to passengers booked to travel on international flights is particularly profitable. The abolition of duty-free sales within the EU in 1999 impacted on airline and airport profitability, but, in the latter case, it was offset as the leading airports directed their marketing efforts into expanding shopping facilities generally, including duty-paid goods. BAA took over the largest company in the USA dealing with duty-free goods to protect profit margins.

Evidence suggests that many travellers are willing to spend time and money on the purchase of goods at airports. One 1997 study found that airport profits rise by 20% for every 10 minutes passengers are kept waiting by delayed aircraft, so it is hardly in an airport's interest to reduce congestion! In the mid-1990s, average 'dwell' time at European airports was 94 minutes – a figure that will doubtless have increased as congestion has worsened, and check-in times have been extended to devote more time to screening passengers and baggage in a world beset by terrorist threats.

EXAMPLE **Time to relax**

Despite the opportunity to check-in online, many travellers are now spending longer at the airport. Queues for the baggage drop and increased security checks have meant that airlines often suggest passengers should arrive three hours in advance of their departure time for an international flight.

So on those days when queues are short and the formalities are processed rapidly, what is done with those extra couple of hours? Airports now provide an extensive range of shopping opportunities to enhance their revenue stream – and with security regulations now restricting liquids in hand luggage, items such as water and toiletries are often important purchases. Once the shopping is over, passengers can also choose to spend their time in the bars and restaurants, also conveniently provided as a revenue-earner for the airport. However, passengers now have an alternative place to spend their time.

Many passengers are choosing to pay to use an airport lounge. Historically, these were operated by airlines (usually one for each alliance) and only accessible to business and first class passengers. However, it is now possible to purchase access through membership schemes or on a one-off basis via travel agents and online.

Earnings from the airlines using the airport are based on a complex set of landing charges, which are designed to cover parking charges, landing fees and a per capita fee for passengers carried, so a jumbo aircraft will be charged a considerably higher landing fee than a small aircraft. In cases where civil aviation authorities pass on the cost of air traffic control to the airports, or where the airport itself is responsible for it (as at Jersey Airport), a share of these costs will also be charged to landing aircraft.

Congestion and airport expansion

Congestion at major international airports is becoming so acute that new technology is being pressed into service to improve ground handling. This is becoming even more urgent as the new generation of superjumbos is phased in. Increased automation is helping to speed up the throughput of passengers, and e-tickets (electronic tickets) issued at the airport against a confirmed reservation – first used widely by the no frills airlines – are rapidly being introduced by all the major airlines to reduce costs while simultaneously speeding up the check-in process.

This process is further speeded up for passengers who travel with airlines that allow them to undertake the check-in process themselves, using computers at the airport, or increasingly, online in advance of arrival at the airport. The budget airlines are moving to a system where passengers can be checked in rapidly when travelling without hold baggage and, in some cases, those passengers travelling with baggage requiring to be checked are charged a supplement for the privilege. This is becoming more common and prices for the 'privilege' are increasing.

Regardless of new technology, there are finite limits to the numbers of passengers that an airport can handle in a given time, and those such as Heathrow, as we have seen, are already close to their capacity. The addition of a further runway and new terminals may postpone the inevitable point where capacity is reached, but air corridors are already over-crowded in many parts of the world and, increasingly, aircraft are forced to 'stack' at busy periods, wasting fuel. This creates a knock-on effect, delaying later take-offs, and the combination of poor weather, lightning air traffic control strikes and the need for increased security in checking luggage at times of terrorist activity have all led to serious problems of congestion at busy airports all over the world.

In the UK, the pressures on London airports have encouraged the government to seek to disperse traffic to regional airports. The importance of major hubs for interline passengers making connections, however, means that delays in expanding Heathrow's capacity have inhibited economic growth. Protests against a fifth terminal at Heathrow, delayed for many years by consultation and lobbying until finally approved in 2001 and opened in 2008 (with disastrous consequences in the opening days, when both BAA and BA were ill-prepared for the change), is expected to allow a capacity increase of 50%. Present runways, however, would be unable to cope with an increase of this magnitude and the pressure is now on for a third runway (as well as a sixth terminal) to be operational by 2020. This would be 2500 metres in length – sufficient for long-haul aircraft such as the Boeing 777 or Airbus 350 to operate – which would theoretically increase maximum flight capacity at the airport to around 702 000 per annum.

Needless to say, there is strong opposition from the environmental lobby to any further expansion, but the UK government fears that refusal to develop will simply divert aircraft to Schiphol Airport, Amsterdam (which has plans to expand to seven runways by 2020, effectively doubling flight capacity). That airport has already benefited from London's congestion by employing the hub-and-spoke system, picking up British regional passengers bound for intercontinental connections. Paris' Charles de Gaulle airport is another major competitor seeking to become a leading European hub, with expansion to seven terminals and capacity for 80 million passengers.

The UK's regional airports have shown their enthusiasm for expansion, but have not always had the support promised by the UK government, which, in the past, was slow to grant approval for American carriers to fly into regional airports; although, in today's more liberal climate of deregulation, we may now anticipate this development. Some airports also face difficulties due to local authorities' unwillingness to expand facilities in the face of opposition from local residents. By contrast, Continental airports have actively sought expansion, with the blessing of their central and local governments, and sometimes with financial incentives for the new carriers developing routes. Such subsidies were considered illegal by the EU, but it has since modified its stand, deciding to permit subsidies normally ranging between 30 and 40%, depending on the economic circumstances of the region. Ryanair and easyJet are two of many no frills airlines that have taken advantage of the relatively low costs associated with regional airports to expand their services. However, Ryanair felt obliged to pull out of Strasbourg and Charleroi (Brussels South) after the EU ruled that its high subsidies were illegal.

At popular and congested airports, gaining take-off and landing slots for new services is extremely difficult, and in consequence they have been traded in recent years at between five and ten million pounds per pair. Slots are awarded to airlines through processes of negotiation, which usually take place in November each year, to cover flights in the following year. Scheduled services receive priority over charter, and the so-called 'grandfather' rights of existing carriers (a concept challenged by the EU) tend to take precedence over new carriers – so much so that, at airports such as Heathrow, a new airline seeking to gain slots may find it necessary to take over an existing airline in order to do so. This can give even financially troubled airlines high paper value if they control a large number of slots at significant airports. The Open Skies agreement which came into force in 2008, liberalizing flights across the North Atlantic, has heightened demand for new services out of Heathrow.

EXAMPLE   **The airport slot**

A slot is an allocation to take off or land at a predetermined time and airport. Getting access to new slots can be expensive and requires lengthy negotiations. The head of BA, Willie Walsh, is reported to have commented that buying Virgin Atlantic would be attractive, just so that BA could obtain the slots (New Europe, 2011).

The importance of slots has grown as airports reach capacity. Airlines are able to keep the same slots, providing they make use of them. Any new slots or unused slots are then distributed to new and existing airlines. Rarely do prime-time, prime location slots come onto the market for redistribution. More commonly, airlines swap slots to improve operating efficiencies or in response to changes in routes served. Monetary payments may accompany these swaps. The EU is investigating this system, concerned over the lack of transparency in these agreements and the restrictions it may cause on free trade, if new airlines are unable to enter the market. The EU reported that the current system led to an inefficient use of capacity as some slots were under-utilized (EC, 2011).

Air navigation and traffic control services

The technical services that are provided on the ground to assist and control aircraft while in the air and landing and taking off are not normally seen as part of the tourism industry, but their role is a key one in the operation of aviation services. Air traffic control (ATC) has the function of guiding aircraft into and out of airports, giving pilots (usually in the form of continually updated automatic recordings) detailed information on ground conditions, windspeed, cloud conditions, runways in use and the state of navigation aids. ATC will instruct pilots on what height and direction to take and be responsible for all flights within a geographically defined area.

In the UK alone, it is estimated that, at any one time during daylight hours, there are some 200 aircraft in the skies. Aircraft movements (take-offs and landings) in the UK exceed 2.9 million annually with over one-third coming from airports in the London area. To cope with the predicted rise in air traffic, ATC systems have been updated throughout Continental Europe to allow many more aircraft movements to take place within a given period, but the introduction of new computers has been fraught with technical problems. The UK's NATS (formerly the National Air Traffic Service) controls take-offs and landings at the 15 largest UK airports, as well as corridors in the skies over the UK and part of the North Atlantic. It handled 2.1 million flights in 2010. Formerly a public service, this became a public–private partnership in 2001, with the government currently controlling 49%, a further 42% owned by seven UK airlines, 4% by BAA and 5% in the hands of the organization's staff.

Eruption closes air space

In April 2010, the eruption in Iceland of the Eyjafjallajoekull volcano sent ash spewing into the air, leading to the grounding of flights across Europe. As the Civil Aviation Authority in the UK – and similar bodies across Europe – closed the air space, air traffic controllers were obliged to accept the situation. NATS estimated that the six-day closure led to a loss in revenue of some £5 million.

Following this event, airspace regulators and aircraft engine manufacturers established detailed volcano guidelines. Interestingly, these were put to the test in May 2011, when a second Icelandic volcano, Grímsvötn, erupted, closing air space for a second time. This eruption, however, had much less impact.

Improvement in altimeters on board newer aircraft has reduced the margin of error from 300 feet to 200 feet. This has allowed airlines to halve the vertical distance between aircraft at cruising speed from 2000- to 1000-foot intervals. Initially introduced on transatlantic routes, this ruling was controversially extended to the European mainland in 2002, virtually doubling the number of flights operating at between 29 000 and 41 000 feet. The present horizontal distance apart that aircraft must maintain, nose to tail, is three miles (at this same cruising height), with aircraft held at least 60 miles apart laterally. If these lateral gaps could also be halved, it would permit an eight-fold increase in the number of flights operating, although the problems of congestion at the airports themselves would still need to be solved. Landing intervals stand at 45 seconds. London's two major airports – Heathrow and Gatwick – are experimenting with cuts to allow intervals of 37 seconds – again, not without controversy.

EXAMPLE   Disruption of services

The impact of an ATC strike can be extensive. For example, a strike of French ATC workers similar to that which occurred in September 2010 would mean that any planes due to fly from or land in France will not be able to take to the skies. Furthermore, any flights which would travel through French airspace en route to their destination would either have to be cancelled or diverted. This means that a plane taking off from Amsterdam to head to Barcelona is likely to have to divert via Germany and Italy to reach the Mediterranean, a far longer route.

Airlines

The services provided by airlines can be divided into three distinct categories:

- scheduled
- charter (in US parlance, supplementals)
- air taxi.

Scheduled services

Scheduled services are provided by some 650 airlines worldwide, of which around 230 are members of the International Air Transport Association (IATA), these representing most of the world's major carriers. They operate on defined routes, domestic or international, for which licences have been granted by the government or governments concerned. The airlines are required to operate on the basis of their published timetables, regardless of passenger load factors (although flights and routes that are not commercially viable throughout the year may be operated during periods of high demand only).

These services may be publicly or privately owned, although there is now a global movement among the developed nations towards private ownership of airlines. Where fully state-owned airlines continue to operate – as in the case of Emirates and Singapore Airlines, as well as in many developing countries – the leading public airline is often recognized as the national 'flag-carrier'. In the UK, all airlines are now in the private sector, although BA, privatized since 1987, is still seen by many as the national flag-carrier. Privatization is not always seen as the best solution and, in one case, that of Air New Zealand, the government reversed earlier privatization by bringing back 80% of the carrier into public ownership after the 9/11 disaster.

The importance of air transport within the national economy is such that even a government committed to private air transport, as the USA is, voted for public funds in the form of compensation and loans to be paid to aid the ailing US carriers in the wake of that crisis.

Airlines operating on major routes between hub airports within a country are known as **trunk route** airlines, while those operating from smaller, generally rural, airports into these hubs are referred to as **regional** or **feeder** airlines. In the case of the USA and certain other regions, these may also be termed **commuter** airlines, as their prime purpose is to serve the needs of commuting businesspeople, many of whom regularly use those routes. The growing development of hub-and-spoke routes will be discussed later in the chapter.

As was discussed earlier in this chapter, the growth of no frills, or budget, carriers – more correctly known as low-cost low-fare (LCLF) carriers – has been the major development in scheduled service operations in the past decade. These airlines have been successful due to a combination of efficient operations and low cost and have, as a result, sharply cut into markets formerly held by the traditional full-cost carriers, even where business traffic is concerned.

Low-cost carriers will typically employ aircraft like Boeing 737s on high-density short-haul routes with one class of seats. Virtually all bookings are taken direct, over the Internet. Tickets are inflexible and generally non-refundable. Passengers turning up late or failing to show lose the entire value of their tickets, often even including taxes – a highly profitable ploy by the airlines. Bookings are usually made and paid for well in advance to take advantage of lower prices, providing helpful cash flow to the companies. If routes prove unprofitable, the carriers pull out quickly – as demonstrated by Ryanair in the aftermath of fuel price increases and declining demand as the recession hit in 2008.

By operating out of secondary, less congested airports, low-cost carriers can reduce times on the ground and operate more flights per day. One study found that easyJet, for example, could employ its aircraft for 11 hours a day, while BA on comparable flights achieved only eight hours (Tarry, 2002). Staff costs are also substantially lower than those of the traditional full-service carriers. For example, staff costs as a share of revenue earned were 25% for BA, compared with 10% for Ryanair. Similarly, the costs of marketing, commission and sales and reservations for the two carriers were very different. Such factors influence profitability (see Table 13.3).

The introduction of no frills flights has resulted in a very pared down service where not only meals and drinks are charged for but also the airlines do little to aid passengers in cases of delayed or missed flights. Extra charges are made for the carriage of items such as skis, golf clubs and surfboards, and Ryanair was the first carrier to impose a charge even for normal baggage carried in the hold – a policy that was then taken up by the other budget carriers – and now some of the full-service carriers have started to charge to transport sporting equipment. Additional costs are imposed for priority boarding and the 'privilege' of couples and families being seated together – and Ryanair has yet to deny that it has been considering the imposition of a charge to use the on-board toilets!

Table 13.3 Profitability of UK scheduled airlines (2009/10)

Airline	Profit (Loss)
British Airways	(£501 906 000)
BMI	(£198 029 000)
Virgin Atlantic	(£180 981 000)
easyJet	£65 700 000
Ryanair	£345 500 000

Source: CAA, 2011, and company annual accounts

The arrivals and departures of new low-cost carriers are now becoming so frequent that any attempt to list current operators would inevitably date this text before it came to print. By way of example, some 20 global airlines collapsed just as the immediate result of the sharp rise in fuel prices in mid-2008. Suffice to say that, throughout the EU, in North America, the Far East and Australasia, new low-cost airlines such as JetBlue in the USA, Virgin Blue in Australia, Volaris in Mexico, Air Berlin in Germany, as well as Hungary and Poland's jointly owned Wizz Air (Eastern Europe's largest low-cost carrier) have appeared on the scene to challenge the longer-established carriers. By no means all will survive – many will merge or be taken over by competitors, as has been reported earlier in the case of Go and Buzz. Others will go under when faced with the cut-throat tactics of better-established and more efficient carriers. Still others will move from ultra-low fare niches to offering a service closer to those of the established airlines, as has been the case with some Air Berlin routes (while another low-cost carrier, Germania, has moved to all-charter operations). Budget carrier easyJet has set a new direction by developing its own holiday website in competition with tour operators and retail agents: **http://holidays.easyjet.com**. It allows its customers to build their own inclusive tours by pairing budget flights with a bedstock of rooms in several thousand European hotels.

Another direction has been taken by new so-called boutique airlines, which focus on niche markets on routes where they can cherry-pick higher fare-paying passengers. A number of these operate in the USA and one or two, such as LyddAir (operating between Lydd and le Touquet in France), have followed suit in the UK. They appeal chiefly to business travellers, for whom superior service and speedier airport check-ins are important.

Mention should be made of there being a move back to seaplane operations, after a gap of many decades. Although amphibious aircraft have been in use continuously for private charter work (particularly in wilderness areas such as exist in Canada, carrying leisure passengers on hunting and fishing holidays to isolated lakes), scheduled seaplane routes were abandoned soon after World War II (Pan American Airways had even operated regular transatlantic services in 1939). Now, both charter and scheduled services are being introduced in the Mediterranean, with Aqua Airlines offering charters between points in mainland Italy, Sicily and the Aeolian Islands.

Charter services

Charter services, by contrast with scheduled services, do not operate according to published timetables, nor are they advertised or promoted by the airlines themselves. Instead, the aircraft are chartered to intermediaries (often tour operators) for a fixed charge and those intermediaries then become responsible for selling the aircraft's seats, leaving the airlines only with the responsibility for operating the aircraft. The intermediaries can change flight departures or even cancel flights, transferring passengers to other flights.

Major tour operators now invariably have their own charter airlines – a relationship that is examined fully in Chapter 18 – and have opened their flights in many instances to bookings on a seat-only basis to increase load factors. This is making the former distinction between scheduled and charter air services less clear-cut, with seat-only sales on charter aircraft now commonplace, former charter airlines operating scheduled services and scheduled carriers operating their own charter subsidiaries. Monarch Airlines in the UK exemplifies this trend, being a former charter carrier, initially servicing the needs of its partner tour operator Cosmos Holidays, but gradually opening its flights to scheduled bookings, to the point where the company now operates a separate scheduled service.

One result of the rapid increase in operating costs in 2008 was an urgent need among charter carriers to cut costs and establish partnerships. German-owned and leading tour operator TUI held talks with Lufthansa in 2008, planning to integrate the latter's German Wings division with its airline. In the same year, Thomas Cook discussed plans to merge its Condor division with Air Berlin. In the event, neither talks were fruitful.

Air taxi services

Air taxis are privately chartered aircraft accommodating between four and 18 people, used particularly by business travellers. They offer the advantages of convenience and flexibility as routings can be tailor-made for passengers (for example, a feasible itinerary for a business day using an air taxi might be London, Paris, Brussels, Amsterdam and London – a near-impossible programme for a scheduled service) and small airfields, close to a company's office or factory, can be used. There are some 350 airfields suitable for air taxis in the UK alone and a further 1300 in Western Europe (see Figure 13.3), compared with only about 200 airports receiving scheduled services. In the USA, where there are over 5400 small local airports catering principally for private and business planes, 98% of the population is said to live within 30 minutes' driving distance of an airport.

The attractiveness of air taxi services using these airports is that flights can be arranged or routings amended at short notice and, with a full flight, the cost for chartering can be commensurate with the combined business class fares of the number of staff travelling.

Aircraft in use range from helicopters such as the Bell Jet Ranger and the piston-engined Piper Twin Comanche (each seating three or four people, with a range of between 350 and 900 miles) up to aircraft such as Embraer's Bandeirante, which is capable of carrying 18 passengers up to 300 miles, and to top-of-the-range Gulfstream V aircraft, costing over $40 million. Larger aircraft can also be chartered as needed. The world's fastest private jet is said to be the Cessna Citation X, which will cruise at Mach 0.92, just short of the sound barrier. It can hold a maximum of 12 passengers, and, with the cost of flying this plane at $3000 per hour (plus crew and airport costs), the hour-long flight from London to Paris would have a minimum operating cost of £500 per person return.

Most air taxi journeys are in the range of 500–600 miles, so these aircraft are ideal for many business trips within Europe. Many business jets find their way into the fleets of the air taxi companies – around 2000 such companies are available to meet the needs of the market.

EXAMPLE **Bringing air taxis to a wider audience**

In 2007, the Air Taxi Association was launched in the USA, subsequently establishing a European arm a year later, aiming to work with the travel industry to support the on-demand air travel sector. To drive demand, this group has worked to add their product to the global distribution systems (GDSs) used to search for airline flights, launched on a trial basis in 2011.

The demand for these taxi services goes beyond the business traveller, however. In 2010, Sri Lanka Airlines launched an air taxi service to provide tourists quick and comfortable access to difficult to reach locations. However, the Sri Lankan Air Taxi uses seaplanes, thus requiring calm, open water as a runway, ultimately limiting the services which can be offered; they provide both charter and scheduled services. Initial promotional fares were set at £30 per person, though this has climbed substantially since; but the opportunity to swap a three-hour car journey for a one-hour plane journey is appealing to many.

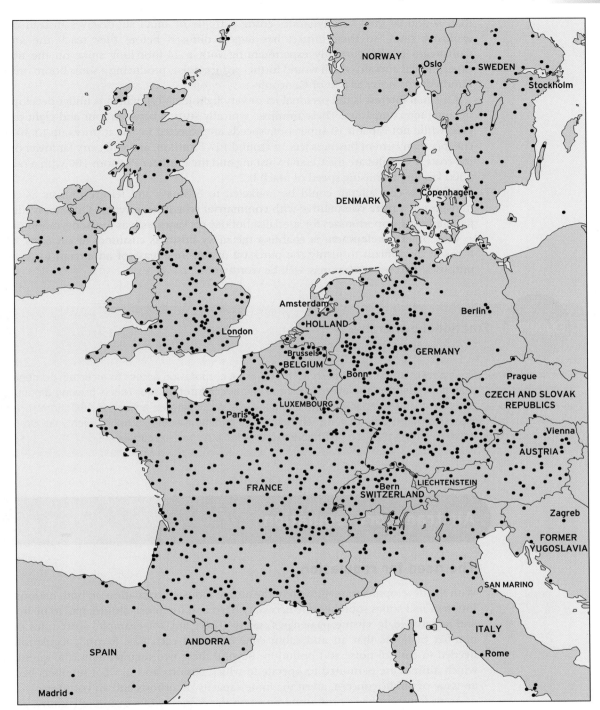

Figure 13.3 Airports and airfields in Europe

A number of manufacturers are looking to develop a new breed of supersonic business jets to satisfy the needs of businesspeople and the very rich who mourn the demise of Concorde. Research by the Teal Group (Dunn, 2007) estimated the immediate demand for supersonic business jets to exceed 400. These smaller aircraft do not cause the same level of disturbance at ground level as the much larger Concorde when travelling faster than sound as their aerodynamics create a ripple of small shockwaves instead of two explosive ones, so their impact has largely diffused before they reach the ground. Gulfstream is also currently experimenting with a 24-foot long spike on the nose of experimental aircraft, which would further reduce noise, producing a sonic boom only one hundredth as noisy as that of Concorde.

Of equal interest is the personal jet or very light jet (VLJ), which is under development in some ten companies. These minijets, typically seating between four and eight passengers, while not capable of supersonic speeds are expected to sell at prices up to 30 times cheaper than current business jets, at around £1–2 million, and will carry far lower operating costs. Examples are the Cessna Mustang and the Embraer Phenom 100 with a range of 2000 km and a cruising speed of Mach 0.7.

Such low-cost aircraft could be marketed to business and leisure tourists as charter transport at a price competitive with commercial scheduled services. One can readily see the marketing opportunities for specialist holiday packages such as the honeymoon market.

One other development is enabling the savvy business customer to cut costs: where it might be difficult to justify the purchase or full-time lease of an aircraft for business purposes, part-ownership may well be worthwhile.

EXAMPLE Fractional ownership

Fractional ownership is a form of aircraft timeshare that gives a corporation access to a certain number of flight hours each year, dependent on the overall share of the aircraft purchased. This is proving a popular alternative to air taxis for many companies. One company, Netjets, operates a fleet of 550 aircraft, and owners can buy amounts of flight time to suit their needs, the minimum being 25 hours each year. On this basis, costs come down to a level that is a justifiable expense for busy top executives.

Air transport regulation

The need for regulation

With the development and growth of the airline industry, regulation on both national and international scales soon became necessary. First and foremost, airlines had to be licensed and supervised to ensure passengers' safety. There are, for example, strict rules on the number of hours that air and cabin crew can work each day. Second, regulations are needed to control noise and pollution. Beyond these two requirements, the question of which airlines are permitted to operate to which airports and in what numbers becomes an issue of public concern, given the finite capacity of airports and air corridors.

As air transport has a profound impact on the economy of a region or country, governments will take steps to encourage the development of routes that appear to offer prospects of economic benefits and discourage those suffering from overcapacity. While the policy of one government may be to encourage competition or intervene where a route monopoly is forcing prices up, another government's policy may be directed at rationalizing excessive competition in order to avoid energy waste or even, in some cases, protecting the profitability of the national flag-carrier.

Some governments are tempted to provide subsidies in order to support inefficient publicly owned flag-carriers. Private airlines in Europe have long complained of this unfair protection against competition, which is contrary to EU regulations, but still survives in isolated cases within Europe. The EU Court of Justice, for example, ruled against Olympic Airlines (62% owned by the Greek state) in 2005 for receiving illegal public aid. However, given that significant shifts in the aviation markets have occurred since the regulations were set in 1994, the European Commission (EC) undertook consultation in 2011 to examine the need for regulation changes. The outcome is eagerly awaited by many struggling airlines.

Another characteristic of such protection is the **pooling** arrangements made between airlines operating on certain international routes, whereby all revenue accruing on that route is apportioned equally between the carriers serving it. This may appear to circumvent competition on a route, but is also one means of safeguarding the viability of the national carrier operating in a strong competitive environment. In developing countries, where governments are anxious to earn hard currency, the support of the national carrier as an earner of that currency through arrangements such as this may be justifiable.

Pooling arrangements are often entered into in cases where the airlines are not of comparable size in order to safeguard the smaller carrier's capacity and revenue. By rationalizing schedules, pressure is reduced on peak time take-off slots and costs reduced. Financial arrangements between the pooled carriers usually limit the amount of revenue transferred from one carrier to the other to a fixed maximum, to reduce what may be seen as unfair government support for an inefficient carrier. Increasingly, such pooling arrangements are no longer acceptable and may indeed be illegal, as is the case in the USA.

In some areas, air transport is an essential public utility that, even where commercially non-viable, is socially desirable in order to provide communications with a region where geographical terrain may make other forms of transport difficult or impossible (New Guinea, Alaska or the Hebrides in Scotland are cases in point). This can result in a government subsidizing one or more of its airlines in order to ensure that a service is maintained. Airlines themselves often argue that they provide vital channels of communication for business, trade and investment essential for the wellbeing of communities and that, therefore, even profitable routes should be exempted from tax (aviation fuel, for example, is currently exempted).

Systems of regulation

Broadly speaking, air transport operations are regulated in three ways.

- Internationally, scheduled routes are assigned on the basis of agreements between governments of the countries concerned.

- Internationally, scheduled air fares are now subject to less and less control and, in both North America and Europe, airlines are free to set their own fares. Governments can still intervene, however, where predatory pricing is involved. Theoretically, governments protect carriers by permitting fares to fluctuate between acceptable maxima and minima, but such constraints have been largely abandoned in the developed countries as low-cost airlines attract passengers with rates that can fall so low that only taxes and administration charges are paid for advance booked seats. In developing areas, however, the extent of regulation is often far greater, with airlines agreeing fares that may then be mediated through the traffic agreements (known as conferences) of the IATA. Agreed tariffs arrived at in this way are then subject to ratification by the governments of the countries concerned. Generally, less direct control is exercised over domestic fares.

- National governments approve and license the carriers that are to operate on scheduled routes, whether domestically or internationally. In the UK, the Civil Aviation Authority (CAA) has this responsibility and is also responsible for the licensing of charter airlines and of tour operators organizing package holidays abroad.

European countries that are members of the EU are now largely subject to its regulations and negotiations regarding the carriage of passengers by air. The EU, for example, has introduced legislation to protect passengers in the event of delays or denied boarding (in the case of an overbooking, for instance) with compensation payable to those affected, but to date the airlines have shown considerable skill in using force majeure rules to avoid payouts.

EXAMPLE **The cost of the closing European airspace**

The rules governing compensation by airlines operating in the EU are complicated. Entitlement to compensation occurs following delays of between two and four hours (depending on the flight distance). At this point, passengers are entitled to refreshments and two telephone calls. A sum of €400 is also possible – unless the airline can prove the delay was not their fault. The airline does, however, have to provide refreshments and accommodation until they are able to get you to your destination.

If an airline has overbooked a flight and a passenger is 'bumped' onto another departure, the airline must refund the price of that part of the ticket price, as well as making alternative arrangements, including providing accommodation.

Having established this, it is clear that the airlines suffered immensely when the ash cloud from the Icelandic volcano closed European airspace for nearly a week. Air France KLM initially announced that it would only pay for one day's expenses, while the head of low-cost carrier Ryanair, Michael O'Leary, claimed that compensation should not be greater than the total cost of the ticket price. Despite delays, eventually most airlines paid according to the terms of the EU regulations. Since this event, however, the EU has been reviewing the need for limits on the liability of the airlines, which may well reduce the rights of the passenger.

One final point needs to be highlighted. Travellers to destinations outside the EU and on airlines which are based outside the EU do not fall under this compensation scheme.

The worldwide trend is to allow market forces to determine the shape and direction of the airline business, so regulation today is less concerned with routes, frequency, capacity and fares and more concerned with aspects of safety. Disagreements between governments over the regulation of routes or airlines can at times lead to major conflict, however, as is the case with the long-standing dispute between the UK and US governments regarding traffic rights across the Atlantic.

Air transport regulations are the result of a number of international agreements between countries dating back over many years. The Warsaw Convention of 1929 first established common agreement on the extent of liability of the airlines in the event of death or injury of passengers or loss of passengers' baggage, with a limit of $10 000 on loss of life and similarly derisory sums for loss of baggage (compensation is payable on weight rather than value). Inflation soon further reduced the value of claims, and liability was reassessed by a number of participating airlines, first at the Hague Protocol in 1955, where the figure was increased to $20 000, and again at the Montreal Agreement in 1966, at which time the USA imposed a $75 000 ceiling on compensation for flights to and from the USA. It was also agreed that the maximum liability would be periodically reviewed.

In 1992, Japan waived all limits for Japanese carriers and, in the following year, the UK government unilaterally required UK carriers to increase their liability to a limit of 100 000 SDRs (Special Drawing Rights – a reserve currency operated by the International Monetary Fund and equivalent at the time to about $160 000).

Finally, in 1995, IATA negotiated an **Intercarrier Agreement on Passenger Liability**, which was designed to enforce blanket coverage for all member airlines, whereby any damages would be determined according to the laws of the country of the airline affected. Not all airlines agreed to implement this, however.

The five freedoms of the air

Further legislation concerning passenger aviation resulted from the Chicago Convention on Civil Aviation held in 1944, at which 80 governments were represented in discussions designed to promote world air services and reach agreement on standard operating procedures for air services between countries. There were two outcomes of this meeting: the founding of the International Civil Aviation Organization (ICAO), now a specialized agency of the United Nations, and the establishment of the so-called **five freedoms of the air**. These privileges are to:

1. fly across a country without landing
2. land in a country for purposes other than the carriage of passengers or freight – to refuel, for example
3. offload passengers, mail or freight from an airline of the country from which those passengers, mail or freight originated
4. load passengers, mail or freight on an airline of the country to which those passengers, mail or freight are destined
5. load passengers, mail or freight on an airline not belonging to the country to which those passengers, mail or freight are destined and offload passengers, mail or freight from an airline not of the country from which they originated.

These privileges were designed to provide the framework for bilateral agreements between countries and ensure that carriage of passengers, mail and freight between any two countries would normally be restricted to the carriers of those countries.

The move to greater freedom of the skies

Other freedoms not discussed by the Convention, but equally pertinent to the question of rights of operation, have been termed the 'sixth and seventh freedoms'. These would cover:

● carrying passengers, mail or freight between any two countries on an airline that is of neither country, but is operating via the airline's own country
● carrying passengers, mail or freight directly between two countries on an airline associated with neither of the two countries.

These various freedoms can best be illustrated using examples (see Figure 13.4).

While a handful of countries expressed a preference for an 'open skies' policy on regulation, most demanded controls. An International Air Services Agreement, to which more than 90 countries became signatories, provided for the mutual exchange of the first two freedoms of the air, while it was left to individual bilateral negotiations between countries to resolve other issues. The Convention agreed not to regulate charter services, allowing countries to impose whatever individual regulations they wished. Few countries, in fact, were willing to allow a total open skies policy for charters.

The Anglo-American agreement which was reached in Bermuda in 1946, following the Convention, set the pattern for many of the bilateral agreements that followed. This so-called **Bermuda Agreement**, while restricting air carriage between the two countries to national carriers, did not impose restrictions on capacity for airlines concerned. This was modified at a second Bermuda Agreement reached in 1977 (and ratified in 1980), however, in line with the tendency of many countries in the intervening years to opt for an agreement that would ensure a percentage of total traffic on a route would be guaranteed for the national carriers of the countries concerned. It was the UK intention, in this renegotiated agreement, to avoid overcapacity on the route by restricting it to two UK and two American carriers.

A further agreement in 1986 extended the agreed capacities across the Atlantic, the tight control of capacity was relaxed and new routes were agreed, although the concept of

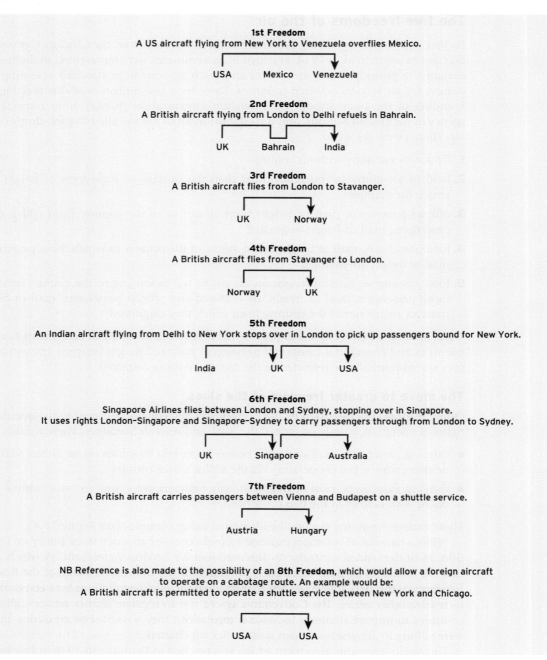

1st Freedom
A US aircraft flying from New York to Venezuela overflies Mexico.

USA   Mexico   Venezuela

2nd Freedom
A British aircraft flying from London to Delhi refuels in Bahrain.

UK   Bahrain   India

3rd Freedom
A British aircraft flies from London to Stavanger.

UK   Norway

4th Freedom
A British aircraft flies from Stavanger to London.

Norway   UK

5th Freedom
An Indian aircraft flying from Delhi to New York stops over in London to pick up passengers bound for New York.

India   UK   USA

6th Freedom
Singapore Airlines flies between London and Sydney, stopping over in Singapore.
It uses rights London–Singapore and Singapore–Sydney to carry passengers through from London to Sydney.

UK   Singapore   Australia

7th Freedom
A British aircraft carries passengers between Vienna and Budapest on a shuttle service.

Austria   Hungary

NB Reference is also made to the possibility of an **8th Freedom**, which would allow a foreign aircraft
to operate on a cabotage route. An example would be:
A British aircraft is permitted to operate a shuttle service between New York and Chicago.

USA   USA

Figure 13.4 Some examples of freedoms of the air

reciprocity remained in force. The UK government was only willing to concede new routes for American carriers if reciprocal routes would be granted to UK carriers. US legislation also limited foreign ownership of American airlines to a minority shareholding, thus effectively restricting operational control to US ownership.

Negotiation on routes and carriers operated by EU member countries subsequently lay in the hands of the EC.

Carriage on routes within the national territory of a country (the so-called **cabotage** routes) is normally restricted to the national carriers of the country concerned. In some cases, however, this provides opportunities for a country's national carriers to operate exclusively on international routes in cases where these countries have overseas possessions. This is the case, for example, on routes out of the UK to destinations such as Gibraltar or on services between France and Réunion Island or the islands of Guadaloupe and Martinique in the Caribbean.

Under the EU's programme of liberalization of the air within member countries, the cabotage regulation – the final barrier to total freedom of operation – was dropped in 1997. Any airline of any member country can now file to operate services between cities within another member's borders. The UK carrier easyJet currently operates flights between many Continental European cities including, for example, between Barcelona and Milan. While this liberalization should, in theory, have opened up competition and encouraged a wealth of new services throughout the EU, in practice, the difficulty of getting slots at congested airports, as well as delaying tactics by some governments attempting to support their own national carriers, have meant that it has taken time for the low-cost carriers to build up competition in some areas and very few are operating out of hub airports.

The role of IATA

For many years, effective control over air fares on international routes was exercised by IATA – a trade body with more than 230 airline members representing most of the leading airlines. The aims of this organization – which was restructured in its present form in 1945, but traces its origins to the very beginning of air transport in 1919 – have been to promote safe, regular and economic air transport, to provide the means for collaboration between the air carriers themselves and cooperate with governments, the ICAO and other international bodies for the promotion of safety and effective communications.

In the past, IATA also had a role in setting tariffs – in effect, operating a legalized cartel. Fares were established at the annual tariff-fixing Traffic Conferences by a process of common agreement between the participating airlines, subject to ratification by the airlines' governments. In practice, most governments merely rubber-stamped the agreements. Critics argued that, as a result, fares became unnecessarily high on many routes and competition was stifled. Often, the agreed fares were the outcome of political considerations in which the less efficient national flag-carriers pushed for prices unrelated to competitive costs.

IATA also controlled many other aspects of airline operation, such as the pitch of passengers' seats, which dictated the amount of legroom they could enjoy, and even the kinds of meals that could be served on board. As a result, the airlines were forced to concentrate their marketing efforts on such aspects of the product as service, punctuality or even the design of cabin crew uniforms, rather than providing a genuine measure of competition.

It was widely felt that this had led to inertia among the participating carriers, with agreements resulting from a desire to avoid controversy. Neither had the cartel ensured profitability for its members as they faced open competition from non-IATA carriers, which successfully competed on both price and added value.

Led by the USA, and soon followed by other countries, airlines chose to withdraw from this tariff-setting mechanism and, as a result, IATA was restructured in 1979 to provide a two-tier organization: a tariff section to deal with fares, for those nations wishing to maintain this role, and a trade section to provide other benefits that an international airline association offered. IATA's role in tariff agreements has become steadily less important and airlines now largely determine their own service and catering arrangements. An interlining agreement also allowed passengers to switch flights to other member airlines freely – an advantage when they were paying full fares for their tickets, but in an age of low-price tickets for all air services, this no longer has the same appeal.

The principal benefit offered by IATA today is its central clearing house system, which makes possible financial settlements between members in the same manner as the UK's clearing banks. Tickets and other documents are standardized and interchangeable between IATA members, while compatibility is established between members in air fare structures and currency exchange rates. Other procedures, too, such as the appointment, through licensing agreements, of IATA-recognized travel agents, are also standardized throughout the world. The computerized Bank Settlement Plan, introduced in the UK in 1984, permits monthly settlement of accounts with appointed agents through a single centre rather than with each individual airline and has enabled financial transactions to keep pace with the enormous growth in airline travel.

UK regulation of air transport

In the UK, the Civil Aviation Act of 1971 led to the establishment of the CAA, which has five regulatory functions:

- responsibility for regulating air navigation services (jointly with the Ministry of Defence), through the UK's ATC services
- responsibility for the regulation of all the UK's civil aviation, including air transport licensing, the award of licences (ATOLs) to air travel organizers and approval of air fares
- responsibility for the airworthiness and operational safety of UK carriers, including certification of airlines, airports, flight crew and engineers
- acting as adviser to the government in matters concerning domestic and international civil aviation
- a number of subsidiary functions, including the research and publication of statistics, and the ownership and management of eight airports in the Highlands and Islands of Scotland.

Prior to the Civil Aviation Act, no clear long-term government policy had been discernible with respect to aviation in the UK. As governments changed, so did attitudes to the public or private ownership of carriers. With the aim of providing some longer-term direction and stability, a committee of enquiry into civil air transport, under the chairmanship of Sir Ronald Edwards, was established.

EXAMPLE **The Edwards Report – UK air transport in the 1970s**

This enquiry recommended that the government should periodically review civil aviation policy and objectives; the long-term aim should be to satisfy air travellers at the lowest economically desirable price and a suitable mix should be agreed between public- and private-sector airlines. The state corporations (BOAC and BEA) were confirmed in their role as flag-carriers, but were recommended to merge and to start charter and inclusive tour operations. The idea of a major second-force airline in the private sector – to complement and compete with the new public airline – was proposed and the suggestion was made that a more liberal policy be adopted towards the licensing of other private airlines. Finally, the report proposed that the economic, safety and regulatory functions carried out by the previous Air Transport Licensing Board, the Board of Trade and the Air Registration Board should thereafter come under the control of a single Civil Aviation Authority.

The Civil Aviation Act, which followed the publication of this report in 1971, accepted most of these proposals. BOAC and BEA were merged into a single corporation – British Airways – while British Caledonian was confirmed as the new second-force airline (following the merger of Caledonian Airways and British United Airways), and the new CAA was formed.

Although it was envisaged by the Edwards Report that British Caledonian would compete with the publicly owned flag-carrier, the CAA redistributed routes, giving British Caledonian South American routes, and restricting the North Atlantic largely to BA.

The CAA is financed by the users of its services, which are mainly the airlines themselves. Any excess profits are expected to be returned to the users through lower charges for its services. A subsidiary of the CAA is the Air Transport Users' Council (AUC), which acts as a watchdog for air transport customers. An international body with similar aims – the International Foundation of Airline Passenger Associations (IFAPA) – is headquartered in Geneva. In 2011, it was announced that the AUC was to be abolished, its functions to be relegated to a body appointed directly by the Transport Secretary, known as Passenger Focus – a body which currently also handles complaints against bus and rail companies.

An open skies policy being favoured by both the US and UK governments in the 1980s led to effective deregulation of fares and capacity across the Atlantic, as well as on domestic routes in both countries. BA was privatized in 1987 and the subsequent redistribution and licensing of routes for smaller UK carriers set the scene for liberalization throughout Europe.

The deregulation of air transport

Deregulation – or 'liberalization' as it has come to be known in Europe – is the deliberate policy of reducing state control over airline operations, allowing market forces to shape the airline industry. The USA led the way with the Airline Deregulation Act of 1978, which abolished collusion in air pricing. The US regulatory body, the Civil Aeronautics Board (CAB), progressively relinquished control over route allocation and fares and was itself disbanded at the end of 1984. Market forces were then to take over, the government expecting that inefficient large carriers would be undercut by smaller airlines that had lower overheads and greater productivity.

In fact, the actual outcome was very different and caused advocates of deregulation in Europe to reconsider the case for total freedom of the air. The opening years of deregulation saw a rapid expansion of airline operations, with a three-fold increase in new airlines. Among the established airlines, those that expanded prudently, such as Delta, prospered, while others, such as Braniff, became overambitious and committed themselves to a programme of expansion that, as fares became more competitive, they could not support financially. While a few routes saw substantial early rises in fares, especially on long-haul domestic flights, on the whole fares fell sharply, attracting a big increase in passengers. This growth was achieved at the expense of profitability, forcing airlines to cut costs in order to survive. New conditions of work and lower pay agreements were negotiated, with some airlines abandoning union recognition altogether. Some airlines reverted to propeller aircraft on short-haul routes to cut costs and worries began to emerge about safety as it was believed that airlines were cutting corners to save on maintenance. Indeed, air safety violations doubled between 1984 and 1987.

Within a decade of deregulation, more than 100 airlines had been forced out of business or absorbed as profits changed to losses. Poor morale among airline crew, due to uncertainty about their future job security, led to indifferent service.

Supplementals, as the charter operators are known in the USA, were particularly badly hit as competing scheduled services dropped their fares. They had neither the public recognition nor the marketing skills to compete openly with the scheduled services and many simply ceased to operate. In the longer term, the 'mega-carriers' were the major beneficiaries. They comprised some ten leading airlines, of which the 'big three' – Delta, American and United – held the lion's share of the air travel market. Far from expanding opportunity, deregulation led to smaller airlines being squeezed out or restricted to less important routes by the marketing power of the big carriers. In 2001 (prior to the 9/11 catastrophe), American Airlines took over TWA, which had been operating under Chapter 11 bankruptcy rules.

A second consequence of deregulation was the development of **hub and spoke** systems of operation – feeder air services from smaller 'spoke' airports provide services into the hubs to connect with the onward long-haul flights of the mega-carriers. This pattern initially enabled the airlines to keep prices down and New York, Chicago, Atlanta, Fort Worth/Dallas and St Louis became major hubs for domestic and international flights, some dominated by a single carrier.

With more liberal policies in force on both sides of the Atlantic, it became clear that renewed talks should take place to negotiate an open skies policy across the Atlantic, too. The Bermuda 2 Agreement having been ruled illegal under EU competition rules and with a further 16 of the 27 EU members having negotiated bilateral agreements directly with the USA, the EU initiated talks with US officials in 2004. The EU pressed for the limitation on foreign ownership of US carriers to be raised to 50% and rights to be granted allowing European carriers to fly on domestic American routes in exchange for opening up inter-European routes to US carriers. US negotiators proved adamant in refusing to accept these terms, however.

Finally, in 2007, after extensive discussion, an **Open Skies Agreement** was reached, which came into force from April 2008. The agreement favoured the USA, in that American airlines are now permitted to operate on EU cabotage routes by extending their trans-atlantic operations (New York–London–Athens, for example) while America has sacrificed none of its closely guarded cabotage rights and foreign airlines are not permitted to secure more than 25% of any American airline's voting rights. The agreement does allow any EU carrier to fly between any EU airport and any US city, however. With these rights, two things become apparent.

- Passengers originating in Africa and the Middle East and using London Heathrow in transit to North America may in future use other carriers on the Continent, to the detriment of Heathrow's transit revenue.
- Slots at Heathrow, already in short supply and estimated to be valued at £25 million per pair, immediately become more valuable. Lufthansa bought, but is currently resell-ing, BMI, whose sale to IAG would increase IAG's slots from 45% to 53% at Heathrow.

EXAMPLE   **Airlines maintain their rights with empty flights**

News reports (Nugent, 2008) highlighted the value of Heathrow slots to BMI – an estimated £770 million. To retain the grandfather rights to these slots, they must be used, and with a downturn in passenger numbers at the end of 2008, BMI took the decision to operate near-empty aircraft to ensure their rights were maintained. BA similarly announced it would not cut transatlantic services to ensure that its Heathrow slots were protected.

Foreign EU airlines based at Heathrow with intra-European routes could now choose to drop them in favour of more lucrative long-haul transatlantic flights. Air France/KLM sought close cooperation with US carrier Delta (they are part of the same airline alliance programme) to run a joint venture that would include common fares, schedules and capacity. The two airlines sought, and received, immunity from US anti-trust laws in estab-lishing this venture.

Lufthansa bought out Swiss carrier Swiss International in 2005, made a substantial investment in US budget carrier JetBlue in 2006 (and still holds 15% of their shares). Both Lufthansa and Air France KLM have expressed interest in joining forces with Polish carrier

LOT, although more recently Lufthansa has distanced itself from this as it integrates Austrian Airlines into its portfolio following takeovers.

BA had also been looking to form closer links with a North American airline and, following abortive talks with Continental Airlines, they renewed talks with American Airlines. BA's first attempt to link with the US carrier dates back to 1997 and further talks were held in 2002, but US anti-trust legislation had inhibited agreements up to that point. Prospects looked rather brighter for a closer partnership with the American carrier by 2008, against a backdrop of rising crisis in the aviation industry. In 2010, BA merged with Spanish airline Iberia, the parent company becoming known as International Airline Group (IAG) and European regulators agreed anti-trust principles under which this expanded European airline was permitted to operate jointly with American Airlines. It now looks inevitable that eventually the two corporations will merge their services and ownership entirely, making the operation a close competitor to become the largest in the world in terms of passenger numbers. If this were coupled with a possible merger between US Airways and American Airlines, rumoured at the time of writing, the new concentration would form a very powerful aviation marketing force, and by far the largest global carrier.

An immediate outcome of the Open Skies Agreement was the rapid increase in capacity as airlines scrambled to introduce new services across the Atlantic. As we have seen earlier, this led to supply rapidly outstripping demand, which, coupled with an escalation in fuel costs, led to difficulties for the airlines on these routes and speeded up merger talks between the larger carriers. In 2008, Delta announced a merger with Northwest Airlines, integrating the latter's name into the Delta brand as Delta Air Lines – effectively creating the world's largest airline. In 2010, Delta carried 111 million passengers, 5 million more than its nearest rival, Southwest and 25 million more than third-placed American Airlines. However, a merger between United and Continental Airlines, currently in process, is likely to put the new greatly enlarged carrier into first place.

With Open Skies successfully concluded across the Atlantic, talks were then held between the USA and Australia, to negotiate a similar liberalization. This led to a similar Open Skies agreement in 2008 for transpacific routes.

Developments in North American air traffic since 1990

Since the early 1990s, the North American airlines' struggle to survive has become more acute. Famous names like Pan American disappeared and, between 1991 and 1993, five airlines were forced to operate under America's Chapter 11 bankruptcy code, which permits an airline to continue to operate, although officially bankrupt, while restructuring its finances. The huge losses sustained by even the biggest airlines led to cancellations of new aircraft orders, the sale of assets and, finally, the formation of alliances with major international carriers – a trend that has become of major importance in the early years of the twenty-first century. Airline retrenchment led in turn to great difficulties for manufacturers of aircraft. They experienced widespread cancellations of orders in favour of leasing or the purchase of second-hand equipment, while the traditional leasing market in turn dried up.

The hub-and-spoke development, after its initial success in the USA, was challenged by new, low-cost regional carriers operating city-to-city on less significant routes. Some of these have been particularly successful – notably Southwest Airlines, a low-cost airline offering no frills flying at budget fares on some 60 routes and operating medium-size aircraft spoke-to-spoke in direct competition with the dominant hub-and-spoke operators. Southwest was the only US airline not to encounter losses after the 9/11 disaster.

By the start of the twenty-first century, some stability had returned, with a pattern emerging of powerful US mega-carriers (which have become known as the 'legacy carriers') on key domestic and international routes seeking alliances with leading foreign airlines in order to offer truly global air services. Most smaller airlines opted to concentrate on niche services, but the growth of no frills airlines in the USA was initially limited, partly owing to effective marketing by the leading carriers, and partly owing to public concern over safety issues (the fatal 1996 crash of no frills carrier Valujet did nothing to reduce this concern). The big carriers established their own low-cost operations – Delta created Delta Express and, later, Song Air (since wound up); American Airlines, its Eagle division; United, Ted. The much-criticized practice of 'bracketing', in which larger carriers lay on cut-price flights departing shortly before and after those of rival cheap carriers, also threatened the survival of many of the new airlines. Only where the airline had sufficient resources to pack a route with flights (as was the case with Southwest Airlines) did this tactic prove impractical.

The 9/11 terrorist attack on New York's Twin Towers and Washington's Pentagon building in 2001 quickly unseated the airlines' economic recovery. In the aftermath, virtually all the leading carriers sought Chapter 11 bankruptcy protection:

- Delta Airlines in 2004
- United Airlines between 2002 and 2006
- ATA Holdings between 2004 and 2006 and again in 2008 (when Southwest acquired their assets and this company ceased to trade)
- US Airways between 2002 and 2003 and again in 2004 and 2005 (when it was absorbed by America West)
- Northwest Airlines in 2005 (subsumed into Delta Air Lines in 2008).

In the decade that has followed the disaster, the legacy carriers have all struggled to survive, let alone return profits. With the consequent downturn in business generally following the crisis, the no frills carriers, led by Southwest Airlines, benefited at the expense of the mega-carriers. Attempts to meet this competition by forming their own budget airlines have not been wholly successful. Song, for example, has been reabsorbed into its parent airline. The big six cannot raise fares, owing to the competition they face from the no frills carriers, but, at the same time, they are faced with high staff pay (which is difficult to renegotiate with strong unions, although United successfully negotiated a five-year contract with its ground workers in 2005, slashing its pay costs), escalating oil prices, which are likely to remain highly volatile for the foreseeable future, and added costs for the extra security that has had to be put in place since 9/11. One result has been a cutting back in service levels, with economy passengers now paying for food and drink on board and refurbishment of aircraft interiors being undertaken less frequently.

In mid-2008, with oil prices at an all-time high, both legacy and budget carriers were facing unprecedented pressures on cost, causing American Airlines to introduce charges for hold baggage – the first legacy carrier to do so – while budget carrier JetBlue announced they would charge a supplement for window seats. While oil prices later fell back, long-term trends anticipate high prices, and the sheer volatility of the market for oil may force leading airlines to start laying up part of their fleets and reducing services.

EXAMPLE **Even more revenue for the airline**

Although JetBlue no longer charges a window seat supplement, they have introduced an upgrade programme for its flights, 'Even More'. This is focused on earning revenue from the seats which offer extra legroom. The Even More offer allowed passengers to chose to pay a premium – around $20 per flight, distance dependent – for these seats when booking the flight online. This upgrade fee would also allow passengers to have early boarding; they specifically draw attention to passengers' advanced access to the overhead storage bins, and access to the fast-track line through security at the departure airport.

The likely direction in the future will be continuation of the current process of integration and, as discussed earlier, this process is now advanced with the major airlines. While in the past legacy carriers have been blocked by the competition authorities, the extreme fluctuation in demand being experienced at the time of writing is likely to mean, inevitably, that fewer airlines will survive and, should the authorities continue to oppose mergers, closer alliances in some shape or form will nevertheless be inevitable.

European liberalization

Elsewhere in the developed world, governments have also supported the steady erosion of state regulatory powers over the airline industry. In Australia, liberalized air policy led to the establishment of new airlines and, for the first time, a competitively priced domestic air service, with JetBlue filling the role formerly occupied by Ansett as Australia's second carrier.

EXAMPLE   The launch and loss of Compass Airlines

Compass Airlines was one of the first low-cost carriers to enter the Australian market following liberalization of the market in 1990. The company set out to compete with the duopoly of Ansett and Australian, bringing down the price of domestic flights significantly. They were said to have 'halved the cost of flying and doubled the number of domestic air passengers' (Yallop, 1992).

Compass suffered difficulties, as do many new airlines, in gaining suitable slots at airports, as well as accessing check-in facilities and other ground-handling services. Ansett and Australian aggressively responded by lowering prices below cost to attract business away from Compass.

Following financial problems at the end of 1991, Compass eventually folded. They were, however, at the forefront of promoting affordable travel and

Figure 13.5 Street protest in Melbourne, encouraging support for Compass airlines in December 1991

Photo by Claire Humphreys

thus were popular with the Australian market. Their closure led to street demonstrations and a petition with over half a million signatures was gathered, both efforts seeking to encourage government support for greater competition in the domestic market (see Figure 13.5).

Europe's airlines were also moving slowly towards a 'market forces' policy, although in those countries where the state retained a financial investment in its airlines, the ethos of liberalization promoted by the EC was resisted. Iberia and Air France, for example, continued to receive public subsidies long after these became technically contrary to EU regulations. The path to liberalization had become irresistible, however, with the EU easing the transition by phasing it in three stages between 1987 and 1997, after which all EU carriers became free to fly anywhere within the EU, including cabotage routes, at fares they themselves determined, hindered only by the lack of slots at the major airports. Other European carriers outside the EU – notably Switzerland, Norway and Iceland – followed suit.

Airline deregulation in the UK had preceded that of other EU countries following a number of individual bilateral agreements with fellow EU members, notably Ireland and the Netherlands. This policy led to a substantial growth in the number of domestic carriers, as well as the numbers of passengers travelling.

No frills airlines were already springing up in the UK by the 1990s, operating chiefly out of regional and secondary airports, especially Luton and Stanstead, which had slots available for expansion and charged lower fees. The less popular regional airports are often keen to subsidize start-up airlines or others developing new routes, with landing charges waived for an initial period and the promise of advertising support. High start-up costs for operators joining dense routes, the big expense of marketing to establish a new name in the public eye and the success of frequent flyer programmes among the large carriers constrained small carriers from directly competing with them. Also, the low prices made levels of commission less attractive to agents, making distribution difficult. All this encouraged the budget carriers to sell their product direct, however, coinciding with the growth in online booking and easier direct distribution. Not all were successful, as we have seen, but the leaders – notably easyJet and Ryanair – were soon undermining even the largest carriers. Irish carrier Ryanair at first successfully competed head-on with Aer Lingus and then massively expanded its route network throughout Europe, to a point where it overtook all European legacy carriers to become the largest airline in Europe, carrying in excess of 72 million passengers in 2010. Inevitably, the large carriers were forced to retaliate, first by launching their own low-cost carriers (BMI launched its offshoot BMIBaby, for example, which continues to trade, although due to be sold by Lufthansa) and subsequently by slashing the prices of economy tickets on their normal flights.

One side-effect of liberalization has been the virtual demise of the **bucket shops** – non-appointed travel agents, selling off illegally discounted airline tickets dumped on the market at short notice by airlines with spare capacity. Their place has been taken by brokers who may legally contract with the airlines for spare capacity and sell this cheaply through travel agents (who were formerly legally forbidden to deal with the bucket shop operators). Increasingly, however, airlines are selling off unsold seats cheaply through website providers. Indeed, the growth in numbers of Internet companies with programmes designed to handle these products is one of the leading characteristics of the airline business at the beginning of the new century. This will be examined later in the chapter.

The potential explosion of passenger traffic resulting from liberalization has been, as we have seen, severely curtailed by problems of congestion. Government statistics have projected flights from the UK to rise from 238 million in 2005 to, according to some estimates (DfT, 2009), 465 million by 2030 – the bulk of this increase arising from demand out of South Eastern airports. Mainland Europe, too, is rapidly approaching saturation.

While the introduction of new fast rail services between the European capitals could theoretically offer some help by reducing demand for air travel on routes of up to about 500 miles, the overall growth in demand for air services poses severe problems for the industry in the long run. Worryingly, in the UK, the high cost of rail fares is tempting people away from rail and towards domestic air travel, with new budget-priced routes between towns as close as Southampton and Newquay (195 miles), Bristol and Plymouth (110 miles) and London and Manchester (even though fast trains operate every half hour on the latter route).

One further worry about the results of liberalization should receive a mention: the issue of air safety. Cost competition is driving some airlines to use older aircraft, including some registered outside the UK. While the CAA has imposed restrictions on UK scheduled airlines using foreign aircraft, there are no restrictions on UK tour operators chartering such aircraft to operate into and out of the UK, nor is any firm control exercised over the use of foreign aircraft registered in other EU countries. Pressures to meet targets on air traffic control and the new compensation regulations introduced in 2005 by the EU against delayed flights have led to further concerns about passenger safety within the EU.

The impact of 9/11 was as keenly felt on European carriers as it was by those in the US, coming as it did on top of an economic downturn that was already depressing airline profitability. Several airlines collapsed, only to return in a new, privatized form, including Sabena, the Belgian flag-carrier (replaced by SN Brussels) and Swissair (now simply Swiss and owned by Lufthansa). Air France and KLM have also merged their operations to improve efficiencies. It has been the no frills carriers, once again, however, that have gained most from the economic climate, undercutting their rivals, opening up new routes and finding new markets for air transport.

The economics of airline operation

The development of an airline route is something of a catch-22 situation. Airlines require some reassurance about traffic demand before they are willing to commit their aircraft to a new route, but air travellers look for regular and frequent flights to a destination before patronizing a route.

There is usually an element of risk involved in initiating any new route, especially as seat prices are likely to be high to compensate for low load factors (the number of seats sold as a percentage of total seats available) and high overheads (for both operating and marketing) before traffic builds up. When a route has proved its popularity, however, the pioneer airline is faced with increasing competition as other airlines are attracted by the increase in traffic – unless governments decide to control market entry. In an open-market economy, the original airline faces lower load factors, as the market is split between a number of carriers, requiring it to either increase the fares or reduce profit margins, although it may well have kept prices artificially low initially in order to build the market and recoup launch costs later.

Key routes, such as those across the North Atlantic, attract levels of competition that can make it difficult to operate any services profitably and many airlines that do operate on these routes have suffered losses and low load factors for many years.

The development of hub-and-spoke systems

Major airlines in the USA recognized that attempting to serve all airports with maximum frequency city-to-city flights was uneconomic, so developed the concept of the **hub-and-spoke system**. The hub airports provide transcontinental and intercontinental services, while the 'spokes' offer connecting flights from regional airports to meet these long-haul services. The latter services can be provided in aircraft that are smaller and cheaper to operate (often turboprops) by low-cost carriers, often working in strategic alliances with the major carriers. Flights are then banked into complexes and, in theory, greater efficiency is achieved. For example, a hub with 55 spokes can create 1500 'city pairs' in this way. Larger aircraft can be used between hubs and higher load factors and better utilization of aircraft are achieved.

EXAMPLE IcelandAir

This airline operates from its hub in Reykjavik and serves 25 airports across Europe, Canada and the USA. This allows passengers from any of eight North American airports to travel to any of 17 European destinations, so potentially creating 136 paired cities for transatlantic flights (see Figure 13.6).

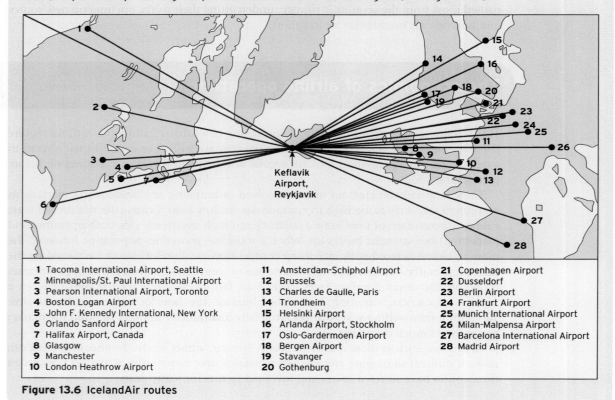

1 Tacoma International Airport, Seattle	**11** Amsterdam-Schiphol Airport	**21** Copenhagen Airport
2 Minneapolis/St. Paul International Airport	**12** Brussels	**22** Dusseldorf
3 Pearson International Airport, Toronto	**13** Charles de Gaulle, Paris	**23** Berlin Airport
4 Boston Logan Airport	**14** Trondheim	**24** Frankfurt Airport
5 John F. Kennedy International, New York	**15** Helsinki Airport	**25** Munich International Airport
6 Orlando Sanford Airport	**16** Arlanda Airport, Stockholm	**26** Milan-Malpensa Airport
7 Halifax Airport, Canada	**17** Oslo-Gardermoen Airport	**27** Barcelona International Airport
8 Glasgow	**18** Bergen Airport	**28** Madrid Airport
9 Manchester	**19** Stavanger	
10 London Heathrow Airport	**20** Gothenburg	

Figure 13.6 IcelandAir routes

Some 40 hubs were soon established in the USA alone, serving 25 of America's largest cities. Within a few years of their introduction, passengers taking advantage of hub-and-spoke systems accounted for three-quarters of the total at Atlanta airport and half at Chicago, Denver and Dallas/Fort Worth. Similarly, in Europe the hub-and-spoke system was brought into operation by leading airlines, notable among them KLM, which, with Schiphol Airport as its hub, had soon built up some ten waves of spoke flights a day to feed into its European and long-haul services. In this way, the airline was able to attract traffic from UK regional airports to connect with its major routes, in direct competition with long-haul flights from London's airports.

Such systems are generally best suited to feeding long-haul flights, as the additional stopover time called for by joining via a spoke is only a small proportion of the total journey. It later became apparent, however, that there are also diseconomies that accrue from operating these systems. The organization of hub-and-spoke flights requires frequent waves of closely spaced banks of arrivals and departures to be established, resulting in peaks and troughs at the hub airports, which puts further pressure on congested air and terminal space and leads to delays. It also requires larger numbers of handling staff on the ground during peaks and involves further peaking expenses. Obviously, on-time performance becomes even more significant under these circumstances, and, if airlines are forced to delay departures while waiting for delayed inbound flights, costs rise.

Some airports are clearly better suited than others to coping with this way of working. Schiphol has benefited from hub-and-spoke flights being based in the same terminal, which means that delays in passengers making their connections are less catastrophic than at Brussels airport, for example, where they have to travel between terminals by airport bus.

There is now growing evidence that, in some circumstances, airlines remaining outside the hub-and-spoke system can be more profitable than those within it. They can do this by charging a higher fare for non-stop services, so even though the demand is not as great, it may still be equally profitable. This applies particularly to business flights, where non-stop services are seen as critical. We have noted elsewhere the success of Southwest Airlines, particularly in gaining market share by flying city-to-city within the USA. There are clear limits on the extent to which city-to-city services can be viable, however; it is dependent on passenger demand and the distances to be travelled.

The growth of strategic alliances

As the problems arising from open competition are obviously going to be long-term ones, the aviation industry has been caught up in a huge global restructuring exercise since the 1990s. European airlines had seen and taken account of developments in the North American market. They recognized that size, which provides economies of scale and scope, would be crucial to survival in the future. They also noted that US domestic carriers were expanding into transatlantic routes and are now benefiting from the five freedoms of the air in Europe, posing further threats to market share. The way forward for the European carriers is seen as lying in either mergers and takeovers or the development of strategic alliances with US carriers.

Alliances are easier to establish, but experience has shown that they can prove less durable. Political differences and differences of management style have frequently hindered effectiveness. The short-lived relationships between BA and United Airlines and between Lufthansa and Air France are cases in point, while the much-vaunted attempt in 1993 to form an alliance between Swissair, Austrian Airlines, SAS and KLM, known as Alcazar, also foundered before being implemented, owing to failure to agree on a US partner. The movement of airlines between the various alliances in order to gain competitive edge also demonstrates the highly fluid nature of these alliances.

Evidence now points to the success of strategic alliances as being dependent on expansion in three stages. First, there is a need to secure a dominant share in the home market. BA undertook expansion specifically through franchising, absorbing 100% of Brymon Airways, and soon held six franchises in the UK, as well as a further four overseas. Air France absorbed a number of domestic French carriers, as did KLM Dutch carriers. More recently, Air Berlin, has expanded rapidly – first by buying DBA (a German domestic carrier first launched by BA) in 2006, followed in 2007 by its purchase of charter operator LTU.

The second step is to gain a strong foothold in the main European countries, especially the UK, France and Germany. This was achieved, for example, by SAS, which controlled 40% of British Midland by the early 1990s, and KLM, which purchased Air UK.

The final stage is the globalization of the carrier, especially through investments in North America and the Asia/Pacific region. BA became a leader in this strategy, taking a minority investment in Australian carrier Qantas in 1992 and seeking similar investments in US carriers, although this is only now becoming realised as links with American Airlines are coming to fruition. The Air France/KLM link-up with Delta is an indication of the achievement of this final step in the process.

Global alliances are now seen as the way forward. They embrace key airlines in Europe, North America and the Asia/Pacific region. While the specific membership of each of these changes quite frequently, the picture in 2011 was as follows:

- *One World* (formed 1998) with current members BA, American Airlines, Qantas, Cathay Pacific, Iberia, Finnair, LAN Chile, Japan Airlines, Malév, Mexicana, Royal Jordanian, S7, together with affiliated regional carriers.
- *Star Alliance* (1997) with Air Canada, Air China, Air New Zealand, ANA, Asiana Airlines, Austrian Airlines, BMI, Continental Airlines, LOT Polish Airlines, Lufthansa, SAS, Singapore Airlines, South African Airways, Spanair, Swiss, TAP Portugal, Thai Airways International, United Airlines, US Airways and associated regional members.
- *Skyteam* (2000) with Aeroflot, Aeromexico, Air Europa, Air France/KLM, Alitalia, China Airlines, China Eastern. China Southern, Czech Airlines, Delta Air Lines, Kenya Airways Korean Air, TAROM and Vietnam Airlines

Two other former alliances – Wings and Qualiflyer – have become defunct as airlines merged or were driven out of service.

EXAMPLE   **Air India alliance on hold**

In the summer of 2011, Star Alliance announced that plans for Air India to join the group had been placed on hold. The airline had been working towards membership since 2007 and it had expected to have completed the process by 2010. However, the minimum terms of membership – which ensure integration of systems between all the alliance airlines – had not been met and therefore existing members of the alliance refused entry to the struggling airline. Air India lost over $1 billion in 2010 and has undertaken debt restructuring in order to continue its operations. Joining the alliance would have helped strengthen its international operations and so this delay in membership will clearly have an impact on its business operations.

Globalization is an inevitable consequence of the growth of the international airline business. A strategic alliance offers opportunities for rapid global growth, coupled with marketing benefits that cannot be achieved as an individual airline. For example, it allows domestic spokes to be tacked on to international routes, as the long-standing alliance between the US carrier Northwest (now part of Delta) and Dutch carrier KLM demonstrated. An effective alliance increases the viability of marginal routes and allows carriers to compete on routes where, separately, they do not hold rights. They also enable companies to reduce costs by using larger aircraft to meet overall demand and sharing operational costs, such as counter space at airports and baggage handling. Marketing costs such as advertising may also be shared. Other operational benefits include control over air terminals. At Heathrow, terminal 5 has become the BA hub, terminal 3 is destined to become a One World hub, while the new terminal soon to replace terminals 1 and 2 will be assigned to Star Alliance carriers.

Alliances may range from the marginal, such as having an interline agreement to accept one another's documentation and transfer of passengers; to marketing agreements, such as joint frequent flyer programmes; and to operational agreements, such as blocking space on one another's aircraft to sell their seats. The commonest advantage to be gained, though, is that of code-sharing.

Code-sharing

Domestic code-sharing was in practice within the USA as long ago as 1967, but was first introduced internationally in 1985, when American Airlines and Qantas agreed to share codes on routes across the Pacific.

Under a code-sharing agreement, two airlines agree to share their codes on through routes – for example, between New York and San Francisco and from San Francisco to

Sydney. This has the marketing advantage of appearing to be a single through flight, but there are also very concrete advantages for passengers, in that flight timings are coordinated, transfer times between stopovers may be reduced (and carriers will often hold flights for up to 20 minutes for passengers connecting from flights that are code-shared) and baggage can be checked through to the final destination, enhancing passenger convenience. Carriers can sell each other's flights as if they were their own and will frequently block off space to do so. A further advantage is that code-shared flights are featured on computer reservations systems before other connections, as these offer passengers the best value. They may also benefit from multiple listing on the computerized reservation system (CRS) as they will be listed under both carriers' services.

EXAMPLE Code-sharing

Although there are said to be benefits of code-sharing for passengers, largely related to convenience in scheduling and baggage arrangements, concern has been raised that such practices can reduce competition on routes. In July 2011, American Airlines announced the expansion of links with Cathay Pacific to add additional flights on the transpacific routes. The agreement, however, was to increase code-sharing activities; no additional planes would be flying. This means there would be a greater chance that passengers booking with Cathay Pacific may end up on a plane owned and crewed by American Airlines, or vice versa – with all the differences in, for example, service quality, safety and customer support that are to be found in two distinct airlines.

The establishment of code-sharing across the Atlantic has been crucial to the successful marketing of long-haul travel and has been extensively used by European carriers to gain access to US domestic destinations. European airlines recognize that US airlines will continue to dominate the global marketplace, partly owing, of course, to the huge demand for both domestic and international travel by American travellers. Success for the European carriers therefore depends on establishing close links with at least one of the leading US carriers.

Airline costs

The selection of suitable aircraft for a route is the outcome of the assessment of relative costs involved (both capital and operating) and the characteristics of the aircraft themselves.

Capital costs

The global growth in demand for passenger services since the turn of the century has averaged between 4 and 7%, and the ICAO has forecast that this pattern will continue up to 2016 at least, with highest growth in the Asia/Pacific region. This growth comes in spite of the impact of the 9/11 tragedy and the subsequent escalation in oil prices. Airlines must therefore plan for continued expansion and regular renewal, with one eye on operating costs while also focusing on customer demand; for example, newer aircraft appeal to passengers in terms of both safety and aesthetics.

With the latest superjumbos costing in excess of $300 million, investment in new aircraft is a huge commitment. Attractive loan terms are likely to be a key factor in closing sales, and some manufacturers are willing to offer very favourable trade-ins on old aircraft in order to sell their new models. Orders for new aircraft are usually a package, embracing not only the aircraft themselves but also the subsequent provision of spares and possibly servicing. Additionally, there are periods when supply will exceed demand and, when there are many second-hand aircraft on the market, the competition between manufacturers for sales enables airlines to drive very hard bargains when purchasing new equipment.

Airlines also have the choice, of course, of leasing aircraft rather than purchasing them and, although they may incur penalties for doing so, if an airline is hit by recession and a sharp drop in demand, it may well cut back on orders already placed, choosing to lease rather than purchase to keep capital costs down. On occasion, this can result in an airline selling existing aircraft and leasing them back to release capital.

Operating costs

Mile for mile, short-haul routes (of up to 1500 miles) overall are more expensive to operate than are long-haul, although this is not simply due to the cost of the fuel used. While the greater frequency of take-offs and landings on short-haul flights will mean high initial fuel consumption on each leg as aircraft gain height, research (Webster, 2002) has shown that an aircraft travelling long distances in a single hop can consume more fuel than one stopping three times on the same route. The example given was of a 9000-mile flight, which, flown non-stop, consumes 120 tonnes of fuel, while an aircraft taking three 3000-mile hops will need only 28 tonnes for each hop – a total of 84 tonnes. The explanation for this is that, ironically, long-haul aircraft use more fuel because they are carrying the weight of the extra fuel needed for the longer journey. When factoring in the additional costs of crewing and landing fees for both forms of travel, however, shorter-haul costs will rise higher than those of long-haul and force up ticket prices.

EXAMPLE The effect of oil price increases

One estimate put the typical fuel burn of flying a Boeing 767 or Airbus A330 between London and New York at 12 800 gallons, reducing to 10 800 gallons for the return flight, due to favourable tail winds (Robertson, 2008). In 2000, with fuel costing just 87 cents a gallon, a return journey would have cost $20 532 in fuel alone. In 2011, aviation fuel had risen to $3.19 a gallon, putting the round trip fuel cost up to $75 284 - almost a four-fold increase. At the same time, intense competition was forcing airlines to keep ticket prices down.

To manage costs, flight planning - determining routes which can in part help maximize operating efficiencies - has become an important activity for airlines, which are now investing in IT technology to enhance this.

Short-haul aircraft also spend a proportionately greater amount of time on the ground than long-haul aircraft. Aircraft are only earning money while they are in the air and depreciation of their capital cost can only be written off against their actual flying time. For this reason, it is important that they are scheduled for the maximum number of flying hours each day. According to the efficiency of the airline and the airports the airline uses, productivity can be increased without impairing the (legally determined) minimum service and maintenance time required (Boeing 747 servicing entails 35–60 work hours, with a complete overhaul, after 6000 hours of flying, involving 10 000 work hours). Here, the American carriers appear to be more successful than the European, with the big three US carriers flying at least ten hours per day on short- and medium-haul flights, against a European average of only seven hours (although there are marked differences between the productivity of the various airlines within Europe). In the USA, aircraft turnarounds (time spent on the ground between landing and take-off) can be as little as 30 minutes, while in Europe a minimum of 45 minutes is the norm. Budget airlines, however, perform significantly better than the traditional carriers, owing in part to their operating out of less congested airports.

Long-haul aircraft normally operate at a ceiling of 30 000–40 000 feet (supersonics were operating at 50 000–60 000 feet), while short- and medium-haul aircraft will operate at lower ceilings. While the cost of getting the long-haul aircraft to its ceiling will be greater than that of a short- and medium-haul aircraft, once at these heights, there is little wind resistance and the rate at which fuel is burned falls considerably.

Improving technology is constantly extending the distances that aircraft can fly non-stop. Singapore Airlines introduced the world's longest non-stop flights in 2003 when they started operating Airbus A345s between Singapore and Los Angeles (16 hours out, 18.5 hours back) and Singapore–New York (18 hours), while Virgin has announced its intention of operating the Boeing Dreamliner 787s direct from London to Perth (17 hours' flying time). The customer appeal of travelling direct and reducing overall travel time is high, but may be offset by concern over very long, uninterrupted flights and growing awareness of the potential dangers of deep vein thrombosis (DVT). Recent research is pointing to a 12% increase in the likelihood of developing DVT among long-haul passengers over other passengers.

Costs can be subdivided into the **direct** costs of operating and **indirect** costs. The former will include flight expenses (salaries of flight crew, fuel, in-flight catering), plus maintenance, depreciation, aircraft insurance and airport and navigation charges. Airport charges will include landing fees, parking charges, navigation charges (where these are passed on to the airline by the airport) and a per capita cost according to the number of passengers carried. Navigation charges vary according to the weight of the aircraft and the distance flown over a particular territory. Many of these charges are incorporated into the price of the ticket or are charged as a supplement to the passenger.

EXAMPLE   **Surcharges to passengers on a return flight from London to New York**

The burden of surcharges is increasing sharply on airline travel. One example, for a BA flight from London Heathrow to New York (JFK) in economy class revealed 11 different taxes surcharges to the basic passenger fare.

Government and Airport fees	£
Air Passenger Duty	60.00
Passenger Service Charge - Heathrow	30.63
Customer User Fee - JFK	3.40
Animal and Plant Heath User Fee - USA	3.10
US Immigration and Naturalization Service user fee	4.30
Passenger Civil Aviation Security Service Fee - USA	1.50
Passenger Facility Charge	2.80
British Airways fees	
Fuel Surcharge	165.00
Insurance and Security Surcharge	10.00
Total	**280.73**

Source: BA website, 2011

Premium class passengers, such as those travelling in business class, are required to pay a higher UK passenger duty, which would add a further £60 to the ticket price.

After 1998, the notional weight of passengers on EU services was increased, adding to costs. The previous 75 kilos for males and 65 kilos for females was replaced by a notional weight of 84 kilos per capita for scheduled flights and 76 kilos for holiday charters, in recognition of the trend for people to have increased in body weight internationally.

This higher figure had already been adopted by US and some other carriers, but, in fact, the US opted for a still higher figure in 2005 – moving from 185 pounds (84 kilos) to 200 pounds (nearly 91 kilos) for males and a slightly lower figure for females. The USA allows a further five pounds per passenger in winter, in recognition of the need for a higher fuel burn than in summer. These figures, however, include carry-on bags, unlike regulations in Europe. Japanese airlines operate on a notional body weight of 73 kilos (regardless of the nationality of those carried), which enables Japanese carriers to gain advantage over others by providing more seats. The tendency towards obesity among the populations of the developed countries is causing concern for airlines anxious to control their costs as the average extra weight now carried increases fuel costs considerably.

EXAMPLE No frills airlines

The no frills airlines have taken steps to recover costs associated with the increasing weight of their passengers. In 2004, Maersk Air introduced three seat sizes: basic fares are paid for the smallest, with a pitch of 70 centimetres on their Boeing 737-700s. For a slightly higher fare, passengers can book a medium seat, with an 80-centimetre pitch, while an upgrade to an X-large seat can be made for an additional payment. Southwest Airlines, on the other hand, require obese passengers (discreetly referred to in the USA as COS – customers of size) to purchase two seats. Air France announced a similar policy early in 2010, offering 25% discount on the second seat. It is a delicate matter for booking and check-in staff to determine how obese a passenger must be before they have to impose the extra charge! The test of obesity is whether or not the armrest between passengers can be dropped - something that would be debateable until the passenger was actually on board.

While the no frills carriers make efforts to improve their slim per capita profits as fuel prices increase, at the other end of the scale equal efforts are being made to reduce aircraft weight in other directions, as we saw earlier in this chapter.

Depreciation is the cost of writing off the original purchase price of the aircraft against the number of hours it flies (which may be as high as 4000 hours per year). Total depreciation periods vary. In the case of smaller, relatively inexpensive aircraft, it may be as short as eight to ten years, while wide-bodied jets may be depreciated over periods as long as 14 to 16 years. A residual value of, typically, 10% of the original purchase price is normally allowed for. In some cases, it might be considered prudent to write off aircraft faster than this because obsolescence can overtake their operating life and airlines must keep up with their competitors by re-equipping at regular intervals. With falling profits, however, few airlines find it easy to re-equip and so the tendency is to extend depreciation time. On top of this, insurance costs will be around 3% per annum of the aircraft's purchase price.

Indirect costs include all non-flight expenses, such as marketing, reservations, ground handling, administration and other insurances, such as passenger liability. These costs will vary very little however many flights are flown, so large airlines will clearly benefit from economies of scale here.

Fuel costs globally are quoted in US dollars and will therefore vary not only according to changing oil prices but also according to changing currency exchange rates. Fuel costs represented about 20% of all operating expenses in 2007, but doubled the following year, hence efforts made by airlines to reduce fuel burn. As we saw earlier, airlines can contract to buy fuel in advance if they fear that prices will rise. Typically, it is the larger airlines with bigger financial reserves that are best placed to do this, but budget airlines, most concerned to control costs, have also hedged. In the USA, Southwest was the sole carrier to cap its fuel costs in 2005, at $26 a barrel, with a contract providing generous terms until 2009. With hindsight, this was an extremely shrewd move. Although hedging does not always save the airline money (oil prices can go down as well as up and the cost of hedging is expensive), it does smooth out cash flow and reduce volatility.

Other ways to trim costs have included reducing the labour force, while renegotiating levels of pay and conditions of service (often at the expense of good staff–management relations), and moving activities to countries where costs are lower. Several companies have moved parts of their administration functions to India, while others have renegotiated contracts for maintenance or cleaning services with other low-cost countries. Savings can also be achieved by forming low-cost subsidiaries – a move taken by several traditionally high-cost European and American carriers. Above all, distribution costs can be trimmed, given the new means of reaching passengers direct. This will be discussed later on in this chapter.

Aircraft characteristics

These will include the aircraft's cruising speed and **block speed** – its average overall speed on a trip – its range and field length requirements, its carrying capacity and customer appeal. In terms of passenger capacities, airline development tends to occur in leaps. Thus, with the introduction of jumbo jets, the number of seats on an aircraft tripled, and with the new generation of superjumbos there has been a further sharp increase in capacity. While average seat costs fall sharply as seat numbers are increased, this can only be reflected in lower prices to passengers if sufficient seats are filled.

Carrying capacity is also influenced by the **payload** that the aircraft is to carry – that is, the balance between fuel, passengers and freight. An aircraft is authorized to 'take off at MTOW' (maximum take-off weight), which is its empty operating weight plus payload. At maximum payload, the aircraft will be limited to a certain range, but can increase this range by sacrificing part of the payload – that is, by carrying fewer passengers. Sacrificing both fuel *and* some passenger capacity may allow some aircraft to operate from smaller regional airports with short runways.

Cost savings can be made in a number of ways when using larger aircraft. It is a curious fact that the relative cost of pushing a large aircraft through the air is less, per unit of weight, than a small one (incidentally, this principle also holds true in shipping operations, in that large ships are cheaper per unit of weight to push through the water than smaller ones). Larger aircraft experience proportionately lower drag per unit of weight; they are more aerodynamic. They can also use larger, more powerful engines. Equally, maintenance and cleaning costs per seat are lower.

Environmental concerns

Airline operations are facing a growing challenge, politically and economically, regarding the concern over aircraft emissions and their impact on the environment. Greenhouse gases – notably CO_2 (carbon dioxide), but also nitrogen oxide and vapour trails that trap heat in the atmosphere when aircraft are flying at height – are now widely acknowledged to add to the problems of global warming. The emissions created by global aircraft movements are estimated to account for around 3% of these gases. As emissions are more damaging at higher altitudes, however, the relative impact may mean that this figure can probably be doubled. Some estimates are far higher. The UK Department for Transport, for example, has placed the figure as high as 13% and believes that, even allowing for a 50% increase in fuel efficiency, emissions will still increase by 50% by 2020, given the projected increase in flights. The UK government is pledged to reduce CO_2 emissions by 20% by 2020 and by 60% by 2050, but there are doubts that these figures are achievable, especially given the same government's expansion plans for, *inter alia*, a third runway at London's Heathrow Airport.

Individual airlines have made some rather half-hearted efforts to offset emissions. BA introduced a 'green fee', ranging from £5 on short-haul flights to £25 for the longest – the money going towards energy-saving projects in developing countries. The disadvantage of the scheme was that it was voluntary and fewer than one in 200 passengers volunteered to pay it when it was first introduced in 2005. Critics have argued in favour of taxation, pointing out that, were aviation fuel to be taxed at the same rate as petrol, a return flight from London to Sydney should attract taxes of £714.

The Chicago Convention precludes the unilateral imposition of fuel taxes by one country and there is little likelihood of obtaining a global agreement to tax aviation fuel. Given the high price of rail tickets in the UK, the final proposal would probably result in encouraging more car traffic on to already congested roads.

Many environmentalists are putting their faith in an emissions trading scheme (ETS). Airlines were required to join this scheme in 2012 and upward of 900 airlines were granted emissions allowances, the majority receiving allowances of approximately 85% of existing levels. The scheme requires organizations, including these airlines, to either reduce their levels or buy carbon allowances at market prices – Air France became the first airline to start trading on the BlueNext emissions exchange (an environmental equivalent of a stock exchange). While some airlines will reduce emissions, this scheme may result in others accepting that they need to purchase additional allowances. In January 2012, Ryanair announced it would raise ticket costs by 25 eurocents to cover the costs of the ETS and there is an expectation that other airlines may well follow suit.

EXAMPLE EU policy to reduce the environmental impact of airlines

An EU policy designed to reduce carbon emissions will have an impact on those airlines flying into European skies. From 1 January 2012, all carriers are required to reduce their emissions or pay a charge, regardless of whether the airline is European or from elsewhere in the world. The reduction in emissions is set at 3% of the average levels between 2004 and 2006 (Rosenthal, 2011).

This policy has attracted criticism – and lawsuits – as airlines argue that the EU should not be able to tax airlines outside Europe for the emissions released into international airspace just because they are en route to a European airport.

Any charges incurred by the airlines are likely to be passed on to passengers in the form of an environmental protection surcharge and this could add as much as £40 to the price of a transatlantic flight.

The marketing of air services

Aside from economic considerations, the customer appeal of an aircraft depends on such factors as seat comfort and pitch, engine quietness, the interior design of cabins and customer service. In a product where, generally speaking, there is a great deal of homogeneity, minor differences such as these can greatly affect the marketing of the aircraft to the airlines and, in turn, the appeal the airline can make to its prospective passengers. For example Air Mauritius (see Figure 13.7) offers business class seats with a 60 inch pitch,

Figure 13.7 Business class seats, Air Mauritius
Photo by Claire Humphreys

comparable with Air France and Emirates which offer similar seat space on their services to Mauritius.

The recent introduction of flat beds in first and business class on long-haul aircraft is an important factor. Some airlines have configured their aircraft to allow only partial recline, such as up to 160°, while others recline a full 180° to make up into a flat bed. Some first class flights now even provide double beds in enclosed suites to provide the ultimate in luxury travel. Such moves are important elements in capturing the key business and celebrity markets.

The marketing division of an airline will play an influential role in determining the destinations to be served, although these decisions are often influenced by government policy and regulation. Marketing personnel must also determine levels of demand for a particular service, the markets to be served and the nature of the competition the airline will face.

Routes are, of course, dependent on freight as well as customer considerations and a decision will have to be reached on the appropriate mix of freight and passengers, as well as the mix of passengers themselves whom the airline is to serve – business, holiday, VFR and so on. An airline can be easily panicked into changing routes unless it recognizes that circumstances can provide opportunities as well as threats. A good example is seen in the collapse of the so-called tiger economies in Asia at the end of the 1990s. In spite of the economic depression experienced by many of these countries, air traffic to the region actually rose because Western travellers took advantage of the currency collapses to increase their leisure travel to the area.

Flight frequencies and timings will be subject to government controls. For example, it is common to find that the government will limit the number of flights it will allow to operate at night. Where long-haul flights and, hence, changing time zones are involved, this can seriously curtail the number of flights an airline can operate. Each individual aircraft is given a quota count (QC) according to the noise it dissipates. The QC of all aircraft flying from an airport at night is totalled and must not exceed the noise quota set by the government for that airport. Boeing 747-400s, for example, are rated at QC2, while the newer 777s and Airbus A340s are quieter, each rated at QC0.5, thus making more night flights possible. Airport and route congestion, of course, will have an additional 'rationing' effect.

It is particularly important for business travellers to be able to make satisfactory connections with other flights. To gain a strategic marketing advantage over competitors, an airline will want to coordinate its flights with complementary carriers, with which it must also have interline agreements (these allow the free interchange of documents and reservations). In planning long-haul flights, the airline must also weigh up whether to operate non-stop flights or provide stopovers to cater for passengers wanting to travel between different legs of the journey (known as 'stage' traffic). Stopovers will permit the airline to cater for, or organize, holiday traffic, as well as allowing additional duty-free shopping opportunities. Alternatively, it may dissuade business passengers from booking if their prime interest is to reach their destination as quickly as possible and another non-stop flight exists. Tahiti experienced a sharp downfall in visitors when the stretched 747-400 was introduced on the transpacific route and it first became possible to fly non-stop between Australia and North America.

Yield management

Following the planning stage, the airline must determine its pricing policy. Fixing the price of a seat is a complex process, involving consideration of:

- the size and type of aircraft operating
- the route traffic density and level of competition
- the regularity of demand flow and the extent to which this demand is balanced in both directions on the route
- the type of demand for air service on the route, taking into account demand for first or business class, economy class, inclusive tour-basing fares and other discounted ticket sales
- the estimated breakeven load factor (the number of seats that must be sold to recover all costs) – typically, this will fall at between 50 and 60% of the aircraft's capacity on scheduled routes and the airline must aim to achieve this level of seat occupancy on average throughout the year (budget airlines will set a much higher load factor as their norm).

The last two points are critical to the success of the airline's marketing. The marketing department is, above all, concerned with **yield management** – the overall revenue that is to be achieved on each route. **Yield** can be defined as the air transport revenue achieved per unit of traffic carried or the total passenger revenue per passenger mile. It is measured by comparing both the cost and revenue achieved per available seat mile (ASM). Balancing the proportion of discounted seats with those for which full fares can be charged, whether in economy or business class, is a highly skilled undertaking as there is a need to ensure that any reduction in full fare will lead to an overall increase in revenue. This is achieved by means of a combination of pricing and the imposition of conditions governing the fares.

Business class, for example, will achieve much higher levels of profit than economy or discounted tickets, so an airline with 10% of its seats given over to business class may achieve 40% of its income from the sale of those seats. The expected demand for the seats on a particular route will call for fine judgement, though. That is because discounted tickets must attract a new market, not draw higher-paying passengers to save money, so they must be hedged with conditions that make them unattractive to prospective business class passengers. Good yield management can, in some cases, even result in full-service airlines undercutting their budget rivals, as the former can charge much higher fares for reservations taken close to departure times, which helps them to offset the discounts given for early bookings.

EXAMPLE | **Changing times and changing cabins**

Budget airlines have, for many years, been successfully balancing revenue maximization and cost reduction through the use of one-class cabins. This has led to a rethink by the full-service carriers. As the business class market has become both more price-sensitive at the bottom end and more likely to use private jets at the top end, so many flag-carrier airlines have chosen to amalgamate their first and business class cabins.

Interestingly, in 2011 American Eagle – the budget arm of American Airlines – announced the introduction of two-cabin services on routes serving the business market. This involved providing larger seats and complementary in-flight catering, and sought to provide superior services for the business and leisure passenger prepared to pay extra for their travel.

One factor that has substantially helped all airlines' yield was the introduction in 2008 of ticketless travel for all IATA carriers. Eliminating the cost of issuing tickets in favour of an e-ticket (with passengers simply being given a reference number for their flights) has been estimated to save carriers an around $3 billion every year.

The growth in bookings using the World Wide Web is a huge bonus for airlines' yield management as, quite apart from avoiding payment of commission, airlines receive payment directly from their passengers when they book, helping cash flow. Previously, payments would be made to travel agents, and payment through the airlines' clearing houses could take up to two months.

Airlines have determined that, in many cases, they can increase yield by downsizing their aircraft and often at the same time increase flight frequency. This increased frequency can also build new passenger traffic, leading to still greater yield – especially where business traffic is concerned. Shuttle services for business travellers were pioneered at one time by Eastern Airlines in the USA, which operated at half-hour intervals between Boston, New York and Washington. These required no advance reservation and the airline guaranteed that a seat would be available. These services were later superseded by no frills carriers.

Boosting yield through frequent flyer programmes

In order to boost overall yield, many airlines have introduced the concept of **frequent flyer** programmes. The idea here is that passengers purchasing airline tickets are entitled to extra free travel, according to the mileage covered. This marketing campaign has been a victim of its own success: over 90 million members worldwide now collect these benefits. One estimate, made in *The Economist* at the end of 2004, claimed that the worldwide stock of airline loyalty schemes, or frequent flyer programmes, was above 14 trillion miles, worth over $700 billion, making them the second-largest convertible currency in the world after the US dollar.

American Airlines was the first to introduce such a scheme in 1981 with its AAdvantage scheme. It is now the biggest scheme in operation, with over 45 million members. Others quickly followed, such as BA's Executive Club, United's Mileage Plus, Virgin Atlantic's Flying Club. The programmes were later extended to allow miles to be accumulated on the value of products purchased at other outlets associated with the airline, such as shops, hotels and petrol stations, as well as partner airlines within the strategic alliances.

The popularity of these schemes has led to so many free seats being offered that airlines are now imposing limitations on their use. (United Airlines, for example, found that, at one point, almost all passengers on its Hawaii-bound flights were frequent flyers, virtually eradicating yield on that route.) While frequent flyers can normally only make use of seats that would otherwise be vacant during the flight, each seat occupied costs the airline the price of the food and fuel consumed and, in total, this still adds up to a substantial cost for the airline.

There is some evidence that airline loyalty schemes are beginning to lose their appeal. Although two-thirds of regular travellers belong to the schemes, a study by Etihad Airways found that only 37% had actually used their frequent flyer points and, by 2005, fewer than one in five were using them. This can be ascribed in part to the restrictions and conditions applied by the airlines to their use.

In recent years airlines have been reducing the generosity of these schemes requiring more miles to be traded for each journey. Furthermore, some airlines, for example, American, have introduced significant charges if passengers wish to use the loyalty points to upgrade to a higher cabin class, making this a far less appealing option.

Deep discounting

All scheduled services operate on the basis of an advance reservations system, with the lowest (APEX) fares being available on routes where the booking can be confirmed some time in advance of departure. This allows the airline to judge its expected load factors with greater accuracy.

To fill up seats that have not been prebooked, the airline offers standby fares – available to passengers without reservations who are prepared to take their chances and turn up in the expectation of a seat being free. On many routes, particularly business routes, the chances of seats being available are good, because business passengers frequently book more than one flight to ensure that they can get back as quickly as possible after the completion of their meeting. Airlines will thus overbook to allow for the high number of no shows (up to 30% on some routes), but must exercise caution in case they end up with more passengers than they can accommodate. If this occurs, they can upgrade them to a better class or compensate them financially and provide seats on another flight, but this may not be sufficient to satisfy an irate business passenger. The EU's insistence on high levels of compensation for these bumped passengers has also caused some airlines to rethink their strategy in permitting business tickets to be refunded without question.

The airline distribution system

The distribution system consists of two elements: the reservation (or booking) and the issue and delivery of a ticket, where pertinent.

Traditionally, air tickets were sold and distributed through travel agents at an agreed rate of commission, with a proportion also sold direct by the airlines to their passengers. In the USA, the high volume of air travel allowed many more airlines to sell direct, through branch offices in the larger cities, than was possible in the UK. The development of the Internet has now changed this pattern of distribution, with a far greater proportion of sales (and, in the case of some no frills airlines, all sales) being made through this channel, either direct with the airlines or via Internet intermediaries' own websites.

In the face of the crises impacting on the airline industry over the past few years, airlines have re-evaluated their distribution systems, seeking to cut costs wherever possible. The first to suffer in this process of re-evaluation has been the travel agent, with commissions first being trimmed, then cut savagely and now largely discontinued, requiring agents to charge their customers a fee for the service they provide. Such a move, however, may further deter customers from booking through intermediaries. As most leading airlines have tended to follow the no commission route, threats by agents to switch-sell air products have had little effect.

Electronic ticketing (commonly referred to as **e-ticketing**) and so-called ticketless travel are now almost universal practices, greatly reducing an airline's costs. This further encourages airlines to push direct sales, with the consequent worrying (for travel agents) fall in the number of airline tickets being booked through intermediaries. There is little doubt that the challenge represented by these moves is requiring agents to rethink their whole rationale and means of operation. All electronic booking systems encourage passengers to book direct and their increasing ease of use, coupled with low fares, pose a major threat to agents.

The EC has been monitoring the websites of airlines to check that the prices advertised were a fair reflection of what the customer could expect to pay. Concern was raised that airlines, particularly low-cost airlines, were not adhering to rules on commercial practices, which had led to a situation where flight prices advertised did not include compulsory fees and surcharges, thus making price comparisons difficult. By 2009, an EC investigation revealed that 57 airlines now abided by the regulations, whilst a further 15 examined had agreed to make appropriate changes. In the longer term, it is likely that these monitoring efforts will ensure more transparent pricing for the consumer.

 EXAMPLE   **Comparing prices**

The Internet has spawned a threat to airlines, with the growth of flight price comparison sites. These sites, examples of which include skyscanner.net and travelsupermarket.com, search GDS systems and tour operator databases to identify the cheapest flights from a number of providers (sometimes limited to those who have agreed terms with the comparison site).

These Internet sites provide customers with a quick way to evaluate the lowest prices for a given route and offer hyperlinks to the site for convenient booking. The comparison sites will earn a fee for each link used, allowing the service to be offered to passengers for free.

The first step in the introduction of high technology to airline distribution systems was the CRS, which provided agents and their clients with a fast and accurate indication of flight availability and fare quotations, coupled with an online reservations service.

The next step was the introduction of the GDS, in which leading airlines themselves held major shareholdings. These rapidly spread to embrace worldwide hotel, car rental and other reservations facilities, and the leading GDSs battled for market leadership in travel agents worldwide. The US systems – notably Sabre, Apollo and Worldspan – either competed against or integrated with the two leading European systems, Galileo and Amadeus.

The key to dominance in this field lies in the way in which agents make use of the information displayed. Access to a large number of major world airlines is possible using these systems and 75–80% of all bookings are made using only the first page of information shown. Formerly, bias in the way information is displayed was declared illegal under US and EU law, but the US Department of Transportation ended restrictive regulations on the GDSs in 2004, as the airlines gradually reduced the stock they sold through this system in the wake of the 9/11 disaster, preferring to sell direct via their own websites.

In the following year, it became EU policy to allow airlines to have commercial agreements with the GDSs that resulted in their favouring certain carriers. While the US carriers no longer have a stake in the GDSs, European carriers Iberia and Lufthansa both hold shares in Amadeus. The GDSs are, in turn, having to face the challenge of new websites – either those of the airlines themselves or intermediaries such as expedia.com, ebookers.com and travelocity.com selling their services. These electronic retailers – the so-called **e-tailers** – have become a major force in the distribution system, particularly for the sale of late availability tickets.

The GDS companies argue that the establishment of websites by intermediaries is unnecessary, given that they themselves are coming to utilize the World Wide Web to provide the same range of travel products, but the intermediaries have successfully challenged these well-established and proven systems.

Apart from their own websites, airlines have also come together to organize joint websites for interactive reservations and information. The US website Orbitz was established in 2000 by five US carriers – American, Delta, United, Northwest and Continental – while the European Opodo network (initially launched by nine European airlines) followed in 2001. These offer access to hotels and car hire, in addition to airline flights.

The extent to which online bookings are replacing traditional channels of distribution may be judged when it is revealed that the leading no frills airlines are becoming almost totally dependent on sales via the Web and promote this medium prominently.

The first decade of the twenty-first century saw the integration of electronic booking agencies. Opodo bought a 74% interest in Amadeus in 2004 (with the balance retained by the original air carriers) and has since moved into tour operating itself, having purchased five travel companies, including long-haul specialist Quest. The travel conglomerate Travelport – its holding company, Blackstone, owning many travel industry companies – owns Galileo, a large part of Orbitz.com and consolidated its hold on the GDS market with the purchase of Worldspan in 2006. The GDS company Sabre (now in private ownership), owns travelocity.com, which itself took over lastminute.com. This process of integration is likely to continue.

Future developments in the technological field are likely to involve expansion into social media, which will provide channels for consumers to communicate with the airlines directly as well as booking their airline tickets electronically. Early initiatives have included mobile phone applications dedicated to providing quotes, taking bookings and managing the online check-in process. More recent developments have seen the introduction of Facebook pages where quotes can be obtained by posting requests onto the provider's wall. Whether these systems will become popular with passengers remains to be seen.

The role of the air broker

One comparatively little-known role in the airline business is that of the **air brokers**. These are the people who act as intermediaries regarding the control of seats rather than merely their sale between aircraft owners and their customers. They provide a level of expertise to business clients, travel agents or tour operators who may have neither the time nor the knowledge to involve themselves in long negotiations for the best deals in chartering aircraft seats. They maintain close contact with both airlines and the charter market and can frequently offer better prices for charters than tour operators could themselves.

They play an important role in securing aircraft seats in times of shortage, and in disposing of spare capacity at times of oversupply. The broker takes charge of the entire operation, booking the aircraft and taking care of any technical requirements, including organizing the contract and arranging any special facilities.

In their role as so-called **consolidators** they purchase seats on scheduled airlines on demand, at discounted rates, and can sell these on to agents at the usual rates of commission. Leading companies in the UK include Gold Medal Travel, Travel 2 and Travel 4. Flight-only operators buy blocks of seats or a whole aircraft to sell wherever they can find a market. Avro is the leading UK company in this field, with over a million passengers every year. These roles are all ones that may be challenged by electronic direct booking systems.

What is the future like for air transport?

In looking to the future, one must take into account both the short and long term. The short term is dominated by the need to reduce operating costs, particularly focusing on fuel burn as oil prices become increasingly volatile.

Despite a global economic downturn, many believe that the habit of going on holiday is so ingrained that it will be one of the last luxuries to be surrendered by consumers. Nevertheless, the short term has seen increased interest in domestic travel, often using land-based, rather than air, transport.

Aviation experts agree that the development of jet aircraft has reached a plateau, productivity and efficiency being unlikely to improve substantially. While costs per seat kilometre may fall as larger aircraft such as the Airbus A380 (seating between 500 and 800 passengers) come onstream, any savings are certain to be outstripped by increases in other costs.

There is growing pressure to reduce the environmental impact of flying, although it is yet to be accompanied by a decision by significant numbers of travellers to switch to alternative methods of transport.

Perhaps, for students, the most interesting area of speculation is the progress towards the development of hypersonic flight. The reality of space flight is on us, albeit still with a substantial cost attached. Virgin Galactic are expecting to start scheduled suborbital flights from the Mojave Desert in 2013, carrying passengers into space, for a one-hour flight, at a cost predicted to be $200 000. Even at this fare, Virgin claim to have nearly 85 000 people registered to fly. Although few would be prepared, or able, to pay the huge sums involved to go on these trips, research carried out by US aeronautical company Futron revealed that, while only 50 people a year would be willing to spend the equivalent of $20 million for a week in space, a further 15 000 a year would be prepared to invest $100 000 for a 20-minute suborbital ride, supporting the applications waitlisted for Branson's project.

EXAMPLE The first space tourists

There is some controversy about how many non-scientists/astronauts have actually travelled into space up to the time of writing.

The American Dennis Tito is unchallenged as the first *tourist* into space, in 2001, followed by Mark Shuttleworth, a South African-born Briton in 2002. The American Greg Olsen took the trip in 2005 and Daisuke Enomoto, who is Japanese, followed in 2006.

Those space travellers are thought to have paid between £11 million and £20 million for the privilege. Others to have taken the ride, however, include Toyoshiro Akiyama, a journalist for the Tokyo Broadcasting System, who did so in 1990 and Prince Sultan bin Salman, the head of the Supreme Commission for Tourism in Saudi Arabia, who became the first Arab in space. American politicians Senator Jake Garn and Congressman Bill Nelson are believed to have travelled there in the 1980s.

There are other organizations also working to enter the space tourism market, despite the huge capital investment costs required and the safety hurdles to be overcome. Investment, encouraged by the Ansari X prize – a $10 million competition for the first non-governmental reusable manned spacecraft (won in 2004 with the successful launch of SpaceShipOne) – has been made by EADS Astrim and Space Adventures, who have announced plans to offer travellers a lunar visit.

Questions and discussion points

1. Fuel surcharges and air passenger taxes now make up a significant share of the total ticket price. Do you think these charges have an impact on whether holidaymakers take short breaks by air? Do you think such charges have an impact on either full-service carriers or low-cost carriers?

2. Some airlines are reducing the size of their in-flight magazines. Do you think customers notice this change? Why do airlines provide these magazines?

3. The quote at the beginning of the chapter identifies problems facing Heathrow, particularly the competition it faces from other European cities. Given this competition, should the British government expand Heathrow as a matter of urgency?

Tasks

1. In groups discuss ways to reduce the environmental impacts of flying. Choose one idea which could best be implemented by airlines. Provide a presentation, aimed at airline CEOs, which explains both how and why your idea should be implemented.

2. Complete a number of interviews with people who have recently taken a flight. Ask them to identify how they spent their time at the airports they travelled though. What facilities and services were provided by the airports? Were their experiences of the airports positive? Write a short summary of your findings.

Bibliography

A.B. (2011) IATA's boss takes on 'potty' Britain, *The Economist*, 10 February.

ACI Europe (2010) *The ownership of Europe's airports*, Brussels, Airports Council International.

CAA (2011) *Airline profit and loss accounts*, available online at: http://www.caa.co.uk/docs/80/aln_financial/2009_2010/Table_06_Major_UK_Airlines_%20Individual_Airline_Profit_and_Loss_Account_2009.pdf (accessed November 2011).

Chance, K. (2010) Aviation has evolved with Airbus's ultra-quiet titan, *Business Day (South Africa)*, 3 March.

DfT (2009) *UK Air Passenger Demand and CO2 Forecasts*, UK, Department for Transport, November.

Dunn, J. (2007) Softening the supersonic boom, *The Sunday Times*, 11 March.

EC (2011) *Impact assessment of revisions to Regulation 95/93*, Brussels, European Commission.

Flightglobal (2011) *Essential guide to low-cost carriers*, available online at: http://www.emagazine.airlinebusiness.com/Low_Cost_Carriers/1A4daff75355558012.cde (accessed November 2011).

IATA (2011) *World Air Transport Statistics – 55th Edition*, Montreal, International Air Transport Association.

Kohlman, M. (2011) Emirates Airline reduces hedging on oil price volatility, *Platts Commodity News (Dubai)*, 17 May.

Mathews, N. (2010) SIA looks at paperless cabin to reduce weight, costs, *Aviation Daily*, **381** (22), 5.

New Europe (2011) The slot machine, Brussels, *New Europe*, 14 March.

Nugent, H. (2008) Planes 'fly empty' to keep slots at Heathrow, *The Times*, 16 July.

Oxera (2009) *What is the contribution of aviation to the UK economy?*, Oxford, Airport Operators Association, November 2009.

Robertson, D. (2008) European airlines facing profit squeeze, *The Times*, 25 April 2008.

Rosenthal, E. (2011) U.S. and Europe Battle Over Carbon Fees for Airlines, *New York Times*, 27 July.

Tarry, C. (2002) Airline Analyst at Commerzbank, reported in 'Flights of fancy', *The Times*, 3 December.

Webster, B. (2002) Long-haul flights on way back to Earth, *The Times*, 17 January.

West, K. (2011) Melted metal cuts plane's fuel bill, *Sunday Times*, 13 February.

Yallop, R. (1992) People come to rescue of the people's airline, *The Observer*, 19 January.

Websites

Airport Operators Association: **www.aoa.org.uk**

Civil Aviation Authority: **www.caa.co.uk**

International Air Transport Association: **www.iata.org**

14

Tourist transport by water

Contents

Learning outcomes

After studying this chapter, you should be able to:

- identify each category of waterborne transport and the role each plays in the tourism industry
- understand the economics of cruise and ferry operations
- identify the markets for cruising and how cruise companies appeal to each
- be aware of principal world cruise routes and the reasons for their popularity
- be familiar with other forms of waterborne leisure transport and their appeal to tourists.

Traditionally cruise holidays cater to the 'well fed, the newly wed and the nearly dead', but such has been the surge in popularity of holidays on the high seas among a new breed of British traveller there is a looming shortage of bunks.

Martin Hickman, Consumer affairs correspondent, *The Independent* (2011), Britons to carrying on cruising in record-size style

Introduction

The increasing demand for cruise holidays, from a wide variety of markets, has led to the construction and launch of vessels designed to reach new destinations, offer new experiences or cater to the requirements of a younger or more active market. No longer are cruise holidays just for honeymooners, the old or the rich.

Although air travel has become by far the most popular means of travel for tourists, very few passengers treat it as anything other than the most convenient means of getting from A to B. Certainly, the frustrations that accompany this form of travel, such as airport delays, queuing, congestion on the ground and in the air and the relative lack of comfort while airborne, tend to detract from the idea that flights are an enjoyable part of a holiday. Transport by water, on the other hand, *can* be enjoyable in its own right and for many it will be the dominant element in the holiday. When cruising, for example, the intention is not necessarily to arrive at a particular destination, but to enjoy getting there. Whether travelling by sea or inland on lakes, rivers and canals, waterborne holidays have never been more popular, and shipping in all its forms plays an important part in the travel industry. According to one survey undertaken by the US Department of Transportation (in 2004), there were at the time 339 active ocean-going passenger ships, just 38 of which carried fewer than 100 passengers – a figure reflecting the importance of this sector to the travel industry in the early twenty-first century. Cruise ships alone provided almost 295 000 passenger berths in 2009 (Euromonitor, 2010).

Travelling by water is inherently relaxing and cruising requires the luxury of free time, whereas air transport's appeal is largely that of speed – often critical when travelling to a long-haul destination. Although cruising tends to be seen as a more expensive form of holiday than air travel, the wide range of prices available today makes it attractive to most markets and comparable in price to many foreign holidays when the all-inclusive nature of a cruise is taken into consideration.

In recent years, cruising has staged an astonishing revival after several decades of decline, and now enjoys a level of popularity not seen since its heyday in the first half of the twentieth century. The advantages of this form of travel are total relaxation and a price that includes all accommodation, food and entertainment (and some cruises now even include drinks and gratuities). Cruises allow the passenger to be carried from one destination to another in comfort and safety, in familiar surroundings and without the need constantly to pack and unpack. Short sea (ferry) vessels have also achieved high levels of comfort and speed on many routes, to a point where they now attract tourists not just as a means of transport, but as an enjoyable 'mini-cruise', with food and entertainment of a standard that a few years ago could be found only on a luxury cruise liner. Technological developments have helped to reduce high operating costs, while new forms of waterborne transport have been developed, such as the hovercraft, jetfoil and twin-hulled catamaran ferry. These have provided rapid communication over short sea routes and sometimes, as in the case of the hovercraft, across difficult terrain.

The pleasure that people find in simply being afloat has spawned many recent tourist developments, from yacht marinas and self-drive motor craft to dinghy sailing in the Mediterranean and narrow boat holidays in the UK and on the European mainland. The continuing fascination with older means of propulsion has led to the renovation and operation of lake steamers in England and on the Continent of Europe, purpose-built and often classic river boats operating on the Rhine and Danube in Europe, the Nile in Egypt and the Irrawaddy in Myanmar, excursion vessels operating out of seaports in many countries and even a paddle steamer plying the Mississippi River in the USA.

In this chapter, we will investigate the appeal and operation of these various forms of water transport. It is convenient to divide them into five distinct categories:

- line voyage shipping
- cruise shipping
- short sea shipping, more familiarly known as ferries
- inland waterway and excursion vessels
- privately chartered or owned pleasure craft.

These categories will be considered in turn.

The ocean liners

Line voyage services are those offering passenger transport on a port-to-port basis rather than as part of a cruise. Ships travelling these routes are known as **liners**. This form of transport has declined to a point where very few such services exist any longer and those that do tend to be operated on a seasonal basis. The reasons for this decline are not hard to identify.

From the 1950s onwards, advances in air transport enabled fares to be reduced, especially on popular routes across the Atlantic, to a point where it became cheaper to travel by air than by ship. The shipping lines, which, until the advent of aircraft, had no competition from alternative forms of transport, could not compete: they faced rapidly rising costs for fuel and labour in a labour-intensive industry. The gradual decline in numbers of passengers as they switched to the airlines led to losses in revenue for the shipping companies that made it impossible to consider renovating ageing fleets or replacing them with new vessels.

By 1957, more passengers were crossing the Atlantic by air than by sea and the demise of the worldwide passenger shipping industry appeared imminent. Leading routes such as Cunard Line's transatlantic services, P&O's services to the Far East and Australia and Union-Castle and British India Lines' services to South and East Africa were either withdrawn or reduced to a skeleton service.

The resulting shake-up in management led to attempts to regenerate passenger demand, mainly by employing the same ships on cruises, but vessels built for fast line voyage services are not ideally suited to alternative uses (many still in service were built for the emigrant trade from Europe and offered four- or six-berth cabins without private facilities), while at the same time the appeal of cruising was beginning to decline. A small but loyal demand for sea transport remained among those (usually older) passengers who feared flying or enjoyed sea voyages and were willing to spend time getting to their destinations. Few lines were able to continue operations to serve such limited markets.

Today, only Cunard Line, among the major carriers, continues to provide a regular summer service across the Atlantic between Southampton and New York; the liner *RMS Queen Mary 2* was introduced in 2005 for this express purpose. The company launched a new vessel in 2008 – a new *Queen Elizabeth*, following the withdrawal of the earlier *Queen Elizabeth 2*. This would enable Cunard to reintroduce a two ship service across the Atlantic, if demand grows sufficiently to profit from this, although the vessel, like her recently introduced companion ship *Queen Victoria*, is currently limited to cruising. Outside of the summer months, *Queen Mary 2* also cruises, although the size of all three ships limits the ports at which they can call.

Apart from this transatlantic service, line voyages technically no longer exist. **Positioning voyages**, in which cruise ships are moved across the Atlantic in the spring and autumn to transfer cruise operations between the Caribbean and Mediterranean for the season, however, do allow these sailings to be sold as line voyages between Europe and Florida or Caribbean ports. Also, a handful of other passenger cargo liners exist around the world, such as the Mauritius Shipping Corporation's services between Mauritius, Réunion Island and South Africa, carrying around 268 passengers, and services from Tahiti carrying up to 60 passengers to the Marquesas islands and Tuamoto atolls in the South Pacific, as well as

Measuring the size of a ship

The size of all vessels is based on their gross registered tonnage (GRT), but it is inaccurate to refer to the 'weight' of a ship. That is because 'gross tonnage' refers to the internal volume of the vessel rather than its weight or displacement. One ton is equal to 100 cubic feet (a measure formally laid down in the Merchant Shipping Act, 1854). Net registered tonnage is the internal volume devoted to passenger and cargo space only, excluding any non-revenue-earning space, such as the engine room, crew accommodation and so on.

As examples, the new Cunarder *RMS Queen Elizabeth* mentioned above has a gross registered tonnage of 90 900 and can carry 2068 passengers, and her sister ship *Queen Mary 2* is 151 400 GRT, accommodating 2620 passengers.

vessels, some carrying nearly 1200 passengers, operated and subsidized by the Indian government, which connect the mainland to the Andaman and Nicobar Islands. The *RMS St Helena* is the sole cargo passenger liner still operating in the Atlantic. At 7000 tons and carrying just 128 passengers, she was built with a UK government subsidy to provide a lifeline to the island dependencies of St Helena and Ascension – the former presently has no airport – and the UK Government continues to subsidize the company. The ship's base has alternated in recent years between Cape Town, South Africa and Portland, in Southern England, making calls at Tenerife and the Ascension Islands en route. This service has always been more important for its freight than its passenger capacity and is expected to be withdrawn when an airport, to be built on St Helena, is eventually opened (a contract to construct the airport was agreed by the UK government in 2011, but construction will take several years).

Apart from these services, there are a number of cargo vessels operating around the world that also accommodate 12 passengers or fewer. This limitation is imposed because the International Maritime Organization (IMO) requires a doctor to be carried as a member of crew if this number is exceeded. Some vessels take as few as two passengers, accommodated in the 'owner's suite', but all are clearly designed for lovers of sea travel for its own sake. Freight demand means that neither departure dates nor ports of call can be guaranteed, nor can it even be certain that passengers will be allowed to disembark at the destinations en route. Entertainment is limited – in some cases, non-existent – on board and passengers dine with the ships' officers. This is not a cheap alternative for long-distance travel – on the contrary, fares on cargo passenger vessels will be comparable to those on cruise ships

Working to keep the coastal waters safe

Trinity House is responsible for the lighthouses in England, Wales and the Channel Islands. As part of their maintenance programme, they operate the THV Patricia, a purpose-built vessel of 2500 tons, designed to service lighthouses, lightships and navigation buoys, all of which are vital to ensure safe navigation in the shipping lanes around the coast of the UK. THV Patricia travels the coast cleaning the buoys, refuelling the lighthouses and even completing testing related to offshore windfarms.

The *Patricia* can accommodate up to 12 passengers in six double cabins, all of which have en suite facilities. Guests on board have their own dedicated chef and steward to ensure a comfortable travel experience – though the nature of being a working vessel means that routes and ports of call will vary, even at late notice. Most trips are week-long, to fit in with crew changeovers, although three and four night options are occasionally available. In 2011, the cost for two people sharing a standard cabin for seven nights was just under £3000.

Further information: www.trinityhouse.co.uk

– but they nevertheless attract an enthusiastic market and passengers frequently have to 'waitlist' their requirements (place their names on a waiting list) a year or more in advance.

The decline of line voyages

The decline of line voyages was not due solely to the rise of air transport. Enterprise was for many years restricted by the so-called 'conferences' (industry agreements) – notably the Transatlantic and Transpacific Passenger Conferences – that governed the operation of fleets worldwide and restrained open competition. Shipping management must also bear much of the blame for its failure to adapt the product to meet changing needs. Ships were built without air conditioning or adequate numbers of cabins with en suite facilities; both essential requirements if ships were to attract the American market. The vessels' specifications and size made them inflexible and unsuitable for routes other than those for which they were built and little was done to adapt them for their new purposes. Shipping managers failed to recognize the extent of the threat posed by the airlines and were too slow to move into that sector themselves. Those that eventually attempted to do so then found that the capital investment required was beyond their available resources.

Traffic conferences were not finally swept away until the 1970s, by which time the market was to all intents lost, and the negative image of cruising, as appealing only to the old and infirm, had become firmly ingrained in the minds of the new generation of travellers. Whether the long-term decline of line voyages anywhere apart from the North Atlantic can ever be reversed is debatable, although tentative proposals have been put forward to build budget ships for transatlantic crossings, as a means of increasing that market, while research is also under way to test the feasibility of developing jet ships, capable of travelling at 40 knots or more. This would allow transatlantic crossings to be completed within 90 hours. The Fjornline Catlink V catamaran made the west–east journey in 1998 at an average speed of 41.3 knots, covering the total distance in two days and 20 hours. The reality is, however, that nothing tangible has emerged that would be capable of sustaining such speeds over these periods of time in the years since jet ship technology was first mooted.

EXAMPLE **The Proteus catamaran**

Currently under test, the prototype for a new form of catamaran, designed in California, gives promise for a new generation of eco-friendly vessels to meet the increasing demands for sustainable sea transport. The light craft uses the WAM-V (Wave Adaptive Modular Vessel) system, in which twin inflatable hulls 'ride' the waves. Modular construction includes use of lightweight material like titanium and aluminium, and a system of springs and ball-joints helps to decrease the impact of rough waters. The prototype is claimed to carry a 12 ton payload at up to 70 mph over a distance of 8000 km. While potentially adaptable for short sea passenger routes, it is questionable whether the vessel could be developed for large vessels, although the company believes it could have potential applications for cruise ships.

Cruising

Although line voyages were also popularly in use for leisure trips, and P&O were marketing their ships for Mediterranean cruises by the mid-nineteenth century, the concept of the purpose-built cruise ship did not arrive until the beginning of the twentieth century.

The first such ship, Hamburg-Amerika Line's 4400-ton *Prinzessin Victoria Luise*, went into service in 1900, but had a lifetime of only six years.

The cruise market emerged gradually, to a point where the ultimate cruise aspiration was a round the world voyage. The 42 300 ton *Empress of Britain* was launched in 1931 specifically to attract passengers to out-of-season round the world voyages, but the intervention of the Depression restricted its appeal. Shorter voyages from US ports became popular around this time, with the advent of Prohibition, as demand was created by the fact that alcohol could be consumed legally once the ship entered international waters. Later, these sailings were extended to Bermuda, Nassau and Havana.

The growth of cruising was delayed by World War II, but, in the immediate aftermath, cruising again became popular, with notable purpose-built ships such as Cunard's *Caronia* entering service in 1949. It went on to achieve enormous popularity, as the 'Green Goddess', for its annual round the world itineraries.

From the 1950s onwards, the passenger shipping industry shifted its emphasis from line voyages to cruising. Initially, this transformation proved difficult, as vessels in service at the time were for the most part too large, too old and too expensive to operate for cruising purposes. Their size was a limiting factor, in terms of the number of ports they could call at, and they were built for speed rather than leisurely cruising. Fuel bills can be cut by operating vessels at slower speeds, but, ideally, cruise ships should be purpose-built to achieve their maximum operational efficiency.

During the 1960s and 1970s, ships of 18 000–22 000 tons, capable of carrying some 650–850 passengers, were built to achieve maximum efficiency. Changes in demand and advances in marine technology, however, enabled later cruise ships to be purpose-built in a variety of sizes. Providing there is sufficient demand, optimum profits can be achieved by employing larger vessels. These do not require any extra deck or engine crew and burn relatively little extra fuel, so adding extra passenger capacity lowers the cost per passenger. The trend since the 1980s has therefore been to build ships of steadily increasing tonnage, first in the range of 50 000–70 000 tons and later in excess of 100 000 tons, capable of carrying as many as 4000–5000 passengers. After the 1970s, it also became popular for companies to return older ships to the shipyards for 'stretching' – that is, cutting the vessel in half and inserting a new section to increase capacity.

There now appears to be a polarization of cruise ships between, on the one hand, very large vessels (see Figure 14.1) and, on the other, much smaller vessels operated by niche companies. This trend towards larger sizes is putting a strain on port facilities and requires

Figure 14.1 Carnival's German managed AIDA operates the *Diva* in the Persian Gulf region, Asia and the Eastern Mediterranean

Photo by Chris Holloway

significantly increased investment, especially in the Caribbean, the cruise market's most important destination.

EXAMPLE   **The largest dominate**

The significance of the move towards larger vessels can be seen when it is realized that four vessels, launched in 2009 and 2010, between them account for 10% of the entire North American capacity. These ships are:

- *Oasis of the Seas* (owned by Royal Caribbean International) with a passenger capacity of 5400
- *Allure of the Seas* (owned by Royal Caribbean International) with a passenger capacity of 5400
- *Norwegian Epic* (owned by Norwegian Cruise Line) with a passenger capacity of 4200
- *Carnival Dream* (owned by Carnival Corporation) with a passenger capacity of 3646

The market is now dominated by only a few players, with the three companies listed above accommodating 96% of all nights spent on board ship.

Source: US DoT, 2011

It has been estimated that, currently, there are well over 340 cruise ships of one type or another operating worldwide, carrying more than 15 million passengers. At the beginning of 2011, a total of 26 new cruise ships were on order for delivery up to 2014, additional to the 12 ships introduced into service in 2010; thus, there is some danger that supply will outstrip demand as new vessels come onstream. However, the phased withdrawal of older vessels will help to compensate for this, and, with demand predicted to grow, particularly in Europe, may well ensure that prices and occupancy rates are retained.

In fact, cruise companies have enjoyed exceptional market growth in recent years, and, with passenger numbers estimated to be around 14 million in 2011, and with forecasts suggesting that the European market will double in size, from 4.9 million to 10 million passengers, by 2020 (British passengers alone will reach 2 million by 2014), prospects remain generally healthy.

More than half of all cruises operate out of US ports, and Americans represent the majority of cruise passengers globally, at around 10.6 million passengers in 2010. In terms of passenger demand, the UK takes second place after the USA, with 1.6 million passengers in 2010, followed by Germany with 1.2 million in 2010 and rather fewer from Italy and Spain (see Table 14.2, on p. 431). All the developed countries are experiencing a marked increase in demand for cruising, after a long period of decline, and growth in this market has averaged between 9 and 15% per annum since the early 1990s. Germany, with a growth rate averaging almost 14% over the five years to 2010, is expected to surpass the UK as European market leader; and the potential long-term market for cruising is predicted to come principally from the European and Asian regions.

The majority of cruise ships are built today by just four West European yards, the leading three companies building nine out of ten of the new cruise ships. Fincantieri in Italy dominates, closely followed by STX Europe (who manage the Aker Yard in Chantiers d'Atlantique, France and the Kvaerner Masa-yards in Finland), Meyer Werft in Germany and Mitsubishi in Japan. Other yards in Finland, South Korea and Japan are responsible for most of the rest of the world's fleet (passenger shipbuilding in the UK having gone into terminal decline in the 1970s). Most new-built vessels will be larger than 60 000 tons and with an average capacity close to 3000 passengers, but, as we have seen some of the largest ships will carry more than 5000 passengers.

The operating costs of these giant vessels are only marginally greater than conventional ships, while the addition of several hundred cabins leads to an increase in onboard spend and boosts overall profitability. With building costs that can go as high as $1 billion – more than twice that of a superjumbo aircraft – these ships represent a huge capital investment for their owners and are something of a gamble, given the volatility of fuel prices.

The whole concept of a cruise holiday has changed from its traditional image. Cruise ships are coming to be seen as floating holiday resorts that conveniently move from one destination to another, offering new scenery every day and non-stop entertainment on board. The very large tonnage allows not only a vast range of public rooms, which on the newest ships include facilities for climbing walls and even ice-skating rinks, but also ensures that passengers have the widest conceivable choice of acquaintances to meet and make friends with on board.

In keeping with this desire to differentiate the product, shipping lines are focusing on novel forms of interior decor. The Norwegian Caribbean Line, to take one example, is restyling its Freestyle ships with cabins that more closely resemble rooms found in the modern art hotels, with curved walls and open bathrooms.

At the other end of the scale, a market has opened for vessels of typically 3000–10 000 tons, carrying around 60–250 passengers. Many of these are aimed at the luxury end of the market, including vessels such as *Le Levant* (90 passengers), the *Clipper Odyssey* (128 passengers) and, slightly larger at 8000 tons, *Le Diamant*, which carries 226 passengers. Many of the smaller ships provide a yacht-like form of cruising for those who are prepared to pay the higher prices these vessels are obliged to charge. They frequently attract wealthier over-55s who seek more adventurous destinations such as Greenland, Antarctica and the Amazon, and often do not accept young children. Many of these ships are able to enter harbours far smaller than would be possible for the traditional cruise ships, opening up new ports of call for cruising, such as Seville on the Guadalquivir River in Spain, Chicoutimi on the Saguenay River in Canada or the further reaches of the Amazon River and Iquitos in Peru. Small ships can also negotiate constricted canals, such as the Corinth Canal in Greece and the Panama Canal, neither of which is navigable by the larger cruise vessels. Small ships with ice-strengthened hulls can penetrate deeper into Antarctica, visiting the Ross ice shelf (see Figure 14.2).

Figure 14.2 Hurtigruten's *MS Fram*, with capacity for 400 passengers, is specially designed for Arctic and Antarctic cruises

Photo by Claire Humphreys

There is another important issue relating to the size of cruise vessels and that is the question of their **sustainability**. It is debatable whether building ever larger cruise ships is an appropriate strategy for the tourism business, even if they could be profitable. In purely practical terms, the effect on small island economies of vessels disgorging up to 4500 passengers simultaneously at port and within a strictly limited time period must be judged against any possible benefits of the visitor spend for the local economy there. Furthermore, the logistics and viability of putting such large numbers of people ashore and organizing shore excursions for them is another factor that will have to be weighed up carefully. Passengers are reluctant to queue up for two hours or more in order to go ashore or return to their vessels.

Cruise routes

Broadly, the world's major cruise routes are located in seven regions of the globe (see Figure 14.3). These are:

- Florida, the Caribbean, Bermuda and the Bahamas, including coastal towns of North, Central and South America
- the West Coast of Mexico, the USA (particularly Alaska) and Canada, plus Panama Canal transit
- the Mediterranean, divided between the western and eastern sectors
- the Pacific islands and Far East
- the Baltic Sea, northern European capitals and the west coast of Norway as far north as the North Cape – extensions to Svalbard, Norwegian island territory north of the Arctic Circle, are rising in popularity, as are cruises to Arctic regions such as Iceland and Greenland, which are easily accessible from both Europe and North America
- West Africa and the Atlantic islands of the Canaries, Madeira and, increasingly, the Azores – occasionally, this is extended to the Cape Verde Islands
- round the world (usually permitting short-leg bookings).

Fly–cruises have enabled long-haul routes to become popular for those with more limited time to spare. These allow the development of routes from Europe and the East Coast of the USA to Central America, especially Costa Rica and the Mexican East Coast, the East Coast of the South American Continent and cruises around New Zealand (the latter being a popular route for the Australian market). Cruise vessels are also being drawn to the attractions of Indian Ocean islands like Madagascar, the Seychelles, Réunion and

EXAMPLE **Cruising in New Zealand**

New Zealand has seen the number of cruise passengers visiting their shores rise five-fold over the past decade, from under 20 000 in 1997 to almost 110 000 in 2009. If forecasts are correct, numbers could reach almost 200 000 over the next few years.

The value of the cruise industry has been the subject of recent research which concluded that this activity brings NZ$176.7 million of direct expenditure into the economy, and supports around 3200 associated jobs (Cruise New Zealand, 2010). Such predictions have stimulated investment, with ports now planning new purpose-built cruise ship berths and passenger facilities. One proposal to fund this is to impose a passenger levy. This has proved problematic elsewhere, however; Alaska reportedly lost a third of the state's cruise business after introducing a US$50 levy designed to help fund, in part, port facilities and environmental improvements.

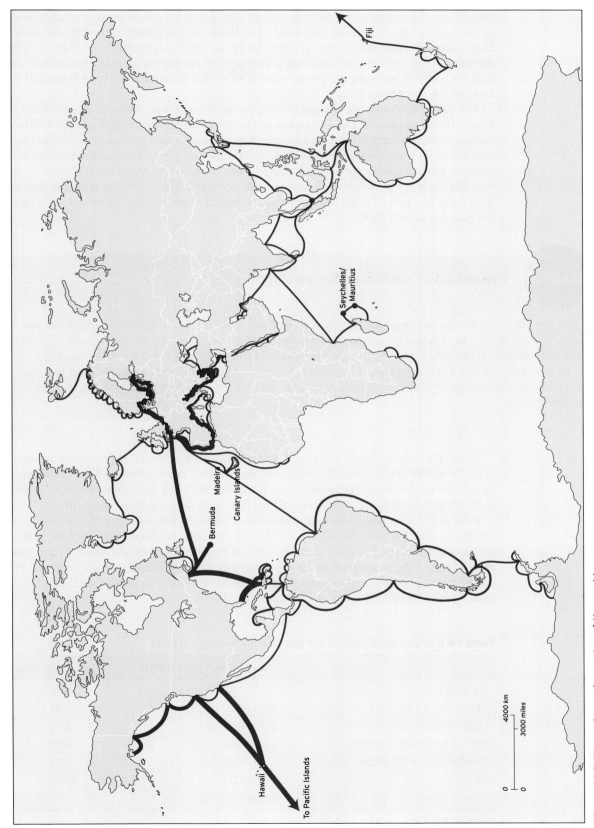

Figure 14.3 The major cruise routes of the world

Mauritius, with the principal port of embarkation being Mombasa in Kenya (small ports of call in this region, such as the island of Aldabra, are beginning to face the threat of a large influx of cruise passengers, as specialist cruise companies seek out ever more novel destinations for their discerning clients). Singapore is promoting itself as a major shipping hub for cruising, with interest rising in ports along the Indian coast, Hong Kong and the Indonesian 'spice islands'.

The Antarctic Peninsula is experiencing strong growth, too, often as an extension to South American ports of call and combined with calls at South Georgia and the Falkland Islands. Vessels bound for Antarctica are expected to meet the requirements of the extreme conditions they will encounter (although these cruises are limited to Southern hemisphere summer periods), with specially reinforced hulls. Ushuaia in Argentina has become the principal base for these vessels and is now of economic importance as a tourist destination, both as a port of departure for Antarctic-bound ships and as a gateway to the Tierra del Fuego National Park.

EXAMPLE The impact of sustainability legislation

In 2011, the IMO introduced important new legislation to regulate ships' emissions. The International Convention for the Prevention of Pollution from Ships will require all ships built after 2013 whose tonnage exceeds 4000 to improve fuel efficiency by 10%. This is to increase to 20% by 2020/24, and by 30% thereafter.

The ruling will have a significant impact on vessels sailing to Antarctica, and has already led to Saga, Swan Hellenic and Voyages of Discovery abandoning their calls, with Hurtigruten reducing their services to that destination.

In the UK, round-Britain cruising has also achieved a measure of popularity in recent years. In addition to calls at the mainland and Ireland, these sailings often include visits to the Shetland, Orkney, Hebridean and Faroe Islands, with occasional forays to remote outposts such as St Kilda, a group of islands now without permanent residents.

Most popular cruising, however, continues to focus on either the Mediterranean or the Caribbean. The European cruise market in 2010 chose the Mediterranean for 60% of their cruises while Northern Europe attracted 17% of European passengers and the Caribbean and the rest of the world making up the remaining 23% of European cruise journeys. The Caribbean is a popular cruise destination for the North American market with over half of passengers cruising in this region (see Table 14.1).

Table 14.1 Cruise destinations for the North American market

	Passenger numbers (2010)	Percentage
US states	1 369 000	13%
Caribbean	5 742 000	54%
Other islands	2 239 000	21%
Central and South America	1 060 000	10%
Transatlantic and Europe	157 000	2%
Other	42 000	0.1%
Total	10 609 000	

Source: US DoT, 2011

Most of these routes are seasonal, which means that shipping companies may be obliged to move their vessels from one region of the globe to another to take advantage of peak periods of cruising demand. These positioning voyages, as we have noted, are then sold as long cruises or even as line voyages where transatlantic sailings are involved, although they might include an en route call at a mid-Atlantic island such as Cape Verde, which is rapidly developing a tourism infrastructure in its own right. Baltic and North Cape cruises are operated during the northern hemisphere's summer period, with visits to the North Cape programmed to coincide with the high summer when passengers can experience the midnight sun. In the western hemisphere, Alaskan cruises are similarly programmed through the summer months, and are of particular appeal to Americans who wish to confine their travels closer to home, at times when political disturbances may be occurring anywhere within the Mediterranean region.

American cruise passengers are generally cautious about foreign travel and, as we can see from the data in Table 14.1, have always shown a preference for cruising in their own waters or those nearby. The onboard culture, and currency, are US-orientated and Americans, until recently, were not required to carry passports for cruises to the Caribbean – an important selling point when only a small minority of the population owned a passport anyway. The Caribbean also benefits from the proximity of the islands to the American mainland, as well as a climate that allows year-round cruising, although the winter's more temperate climate attracts the highest level of demand. Ports in Florida, such as Fort Lauderdale, Miami/Port Everglades and Port Canaveral, have become key bases for cruise ships, with Port Canaveral alone embarking over 2 million passengers every year. Demand from Europe, too, is such that charter flights from Europe now provide connections with many of the vessels sailing from Florida's ports.

Fly–cruising has made a significant contribution to the growth of cruising from European countries. Passengers are carried by the cruise company on chartered aircraft to a warm-water base port from which they can directly embark on their cruise or spend a few days at a nearby resort before or after the cruise. This overcomes the problem of poor weather and rough seas (the Bay of Biscay, off northern Spain, can be a notoriously unpleasant stretch of water to cross at any time of the year) and ensures that passengers can be enjoying the sunshine and calm seas of the Mediterranean or Caribbean from day one of their cruise holiday. Cruise and stay – with a week ashore at a Caribbean hotel, followed or preceded by a week cruising – is another popular option for the European markets. Although many traditional, often older, cruise passengers still reveal a preference for embarking directly onto their cruise ship at a European port, it has proved a popular development among younger cruise passengers. In recent years, however, the demand for direct embarkation has remained strong enough within Europe for several companies to position their vessels at ports such as Southampton or Bremen, at least for the summer season. In 2010, 653 000 of all UK and Irish cruise passengers chose a cruise that sailed directly from a UK port against a total of 969 000 choosing a fly–cruise holiday (Passenger Shipping Association, 2011).

The search for new destinations has led to the opening up of ever more adventurous cruise routes. Emulating American adventure cruises, companies such as Noble Caledonia and Jules Verne pioneered Pacific inter-island cruises and voyages in the Arctic and Antarctic regions, often using smaller, purpose-built vessels (such as the former company's *Island Sky*, see Figure 14.4). They and other specialist operators also charter Russian vessels with specially strengthened hulls to penetrate further south along the Antarctic shores.

Such cruises are still largely aimed at the top end of the market, though, with prices starting as high as £500 or more a day. The Passenger Shipping Association (PSA), the UK cruise association, categorizes the top cruise vessels as 'ultra luxury', with criteria that include passenger capacity (between 100 and 1000), a crew to passenger ratio of 1:2 and at least 40 square metres of space for every passenger. In the UK, 2% of cruise customers are in this market, paying over £5000 for their cruise.

Figure 14.4 The *Island Sky* carries a maximum 116 passengers on upmarket cruises
Photo by Chris Holloway

EXAMPLE New concepts in cruising

The World – a £182-million investment project by ResidenSea – represents a new departure for the cruise industry. This 43 500 ton ship (see Figure 14.5) was built in 2002 as a floating apartment block, with individual apartments priced between £1.5 million and £5 million sold off to wealthy investors as second homes. The original intention was that these were to be used mainly for their own pleasure, with the owners joining the ship at any point during its continuous round the world itinerary.

Initial sales were slow, so it was decided that some of the apartments would be sold for short legs only, while others would be made available for commercial rent to cruise passengers. Prices were set at the highest end of the scale, but resident owners were disappointed at the resultant mix of private ownership and commercial rental. The original financial backers were bought out by the owners, who now administer the ship's operations themselves. Over 100 families, from 19 countries, own the 165 apartments and decide upon the itinerary for the vessel. The average stay on board is four months. 2011 included visits to 53 countries,

Figure 14.5 *The World*, cruising into London
Photo by Claire Humphreys

primarily in South America, Europe and Africa, while 2012 will see *The World* visit North America and Australia. Although this would be considered an 'all-inclusive' holiday, the fees for apartment owners are believed to be in the region of $20 000 per month.

An alternative development has recently been announced, involving the construction of *Quintessentially One*, a 45 000 ton vessel to be launched in 2013 and promoted as a members-only cruise ship. Carrying 500 passengers, the vessel is designed to serve the needs of a total of just 4000 members, each paying an annual fee.

Further information: www.aboardtheworld.com; Quintessentiallyone.com

Table 14.2 Leading sources of European cruise passengers, 2010

Market	Passengers ('000)
UK and Ireland	1622
Germany	1219
Italy	889
Spain	645
France	387
Scandinavia	168
Rest of Europe	522
Total	5452

Source: European Cruise Council, 2011

While the US market dominates the global demand for cruising, with over 10 million cruise passengers annually, now more than 5 million Western Europeans cruise each year. Together, the UK, Germany and Italy account for 68% of the European cruise market (see Table 14.2).

Among European passengers, the average length of a cruise was between five and 14 days, with nearly 60% choosing routes in the Mediterranean or near-Atlantic (such as the Canary Islands and Madeira). In the UK, the average duration was just under 11 nights, although 44% booked a cruise lasting a week or less. This is similar to the North American market, where passengers had an average cruise length of seven days in 2009, with just over one-third of passengers falling into the two to five day cruise category.

Other strong growth areas are river cruising and cheaper cruises on ships chartered by tour operators. The demand for river cruising will be looked at in more detail a little later in this chapter.

The nature of the cruise market

The thought of a cruise still carries, for many holidaymakers, two distinctly negative images. On the one hand, cruise ships are thought to be peopled by conservative, rather elderly passengers who choose to spend their days at sea playing bridge or sitting on steamer chairs covered with blankets, watching the horizon and drinking cups of bouillon, while, on the other hand, at the cheaper end of the market, the image is of ships as floating holiday camps, peopled by hyperactive, extrovert middle-aged passengers propping up the bars, looking for non-stop entertainment and enjoying five-times-a-day opportunities to eat, in between shipboard romances. While undoubtedly such stereotypes exist, and some shipping lines cater for each of these, such images are far from being an accurate general picture of cruising today.

The key factors that determine cruise demand can be identified as price, length of cruise and ports visited, but there are a number of other factors contributing to people choosing one cruise over another, not least the efforts made by the shipping companies to appeal to niche markets through their ships, onboard activities and destinations. Unlike other sectors of the travel industry, cruising is a product that enjoys strong brand loyalty, with well-established brands claiming a high proportion of repeat bookings, many of which are rewarded by deep discounts. With the rapid expansion of interest in cruising (which, in the UK, accounted for 4.5% of all foreign holidays in 2010), the importance of niche marketing has never been so strong.

Cruise companies

Three distinct forms of cruise company have emerged to cater for this global demand.

1. There are the major international cruise companies that draw on global markets and are tending to dominate the industry. The three leaders in this sector are the US-owned Carnival, by far the world's largest cruise company, which, over recent years, has absorbed many other leading cruise brands, including the former UK companies P&O and Cunard. Its nearest competitors are RCI (Royal Caribbean International) and Star Cruise Line, which includes in its portfolio Norwegian Cruise Line. These three carriers are estimated to control 80% of the global cruise market; the first two focus largely on the North American and European markets, while Star cruises has a 70% share of the Asian market. A fourth company, MSC, is expanding rapidly, and together these four controlled 87% of the cruise market passenger berths in 2010 (see Table 14.3).

2. There is a handful of long-established lines with few vessels, such as Hapag-Lloyd and Fred Olsen, that are strongly dependent on their home markets and to which cruise passengers demonstrate strong brand loyalty. Customer commitment may be to companies, but, in some cases, it may be to individual ships. This category also includes the

Table 14.3 Ships operated by major cruise companies

Company	No of ships	Passenger berths
Carnival Corporation (Carnival Cruise Lines, Princess Cruises, Costa Cruise Lines, Holland America, Cunard Line, Seabourn Cruise Line, P&O Cruises, AIDA, Ibero)	104	214 590
Royal Caribbean International (Royal Caribbean, Celebrity, Azamara, Pullmantur, CDF)	42	100 030
Star Cruises / Norwegian Cruise Lines	17	33 534
MSC Cruises	11	26 071
Louis Cruise Lines	8	10 173
Disney Cruise Line	3	7 300
Thomson	5	7 153
Hurtigruten	13	5 923
Fred Olsen Cruise Lines	5	4 567
Oceania Cruises, Inc.	4	3 312
Regent SevenSeas Cruises	4	2 222
Silversea Cruises	6	2 028
Crystal Cruises	2	2 014
Saga Cruises	2	1 275
Hapag-Lloyd	4	1 176

Source: Cruise Market Watch, 2011

three Disney cruise ships, aimed particularly at the family market, and a cluster of companies operating super-luxury vessels that have a more international appeal, such as Regent SevenSeas Cruises and Crystal Cruises. It also includes the ships run by Saga, which have been largely aimed at the senior citizens market, although the company is seeking to widen its appeal with its latest ship, *Spirit of Adventure*. These carriers operate large vessels, but they are not behemoths, so are unable to offer the range of activities and entertainment on board that are to be found on ships operated by the leading carriers. Their survival is due in part to the strong financial support they receive from their parent organizations. For example, the Disney Cruise Line is part of the Disney entertainment empire, Crystal Cruises has the backing of the leading Japanese shipping company NYK, Regent SevenSeas is part of Carlson, the American travel conglomerate, and Hapag-Lloyd belongs to the TUI travel empire (although, at the time of writing, some of the stake owned by TUI was being sold to other investors).

3. There are niche cruise operators, generally operating much smaller vessels and with a narrower focus. Typically, these offer more adventurous destinations or activities designed to appeal to particular markets. These operators also have intensely loyal passengers. Examples include Swan Hellenic's *Minerva*, Noble Caledonia's *Island Sky* (see Figure 14.4), Voyages of Discovery's *Discovery*, Silversea Cruises' *HAS Prince Albert II* and Hebridean Island Cruises' *Hebridean Princess*. Sailings are aimed at the more sophisticated traveller and are frequently sold as cultural cruises, accompanied by experienced guides and lecturers. Smaller vessels are well suited to itineraries such as summer cruises in the Baltic, with destinations that appeal to upmarket audiences with an interest in culture. Expedition cruising, offering more adventurous destinations such as the Chilean fjords and Antarctica, in which landings are made by Zodiac tenders, calls for a more energetic (although not necessarily younger) market. These ships are often chartered or part-chartered to specialist tour operators that search out and organize ever more adventurous holiday destinations. In 2006, three times as many British passengers travelled on ships carrying fewer than 1100 passengers as had travelled in 1999.

EXAMPLE **Sailing first class**

Historically, transatlantic crossings operated with different classes of ticket, providing different facilities and spaces to each class of passenger. MSC Cruises has resurrected this approach, through the introduction of the MSC Yacht Club.

This cruise company has allocated areas of the ship accessible to Yacht Club members only, providing a pool, separate lounge and dining area and offering additional services such as in-room dining, a butler service, free drinks and minibar, and priority embarkation and disembarkation. The Yacht Club is only available for those staying in the luxury suites, and non-members are unable to access this accommodation area. MSC Cruises claims that this 'ship within a ship' allows Yacht Club members to benefit from big ship facilities while experiencing the personalized service that smaller ships can provide.

This approach is not unique to MSC Cruises. Norwegian Cruise Lines has introduced a Villa Complex, which house private facilities while Cunard's three *Queens* and Royal Caribbean's *Allure of the Seas* offer premium status guests access to exclusive areas.

The economics of cruising

The present variation in the size of cruise vessels is a natural development, arising from the competition that emerged during the late 1980s as cruising once again became a popular form of travel. The losers in this competitive market were the higher-cost companies, particularly the US-owned ones. High labour costs and expenses incidental to flagging vessels in the developed countries led to the demise of a number of carriers, among them Regency, Dolphin, Premier, Commodore, Crown, Renaissance, Royal Olympic and American Classic Voyages. Through growth, mergers and acquisitions, the current three market leaders came to dominate the global cruise market, taking advantage of economies of scale (for example, Carnival provides identical meals on all brands of its ships operating in the Caribbean), typically flagging their vessels in countries offering substantial tax benefits, such as the Bahamas and Panama, and recruiting cheap labour from low-cost developing countries (the International Transport Workers' Federation estimates that more than half of all the world's cruise fleet now operate under flags of convenience (FOC), where taxation is either low or, in some cases, nil). Carnival has also diversified horizontally, with investments in hotels, lodges, luxury trains and motor coaches. The huge investments that these giant corporations can make in new vessels have led to a new form of cruising holiday – the ship itself becoming the destination, with an ever-widening range of activities and attractions on board, so that calls at ports en route become almost incidental to the shipboard experience.

Cruising appeals on a number of levels. The all-inclusive nature of a cruise, in which unlimited, and often excellent, food is on offer; the general ambience on board; the high levels of security that isolation on a ship can provide; the attraction of travelling with 'like-minded people' with whom it is easy to make friends, being thrown together within a confined space; the absence of constraint on the amount of baggage carried (other than on fly–cruises); all these offer significant benefits. Indeed, for those with a real fear of flying, cruising directly from home ports provides one means of travelling to far-flung places abroad.

While the concept of a floating hotel has become important as a way to sell cruises, many more traditional passengers still expect ships to look like ships. A great deal of care goes into the design of a modern cruise liner, in order to create the illusion of greater space while still including all the facilities that maximize the revenue-earning opportunities for the shipping company, in the form of shops, hairdressing facilities, casinos and bars. The design also takes account of the preferences of the nationalities of those travelling. Cruise ships aimed predominantly at the US market, for example, tend to make greater use of plastics, gilt stairways, mirrors, neon lights and bright colours, while the more traditional European, and particularly British, market will expect greater use of wood (although safety standards at sea encourage the use of more fire-retardant materials today) and quieter, more refined decoration.

The image of cruising as an older person's holiday is finally beginning to fade as companies such as Carnival and the Thomson-owned Island Cruises encroach on the traditional cruise market and reach a younger group of holidaymakers. According to the PSA, the average age of British cruise passengers in 2010 was 54 years, with around 13% under the age of 35. Vessels appealing to the family market, such as those operated by the Walt Disney Company, are undoubtedly contributing to a lowering of these averages, while the more price-sensitive ships operated by the large tour operators will also attract a younger market. In the USA in particular, cruises are marketed as just another form of package holiday, comparable to an all-inclusive holiday on land. This has resulted in some 20% of all Americans having taken a cruise (CLIA, 2010).

Shipping companies have recognized the difficulty of appealing to varied markets and varied nationalities on the same vessel, however appealing this might be economically. Multinational passenger mixes call for multilingual announcements and entertainment on board, which will not be an attractive selling point. Passengers from different countries have differing habits and preferences in onboard food and entertainment. Those from Latin countries, for instance, prefer to take dinner later than those from the UK or USA. These differences lead cruise companies to niche market, whether by price, brand, market or type of cruise offered. Saga Holidays caters extensively for the upper end of the age market, P&O's vessel *Adonia* is reserved for adults only, while their *Oceania* was designed to appeal to passengers new to cruising, both in its style and routes. *Artemis*, introduced in

2005, is a smaller vessel of 45 000 tons with more traditional décor, designed to appeal to a conservative market.

Competition encourages shipping companies to emphasize product differentiation, while striving to build the newest ships, and to offer the latest onboard facilities to meet the expectations of an increasingly sophisticated cruise market. Entertainment has become increasingly varied, with Cordon Bleu cookery courses, acting classes, wellness at sea programmes and a golf academy. One noted trend is to have greater variety in catering on board. P&O's *Oriana*, to take one example, has introduced a pizzeria on board, while Crystal Cruises offers a choice of Italian, Japanese and Chinese restaurants on its vessels. A notable feature of catering on board the most recent ships has been the appointment of celebrity chefs to oversee the restaurant menus.

EXAMPLE   Themed cruises

For special events such as a product launch, it is possible to charter an entire vessel and introduce onboard activities focused around a particular theme. Yet more common is the development of the theme by the cruise companies themselves. These themes are designed to attract specialist audiences who will book to share the experience with other 'like-minded' passengers.

One example of this is the 2012 Great Barrier Reef Solar Eclipse cruise promoted by Coral Princess cruises. The ship, with a capacity for only 72 passengers, regularly visits the Great Barrier Reef, but for this trip the itinerary was arranged to maximize the opportunity to view this rare natural phenomenon.

Other themed events have included Holland America Line's Alaska Knitting Cruise and that company's History and Genealogy cruise, Royal Caribbean's Film Festival at Sea and Crystal Cruise's Forbes Cruise for Investors. This last provides an example where external providers and cruise companies can work together for mutual benefit.

In spite of the rise in popularity of cruising, it remains a highly volatile market and is quickly affected by adverse events, such as terrorist activities or upheavals in the Middle East. Americans in particular, as noted earlier, are cautious travellers and seek security abroad. The perception of danger in the Mediterranean will cause many to switch bookings to safer home waters in the Caribbean or Alaska – evidenced by there being something of a boom for those destinations whenever bookings to the Mediterranean decline. Cruise companies can also be forced, in these circumstances, to reposition their vessels to the already congested Caribbean, as a result of which, even with rising demand, oversupply leads to deep discounting for all cruise ships and hence profits fall.

Cabotage rights (controlling companies from transporting passengers within a foreign territory) extend to shipping operations as much as they do to airline operations (although these rights have been abandoned within the EU, with cruise companies of member states being free to determine their own routes within the EU). In other parts of the world, vessels of foreign registry are not permitted to carry passengers between two ports within the same country, nor to carry passengers from and back to the same port without an intermediate port of call in a foreign country.

American legislation is contained in the Merchant Marine Act (1920), better known as the Jones Act, which prohibits non-US-registered vessels from carrying passengers between two US ports without a call at a 'distant foreign port' (Canadian ports are close and therefore not counted as foreign for the purpose of the Act). The Act also requires ships travelling on cabotage routes to be US-flagged, US-crewed, US-built and subject to US domestic labour laws (although the Act has been amended to exempt certain routes and industries). Efforts to repeal the Jones Act and open up American coastal waters were lodged in 2010, although any changes have yet to be agreed by the legislature.

Norwegian Caribbean Line (NCL)

Following the collapse of American Classic Voyages in the wake of the 9/11 tragedy, Hawaii found itself with no major US-flagged cruise line.

NCL had been operating cruises from the Hawaiian Islands for a number of years, but was obliged to call at a foreign port under cabotage regulations. It programmed a call at Fanning Island (Tabuaeran) in Kiribati, the nearest non-US port, to satisfy the Jones Act, even though the call had little passenger appeal.

The company won exemption from the Act after reflagging its vessels, agreeing to build new vessels in US shipyards and abiding by US labour regulations. Subsequently, the company formed a new US-registered company, NCL America, and since 2004 its vessels have sailed under the American flag, allowing them to operate their Hawaiian cruises without the need to make an intermediate call at a foreign port.

More than 40 countries around the world continue to enforce cabotage rules, including Canada, Mexico and Japan.

Managing costs

Cruising is both capital-intensive and labour-intensive. A modern cruise liner can easily cost more than $250 million to build, with some, such as the *Queen Mary 2* costing in excess of $500 million (costs for a 222 000 ton vessel such as the new *Oasis of the Seas* exceeded $1.3 billion). The life expectancy of a cruise ship is fortunately far longer than that of an aircraft and, allowing for some rebuilding and complete interior renovation, a 50-year productive life would not be unusual. The *Queen Elizabeth 2* enjoyed a life of more than 40 years before her withdrawal from service in 2008.

Fuel burn is obviously an important consideration in overall operating costs, although perhaps not as critical as one might expect. Although oil prices have typically represented only a small proportion of overall costs, in recent years rising prices has led to this reaching levels of 9% or more. To offset this increase, efforts have been made to reduce fuel burn. Royal Caribbean's Celebrity Cruise Line has repainted the hulls of their vessels with a low-drag silicone coating, reducing fuel use by 3%. New, more efficient marine engines are making an appearance, burning liquefied natural gas, which emit much lower levels of carbon dioxide and nitrous oxide, although, so far, these engines are more suitable for ferry operations than cruising. Furthermore, only half of the fuel used is for propulsion; the rest is used to provide electricity for air-conditioning, catering and other onboard necessities.

Further economies are obtained by calling at a greater number of ports on any one itinerary and spending more time in port, both of which help to reduce fuel burn, while at the same time increasing the passengers' satisfaction. A reduction in speed also saves on fuel, but, if vessels are to travel slowly and call at numerous ports, it is essential that the ports are grouped closely together. For this reason, the Caribbean, with its many islands of differing nationality, makes an ideal cruise destination. At times of rapid escalation in fuel prices, as in recent years, the operating costs will rise sharply as a result, but competition and oversupply make a parallel rise in prices difficult to enforce, although some companies have taken to imposing an oil surcharge, in line with airline policy.

The global political situation has not only led to higher fuel costs; ships and seaports also now need heightened security, just as do aircraft and airports. Passengers and their luggage have to be checked more carefully as they board and the vessels must be guarded around the clock while in port and under way.

Vessels also need a substantial number of crew, both in passenger service and below deck – a 4- or 5-star cruise ship would carry as many as one member of crew for every two passengers, and a ratio of one to one is not unknown for the luxury top end of the market. With such labour costs, it is not difficult to see why luxury cruises are selling for up to

Cunard's transatlantic service

One example of effective cost-reduction in shipping operations was demonstrated by Cunard, which, in 1996, took the decision to extend the journey time for its *Queen Elizabeth 2* between the UK and New York from five to six days.

While this achieved significant savings in terms of fuel burn, reducing the average speed from 28.5 knots to 23 knots, it also offered other advantages, in marketing terms. A higher onboard spend was encouraged, while the passengers themselves saw an additional day's cruising as an added benefit. It also allowed the ship to arrive at a more convenient time of day for those with onward travel arrangements. This policy remained in force with the introduction of the *Queen Mary 2*, and its economic success encouraged Cunard to add a further day to some crossings during 2010, and to make all crossings from 2011 onwards seven-night voyages.

$1000 a day. The decline in the fleets of the established maritime nations, such as the UK, can be partly accounted for by their uncompetitive operating costs compared with their cheaper competitors. Lower-cost nations like Greece and Russia built up their own fleets, while, as we have seen, the more expensive nations were obliged to trim costs by registering their fleets in developing countries such as Panama, the Bahamas or Liberia and recruiting crews from countries where labour costs are low, such as the Philippines, Indonesia or India, to the chagrin of trade unions representing maritime crews in the developed nations. Virtually all leading cruise companies today recruit a substantial proportion of their deck staff from the Philippines, where lower salaries are acceptable. A study completed in 2000 reported that more than half of cruise ship employees earned less than $1000 a month (Klein, 2006). Some large companies have also reduced the ratio of crew to passengers, aiming to deliver a 3-star, rather than 4- or 5-star, service.

Costs can be reduced by putting passengers ashore by tender (ship's launches), rather than tying up alongside. This may be a practical alternative when islands are pushing up mooring fees, but it does delay disembarkation and is a less attractive selling point. Furthermore, competition has forced the leading companies to speed up their turnaround times at their home ports between cruises. Some turnarounds have been reduced to as little as 12 hours, although concern has been expressed that such tight scheduling does not allow for adequate cleaning between cruises, risking the spread of onboard diseases such as the Norovirus, which has plagued the shipping companies in recent years.

Companies operating large fleets can also obtain some economies of scale by reducing the cost per unit of their marketing and administration. It has also become more economical to operate large ships rather than small ones and the trend is to build bigger and bigger vessels, to take advantage of this and maximize onboard spend. Five-star operators such as Silversea Cruises face a different problem, however. While high levels of profitability are hard to achieve for these vessels when capacity is low, any increase leads to difficulties in delivering the expected high standards of service. Optimum viability for the luxury end of the market is believed to be achieved, therefore, with vessels of around 25 000 tons, carrying a maximum of 400 passengers.

The largest ships are able to pare costs by providing smaller cabins with larger areas given over to public use. This provides space for shopping and other sales opportunities that, together with shore excursions, make up around one-third of a cruise line's revenue. Dining rooms accommodate large numbers within relatively confined spaces, either by having two sittings for meals or providing only large tables (tables for two are rare on board many ships). Some companies have capitalized on this, however, by designing their ships to permit *all* passengers to be accommodated in the restaurant at a single sitting – an attractive marketing advantage.

Earning revenue

One feature of shipping that it shares with the airline industry is the highly fluid pricing structure that the industry now finds necessary to adopt. Deep discounting has become the norm for nearly all cruise lines, with discounts for early bookers, last-minute bookers, loyal clients, even for readers of certain newspapers and magazines. Identical cabins will be sold at different fares in the UK, on the Continent and in North America – the result, the shipping companies insist, of market conditions, although website searches by passengers are reducing this differential. Most cruises (more than three-quarters of bookings in the UK) are still sold through travel agents and they, in turn, may offer discounts and incentives to secure the booking, on top of any discounts offered by the principal; however, shipping companies are in many cases now resorting to selling accommodation to agents at the full retail price, limiting opportunities for the agent to undercut direct sales. With a wide variety of cabin types, and only minimal distinction between each, opportunities for 'up-selling' are provided if lower quality cabins are unavailable.

One impact on the total revenue to be earned from cabin sales is set by the lifeboat capacity. Occupancy rates for cruise ships often exceed 100% because cabins are designated as holding two people, yet often children are accommodated in the same cabin. However, every ship is allocated a maximum capacity based on lifeboat seats. This means that if large numbers of cabins are reserved with more than two adults, the capacity can be reached well before all cabins are sold. This is factored into the design of the ship; for example, the Disney Magic ship has 877 cabins and 2713 lifeboat seats (Biehn, 2006) – this must also be factored into the fluid pricing calculations.

Cruise lines have to ensure that their ships are used for the maximum amount of time during the year (just as airlines do) although this does not necessarily mean that they are used only for cruising. Some companies charter cruise ships to tour operators, while others have successfully chartered ships for use as floating hotels when accommodation pressures force tourist destinations to find alternative accommodation for special events. Cunard was even successful a few years ago in chartering its largest vessel, the *Queen Elizabeth 2*, for a period for Japan to use as a hotel, and German passenger ship *Deutschland* will be berthed in London during the 2012 Olympics to accommodate guests of the German Olympic Sports Confederation. This represents a substantial saving on operating costs for the companies concerned as the period of charter requires no use of fuel.

Onboard sales can account for a quarter of revenue earned by many cruise companies. Predominantly this is achieved through bars and casinos. Historically the prices of drinks on board were kept low as companies passed on the duty-free discounts, but now it is more common for the prices to be in line with those found in hotel bars. Estimates have put profits as high as 80% on the price of drinks, and this is maximized by the ban many cruise lines set on passengers bringing onboard their own refreshments. Casinos, now a frequent addition to ships, are often operated by a concessionaire, who pays a fee and a percentage of the profits to the cruise operator.

Onboard sales will be also made in the shopping malls now common on the large ships, many of which are also operated as concessions. Revenue also comes from providing communications (such as telephone and Internet access), spa facilities and some leisure activities which charge a fee – using golf ranges or rock climbing walls, or participating in cookery lessons, for example. Some ships have also introduced 'extra tariff' restaurants and coffee bars, which can also encourage passengers to spend on board; cover charges are payable, for example, in the Todd English Restaurants on board Cunard's *Queen Mary 2* and *Queen Victoria*, and in the Verandah Restaurant of the *Queen Elizabeth*.

One other important income stream is shore excursions. It is common for more than half of passengers to disembark at ports, and many take pre-arranged excursions booked on board prior to arrival. The cruise companies, working with the providers onshore, will charge a premium rate for the convenience of tying into the schedule of the ship. Anecdotal evidence suggests that the cruise company's share of the profits can be as high as one-third of the excursion price.

EXAMPLE Buying excursions

Shore excursions are considered such a profitable element of the cruise industry that competition is entering this sector. Passenger will often take an excursion at each port of call and this can add significantly to the overall cost of the holiday.

To provide an alternative to those excursions offered for sale on board ship, a new online company – Cruising Excursions – has been established. Cruise passengers can visit their website prior to the start of their holiday and view a range of excursions specifically tailored to fit with their ship's itinerary. The company claims that prices will be up to 60% lower than onboard prices. This is not the first company to venture into this market; in the USA, several companies exist to provide a similar service both for travel agents and to travellers directly.

EXAMPLE The bottom line

Carnival Cruise Line is by far the largest cruise company, with brands which include Princess Cruises, Costa Cruise Lines, Holland America, Cunard, Seabourn Cruise Line, P&O Cruises, AIDA and Ibero. In 2010, it declared a profit of almost $2 billion on revues of over $14 billion having carried over 9 million passengers. Its operational costs and revenue is broken down in Table 14.4.

We can see from this the importance of the onboard and excursion revenue (adding over £3 billion) and the impact of high fuel prices, accounting for over 13% of operating costs.

Table 14.4 Consolidated statement of income for Carnival Corporation

	2010 ($million)	%
Revenue		
Passenger tickets	11 084	77%
Onboard revenue	3 104	21%
Tours, excursions and other	281	2%
Total revenue	14 469	
Costs		
Commission and transportation	2 272	19%
Fuel	1 622	13%
Food	869	7%
Other onboard costs	474	4%
Tour costs	212	2%
Payroll	1 611	13%
Sales, marketing and administrative	1 614	13%
Other shipping costs	2 032	17%
Depreciation/amortization	1 416	12%
Total costs	12 122	

Source: Carnival Corporation Annual Report, 2010: http://phx.corporate-ir.net/phoenix.zhtml?c=140690&p=irol-reportsAnnual

Finally, one other revenue stream for the large cruise lines is from the destinations visited. Ports have been known to pay bounties for landing passengers ashore. One example was Panama, who announced in 2000 that it would pay cruise companies a fee for every passenger, with the amount per head escalating as more passengers were landed.

This five-year scheme resulted in more than a dozen ships introducing a stop in their itinerary. Schemes in the Bahamas and Puerto Rico have also operated (Klein, 2006).

The cruising business

A useful rule of thumb in judging the relative luxury and spaciousness on board ship is to ascertain the size to passenger ratio (SPR), sometimes referred to as the passenger–space ratio (PSR). This is based on the vessel's gross registered tonnage divided by the number of passengers carried. If this amounts to 20 or fewer, the ship is likely to appear crowded, while a figure approaching 60 would be considered luxurious and command high daily rates (see Table 14.5). Tonnage alone is not a good guide as to the amount of space per passenger, however. *World of Cruising* magazine points out that the *Lirica*, at 60 000 tons, has a PSR of 25.42, while the *Discovery* at 19 900 tons offers a PSR of 32.6, yet both are classed as 4-star ships.

Distribution is all important in this competitive sector, and, although cruise operators have made full use of the World Wide Web to market their products, the complexity of cruising makes it difficult for sales staff to acquire adequate knowledge of the variety of types of accommodation and ships available without gaining first-hand experience. In recent years, the PSA, marketing arm of the passenger shipping business in the UK, has attempted to overcome this problem by mounting special campaigns to train agents through its training subsidiary Association of Cruise Experts (ACE) and has some 2300 travel agency members and 38 cruise line members to date.

The larger shipping companies tend to receive greater support from travel agents, who find it easier to deal with companies owning a greater number and variety of ships and, therefore, a larger choice of both sailings and destinations. A growing number of agents, seeking ways to specialize as the commission received for other services has reduced, have switched their focus to the cruise sector, developing their competence in selling in this sector. A Leading Cruise Agents' Alliance (LCA) has been formed in the UK to bring these specialists together.

Although demand has been rising strongly for more than a decade, it has barely kept pace with the growth in supply, in terms of both the number of vessels and their overall size and capacity. This has led to fierce competition in the industry, artificially high 'brochure prices' allowing the maximum price flexibility and deep discounting to clear unsold accommodation. Escalating costs, for both shipbuilding and operating (notably increases in oil price), have led to some retrenchment and slimmer profits have been followed by market concentration – a trend now familiar in many sectors of the tourism industry.

Table 14.5 Comparing size and comfort of some leading cruise ships

Ships	Tonnage	Star rating	Space ratio	Passenger to crew ratio
Grandeur of the Seas	74 137	★★★★	38.00	2100/760
Oriana	69 000	★★★★	37.80	1830/760
MSC Lirica	60 000	★★★★	25.42	1600/760
Island Escape	40 132	★★★	26.50	1600/612
Black Watch	28 500	★★★★	37.45	761/310
Emerald	26 431	★★★	26.60	1100/420
Marco Polo	21 000	★★★★	24.10	800/356
Discovery	19 900	★★★★	32.60	600/325
Braemar	19 900	★★★★	26.10	727/320

Source: modified from Voyages of Discovery brochure, 2005, based on September 2004 edition of *World of Cruising*

Over-tonnage in American waters has forced cruise companies to turn to Europe to fill ships and several companies now offer free flights to the Caribbean to join their cruise ships based there.

Carnival, in particular, has been able to attract a much younger than average market for its major division, Carnival Cruises, which offers relatively cheap cruises of short duration, using large vessels of, typically, 70 000–100 000 tons or more. Its most recent vessels accommodate, usually, between 2000 and 3000 passengers. The fanciful names of the ships (*Paradise, Elation, Ecstasy, Sensation* and *Imagination*, for example) are pointers to the expectations their passengers will have of the kinds of experiences these cruise ships promise. They are sold as 'fun cruises', offering a wide range of onboard facilities, including shops and casinos.

Carnival has also identified smaller niches. Its Fiesta Marina division of Hispanic-orientated tours was developed to tap into Spanish- and Portuguese-speaking markets in the USA and Latin America, based at a home port of San Juan, Puerto Rico, an island commonwealth of the USA. Food, wine and entertainment on board were designed to suit Hispanic tastes, and dining hours are later than usual, in accordance with Hispanic preferences.

Niche markets are being tapped by both the shipping companies themselves and specialist operators around the world, often using chartered vessels. Even the largest vessels find their specialist markets. For example, in 2006, the *Ocean Majesty* was chartered by Just You, for single passengers only. In the USA, operators Atlantis and RSVP offer exclusively gay cruises, while Alternative Holidays caters to a similar market in the UK. Olivia, an operator in San Francisco, has chartered ships exclusively for lesbian passengers. The *Queen Mary 2* was sold as a gay transatlantic crossing for one sailing in 2007.

Health, safety and the environment

Health and safety issues are controlled by the IMO, which requires ships and ports to conform to internationally set standards, and regulations pertaining to these issues are constantly being tightened up. The International Convention for the Safety of Life at Sea (SOLAS) (1974) is the principal regulation governing standards for ships and their crew and its directives are widely adhered to throughout the world, but the dominance of the Americans in the world cruise market and American concerns about both safety and hygiene have also resulted in strict standards being imposed on all foreign flag-carriers operating out of, or calling at, US ports. All such ships are subject to unannounced inspections by the US Vessel Sanitation Program. Vessels are rated for the quality of their water, food preparation, cleanliness, storage and repairs. An acceptable rating is 86 points out of 100, but it is not uncommon for even leading cruise ships of the world to be given grades considerably lower than this. Owners are then required to raise their standards. Adverse publicity in the press is a further incentive not to fail these tests. Over the past decade, there have been numerous outbreaks of contagious diseases on board cruise ships, ranging from viral gastroenteritis to the Norwalk virus (Norovirus) and such outbreaks get maximum publicity in the world's press.

EXAMPLE   **Sea sickness**

Between 2009 and 2010 press attention was brought to many case of Norovirus contracted while on board cruise ships. In September 2009, the *Balmoral* required 18 passengers to be confined to their cabins, and a month later 16 passengers were restricted aboard the *Boudicca* (both vessels operated by Fred Olsen Cruises). Larger scale outbreaks have been witnessed, with 400 passengers aboard Transocean's *Marco Polo* hit by the virus and more than 130 passengers aboard Thomson's *Escape* sought compensation after they contracted the virus.

Such outbreaks can be difficult to manage and crews must be vigilant to reduce the likelihood of an epidemic.

New regulations governing environmental protection are also affecting the shipping industry. The IMO has recognized that global shipping emissions are much higher than had earlier been estimated and are now put at some 1.2 billion tonnes a year, against 650 million tonnes produced by the aviation industry (although this figure, of course, includes all maritime craft – container ships, tankers and so on). This represents around 4.5% of all global CO_2 emissions. The environmental agency Climate Care estimates that larger cruise ships emit some 0.43 kg of CO_2 per passenger mile, compared with long-haul flights, even at high altitude, of 0.26 kg, although the PSA insists that passenger ships are globally responsible for only 1.4% of greenhouse gases. Illegal cleaning of tanks at sea, discharge of oil and pumping of raw sewage into the oceans are of increasing concern in terms of their effect on the environment. The waste produced on board ships is extensive, with estimates by an ocean conservation organization suggesting that 168 000 gallons of sewage and seven tons of garbage and solid waste is produced daily on board a cruise ship (Euromonitor, 2010). Cruise companies are responding by making investments in their waste treatments systems and engine efficiencies and through improvements to their power sources.

The original International Convention for the Prevention of Pollution from Ships, adopted in 1973 and modified in 1978 (now known as MARPOL 73/78), laid down strict controls governing the disposal of waste at sea and was adopted by 136 maritime countries. Further rulings on environmental pollution came into force in 2004 and other measures have followed since, in 2010/11, as indicated earlier in this chapter. As a result, shipowners will increasingly expect to have to upgrade older vessels or invest in newer ones with more efficient engines.

The PSA claims that large cruise vessels now recycle 60–65% of their waste and many ships (and all ships of Holland-America Line) have environmental officers on board to ensure compliance with rules and standards laid down by the US body CLIA.

More recently constructed vessels, designed to achieve higher standards of safety, can attract lower insurance premiums. These vessels are also more technically advanced and have lower operating costs, resulting in older ships finding it difficult to compete. On top of this, owners are also required to be bonded against financial collapse, adding to costs. In this respect, the shipping and airline businesses face similar problems. Medium-sized operators are likely to be absorbed over the next few years by the three or four largest companies, leaving only the niche market cruise operators to remain as independents in the field.

EXAMPLE   Clean up cruises

The *Star Cipper* is a tall ship, with a maximum capacity of 170 guests and a passenger profile younger than that of many cruise companies, with an average age of around 45 years. The sailing ship operates under wind power for 70% of its journeys. Clearly, this is not the usual cruise, and the activities undertaken in port highlight this.

On a visit to St Kitts in 2011, the ship's passengers took part in a rubbish collection exercise, managing to gather three-quarters of a ton of rubbish from local beaches. This is part of an eco-awareness programme offered on board the ship.

The expansion of the cruise business has been welcomed for the benefits it can bring to holidaymakers, shipping companies and cruise destinations alike, but there can be less attractive consequences for some popular cruise ship destinations. Responsible cruising suggests not only environmental concern but also the need to ensure that destinations receive adequate financial rewards from ships' visits. The large shipping companies, however, are stressing onboard spend, and the construction of ships that have become virtual leisure complexes in their own right has resulted in many port destinations experiencing a decline in onshore spend, which parallels the problem faced by other destinations that have encouraged expansion by tour operators of the all-inclusive holiday concept. Bigger onboard spend equates to less being spent ashore – less money going into local shops, bars and transport companies. Some shipping companies have purchased their own, frequently deserted, islands on which they can land their passengers for barbecues and lazy beach days, ensuring, once again, that no revenue goes into the local economy. Private islands that are either owned or rented include:

- Great Stirrup Cay (NCL/Star Cruises)
- Coco Cay (RCI)
- Half Moon Cay (HAL/Carnival)
- Princess Cay (Princess Cruises/Carnival).

Larger ships also tend to attract passengers with lower incomes, resulting in a further reduction in the per person spend at ports of call, while the growth in size of cruise vessels, as we have seen, threatens massive congestion at small island ports.

Health and safety issues affect the carriage of disabled passengers, too. In 2006, the US Supreme Court ruled that the Americans with Disabilities Act applied equally to US and foreign cruise ships operating within US waters (contrary to UK regulations, where the Disability Discrimination Act does not yet apply to shipping). As is the case with hotels, in order to comply with the Act, some cabins must be equipped to meet the needs of physically disabled passengers, including wider doorways for entry to the cabin and bathroom, while gangplanks have to accept wheelchairs. Currently, not all cruise lines accept guide dogs for the blind and some insist on disabled passengers being accompanied by fare-paying, fully able-bodied escorts to look after them. There are ample lifts on large cruise ships, but this is not always the case where river cruising is concerned, making these vessels far from ideal for disabled bookings, even though this is a form of travel likely to be favoured by both disabled and elderly tourists. Further complications arise in the case of cruise ships if landings have to be made by tender or zodiac (the latter hazardous even for the able-bodied in swells, and more so for elderly passengers). Encountering rough seas can pose a threat to the disabled, whether or not they are wheelchair-bound. The question of compensation in the event of injuries then arises and whether or not exclusion clauses in contracts can overcome such threats.

The UK government is expected to legislate to do away with the current legal exemptions on disabilities applying to cruise ships and the lines are taking steps to keep ahead of the legislation. The Fred Olsen Line, to take one example, has purchased stair walkers to help disabled passengers when embarking and disembarking.

Budget cruising

Although cruises are sold as package holidays in the USA and tour operators there have also played their part as intermediaries in bringing the product to the notice of the travelling public, UK tour operators, on the other hand, were in general slower to move into the cruise market. Some early attempts were made during the 1970s, when operators, including market leader Thomson Holidays, started to charter or part-charter cruise ships that they incorporated into their programme of inclusive tours, but efforts to bring down the overall prices of cruising led to dissatisfaction with standards of service and operation. Two decades later, Airtours, one of the leading operators, introduced its own ship, *Carousel*, with low lead-in prices and, for the first time, cruises were marketed as just another package holiday, with all meals and entertainment thrown in. Other leading operators soon entered the competition and, in 2000, Royal Caribbean International bought a 20% stake in tour operator First Choice to form a joint cruise company, Island Cruises, with the clear intention of using the operator's retail outlets to push cruise sales in the UK.

The entrance of these tour operators into the mass market cruise business changed the face of cruising in the UK. Not only did the average age of cruise passengers come down but also a whole new market was introduced to cruising. One major budget cruise company, Ocean Village, claimed that 60% of its passengers were first-time cruisers. Undoubtedly, the budget cruise companies helped to account for the fact that one in nine of all foreign package holidays booked in the UK in 2010 was a cruise. Tour operators also helped to popularize the short cruise in the British mass market, which brought down cruise prices, and the seven-day, or shorter, cruise has since enhanced the appeal of this form of holiday for both European and American passengers. A Cyprus-based company, Louis Cruises, further boosted the appeal of short cruises by offering two-night voyages from Limassol to Egypt and the Lebanon, mainly as excursions for holidaymakers staying on the island. Since then, the company has expanded its programme of short cruises to include sailings from Genoa, Piraeus and Marseilles, having taken over the MyTravel (formerly Airtours) vessels when that company withdrew from the cruise business. With the merger between MyTravel and Thomas Cook, cruises are now marketed under the Cruise Thomas Cook label, but the operator neither owns nor charters vessels on its own account. Thomson, however, has expanded its cruise division and now operates four vessels.

EXAMPLE **easyCruise**

In 2005, easyJet founder Stelios Hadji-Ioannou announced his foray into the cruise industry with the launch of easyCruise. This was an entirely new concept in cruising. Working on a low-cost model, customers could book cabins for any variety of legs between ports around the Mediterranean, with a minimum of two nights on board. The cabins, which were very small, were initially sold at a rate of just £29 per double per night. Similar to the easyJet model, any extras required were at a supplement and several charges could not be avoided; for example, a supplement for departure cleaning was payable. Food was not included in the price. Customers were able to make their own connecting flight arrangements, or pay extra for flights to and from their departure points.

As an alternative to the more usual cruise itineraries, the ship would not leave port until the early hours of the morning, thus allowing passengers the opportunity to spend the evening onshore, perhaps eating in the local restaurants or exploring the local bars and clubs. On its maiden voyage, it attracted passengers with an average age of just 35.

Yet the success of this business has been relatively short-lived. easyCruise was sold to Hellenic Seaways in 2009 who suspended operations soon afterwards, struggling to make money from the low cabin rates and low passenger spend on board – an issue highlighting the importance of this revenue stream.

The future of the cruise business

For all the contributions made by the mass market tour operators, it is anticipated that most cruising will retain its upmarket image, at least within Europe. Both luxury and middle-priced cruising have been experiencing sharp rises in demand, in spite of deep discounting, and it is these that are seen as offering the best opportunity for long-term profitability. The market for this price bracket is very loyal – both P&O and Cunard have claimed that 60–70% of their market is repeat bookings. The future of the cruise industry in general also looks healthy in terms of growth in demand, but perhaps less so in terms of profitability, especially given the expectation of rises in oil prices. One study by the PSA found that fewer than one in 60 British travellers has ever taken a cruise, far fewer than among the US population. That would suggest there is considerable scope for growth, but also points up the fact that cruise numbers, while growing fast, would have to rise substantially in order to match the levels achieved in the USA.

As we have noted, brand loyalty is strong among cruise passengers and great efforts are now made to differentiate individual ships as well, rather than depending on discounting to sell unsold cabins. Certainly Carnival, with its niche marketing to the younger holiday-makers in the USA, has led the way in this direction, while other companies have focused on theme cruising to survive. Indeed, cruise lines now offer a huge variety of special interest cruises, ranging from botanical cruises to classical civilizations cruising in the Mediterranean, accompanied by specialist, often well-known, guest lecturers, and from classical music cruises to jazz cruises, with onboard orchestras. Some shipping operators have experimented with new types of vessel. Radisson, for example, introduced twin-hull catamaran vessels, while both Windstar Cruises and Club Méditerranée offer luxury sail-assisted ships to widen the appeal of cruising. Small luxury ships are also in vogue. Society Expedition Cruises offer luxury cruising for around 100 passengers to exotic destinations such as the Amazon and Antarctic, while the similarly small (4260 gross tons) Sea Dream Yacht Club ships offer unparalleled luxury to more traditional destinations in the Caribbean and Mediterranean for just 110 passengers, with a crew of just 90 and a retractable platform at the stern from which passengers may swim, snorkel or sail while the ship lies at anchor. Diving holidays from even smaller ships are also growing in popularity, with vessels such as *SY Siren*, based in Thailand, *Four Seasons Explore* in the Maldives, *Komodo Dancer* in Bali and *Aqua Cat* in the Bahamas. These small vessels typically carry fewer than a dozen passengers in extreme luxury. Their popularity is likely to increase.

Looking to the longer term, research is continuing on designs for more fuel-efficient craft. Successful sea trials have taken place of vessels that complement the use of their engines with metal sails, increasing the overall speed while reducing costs – an important consideration at a time when fuel prices are rising sharply. Marine research in the short term is focusing on greater efficiency in engines to reduce pollution and improving designs and finishes to reduce drag. The pressure must also be on to develop new forms of energy to propel ships, given the continuing rise in oil prices. As we saw earlier, liquefied natural gas is already in use for ships on short sea routes, but, unlike the automobile industry, the development of hydrogen power for seagoing vessels does not appear to be imminent.

The appeal of cruise ships that resemble floating hotels with a full range of leisure facilities has led to the construction of ever larger vessels, but whether *Oasis of the Seas* will see this trend taper off is debatable. One forecast (by Tillberg Design – the company responsible for designing the *Queen Elizabeth 2* and *Queen Mary 2*) expects to see even larger vessels, carrying between 5000 and 7000 passengers, who would be carried to shore in smaller vessels, as the mother ship would be too large to enter most existing ports. Such ships would indeed be veritable floating hotels, with gardens on the top deck and a range of environmentally-friendly additions, including solar panels to generate hot water on board.

Proposals have also been advanced for much larger catamarans and trimarans (twin-hulled and triple-hulled vessels) than those currently in existence, capable of transporting large numbers of passengers at high speed and with far more comfort, without the customary problems of motion sickness experienced with single-hull ships. It is conceivable that the construction of such vessels would allow transatlantic crossings to be completed in under 48 hours.

Finally, the impact of piracy will continue to be an issue for many cruise companies. Attacks on merchant navy vessels in the Gulf of Aden, off the coast of Somalia and increasingly further south off the African coast have led to the payment of ransoms, encouraging yet further attacks. The cost of security for ships passing though this area is significant and the impact on company image can be devastating when attacks on passenger ships occur. Some UK cruise ships travelling through the area have now armed themselves with high-pressure water-canon to prevent pirates boarding the ship. Frequent attacks in this area has already had an impact on the Kenyan tourism industry, with cruise passenger numbers in the first half of 2011 declining from 11 000 passengers to just 500. This is by no means the only area where piracy attacks occur and cruise companies are changing routes and itineraries to avoid known hotspots.

Ferry services

The term 'ferry' is one that embraces a variety of forms of short-distance waterborne transport. This includes urban transport in cities such as Stockholm, where people travel from the city centre to outlying suburbs and surrounding towns by water. Ferries of this type also attract tourists, who use it as either a convenient form of local transport or an original way to view the city. Some ferries, such as the Staten Island ferry (Figure 14.6), which links Manhattan with the borough of Staten Island in New York, and Hong Kong's Star Ferry, have become world famous and a 'must' for visiting tourists. Other notable ferry rides that serve the needs of both locals and tourists include the Bosporus ferries linking Europe and Asia in Istanbul, the many island ferries in Greece and Indonesia, the Manly ferry between Sydney and Manly in Australia, the Niteroi ferry crossing Guanabara Bay in Rio de Janeiro, the Mersey ferry in Liverpool (immortalized in various songs), the Bainbridge Island ferry in Seattle, the Alameda–Oakland ferry in San Francisco, the Devonport and Waiheke inland ferries in Auckland, New Zealand, and the Barreiro and Cacilhas ferries crossing the River Tagus in Lisbon. Most of these, of course, have been designed primarily to provide essential links for local commuters, but, inevitably, they also provide important attractions for tourists either wishing to get a different view of a city or planning to visit more remote areas of a country, where convenient links by air may not be possible. Examples of the latter include the Greek islands, the Hebrides off the west coast of Scotland, the Isle of Wight off the south coast of England and crossing the Strait of Messina, between Italy and Sicily.

Figure 14.6 New York's renowned Staten Island ferry

Photo by Chris Holloway

The key ferry routes for tourists, however, are those that are major links between countries separated by water, such as across the English Channel, between countries in the Baltic Sea, between Corsica and Sardinia and across the Adriatic between Italy, Greece and the Balkan countries. These routes may be vital for those wishing to take their car on holiday, but also provide an attractive alternative to flying for those with time to spare. Additionally, there are many places in the world where transport is dependent on good national ferry services, owing either to the number of islands belonging to the territory or the difficulty of reaching coastal destinations by air or sea. A notable example is the west coast of Norway, where small towns cut off from land routes and air connections depend on the Hurtigruten, or fast route, where daily ferries call at dozens of ports between Bergen and the North Cape. This itinerary has become so popular with tourists that full-size cruise vessels now ply the route. Other popular routes include the west coast of Canada and Alaska and the Hebridean islands off mainland Scotland's western coast.

EXAMPLE   Dubai introduces ferry services

Traffic congestion has become problematic in Dubai. To ease the problem, public transport infrastructure has been developing at a rapid pace, with a second Metro line constructed. But to further serve the local commuters and tourists to the city, Ferry Dubai has been launched. Initially operating on a tourist route - cruising Dubai Creek and returning to the same port station where it started - this service will eventually link Jumeirah Beach with Dubai Marina and other waterfront locations. Up to 40 ferry stations are planned, being served by 10 ferries, each capable of transporting 100 passengers.

This development is not entirely new to the emirate. Dubai has long been served by Abras, long narrow wooden boats, which can each carry about 20 passengers. The boats, while fairly basic, are believed to transport 16 million passengers a year across Dubai Creek (Eagles, 2011). To manage safety issues, Dubai Roads and Transport Authority has provided six official boarding stations and Abra operators must be licensed.

The significance of the short sea ferry market can be appreciated when it is learned that, by the end of the last century, some 2150 ro–ro (roll-on–roll-off) ferries were estimated to be in operation worldwide, and demand shows no signs of slackening. Almost 22 million international ferry passengers travelled to and from the UK in 2010 (DfT, 2011). Of course, not all these passengers will be counted as tourists, an important point to remember. Typically, ferry services are designed to provide a communication network for local populations, while taking advantage of visitors to boost numbers and become profitable.

The rise in demand for ferries over the past half century can be partly attributed to the general growth of tourism and trade in the region, especially between EU countries, but the growth of private car ownership and independent travel have also played a significant part in raising demand. France, in particular, has always been a destination with a strong attraction for British holidaymakers travelling independently with their cars, although the relative strength of the pound to the euro is a key factor in influencing demand between the UK and the Continent. There has also been a steady rise in coach transport between the UK and the Continent, as coach companies introduced long-distance coach routes linking London with the capitals and cities of Continental Europe. Despite the challenge offered by the Channel Tunnel linking the UK and France since 1994, Dover remains by far the most important of the ports serving the Continent, with P&O currently offering cross-Channel services from this port (see Table 14.6). Since the end of the last century, when passenger numbers peaked at 36 million there has been a steady decline in passenger numbers, perhaps partly as a result of the abolition of duty-free shopping in 1999, which reduced the number of passengers taking daytrips across the channel.

Table 14.6 Ro-ro ferry journeys from UK ports

Port	Passenger numbers 1980	Passenger numbers 2000	Passenger numbers 2010
Dover	10 965 000	16 078 000	13 125 000
Portsmouth	722 000	3 176 000	2 212 000
Holyhead	1 142 000	2 518 000	2 073 000
Hull	484 000	972 000	950 000
Harwich	1 669 000	1 335 000	620 000
All short-sea routes	23 395 000	28 517 000	21 883 000

Source: DfT, 2011

Good marketing by the ferry companies has played a part in stimulating traffic over the years. New routes have been developed to tap regional markets and provide greater choice, so passengers have been able to choose to travel to the Continent from a variety of ports along the south coast of England (Figure 14.7). Not all new routes have proved viable, as price competition attracts tourists to the most popular routes even if they are not the most convenient. The generally high prices charged by ferries out of Kent to the Continent (claimed to be the highest fares per mile anywhere in the world) were challenged by Danish company Speedferries, which undercut the prices of the established lines operating across the Channel but foundered in the current economic recession. Eurotunnel, too, has slashed prices to attract more passengers to the land link with the Continent.

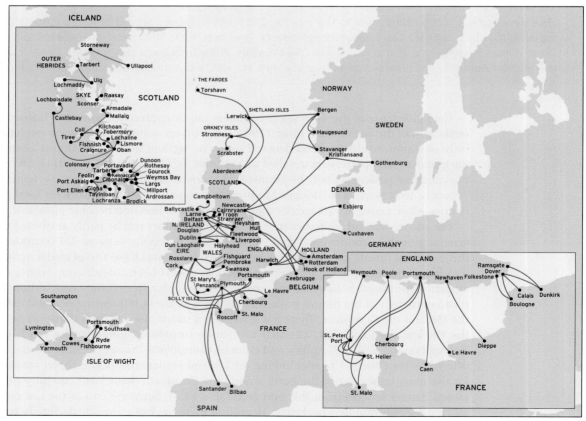

Figure 14.7 The major passenger car ferry services operating from ports in the UK
Courtesy of Travel Weekly

From the UK, routes can be conveniently grouped into four geographical regions:

- English Channel (short sea crossing) routes, including services from ports such as Ramsgate, Dover, Folkestone and Newhaven
- Western Channel routes, including services from Portsmouth, Southampton, Poole, Weymouth and Plymouth
- North Sea routes, including services from Newcastle/North Shields, Hull, Felixstowe, Harwich and Sheerness
- Irish Sea routes, including services from Swansea, Pembroke, Fishguard, Holyhead, Liverpool, Stranraer, Cairnryan and the Isle of Man.

It should be stressed that, while these have been identified as key ports, services operating out of them do vary from time to time as competition forces out some companies and others attempt to operate new routes in their place. The expectation that a route, once announced, will continue to operate for many years is no longer true. Recent years have seen a number of companies' routes fail, while others have withdrawn services or reverted to alternative ports. Even one of the oldest ferry routes, that between Newhaven and Dieppe, with a history of service stretching back to 1825, was briefly without a ferry connection until new services were introduced earlier this century.

In addition to the UK's ferry connections to the Continental and Irish ports, a number of important smaller ferry services provide internal links to the Hebridean islands of Scotland, the Orkney and Shetland islands, and to the Isle of Wight, the Isle of Man, the Scilly Isles and Lundy Island in the Severn Channel.

The economics of operating ferries

As with cruising, operating short sea ferry routes is expensive, in terms of both capital investment and direct operating costs. Modern ferries on many routes are now nearly as large and sumptuous as cruise ships and building costs can run into hundreds of millions of pounds. Within the EU, ferries are expected to be written off over a 27-year timespan, although Greece has traditionally operated its ferries for as long as 35 years.

Profitability is achieved through a combination of maximum usage of equipment and onboard sales. The termination in 1999 of duty-free sales within the EU had a significant impact on cross-Channel revenue – it had accounted for up to 50% of ferry companies' turnover, so ticket prices were forced up. Rapid turnarounds in port at the end of each journey are essential, as are round-the-clock sailings, with, ideally, an even volume of business all year round and a balanced flow of demand in both directions. In practice, this is, of course, impossible to achieve. In winter, when much of the pure holiday traffic dries up, the ferry services become very dependent on freight to contribute to their costs. Despite transporting almost 3 million passengers annually, Seafrance was declared bankrupt in 2012, although DFDS has expressed an interest in taking over their operations with a view to amalgamating this with its existing routes out of Dover, adding to their recent acquisition of Norfolkline, a competitor on the cross-Channel route.

The shorter sailings to France, Belgium and Holland attract much better market demand than do the longer routes to Scandinavia, Germany and northern Spain, although the ferry companies on the latter routes have achieved considerable success in marketing the longer (24 hours or more) sailings as mini-cruises. Their success is modelled on the enormously popular service between Stockholm, Sweden and either Turku or Helsinki, Finland, which, in addition to providing one of the most scenic routes anywhere in Europe for a ferry service, also attracts customers through the sale of relatively cheap onboard drinks in a region where alcohol is prohibitively expensive. As a result, the ferry market between these two countries has grown to a point where the two major carriers, Silja Line and Viking Line, can support a string of superferries, the largest of which, at 60 000 tons, is capable of carrying in excess of 3000 passengers. By including a stop at the Finnish-owned Åland Islands, which have special status within the European Community, duty-free goods can continue to be sold on board these vessels, maintaining their popularity with the short-break market.

Off-peak sailings on shorter routes can be boosted by low fares, aiming a wide range of discounted prices at differing market segments. Quick round trips on the same vessel or short stopovers of one to three nights have expanded, while shopping expeditions to the French hypermarkets for food and alcohol prove popular, especially in the run-up to Christmas. While the termination of duty-free goods on these routes initially cut the market for short trips to France, the removal of customs barriers on duty-paid goods within the EU and the relatively low cost of duty-paid alcoholic drinks in France compared with the UK has helped to boost sales on cross-Channel vessels.

At extreme off-peak periods and for night sailings, which attract fewer bookings, some ferry companies will price their sailings to make a contribution to fixed costs rather than attempt to cover all costs on every crossing. Low fares will stimulate onboard spend, making a useful contribution to total revenues. The ferry companies have increased their general shopping facilities in their newer ships in order to boost onboard sales. While this has not fully made up for the loss of duty-free revenue, it has helped to reduce the impact of the withdrawal of this facility.

Leading ferry companies have made strenuous efforts to cut their operating costs in recent years, particularly their labour costs. New labour practices were introduced to increase the efficiency of crewing, but only after serious confrontations with the seamen's union. As with cruising, many staff from developing countries are now recruited. At the same time, SOLAS regulations, which came into effect at the end of 2004 following the Stockholm Agreement signed in 1997 between the UK and six northern European countries, have substantially added to building costs.

The objective of these regulations was to increase the safety and stability of ro–ro ferries following the *Herald of Free Enterprise* disaster, when it sank at Zeebrugge in 1987 and nearly 200 people died, and the subsequent sinking of the ferry *Estonia* in the Baltic in 1994, with the loss of 850 lives. The Stockholm Agreement requires vessels operating into and out of ports in the seven countries to be capable of remaining upright in waves up to 4 metres high and with 50 centimetres of floodwater on the car deck. It called for transverse bulkheads to be fitted on all ships to improve stability in rough seas, but these obligatory modifications can reduce car capacity and slow down the loading and unloading of vessels, leading to delays in turnarounds.

One study, by the DK Group, found that the global shipping industry wastes almost 3 million barrels of oil daily as a result of ageing vessels not having been upgraded with fuel-saving technology, and certainly the global ferry market has made a contribution to this wastage. The research suggests that upgrading vessels by fitting new propellers and engines and installing new technology could reduce global marine fuel consumption by as much as 40%.

The Channel Tunnel and ferry services

The Channel Tunnel was viewed initially as the single greatest threat to cross-Channel ferries since their inception. Opened to passenger traffic in 1994, the Tunnel has attracted the lion's share of the cross-Channel market, but has failed to drive the ferries out of business. In recent years it has even come close to financial collapse itself, due to the huge burden of capital debts it bears. The background to this problem is described more fully in Chapter 15, but here we will take account of the impact of this land link on ferry services.

Groupe Eurotunnel, which operates the Channel Tunnel, suffered a number of setbacks in building and operating the Tunnel, including repeated delays in opening, delays in obtaining equipment to run through the Tunnel and a disastrous and costly fire in a freight wagon at the end of 1996. Eurotunnel's original estimates of passenger numbers proved wildly optimistic, but nonetheless the company achieved a 51% share of the Dover Straits traffic (Dover/Folkestone to Calais/Boulogne) within its first five years of operation. Eurostar, which offers rail connections between London, Lille, Paris and Brussels via the Tunnel, has also been successful in diverting a substantial number of air travellers back to rail between these destinations.

The ferries were quick to retaliate. P&O and Stena invested heavily in their short sea operations and merged their services on the route between Dover and Calais, following investigation by the Monopolies and Mergers Commission (MMC) (now the Competition Commission). Improvements in passenger-handling facilities at Dover were introduced, allowing passengers to check in just 20 minutes before sailing. A 'turn up and go' service obviated the need for reservations, while, curiously, Eurotunnel itself withdrew this same benefit, obliging its passengers to hold a reservation before arrival at the terminal. New, faster ferries were introduced, with the travel time between Dover and Calais reduced from 90 minutes to 75 minutes. The emphasis of its marketing shifted, selling the crossing as part of a holiday, with time to relax and unwind on board. The Tunnel was disparaged as offering no more than 'a toilet and a light bulb'. Larger, more luxurious ships on the route helped reinforce the concept of a mini-cruise, with the result that the short sea routes have held up well, although the other longer routes suffered badly from the competition.

On the medium-distance crossings, a new generation of fast ships and catamarans came onstream. This resulted in the crossing time from Portsmouth to Cherbourg, for example, being reduced from five hours to two hours 45 minutes.

The problem for the ferry services is attracting sufficient trade during the winter months, when the Tunnel is seen by many passengers as preferable to a rough sea crossing, and a longer journey time. Eurotunnel now appears to have established itself more securely in the market, and in 2010 carried a total of 2 125 000 cars through the tunnel (in addition to the 9.5 million passengers who travelled by Eurostar), accounting for 43% of the Dover–Calais market.

 EXAMPLE **Contrasting fortunes**

Competition between Eurotunnel and the Port of Dover has been intense, ever since the Channel Tunnel opened. While tourists travelling abroad in their own cars are important, equally so is freight traffic. The port also received 167 visits from cruise ships in 2010.

Table 14.7 Operating data for Eurotunnel and the Port of Dover

	Eurotunnel (2010)	Port of Dover (2010)
Cars	2.1 million	2.8 million
Lorries	1.08 million (up 42% on 2009)	2.09 million (down 10% on 2009)
Revenue	£630 million	£57 million
Net profit (loss)	(£48.7 million)	£7.8 million

Source: Company Annual Reports

Any comparison of these two entities should note that Eurotunnel acts both as port and as transport operator, while the Port of Dover relies on ferry and cruise companies to provide the sea crossings. In addition to this, the costs of constructing the Channel Tunnel weigh heavily on the balance sheet for Eurotunnel – servicing that debt cost almost £250 million in 2010, accounting for their loss-making position.

New modes of crossing

Alongside the introduction of the new fast ferries, alternative and still faster forms of water transport have become popular on many short- and medium-range routes. First hovercraft, then hydrofoils and, finally, catamarans entered service, with the benefits of speed and a certain degree of novelty.

Hovercraft were used to initiate the first fast ferry crossings across the Channel as early as 1968. They offered several advantages over the traditional ferries. Riding on a cushion of air just above the surface of the water and able to travel over land as well as water, they avoided the usual capital costs associated with dock facilities, as the craft could simply be beached on any convenient and obstacle-free foreshore. Unfortunately, they also offered their passengers a somewhat bouncy and noisy ride by comparison with the more traditional ferries, and could not operate in seas with waves greater than 2.5 metres. The vessels also suffered many technical problems in their development and throughout the years of their operation, so were finally withdrawn from service in 2000, being replaced by catamarans.

The hydrofoil offers better prospects for future development, even though it, too, suffered initial teething problems. This vessel operates with a conventional hull design, but when travelling at speed the hull is raised above the surface of the water on blades, or, 'foils'. This enables the vessel to travel at speeds of up to 60 knots. Recent models have been powered by jet engines (jetfoils), but their unreliability on open waters and inability to contend with high waves have hindered their adoption in UK waters.

The most promising recent development in ferry operations has been the high-speed, wave-piercing catamaran (WPC). These have been operating on cross-Channel services since 1991 and have now replaced the hovercraft. They are mainly twin-hulled vessels, large enough to accommodate cars, travelling at speeds of up to 40 knots. This type of vessel has now proved reliable in most weathers, operating successfully from the UK to Ireland and the Continent, as well as on key routes such as Dover–Calais and Harwich–Hook of Holland. Catamarans have also proved popular on routes across the Baltic Sea and other key European routes.

The popular Seacats (twin-hull) and Superseacats (monohull) offer a valuable service for passengers wanting the fastest possible crossing to the Continent but who might find the Channel Tunnel claustrophobic. The latest HSS (high-speed sea service) twin-hull ferries introduced by Stena have further stretched capacity, carrying up to 1500 passengers and 375 cars. The downside, however, is that some constraints still remain on their operation in rough weather – waves above 4 metres can lead to cancellations, which is a serious constraint in the winter months. Additionally, the higher fuel burn of all these craft impacts on their operating costs more severely than on other forms of ferry. As a result, Stena Line took the decision to extend its crossing times on some routes from the UK, reducing fuel consumption by 8%. Whether these catamarans have a long-term future is questionable at this point, as long as oil prices remain high. Some HSSs are already being laid up, to be replaced by more traditional vessels.

With growing concern over fuel prices, alternative forms of energy for marine vessels are receiving attention. One interesting development is that of the *Solar Sailor* – a 100-passenger catamaran ferry that went into service in Sydney Harbour in 2000. This vessel operates with solar and wind power, with a back-up electric motor running from batteries that store the energy the craft collects while running on the alternative energy sources. It is silent, smooth, creates no pollution whatsoever and its photocells are boosted 20% by the sun's reflection in the water. A similar vessel is being trailed for operation, to transport golfers between three island-based courses located off the coast of Hong Kong Island; and a solar-powered 'hotel boat' also operates on France's Canal du Midi between Carcassonne and Beziers, a distance of some 75 km.

Other European ferry operations

While the focus here has been primarily on connections between the UK and its Continental neighbours, the continuing importance of other routes, especially within Europe, must be recognized. In the Mediterranean, ferries provide not only vital connections to travellers on a port-to-port basis, but also the opportunity to package these routes as mini-cruises, calling at a variety of different countries. By way of example, services are available in the eastern Mediterranean between Venice, Dubrovnik, Piraeus, Iraklion and Alexandria or between Istanbul, Piraeus, Larnaca, Lattakia (Syria) and Alexandria. Other important routes include those between Patras (Greece) and Ascona (Italy) and between Nice and Corsica. Tourists who traditionally think only of travelling by air to Majorca may be unaware of the alternatives – travelling from Barcelona by catamaran with Trasmediterranea, for example.

The Greek economy is heavily dependent on its shipping interests, with some 10 million passengers using ferries within the country each year. The significance of this area of the economy to Greece was such that EU cabotage restrictions were permitted to remain in place until 2004. The disastrous sinking of the poorly maintained and elderly ferry *Express Samina* in 2000, however, led the Greek government to withdraw the licences of some older vessels and bring deregulation forward by two years. Vessels from other countries are now allowed to operate freely in Greek waters (although few have taken up this challenge to date). This has spurred Greek shipowners to invest heavily in new equipment, as well as expanding their own activities outside the country.

Ferry operations in the Baltic call for special mention. Services here connect the Scandinavian countries and, in turn, provide vital connections for travellers between these countries and Germany. Independence for the three Baltic states of Latvia, Estonia and Lithuania, the entry of these countries into the EU, the rebuilding of the historic port of Gdansk (formerly Danzig) in Poland and the reunification of Germany have all renewed interest in these destinations for tourists, and both cruise ships and ferry crossings have achieved considerable growth in this area. The benefit of having St Petersburg in Russia as a major port in the Baltic has further stimulated interest in the region. With the enormous popularity of Tallinn as a tourist venue since EU accession and the short ferry journey between Helsinki and Tallinn – just one hour and 40 minutes by fast ferry – it has become a key route in the Baltic. It provides tourists with the opportunity for an attractive mini-cruise, coupled with bargain-priced shopping. Reference has already been made to the equally popular route between Stockholm and Helsinki. An overnight sailing can be treated as a mini-cruise, the 60 000-ton superferries carrying up to 2800 passengers at a time. The obvious success in this region of selling what were originally merely transport connections as luxury mini-cruises has established a trend that other ferry operators are keen to emulate.

The future of ferry operations

Work on still more advanced vessels is under way. Yet another form of fast ferry, the hoverplane, combines elements of catamaran, hovercraft and wing-in-ground (WIG) in its design. 'Wingboats' built on the WIG principle operate by generating a stable cushion of air under the wing as the craft 'flies' close to ground or water. By travelling on this dense layer of air, the craft benefits from reduced drag and increased lift, thus achieving high levels of fuel economy. Exceptionally high speeds are anticipated at one-fifth of the normal fuel cost of a ferry, which should enable prices to be much lower than at present. It is expected that these craft, in their initial development, should be capable of carrying between 80 and 150 passengers over distances of up to 250 miles. An added advantage of such a vessel is that it requires neither runway nor port in the accepted sense of the words. The *Airfish8*, registered in Singapore in 2010, is the first WIG craft to be registered as a commercial vessel. It has a speed of 90 knots and travels 6 metres above the surface of the water. The nature of the design does, however, limit its operations in high winds or over seas with high waves.

More sustainable options are also being developed. In Japan, work to develop a 'zero-emissions' car ferry has commenced. This will use solar panels on its upper deck to generate energy, which can be stored in lithium batteries, to be used while the vessel is berthed in port. The batteries have been designed as a part of the fixed ballast, thus not reducing the number of cars which can be transported. Similar efforts to use low-emission technology has been employed by Stena on their Jutlandica ferry, operating the Sweden–Denmark route. Two wind turbines have been installed to provide electricity for the ship.

Coastal and inland waterways tourism

The attraction of water offers many other opportunities for tourist activity, both independently and in forms that have been commoditized and packaged for visitors. Inland waterways, in particular, lakes, rivers and canals, provide exceptional opportunities for recreation and tourism, and in the UK the renovation of former canals, derelict locks and similar watersites has added in recent years to the many opportunities for river and lake recreational travel.

The major waterways of the world have long attracted tourists. The Nile River in Egypt has provided inland waterway cruising for many decades and, in recent years, the popularity of this stretch of waterway led to an enormous expansion in the number and size of cruise ships operating as part of package holidays up to the early years of the 1990s. The volatility of the tourism business is well illustrated by the collapse of the Egyptian inland cruise market in the mid-1990s, when the country was hit first by terrorism in which tourists were targeted explicitly, and then drought, which caused navigational difficulties in the upper Nile region. In 2000, the Nile came back into favour briefly, until the advent of 9/11 and then the Iraqi war once again discouraged tourists from travelling to the Middle East. Civil uprising in 2011 and the overthrow of the Egyptian government led to further questions over the viability of tourism to the area, although the subsequent desperately low prices offered to tempt visitors back helped to boost the Western markets searching for bargains in a time of severe recession.

Popular European river cruises include the Rhine/Danube (between Amsterdam, Holland and Passau in Germany, thence to Constanta in Romania), the Douro in Portugal and the French rivers Seine and Rhone. Elsewhere, rivers with strong tourist appeal include the Mississippi in the USA (where traditional paddle steamers offer a nostalgic cruise experience) and the Yangtze and Li Rivers in China, while the Volga and Russian waterways linking St Petersburg with Moscow, the Italian River Po and the German Elbe are all increasing in popularity. The Guadalquivir River in Spain allows small passenger craft to travel from the port of Cadiz as far inland as Seville and this has become one of the more recent innovations in river cruising. In South America, the Amazon River is sufficiently large to allow ocean-going ships to navigate as far inland as Iquitos in Peru. All of these river journeys have been packaged as tours and sold to tourists throughout the world.

Public craft are employed on coastal trips as well as on inland waterways. The popular excursion boats *Waverley* – one of the few remaining paddle steamers in the world – and *Balmoral* carry tourists on trips along the coast in the UK during the summer from ports in Scotland, South Wales and the West Country.

Others travel across the Scottish lochs (Figure 14.8) and along the Caledonian Canal. The lakes steamer remains a familiar sight in many parts of the world, providing an important tourist attraction in the US and Canadian Great Lakes, the Swiss and south German lakes, the islands of southern Sweden around Stockholm and the Scottish lochs and

Figure 14.8 Steamship *Sir Walter Scott* coming into berth on Loch Katrine, Scotland

Photo by Claire Humphreys

English Lake District in the UK. Many of these are elderly craft that have been restored and are kept in tiptop condition because of their appeal to tourists. The Swiss, for instance, have recently restored their classic (1909 built) *Stadt Rapperswil* and *Stadt Zürich* operating on the Zürichsee, while the Bodensee (Lake Constance) has 34 lakes steamers owned by five different companies operating between the ports of Germany, Switzerland and Austria. Both these lakes employ steamers essentially as regular transport for residents, but, because of their appeal as iconic tourist symbols, they are just as important to tourism as are the famous red double-decker buses of London.

It is the growing attraction of rivers and canals for the independent boating enthusiast that perhaps holds the greatest potential for development over the next few years. The networks of rivers and canals in countries such as the UK, Holland and France have been redeveloped and exploited for tourism, and canals such as the Burgundy canals and the Canal du Midi in the South of France, as well as the Gota Canal in Sweden, are being discovered by British tourists in growing numbers. In 2011, it was announced that Italy plans to reopen its inland waterway between Locarno in Switzerland, on Lake Maggiore, and Venice, via Milan, a distance of some 500 km.

EXAMPLE   **Opening up to river tourism**

The waterways of Russia have now been opened up to sailors from across the globe. In July 2011, the President, Dmitry Medvedev, signed a bill which permitted foreign pleasure yachts to sail on the inland rivers, providing the vessels travel for sports, cultural or recreational purposes. There are still some limitations to this, however. The yachts can have no more than 18 people on board and some ports and rivers may still remain restricted areas.

This amendment will help to encourage the development of river tourism. Yet other facilities, such as suitable moorings, dock families and fuelling stations, will all need to be provided if this form of tourism is to develop. One motivation for using the rivers is that they provide access to regions notoriously difficult to reach by road. It is also possible that the market attracted to this is likely to have a high level of spend.

The UK itself is particularly well endowed with canals and rivers suitable for navigation. In the mid-1800s, the nation could boast of some 4250 miles of navigable inland waterways, many of which had been developed for the movement of freight. As these became redundant with the advent of the railways, they fell into disrepair until many stretches became no longer navigable. In recent years, however, British Waterways (BW) has encouraged the development and use of these waterways for pleasure purposes, and, in partnership with private enterprise, aided by voluntary bodies, it has helped to restore and reopen many formerly derelict canals.

Today, some 2200 miles of navigable British waterways are open (Figure 14.9) and maintained by BW, and the Board licenses 35 000 boats to use its network and just under 13 million tourists use the waterways and its towpaths for recreational purposes, whether for angling, walking or cycling. Previously a public body, BW now has charitable status and funding for its activities will come from donations, sponsorship and, increasingly, commercialization of its activities. There are hopes that eventually well over 4000 miles of the network can be reopened.

Additionally, the Norfolk and Suffolk Broads offer 125 miles of river cruising and have been catering for thousands of holidaymakers in private or hired vessels every year since the early twentieth century. The reopening of many formerly derelict waterways has made it possible for boat hire companies to organize packages that allow enthusiasts to follow a circular route during a one- or two-week holiday, without the need to travel over the same stretch of water twice.

A further 1250 miles of navigable waterways are preserved by other bodies, largely under the supervision of the Waterways Trust – an organization expected to merge with BW once charitable status for the latter is settled. In 2002, a long-term investment of £500 million was raised to go towards reopening derelict canals, and nine schemes are in place to return another 300 miles to public use, under the Trust's guidance. Now foreign as well as British tourists are becoming attracted to the tourism potential these waterways offer.

EXAMPLE **Sailing to the Olympics**

Running through the Olympic Park in London are several canals. In 2010, BW completed the repairs to a derelict lock, opening up the waterways of the Olympic Park to the canal and river network across the UK. Waterways regeneration has also included upgrading a three-mile loop running in and around the park.

BW also established a booking system for temporary moorings around the capital as vessels from across the UK and abroad brought visitors to this global event. Narrowboats, whose usual home is on one of the inland canals of England, berthed alongside superyachts more at home in the marinas of Cannes and Monaco.

Boat rental is a highly competitive business, and in the UK the season is relatively short. Most pleasure boat companies are small, family-run concerns, achieving low returns on capital invested and generally low profits. Effective marketing, especially to overseas tourists, is a problem when companies' budgets for promotion are small and the destination being sold is linear (the Kennet and Avon Canal, for instance, runs through a number of different regions, making unified marketing difficult).

In such circumstances, cooperative promotion between the small boat companies themselves, working with other private-sector interests, is generally the best solution. A star rating for boat hire companies, along similar lines to that used for hotels, has been introduced in the UK, helping direct boat hire customers to their preferred products.

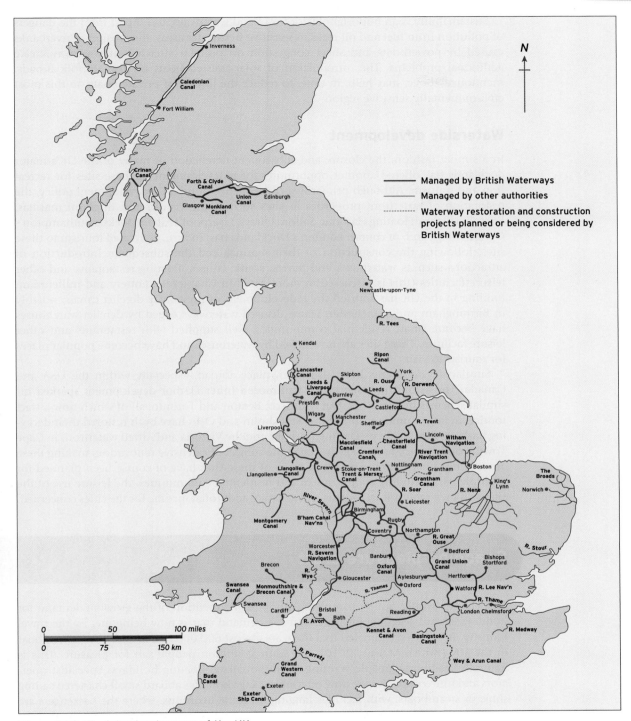

Figure 14.9 The inland waterways of the UK

Courtesy of British Waterways

Consortia like Blakes and Hoseasons offer the power of centralized marketing for small companies and, for others, the World Wide Web is making direct selling easier. Some tour operators have also taken an interest in this sector and are packaging holidays on inland waterways across Europe and in the USA.

Sustainability is an important factor for inland waterways, too. Apart from the dangers of pollution from fuel and oil leaks in sensitive freshwater areas, the erosion of riverbanks caused by powerboats and sheer congestion on popular stretches of waterway create additional problems. The introduction of solar-assisted boats on the Norfolk Broads, mentioned above, may help, in time, to reduce the impact of private boats on this most environmentally sensitive region.

Waterside development

In a similar fashion, the closure and subsequent dereliction of many of the UK's major docklands has offered another opportunity for redevelopment of these sites for recreation and tourism. Although primarily a consequence of urban redevelopment policy, the restoration of waterfront properties in sites such as the Cardiff and Brighton marinas, Bristol's Historic Floating Harbour, Salford Quays, Liverpool's Albert Docks, Southampton's Ocean Village and, of course, London's Docklands has, in turn, generated tourism to these sites, following the construction of their marinas and the subsequent introduction of attractions such as waterbuses and ferries, scenic cruises, floating restaurants and other leisure facilities (this is discussed in more detail in Chapter 9). Lottery and millennium funding in the UK has spurred the redevelopment of previously derelict canals, notably in Birmingham and Manchester, where disused waterways edged by derelict warehouses have become smart residential communities, well supplied with restaurants and other leisure facilities. These sites are now linked by waterbuses and have become popular places for tourists to visit.

Similar developments have also taken place abroad, especially within the USA and Canada. The astonishing success of Baltimore's Inner Harbor development sparked off similar schemes in New York, San Francisco, Boston and Toronto, all of which now attract tourists in large numbers. In Europe, Stockholm and Oslo have both restored their decaying harbour sites. Sydney's Darling Harbour and the Victoria and Alfred waterfront in Cape Town, South Africa, have, likewise, been the subject of extensive renovation, making these areas honey pots for tourism. While most of these sites have of course been planned for multiple use, including shops, offices and residential communities, the leisure use of the sites will inevitably attract tourists and generate additional income for the cities concerned.

Seagoing pleasure craft

This chapter would not be complete without some mention of the growing demand for holidays aboard seagoing pleasure craft – a demand that is now being met by the travel industry. It has been estimated that there are almost 600 000 households who own a boat in the UK (British Marine, 2010) and some 2 million people sail for pleasure. This is naturally leading to people wanting institutionalized boating holidays. Specialist operators and hire companies are now offering package holidays aboard small chartered sailing ships or steamboats, with facilities ranging from the luxurious, where the passengers are guests, to the more basic, where passengers play an active part in crewing the boat. Tour operators also cater for this growing demand for boating holidays with flotilla cruising holidays, especially in areas with numerous small islands where sheltered anchorage and fair weather conditions can be found. The Greek islands and certain Caribbean islands, such as the Windward and Leeward groups, offer ideal conditions for these types of packages, in which individually hired yachts sail together in flotilla formation from island to island. In this manner, tourists have the benefits of independent use of the yacht while also enjoying the social life of the group when together at anchor.

EXAMPLE **Sailing holidays**

The variety of sailing opportunities is extensive – as is demonstrated in this example of programmes organized by Neilson, a tour operator now part of the Thomas Cook Group.

- Firstly, Neilson offers yacht training courses, where holidaymakers can learn the complexities of sailing and marine navigation. The culmination of this can be certification by the Royal Yacht Association. Such courses are designed either for the individual enthusiast or as a family holiday.

- Alternatively, Neilson offer flotilla holidays, where each group of holidaymakers can rent their own craft and sail in a group between ports – with a lead crew in a separate boat to offer guidance and assistance. This provides the opportunity for sailors to travel at their own pace and join with others only when they feel the desire for company.

- A third option – one designed for the more experienced sailor – is a bareboat holiday. Neilson provides the boat, marine equipment and a briefing on the local routes, but the rest is down to the sailor. This gives a freedom to sail unfettered by the itineraries of others.

- Finally, again for the experienced sailor, is the Neilson Delivery Trip. This offers a two-week sailing experience moving the fleet of yachts between their winter home and their summer flotilla base.

The influential factor in selecting the type of holiday is likely to be the level of sailing experience and the desire to balance independence with group interaction.

Further information: www.neilson.co.uk/yacht-home

A phenomenon of the early twenty-first century has been the rapid expansion in ownership of superyachts around the world. These are categorized as vessels exceeding 30 metres in length, and it has been estimated that around 5000 such vessels were in service in 2010. There is a substantial economic benefit to ports harbouring these vessels, including mooring fees, labour, maintenance and leisure spend ashore by owners and their guests, although estimates have yet to be made of the contribution this business makes to the local economies.

Many superyachts are used only by their owners, but some are purchased specifically for the charter market while others are available for rental from the owners for part of the year. Costs of renting a superyacht can be as high as £500 000 for a week's rental but typically will be between £50 000 and £250 000 per week.

As with much larger ships, fractional ownership is now emerging as a new means of owning leisure craft for holidays. Luxury yachts cost many millions and require expensive upkeep, but owning a *share* of one will cost only a fraction of the price and enable the owner to buy one or more weeks each year to enjoy holidays on board a luxury yacht with a full crew. One company, for example, offers a one-eighth stake in a £7 million yacht and owners may rent out some or all of their weeks to earn income.

What does the future hold for water transport?

Research is underway on more advanced forms of sea transport, which much of it focused on improving efficiencies in order to reduce costs and damage to the environment. Increasing speed is also a focus as it becomes clear that, for a great many holidaymakers, faster transport times to reach their holiday destination become important.

The appeal of cruise ships that resemble floating hotels with a full range of leisure facilities is leading to the construction of ever-larger vessels, providing activities, some of which are often more suited to onshore holidays. At the same time, the demand for holidays which appeal to particular niche markets is encouraging the development of smaller vessels able to access more remote locations. It is likely that this sector in particular will see significant growth.

Finally, inland waterways will provide new opportunities for newly developing destinations as the desire to develop river tourism is incorporated into the activities of destination marketing organizations. One example is that of Vietnam, where the Ho Chi Minh City Tourism Association has established the Vietnam Yacht Club with the aim of facilitating the development of river tourism in the city. The infrastructure required, such as dock facilities and marinas, although substantial, may well be justified by the typically higher spend of this type of tourist. There are many existing tourism destinations also looking to reinvigorate their river tourism to boost earnings from visitors. Australia's Murray River has long been a popular holiday spot for domestic tourists, but improvements are now being encouraged in order to attract the international visitor. Whether this sector experiences significant growth may well be determined by the ability to link the attraction of the riverside with the quality of the facilities on board the riverboat and market this to a receptive audience.

Questions and discussion points

1. One example in the chapter highlighted the fact that MSC Cruises has set aside parts of their ship for premium class passengers only. Why might they have offered this? Do you think this will become commonplace for all cruise companies?

2. Why might a family taking a self-drive holiday from the UK to France decide to use the ferry rather than the channel tunnel? Alternatively, what are the benefits of using Eurotunnel to cross to the Continent?

3. What factors may influence the demand for sailing and boating holidays where the vessel is hired and the holidaymakers skipper it to the destination?

Tasks

1. As marketing officer for a river cruise company, you have been asked to explore the potential for expanding your cruise programmes to new destinations. Firstly identify a suitable destination which could offer suitable attractions for your customers and secondly identify the facilities which exist and those which may need to be constructed, if you are to operate cruises on a regular basis. Write a briefing paper for your manager, summarizing your findings.

2. The impact of the tourism industry on the environment is always a concern. Identify the damage that cruises can cause the environment and then detail the actions that the cruise industry, and others, are taking to reduce these impacts.

Bibliography

Biehn, N. (2006) A cruise ship is not a floating hotel, *Journal of Revenue and Pricing Management*, **5** (2), 135–142.

British Marine (2010) *Watersports and Leisure Participation Survey*, available online at http://www.britishmarine.co.uk/upload_pub/WatersportsandLeisureOmnibusreport2010.pdf (accessed November 2011).

CLIA (2010) *CLIA Cruise Market Overview 2010*, Cruise Lines International Association, available online at: http://www2.cruising.org/press/overview2010/ (accessed November 2011).

Cruise Market Watch (2011) *Passenger Capacity*, available online at: http://www.cruisemarket-watch.com/blog1/capacity/ (accessed November 2011).

Cruise New Zealand (2010) *New Zealand Regional Cruise Industry Study*, Auckland, Market Economics.

DfT (2011) *Sea Passenger Statistics*, London, Department for Transport.

Eagles, J. (2011) A transport of delight in Dubai, *New Zealand Herald*, 28 June.

Euromonitor (2010) *Global Cruise Briefing: Sailing to Opportunities*, London, Euromonitor, 17 November.

European Cruise Council (2011) *Statistics and source markets 2010*, Birmingham, IRN Research.

Hickman, M. (2011) Britons to carry on cruising in record-size style, *The Independent*, 2 June.

Klein, R. A. (2006) Turning water into money: the economics of the cruise industry, in Dowling, R. *Cruise Ship Tourism*, Wallingford, CABI, 261–269.

Passenger Shipping Association (2011) *The Cruise Review*, available online at: http://www.the-psa.co.uk/downloads/PSA_Cruise_Review_2011.pdf (accessed November 2011).

US DoT (2011) *North American Cruise Statistical Snapshot – 2010*, Washington, DC, US Department of Transportation.

Further reading

Chin, C. B. N. (2008) *Cruising in the Global Economy: Profits, pleasure and work at sea*, Aldershot, Ashgate.

Dickinson, B. and Vladimir, A. (1997) *Selling the Sea: An inside look at the cruise industry*, New York, Wiley.

Prideaux, B. and Cooper, M. (2009) *River Tourism*, Wallingford, CABI.

Websites

British Waterways: **www.britishwaterways.co.uk**

Cruise Lines International Association: **www.cruising.org**

European Cruise Council: **www.europeancruisecouncil.com**

Inland Waterways Association: **www.waterways.org.uk**

Passenger Shipping Association (PSA) statistics: **www.the-psa-co.uk**

Seatrade magazine: **www.seatrade-global.com**

Staten Island Ferry: **www.siferry.com**

World Shipping Council: **www.worldshipping.org**

Tourist transport on land

Contents

Learning outcomes

After studying this chapter, you should be able to:

- understand the role and scope of railways and their place in tourist travel
- be aware of the role and significance of the coach industry in tourism
- recognize the importance of the private car to tourist travel
- understand the role of car hire in domestic and foreign tourism
- be aware of the growing importance of tourist travel by bicycle and on foot.

My earliest recollection in connection with railways is my first railway journey. I recollect it well. How the wonder of it all impressed me! Railways were new and railway travelling was, to most people, an event.

Joseph Tatlow, Director – Midland Great Western Railway (1920) *Fifty Years of Railway Life in England, Scotland and Ireland*

Introduction

Rail travel for many commuters today may not seem to be the memorable event that Tatlow describes, but there are many train journeys that still enthrall their travelling audience. In this chapter we will explore the different forms of land transport that help tourists reach their destination, though we must not forget that, as we highlighted in Chapter 9, some transport can form part of the attraction and become the destination, as it can offer visitors a unique and memorable experience. Typical examples of this would be a rail journey on the Orient Express through Europe or the Blue Train through the African countryside.

The role of the railways in tourism

Given the length of time that railways have been a part of the public transport system, it may be thought surprising that they have been so slow to take advantage of the growth of mass market tourism that followed World War II (1939–1945). It is all the more surprising when one considers the important role played by the railways in their 100 years of existence up to that point, at a time when rail transport was the principal means by which people took their annual holidays, travelling either to the coasts of their own countries or across the face of Europe to the Mediterranean. Rail transport's decline in popularity paralleled the rise in ownership of private cars, and rail companies appeared content to focus on what they saw as their prime markets – commuters and business travellers – and, of course, freight. Even before the outbreak of war, the decline in tourist travel by rail had been noticeable and the process only accelerated in the UK after 1947, when the railways were nationalized.

Improvements in coach transport, as public road vehicles become more comfortable, faster and more reliable, and the significant gap in price between road and rail, encouraged those without private vehicles to switch to road transport for their holidays, while the better-off made increasing use of their private cars. A similar pattern occurred in the USA, where the switch was to domestic air travel alongside the growth in private car usage.

Instead of fighting back, the railways retrenched, cutting services and routes and concentrating on the main intercity routes. The US railway companies switched their focus to more remunerative freight, with passenger services largely restricted to a handful of well-established intercity routes – a strategy that continues to this day, despite the formation of Amtrak as a public service railroad system, with government subsidies to encourage regeneration of the rail services.

Unprofitable branch lines were closed, especially in the UK following the Beeching Report in the 1960s, and, as a result, many smaller UK coastal resorts and other rural destinations that attracted tourists became inaccessible by rail. The alternative of coach services linking with rail termini made tourist travel inconvenient and time-consuming and this, coupled with continuing disparities in fares and the relative decline in the cost of car travel, soon made the railways an unattractive choice for many destinations.

Privatization of the railways in the UK in the late twentieth century, which resulted in higher fares and inferior service, and the previous long-term lack of investment in track and signalling under public ownership, all made rail travel still less attractive for tourists. This was in contrast to developments on the Continent, where investment in high-speed rail over the past two decades has brought many tourists back on to the trains.

Table 15.1 Top 10 countries for travel by rail

Domestic leisure travel by rail (millions)		International inbound rail passengers (millions)		International outbound rail passengers (millions)	
China	361.3	Ukraine	12.6	Russia	10.2
India	104.2	France	11.8	Hong Kong	9.6
Japan	84.6	Russia	10.1	Ukraine	6.5
USA	62.8	Hong Kong	4.8	Belarus	4.8
Russia	30.5	Hungary	2.9	China	3.4
Indonesia	29.4	UK	2.7	UK	3.2
France	28.4	Belarus	2.5	Germany	3.1
Germany	21.6	Austria	2.3	Hungary	2.4
Egypt	20.6	Italy	2.0	Switzerland	2.3
Ukraine	15.0	Belgium	1.8	France	2.2

Source: Euromonitor, 2010

Rail travel cannot be dismissed as no longer important to tourism, and within Europe the rail companies themselves are now actively pursuing tourist markets over distances of up to 500 miles and, in some instances further, in open competition with the airlines. Rail travel is particularly significant for domestic travel (see Table 15.1).

Improvements in rail services within the UK are gradually enabling the railways to win back tourists from air and from other surface transport, aided by growing road congestion and crowded airports. Some services in the UK remain popular, transporting domestic tourists from the major conurbations to key English resorts like Brighton, Bournemouth and Torquay. Faster services with Eurostar – which uses the Channel Tunnel high-speed rail link to connect London with the high-speed network on the Continent – are attracting British tourists not just to Paris and Brussels but also to other popular tourist destinations such as Cologne, Lille and even the Côte d'Azur in the summer, with special through services operating to the French ski resorts in winter.

Sharp fuel price increases like those which occurred in the 1970s and again since the beginning of the current century helped to win back some domestic tourists from private car travel. Rail companies have become more marketing-orientated, often partnering specialist tour operators to target tourists. Rail and hotel packages in the UK have proved popular for the short-break market, particularly to London and capital cities on the Continent. Efforts to entice rail travel enthusiasts have also met with some success, even though this is on a limited scale. Nostalgic day trips and excursions using old steam engines are popular, as are packages aimed at the over-55s. Recognizing that unsold off-peak seats represent substantial lost revenue, the railways have used variable pricing policies and promotions, sometimes in cooperation with well-known retail stores, to attract tourists and excursionists back to the railways.

Tickets offering unlimited travel by train, sold to inbound tourists only before their departure from their own countries, are yet another means of boosting rail travel. These include the Britrail pass within the UK and Eurailpass on the Continental mainland, while a Scanrail pass provides unlimited travel within the Nordic countries, coupled with a 50% reduction on interconnecting ferry services. Such schemes are aimed at tourists, particularly those from the USA and Australia visiting Europe independently or on tailor-made itineraries, and appeal to the young backpacker market. Similar Railpass schemes are on offer on Amtrak services in the USA, and in Australia; however, the distances involved, some less than adequate services and budget transcontinental air fares make rail travel in these countries less attractive to tourists.

The privatization of rail transport in the UK

Towards the end of the twentieth century, it became clear that action would have to be taken to improve the railway systems, both in Europe and North America. Heavily subsidized and lacking adequate investment over many years, railways were in a parlous state. Two alternatives presented themselves: either the state could move railways out of public ownership or it could agree to a programme of massive state investment to increase the appeal of the railways as a form of public transport.

In the UK, the Conservative government then in power took the decision to denationalize the railways. Private companies were to be allowed to bid to run parts of the British Rail system, while the maintenance and operation of all track, signalling and stations were to be hived off to a separate company called Railtrack. The government's belief was that a privatized railway system would become more efficient, ending the drain on government funds through subsidies, and competing more effectively with other forms of transport through new private investment that would attract travellers back to the railways. Privatization was initiated in 1993 and, by early 1997, 25 train-operating units in the UK had replaced the former monolithic rail system and a further three companies were formed to control rolling-stock.

While passenger traffic did increase on most services, partly as a result of better marketing, passengers became confused about the range of choice and fares facing them and journeys involving the services of more than one rail company became more complex. Competition between the rail companies led to passengers not being fully informed about the range of services available or the cheapest fares for their itineraries. Concern rose over the lack of promised investment by the rail companies and the impact of cost-cutting by some companies in order to boost profits, which, in some instances, led to safety violations and even accidents. Some disastrous mishaps arising from broken rails forced Railtrack into expensive investment in updating track and signals, severely disrupting mainline services. Distribution systems for rail tickets also suffered. Travel agents were already abandoning the sale of rail tickets as unprofitable before the advent of privatization and this was hastened by the additional complexities of dealing with a score of different rail companies.

The rail companies have been less innovative in seeking improvements in their distribution systems, although a computerized reservations and ticketing system, ELGAR, was developed – initially to handle bookings for the Channel Tunnel's Eurostar service and later extended to all members of the Association of Train Operating Companies (ATOC).

Eurostar's marketing and distribution was strongly criticized. Onward bookings beyond Paris and Brussels could no longer be made to any European destination, but were instead limited to major railway stations. Systems to sell tickets to the public via the Internet replaced the role of many travel agents, with companies such as thetrainline.com (owned by Virgin Rail and the National Express bus group) acting as electronic intermediaries for the sale of rail tickets. In 2008, agents' rail commission was cut from 9 to 5% and, at the same time, Eurostar abandoned the ELGAR distribution system, further disincentivizing the retailing of rail tickets.

Continued criticism of rail services in the UK led eventually to changes in the structure of the organization. Network Rail replaced Railtrack as owners of track, signals and stations, with 27 rail companies gaining franchises to control the rolling-stock, usually under contracts of five to eight years, although some were extended up to 20 years (curiously, these sometimes fell into public ownership once again – for example, Deutsche Bahn, owned by the German state, bought the franchise for Chiltern Railway in 2007 and East Coast was established as a subsidiary of the Department of Transport, when the route was re-nationalized after failure of the National Express East Coast company to profitably operate this route).

EXAMPLE Will the UK ever get domestic high-speed rail services?

Investment overruns in upgrading UK rail services have resulted in cutbacks to the more ambitious schemes to improve electrification and operate high-speed trains. The planned upgrade of the West Coast main line escalated from an initial £2 billion to £12 billion, while the idea proposed in 2002 of a dedicated TGV (Train à Grande Vitesse)-style track between London and Glasgow, which would cut the journey time from six hours to three, was shelved. A new proposal in 2005, however, for an ultra-high-speed railway between London and Edinburgh to replace the plans for upgrading the East Coast main line, offered hope that the UK could have a service to match those on the Continent. Initially estimated to cost £33 billion, this would require depreciation over at least a 50-year period (as for TGV lines on the Continent), rather than the 30 years current in the UK. If it were to have gone ahead, it would have cut the journey time from four and a half to two and a half hours and be competitive with the no frills airlines. Currently it is quicker to travel from London to Brussels than to travel to Liverpool, and it takes an hour less to travel from London to Rotterdam than it does to reach Glasgow from London by train (Elan Jones, 2011).

In 2008, the Department for Transport decided to abandon any plans for high-speed domestic services, citing the increased pollution resulting from their operation as the reason. Also, in the view of the Rail Minister, Tom Harris, the UK's economic geography did not call for a high-speed network, the priority being to improve on congestion and reliability. This conflicts with government's stated intention to move people away from air travel to rail and ignores the much higher pollution levels of domestic air travel.

There has been extensive debate about the benefits of developing HS2 – the high-speed line to operate initially between London and Birmingham (due to open in 2026), with extensions to Manchester and Leeds in latter phases (opening by 2032). Government estimates suggest that its development will bring £44 billion in returns to the regional economies of the areas opened up by the new route, and is therefore pushing for this development to happen. Others, concerned about the economic, social and environmental impacts along the planned route, suggest this is not the case – for example, the Institute for Economic Affairs, an independent research organization, suggests that these figures are flawed and the benefits will in fact be far less (Milmo, 2011).

Consequently, as matters stand, the only truly modern high-speed rail line in the UK to be recognized by the Union of International Railways is the Channel Tunnel rail link – now rebranded as HighSpeed One – developed to provide Eurostar with high-speed services between London and the Channel Tunnel at Folkestone. This track is also used by Southeastern to provide high-speed services between St Pancras and major towns in Kent.

EXAMPLE The pressures of high-speed rail travel in Kent

The high-speed routes from Kent to London have been operating since 2009, and those passengers who take this route – and pay the premium ticket price – will find this a quiet and comfortable experience. Finding a seat is usually not difficult because these trains are rarely full, anecdotal evidence suggesting that off-peak trains are operating 90% empty (Gilligan, 2011). Yet existing trains operating on the older network now seem to be packed with travellers, as there are fewer peak-time trains and those that operate now take longer as the schedules make way for the faster trains.

There have also been accusations that passengers searching for tickets to the Kent region are being offered only the more expensive high-speed options. Although this may mean tourists get the benefit of quicker journey times, the price of these journeys can increase the cost of a family day out, deterring an important tourism market to popular destinations like Canterbury.

Although the potential exists for a greatly expanded market for rail travel within the EU, the full potential of this is only just beginning to be tapped in the UK with Eurostar's connections to the new high-speed train services onwards from Brussels and Paris. Marketing agreements between the European train operators and the interest in high-speed trains is changing attitudes to rail travel. An agreement between Eurostar and the Thalys international rail network helped boost rail travel between London and Amsterdam, and this was followed by the establishment of a marketing alliance of the high-speed railways in the UK, France, Belgium, The Netherlands, Germany, Switzerland and Austria, under the brand name Railteam (see the Example on p. 470). Train timetables throughout the region are now synchronized, a single timetable produced and common regulations (such as for children's fares) introduced. Most importantly, a single website provides access to all these integrated services.

The Channel Tunnel and the railways

In Chapter 14, we examined the impact of the Channel Tunnel on ferry operations from the UK. Here, we must examine its impact on, and relationship to, land transport services elsewhere in the UK and in mainland Europe.

The Channel Tunnel is one of the great engineering feats of the twentieth century. With 37.8 km of its 50 km length under water, it takes pride of place as being the longest underwater rail tunnel in the world. While Japan's Seikan Tunnel between Tappisaki, Honshu Island, and Fukushima, Hokkaido Island, has the honour of being the longest rail tunnel at 53.8 km, the section underwater is shorter, at 23.3 km.

The first direct rail link between the UK and France was completed and opened to traffic in 1994, after frequent delays. It offers passengers the choice of two forms of transport: passenger travel on Eurostar from London to either Paris or Brussels, calling at Ebbsfleet (and, less frequently, Ashford in Kent) and Lille in northern France (with opportunities to transfer to high-speed trains for onward travel in Europe); and Groupe Eurotunnel's vehicle-carrying flatbed rail service, operating between Cheriton (near Folkestone) and les Coquelles (near Calais). Cars are driven on to double-decker carriages (taller cars, those with trailers and coaches are accommodated in single-deck carriages). These are then transported across the Channel and passengers can drive off to connect directly with the French motorway system in just a little over 30 minutes after leaving England.

Rail connections between London and the Continent have been firmly pitched at the business traveller. A fast line, known as High Speed 1, from the newly renovated St Pancras Station in London (see Figure 15.1) through Kent, which was fully opened in late 2007, allows Eurostar to operate at speeds up to 186 mph, cutting the overall journey time between London and Paris to two hours and 15 minutes (a little under two hours to Brussels). This compares with closer to four hours by air, when allowance is made for check-in times and the inevitable delayed departure, making journeys by rail a viable alternative for the business traveller as well as leisure tourists. Using the High Speed 1 line shortened journey times by 20 minutes and led to a 25% increase in income and a 21% increase in traffic in the first quarter of its opening.

Eurostar carried 9.5 million passengers between London and Paris or Brussels in 2010, having carried its 100 millionth customer the previous year. Rail is now the main option for travel between London and both Paris and Brussels, with a market share in excess of 75% (Eurostar, 2009). A two-hour trip from London St Pancras to Lille also enables the leisure tourist to connect with the French TGV high-speed trains for onward travel to southern France or adjoining European countries, making Lille to Bordeaux a five-hour trip, while Calais to Marseille is of similar duration. This brings Marseille just over seven hours from London, making the journey competitive with air travel (typically five hours when considering connections to and from local airports). Lille itself, heavily promoted as a destination in its own right, has become an important city-break market for British tourists

Figure 15.1 Eurostar trains at the newly renovated St Pancras station
Photo by Claire Humphreys

to France. Such important routes as London to Amsterdam or Frankfurt take almost the same time by train, city centre to city centre, as by plane (see p. 471 for comparisons).

At the insistence of the Conservative government, the Channel Tunnel was privately financed, with no public contribution. Its construction involved leading-edge technology, and the project ran into delays and huge cost overruns, leaving the parent company, Eurotunnel, with debts amounting to some £9 billion. Overambitious estimates of traffic and revenue were not realized, but this is not to say that the Tunnel has been a failure. Within two years of operation, it had made sufficient inroads into the share of the short sea market to badly worry the ferry companies, which were obliged to slash their prices to compete. A fire in the Tunnel in 1996 was a serious setback, but, despite this, Eurostar was carrying 66% of all passenger traffic between London and Paris by 2003, while Eurotunnel itself has made similar inroads into the cross-Channel car market between Dover and Calais. An ash cloud, due to the eruption of the Eyjafjallajoekull volcano in April 2010, caused the closure of European airspace, grounding flights for several days. This benefited Eurostar greatly as customers switched travel plans to the rail network. A similar, although much shorter, event in May 2011 further increased passenger numbers. It hasn't all been good news for Eurostar, though. Bad weather significantly disrupted services in 2009, while a fatal rail accident in Belgium in 2010 led to line closures on the London to Brussels route.

When it was established, control of the Eurostar rail services was the responsibility of each national railway (SNCF in France, SNCB in Belgium and Eurostar UK in the UK). Since September 2010, a separate business entity, Eurostar International, has been responsible for operations. This entity is owned by three shareholders: SNCF (55%), SNCB (5%) and LCR (40%) – although, since 2009, LCR has been under the control of the UK government, so their shares may well be sold in the near future.

The minimum usage charge paid by Eurostar to Eurotunnel, agreed in the initial contract with the company, ended in 2006; but, despite this loss, the newly restructured

Groupe Eurotunnel has succeeded in taking control of its finances, paying off some of its huge burden of debts and increasing load factors to a point where it became operationally profitable in 2007. The ferry operators must be drawing a communal sigh of relief as the prospect of a takeover of a bankrupt Eurotunnel would be their worst nightmare. That is because a mode of cross-Channel transport that would have the bulk of its capital costs erased and with far lower operating costs than those of any shipping company would make competition extremely difficult for the surface operators. If Eurotunnel continues its success in drawing the cross-Channel market away from both the airlines and ferry companies, long-term demand will rise substantially, to a point where capacity in the present tunnel could even be reached by 2025 and original projections start to become realistic forecasts again.

Rail travel on the Continent

Railway investment on the Continent is in marked contrast to investment in the UK's railways, whether under public or private administration. Continental rail companies and their governments recognized that investment in high-speed rail would encourage regional investment, giving rise to increased property prices and at the same time boosting tourism. In 1990, the EU approved the formation of a Trans-European Network for Transport (TEN-T) of high-speed road and rail links, the bulk of which were to be in place by 2005 (the full network to be completed by 2020). The initiative was supported by the European Commissioners in the expectation that rail would account for more than 23% of all passenger kilometres travelled in Western Europe by 2010, alleviating the pressure on air and road services. Total investment in rail services will approach 225 billion euros, 80% of which will be found from EU and national budgets, with the balance raised privately. By completion, nearly 94 000 km of rail track will be in place throughout the EU.

In France alone, SNCF, the publicly operated rail service, and RFF, which is responsible for building and maintaining tracks, invested more than £22 billion of public money to build its 300-kph TGV service. France now has over 1100 miles of high-speed track, while its latest TGV, in a test run in 2007, achieved a record speed of 357 mph (although such speeds are not sustainable with existing equipment). Payback on the investment is unlikely to be realized for up to 50 years (and local lines have been starved of funds while the new high-speed network was being established). There are savings to be achieved by improved connections and communications, however, and switching passengers and freight from road and air services to rail will help to meet the EU's target to reduce CO_2 emissions.

Germany found £54 billion to build its own network of 280-kph ICE (Intercity Express) trains (see Figure 15.2), with an even faster route between Cologne and Frankfurt, allowing the ICE3 330-kph train to halve the previous journey time. Italy introduced its Pendolino 250-kph tilt-body train on the Milan to Rome route, while Spain's AVE (Alta Velocidad Espagnola) offers a high-speed, two hours and 15 minutes service between Madrid and Seville.

In 2008, RENFE, the Spanish railways operator, also brought into service a high-speed line for the Madrid to Barcelona service. The VelaroE travels at speeds up to 350 kph, cutting the 410 mile journey to just $2^{1}/_{2}$ hours. High-speed routes from Madrid to Málaga opened in 2007 and in 2011 the Spanish network linked with the TGV services at Perpignan. There are further ambitious plans for a total of 10 000 km of high-speed track by 2020, with better signalling, which will allow speeds of up to 220 mph. The prospect of luxury trains running continuously between Northern Europe (including the UK) and the French Riviera or Spanish coastal resorts is a tantalizing one for the future of tourism.

Within Northern Europe, Thalys – a consortium of Belgian, French and Dutch rail interests – has enabled similar high-speed links to be developed between the member countries and Germany, with the popular Paris–Brussels route coming down to a mere one hour and 25 minutes. Sweden's hugely successful X2000 high-speed train has reduced the journey

Figure 15.2 The ICE train at Düsseldorf Station, Germany
Photo by Chris Holloway

between Stockholm and Gothenburg to less than three hours, increasing rail's share on this route from 30% to over 50% and leading to the extension of the service to other Swedish cities as well as to Oslo, in Norway. In the latter country, the Signatur tilting train, introduced between Oslo and Kristiansand in 1999, gained sufficient popularity to ensure other routes were opened up throughout Norway. High-speed services of NS HiSpeed, The Netherlands rail company, joined the network in 2007.

The advent of these high-speed networks is changing the face of European transport. Even allowing for the success of the budget airlines, rail services are finding that, if they can provide the reliability, comfort and speed at the right price, they can attract markets from other modes of transport. There is no uniform agreement that these new high-speed rail services can force airlines to withdraw from the routes, however.

EXAMPLE **A rail alliance**

In 2007, European high-speed rail operators launched an alliance to enhance their rail product. Railteam is a cooperation between Deutsche Bahn (Germany), SNCF (France), Eurostar (UK, France and Belgium), NS Hispeed (The Netherlands), ÖBB (Austria), SBB (Switzerland), SNCB (Belgium) and their subsidiaries Thalys and Lyria.

Established to coordinate rail links that will stretch from London to Hamburg in the north, Vienna in the east and Marseille in the south, the alliance aims to ensure a smooth journey when using connecting rail networks, the booking and ticketing covering the entire journey (if one part of the service is delayed, then tickets will still remain valid on connecting journeys). They have also introduced a 'frequent traveller' scheme, providing reward tickets and access to business lounges.

As high-speed networks expand across Europe over the next decade, so the possibility of travelling to ever greater numbers of destinations will see the demand for rail increase. Railteam forecasts that, by 2020, high-speed rail journeys on their network will have increased by 50%, with 68 million international trips being made annually (Railteam, 2009).

It is likely that other factors are at work to determine modes of transport, including status, place of residence and attitudes within the business world – even habit. It is certainly the case, however, that demand from tourists, both business and leisure, for the new high-speed services from London to destinations on the Continent has increased, paralleling a rise in demand for new budget air routes. Minimum travel times by rail from London to key destinations on the Continent (sometimes entailing connections at Lille) are now given as:

- London to Brussels   one hour 51 minutes
- London to Paris   two hours 15 minutes
- London to Amsterdam   three hours 30 minutes
- London to Cologne   three hours 30 minutes
- London to Frankfurt   four hours 40 minutes
- London to Geneva   five hours 15 minutes
- London to Marseilles   six hours 45 minutes.

Even popular Mediterranean resorts such as Cannes are now a comfortable day's journey away, at just over eight hours. These timings ensure that, in many cases, both business and leisure travellers can be tempted back on to rail services – as can travellers from Paris, who can now reach Stuttgart in three hours 39 minutes, while the popular short-break city of Munich lies a little over six hours away.

Where formerly water acted as a barrier to fast surface transport, new bridges have helped to increase demand for the European rail networks, especially in Scandinavia. In Denmark, bridges across the Great Belt and the Øresund between Denmark and Sweden have opened up continuous rail travel between London and either Stockholm or Copenhagen for the first time. The surface link that has brought Copenhagen and Malmö closer together has led to a partnership between the regions, encouraging international tourism to what was formerly a somewhat isolated and economically deprived region of southern Sweden.

Where bridge construction is impracticable, tunnels are opening up other fast track routes through Europe, notably through the Alps. In 2006, work started on the world's longest tunnel, which will link Innsbruck in Austria with Fortezza in Italy, following the EU's plan to provide a continuous link between Munich and Palermo. The Brenner Base Tunnel will be 63 km long (the length of the existing Gothard Base is just 57 km) and is planned to cut the 2 million vehicles currently travelling every year from Germany and the North to the Mediterranean resorts – this flow of traffic is said to account for substantial levels of pollution as it makes its way through the mountains. The new twin tunnels through the Alps, due for completion in 2025, will be capable of carrying up to 400 trains a day.

Another major engineering project is the planned TAV rail link between Lisbon and Kiev, which will connect via Madrid, Barcelona, Lyon, Turin, Trieste and Budapest, but involves the construction of yet another 53 km tunnel through the Alps, to carry up to 300 goods and passenger trains daily. Consequently, the programme has been delayed while environmentalists fight the noise, disruption and environmental damage that could potentially result from the line's construction.

Improved equipment and service, rapid connections between major cities and the avoidance of delays in congested airports are making European rail services appear increasingly attractive to the tourist market, and there is little doubt that rail services will figure prominently in the future of European tourism. Moreover, under EU liberalization rules, present train companies within the member countries now face open competition, with non-EU companies being permitted to run international train services anywhere within the Community. By 2020, the amount of high-speed rail track is expected to further increase three-fold, to some 15 000 km.

Competition for Eurostar

In October 2010, the first ever non-French train on the route made a test run from mainland Europe though the Channel Tunnel to the UK. Train operator Deutsche Bahn ran this test-train as part of its plans to compete with Eurostar on the London to Brussels route in 2013, extending the route to Frankfurt by 2014.

The Tunnel currently operates at about 50% capacity, so allowing the German train operator to use this route could help to boost Eurotunnel's revenue with a predicted 36% increase in passenger traffic (Wall Street Journal, 2010).

While the introduction of competition will affect Eurostar's activities, the removal of sole rights to the operation of passenger services has led to a reduction in the fees (by 23%) that Eurostar has to pay to Eurotunnel (Sylt and Reid, 2010). This has helped to balance the losses of previous years.

Rapid transit services in the Far East

In Japan, the Shinkansen (popularly known as the bullet train) has changed the face of high-speed transport, and its reliability and high levels of service have proved immensely popular with tourists. The journey between Tokyo and Osaka, for example, usually takes three hours city centre to city centre by train, compared with an hour's flying time between airports, so 80% of all passengers now use the train for this journey.

Japan takes immense pride in its bullet trains – any delays are counted in seconds rather than minutes and the technical specifications of the trains are constantly improved. The most recently developed model is the Nozomi Series 800, introduced in 2004 and designed to travel at 260 kph – slightly slower than the earlier 500 series, which holds the record for normal operations at 300 kph.

Changes to rail travel in Japan

The opening in December 2010 of the Tohoku Shinkansen line between Tokyo and Aomori means that the bullet trains now run the entire length of Honshu and Kyushu, Japan's main islands. Travelling at speeds of up to 300 kph, a journey the full length of the Tohoku Shinkansen takes just over three hours. Additional Shinkansen lines are due to open between Nagano and Kanazawa (in 2015) in the south and between Aomori and Hakodate (in 2016) in the north. These current and future developments will further increase the rivalry between air and rail travel in the country.

Amongst the extensive damage caused by the tsunami which struck Japan in March 2011 was the loss of a bullet train, swept away by the rising waters. Extensive damage to bridges, overhead wires and rails was also experienced, closing parts of the high-speed routes while repairs were made. It took 6 weeks for the entire network to be reopened.

Conventional railway lines serving local areas hit by the tsunami have yet to see such efforts for repair. The cost of rebuilding the infrastructure is shared between the local train operator and the government, and for many of the train companies it is proving difficult to find the necessary funds. One other factor delaying the reconstruction lies with town planning. As devastated towns review their urban layout, so the location of the rail infrastructure may need to be moved to ensure that rail services remain convenient to business and residential neighbourhoods.

Despite Japan's record, the award for fastest train service in the world now goes to the high-speed rail service built by the Chinese to link its two Olympic host cities, Beijing and Tianjin, in 2008. This service covers the 70 miles in just half an hour, at speeds up to 350 kph (217 mph), giving a taste of what can be anticipated in terms of global high-speed rail services later this century. With 7500 km of track, China has the world's largest high-speed network, with planned investments expecting to double this in the near future. However, concern regarding the safety of these new services has been raised, following the serious derailment of a train in 2011, thought to have been the result of pressure to deliver new routes too quickly.

Classic rail journeys around the world

There remains a strong body of transport enthusiasts throughout the world for whom the 'romance of steam' remains a major attraction, and they are willing to travel anywhere in the world for the privilege of taking a journey on one of the few remaining steam trains. Some of these have been reconditioned, with lines re-laid or reopened to cater to tourist demand, although others are often mere shadows of their former selves, but continue to appeal either through their exotic routing or due to nothing more than their romantic titles. Consequently, we now have two distinct forms of 'nostalgic rail' journey – on classic trains or on classic routes. In rare cases, the two coincide.

Classic train journeys are generally provided in reconditioned or reconstructed period coaches and are sometimes still drawn by steam engines. The *Venice Simplon-Orient-Express* is a leader in such nostalgic journeys, drawing on the appeal of its name and the image of ultimate luxury. The company now trades on that name, operating not only on the Continent, but also in the UK, the Far East and Australia.

At the top end of the market, such luxurious journeys in reconditioned trains or carriages are very attractive to tourists, who will build their itinerary around their rail journey. An example is the *El Andalus Express*, a vintage train comprising 12 carriages built in the 1920s and 1930s, operating between major tourist centres in southern Spain, including Seville, Jerez and Granada, during spring and autumn. This itinerary and others like it are featured in upmarket programmes of specialist tour operators like Great Rail Journeys of the World and Travelsphere. Hungary has introduced the *Royal Hungarian Express*, employing carriages built originally for the use of high-level party members under the communist regime, as a feature to attract tourists to destinations outside Budapest. The *Danube Express* is a recent introduction, operating between Berlin, Cracow, Prague and Istanbul.

Further afield, countries in which steam engines still operate, such as India and China (although, sadly, these are being largely phased out), attract both independent travellers and package tourists. Regular steam services in India may be mostly a memory, but *The Palace on Wheels* keeps that memory alive for those still anxious to experience the classic trains of imperial India.

In the Far East, a few steam-hauled trains still operate in Cambodia's highlands, while luxury trains designed to cater for the growing flood of tourists to Vietnam include the *Victoria Express* between Hanoi and Sapa and the *Reunification Express* from Hanoi to Saigon. The single-line track, running for over 1700 km, means that the train journey is interspersed with waits at key passing points for the train service running in the opposite direction (see Figure 15.3). These all add to the journey experience.

In South Africa, the *Union Limited* is still steam-hauled, and the famous *Blue Train* continues to cater to the top end of the market, while Rovos Rail's *Pride of Africa*, a train with 1930s carriages, is chartered out to tour operators to provide an equally luxurious service between East and South Africa, via Victoria Falls. A popular and more modestly priced addition to the tourist trail, the *Outeniqua Choo-Tjoe* is a 1920s steam-hauled train (the last

Figure 15.3 Vietnamese hawkers serve food and other wares to train passengers as they stop at a passing point between Saigon and Hanoi

Photo by Claire Humphreys

scheduled steam service in South Africa) operating between George and Knysna, which travels through the scenic Wilderness National Park. Namibia, emulating the success of its neighbour, has introduced its own luxury train, the *Desert Express*, which operates out of the capital, Windhoek, to the coast and Etosha National Park.

Australia has extensively promoted its famous trains – the *Indian Pacific* (a three-day service across the country between Perth and Melbourne) and *The Ghan* (from Adelaide across the red centre to Darwin via Alice Springs), while the Orient-Express company runs another luxury tourist train, the *Great South Pacific Express*, between Cairns and Sydney. The tilt train between Brisbane and Rockhampton is also proving popular, with tourists visiting the resorts of the East Coast and the Great Barrier Reef.

Longer rail journeys across the continents of Europe and Asia, while far from luxurious, fulfil the ambitions of true rail aficionados, who can choose between the *Trans-Mongolian Express*, *Trans-Manchurian Express* and *Rossiya*, or *Trans-Siberian Express*, and these too have been incorporated into programmes by specialist operators.

A recent introduction is the trans-Asia railway route, from Istanbul to Dhaka, linking in with European tracks. A tunnel across the Bosporus is planned to replace the ferry, which will form one of the final rail links in this 7000-mile journey, and the line, it is hoped, will eventually be extended to Singapore.

Finally, worthy of a mention is the SNIM service from Morocco via Western Sahara to Mauritania. Essentially a service to carry iron ore to the coast, it is supposedly the world's longest train – some 250 freight cars, with a total length of up to 2.5 km. Tourist interest encouraged the authorities to attach two passenger carriages twice daily for the 700 km run, and rail enthusiasts are now eager to book this very basic service between Nouadhibou and Zouerate – the one opportunity to experience the Sahara Desert by rail.

EXAMPLE   **The highest railway in the world**

In 2006, the Chinese completed the highest railway in the world, between Beijing and Lhasa in Tibet. At its highest point, the Tangula Pass, the train reaches a height of 5070 (over 16 000 feet) and, at this height, the carriage compartments are pressurized, owing to the thin air. Oxygen cylinders are also carried on board to cater for emergencies, which are not uncommon.

The construction of the rail track was in itself a major engineering feat, as much of the route is across permafrost, requiring the track to be laid on causeways raised above the unstable ground. The diesel engines were specially designed so they could operate efficiently at this three-mile high altitude.

Curiously, to date no iconic name has been chosen for the train, but this has not stopped a surge of bookings from intrepid passengers from all over the world, and the journey has been rapidly incorporated into specialist operators' rail itineraries.

Rail services in North America

In North America, rail travel in the 1960s and 1970s declined in the face of lower air fares and poor marketing by the railway companies themselves, which chose to concentrate on freight revenue at the expense of their passenger services. The continuing losses suffered by most US rail companies, and the importance of the rail network in social communications, led the government to integrate rail services in the country into a centrally funded public corporation known as Amtrak. This organization has achieved some success in reversing the decline of passenger traffic and achieved some benefit after a rise in bookings by Americans nervous about flying following the 9/11 disaster, although additional security measures, commensurate with those offered on airline flights, have added to the journey times. The Obama administration has been vocal about investing in high-speed rail, with plans for $53 billion to be invested over six years (although senate and state support may restrict this – Florida, Wisconsin and Ohio all refused public funds, asserting that development costs for high-speed rail could not be justified). Funding has been awarded, however, for improvements to the North-East corridor (Washington–New York–Boston), San Francisco to Los Angeles and between Chicago and Detroit.

While many of the famous names of the past, such as the Santa Fé *Superchief* and the *20th Century Ltd*, have gone for ever, the mystique of rail travel is maintained, at least in name, by others that *have* survived, including the *Lake Shore Ltd* on the Boston–New York–Chicago route, the *South West Chief* from Chicago to Los Angeles, the *Capitol Limited* from Washington to Chicago, the *California Zephyr* between Chicago and San Francisco, the *Empire Builder* between Seattle/Portland and Chicago and the *Coast Starlight* between San Francisco and Los Angeles. The only fully transcontinental service, the *Sunset Limited* operating from Florida to California, was severely disrupted by the flooding in Louisiana in 2005 caused by Hurricane Katrina. Although the section of the route from Florida to New Orleans has yet to be resumed, demand for the New Orleans–Los Angeles route is still popular, with 91 600 passengers carried in 2009/10 (Amtrak, 2010).

North American railways pass through some of the finest scenery in the world, and both USA and Canada exploit this in their rail journeys. Rail journeys to the Rockies already form an important element in excursions for those booking cruises out of North American ports on the west coast. The *Rocky Mountaineer* provides an opportunity to package scenic local transport when visitors travel to this region, while *The Canadian*, operating between Toronto and Vancouver via Jasper, has been restored to its original 1950s style, with an observation dome on the rear carriage, giving tourists spectacular views of the passing scenery.

Tourists are also attracted to the restored or reconstructed nineteenth-century trains operating within the regions, notably in the Far West, such as the Silverton and Durango Railroad's steam train to Durango and the steam-hauled Grand Canyon Railway's trains. GrandLuxe Rail Journeys have introduced vintage Pullman carriages for their luxury scenic tours of the mainly western states.

By no means period or traditional, but nevertheless offering tourists memorable transport experiences, the *Talgo* tilting express travels from Seattle down the west coast, while on the eastern seaboard the *Acela* high-speed rail link between Boston, New York and Washington cuts the journey between Boston and New York from five hours to just over three (although even these services can be affected by the priority given to freight, which can lead to delays to passengers' schedules).

Mexico has entered the market for tourist passengers, the privately run *Maya Express* in Yucatán taking tourists between Cancún and other popular coastal resorts.

Rail nostalgia in the UK

In the UK, nostalgic rail enthusiasts are being given the opportunity to enjoy rail services that conjure up a period when travel by train was, in many cases, a luxury for the well-heeled. Among others on offer in recent times have been the:

- *Shakespeare Express*, between Birmingham and Stratford
- *British Pullman*, between London and Bath (operated by Orient-Express)
- *Cathedrals Express*, between London and Salisbury (and other cathedral cities)
- *Jacobite*, between Fort William and Mallaig (operated by West Coast Railways).

In Scotland, another successful venture has been the introduction of the *Royal Scotsman*. Although without the benefit of a genuine pedigree, the 1920s-style train, part-owned by Orient-Express, has been packaged with success in the American market, offering a very upmarket tour of the Scottish Highlands. These enterprises demonstrate that market niches exist for unusual rail programmes, which can undoubtedly be emulated in other tourist regions.

The continuing appeal of steam trains has led to a new steam train, built in 2008 by the A1 Steam Locomotive Trust, to operate classic rail excursion services on the national rail network in the UK.

The 'little railways' as tourist attractions

With the electrification of the railways in the UK, nostalgia for the steam trains of the pre-war period has led to the re-emergence of many small private railways. Using obsolete track and former British Rail rolling stock, enthusiasts have painstakingly restored a number of branch lines to provide one more type of attraction for domestic and overseas tourists.

In the UK alone, there are over 250 railway preservation societies and more than 50 private lines in operation, with many other projects either in hand or under consideration. Some of these depend largely on tourist patronage, while others principally serve the needs of the local community. Their profitability, however, is often dependent on a great deal of voluntary labour, especially in the restoration of track, stations and rolling stock to service-able condition. As these services are generally routed through some of the most scenic areas of the UK, they attract both railway enthusiasts and tourists of all kinds and undoubtedly enhance the attractiveness of a region for tourism generally. Notable examples include the Ffestiniog Railway and the Romney–Hythe service in Kent. A route now devoted exclusively to serving the needs of tourists is the Snowdonia Mountain Railway, which has been in continuous service since the nineteenth century, transporting tourists to the highest point in England and Wales.

The future of rail travel for tourists

The future holds the promise of trains travelling at much higher speeds than even the fastest in operation today. Magnetic levitation (Maglev) offers the prospect of rail journeys at speeds of up to 360 mph, but the cost of building these is prohibitive. This form of propulsion offers high speed coupled with exceptional quietness, the track consisting of a metal trough generating a magnetic field that repels magnets on the train, causing the vehicle to ride 10 cm above the track. There is therefore little wear and tear and, in consequence, the cost of maintenance is much reduced.

The Germans and the Japanese have led the research into developing Maglev propulsion, and the first working line, constructed by a German engineering firm for the Chinese government, is the 270 mph route between Shanghai's Loyang Road Station and Pudong International Airport, covering the 19 miles in just eight minutes. The company estimated that 20% of its passengers in the initial years were coming aboard purely for the ride. It is intended that this line will be extended to Hangzhou, 105 miles to the south. Building costs will be high, but are estimated, per kilometre, to be less than half of those for building the Channel Tunnel. It has also approved construction of a high-speed traditional route between Beijing and Shanghai, which will reduce travel time for the 820-mile journey from 13 hours to five.

In Japan, the Central Japan Railway's Maglev MLX-01, when it was tested, achieved a top speed of 361 mph (581 kph) in 2003. The country has firm plans to build a *Linear Express* Maglev railway between Tokyo and Nagoya – a distance of 180 miles, which the new train would cover in just 40 minutes. The target for completion of this line is 2025. There are also further proposals to build between Tokyo and Osaka, a distance of 300 miles. While building costs would be 30% higher than for the Shinkansen, and electricity costs three times as much to run, maintenance costs would be extremely low and the speed would enable the line to compete even more effectively against air services. Whether this project gets beyond the planning stage will again depend on the availability of public finance – and the reconstruction costs for existing rail routes following the 2011 tsunami are likely to affect this greatly.

Although an earlier experimental route was built in England, linking Birmingham station with its airport in 1983, unreliability led to its closure in 1995 and, since then, the UK has been slower to research and develop Maglev or other advanced forms of surface propulsion. The UK government has, however, put forward proposals to consider the feasibility of establishing a public–private partnership with Ultraspeed (the private sector investing 70% of the cost), the aim being to build a 300 mph 'hovertrain', which would operate between London and Glasgow via Manchester. The cost was originally estimated at £30–33 billion, with an anticipated construction period of 12 years. Both the cost estimate and construction period are probably optimistic, given the cost and time overruns on other ventures of this kind, and, in view of current government hesitancy over far less ambitious schemes for the West Coast line, the reality is that this scheme is likely to take decades rather than years to come to fruition.

In the USA, more prosaic schemes are being researched. Rail authorities have tested the CyberTran – a cross between a high-speed train and a light railway system – designed to provide fast, non-stop services at speeds of up to 150 mph between US cities.

One system even more advanced than the Maglev, however, is being explored in New Mexico. The Hypersonic Upgrade Programme (HUP) is supposedly capable of speeds up to an incredible 6500 mph (and has, in fact, achieved a speed of just 20 mph short of this in tests conducted during 2004), but the development and application of such a project for commercial use clearly lies some way in the future.

Russia and America have held talks to discuss the construction of a 50-mile tunnel under the Bering Strait and a 4600-mile rail track to provide a surface transport link between the two countries. While designed primarily as a means of competing with shipping across the Pacific for the carriage of freight, it would also enable the rail enthusiast to travel by rail between London and New York in 14 days. However, the costs of all these developments are substantial (the US–Russian project alone is estimated at £27 billion) so they are unlikely to materialize until much later this century.

Several of these initiatives will provide strong competition for short-haul air services, particularly on major business routes. In view of the existing congestion of many air routes and growing concern about aviation's pollution of the atmosphere, the development of alternative high-speed land routes is vital if trade – and tourism – are to prosper.

Coach travel

The term **coach** is used to describe any form of publicly or privately operated road service for passengers, other than local scheduled bus services (although Americans still use the term 'bus' to apply to their long-distance vehicles). It thus embraces a wide range of tourist services that are sold to the public, both directly and through other sectors of the travel industry, and these may be categorized under the following headings:

- express coach routes, both domestic and international
- private hire services
- tour and excursion operations
- transfer services.

Long-distance coach services provide a cheap alternative to rail and air travel, and the extension of these services, both within the UK and from the UK to points in Europe and beyond, has drawn an increasing number of tourists at the cheaper end of the market, particularly those in the younger age groups. Younger passengers have also been attracted to adventurous transcontinental coach packages that provide, for a low all-in price, both transport and minimal food and lodging en route (often under canvas). These long-distance services were curtailed to some extent owing to political problems in the Middle East and beyond, but some have since been reintroduced, skirting major trouble spots, while others have been diverted to the African continent. Another form of cheap coach tourism is the Rotel sleeper coach (Figure 15.4), an innovation scarcely known in the UK, although, on the Continent, particularly in the German market, this is a popular form of budget long-distance coach holiday. In this form of transport, the coach either has built-in sleeping berths or pulls a sleeper trailer that, at night, can accommodate all the passengers in sleeping bunks.

Apart from these exceptions, for the most part coach travel obstinately remains the mode of transport of the older traveller, despite efforts by coach companies to widen their market. In the UK, most coach holidays are taken by those aged between 55 and 64, with around two out of every three booked by the over 45s. This is perhaps unsurprising, given the advantages that coach services offer to the older market – not just low prices (reflecting low operating costs vis-à-vis other forms of transport) but also the convenience of door-to-door travel when touring, overcoming baggage and transfer problems, and courier assistance, especially overseas where the elderly prefer to avoid problems of language and handling documentation. Additionally, coach operators frequently make arrangements to pick up and drop off passengers at points convenient to their homes. One result of this is that coach companies traditionally benefit from high levels of repeat business, often supported by loyalty rewards such as discounts, or special treatment like preferential hotel rooms.

Figure 15.4 A Rotel sleeper coach in India
Photo by Chris Holloway

Coach companies are now taking the view that their marketing efforts are best spent on raising the frequency of sales to the older market, rather than trying to attract a new younger market, given that the former market is expanding rapidly, as more people retire early. The most popular holiday destinations for British clients are Germany's Rhineland and Bavarian regions, the Austrian Tyrol and the Swiss Alps. While the long-distance coach market on the Continent is holding up reasonably well, the trend is towards short-break holidays by coach, in keeping with the growth of short-break holidays in general.

The operation of coach tours is a highly seasonal business, however, and companies are often forced to lay off drivers and staff out of season, unless they can obtain sufficient *ad hoc* charters or contract work (such as school bussing, useful for the coach companies as these commitments do not coincide with their busy holiday periods). Other out-of-season opportunities have been successfully marketed, however – notably Christmas market trips for British tourists to the Continent, pre-Christmas shopping trips to major cities and across the Channel, pantomime visits in the early part of the New Year and, of course, bank holiday trips.

Most coach companies specialize in certain spheres of activity. While some operate and market their tours nationally, others may concentrate on serving the needs of incoming tourists and tour operators by providing excursion programmes, transfers between airports and hotels or complete coach tours for overseas visitors. These coach companies must build up good relations and work closely with tour operators and other intermediaries abroad or in the home country.

Coach regulations in the UK

Coach operators are now governed by EU directives, which are designed to ensure adequate safety provisions for passengers. The concern with safety has been highlighted by recent incidents in the coaching industry, most notably some serious accidents on the

Continent involving holiday coaches. The maximum number of hours' driving permitted for each driver per day are stipulated for all express journeys by coach, with stages over 50 km. The controversial tachograph provides recorded evidence of the hours of operation and vehicle speeds of individual drivers. However, accidents, often involving fatalities, are a feature of coach travel in some developing countries where regulations are less strict, or inadequately enforced.

While there can be little doubt that implementation of regulations has led to higher safety standards in the industry, the effect has also been to increase the cost of long-haul coaching operations, making it more difficult for them to compete with rail or air services. To permit through journeys without expensive stopovers, two drivers must be carried or, more commonly, as rest periods must be taken off the coach, drivers are exchanged at various stages of the journey. With the constraint of a limited number of seats on each coach, this has the effect of pushing up costs per seat.

In the UK, under the terms of the Transport Act 1980, coach operators must apply to the Transport Commissioners for a licence, which will normally remain in force for five years and limit the operator to a specific number of vehicles. Applicants must have a good financial record and demonstrate adequate resources, including professional competence based on management experience and appropriate educational qualifications, for example, membership of the Chartered Institute of Logistics and Transport (CILT). Members of the Confederation of Passenger Transport (CPT) UK, which represents bus, coach and light rail companies, must also be bonded for 10% of their touring turnover as insurance against financial collapse.

EXAMPLE ⬤ **The dominance of National Express in the UK**

The 1980 Transport Act in the UK ended many of the restrictions on express coach services on routes of more than 30 miles. This led to a spate of new coach services of all types being introduced in 1981. A period of intense competition followed, in which the National Bus Company (NBC) (originally state-run) emerged as the chief beneficiary, using the National Express brand name. Its dominant size offered it an advantage over its rivals as it was able to offer greater frequency of services and flexibility. With its huge fleet of coaches and a national network of routes, it was able to replace a defective vehicle at short notice with little inconvenience to its passengers – an advantage denied to its smaller rivals. Some new companies attempted to find niches by operating newer or unusual vehicles (such as luxurious foreign-built coaches). While this enabled them to compete in the short term, over time, most found that, given the prices they were forced to charge to recover their investments, they simply could not generate adequate demand for the luxury coaches and so they were forced out.

The 1985 Transport Act set the scene for almost total deregulation of the UK bus industry the following year. This required the break-up and privatization of the National Bus Company, providing small bus and coach operators with greater scope to compete, and many new companies emerged. The newly privatized National Express, however, soon re-established its lead in the long-distance market as the National Express Group, establishing a partnership with Continental operators to create Eurolines (which it purchased in 1993), operating long-distance services between the UK and major cities in mainland Europe. The company also invested in the UK railways (including a share in Eurostar) and in North American and Spanish coach operations.

Competing with National Express is Stagecoach, a small private company that, through aggressive acquisitions, became one of the UK's leading bus and coach companies, with interests in trams and ferries as well as the largest rail franchise in the UK, South West

Trains. In 2003, the company also launched a popular low-budget coach service, Megabus, in the UK, later expanded to the USA. A third company, First Bus (later renamed FirstGroup), acquired prominent local bus companies and also successfully bid for train franchises, including the operator First Great Western, to become the third member of the triumvirate. All three have interests in overseas transport services.

Two other medium-size operators, Go-Ahead and Arriva, have joined the triumvirate and combined they now effectively control the scheduled bus and coach industry in the UK; all have made substantial investments in the UK rail services as well. This process of concentration in transport, both at home and abroad, is the direct outcome of the move to privatization – a move that has been watched with interest by companies and governments abroad, several of which have their own plans to move transport to the private sector. In common with the US airline industry a decade earlier, deregulation of the bus and coach industry appears to have had the opposite effect from that intended, with the growth of a handful of powerful oligopolistic scheduled carriers. Other coaching companies have found it easier to specialize in the inclusive tour markets, rather than compete openly with the leading carriers.

Coach tour-operating companies

Despite its rather archaic image, the coach tour remains popular with British travellers. Operators best known for organizing package tours by coach have also tended to amalgamate since deregulation. Initially, two market leaders emerged from the string of takeovers – Wallace Arnold and Shearings – and these, in turn, merged in 2005, to form WA Shearings (and since 2007 the company has been known only as Shearings Holidays), which is now by far the largest coach tour operator in the UK, with well over a million passengers (principally the over-55s) each year. The company packages tours throughout Europe and in North America, Australia and New Zealand, acts as a travel agency for air and cruise holidays and has a string of shops. In addition to its fleet of coaches, it also owns 50 hotels, operating under the Bay and Coast brand. This is typical of the movement towards horizontal integration among the coach companies, and vertical integration between the coach companies and the hotels they use. Smaller companies are finding it ever more difficult to compete and will have to find niche markets if they are to survive.

EXAMPLE   **Guide Friday**

A good example of a niche operator, Guide Friday set out to become the leading sightseeing bus operator in cities throughout the UK. Starting up in Stratford-upon-Avon, it expanded to operate in 29 different locations. Older open-top buses were purchased to keep costs down and reduce depreciation. As a result, the company was able to ensure profitablity even when operating for just the three busy months of the year.

Its success attracted attention from larger competitors, and Guide Friday was taken over in 2002 by City Sightseeing, the world's largest open-top bus operator. The expansion of City Sightseeing has been achieved in part by such buy-outs, but to an even greater extent by offering franchises. The company now offers 32 tours in the UK, 42 tours in Europe and also operates in 15 other cities across the world.

Some specialists have chosen to move upmarket rather than attempt to compete directly with the market leaders. Coach charters are a popular means of achieving this. By purchasing luxury vehicles and fitting these out with videos, bar and catering facilities, more luxurious seating and accompanying hostesses, the coach companies can target niche markets for business routes, charters or long-distance luxury travel to compete with trains.

Some operators have opted to provide coaches with sleeping accommodation. Unlike the Rotel coaches, these are used for charters, principally by the music and entertainment industry, for artists and crews touring to play gigs. Typically, they have sleeping facilities for between eight and 16 passengers in comfortable, curtained-off bunk beds, with seating areas at the rear; some also include full catering facilities, along with an accompanying hostess.

At the other end of the market, many small independent operators are engaged in small-scale enterprises that include transfers between airports and hotels, local excursions and city tours.

International long-distance scheduled operations form another sector of the budget coach market. The growth of shuttle services between the UK and the Continent, led by the Eurolines service, has been a prominent feature of budget travel for tourists within Europe (and the movement of labour between the EU member countries has fuelled demand for these services in recent years). These international stage journeys travel as far afield as Poland, Hungary, Greece, Finland and Turkey, their success varying according to the relative strength of sterling against other European currencies and the differential between air and coach fares.

EXAMPLE **Transcontinental coach travel**

The extreme scheduled coach route must be the OzBus, launched in 2007. It involves a 13-week journey between London and Sydney, with only the section between Bali and Darwin requiring a transfer to air services (the bus is shipped by sea). Its relatively high cost (over £4500) has not appeared to discourage bookings (the price does include primitive accommodation and most food). The company has expanded to offer coach routes between London and New York (via eastern Europe, Russia and China) and around southern Africa. This marks the first return to the hippy trail ventures popular in the mid-twentieth century and is proving popular with the backpacker market and returning Australians.

Coach operations in North America have become equally concentrated. For many years, two powerful coach companies – Greyhound Lines and Trailways – dominated the domestic coach market, and their low fares enabled them to compete successfully against both the huge network of domestic air services and the private car. In 1982, however, road passenger transport was also deregulated in the USA, leading to a flood of small, low-priced coach companies, against which, in marked contrast to events in the UK, neither of the two giants seemed able to compete.

Trailways cut services in an effort to remain profitable, but, ultimately, merged, under new management, with Greyhound in 1987. Despite this move, the amalgamated company went into bankruptcy three years later. After further restructuring and the introduction of new vehicles, including minibuses, Greyhound emerged from bankruptcy to face new challengers from other small companies – notably US Bus, launched in 1998 with smaller, more comfortable vehicles.

Greyhound's problem was its dependence on low-budget travellers and the fact that many of its city termini were in run-down and depressed areas of the city. Although now out of bankruptcy and under the ownership of the UK's FirstGroup, the company has been forced to cut many of its services, having to compete not only with budget bus companies but also no frills budget airlines (notably SouthWest) and the Amtrak rail services, which are locally subsidized and have become more attractively priced. It has recently started to fight back with its own budget offshoot, BoltBus, offering cheap but relatively luxurious interiors.

The proliferation of small, low-priced bus companies over the past decade is a phenomenon of US travel. Stagecoach's Megabus, with its minimum $1 rides, has made an impact since its introduction to the USA, while other companies such as Chinatown Bus and Today's Bus have arrived on the scene to take on the national carrier on key routes. Also, online ticketing agency Gotobus has enabled passengers to book their tickets on the Web, so they can choose on the basis of price from a range of bus companies. All these companies operate in the heavily travelled north-eastern corridor of the USA.

Finally, mention should be made at this point of the Gray Line organization – an American franchise offering coach excursions and tours not only within the USA and Canada but also in many other countries. Franchising globally on this scale is relatively uncommon within tourism, but offers a pointer to the possible direction the industry will take in the future, as large companies go multinational.

It must not be forgotten that, in many countries, vehicles in common use for local residents are attractions for visiting tourists, too. Just as some ferries across the world are must-see attractions, so famous local services will attract tourists just to sample the experience. Examples include London's double-decker buses and vintage buses in countries such as Malta and the Philippines, but this phenomenon is by no means limited to buses and coaches. The San Francisco cable cars, the tram and gondola rides to mountain tops in Hong Kong and Cape Town, black cabs in London, yellow cabs in New York, tuc tucs in Bangkok, tricycles and rickshaws in the Far East (and now spreading to Europe as we can see in Figure 15.5) – these are all essential elements of the tourist experience of the destination and contribute to tourism revenue as well as forming the ideal way in which to see the sights of the city.

For every country with a well-developed tourism market, however, there are many others that make little effort to bring their local bus and coach services to the attention of visitors. Buying bus and tram tickets can be a daunting experience for those visiting a

Figure 15.5 Cycle rickshaws waiting for passengers on the Champs Elysées, Paris
Photo by Claire Humphreys

foreign city for the first time, where tickets often have to be purchased in advance from kiosks, then punched in a machine on board the vehicle, yet all too often instructions are only available in the local language. Visitor passes and pre-purchase tickets, often available online, all help to make this process simpler. One example is Eurostar's sale of Paris Metro tickets at the St Pancras terminal in London, reducing the need to queue for tickets on arrival in France and thus speeding the onward journey of passengers.

Promoting public transport encourages tourists to stay longer as they can be told how to visit attractions away from the town centre; transport costs are often very cheap, so they need never fear being overcharged. In Finland, Helsinki has successfully marketed the internationally renowned Arabia ceramic factory, museum and showroom located out of town at the end of a tram route. By contrast, visitors to Tallinn in Estonia are offered no guidance in other languages on how to use public transport, despite the rapid growth in their numbers. Similarly, visitors to Beijing in China receive little guidance on the use of local buses, even though they are cheap and frequent.

EXAMPLE New ticketing system ignores tourists

In 2010, Sydney introduced a new ticketing system for local bus, rail and ferry transport; yet the system offers little for the tourist seeking to explore the central attractions of this popular destination. Tourists currently have to buy a separate ticket for each leg of their journey, or pay for a MyZone day pass which covers the entire city and suburbs area – at AUS$20 for adults this can prove to be an expensive, albeit perhaps more convenient, option. However, perhaps not so convenient for any tourists who want to travel on the monorail to the popular Darling Harbour attraction – this mode of transport is not included in the MyZone pass.

Before leaving the coach sector, we must look at a few examples where other road vehicles are pressed into service to transport tourists. Between the coach and the private hire car, a variety of sometimes unusual, if not bizarre, vehicles serve tourist needs; for instance, specially constructed four-wheel vehicles are used by tourists in rough terrain or wilderness areas (Figure 15.6).

In some countries, the postbus fulfils the need for public transport where traffic is too limited to sustain a scheduled bus route. These are postal delivery vehicles that are also equipped to carry a limited number of passengers. They have long been popular in mountainous areas such as Austria (where they are operated by the Austrian Railways) and Switzerland but are also used extensively by adventure tourists and backpackers travelling independently.

The UK introduced these passenger-carrying vehicles for the first time in 1967, serving the community around Llanidloes in Wales, and, over time, some 200 postbus routes were established, principally in the less-populated communities in Scotland. Sadly, they are being phased out to a large extent, with only some 12 routes still functioning at the time of writing – although Royal Mail claims to carry 50 000 on these routes annually. Such a service is vital in regions such as the Western Isles, and vehicles in use range from four-passenger Land Rovers to 14-seat minibuses.

In Australia, similar services are provided by the mail planes. Tourists travelling on foot are finding these useful means of getting about where other forms of public transport are limited or non-existent and, in turn, these services are learning to attract visitors as well as locals – see for example Westwing Aviation, which operates in the Northern Territories. Indeed, the mail services in Australia have gone as far as packaging tours around their mail runs in the remote Flinders Range, including accommodation and meals.

Figure 15.6 Safari vehicles at Etosha National Park, Namibia
Photo by Chris Holloway

Finally, mention must be made of the curious, not to say bizarre, use to which some vehicles are put to give rides to tourists. While they are too numerous to list extensively, one good example, from a nation for which bizarre tourism is the norm, will serve the purpose. In San Francisco, among other exotic transport modes such as duck boat trips in the harbour and antique car tours, visitors can take a 75-minute ride over the Golden Gate Bridge on an authentic antique fire engine, dressed in firefighter gear. More demure transport is on offer in Australia, where wine lovers are offered an opportunity to tour the wine-growing area of Margaret River, Western Australia, in chauffeur-driven classic Bentley cars.

The private car

Undoubtedly, the increase in private car ownership has done more to change travel habits than any other factor in tourism. It has provided families in particular with a new freedom of movement, increasing opportunities to take day excursions as well as longer trips. From the 1950s onwards, the costs of motoring have been falling in relative terms, and car owners also tend to take into account only the direct costs of a motoring trip, rather than the full cost, which would include depreciation and wear and tear. Thus, car transport has long been favoured over public transport.

The effect of this preference on the travel industry has been considerable. Over the years, the hotel and catering industries responded by building motels, roadside cafés and restaurants, while formerly remote hotels and restaurants suddenly benefited from their new accessibility to these tourists. Car ferry services all over Europe flourished, and countries linked by such services experienced a visitor boom. France remains, for the British, the leading holiday destination, being seen primarily as a destination for the independent and mobile tourist.

Camping holidays also boomed, and tour operators reacted by creating flexible self-drive car packages, including packaged camping holidays in tents or mobile homes.

The rented cottage industry took off, the gîte holidays in France soon being followed by cottage and villa rentals in many other countries.

Fly–drive and rail–drive packages were introduced. The railways, too, adapted to meet the needs of motoring tourists, introducing motorail services that allowed people to take their cars with them on longer journeys, such as to the south of France and Spain.

In the twenty-first century, the desire for greater flexibility has to be weighed against the burden of a rapid escalation in the cost of motoring, particularly in terms of fuel. If those costs continue to rise, this may well curtail demand for motoring holidays, with serious implications for the types of holiday chosen. Many British-owned second homes, for instance, are in fairly isolated regions on the Continent, so access would be difficult without personal transport.

A decline in car usage may be beneficial for some aspects of tourism. New roads catering for mass travel include bypasses that encourage touring drivers to sideline small towns and villages. One example of this was the construction of the second Severn crossing into Wales, which sidelined Chepstow and led to a marked decline in visits to the town. Constructing new roads causes additional environmental damage to the countryside, but the expansion of motoring and private car ownership in a small country such as the UK is leading to enormous problems of pollution and congestion, creating pressure to upgrade existing roads and build new bypasses. With car ownership in the UK standing at well over 30 million and rising, the country is rapidly approaching a standstill – literally the case on major motorways on bank holidays in the summer.

This is creating problems as small resorts and scenic attractions are often unable to expand sufficiently to meet the demand for access and parking facilities without damaging the very environment that the motorists have come to see.

The growing interest in our society in ecologically friendly tourism will inevitably discourage motorists from taking their cars to such destinations. Greater control can be expected in the future in the form of developments such as park and ride schemes, already provided at congested resorts such as Bath, Canterbury, Cambridge, Oxford and St Ives, as well as Polperro in Cornwall, where visitors are encouraged, and sometimes required, to park their cars at car parks on the outskirts and either walk or use public transport to travel in to the centre. Rationing by charging high prices for car parking (as has been introduced in both Oxford and Cambridge) or limiting access or denying facilities for car parking (as occurs at the more popular US national parks and is now finding favour in some of the UK's National Parks) will inevitably become a characteristic of future tourist destinations when demand rises to a point where there is insufficient physical space to accommodate

EXAMPLE   Is congestion charging the solution to overcrowded cities?

Faced with massive congestion and resulting pollution from traffic fumes, the then mayor of London decided to introduce congestion charges in an effort to resolve the problem. These charges were ring-fenced, with the income earned being dedicated to improvements in public transport. Other cities, both in the UK and abroad, have also mooted the idea of charging private vehicles to travel into city centres.

Stockholm introduced a scheme in 2007, charging for each journey into the city, with a maximum daily cap when upwards of four visits have been made in a single day. The level of charge varies according to time of day, and, since its introduction, traffic levels have dropped by 18%. Although the profits raised from the scheme were due to fund improvements in public transport, the scheme has yet to make a surplus.

A similar scheme has been proposed for Gothenburg, with charges levied on vehicles entering the city between 6 am and 6.30 pm. Weekends, public holidays and the month of July are free.

all who wish to arrive in their private cars. Many towns in the UK now adopt a variable pricing policy for parking, with comparatively low prices for parking up to two or three hours, to encourage shoppers and short-stay visitors, but rising sharply thereafter to discourage commuter parking. Prices then drop in the evening to encourage leisure visitors after the business traffic has left. On the other hand, pressure to raise revenues at local authority level is encouraging some communities (noticeably London) to impose meter parking charges even during evening hours and on Sundays.

While congestion charges are predominantly aimed at encouraging commuters back on to public transport, the impact on tourism also has to be taken into account. To what extent is private car usage vital to either domestic or inbound tourist markets? Are tourist car rentals largely restricted to rural areas, limiting their impact on the economy? Would tourists visiting London actually prefer a vastly improved public transport system to the current chaos, even if it inhibited their ability to drive in the city? Do inbound tourists actually consider changing their holiday destinations on the strength of the congestion problems they might face?

These are highly relevant questions for the industry, but they have been inadequately researched. The next development to discourage car use is likely to be road pricing, with drivers paying a set fee per mile of the roadways they drive on. Tentatively, officials in the UK have talked of figures of £1.30 per mile in the cities, with a nominal figure of perhaps 2 pence in rural areas. Again, little is known about the possible impact of such a move on tourism. Road pricing for motorway driving is common in Europe, with tolls on French motorways, for example, costing about €1 for every 10 miles. Tolls for bridges and tunnel crossings also add to the cost of road travel.

Caravan holidays

Caravanning has always been popular in the UK, since the manufacture of the first leisure caravan, the Bristol Carriage Company's 'Wanderer', in 1880. Today, there are some 3500 caravan parks in the UK and over 500 000 privately owned mobile caravans. The Caravan Club boasts 388 000 members and between 1 and 2 million people take caravan holidays every year. Caravan holidays have been falling relative to other forms of holidaymaking, however, largely as a result of the introduction of cheap air fares to the Continent.

In the USA, sales of trailers (the American term for caravans) have declined as motorhomes or campervans (motorized caravans) have found favour. These vehicles are widely known in the USA as recreational vehicles (RVs). Originating with the invention of the Curtiss Aerocar in the 1930s, they have steadily grown in popularity to a point where, today, more than 25 million Americans make use of them each year.

The industry responded by providing new and more luxurious camping facilities, with the franchise company Kampgrounds of America ensuring water and electricity were available at all its sites. RVs are widely available for rental, too, and are popular among European visitors touring the USA, especially in the far west. While not cheap to rent, they are luxurious by any standards, with amenities that compare well with many hotel rooms, including en suite showers. While some have been imported into the UK, their sheer size makes them unsuitable for use on most of the UK's roads. There are, however, specialist holiday companies that rent out motorhomes (see the website addresses at the end of this chapter) and they are becoming popular on the Continent where, in many countries, the roads are not too crowded and there are adequate facilities to park overnight.

The car rental business

It has been estimated that there are over 1000 car hire companies operating in the UK, with more than 130 000 cars available for hire (many being fleet cars on hire to private companies). The car rental business owes a substantial proportion of its revenue (and, in many resorts, virtually all its revenue) to tourists. While in total only 30–40% of car hire is associated with leisure, small companies and local car hire operators get a disproportionate share of this, while the large corporations have the lion's share of the business travel market.

Car rental companies can be divided into two categories:

- large international companies or franchise operators
- small, generally locally based, independent hire companies.

Most of the larger companies charge broadly similar prices, but offer a choice of cars, hiring locations and flexibility (for example, the ability to pick up a car at one location and drop it off at another). This flexibility and convenience makes them attractive to business travellers, who are less sensitive to price, but insist on speed of service, reliability and a more luxurious standard of car. Contracts with suppliers generally tie them to favouring a particular make of car, on which they are given advantageous prices. Several of the large international chains now offer a home delivery service.

Hertz is the largest car rental agency in the world, with over 8000 outlets, while Avis, which also owns Budget Rent-a-car, is the largest car hire company in Europe. Ownership of these two companies has changed frequently over the years and their operation now appears secondary to the perceived value of the asset. Hertz was sold in 2005 to a group of private equity firms, while AvisBudget group was purchased by travel conglomerate Cendant and separated into an independent entity. In 2011, AvisBudget Group purchased Avis Europe, a separate organization which has purchased the franchise rights to operate under the Avis and Budget brands in Europe, Middle East and Asia. This will bring the two organizations under one worldwide operation.

In the UK, Europcar dominates the market, earning almost one-quarter of the total sales revenue. They operate in an alliance with Enterprise Car Hire and this ensures they are the largest car rental company in Europe, drawing on a fleet of 1.2 million cars. However, they, along with Hertz and Avis Budget, have been reducing fleet size over the past few years in cost-cutting measures designed to respond to the decline in demand for car rental.

As to the second category, there are literally hundreds of small, local car rental companies that generally offer limited choice but low price and the convenience of a local pick-up, although perhaps from only one or two locations. Because of their reliance on the leisure market, these companies work in a highly seasonal business, where they may be unable to maximize their opportunities for business in summer because they have insufficient vehicles. In addition, there are some specialist car hire operators that provide very luxurious vehicles, high-powered sports cars or even classic vehicles, for a small upmarket leisure or business clientele.

The competitive nature of the industry has once again resulted in good marketing playing a key role in the success of individual car rental companies. The expansion of outlets has been greatly aided by the introduction of franchising in the 1960s – a means of distribution now used by all the large companies. Three other factors have been critical.

- *Contracts with airports and railways.* These allow car rental companies to maintain a desk at airport or rail terminals. The opportunities for business that are provided by having desk space in these locations make these contracts very lucrative and they are fought for by the major companies, occasionally changing as competitors offer higher bids at the termination of a contract agreement.
- *Links with airlines and hotels.* This establishes good relations with – and, hence, referrals from – hotel chains and larger airlines, generates huge volumes of business and is critical for maximizing sales opportunities for business travel bookings. Large hotel chains may also offer desk space for the car rental company in reception areas. The independent travel behaviour of many of their passengers has meant that budget airlines have

provided direct links from their website to their car hire partners – and receive a small commission on every rental.

- *Computer reservations systems (CRS).* The development of a good CRS (and, increasingly, global distribution systems, GDSs), together with accessibility via the websites of major airlines or intermediaries, plays an increasingly important role in the success of the larger car rental companies, which cannot afford not to be linked to such major systems. Equally, these information providers need car hire as an adjunct to their flight and accommodation sales via the Web. One company that has recognized this is online agency lastminute.com, which acquired the fast-growing leisure rental company Holiday Autos to complement its website operations.

Historically, car rental companies have also courted travel agents, which provide a good proportion of advance sales for business and leisure travel. Attractive rates of commission of 15% or more are still on offer to gain agency support. Car rental through the trade, however, is less common in the UK than in the USA. The growing 'seat only' airline reservations market helped to expand the demand for car hire overseas, as has the huge demand generated by second home owners travelling to their holiday homes across Europe.

Trading conditions for the car rental companies have been particularly difficult in the face of continuing high levels of competition in the trade and the terrorism threat since 9/11, which, coupled with adverse movements of European currencies against the dollar, have affected demand from Americans visiting Europe. While profits are thin for the leading franchises, others, including those associated with or owned by air carriers, have benefited from the introduction of low-cost air fares within Europe, which now make it cheaper for tourists to fly to their destination and hire a car there rather than drive all the way.

A recent development – and the direct outcome of website bookings – has been the introduction of companies organizing private transfers. With the growth of independent travel, more holidaymakers are putting together their own packages by searching the Web, and this includes arranging transfers to their hotel abroad. Specialist companies are arranging transfers by taxi, mini-coach, private limousine – even helicopter – for customers on their arrival at airports abroad. These services can also be incorporated into dynamic packaging programmes by agents.

Cycling and tourism

Over the past three decades, holidaymakers have shown a much greater interest in cycling holidays than in the past, partly on the grounds of their ecological sustainability. The Cyclists' Touring Club boasts some 70 000 members in the UK, and several specialist holiday firms have been established in recent years to cater for those seeking organized cycling holidays in the UK, on the Continent and even further afield. These include both leisure and sporting (off-road) pursuits, reflecting the growth in ownership of hi-tech equipment such as mountain bikes. Tour operators like Cycling for Softies, which specializes in cycling holidays in France, provide vehicles for the transfer of cyclists' baggage between accommodation stops, leaving their clients to travel light. This form of touring has proved very popular, falling into the 'Hilton hippies' category of demand, where roughing it by day is compensated by enjoying comfortable accommodation and gourmet food at night.

Rural destinations, particularly those in relatively flat but attractive landscapes, have recognized the growing popularity of cycling as an activity for visitors and encouraged cyclists by providing suitable trails and informative leaflets about the surrounding countryside. Small businesses, such as cycle hire companies, have sprung up to serve these visitors. An example is that of the village of Worpswede, north of Bremen in Germany, which is a popular venue for domestic cycling tourists. The village lies on the edge of the famed Teufelsmoor, a nature reserve, and the Worpswede Radtour offers five themed cycle rides through the region, ranging in length from 19 to 45 km. France, too, has long popularized holidays by bicycle.

The interest in off-road biking has led to tour programmes catering for mountain bike tours in distant countries. Morocco, South Africa, New Zealand, the USA, Kyrgyzstan and Kazakhstan are just a few of the countries now offering mountain bike adventure tours.

EXAMPLE **Cycle routes in Europe**

Eurovelo6 is one of a dozen long-distance cycle routes planned for Europe. This route takes cyclists from the west coast of France, following the Loire, Rhine and Danube rivers, to the Black Sea in Romania. The total distance of the route is over 2200 miles, and it passes through Vienna, Bratislava, Budapest and Belgrade.

In funding these routes, EU government research identified that 'the number of cycle overnight tourists is 25.6 million or about 3% of the total number of tourist trips generated by the EU population' (European Parliament, 2009).

The entire Eurovelo network covers more than 37 000 miles of cycle paths and existing road network (although, at the time of writing, none of the routes had been fully completed), although, to make the routes suitable for cyclists, roads must have very low levels of traffic usage and hills cannot have steep gradients. Other planned Eurovelo routes run from the Norwegian coast to Portugal, from Ireland, though the UK, Germany and Poland to Russia, and from London to Italy.

There are fears that the rise in the numbers of cars on rural roads, resulting from drivers seeking relief from the growing congestion on trunk roads in the UK, will make cycling far more dangerous where there is no dedicated cycle path, discouraging people from taking cycling holidays.

The UK is now following the lead of other European countries like The Netherlands and Denmark, in providing dedicated paths for cyclists in and around towns, and new traffic-free long-distance cycle routes are also being established. Lottery funding of more than £90 million has been made available to the charity Sustrans to complete the National Cycle Network, consisting of 12 000 miles of dedicated cycleways (coupled with walk-ways) throughout the UK, emulating similar cycle routes across Europe. There is clearly high demand for this amenity as, according to Sustrans, over 420 million trips were made on the existing stretches of the National Cycle Network in 2010, with 216 million on bikes and the others on foot. Cycling still accounts for less than 2% of all trips in the UK, compared with 18% in Denmark and 11% in Germany, but efforts are being made to increase cycle use, both as a means of local transport and for tourism.

Cycling has been encouraged in cities and towns through the introduction of convenient cycle hire points, which do not require the user to return the cycle to the start point. London introduced these in 2010, although non-residents were unable to use the system for the first six months of its operation, as computer and docking stations were trialled. The London system offers a low daily rate for the occasional user (currently £1) with additional hire costs based on the time the cycle is used – the first 30 minutes being free. Similar schemes are in operation in Paris and other provincial cities across France (for example, see Figure 15.7) as well as Barcelona and Copenhagen.

Figure 15.7 The Bordeaux cycle hire scheme, known as V-Cub, provides convenient docking stations across the city centre

Photo by Claire Humphreys

In the interests of improving the environment, efforts are also being made to improve opportunities for cyclists in the UK to take their cycles on trains, which would encourage rural tourism by bike. While train services in the UK have offered this facility in the past, commercial concerns are making rail companies more reluctant to allow bicycles to be carried free and rules governing their carriage differ for each of the 27 railway companies and on every route, discouraging the practice. Integrated transport planning should include and facilitate this opportunity, but the privatization of the railways has made this difficult to enforce.

Tourists on foot

In examining the role of transport, one must not forget tourists who travel mainly on foot. The destinations that draw such tourists were touched on earlier in Chapter 9, but let us look at this area a little more here.

Walking holidays in the mountains have a long tradition, and hiking and trekking have both grown in popularity in recent years. Ramblers' associations represent the interests of these long-distance walkers, working to ensure that rights of way over both public and private land in the UK are protected. The European Ramblers' Association was established in 1969, and, since that time, 11 European long-distance paths – the longest, from Norway to Turkey, stretching some 4500 miles – have been established, often refurbished long-existing routes. Some of these, such as the E2 Grande Traversée des Alpes or the five pathways through the Austrian Alps, are well maintained and extensively used, while others, such as those in southern Italy, Romania, the Ukraine and Turkey, have yet to be opened officially, although they are in use. Two of these European footpaths extend into England and Scotland – the route E2-GB stretching from Stranraer to Dover and eventually connecting with the Grande Traversée des Alpes. Such routes are particularly popular with German and Dutch hikers and are expected to attract growing numbers of British tourists.

EXAMPLE   The Iron Curtain trail

In 2005, it was announced that a 4250-mile tourist trail would be developed to follow the route of the 'Iron Curtain' – a term denoting the border separating the West from the former Soviet Union. Stretching from the Arctic Ocean to the Black Sea, this former border snakes through scenic countryside that it is ideal to incorporate into cycling and walking holidays.

EU funding is being provided and each country along the route will make its own contribution to developing the infrastructure and superstructure needed to support the trail.

Tourism on foot is also important to towns and cities. In the most popular urban destinations, trails are often marked out by means of symbols on pavements or signposts, just as markers on trees enable visitors to find their way along forest trails. Apart from the obvious attractions identified by these trails, promotional bodies are recognizing that walking tours provide the opportunity to introduce tourists to little-known regions of the town, allowing poorer districts to benefit from the influx of visitors. Liège, in Belgium, offers a ten-day Festival de Promenade for tourists visiting the city in August, with more than 40 different walks of varying lengths, appealing to a variety of different tastes. The UK's cities are increasingly recognizing the value of such initiatives.

EXAMPLE   Discover Toronto on foot

Self-guided walking tours are a common feature of many tourist destinations. Visitors may use a guidebook or specially produced brochure to help them discover the attractions and history of the local neighbourhood.

Toronto Tourism has developed 26 self-guided walking tours which highlight many different aspects of their urban landscape, thus appealing to a variety of audiences. The tours, likely to last between 30 minutes and two hours depending on the speed of the walker, are supported by a brochure containing a map of the area and a brief overview of the attraction. The information is available to download on the Internet (although it is not yet easily available via a smartphone application).

Such initiatives can help to encourage dwell time in a city as well as enhancing the overall experience of the visitor.

Further information: **www.toronto.ca/transportation/walking/walking_tours.htm**

An interesting development in urban tourism has been the concept of **sightjogging**, in which joggers accompany tour guides on a run while key attractions are pointed out to them. Berlin offers 90-minute tours, which have proved popular, while similar tours are on offer in the USA in New York, Washington, DC, San Diego and Charleston. Purists might disparage this limited form of sightseeing, but, as an encouragement to exercise, the concept has its merits!

Future developments in land transport

In terms of future development, railways in particular are making substantial progress. Japan's Linear Express, capable of cruising at speeds up to 300 mph, has already reached the prototype stage. This train has the advantage of superspeed while being super quiet, and, if the technology proves successful, rail services could certainly pose a major threat to air routes of distances over land up to 1000 miles.

The costs of fuel, and the environmental impact of creating and burning fuel for transport, are frequently in the news. The introduction of transport which uses biofuels, and hybrid systems, are growing in number and it is likely that investment in this area will continue to grow. The introduction of electric systems – especially in situations where journeys are short and don't require high speeds – has already been seen, for example in the shuttle buses taking tourists up the mountain to Machu Picchu from the base at Aguas Calientes.

The growing awareness of the health benefits of exercise is encouraging more tourists to be active and include walking and cycling as part of their holidays. The EU, among others, is promoting such exercise as part of a healthy lifestyle, and, as demand increases, we may see a greater variety of facilities conveniently available to tourists.

Finally, there has been much improvement in information about transport; for instance, the electronic noticeboards at bus stops that detail the arrival of the next bus. Moves are also afoot to ensure that all transport networks will eventually be linked by global positioning software, enabling travellers to track the current location of any form of transport using smartphone technology.

Questions and discussion points

1. What are the advantages of travelling by rail rather than air between London and Paris? Would these same advantages exist if you were travelling between London and Avignon in the south of France?

2. How might the development of long-distance cycle and walking trails (such as the Eurovelo and the E2 Grande Traversée des Alpes) help to develop tourism in rural areas traversed by these routes?

3. This chapter has highlighted the example of Toronto Tourism, who developed freely available materials to encourage visitors to take self-guided walking tours. Can the cost of designing such materials be justified? Who might oppose the production of such resources?

Tasks

1. Complete five interviews with people who have recently taken a holiday. Ask the holiday-maker to identify the different types of land transport used throughout their trip. Report on the most popular modes of transport used as well as the transport costs as a share of their overall holiday spends. Explain why the modes of transport used were chosen.

2. You are the owner of a successful coach company offering tours across Europe. Currently your market is mostly over the age of 60. However, you would like to expand your business to attract a younger audience - those aged 18-28. Write a report which details how the different aspects of the tours you currently offer many need to be changed to attract this new market.

3. In the UK, free local bus transport is available for the over-sixties throughout the country (although Scotland and Wales operate their own versions for their residents), aided by government subsidies. This has encouraged many more elderly travellers, especially those living near to the coast, to take days out. Many are questioning this benefit in the face of the current recession. Do the social benefits outweigh the economic costs involved? Do these benefits increase the spend by tourists? Interview a selection of residents in your area to find out the potential value, both social and economic, of this benefit, and write a report which also identifies any drawbacks, apart from that of cost, which this might involve. Can these drawbacks be overcome?

Bibliography

Amtrak (2010) *Amtrak sets new ridership record, thanks passengers for taking the train*, Press Release, 11 October.

Elan Jones, S. (2011) High Speed Rail, *Hansard*, 13 July.

Euromonitor (2010) *Global Rail Transportation – Picking Up Speed*, London, Euromonitor, March.

European Parliament (2009) *The European Cycle Network: Eurovelo*, Brussels, European Parliament's Committee on Transport and Tourism.

Eurostar (2009) Memorandum from Eurostar (PIR 43), *Submission to House of Commons Transport Committee Report, Priorities for Investment in the Railways*, available online at: http://www.publications.parliament.uk/pa/cm200910/cmselect/cmtran/38/38we51.htm (accessed November 2011).

Gilligan, A. (2011) A portrait of high-speed rail, *The Sunday Telegraph*, 3 April.

Milmo, D. (2011) HS2 high-speed rail plans 'a recipe for disaster', *The Guardian*, 20 July.

Railteam (2009) *European high speed rail travel in 2020*, Press Release, 26 November.

Sylt, C. and Reid, C. (2010) Eurostar narrows losses ahead of Deutsche Bahn competition, *Independent On Sunday*, 19 December.

Tatlow, J. (1920) *Fifty Years of Railway Life in England, Scotland and Ireland*, London, The Railway Gazette.

Wall Street Journal (2010) High-Speed Competition; Deutsche Bahn versus Eurostar, thanks to Margaret Thatcher, *Wall Street Journal*, 22 October.

Further reading

Penn, R. (2005) *A Place to Cycle: Amazing rides from around the world*, London, Conran Octopus.

Websites

Railways

Amtrak: **www.amtrak.com**

Rail Europe: **www.raileurope.com**

The Man in Seat 61 (advice on planning train journeys): **www.seat61.com**

UKsteam Info (steam train excursions in the UK): **www.uksteam.info**

Coaches

Coaches offering sleeper accommodation: **www.sleepercoaches.co.uk; www.jumbocruiser.com; www.silvergray.co.uk**

Westwing Aviation: **www.westwing.com.au/mail-runs**

Cars

HolidayTaxis.com: **www.holidaytaxis.com**

Motorhome rentals: **www.abacusmotorhomehire.co.uk; www.international-motorhome-hire.com**

resorthoppa.com: **www.resorthoppa.com**

resorttaxis.com: **www.resorttaxis.com**

Cycling

Cycling for Softies: **www.cycling-for-softies.com**

Mountain bike holidays: **www.exodus.co.uk**

Sustrans (map of National Cycle Network): **www.sustrans.org.uk**

On foot

City Running Tours: **www.cityrunningtours.com**

Sightjogging: **www.sightjogging-berlin.de**

Part 3

Intermediaries in the provision of travel and tourism services

16

The management of visitors

Contents

Learning outcomes

After studying this chapter, you should be able to:

- explain the concept of visitor management
- identify different techniques employed to manage tourists
- understand the role of interpretation in visitor management
- be aware of the controls that can be implemented to protect the physical environment.

As Hawaii's visitor counts once again hit record levels, state officials grappled with the issue of visitor management and the impact of the visitor industry on the state's environment and residents. Attention centered on restricting tour bus access to public places, legislating limitations on thrill-craft to protect breeding whales and assessing resident's attitudes toward the visitor industry.

Long (1990), Hawaii studies visitor management

Introduction

As can be seen in the case of Hawaii above, the pressure of excessive numbers of visitors has long caused concern, and the need to manage the impacts has been recognized. The global growth of the tourism industry has exacerbated this problem as more destinations consider the opportunities offered by attracting tourists to their area. As tourists seek new experiences, so the frequency of both short and long breaks has increased and the numbers of leisure tourists have increased (and management problems are evident in Figure 16.1). Destinations not traditionally seen as tourist resorts are becoming popular places to visit, and consequently pressure to respond to an influx of people lies at the heart of visitor management.

Visitor management involves finding ways to regulate visitors in order to minimize negative impacts and, where possible, maximize the benefits of tourism (Mason, 2005). This chapter examines the range of techniques that can be employed by tourist businesses and destinations in order to control and manage visitors and, in consequence, their impacts. These impacts extend beyond placing pressure on the physical environment – large numbers of tourists can also impact on the host community and its way of life. Furthermore, large tourist numbers can place pressure on infrastructure and superstructure, impacting on the economic balance of the destination.

Figure 16.1 A logistical nightmare: organizing baggage for QM2 passengers disembarking at Southampton
Photo by Chris Holloway

Controlling the impacts of visitors

A great deal has been written over the past few decades, acknowledging the diverse impacts of tourism and, importantly, considering the ways in which negative impacts can be prevented. Visitor management can help to ensure that the expectations of tourists are balanced against the demands of the host environment, community and tourist businesses. Thus, successful visitor management requires a clear understanding of the demands of these groups and the extent to which they are prepared to compromise their positions in order to achieve a balanced outcome for all stakeholders.

A variety of visitor management strategy models have been employed over the years, including the Recreation Opportunity Spectrum, Visitor Impact Management model, Visitor Experience and Resource Protection model and Visitor Activity Management Program (Richardson and Fluker, 2004). The approaches of these models are underpinned by an appreciation of the need to control negative impacts by establishing limits for tourism, embracing two key principles – carrying capacity and the limits of acceptable change.

Carrying capacity

This concept proposes that there is a finite capacity for a tourist facility or destination and what that is should be established in order to restrict any detrimental impacts. Specifically, this can be defined as 'the maximum use of any site without causing negative effects on the resources, reducing visitor satisfactions, or exerting adverse impacts upon the society, economy or culture of the area' (McIntyre, 1993, 23).

The origins of this concept derive from wildlife management, where it has been recognized that plants and animals require certain physical conditions to survive. Once an environment has been altered to a point where those conditions no longer exist, the wildlife populations cannot be sustained. This principle makes the assumption that impacts are likely to be relatively gradual, until a point is reached at which intense changes occur. For the principle of carrying capacity to be effective, clearly the limiting point should be set somewhere before such changes happen. One critique of this approach takes the view that intense impact on environments occurs when use of them first begins, with increased use only adding marginally to that impact. If that is the case, unless all tourists are banned, an increase in visitor numbers will cause little marginal distress to the landscape. While both perspectives may have validity, it is achieving an understanding of the impacts of use that is the underlying principle here.

Although the initial focus of carrying capacity may have been on damage to the physical environment, there is now greater awareness of other carrying capacities. Richardson and Fluker (2004) identify five subtypes of carrying capacity:

- *physical* – the number of visitors that the site was designed for or has the ability to accommodate
- *economic* – the level at which the tourism business can operate before other industries are squeezed out by the competition for resources
- *perceptual* – the level of use that can be accommodated before the psychological experience of visitors is negatively affected
- *social* – the numbers of visitors that can be tolerated by the host community
- *ecological* – the numbers of tourists that can use an area before damage is done to the natural or biological environment.

For some attractions, such as a staged Wild West show or a city bus tour, the maximum capacity may be fairly easy to determine, based perhaps on the numbers of seats in an auditorium or on the vehicle. For many other attractions, however, such a finite number is often difficult to establish.

Social carrying capacity for Cyprus

Research in 2000 explored the attitudes towards tourism of the local population of the Mediterranean island of Cyprus. Many respondents recognized the economic importance of the industry but also high-lighted the changes to customs and social practices. Interestingly, tourism was seen as promoting Cypriot culture, arts and crafts, resulting in housewives taking up embroidery to help meet the demand for souvenirs, and traditional wedding ceremonies being staged for tourists to observe.

Few locals expressed an opinion that tourism numbers should be reduced, and generally enthusiasm for, rather than apathy towards, tourism was expressed. Of those who felt that tourism impeded their lives, generally this was attributed to price inflation, beach congestion and restaurant service. Tourism was also held partly responsible for a shift in moral standards, increased divorce levels and drug-taking.

However, despite these concerns, and the heavily crowded tourist region, few local residents feel overwhelmed by visitor numbers, suggesting that the social carrying capacity has yet to be exceeded.

Source: Edited from Saveriades, 2000

It is worth commenting that it is difficult to establish one numerical capacity point as various stakeholders are likely to have different perspectives on where the limit lies. For the planners and managers of popular tourist destinations, objectives to protect animal and plant life will need to be balanced with objectives to maintain an environment acceptable to the host community, the tourists and the businesses seeking to profit from visitors. This may lead to conflicting pressures when considering maximum capacity.

Finally, even if an exact number is precisely established, it may then be hard to control numbers so that they remain within that capacity limit. For example, attractions such as national parks may have several entry points, which makes restricting numbers difficult. Furthermore, fundamental principles such as the right to access national parks may make closure or restrictions unpopular or unenforceable in law. In such cases, a range of more subtle visitor management techniques, discussed in detail later in this chapter, may help to control demand.

As it may be impossible to establish and implement an exact carrying capacity, an alternative approach may be to determine the level of impact or alteration that is acceptable to these user groups, through compromise and negotiation, accepting that some change to the environment will occur.

The limits of acceptable change

This principle acknowledges that humans' use of the natural environment will ultimately lead to change. Therefore, the aim is to manage the destination or attraction through this change, acknowledging that impacts beyond a pre-established level will not be tolerated and responses will be implemented to ensure that the limits of acceptable change (LAC) are not exceeded. The management challenge 'is not one of how to prevent any human-induced change, but rather one of deciding how much change will be allowed to occur, where, and the actions needed to control it' (Stankey *et al.* 1985, 1).

The LAC approach requires that the nature of different types of impacts is identified as well as noting where those impacts occur. Managers of the destination or site must then determine the levels of impacts that are acceptable and introduce initiatives to ensure that actual impacts remain within these boundaries or limits. Stankey *et al.* (1985) propose that the LAC process consists of four major components:

1. the specification of acceptable and achievable resource and social conditions, defined by a series of measurable parameters
2. an analysis of the relationship between existing conditions and those judged acceptable
3. identification of management actions necessary to achieve these conditions
4. a programme of monitoring and evaluation of management effectiveness.

Over the years, this approach has been implemented at a variety of destinations and tourist sites, especially in wilderness areas in the USA.

Meeting the cost of visitor management

Both the strategic process of creating a visitor management plan and the implementation of operational methods to control visitors have an inherent cost. For example, there are likely to be significant costs involved in adapting the physical environment – such as constructing paths, a visitor management centre or signage – to control the behaviour of tourists. The costs may be passed on to the visitors, borne by the host community or met by local tourism businesses. In cases where the tourists are expected to meet (or pay a contribution towards) the cost of managing the impact of their activities, a direct charge for access may be made, perhaps in the form of entry charges. Many popular heritage sites charge entry fees that contribute towards the costs of maintaining the site and making it accessible to visitors. In order to ensure that the local population is not excluded from accessing its local heritage site, a reduced charge or discounted annual fee may be offered.

EXAMPLE   Entry fees for Canterbury Cathedral

The historic city of Canterbury, located in the south east of England, is home to this popular tourist attraction, now receiving around a million visitors, annually. To help manage visitors, an entry charge is levied. First introduced in 1995, this charge was seen as a means to address two problems: the overwhelming visitor numbers (believed to be in excess of 2 million at the time) and the limited financial resources available leading to a deficit. Today, the money raised from this charge helps to maintain the upkeep of the building as well as providing information and other facilities for tourists.

To ensure that this does not exclude the local population, entry is free to those who work in the old city or live within four miles of the cathedral.

As an alternative to entry fees, tourists may be required to purchase a licence to gain access to a destination. Limiting licences will further control the number of tourists accessing the protected area. An example of the requirement to obtain a licence is the trekking permit required to enter the Annapurna conservation area in Nepal. More than 25 000 trekkers visit this area annually, and the fees collected for the permit to trek are estimated to improve the living standards of around 40 000 local people, as well as funding environmental protection and sustainable tourism initiatives.

Trekking permits are also required for the popular trail to Machu Picchu, Peru. Passes are limited to around 500 permits per day, although it is estimated that more than half of these are allocated to the guides, cooks and porters (see Figure 16.2) who support the tourists trekking the Inca Trail.

Figure 16.2 Porters making preparations for Machu Picchu trek

Photo by Claire Humphreys

The host community may cover the costs of managing local resources, perhaps through the level of state or council taxes that they are required to pay, while businesses may be required to make a contribution through their business rates. Tourism companies may foot the bill for visitor management through demands to adapt their operations, perhaps by constructing supporting infrastructure, funding information provision, marketing campaigns or other similar activities.

While many tourist attractions are commercially operated businesses, some resources are under the control of governments. Natural environments, such as national parks and wilderness areas, as well as some built heritage sites, may be the responsibility of governments, who must provide the funding to protect, maintain and manage them. In such cases, governments may open such resources to the public and tourists as part of a remit to provide access. The costs of implementing effective visitor management are likely to be borne by the public purse.

Operational approaches to visitor management

The operational techniques employed to manage visitors and their impacts can be broadly separated into two categories: 'hard' and 'soft' management. The **hard management** techniques are those methods that restrict tourists' activities, perhaps through financial or physical controls. **Soft management** techniques focus on encouraging a change in behaviour, through design or subtle persuasion.

While hard techniques have been a common approach employed to protect the environment and resources from the pressures of tourism, the use of soft techniques can help to balance the need to protect with the need to provide positive experiences for visitors. For example, educating visitors about the impacts they have and the ways in which these

Table 16.1 Examples of hard and soft visitor management techniques

Hard techniques	Soft techniques
Closure of attraction or areas within an attraction	Marketing
Zoning	Directional signage
Permits and licences	Limited infrastructure development
Vehicle bans	Codes of conduct
Entrance fees	Education and information provision

effects can be minimized can serve not only to encourage improved behaviour but also to provide a greater engagement with the activities undertaken to protect resources from demand pressures.

More than 20 years ago, the Department of Employment and the English Tourist Board (DOE/ETB, 1991) produced a report, 'Tourism and the environment: maintaining the balance', designed to encourage improved management of tourism resources. This identified the following three key areas for managing visitors.

● *Controlling demand* may be achieved by attempting to spread the arrival of visitors throughout the year. Furthermore, it may be possible to control the areas that are accessed by visitors. This can ensure that tourism is more evenly spread across the area (reducing the intensity of pressure). An alternative may be to contain visitors in one location that, while intensifying the pressure in that specific location, does allow protection of other areas left untouched by the tourists. Ultimately, control may be achieved by limiting total numbers, the amount of time that tourists can spend at a location or banning access altogether.

● *Altering visitors' behaviour* may be possible through increased awareness. Encouraging tourists to understand the impact of their presence and to take responsibility for this may lead to improved behaviour, thus reducing the impact. Codes of conduct are often designed to encourage such responsibility.

● *Adapting supply* can ensure that the resources are better placed to cope with demand. This may include developing supporting infrastructure, such as roads and paths, toilets and information centres.

It should be appreciated that these areas are interlinked, and employing initiatives that seek to consider all three areas can provide greater benefits than just attempting to address one area alone. Therefore, the techniques identified in the following sections recognize the effects on all three realms.

Controlling demand and flows of visitors

All too often, discussion relating to visitor management at a destination only arises when problems start to emerge, yet it is vital that policies and the actions required to successfully manage the impacts of tourism should be introduced as soon as visitor flows begin. As demand levels change, so the strategies for managing visitors should be revisited. A variety of initiatives can be implemented to adjust the flows of visitors.

Pricing policies and strategies

As highlighted in the example of Canterbury Cathedral above, price mechanisms are often proposed as means of controlling tourist demand, with an increase in prices expected to reduce the number of visitors attracted. As prices are often relatively inelastic where major tourist attractions are concerned, however, this may not always have the desired limiting effect.

The benefit of employing a pricing policy is that it raises revenue that can help to finance the implementation of visitor management. Selective taxation on hotel accommodation or higher charges for parking can also be imposed, but some criticize this as a regressive tax, affecting the less well-off but having little effect on the wealthy.

For some attractions, the use of pricing as a means of controlling demand can be controversial. Several religious buildings (including St Paul's Cathedral in London and St Basil's Cathedral in Moscow) have introduced entry charges, often using the funds to assist with the costs of maintenance, but the charge does not sit easily with many, who feel that places designed for religious worship should not be limiting entry to those who can afford the charge.

Controlling access through ticketing and licensing

Limiting entry through some form of visa or licence is another practical alternative. Requiring prior application in order to gain access can allow destination managers or tourism businesses the chance to deter arrivals. The number of visas or licences can be restricted, both in total and across time periods – the latter helping to manage seasonality. An example is that implemented by the government of Bhutan, which limits tourists to a few thousand every year, each of whom is required to meet a minimum daily spend on their travel arrangements. Thus, control by licence simultaneously restricts tourists and provides the government with useful revenue, directly and indirectly.

 Timed tickets for blockbuster art shows

Highly popular exhibitions draw huge crowds, and, in cases where the object is to look at artwork, the result can be extremely unsatisfying. A case in point was the Paul Gauguin exhibition held at the Tate Modern in London in 2010/11, which attracted so many visitors that it became almost impossible to see individual works of art. It became clear that simply restricting visitors to limits dictated by health and safety regulations was inadequate. London's National Gallery learned the lesson for their blockbuster Leonardo da Vinci exhibition in 2011; only 180 visitors were admitted at a time, instead of the maximum of 230 permissible under health and safety regulations, and timed tickets were restricted to a half an hour.

Timed tickets, which allocate visitors to a particular time of day, help to spread demand for the resource, while providing tourists with an opportunity to participate in other activities in the meantime. This can significantly enhance the visitors' experience as well as benefiting the destination – visitors can see other attractions in the area as well as using the time to eat and shop, which can substantially increase their spend.

Restricting activities

In order to control the impacts of tourist demand, it may be necessary to set regulations or policies that restrict the use of tourist resources. There are various ways in which restrictions can be implemented. Failing to expand supporting infrastructure is an option sometimes chosen by local authorities in an attempt to discourage visitors. This can be effective, but, unfortunately, it can impact on local residents equally, whose frustrations with, say, inadequate road systems may lead to a political backlash.

Ban the tourist buses from the volcano

From the summit of Mount Eden, in Auckland, New Zealand, there are great panoramic views across the city. This extinct volcano is a popular tourist attraction, with an estimated 1.2 million visitors a year and 275 000 vehicles climbing the road to the summit – 9% of these are tourist buses (NZ Herald, 2006)

Now calls to ban large vehicles from the summit have been proposed. Following two surface-slips in the past three years, concern is raised that slope failure would cause the roadway leading to the summit to collapse with the potential for a serious accident.

Furthermore, conflict can arise between pedestrians walking to the summit and the buses. Heritage manager for the local indigenous population, Ngarimu Blair says, 'the greatest danger to pedestrians is buses and for this reason alone we have to question why we allow vehicles to the summit'.

However, it has been more than five years since the first call for a ban on tourist buses and the lack of a management plan for the area suggests that this debate will continue to rage.

Source: Spyksma, 2011

Additionally, it may be considered appropriate to control the length of time tourists spend at the destination. This may be vitally important in popular locations, where keeping the visitors flowing is vital. Linked to this is a management approach that can restrict the use of sites at particular times.

In addition to restricting the time spent at an attraction, it may be helpful to restrict access by groups or the range of activities allowed at particular sites. For example, camping and campfires may be banned in fragile forest areas of some national parks.

Marketing

Another form of control can be achieved through marketing, concentrating publicity on less popular attractions or geographical regions and promoting the low season. For example, the national tourist board VisitBritain might stress the appeal of the north-east of England in its marketing abroad, making little reference to the south west, which already attracts a high proportion of domestic tourists.

Attempts to do this may be frustrated by private-sector promotions, however. Airlines, for example, may prefer to concentrate on promoting those destinations for which they already have strong demand, although credit must be given to the no frills carriers, which have opened up new areas by flying to small provincial airports. There is always a danger that if the public-sector strategy is too successful and tourists are siphoned off to the new regions, the amenities and attractions at more popular sites could suffer a downturn in business. These popular sites may be better able to cope with large levels of tourism, while the diversion of visitors to other areas less able to cope with a large influx may cause new problems for both the established and the new destination.

Niche markets

To ensure a consistent demand for tourism all year round, it may be advisable for marketing efforts to try to attract specific niche sectors. For example, the conference market may be sought by a seaside resort destination as these events tend to take place outside the traditional summer holiday period. Thus, a large conference can fill bed spaces and use restaurants, transport and meetings venues at a time when other holiday markets are scarce.

Alternatively, marketing activities may focus on encouraging the traditional holiday-makers to visit at less popular times of the year. In some cases, external factors, such as school and public holidays, mean that some people cannot be encouraged to alter the time they travel, but other travellers may not be restricted by such factors. To take one example, retired or childless travellers may be encouraged to adjust their travel plans to the shoulder season, spreading demand and reducing congestion.

Dispersal of tourists into less congested areas may be a valuable strategy in other ways, too. Changing the behaviour of the more flexible traveller may be achieved by offering lower prices, but, importantly, this can also be achieved through marketing and information provision, making the traveller aware of the benefits of travelling to the destination at a quieter time or to a less popular area of the destination. While the benefits for the traveller may include less congestion, fewer queues, lower prices and improved service as staff are less pressured, it is also useful to highlight that such a shift in behaviour can help to protect resources, limiting pressure on the natural environment, reducing the likelihood of accidents and limiting other pressures that may affect the quality of life for the host community. In this way, tourists may be encouraged to adjust their travel patterns to protect the destination.

Demarketing

It may seem unimaginable to some businesses or destinations, but there are several examples where too many tourists wish to visit a place, leading to marketing activities being undertaken to deter visitors. Efforts may focus on trying to discourage visitors during peak times or dissuade those tourists who will be less profitable. Kotler and Levy defined the concept of demarketing as 'that aspect of marketing that deals with discouraging customers in general or a certain class of customers in particular on either a temporary or permanent basis' (1971, 75).

A variety of adjustments to the marketing mix can be employed in demarketing, including increasing the price for some or all of the market, reducing promotional activities and limiting sales outlets offering access to the product. Such actions can be controversial, however. Restricting access to those who can afford the higher price may be perceived as elitist, while a reduction in promotional efforts by a destination management organization (DMO) may not be popular with local tourist businesses.

Altering visitors' behaviour

While acknowledging the benefits of reducing the impact of tourism through restrictions on demand, it is also helpful to appreciate that management of those tourists who do visit can also help to control the pressures caused. This will improve the tourists' experience, as it can reduce conflicts between different stakeholder groups.

Interpretation, information and education

Information can be provided in a variety of ways, both prior to visiting and on reaching the attraction or destination.

One reason for providing information to visitors may be to meet obligations to educate – often an important remit for attractions funded by governments, such as galleries and museums. Providing an interpretation of exhibits or information about landscapes and buildings can help to fulfil this obligation.

Adequate information can also help to change the behaviour of visitors. For example, telling them about the pressures caused by tourism and the ways in which such pressures can be reduced can encourage visitors to develop an awareness of their responsibility and the impact of their activities (see Figure 16.3), but it is important to stress that the majority of tourists do not set out to harm or damage the destination they visit. Cole reports that, 'while some tourists may be open to learning, they are often unaware of appropriate behaviour and have little guidance on how to behave' (2007, 443).

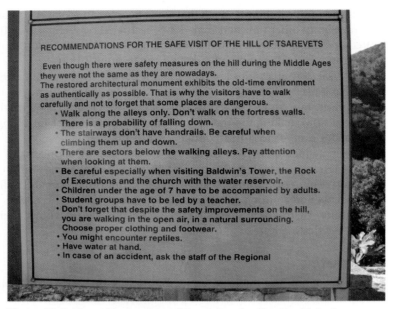

Figure 16.3 Managing tourist safety and protecting the historic medieval stronghold of Tsarevets, Bulgaria

Photo by Chris Holloway

It is often the combined activities of tourists *en masse* that cause significant pressures and problems for destinations. It is possible to adjust the behaviour of each tourist, however, through education and information, leading to considerable adjustments to the overall impact for the destinations. There is a variety of ways in which visitors can be informed, including signage, guides and codes of conduct.

Signs and guides

There is an extensive diversity in the signs and guides available to inform and educate tourists. The reasons for their provision are also varied, and they may be funded either by tourism businesses or governments at local or regional level.

Signposting can fall into two categories – informational or directional. Informational signs can provide interpretation of a particular point of interest or act as a marker, pointing it out. An example of this may be a blue plaque on a building identifying a location as the place of birth of a noteworthy person in history. Informational signing is used to add to the knowledge of visitors, thus enhancing their experience.

Directional signposting is used to assist tourists to navigate, perhaps finding their way to a tourist attraction or locating particular amenities or facilities, such as toilets. Directional signage needs to be clear, consistent in style and suitably positioned (Figure 16.4).

Early warning is vital for car drivers navigating unknown routes, so signs must be positioned well in advance of junctions and repetition of signs may be needed. Directional signs may not necessarily take car drivers on the shortest or most direct route. Often routes are designed to encourage the use of bypass or ring roads, as well as keeping tourist traffic away from commonly congested areas. The growing popularity of satellite navigation systems, however, may lead to many of these diversionary tactics becoming ineffective.

Signs aimed at pedestrians must generally provide the most convenient and safest routes, taking into consideration the needs of those with pushchairs, in wheelchairs or those less stable on their feet. Directional signs may also be provided for specific groups, such as walkers, cyclists or horse riders, each having their own requirements for convenient routes.

Figure 16.4 Directional and safety information signage at Herne Bay beachfront

Photo by Claire Humphreys

For a less well-known destination or visitor attraction it may be necessary to provide guides to help interpret the nature and importance of the place. Guides can play a very important visitor management role, however, so even well-known or established destinations use them to inform visitors, seeking to influence their behaviour.

Perhaps the commonest type of guide is the tour guide – a person who takes on an explanatory role, providing information about the heritage and history of a destination as well as describing the operation of machinery at an attraction or topics relating to the local population. An example may be seen in the case of the guide who takes a small group on a factory tour of the Ferrari car plant in Italy, explaining the equipment or processes en route. Alternatively an explanatory guide may be tasked with explaining the different stages of a religious service to observers witnessing it for the first time.

Guides may also take on the role of wardens, controlling the behaviour of tourists at the destination. In such cases, the guide may inform the visitor of expected modes of behaviour and remove or chastise tourists who do not conform. In that way, the guide acts to protect the resources by reducing or removing threats caused by those tourists who may be ignorant of the effects of their actions. While the role of such a guide may sound severe, in reality it may only require him or her to ask and visitors will respond. For example, guides will commonly ask visitors to dress suitably when entering religious buildings, be quieter when walking through areas where rare animals may be spotted and avoid entering buildings if they are residences of the local population. In such cases, only when tourists ignore the advice is there a need for the guide to take more severe action.

A guide can also take the role of a director or leader, selecting routes that can take tourists to less congested areas or less well-known attractions, helping to relieve pressures on the destination. The guide can also determine the length of time spent at particular sites, which may be vital at popular sites as it ensures that a turnover of visitors is achieved. The guide who acts as a group leader may also be able to divert tourists to other attractions. There have been many examples of tour groups being taken to 'attractions' that offer little more than shopping opportunities (for which the tour guide may be provided with a financial reward for bringing the group there). While many tourists have negative reactions to such actions, the practice remains widespread.

EXAMPLE — Tourists forced to shop by rogue tour guide

A fight broke out between two tourists and their tour guide during a visit to Hong Kong. The dispute arose after the tour guide berated the tourists for not shopping at a jewellery store, having been forced to stay there for two hours.

One underlying cause is the low basic income for guides, forcing them to rely on commission from the shops they bring custom to.

Following worldwide publicity of the problem in July 2010 – when an Internet video clip was circulated, showing a Hong Kong tour guide abusing Chinese mainland visitors and forcing them to shop – the local tourist authorities vowed to stamp out this problem. Yet rules to restrict this are clearly yet to have an effect.

Source: Shanghai Daily, 2011

A final role for the tour guide may be that of public relations. Given that guides have the tourists in their company often for an hour or more, they have an extensive opportunity to provide positive information in order to enhance the image of the destination.

Travel guidebooks conveniently provide tourists with details about the destinations they are visiting. Books can include information on the history, attractions, facilities and amenities in the area, as well as some key phrases or words in the local language. The German publisher Baedeker set the standards when it started to print travel books over 150 years ago, providing accurate, detailed information in its travel guides, and, since then, companies such as Lonely Planet, Rough Guide, Frommer's, Fodor, Insights and numerous others have produced their own city and country guides covering the globe.

Information provided to visitors in the form of guides can have an impact on their behaviour at destinations. Written guides can be designed to highlight the range of facilities or attractions in an area, which can in turn encourage a longer dwell time. Guides can also be published to provide information about a specific attraction, detailing the history and enhancing the visitors' interpretation of exhibits. They can also act as a souvenir of a visit.

Difficulties faced when deciding to publish guides are extensive. If guides are to be sold to tourists, then the amount of information included must justify the price to be paid. Major attractions or destinations will need to consider several versions in different languages to serve their most popular markets. Adaptations for different markets may involve adjusting the content by identifying relevant areas of interest. If guides are to be provided free to visitors, then the costs of their production may need to be controlled, which may limit the size and quality of the guide. If free guides are to be offered, it may be necessary to consider how these complement any other guides available for purchase.

Technology has been successfully developed which means audio guides have become commonplace at tourist attractions. The use of human guides has been discussed above, but here we need to consider prerecorded commentaries available in places such as museums, tourist attractions and now, more commonly, on city bus tours.

Audio guides can provide an extensive range of information on specific topics, but, unlike a human guide, offer no opportunity for questions to be answered. They are often available in a variety of languages and can be programmed to provide segments of information at particular locations. In museums, signs close to exhibits can show codes that can be entered into an audio guide for the visitor to hear the relevant segment of explanation. Technology thus allows prerecorded guides to offer a level of control over the information provided to visitors.

The rapid growth in popularity of digital music players (including iPods and telephones that can play MP3 audio recordings) has also provided visitors with the opportunity to download files containing information designed to enhance their visit.

EXAMPLE   **Bring your own guide**

As more and more travellers take their music players (and smartphones) with them on holiday, so the online market for downloadable audio guides of city destinations has taken off. There are many different companies offering prerecorded information, often structured as a walking tour of the city with a charge being made for each download. Examples include Tourist Tracks (**www.tourist-tracks.com**), Audio Steps (**www.audiosteps.com**) and Tourcaster (**www.tourcaster.com**).

In 2007, the brewer, Guinness, introduced two walking tour podcasts. The first provides a guided walk between Dublin city centre and the Guinness Storehouse (see Figure 16.5), location of its tourist attraction. The second provides information guiding the visitor around the attraction. By the end of the first year, more than 10 000 downloads had taken place, in a variety of European languages.

Whilst these guides are available freely from their website, their provision can help to encourage visitors to both find and pay to enter this popular attraction. Surely, a great move by the marketing managers at Guinness.

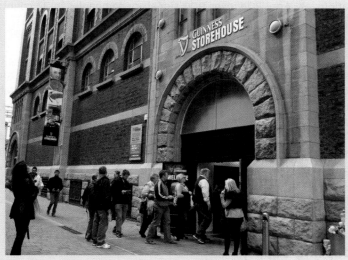

Figure 16.5 Guinness Storehouse, Dublin
Photo by Claire Humphreys

Codes of conduct

The creation of codes of conduct can place responsibility for the impact and problems caused by tourism on those who cause them or have a role to play in reducing them. The existence of such codes is more than just regulation of behaviour – it also plays a role in education, raising awareness of the problems and issues. While codes of conduct are often aimed at tourists, there are many cases where host communities and tourism businesses are encouraged to agree to codes of conduct to ensure that their actions and operations are responsible.

EXAMPLE **Code of conduct against the sexual exploitation of children in tourism**

In 2004, the United Nations World Tourism Organization, together with End Child Prostitution, Child Pornography and the Trafficking of Children for Sexual Purposes (ECPAT) and UNICEF, introduced a code of conduct for the travel industry that is designed to protect children from commercial exploitation, especially in the sex tourism industry.

In agreeing to abide by the code of conduct to protect children, the tourist organization agrees to:

- establish an ethical corporate policy against commercial sexual exploitation of children
- train personnel in the country of origin and where children are sexually exploited
- introduce clauses in contracts with suppliers, stating a common repudiation of sexual exploitation of children
- provide information to travellers on the sexual exploitation of children
- provide information to local 'key persons' at destinations
- report annually.

This code of conduct has become a key instrument in the prevention of child sex tourism worldwide. The initiative is recognized by the travel industry, child protection organizations, several governments and international organizations. By April 2011, over 900 signatory companies in 37 countries on all continents had signed up to the code.

Codes of conduct are suggested as being relatively easy to introduce as well as effective (Cole, 2007). This is especially true in cases that include considerable levels of restrictions, which, if implemented through local legislation, may take years to reach the statute books (Garrod and Fennell, 2004).

The disadvantage of voluntary codes of conduct, however, is that they may have limitations, such as being unable to effectively penalize offenders when the regulations are breached or ignored. To be successful, such codes rely on a moral consensus being reached to abide by the principles in order to achieve the desired goals. As companies are being encouraged to consider their social responsibility roles, so greater pressure to abide by codes of conduct may be felt.

Adapting supply

In order to protect attractions such as natural and heritage areas, there is often a need to make changes or adaptations to the supporting infrastructure. This can help to ensure that the demands of tourists are best served, while reducing negative pressures on the resource itself.

Queuing

In many areas of life there is the need to queue – perhaps in a post office, a supermarket, to be served in a bar or café, waiting for a customer service assistant on the telephone.

Unsurprisingly, queues are every bit as evident in the tourism business. While there are many initiatives aimed at reducing or dispensing with them, in some cases queues can be seen as a sign of popularity, attracting attention and, on occasion, they may even be encouraged.

Queues form when the arrival rate is higher than the time taken to service those arrivals. For example, passengers on a plane landing at an airport will disembark at the same time and reach customs together. As it takes time for the border security staff to process each of these passengers, the outcome will be the formation of a queue.

Having to queue can create a negative impression, affecting the visitors' experience. There has been extensive research into ways to shorten wait times as well as understanding attitudes towards waiting. Over 20 years ago, David Maister (1985) explored the psychology of waiting and suggested eight propositions:

- occupied time feels shorter than unoccupied time
- an 'in process' wait feels shorter than waiting to get started
- stress and anxiety can make the wait feel longer
- uncertain waits feel longer than finite, known waits
- unexplained waits can appear longer than explained delays
- unfair waits appear longer than equitable waits
- waiting alone seems longer than waiting with a group
- the more valuable the service, the longer the customer will wait.

These propositions can give insight into strategies that can be introduced to manage the experience of waiting visitors. They can be commonly seen in the activities of those tourist operations where queues are prevalent – theme parks, airports, catering establishments and hotel receptions, for example. Here are some responses to managing queues.

- *Entertaining visitors while they wait.* This can be achieved through a range of distractions, such as providing entertainers to amuse a queue waiting for a theme park ride. This does not necessarily have to be expensive or high-tech – for example, a wall of mirrors that distort the image can entertain visitors as they move slowly along the queue. A restaurant may ask customers to wait in the bar while their table is prepared or peruse the menu. While distracting customers from the wait, this can also provide the impression that they are in process, that their presence has been acknowledged and they will be seated in the restaurant in due course.

- *Start the process.* It is useful to greet customers and assess their needs. This can ensure that customers have not waited only to discover later that they are in the wrong place or that they need not have joined the queue. This can help service providers identify VIP customers – the business may have a policy to service these customers in a different manner. For example, the airline easyJet has introduced a 'speedy boarding' ticket that customers can purchase when booking their tickets. The ticket allows travellers to use a dedicated check-in desk, generally with shorter queues, and board the plane first. While such tickets can be lucrative for the airline, they can help reduce perceived waiting times for passengers, which, in turn, may help to reduce anxiety and stress.

- *Use customers as a resource.* Asking customers to complete paperwork while they are in the queue or even prior to arrival may reduce the time needed to service each customer, thus shortening the length of queues. Car hire company Avis offers frequent customers the opportunity to complete a hire agreement form in advance that can then be applied to all their rentals. This reduces the need for paperwork for each occasion and allows customers to bypass the hire desk, going straight to the parking lot to collect their pre-booked car. This benefits both the frequent traveller as well as other customers as it reduces the queue at the service counter.

- *Informing customers of the length of time they can expect to wait*. This is an important factor in enhancing customers' experience. While many flyers may be happy to wait an hour or more at an airport, often being entertained by the duty-free shopping or restaurants, once their expected departure time has passed, only short waits will be tolerated before their level of satisfaction is affected. Keeping customers informed of delays can allow each individual to make a choice about how the time is to be spent. For instance, advising that the plane will be delayed by an hour may allow the customer the chance to go to a bookshop to purchase reading matter, check e-mails or make business calls, have something to eat or grab a last-minute gift from a souvenir shop. While companies are encouraged to be honest about waiting times, there are occasions when expected delays are exaggerated so customers are pleasantly surprised when they experience a shorter delay than they had prepared themselves for. Restaurants, especially, may employ this tactic. Many theme parks, too, manage their queues by informing visitors of the time it will take to reach the front of the line.

- *Use equitable queuing systems*. Confronting customers with several queues requiring them to make a decision can cause anxiety that other queues will move faster or the queue joined may be the wrong one. A common resolution to this problem is to create one long queue, with customers being allocated to a service agent only when they reach the front. This can encourage a sense of fairness. Signs are also important. Customers need to know that their particular need can be addressed by the service agents once they reach the front of the queue.

- *Introduce separate queues for those customers who can be serviced quickly*. Cafés may create a separate counter for takeaway service, separating these customers from others who may need to wait for a table. Ski resorts and theme parks often employ a similar system for 'singles' or customers prepared to ride the ski-lift or rollercoaster without their friends alongside them. Such an initiative allows every seat to be filled, thus moving more passengers through the system, shortening the waiting time for all customers.

- *Consider the use of booking systems*. Allocating fixed time slots can spread the arrivals of customers, but it is vital that the time between those slots is appropriate. If the slots are too far apart, then resources may be left idle, but, if it is too short, then a backlog will build, frustrating later arrivals. Booking systems may also fail if customers do not show for their appointments, so it may be necessary to impose penalties on customers who fail to come at their allocated time. Applying penalties may be problematic, however. The causes of delays or missed appointments may be beyond the control of customers, who will have already suffered stress, so penalizing them still further can create antagonism towards the business. Flexibility regarding imposing penalties may be needed.

While businesses should evaluate *actual* waiting times, analysing what may cause congestion points within their operations, using a range of strategies to reduce the *perceived* time spent queuing to be served can be an important factor in enhancing customer satisfaction and effectively managing visitors.

Zoning

For popular destinations that receive large numbers of tourists, it may be beneficial to group together those who have similar expectations or patterns of behaviour. For example, those tourists who wish to relax and sunbathe on a beach may be separated from those who wish to play ball sports. This can be achieved by providing volleyball nets, goals and other such facilities in one area, making it attractive for those playing sports to move to that location. Similarly, at seashores or lakes, areas allocated to sailors, windsurfers and so on may be separated from those allocated to swimmers.

While zoning is an effective tool for managing a variety of demands for resources and reducing the potential for conflicts between users, it is also used to balance the demands of users with conservation ideals, protecting the natural environment. This has been seen in relation to the protection of marine parks as well as national parks (Geneletti and van Duren, 2008).

Zoning has also been used to balance conflicting demands of tourists and the host population. This may be achieved through planning policy and is used in urban as well as rural locations. Tourist zones are often prevalent in cities, where attractions, accommodation, amenities such as bars, restaurants, currency exchange facilities and so on are clustered together, all benefiting from the large numbers of tourists drawn to these areas.

EXAMPLE **Zoning to protect the natural environment**

The coastal resort of Phuket, Thailand, has long been popular with divers as well as other water-sports enthusiasts. However, its coral reefs are suffering from the damage caused by, amongst other things, tourism – the very thing that values its existence.

In 2007, a summit attended by government officials, tourism operators and local fisherman led to the agreement that the areas would be zoned. This would designate separate areas for preservation, diving and fishing.

As an alternative to diving on the natural coral, the Department of Marine and Coastal Resources sank two boats, to create an artificial reef and by 2010 it was estimated that it attracted about 100 divers a day – and had become the home of turtles, eels and blowfish.

Source: Thai News Service, 2010

Closure

While zoning areas for particular use can help to balance the conflicting demands of users, in some cases protection and visitor management can only be achieved by means of closure. One approach may be to close an area by erecting fences and security, refusing entry to the site. This can achieve a maximum reduction in access and ensure that an area is protected from the demands of tourists. Refusing entry to all visitors, including the local population, however, may be seen as extreme and a more moderate form of restriction may be desired.

Protection of some attractions or destinations may be achieved by restricting opening hours – perhaps only allowing afternoon visits or access just at weekends. This can significantly reduce the impact of visitors. If such an approach is to be employed, it is necessary to provide tourists and tour operators with information about the restricted hours. This ensures that tourists are not disappointed by arriving and finding that the attraction is closed. In such situations, marketing efforts should focus on explaining that the closure provides a means of protection.

The pressure caused by the excessive demands of tourism may also be managed by the use of selective closure. This may restrict access to particular parts of the destination or attraction, perhaps by means of a zoning policy, marketing efforts to divert attention or changes to the infrastructure. An example of limited closure to protect a site from the impact of visitors can be seen in the case of Stonehenge – a World Heritage site in the south west of England. The site introduced a rope fence around the stones, keeping tourists some distance from the historic stones. This has reduced the amount of erosion previously resulting from visitors touching and walking through the circle.

Pedestrianization

In recent years, it has become increasingly common to protect the central areas of towns and cities by restricting access by cars – in effect, pedestrianizing the area. Changing road systems is a complex and expensive task, but the rapid increase in car ownership has required cities – especially those with historic centres not designed to cope with modern-day traffic – to impose measures to control traffic flows. This has the added benefit of enhancing the experience of both locals and visitors, who no longer have to compete with the traffic for space. The absence of cars parked in historic city centres also enhances the visual experience of the site.

While it is common for pedestrianization to be a permanent feature, in some cases the closure may be for only short periods of time. For example, there are several provincial towns in France that close the central streets in order to allow street markets to take place. In Cambridge, England, closure of parts of the central area occur between 10 am and 4 pm, achieved by closing gates located at key entrance points to the central area.

When implementing pedestrianization, it is important to ensure that the improved environment also addresses health and safety demands. This may mean ensuring that emergency vehicles can gain access to the enclosed area if required. Areas must be made safe for all users, especially those who may have visual or mobility impairments. Pedestrianized areas can be used as social and event spaces for the local community, but, however used, it is vital that the area is perceived to be safe and free from crime.

EXAMPLE ## Pedestrianization requires more than just a ban on cars

In Hyderabad, there have been frequent complaints that the Charminar Pedestrianization Project was moving at too slow a pace. However, this development project reveals that turning over the area to those on foot takes time. The initial phase required the relocation of bus stands and cabling. In addition, the tourism department then needed to erect directional and informational signage.

However, it is also vital to ensure that the human factor is taken into consideration. The shopkeepers and hawkers must also be consulted to ensure that their livelihoods are not negatively affected. As a consequence, the streetscaping will provide a demarcation of space for the hawkers to trade, whilst bollards will mark areas on which they cannot encroach.

The project also required consultation and negotiation with local business to develop uniform signage, the removal of advertising boards and façade improvements. Finally, after 11 years the project is nearing fruition.

Source: The Times of India, 2010

Research into pedestrianization schemes in a selection of German and UK cities (Hass-Klau, 1993) revealed that, while pedestrianization of areas can lead, in the short term, to a downturn in trade for local shops, in the longer term it can lead to improvements in turnover. Thus, pedestrianization can gain great support from local enterprises, as well as being beneficial for locals and visitors who use the area.

Gateways

It is possible to manage the pressure caused by the influx of tourists by creating gateways. These are conveniently accessible routes providing access to popular areas, directing demand through those areas best able to cope with it, and they are designed to manage the impacts of that demand. Encouraging tourists to use specific gateways to tourist areas can be achieved by good signs, marketing, the location of convenient coach drop-off points and the creation of facilitating resources, such as visitor centres and parking spaces.

Visitor and tourist information centres (TICs)

Visitor and tourist information centres can play many roles: they can be used to educate visitors, perhaps affecting their behaviour, granting protection to the resource, and they can become an attraction in their own right.

In this way, visitor centres may provide convenient parking points for visitors, attracting tourists in a way that can then be conveniently managed. For example, in areas of natural beauty, they may act as a gateway or starting point for tourists' exploration of the area, perhaps on foot or by other transport. This role as a hub means that trails (walking, cycling and driving routes) can be constructed, influencing the behaviour of the visitors.

Trails and pathways

Trails may be used to disperse tourists, relieving pressure on an area and encouraging less well-known areas to be accessed. Alternatively, trails may be designed to cope with large numbers of visitors – perhaps by constructing surfaced paths, informative signs and toilet facilities. While such approaches may *increase* various impacts on these routes, they also serve to protect those areas that are less able to cope with such influxes of visitors. They can often be controversial, however, as the amount of construction necessary to hard-surface paths to manage the footfall of the many visitors can mar the landscape, affecting its natural beauty. This has to be balanced with the fact that, in many cases, constructing such paths can control erosion of the land, as well as control the spread of damage. Furthermore, the surfacing of paths can create an environment that is better able to cope with increased numbers of tourists. The downside is that this ultimately makes access easier, further stimulating increases in demand (Mason, 2005).

 Tennessee Trails

The state tourism organization has established a project to create 16 driving trails across the region. The circular routes include visits to historical and cultural locations as well as identifying restaurants and rest stops along the way. Each trail has a series of interpretive markers, designed to provide information to those with only limited knowledge of the region.

The 5th route, launched in December 2010, is the 'Walking Tall trail' (in reference to the 1973 movie based on the life of a Tennessee Sheriff). The 360-mile route includes Gracelands, the home of Elvis Presley, the Lorraine motel in Memphis (where Martin Luther King was assassinated), Shiloh, site of a key Civil War battle, as well as Adamsville, the home of the famed Sheriff Pusser.

Tourist officials have established the trails with the expectation that those who drive the routes will see the markers and stop at the attractions. Their goal is to increase tourism spend as well as helping spread the benefits of tourism to more counties. The trails are also aimed at encouraging visitors to the metropolitan regions to stay longer and discover the surrounding areas.

As part of the Discover Tennessee Trail and Byways programme, these routes use existing roads, attractions and facilities which has minimized the need for large-scale investment. The cost of the markers is being borne by the transportation department whilst the marketing of the trails is coming from the state tourism budget. Information about these trails is available online at **http://tntrailsandbyways.com**.

Source: Sainz, 2010

Transport links

Gateways can be linked with supporting transport services. This may include park and ride options, which can provide mass transport services to sensitive areas. These may exist in both urban and rural areas. Many historic cities have set up park and ride facilities to cope with the demand for access from the local population as well as visitors, while, in rural locations, including national parks, such schemes can limit the need for car journeys into wilderness or natural areas.

Technology that can assist in visitor management

Many tourist businesses have employed a variety of technological methods to examine visitor behaviour in order to improve the experience for their customers. To take one example, Alton Towers, one of the largest theme parks in the UK, provided selected visitors with an electronic badge that used tracking technology to monitor the time they spent in particular areas of the park and the routes they took. This provided the park managers with information that could help them decide where to site new rides or catering facilities. Badge monitoring is often used at business events such as conferences and exhibitions, too, tracking the movements of visitors. Camera technology is also used to monitor visitor behaviour, identifying areas where queues might build up or tourists are reacting negatively to particular resources.

The Internet can provide a variety of opportunities to enhance visitor management, including the dissemination of information and the means to conveniently prebook tickets, thus allowing the flow of visitor arrivals to be managed. An example of this is the use of the Internet by airlines to manage visitors through the provision of online check-in. This can help to speed visitors through the airport system.

Future issues

With ever-growing visitor numbers, the need to manage the pressures caused by tourism is significant. Importantly, however, is the realization that for many tourists their expectations are also changing. As more visitors demand 'experiences' which can provide special memories, so there is a need to ensure that the management and control of visitors does not detract from the overall encounter. This may require excellent communication to inform and establish expectations.

The rapid development of mobile technology may offer an opportunity here. The provision of information and opportunities to reserve tickets conveniently using dedicated phone software or 'Apps' may help to ensure that tourists are able to plan their travels with greater convenience. Furthermore, GPS systems on phones can also provide updated information about attractions in the immediate vicinity. For example, Alton Towers, the theme park mentioned earlier, has developed an App which allows visitors to obtain walking directions to any of their rides when they are inside the park.

Finally, as budgets tighten for many attractions, the cost of visitor management may become a greater issue. It is vital to recognize that successful visitor management can ensure that resources are protected, thus reducing the likelihood that costs will be encountered at a later date repairing damaged facilities. Furthermore, improved visitor experiences may well increase dwell time as well as enhancing positive word-of-mouth reviews, both of which can potentially increase visitor spend.

Questions and discussion points

1. Do you think it is beneficial to use soft rather than hard visitor management techniques? Is there always a choice?

2. Printed, audio and digital tour guides are now widely available. Do you think this spells the end of the human tour guide?

3. Signage can be directional or informational. How do these different types of signage play a role in visitor management?

Tasks

1. Visit a popular tourist attraction and identify the different ways they manage visitors. Write a report which explains why they use these different techniques.

2. Obtain a brochure or information leaflet which promotes a walking or driving trail. Consider the reasons why this trail has been established. Discuss how it helps the tourism businesses listed on the route.

Bibliography

Cole, S. (2007) Implementing and evaluating a code of conduct for visitors, *Tourism Management*, 28, 443–445.

DOE/ETB (1991) Tourism and the environment: maintaining the balance, London, Department of Employment and English Tourist Board.

Garrod, B. and Fennell, D. A. (2004) An analysis of whalewatching codes of conduct, *Annals of Tourism Research*, **31** (2), 334–352.

Geneletti, D. and van Duren, I. (2008) Protected area zoning for conservation and use: a combination of spatial multicriteria and multiobjective evaluation, *Landscape and Urban Planning*, **85** (2), 97–110.

Hass-Klau, C. (1993) Impact of pedestrianization and traffic calming on retailing, *Transport Policy*, **1** (1), 21–31.

Kotler, P. and Levy, S. J. (1971) Demarketing? Yes, demarketing!, *Harvard Business Review*, **49** (6), 74–80.

Long, D. (1990) Hawaii studies visitor management, *Tour and Travel News*, 31 December.

Maister, D. (1985) *The psychology of waiting lines*, Harvard Business School, Note 9, May, 2–3.

Mason, P. (2005) Visitor management in protected areas: from hard to soft approaches, *Current Issues in Tourism*, **8** (2&3), 181–194.

McIntyre, G. (1993) Sustainable Tourism Development, World Tourism Organization, cited in McCool, S. F. and Lime, D. W. (2001), Tourism carrying capacity: tempting fantasy or useful reality?', *Journal of Sustainable Tourism*, **9** (5), 372–388.

NZ Herald (2006) Vehicles set to be banned from 'eroding' Mt Eden, *Bay of Plenty Times*, 5 August.

Richardson, J. I. and Fluker, M. (2004) *Understanding and Managing Tourism*, French's Forest, Pearson Hospitality Press.

Sainz, A. (2010) New Tourism Trail created in West Tennessee, *Associated Press*, 1 December.

Saveriades, A. (2000) Establishing the social tourism carrying capacity for the tourist resorts of the east coast of the Republic of Cyprus, *Tourism Management*, **21** (2), 147–156.

Shanghai Daily (2011) Tourists, guide fined following fight over HK forced shopping, *Shanghai Daily*, 8 February.

Spyksma, H. (2011) A mountain of concern, *Central Leader*, 8 April.

Stankey, G. H., Cole, D. N., Lucas, R. C., Petersen, M. E. and Frissell, S. S. (1985) *The limits of acceptable change (LAC) system for wilderness planning*, Ogden, UT, United States Department of Agriculture: Forest Service.

Thai News Service (2010) Tourists flock to see artificial coral in Phuket, *Thai-Asean News Network*, 3 September.

The Times of India (2010) Charminar project to be launched soon, *Times of India*, 8 December.

Further reading

Beunen, R., Regnerus, H. D. and Jaarsma, C. F. (2008) Gateways as a means of visitor management in national parks and protected areas, *Tourism Management*, **29** (1), 138–145.

Richardson, J. I. and Fluker, M. (2004) *Understanding and Managing Tourism*. French's Forest, Pearson Hospitality Press.

Websites

VisitEngland – Developing visitor management plans: **www.visitengland.org/england-tourism-industry/DestinationManagerToolkit/Destinationdevelopment%5C2HDevelopingVisitorManagementPlans.aspx?title=2H%3a+Developing+Visitor+Management+Plans**

Wilderness.net, Visitor Use Management Toolbox: **www.wilderness.net/index.cfm?fuse=toolboxes&sec=vum**

17

The structure and role of the public sector in tourism

Contents

Learning outcomes

After studying this chapter, you should be able to:

- understand the part played by local, regional and central governments and their agencies in the planning and promotion of tourism in a country
- recognize the growing importance of the public sector in all aspects of tourism and its role in public–private partnerships
- define the term 'social tourism' and understand its significance for disadvantaged populations
- explain how governments and local authorities in the UK and elsewhere supervise and exercise control over tourism
- appreciate the changing role of public-sector tourism in the UK.

The focus was on the tourist industry and of course what we really need is for people to go into the shops and start buying again. If that starts, with tourists visiting our shores stimulating the retail side, and is followed by our own ordinary citizens going about their shopping and beginning to spend again, then we begin to lift out of the crisis.

Michael Noonan, Irish Finance Minister, discussing the economic crisis impacting on Ireland (Carty *et al.* 2011)

Introduction

Tourism often plays an important part in a nation's economy by providing opportunities for regional employment, contributing to the balance of payments and stimulating economic growth. Countries that experience an influx of large numbers of tourists, however, also suffer the environmental and social consequences of mass tourism, unless care is taken to plan for and control the flow of tourists. Any economy that has become overly dependent on tourism can be massively weakened by a single political or natural disaster which dissuades tourists from visiting – as the chaos created in Bali following the terrorist strike there has shown. Tourists in the generating countries were 'strongly advised' against travelling to Indonesia for a whole year after the event and, as a result, tourism virtually came to a halt. Neither does it necessarily benefit a country to switch labour and other resources away from, say, agriculture towards tourism. For both economic and social reasons, therefore, governments cannot let market forces rule – they must take a direct interest in the ways tourism affects their country. The more dependent a nation becomes on tourism, whether domestic, inbound or outbound, the more likely it is that the government will intervene in the industry's activities.

The nature of government involvement

A country's system of government will, of course, be reflected in the mode and extent of public intervention. At one end of the scale, centrally planned economies may choose to exercise virtually complete control, from policy-making and planning to the building and operating of tourist facilities, the organization of tourist movements and the promotion of tourism at home and abroad. Since the collapse of the Soviet Union, such central control is now limited to a very few countries and even some of those nations still ostensibly operating centrally planned economies – China, Cuba and Vietnam, for example – recognize and accept the importance of private enterprise, and the benefits of private investment, in their tourism planning. China, ostensibly a centrally controlled economy, happily co-operates with privately owned American hotel interests to establish chains of hotels in popular tourist destinations throughout the country and accepts the independent movement of tourists on itineraries tailor-made by Western operators. Even Saudi Arabia, which for cultural and political reasons has long restricted the movement of independent Western tourists, is easing its constraints and allowing some freedom of movement for foreign tourists. Only North Korea and Turkmenistan still control tourism so rigidly that independent travel around either country is impossible.

Most other nations have mixed economies, in which public and private sectors coexist and collaborate in the development of tourism within their borders; only the balance of public versus private involvement will vary. The USA, with its belief in a free enterprise system and a federal constitution, delegates much of the responsibility for overseas promotion of the nation either to individual states or even to private organizations created for the purpose. Central government intervention in the USA is limited to measures designed to protect the health and safety of its citizens (such as aircraft safety and air traffic control). It even disbanded its public tourism body, the US Travel and Tourism Administration, in 1996, allowing private enterprise to fund overseas marketing. The public body has been replaced by the privately sponsored US Travel Association, which markets the USA abroad under a number of brands, including the Visit USA Association, Discover USA and Discover America, in some cases maintaining an office abroad to serve the trade's (but not the public's) needs.

Table 17.1 Government departments responsible for tourism in a selection of countries

	Country	Government department
Tourism	India	Ministry of Tourism
	Malaysia	Ministry of Tourism
	Kenya	Ministry of Tourism
Industry/economy	France	Economy, Finance and Industry
	Germany	Economics and Technology
	Hong Kong	Commerce and Economic Development Bureau
Environment	Namibia	Ministry of Environment and Tourism
	Tanzania	Minister for Natural Resources and Tourism
	Bosnia and Herzegovina	Ministry of Environment and Tourism
Art and culture	Maldives	Ministry of Tourism, Arts and Culture
	Korea (republic)	Ministry of Culture, Sports and Tourism
	UK	Department for Culture, Media and Sport
Other fields	Australia	Department for Resources, Energy and Tourism
	Greece	Ministry of Development
	Ireland	Department of Transport, Tourism and Sport

Source: C. Humphreys, author's own research based on ministry of tourism websites, 2011

Public ownership of transport is also generally declining, as rail and air services are denationalized, but in some developed countries there are still examples of widespread public ownership. The French government, to cite one example, owns 100% of SNCF, the French rail network, and 18.6% of Air France–KLM, while the majority of French airports are in public ownership (ACI Europe, 2010). Public ownership of the railways undoubtedly made it easier to invest in the hugely expensive TGV network for which the country is now famous.

The system of government is not the only factor dictating the extent of state intervention. If a country is highly dependent on tourism for its economic survival, its government is likely to become far more involved in the industry than would be the case if it were less important. The government department to which the responsibility for tourism is allocated can highlight the perspective and importance placed on tourism by its government (see Table 17.1).

The relative importance attached by government to tourism in the UK can be judged by the amalgam of responsibilities assigned to the Department for Culture, Media and Sport. Not only does tourism not appear in the title of the department, the job title of the minister within the department is Minister for Tourism and Heritage; this minister is now responsible for Heritage and the Built Environment, the Royal Parks and Royal Household, the National Lottery, Licensing, Gambling and Horseracing, in addition to tourism.

Countries where tourism has only relatively recently become a significant factor in the economy, and where that sudden growth has become problematic, are likely to exercise stronger control over the development of tourism than are those where tourism is either in its early stages of development or has developed slowly over a long period of time. Mauritius, for example, recognized that the wave of visitors it experienced in the early 1980s could soon lead to the country being swamped by tourists, destroying the very attractions that had brought them to the islands in the first place, unless the government took steps to control such key activities as hotel construction. Tunisia, too, learned that lesson and introduced control over hotel and other construction related to tourism early in the development of mass tourism to that destination.

Unfortunately, the potential for quick riches can exercise a greater influence than the long-term interests of the country, and there are all too many examples of countries that have suffered from lack of sufficient control over building and development, leading eventually to a drop in visits as tourists turn to less exploited destinations. Overbuilding in Spain was held up as an example in the late 1960s and could have influenced subsequent development in other Mediterranean countries to which tourists turned *en masse* somewhat later. Nevertheless, the 1980s and 1990s witnessed overdevelopment in some key regions – first in Greece, then in the Portuguese Algarve and, later (despite initial efforts to control hotel-building), in Turkey. Corruption and nepotism – the significance of having influential 'connections' to overcome planning controls should never be underestimated – are very real enemies of sustainable tourism policies.

All countries require reliable supporting infrastructure in order to encourage tourism in the first place, which will inevitably involve local and central government. Adequate public services, roads, railways, harbours and airports must all be in place before the private sector will be interested in investing in the equally necessary superstructure of hotels, restaurants, entertainment, attractions and other facilities that will bring in the tourists.

EXAMPLE   **Investing in tourism for Vietnam**

Tourism is vital to the economy of Vietnam, but its ability to attract international visitors is seen to be lagging behind its regional competitors (WEF, 2011) despite its diverse culture and natural environments.

Anecdotal evidence (Modler, 2011) suggests that the majority of visitors to the country would be unlikely to return, put off by key infrastructure issues such as:

- severe traffic congestion and lack of pedestrianization which made cities such as Hanoi and Saigon rather unfriendly to visitors
- excessive air pollution marring the overall tourist experience
- rail and road travel that is slow and often uncomfortable, making some interesting tourist areas difficult to access
- scarcity of Midrange and luxury accommodation outside of main cities – although budget accommodation is plentiful and competitively priced
- international arrival by air only possible into major hub airports, restricting regional travel.

To try to attract more international visitors, including the higher-spending markets, the national government has invested 4 trillion VND (US$204 million) in enhancing infrastructure designed to benefit the local tourism industry.

The Ministry of Culture, Sports and Tourism has submitted plans to the central government to gain funding for investments which would see the development of rail links across the country, enhancement of the waterways of the Mekong Delta and improvement to the routes linking World Heritage sites in the country.

Developing nations may have a further incentive for involving government. Private developers may be reluctant to invest in speculative tourist ventures, preferring to concentrate their resources in countries where there is already proven demand. In this case, it may fall to the government to either aid private developers (in the form of grants or loans for hotel construction) or even to build and operate the hotels and other tourist amenities that will first attract tourists. Where the private sector can be persuaded to invest, it is often companies from the generating countries that first show interest, with the result that most of the profits are repatriated rather than benefiting the local economy. There is also the danger that private speculators will be more concerned with achieving a quick return on their investment rather than the slow but secure long-term development that will benefit the country most.

The state is often called on to play a coordinating role in planning the provision of tourist amenities and attractions. Supply should match demand as closely as possible, and only the state can ensure that facilities are available when and where required and that they are of the right standard.

As tourism grows in an economy, so its organization, if uncontrolled, can result in the domination of the market by a handful of large companies. Even in a capitalist system, the state has the duty to restrict the power of monopolies, to protect consumers from malpractices such as unfair constraints on trade or exorbitant prices.

Apart from these economic reasons for governments becoming involved in tourism, there are also social and political reasons. In many countries, especially in developing nations, national airlines are state-owned and operated. While, of course, the income accruing from the operation of the airline is important to the state, there is also the political prestige of operating an airline, even if the national flag-carrier is not economically viable. In other situations, certain airline routes may be unprofitable, but, if they provide a vital economic lifeline to the communities they serve, they will need to be subsidized by the government.

Governments also have a duty to safeguard a nation's heritage. Buildings of historical or architectural interest (particularly UNESCO World Heritage sites and others of international importance) have to be protected and maintained, as must landscapes of exceptional merit. The state will therefore fund national heritage agencies (such as English Heritage, Historic Scotland and CADW in Wales) and establish national parks to protect sensitive sites and buildings.

EXAMPLE

The US Forest Service enhances visitor appeal for Columbia River Gorge

Over the past 25 years, the US Forest Service has spent US$67 million purchasing land on the Oregon-Washington state border to enhance the Columbia River Gorge National Scenic Area. As part of its activities, the Forest Service has improved the woodland, removed an airstrip and rubbish dump, and constructed miles of cycling and hiking trails.

The Forest Service has also recognized the increased demand for recreation in the Gorge, and has been involved in balancing the demands from rock-climbers, mountain bikers and sailboards, with the need to protect the fragile plants and cultural sites. An estimated 2 million visitors head to the area annually, and persuading users to protect the very area they came to enjoy can be a challenge. Balancing protection with access - deciding where mountain biking or horse riding can take place, for example - is a difficult decision and one which can bring intense debate. The right to access public lands without restriction is an ideal which does not always fit with environmental protection and sustainability.

The Forest service also works with the Gorge Commission (a bi-state regional planning agency) to control - and enforce - planned development in the area, especially in the most visually and environmentally sensitive areas.

Source: Durbin, 2011

The long search for a third London airport was extended by several years while the government weighed up the relative merits of the economic benefits of a particular site and the environmental damage that the development would cause. Still more recently, a long-running conflict emerged in the UK between conservation and economic development over the construction of a fifth terminal at London's Heathrow Airport. Economics won out, but not before the construction had been delayed for many years, undermining the strategic importance of the airport vis-à-vis its competitors on the Continent. Needless to say, the power of political lobbying may be the critical factor in any decision made by the public authorities.

We can sum up by saying that a national government's role in tourism can be manifested in the following ways:

- in the planning and facilitating of tourism, including the provision of financial and other aid
- in the supervision and control of the component sectors of the tourism industry
- in direct ownership and operation of components of the industry
- in the promotion of the nation and its tourist products to home and overseas markets
- in supporting key tourism interests in a time of crisis.

This clarification of the range of activities that need to be undertaken by national governments is helpful when they are considering their own responsibilities in relation to the provision and management of tourism.

Planning and facilitating tourism

Any country in which tourism plays a prominent role in national income and employment can expect its government to devise policies and plans for the development of tourism. This will include generating guidelines and objectives for the growth and management of tourism, both in the short and long term, and devising strategies designed to achieve those objectives.

It may be the case that the government feels the need to invest in the tourism industry in order to 'pump-prime' or stimulate investment, development and growth in a sector of the economy. For example, UK government policy on tourism favoured investment in tourism to create employment opportunities, although the cost on the public purse was seen as a concern. While support for tourism was initially through grant aid, by the 1990s the government took the view that the industry was now 'mature' and further investment should be left to the private sector.

VisitBritain, as a quasi-autonomous national government organization with the responsibility to promote the UK abroad, has as its aims not just to increase the total number of tourists to the UK but also to spread visitors more evenly throughout the regions and across the months, to avoid the congestion of demand in the south and during the summer months. In Spain, as demand had already been created by the private sector for the popular east coast resorts and the Balearic and Canary Islands, its national tourist office policy has focused on promoting the less familiar north-west coast and central regions of the country, while coastal development has become subject to increasing control.

Tourism planning calls for research – first, to assess the level of demand or potential demand to a particular region; second, to estimate the resources required in order to cater for that demand; and, finally, to determine how those resources should best be distributed. As we have seen, demand is unlikely to be generated to any extent until an adequate infrastructure and superstructure are in place, but it is not sufficient simply to provide these amenities. Tourists also need staff to service the facilities – hotel workers, travel agents, guides – trained to an acceptable level of performance. Planning therefore implicitly includes ensuring the availability of a pool of labour, as well as the provision of apprenticeship schemes or training through hotel, catering and tourism schools and colleges to provide the skills and knowledge the industry requires.

In some cases, providing the facilities that tourists want can actually have a negative impact on tourism to the region. To take one example, while the building of airports on some of the smaller islands in Greece opened up these islands to larger flows of tourists, it made the islands less attractive to the upmarket high-spending tourists, who preferred the relative isolation that existed when accessibility was limited to ferry operations.

Government control over entry

Accessibility is a key factor in the development of tourism. It relies on both adequate transport and the absence of any political barriers to travel. If visas are required for entry to a country, this will discourage incoming tourism. At the beginning of the 1990s the UK imposed a visa requirement on citizens of Turkey seeking to enter the country. The Turkish retaliated by imposing a visa requirement on British visitors to their country. The flow of tourists was almost entirely one way, however, so the Turkish emerged as the clear losers, the visa requirement dissuading tourists from visiting their country.

EXAMPLE **Entry to the USA**

In 1988, the USA abandoned the requirement for visas for many visitors from Western Europe (albeit with some limitations that continued to hinder the free flow of tourism), having recognized the barrier that this bureaucratic constraint created at a time when other factors, such as relative exchange rates, were favouring the rapid expansion of tourism to North America. The political panic that followed the 9/11 disaster changed attitudes, however, and the US government tightened entry requirements, including the need for computer-scanning of passports. Biometric data (including fingerprinting and iris-scans) were taken on entry and visas, where required, became more difficult to obtain, with prospective tourists having to travel long distances to attend interviews at US embassies.

Since October 2005, the Department of Homeland Security requires airlines and cruise ships to provide details of their passengers, prior to arrival. The information required includes each passenger's full name, date of birth, gender, citizenship, passport details, country of residence, address while in the USA and arrival and departure transport details. This has raised debate regarding the rights to privacy, as well as concerns over protection and security of the data provided.

In additional to the information provided by the airline, from 2009 all visitors using the visa-waiver scheme had to apply for travel authorization prior to arrival. This operated though an online system called ESTA (Electronic System for Travel Authorization) and, although this service was initially free, a charge of $14 was introduced in September 2010 – $10 of which was used to fund promotional campaigns to attract more visitors to the USA.

The difficulty in obtaining visas and concerns that the increased security will cause problems for arriving travellers have combined with other factors to influence arrival figures. Despite a weak dollar, international arrival figures (excluding those coming from Mexico and Canada) took until 2010 to reach the levels that existed prior to the terrorist attacks of 2001, despite global international tourism arrivals increasing by almost 40% over the same period.

The ending of visa requirements for trips to the Baltic states following the collapse of communism in Russia and the satellite countries led to a substantial increase in tourist visits. Russia, by contrast, continued to insist on visas. The predictable result has been a drop in the numbers of visitors to Russia while the Baltic states have enjoyed a significant rise, which has accelerated since their entry into the EU. Ukraine and Georgia have also both since abandoned the need for visas for EU nationals, which will further encourage demand for visits to Russia.

Maximizing revenue from inbound tourism flows is always a temptation for governments, but it is a practice that backfires if visitors can simply switch to alternative destinations offering similar attractions. Arguably, long-haul travellers will be more willing to accept reasonably high visa costs when travelling extensively in a country, but such costs are offputting for short-break visits or calls by cruise liner (and St Petersburg has become an important port for cruises in the Baltic region).

China restricted access to leisure travel for its citizens by granting visas only for selected destinations, with only six countries having approved destination status (ADS) by the end of the 1990s. ADS allows Chinese visitors to participate in group tours for reasons other than business or education. The list of countries gaining ADS has expanded rapidly, however; at the end of 2007 the USA became the 95th country to be added, and there are now over 100 countries holding ADS. With 31.7 million Chinese taking trips overseas in 2010 and in excess of 50 million forecast to do so annually by 2015 (Euromonitor, 2011), countries gaining ADS are hoping to gain a significant share of this massive market. Importantly, although ADS allows Chinese companies to offer tours to the overseas country, the travellers still require entry visas and these are not always easy to obtain.

The benefits of expansion of the EU's Schengen Agreement for non-EU visitors

The Schengen zone has been significantly expanded since its introduction – eight eastern European countries and Malta were added in 2007 and Bosnia and Albania were included at the end of 2010 – so the Agreement now covers travel across 26 European countries. Border controls have eased for travellers between these countries. While EU travellers and visitors from the USA and Japan can travel without a visa in the EU zone, other travellers moving around Europe would have required a separate visa for each country they entered. Now, a single Schengen visa can provide access to all 24 countries, saving money as well as making travel across Europe more convenient, thus making Europe a more attractive destination for some international tourists.

It has been claimed that Chinese tourists are deterred from visiting the UK because it is outside the Schengen zone and therefore requires a separate visa. Additionally, the process is complex for the incoming Chinese visitor - applying for a Schengen visa costs approximately £55 at the time of writing and is valid across Europe, while a UK tourist visa costs £100, requires travellers to give a full set of fingerprints and takes four times as long to process. In 2009, 110 000 Chinese visitors came to the UK, compared with 2 million travelling to the Schengen counties (Foster and Moore, 2011).

The cost of obtaining visas as well as the complexity of applications can encourage travellers to choose to travel to countries that do *not* require visas.

Taxation policy

Government policies on taxation can impact on tourism, whether the taxes are applied directly to tourists (such as an entry or exit tax), the industry (such as on hotel accommodation) or indirectly (such as VAT or sales taxes, which can discourage shopping and benefit countries with lower taxes). It may even encourage day trips across borders to shop in areas where taxes are lower.

Transportation taxes, such as those introduced in 1997 both into and out of the state of Florida, increasing the cost of an airline journey for a family of four travelling to the Walt Disney World Resort by some £70 – a substantial percentage of their total flight costs – can have a significant impact on demand for a destination. Even within the EU, variations in taxation can have an impact on tourism flows. To take just one example, in 1993 Greece increased its airport departure tax threefold, to 5200 drachmas (roughly £15), a sum sufficient both to antagonize tour operators and to persuade the 'marginal' tourists to switch to other Mediterranean destinations.

The UK government's imposition in the 1993 Budget of an airport departure tax (Air Passenger Duty, or, APD) of £5 in the EU and £10 elsewhere was widely criticized in the press, and the decision to double this rate from November 1997 provoked fury in the trade. A further increase followed in February 2007, and in 2010 APD was calculated by using bands, based on distance and class of service. Band A (2000 miles) incurred a levy of £13.85, while at the top end of the scale band D (over 6000 miles) cost the passenger £98. Business class passengers are additionally penalized, paying double these rates. There are also some anomalies, caused because the band is calculated not on actual journey distance but by taking the mileage between London and the capital city of the country being visited. Thus trips to Los Angeles on the west coast of the USA are considered band B (determined by the distance between London and Washington, DC), although destinations in the Caribbean, a far shorter flight, are treated as band C (Ryan, 2010).

If the revenue raised by such taxation were to be reinvested in the tourism industry, there would be less of a sense of outrage, but when it is introduced purely as a convenient means of raising taxation, travellers often feel that it is an injustice.

More recently the government has proposed removing the APD, replacing it with an aircraft tax (paid on each flight, rather than on the number of passengers), which is aimed at encouraging airlines to ensure flights operate close to full capacity. This is seen as a small step towards making the industry 'greener'. A variable departure tax, to encourage passengers to make greater use of regional airports, rather than congested hubs such as Heathrow, has also been suggested. There has been some shift in government attitude towards these taxes, with the reduction in APD for long-haul flights out of Northern Ireland. However, whether this paves the way for further changes remains to be seen. Overall, when one considers the level of taxes paid against the low-cost fares offered within Europe by carriers such as easyJet, it is apparent that taxes can regularly account for as much as 25% of air transport costs.

EXAMPLE   **The Balearic Islands eco-tax**

In 2002, the Balearic Islands' government, composed of a coalition of Socialist and Green parties, introduced an eco-tax as a means of discouraging low-spending visitors and funding enhancements of the islands' infrastructure to attract more upmarket visitors. The local government was concerned that the islands were attracting some 7 million visitors a year, swamping the resident island population of 600 000. The tax was imposed on hotel accommodation, ranging from €0.25 to €1.00 per night for hotels up to the 4-star category, €2.00 for the 5-star category.

There was an immediate negative reaction from the tourist trade abroad, which argued that sales for flights and package tours would drop and it had been introduced too quickly for tour operators to add to their brochures. There were also complaints that the tax was unfair as it applied only to hotels, not unlicensed accommodation, villas, B&Bs or privately owned second homes. As a direct result, it was eventually agreed that the tax be collected directly from travellers at their hotels.

A year later, the tax was scrapped, when a new centre-right government was voted into power. During the time in which it was in operation, however, it is estimated that the tax raised more than £25 million to help fund tourism projects. While the overall number of visitors to the Balearics did drop 7% compared with the previous year, this could not be ascribed solely to the effect of the tax; visitors to the Canary Islands dropped a similar amount, and those from the UK actually increased by some 8%.

Facilitating training

Another important factor determining tourism flow is the attitude of nationals in the host country towards visitors in general and those from specific countries in particular. Governments in countries heavily dependent on tourism must mould the social attitudes of their populations, as well as ensuring that those coming into contact with tourists have the necessary skills to deal with them. Customs officers, immigration officials, shopkeepers, hotel staff, bus and taxi drivers must not only be competent at their jobs but also trained to be polite and friendly, as first impressions are vitally important for the long-term image of a country.

The USA is one of several countries that have found it necessary to mount campaigns to improve the politeness and friendliness of officials dealing with incoming visitors, while some Caribbean governments have run training programmes to reduce xenophobia among the local populations and make residents aware that their economy depends on incoming tourism. In the UK, the government has supported industry moves to improve social and personal skills in handling foreign tourists, with training programmes such as Welcome Host, International Welcome Host and Welcome Management. Encouragement has also been given to learning foreign languages – a major weakness among personnel in the UK's tourism industry.

The responsibilities of central and local government

The very complexity of tourism makes its administration difficult as it does not sit easily in any one sector of government. For example, although responsibility for tourism in the UK lies with the Department for Culture, Media and Sport (DCMS), there are clearly other departments with a direct interest in the industry, including the Department for Environment, Food and Rural Affairs (DEFRA), the Department for Transport (DfT), and the Department for Business, Innovation and Skills (BIS) (its responsibilities include consumer affairs, employment relations and higher education). In practice, coordination between these various departments is difficult to achieve, hindering the effectiveness of the overall planning of tourism initiatives within the country. It is further hindered by the fact that the Scottish Parliament and the Welsh Assembly have responsibility for tourism within their own region.

The responsibilities of central and local governments will also differ with respect to issues affecting tourism. Local government may be responsible for planning, policy and infra-structure and, as a consequence, have to address a number of issues that directly affect visiting tourists, including the provision of car and coach parking, litter control, maintenance of footpaths and promenades, public parks and gardens and, where appropriate, beach management and monitoring of seawater for bathing. These responsibilities are, to some extent, split between city and regional councils, and conflicting views may surface between local authorities, as well as between local and central government. Local authorities are, of course, greatly influenced by the views of their local taxpayers, who are often unsympathetic to the expansion of tourism in their area, particularly if it is already popular with tourists. In countries where tourism is not a statutory obligation of local authorities (and the UK is one such example), they may not legally have to include tourism in their plans or provide funding for resources for tourists. This issue comes to the fore in times of cutbacks, when funding of non-statutory activities is often closely reviewed. To take one example, in 2010, as part of wider government cuts, it was announced that VisitBritain, the national tourism organization, would lose 34% of its funding over the period to 2014.

Financial aid for tourism

Governments contribute to the growth of tourism by financing the development of new projects. On a massive scale, tourist resorts have been constructed around Cancún on

Mexico's eastern coast, while in the 1970s the Languedoc–Roussillon area in the south of France was the subject of development that included draining swampland and eradicating mosquitoes in order to build five new tourist resorts, including the now well-established Cap d'Agde and la Grande Motte. The success of these ventures demonstrates the effectiveness of large-scale private/public-sector cooperation in building new tourism resorts from scratch, with the public sector providing the huge funds necessary to acquire land and build the necessary infrastructure.

On a smaller scale, governments may also provide assistance to the private sector in the form of financial aid, offering loans at preferential rates of interest or outright grants for schemes that are in keeping with government policy. One example of the way in which such schemes operate in developing countries is for loans to be made on which interest only is paid during the first few years, with repayment of capital postponed until the later years of the project, by which time it should have become self-financing.

Other forms of government aid include subsidies such as tax rebates or tax relief on operating expenses.

EXAMPLE   **India subsidizes hotel improvement for the Commonwealth Games**

In October 2010, India hosted this international event, with extensive press coverage raising concerns in the run up to the Games that facilities and infrastructure would not be ready, particularly focusing on problems with stadiums and the athletes' village.

In June 2010, just four months prior to the opening ceremony, the Indian Ministry of Tourism announced some interest subsidies for hotel and guest house owners wanting to take on loans which would upgrade the quality of their bedrooms and communal areas. The goal was to encourage improvements in facilities in time for the Games. Improvements could include providing new flooring, room furniture (such as new beds, tables and chairs, cupboards and luggage racks), bathroom fixtures and air conditioning. Interestingly, a minimum of 7.5% of the loan had to be spent on improving the external façade of the building. The subsidy was only available to licensed accommodation, approved by the Ministry of Tourism.

Perhaps the biggest issue with this proposal related to the very tight timeframe – as the goal was to encourage improvements in time for the Games, all works were required to be completed by September 2010, even though, in some cases, local planning permission for the exterior work was necessary.

Government support is also necessary at a time of catastrophe. The recovery of popular Asiatic resorts following the disastrous tsunami in 2004 has depended on a programme of massive international government aid, supported by direct contributions from millions of ordinary people around the world. Similarly, in the UK, after the devastating outbreak of foot and mouth disease in 2001, the government stepped in to offer financial aid to small tourism businesses in rural areas; they were granted 95% tax relief, and the Welsh Assembly extended 100% rate relief to Welsh businesses with higher rateable values. Central government grants were also made available in the affected areas for marketing and investment in information technology.

Apart from financial aid from a country's own government, public-sector funds are also available from sources overseas. Within Europe, the European Investment Bank (EIB) provides loans at commercial rates of interest to small companies (normally those employing fewer than 500 staff). These loans have been provided for up to 50% of fixed asset costs, with repayment terms of up to eight years, and the interest rates may be slightly lower in the EU's designated 'Assisted Areas'.

The European Regional Development Fund (ERDF) offers financial assistance for a range of initiatives, including many tourism projects. Between 2000 and 2006, funding was provided based on three objectives: focusing on promoting development in impoverished areas, supporting areas facing structural difficulties and supporting the modernization of training and education.

The 2007/13 plans focus on three new objectives: convergence, regional competitiveness and employment and territorial cooperation. Funds of €308 billion are to be allocated. Convergence (perhaps closest to 2000/06's first objective) seeks to assist the least-developed regions, and the bulk of the funding (over 80%) is allocated to this goal. The funding to address these three objectives can be used not only as pump-priming for attractions directly aimed at tourists, such as museums, but also for infrastructure to support tourism, such as airports or car parking facilities.

To be eligible to receive ERDF convergence funding, regions must have incomes lower than 75% of the EU average (although there is some funding available under the European Cohesion Fund for areas where income is below 90% of European average). Areas that are eligible include the recent accession countries as well as:

- Germany – Brandenburg-Nordost, Mecklenburg–Vorpommern, Chemnitz, Dresden, Dessau, Magdeburg, Thüringen
- France – Guadeloupe, Martinique, Guyane, Réunion
- Italy – Campania, Puglia, Calabria, Sicilia
- Spain – Galicia, Castilla-La Mancha, Extremadura, Andalucía
- UK – Cornwall and Isles of Scilly, West Wales and the Valleys.

EXAMPLE · Tourism projects receiving ERDF funding

Location	Project	ERDF contribution
Belarus, Latvia and Lithuania	Exciting Cycling Net - developing cycle tourism routes, information panels and signage, and almost 100 rest areas.	€775 000 between November 2005 and October 2007
Province de Hainaut, Belgium	Restore the former colliery at Bois du Cazier as a visitor facility, attracting 30 000 tourists annually. This included developing displays of ironworking and museum artefacts.	€15 798 800 between 1994 and 2006
Bramsche, Niedersachsen, Germany	Developing a new visitor centre located at the entrance to Kalkriese Museum and Park. This provides amenities and a shop as well as space for exhibitions and events linked to the surrounding sites.	€1 500 000 between July 2007 and March 2009
Hagar Qim and Mnajdra, Malta	Temporary shelters were provided to cover the sites of two Maltese megalithic temples. These shelters ensure long-term conservation of the temples as well as offering shelter to visitors on hot or rainy days.	€3 220 000 between 2004 and 2006
Praha, Czech Republic	Reviving gardens in the heart of Prague to provide visitors with a unique place to relax. Statistics indicate that visitors paying to see the gardens doubled to 6500 in 2009.	€5 627 600 between 2004 and 2006

Source: EU, 2011

Social tourism

One aspect of public-sector support for tourism is to be found in the encouragement offered by way of **social tourism** – little-known, at least in the UK, but now receiving greater attention in academic literature and tourism education.

The concept of social tourism has been used in several contexts, so it is difficult to provide one specific definition. In some cases, this term is used to propose the idea that the opportunity to take a holiday is a human right and there should be provision by the welfare state for those unable to afford to take a holiday. From a supply side, the term is often used when considering circumstances in which governments encourage tourism to specific areas in order to promote economic development. To provide an encompassing definition, Minnaert *et al.* suggest that 'social tourism is about encouraging those who can benefit from tourism to do so. This may represent a wide variety of groups, such as the host population of an exotic destination, tourists on a cultural holiday, persons with disabilities, their carers, the socially excluded and other disadvantaged groups' (2006, 9).

Economic support to encourage social tourism may be offered in the form of finance (grants, low-interest loans and the like) or direct support, such as the provision of free coach trips or holiday accommodation. One might also use this generic term to include the public funding of health tourism, which some countries' governments have subsidized as part of the general public health and wellbeing of its population. This is often the case for countries which have planned economies. In mixed economies like those in Europe, several countries have been active in providing subsidized tourism for their deprived citizens, led by Belgium, France and the southern countries of the EU. Indeed, the Brussels-based International Organization of Social Tourism (OITS) – formerly the International Bureau of Social Tourism (BITS) – has been active since 1963 as a base for the study and debate of social tourism issues and maintains a data bank, issues publications and conducts seminars on the subject.

EXAMPLE **EU funds social tourism development**

Calypso is a European Commission (EC) project focused on promoting social tourism. It aims to extend travel opportunities to under-privileged groups as well as boosting local economies and employment opportunities (Calypso, 2011). It is particularly interested in expanding demand in off-peak periods to overcome the problems caused by intense seasonality.

It particularly focuses efforts on four target groups:

- seniors
- youths (18–30)
- people with disabilities
- families on low incomes.

The aim is to encourage these target groups to participate in cross-border tourism, in order to experience the different cultures and lifestyles of European neighbours.

To achieve this, the Calypso project has sought to bring together experts in this field to catalogue best practice, to survey existing provision and impacts and to suggest ways in which to develop schemes for social tourism. The budget for these activities is now €1.5 million, funding the three phases running from 2009-11.

There are well-established programmes of aid on the Continent for holidays for the mentally, physically and socially handicapped, although financial pressures are reducing these opportunities. The French government, for example, terminated its programme of welfare-funded spa holidays in 1999 – a severe blow to the spa tourism industry, which hosted over 600 000 French visitors who had been able to recover up to 70% of their costs through their social security system. Other now well-established programmes of social tourism remain in place, however.

Little support of this kind is provided in the UK for the disadvantaged, although the UK has over 6 million registered disabled people. Responsibility for providing this service is delegated to local authorities (the Chronically Sick and Disabled Act 1970 imposed a statutory duty on local authorities to fund holidays for the disabled). Many authorities used to provide coach outings for the elderly and other disadvantaged groups, but, over the past 20 years, cutbacks in local authority funding have sharply reduced these services, and the number of those receiving financial help from local councils has slumped. The result has been that social tourism has largely become the responsibility of the private sector.

Sponsored by the then English Tourist Board, and with the full support of the travel industry in the UK, the Holiday Care Service was set up in 1981. Essentially, it provided information about holiday opportunities for the disadvantaged; later, this was expanded to include training programmes for members of the tourism industry. A number of specialist operators then turned to catering for the needs of these groups or providing discounted holidays for those with limited means. These responsibilities are now vested in Tourism for All, which is a national charity. The Travel Foundation also provides help for disadvantaged holidaymakers with financial support from the industry.

EXAMPLE   The Family Holiday Association

A UK national charity, the Family Holiday Association (FHA), promotes holidays for disadvantaged families. It suggests that holidays benefit individuals as well as wider society, through:

- improving wellbeing and reduce stress
- increasing self-esteem and confidence
- strengthening family communication and bonding
- providing new skills, widening perspectives and enhancing employability
- giving long-lasting, treasured memories
- resulting in happier, stronger families and a more inclusive society.

Poverty is the principal reason for one out of three people in the UK not going on holiday at all. The FHA was set up in 1975 to provide grants that would make a holiday possible for this group. The FHA evaluated government data to estimate that 2.2 million families don't go on holiday each year because they are unable to afford the cost. With a budget of just over £1 million, in 2009 the FHA enabled around 1600 families to enjoy a holiday, and over 100 000 people have been helped since its foundation.

The FHA has a high profile in the industry, with strong support from ABTA and AITO. It is funded largely by individual donations, but is also helped by trusts, corporate donations and income received from fundraising events.

Further information: **www.fhaonline.org.uk**

Holidays are also organized by the trade unions in the UK, which have established holiday homes and subsidize holidays for their members. Other bodies arranging holidays for the disadvantaged include Mencap, the Red Cross, Multiple Sclerosis Society and Winged Fellowship Trust. Both SCOPE (formerly the Spastics Society) and the Spina Bifida Association also own holiday homes where holidays can be provided for those suffering from these illnesses.

The UK government's involvement in helping the disadvantaged in this area is largely restricted to ensuring adequate access to tourism attractions, hotels and so on for the disabled. The Disability Discrimination Act (1995) (DDA) has had a profound effect on tourist facilities in the UK, necessitating their making substantial investments to meet the conditions of the Act. Services (including the provision of information for the blind and deaf, for example) have had to be accessible to the disabled since the final part of the Act came into effect towards the end of 2004, although there are exemptions granted in the case of heritage buildings that are impractical to convert. In 2010, the Equality Act replaced most of the DDA, further extending the rights of people with disabilities, and their carers.

Supervision and control of tourism

The state plays an important part in controlling and supervising tourism, as well as helping to facilitate it, where it is deemed necessary. It will, for example, intervene to restrain undesirable growth or unfair competition or, alternatively, help to generate demand by improving infrastructure or encouraging the building of hotels (as the Development of Tourism Act did in the UK in 1969). Governments also play a role in maintaining quality standards and protecting all consumers (in this case, tourists) from business malpractice or failure.

Local government may introduce visitor management policies (details of which are provided in Chapter 16) to control both the numbers visiting destinations and their actions and behaviour there. Visitor management may be enforced by local government, but it is often implemented both by government initiatives and the activities of private-sector tourism businesses.

A government can act to restrain tourism in a number of ways, whether through central directives or local authority control. Refusal of planning permission is an obvious example exercising control over the development of tourism. This is seldom totally effective as a mechanism, however, as when an area is a major attraction for tourists, the authorities will be unlikely to dissuade visitors simply by, say, refusing planning permission for new hotels. The result of such actions may simply be that overnight visitors are replaced by excursionists, or private bed-and-breakfast accommodation moves in to fill the gap left by the lack of hotel beds. For example, Cornwall has had measures to control caravan sites since 1954, but the local authority has still found it difficult to prevent the growth of unlicensed sites.

Up to a point, planning for the more extensive use of existing facilities can delay the need to de-market certain attractions or destinations, but it is undoubtedly true that some tourist destinations are victims of their own success. Only in extreme cases are tourists totally denied access to destinations or attractions. In France, the prehistoric cave paintings at Lascaux have been so damaged by the effect of countless visitors' breath changing the climate in the caves that the French government has been obliged to introduce a total ban on entry to the site. An artificial replica has been built on an adjacent site, however, and it continues to attract many visitors.

In recent years, the UK has debated the need to follow the example of some of its other European neighbours in attempting to stagger holidays, by means of legislation, with the Government's Educational Secretary, Michael Gove, suggesting, in 2011, that schools

Table 17.2 School holidays across Europe

Country	School summer vacation period
Austria	9 weeks between early July and early September
Denmark	6 weeks between end of June and early August
England and Wales	6 weeks between mid July and early September
France	9 weeks between early July and early September
Germany	6 weeks – staggered – between end of June and mid-September
Greece	12 weeks between mid-June and mid-September
Italy	12 weeks between June and September
Portugal	12 weeks between mid-June and early September
Spain	11 weeks between late June and mid-September

Source: Loveys, 2011

should move to a six-term academic calendar, allowing staggered summer breaks which would fall between the beginning of July and the end of September. Even though holiday periods vary across Europe, it is clear from Table 17.2 that July and August will always see demand peak.

The staggering of school holiday periods is expected to aid the tourism industry and help avoid the worst peaking problems of the summer months. On the Continent, not only educational holidays but also industry holidays are staggered. In Germany, the *Länder* (individual states) are required to take their holidays on a rota basis over an 11-year cycle, thus avoiding the holiday rush that is common in the UK at the end of the school summer term. Factories, schools and businesses all plan their closures in keeping with the rota. France, too, divides the country into three zones, each of which takes the summer holiday at a different time. While this helps to avoid national peaking, it is not without drawbacks – for example, the mass exodus of German holidaymakers clogging the motorways from their particular *Länd* when their turn arrives!

Sometimes governments exercise control over tourism flows for economic reasons. Governments may attempt to protect their balance of payments by imposing currency restrictions or banning the export of foreign currency in an attempt to reduce the numbers of its citizens travelling abroad. The last significant control of this kind in the UK occurred in 1966, when the government of the day imposed a £50 travel allowance and France also imposed restrictions on the amount of currency that could be exported in the early 1980s. There is little evidence to suggest such controls are particularly effective in preventing the outflow of foreign currency and, since the advent of the free movement of currency within the EU, the right of its members to travel within the EU can no longer be restricted.

Whatever one's view of the euro, its introduction has benefited tourists, including the British and others who remain outside the common currency agreement, but who no longer have to change their holiday money as they move from one euro country to another.

Concern over safety is a government responsibility and all governments will take measures to enforce standards of safety and prosecute breaches of safe practice. Transport companies are obliged to meet the necessary criteria to obtain licences to carry passengers, and tour operators are also subject to certain controls through the imposition of Air Travel Organizers' Licences (ATOLs). In many countries (although not yet in the UK), travel agencies are required to have a government licence to operate, and in others tour guides are licensed by the government or a local authority. In France, motorboats must also be licensed, even in the case of visitors from abroad, following a spate of accidents caused by poor navigation.

EXAMPLE   **Airline safety a priority**

Tiger Airways Australia, a subsidiary part-owned by Singapore Airlines, was banned from operating flights to and within Australia by the Civil Aviation Safety Authority (CASA). The ban was introduced because of concerns over 'serious and imminent' safety risks (Parry, 2011). These particularly focused on pilot proficiency and fatigue management.

At a cost to this budget airline of US$1.6 million per week, the grounding has damaged the airline's reputation and impacted on those holidaymakers holding reservations. Although refunds were promised, this could take several weeks and meanwhile the cancellation of flights – more than 50 flights a day were due to take off – means that many won't make it to their holiday destinations (Heasley, 2011).

EU legislation protects tourists in a variety of ways, taking precedence over national laws. Legislation introduced in 2005, for instance, requires airlines to pay compensation to passengers for delayed flights, with the extent of compensation varying according to the length of the flight. Prosecution is enforced through the CAA.

Governments will intervene where it is thought that the takeover or merger of large companies could result in the emergence of a monopoly. In UK, the Competition Commission exists to investigate such situations, but, in general, it has taken a relaxed attitude towards horizontal integration on the grounds that tourists have not been disadvantaged by the moves. The EU, however, has tended to take a stronger line on this issue and has interceded in a number of cases in recent years, notably that of the proposed merger between BA and American Airlines.

Perhaps the most common form of government supervision within the tourism industry in all countries is to be found in the hotel sector. Apart from safety and hygiene requirements, many governments also require hotels to be compulsorily registered and graded; prices must be displayed, and buildings are subject to regular inspection. Camping and caravan sites may also be subject to inspection to ensure consistent standards and acceptable operating conditions.

Finally, the government's concern with quality will lead to setting up systems of inspection, where safety is concerned, or training programmes and other means to enhance quality where it is seen as sub-standard. Again, the UK has recently promoted schemes leading to publicly recognized standards of quality, including the National Quality Assurance Schemes (NQAS) and Visitor Attraction Quality Assurance Scheme (VAQAS).

The organization of public-sector tourism

Having looked at the various ways in which public-sector bodies concern themselves with tourism, we can now usefully summarize their main activities below.

For the most part, government policies and objectives for tourism are defined and implemented through national tourist boards, although, as we have seen, in many cases other bodies directly concerned with recreation or environmental planning will also have a hand in the development of tourism. These boards are normally funded by government grants and their functional responsibilities are likely to include all or most of the following:

- *Planning and control functions*
  - product research and planning for tourism plant and facilities
  - protection or restoration of tourism assets
  - human resources planning and training
  - licensing and supervision of sectors of the industry
  - implementation of pricing or other regulations affecting tourism.
- *Marketing functions*
  - representing the nation as a tourist destination
  - undertaking market research, forecasting trends and collecting and publishing relevant statistics
  - producing and distributing tourism literature
  - providing and staffing tourist information centres (TICs)
  - advertising, sales promotion and public relations activities directed at home and overseas markets.
- *Financial functions*
  - advising industry on capital investment and development
  - directing, approving and controlling programmes of government aid for tourism projects.
- *Coordinating functions*
  - linking with trade and professional bodies, government and regional or local tourist organizations
  - undertaking coordinated marketing activities with private tourist enterprises
  - organizing workshops or similar opportunities for buyers and sellers of travel and tourism to meet and do business.

National tourist boards will generally establish offices overseas in those countries from which they can attract the most tourists, while their head office in the home country will be organized along functional lines. This is demonstrated in Figure 17.1, taking the example of the Korea Tourism Organization. It has structured the responsibility for marketing tourism by generating regions, providing teams dedicated solely to the dominant markets of Japan and China, whilst the entire continents of North and South America, as well as Europe, are covered by one team. Domestic tourism is managed under the banner of 'tourism competitiveness', which includes the infrastructure development and investment teams, whilst the planning and administrative functions are managed within specialist departments.

In some countries, some of these activities may be delegated to regional tourist offices, with the national board coordinating or overseeing their implementation.

EXAMPLE **Washington is closed**

The Pacific coastal state of Washington has many attractions to bring the visitor to this part of the USA, including the landmark Seattle Space Needle or Mount Rainier; but a cut in budget from $7 million in 2009 to zero in 2011 has led to the closure of its State Tourism Office. Whilst many states are facing cutbacks in their government spending, the importance of tourism is often recognized, especially in areas where traditional manufacturing industries are in decline – Michigan, for example is launching the 'Pure Michigan' campaign to attract visitors to Detroit and the regions. Tourism is the fourth largest industry in Washington State, but tourism promotion will now be the responsibility of an alliance of members from the local tourism industry. Whether it can raise the funds needed for successful international marketing remains to be seen.

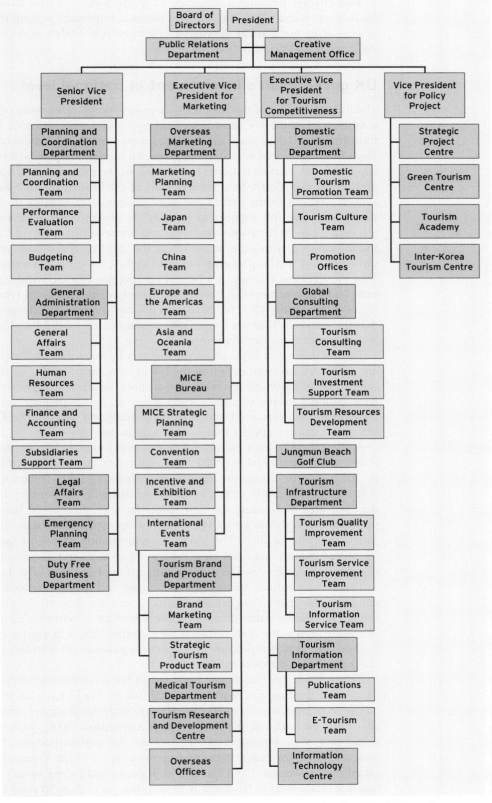

Figure 17.1 Organizational chart for the Korea Tourism Organization (South Korea)

This chapter provides a snapshot of public-sector tourism structure and operations by looking at the UK as an example, but it is important to note that the picture is not dissimilar in many other developed countries. It considers government involvement at national, regional and local levels.

UK government's involvement at national level

The illogical nature of the UK's tourism policy has been a feature of UK governments for a number of years. The promises of support and a recognition of the contribution that tourism can and does make to the UK economy, coupled with simultaneous cuts in government funding, lack of development grants for tourism in depressed regions, the decline in support for an English national board vis-à-vis the other national boards and its eventual absorption into VisitBritain, subsequently re-established in 2009 following a review, all suggest a failure on the part of successive governments to think through rational policies that would give full support to tourism. As evidence, we need to go no further than a speech given by the then recently elected Prime Minister, David Cameron, highlighting the importance of tourism in the UK as the third biggest export earner for the UK. Said Cameron, 'For too long tourism has been looked down on as a second class service sector. That's just wrong. Tourism is a fiercely competitive market, requiring skills, talent, enterprise and a government that backs Britain. It's fundamental to the rebuilding and rebalancing of our economy' (No. 10, 2010). Yet just two months later the government announced that the National Tourism Organization, VisitBritain, would lose more than a quarter of its funding over the next four years.

Further damage is imposed on the industry by the unfavourable rate of VAT on restaurant and hotel accommodation in the UK in comparison with that in other countries, the imposition of passenger levies on air transport (now seen by governments as a comparatively painless means of raising extra revenue), an inadequate transport infrastructure (notably the railways and London Underground) and the continued failure to provide an integrated transport policy that would facilitate tourism.

Against these failures, however, one can point to one clear success achieved through a public–private partnership (PPP) – that of the awarding of the Olympic Games to London in 2012. Against what were seen as overwhelming odds favouring Paris, the PPP was able to make an effective case, based substantially on the benefits that would accrue to a deprived area of London, the new sports facilities that would become available to the population and the increase in permanent employment for locals resulting from the construction of the facilities. The long-term rejuvenation of one of the most impoverished regions of London has been viewed by many as sufficient justification for the enormous expense that was incurred to develop the facilities needed to host the games.

This one important success in encouraging and supporting tourism is unlikely to be emulated elsewhere. Government efforts to increase domestic tourism have been largely limited to rhetoric rather than hard cash. While the government advocates a regeneration of seaside resorts, the costs involved are such that little is being done to halt their decline. In short, the increased pressure to cut back on government spending makes it unlikely that the policy of self-support will be reversed.

Before 1969, tourism played little part in UK government policymaking. Prior to that time, some funding was provided to establish the Travel Association of Great Britain and Northern Ireland in order to encourage travel to the UK from overseas. During the interwar years, this evolved into the British Travel Association (BTA), which was given the additional task of promoting domestic holidays for British residents, but no clear policies were laid down for its activities and its powers were limited. Voluntary tourist boards were established in Scotland in 1930 and in Wales in 1948 – the same year in which a board was first established in Northern Ireland. It was more than 20 years later, however, before a coordinated framework for public-sector tourism was established in the UK as a whole.

The Development of Tourism Act 1969 provided the first statutory legislation in the country specifically concerned with tourism. It dealt with the organization of public-sector tourism, providing financial assistance for much-needed hotel development and a system of compulsory registration of tourist accommodation.

National tourism boards in the UK

The first part of the 1969 Act called for the establishment of four national boards to be responsible for tourism and defined the structure and responsibilities of each of them. Initially, both the BTA and the English Tourist Board (ETB) were responsible to the Board of Trade, while the Scottish and Wales Boards were responsible to their respective secretaries of state.

All four bodies were established by the Act as independent statutory bodies and were to be financed by grants-in-aid from central government. Later, responsibility for the BTA and ETB passed to, first, the Department of Employment, and subsequently, in 1992, to the newly created Department of National Heritage, which absorbed a number of other related interests, including the royal parks and palaces, arts and libraries, sport, broadcasting and the press, as well as heritage sites. This department became known as the Department for Culture, Media and Sport when the Labour government came to power in 1997.

Further structural and cosmetic changes have since occurred. In 1999, the ETB's title was changed, to the English Tourism Council, and, in 2003, it was abolished as a separate entity altogether – its functions being integrated with those of VisitBritain, the new brand name for the BTA. Finally, it was again recreated in 2009 as a separate entity, VisitEngland.

EXAMPLE   The role of VisitBritain

With general responsibility for tourism throughout the UK, VisitBritain acts as an adviser to the government on tourism issues and is financed by an annual grant-in-aid from the Treasury, channelled through the Department for Culture, Media and Sport. Its mission is to 'build the value of tourism to Britain, working in partnership with the industry and nations and regions – in order to increase overseas visitor spend to all parts of Britain and improve Britain's ranking on the destination wishlist for international travellers' (VisitBritain, 2011). A recent report, commissed by VisitBritain to evaluate their work, suggests that they create £430 million in direct economic contribution to the visitor economy (Deloitte, 2010).

In light of funding changes announced in 2007, a review of the framework of public-sector provisions was undertaken. VisitBritain is represented in 36 markets globally, but, by 2008, they were reorganized into three regional hubs: Americas, Asia-Pacific and Europe.

In addition to marketing activities, VisitBritain also carries out research and liaises with the other tourism bodies in the UK. Unfortunately, funding cuts have led to staff reductions in both the UK and overseas, leading to some concern among industry professionals who believe that it may now be difficult for the organization to fulfil its role.

Following the devolution of power to Scotland and Wales, responsibility for tourism in these parts of the UK was placed directly in the hands of the Scottish Parliamentary and Welsh Assembly governments. In Ireland, following the 1998 Good Friday Agreement, The Northern Ireland Tourist Board, which reports to the Northern Ireland Office, united in 2002 with its opposite number south of the border, the Irish Tourist Board, to form Tourism Ireland for marketing purposes.

UK government's involvement at regional level

The changes in structure outlined above heralded even greater upheavals that were to affect the UK's public-sector tourism in the twenty-first century. One of the most significant changes was the rerouting of DCMS funds for the English board direct to the regional development agencies (RDAs), which were responsible for all economic strategy in the regions. However, government funding cuts led to the planned abolition of the RDAs (with a deadline for closure of April 2012), with government asserting that 'tourism, previously the responsibility of regional tourist boards within RDAs, will be passed to new Destination Management Organisations, which will be formed through existing tourism support bodies, councils, local business networks and new local enterprise partnerships' (Sandford, 2011).

The nine RDAs were set up in 1998, funded directly by the Department for Trade and Industry (DTI). Tourism was only one of the RDAs' remits, resulting in impacts in funding and support for organizations like the Regional Tourist Boards (RTBs). Historically, the RTBs supported the RDAs to produce a coordinated regional strategy for tourism, market tourism in the region and encourage the development and improvement of tourist amenities and facilities that meet the changing needs of the market. In the wake of the closure of the RDAs, several RTBs were closed, being unable to obtain government funding beyond March 2011. The full impact of this is yet to be seen, but in some cases Destination Management Organizations (DMOs), already in existence, are likely to become more prominent in tourism marketing and development. The North West RDA, for example, had established five DMOs, focusing on particular areas in their region:

● Visit Chester and Cheshire
● Cumbria Tourism
● Lancashire and Blackpool Tourist Board
● Marketing Manchester
● Mersey Partnership.

These bodies are designed to emphasize the importance of the destinations in marketing the region.

EXAMPLE **Supporting tourism in the Liverpool region**

The Mersey Partnership (TMP), acts to enhance the economy of the Liverpool region. Established in 1993, its mission is to support economic development, encourage inward investment and promote tourism in order to increase visitor numbers.

TMP is a membership organization, with over 500 affiliates, including:

● guest houses and hotels – chain and independently owned
● Liverpool John Lennon Airport
● Merseyside Guides Association
● sports organizations – for example, Liverpool and Everton football clubs, Formby golf course and Aintree and Haydock Park racecourses
● restaurants and bars – chain and independently owned
● Arena and Convention Centre Liverpool
● British Waterways
● visitor attractions – for example, Knowsley Safari Park and National Museums Liverpool.

TMP acts as a coordinating body (spanning six local authority areas) to speak on behalf of the region, seeking efficiencies in promotional and development activities to improve the image of the region as a place for business and to visit. In terms of the visitor economy specifically, they work to market the Liverpool Region as a tourist and conference destination, managing the **www.visitliverpool.com** website, which provides support and information for business and leisure travellers as well as conference organizers. The city's status as 2008 Capital of Culture provided a strong grounding for their promotional activities.

VisitWales, located in the Welsh government's Department for Business, Enterprise Technology and Science, acts as the country's tourist board, responsible for the promotion and development of tourism. They work with four regional tourism partnerships. These are:

- Tourism Partnership North Wales
- Tourism Partnership Mid Wales
- South West Wales Tourism Partnership
- Capital Region Tourism.

The principal role of these four organizations is to improve the competitive performance of tourism in Wales so that it better contributes to the economic and social prosperity of the area. Each organization works in partnership with VisitWales, local authorities and tourism businesses to market their respective destinations, as well as encouraging new product development and the enhancement of existing resources.

In Scotland, 15 area tourism partnerships now exist to address local tourism priorities in an integrated manner. The partnerships bring together representatives from the private and public sectors, such as tourism operators, local tourism groups, Chambers of Commerce, local authorities and VisitScotland. The partnerships are:

- Angus and Dundee
- Argyll and the Isles Strategic Tourism Partnership
- Ayrshire and Arran
- Borders
- Dumfries and Galloway
- Edinburgh and Lothians
- Fife
- Forth Valley Tourism Partnership
- Glasgow
- Highlands
- Lanarkshire
- North East Scotland
- Orkney
- Outer Hebrides
- Perthshire.

These area tourism partnerships are expected to design and implement plans which focus on the development and marketing of tourism in their region. These plans should work in alignment with the national tourism strategy. Funding these activities is achieved by encouraging the private sector to invest in initiatives which will ultimately assist in enhancing the profitability of their operations. The area partnerships also act as a lobby group, to actively voice the interests of tourism in the area.

Northern Ireland, in addition to its forming one region within the all-Ireland marketing consortium Tourism Ireland, also has regional-level organizations, although the current policy to remove regional level governance may well impact on this in the longer term. Currently four regional tourism partnerships exist, namely:

- Armagh Down Regional Tourism Partnership
- Belfast Visitor & Convention Bureau
- Causeway Coast & Glens Regional Tourism Partnership
- Western Regional Tourism Partnership.

The aim of these regional tourism partnerships is to 'support each destination in the achievement of its potential, through the delivery of a coordinated, customer focused approach to product development, industry development, visitor servicing and marketing communications' (NITB, 2011).

UK government's involvement at local level

We have now examined how tourism is structured at both national and regional levels, with particular reference to the structure in the UK. The third tier in this structure is the local authority level, where town, county and district councils also have statutory responsibilities and interests when it comes to providing tourist facilities – or, at very least, encouraging inbound tourism where the potential for it exists, as part of the economic development plans for the area. This will generally include the provision of TICs.

In the UK, the Local Government Act 1948 empowered local authorities to set up information and publicity services for tourism. This Act was reinforced by the Local Government Act of 1972, giving local authorities the power (but not the obligation) to encourage visitors to their area and provide suitable facilities for them.

Historically, the organization of tourism at local level has been piecemeal. Councils at county or district level on the whole relegate responsibility for tourism to departments that are also concerned with a range of other activities, with the result that it is seldom given the significance that its economic impact on the area merits. Up until 25 years ago, fewer than half of the local authorities in England included any strategy relating to tourism in their planning. Now this has changed. Research published in 2002 revealed that 80% of local authorities surveyed had a written tourism policy, with nearly all (98%) having a tourism strategy (Stevenson, 2002). The then ETB had offered guidelines for local authorities to follow when drawing up such plans. The following key points were emphasized:

- assess the number and distribution of tourists in the area
- estimate future changes in tourism flows and implications of this for land use
- identify growth opportunities
- assess the impact of tourism on employment and income in the area
- assess the tourists' effect on traffic flows
- assess the tourists' demand for leisure and recreation
- identify the need for conservation and protection
- evaluate the contribution tourism could make to development, especially in the use of derelict land and obsolete buildings.

Local plans should take into account the impact of tourism and the resultant need for car and coach parks, toilets, information centres, tourist attractions and local accommodation. The inadequacy of parking and toilet facilities in resorts has been a frequent topic of criticism, and cutbacks in local funding have magnified the problem recently.

The principal responsibilities of county and district authorities that bear on tourism are as follows:

- provision of leisure facilities for tourists (such as conference centres) and residents (theatres, parks, sports centres, museums and so on)
- planning (under town and country planning policies) – note that district councils produce local plans to fit the broad strategy of the county councils' structure plans and those plans are certified by the county councils
- powers to control development and land use
- provision of visitor services (usually in conjunction with tourist bodies)
- parking for coaches and cars

- provision of caravan sites (with licensing and management the responsibility of district councils)
- production of statistics on tourism, for use by the regional tourist bodies
- marketing the area
- upkeep of historic buildings
- public health, including food hygiene and safety issues, as well as litter disposal and the provision of public toilet facilities.

Local authorities may also own and operate local airports, although in many cases these are now in private hands. The provision of visitor services will normally include helping to fund and manage TICs, in cooperation with the regional tourist boards, which set and monitor standards. Local authorities will also fund tourist information points (TIPs), and information boards found at lay-bys, car parks and city centres.

The national Government Tourism Policy, launched in 2011, pays particular attention to local tourism provision – at the expense of regional tourism organizations – to encourage increased links between the public and private sectors. The policy aims to 'modernise and update local tourism bodies to become focused and efficient DMOs which are led by and, increasingly funded through, partnership with the tourism industry itself' (DCMS, 2011, 21). The expectation is that these DMOs will not be confined by the boundaries of the local and district councils, but work with all local authorities and tourism organizations at the destination.

Any DMO established is likely to act as a coordinator for tourism in the area, advising on development and grant-aided opportunities, and carry out research related to tourism in their area. They may become involved in the provision and training of tourist guides; and provide training in areas such as service quality and business development for SMEs – especially small businesses such as guest houses or cafés.

The DMO will also undertake a range of promotional and publicity functions, including the preparation of publications such as guides to the district, accommodation guides, information on current events and entertainment and specialist brochures listing, for example, local walks, shopping, restaurants and pubs. The cost of most of these publications will be met in part by contributions from the private sector, either through advertising or, as in the case of the accommodation brochures, through a charge for being listed.

DMOs may also organize familiarization trips for the travel trade and the media, and, if the resort shows sufficient potential, may invite representatives of the overseas trade and media. They frequently play a part in setting up and operating the local TIC, which may include a local accommodation-booking service. They may also produce a trade manual, aimed at the travel trade and giving information on trade prices, conference facilities and local attractions.

EXAMPLE   ## Local authorities encourage investment in tourism

Tourism planning and sustainable development form key elements of a local authority's functions. They may be as concerned to reduce or stabilize tourism as to develop it, particularly when local residents are opposed to any increase in the numbers of tourists attracted. For this reason, the authorities must be as sensitive to local residents' needs as they are to those of incoming tourists. They must convince the residents of the merits of public investment in tourist projects.

The development of conference centres in popular resorts such as Bournemouth and Harrogate was a controversial issue with local residents as very few private investors were willing to put money into centres such as these, but using public funds would have greatly increased the burden of debt on the councils initially. It is hard to convince local residents of the wisdom of investments that do not appear to provide a direct profit, but conferences do generate a healthy flow of indirect revenue as delegates spend money in local shops, hotels and restaurants. The added bonus is that much of this revenue will accrue outside the traditional holiday season.

It is not always easily achieved. The ill-fated regeneration of Bath Spa, where cost overruns spiralled to some £50 million as a result of mistakes in construction, led to a massive debt burden for local taxpayers, and delayed the opening years beyond the proposed completion date.

Tourist information centres (TICs)

TICs play a particularly important role in disseminating information about tourism, in the UK as elsewhere. There are well over 800 official TICs in the UK, with some 600 in England alone. Many TICs have been forced to become more commercial due to government policy and the decline in funding by cash-strapped local authorities, which do not, in fact, have a statutory duty to provide these services. Apart from the now well-established Book a Bed Ahead scheme, TICs are increasingly introducing commercial products for sale within their shops, while seeking ways to cut costs to remain viable. Cafés and shops have been combined with exhibition and interpretation galleries in many TICs to attract tourists and get them to spend money in the centres.

EXAMPLE **Funding cuts impact on the UK's tourism information centres**

One of the casualties of the UK government's funding cuts are the local TICs – between the summer of 2010 and the summer of 2011, 30 TICs closed (Rowe, 2011). As mentioned earlier, tourism is a non-statutory service – that is to say, it is not compulsory for local authorities to provide support for this sector. Although many local councils do recognize the economic benefit of promoting tourism, when funding is tight it is hard to justify financial support in marketing their destination when the private sector – attractions and hotels, for example – could fund their own marketing to tourists. This is not to say that the local authorities are entirely to blame; the loss of the RDAs has also reduced funding available for regional promotion.

One example is Cornwall, where the tourism budget was cut by 35% and three TICs were closed. In order for these to reopen, there is a need to adjust their operational model, ensuring that they can establish new income streams, becoming self-financing. Whether this is possible is questionable, especially in less-established tourism destinations.

A final point to make is the valuable contribution that TICs can make to tourism through the buildings they occupy. In many cases, TICs are housed in buildings of outstanding architectural or historic interest in a city (see Figure 17.2) and their careful preservation and adaptation for this purpose has ensured that the buildings are not only put to good use but also provide an additional point of focus for visiting tourists who are able to see the interior of a building that might otherwise be restricted. Increasingly, local authorities have come to recognize the important role that the TIC can play in drawing attention to modern design as well, whether in the traditional style and materials of local buildings, or in a more modern concept where the new building can itself become a stimulus for tourist interest.

Figure 17.2 Traditional architecture enhances a TIC in Mayrhofen, Austria
Photo by Chris Holloway

Information technology initiatives in the public sector

One means of providing tourist information cheaply is to have tourist information points (TIPs) – unattended stands providing information about local facilities. In many cases these will be located in TICs, but in some cases they are placed in popular tourist spots and can include sophisticated booking systems for local hotels, either using telephone connections or computer links (see Figure 17.3).

The computer-linked accommodation reservation system was just the first step into IT taken by the public sector. The UK boards have moved steadily towards developing and expanding their websites and now provide the public with a comprehensive package of information and booking services. The BTA devised its first VisitBritain website in 1997, incorporating details of tourist attractions, events and hotels, with accompanying advertisements. These have been complemented by national and regional boards' websites and, more recently, the development of an all-encompassing site known as EnglandNet.

EnglandNet has proved to be one of the most ambitious schemes undertaken by VisitBritain, originally in collaboration with the RDAs. This system allows companies to enter up-to-date information about their organizations into a central database, which is then used to provide website information for linked websites such as **www.enjoyengland.com** and **www.visitbritain.com**. This is of particular value to SMEs, enabling them to reach their customers more effectively online. The UK government provided grants totalling more than £3 million through the DCMS, but, following a spending review in April 2011, direct funding from VisitBritain was withdrawn.

Few can doubt that websites will become one of the most popular means of accessing information about tourism products and making accommodation bookings within the space of the next few years. Some local authorities are involved with plans to allocate rooms within their districts to tour operators for package tour arrangements. Although national tourist boards frequently provide information for the tourist – the VisitBritain

Figure 17.3 Roadside hotel telephone booking system, Mayrhofen, Austria
Photo by Chris Holloway

family of websites has reached 17 million potential visitors – it is likely to be the newly emerging DMOs that further the efforts to provide up-to-date information on attractions, accommodation and local events, all of which will encourage tourists to visit.

The wider influences of the public sector on tourism in the UK

While departments with a specific responsibility for tourism play a major influential role in the development and management of the industry, the diverse nature of tourism and its impacts on so many different facets of the economy mean that there are often other government departments that have a vested interest in the way in which tourism is planned and managed. Furthermore, there are also public or quasi-public bodies that, owing to their roles, impinge in one way or another on tourism.

EXAMPLE   **Transport and tourism**

The Department for Transport, quite apart from its public transport responsibilities, exercises control over certain types of signposting, and the signposting of attractions is of immense importance to the success of tourism. In January 1996, the relaxation of control over brown and white road signs for tourist sites led to information about these sites becoming far more readily available to passing tourists, enhancing tourist spend.

In 2005, the Peak District National Park, concerned about the increasing numbers of visitors it received each year (22 million at the time), proposed an environmental levy on cars visiting the park, but this was rejected by the Department for Transport (DfT).

The water authorities offer just one example among many non-government interests that relate to tourism, as water-based recreation has come to play an important part in leisure and tourism planning. Local authorities and water authorities are now fully aware of the commercial leisure opportunities associated with open expanses of water. In this respect, it is interesting to note the extent to which tourism was taken into account in the planning and development of the Kielder Reservoir in Northumbria compared with earlier reservoir development.

Opened in 1982, Kielder is the largest man-made lake in Europe, with a shoreline 27 miles long, and is set within the largest man-made forest in the UK, Kielder Forest (which is managed by the Forestry Commission). Accordingly, the area has huge tourism potential and facilities to attract tourists were planned from the outset, including picnic areas, campsites, water sports, fishing and mountain bike hire.

EXAMPLE   Licensing the waterways of the UK

Sailors bringing their own boats into UK waters and wishing to cruise the inland rivers and canals of England and Wales must obtain a tourist licence. The scheme is administered by British Waterways, a quasi-public organization, funded in part by DEFRA, in England and Wales, and in Scotland, the Department of Transport, Infrastructure and Climate Change. British Waterways looks after more than 2000 miles of rivers and canals, protecting both the heritage and built infrastructure as well as the surrounding flora and fauna.

The licence scheme for visiting boats offers daily, weekly and month-long permits, with a one-week pass costing between £20 and £50 depending on the size of the boat. This suggests that the organization is not seeking to raise huge sums from its visitors, but wishes to ensure boat regulation and safety on its waterways.

It is not just waterborne transport which must hold a licence. The canal-paths are a popular location for cycling and riders must also hold a permit – free to obtain, but which requires holders to agree to abide by a code of conduct aiming to protect the safety of all users and safeguarding the environment.

Other quasi- or non-governmental bodies with interests that touch on tourism include Natural England (incorporating the former Countryside Agency and English Nature), the Forestry Commission, the Arts Council, the National Trust and SportEngland; yet there is no common coordinating body to bring these interests together.

National heritage bodies

Heritage plays a particularly important role in tourism – monuments, historic homes and cathedrals make a substantial contribution to many areas' tourist attractions. Although many of these resources remain in private hands or are the responsibility of bodies such as the Church Commissioners, a number of quasi-public or voluntary organizations exist to protect and enhance these heritage sites. These bodies, therefore, fulfil an important role in the tourism industry. Even when heritage buildings are not open to the public, they still form an attractive backdrop to any townscape for passing tourists.

Internationally renowned UNESCO World Heritage sites draw people from all over the world, and are carefully protected. UNESCO works to protect sites of international importance, encouraging management plans to be developed to ensure the protection and conservation of its recognized sites (more than 930 were recognized in 2011). It also provides around US$4 million annually in funding support.

Public/private-sector cooperation

Due to the sheer complexity of tourism, there is frequently a lack of coordinated tourism policy at government level, while, at the same time, financial constraints are restricting public expenditure on tourism. As we have seen in the case of the UK, increasingly, the view is being taken that the public sector can best assist a country's prospects for tourism by reducing its role in development and promotion and entering into partnership with the private sector.

The desire to turn national tourism promotion over to the private sector or develop partnerships with the private sector has been led by developments in North America, where the USA abandoned its public-sector body in favour of the privately sponsored Travel Industry Association of America. Individual states have also gone down this road: Visit Florida is a public/private-sector partnership that is funded in part by taxation on car hire within the state and sponsorship from some 3000 members of the industry.

Regions, sometimes transnational, are also opting for a collaborative approach. An interesting example is that of the Øresund region, where Denmark is geographically separated from southern Sweden. The construction of a bridge linking the two countries has led to the formation of a joint marketing organization – the Øresund network – to promote the Danish islands of Zealand, Lolland-Falster, Møn and Bornholm and the Swedish region of Skåne. One notable effect of this marketing drive has been the economic improvement resulting from tourist flows into Malmø and southern Sweden, an economically depressed region. This exemplifies a general move to introduce DMOs that work to encourage partnerships between the public and private sectors in order to promote tourism to a region more effectively.

In the UK, Plymouth was the first city to launch a public/private marketing partnership, back in 1977. The city's marketing bureau draws its members from those nominated by the city council and others elected by the private sector. The bureau is financed by a grant from the city's council, membership subscriptions and commercial activities. Other cities and districts to have followed suit include Merseyside, Birmingham, Greater Glasgow, Sheffield and Manchester. Not all these public/private partnerships or private initiatives have proved successful; notable failures include the marketing bureaux of Chester and Bristol. There can be no denying, however, that the lack of collaboration between the sectors prior to the new partnerships was limiting tourism opportunities.

It should be stressed that public funds for private tourism projects have not ceased entirely. Many countries still offer subsidies in the form of grants, loans or other financial incentives that help to reduce costs for entrepreneurs in tourism. Where the state remains keen to see the development of private tourism, and funding for such development would not be forthcoming without direct public assistance, both central and local governments will still offer some measures of help.

Town twinning and tourism

No discussion of public-sector tourism can be complete without exploring the development of town twinning, even though the impact of this relationship between towns is seldom considered as an element of the tourism business.

The concept of town twinning emerged in the aftermath of World War II, as a means of overcoming hostilities between the warring nations and forging greater understanding between communities in different countries. Usually, the selection of a twin town is based on some common characteristics, such as population size, geographical features or commercial similarities. Local authorities and chambers of commerce arrange for the exchange of visits by residents of the twinned towns.

Although conceived as a gesture of friendship and goodwill, the outcome has commercial implications for tourism, as visitor flows increase between the twinned towns. While accommodation is normally provided in private homes, expenditure on transport, shopping and sightseeing can have a significant impact on the inflow of tourist revenue for the towns concerned, some of which may have little other tourist traffic. Friendships formed as a result of these links also lead to subsequent demand for travel. So far, no studies appear to have been made as to the financial contribution resulting from these links, but it is likely to be considerable overall.

EXAMPLE   Towns are searching for partners

Town twinning has been in existence for more than 60 years, and new relationships are frequently being established. In 2011, Dublin, Ireland, confirmed a link with Beijing, China. More than 900 UK towns have partners in France, 445 towns have counterparts in Germany and the USA has over 100 towns twinned with the UK (Baden, 2011).

Much of the enthusiasm for links is maintained within Europe. Supported, and partially funded, by the EC, through their 'Europe for Citizens' programme, towns and cities are uniting with a partner to encourage cross-border cultural connections. To help in the search for a suitable partner, the EC has developed a website **www.twinning.org** which lists more than 500 requests for partners.

The links provide more than an opportunity for the respective local government officials to travel abroad; local community groups are encouraged to establish links, and often schools develop associations to support educational trips. Often tourism can be encouraged – to take one example, in June 2011 more than 60 French tourists arrived in Lymm, Cheshire, from Meung-sur-Loire, their French twin. The visitors stayed for four days, taking trips into the surrounding region.

The role of the European Union (EU)

By contrast with some EU nations where tourism makes an equally important contribution to the economy, the UK has chosen, largely, to allow the free-market economy to operate in the tourism field, with little attempt to centralize policy-making. As the UK becomes more closely integrated with the EU, however, UK travel and tourism interests have become subject to EU legislation. Most importantly, since harmonization came into force at the beginning of 1993, any constraints of trade have been largely abolished, allowing travel firms to compete within the EU on an equal footing and without legal hindrance.

Within the EC, almost half of directorates general (the Commission's departments) have some responsibilities that impact on the tourism industry, although the Tourism Unit itself is allocated to the Directorate General for Enterprise and Industry. As with government departments in the UK, there is no system for coordinating tourism interests across the directorates general.

In 2010, the EC announced efforts to develop a new political framework to support tourism across member states. This recognized that the 'main aim of European tourism policy is to stimulate competitiveness in the sector, while being aware that in the long term, competitiveness is closely linked to the "sustainable" way in which it is developed'. The EC (2010) identified a number of planned actions including:

● developing a coordinated strategy to promote European heritage and the natural environment

- providing an information technology platform for tourism, which would seek to improve industry competitiveness
- promoting existing skills training programmes
- supporting a social tourism programme to encourage mobility
- developing an online information source to improve the coordination of school holidays
- improving research networks for tourism
- developing a 'Qualité Tourisme' brand to enhance consumer confidence and safety
- creating a 'Europe brand' and promoting the **www.visiteurope.com** website.

The future role of the public sector in tourism

It seems that there is greater recognition today, by governments across the globe, of the economic benefits of tourism. However, the recent economic downturn has left many governments seeking to make cutbacks, and for nations with a mature industry especially, funding the support for tourism now is an endeavour they wish to share with the private sector. There are, of course, still examples where governments are giving extensive financial support, often to develop a fledgling industry; the Chinese government, for instance, is offering financial support in order both to develop their domestic industry and to attract the international inbound visitor.

Security and cross-border travel remain important issues for many nations, as immigration and anti-terrorism legislation heightens awareness of homeland threats. Increased security at airports has lengthened the time required to reach the departure gate and this may, in the short term, lead to some travellers choosing domestic rather than international travel. Complex and expensive passport and visa requirements can deter travellers, leading them to choose alternative destinations with fewer restrictions, or to refrain from travelling at all if the problems are created by their home government.

The continued expansion of the EU may make cross-border travel more difficult to monitor – research into international tourism in countries with open borders has often had to rely on the accommodation sector for estimates of international tourism arrivals. Whether the borders continue to be truly open remains to be seen. A recent move by the government of Denmark has seen the reintroduction of border checks, though these are claimed to be only 'spot-checks' designed to restrict illegal importing, to avoid falling foul of EU regulations on the free movement of European citizens.

Summary

Governments across the globe are often interested in reaping the economic benefits that the domestic and inbound tourism industry can bring. We have also seen that, through social tourism initiatives, tourism can bring health benefits to disadvantaged members of the population. How, and whether, tourism is supported by government depends often on the ideological policies of government. Yet even in a free-market economy like the USA, we see governments, often at state level, providing support for the industry. The government department given responsibility for tourism can often say much about the attitude of government towards the industry.

A government becomes involved in tourism through the taxation policy it sets, the financial support it offers and the planning policies it provides, all of which may discourage or encourage tourism to take place. The government may also provide support for tourism development through training schemes and licensing programmes, which can often help to improve the quality of the tourist experience. These activities may take place at national, regional or local level, although we have seen in the case of the UK that the regional level of governance is being reduced in favour of greater local initiatives between the public and the private sector. Efforts to encourage partnerships with the private sector are likely to continue.

Questions and discussion points

1. The development of social tourism is encouraged through the EU Calypso programme. This suggests that it is beneficial for both the local population and for regions which host tourism. What are the main benefits of introducing a social tourism programme? Should tourism be considered a necessity, with holidays paid for by the state?

2. One activity historically undertaken by local government tourism organizations is that of marketing. In established and popular destinations, should spending on marketing and promotion now be left in the hands of the private sector, which are the businesses that gain from tourism spend?

3. In what ways has tourism in Europe changed as a result of the expansion of the EU?

Tasks

1. Select a country to investigate and produce a presentation which addresses the following three questions:

   (a) How are tourists or the tourism industry specifically being taxed by government?

   (b) How is the government financially supporting tourism activity?

   (c) Does the government encourage the improvement of the industry though schemes designed to enhance the quality of the visitor experience?

2. Explore the EU town twinning website **www.twinning.org**. This resource contains information about the towns and cities seeking partners, their characteristics and twinning preferences. Using the partners list, suggest an ideal match for your own town. Write a brief report which highlights why this is a good match and what benefits may accrue from creating this relationship.

Bibliography

ACI Europe (2010) *The ownership of Europe's airports*, available online at: http://ir.oma.aero/partners.cfm (accessed November 2011).

Baden, S. (2011) Twinning can boost economy, *Nottingham Evening Post*, 16 June.

Calypso (2011) *Calypso means tourism for all*, Luxembourg, European Union.

Carty, E., O'Mahony, B., McEnroe, J. and Cahill, A. (2011) Noonan calls on shoppers to save economy, *Irish Examiner*, 24 June.

DCMS (2011) *Government Tourism Policy*, London, Department for Culture Media and Sport.

Deloitte (2010) *The economic contribution of VisitBritain: Promoting investment, delivering value*, London, Deloitte, March.

Durbin, K. (2011) Forest Service land purchases heighten area's appeal, *The Columbian*, 3 July.

EC (2010) *Europe, the world's No 1 tourist destination – a new political framework for tourism in Europe*, Communication, COM (2010) 352 final, 30 June.

EU (2011) *Regional Policy – Project examples*, available online at: http://ec.europa.eu/regional_policy/projects/stories/search.cfm?LAN=EN&pay=ALL&region=ALL&the=79&type=ALL&per=2 (accessed November 2011).

Euromonitor (2011) *Tourism Flows Outbound in China*, London, Euromonitor.

Foster, P. and Moore, M. (2011) Red tape keeps Chinese tourists out of Britain, *The Daily Telegraph*, 15 February.

Heasley, A. (2011) Tiger boss quits as flying ban to be extended, *The Sydney Morning Herald*, 7 July.

Loveys, K. (2011) Summer school holidays could be slashed to just four weeks, says Michael Gove, *Daily Mail*, 21 June.

Minnaert, L., Maitland, R. and Miller, G. (2006) Social tourism and its ethical foundations, *Tourism, Culture and Communications*, **7**(1), 7–17.

Modler, M. (2011) A return trip too far, *Saigon Times Weekly*, 4 June.

NITB (2011) *Regional Tourism Partnerships*, available online at: http://www.nitb.com/DocumentPage.aspx?path=b019d219-34a1-48eb-8e21-900525c4e543,7cf01d89-6b8a-4a6f-a350-7005ea7a41c2,3502cb32-feb9-4819-8db3-819d14ad2d38,caa968c9-f7df-4cbb-9afc-48b523d8df55,87de4ebe-068b-4163-8972-cd62a64ffadd,d47a7151-124e-4454-9703-b0f3474198b8,800b2cf9-0f89-4ebb-bead-3388b4744d29 (accessed November 2011).

No. 10 (2010) *PM's speech on tourism – 12 August* available online at: http://www.number10.gov.uk/news/pms-speech-on-tourism/ (accessed November 2011).

Parry, M. (2011) Grounded Tiger Airways' future in doubt, *Agence France Presse*, 7 July.

Rowe, M. (2011) Will the big society fill the tourism gap?, *Independent On Sunday*, 26 June.

Ryan, R. (2010) Premium economy passengers hit by APD, *The Sunday Times*, 31 October.

Sandford, M. (2011) *The abolition of regional government*, House of Commons Library, 17 March, Standard Note: SN/PC/05842.

Stevenson, N. (2002) The role of English local authorities in tourism, *Tourism Insights*, January.

VisitBritain (2011) *Our strategy*, available online at: http://www.visitbritain.org/aboutus/ourstrategy

WEF (2011) *The Travel and Tourism Competitive Report*, Geneva, World Economic Forum.

Websites

enjoyEngland: **www.enjoyengland.com**

Family Holiday Association: **www.fhaonline.org.uk**

Tourism For All: **www.tourismforall.org.uk**

Town Twinning: **www.twinning.org**

VisitBritain: **www.visitbritain.com**

18

Tour operating

Contents

Learning outcomes

After studying this chapter, you should be able to:

- define the role of a tour operator and distinguish between different types of operator
- explain the functions of each type of operator
- understand how operators interact with other sectors of industry
- understand how the activities of operators are constrained
- understand the basic principles behind the construction and marketing of a package tour
- understand the appeal of the package tour to its various markets
- evaluate alternative methods of tour distribution and recognize the importance of new forms of electronic reservations and sales systems for operators and their clients.

Bare electric wires, Heath Robinson lifts and the absence of any real fire precautions or escapes are all part of the 'charm' of any holiday spent in a traditional hotel in many parts of Europe. Package holiday makers, cocooned in a more British-style modern hotel environment throughout their whole holiday, feel protected from such primitive risks.

Hope (1974) Holidays with risk, 371

Introduction

The package holiday has today made both the experience while away and the process of organizing holidays much more straightforward than in earlier times. For many holiday-makers, the convenience of booking a package, which provides all the component parts of the holiday, has encouraged travel to locations that otherwise they would not have considered. This has overcome language barriers, as well as concerns regarding the suitability of the products such as accommodation, airport transfers or tours; and all at a competitive price. Thus, the demand for packages has ensured that tour operators continue to have a significant role in the tourism industry.

Tour operators - why a European perspective?

The use of the tour operator as an intermediary in the travel booking process varies across nations. The decision whether or not to use intermediaries is influenced by a wide variety of factors, including the nature of travel (domestic or international) as well as the experience of the traveller.

It is often reported that the first tour operator was established in the UK, through the activities of Thomas Cook back in the nineteenth century. Many tour operators today, however, are mainland European companies; for example, both Thomas Cook and TUI are German-owned, while Kuoni, a leading long-haul operator, is Swiss. Furthermore, the largest outbound travel market by far is the European region. The United Nations World Tourism Organization (UNWTO) reported that in 2010 over 52% of global arrivals were from Europe, the next largest markets being the Asia-Pacific region and the Americas, with 21% and 16%, respectively (UNWTO, 2011).

The number of travellers from the European region has seen a slow but steady growth over the past decade (27% since 2000), but the Asia-Pacific region has experienced much more rapid growth, almost doubling over the same period (from 113 million in 2000 to 197 million in 2010). This region is dominated by the markets of Japan, South Korea and China, the latter moving to number three in the world outbound markets (by spend). That said, the spend from Chinese holidaymakers is still less than three quarters of that of German travellers (see Table 18.1). The North American market shows high levels of international spend, but much of this is inter-regional; in 2011, over 70% of Canadian international travel was to the USA.

For these reasons, this chapter is focused largely on the European tour operator industry, acknowledging the traditional role of the tour operator as well as changing trends that are placing great pressure on tour operators to adapt their activities.

Table 18.1 Tourism spend by top seven outbound markets, 2010

Europe	$US billion	Asia-Pacific	$US billion	Americas	$US billion
Germany	77.7	China	54.9	USA	75.5
UK	48.6	Japan	27.9	Canada	29.5
France	39.4				

Source: UNWTO, 2011

The role of the tour operator

For many years, tour operators have formed the core of what we understand as the travel industry, and, to a large extent, they can be said to have moulded the industry into the form familiar to us today. Traditionally, they provided an essential bridge between travel suppliers and customers, purchasing separately the elements of transport, accommodation and other services and combining them into a package that they then sold direct (or through travel agents) to consumers. Their position in the tourism distribution system is demonstrated by Figure 18.1.

Some take the view that tour operators are essentially wholesalers, as they purchase services from the principals in large quantities and break these into individual units to sell to customers. Wholesalers, however, are not normally known to change the product they buy before distributing it, so for this reason some argue that tour operators should be classed as principals in their own right, rather than simply intermediaries. Their argument is based on the premise that, by packaging a series of individual tourism elements into a single whole new product – the **inclusive tour** – the operator is actually changing the nature of those products. The service the tour operator provides is that of buying in bulk, thus in theory securing considerable discounts from the suppliers that could not normally be matched by customers buying direct. The operator is able consequently to assemble and present to the customer a package – the inclusive tour – that is both convenient to purchase and competitively priced.

Recent years have witnessed a change to the ways in which travel products are bought and sold by operators. In the last quarter of the twentieth century, operators had begun to sell unpackaged 'seat only' flights to agents and customers in order to fill seats on their charter flights, and, with the advent of the World Wide Web, which encouraged principals to sell travel arrangements direct to customers, operators have become far more flexible in marketing their products. Many now offer each element of their packages separately or give their clients the opportunity to book their flights direct while helping them to organize the remaining elements of their holiday separately. While traditional 7- and 14-day packages will remain a popular feature in most operators' brochures, more flexible durations as well

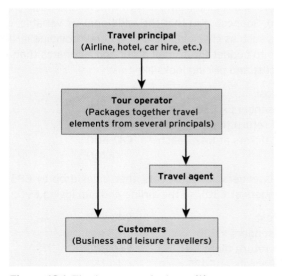

Figure 18.1 The tour operator's position in the chain of distribution

as tailor-made arrangements and individual elements of the package are now negotiable. The evidence in the UK is of a decline in the percentage of package overseas holidays – from 52% in 2002 to 38% by 2009 (ONS, 2011).

The packaging of travel elements by tour operators is also valuable to principals in the travel and tourism industry. The travel industry operates in a business environment where supply and demand are seldom in balance; neither can supply expand or contract quickly to take advantage of changes in demand. Both the airline and hotel businesses operate in circumstances that make it difficult to adjust their capacity in the short term.

The advantage of working with a tour operator – the case for airlines

Once a flight takes off, the airline has lost the opportunity to sell any empty seats on the plane, and therefore any potential revenue for those seats. Maximizing the load factor (the percentage of available seats filled by passengers) is therefore key to maximizing revenue. Tour operators can help ensure that more seats are sold.

A charter airline with a single type of aircraft – say, a Boeing 757–200 with a maximum capacity of 233 passengers – can neither expand the number of seats to take advantage of peak opportunities, nor reduce capacity if demand falls slightly. We say that supply is **lumpy**; that is, it cannot be expanded by a *single* seat, but must be expanded in *blocks* of seats – perhaps as many as 150 at a time in the case of aircraft. Carriers, therefore, seek ways to adjust demand to fill the available seats. It is important to do this to keep down costs per passenger and reduce the waste of resources, as flying an aircraft involves fixed costs regardless of the number of passengers on board, and those fixed costs are likely to be the major element in any transport costs. Tour operators have played a very useful role in helping to achieve this for the scheduled airlines, and, in return, the airlines can offer substantial discounts on seats that they know they themselves cannot fill. Example A demonstrates this.

EXAMPLE **A. Costing a scheduled flight**

Suppose that the fixed cost of flying a 140-seat plane from Paris to Athens and back is €43 540 (including capital costs, fuel, crew's pay and so on). Suppose also that the additional, or variable, cost per passenger is €30 (to cover administrative expenses such as check-in, the e-ticket and providing in-flight refreshments, extra fuel and so on). If the airline wants to budget for a small profit and estimates that, at a price of €425, it can expect to sell 112 seats, then the cost and pricing looks like this:

Fixed cost	€43 540
112 passengers × €30	€3360
Cost of return flight	€46 900
Sell 112 tickets at €425 each	€47 600
Profit	€700

Of course, in the example, if only 110 passengers are sold seats, then sales drop by €850 (two passengers at €425), costs by only €60 (two passengers at €30), so the airline ends up losing €90:

Fixed cost	€43 540
110 passengers × €30	€3300
Cost of return flight	€46 840
Sell 110 tickets at €425 each	€46 750
Profit/loss	–€90

The example shows a very simplified picture of pricing on a single route, but the complexity of pricing has substantially increased since the no frills airlines came into service, with the variations in prices becoming far wider (see Chapter 13 for a fuller discussion of this). Airlines also overbook in the expectation that a few passengers will not turn up in time for their flights, or will cancel without refund. Airlines retain the revenue (including tax, although this is only applied if passengers actually travel and, therefore, theoretically should be refundable), making a significant contribution to overall profit, especially if the seat can be resold.

Tour operators prove themselves useful to airlines by agreeing to purchase in bulk, say, 25 seats, which can virtually ensure that the airline will fly at a profit. The amount of discount that airlines give to tour operators must be considered, however. For example, if we continue with the example above, as far as the airline is concerned, anything above €30 a head will be profitable, as the fixed costs are already paid for. Tour operators will want the lowest price possible to ensure that they can resell all 25 seats. Obviously, customers are unwilling to pay anything like the original €425 that was being asked or they would have already booked with the airline itself. Let's say that, after negotiating, the airline agrees to sell the seats to a tour operator at a net price of €225 each. The airline's budget for this case is shown in Example B.

EXAMPLE B. Costing a scheduled flight with a tour operator

Fixed cost	€43 540
137 passengers × €30*	€4 110
Cost of return flight	€47 650
Sell 112 tickets at €425 each	€47 600
Sell 25 tickets at €225 each	€5 625
Revenue	€53 225
Profit	€5 575

* Assumes all 25 seats are sold by the tour operator.

The airline will now achieve a greater profit from this flight than before. What is more, it does not have to take responsibility for marketing the 25 seats, which the tour operator now must sell. This may involve heavy selling costs for the operator, but, as long as it sets a sensible price for each seat which will still deliver a profit for the company after paying overhead costs, the customers are able to buy seats that represent good value. A figure of €299 might be considered reasonable under these circumstances. To ensure that tour operators do not poach existing passengers, airlines usually impose various conditions on the resale of tickets. The main condition is that the tour operator must build the trip into a package, or inclusive tour, and publish a number of brochures to prove it.

As tour operators build their markets, they can eventually decide that they will have enough customers to fill an aircraft and consider either part-chartering a plane with other operators or even chartering a whole plane themselves. Eventually, they may be in a position to buy and operate their own airline to carry their customers, as do the leading tour operators in Europe.

EXAMPLE   **World of TUI Airlines**

European tour operator TUI owns several airlines, which provide charter flights to service their package holiday operations. In recent years, rebranding has led to the renaming of some of these operations and now TUI has more than 140 aircraft serving destinations both within and outside Europe. TUI-owned airlines include: TUIfly (Hapag-Lloyd Flug and Hapag-Lloyd Express), Thomson Airways (merging Thomsonfly and First Choice Airways) (ex-Britannia UK), TUIfly Nordic (Britannia Nordic), TUIfly Nederland (Arkefly), TUIfly Belgium (Jetairfly), Corsair.

Source: www.tui-group.com

The advantage of working with a tour operator – the case for hotels

In exactly the same way, hoteliers attempt to use tour operators to fill their unsold bedrooms. They, too, have substantial fixed costs in relation to operating their properties and so are willing to provide substantial discounts to operators and others willing to commit themselves to buying rooms in bulk. This is because, as with airlines, once the fixed costs of the property have been covered by revenue, any price that is greater than the variable cost will represent pure profit for the hotel, which will also then have the opportunity to sell extra services to its clients, such as drinks, entertainment and meals, those profits compensating for the low room rates that the operators have paid them. Furthermore, if the price is sufficiently attractive, the tour operator may even be able to provide the hotel with guests at times other than peak season. This will allow the hotel to operate all year round rather than have to consider closing during the off-peak period (closure means that no revenue is coming in at all, while the hotel will still attract costs for permanent staff, maintenance and so on).

Hotels in the Mediterranean have, historically, found it difficult to reach the North American market direct, so have been delighted for their hotels to be marketed by tour operators in those countries. As a result, they came to depend largely, and in some cases entirely, on tour operators to sell their rooms.

Some of the larger tour operators started to own and run their own accommodation, but in practice this proved more difficult, and most operators eventually divested themselves of their overseas properties, preferring to sign contracts with overseas proprietors, often for the entire capacity of the hotel and sometimes for several years in advance. The hoteliers' dependence on those contracts and their inability to reach the marketplace in any other way made them overly dependent on tour operators, which, in turn, used their dominant positions in the market to force down prices. Consequently, the low profit levels achieved by the hoteliers led some to implement cost-cutting measures in the level of service they provided. The number of customer complaints rose as a result.

EXAMPLE TUI hotels and resorts

TUI owns or has management agreements with many hotels across Europe, which operate under brand names such as Rui, Grecotel, Grupotel, Magic Life, Iberotel, Paladian and Robinson Clubs. With more than 260 hotels providing around 170 000 bed spaces, TUI is the largest leisure hotelier in Europe. TUI also controls around 21% of hotel beds in the Caribbean and 25% of beds in the North Africa/Egypt region. The majority of their hotels (60%) are rated 4-star. The average revenue earned in these hotel chains varies from a low of €35 (for the Dorfhotel group) to a high of €80 in the Robinson hotels group.

Source: www.tui-group.com

While parts of the package market appear to be unwilling to pay higher prices for better standards of service, there is some evidence that higher-quality accommodation is being demanded, with customers being prepared to pay slightly higher prices for the opportunity to upgrade. In light of this, some tour operators (such as Club Mediterranée) have elected to upgrade the quality of the accommodation they offer.

The growth of independent websites is beginning to change this picture. Not only can hoteliers now market their product direct to the public at prices that are competitive with those they offer tour operators, but they can also work with other intermediaries like website accommodation providers, hotel.com being one such example. These are important opportunities for the hotel sector, which is gradually relinquishing its sales dependence on tour operators.

The specialized roles of tour operators

The domestic operator

Tour operators fulfil a number of roles; they do not only carry traffic out of the country, although this is the role with which we most frequently associate them. Operators also exist to organize package holidays domestically; that is, to a destination within the country in which the tourists reside. For many countries, the numbers for domestic travel exceed those for international outbound travel (see Table 18.2).

Traditionally, tour operators that served the domestic market have formed just a small part of the travel and tourism industry, because it is relatively simple for tourists to make their own arrangements within their own country. In the past, it was uncommon to find a tour operator that simultaneously organized both domestic and foreign package holidays

Table 18.2 Domestic tourism in Europe

Countries	Domestic trips 2010 (as a percentage of total domestic and international trips)
Austria	53
Belgium	32
Bulgaria	78
Croatia	20
Czech Republic	75
Denmark	51
Finland	85
France	89
Germany	57
Greece	89
Hungary	79
Italy	80
Netherlands	50
Norway	71
Poland	82
Portugal	90
Romania	49
Russia	71
Slovakia	74
Slovenia	48
Spain	92
Sweden	76
Switzerland	48
Turkey	72
UK	71

Source: calculated from data supplied by Euromonitor, 2011

(although, of course, the originator of the package tour, Thomas Cook, started as a domestic holiday organizer, only later expanding into foreign holidays). As concentration in the industry develops and competition becomes fiercer, however, the larger operators are tending to expand into the domestic market. Despite this, most companies in this sector are relatively small, often dealing directly with the public, and are therefore not involved in retailing through the trade.

The longest established domestic programmes are coach tours operated by companies such as Shearings, based in the UK, OAD Reizen, which operates in The Netherlands, and Orbis Transport in Poland.

The incoming operator

Those countries such as Spain and Greece, which are predominantly destination rather than generating countries, will have an incoming travel sector that is as important as the outgoing sector. Organizations specializing in handling incoming foreign holidaymakers have a rather different role from that of outbound operators. Some are merely ground-handling agents, so their role may be limited to organizing hotel accommodation on behalf of an overseas tour operator or greeting incoming visitors and transferring them, often by coach, to their hotels. Other companies, however, will offer a comprehensive range of services, which may include negotiating with coach companies and hotels to secure the best quotations for contracts, organizing special interest holidays or study tours or providing dining or theatre arrangements. In some cases, companies specialize according to the markets they serve, catering for the inbound Japanese or Israeli markets, for example.

EXAMPLE Incoming sport tours

Tours 4 Sport is an incoming operator specializing in travel for sports teams and schools. The organization can make travel arrangements which include accommodation reservations, airport transfers and sightseeing tours with guides. However, their specialism in the sports tours market means that they also provide services such as organizing tickets to professional sports events, team entry into amateur tournaments, arranging sports fixtures against teams of a similar calibre and educational visits to sports venues.

Understanding their sport tourism market has allowed them also to select a range of additional tourist activities most likely to suit the customer base; this can include paintballing, karting, shooting or bowling. They also arrange social evenings. Such activities provide additional sources of revenue for the company.

In Britain, there are more than 300 tour companies that derive a major part of their revenue from handling incoming business. As with domestic operators, most of them are small companies and many of them are members of UKinbound, the aim of which is to provide a forum for the exchange of information and ideas among members, maintain standards of service and act as a pressure group in dealing with other bodies in the UK who have a role to play in the country's tourism industry.

Incoming tour operators' services are marketed largely through the trade, and organizations work closely with public-sector bodies such as national tourist boards in order to promote their services.

Other specializations

Many operators recognize that their strengths lie in specializing in a particular niche. For example, some outbound operators choose to specialize according to the **mode of transport** used by their clients, such as coach tours, rail travel or self-drive holidays. Naturally, such tour operators are in competition with the transport companies that seek to boost their carryings by building inclusive tours around their own forms of transport.

Alternatively, specialization can be based on the markets they serve or the products they develop. The commonest distinction is between, on the one hand, the **mass market operators** that have as their products, typically, the sun, sea and sand holiday, designed to appeal to a very broad segment of the market, and, on the other hand, the **specialist operator**, which targets a particular niche market. By trying to distinguish their products from those of their competitors, these operators are not in such intense competition with each other, or with other operators, and their market product is often less price-sensitive as a result.

Specialists have a number of advantages over mass market companies in the marketplace. Most carry small numbers of tourists and can therefore use smaller accommodation units, such as the many small, family-run hotels in Greece which are popular with tourists but individually too small to interest the larger operators. As the specialist companies generally use scheduled carriers and do not have the level of commitment to a particular destination that their larger colleagues have, they can be more flexible, switching to other destinations if market demand changes for any reason. Staff can generally be expected to have a good knowledge of the products and, as the market is less price-sensitive, the intense price competition found in the mass marketplace is absent, allowing companies to make reasonable profits. If they are successful, however, there is always the danger that one of the larger operators will be attracted to their market and either undercut them or attempt to buy the company. This has been a feature of the UK tour operating market in recent years, with the largest brands buying out medium-sized niche operators and fitting them into their own specialist products division (sometimes, later dropping the brand altogether or integrating it into their own mainstream brands).

 EXAMPLE **First Choice brands**

One of the attractions of merging TUI with First Choice was the dominance of the latter in serving specialist niche markets. Prior to the merger, First Choice reportedly owned 96 specialist brands, but, following the merger, they were separated into three specialist sectors and three activity sectors. The specialist sectors focused on the following.

Sector	Area of focus	Brands include
Specialist – destination	These brands focus on providing a range of products and experiences at a few key destinations	Marmara, Turchese, Signature Vacations
Specialist – premium	This sector focuses on premium leisure travel experiences serving destinations across Asia, Europe and the Caribbean	Hayes & Jarvis, Sovereign, Citalia, Meonvillas
Specialist – life stages	These serve specific markets segmented by demographics, such as age	Student City.com, Young Explorers, Jumpstreet
Activity – marine	This division operates over 2400 yachts and motor boats	Sunsail clubs, The Moorings, Crown Blue Line, Connoisseur, Emerald Star
Activity – adventure	This sector focuses on providing a variety of adventure travel opportunities, including trekking and expeditions	Exodus, Imaginative Traveller, Trek America, Waymark, Flexiski, Travelbound
Activity – experiential	This division provides cultural and luxury escorted tours, primarily for the US market	Travcoa, Brian Moore International Tours, Europe Express, Starquest Expeditions

Source: e-mail correspondence with TUI corporate communications, 2008

Many of these brands have remained separate from the TUI trade name, as many of the customers served are likely to be deterred by the mass market connotations associated with the parent company.

Many companies seek to specialize by geographic destination, but this can be a high-risk decision, as exemplified by the collapse of markets due to factors affecting one country or region. The SARS outbreak in 2003 caused some operators to withdraw their entire China programmes, while the unstable political situation in the Middle East has frequently affected operators specializing in holidays to Israel and neighbouring Arab countries. An extreme example is that of Yugotours. When civil war fractured the former Yugoslavia in the 1990s, Yugotours, which specialized almost exclusively in that destination, was forced to change not only its destinations but also even its brand name in order to build a new market. It failed to re-establish itself and the brand disappeared.

Specialization by market is common. Some companies choose to appeal to a particular age group, as does Saga Holidays, which has for many years been the UK's market leader in holidays for the over-50s. The company faced a challenge from Travelsphere's takeover in 2004 of Page and Moy, which, with 4 million customers, targets the over 45s to widen the potential market. Others target the younger markets, such as Club 18–30 and 2wenties. The singles market – fast growing as social changes have increased the proportion of divorced people in our society – is served by specialists like Solo Holidays and Page and Moy Group's Just You brand. Other operators specialize by gender. WalkingWomen, for example, as the name implies, offers walking tours for females only. Targets are becoming increasingly tightly focused. One example is Small Families which targets one-parent families, providing escorted group tours.

Obviously, there is ample opportunity to specialize according to the specific interests, activities or hobbies of clients, and tour companies have been established to cater for such diverse needs as those of vegetarians, those with an interest in various cultural activities, golfing or angling enthusiasts; even such highly specialized activities as textile weaving. One company that has proved itself highly successful in its targeting is Cycling for Softies, which caters for tourists interested in using bicycles as a mode of transport but still seeking comfortable and well-equipped overnight accommodation. This company's main focus is on travel in France and it therefore specializes in both the destination and the market it serves.

Activity and adventure holidays together form one of the fastest-growing areas of specialization. This sector has been hit, somewhat, by the global economic downturn which occurred at the end of last decade, but estimates still forecast that the number of activity holidays will have increased by almost 50% in the decade to 2013 (Mintel, 2009). This market is no longer the preserve of the young, attracting more over-50s.

EXAMPLE Greycations

One organization providing adventure holidays for the older age group is ElderTreks. Based in Canada, this tour operator has been operating for 25 years, and now provides small-group trips to over 100 countries. This includes safaris, hiking in the Himalayas, the Andes and the Rockies, and expeditions by icebreaker to the Arctic and Antarctic.

The only concession made to accommodate the mature clientele is that the tours take place at a slightly slower pace, and where possible avoid single-night stops. The company also reserves rooms with en suite bathrooms - something that is appreciated more acutely by the older customer!

Further Information: **www.eldertreks.com**

The role of air brokers

One other role should be examined here; that of those who specialize in providing airline seats in bulk to other tour operators. These specialists are known as **air brokers** or, where their business is principally concerned with consolidating flights on behalf of operators that have not achieved good load factors for their charters, **consolidators**.

Air brokers negotiate directly with airlines, buying seats in bulk and arranging to sell them, either in smaller blocks or even individually to tour operators or travel agents. They provide the airlines, especially those companies that may find it difficult to obtain good load factors on some legs of their operations, with a good distribution service and, in return, the airlines are willing to offer very low net rates to fill their remaining seats. The brokers put their own mark-up on the seats and take on the responsibility of marketing them for whatever price they can get. Their operations led to the demise of the former bucket shop operators, who performed a similar function but often infringed International Air Transport Association (IATA) regulations by 'dumping' tickets at discounted prices on the market. Deregulation on an international scale has now virtually eradicated the former illegal operations and made ticket discounting 'respectable'. Many mark-ups are very low, with the broker making money on the huge turnover of seats they achieve.

Online intermediaries reflect the growth in modern air brokerage, with companies such as ebookers and Opodo becoming major players in the field.

Integration in the industry

There have been extensive changes within the competitive environment of the tourism industry. Mergers and takeovers became commonplace, coupled with an increasingly international perspective in the tour operating business, as operators have come to look abroad for opportunities to expand and dominate the market through purchasing power. The leading European tour operators' attempts to enter the difficult and highly competitive North American markets have tended to prove abortive, although the rationale behind the move was clear: a desire to spread the seasonal flow of traffic, thus obtaining better year-round usage of aircraft. The risk would also be reduced by ensuring a more even spread of revenue between markets in North America, the UK and mainland Europe.

The takeover or merger of businesses is termed **integration**, and it can take place either at the same stage of the supply chain – horizontal integration – or at different stages of the supply chain – vertical integration.

Horizontal integration

The amalgamation of two businesses which operate within the same part of the supply chain (such as a tour operator merging with or buying out another tour operator) is called **horizontal integration**.

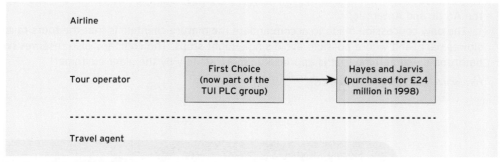

Horizontal integration

The reasons for horizontal integration may include the ability to gain economies of scale in operations as well as increase purchasing power, the opportunity to gain greater market share, acquire or share a wider range of products and increase the market value of the company. It can also reduce competition as the merged businesses then work together.

Vertical integration

The amalgamation of companies at different stages of the distribution chain is termed **vertical integration**. In cases where control of suppliers is achieved, backward vertical integration is said to have occurred; where control of the buyer of the product has been achieved this is termed forward vertical integration.

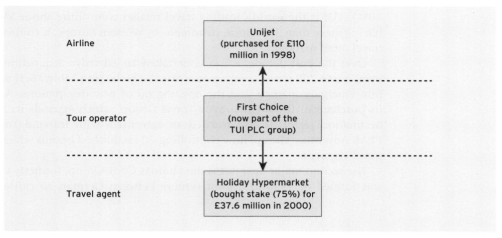

Vertical integration

Even with the much greater levels of concentration in the industry found in the late twentieth century, the European Commission (EC) has suggested that the growth of Internet travel providers as well as the existence of low-cost airlines has meant that the market remains competitive as smaller tour operators have been able to gain market awareness, travel agents have been able to dynamically package travel (explained in Chapter 19) and consumers have been able to access travel components directly. Thus, it has been accepted that integration is not against the public interest, given that competition still ensures prices are kept down.

Tour operating within the European Union (EU)

The process of integration has been witnessed extensively across Europe, but some reports have suggested that it may be on the decline in some regions. For instance, established budget airline networks and high levels of Internet use in both the UK and Scandinavia have led business operations in these areas to provide strong challenges to the vertically integrated tour operator model. The integration of travel companies across European borders remains prevalent, however.

Investment companies appear interested in many vertically integrated travel groups. For example, Spain's Orizonia was sold in 2007 to private equity groups Carlyle and Vista, while Blackstone purchased Travelport (which includes ebookers, Orbitz and Octopus Travel among its brands). Furthermore, businesses operating in other industry sectors are being attracted to large travel companies. For instance, the German department store and mail-order company Arcandor AG (formerly KarstadtQuelle AG) owns a majority stake in the Thomas Cook Group, while the large German tour operator Rewe Touristik is owned by a food retailer and Hotelplan is a subsidiary of Switzerland's largest supermarket chain, Migros.

The dominance of a few mega-tour operators means that, for many European countries, their largest operators are not nationally owned. Some countries, for example Belgium, have no major locally owned tour operator. Perhaps the most dominant is TUI, which is the leading tour brand in several European countries, including the UK and Germany.

Following its merger with UK-based First Choice in the summer of 2007, the TUI group was formed (with TUI AG owning 51% of the shares and First Choice shareholders owning 49%). TUI is the world's leading travel retailer controlling about 5% of world sales and having more than 30 million customers. In Western Europe, it controls almost 14% of the travel retail market.

Over the past decade, it has undertaken an extensive acquisition strategy – TUI now owns some 700 travel companies across the globe (see Table 18.3) to assist its expansion into emerging markets and the opening up of new destinations. A recent example was its purchase of the Russian Svoy Travel Group, which expands its accommodation and destination sector. It also reached an agreement with Intrepid Travel to establish the PEAK Adventure Group, now controlling 20 established brands which serve the adventure travel segment.

The second major operator is the Thomas Cook Group, formerly C&N Touristik, which was formed in 1998 as a joint venture between German air carrier Lufthansa and the

Table 18.3 A selection of TUI owned companies

Country	Company
Austria	TUI Austria, Thomson Reisen, Magic Life, Dorfhotel, Robinson Austria
Belgium	TUI Travel Belgium, JetAir, Nouvelles Frontières Belgique, Connoisseur Belgium
Bulgaria	Travel Partner Bulgaria, Apart Hotel Zarevo
Croatia	Gulliver Travel, Sunsail Adriatic, The Moorings
Denmark	TUI Denmark, MyPlanet, Star Tour, Travel Sense
France	First Choice, Corsair, Groupe Marmara, Nouvelles Frontières
Germany	TUI Deutschland, TUI Cruises, Hapag-Lloyd Kreuzfahrten, First Choice Deutschland
Greece	TUI Hellas, Hellenic Sailing, Magic Life
Ireland	TUI Travel, Prestige Boating Holidays, First Choice
Italy	TUI Italia, I Viaggi des Turchese, Vacanze Thomson
Netherlands	TUI Nederland, First Choice, Le Boat, Sunsail
Norway	TUI Norway, Startour, MyPlanet
Poland	TUI Poland
Portugal	TUI Portugal, Thomson Viagens e Turismo
Spain	TUI España , Fritidsresor, First Choice, Hotelbeds, Ambassador Tours
Sweden	TUI Nordic, Fritidsresor, Britannia, MyPlanet
Switzerland	TUI Suisse, Thomson Travel, Robinson Club TUI Travel, Thomson Holidays, First Choice, Bakers Dolphin, Crystal Holidays, Exodus Travel, Gap Year for Grown Ups, Hayes & Jarvis , Portland Holidays
UK	Sovereign, Sportsworld, Sunsail, TUI UK/Thomson

Source: TUI Annual Reports

Karstadt/Quelle department store organization. Like the TUI group, Thomas Cook also undertook a major merger, joining with MyTravel in 2007. The merged company now achieves sales of approximately £9 billion annually, with Thomas Cook a major operator in the UK, Germany and Scandinavia. The group serves 22.5 million customers globally and has some strong brands including:

- Thomas Cook
- Airtours
- Cruise Thomas Cook
- Direct Holidays
- Neilson
- Flythomascook.com
- Sunset
- Thomas Cook Signature
- Thomas Cook Sport.

Despite a 4% decrease in turnover in 2010, largely resulting from the challenging conditions in the UK – £80 million in revenue lost due to the 2010 ash cloud crisis alone – and US holiday markets, they made an operating profit of £397 million. As with TUI, acquisitions were also important for Thomas Cook. They purchased the German travel operator Oger Tours, specialists in packages to Turkey, Thailand and Cuba, and agreed a merger with the Co-operative Group in the UK which will bring economies of scale, and hence efficiencies, in their travel agency operations. Furthermore, a joint venture with Russian company Intourist, a tour operator, travel agency and hotel management organization, will open up Russia as a market as well as expanding destination opportunities there. Thomas Cook has also announced plans to develop its operations in China to attract the growing outbound market. This is important because the mainstream travel sector of its business is expected to see limited expansion in the immediate future.

A third major player is Rewe, a leading supermarket chain that controls tour operator LTU-Touristik and other tour operator brands including ITS, Jahn Reisen, Tjaereborg, Dertour, Meier's Weltreisen and ADAC Reisen, together with over 2600 retail travel agencies. Rewe is active in Germany, Austria and Switzerland, and is expanding in the Czech Republic, Poland and Russia. The company dominates in Germany, gaining 14% of the market, ahead of TUI Deutschland, with 9%.

The fourth major player in the European tour operator industry is Swiss-based Kuoni. A long-established brand, founded more than 100 years ago, it has sought to provide specialist products, allowing the company to achieve premium prices for its products. In recent years, the company has sold some non-core subsidiaries in an effort to streamline its operations, but has also purchased a 70% shareholding in Norwegian-based Reisetorget AS, an Internet retail specialist for travel products, which was sought to enhance Kuoni's online sales. The company focuses on leisure travel, destination management activities, and (though to a lesser extent) the meetings and incentive travel sector. The leisure travel sector accounts for 85% of company revenues. Although Kuoni weathered the economic downturn at the end of the last decade, largely due to positive results in the Scandinavian and Asian markets, it has announced significant retrenchment as part of a management-cost drive. Expansion into China has occurred with investment in Et China.

All these operators have recognized the importance of gaining customer numbers to increase the scale of their operations, thus allowing them to buy at the lowest price and control the markets. Transnational mergers and joint ventures will remain increasingly common, limited only by the anti-monopoly forces of the EC.

EXAMPLE   The structure of the outbound tour-operating business in the UK

There are, at the time of writing, 750 tour operators in the UK which are members of ABTA, representing a steady decline from the peak level of 866 in 2004. The market is dominated by two main operators, TUI and Thomas Cook. Both companies have expanded their operations by purchasing smaller tour operating businesses; between them, they now control hundreds of popular holiday brands including:

● TUI PLC – First Choice, Airtours, Crystal, Thomson, Hayes & Jarvis, Austravel, Exodus

● Thomas Cook Group – Airtours, Club 18-30, Cresta, Direct Holidays, Going Places, Neilson, Panorama, Sunset, Thomas Cook.

This horizontal integration has been a dominant feature of the UK tour operator sector for over 20 years. Vertical integration has also been prominent, with the largest companies owning and/or controlling their own airlines, ground-handling agents at airports, electronic distribution channels and retail travel agencies. The initial phases of sector concentration can be traced back to the rapid expansion that took place in the tour operating business in Britain after the 1960s (this occurred slightly later in other parts of Western Europe and North America).

Apart from TUI and Thomas Cook, most UK operators are very small companies. Tour operator ATOL-licensing data for the number of passengers carried shows that TUI and Thomas Cook dominated, both with licenses to carry 4.3 million passengers and only one other organization carrying more than half a million passengers (Gold Medal Travel). The 25 next largest operators carried an average of 235 000 passengers (CAA, 2011).

Efforts have been made in recent years by the smaller operators to gain market share by impressing on the public their more personal levels of service and greater expertise, in this way distancing themselves from the mass market operators. The Association of Independent Tour Operators (AITO), with a membership of some 150, works closely with the independent travel agents to sell distinctive products.

The changing marketplace in tour operating

Three factors were at work in the second half of the twentieth century that encouraged the growth of the package holiday in Europe.

● The expansion of leisure time in the developed countries.

● This was accompanied by greater discretionary income in those countries.

● Package holiday costs were low, both in themselves and in comparison to similar holidays in the home country. This was due to the relatively low costs of accommodation and food in the Mediterranean countries, reductions in air transport costs due to advancing technology, liberalization of air transport regulations, the introduction of year-round operations, covering both summer and winter seasons, and bulk purchasing by tour operators.

The operators, recognizing the strong growth potential in the overseas holiday market, sought to expand their market shares and, at the same time, attempted to increase the total size of the market by encouraging those who traditionally took domestic holidays to travel abroad. To achieve this, they slashed prices. Large companies used their purchasing muscle to drive down suppliers' prices (at some cost to quality in a number of cases). They introduced cheap, 'no frills' holidays and, more recently, budget holidays that offered no transfers, no in-flight meals and no resort representatives. Arguably, this new offering can barely be considered a package, in the traditional sense of the word, but budget-conscious consumers have been attracted to it all the same.

Additionally, profit margins were trimmed. Leading tour operators, each determined not to be undersold, engaged in the periodic re-pricing of their holidays throughout the season, using the strategy of brochure reissues with cheaper prices to try to outpace their competitors, but operators always held to the hope that, given the right conditions, prices could be increased rather than decreased in the later editions.

In the past, overly optimistic forecasts of market growth led to surpluses in supply. Capacity generally exceeded demand each year and operators were then forced into offloading holidays at bargain basement prices. Not surprisingly, this led to a good deal of dissatisfaction among clients who had booked earlier when the prices were higher. This factor was key to the growth in late bookings.

Traditionally, bookings for package holidays had occurred in the weeks immediately following Christmas, allowing operators time to balance supply and demand and aiding their cash flow – deposits paid by clients in January would be invested and earn interest for the company until its bills had to be paid, which, in some cases, could be as late as September or October. Demanding full balances eight to ten weeks before departure proved similarly lucrative for operators.

Holidaymakers soon came to realize, however, that, if they refrained from booking holidays until much nearer to the dates they wanted to travel, they could snap up late booking bargains. The development of computerized reservations systems allowed operators to update their late availability opportunities quickly, putting cheap offers on the market at very short notice, which made late bookings convenient as well as attractively priced.

The early twenty-first century has seen the introduction of online booking, with websites accessible to both retail agents and the general public. This has further promoted the attraction of late booking, reducing the gap between deposits and final payments from months to a matter of weeks, or even removing this gap altogether. The uncertainty caused by this volume of late bookings also made tour operations management more difficult.

The year 2005 appears to have marked the first change of direction; the leading operators reduced their capacity compared with the previous year to reduce the likelihood of overcapacity. In addition, the new technology allowed operators to counteract late booking trends through the introduction of a policy of fluid pricing. First introduced by Thomson Holidays in 1996 and soon copied by the other leading operators, this entails offering holidays that are detailed in the brochures for different prices – large discounts being given for early bookings and lower or no discounts for booking nearer the time of the holiday. Some operators (and their agents) have even quoted prices above the standard brochure price where demand is sufficiently strong, although the legality of this move has been questioned.

EXAMPLE Holiday pricing and Thomson Holidays

The brochures produced by Thomson Holidays include prices for each hotel they feature. However, brochures now clearly state that prices are a guide only. The customer is reminded that 'all prices can go up or down'.

As well as the fluid pricing of the basic holiday price, the total cost of the holiday will also be affected by under-occupancy charges. In many cases the hotel room may be expected to accommodate two or four adults (in the case of ski accommodation this may even be higher) and a charge is payable if the rooms are not at maximum capacity.

Prices will also be influenced by the departure airport. Flight premiums are paid for flights operating during the day (rather than late at night or early in the morning). Supplements are also added if flights are from smaller regional airports; for example, flying from Norwich Airport can add between £30 and £95 depending on season and destination.

Finally, the total cost of the holiday will include any 'extras' selected to improve the service. To take one example, Thomson offers passengers the opportunity to pay £12 each to select their seat, ensuring that a family will be able to sit together – something that, generally, frequently happened but could not always be guaranteed on busy flights. Passengers can also choose a host of upgrades. Passengers may choose to have a taxi transfer to their accommodation on arrival (£29), rather than wait for a coachful of passengers to be delivered to their respective hotels in turn. A garden view room would add, typically, £14 per week per person or an upgrade to a suite an extra £140.

When all these additional charges and supplements are added, the final price is likely to be nothing close to the basic holiday price. They are, however relatively transparent and travel agents or online bookings will display these additional costs separately so passengers can clearly see how the overall cost of the holiday is determined.

Starting in the late 1990s, there was a tendency among operators to launch brochures for the upcoming year at ever earlier dates, resulting, at times, in agents having to find room for brochures covering three different periods – summer and winter of the current year, as well as summer of the following year. More recently, some sense has prevailed and a more rational approach has been apparent. While printed brochures may not be available far in advance, brochures provided electronically online are often available up to 16 months before the holiday period. There is evidence that early launches of brochures did benefit operators, by boosting sales.

The cost to the tour operator of creating travel packages is affected by changes in the inflation rate, exchange rates or costs of supplies, particularly aviation fuel, which is priced in US dollars on the world market and is therefore affected by either increased costs or changes in the relative values of the local currency and the dollar.

Tour operators have to estimate their costs for all services up to a year ahead of time. They can anticipate higher costs by raising prices, but this may make them uncompetitive; alternatively, they can take an optimistic approach and price low, in the expectation of stable or declining costs. Originally, the latter was more attractive as moderate cost increases could be passed on to customers (within established limits) in the form of surcharges. Within Europe, however, such surcharges are now no longer acceptable. Legislation implemented by member states in response to the 1992 Directive on Package Travel states that 'a price revision is possible only for variations in transportation costs (including the costs of fuel), dues, taxes or fees chargeable for certain services (such as landing taxes or embarkation or disembarkation fees at ports) and the exchange rates applied to the particular package' (Schulte-Nölke *et al.*, 2006, 288).

Stability in price can be obtained by 'buying forward' the fuel required for the following year, but this is only practical for the largest operators with sufficient financial reserves. While there is no formal 'futures' market in aviation fuel, negotiation is possible on future purchases of fuel on an *ad hoc* basis, but clearly at a premium, so purchasing forward will further affect the operators' cash flow.

The introduction of government taxes can also affect the total price paid by tourists. Such taxes might include hotel or bed taxes or departure taxes at ports. In 1996, the UK Government introduced an 'exit tax', in the form of Air Passenger Duty (APD), for all flights out of the UK, amounting initially to £5 within the EU and £10 outside the EU (a rate that doubled at the end of 1997, and increased again in 2001, this time requiring business and first class passengers to pay a higher APD levy). This resurrected the issue of hidden charges, with many tour operators not absorbing these taxes in their total price structures. Some claimed that to do so would make their prices unattractive against scheduled air rivals such as low-cost carriers, which have traditionally promoted their flight prices separately from taxes and charges. Nevertheless, greater pressure is now being placed on these airlines to promote the price inclusive of taxes rather than headline fares.

The long-haul market

The tendency for all mass-market operators to focus on low price rather than quality or value for money led to this type of tour moving downmarket. As it did so, tourists at the top end of the market, particularly those who had travelled frequently, began to travel independently more often and to more distant destinations.

The demand for long-haul packages has expanded much faster than that for short-haul. More than 20% of all holidays are now taken to long-haul destinations annually, and, although travel declined at the end of the last decade largely as a result of the recession, long-haul travel remained robust, with trips outside of Europe actually increasing in 2010 (ONS, 2011). In the longer term, this sector is expected to see significant growth, particular among the 50–64 age group. The USA (with its particular appeal of the Walt Disney World resort in Florida), New Zealand and Australia have all witnessed mass market long-haul growth, while Thailand and Bali have successfully sold the idea of long-haul sun, sea and sand holidays. South Africa, India and the Middle East (notably Dubai), even Cuba in the Caribbean, have all seen substantial growth in visitors from Western Europe. All of those increases can be directly ascribed to the huge drop in air fares relative to other prices in the past decade.

The market leader for long-haul packages is Swiss-owned Kuoni Travel, with TUI and Thomas Cook also competing strongly for such destinations with their specialist divisions.

Seat-only sales

The introduction of low-cost carriers into the aviation markets has encouraged travellers to consider booking travel components separately. In addition, as growing numbers of British holidaymakers are either prepared to find their own accommodation abroad or are seeking flights to carry them to their second homes, timeshare apartments or friends' accommodation on the Continent, changes in the accommodation sector have further affected demand for traditional packages. As a consequence, some tour operators owning airlines which provide charter flights to service their packages now offer seat-only sales, in which passengers, although ostensibly buying a package, are, in fact, only using the air travel portion of the tour.

This type of 'package' was originally introduced by operators to fill surplus charter seats. Technically, to abide by international regulations, some form of basic accommodation had to be included in the package, although this was seldom used. After January 1993, EU legislation swept away the requirement to book accommodation within EU destinations, leading to seat-only sales becoming an important feature of the travel industry.

Recent factors influencing demand for package travel

There is little let-up in the volatility of the tour operating business. Political conflicts in the Balkans and Turkey at the end of the last century, wars in the Gulf and fears of terrorism that were heightened after the 9/11 tragedy, Bali, Madrid and London bombings, and civil uprisings in northern Africa and the Middle East, have all unsettled global travel and tour operations. Natural disasters like the earthquake and subsequent tsunami in the Far East at the end of 2004 and in Japan in 2011 similarly reduced long-haul travel to the affected regions severely. In spite of this catalogue of crises, the sector has shown itself in the past to be resilient and, while in the short term cancelled bookings and hotel reservations would impact severely on these destinations, recovery from even the worst disasters would normally be expected within a year of the event.

European operators have sought new locations to develop where hotel capacity is cheap and readily available, as traditional resorts began to price themselves out of the market. First, the more remote areas of Greece, then Turkey, became boom destinations for Western Europeans seeking sun at rock-bottom prices. The evidence suggests, however, that the inclusive tour market for the traditional sun, sea and sand destinations has probably peaked. For example, in the UK today fewer than half of the population choose a package when buying an overseas holiday to Europe. Even in recent years, when package sales have shown an upturn, owing to the value and financial protection they provide, the share of package holidays by British residents remains below 40% (ONS, 2011).

Second home ownership has also had a marked effect on patterns of holidaymaking. Many owners disappear from the inclusive tours (IT) market, tending to take most, if not all, of their overseas holidays in their own properties. This, however, has fuelled the growth of the no frills airlines and the benefits of travel are by no means lost to other sectors of the industry, because second home owners purchase local products and services at their destinations, invite friends and others to their homes, rent out their properties either privately or through operators and participate in home exchange opportunities around the world.

In Europe, many in the population have now experienced a foreign holiday at some point in their lives. For example, over 70% of the UK population has travelled overseas. Thus, it is reasonable to assume that the first-time market has been captured and the future growth of the IT market is likely to be concentrated on selling a greater frequency of holidays, with a focus on the variety of holidays offered.

The changing nature and demographics of European society is throwing up demand for new kinds of holiday. Growth areas include the following.

- Short breaks and city breaks, especially to more exotic destinations. Reykjavik, Barcelona and New York have become popular destinations for short-stay tourism. The entry of the Baltic States into the EU has boosted short breaks to Tallinn and Riga, just as the earlier entry of the Czech Republic boosted Prague as the city break of choice.

- Expansion of the EU has led to increased mobility of the residents of the new accession states. This has the potential to encourage greater VFR (visiting friends and relatives) travel as some choose to work outside their home country, as well as offering wider travel opportunities due to the removal or reduction of visa restrictions, which allows convenient travel to countries across the Continent and further afield.

- In the field of exotic long-haul, activity and adventure holidays, elderly travellers are now far more active than formerly and packages catering to their needs and interests are now common. Early retirement packages at one end of the third age and longer lifespans at the other contribute to this trend.

- Changing attitudes have meant that many tourists are seeking out experiences rather than just material products. A greater focus on self-development, culture and health is likely to see customers demanding specialist activities and experiential holidays.

Including more or less?

All-inclusive holidays have grown in popularity. Introduced in the Caribbean, the concept has now expanded to many European destinations too, primarily to Mediterranean coastal resorts. These are fully inclusive packages, even down to alcohol and all entertainment at the resort.

First Choice goes all-inclusive

Having merged with Thomson Holidays in 2007, First Choice announced in April 2011 that, from the spring of 2012 it would only offer all-inclusive holidays. Any customers wishing to travel on bed-and-breakfast or half-board rates would have to book holidays via the Thomson portfolio. The all-inclusive rates would include all flights, accommodation, meals and drinks in the price of the holiday. Between 2004 and 2009, the all-inclusive market grew by a third. This was viewed as a particularly cost-effective option, especially for a family seeking to control costs once on holiday.

Of course, the tour operator does charge a higher price for such vacations, and, although the accommodation resort will have negotiated a higher rate with the tour operator to provide an all-inclusive service, the tour operator will gain more of the travellers' holiday spend, which can add to profitability. The sustainability of all-inclusive holidays for destinations is questionable, however, given that customers do not need to go out of their complex to buy anything while they are on holiday; consequently, local shops and services fail to obtain the benefits of the tourists' visit.

At the same time, some operators are electing to 'unpackage' elements of the package holiday that would have traditionally been included, such as airport transfers and in-flight catering. The operators are then able to increase their revenue by selling these as 'add-ons', especially common when customers buy no frills packages. Operators are also making additional charges for early check-in or late check-out of rooms, prebookable seats or upgraded seats (as several charter airlines have introduced a premium economy cabin on their planes), the use of prestigious airport lounges and even for guaranteeing a seat next to a friend or relative.

Of course, traditional sales of excursions and car hire at the destination are also lucrative, and resort representatives are actively encouraged to make such sales to the tourists. A further boost to operators' profits can come through the imposition of high cancellation charges as operators retain the revenue while remaining free to sell the same holiday subsequently to other holidaymakers.

Consumer complaints

One inevitable consequence of the process of 'trading down' to cheaper package travel has been an increase in customer complaints. Studies have revealed that some 40% of complaints arose from budget holidays – often based on late availability that came without prior identification of exactly what accommodation was to be provided (often only a guarantee of a level of star rating would be offered). While operators were responding to consumer pressure for low-cost packages, consumers were unwilling to accept the very rational argument that they got what they paid for; the minimum standards provided simply failed too often to meet consumers' expectations. Even more worrying to operators was the fact that only 40% of those dissatisfied were prepared to make an official complaint; others simply refrained from booking with the company again.

Another source of customer irritation has been the practice of operators applying surcharges to their final invoices. These surcharges are resented by travellers and are in any case not applied to scheduled fares (which can respond to market prices more quickly). It also became apparent that a handful of operators were misusing this facility and adding fuel surcharges in excess of actual increases in cost, or even when actual fuel costs had not increased at all, as a means of raising profits that had been slashed by open competition. The leading tour operators themselves helped to phase out surcharges by guaranteeing prices, while legislation also restricted the use of surcharges.

The nature of tour operating

An inclusive tour programme, as we have seen, is composed of a series of integrated travel services, each of which is purchased by a tour operator in bulk and resold as part of a package at an all-inclusive price. These integrated services usually consist of an aircraft seat, accommodation at the destination and transfers between the accommodation and the airport on arrival and departure. They may also include other services, such as excursions or car hire.

The inclusive tour is commonly referred to as a package tour and most are single-destination, resort-based holidays. Tours comprising two or more destinations are by no means uncommon, however, and long-haul operators frequently build in optional extensions to another destination in their itineraries – a beach holiday in Kenya might offer an optional extension to one of the game parks, for example; or a visit to the Chilean fjords, flying to Santiago, might offer tourists the opportunity to extend the itinerary to Chilean-owned Easter Island.

In East Asia, multicentre holidays are very common, as many capital cities in the area are seen as meriting only relatively short stays of three to four nights. Increasingly, itineraries other than the most basic are tailor-made for clients, in terms of length of stay, accommodation, flights and activities at the resort. Dynamic packaging (see Chapter 19) has become a more common booking approach, and it permits either operators or their travel agents to put together tour programmes tailor-made especially to meet the demands of each individual client, using websites to contact suppliers.

Linear tours, such as those offered by coach companies that carry people to different destinations or even through several countries, were at one time the most popular form of trip and still retain a loyal following, but mainly among older clients. Even they lend themselves to tailor-made adaptation, with alternative flights to connect with the tours and short-stay extensions being arranged at the beginning or end of the holiday.

The success of the operator usually depends on an ability to buy a combination of products, put them together and sell them at an inclusive price that is lower than the customers could obtain themselves. The major international operators may book several million hotel beds for a season, thus negotiating very low prices from the hotel owners. Similarly, they bulk-buy seats on aircraft or charter whole aircraft at the best prices they can secure. The end result must be seen by the customers as offering value for money, either in terms of the final price paid or time saved shopping around. With package holidays becoming more and more a standardized product, not changing much for different destinations, the destination or country has come to play a lesser part in customers' decision-making. Destinations will be readily substituted if customers feel that their first choice is overpriced.

Managing air transport

Tour operators can lower prices by either reducing their profit margins or cutting costs. Cost savings can be achieved initially by chartering whole aircraft instead of merely purchasing a block of seats on a scheduled flight. Further savings can be made by chartering the aircraft over a lengthy period of time, such as a whole season, rather than on an *ad hoc* basis, this now being the normal pattern of operating for the large companies. Ultimately, the largest operators reduce costs to the minimum by running their own airlines, which allows them to exercise better control over their operations and the standards of their products.

Owning your own aircraft ensures that, when the demand is there, you have the aircraft to meet it at a price you can afford. Emphasis then shifts to ensuring that the highest possible load factors – the percentage of seats sold to seats available – are achieved and the aircraft are kept flying for the maximum number of hours each day as they are not earning

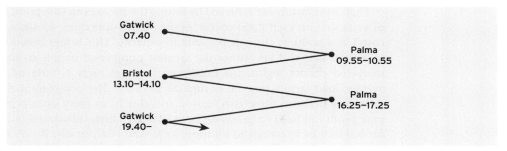

Figure 18.2 A typical 'W' flight pattern

revenue while stationary on the ground, and parking fees can amount to hundreds of pounds every hour.

This requires careful planning to ensure that **turnarounds** (the time spent between arriving with one load of passengers and taking off with another) are as rapid as possible, commensurate with good standards of safety. Typically, this will result in up to three rotations in a single day, say, between a Northern European point of origin and a Mediterranean destination. These rotations may be made from a single point of origin (an airport) to a number of different destinations abroad or from several points of origin to a single destination abroad or from different points of origin to different foreign destinations. The latter flight plan is commonly known as a 'W' flight pattern (see Figure 18.2), which can be programmed to produce the maximum aircraft usage during a 24-hour period.

W-pattern flights are not necessarily carrying the customers of a single operator (even where the carrier is owned by one of the operators). Charters can be contracted to carry the passengers of a number of different operators between the same points of origin and destination, either sharing the flights or filling different flights. This can give rise to problems, one of which will occur when different operators contract for morning, afternoon and evening flights. If one operator decides to cancel, the airline concerned has to find alternative users for the aircraft, which may mean a longer flight commitment, causing delays or a change of flights to those passengers already booked on that flight. The knock-on effect of delays can become very apparent if there is a minor maintenance issue with the plane or air traffic controllers go on strike. Tight flight scheduling, particularly into busy airports at the height of the season, can mean that delays on one flight can have repercussions on tour operator movements using the same aircraft over the next two or three days.

EXAMPLE   Aircraft position

The six-day closure of European airspace as a result of the eruption of the Icelandic volcano Eyjafjallajoekull caused many problems for tour operators, with passengers unable to fly out to their holiday destinations, or stranded in destinations unable to return home.

But the opening of airspace was not the end of the problems. The cancellation of many flights had left airlines significantly out of position, at the airports where they were grounded when the ash cloud rolled in. And with aircraft of various sizes, capable of travelling different distances, it was important that they were quickly returned to their schedule as this had an impact not just on the immediate flight but also on those for several weeks ahead.

Not only were aircraft out of position; so too were the crew. Each aircraft requires a set number of cabin staff, based on safely rules linked to capacity. Therefore crew scheduling also had to be reconfigured to ensure the planes were allowed to take off. Getting both aircraft and crew back on schedule took several weeks.

High load factors are achieved by setting the **breakeven** (the point at which the number of seats sold on each flight covers all the flight's operating, administrative and marketing costs) at a point as close as possible to capacity. This brings down the average seat cost to a level that will encourage the greatest number of people to travel. On many well-marketed charter flights, the breakeven is set as high as 90% or higher, while actual average load factors may be as high as 96–98%. The company makes its profits on the difference between those two figures, and clearly, as every extra person carried is almost pure profit (all fixed costs having been covered), then substantial reductions can be made for last minute bookings to fill those final seats. Conversely, if very few seats remain, the company may even choose to inflate the price, in the knowledge that there are always a few passengers who are willing to pay for a very specific flight at short notice. Of course, if the breakeven load factors have not been reached, the operator will not cover all costs, but it will still be better to attract as many people as possible for the flight, because they will at least make a contribution to the fixed costs of operating the flight, even if all the costs are not recovered. Passengers may also buy duty-free goods on board (if travelling outside the EU countries), and an increasing number of short-haul airlines no longer serve food and drink free of charge, so the sale of these items on board becomes another important source of revenue, making a further contribution to profit for the airline – or, taking a broader view, for the parent company of the jointly owned airline/tour operator. Furthermore, if the operator has contracted for a set number of beds and is committed to pay for that number, it is better to carry passengers to fill those beds than for them to be empty.

Productivity in airline operations can be aided by the procedure of **consolidating flights**. Charter flights with unacceptably low load factors can be cancelled and their passengers transferred to other flights or even departures from other airports. This helps to reduce the element of risk for the tour operator, otherwise breakevens would have to be set at a lower level of capacity, so fares would be higher. Such consolidations are not available for groups carried on scheduled airline services and are, in any case, subject to considerable restrictions, such as adequate advance notice being given to the clients. Inevitably, they are unpopular with clients, so many companies now try to avoid them.

The problem of seasonality

A problem facing all sectors of tourism is the highly seasonal nature of most tourist traffic. Nowhere is this more apparent than in the demand for package holidays in Europe. This market, however, is also highly price-sensitive and longer periods of holiday entitlement over the past 20 years have helped to encourage many people to take their second holiday abroad too, often outside of the peak periods. This has meant that operators can spread their fixed costs more evenly over the entire year, rather than concentrating them in the summer period, helping to reduce prices further. Most importantly, it has allowed the operators to contract for aircraft and hotels on a year-round basis.

If only a summer season is programmed, any tour operator running a charter airline to service its needs is left with a 'dead leg' twice in the year (an aircraft returning empty after the first flight of the season because it has no passengers to pick up and an empty outbound flight at the end of the season to pick up the last clients returning home). The costs of those empty flights have to be built into the overall pricing structure of the operation, but, if they can be avoided by offering year-round programmes, clearly the savings made can be passed on to customers.

Accounting for dead legs

A tour operator is offering a holiday package flying from Edinburgh to Alicante in Spain. It estimates the cost of the flight is €12 000 for each segment flown. Each flight has capacity for 160 passengers.

Initially, the cost per passenger for this holiday may appear to be €150 (return flight €24 000 ÷ 160 passengers). However, the tour operator has chosen to operate only in the summer months (12 separate holiday weeks) and therefore has contracted an airline to serve for 13 weeks – the last week is needed to fly the holidaymakers who travelled in week 12 home. Through successful marketing efforts, all 160 holidays available have been sold so they are operating on 100% capacity (in reality tour operators may operate on load factors closer to 95%).

	Week 1	Week 2	Week 3–12	Week 13
Number of passengers flying out to Alicante	160	160	160	0 (dead-leg)
Number of passengers returning from Alicante to Edinburgh	0 (dead leg)	160	160	160

As we can see from the table above, the total number of flight segments is 26 (including the two dead legs) so at €12 000 per flight segment the total cost is €312 000. The total passenger numbers sold holidays for the 12 weeks is 1920 and therefore the flight cost per passenger is €162.50.

Operators also use marginal costing techniques to attract clients out of season. This means that the holidays need to be priced to cover their variable costs and make some contribution to fixed costs. This recognizes that many costs, such as those encountered in operating hotels, continue whether the hotel is open or closed, so any guests that the hotel can attract will help to pay the bills. They will also enable the hotel to keep its staff all year round, thus making it easier to retain good staff. Some market segments – the retired, for example – can be attracted to the idea of spending the entire winter abroad if prices are low enough, and hoteliers welcome these budget clients as they can still be expected to spend some additional money in the hotel bars or restaurants.

Operating scheduled programmes

Not all destinations allow charter flights to operate into their territory (often, in order to protect bookings on the scheduled flights of the country's airline); neither will there be sufficient demand for flights to many destinations (such as those served by most long-haul programmes) to merit chartering an entire aircraft. For those forms of packaging, the tour operator can arrange the transport element through schedule airlines, using net inclusive tour-basing excursion fares (ITX) or group inclusive tour-basing (GIT) fares, either contracting individual seats based on client demand (around which a tailor-made holiday can be constructed) or contracting a block of seats on flights to satisfy the needs of a brochure programme.

Airlines will allow ITX fares to be applied subject to certain conditions attached to the programmes, primarily that it must be packaged with land arrangements. Tour operators may also have access to some seat-only special price fares offered by airlines to tactically stimulate demand on particular routes. Such fares, while often very competitive, tend to

Table 18.4 Examples of EU regulation of tour operators

Countries	Type of documentation required
Czech Republic, France, Portugal, Slovakia,	Trade Licence
Hungary	Statutory Public Register – managed by the Hungarian Trade Licensing Office
Italy	Licence – procedure managed by regional governments
Malta	Licensed by the National Tourism Authority
Poland	Register for organizers of tourism and tourism intermediaries
Slovenia	Licensed by the Chamber of Commerce
Spain	Qualify as travel agent according to administrative legislation
UK	Air Travel Organizer Licence (ATOL) – managed by the CAA

Source: Schulte-Nölke *et al.*, 2008

have strict ticketing guidelines deigned to achieve the market objectives. Tour operators in the UK making a forward commitment on seats must also obtain an Air Travel Organizers' Licence (ATOL) through the CAA.

Control over tour operating

In order to protect both consumers and the wider tourism industry from rogue operators, a variety of regulations have been used. In some cases, these have come into force to protect consumers and their money, but in other cases they protect the commercial operations of scheduled airlines or the destinations and regions they serve. Many countries within the EU require some form of licensing or qualification for tour operators (see Table 18.4).

The EU and legal issues relating to package holiday operations

Concern was shared by the European Commissioners, who were also looking at the problems of protecting consumers in member states. As a result, the 1992 EC Directive on Package Travel was published, designed to clarify and extend responsibility to all sectors of the industry involved in providing and retailing package travel. Those regulations, which each member state was required to introduce into law, covered non-air-based holidays also. The measures included the following obligations (Schulte-Nölke *et al.*, 2006):

● *Information duties*
  ● To provide a travel brochure, pre-contractual information and details of elements included in the contract, as well as information before the start of the journey. All information must be accurate as the directive specifically references the prohibition of misleading information.
● *Limitation of price revision*
  ● To provide regulation of the situations when an increase in price (or, for some countries, also a decrease in price) may be possible while identifying the conditions for price revision.
● *Consumer rights*
  ● To identify the right of the purchaser to transfer the booking as well as clarifying consumer rights in case of significant alterations to the package.

- *Additional duties of the organizer*
  - These include obligations to make alternative arrangements if the original package cannot be provided as planned, providing consumers with equivalent transport back to their point of origin and compensation when the product cannot be delivered as planned.
  - The operator also has a duty to provide assistance to consumers if they experience emergencies or difficulties while on holiday and, in the case of complaints, to undertake prompt efforts to resolve issues.
- *Liability*
  - To clarify the organizer's and/or retailers' limits of liability in cases where the package is not delivered according to plan or where the consumer has experienced a loss of enjoyment.
  - Schemes to provide security in case of insolvency of the tour operator are also considered.

Initially, the imposition of these regulations brought considerable problems for many tour operators and travel agents, not least because the interpretation of the regulations was unclear. In particular, it remained unclear what exactly constituted a 'package holiday' – was this to include business trips and tailor-made holidays? Would all organizers of packages, such as clubs or schoolteachers organizing educational trips, be included? 'Occasional' organizers were to be excluded, but the interpretation of what constituted 'occasional' posed further problems.

What does appear clear is that the additional burden of responsibility placed on tour operators led to some increases in cost for consumers, as operators attempted to cover themselves against any threat of legislation. The regulations imposed much greater responsibility on operators. For example, they directly penalize an operator if there is any dissemination of misleading information and provide for compensation to be paid for any loss suffered by consumers as a result of being misled. Furthermore, they make the tour operator directly responsible if hotels or other suppliers fail to provide the accommodation or services contracted for.

EXAMPLE　**The changing regulations for the UK-based tour operator**

Regulating air travel packages

Regulations restricting tour operators were very limiting when the mass tour market developed in the 1960s. In particular, the regulation known as Provision 1 made it impossible to price package tours lower than the cheapest regular return air fare to a destination. The sole exceptions to this rule were in the case of affinity groups, which involved charters arranged for associations that exist for a purpose other than that of obtaining cheap travel. Travellers were obliged to have been members of the organization for at least six months before they became eligible for low-cost flights. The rule was designed to protect scheduled carriers and ensure adequate profit for tour operators, but it severely hindered the expansion of the package tour business. It was also widely abused by club secretaries, who backdated membership, and many spurious clubs were formed in order to provide the benefits of cheap travel.

When the CAA was established in 1971, restrictions were lifted, initially only during the winter months (leading to a huge increase in out-of-season travel), but, by 1973, this was extended to all seasons. At the same time, however, the CAA tightened up control on tour operators themselves, introducing in 1972 the requirement to hold ATOLs for charters and block-booked scheduled seats, and, at the same time, introducing a system for vetting operators on their financial viability. By 1995, all tour operators were required to hold ATOLs when selling any flights or air holidays abroad. Licences are not required, however, for domestic air tours or for travel abroad using sea or land transport.

Regulating to ensure financial protection of the industry

Following the collapse of an important tour operator, Fiesta Tours, in 1964, which left some 5000 tourists stranded abroad, the industry and its customers came to recognize the importance of introducing protection against financial failure.

On the whole, in the UK, successive governments have preferred to allow the industry to police itself rather than impose additional controls and so it was initially undertaken relatively effectively by ABTA on behalf of tour operators and travel agents. In 1965, ABTA set up a Common Fund for this purpose, anticipating that there would be legislation for the compulsory registration of tour operators. When this did not materialize, ABTA introduced its stabilizer regulation, restricting ABTA tour operators to selling their package holidays exclusively through ABTA travel agents. In turn, ABTA agents were restricted to selling tours operated by ABTA tour operators. Many agents, however, resented having to contribute to a fund to insure operators and it also became clear that the provisions against collapse were inadequate.

In 1967, the Tour Operators' Study Group (TOSG – later to become the Federation of Tour Operators, FTO), established its own bonding scheme. A bond is a guarantee given by a third party (usually a bank or insurance company) to pay a sum of money, up to a specified maximum, in the event that the company becomes insolvent. That money would be used to meet the immediate financial obligations arising from the collapse, such as repatriating tourists stranded at overseas resorts and reimbursing clients booked to travel later with the company.

Later, ABTA itself introduced its own bonding scheme for all tour operating (and retail agency) members. The collapse in 1974, in the height of summer, of the Court Line group brought down Clarksons Holidays – then Britain's leading tour operator – and revealed, once again, that the level of protection was inadequate.

The government introduced an obligatory levy of 2% of operators' turnover between 1975 and 1977, which established the Air Travel Trust Fund (ATTF). These reserves were severely depleted, however, by collapses throughout the 1990s, particularly that of the International Leisure Group at the beginning of that decade, and the ATTF was obliged to call on the government for additional borrowing facilities when reserves ran dry. Since then, a number of alternative schemes have been introduced, in the form of either bonds or trustee accounts, including those schemes operated by the AITO Trust, the Travel Trust Association (TTA) and the Association of Bonded Travel Organizers Trust (ABTOT) for smaller operators. The Confederation of Passenger Transport (CPT), Passenger Shipping Association (PSA) and Yacht Charter Association operate their own schemes.

In July 2008, ABTA and FTO merged, thus providing combined expertise to better serve their tour operator members, while providing comprehensive protection schemes for their customers.

Regulating to manage complaints

ABTA operates its own arbitration scheme to resolve complaints by customers about its members. This is at a low cost to claimants, who are successful in about half of all cases brought. AITO provides a similar scheme. Alternatively, claims can be made through the courts under a new tracking system, which entails only moderate costs for plaintiffs.

Planning and marketing of package tours

Planning for the introduction of a new tour programme or destination is likely to take place over a lengthy span of time, sometimes as long as two years. A typical timescale for a programme of summer tours is shown in Figure 18.3.

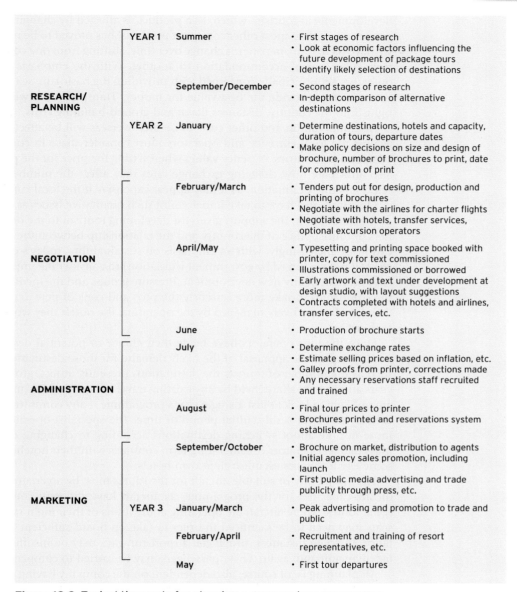

RESEARCH/ PLANNING	YEAR 1	Summer	• First stages of research • Look at economic factors influencing the future development of package tours • Identify likely selection of destinations
		September/December	• Second stages of research • In-depth comparison of alternative destinations
	YEAR 2	January	• Determine destinations, hotels and capacity, duration of tours, departure dates • Make policy decisions on size and design of brochure, number of brochures to print, date for completion of print
NEGOTIATION		February/March	• Tenders put out for design, production and printing of brochures • Negotiate with the airlines for charter flights • Negotiate with hotels, transfer services, optional excursion operators
		April/May	• Typesetting and printing space booked with printer, copy for text commissioned • Illustrations commissioned or borrowed • Early artwork and text under development at design studio, with layout suggestions • Contracts completed with hotels and airlines, transfer services, etc.
		June	• Production of brochure starts
ADMINISTRATION		July	• Determine exchange rates • Estimate selling prices based on inflation, etc. • Galley proofs from printer, corrections made • Any necessary reservations staff recruited and trained
		August	• Final tour prices to printer • Brochures printed and reservations system established
MARKETING		September/October	• Brochure on market, distribution to agents • Initial agency sales promotion, including launch • First public media advertising and trade publicity through press, etc.
	YEAR 3	January/March	• Peak advertising and promotion to trade and public
		February/April	• Recruitment and training of resort representatives, etc.
		May	• First tour departures

Figure 18.3 Typical timescale for planning a summer tour programme

In planning deadlines for the programme, it is necessary to work backwards from the planned launch dates. One critical problem is when to determine prices. These have to be established at the last minute before material goes to be printed, but inevitably this will be several months before the tour programme starts, so entails a good understanding (and some luck!) with regard to the movement of currency and the foreign exchange markets in the intervening period. Assessments must also be made of what the competition is likely to charge for similar products. The introduction of fluid pricing has eased the former inflexibility of brochure prices, although any changes made immediately after publication would be frowned on.

Market research

In practice, the decision to exploit a destination or region for package tours is as much an act of faith as it is the outcome of carefully considered research. Forecasting future developments in tourism, which, as a product, is affected by changing circumstances to a greater extent than most other consumer products, has proved to be notably inaccurate. As we have seen, tourism patterns change over time, shifting from one country to another and from one form of accommodation to another. With the emphasis on price, mass tour operators are principally concerned with providing the basic sun, sea and sand package in countries that provide the best value for money. Transport costs will depend on charter rights into the country, distances flown and ground-handling costs.

Accommodation and other costs to be met overseas will be affected by exchange rates against the local currency and operators must consider these in comparison with other competitive countries' currency values when setting the price for the package. They should also anticipate how changing exchange rates may affect the number of clients likely to select any one destination, as it may appear expensive if the local currency is strong.

Operators also have to take into account such qualitative issues as the political stability of the destination, the support given for developing tourism to the destination by the carriers or tourist office of the country and the relationship between the host and destination countries. Increasingly, with an emphasis on sustainability, today's operators are encouraged (if not yet forced by government legislation) to consider the impact on locals and the environment of any new development. Pressure groups and the media are slowly persuading companies to take more seriously the pros and cons of new developments and how these can be effectively managed by the operators, the hotels they work with and the local authorities.

Once the tour operators have made their choice of potential destinations, they must produce a realistic appraisal of the likely demand for those destinations, based on factors such as the number of tourists the destinations presently attract, growth rates over recent years and present shares held by any existing travel companies. The mass market operators are unlikely to look at just a single year's programme – any commitment to a destination is likely to be for a substantial period of time. The specialist operator, however, may be more flexible about switching destinations according to changing demand. In contrast, mass market operators consider long-term contracts with their hoteliers abroad or even in some circumstances establish their own hotels.

The availability of suitable aircraft for the routes must be ascertained. This will, in part, dictate capacities for the programme, as aircraft have different configurations, and, on some routes, where aircraft are operating at the limits of their flight range, some passenger seats may need to be sacrificed in order to take on board sufficient fuel to cover the distance. In some instances, provincial airport runways may be insufficient for larger, fully laden aircraft and, again, fewer passengers may be carried to compensate.

All planning is, of course, also dependent on the company having the necessary finance available to operate and market the programme.

The process of negotiating

Once the decisions have been made as to destinations to be served, numbers of passengers to be carried during the season and dates of departure, serious negotiations can get underway with airlines, hotels and other principals, leading to formal contracts. Those contracts will spell out payment due dates as well as the conditions for the release of unsold accommodation or the cancellation of chartered aircraft flights (or, in the case of block bookings on scheduled services, the aircraft seats), along with details of any penalties that the tour operator will incur for cancellation.

Airline negotiations

Normal terms for aircraft chartering are for a deposit to be paid on signing the contract (generally 10% of the total cost), with the balance becoming due on each flight after it takes place. In negotiating for charter services, the reputation of the tour operator is of paramount importance. If they have worked with that airline or with similar charters in previous years, that will be taken into account when determining the terms and price for the contract. Relationships between the sectors of the industry are still based predominantly on trust, as the threat of legal action, perhaps months after a dispute such as an overbooking problem has arisen, will do little to resolve problems at the time.

Part and parcel of the negotiations is the setting up of the tour operating flight plan, with decisions being made on the dates and frequency of operations, airports to be used and times of arrival and departure. All of this information will have to be consolidated into a form suitable for publication and easy to understand in the tour brochure.

A well-established operator does not wish to be at the mercy of market forces when dealing with charter airlines. In any given year, the demand for suitable aircraft may exceed the supply, which has encouraged the larger tour operators to form or buy their own airline, just to ensure that the capacity they need is available to them.

Hotel negotiations

Hotel negotiations – other than in the case of large tour operators, which may negotiate contracts for an entire hotel – are generally far more informal than are airline negotiations. Small and specialist tour operators selling independent inclusive tours may have no more than a **free sale** (or **sell and report**) agreement with hoteliers. These involve the hotel agreeing to guarantee accommodation for a specified maximum number of tourists (usually at least four, although it may be higher in large hotels with plenty of availability for certain days of the week) merely on receipt of the notification of a booking from the tour operator, whether by phone, fax or e-mail. This arrangement may be quite suitable for small tour programmes, but it suffers from the disadvantage that, at times, hoteliers will retain the right to close out certain dates. As these are likely to be the most popular dates in the calendar, the operator stands to lose both potential business and goodwill. The alternative is for the operator to contract for an allocation of rooms in the hotel, with dates agreed for the release of those unsold that are well in advance of the anticipated arrival dates.

Long-term contracts, either for a block of rooms or the entire hotel, have the attraction of providing the operator with the lowest possible prices, but they carry a higher element of risk. Some contracts have been drawn up by operators to cover periods as long as five years and, while at first glance such long fixed-term price contracts may seem attractive, they are seldom realistic and, in an inflationary period, may well have to be renegotiated to avoid bankrupting the hotelier (such an event would obviously not be in the operator's interest).

In addition to the operator spelling out exact requirements in terms of rooms – required numbers of singles, doubles, twins, with or without private facilities, whether with balconies or sea views and with what catering provision (room only, with breakfast, half or full board) – it must also clarify a number of other facts, including:

- reservations and registration procedures, including whether or not hotel vouchers are to be issued
- accommodation requirements for any representatives or couriers (usually provided free)
- handling procedures and fees charged for porterage
- special facilities available or needed, such as air-conditioned or non-smoking rooms, facilities for handicapped customers or special catering requirements, such as kosher or vegetarian food
- languages spoken by hotel staff
- systems of payment by guests for drinks or other extras

Figure 18.4 A typical representatives' hotel noticeboard

Photo by Chris Holloway

- reassurance on suitable fire and safety precautions (tour operators based in the EU have responsibility (and liability) for protecting their customers under the package travel directive, no matter where the hotel is situated)
- if appropriate, suitable space for a representative's desk and noticeboard (see Figure 18.4).

In negotiations, consideration may also be given to the availability of alternative hotel accommodation of a comparable standard in the event of overbooking. Of course, a hotel with a reputation for overbooking is to be avoided, but, over the course of time, some errors are bound to occur and so guests will need to be transferred to other hotels. Tour operators must satisfy themselves that the arrangements made by the hotelier for taking care of clients in these circumstances are adequate. Any operator negotiating with a hotelier will be aware that they are likely to be sharing contracted space with other operators, not only within their own country but also from other countries. It is as well to be aware of one's own standing with the hotelier in relation to those other companies. For example, in Spain it was not uncommon in the past to find that the German operators, which tended to pay higher prices for their rooms than did the British, would have their rooms protected in preference to UK operators when overbookings occurred.

Independent companies can find themselves squeezed out of the market for European bed stock in popular resorts and, at times, even the mass market operators become aware that greater concentration in the industry can lead to more difficulty in tying up contracts with popular hotels. For this reason, as demand rises for key Mediterranean destinations – and also to ensure greater control over the major elements in the package – some operators turn to owning hotels at the destinations or, at the very least, having far more say in their management. First Choice announced in 2000 its intention to play a part in designing new hotels and influencing their layout, when long-term contracts are envisaged.

EXAMPLE ## TUI buys up an Italian village

In May 2007, TUI announced that it had purchased a Tuscan village – Tenuta di Castelfalfi, located between the popular tourism destinations of Florence, Pisa and Siena. The land, covering 11 square kilometres, includes a mediaeval castle and golf course, as well as arable land. However, the local population amounted to just two persons. The reported cost of purchasing the village was some $340 million.

Development of the area began in 2011, with phase one comprising a 32-room boutique hotel, a golf course and restaurants. Eventually the entire redevelopment is expected to include renovation of the main village, as well as the addition of other hotels (all TUI brands), villas, apartments, spa and shopping facilities.

To gain permission for these developments, TUI has incorporated ecological protection into the plans – particularly linked to energy and water use – with expectations that the construction footprint will cover less than 1% of the total land purchased.

Destination services negotiations

Similar negotiations will take place with locally based incoming operators and coach companies to provide transfers between airports and hotels and any optional excursions. Car hire companies may also be approached so as to negotiate commission rates on sales to the tour operator's clients and tailor-made transfers between airports and hotels.

The reliability and honesty of local operators is an important issue here. Some smaller tour operators may not be in a position to employ their own resort representatives initially, so their image will depend on the level of service provided by the local operators' staff.

If a local company is also operating optional sightseeing excursions, procedures for booking these and handling the finances involved must be established. It should also be clarified whether qualified guides with a sound knowledge of the clients' language are to be employed on the excursions.

The role of the resort representative

Tour operators carrying large numbers of package tourists to a destination are in a position to employ their own resort representatives. This has obvious advantages in that the company can count on the loyalty and total commitment of its own staff. A decision must be made as to whether to employ a national of the host country or of the generating country (although it should be acknowledged that, in some cases, the destination may receive customers from several generating countries and the representative will need to be able to serve all customers effectively). The advantage of hiring a representative from the local community is that he or she will be fully acquainted with the local customs and geography, fluent in the language of the country and have good local contacts, which may make it easier to take care of problems effectively (such as dealing with the police, local shopkeepers or hoteliers). The flipside of this is that he or she is likely to be less familiar with the culture, customs or language of the clients, which can act as a negative point for tourists, especially for those on first visits abroad. Exceptional local representatives have been able to overcome this problem and, if they themselves have some common background with their clients, such as having lived for some years in the incoming tourists' country, they can often function as effectively as would representatives from the generating country.

Furthermore, some countries impose restrictions on the employment of foreign nationals at resorts, which is a point that must be clarified before employing any representatives. This used to be a problem at the popular Mediterranean resorts, but, with the development of freedom of labour movement within the EU, tour operators are now free to decide for themselves what should be the background and nationality of their representatives.

The representatives' role is far more demanding than is commonly thought. During the high season, they can be expected to work a seven-day week and will need to be on call for 24 hours each day to cope with any emergencies. Resort representatives are usually given a desk in the hotel lobby from which to work, but, in cases where tour operators have their clients in two or more hotels in the resort, they may have to visit each of these hotels during some part of the day. Their principal functions include:

- handling general enquiries
- advising on currency exchange, shopping and so on
- organizing and supervising social activities at the hotels
- publicizing, selling and booking optional excursions
- handling special requirements and complaints and acting as an intermediary for clients, interceding with the hotel proprietor, the police or other local authorities as necessary.

These routine functions are supplemented by problems arising from lost baggage, ill health (needing to refer clients to local dentists or doctors) and even, occasionally, deaths, although serious problems such as these are often referred to area managers, who may oversee and manage representatives across several resorts in a region or country. The representatives must also relocate clients whose accommodation is for any reason inadequate or when overbookings have occurred and may also have to rebook flights for their clients whose plans change as a result of emergencies.

The representatives' busiest days are when groups are arriving or leaving the resort. They will accompany groups returning home on the coach to the airport, ensuring that departure formalities at the hotel have been complied with, arrange to pay any airport or departure taxes due and then wait to greet incoming clients and accompany them, in turn, to their hotels on the transfer coaches. In the not uncommon situation where flights are delayed, this can result in representatives having to spend very long hours at the airport, sometimes missing a night's sleep. On their return to the hotels, they must also ensure that check-in procedures operate smoothly, going over rooming lists with the hotel managers before the latter bill the company.

Most operators also provide a welcome party for their clients on the first or second night of their holiday and it is the representatives' task to organize and host this. It also provides an important opportunity to sell excursions to the newly arrived guests. As profit margins are often tight for tour operators, there has been more emphasis placed on the sale of excursions in recent years. Many representatives have in the past been given sales targets to achieve and rewarded financially for good performance in this area.

The commercialization of the resort representative's role became steadily more marked, to a point where their duty to interact socially with the customers became less important to their managers. This led, eventually, to substantial reductions in the numbers of representatives employed and in some cases to their disappearance entirely. The explanation for this move comes partly from the increasing sophistication of the customers, many of whom are well travelled and no longer feel that they need a rep's help at the destination, as long as a company rep is available at the end of a phone.

Arguably, this development leads to two weaknesses in promoting a brand. First, it may reduce the opportunities for clients to engage in commercial transactions that will benefit the company and, second, it devalues the image of the company, in the sense that a representative is, in many cases, the only personal contact a tour operator has with its clients and, therefore, represents the brand. Smaller operators have not been slow to recognize that they now hold a significant advantage over the leaders if they simply employ personable individuals to represent them.

Reviewing the need for holiday reps

Both Thomson Holidays and Cosmos announced in 2004 that they were reviewing the role of resort representatives. This recognized that alternative arrangements were more suitable to some markets. Thomson had provided emergency contact numbers for their guests, providing 24-hour support; therefore having to wait until the resort rep arrived at the hotel was no longer necessary.

Travellers on packages which were last-minute deals, or those tours more suited to experienced vacationers, were seen to have less need for face-to-face meetings with representatives. Reps were not phased out completely – the changes meant merely that fewer were provided, and they were targeted at those holidaymakers most needing their skills and expertise.

Where representatives continue to be favoured, they can expect to spend some time at their resort bases before the start of the season, not only to get to know the site but also report back to their companies on the standards of tourist facilities and pinpoint any discrepancies between descriptions in the brochures and reality. This has become increasingly important since the regulations imposed by the EU Directive on Package Holidays came into force. Representatives may also be expected to inform their companies if any changes occur during the season about which clients must be notified at the time of booking. In an effort to reduce complaints and handle them at source, some operators give representatives the authority to compensate their clients on the spot for minor claims and complaints.

Today some operators employ full-time staff who spend part of the year as representatives at their resorts, either in the summer or winter, while at other times they are brought back to head office to handle reservations or other administrative work. The job of a representative seldom offers genuine career opportunities, but, for some, there is the opportunity to progress, starting with positions as children's representatives and moving on to adult representative, senior representative, area supervisor and eventually area manager. Ultimately, the opportunity for progression lies back at head office, where the managers having overall responsibility for resort representatives recruit and train staff, organize holiday rosters, provide uniforms and handle the administration of the representatives' department. Nevertheless, for the large majority, opportunities for employment are limited to the high season.

Pricing the package tour

Key to the success of a tour operator's programme is getting the price right. It must be right for the market, right compared with the prices of competitors' package tours and right compared with the prices of other tours offered by the company.

Table 18.5 The typical cost structure of an inclusive tour using charter air services

Costs	Percentage of overall costs
Charter air seat	45
Hotel accommodation	37
Other services at destination	3
Head office overheads	5
Travel agencies' commission	10

Costing the package

A tour operator will, as we have noted, normally purchase three main inputs to create inclusive tours: transport, accommodation and services. The latter will include transfers between airports and accommodation abroad and, possibly, the services of the company's resort representative at the site. The operator will also, of course, have to cover costs that arise within the company's headquarters, such as administration, reservations, marketing and advertising. Finally, the operator will have to cover the cost of commission paid to retailers and servicing those retailers. A typical inclusive tour from the UK might well have the kind of cost structure outlined in Table 18.5.

As the profits achieved by most operators after allowing for agencies' commission are actually quite narrow – perhaps as little as 1–3% of revenue, after covering all costs – operators will seek to top up their revenue in any other way possible. For mass market operators, the bulk of their revenue – in excess of 50%, normally – is achieved through the sales of summer holidays. Perhaps another 15–20% will be achieved through a winter tour programme and the balance through a mix of sales of excursions at the destination, the interest received on deposits and final payments invested, foreign currency speculation and sale of insurance policies.

One contribution to revenue is achieved by imposing cancellation charges. These charges will often substantially exceed any costs borne by the operator resulting from that cancellation and, indeed, the operator may well be able to sell the cancelled accommodation again, gaining twice. The EU Directive on Package Holidays now allows, in theory, the substitution of names by the clients to replace cancelled bookings, but this is impossible to enforce where many airlines do not accept name changes and countries require arriving passengers to hold visas.

Specialist operators that offer a unique product may have more flexibility and the freedom to determine their prices based on cost plus a mark-up that is sufficient to cover overheads and provide a satisfactory level of profit. The mass operators, however, must take greater account of their competitors' prices as demand for package tours is, as we have seen, extremely price-sensitive, especially for programmes offered in the shoulder or low season.

In the following section we will examine two alternative, but typical, examples of cost-determined tour pricing. The first will consider pricing for the mass market, the second, pricing for the specialist operator.

Mass market tour pricing

The first example is based on a German company providing time series charter travel and a two-week hotel stay at a Mediterranean beach resort destination, such as those found on the island of Majorca, Spain.

EXAMPLE **Mass market operator pricing**

	Flight costs €	Package costs (including flight costs) €
Flight costs, based on 15 holiday departures (back to back) on Boeing 737-800, 189-seat aircraft at €20 725 per flight	621 750	
Plus one empty leg each way at beginning and end of the season;		
out	20 725	
home	20 725	
Total flight costs	663 200	
Total cost per flight:		
(€663 200 ÷ 15 holiday departures)	44 213.33	
Cost per seat at 90% occupancy (170 seats), i.e. €44 213.33 ÷ 170		260.08
Plus passenger charges (e.g. airport fees at outbound and inbound airports, government taxes, security fees)		40.00
Net hotel cost per person, 14 nights half-board		245.00
Resort agent's handling fees and transfers, per person		10.00
Gratuities, porterage		5.00
Total cost per person		560.08
Add mark-up of approx. 30% on cost price to cover agency commission, marketing costs (including brochure production, advertising, etc.), head office administrative costs and profit		168.02
Selling price (rounded up)		730.00

Many companies would add a small fee, say €15, in order to build in a no surcharge guarantee, especially in times of economic instability. Holidays that are cancelled are presently resold to the public – as mentioned, a source of considerable extra income as full refunds do not have to be made to the original customer (who recovers these costs from insurance, if there is a valid claim).

In estimating the cost of a seat on the aircraft, operators must not only calculate the load factor on which this cost is to be based but must also aim to achieve this load factor on average throughout the series of tours they will be operating. This must depend on their estimates of the market demand for each destination and the current supply of aircraft seats available to their competitors. Remember that one flight route may service several destinations; for example, a flight taking skiers to the USA may land in Denver and serve holidaymakers visiting the popular resorts of Vail, Breckenridge or Keystone as well as transferring other passengers onto a short internal flight serving Steamboat Springs. Similarly, flights to Geneva may serve alpine resorts in France, Switzerland and Italy. As the demand at high season will frequently exceed the supply of seats to the destinations, there is scope to increase the above price, and hence profits, for those months of the year, even if that results in the company being uncompetitive compared with other leading operators. As operators have in the past tended to overestimate demand, however, this is becoming a risky procedure. In the low season, meanwhile, supply is likely to exceed the demand for available packages, so companies may set their prices so low that only the variable costs are covered, with a very small contribution made to the fixed costs (marketing, administration and so on), in order to fill the seats.

Each tour operator must carefully consider what proportion of its overheads is to be allocated to each tour and destination. As long as the expenses are recovered in full during the term of operation, the allocation of costs can be made on the basis of market forces and need not necessarily be apportioned equally to each programme and destination. In practice, most operators now recover their overheads by determining a per capita contribution, based on anticipated head office costs for the year and the total number of passengers the company expects to carry. Under this system, of course, each tour carries the same burden of office costs regardless of destination or price. There is a case for a more marketing-orientated approach to pricing, however, based on a consideration of market prices and the company's long-term objectives. In entering a new market, for instance, it may be that the principal objective is to penetrate and obtain a targeted share of that market in the first year of operating, which may be achieved by reducing or even forgoing profits during the first year and/or reducing the per capita contribution to corporate costs. Indeed, to some destinations the operator may introduce loss-leader pricing policies, other more profitable routes subsidizing the cost of this policy in order to get a footing in the market to a new destination.

Specialist tour pricing

The second example is of a specialist French long-haul operator that uses the services of scheduled carriers to Hong Kong, with a GIT.

It will be noted that, in the case of this specialist operator, prices reflect market demand at different periods of the year and there is no equal distribution of office overheads as the profits and most overheads are recoverable in the high-season prices charged to the market. The lead price gives very little profit for bookings made through the trade, but is strictly limited to one or two weeks of the year. Large profits can be obtained, however, over Christmas, Chinese New Year, during conferences and for other business committed to specific dates. There is a tendency to be cautious about milking excess profits from periods of increased demand. Several Gulf States carriers, for example, offer much lower prices to offset the need to change flights, so competition at all times of the year is quite high. If charges are set too high, operators may be left with availability during peak times.

The pricing policy shown here is common among the smaller specialist operators, which tend to use less sophisticated pricing techniques when fixing target profits. Many specialists operating in a climate where there is no exact competition for their product could be expected to charge a price that would give them an overall gross profit of 25% or more, while most mass market operators, and some specialists, will be forced by market conditions to settle for much lower margins.

EXAMPLE **Specialist operator pricing**

	Package costs (including flight costs) €
Flight cost, based on net group air fares, per person	470
Plus air charges	70
Net hotel cost per person, 7 nights, twin room (HK$720 per room = HK$360 per person per night; HK$12 = €1)	210
Transfers HK$90 each way (equating to €7.50 each way)	15
Subtotal	765
Add agent's commission	85
Total cost per person	850
Selling prices	
'Lead price' (offered on only one or two low season flights)	859
Shoulder season price	899
High season price (summer, Christmas and Easter holiday periods)	1049

In developing a pricing strategy for package tours, operators must take into account a number of other variables in addition to those shown above. Earlier, the point was made that the price had to be right compared with all competing products on the market. For example, when setting a price for a departure from a regional airport, the operator will look at how much more the client will be willing to pay to avoid a long trip to a major airport. In the example given above, for flights from France to Hong Kong, a traveller living near Strasbourg may prefer to fly from a regional airport to Hong Kong via Frankfurt with Lufthansa rather than make the journey to Paris in order to access an Air France flight. Equally, if a flight is to leave at two o'clock in the morning, the price must be sufficiently attractive compared with others leaving during the day to make people willing to suffer the inconvenience of travelling at that time. What special reductions are to be offered to children or for group bookings? As seat and other costs will be unaffected, whatever reductions the company makes for these bookings will have to be recovered in profits achieved through sales to other customers.

Discounting strategies

Discounts on published tour prices have become a widely accepted practice in the industry. Originally applied to late bookings in order to clear seats, the technique has more recently been used by the larger operators to persuade members of the public to book earlier, using a system of fluid pricing – the practice of prices for travel products altering as demand levels change, discussed earlier. Other operators prefer to offer guarantees to those who book early that there will be no increases in price prior to their departure.

Discounting is also influenced by travel retailers – they may elect to sell packages below the prices determined by the operators themselves by passing on to the clients a proportion of their commission. In practice, this has meant that the largest discounts can be allowed by the largest multiple travel agencies, as they can negotiate larger commissions, well above the 10% norm, as they achieve higher sales levels and, in effect, can pass on to their clients almost all the 10% basic commission. As this percentage represents the total commission that most independent agents receive from operators, the independents cannot match their prices and therefore find it impossible to compete on price alone. Instead, many will offer alternative benefits, such as free insurance to secure a sale or an extra service, such as a free taxi transfer to the local airport.

Heavy discounting by the market leaders through their own retail chains has been a major factor in boosting their share of the mass market. Given the problems that have faced the industry over the past few years and the strong competition between operators to survive in a difficult marketplace, there is little likelihood of the industry moving away from deep discounting in the foreseeable future.

Cash flow

The normal booking season for summer holidays starts in the autumn of the preceding year, reaching its peak in the three months following Christmas, so a large proportion of deposits will have been paid by the end of March. Although the operators themselves will have had to make deposits for aircraft charters at the beginning of the season and may also have had to make some advances to hoteliers to ensure that the rooms they need are held, the final account for these services will not fall due until after the clients have completed their holiday. Operators will have the use of deposit payments for anything up to a year in advance and will have clients' final payments at least eight weeks before they themselves have to settle their accounts. This money is invested to earn interest and, in some cases, that interest will actually exceed the net profits made by tour operating itself. Clearly, one effect of the tendency of holidaymakers to book their holidays later and pay by credit card will be a fall in interest earnings by the operators.

Yield management

The high levels of competition for summer holiday sales require operators to take a great deal of care to get the prices of their packages right, so that sufficient demand is generated to fill available seats. At the same time, they must not be so cheap as to threaten their profitability.

Yield management has been a key tool to this end for the airline industry, allowing each fare category to be allocated to a set number of seats, with the number of seats in each category being determined by the demand for any flight. Typically operating with a tiered pricing system for their fixed capacity, with early bookers able to purchase the cheaper seats, the price for seats moves up with the scarcity of seats (as the flight nears capacity). Such a technique is now being applied across the industry, including sectors such as hotels, car hire and tour operators.

For tour operators, the smooth running of yield management is frequently defeated by the excess capacity available in the market, forcing companies to 'dump' packages at whatever price they can achieve in order to help make a contribution to their overheads. There is some evidence that companies are improving their skills at yield management by improving their forecasting or a willingness to reduce capacity in order to achieve a better balance between supply and demand. While such actions have been taken largely in the form of implicit agreements between the major operators, there is always the risk that the smaller operators will see this as an opportunity to steal some market share from the brand leaders and increase their own capacity.

If prices are set too low initially and late demand in the season results in a 'sold out' situation, the company will not have maximized its profit opportunities. At the same time, if the company finds itself involved in added expenditure in the course of the summer – for example, providing accommodation and meals for clients delayed by air traffic control strikes (which cannot be foreseen a year in advance but occur not infrequently in Europe) – what might have been a slim but acceptable profit can soon be turned into an overall loss.

Another aspect to consider is when to launch the new holiday programme. In the past, some operators have even launched programmes more than a year in advance. Companies launching their programmes ahead of their rivals will always hope to steal a larger proportion of the early booking market and, of course, have the consequent revenue that can be invested over a longer period. It is unclear, however, if the advantages of early sales achieved in this way are sufficient to offset the drawbacks, not least of confusing both agents and customers through the range of choice on offer at any given time. A further issue is that publishing this far in advance gives competitors full view of your prices, hotels and sales techniques, giving them an opportunity to adjust their marketing when they launch their own programmes.

The tour brochure

For many years, the tour operator's brochure was the critical marketing tool and the main influence on customers' decisions to buy. Tourism is an intangible product that customers are obliged to purchase without having the opportunity to inspect it, and often from a base of very inadequate knowledge. In these circumstances – and given the often limited personal knowledge of products and destinations held by travel agents – the brochure became the principal means of both informing customers about the product and persuading them to purchase it.

For most companies, very large sums are still invested in the brochure itself, as well as advertising designed to persuade customers to visit travel agents to pick one up or order a copy to be delivered to their homes. In particular, the production of the brochure is likely to represent a very significant proportion of the total marketing budget for the year, with print runs, in the case of the largest operators, running into tens of millions, at a unit cost of well over £2 a copy. Industry estimates suggest that tour operators typically produce 20–25 brochures for every holiday sold.

Accordingly, it is essential for operators to ensure that this large expenditure achieves its intended results. Despite this, however, there is considerable wastage. In one study undertaken by the environmental lobby Green Flag International, it was estimated that of 120 million travel brochures printed in the UK in one year, 48 million were never used. This wastage rate, coupled with the high cost of printing and distributing each copy, was estimated to add approximately £20 to the price of the average package holiday. More recently, tour operators have taken to providing brochures electronically, allowing customers to collect a DVD from retail outlets or, more commonly, to download copies directly from their websites. Such moves can help to reduce the high costs of distributing paper brochures, as well as reducing waste. Also, when a price update needs to be made, the online brochure can be quickly updated and made available to customers.

Despite the cost advantages of producing electronic brochures, the demand for a printed version is still high. The opportunity to mark up pages with notes about particular products, to share these brochures with others travelling in the group and to repeatedly review the product as the holiday decision is being made, still remain important actions for many holidaymakers. Personalized brochures sent by e-mail at the request of the traveller may help here, as the brochure can be printed if necessary and shared with others electronically – important if the travellers are geographically spread. One downside of the personalized brochure containing only the sections requested by the holidaymaker is that this may limit the opportunity to cross-sell products; a multidestination printed brochure provides an opportunity to inspire travellers to consider alternative destinations which may also meet their desires.

The brochure is no longer the critical tool it once was, as many operators now sell directly from their websites. Indeed, some small companies no longer print brochures at all, simply printing off relevant pages from their websites for those customers wanting a paper copy of their holiday arrangements. While this trend is likely to accelerate, for the present the brochure still remains an important tool, so must be considered here.

Brochure design and format

Larger companies will either have their brochures designed and prepared in their own advertising department or coordinate the production with a design studio, often associated with the advertising agency they use. The agency will help to negotiate with printers to obtain the best quotation for producing the brochure and ensure that print deadlines are met. In other cases, tour operators will tackle the design of the brochure themselves – a process that is being increasingly aided by computer programs that allow desktop publishing, which means that the operator is able to produce the entire contents of the brochure, including all the illustrations, on an inhouse computer. The computer will organize the layout, selecting the best locations for text and illustrations to minimize use of space, thus helping to reduce the cost. Naturally, the financial investment in the technology necessary to undertake this work is considerable.

Smaller operators tackling the design of the brochure themselves are best advised to use the help of an independent design studio, which can provide the professional expertise required in relation to the brochure's layout, artwork and copy that are so important to ensuring that the result is a professional piece of publicity material. Most printers have their own design departments that can undertake this work for their clients, but, unless the company has had experience of the standards of work of a printer, they are probably better advised to approach an independent studio to do this work.

The purposes the brochure serves will dictate its design and format. A single *ad hoc* programme, for example, to a foreign trade exhibition, may require nothing more than a leaflet, while a limited programme of tours may be laid out in the form of a simple folder.

Folders can take a number of different forms, ranging from a **centrefold** to more complicated folds. Larger brochures (or, in printing terminology, **booklets**) consist of eight or more pages, printed in multiples of four sheets that need to be bound together in some manner. Smaller brochures are usually machine-bound by **saddle-stitching** (stapling through the spine), while larger brochures may be **side-stitched** with a glue-on cover or bound as a book. It is not the aim here to discuss printing methods in detail, so, for further reading in the subject, see the many excellent books on print publicity.

Purpose-designed brochures will usually include all of an operator's summer or winter tours within a single brochure. However, many larger operators have diversified into a great many different types of holiday – long-haul and short-haul, coach tours as well as air holidays, lake and mountain resorts as well as seaside resorts – and if all these were to be combined into a single brochure, it would run to hundreds of pages and be both clumsy to handle and very expensive to produce. There would also be high wastage, as clients who know the type of holiday they want will have to pick up the entire programme just to get details of the particular product they are interested in. Operators therefore produce individual brochures, even in some cases separating brochures by destination. This has the added advantage of filling more of the agents' rack space, leaving less available space for competitors. If the leading half-dozen operators produce as many as 70–80 different brochures – all top sellers for agents – this will require the agency to devote as much as half their rack space to these brands.

EXAMPLE   Pick a colour

First Choice holidays designed their summer 2012 brochures using three colour categories – silver, orange and jade. The colour coding of brochures is designed to make it easier for holidaymakers and travel agents to find suitable holiday accommodation.

Silver brochures contain premium hotels and resorts, orange brochures are for holiday villages and resorts with SplashWorld (waterpark) facilities while jade brochures are filled with standard all inclusive hotels and resorts.

The first task of a brochure is to attract attention. Operators have often developed a **house style** for the covers of their brochures, which means that they have the same sorts of covers each time so that they are quickly recognized by customers when they are looking through the agents' racks. They usually have images of attractive models in beachwear combined with an eye-catching symbol and brand name across the top of the brochure. In trying to get away from the stereotypical images, one holiday company, Cornwall Traditional Cottages, as part of a rebranding exercise launched a photographic competition with the winning entry becoming the cover of their 2012 brochure. This encouraged entrants to submit eye-catching and inspiring images of Cornwall.

While some might contend that there is a disappointing sameness to the leading operators' brochures today, taken individually the quality and professionalism of modern brochure design and printing is outstanding. As brochures must also reinforce an image of quality and reliability, the text and images contained in brochures must not only be attractive but also truthful, accurate and easily understood. Good layout, high-quality photography and suitable paper are all essential if a brochure is to do its job effectively.

Obligations affecting tour brochures

Tour operators are selling dreams, and their brochures must allow consumers to fantasize a little about their holidays. It is also vitally important, however, that consumers are not misled about any aspect of their holiday. Care must be taken not to infringe the EU Directive on Package Holidays, which explicitly makes it an offence to make misleading or false statements concerning the provision of services. Legislation introduced in European countries to comply with the Directive clarified operators' responsibilities regarding misrepresentations of elements of the travel product, which has simplified proceedings for tourists, who can sue an operator for offences for which their suppliers abroad are responsible, requiring the operator, in turn, to sue suppliers in the destination country to recover their costs.

Information required in the brochure

The EU Directive on Package Holidays established requirements for the minimum information to be provided in brochures. Since its introduction, the growth in online sales has led to this being reviewed, and currently the EU is canvassing opinion on whether the list is up to date.

Article 3.2, which details the content required, recognizes that any descriptive material concerning a package should not contain any misleading information and that the brochure should indicate:

- the price
- the characteristics and categories of transport used
- the type of accommodation, its location, quality rating and main features
- the meal plan
- the travel itinerary
- passport and visa requirements
- any health formalities required for the journey and the stay
- the amount of the deposit and timetable for payment of the final balance
- whether a minimum number of persons is required for the package to operate
- the arrangements in the case of travel delays
- the arrangements for financial protection against insolvency of the tour operator.

Discussions related to this legislation are ongoing, particularly in regard to the inclusion of the price of a holiday in the brochure. Fluctuating prices, perhaps due to shifting exchange rates or fuel prices, have had an impact on the accuracy of this, and tour operators argue that the cost to reprint brochures adds unnecessary cost to the travel sector. With more travellers booking online there is pressure to remove this requirement. However, concern that removing prices would make it more difficult for the consumer to compare alternative holiday products has meant that brochures still have prices included (EU, 2007).

The e-brochure

Websites now frequently replace some elements of the traditional brochure, but the preparation of web pages has to be undertaken as carefully as that for brochures. While a website will share many characteristics with a brochure, there are important differences. Customers will read fewer words on a screen than on the printed page, so the visual elements take on greater significance. The particular advantage of a website is that it can be changed frequently and at short notice – in fact, it is critical that the site is always up to date, as this will be expected. Staff must be trained to undertake this and assess what changes have to be carried out. Sometimes whole programmes will need to be withdrawn or added. Many companies use their websites to personalize their approach to clients, giving portraits of staff and adding comments from tourists on the resort pages.

In many cases, tour operators will offer visitors to their website the opportunity to download all or part of their brochure. In most cases, the format used is a PDF file (which can be read using widely available free software). In the past, it was common to allow the brochure to be downloaded through a hyperlink on the website. More and more, however, tour operators are realizing that they can make contact with those customers reading their brochures by sending the requested information as an attachment to an e-mail address. This provides the tour operator with the opportunity to follow up the brochure request with relevant e-mails to try to encourage the customer to book with them. This latter approach also allows customers to request only the parts of the brochure in which they are interested.

EXAMPLE **Accessing brochures online**

Kuoni's 2012 Worldwide brochure is split by geographic region (Indian subcontinent and Ocean – 96 pages; Far East and Pacific – 134 pages; Egypt, Dubai and Arabia – 56 pages; Africa – 44 pages; Caribbean – 72 pages; Americas – 24 pages), and its website (**www.kuoni.co.uk/brochures**) allows customers to select a region to download or even a country within that region. This is important as the entire brochure covers several hundred pages, many of which may not be of interest to customers. The information received by customers will always include booking information, giving details of the terms and conditions, too.

To download the brochure, customers select the regions that they are interested in and are asked to enter an e-mail address. The selected pages are compiled as a PDF document, with important legal information and flight details included, which is then sent to the e-mail address almost instantaneously.

Negotiating with printers

Printers do not expect their clients to be experts in printing methods, but those involved with the processing and production of a brochure should be reasonably familiar with current techniques in printing and common terms used. Printers need the following information:

- The number of brochures required.
- The number of colours to be used in the printing. Full-colour work normally involves four colours, but some cost savings should be possible if colour photography is not to be included.
- The paper to be used – size, format, quality and weight. The choice of paper will be influenced by several factors, including the printing process used. Size may be dictated by the industry's requirements. For example, a tour operator's brochure needs to fit a standard travel agents' rack. Paper quality varies according to the material from which it is made. It may be glossy or matt, but will be selected for its whiteness and opacity. Inevitably, there is an element of compromise here as very white paper tends to be less opaque and one must avoid print showing through on the other side of the sheet. The weight of paper chosen will of course depend on its effect on the overall weight of the brochure, if it is to be mailed in quantity. Operators may well cut the size of a brochure if it reduces postage costs to a lower band.

- The number and positions of illustrations (photos, artwork, maps and so on) used.
- Typesetting needs. There are over 6000 typefaces from which to choose, and the style of type chosen should reflect the theme of the brochure, its subject and the image of the company.
- Completion and delivery dates.

When obtaining prices for printing, operators should approach several companies, as quotes can vary substantially from one printer to another. Many operators choose to have their brochures printed abroad. Good-quality work can be produced at very competitive prices for long print runs, but, obviously, the operator will want to see whether or not domestic printers can match the prices quoted by printers abroad as using a local printer will reduce transport costs. Most importantly, operators must avoid cutting corners to save money as an inferior print job can threaten the whole success of the tour programme.

The progress of the printing must be supervised throughout, either by the operator or its advertising agency. Proofs should be submitted at each stage of production to check on accuracy and a final corrected proof should be seen before the actual print run to ensure that there are no outstanding errors. As the brochure is such a crucial legal document, generally several members of staff will read it through before the final proof is passed for printing.

 EXAMPLE   **Accuracy is everything**

Checking the content of a holiday brochure is vital. While ensuring that printers do not make mistakes is important, it is also vital to ensure accuracy in the information provided to the printers – they are unlikely to question the content provided, especially if it is specific to a particular product or destination.

UK holiday company Warner Leisure should have double-checked the content of their 2010 brochures before mailing these to their clients. A case of mistaken identity led to the embarrassing admission that the promotional text encouraging visitors to their Norton Grange venue, in Yarmouth, Isle of Wight, was actually referring to a range of attractions and events taking place in Great Yarmouth – a seaside destination in Norfolk, some 250 miles away!

The printer should be asked to quote for not only the actual number of brochures that are expected to be required but also the run-on price for additional copies. Once a brochure is set up for printing, the cost of running off a few extra thousand is very small compared to the initial price, and it may be better to do this rather than have to reorder copies at a later date.

Brochure distribution and control

Tour operators must make the decision to either use all of the retail agencies available to them or select those that they feel will be most productive for the company. Whatever decision is made, operators must also establish a policy for distributing their brochures to these agents. If equal numbers of brochures are distributed to every agent, many copies will be wasted.

Wastage can be reduced by establishing standards against which to monitor the performance of travel agents. A key ratio is that of brochures given out to bookings received. 'Average' figures tend to vary considerably for different operators, so, while one will expect

Table 18.6 Example categories reflecting sales productivity

Agents	Bookings per year
Category A: top, most productive agents, multiples	100+
Category B: good agents	50-99
Category C: fair agents	20-49
Category D: below average agents	6-19
Category E: poor agents, producing little	0-5

to gain a booking for every three to four brochures given out (which may still mean that every booking carries the burden of some £10 in brochure production costs), specialist operators may have to give out as many as 25–30 brochures to obtain a single booking. The position is slightly better than this suggests, as each booking will involve typically between two and four people.

If figures consistently poorer than these are achieved by any of its agents, the operator should look to them for an explanation. The problem could be accounted for by an agent's lack of control over their own brochure distribution – do they merely stock their display racks and leave clients to pick up whatever numbers of brochures they wish or do they make a serious attempt to sell to 'browsers'? Some agents retain all stocks of brochures except a display copy, so that customers have to ask for copies of the brochures they require. This is instrumental in cutting down waste and it increases the number of sales opportunities.

It is now the practice of most operators to categorize their agents in some way, in terms of their productivity. This could typically take the form shown in Table 18.6.

Of course, for a specialist operator, the numbers of sales per category might be considerably smaller – a good agent may produce as few as ten bookings a year. The principle remains the same, however: the operator will determine, on the strengths of these categories, what level of support to give each of the agents. Those agents at the top of the scale can expect to receive as many brochures as they ask for, while at the other end, perhaps the operator will be willing to provide only a file copy or two to three brochures to work with. Many new or independent agents are finding it increasingly difficult to obtain any supplies of brochures from the major operators, which are tending to narrow the focus of their distribution policy.

The reservations system

In order to put a package tour programme into operation, a reservations system must be developed and implemented. The design of the system will depend on whether reservations are to be handled manually or by computer and on whether the operator plans to sell through agents or direct to the public.

Many tour operators still sell their tours principally through the high street travel agents, although direct sales through the leading operators' websites are increasing rapidly. In the UK, the multiples – retail chains owned by the lead operators – are responsible for over 50% of all package holidays sold by agents.

Manual systems have almost entirely disappeared in favour of computer reservation systems (CRS), which offer a faster, more efficient service at a much cheaper price for the operator. A travel agent needs to contact the operator quickly when serving a client at the counter. If telephone lines are engaged, or not answered for long periods of time, the agent could become frustrated and decide to deal with a competitor who is easier to contact or the client will go home and then simply search for a holiday on a website.

Initially, the CRS operated only inhouse – that is, on the operator's own premises. Agents seeking to make a booking would telephone the operator, who tapped into the company's computer to check on availability. It was but a short step from this to link the agent directly to the CRS, providing a visual display unit (VDU) in the agent's office.

In the UK, Thomson – the market leader – was the first operator to decide that all bookings through agents should be handled by a specially developed system called TOPS, forcing agents to invest in the appropriate hardware if they wished to book holidays from this major player. Most other large companies rapidly followed suit.

These connections originally depended on the use of telephone lines to link the agent's VDU to the operator's CRS. This posed problems of cost and time-wasting for the agent if lines were busy and there was difficulty in accessing a CRS. Subsequently, agents were 'hard-wired' directly into the operators' CRS, reducing the time taken to make bookings and allowing the agent to switch directly from one CRS to another without redialling.

Making a reservation

The computer will allow the agent to see whether or not the particular tour required by the client is available. If it is not, it will automatically display other dates or destinations that match the client's needs as closely as possible. Once the agent has established that a package is acceptable to the client, a booking is made (sometimes an option can be taken for 24 hours, but operators are now tending to accept only firm bookings). Any late changes to the holiday that are not in the brochure can be drawn to the attention of the client and agent on the screen at this time. The agent is provided with a code number to identify the booking and obtains a completed booking form from the client, together with a deposit.

The computer booking alone is sufficient to hold the reservation, so booking forms are now held in the agent's files rather than, as formerly, sent to the operator with the deposit. The operator will issue an interim invoice to confirm the booking, on receipt of the deposit, and a final invoice will be issued, normally about ten weeks before the client is due to leave, requesting that full payment is made eight weeks before departure. Changes to the holiday cannot be made once the final invoice has been issued. After receipt of the final payment, the tour operator will issue all tickets, itineraries and, where necessary, vouchers and despatch them to the agent, who will forward them to the client. The advent of e-tickets and vouchers, however, is dramatically reducing the amount of paperwork sent by operators to their clients.

Prior to each departure, a flight manifest is prepared for the airline, with the names of all those booked on it. In the case of flights using US airspace, a considerable amount of personal information has to be supplied for every passenger – a security measure introduced after 9/11. Also, a rooming list is sent to the hotels concerned and resort representatives where appropriate. The latter should go over the rooming list with the hotelier to ensure that all is in order prior to the clients' arrival.

Larger tour operators will have a customer relations department. Its function is to monitor and handle passenger and agency complaints and administer quality control measures in the operation of the tour programme. It monitors the questionnaires that most operators give to their clients to complete at the end of the holiday. These provide regular statistical information that can be analysed to assess which hotels are meeting clients' expectations and which ones are failing to do so.

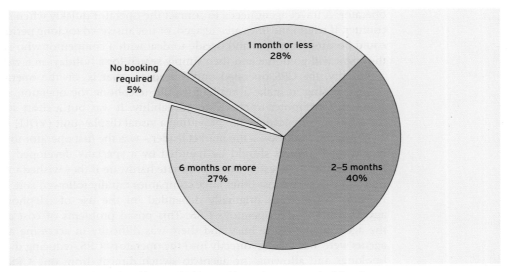

Figure 18.5 Holiday booking – UK (domestic and overseas holidays)
Source: edited from data provided by Mintel, 2010

Late bookings

Tour operators are anxious to sell every one of their holidays. The ability to react quickly to deal with last minute demand for bookings plays a key role in fulfilling this objective. In the UK, more than a quarter of holidays are booked within a month of departure (see Figure 18.5). Coupled with the offer of last-minute discounts, many operators have introduced procedures designed to pick up these late bookings, including the rapid updating of availability on computer reservations systems and a booking procedure that allows tickets to be collected at the airport on departure or, more commonly now, e-tickets to be used, which can be forwarded directly to the customer electronically. The new dot.com agents provide an excellent new medium for selling off unsold flights and accommodation at short notice.

The distribution network

Selecting retailers

Essentially, tour operators have to choose between two alternative methods for selling their holidays: retail travel agents or direct to the public (although websites can have a role in either of these approaches). Larger operators that have products with universal appeal and the market for which is national in scope have tended to sell the bulk of their holidays through the retail trade, but the development of websites has encouraged an increasing number of sales to be made direct – a development welcomed by the operators as they can thus save paying agents' commissions. Websites also aid retailers, in that agents now need to spend less time talking to their clients about the products or ordering brochures and can therefore stress their role as a personal link, which offers clients a sense of security. Companies with a policy of selling direct to the public will be examined in the next main section.

Few operators deal indiscriminately with all retail agents. The cost of servicing the less productive agents is often greater than the revenue they produce as they must not only be provided with expensive brochures but also receive regular mailings to update their information and be supported by sales material and even, in some cases, visits from the operators' sales representatives. Even in the era of websites, many operators still find that the personal contacts established by a good sales representative lead to more sales than do mail-shots or phone calls. The operators must therefore decide whether to vary the support they offer to different agents, or even dispense with the services of some agents altogether.

We have already seen how brochure supplies are varied according to the productivity of agents. It has also been the practice of operators to support their best agents by offering them an overriding commission of between 1 and 5%, in addition to the basic 10%, for achieving target sales figures. The large multiples, due to the strength of their position in the retail trade, can negotiate the highest overrides, giving them the ability to discount substantially in order to attract yet more business.

Leading operators have reduced both support and commission to their agents in recent years, and their process of directional selling has favoured sales through their own chains. This is proving a challenge for the independent agents, which will often work with independent tour operators and other small operators to make up for the shortfall in their sales of mass market tours.

The smaller operators – those which are strong in certain geographic regions or cater for specific niche markets, often involving quite a small number of customers in total – are obviously not in a position to support a national network of retailers. Most of them will therefore choose to sell direct to their customers, although a handful may try to concentrate sales through a limited number of supportive agents.

Relationships with travel agents

It is customary for tour operators to draw up a formal agreement with the travel agents they appoint to sell their services. Those agreements specify the terms and conditions of trading, including such issues as the normal rates of commission paid and whether or not credit will be extended to the agent or settlement of accounts must be made in cash.

Under the terms of these agreements, the agents agree to support and promote the sale of their principals' services. In return, the operators agree to provide the support and co-operation necessary for the successful merchandising of the companies' products – that is, providing adequate supplies of brochures, sales promotion material and sometimes finance for cooperative regional advertising or promotion campaigns. Operators will also try to ensure that their retailers are knowledgeable about the products they sell. This will be achieved through the circulation of sales letters or mailshots, invitations to workshops or other presentations and inviting selected agents on educational study trips.

The educational study trip

The **educational study trip (familiarization trip**, or, 'fam' trip, as it is known in North America) is a trip organized by principals (whether tour operators, carriers or tourist offices of the regions involved) for a variety of purposes. For example, members of the media or travel writers will be taken to tourist destinations in order for the principals to gain free – and, hopefully, positive – media coverage. Travel agents are also offered opportunities to undertake trips in order to improve their knowledge of the destinations or encourage them to sell the region or product. Sometimes, these trips are used by tour operators as incentives to agents – that is, if certain targets are reached, trips will be provided as a reward.

Visits to a destination are known to be one of the most effective means of encouraging agents to sell a particular package. These organized trips also have a social function, enabling the operators to get to know their agents better and to obtain feedback from them. The cost of mounting educational trips, however, is high, even if a proportion of the costs is met by the hotels at the destination or the national tourist offices and carriers helping to organize the holidays, so principals will try to do everything they can to ensure that the trips give them value for money. This was not always the case in the past, where such visits abroad were often treated as purely social events, attractive as a travel perk rather than an educational experience.

The effectiveness of the trips has been improved by selecting the candidates more carefully, providing a more balanced mix of visits, working sessions and social activities and imposing a small charge for attendance, so that the managers of travel agencies will take care to ensure that the expense is justified in terms of an increased productivity and expertise of their staff.

EXAMPLE   Fam trips

The specialist holidays division of TUI launched one of the biggest fam trip programmes in years. The division – which includes Hayes & Jarvis, Austravel, Sovereign, Citalia, Meon Villas and Crystal – provided 200 places on seven multicentre trips. Operated as a competition, this programme particularly targeted independent agents in an effort to enhance links with this sector following many years of focusing on inhouse agents.

The fam trips were planned to support expansion of the long-haul programmes in the 2012–13 season when Thomson Airways is due to introduce the Boeing 787 Dreamliner aircraft into its fleet, offering faster travel to the Far East. These fam trips are operated during the quieter periods of the year for the tour operator.

The careful selection of candidates will ensure that all those attending share common objectives. Monitoring performance, by soliciting reports from those attending and checking the sales of staff from those agencies invited to participate, will help to ensure that the operators' money has been well spent.

The sales representative

Tour operators, like most larger travel principals, employ sales representatives to maintain and develop their business through travel agents and solicit new sources of business. The functions of the sales representatives are to call on travel agents (and others) to give advice about the products and services they offer and support their agents with suitable merchandising material.

These representatives act as one point of personal contact between the agent and operator when problems or complaints are raised, and the often close relationships that develop between representatives and their contacts are valuable in helping to build brand loyalty for the company. They enable them to receive direct feedback from the marketplace about client and agency attitudes to the companies and their products. Representatives are also likely to play a valuable role in categorizing agents in terms of their potential, and selecting sales staff for educational study trips.

Making sales calls in person is expensive, however, and most companies have now switched to using telephone sales calls to keep in touch with all but their most productive agents. As with the resort representatives abroad, however, the sales representative is another means by which the company can be distinguished from its competitors and the appropriateness of this trend towards less personal contact is questionable. It is true that many agents have mixed feelings about the merits of sales representatives, who are seen by some as time-wasting socializers. It goes without saying that if the representatives are to do their job effectively, they must be well trained; those who are not sufficiently knowledgeable about their companies' or competitors' products will relay a poor image of the company to the agent.

Operators selling direct

Apart from those operators that will inevitably sell direct to their clients, for the reasons outlined above, a handful of larger tour operators have chosen deliberately to market their products direct to the public. This movement was spearheaded by the Danish company Tjaereborg, which entered the UK market in the late 1970s with a promotional strategy that asserted that if customers booked holidays direct, by cutting out the agents' commission, they would save money. While isolated bargains were certainly on offer, many holidays were no cheaper and sometimes more expensive than similar packages booked through an agent.

The reasons for this are not hard to understand. While travel agency commissions were indeed saved, huge budgets were required to inform and promote the holidays to the general public. The company had to invest millions in heavy advertising in the media, and similar high costs were incurred by the need to have a large reservations staff and multiple telephone lines to answer queries from the public. Those costs were, of course, fixed, while commissions are only paid to agents when they achieve a sale.

Tjaereborg soon found that, after initial success, which was probably the outcome of curiosity, it was unable to achieve greater market penetration – especially as Thomson Holidays had rapidly joined the competition with a direct sell division, Portland Holidays. Tjaereborg, after turning in an indifferent performance for several years, was sold to First Choice (then called Owners Abroad), which eventually replaced the brand with another direct sell operation, Eclipse.

Whether holidaymakers choose to buy direct or use an intermediary is often dependent on cultural influences related to traditional buying habits for travel products. In the UK, evidence suggests that many British holidaymakers still seek the assurance of face-to-face contact with an agent, even if the product knowledge of that agent is limited. There are some interesting variations in the pattern of agency sales, however. For example, people in the London area demonstrate a higher propensity to buy their holidays direct than do those in other parts of Britain, and certain types of package tour, such as ski holidays and coach tours, also experience a higher proportion of direct bookings than others. The advent of interactive booking of travel arrangements using the Internet is now changing this pattern dramatically.

The German market is also experiencing changes in booking behaviour, with holiday-makers bypassing the agency channel to book direct (leading to a decline in the number of travel agencies in operation). The Internet has heavily influenced booking habits there, too, with consumers increasingly booking individual services directly with principals, but the news is not so good for *tour operators* hoping to sell directly to customers. The prevalence for both self-booking and self-organization has increased considerably, with nearly two-thirds of holidays now being organized directly by the German holidaymaker (Euromonitor, 2011a).

In France, the high levels of Internet access, as well as changing consumer profiles, meant that in 2010 almost half of French travellers compared prices on the Internet, regardless of the mode of booking used (Euromonitor, 2011b). The positive aspect for tour operators serving this market is that the French continue to demand packages – particularly all-inclusive holidays. More than 10 million French people arranged their travel and holidays online, benefiting both tour operators and principals directly.

While every country has its own unique patterns, many follow similar patterns to those of the UK and Germany regarding package travel. In Belgium, package holidays make up about one-quarter of the total spent on holiday travel. In 2006, only 14% of retail sales value was earned via the Internet. In The Netherlands, it is reported that online sales are growing in importance, particularly for accommodation, airlines and car rental – suggesting a greater emphasis on self-organization rather than booking the package holidays traditionally demanded by Dutch tourists, the majority being booked through travel agents. Domestic travel for the Dutch, however, tends to be booked directly with the principals. This growing popularity for dynamic packaging is likely to lead to the decline of standardized package trips, which may further affect booking patterns.

The information technology revolution and its impact on tour operating

No business is being transformed by information technology (IT) faster or more radically than the business of travel; and tour operating, of all the sectors of this business, is arguably the most affected by developments. Of course, the advent of modern technology is no longer a recent phenomenon – after all, computers were widely introduced into the trade as early as the 1960s, hastening the demise of the traditional manual booking system. It is the scale and pace of development, however, that is proving so disruptive for the industry, as new forms of booking and information facility become available to both the trade and customers. Even the telephone has become a tool for providing new ways to book holidays, with the growth of call centres and the development of smartphone applications, which allows customers to access material quickly from various information sources onto their mobile phones.

The key question is not whether such new techniques will start to replace traditional methods of booking holidays, but rather how quickly the transition will occur and how completely it will come to dominate distribution. One can only speculate on what kind of future the traditional agency channels will have – or even traditional tour operators, given that suppliers can now reach their customers directly through websites and e-mail, and customers are not slow to recognize that they can put together their own packages as well as any operator. The number of holiday sales that are made online through the World Wide Web is growing rapidly each year, with both packages and travel components being purchased.

As can be seen from Table 18.7, the use of the Internet to book package holidays varies enormously across countries, with the UK and Poland both being high users of this approach, while the French and Portuguese are more likely to use the Internet to book flights, and the Germans and Greeks go online to book flights and accommodation separately.

Table 18.7 Percentages of Internet sales for each travel sector for selected European countries

	France	Germany	Greece	Italy	Poland	Portugal	Spain	Sweden	UK
Accommodation only	18.1	30.1	25.5	23.8	8.3	9.8	23.1	19.8	9.5
Car rental only	2.8	1.2	3.8	3.5	4.5	7.3	6.9	0.1	1.6
Dynamic packaging	8.6	16.1	4.3	6.5	7.9	2.2	6.4	7.1	19.4
Flight only	51.1	37.7	55.3	45.3	29.8	53.2	36.9	42.8	29.1
Traditional package holiday	16.5	12.4	10.1	12.6	47.4	25.4	20.0	25.9	37.1
Other online transport only	1.9	1.5	0.3	0.9	2.1	1.3	1.5	3.4	2.1
Other travel retail online sales	0.9	1.0	0.7	7.4	0.0	0.8	5.3	0.8	1.2

Source: edited from national travel retail reports provided by Euromonitor, 2010/2011

The leading operators have responded to the growth in Internet booking of travel products, often with the introduction of their own booking sites. This is true not just for package holidays but also for their efforts in trying to capture the growing numbers wishing to use dynamic packaging.

Some observers in the industry are adamant that the growth in online booking will neither lead to the closure of tour operators nor eradicate the travel agent, and have pointed to the relatively slow takeup of this method of distribution among some parts of the European market. Some believe that the caution of some consumers, the lack of IT knowledge and skills among the older generation as well as uncertainty about the reliability of the many new dot.com companies will ensure that support for more traditional means of booking will continue. Others, aware of the rise in criminal activity associated with credit cards, are also reluctant to provide their card details over the Internet. Still others believe that independent agents will be more impartial in giving advice about travel products than will the suppliers' websites, as well as providing greater expertise in recommending holidays.

Undoubtedly, all of these views have some validity, discouraging sales through new channels. Operators and agents fight back by pointing out to the independent travel bookers that they will have no one to turn to when things go wrong (a message strongly reinforced when the Asian tsunami struck in 2004) and that accommodation and flights booked separately will not have the level of protection offered by a package in the event of the collapse of suppliers or some other disaster.

EXAMPLE The European Directive on Package Travel

Rapid changes in travel retail – particularly the growth in dynamic packaging – led the EC to review this two-decade-old legislation. Their justification for the review lay in the acknowledgement that the Internet now provided customers with the opportunity to book travel components separately, rather than use packages organized by tour operators. One consequence of this is the lack of clarity regarding which travel arrangements are covered by the legislation.

The EC review particularly focused on the need for clarification of which holiday bookings would be protected by the legislation and whether definitions related to the term 'packages' and 'organizer' needed reviewing. The review also considered the range of information required in brochures and how information requirements could be adapted for Internet sales channels. Examination of pricing and supplementary charges was considered alongside cancellation policies and compensation rights. Finally, the review considered the financial protection schemes required by the scheme.

At the time of writing, the outcome of this review has not been revealed, but it is likely that legislation will be updated to better reflect needs of the retail travel industry and the customer today.

The new IT systems of distribution can broadly be described as falling into one of the following three categories:

- information and reservations systems offered by the suppliers of travel products and available to travel agents or other retailers
- similar systems offered by intermediaries on behalf of travel suppliers
- similar systems offered by either suppliers or, through intermediaries, direct to consumers.

The principal means of delivering these new systems include Internet services on the World Wide Web via computers and the increasingly sophisticated mobile telephones.

smartphone applications, whether on iPhone, Android or Blackberry, provide convenient tailored access to reservation systems. With more than 10 billion apps downloaded since 2008, this is extremely popular with users, yet to date this approach has been more successful for airlines and hotels, with few tour operators offering their own reservation app.

A feature of the rapid escalation of online providers was the subsequent and equally rapid collapse of many of these same companies – largely those acting as intermediaries for the travel suppliers. Inevitably, as suppliers set up their own communication networks to service the public directly, this threatens to undermine intermediaries. The intermediaries' role is assured, however, as long as they can continue to offer a wide range of products at competitive prices and are judged by the public to be at least as impartial as the more traditional outlets in providing these services. Whether or not major suppliers will be willing to continue to offer their products through intermediaries if they can satisfactorily sell a sufficient majority of them direct to the public is a matter that will determine the future of those intermediaries.

What we are seeing at this point is a gradual concentration of the intermediaries to a point where a bare handful will emerge as market leaders, just as occurred among traditional tour operators at an earlier stage. Companies such as Opodo, ebookers.com, lastminute.com, expedia.com and travelocity.com are reinforcing their strong positions in the market, but there has been consolidation within larger companies seeking to take control of those which have greater success (and regularly achieve high levels of hit rates from consumers).

The development of alternative channels is hindered by two factors. Operators have been slow to realize the potential of the new technology and, in general, marketing costs remain high for suppliers attempting to sell direct to the public. Nonetheless, more and more operators are becoming aware that selling via the Internet allows suppliers to trim, and possibly even eradicate, their two major sources of expenditure – commission and brochures. Already much information on destinations and facilities is available for public viewing on the Internet, and before long all holiday information currently provided by operators through the medium of brochures will become accessible in this way.

Call centres, set up to take bookings over the phone, provide another convenient means of enabling operators to reach their customers cheaply while offering very competitive prices. Technology that allows tour operators to employ fluid pricing strategies means holidays can be more readily retailed through these call centres (or via the Internet) than through traditional channels. As a result, call centres have already led to reductions in the number of outlets operated by the retail chains, which cannot directly compete with this form of distribution.

The growth of technological development in this field is too rapid to allow a thorough treatment of the subject in a textbook. Students of tour operating must keep abreast of such developments through the trade press or other media. Suffice to say that, in addition to reservations systems, computers are now used widely to provide accounts and management information quickly and accurately to both operators and agents, while larger operators have also introduced accounting systems that allow the direct transfer of agency payments from agents' bank accounts to the operators'.

In any examination of the influence of new technology in industry, it would be facile to ignore the counter-argument that impersonal means of communication can only go so far in satisfying consumers' needs. It is helpful to look at parallels in other industries. In the world of print, for example, newspapers remain popular even though their data are available online and, despite the growth of online banking, customers still value direct contact with their bank. Operators would do well to look at developments in other fields and see what lessons can be learned to improve their own means of communication with their clients.

The future for tour operators

Consolidation within this sector is likely to continue. The merging of companies that has been experienced over the past two decades will also be seen with many online operators, as they seek to establish greater turnover as well as try to control a larger share of loyal customers. The growing popularity of dynamic packaging will give travel agents the opportunity to provide a tailored holiday product to their customers, drawing on travel elements from a range of suppliers. This may require a response from tour operators as demand for package holidays declines.

As tourists become more experienced and seek out more unusual or exotic experiences, specialist niche products are likely to become more popular. This may provide a distinct opportunity for smaller, independent tour operators, although already it is possible to see that the mega-operators are trying to serve this market, focusing attention on the specialist brands within their operations.

Questions and discussion points

1. The travel trade press continues to report that brochures are still in demand by holidaymakers, regardless of whether they choose to book online or via travel agents. Why is this still the case?

2. The vertical and horizontal integration undertaken by major European tour operators have brought the companies involved many benefits. Identify both the benefits and disadvantages that this integration can bring for consumers.

3. Mobile phone applications have been created to support many aspects of travel, including travel guides, customer reviews and hotel and flight reservations. Yet, at the time of writing, few tour operators offer online booking for their packages. What factors may be influencing this?

Tasks

1. Select a small independent tour operator – the AITO website can help here – and examine the company and its operations. Write a brief report which identifies the products they offer and the markets they target. How does the organization differentiate itself from large mass-market tour operators?

2. Interview five people who have recently booked a holiday. Inquire as to whether they used a tour operator and ask them about the reason for this choice. Summarize your findings in a presentation to your colleagues.

Bibliography

CAA (2011) *Top ATOL Holders Reports*, available online at: http://www.caa.co.uk/application. aspx?catid=490&pagetype=65&appid=4 (accessed November 2011).

EU (2007) Working Document on package travel, package holidays and package tours, available online at: http://ec.europa.eu/consumers/cons_int/safe_shop/pack_trav/comm_wd_ 20072007_en.pdf (accessed November 2011).

Euromonitor (2011a) *Travel and Tourism in Germany*, London, Euromonitor, July.

Euromonitor (2011b) *Travel and Tourism – France*, London, Euromonitor, April.

Hope, A. (1974) Holidays with risk, *New Scientist*, 16 May, 371.

Mintel (2010) *Holiday Booking Process – UK*, UK, Mintel, March.

Mintel (2009) *Market re-forecasts – Travel UK*, UK, Mintel, March.

ONS (2011) *Travel Trends 2010*, London, Office of National Statistics.

Schulte-Nölke, H., Twigg-Flesner, C. and Ebers, M. (2008) *EC Consumer Law Compendium: Comparative analysis*, Germany, Bielefeld University.

UNWTO (2011) *Tourism Highlights*, Madrid, World Tourism Organization.

Websites

Association of Independent Tour Operators: **www.aito.co.uk**

EC Package Travel Directive (90/314/EEC): **ec.europa.eu**

European Tour Operators Association: **www.etoa.org**

TUI AG: **www.tui-group.com**

WalkingWomen: **www.walkingwomen.com**

Selling and distributing travel and tourism

Contents

Learning outcomes

After studying this chapter, you should be able to:

- explain the role of travel agents as a component of the tourism industry and their relationship with other sectors
- identify the functions performed by an agent
- be aware of the qualities necessary for effective agency management and service
- understand the considerations and the requirements for establishing and running a travel agency
- be aware of the constraints and threats to agents' operations and evaluate alternative solutions for their survival.

Today, although I have travelled to all parts of the world during the last twenty years – and therefore could be called 'experienced' – I wouldn't think of taking any kind of trip without first consulting a travel agent.

Reynolds (1958), Bless that travel agent, 36

Introduction

Half a century ago, as mass market travel was starting to boom, travellers would actively discuss the use of travel agents vis-à-vis making arrangements independently. Today, as we will discover throughout this chapter, that same debate continues.

The European Commission (1999) has defined **travel agents** as retailers to leisure and business travellers, selling flights (charter or scheduled), accommodation, car hire, foreign currency, travel insurance and other travel services. They are generally paid a commission by the supplier of the service or, in the case of a package holiday, by the operator. In some countries, the term 'travel agent' is used more generally, to refer to an organization operating in the travel industry (this may be as a retailer but also includes those acting as tour operators or tour providers). This chapter, however, specifically focuses on the travel agent as a retailer. The travel agent acts as an intermediary, conveniently linking customers with the providers of travel products. Providers of travel products are often termed **principals**, owning specific travel elements, such as hotels or airlines, as well as tour operators, which put together packages that combine several travel elements (see Figure 19.1).

Most travel principals continue to rely, to a greater or lesser extent, on travel agents as an important source of distribution, and retailers continue to play a key role in the structure of the industry. Their share of business, however, is declining, even in the key area of inclusive tours, as customers turn to booking direct. The agent's role is changing, but there are grounds for belief that it is far from collapsing, providing agents are willing to adapt.

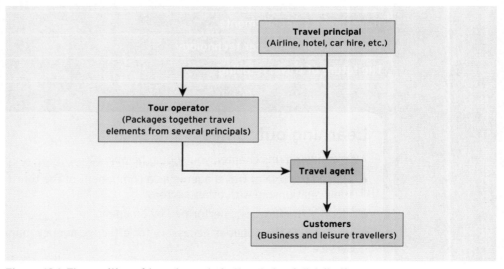

Figure 19.1 The position of travel agents in the chain of distribution

Historical context

Agents selling travel arrangements have been in existence in the UK for well over 100 years. Indeed, the oldest – now the tour operator Cox and Kings – traces its origins back to the eighteenth century. The travel agent's principal role in earlier times was to sell shipping and rail services, but, with the coming of air transport and the development of the package tour business after World War II, their product range expanded.

Before World War II, shipping companies had been able to provide a good reservations and ticketing service direct to the public, with sales outlets in their city offices and at leading ports. Railways and coach operators had similarly established city centre terminals from which they could dispense tickets direct to the public. When the airlines arrived on the scene, however, their airport terminals were situated well away from centres of population, and, as a convenient network of travel agents was in place by that time, they did not face the same pressure to establish their own sales offices. Although most leading airlines did establish a main selling office in capital cities and many also opened offices in other leading cities, the new demand for air tickets encouraged travel agents to expand their distribution outlets further. With the deregulation of air travel and a greater willingness on the part of passengers to book direct (first by phone or fax, later via the Internet), many airlines closed their town centre sales offices. Travel agents have similarly experienced a fall in air ticket sales in the past few years.

It was the travel agents themselves that developed the first air package tours. Retail entrepreneurs had the vision to see that, if they could buy seats on flights in bulk at discounted prices, they could reduce the cost of air fares and, thus, a huge mass market for foreign tours would develop. The packages they developed were, in turn, sold through other agents, eventually to become the retailers' principal source of revenue.

The scale of the retail sector

It is difficult to estimate the number of travel agents in existence globally. Many become members of their national association bodies, but, as such organizations often allow those tour operators who also provide retail services to join, their membership statistics can provide only limited detail regarding the numbers of businesses operating primarily as travel agents (see Table 19.1). While some countries require agents to be licensed, many have no

Table 19.1 Membership of travel agent associations

Association	Membership (percentage of total travel agency sales attributed to members)
Algemeen Nederlands Verbond van Reisondernemingen (ANVR) – Netherlands	330 – with 1080 branches
Association of Croatian Travel Agencies (UHPA)	207
Association of Danish Travel Agents and Tour Operators	140 (70% of sales)
Association of Finnish Travel Agents	160 (95% of sales)
Association of South African Travel Agents	409
Association of Turkish Travel Agencies (TURSAB)	6221
Federation of Associations of Travel & Tourism Agents – Malta	65
Deutscher Reisebüroverband (DRV – German Travel Association)	2247
Österreichischer Reisebüroverband (ÖRV) – Austria	420
Svenska Resebyråföreningen (SRF) – Sweden	120 (85% of sales)
Swiss Federation of Travel Agencies	830
Travel Agents Federation of India	1400
Travel Agents' Association New Zealand	340

Source: C. Humphreys, correspondence with membership managers of travel agents' associations, 2011

Table 19.2 Booking overseas holidays using travel agents

Year	Total overseas holidays	Overseas holidays booked through travel agents	Travel agents share of total market (%)
2005	44.2	20.7	46.8
2006	45.3	20.6	45.5
2007	45.4	20.7	45.6
2008	45.5	19.8	43.5
2009	38.5	17.6	45.7
2010 (estimate)	36.8	16.7	45.4

Source: Mintel, 2010

compulsory registration scheme. Licensing schemes can vary in their format. For instance, in Ireland, the licensing of travel agents and tour operators is undertaken by the Commission for Aviation Regulation (239 travel agents were licensed to trade during the last quarter of 2009). Alternatively, licensing may be through government bodies or linked to customer financial protection schemes. An example of both approaches is seen in Australia, where travel agents are licensed through their state governments but the state also requires them to be members of a travel compensation fund (which provides financial protection for customers should a travel agency collapse). At the end of 2010, over 3000 head office and 1600 branch office travel agents were members of this scheme.

It should also be noted that customers' use of travel agents varies from country to country. Research (Dumazel and Humphreys, 1999) found that, while 80% of travel purchases in the UK were through travel agents, Belgium, The Netherlands and Switzerland recorded levels closer to 25%. While the market has changed significantly since that time, it highlights the fact that different distribution channels are used in different nations.

The number of travel retail outlets in the UK declined by 5% in 2010 alone (Euromonitor, 2011), while agents affiliated to the Association of British Travel Agents (ABTA) – the leading trade body representing both tour operators and travel agents in the UK – has seen a decline in total travel agency members of more than a third since 1991. However, the use of travel agents by holidaymakers has not significantly shifted over the past five years (see Table 19.2), with only a weak decline in travel agents market share for overseas holidays.

The power of the travel agency chains

As the demand for travel services grew in the UK, travel agencies expanded their operation, opening new premises (or, in some cases, acquired smaller existing businesses) in order to service more customers. In addition, several tour operators sought to take control of the retailing element of their business so they also established large networks of outlets. For example, the purchase in the 1970s of the Lunn Poly travel agency chain by Thomson Holidays (now part of the TUI group) ensured that the tour operator could provide an expanded network of retail outlets. These **multiples** could achieve business advantages through their centralized marketing activities, negotiating higher commission rates based on sales across the group and reduced costs through mass development and purchasing of key resources (such as computer systems).

The concern that the multiples would expand to a point where independents would be squeezed out of the market has receded to some extent in recent years. Indeed, the composition of the travel agency industry has changed dramatically over time. There was a fall in independent agencies (small privately owned businesses with only a few outlets) as the travel agency chains (with multiple outlets) expanded under the ownership of major tour operators like Thomas Cook and TUI, but, with the growth in call centres and electronic booking, the multiples are now starting to reduce the number of their own high street outlets.

EXAMPLE   **Two travel giants merge**

After almost a year of negotiations, plans were finally agreed in 2011 to merge two of the largest UK travel agents. Thomas Cook, operating 780 high street shops, confirmed plans to merge with the Co-operative Travel (see Figure 19.2), operating 460 branches. Thomas Cook's 'Going Places' outlets were to be rebranded to be Co-operative Travel. Some closures of existing shops were anticipated.

The Competition Commission reviewed the planned merger, and allowed it to proceed as it considered there was sufficient competition within the travel retail sector to ensure that customers would not be disadvantaged.

Figure 19.2 A Co-operative Travel outlet
Photo by Claire Humphreys

Competing with the multiples

Although the large number of branches owned by the leading chains appears to give them an insuperable advantage over the independents, this is not always the case. Medium-sized chains (often operating only in a limited geographic region) can provide strong competition. These chains, commonly known as **miniples**, typically control between 40 and 100 shops. They are, however, vulnerable to takeovers, and some of the major players have been absorbed into leading operators' retailing organizations.

The independents have recognized that, on their own, they face an almost impossible task in competing with the multiples for the sale of mass market holidays. Since it became legal to discount the price of travel products at the point of sale, the independent agents have been under particular pressure from discounting undertaken by the multiples. Such large chains, because of their substantial buying power, can negotiate commission overrides (an additional percentage of commission paid when higher sales targets are achieved), making it easier to undercut independent agents on price. The multiples can also invest more in the latest technology, and in national advertising campaigns, than can the independents.

Independent travel agents have realized that, in order to compete on price, they need to collaborate with other travel agencies. This allows them to negotiate for higher commissions based on their joint buying power. As a result, there has been massive growth in alliances, particularly through the establishment of consortia. An example is the North American-based Vacation.com, which has a network of over 5000 agencies across the USA and Canada and combined sales of more than $18 billion.

EXAMPLE Consortia

Travelsavers International
Formed in the USA in 1970, this marketing group has some 3000 branches in 14 countries worldwide. The travel agencies are not marketed under this brand name – all the agents retain their own identities. In the UK, they must hold ABTA or IATA membership to operate within this group.

Advantage
Established in 1978 and known initially as the National Association of Independent Travel Agents (NAITA), then as Advantage Travel Centres, this consortium supports around 800 branches which have a combined turnover of £3 billion. Agents may use their own trading names, but around half of the members have chosen to emphasize the Advantage brand in their names.

WorldChoice
Formed in 1976, this group operated initially as the Association of Retail Travel Agents' Consortia (ARTAC). Following a merger with the Travel Trust Assocation (TTA) in 2008, this group is one of the largest consortia of independent travel agents in the UK, with 800 members.

Global Travel Group
Formed in 1993, this group has 800 members and operates its own bonding system. The consortium was purchased by Stella Travel Services, owners of Travelbag and Travel 2. They are particularly keen to see new agencies established and operate their own training academy for those just starting out.

Elite Travel Group
Established in 1977, this small consortium was formerly known as Midconsort Travel Group (reflecting its geographical focus on the Midlands region of England). This group is owned by those travel agencies who are its members.

Freedom Travel Group
Established in 2001, as the trading arm of the Co-operative Travel Group, its members have combined sales of £1.5 billion. This group charges members a management fee based on the commission earned.

In 2005, three UK-based consortia – Advantage, WorldChoice and Global – reached an agreement to unite, creating a super-consortium, the Triton Travel Group, which served, at that time, around 2300 branches. In 2008, Advantage announced it would leave the group and now Triton provides a centralized purchasing organization for the two remaining consortia, with its combined purchasing power enhancing its position in negotiations with suppliers. A full merger of these two consortia is not currently planned, however.

The potential buying power of such groupings of independent agencies provides them with a very real chance of being able to compete with the large chains as they can share marketing costs as well as work with the smaller tour operators to ensure that they are represented in the high street. In addition, consortium membership can avoid the necessity for each agency to have separate licences when putting different components of a package together.

Franchising has generally been less successful as a strategy for competing with the multiples. The first chain in the UK to attempt to franchise on a wide scale, Exchange Travel, went into liquidation in 1990 and the Canadian-based Uniglobe chain has similarly found it difficult to establish itself in the UK, despite having a chain of offices in 54 countries worldwide. Travel Leaders, based in the USA, has over 1200 franchised locations, suggesting that markets outside of the UK can operate travel franchises more successfully.

The profitability of travel agents

Surprisingly few studies of travel agency productivity and profitability exist. One way to measure these is to examine their profit levels and turnover per employee. Earlier studies have generally found multiples to be more profitable than independents. Annual reports allow comparisons to be made between multiples and independent agents (see Table 19.3).

Some agencies have been successful in increasing profits through a supermarket approach to sales. For example, First Choice introduced the Holiday Hypermarket brand, with superstores primarily located at out-of-town retail parks. Thomas Cook has introduced Thomas Cook Direct, to sell its products direct to consumers, and many others have followed suit with a call centre approach, abandoning face-to-face contact with customers to keep down costs. The UK's two leading tour operator chains have both tried selling their products through interactive TV; however, despite more customers having access to interactive TV it has not really seen success. In 2005, Expedia's TV travel shop failed, following losses of more than $46 million and, as Internet opportunities have expanded, so efforts to achieve sales via interactive TV have declined.

Table 19.3 The profitability of UK travel agents, 2009–2010

Company name	Turnover (£000)	Profit (loss) before taxation (£000)	Profit (loss) as % of turnover	Number of employees	Profit (loss) per employee (£)
Multiples					
Thomas Cook Retail Limited	455 519.00	(35 989.00)	(7.90)	6799	(5 293.28)
Trailfinders Group Limited	483 345.00	12 455.00	2.58	981	12 696.23
Travelbag Limited	52 837.00	(511.00)	(0.97)	165	(3 096.97)
Flight centre	204 446.00	3 002.00	1.47	773	3 883.57
Independent					
Haslemere Travel Limited	2 939.40	19.14	0.65	7	2 734.29

Source: company reports

The role of travel agents

The travel agent's role is dissimilar to that of most other retailers, in that agents do not purchase products for resale to their customers. Only when a customer has decided on buying a particular holiday do agents approach their principal on their customer's behalf to make a purchase. The travel agent does not, therefore, carry stock. This has three important implications for the business of travel distribution:

1. The cost of setting up in business is relatively small compared to that of other retail businesses.
2. Agents are only able to sell products made available by the tour operators or principals, so in times of peak demand they may be competing with other agencies to find the products that the customers wish to purchase.

3. Agents are not seeking to dispose of products that they have already purchased, so may display less brand loyalty towards a particular product or company.

Arguably, the main role of a travel agent has always been to provide a convenient location for the purchase of travel. At those locations, they act as booking agents for holidays and travel, as well as a source of information and advice on travel services. Their customers look to them for expert product knowledge and objectivity in the advice they offer. However, as agents choose to deal with an increasingly limited range of products on which they can maximize their revenue (the competitive nature of retail travel is such that profit margins are small and agents must find whatever means they can of surviving), objectivity in recommendations and travel advice may not be possible. Nor is it realistic to imagine that sales staff – who are often young and generally inexperienced in travel themselves – can have a thorough knowledge of every product available, and this limits their value as a source of information. In recent years, the number of people using travel agency shops to gather research for their holiday has declined, from 27% in 2005 to less than 20% in 2010 (Mintel, 2010).

The range of products that an agent will choose to offer will vary not only on the basis of the commission each earns but also on the nature of demand within the catchment area, the degree of specialization of the agency and the preferences and marketing policies of the proprietor. An agency that is attempting to provide a full range of services to the public would sell air tickets, cruise and ferry tickets, rail and coach transport, car hire, hotel accommodation and package tours (which might include domestic travel). Additional services, such as travel insurance, traveller's cheques and foreign exchange may also be offered, and some agents will also undertake to arrange travel documentation (such as arranging visas) for their clients. Some will even deal with theatre tickets.

Such all-round agents are rapidly disappearing in the face of commercial pressures, however. Owing to the small amount of revenue achieved on the sale of coach or rail tickets, many agents are now forgoing sales of these types, although some still believe that it is better to offer a full range of services, even if some offer little or no profit, on the grounds that customers may return to buy other travel arrangements later.

An alternative to providing a full range of products is for the agency to specialize in a niche product, such as cruising (see Figure 19.3 and the Example below). Agents may specialize not only in the selection of products they offer, but also in the markets they serve. The clearest distinction is between those which focus on business travel (serving the travel needs of the local, and in some cases national, business community) and those that concentrate on leisure travel.

EXAMPLE **Accessible travel**

Wheelchair Escapes is based in the USA and is a travel agency serving a market requiring accessible travel. This agency makes travel arrangements that go far beyond the mainstream. This can include arranging wheelchair accessible hire cars, wheelchair transportation at airports and mobility scooter hire to help travellers get around their holiday destinations.

The owner of the company, Kristy Lacroix, is a member of The Society for Accessible Travel & Hospitality (SATH), an organization dedicated to expanding travel opportunities in the USA and abroad for people with disabilities.

In 2009, a UK travel trade magazine completed a mystery shopper exercise for a seven-night holiday for two adults, one of whom was in a wheelchair. The response by travel agents was generally poor, with little detailed information sought from the customer about specific needs and a lack of product knowledge on accessibility issues. With 10 million disabled travellers in the UK, this is clearly a substantial niche.

Figure 19.3 A travel agency in Krefeld, Germany, specializing in late bookings for holidays
Photo by Chris Holloway

Distribution trends

It is becoming clear that the retail sector of the leisure tourism industry is now moving in two distinct directions: towards the fast turnover 'leisure sales shop', a feature of the multiples' approach, which is essentially a booking service offering rock-bottom prices; or towards a more specialized advisory service for complex or expensive tailor-made travel arrangements, which allows the agency to charge fees for their services and avoid the usual pressure to discount.

The move towards charging fees for services has its precedent in the USA, where, for a number of years, travel experts holding the Certified Travel Counsellor (CTC) qualification have dealt with the more lucrative end of the package tour business. It is these operations that seem most likely to benefit if suppliers move to contracts with lower or zero commissions, as their customers will be more disposed to pay fees for the services that are rendered.

Charging fees is common in the USA, with the American Society of Travel Agents (ASTA) reporting that, by 2009, 91% of their members charged service fees. In 2008, both Co-operative Travel and Thomson announced that some services would incur a service charge. However, the UK has yet to see extensive introduction of service fees by travel agents.

Meanwhile, the traditional travel agent, attempting to provide a wide range of services with little discounting, faces a future that is increasingly uncertain as there are increasing opportunities for members of the public to book direct with the suppliers using the Internet. While the Internet has been seen as a major threat, the high profile failure of some tour operators has led to customers using travel agencies, aware of the financial protection they provide, and there is a suggestion that online sales are now hitting a peak in terms of market share, as growth rates slow. Still, in the UK, online bookings accounted for one third of total travel sales in 2010 (Euromonitor, 2011).

The policy of mass market tour operators as well as airlines in recent years has been based on selective distribution – that is, favouring a smaller number of highly productive agents rather than dealing with all retail agencies. This policy has also been favoured by the multiple agents themselves, which choose to stock the products of a few key operators responsible for perhaps 80% of the total revenue in the mass market. Thomas Cook, to take one example, introduced a policy to work with only about 400 companies, of which 30 were identified as 'premium selection'. If this tendency becomes widespread over the next few years, smaller tour operators will have to find other means of reaching their customers.

The tour operator-owned multiples also engage in **directional selling** – that is, they recommend their own companies' products to customers at the expense of those from other suppliers. This ensures that the majority of the sales of the larger tour operators' products are achieved through their own travel agencies. The UK's Foreign Package Holidays (Tour Operators and Travel Agents) Order (2000) requires that the links between operators and their agencies are made clear to customers. Publicizing such links will not necessarily work to the advantage of the independent agents, however – it may encourage the public to believe that the leading tour operators' programmes can *only* be purchased from the retail branches of those operators. While some independents are concerned that tour operators will eventually choose to retail their products exclusively through their own retail chains, currently this is thought unlikely.

EXAMPLE · Agents involved in directional selling

In 2004, Amadeus, the travel technology provider, surveyed British holidaymakers and reported that more than two-thirds of travel agents had tried to encourage their customers to switch from the holiday company they originally requested to other providers.

With over 70% of travel agents admitting that they are likely to push companies paying them higher levels of commission, such directional selling was seen to be a strategic business decision by the management of those travel agents. As tour operators drive customers towards direct sell channels and lower commission levels, the fight for customer business has become competitive. Even independent agents are not immune from such behaviour. In many cases, encouraged by their management, they also make their selections from companies offering them the most favourable commissions. There has been criticism of this, suggesting such activities fly in the face of customer expectations that agents are offering independent advice.

There have frequently been suggestions that directional selling increases when markets are difficult, as pressure is placed on agents by tour operators to offload excess stock in order to reduce potential risk of losses – Thomas Cook confirmed that it increases the commission earned by its own agents, when selling inhouse products to encourage this. The extent to which directional selling occurs can be seen with the announcement by Thomson that 80% of their shops' sales are now for their own products; in 2005, this was 60%. Two UK trade magazines (*Travel Weekly* and *Travel Trade Gazette*) reported that directional selling at TUI and Thomas Cook outlets was prevalent in 2011.

Changes to retail distribution

A number of other notable developments in travel retailing have taken place in the past few years in addition to those already described above.

Home-based sales agents

The field of home selling has expanded rapidly in recent years. Personal travel counsellors and online travel counsellors who work on a freelance basis sell on behalf of an agency and earn commission from that agency. That commission is then shared, with the travel counsellor receiving between 30 and 100% of the total commission earned, depending on the level of support service provided by their host agency.

EXAMPLE **Travel Counsellors**

Travel Counsellors is one company that has built up a major retailing base in travel, with more than 1100 home-based employees operating in the UK, The Netherlands, Ireland, Australia, South Africa and Canada. Turnover in 2009 was in excess of £250 million and its recent growth has moved it into the UK's top 100 private firms.

In 2006, Travel Counsellors reported that over 40% of its UK-based agents earned more than £300 per week in commission, but acknowledged that more than a third of their counsellors worked between 40 and 60 hours per week to gain such returns. Agents are encouraged to build positive business relationships with their customers, as trust becomes important in developing repeat custom, and developing a loyal customer base can enhance earnings for both the agent and the company.

Diversification into travel retailing by non-tourism businesses

The threat always remains of organizations outside the travel industry taking an interest in diversifying into travel retailing, especially where this is seen as a logical expansion of their existing activities and they have a retailing operation that can be easily adapted to take on these extra travel services. The highly competitive marketplace and legislation relating to financial and consumer protection, however, has added complexity to the business of selling travel, which may well be a factor in the decision of so many other retail organizations to avoid the travel business. Yet, in The Netherlands, the sale of holidays through banks is a long-established practice and, in Germany, large department stores have played a major role in travel retailing for many years.

Direct sales

Perhaps the greatest threat that travel agencies face in the short term is the move to direct selling which is now accelerating as use of the Internet expands. Can travel principals sell their products directly to the public at a lower cost? That is a vital question for both principals and tour operators.

On the one hand, selling direct to customers cuts out the high cost of servicing intermediaries as well as having to pay commission on each sale. On the other hand, it can involve substantial capital investment to set up sales offices and direct marketing costs can be high, especially if national advertising campaigns have to be mounted. Additional staff must be employed to operate call centres, too, and these must be adequately trained for the job.

Currently, many products available to customers direct on the principals' websites are offered at prices below those quoted to travel agents, leaving customers with little incentive to book through an agent. Companies that occasionally accept bookings from agents, even when selling most of their product direct (small hotels are a good example), however, usually recognize that to deliberately undermine the retail trade by, for instance, charging a lower price when accepting direct business from their customers, can jeopardize their relationship with travel agents, thus impacting on future business.

EXAMPLE **Online retailers and American Airlines do battle**

A contretemps over terms between American Airlines and Expedia led to the latter restricting sales of the airline's flights. This follows a similar response by online retailer Orbitz.

American Airlines has been making moves to encourage its online retailers to connect to the American Airlines flight database directly – rather than through global distribution systems (GDS) – and to pay a lower commission on the sale. In response, Expedia ensured that customer's search results showed American flights a long way down the list, thus reducing the likelihood that these would be chosen. Expedia argued that American Airlines strategy is against the interest of the consumer as it restricts opportunities for price comparisons to be made.

It took nearly four months of negotiations to reach a compromise; one which will help American to reduce its distribution costs while allowing Expedia continued access via GDS technology.

However, some travel firms have little choice other than to sell their products direct as their total capacity is too small for it to be considered by the retail distribution network. Consequently, such operators may adopt one of two distributive strategies: find a selection of key agents (likely to be independents rather than chains) that are willing to stock the product or sell all their holidays direct to the public. The AITO Special Agents Scheme is an example of the former. The small specialist operators that form the membership of the association have identified some 140 specialist agencies to handle their bookings.

Travel agents today have much more to fear from advances in technology that will allow the travelling public to access operations' computer reservation systems (CRSs). This is a reality in the USA and France and it is already available for business travellers in the UK. Such access lets customers compare the availability and price of travel products in real time.

Changes in access to brochures

The proliferation of brochures and the policy of leading tour operators to produce a range of different, branded products, each in their own brochure, has forced travel agents to re-evaluate their policies on stocking brochures for customers. With the typical travel agency only having rack space for around 150 brochures, of which up to 20% may be filled with the products of the leading operators, there is little opportunity for the smaller and specialist operators to get their brochures on those racks. While a few years ago that would have been disastrous for their trade, the introduction of the Internet has led to companies becoming far more dependent instead on their websites to sell their products, and many companies now make brochures available to download.

EXAMPLE **Thomson brochures**

The production of holiday brochures can be a costly affair, especially for the environment. In 2010, Thomson produced nine brochures for its First Choice brand and a further 11 brochures covering the Thomson range of products – and with summer sun brochures often containing hundreds of pages, this is a lot of paper! Each brochure is designed to appeal to different markets, and travel agents are expected to stock those brochures most suited to their local market. Having the right brochure may have an impact on whether a sale is made.

Thomson also makes its brochures available online – in 2011 there were 27 different types. The company also provides an e-mail facility, allowing the customer to receive a copy of the brochure electronically via their inbox. These online brochures are also accessible to travel agents, so they are always able to access a copy of the brochure to help persuade customers of the suitability of a suggested holiday.

The product portfolio

The decision about which products to stock is taken not only on the basis of what it is thought will sell quickest or easiest. The introduction of tighter EU legislation over quality and safety has forced many Europe-based agents to reconsider the companies with which they deal and, while override commissions undoubtedly play a role in the decision, equally the service the operator provides to the agent is taken into consideration. Agents that encounter difficulties in getting through to operators on the telephone or who find their e-mail communications or complaints are not answered quickly are less inclined to stock that operator's products. Companies insisting, for example, that agents use high-cost phone numbers when telephoning, and then keep agents waiting on the line for extended periods, can antagonize the retailers.

While the apparently unbiased service provided by independent travel agents appears to be a marketing advantage, it is questionable whether or not clients themselves actually deal through an agent to gain this benefit, as the proportion of sales through travel agents is highest for the standard package holidays, which could, arguably, be booked direct with equal simplicity. This supports the view of many that travel agents represent only a convenient outlet for buying a holiday rather than an advisory service. One should also not dismiss the value of personal contact when making bookings. Many customers are still reluctant to make such a high-price purchase on the Web – there is a growing fear of fraud when offering credit card details over the Web and so agents still offer some guarantee of financial security, which customers see as an advantage. Furthermore, concerns that they may make mistakes or misunderstand booking conditions encourage customers to use the expertise of travel agents. Examples of such mistakes include the traveller who mistyped Sydney and, instead of ending up in Australia, flew to the small mining town of Sidney, in Montana, USA, and the American customer who mistook the currency used in quotations and found the price quoted for a booked tour was not €789 but, in fact, £789 sterling – at that time meaning that it cost about 40% more than expected.

The low proportion of bookings achieved by travel agents for domestic holidays owes much to the traditional pattern of booking holidays in the UK. Domestic holidaymakers have tended in the past to contact principals directly, often by writing to resort tourist offices for brochures and details of hotels. Holidays in the UK were neither conveniently packaged nor seen by travel agents as sufficiently remunerative to justify devoting precious rack space to brochures about them, or training staff in domestic product knowledge. Two factors have tended to increase sales through agencies more recently, however.

First, domestic holidays have risen in price in comparison with foreign holidays, so sales of holidays at home can equal or exceed the 'bargain basement' prices now offered overseas. Therefore holidaymakers wish to be sure that the purchase they make is providing good value and is suitable to their needs. Second, UK holidays are now better packaged by the tour operators, with the larger companies now including domestic holidays in their product portfolios. Combined, these factors provide travel agents with greater opportunity for earning higher returns on conveniently booked packages. As a result, the UK has experienced fluctuations in the use of travel agents to book domestic holidays (see Table 19.4).

Dynamic packaging

The growth of low-cost carriers has encouraged travellers to consider purchasing individual elements of their holiday, allowing greater flexibility in design. Accommodation suppliers

Table 19.4 Domestic holidays booked using a travel agent

Year	2001	2005	2006	2007	2008	2009
Percentage	17.6	19.2	15.0	12.7	15.3	22.4

Source: Mintel, 2009

and transfer companies have recognized this demand and have ensured their products are now available for independent bookings. Agents have realized this opportunity and are using dynamic packaging to become tailor-made operators for their clients. The Web, which threatens their livelihoods, also offers the best prospect for their survival, if they adapt.

By accessing the websites of reliable suppliers, putting together a package of components that exactly meets a customer's needs and adding a mark-up allowing them a reasonable level of profit for the expertise they are delivering, agents are fulfilling a new role. Here, the consortia were able to help. Worldchoice, for instance, struck a deal with Thomas Cook that allows it to sell Thomas Cook's products under its own label. Members of the consortium are able to access its Cook's Flexible Trips dynamic packaging operation and are also protected under Cook's Air Travel Organizer's Licence (ATOL) for the resultant package they create.

Initially, much of the dynamic packaging market focused on short-haul trips, often providing facilities similar to those offered by packages. However, customers are now expecting similar flexibility across all their travel experiences, and this has seen greater demand for dynamic packaging in product areas such as skiing and cruise holidays, where flights, transfers, cruises and shore excursions are packaged to create a tailor-made holiday.

In the UK, ATOL regulations were amended in 2003 so that agents could no longer buy the separate components of an inclusive tour and package them without possession of an ATOL. Agents were faced with the choice of either buying the components from an existing ATOL holder (such as a tour operator's dynamic packaging website) or applying for a mini-ATOL to set themselves up as package operators. Consortia often hold an ATOL licence to cover all members of their group. If flights are not included in the package, an ATOL is not obligatory, but, if bundling other components, the agent must still comply with the conditions of the European Package Travel Regulations. This includes providing clear booking conditions, the service of a representative or 24-hour telephone assistance and accepting liability for damages, so business insurance is a must.

More recently, the government has revisited this legislation. To provide better consumer protection for British travellers, the Department for Transport (DfT) announced a review of regulations for what are called 'flight-plus' holidays. The DfT defines this as 'holidays composed of a flight and other key components bought together (within two successive days)' (DfT, 2011). The changes are needed to clarify the responsibility of the agent booking the components as well as ensuring liabilities are clear. At the time of writing, the industry was being consulted on the impact of these new regulations and it is envisaged that they will be in force by the end of 2012.

While dynamic packaging has been important in the UK market for some time, the recession which hit the end of the last decade led to a slowdown in this form of travel booking. The failure of several airlines and travel operators, coupled with events like the Icelandic ash cloud and political unrest in holiday destinations such as Egypt and Greece, led to concerns over financial protection and personal safety. The outcome is that many travel agents are again finding that package holidays are increasing their share of the market (Mintel, 2011).

Disintermediation and reintermediation

The growing use of the Internet to purchase travel products direct from the provider has meant that consumers have begun to bypass intermediaries. This removal of travel agents (as well as tour operators in some cases) from the chain of distribution is termed **disintermediation**.

This has caused obvious concern for travel agents, and their response has been to reinforce their role in the chain of distribution by providing customers with an enhanced travel booking experience. Agents have reinforced awareness of their role in providing information, convenient booking and problem-solving in times of crisis.

Many specialist travel organizations (often online) have been established to support customers in purchasing various elements of their travel at their convenience. Such companies allow different elements to be purchased through one site, often providing discounts when more than one element is purchased. The advantage of these websites to consumers is that they are independent of the suppliers and viewed as unbiased in terms of the range of products they offer. Airlines also value these outlets as a means of unloading surplus stock without degrading the brand. There have been a few great successes in such travel businesses, including Expedia, lastminute.com, travelocity.com and ebookers, which sell, among other things, discounted and late availability travel – mainly airline seats, hotel accommodation and car rental – rather than focusing on package holidays.

The growing inclusion of such businesses within the chain of distribution has been termed **reintermediation**. This century has seen reintermediation grow, as specialist online providers offer customers improved price comparison opportunities as well as greater efficiencies in the time spent booking travel products.

Setting up and running a travel agency

The leisure travel agency

Traditionally, travel agents are located in major city centres, in the suburbs of large towns and, less frequently, in smaller towns. They are often termed 'bricks and mortar' or 'high street' agents, reflecting the locations of their buildings. To be successful, they tend be sited at street level and close to the centre of main shopping areas. They compete against the other agents drawing on the market within the local area. In the case of a large city, that area may extend only to the surrounding streets, but, in the case of an important market town, it may draw on residents living within a radius of 30 or 40 miles. There was also noticeable growth in travel hypermarkets, located at the out-of-town retail parks. They attract high levels of trade as customers incorporate travel purchases into their other leisure shopping in these locations with convenient parking.

It is also worth noting that agents in city centres attract as their clients not only local residents but also workers employed in the area who may find it more convenient to make their travel arrangements close to their place of work than to do so nearer to their homes. It may also be the case, however, that a number of workers in the area will choose to pick up their brochures from the city branch, but make their reservations at an agency near their homes, where bookings can be arranged together with their spouse or partner. This may mean a high turnover of brochures with little return for the city agency – a problem particularly common in a major city like London.

As noted earlier, since holiday brochures can be downloaded by customers from the websites of tour operators there has been a reduction in the printing of brochures and these people will not be calling in to a travel agent. In some cases, too, travel agencies themselves may hold only electronic copies of brochures, just printing the required pages for their customers. This has the benefit of reducing the need to stock all brochures, and may mean that customers are not distracted by other products within the brochure, but this switches printing costs onto the travel agent.

A recent development among specialized agencies is to focus on contacting their clients through websites or recommendation by word of mouth, thus making them less dependent on expensive street-level premises. These agents generally avoid the problem of timewasters – people who pop in to pick up brochures from which they will later book direct online or merely wish to get quotations to compare with those obtained from several other agencies in the area.

Setting up a travel agency requires little capital, although in some countries formal qualifications are a prerequisite. The International Air Transport Association (IATA) also requires that a suitably qualified and experienced staff member is employed if the agency wishes to sell air tickets. As not every staff member has to be suitably qualified when the business is established, however, it is possible to operate with only one or two experienced employees. Consequently, the business appears extremely attractive to outsiders, who see it as a glamorous occupation with wonderful opportunities for cheap travel.

Establish a new business or purchase an existing agency?

Anyone contemplating opening a travel agency will have to consider the merits of buying an existing agency against those of establishing a new one.

There are considerable advantages to taking over an existing agency. To begin with, trading figures for recent years can be examined and the viability of the agency evaluated in relation to the purchase price. An agency that is operating successfully can be expected to retain its loyal clientele, if service remains comparable in the future. Against this, if there is a strong and loyal market already, the price for the agency may be high, to include the goodwill. **Goodwill** embraces the reputation of the business and the expectation that existing customers will continue to buy from there.

Another advantage of buying an existing agency is that licences and **appointments** (agreements with tour operators to sell their products) are generally retained by the new management. Staff, too, can be retained and good, qualified and experienced staff are often not easy to find, especially for those seeking to set up a new agency.

EXAMPLE   Travel agency for sale

There are specialist companies, many of whom advertise online, who sell businesses on behalf of the owner. These companies can offer a wide variety of online and 'bricks-and-mortar' businesses. Here we look at one example to provide an insight to the market for purchasing an established business.

This is the example of 'TA', an agency based in North London. The business consists of one outlet, located in a parade of shops, set on a busy main road. The location is in a densely populated area, and a nearby shopping centre brings people past the door. The store front provides a display area so passers-by can be tempted by special offers and late-deals. Inside there are five desks, brochure display units and a separate storage area. Staff facilities include an office and kitchen.

The premises are 600 square feet and the lease on this property has just under ten years to run. The annual rental costs are £10 400 while business rates add another £3200 to operating costs. Historically, turnover has been in excess of £600 000 and profit before tax runs at 8%. The business employs three people full-time and one part-time. The business currently holds ABTA, ATOL and IATA licenses.

The cost to purchase this business is £50 000.

The attraction of starting from scratch is mainly a financial one: the capital cost will be limited to office furnishings, fixtures, computers, phones and perhaps a new external fascia. Persuading principals to provide you with brochures, offer you appointments and pay commission on sales, however, may prove difficult, especially if the area concerned is already well served by existing agents.

Location, location, location

A popular phrase may be adapted here: 'There are only three things that are important when setting up an agency: location, location, location'. This drives home the fundamental point that, from your customers' point of view, the convenience of the location is the main criterion in their choice of a travel agent, especially if they require little more than a simple holiday booking service offering the best possible price.

Sites need to be researched carefully. Existing pedestrian flows should be noted, as should barriers, whether physical or psychological. For instance, shops on traffic 'islands' where pedestrians have to use subways to cross the road will find it difficult to attract passing trade. Parking is often difficult in town centres, so if there are too many restrictions and no nearby car parks, this can be a further important disincentive to your customers. The local planning office should be consulted to examine any plans for redevelopment in the area. Residential redevelopment in the immediate area could be an important plus for the site, while commercial redevelopment nearby may pose a threat.

Any agent expecting to attract casual passing trade who chooses a little-used side street away from the main shopping area merely because rents or rates are lower will be at a major trading disadvantage. If, however, the agent aims to serve clients seeking a professional agency via the Internet or those seeking a specialist to advise on a complex travel itinerary, then that side street, or even an upper floor, may adequately serve the purpose.

Clients are attracted to roomy shops with plenty of rack space and a bright, cheerful, inviting atmosphere to tempt them in. Increasingly, windows are designed not as settings to display brochures or destination publicity (although, as can be seen in Figure 19.4, some agencies do still take this approach), but as living advertisements for the shop's interior. Good lighting, warm colours, comfortable chairs, desks rather than impersonal counters, all affect clients' perceptions of the agency and their motivation to enter the shop. Once inside, the good agent takes advantage of the opportunity to make a sale, but enticing clients through the door is the first step in selling.

Figure 19.4 Window display promoting UK and European holidays suited to a variety of markets

Photo by Claire Humphreys

EXAMPLE Shop design

Customers may be tempted by the special offers promoted in the storefront, but, unless the atmosphere and the service live up to their expectations, they are unlikely to buy. Current thinking is that a comfortable environment will help to build a relationship with the customer and it is the trust developed by this relationship which converts the sale.

To improve the shop environment, some agencies have included coffee facilities, provided wireless Internet and included sofas and armchairs to encourage a longer dwell time – especially important if the shop is busy.

Historically, customers sat across a desk from the agent, who faced a terminal screen, hiding the 'secrets' of the travel industry. Now it is more likely that the screens are visible to the customer, making it easier for the agent to explain details; it is possible today to find that the desk has been replaced by a small table surrounded by comfortable chairs. Finally, it is equally important to get the heating, ventilation and lighting right.

Operations

In the UK, Sunday trading has become much more common in recent years, although it is often restricted to key booking periods of the year, such as the post-Christmas booking season. Longer opening hours are now deemed necessary to compete with the facility to make bookings on the Internet, which can be made at any time of the day or night.

In the past, agents earned their revenue largely in the form of commissions on sales. Levels of commission have varied over time and according to the travel product sold, but typically have been highest for package tour sales (between 10 and 15%), with transportation companies paying slightly lower rates and other services even less. This pattern has changed radically within the past few years, as principals have sought to remain profitable by cutting costs and finding cheaper means of distributing their products.

Many airlines have changed their payment structures to agents, often withdrawing commissions entirely, forcing the agents to charge a service fee to their customers for the sale of tickets. This has been a noted practice of the low-cost carriers, led by Ryanair, whose bookings are almost entirely via the Internet, but this soon became the practice of many more traditional international carriers, too. In September 2007, Qatar Airlines announced that they would be eliminating commission payments (they had been 9% in 2004). This followed an announcement by its rival, Emirates, which chose to reduce its commission payments to 5%. Some airlines pay a fixed-level fee according to the class of ticket purchased (paying higher fees for business or first-class tickets). KLM moved from paying 7% commission to a fixed fee in January 2001, while Lufthansa moved to a service fee in January 2002. BA (now taking over half its bookings via the Internet) has moved in a similar direction, not only reducing commissions, but also withdrawing ticketing and GDS privileges for agents achieving less than £50 000 worth of sales.

The nature of the local market significantly affects such decisions, however. For example, in India, the use of travel agents is high, so the decision to reduce commissions in India was only announced in the summer of 2008, although neither SpiceJet nor GoAir, both low-cost airlines, have paid commission in recent years. In 2006, Kingfisher bucked the trend and announced that it would double the commission it paid (to 10%), recognizing that it sold 60% of its tickets through travel agents in India. In the summer of 2008, however, it too announced a plan to bring in zero commission, after its competitor Air

India implemented such a policy. By 2010, most travel agents were earning little more than 3% commission on domestic flights and little or no commission on international flights. As a response, they now charge transaction fees, varied according to the type of airline ticket purchased.

Among tour operators, Thomson led the way in reducing the basic rates of commission paid to its agents and introducing a complex reward system for greater sales effort, including directional selling. However, there appears to be a general move towards increasing commission levels again to encourage loyalty from agents. Those principals that do pay commissions will generally offer higher levels to agents that are members of consortia – that is, they have banded together to achieve agreed sales targets in order to compete with the multiples. This can add 2.5% or more to the earnings of the agent, particularly for the sale of package tours. It is still rare, though, to find an agent averaging earnings of more than 10–11% on the total of the revenue achieved during the year. The likelihood is that, eventually, commissions will cease to be paid, with agents initiating fees to cover their expenses.

EXAMPLE It's not just commission that is important

The reality is that many travel agents earn their money though commission and therefore their turnover will be affected by total sales and which companies' holidays they sell.

However, to succeed in the long term, repeat business from customers is critical, and selling them the right holiday is vital if this is to be achieved. Two industry professionals working in the luxury sector of the industry suggest that having a good rapport with the principal to access the right product, and confidence in the service delivery both play an important role in the decision (TTG, 2011).

Agents at first resisted changes to the commission structure, arguing that their customers would be angered by attempts to charge a transaction fee and would therefore be more likely to book direct with the airlines. The introduction of ticketless travel by some airlines, which not only saves airlines and other travel suppliers the cost of issuing tickets, but also encourages direct bookings, has further reduced agency revenue.

Evidence from the USA tends to support the agents in their view that service charges have been difficult to impose. Commissions were capped by the airlines there in the mid-1990s, but the public initially resisted attempts to impose fees, turning to book on the Internet. In 1995, 70% of all airline tickets issued in the USA were sold through agents, but this had dropped to just 30% a decade later. Some 40% of agents have left their jobs in the interim as a result, with many turning to working as home-based agents. Virtually all US agents now charge transaction fees, while attempting to increase sales of package holidays and cruises to maintain revenues. Furthermore around 40% charge consultation fees, payable even if no booking is made. Research by ASTA suggests that fees are usually around $35 for arranging air travel.

In the UK, package tours represent by far the largest proportion of all agents' sales, although an increasing proportion of these involve some tailor-made elements. Typically, overseas holidays account for the majority of those sales, with air transport a declining element. Domestic holidays, a growing area of potential sales, have been estimated to take up to 4%, while the remainder is divided between cruises, rail and coach bookings and miscellaneous services. Tailor-made packages, or dynamic packaging, are steadily eroding the traditional tour operator-based package tour product for many agencies.

The business travel agency

Those agents located close to city centres or other centres of business and industry, such as an industrial estate, may also try to capture the business travellers within their territory. This is a highly specialized market, however, for which staff must have greater skills and will be competing against the large business travel corporations that have contacts with suppliers, allowing them greater flexibility in negotiating prices.

Any commissions earned from suppliers may have to be split with business clients, as part of the contract to act as the travel agency for the company. It is increasingly common for business travel agents to negotiate discounted travel with the principal (receiving no commission), then pass on those improved rates to the company they serve, but charge a management fee for the service.

There are a number of approaches that these travel management companies (TMCs) use in fee-based contracts, the most common being:

- a flat fee, usually payable per month, based on predicted levels of business
- rebate of any commission paid to the agency, the agency charging a fixed amount per transaction
- a simple fee per ticket set-up
- variable fees charged according to the complexity of the transaction
- a minimum fee charged per transaction with the guarantee of there being a minimum number of transactions per month.

It is also common to find contracts drawn up based on fees that depend on the agency achieving a certain level of cost savings for the company. Agreements will also generally include extended credit terms, whereby accounts do not have to be settled until 10–12 weeks after the receipt of tickets. One drawback of a system in which commission is fully rebated to the client is that the supplier, such as a hotel, gains no sales benefit from increasing its commission rates to its distributors, so must look for other strategies to gain the agency's support.

Management issues

Businesses are extremely demanding customers. The level of service that agencies must offer to retain their patronage is considerable. Focusing on the business community requires not only additional skills and knowledge but also a willingness to provide extended hours of service (for the convenience of the businesses) and a level of service far beyond what would be expected of counter staff in a leisure agency. Documentation such as visas may have to be arranged for clients, often at short notice, then delivered to the customer, possibly out of normal business hours. Senior staff must be accessible at any time to arrange last-minute travel. Professional business travel staff will expect to be paid well above the rates paid to counter staff in leisure agencies, yet the margins may be slimmer. The additional costs of handling these arrangements must be considered by the agent, particularly where credit is offered to businesses. It is not unusual for companies to delay payments until well beyond the dates they were due, while the agent is still obliged to make payments to principals on time. Thus the agency is helping to fund those companies' cash flow at its own expense.

All of this makes business travel a difficult field for an independent operator to enter, regardless of the level of personal service it is willing to offer. The financial attraction of the larger business accounts, which often exceed a million pounds a year, nevertheless results in many agents competing for the business by offering extra levels of service, fares expertise to guarantee lowest prices and implant offices.

Implant offices are those based in the business client's own premises but staffed by the agency, specifically to handle the company's travel needs exclusively. To justify this, the company must be certain that the revenue generated will be sufficient to cover the high costs of setting up and operating such an additional branch.

As the highest discounts can be offered by agents negotiating the best deals with their principals, this has once again led to the multiple branch agencies dominating the business travel agency market – American Express, Carlson Wagonlit, BCD, Hogg Robinson, FCm and Omega World Travel. Furthermore, some business travel agents are also members of international consortia (for example, Advantage Business Travel), which offer them even greater influence and purchasing power with the principals. With the global buying power of such groups, airline and other tickets can be purchased at the lowest possible price for business house clients.

EXAMPLE   **Tripcase**

Sabre has created a mobile phone application specifically aimed at the customers of TMCs. Both Hogg Robinson and Omega World supported this for their business clients.

The app allows the TMC to communicate with the traveller directly, providing travel itineraries and updates, as well helping the traveller ensure any amendments to travel plans fit within corporate travel policy. The system also sends flight updates to the phone so that travellers can arrange their meetings and schedule accordingly.

Such technology has proved popular, and this allows TMCs the opportunity to enhance their offering to the client. It also ensures they can directly communicate with the customer improving efficiencies in dealing with client employees.

The Guild of Travel Management Companies, established in 1967, is the professional body representing the leading business travel agents in the UK and accounts for some 75–80% of all the airline tickets sold in the UK. The Guild's role is to represent the interests of business agents and their clients and improve the standards and quality of travel for its members through negotiation with suppliers such as airlines, airports and hotel chains. With its encouragement, associations have been established in Germany, Ireland, Italy, The Netherlands, Portugal and Spain, and these groups work together as the Guild of European Business Travel Agents.

Large companies often employ specialist travel managers, who act as buyers of travel products for their employees and liaise between the employees and travel agency. Purchases arranged centrally allow the company to manage travel arrangements (perhaps to adhere to company travel policies) and use the specialist knowledge of the travel manager to gain better prices. These managers have their own professional body in the UK – the Institute of Travel Management (ITM). This organization seeks to use its influence to obtain better deals for its members, while acting as a mouthpiece and watchdog for this section of the industry.

There is an equivalent organization in the USA – the National Passenger Traffic Association (NPTA) – which has actually set up its own travel agency to make further cost savings for its members. Both the ITM and NPTA are represented in the International Business Travel Association (IBTA), which includes a number of Continental European organizations among its members.

Some large corporations have gone a stage further. Recognizing that they have the buying power to organize their own travel arrangements without the intercession of a travel agent, they will negotiate direct with airlines for their tickets and discount agreements, cutting out intermediaries entirely. Once again, the online suppliers and agencies are making it easier for the customer to benefit by going direct.

Travel agency skills and competences

Due to the extremely competitive nature of the retail travel business, two factors become important if the agency is to succeed: good management and good service. Good management will ensure that costs are kept under control, members of staff are motivated and the agency goes out actively to seek customers rather than wait for them to come through the door. Good service will ensure satisfied clients, help to build a loyal clientele and encourage word-of-mouth recommendation, which will increase the local share of the market for the agency.

Despite the expansion of the large multiples, most independent travel agents are still small businesses, in which the owner acts as manager and employs two or three members of staff. In such an agency, there is little specialization in terms of the usual division of labour, and staff will be expected to cope with all the activities normally associated with the booking of travel, which will include:

- advising potential travellers about resorts, carriers, travel companies and travel facilities worldwide
- making reservations for all travel requirements
- planning itineraries of all kinds, including complex, multi-stopover independent tours
- accessing relevant supplier and destination websites
- issuing documentation, including travel tickets and vouchers
- communicating by telephone, e-mail and letter with travel principals, tour operators and customers
- maintaining accurate files on reservations
- maintaining and displaying stocks of travel brochures
- mediating and negotiating with suppliers in the event of customer complaints.

It is ironic that the travel product requires perhaps greater knowledge on the part of retail staff than does virtually any other product, yet in many countries travel agents' salaries still lag behind those of others in the retail industry. This makes it particularly hard for agency managers to attract and retain skilled staff. Agents argue that competition and discounted prices make it impossible to pay higher salaries, although the opportunity for free or discounted travel does provide an additional employee benefit. Principals have come to accept that their retailers cannot be expected to have detailed knowledge of every product and concentrate instead on providing agents with easier access to information through websites, reservation systems and brochures.

In addition to product knowledge, therefore, the main skills that counter staff require include the ability to read timetables and other data sources, source 'best buy' airline fares, complete tickets and have sufficient knowledge of their customers to be able to match customers' needs with the products available. All staff today are also required to be familiar with the latest technology, including the use of e-mail, fax and accessing websites and CRSs of all types.

The ticketing function is largely undertaken via computers and, arguably, fare quotations and ticketing skills are becoming less important for most agency staff, apart from those dealing with business travel. An understanding of the principles underlying the construction of fares, however, can be helpful – for example, so that staff can explain complex fares to customers; and, of course, there will be a continuing need for fares experts in the industry.

EXAMPLE   Fares expertise

Constructing fares is a complex subject and entails a lengthy period of training, coupled with continuous exercise of these skills. A number of internationally recognized courses are available to provide these skills, including, in the UK, those offered by BA, which meet IATA requirements and can be taken up to the BA Fares and Ticketing Part II level, indicating full competence in meeting any requirement for fare construction and ticketing.

In some cases, large travel agency chains have centralized the fare calculation role so that a handful of experts can quickly determine the lowest prices for a particular journey by air when requested by a member of their counter staff. For most air fares, however, agents are now dependent on quotations given by carriers or intermediaries via the CRS and websites.

Travel management companies, who are serving the needs of corporate clients with complex travel demands, are likely to need excellent fare calculation skills. In 2005, FCm launched its own training academy, providing fares and ticketing education for its agents, as well as other training programmes for its staff.

In addition to the counter staff functions, agency managers (who frequently spend time at the counter themselves) are required to fulfil a number of administrative functions. On the financial side, these will include:

- maintenance and control of the agency's accounts
- invoicing clients
- effecting bank reconciliations (matching payments made and received on the bank statement with those in the customer and supplier accounts records)
- preparing and controlling budgets
- providing an estimate of the cash flow in the company on a month-by-month basis
- controlling expenditure.

Sales records must be kept and sales returns completed regularly for travel principals. All these back office jobs are often computerized, even in the case of smaller independent agencies.

Managers are also responsible for safeguarding access to their booking systems, promoting their business and recruiting, training and supervising office staff. Managers will try to ensure that staff are motivated – in general, to provide good customer service and, specifically, to achieve particular sales targets or goals. Managers will often use educational study or familiarization (fam) trips and training programmes as well as commission bonuses to enhance staff knowledge and motivation. Trips are usually provided by tour operators or destination marketing organizations (DMOs) in order to enhance the product awareness of travel agents, and thus increase sales. There is now much greater emphasis on the educational element of such trips, rather than these being free holidays with little opportunity to develop product knowledge.

Finally, managers need to control and regularly update their websites and oversee the preparation and distribution of e-newsletters to clients. Regular contact with clients via the Internet or by post is now essential if business is to be retained and clients discouraged from booking direct on the Web.

Customer contact skills

The way in which staff communicate with clients is, together with the essential product knowledge they display, a key ingredient in an agency's success. These communication skills can be divided into three distinct categories:

- language skills
- personal and social skills
- sales skills.

Written communications with clients that demonstrate poor sentence construction, grammar or spelling reflect not just on the employee but also on the company itself. When such correspondence goes out under the signature of a senior member of staff, the image of the company suffers a still more serious blow.

Personal and social skills are also very important. Serving the public should not be confused with servility (being a servant). The key is ensuring that customers are served effectively and with respect. Customers expect to be received warmly, with a genuine smile of greeting. Staff are expected to be unfailingly calm and cheerful, whatever stress they may be experiencing during their working day. These qualities need to become second nature to counter staff.

First impressions weigh heavily and staff will be judged by their dress and appearance. Tourism employees must be prepared to adjust to the constraints that the job imposes if they wish to succeed in the industry. Employers will insist on neat hairstyles, suitably discreet makeup for female staff and high overall standards of grooming and appearance – often to the extent that counter staff in the agency chains will be required to wear a uniform. Personal hygiene is, of course, essential.

The way employees sit, stand or walk says a great deal about them and their attitude towards their customers. Staff who meet face-to-face with customers will be expected to look alert and interested, avoid slouching when they walk and sit upright rather than slump in their chairs. These non-verbal signals all say a lot about the attitude of the company to its customers. The scene of employees filing their nails or talking to their friends on the telephone while customers try to attract their attention is a common one in training videos and one that encourages us to think about how we present ourselves in public.

A warm, welcoming smile and friendly manner when greeting a customer approaching the desk will convey a positive view of the company and make the customer feel at home and in a buying frame of mind. Attentiveness to the customer is not only polite, it ensures that vital client needs are recognized, enabling the employee to match needs with products. When talking to customers and greeting them, the employee should maintain eye contact and a manner that will breed confidence in the agency and its staff's product knowledge. Even handshakes are important cues to confidence – they should be firm and offered willingly. Use of the client's name enhances the relationship.

Even the way in which staff answer the telephone can help to generate the right image of the company. Telephones should be answered quickly and competently. As there are no dress and appearance cues that enable the client to make a judgement, the voice becomes the sole factor. Trainers emphasize the need to smile, even when on the telephone, as an impression of friendliness can still be conveyed in the voice. If clients are asked to hold, they should be given the reason and regularly checked to ensure that they are still holding. If the person they are trying to reach is busy, an offer should be made to call them back and this should be followed up to ensure that they have been called back. Similarly, if employees cannot give an answer immediately to a problem, they should offer to call the client back with the answer in a short while and then ensure that they do so. Failure to call back is one of the commonest sources of frustration for clients and can easily lead to the loss of their business to a competitor.

The e-mail has become a significant mode of communication with customers. Research suggests that, as a booking tool, an e-mail takes 30% less staff time than the telephone, but it is vital that e-mails are dealt with promptly and accurately to ensure that customers feel they are receiving a high quality of service.

It's a mystery

For many years the UK travel trade magazines have operated a mystery shopper programme, reporting the results in their publications.

Historically, TTG would compare different high-street agents in the same locality. Now, however, they test online agents alongside high-street agents. TTG assesses the staff on four criteria: first impressions, sales process, product and budget match and incentive and extras offered to encourage booking.

Travel Weekly uses a similar approach, scoring agency appearance (15%), brochure racking (10%), product knowledge (25%), sales technique (25%) and staff attitude (25%). They currently focus on visiting high-street agents and ensure both independent and tour-operator owned agencies are examined.

Both magazines assert that these mystery shopper exercises are not designed to cause detriment to businesses receiving a low score – rather, they are designed to encourage improvements in service quality and to give recognition to high performers.

Good customer contact is deemed so important that many of the multiples use mystery shoppers to monitor the experience provided to customers. In such cases, mystery shoppers will telephone or visit the shop to make travel arrangements. After the visit, they will report back to management regarding the quality of the service they received. This technique can be used to identify weak points in service delivery and encourage staff to maintain or improve service levels by linking assessment to bonuses. It can also be used to evaluate the services of competitors, too, and establish comparison benchmarks.

The national tourist board for Australia has also used mystery shoppers to test agencies that specialize in selling holidays to their country in order to encourage accurate product knowledge.

The sales sequence

Good social skills and high-quality customer service can build an atmosphere that encourages buying, but closing a sale requires an understanding of the techniques involved. Effective selling is the outcome of four stages in the selling process, which together make up the sales sequence:

- establishing **rapport** with clients
- **investigating** clients' needs
- **presenting** the product to the clients
- getting clients to take action by **committing** themselves to the purchase.

Below, each of these stages is examined in more detail.

Rapport

To sell products successfully, one must first match them to the customers' needs. If the clients buy a product that they do not really want or which does not provide the satisfaction they were looking for, they simply will not come back again. As no travel agency can survive without a high level of repeat business, achieving one-time sales is clearly not enough; customers must be satisfied in the longer term.

To achieve this, the first step is to build **rapport** (a trusting relationship), by engaging clients in conversation, gaining their trust and learning about their needs. This process also allows the salesperson to judge how receptive clients are to new ideas and how willing they are to have products sold to them. Some customers prefer to self-select, so should not be badgered into a sale, while others need and seek advice more openly.

To generate a two-way conversation, the opening phrase 'Can I help you?' has to be avoided – it simply invites the reply, 'No thanks, I'm just looking'. A more useful way of opening a conversation would be to use a phrase such as, 'Do you have a particular type of holiday in mind?' or, to a customer who has just picked up a brochure, 'Were you just looking for sun, sea and sand holidays or had you something more adventurous in mind?' This forces a reply, and encourages the client to open a conversation.

Investigation

Once you have gained clients' trust, the next step is to **investigate** their needs more thoroughly. Once again, it is necessary to ask open questions that elicit full answers rather than a simple 'yes' or 'no'. The sort of information needed to draw out the client will include:

- who is travelling and the number in the group
- when they wish to travel and how long they want to stay at a destination
- their preferred mode of travel
- their choice of destination
- what they expect to pay.

The last is one of the hardest for junior staff. It requires good judgement to know whether the cost of the holiday is critical and, if so, what the limits might be. If customers mention a figure, one should not take it for granted that this is the maximum they are willing to pay. The industry has encouraged holidaymakers to believe that holidays are invariably cheap, but one is doing clients a disservice not to point out that cheapness is not necessarily value for money and, by paying a little more, one might have a better guarantee of satisfaction. The good salesperson is one who can encourage clients to consider products at a higher price while reassuring them that their best interests are being considered. It is generally better to wait for clients to give an indication of their budget than to question them directly on this point.

Clients may have only the vaguest idea about where they want to go, what they want to do, even what they expect to pay. Needs must never be assumed, even when there is a clear statement of intent. For example, clients who say that they do not want to go on a package holiday may merely be revealing a deep-seated prejudice that such holidays are down-market. Alternatively, they may have had a bad experience of earlier such holidays. The salesperson's task is to tease out the real reason so that the appropriate product can be offered. For example, a tailor-made independent inclusive tour may offer the best solution, as the client would not be part of a crowd.

Sometimes it will be clear to the salesperson that the client has superior knowledge about the destination or is seeking information about a little-known destination. In these conditions, it is preferable to admit ignorance and either offer an introduction to another member of staff with better knowledge of the destination or offer to obtain more information for them.

Presentation

Once the salesperson is satisfied that they know exactly what the client needs, they may go on to the next stage – **presenting** the products that they feel will suit the client. The aim will be to present not only the features of the holiday being offered, but also their benefits:

> Travelling in the early spring, you have the advantage of lower prices *and* this can be the nicest time of the year in the Austrian valleys, as the blossom is out and it is before the mass of tourists arrive at the height of the season.

It has more recently been suggested that the presentation is about telling the customer the story about the product and how it is suited to them. It is not about a 'hard-sell' but about buying into the life of the customer and placing them at the centre of the holiday search. Thus, the customer can feel that purchasing a holiday is a positive experience, rather than merely a transaction.

Product knowledge is, of course, critical for success in gaining clients' confidence to the point where they will be willing to accept the salesperson's recommendations. Even if they feel that what they are offering is exactly suitable for their client, it is always a good idea to offer an alternative, so that the client has the opportunity to choose. If the salesperson then demonstrates just how one holiday is a better buy than the other, this will make it easier for the client to understand the options being recommended.

At this stage in the sales sequence, the salesperson will often have to handle objections. Sometimes, objections are voiced only because the client needs reassurance or they have not yet fully understood the benefits being offered to them. At other times, objections occur because not all the client's needs have yet been met and then a process of patient questioning may be needed once again to draw out the possibly hidden motives for the objections.

Commitment

This final stage closes the sale. This means getting clients to take action – ideally, to buy, but, of course, some clients will need more time to consider the offer. The aim of the salesperson is to get the best possible outcome from the sales sequence – taking an option (placing the required product on hold for the customer), getting the clients to call back later or getting them to agree that the salesperson may call them later to follow up the sale.

The good salesperson is always looking for the buying signals that reveal clients are ready to buy: 'Would you like me to see if I can get you a reservation for that date?' can prompt clients who are dithering about taking action. Care must be taken, however – never push clients into a sale before they are ready to buy or they may be lost forever.

In some cases, offering extras, such as access to an airport lounge, may be enough to encourage purchase. Here again, knowing the customer – and the things they prize – can help to ensure the right extras are offered. For example, there is little benefit in offering an upgrade to a larger hire car if the customer plans to spend little time driving.

After-sales service

Finally, having received the deposit for a firm booking, the salesperson must remember that the sales job is not yet finished. Different countries place various legal obligations on travel agents, so it may be necessary to provide customers with detailed information on visas or other terms and conditions of the booking (such as rights with regard to cancellation). Even after the booking has been confirmed, the tour operator or principal may make changes (such as altering flight times) and customers will need to be notified of these by the agent. In some cases, flights may be cancelled and alternative arrangements will need to be discussed and agreed with the travellers. Clients may also want to make changes to bookings and will expect the salesperson to provide advice and make the arrangements accordingly.

It is beneficial for agencies to try to gain the loyalty of customers, so the salesperson must continue to show interest and concern for clients, helping to reinforce the sale and their commitment to return to make future travel arrangements. Many agents now send a 'welcome home' card to their clients after their return from holiday, to invite them to come into the agency to talk about their experiences and ensure they will remember the agency in the future. The medium of e-mail is invaluable for keeping in touch with clients – communication is immediate and there is minimal cost involved.

Training and qualifications

Formal training qualifications for the industry are both diverse and confusing. Not all courses that have been introduced are universally welcomed or understood by the industry. Some national associations provide professional development training, which can help to maintain quality within the industry as well as enhancing the career opportunities of their members.

In the USA, ASTA operates Model Agency courses, which encourage agency managers to evaluate their business operations and improve their services.

The Australian Federation of Travel Agents (AFTA) offers certificated courses to develop the knowledge and skills of those entering the industry, as well as continuous professional development through a skills accreditation initiative – the Australian Travel Professionals Program, which replaced their travel agents' qualification (ATAQ).

In the UK, ABTA has supported professional qualifications and life-long learning in the travel industry and has established the Accredited Travel Professional (ATP) scheme. This scheme allows agents to gain recognition for their qualifications and training programmes they attend throughout their years of employment. Once ATP status has been achieved, members must continue to undertake relevant training to further enhance their knowledge and skills.

 The ABTA-Accredited Travel Professional programme in detail

After numerous changes to qualifications, both professional and academic, over the past few years, training provision in the UK is now overseen by People 1st, a government-sponsored skills body. They have been working with ABTA to establish the ATP scheme.

The scheme provides three levels of membership based on experience and qualifications, with the minimum entry criteria being either one year's experience and a level 2 national qualification (such as an NVQ) or two years' work experience.

ATP has evaluated the many different qualifications and skills training programmes available and awarded them points. To continue to hold ATP status, members must earn a minimum of 20 credit points annually, which encourages continuous professional development (CPD). Table 19.5 provides examples of the points earned through a variety of inhouse or national qualifications.

Table 19.5 ATP accredited training

Training course and qualification	Points earned
A Level in Travel and Tourism	119
ABTA seminar – Extreme weather patterns	5
Abu Dhabi Champions Training Programme	3
Certificate in Air Fares & Ticketing IATA – level 1	13
ECPAT – Following Child Protection Policies and Procedures	20
Fam trip attendance	5
Hoseasons – Dealing with a complaint call	8
Superbreak Product Knowledge and Travel Geography Quizzes	2
Worldchoice – Action plan for profit	15

Source: ATP website

Travel agency appointments

Most principals license the sale of their services through a process of contractual agreements with travel agencies, which, as noted earlier, are called **appointments**. In effect, these are a licence to trade and receive commission for sales achieved. Some principals dispense with this formality – hotels, for example, will normally pay commission on any sales made through a reputable travel agency without any formal agreement. In addition, agents may join trade associations to gain formal national recognition as travel agents.

Dealing with principals

Most contracts with principals are non-exclusive – that is, they do not prevent an agent from dealing with the principal's competitors. Occasionally, however, a contract may offer an agency the exclusive right to sell a product, and may furthermore restrict an agent's ability to deal with other directly competing companies.

Unless expressly stated in a contract, agents do not have the automatic right to deduct their commission from the monies due to principals. If bonus commissions are paid for targets achieved, it is generally the case that these sums of money are paid to agents at the end of the season, rather than immediately following the achievement of a target. These facts must be kept in mind by agents when estimating their business cash flow.

A licence is required if commission is to be paid on the sale of services of members of IATA (apart from sales of purely domestic tickets). Although IATA carriers have been reducing or eliminating commissions for agents, some are continuing to pay them, and it is important for travel agents which wish to offer a full range of services either to hold the necessary IATA appointment or to have an arrangement with another agency that does so – that agent issuing tickets on their behalf. New agents are permitted to sell air tickets and earn income by sharing commission with an established IATA agent.

There are around 3000 IATA-accredited agencies in the UK. IATA's Agency Distribution Office deals with applications for licences, a process that can take up to 45 days. The cost of application is in the region of £1000 for a new travel agency (slightly less if the application is to add a new branch to an existing agency).

A representative from IATA's Agency Investigation Panel visits the agent to judge whether or not the site is easily identified as a travel centre and suitable for the sale of tickets (while proof of turnover is no longer required of agents, IATA wishes to satisfy itself that the agency has the scope to generate business). The number and competence of staff will be judged, with at least one member of staff being expected to have two years' agency experience and, preferably, to hold a Certificate in Travel Services or an equivalent qualification in fares and ticketing. The representative must also be satisfied that the agency premises are secure and any ticket stock held can be safeguarded, although this is becoming less of an issue with the growing use of e-tickets. These in turn are posing new security problems, as IATA must now take steps to reassure themselves that the agent will not issue hundreds of e-tickets and disappear with the clients' money.

If approved, a bond is taken out to cover the agency's anticipated monthly IATA turnover. There is a small annual subscription. This approval enables the agent to sell the services of all IATA members.

Approval is also required to make commissionable sales on the services of railways, coach tickets, domestic airline services and other principals, such as shipping and car hire firms. Obtaining approval for most of these has been largely a formality for agents holding ABTA and IATA appointments. Appointments to sell travel insurance, however, involve closer scrutiny as the agent will be acting as a broker for the insurance service concerned.

Table 19.6 Travel agency licensing requirements

Country	Regulation
Association of Croatian Travel Agencies (UHPA)	• Must register and obtain identification code
Association of Danish Travel Agents and Tour Operators	• Must register with Travel Guarantee Fund if selling packages
Association of Finnish Travel agents	• Required to register with Consumer Agency and protect against financial insolvency
Association of Turkish Travel Agencies (TURSAB)	• Must register with TURSAB
Federation of Associations of Travel & Tourism Agents, Malta	• Required to hold licence issued by Malta Tourism Authority
Swiss Federation of Travel Agencies	• No licence is required but customer payments must be protected
Travel Agents' Association New Zealand	• No licence, but must have financial bond

Source: C. Humphreys, correspondence with membership managers of travel agents' associations, 2011

Insurance companies have generally tightened up on standards for their brokers, including those retailers operating in the travel industry.

Membership of trade bodies

In the UK, there are no legal requirements to meet when setting up as a travel agent, but, in some countries, including many of those within the EU, governments do exercise licensing control over agencies (see Table 19.6). In some cases, licensing is carried out at government level (as in Australia and some parts of the USA). In addition to government licensing, many countries also have national associations, established to promote the interests of their members, which establish standards of practice to protect customers and the industry, as well as lobbying government on policy affecting travel agents and their customers.

The role of trade associations – the case of the Association of British Travel Agents (ABTA)

Until 1993, any travel agent wishing to sell the products of an ABTA tour operator had to be a member of ABTA. In turn, ABTA tour operators could only sell their services through ABTA retailers. This reciprocal agreement, known as Stabiliser, was technically a constraint on trade and, as such, was challenged by the Office of Fair Trading. The Restrictive Practices Court upheld the agreement in 1982, however, after an appeal by ABTA, on the grounds that it was in the public interest, as ABTA's inhouse scheme of protection for consumers against the collapse of a member company was recognized as one of the best in the world. A Common Fund, provided out of membership subscriptions, allowed clients of a travel agency to continue with their holidays even if the travel agency they had booked with went into liquidation before the tour operator received payment for the tour. This complemented the protection offered by ABTA against the collapse of a tour operator. Many earlier conditions imposed on members by ABTA, however, such as a prohibition on discounting and the sale of non-travel products ('mixed selling'), were overturned by the Restrictive Practices Court.

In 2000, ABTA also removed the distinction between tour operator and retail agent membership, absorbing members into a single class. In July 2008, ABTA merged with the Federation of Tour Operators (FTO) to enhance its ability to support its members across the industry.

Membership of ABTA provided many advantages, but it also imposed various obligations. Premises were open to inspection and agents were obliged to abide by a strict Code of Conduct complementing that of the tour operator. Some key regulations remain. Members must satisfy ABTA about their financial standing and qualifications. ABTA also requires its members to have at least one member of its customer-facing staff with a minimum of two years' experience (reduced by six months for staff holding formal qualifications).

Some independent agents operate outside the ABTA framework. Regulations that previously constrained non-ABTA agents effectively limited them to selling fringe services, such as coach trips, or operating as so-called bucket shops (a term we met earlier, meaning outlets used by airlines to dump unsold tickets on the market at short notice and at heavily discounted prices). The abolition of the Stabiliser agreement and the introduction of the EU's Package Travel Directive led to much greater freedom for agents to operate outside of ABTA membership, however, and so it lost many of its controlling functions. Agents became free to trade with all ABTA and non-ABTA tour operators and are now subject only to legal requirements to carry satisfactory bonds against financial collapse. These changes did not lead to the wholesale withdrawal of members from ABTA.

ABTA represents the interests of both tour operators and travel agents. Given the potential conflicts of interest between these two groups, and other conflicts that can arise between the multiples and independent agencies, the continuing support for ABTA within the trade may seem surprising, but the importance of having a strong body to represent trade interests in consultations with government and other industry bodies and the organization's role as a mouthpiece for the industry have ensured its survival.

Customer recognition of the financial protection afforded to ABTA members is extensive (70% of customers booking holidays see it as essential that their travel providers are ABTA members) and retailers benefit from this brand recognition. Retailers also benefit from the clearing house that processes payments to tour operators.

Bonding

The introduction of the European Package Travel Directive meant that member states were required to incorporate financial protection within their legislation on travel operations. It should be noted that bonding is also often a requirement of operating as a travel agent in many non-European countries.

Bonding may be undertaken in one of three ways:

1. A sum of money equal to the value of the bond can be placed in a trust account. The agent can benefit from the interest accruing on the account, but cannot touch the capital itself. As this could involve putting up a substantial amount of money, it is rarely chosen except by the largest corporations.

2. The agent can obtain an insurance policy for the amount required, paying an annual premium.

3. The agent has the bank put up the bond, either against company assets or, more commonly, the personal guarantees of the directors. A fee is charged that is substantially less than the premium paid for an insurance policy, but the directors become personally liable for the amount of the bond in the event of the company's failure.

Following the introduction of the EU Directive that made bonding compulsory for any EU tour operator or agent, agents have made their own bonding arrangements, generally through banks or other organizations. In addition to this, any retail agent that operates tours will also be required to put up a tour operating bond.

Australia's Travel Compensation Fund (TCF)

To offer financial protection to customers, most Australian travel agents are required to participate in the Travel Compensation Fund (TCF), in addition to holding a licence from their state government (apart from the Northern Territory, which does not yet participate in this national scheme for regulating travel agents).

The TCF was established to provide financial compensation to consumers in the event of the collapse of a travel agent. The organization also monitors the financial viability of licensed travel agents, both when these businesses are first established and through an annual renewal process, to ensure that this sector of the industry is financially stable, reinforcing consumer confidence. The organization also maintains a register of licensed agents to provide information to government and consumers.

By 2010, more than 4600 agency outlets were participants in the scheme, each being required to pay into the compensation fund. Recent changes to the regulations of the scheme mean that now the charge made is based on an assessment of the level of risk inherent in each organization. The renewal fee paid by members amounts to around AUS$350. The annual financial review submitted by the agents assists with assessment, as well as encouraging the financial monitoring of companies (in areas such as record keeping and managing client monies correctly).

In 2010, 19 travel agencies collapsed, leading to 340 claims affecting more than 1500 travellers. This is significantly down on the levels experienced in 2008 and 2009. Almost AUS$1.5 million was paid in compensation, with average compensation amounting to $2786, a figure in line with the previous three years.

In order to recover some of the costs of this compensation, the Fund uses litigation and legal negotiation in relation to any collapsed business, though this can often take many years. Compensation for the customer, however, is provided swiftly – often within days of the claim being received – thus allowing customers the opportunity to book alternative travel.

Note though that TCF does not cover the Northern Territories (NT). The NT came close to joining the scheme in 1996 but was not prepared to make this mandatory for travel agents and thus was not able to join. This anomaly was evident when a large NT agency, Top End Escapes, collapsed in December 2010, and consequently client losses, estimated to be in the region of AUS$680 000, were not covered by the scheme.

Source: TCF, 2010

The impact of computer technology

As we saw earlier, the industry has been profoundly affected by developments in technology over the past decade, particularly computers. As innovations in this field are constantly being launched or improved, information about this sphere of travel activity tends to date very quickly, so there will be little benefit to be gained from examining the detailed merits of any existing system here, but this section of the chapter will provide an overview of the topic.

Computer systems in travel agencies are designed to offer three distinct facilities:

- front-office 'client relations' systems, enabling staff to access principals' CRS/GDS and websites, check availability and make reservations
- back-office systems, enabling documents such as invoices, vouchers, tickets and itineraries to be issued and accounts to be processed with principals
- management systems, producing updated figures on the company's performance to assist managers in guiding and controlling operations.

Systems have now been developed that will provide all three facilities for even the smallest independent agent, at prices that continue to fall. Alternatively, equipment can be leased to reduce capital investment and spread costs.

With regard to front-office sales and reservation activities, it is now mandatory to use computers rather than the telephone to make bookings with the leading tour operators and many principals. The retail travel sector is ideally suited to benefit from the use of computer technology. The products sold cannot be inspected directly before purchase, but may be viewed with the use of brochures or on TV or computer screens; sales outlets require systems for determining the availability of transport and accommodation, often at short notice, and the ability to make immediate reservations, amendments or cancellations; complex fares and conditions of travel must be accessed in order to provide customers with accurate and current quotes.

Back-office functions can be greatly assisted by computer technology. It can produce travel documents such as tickets, invoices, vouchers and itineraries, all which can now be processed efficiently and, when needed, quite rapidly (many providers are moving towards computer-generated e-tickets, which can further enhance this process).

The travel agent also needs to process an ever increasing amount of accounting and management information quickly and computers are invaluable for this. Computers can also assist with processing customer payments, chasing customers for balances on their travel accounts, as well as managing supplier accounts. Storing customer details using database technology means they can easily now be used to support marketing activities such as mailshots. It is common now to e-mail newsletters and special offers to customer e-mail addresses, to maintain contact and stimulate a purchase. More general office administration, such as personnel and payroll functions, can also be performed easily using dedicated software. In addition, business performance data can be retrieved to quickly assess areas such as sales levels and profit margins.

Global distribution systems (GDS)

In considering systems that are designed to access travel principals' reservations systems, one can distinguish between those developed by airlines and those developed by tour operators.

The airlines' travel reservation systems must be capable of booking seats on a large number of different airlines to allow maximum flexibility regarding route options (to allow a variety of origin and destination options to be available to customers). Agents currently achieve this principally by using one of the four major global distribution systems: Galileo, Amadeus, Sabre or Worldspan. In 2007, Galileo merged with Worldspan, although this is not predicted to have negative effects on users as travel agents can move quite easily between GDS suppliers, thus encouraging competition between the three providers. In recent years, there has been an effort to increase the range of products available through such systems, possibly including low-cost airlines, and this may further increase the use of GDS by travel agents.

American Airlines (AA) has rocked this approach, placing pressure on agents to connect directly to the AA system rather than via GDS. AA sees this as a key way of reducing distribution costs, but, at the time of writing, this has led to some industry recriminations (and lawsuits in US courts), with AA battling with Travelport, Orbitz and Expedia, supported by GDS provider Sabre, which argues that it is illegal for AA to force agencies to tie into the AA direct connect system. The outcome of this battle is likely to have repercussions for both travel agencies and GDS providers.

Tour operators' reservation systems

Systems to reserve products from the major tour operators are likewise accessed live on the computer. In the past this was done though a direct connection to the system using a specially designed terminal system known as Viewdata. More recently, however, many tour operators (as well as principals) have moved their operations to Internet-based systems, often incorporating specially designed reservations systems, such as the 'I-tour' system developed for Thomas Cook.

Technology providing new retailing systems

Although connections between suppliers and agents are being made simpler, there is still the need to provide travel agents with computer training to operate the many different systems used by suppliers (such training may be provided by the supplier). Many of those agents who have embraced technology wholeheartedly have also recognized the advantage of becoming electronic retailers, or, e-tailers (the term e-travel agent is beginning to be used to describe this function). Such agencies are adapting new technology to reach their clients online through the Web.

Web-based travel retailers are also providing other Internet companies with the capability to sell travel products, by embedding their search and booking facilities within the host's website. In such cases, the design of the site is dictated by the host company, while the travel content is externally provided by the travel retailer. This allows the host the opportunity to offer its customers a range of travel products, while the Web retailer expands its sales opportunities. The host provider may also earn a small fee for each booking made through its portal.

Technology helps suppliers to serve customers directly

Suppliers, notably the airlines, are creating their own websites, and it is against these that the e-tailers will have to compete. More widely, there is a rapid growth in business-to-consumer (B2C) sites, which are designed to cut out the intermediaries and sell direct to the public. In 2007, the UK tour operator Thomson reported that 60% of its holidays were booked online (thus reducing its reliance on traditional travel agents). The airlines have formed their own intermediaries, as with Opodo and Orbitz, while their own websites attract consumers with competitive prices, both of which challenge sales through agents using the traditional GDSs.

The critical question is whether or not the high street agent can survive in the face of these new methods of distribution. There are claims that, while the World Wide Web offers more options to customers, it does not necessarily replace existing forms of distribution as answers to specific questions will need to be raised with agents. The question remains as to how agents can avoid clients coming to them to pick their brains and then going home to book their holidays on the Internet. In addition, the growth of sites such as tripadvisor.com, which allows travellers to post reports on travel products such as hotels, provides customers with extensive information to aid their decisions. However, the Advertising Standards Authority (ASA) has expressed concern about fake or misleading reviews on TripAdvisor, which include favourable reviews paid for by principals and cases where customers have threatened to write bad reviews unless compensated.

Technology and generating markets for travel products

Not all markets are currently threatened by the changes in distribution network that have occurred though the development of technology and use of the Internet. While access to computers as well as connection to the Internet have occurred in many key markets, it has not penetrated all areas – in the Asia region around 17% of the population currently have access to the Internet, although this area is seeking a rapid growth in access, second only to the Middle East. For example, it has been reported that in India, although online travel companies exist, low Internet usage, limited access to credit cards (with sufficiently high credit limits) and concern over payment security have restricted online sales. To counter this, some online companies are considering opening high-street outlets.

Opinion is divided on whether the majority of agents or only a handful of the most adaptable can survive the Internet explosion that has occurred in major travel-generating markets. Mandelbaum (2004) proposed that demand for good travel agents will continue, as these can assist clients when travel problems occur; they are aware of the track records of products and can locate the latest special deals, often more quickly than a customer can find products though Internet searches. This suggests that those who are the most adaptable, offering a personal service, including expert advice, will be the ones which survive. The fact remains, however, that most agents have neither the knowledge nor the resources to undertake major change. Salaries are already low in the industry and the level of expertise among agents is questionable when confronted with an increasingly sophisticated and well-travelled clientele. The move to cutting commissions and, in the case of the airlines, withdrawing commission entirely, must encourage many agents to charge fees. If agents are to become professionals, like solicitors, as many are arguing, how do they pay the salaries and obtain the staff with the qualifications that will be required to deliver this level of expertise?

The future of travel retailing

Not only travel agents, but the entire travel industry faces greater uncertainty than ever before. The introduction of B2C in travel – suppliers providing a direct interface with their clients – threatens both agents and tour operators. This is because, if customers are encouraged to book flights and hotels direct for less than is possible through intermediaries, how long will it be before it becomes customary for those same customers to put together their own packages?

To meet the demands of more experienced travellers who seek tailor-made trips, dynamic packaging has grown rapidly, the technology now allowing travel agents to conveniently create packages at cheaper overall prices than by purchasing products separately. Legislation is starting to catch up, providing greater protection to customers taking this approach to travel booking and, once in place and publicized, it is likely that dynamic packaging will expand further.

Two factors may help to save the traditional high-street travel agent. The first is the impact of the global recession, which has hit demand for holidays and led many holiday-makers to re-evaluate whether holidays are considered a necessity or a luxury they can forego. The second factor, in part linked to the first, is the failure of many travel businesses. This has led to passengers relying on compensation schemes to refund lost monies and, if they are stranded overseas, to fly them home. Events like the Icelandic ash cloud have also highlighted the need for support in troubled times. As customers seek greater value for their money, financial protection and support in emergencies, so the traditional travel agent may benefit from the return of customers to their doors.

However, the traditional corner-shop-type travel agent that we have known in the past has already largely disappeared. The successful agents of the future will be flexible and innovative, willing to move with the times and to make use of the new tools of marketing that technology makes available.

Questions and discussion points

1. Do you think it is a good time to open your own high street travel agency? What could you do to ensure that your agency attracted enough business to be successful?

2. What are the benefits of using travel agents today? Are there any drawbacks?

3. Some countries require travel agencies to hold licences (in addition to licence requirements set by organizations such as IATA). Do you think this is necessary? Does this help to protect the customer? Does it help to protect the industry?

Tasks

1. Obtain a holiday brochure and review the holidays it offers. Write a brief report which highlights the market that this brochure is targeting. Provide evidence from the brochure to justify your assumption.

2. Visit a high street travel agent in your area and view the information provided in the window. Now visit a travel agent's website and view the information available on the home page. Compare and contrast the information you have seen. Give a presentation which identifies the different types of information displayed and explain why this information is provided.

Bibliography

DfT (2011) *ATOL reform consultation document*, London, Department for Transport, June.

Dumazel, R. and Humphreys, I. (1999) Travel agent monitoring and management, *Journal of Air Transport Management*, **5** (2), 63–72.

Euromonitor (2011) *Travel Retail in the United Kingdom*, London, *Euromonitor*, 1 June.

European Commission (1999) *Commission decision – declaring a concentration to be incompatible with the common market and the EEA Agreement: Case No. IV/M.1524 – Airtours/First Choice*, EC, C (1999) 3022 final – EN, 22 September.

Mandelbaum, R. (2004) Travel agents – it still pays to hire one, even in the Internet age, *Money*, April.

Mintel (2009) *Domestic Tourism – UK*, London, Mintel, December.

Mintel (2010) *Travel Agents – UK*, London, Mintel, December.

Mintel (2011) *Package vs Independent Holidays – UK*, London, Mintel, May.

Reynolds, W. H. (1958) Bless that travel agent, *The Rotarian*, January, 36–37.

TCF (2010) *Travel Compensation Fund Annual Report 2010*, available online at: http://www.tcf.org.au/downloads/annualreports/2010_Annual_Report.pdf (accessed November 2011).

TTG (2011) Commission not king for agents, *Travel Trade Gazette*, 4 February.

Websites

ABTA: **www.abta.com**

European Travel Agents' and Tour Operators' Associations: **www.ectaa.org**

IATA: **www.iata.org**

Travel Compensation Fund, Australia: **www.tcf.org.au**

20

Ancillary tourism services

Contents

Learning outcomes

After studying this chapter, you should be able to:

- understand the roles of guides, couriers and animateurs in meeting tourists' needs
- appreciate the use of insurance and financial services to assist the tourist
- identify the principal sources of information in use by travel agents
- be aware of marketing and consultancy services available to the tourism industry.

Travelers differ. At one extreme are random travelers who see what they accidentally bump into. At the other extreme are the lock-step travelers who follow a banner (or a red umbrella) and look when and where a voice tells them to look. Between these extremes are the guide-book travelers who identify the whereabouts of those sites that interest them and they plan their sightseeing accordingly.

Rigden and Stuewer (2009) *The Physical Tourist: A science guide for the traveler*, vii

Introduction

As we can see from the quote above, different types of tourist guide lead to varied encounters of the tourist destination, as the number and overall experience of local attractions is influenced by the information provided to the visitor. In fact, guides can manipulate many aspects of visitor behaviour, through their recommendations of places to eat, stay, be entertained and shop. The guide may provide directions to a supermarket for provisions or a bank for local currency, highlighting that there are many facilities and services used by tourists which are seldom considered to be part of the tourism industry itself – customs services or visa issuing offices, for example. Other services that derive much of their revenue from tourism and yet are clearly not part of the industry include companies specializing in the design and construction of hotels, theatres, restaurants and other centres of entertainment.

Consequently, there is a further category of miscellaneous tourism services that deserves to be examined more closely here. We will call these **ancillary services** – these are provided either to the tourist or to the suppliers of tourist services. Each of these will be dealt with in turn.

Services to the tourist

Guides and courier services

Unfortunately, there is as yet no term that conveniently embraces all the mediators whose function it is to shepherd, guide, inform and interpret for groups of tourists; nor can one conveniently link their functions to one particular sector of the industry. Some are employed by transport providers and tour operators; others work independently or provide their services freelance to companies in the industry.

In an industry that is becoming increasingly impersonal, as companies grow in size and tourism products themselves become more homogeneous, the role of those who interface with tourists becomes more and more important. Indeed, it may be the only feature of a package tour that distinguishes one product from another, yet curiously it is a role that has been progressively downgraded by the larger companies, often as a means of cutting costs. As experienced travellers see the provision of such support as less important, many tour operators have reduced the numbers of representatives in resorts, often providing any emergency assistance via telephone contacts instead. There are some areas where the use of support personnel is still popular, however, so we will examine these two similar roles – the courier and the guide. Couriers differ from guides in the sense that the latter lay stress on imparting information as the most important function of their job, while couriers may attach more importance to their social and people management functions.

Couriers

Couriers are employed by coach companies or tour operators to supervise and shepherd groups of tourists participating in tours (either on extended tours or day excursions). As well as being called couriers, they may be known as tour escorts, tour leaders, tour managers or tour directors (the latter terms imply greater levels of responsibility and status).

One of their functions is to offer a sightseeing commentary on the country or region through which tourists are travelling and to act as a source of information.

Some companies dispense with the separate services of a courier in favour of a driver who is also a courier, taking on the responsibility of both driving the coach and looking after the passengers. Many drivers, however, have neither adequate general knowledge nor the necessary training to offer a truly professional guiding service and they should not, in any case, be diverted from their prime responsibility – that of driving the coach safely and expertly. Some countries frown on coach drivers who give commentaries while their coach is in motion, sometimes going as far as to forbid the practice.

Courier work is often freelance and offers little opportunity to develop a career. Apart from a handful of destinations that have truly year-round appeal (such as capital cities), most guiding work is temporary and seasonal, even though many professional guides choose to return to the job year after year. Some are able to find a combination of posts in summer and winter resorts, enabling them to take up paid employment for most of the year.

Prior experience is the principal criterion in gaining employment. While qualifications exist in many countries, they are not always essential to the role, and in the UK professional training is available but by no means obligatory. The role attracts graduates with relevant qualifications such as languages or history, but many companies prefer to recruit couriers largely on the strength of their personality, ability to handle clients with sensitivity and tact, and stamina – both physical and mental. In some posts, employers will lay emphasis on sales ability, as couriers may be required to sell supplementary services such as optional excursions. Arguably, this is changing the nature of the role – commercial acumen replacing sociability.

Guides

Guides, or guide lecturers as they are frequently known, are retained by principals for their expertise in general or specialist subjects. Employment tends to be freelance and intermittent, with low-season jobs rare outside the large cities. Guides take pride in their professionalism and will often have well-established regional and national bodies to represent their interests.

In the UK, the Blue Badge is seen as the mark of attainment of professional status. It is awarded following formal periods of training and examinations, the wearer having passed national level 4 exams. The Green Badge is awarded for Associate status at level 3.

EXAMPLE **The Blue Badge scheme**

In the UK, there are approximately 1400 members of the Institute of Tourist Guiding (ITG) who hold the Blue Badge qualification, the majority of them based in London where guiding work is easiest to find.

The ITG was formed in 2002 and represents guides in England, Wales, Northern Ireland, the Isle of Man and the Channel Islands (the Scottish Tourist Guides Association fulfils a similar function in Scotland). While the ITG does not itself run training courses, it oversees those operated in colleges and by other training providers and sets the standard for Blue Badge and other guides.

The Guild of Registered Tour Guides is the sector's professional wing and campaigns for professional recognition and the implementation of Blue Badge standards throughout the industry.

This is a rather different picture from that in other European countries, where professional qualifications are often essential to secure a licence to operate. In France, for example, a local guide must be employed to guide in Paris, having demonstrated local knowledge in formally approved qualifications (although such qualifications can also be obtained by workers from other EU member countries, of course).

While qualified guides offer high levels of quality, many companies running coach sightseeing tours prefer to recruit amateur guides without qualifications to keep down costs. The 'added value' of a qualified guide is still seen by many employers as a luxury they cannot afford in a climate where cutting costs to achieve sales is imperative.

A separate category of guide is the *driver* who is also a *guide*. These are professional guides who operate on a freelance basis, taking up to four individuals on tour in their own vehicles. The close personal relationship that is built up on these tours between guide and clients is valued on both sides. This form of tailor-made package is popular with wealthier visitors to the UK.

EXAMPLE **International Tour Guide Day**

The importance of tour guides to the image and reputation of a destination has not always been overtly recognized; yet, they are 'of critical importance in the smooth and successful running of the tourism industry because their contact with tourists often has direct influence on the tourist's experience in the country' (Business Day, 2009). Efforts to increase awareness of their activities has come with greater media reporting of the official 'International Tour Guide Day'.

Developed at the 1987 summit of the World Federation of Tourist Guide Associations, in order to raise the profile of their profession, the International Tour Guide Day – on 21st February – often sees tour guides providing events for their local communities and tourism industry representatives, or participating in training events for themselves.

The role of the guide

Not only should the guide have extensive knowledge of the attraction or destination linked to their work (see Figure 20.1), they take on a number of other roles. Firstly, they will act not just as an educator but also may need to provide translations – including information and directional signage as well as menus and other documents. This is important in enhancing visitor experience as well as ensuring safety. Maintaining control over visiting groups, selecting the direction of walking routes, timings of visits and the speed of movement around attractions can ensure safety as well as ensuring visitor flow which can be beneficial to the attraction, other visitors and possibly the local population. Control can also ensure that tourists are kept away from high-crime areas reducing overall risk of danger. Finally the tour guide may take on a social role, perhaps as entertainer or as mediator between visitors within the group. Taking the opportunity to dine with the tour party may enhance the experience of the tourist as they feel they have had opportunities to interact with a member of the local community.

Figure 20.1 Guide at a Sheikh's Villa, Abu Dhabi, UAE

Photo by Chris Holloway

The role of the animateur

The term **animateur** is now becoming more widely known within the tourism industry. It applies to those members of the industry who entertain tourists, either by acting out a role or providing entertainment or instruction. The English term 'entertainer' is not strictly comparable as this tends to be associated with either a stage role or **street entertainers**, who are typically jugglers, acrobats, fire-eaters or, increasingly popular in leading resorts, 'living sculptures'.

The French term, however, relates to those whose task it is to interact with tourists in a broad range of roles that will enhance the destination or attraction where they work. It applies to the British role of the Butlin's holiday camp redcoat and to the US camp counsellor, as well as the compère on stage on a cruise ship. Other tasks include instructing tourists in sports or hobbies (ski instructors, surfing instructors), lecturing to cruise passengers or teaching them how to play bridge or other card games. Resort representatives are often expected to take on the role of animateurs when they form part of the evening's entertainment on stage at European camp sites. In Disney's theme parks there are a variety of animateur roles, the best-known of which is Mickey Mouse, but a host of other Disney characters are to be found on site, such as Alice in Wonderland, Snow White and even the Chipmunks. These workers normally have no speaking role and are there to make friends with younger visitors, posing for photographs and so on. Elsewhere, you might find animateurs dressed as historical figures at a heritage site. For example, at Williamsburg in Virginia, a number of staff are dressed in eighteenth-century costumes and will maintain their roles if questioned by visitors.

The job might be thought of as fairly basic, in terms of skills, but Continental Europeans take a different view – animation appears on the syllabus of French tourism and leisure qualifications, to cite just one example. This reflects the seriousness with which Continental tourism employees and employers view the role – it is one way to provide a professional service for the industry.

Animateurs add to the theme park experience

Warner Bros Movie World, located on Queensland's Gold Coast, is Australia's only movie-related theme park. It opened 20 years ago and, throughout this time, it has included shows related to the long-time favourite Looney Tunes cartoon characters as well as hit movies – attractions have included the Police Academy stunt show, Batman Adventure and the Harry Potter magical experience.

Like its well-known rival, Disney, the park employs staff to dress in costume and entertain the visitors. This can help add to the excitement, providing picture opportunities for children and adults alike. However, it can be hard work for the actors inside the costumes – being mobbed by eager parents keen to get photo opportunities of their offspring; remaining in character despite being prodded, mauled and kicked; and dealing with the heat inside large and unwieldy costumes.

The actors may form part of a stage show (see Figure 20.2) or wander around the park, interacting with the visitors. In some cases, their work may take them further afield – the airline Etihad, as a promotional campaign for their Queensland route, provided customers to their holiday shop in Abu Dhabi with the opportunity to have their photo taken with Tweety Bird and Bugs Bunny.

Figure 20.2 Looney Tunes stage show – Movie World
Photo by Claire Humphreys

Financial services

This section will deal with financial services offered to tourists – insurance, foreign exchange and credit.

Insurance

Insurance is an important, very often obligatory, aspect of a tourist's travel arrangements, embracing coverage for one or more of the following contingencies:

- medical care and hospitalization (and, where necessary, repatriation – important where hospital services are of a low standard)
- personal accident
- cancellation or curtailment of holiday
- delayed departure
- baggage loss or delay
- money loss
- personal liability.

Some policies now also include coverage for the collapse of the travel agent or tour operator through which the tour was purchased – an increasingly important option in view of the growing instability in the industry, although bonded tours should be refundable in the event of a cancellation. The growth of budget airlines and their not infrequent demise point to the importance of adequate insurance, as scheduled air travel, apart from that in a package tour, is not currently protected by bonding. The inclusion of Airline Failure Insurance (AFI) is now commonly also offered to travellers when booking flights online.

Tourists may purchase insurance either in the form of a selective policy, covering one or more of the above items, or, more commonly, in the form of a standard 'package', which will include all or most of the above. The latter policy, although inflexible in its coverage, invariably offers the best value if comprehensive coverage is sought. Although most tour operators encourage their clients to buy their company's comprehensive policies, they are often more expensive than a comprehensive policy arranged by an independent insurance company. Travel agents may offer better-value insurance policies than those of an operator, but they, too, may be biased in favour of schemes paying them higher levels of commission. It is no longer legal to force clients to purchase a particular policy, although operators can demand evidence that customers are insured. Free insurance has become an attractive incentive in marketing package tours.

Other retailers are now competing with travel agents to sell travel insurance, including supermarkets, banks and high street shops, such as Marks & Spencer, while cut-price annual policies are marketed direct by insurance agents, so travel agents are faced with a very competitive environment in which to sell their products notwithstanding the attractive commissions paid.

Key issues in choosing a policy are to ensure that medical coverage is sufficient to meet the needs (in the USA, bills in excess of $1 million are not uncommon for serious illnesses) and loss of any treasured individual items will be covered in full. The normal comprehensive coverage will limit compensation for total valuables and may restrict claims for any individual item lost or stolen to a figure that will be unlikely to cover the cost of an average tourist's camera, so it is important for holidaymakers to consider covering such valuables within their house contents insurance. Insurance at reasonable cost for older travellers is becoming harder to find as they are travelling more frequently but are also more likely to suffer medical difficulties than younger travellers. Doubling, or even tripling, the price of a policy is common for this group above the age of 65. Of equal concern are the high numbers of travellers who fail to insure themselves when travelling abroad. The availability of cheap flights through budget airlines and ownership of second homes abroad has encouraged people to take more short breaks but a UK study has revealed that one-third of travellers would consider going abroad without insurance (Mintel, 2011).

The cost of not having travel insurance

The volcano ash cloud, which affected European travel in 2010, and briefly again in 2011, helped to highlight the importance of travel insurance, as vacationers were stranded overseas with little help and unexpected cost. Efforts by governments in the UK, USA, Australia, Ireland and Germany amongst others have sought to encourage travellers to take out insurance in case the worst happens.

The UK Foreign and Commonwealth Office reported that although many of its nationals consider insurance for package trips, nearly half did not take out cover when travelling abroad to visit friends and family; yet costs of illness, such as a heart attack, could be as much as £25 000 (Smithers, 2011). The Department of Foreign Affairs in Australia reported that hospital stays in south-east Asia can amount to more than $800 a day, with medical evacuation from Bali to Australia costing up to AUS$60 000 (Clitheroe, 2011).

Insurance remains a lucrative business for both operators and agents, although claims have been rising in recent years. Some reports estimate that 10% of holidaymakers make claims, often fraudulently, against their policies and this has led insurers to increase premiums to offset those losses.

Foreign transactions

Travellers today have an ever widening choice of ways in which they can pay for services and goods while abroad. These include:

- taking sterling or foreign banknotes with them – however, this can lead to loss or theft, and certain foreign countries have restrictions on the import or export of their currencies
- taking traveller's cheques, in sterling or currency such as US dollars or euros
- arranging for the advance transfer of funds to a specified foreign bank or an open credit to be made available, through their own bank, at a foreign bank
- using credit cards or charge cards
- travel money cards.

The introduction of the euro as common currency in many EU countries has made life easier for visitors touring a number of countries on the Continent. Purchasing foreign currency is relatively convenient, with many outlets offering exchange facilities (see Figure 20.3). Leading travel agency chains operate their own foreign exchange desks, as do the high street banks, and the Post Office has also introduced a foreign exchange desk offering highly competitive rates. Some large department stores, for example Marks & Spencer, also provide currency exchange facilities in their major branches. Companies such as Travelex and TTT Moneycorp provide such facilities at airports and other transport hubs. The large number of foreign exchange facilities available provide people with a very wide choice, but charges fluctuate considerably and both rates of conversion and fixed charges need to be compared to judge what represents best value for money.

Traveller's cheques are also still widely used, being readily accepted throughout the world by banks and commercial institutions. They offer the holder guaranteed security, with rapid compensation for theft or loss – an advantage that outweighs the standard premium charged of 1% of face value. The value of the system for suppliers is that there is generally a considerable lapse of time between the tourist purchasing traveller's cheques and encashing them. The money invested in the interim at market rates of interest provides the supplier with substantial profits. Market leaders in traveller's cheque sales in the UK are

Figure 20.3 A currency exchange outlet caters for incoming visitors as well as the local population looking to purchase currency for their own holidays

Photo by Claire Humphreys

Thomas Cook (whose 'circular note', the predecessor of the traveller's cheque, originated in 1873) and American Express, which first introduced the concept in 1891. US$ traveller's cheques are useful almost anywhere in the world, and may be used as freely as cash itself within the USA.

Sending money abroad in advance of travel is useful when planning to spend some time in the same place, but it is expensive, unless electronic transfer is insisted on. It pays to shop around for the cheapest deal.

Credit cards such as those of Visa and Mastercard (Eurocard on the Continent) are widely accepted throughout the world, but, as transactions can take some time to filter through to one's bank account, users take a chance on the fluctuation in exchange rates. Some retailers, however, will now quote their prices either in local currency (such as Swiss francs) or pounds sterling and will debit accounts accordingly, so that British purchasers abroad will be aware of the actual cost for the item in their own currency. Bank charges for drawing cash abroad against both credit and debit cards can also be high. Charge cards such as American Express or Diners Club provide similar advantages and drawbacks (charge cards differ from credit cards in that accounts are due for settlement in full after receipt of an invoice from the company – credit is not extended – but the limit on charge card transactions is generally much higher than on credit cards; indeed, the company may impose no ceiling on the amount the holder may charge to their account).

As agents are required to pay a fee to the card companies when accepting credit cards in payment for travel, there has been some reluctance in the past to accept them, but credit card sales are increasing at such a rate that no agent can afford to turn this form of business away. For the most part, however, they do pass these costs on to their clients.

In the UK, payment by credit card offers the additional advantage to the traveller of the funds being protected by the card companies on amounts in excess of £100 in the event of the collapse of the agent, operator or airline with which they are dealing. The special free insurance coverage offered by some banks against the use of their cards has largely been withdrawn, however, due to the cost of servicing claims.

Another alternative recently introduced to the marketplace is travel money cards, provided by companies like Western Union, American Express, Mastercard and Fexco. These are prepaid cards loaded with a fixed sum of euros, dollars or sterling in the form of 'e-money' and a PIN code. Additional amounts may be loaded on to the card at any point, subject to an authorized maximum. The card can then be tendered for purchases or used to withdraw cash from ATMs abroad. They have already proved popular in the USA and are rapidly catching on in the UK. Their clear value is their relative protection against theft and fraudulent misuse as they cannot be used to clear a bank account and they also make it impossible for the holidaymaker to overspend. They are, however, rather expensive to use for withdrawing cash abroad and charges are made for encashing any unused balances after completing a journey.

Many countries now use chip and PIN cards, although, when used abroad, a signature is often required instead, which is felt to be less secure. Theft and the fraudulent use of cards is discouraging total reliance on plastic to make purchases and draw money when abroad. Tourists are now recommended to carry an assortment of small denomination notes, traveller's cheques and plastic cards when travelling.

Incentive travel vouchers

Incentive travel has shown considerable growth over the past few years, with companies providing their employees or dealers with attractive travel packages as rewards for achievement.

One option taken up by some companies is travel vouchers, issued in various denominations, which allow the recipient to choose their own travel arrangements. This is simply monetary reward for achievement in another form, but the appeal of travel has proved to be a stronger motivator than either cash or consumer durables. The vouchers offer greater flexibility and can be given in smaller denominations – to reward, for example, low absenteeism or the achievement of weekly targets. Some of these vouchers can only be exchanged against specific travel products or through certain travel agents, while others can be used to pay for any holiday arrangements purchased through any agent.

Duty-free shopping

Under the category of services to tourists, mention should also be made of duty-free shopping facilities, although the subject has been discussed elsewhere in this text. The purchase of duty-free goods at airports, on board ships and aircraft or at specially designated duty-free ports has been a strong attraction for tourists for a very long time.

Introduced during the first half of the twentieth century, mainly to satisfy the demands of travellers on the great ocean liners, it was extended to aircraft in 1944. The first airport duty-free shop arrived in 1947, when the Irish parliament passed the Custom-free Airport Act, giving Shannon this honour. Since those days, duty-free purchases of spirits and tobacco in particular have been effectively marketed by airports and carriers alike and the profits and sales of such items have always been substantial, accounting for large shares in the profits of many companies. Airports have achieved up to half their total operating profits through such sales, while some Scandinavian ferry companies obtain up to 70% of their income in this manner.

This has led in some quarters to criticisms of profiteering, but airports reply to such criticisms by claiming that, without these profits, they would be forced to increase their landing charges, which would have a knock-on effect on carriers, forcing these in turn to raise their fares. Without the benefit of duty-free shopping, transport fares do tend to rise appreciably – estimates typically point to increases ranging from 10% to as high as 30%. Rising congestion at airports, the requirement for earlier check-in times and flight delays all tend to enhance sales in airport shops. The high value of return in airport outlets can be seen in the announcement in 2008 that BAA would sell its duty-free shops for £546 million, providing the purchaser, Italian company Autogrill, with a 12-year concession to operate these outlets at its seven UK airports.

Tax harmonization in the EU led to the withdrawal of duty-free privileges for travel between member states in July 1999 and many companies were badly hit by the move. To take one example, Eurotunnel alone saw a 72% fall in its retail revenues in the months following the ending of duty-free sales across the Channel. Fares on cross-Channel services were raised sharply, although heightened competition succeeded in pushing them down again. In response to the decline in sales at UK ports, marketing efforts highlighted the opportunities to purchase duty-paid goods, often at French prices, which substantially undercut those in the UK. Countries such as Tunisia, Morocco and Turkey are close enough to provide alternatives for tourists for whom duty-free sales are an important component of the holiday, but with Malta and Cyprus both now drawn into the EU, the opportunity for duty-free visits to cheap holiday islands in the Mediterranean has dried up.

EXAMPLE **Tax-free shopping boosts domestic tourism**

Sanya, one of the southernmost cities in China, launched a 'duty-free' policy in April 2011. Popular with Chinese residents, this led to a rapid increase in visitors to the city, with many spending two to three hours in the specially designated duty-free shops. The purchases are sent to the airport, where the tourist can collect them on departure.

Early reports suggest that tourist numbers may increase by as much as 20% on the back of this decision by local authorities who have promised to build the world's largest duty-free complex to take advantage of new tax-free shopping rules.

Services to the supplier

Education and training

Historically, the approach to training in the tourism industry has been a sectoral one. In the past, each sector of the industry was primarily concerned with training staff to become competent within its own sector, focusing on narrow job-specific abilities. In an industry comprising mainly small units with entrepreneurial styles of management, the benefits of formal education and training have seldom been acknowledged. Most employees of travel agencies, tour operators and hotels were trained on the job, often by observing supervisors at work. A handful of companies, such as Thomas Cook, however, were notable for their early recognition of the need for more formal, although still inhouse, training.

With the growing institutionalization of sectors, greater emphasis is placed on professionalism, the introduction of national standards and more formal modes of training. The difficulty of organizing day release for employees of smaller travel companies encouraged the development of distance learning packages. BA fares and ticketing courses, for example, which are offered either full-time or through self-study packs, have found national acceptance as a standard for those seeking to work in travel agencies and airlines, while Lufthansa provides similar nationally accepted courses in Germany, and the United

Nations World Tourism Organization (UNWTO) and International Air Transport Association (IATA) organize internationally recognized distance learning packs for students of tourism throughout the world.

With vocational courses of this nature, the question of balance between job-specific skills and broader conceptual knowledge has long taxed employers and educationalists alike. Unlike most countries in Europe, many tourism employers in the UK still do not hold formal qualifications in high regard, still preferring to provide the job skills that are seen as essential to fulfil basic, sector-specific roles in the industry. Across the globe, however, universities and colleges now offer courses designed to provide not just essential skills but also a broader knowledge of the industry and the world of business. This includes undergraduate studies as well as postgraduate diplomas and Master's qualifications in tourism-related studies (including specialist areas, such as e-tourism, events and conference management).

EXAMPLE Tourism skills training in the UK

In the UK, the professional bodies in the industry introduced their own programmes of training and vocational education leading to membership, often carried out through full-time or part-time courses at local colleges of further or higher education. Examples of these early developments included courses offered by the Hotel and Catering International Management Association (HCIMA – now the Institute of Hospitality), the Chartered Institute of Logistics and Transport (CILT) and the Institute of Travel and Tourism (ITT). However, with the rapid expansion of nationally validated travel and tourism courses in colleges of further and higher education which occurred from the 1970s onwards, there was a move to recognize formal qualifications, especially those offered by such bodies as the City and Guilds of London Institute. In 2004, the government-funded Sector Skills Council licensed People 1st as the official body to develop training programmes for the hospitality, leisure and tourism industries. This body encourages the training organizations to provide what are perceived to be the right courses for the industry.

Within the school system itself, GCSEs at ordinary and advanced level specializing in leisure and tourism have also been introduced, with the support of key members of the industry, in order to interest school leavers in careers in travel. Attitudes among careers counsellors in schools, however, are slow to change and tourism continues to be seen by many, inaccurately, as a career for the less academically able.

The trade press

In addition to specialist academic journals, there is a large selection of weekly and monthly journals devoted to the travel and tourism industry. The weekly trade papers *Travel Trade Gazette* and *Travel Weekly* provide an invaluable service to the industry, covering news of both social and commercial activities, as well as providing the heaviest concentration of advertisements for jobs in the industry. Updates on the industry are also available to readers online.

In an industry as fast-moving as tourism, employees can only update their knowledge of travel products by regularly reading the trade press, whether in hard copy or online. The newspapers complement the work of the training bodies, while, for untrained staff, they may well act as the principal source of new information.

The trade press depends largely on advertising for its revenue, as the two weeklies are distributed free to members of the industry. In return, they support the industry by sponsoring trade fairs, seminars and other events. Today these trade journals also provide a significant amount of their news content online (**www.ttgdigital.com** and **www.travelweekly.co.uk**).

Table 20.1 Examples of travel publications

Publication	Details
Industry guides	
OAG flight guide	Printed guide providing information on airline schedules. This guide supports the online database of flight details
World Travel Guide	Detailed country information, including details of passports and visas, health and climate, as well as resorts and excursions
Travel magazines	
Business Traveller	A magazine aimed at the frequent business traveller, published worldwide
Condé Nast Traveller	Aimed at the upmarket leisure sector, this magazine provides information on upcoming destinations and resorts as well as current issues for travellers
National Geographic	An international magazine focusing on the environment and landscape across the globe
In-flight magazines	
American Way	American Airlines
Discovery	Cathay Pacific
High Life	British Airways
Sky	Delta Airlines
The Australian Way	Qantas Airlines
Destination travel guides	
Lonely Planet	Country and destination travel guides, often used by budget and gap year travellers
Fodor's	Country and city guides, aimed at a discerning travellers
Michelin Red and Green guides	Guides to restaurants, travel and tourism businesses and sites of interest

Note: Many agents now buy their guides and directories on DVD or use the Internet to access directories instead of subscribing to hard copies

Within the general category of the press, one must also include those who are responsible for the publication of travel guides and timetables. The task of updating this information is obviously immense, especially in view of the worldwide scope of many of these publications. As their production becomes more complex each year, this is also a field that lends itself to computerization. Most guides now provide access for agents – and the public – electronically and it is questionable whether there will still be a demand for hard-copy guides of this nature for very much longer.

Many travel guides are bought by both the trade and the travelling public (see Table 20.1). Corporate travel managers and frequent travellers on business are likely to want their own copies of guides, and agents may want hard copies to show to their customers when discussing alternatives.

Hotel guidebooks

Hotel guides, of course, have always served the needs of both the trade and the public, although many are produced commercially for purchase by the travelling public. They fall into three distinct categories:

- independent guides which do not charge for entries and inspections are made anonymously – examples include the *Michelin Red Guide* and the *Good Hotel Guide*
- paid-entry guides which make a charge for listing – examples include Alastair Sawday's *Special Places to Stay* and Condé Nast Johansen's *Recommended Hotels*
- registration guides which are funded by membership fees – examples include the AA and RAC handbooks.

The Internet has had an impact on the information available for this sector particularly, with many websites – Trip Advisor being one such example – encouraging guests who have stayed at hotels to post their own reviews, rating the performance and overall quality of the accommodation. As these data become conveniently available, both online and through mobile phone apps, hotels will need to be ever more responsive in their monitoring of information published about their properties.

Travel guidebooks

Travel guidebooks are enjoying huge popularity as more and more holidaymakers travel further afield each year and specialist book shops, such as Stanfords, have sprung up to cater for this growing demand. Such guidebooks must be updated frequently if they are to remain of any value, so many are produced on an annual basis. This, again, is an area that lends itself to computerization, and much of the information held in guidebooks can be readily accessed using a computer. Travel guides for longer trips, such as Lonely Planet or Rough Guides, or for cities, such as Dorling Kindersley's Eyewitness series, include accommodation and transport details alongside historical details of destinations, places to visit and restaurant recommendations for a variety of budgets.

EXAMPLE **Mobile phones as travel guides**

Although mobile phone city guides are not new, Dublin Tourism is at the forefront with an augmented reality application which provides a wealth of information for visitors (see Figure 20.4).

Impressively it uses GPS directional technology to allow the user to point their phone at buildings and landmarks and answer the 'what's that?' dilemma, receiving details of the attraction, sometimes with additional audio commentary. It also provides contact phone numbers and website links. In addition to this, the application provides suggestions about things to see, places to eat and events happening in the city.

Importantly for many overseas tourists, the application can operate without needing phone network connections, thus avoiding international data roaming charges.

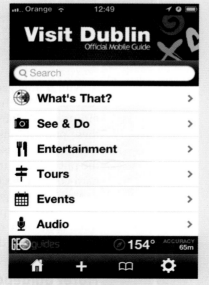

Figure 20.4 Screenshot of the Visit Dublin phone application

Image courtesy of Fáilte Ireland

Marketing services

A number of services exist to provide marketing support, either wholly or in part, to members of the travel industry. These include marketing consultants, representative agencies, advertising agencies, brochure design, printing and distribution services, suppliers of travel point-of-sale material and research and public relations organizations. To this list must be added the organizations that provide the hardware and software for the travel industry's computer systems.

This book does not propose to discuss in depth the marketing of tourism as the subject is comprehensively covered in a companion book (Holloway, 2004). Other books dealing with the topic can be found in the bibliography at the end of this book. The point to be made here is that both large and small companies in the industry can benefit from employing these specialist agencies and, in some instances, their services are, in fact, indispensable.

Tourism consultants

Management and marketing consultants offer advice to companies on the organization and operation of their businesses. They bring to the task two valuable attributes: expertise and objectivity.

Most tourism consultants will have had years of experience in the industry on which to draw, having been successful in their own fields before turning to consultancy, but, with the economic and political crises that have occurred over the past two decades and the resultant mergers and takeovers that have led to downsizing in the industry, it is inevitable that the pool of former executives in the industry have turned to consultancy work. The consultants' group affiliated to the Tourism Society alone lists over 100 individuals.

Consultants, not being directly involved in the day-to-day running of the companies they are employed to help, can approach their task without any preconceived ideas. They can therefore advise companies on either the general reorganization of the business or on some *ad hoc* issue, such as undertaking a feasibility study or the introduction of a new computer system.

Representative agencies

For a retainer or payment of royalties on sales, these organizations act as general sales agents for a company within a defined territory. This is a valuable service for smaller companies seeking representation abroad, for example. In the travel industry, it is most commonly found in the hotel sector, but carriers, excursion operators and public-sector tourist offices all make use of the facility in marketing their services in other countries. As with consultants, many of the employees of these agencies will have had prior work experience in the sector that they represent.

Advertising and promotional agencies

Many large travel companies – and an increasing number of smaller ones – retain an advertising agency. A number of these specialize in handling travel accounts.

Advertising agents do much more than design advertisements and place them in the media. They should be closely involved in the entire marketing strategy of the company and will be involved with the design and production of travel brochures. Many are equipped to carry out market research, the production of publicity material and merchandising or public relations activities. Some larger agencies also produce their own hotel/resort guides, using their own staff's extensive knowledge.

Travel companies may have their brochures designed by the design studio of their advertising agent, arrange for them to be produced by an independent design studio or, in some cases, their printer's studio may undertake the work. A growing number of brochures are now put together inhouse instead, however, with the aid of sophisticated computer software available to allow desktop publishing. Advertising agents can also help and advise in the selection of a printer for the production of brochures or other publicity material.

Innovation in publicity material for the trade saw the use of technology to replace the printed travel brochure. Initially, this took the form of video cassettes, but these gave way to CD-ROMs and, more recently, DVDs. These are designed to help customers reach a decision on holiday destinations, facilities and services. They are sometimes produced by tour operators, who make them available on loan to their customers through travel agents. The production costs are borne by the principals – operators, hotels, airlines – whose services are promoted. A number of companies now specialize in the production of these travel aids.

There was some initial concern that they might come to replace the brochure entirely, but, to date, there is little evidence to suggest that this is occurring – holidaymakers still like something tangible to flick through and refer to. With the development of direct communication between principals and consumers via the Internet and digital TV channels, if brochures are ever to be replaced, it is more likely that it will be by computer-accessed text and illustrations, which can be quickly updated and re-priced. Changes affecting the tour brochure are discussed in more detail in Chapter 18.

Finally, mention should be made of direct mail and distribution services, some of which specialize in handling travel accounts. Some of these companies design and organize direct mail promotional literature aimed at specific target markets or travel retailers. They will also undertake distribution of a principal's brochures to travel agents.

Technical services

The rapid spread of the computer within all sectors of the travel industry has led to the establishment of specialist computer experts, who concentrate on designing and implementing purpose-made systems for their travel industry clients. Such systems include not only travel information and reservations functions but also accounting and management information.

Other computer organizations have been set up to provide networks that allow agents to access principals' computer reservations systems. With the pace of change that one has come to expect of this field, updating equipment and software is a regular function of the modern business, and these organizations fulfil a vital role in ensuring that businesses are up to date and efficient in improving their service while keeping costs under control.

The future of ancillary services

For more than a decade, academics have been reporting that tourists are changing, seeking out travel opportunities that allow them to experience the unusual, rare or even provide for self-development and education. While the concept of a tourist guide may have often been seen as old-fashioned or outdated, as these tourists seek out such personal experiences, the role of the animateur or guide will remain important. The provision of human interaction to inform and entertain will provide opportunities for attractions, destinations and tourist resorts to enhance their offering.

Furthermore, as tourists gain greater access to information (with access to the Web expanding to all corners of the globe and via mobile technology), the need to provide knowledge in a format that adds to the experience of visiting a place will become ever more important. Walking tours that can be downloaded on to MP3 players and virtual tours online will provide many visitors with a perception of the destination, but it will be the guides or animateurs who can bring the visit to life and make the experience memorable.

While modern film technology, including virtual reality animation, can provide stunts and scenes that are nearly impossible to achieve in real life (certainly not on a budget that most tourist attractions or destinations can afford), it is noticeable that many tourists still seek out 'low-tech' experiences where their interaction with humans (often perceived as 'locals') is a main attraction.

Mobile technology and social media systems have provided convenient opportunities for customers to feedback their opinions on the products they experience – whether it is choosing to 'like' a company on Facebook or tweeting about the poor experience received at the reception desk of a hotel. The consequence is that companies will need to monitor, and respond to, the feedback they are receiving from their customers in a timely and professional manner – thus requiring a familiarity with the ever-advancing technology.

Questions and discussion points

1. Tourists can gather their information using a variety of guides. For each form of guide listed below, explain why it might be beneficial for a tourist to use such an information source:

   (a) electronic audio guide in a museum

   (b) printed guide book for a destination

   (c) a trained human guide (such as Blue Badge guide) providing a walking tour.

2. List the different items covered on a travel insurance policy. Do you think the areas covered are as important for domestic tourism trips as they are for international tourism trips?

3. Both academic education and vocational training related to tourism and the travel industry are widely available. How can this help to improve the industry?

Tasks

1. Read some of the articles published in the in-flight magazines published by airlines (if you cannot obtain a printed version, many airlines publish these online). Compare the articles published. Produce a short presentation which explains the factors influencing the topic areas covered in the magazine. Provide a conclusion which considers why airlines produce these magazines.

2. Complete a small piece of research, asking travellers if they have used any travel-related mobile phone applications. Find out whether this helped them to book travel, guide them to or around the destination or to provide feedback on their travel experiences. Which applications proved most popular? Write a report which summarizes these findings.

Bibliography

Business Day (2009) Guiding lights gather, South Africa, *Business Day*, 6 March.

Clitheroe, P. (2011) Travel insurance is essential part of your luggage, *Coffs Coast Advocate*, 17 May.

Holloway, J. C. (2004) *Marketing for Tourism*, 4th edn, Harlow, Prentice Hall.

Mintel (2011) *UK Travel Insurance*, London, Mintel, February 2011.

Rigden, J. S. and Stuewer, R. H. (2009) *The Physical Tourist: A science guide for the traveler*, Basel, Birkhäuser Verlag, AG.

Smithers, R. (2011) Britons urged to take out travel insurance if visiting family abroad, *The Guardian*, 2 June.

Websites

Foreign and Commonwealth Office (travel insurance advice): **www.fco.gov.uk/en/travelling-and-living-overseas/staying-safe/travel-insurance**

Institute of Tourist Guiding: **www.itg.org.uk**

People 1st: **www.people1st.co.uk**

Travel Trade Gazette: **www.ttglive.com**

Travel Weekly: **www.travelweekly.com**

Part 4

Case studies

Pro-poor tourism

Prepared by Dr Lynn Minnaert, University of Surrey

In Chapter 6 we highlighted the impact of tourists specifically, and tourism generally, on the host population. This included discussion on the benefits that host–guest interaction can bring. Furthermore, in Chapter 5 we discussed the potential for positive economic impact, noting examples in the developing world, where governments have sought to expand the tourism product as a means of economic development. However, economic leakages (caused, for example, by the repatriation of profits by foreign tour operators or hotel chains) reduce the overall effect of such initiatives. To counter some of these problems we have, in recent years, given greater attention to the concept of pro-poor tourism.

What is pro-poor tourism?

Ashley *et al.* (2001, viii) define pro-poor tourism as tourism interventions that 'aim to increase the net benefits for the poor from tourism, and ensure that tourism growth contributes to poverty reduction'. Pro-poor tourism is not a specific tourism product – different tourism businesses and types of holiday can be included under its banner – but rather an approach to tourism management that improves the socio-economic and sociocultural quality of life for poor persons in the host community. In other words, pro-poor tourism is not a new type of holiday, but rather a way of doing business differently. It focuses on giving poor communities a place in the market, a role in the provision of goods and services to tourists. This means that pro-poor tourism is different from many other types of tourism such as:

- *Sustainable tourism.* Although pro-poor tourism has overlaps with the social aspect of sustainability, it is focused primarily on poverty reduction.
- *Community-based tourism.* Pro-poor tourism projects are active in local communities, but require actions that surmount the community level in terms of product development, marketing, planning and investment (Ashley *et al.*, 2001).
- *Responsible tourism.* Responsible tourism strategies are usually focused on the behaviour of the tourists, not the host community. Responsible tourists, however, may decide to buy pro-poor tourism products.

What are the potential benefits of pro-poor tourism?

Pro-poor tourism initiatives can have economic and sociocultural impacts. From an economic perspective, pro-poor tourism initiatives often focus on building linkages with local suppliers. Hotels, for example, may be encouraged to buy products locally, rather than relying on imports from abroad. They could be encouraged to serve local, seasonal ingredients in their menus that can be bought from local suppliers, rather than using ingredients imported from further afield. Local industries, such as transport, retail, catering, agriculture and arts and crafts, can benefit from linkages with tourism – businesses in all these sectors can potentially benefit from linkages with pro-poor tourism initiatives.

Although building linkages with local suppliers may seem like a simple measure to implement, small local businesses often find it hard to compete with well-established, international operators. The success of the pro-poor tourism scheme therefore depends on how competitive it can be in the face of existing providers.

Another potential economic impact of pro-poor tourism is job creation for the local community: the businesses that are created via pro-poor initiatives employ local staff, train them and pay them a fair salary. Pro-poor tourism initiatives may provide jobs where these are otherwise not available, and can reduce the level of poverty for the workers. It should, however, be noted that pro-poor tourism rarely lifts people out of poverty altogether – many workers and their families are still on low incomes, but the income of pro-poor tourism employment can ensure that basic needs are met more continuously (Ashley *et al.*, 2001).

The increased income for the local community can lead to sociocultural improvements such as better infrastructure and quality of life. Another sociocultural aspect of pro-poor tourism can be the development of excursions and cultural attractions in the local area, increasing the local population's opportunities for finding pride in their culture and developing their own businesses. This can increase positive contacts between hosts and visitors, encourage capacity building within the poor population and improve the balance between tourism and other forms of resource use.

Pro-poor tourism actions

Pro-poor tourism is about doing business differently – working with local people and local suppliers can require additional help and support, particularly at the beginning of the partnership. Ashley and Mitchell (2005), for example, highlight that for pro-poor tourism to flourish in Africa, critical investments are needed to unlock opportunities – these refer to education to establish basic hospitality skills, strengthening community or local tenure over resources, small business support and infrastructure for tourist transport and services in poor areas with potential. Braman and the Fundación Acción Amazonia (2001), discussing pro-poor tourism in Ecuador, also highlight that it is important to keep up the momentum with tourism projects so that the local community does not lose faith in the potential benefits of tourism: tourism developments can take a lot of time to build and promote, and poor communities are often looking for immediate income to alleviate poverty. The Pro-Poor Tourism Partnership, in co-operation with the Caribbean Tourism Organization, has compiled a report with guidelines for pro-poor projects in the Caribbean (Ashley *et al.*, 2006). Examples of the actions in these guidelines include:

- Pay smaller, local suppliers frequently. Hotels often pay for goods 30–90 days after these have been delivered, but small producers do not always have the working capital to wait for payment that long.

- Local producers often produce goods that can be used in hotels, but the quantity, quality and reliability of the supply are often inadequate. Consider working with smaller contracts, and appointing a facilitator who can inform and work with the local suppliers.

- Develop and implement a policy which encourages openness and lack of stigma towards HIV. Educate managers as well as staff about HIV/AIDS, safety in the workplace and working with colleagues who have HIV.

- Integrate local interaction and local shopping into existing tourist excursions. Visiting local craft markets or workshops can enhance tourists' experience and expenditure. Offer retail space to local craftspeople and advertising space to local taxis, excursions and guides.

- Find out what goals local people have: they may be different to what tourism operators expect. In several pro-poor tourism projects, local income has been welcome, but poor people also have non-financial priorities such as training, dignity, access to natural resources, access to infrastructure and ability to participate in decisions.

Examples of pro-poor tourism initiatives

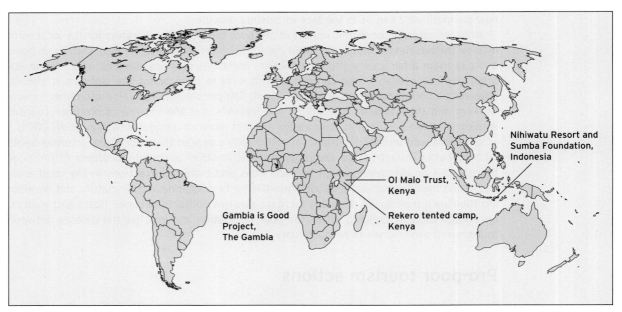

Figure 1 Location of pro-poor initiatives

Nihiwatu Resort and Sumba Foundation, Indonesia

The Nihiwatu Resort (**www.nihiwatu.com**) is located on a small and remote island in the Indonesian archipelago. It is a luxury resort with seven bungalows and two villas, located in 438 acres of tropical forest and wrapped around Nihiwatu beach. The Resort is linked to the Sumba Foundation, a charity that aims to reduce the poverty on the island of Sumba. The Resort and the Foundation look to tourism as a generator of employment and income in the community. The Sumba Foundation, for example, supports agrobusiness programmes that train and encourage business partnerships with the newly started tourism industry. They also work with environmental organizations to teach bird trappers the language skills necessary to become tour guides for bird watching tours. Scholarships are provided for children to attend the hotel school, and the Resort hopes to provide future employment opportunities for graduates.

The Sumba Foundation (**www.sumbafoundation.org**) also supports non-tourism employment and business projects such as farming and biodiesel production. As Sumba is a dry island, wells have been built to improve irrigation. The staple food in Sumba is cassava: cassava, however, is a low-protein food that is not very nutritious. Seeds for other crops have therefore been provided to improve the diet of the local population. The biodiesel project is another initiative that helps local farmers: the biodiesel is made of copra (dried coconut), a commodity that is locally available but for which demand has diminished. The biodiesel project has re-established a market for local copra and has provided a new source of income for hundreds of families.

Rekero tented camp – Kenya

The Rekero tented camp (**http://asiliaafrica.com/Rekero**) is a temporary accommodation facility in the heart of the Masai Maara National Reserve. The small and exclusive camp of seven tents offers space for 18 guests and is set up seasonally (June–October and

December–March). The tents are furnished to a high standard and great emphasis is placed on service quality.

The former owner of Rekero Tented Camp, Ron Beaton, was integral in the setting up of the Koyiaki Guiding School, the aim being to provide local Masai with employment opportunities within the tourism industry – in the Rekero camp or in other safari lodges in the area. Rekero was one of the first to employ only Masai tour guides.

Rekero not only supports the local community via direct employment opportunities, it also supports local education to improve the employability of the Masai community. The camp remains a committed supporter of the Koyiaki Guiding School, sponsoring and employing students and continuing their training following graduation. Additionally, the camp provides support for the local Ngousani Primary School, providing bursaries for more than 20 children, a rainwater collection system and donations in books and sports equipment. At the trust headquarters, there is a modern computer classroom for the local schools and communities that includes 12 laptops, some with wireless connection via a satellite. It offers a fully funded 10-day course for local schools and institutions, and has already paid for 12 groups to attend. In 2006–07, the trust built the 'Bwana Phil' building that provides accommodation for up to 18 students and two instructors, with shower and toilet facilities as well as a kitchen and a dining room.

Gambia is Good Project, The Gambia

The Gambia is a popular destination that receives more than 100 000 visitors every year. Tourism in the Gambia, however, is largely managed by foreign corporations offering package holidays, which means that the economic leakages are considerable and relatively few local businesses supply the tourism sector. Local food producers, for example, were rarely used because of irregular supplies, problems with product quality and shortages during dry periods – instead, most produce was imported from The Netherlands, France, Spain and Senegal. In 2004, a partnership was established between Haygrove, a UK fruit and flower grower which supplies major UK supermarkets, the international charity Concern Universal and local groups in the Gambia, with the aim of ensuring that local farmers in the Gambia could trade with high-value tourist hotels and restaurants (Concern Universal, 2011).

A fair-trade company, Gambia is Good, was set up to help local farmers improve their product and become more competitive. Haygrove worked with local growers to improve irrigation, distribution and marketing. The local farmers were also given access to training and capacity building, quality seeds, pesticides and fertilizers that were not previously available. Advice was also provided on which crops to grow: certain produce, such as courgettes and broccoli, was encouraged. As a result of these efforts, Gambia is Good now works with over 1000 producers, most of whom are women. Of the hotels in the area 80% are participating and now buy 20 tonnes of produce during the season. Agriculture has not only been turned into a source of income, but also into a tourist attraction. Gambia is Good has linked up with the Travel Foundation, and now has a farmyard that is open to visitors.

Ol Malo Trust – Kenya

Ol Malo Eco-Lodge is situated in the deserts of Samburuland, Northern Kenya. The lodge is an accommodation facility that focuses on low-impact nature tourism, and attracts responsible tourists from all over the world. The Ol Malo Trust (**www.olmalo.com**) was established during the drought of 1999–2000, when the surrounding tribal communities (Samburu) lost over 80% of their cattle. The trust first focused on the eradication of trachoma, an infectious illness that leads to painful blindness. Ol Malo then developed pro-poor tourism projects, based on the trust relationship with the tribal elders and the tribe members.

The Sayen E Ndaa 'Beads for Food' programme was set up to provide the women of the tribe with an opportunity to trade traditional beads for food. For every old bead the women bring in, they receive two beads and the equivalent in food items (such as maize, beans, sugar, tea and cooking fat). The beads are used by the women to produce jewellery, which is for sale in the Ol Malo Lodge and a showroom in Nairobi. Every day, around 30 women come to the Ol Malo Trust to produce their colourful beadwork in modern designs. The women are paid for their work, and the profits invested in the work of the trust. Not only does the Beads for Food programme provide the tribal women with a source of income, it also helped build a trust relationship between them and the Ol Malo Trust, which in turn helped to expand the eye clinic programme.

Limitations of pro-poor tourism

Pro-poor tourism, although strongly supported by organizations such as the Pro-Poor Tourism Partnership, has become increasingly open to criticism. Hall and Brown (2006, 13) ask if 'pro-poor tourism simply offers another route by which economic imperialism, through tourism, may extend its tentacles?' It could be argued that providing employment and income opportunities for poor people is only one aspect of reducing poverty: poverty has many other aspects, such as a lack of education and healthcare facilities, lack of political voice, lack of empowerment to name but a few. Not everybody would agree that the social responsibility of companies in developing countries ends with the provision of work and income opportunities. The examples provided above are examples of good practice, where employment and income generation are linked to training, wellbeing, education and other aspects of life. The examples are mostly of small companies with very close links to the communities in which they are based. Often the tourism business and the charitable trust are separate entities. One can wonder, however, if it is realistic to expect that multinational tourism companies could achieve similar close ties with communities given the global scale on which they operate. In that case, is involvement in pro-poor tourism merely a way to get positive PR? Can the social goals of pro-poor tourism really compete with the need to make a profit?

Critics of pro-poor tourism have therefore argued that the provision of jobs and income generation does not go far enough – they argue that tourism needs to change on a much more fundamental level. Pro-poor tourism still takes place within a context of free trade (Hall, 2007) – in this context, people in developing nations will find it very difficult to participate as equal partners because of their lack of knowledge and resources. Critics of pro-poor tourism therefore often highlight the fact that pro-poor tourism is a form of imperialism: poor communities in developing countries are given an opportunity to improve their economic situation, but only as long as the investor can make a profit (Hall, 2007). Small-scale initiatives may be possible, but it is unlikely that any of the initiatives mentioned as examples in this case study could compete with multinational tourism suppliers on a large scale. In this bigger picture, the contributions pro-poor tourism can make to poverty alleviation in developing countries in general is necessarily limited: not only are they small players in the tourism sector, tourism initiatives are by nature limited by location – only poor communities in locations attractive to tourists can benefit from it.

Summary

Although there may be limits to the role pro-poor tourism can play in reducing poverty in general, it is equally important to highlight that some pro-poor tourism initiatives (for example, those mentioned in this case study) can have a fundamental impact on the lives of poor people in tourism destinations. Even though pro-poor tourism may not be able to eradicate all inequalities (and it is doubtful tourism alone ever could), their value and innovative forms of combining business and human welfare is by no means marginal.

Questions and discussion points

1. Imagine that you run a small hotel in Tanzania, in the vicinity of a poor community. What could you do to engage in pro-poor tourism? Which areas of your business would be particularly suitable for achieving the aims of pro-poor tourism? Which challenges are you likely to encounter?

2. Why would tourism businesses choose to engage with pro-poor initiatives, given that these may require intensive support to set up and operate? Why, for example, would a tourism business choose to hire local people who need to be trained, rather than recruiting staff members from abroad who have the necessary skills and experience?

3. Hall (2007) challenges the idea that tourism exchanges mainly benefit countries in the 'global South' – this term refers to developing nations in Asia, Africa and Latin America. Hall argues that this statement is incorrect, because 'not only is the consumption of tourism the domain of the wealthy, but in many ways so is its production' (2007, 6). What does this statement mean?

Bibliography

Ashley, C. and Mitchell, J. (2005) Can tourism accelerate pro-poor growth in Africa? *ODI Opinions,* **60,** available online at: www.odi.org.uk/resources/download/504.pdf (accessed November 2011).

Ashley, C., Goodwin, H., McNab, D., Scott, M. and Chaves, L. (2006) *Making Tourism Count for the Local Economy in the Caribbean. Guidelines for Good Practice,* Pro-poor Tourism Partnership/ Caribbean Tourism Organization.

Ashley, C., Roe, D., and Goodwin, H. (2001) *Pro-Poor Tourism Strategies: Making Tourism Work For The Poor,* London, Overseas Development Institute.

Braman S. and Fundación Acción Amazonia (2001) *Practical strategies for pro-poor tourism: TROPIC Ecological Adventures – Ecuador,* Pro-Poor Tourism Working Paper number 6, available online at http://www.propoortourism.org.uk/ecuador_cs.pdf (accessed November 2011).

Concern Universal (2011) How Gambia eased its growing pains, available online at: http://www. concern-universal.org/files/rta_magazine_article.pdf (accessed November 2011).

Hall, C. (ed.) (2007) *Pro-Poor Tourism: Who Benefits? Perspectives on Tourism and Poverty reduction,* Clevedon, Channel View.

Hall, C. and Brown, F. (2006) *Tourism and Welfare: Ethics, Responsibility and Sustained Well-being,* Wallingford, CABI.

Medical tourism: Surgical Bliss

Prepared by Claire Humphreys with information and insights provided by
Denise Hoogervorst, Director, Surgical Bliss

This case examines the niche sector of medical tourism. As has been discussed in Chapter 9, the demand for travel which includes a planned medical intervention has been growing rapidly over the past decade. Focusing on a company based in South Africa – a popular medical tourism destination – we examine here the services provided by Surgical Bliss and consider the benefits of travelling for medical treatment as well as the issues South Africa faces in maintaining its medical tourism market.

What is medical tourism?

Some of the earliest forms of tourism were motivated by the desire to improve one's health and wellbeing. We see similar motivations today in the niche market that is medical tourism. This sector has 'grown dramatically in recent years primarily because of the high costs of treatment in rich world countries, long waiting lists (for what is not always seen institutionally as priority surgery), the relative affordability of international air travel and favourable economic exchange rates, and the ageing of the, often affluent, post-war baby-boom generation' (Connell, 2006, 1094). It is reportedly growing at a rate of 15% annually (Rickard, 2011) and now has consumer guides dedicated to advising patients on destinations and medical institutions (see **www.patientsbeyondborders.com**). However, there is significant concern (Crooks and Snyder, 2010; Shetty, 2010) that little in the way controls or regulation have been introduced to protect the interests and welfare of the patient.

Medical tourism can be defined as 'the movement of patients across an international border for the purposes of obtaining healthcare' (Álvarez *et al.*, 2011), and it occurs when citizens, typically from industrial nations, bypass local healthcare services and travel to receive faster and/or more affordable treatment overseas (Horowitz *et al.*, 2007). In many cases, the cost of care is covered by the patient, but in fact the cost can in some cases be covered by the citizen's own government or by insurance companies.

Within the medical tourism industry sector, there exists a number of companies which act as intermediaries, facilitating the link between the patient and the medical professionals. The extent of their involvement may vary from country to country and by company, with some acting merely as an initial contact point while others offer a full service acting as travel arranger as well as advocate for the patient (Snyder *et al.*, 2011). This latter role is played by companies such as Surgical Bliss.

Background to the company

Surgical Bliss (see Figure 1) is a South African medical tourism company based in Cape Town. It was established in 2008 by owner and CEO Denise Milner, who identified a niche in the global market for a medical tourism company that operated ethically and in the best interest of the patient. South Africa has spectacular tourism attractions and resources, and these have been coupled with highly regarded healthcare facilities to attract medical tourists. Doctors and dentists in South Africa are registered with the Health Professionals Council of

Figure 1 Surgical Bliss banner
Reproduced courtesy of Surgical Bliss

South Africa and are part of the Continuing Professional Development System, which compels them to attend regular courses in order to retain their yearly registration.

A wide range of procedures and treatments may be sought by medical tourists. Surgical Bliss offers its clients the following:

- *in vitro* fertilization
- plastic and cosmetic surgery
- orthopaedic surgery
- general surgery
- dental surgery
- ophthalmology.

Medical tourists come from all over the globe. For Surgical Bliss, key markets are: African citizens from countries such as Gabon, Nigeria and Zimbabwe, Angola and Cameroon; the USA, Britain and Australia; Norway and Russia.

An important aspect to understand in the industry is that each person is an individual. No two people or procedures are alike. Furthermore, clients who opt to travel in order to access medical treatment are generally knowledgeable and well-informed in regard to the quality and standards of medical facilities, both in their home country and, in the case of clients of Surgical Bliss, those in South Africa.

Key services provided

Cosmetic and plastic surgeries such as breast augmentation, tummy tucks, liposuction and face lifts make up a large portion of the procedures offered by Surgical Bliss. Second to this are procedures linked to *in vitro* fertilization.

On average a Surgical Bliss client flies into Cape Town and stays in the city for two to three weeks. However, this depends on the type of surgery and whether the client has decided to stay for an extended period following the procedure, to enjoy a holiday. Generally, orthopaedic surgery requires the patient to stay on longer.

The demand for an individually tailored service directly impacts upon how Surgical Bliss can approach each enquiry. The company plans and coordinates both the surgery and the post-treatment recovery programme, with or without a holiday component. It offers packages inclusive of accommodation (offering a variety of types and quality standards to meet the different budgetary limitations of customers), post-operative nursing and ground transportation. It can also provide post-treatment excursions and tours for those patients wishing to stay longer and make the trip a holiday.

Organizing the medical tourism trip

Surgical Bliss receives medical queries directly through their company website. It also contracts with online medical tourism referral companies and may also receive referrals from doctors, clinics and past patients who are aware of its services.

Once the patient has contacted Surgical Bliss, a consultant will review the medical aspects of the enquiry and respond to the client – usually within 24 hours. The company will then liaise between the client and the specialist surgeon providing the treatment, forwarding the client's treatment description, doctor's referral letter, x-rays and photographs as appropriate. Often Surgical Bliss will meet face to face with the doctor on behalf of the company's client. The specialist surgeon then makes recommendations specific to the patient's medical history and case notes, and Surgical Bliss subsequently supplies the client with a comprehensive quotation inclusive of hospital, theatre and anaesthesiologist's fees.

Surgical Bliss facilitates the entire process, coordinating the medical logistics, booking consultations and the procedure according to the timeframe of the client and availability of the surgeon, offering advice on payment for treatment, and managing any travel and accommodation arrangements necessary, including assisting with visa applications.

For some medical tourists, it can be daunting being in a strange country and dealing with different healthcare systems, when they are already anxious about the surgical procedures to come. Therefore, one important aspect is the personal service and support provided by Surgical Bliss; taking a sincere personal interest in the wellbeing of a client is core to their business and encourages word of mouth referrals.

Benefits of travelling for medical treatment

There are many benefits to be gained by medical tourists opting for surgery in South Africa apart from the affordability involved. The services are outstanding and the people are extremely friendly and helpful. The UEFA World Cup, hosted in 2010, provided extensive media coverage of the country and this has added to the appeal as a place to visit. Furthermore, the country is very beautiful with splendid weather conditions and, as a result, is a popular tourist destination. Hospitality in South Africa is at a very high standard as controlled by the Tourism Grading Council of South Africa.

The variety of tourist sites and landscapes (from the mountainous beauty of the Western Cape, the ocean views along the Garden Route to the wildlife of the north eastern parts of the country including the world famous Kruger National Park) add to the appeal of the destination, perhaps over other countries offering medical tourism services.

For some patients, the decision to travel for treatment is based on the fact that there is no wait for consultations, or delays in surgery; Surgical Bliss highlights the fact that it can provide appointments organized to meet the needs of the client, rather than waiting to reach the top of a long NHS waiting list.

In some cases, clients opt for treatment abroad for the anonymity it offers. Patients who wish to keep cosmetic surgery private from their friends may claim they are taking a relaxing holiday and attribute their improved 'overall appearance' to this rejuvenating experience.

It should also be noted that, while much of the demand may come from the developed world, there are cases where medical tourists travel to South Africa because there is a lack of resources, surgical skills and technology for the treatment they require in their own countries.

Issues linked to medical tourism in South Africa

In the South African marketplace, the global recession has presented difficulties to the medical tourism industry. With a weak dollar, the exchange rate is less favourable then when the dollar is stronger and, as a result, there are fewer foreigners able to afford surgery abroad as the cost benefit decreases with the value of the dollar.

Private surgical tourism is less favoured in the European Union (EU), as citizens are often entitled to free medical care under the countries' national health systems. The NHS is also loath to release medical records comprising scans and blood results required by the South African doctors for procedures such as fertility treatments, while clients may also find it difficult to attain the necessary medical documentation needed to obtain quotes for medical treatment overseas.

The perceived level of crime in South Africa has historically proved a deterrent for some medical tourists. A widespread belief that South Africa is an underdeveloped nation is a setback when trying to encourage potential medical tourists to visit for treatment and a holiday.

Finally, convincing patients that medical care overseas, not just in South Africa, would be of a standard as good, if not exceeding, the quality of care offered at home, will always remain a challenge. Media coverage of botched operations or poor aftercare impacts on confidence and there is limited evidence that the travelling public would bother to distinguish between medical tourism experiences in South Africa, South Korea or South America – despite the significant differences in provision between these regions.

Summary

Overall, the relative costs of surgery in South Africa are often reasonable, due to low medical tariffs and a current exchange rate which favours the foreign visitor. The popularity of the country as a tourism destination, a pleasing climate and warm hospitality can all add to the attractiveness of the country as a successful medical tourism destination.

The future is bright for medical tourism generally, as people have more convenient access to the Internet to investigate the medical options open to them. Furthermore, patients are also taking responsibility for their health and are increasingly investing in their own looks, fitness and wellbeing.

Questions and discussion points

1. What factors may affect the demand for planned medical treatment overseas?

2. How might an understanding of tourism typologies help to differentiate between different medical tourists? What might these differences in characteristics mean for supply?

3. Is there an ethical issue to consider when foreign tourists obtain treatment in countries where the local population is not provided with adequate healthcare services?

Bibliography

Álvarez, M. M., Chanda, R. and Smith, R. D. (2011) The potential for bi-lateral agreements in medical tourism: A qualitative study of stakeholder perspectives from the UK and India, *Globalization and Health*, **7** (11): http://www.globalizationandhealth.com/content/pdf/1744-8603-7-11.pdf.

Connell, J. (2006) Medical tourism: sea, sun, sand and surgery, *Tourism Management*, **27** (6), 1093–1100.

Crooks, V. A. and Snyder, J. (2010) regulating medical tourism, *The Lancet*, **376** (9751), 1465–1466.

Horowitz, M. D., Rosensweig, J. A. and Jones, C. A. (2007) Medical tourism: globalization of the healthcare marketplace, *Medscape General Medicine*, **9** (4), 33.

Rickard, A. (2011) Sink teeth into medical tourism, *The Queensland Times*, 17 September.

Snyder, J., Adams, K., Kingsbury, P. and Johnston, R. (2011) The 'patient's physician one-step removed': the evolving roles of medical tourism facilitators, *Journal of Medical Ethics*, **37** (9), 530–534.

Shetty, P. (2010) Medical tourism booms in India, but at what cost?, *The Lancet*, **376** (9742), 671–672.

The Pro Sky Airliner Conference

Prepared by Rob Davidson with the kind assistance of Torben Lenz of Pro Sky AG

This case study provides a brief overview of an event organized to serve a particular segment of the aviation industry. The organization of conferences is discussed in detail in Chapter 11 and some of the trends facing the industry are noted in this case study.

Background to the conference

Pro Sky, the initiator of the annual Pro Sky Airliner Conference, is a company specializing in customized flight services for groups and individuals, and aviation advertising. Its portfolio of services includes aircraft charters, scheduled tickets for groups, private jets, airport and in-flight services and media solutions. Pro Sky has offices in Cologne, Paris, São Paulo and Zurich.

The one-day Pro Sky Airliner Conference is described by the company as 'the leading networking platform for the ad-hoc (sic) aircraft charter business and customised aviation'. It is an event that has been held every year since 2001. In its first year it attracted 30 delegates; by 2011, that number had risen to 100. The delegates are managers, executives and owners of airlines that have an on-going or potential business relationship with Pro Sky. They come from all over the world, although mainly from Europe. There are generally more men participating than women, but the age-range of participants is wide, with some on the threshold of retirement and others just beginning their careers in the aviation industry. Pro Sky funds all costs of the conference programme itself; the delegates merely cover travel and accommodation costs resulting from attendance at the event.

Objectives of the conference

An important objective of the conference is to bring together Pro Sky and its stakeholders, in particular the airlines, which are among the company's key suppliers. In that sense, the conference forms part of Pro Sky's relationship management strategy, allowing the company to get to know its suppliers and business partners in a personal way, and to position itself as a competent, approachable and innovative partner. The conference also enables Pro Sky to communicate its clients' specific needs to the airlines in a relaxed, face-to-face setting.

Organization of the conference

For the first few years, when the Airliner Conference was smaller and less complex than it is today, Pro Sky's own staff organized the event, with no use of external agencies. Latterly, as the conference has grown, some tasks have been outsourced to an external communication agency. As a medium-sized company, Pro Sky lacks the capacity to employ members of staff to work only on the annual conference; however, by sharing out the tasks among many colleagues, much of the organizing of the event can be done internally. The different tasks include, for example, creating the conference programme, planning the different workshops, communicating with the conference hotel, choosing the evening venue and communicating with the evening venue and entertainers.

Destination and venue

As the home city of Pro Sky, Cologne is a natural choice of destination for this event. Over the years, several different conference hotels have been used as the venue for the daytime proceedings. For the evening venue, Pro Sky chooses locations that change every year to provide a surprise for the delegates and encourage them to see Cologne through different eyes. In the past, these have included Butzweilerhof (Cologne's former civil airport, where the main airport terminal building, opened in 1926, is now protected as a listed building), the German Sports and Olympia Museum and the Cologne Tower.

The programme

The storyboard of the 2011 conference (produced for internal use by Pro Sky staff) appears in Table 1. No official programme is issued to delegates, because the evening venue is always kept secret in order to surprise them.

Table 1 Pro Sky Conference Programme 2011

Date	Time	Place	Task
13/01/2011	12:30	Conference foyer	Get-together of all Pro Sky team members
13/01/2011	13:00	Conference foyer	Pro Sky team will welcome guests and distribute name badges
13/01/2011	13:30	Hotel	Start of welcome reception
13/01/2011	14:25	Hotel	Pro Sky staff go into the conference room to take seats first
13/01/2011	14:30	Hotel	Welcome by Armin Truger (CEO) and Gilles Meynard (General Manager France)
13/01/2011	14:40	Hotel	Presentation of award entries
13/01/2011	15:00	Hotel	Start of workshops. Topics:
			'It's a Revolution' – what is the state-of-the-art way of selling aircraft charters to clients?
			'Thinking out of the Box' – how do you generate additional revenue by customizing flights?
			'IATA' – current state of affairs in the German market for groups on scheduled flights
13/01/2011	16:00	Hotel	Start of coffee break
13/01/2011	17:00	Hotel	Presentation by John Trevett of FlightSafe Consultants Ltd: 'Airline Safety and Ranking Systems'
13/01/2011	17:30	Hotel	Presentation by Stefan Buschle of Omni Aviation: 'The Portuguese Ad Hoc Charter Market and Omni Aviation'
13/01/2011	17:50	Hotel	Pro Sky Aviation Excellence Award ceremony
13/01/2011	18:15	Hotel	Information about the evening programme and closing of the conference
13/01/2011	19:15	Hotel	Start of bus transfer and head-count of participants
13/01/2011	19:30	Hotel	Final bus to evening location and information to reception about last minute taxi transfers to location for any latecomers

Table 1 *continued*

Date	Time	Place	Task
13/01/2011	19:35	Evening location	Start of welcome drink & flying buffet
13/01/2011	20:00	Evening location	Admission to location, open the doors
13/01/2011	20:00	Evening location	Ask guests to take seats / wardrobe
13/01/2011	20:15	Evening location	Speech by Uli Stiller
13/01/2011	20:30	Evening location	First course
13/01/2011	20:55	Evening location	Main course
13/01/2011	21:30	Evening location	Armin & Gilles introduction to Lipdub
13/01/2011	21:40	Evening location	Drum Café
13/01/2011	22:30	Evening location	Speech by Armin & Gilles
13/01/2011	22:35	Evening location	Dessert buffet
13/01/2011	22:35	Evening location	Opening of Pro Sky Cocktail Lounge
13/01/2011	22:35	Evening location	Pro Sky Cocktail Lounge

Changing trends in the Pro Sky Conference

More interactive

In recent years, there has been more focus on the workshops, with these becoming increasingly interactive. There are still some keynote speakers, but these are fewer in number than before and are gradually being replaced by more interactive sessions. An example of delegate participation is the Pro Sky Aviation Excellence Award – during the conference the delegates are given the opportunity to present examples of their airlines' services in the field of group travel and the most outstanding example is chosen by the delegates as a whole, through a voting system (Pro Sky participants do not vote).

The airline Omni Aviation has just received the renowned Pro Sky Aviation Excellence Award (see Figure 1) for an extraordinary tour through Africa described in this extract from Pro Sky's own website (**http://www.pro-sky.com/detailansicht/items/award_2011.html**).

Figure 1 Omni Aviation receive the Pro Sky Aviation Excellence Award
Photo courtesy of Pro Sky

650 bottles of wine and champagne for an 'African cruise' by air

Cruise ships stop off at the most beautiful ports in the world. But what about the exotic pearls to be found inland? A clear case for air cruises. These luxury flights are enjoying increasing popularity. The airline Omni Aviation has just received the renowned Pro Sky Aviation Excellence Award for an extraordinary tour through Africa. There were 650 bottles of wine in the hold and, behind the scenes, Omni Aviation had pulled out all the stops to ensure the guests a wonderful travel experience.

Dire Dawa in Ethiopia, Lilongwe in Malawi or Mopti in Mali: the route reads like a globetrotter's expedition diary. For 48 guests from Germany, Austria and Switzerland, these sounded like perfect places to visit on an unusual trip: an air cruise over Africa. They spent 17 days travelling across the continent on their own chartered plane. 'Like on a luxury cruise ship, our guests demand top service even in exotic destinations', was how Stefan Buschle from the airline Omni Aviation explained the challenge. Therefore, behind the scenes, mountains were moved in order to meet the customers' requirements. For example, the crew in Vienna took 650 bottles of wine and champagne on board with them, and their own chef conjured up exquisite menus en route.

More use of technology

Each year, more use is made of the Internet as a means of extending the life of this live, face-to-face event, meaning that it is no longer simply a one-day conference, but an all-year event, using blogs and other social media to maintain an on-going dialogue between Pro Sky and its partners.

More corporate branding

The Pro Sky Airliner Conference is developing into a brand, with its own distinctive corporate design used on name badges, presentation slides and on their website.

Measuring the return-on-investment of the Pro Sky Conference

The success of the Pro Sky Airliner Conference is measured using a number of key performance indicators. These include feedback from the delegates regarding the content of the workshops, the level of attendance and the benefits of the networking sessions.

Summary

This conference has become a significant element in building stakeholder relationships for Pro Sky. Although expansion has led to some tasks being handed over to an external agency, much of the organization of this event remains inhouse.

Questions and discussion points

1. What are the benefits of having the event organized directly by employees of Pro Sky? What benefits may be gained by allowing a professional conference organizer to manage the event?

2. To what extent is the trend towards greater use of technology and interactivity in this conference unique?

3. The decision to keep the evening venue a secret in order to surprise attendees is a bold one. What problems are likely to arise from this decision?

Travel for education: Quest Overseas

Prepared by Claire Humphreys, with the kind assistance of Jon Cassidy, Managing Director, Quest Overseas (**www.questoverseas.com**)

This case examines the realm of educational travel, specifically looking at the case of gap-year travel. This is a sector which has experienced rapid growth over the past decade, but predictions are that it is entering a rather more turbulent period over the coming few years. The focus is on one company, Quest Overseas, and their activities in providing volunteer projects and travel expeditions for the 17–24 year-old market.

The case links with points discussed in Chapter 4 related to travel motivations as well as some of the issues linked to social and environmental impacts identified in Chapters 6 and 7. This organization is particularly interesting in the way it selects volunteers in order to protect as well as enhance established relationships with charity projects.

The historical perspective

Travel provides the opportunity not just to explore the world but to experience a journey of self-discovery. This is, of course, by no means a recent concept; the Grand Tour, for example, provided wealthy Europeans with an opportunity to learn about different cultures, languages and the arts. It also provided opportunities to expand networks and contacts with other aristocratic families across the European Continent. Today, travel for education and self-development remains popular, particularly among young adults taking time out following long periods of formal schooling. Gap-year travel has been particularly popular in Europe and Australia for a number of years, and is now becoming more common in North America.

The existence of gap-year travel, designed to enhance both educational and social opportunity, can draw on the established backpacker tourism to understand its growth and social acceptability. As a form of 'long-term independent travel' (O'Reilly, 2006) backpacking provided an opportunity to travel which would be measured in months rather than weeks and relied on low-cost transport, accommodation and catering to ensure a small budget could last for years. These provided the traveller with the opportunity to meet others – often staying in the same budget hostels – and discuss their travel experiences, draw contrast with their own cultures and practices and develop shared experiences with an international and cosmopolitan group.

In recent years, technology has allowed backpackers to share their experiences and tales more widely via commercial websites and forums (such as the Lonely Planet's Thorn Tree). In some cases, backpackers have created their own website, posting images and diary updates regularly, occasionally publishing these at the end of their trip as a permanent record of their exploits, conveniently accessible for wider audiences.

Historically, such travel occurred either to delineate the end of university education and the start of a career, or as a career break or prelude to a change in career direction. However, in the past decade there has been growing demand for gap-year travel falling between the end of school education and the start of a university education. Often the gap-year experience was seen by universities and employers as an advantage, the traveller having gained greater independence, cultural awareness and improved communication skills. Research (Anon, 2011) has highlighted that gap-year students entering education were more focused, wasted less money and were more likely to be employed because of their travel experience.

Such travel has been aided by a growing affluence in the western world combined with a relative fall in airfares, making long-haul travel more affordable. Coupled with this was a growing acceptability among employers which led to sabbaticals and long-term unpaid leave becoming more widely available. The growing number taking a 'year out' meant popular routes were established which were considered to be safe and easy to travel. These routes provided affordable transport, an excess of cheap and clean hostel accommodation and popular attractions – some cultural, others linked to activities such as bungee-jumping and diving, a lively nightlife, drinking, drug-taking and partying.

Although many gap-year trips remain within the backpacking sector, we have seen the introduction of a more formalized range of activities to be included in the travel experience. This may be as a result of the younger demographic of traveller; alternatively, it may be an attempt to ensure that gap-year travel enhances the CV, thus increasing career prospects. Research of employers has highlighted that half of business managers believe gap year experiences are as important as university degrees when selecting interview candidates.

The changing market for educational gap-year travel

The growth of the gap-year travel sector has been rapid in the UK. It was estimated that in 2001 some 50 000 UK students took a year out – including the future heir to the throne, Prince William. The gap-year travel business is an important sector of the travel industry in the UK, and for many developed countries across the globe. In 2008, research estimated that the global gap year market involved 1.6 million volunteer trips (TRAM, 2008).

There are flourishing debates criticizing organized gap-year travel as largely the domain of the white middle class. In an effort to provide the benefits of such experience to low-income groups, a UK government initiative – the International Citizen Service – has been launched to offer some 1000 young people a volunteering experience designed to help poor people across the world. The pilot project for this scheme secured the first placements in June 2011.

Gap-year travel is no longer just the preserve of the young. There is increasing demand from the middle-age and senior market, as redundancy, divorce and other events encourage a career break and life changes. In such cases, the demand for education and self-development forms a significant part of the motivation to take time out. Saga, a holiday company specialist in travel for the over-50s age group, reported a 300% increase in sales for longer, more adventurous holidays. One justification for this growing desire to participate in longer and more adventurous travel lies in the realization that for many in this age sector gap-year travel was not an option in their youth. Travel organizer Bridge the World estimates that they will take 50 000 passengers on 'grey gap-years' in 2011 (Goodley, 2010). This market is growing in importance, as the size and spend levels can be greater than those for the student gap-year traveller. Senior gap-year travellers tend to use more luxurious accommodation and higher classes of transport, drawing on savings and pensions to fund their travel costs.

The supply of gap-year travel

The gap-year travel industry is reportedly worth £6 billion a year for western companies, with many volunteers paying between £1500 and £4500 for a two-month experience (Boffey, 2011). The increase in supply has been coupled with many negative press reports on the benefits of the projects offered and the cost of participation. Some reports suggest that this is just a new form of western colonialism (Urwin, 2011) and companies have worked to

Table 1 Examples of gap-year travel organizations

Camp America	Operating since 1969, the organization sends 7000 young people to work in camps across the USA. The focus is to work with young people staying in the camps over their school summer holiday.
Lattitude Global Volunteering	Established as Gap Activity Projects in 1972, the focus is on community projects linked to healthcare, teaching and conservation.
The Year in Industry	Provides paid work placements in the UK. Focusing on engineering, science, IT, business and logistics and last about 10 months. Students can combine these with travel experiences abroad as the organization works with BUNAC and Raleigh International.
Raleigh International	This is a youth education charity, established almost 30 years ago. Over this period more than 30 000 people have participated in expeditions which have developed a variety of community facilities across the globe.
BUNAC	Operating to provide overseas work and volunteering opportunities in traditional gap-year travel destinations such as the USA, Canada, Australia and New Zealand as well as more adventurous locations like Ghana, Cambodia, India, China, Peru and Costa Rica, this enterprise has been operating for more than half a century.

reduce the negative image; to promote best practice in the industry, organizations like the Year Out Group have been established, requiring members to adhere to codes of practice which protect the traveller and the host destination.

Table 1 identifies some key players serving the gap year market. When examining the industry more extensively we see that there are many companies which have chosen to specialize, perhaps by geographic region or perhaps by the type of activities and experiences they offer. Others may serve a particular segment of the market, for example the older traveller. Some provide projects which last much of the year while others offer shorter experiences, perhaps lasting only a few weeks, which are designed to be embedded into a wider plan for travel.

The rapid growth in the gap-year travel sector experienced during the past decade has not escaped the notice of the mainstream tour operators. Successful businesses have been bought out by major tour operators like TUI (see Table 2).

Interestingly, many organizations, including Quest Expeditions, the focus of this case study, now offer gap-year travellers the opportunity to obtain a qualification linked to their volunteering experiences. The Certificate of Personal Effectiveness (CoPE) is worth 70 UCAS (UK university admissions) points and requires that students demonstrate through a portfolio that they possess a range of skills, including working with others, problem-solving,

Table 2 Adventure travel and gap-year travel organizations owned by TUI AG

Real Gap Experience	Claims to be the largest gap-year travel company, with over 200 projects in 35 countries across five continents.
i to i	Specializes in providing Teaching English as a Foreign Language (TEFL) teacher training alongside volunteering programmes as part of travel experiences.
International Academy	Provides ski and snowboard instructor training taken as part of a gap-year or career break.
Exodus	Provides adventure and active holidays including trekking, rafting and mountain biking.
Gecko's	Claims to provide authentic travel experiences which benefit local communities.

research planning and communication. University recognition of this qualification has been muted in enthusiasm, but it is seen as a useful way of differentiating between university candidates.

Quest Overseas

In the 1990s, Michael Amphlet was involved in organizing solo travel experiences for young-sters which took them to remote and deprived areas of India. The culture shock experienced by many of the young travellers was felt to deter their desires to explore the developing world, so Quest Overseas was born, providing organized group travel linked to development projects which sought to encourage travellers to be community-driven global citizens, while supporting their discovery of poverty-stricken areas of the world, and ensuring they returned home having had a positive and rewarding experience.

History and background

Quest Overseas started operating in 1996, with a 10-week adventure tour in Peru; this included six weeks working on a children's project followed by four weeks travelling through-out the country. The success of this adventure tour led to the provision of further trips, some including language courses at the start of the journey to improve the interaction that the travellers – or 'volunteers' as they are known – could achieve during the three-month experience.

In the early years, Quest worked with a project in the Villa Maria shanty town area of Peru which sought to improve the lives of children affected by crime and poverty. This relation-ship continues today, and over the years Quest volunteers have provided recreation and cultural activities as well as constructing playgrounds, houses and, more recently, school facilities through this project. Another charity initiative with which Quest has developed long-term links is the Inti Wara Yassi animal sanctuary in Bolivia, where volunteers care for rescued animals, helping rehabilitate them for release back into the wild. Again, volunteers have provided labour to construct animal enclosures and other infrastructure needed.

Currently, Quest works directly with four projects in South America and a similar number in Africa. In South America, the two long-standing projects discussed above have been complemented with a community project linked to Rio Carnival and a conservation project protecting the Peruvian Amazon. In Africa, the volunteers work on an orphan and commun-ity project in Malawi, a community development project in Tanzania, a water relief project in Kenya (see Figure 1) and a children's project in Rwanda. To enhance their efforts to support these projects a charitable organization – Quest4change – was established. All volunteers taking trips with Quest are required to provide a donation to the project in which they are involved, and the charitable status of Quest4change allows that to be achieved more effectively and transparently. Donations are currently between £650 and £850 for each gap-year trip.

The donations help to ensure the long-term viability of the projects, including funding salaries for the local employees who are running the projects year-round. This ensures that the initiatives can operate even when no Quest volunteers are in town; for example, the Villa Maria project provides year-round support sessions and activity workshops for the local community. Quest have chosen their projects cautiously and ensure that the projects are viable in their own right – the support from the volunteers is seen as a way of enhancing the offering, not one which encourages an over-reliance on charity support.

The third arm of the operation is Experience Quest. Launched following the request of parents of some volunteers to allow them a similar experience, this sector of the business now provides school expeditions, corporate challenges and adventure holidays, linking the projects with tailor-made travel plans for each group. Although three-quarters of Quest

Figure 1 Quest volunteers work with the local population on a construction project in Kenya
Photo by Jon Cassidy

business is gap-year travel arranged by Quest Overseas, the Experience Quest development has allowed older travellers and school parties to experience the product, whilst providing increased resources and financial benefits for the charity projects.

In summary, Quest operates:

1. Quest Overseas

  (a) Gap-year travel – lasting three months and including language classes, volunteering with a project, then taking a challenging expedition.

  (b) Project trips – working on just the volunteering aspect of the gap-year travel package, lasting six weeks.

  (c) Expeditions – participating in just the expedition aspect of the gap-year travel package, six weeks in duration.

2. Experience Quest – tailor-made school or corporate trips combining a short volunteering experience with a short tour, the entire trip lasting only two to three weeks.

3. Quest4change – charitable arm providing funding streams to support projects linked with volunteering for Quest Overseas clientele.

Whether it is tailor-made trips organized by Experience Quest or the gap-year travel organized by Quest Overseas, the business model is largely focused on combining voluntary work, language training and adventurous expeditions.

Quest's gap-year market

The company caters to travellers in an age range 17–24, yet by far the majority of the volunteers are recent school leavers, and thus at the lower end of this age range. Two-thirds of places on the gap-year experiences (which includes language classes, volunteering for the project, followed by an expedition) are filled by students taking time out between school and university, and are thus aged 18–19.

The overall cost of a three-month trip is about £4000, not including the project donation or international flights. This has a significant impact on the market able to participate, with many coming from wealthy backgrounds, often schooled in private rather than state institutions. Occasionally, some choose only to participate in the projects, while others only participate in expeditions. In such cases these shorter trips draw on a slightly more diverse market, including some taking breaks between their first and second year at university.

Historically, nearly all customers were from the UK, perhaps as a result of the company being based there, but also perhaps acknowledging that gap-year travel is well-established as a concept. The US market is now growing, as gap-year travel becomes more widely accepted and encouraged there. Quest estimates that now 10–20% of their volunteers come from Australia, mainland Europe and the USA.

The motivations for taking an organized gap-year trip, rather than travelling independently, are as diverse as the individuals. However, the key reason may be that the gap-year traveller:

● Wants to get involved in something which is 'genuinely worthwhile', and travelling to developing world areas for the first time may mean they feel they don't have the knowledge or experience to know what is 'worthwhile' work.

● Wants to know that the project they contribute to will continue to benefit after their contribution has been made. Quest highlights in their marketing and promotional materials that projects are long-term and will continue after the gap-year visitor has moved on.

● Looks for a degree of safety and security, gaining peace of mind that they can easily access support and help if things go wrong.

● Enjoys the company of others and is looking to be a part of a team, to gain a new network of friends and colleagues who will share their experiences.

Between the charitable projects and Quest volunteers, it is clear from the outset that there is both a mutual need and a mutual benefit; the project gets assistance both in terms of labour and donations while the volunteer gets an unusual and memorable positive experience. Experience is high on the agenda for Quest, and positive recommendations from participants bring two-thirds of new volunteers to Quest's door.

Operations

The size of the operations remains small. The company employs six full-time staff in the UK and 12 project and tour leaders based in Africa and South America. The company has focused on a limited number of geographic areas, developing extensive networks and contacts in these locations to ensure that community needs are understood and community support is given. Each charity project annually receives visits from about five volunteer groups, some there for several weeks, others working on smaller projects for just a few days before continuing their trip. The group size is a maximum of 16, accompanied by a tour leader and an assistant tour leader.

Separate from work with the charity projects is a range of expeditions (see Figure 2). These provide a series of challenging trips which include activities such as summiting Kilimanjaro, learning scuba diving in Kenya, white-water rafting, trekking to Machu Picchu, ice-climbing in the Andes and canoeing down the Amazon. Each expedition lasts six weeks. Customers can book these trips without participating in any projects. They do, however, have to make a small donation which goes to Quest4change and helps to fund the local projects. Currently the donation is £75.

Recruiting volunteers

Quest highly prize the relationships they have developed with their projects – and the communities they work with – so have established an application process for the volunteers.

Figure 2 Visiting Colca Canyon, Peru as part of the Andean Expedition
Photo by Jon Cassidy

Each applicant is interviewed, usually face-to-face but occasionally by telephone, to establish their suitability to participate. The purpose of this is not for Quest to put together an 'elite task-force of superb gap-year students' but to ensure that volunteers understand what they are taking on by participating in such a trip, both in terms of the physical expectations and the underpinning project philosophies. Quest highlight at this point that their trips are not about 'saving the world in two weeks and then sitting on a beach'! Quest need to ensure that the volunteer is not likely to damage relationships with the projects, which have often taken years to establish. Once selected, the volunteer is likely to be in frequent contact with Quest prior to travel, including participating in pre-departure training camps. Each year about a quarter of applicants are not accepted.

Interviewing is not common in this sector of the travel industry now – just a handful of operators do this, though a few more may well ask for application forms to be completed. Less rigorous companies allow travellers to pay their deposit online and that is all that is required. Interestingly BS8848 (a British Standard for Overseas Expeditions, discussed later) requires that companies have a clear selection process which examines an applicant's capability to participate in the adventure activities planned.

Applications are received as much as 18 months in advance, with women more than men organizing their travel plans early. Occasionally, late applications (one month from departure) are received, although this is unusual and limits the opportunity for pre-departure preparations and training.

Volunteers are encouraged to fundraise in order to gain financial support for the charity donation they must make via the Quest4change charity. Quest help the volunteer with this, making suggestions on successful fundraising activities of the past. Some students can also access grants and bursaries, and Quest maintain a database of these, to help guide the volunteer towards funding which may help to cover some of their own trip costs. Funding for the project elements or the language courses is more likely than funding for the expedition elements of the trip, and Quest provide a transparent breakdown of costs to increase the opportunities of such grants being accessed.

Travel arrangements

Quest do not make any of the international flight arrangements directly and therefore do not need to be ATOL bonded. They work with a local flight agent who is recommended to the volunteers, and, although many use this service, some choose to book independently or make use of airmiles or other benefits they have to access cheap travel to the startpoint. It is estimated that about two-thirds of volunteers take the recommended flights for peace of mind or the desire to travel out with the group.

The pre-departure training camps include information sessions on medical injections and travel practicalities. Quest provide travel insurance as part of the trip.

Recruiting staff

On average, the tour leaders work for the company for over three years. About a half of these employees first came to Quest as volunteers, themselves taking a gap-year trip. They have then come to work for the organization after graduating from university. It is important to note that Quest is unable to offer year-round work for many of the tour or expedition leaders because they offer only a limited number of trips annually. In many cases, the tour leaders get involved in working with other local organizations, often through links with the charity projects.

The characteristics and personalities of the staff are one key to the success of the trips. Staff need to be sensitive to the local cultures, balanced with the need to lead the group effectively. It is absolutely vital that they do not have a 'colonial approach' which can antagonize the local community and the project staff, some of whom have been involved with Quest for a decade or more. The tour leader must be able to motivate the volunteers to work hard all day, to interact effectively with the local project staff and, in some cases, the people they are helping, to ensure conflicts with the local community don't arise, all the while ensuring that the volunteers have a memorable and enjoyable experience.

Codes of Practice

Quest have been a member of the Year Out Group for several years and, as such, agree to abide by its voluntary code of practice. This sets out criteria to ensure financial security, accuracy in promotional literature, high standards of service, safety and security, and consideration of the social and environmental impact of the operations. This code of conduct is not examined; rather, members are taken on trust that they will adhere to these requirements. One code of practice which is more robust is the BS8848 specification for overseas expeditions, and Quest achieved this accreditation in 2009. This required the organization to formalize the processes and procedures of its operations to confirm that participants are effectively supervised, planning and preparation is appropriate and staff are suitably trained – in the case of Quest, all overseas staff must hold a Wilderness First Aid certificate, while expedition leaders must also hold a Mountain Leader qualification.

There is some question as to the value of these codes of practice. It seems that few 18 year-olds worry about such things, so these may be more important to the parents of the volunteers. Furthermore, little promotion of the BS8848 standard has been undertaken so few seek out organizations holding this accreditation.

Quest have also been involved in the establishment of Fair Trade Volunteering (FTV), an organization seeking 'to give volunteer placement organizations a benchmark by which to operate, as well as giving prospective volunteers a way to understand what they should be looking for in a Fair Trade Volunteering placement' (**www.fairtradevolunteening.org**).

Problems and difficulties

Whilst problems can occur at any time, the pre-departure training is designed to reduce the likelihood of difficulties arising. One area which is often necessary to manage is the expectations of the volunteers and of those involved only in the expeditions. For young and perhaps slightly naive travellers, seeing something which on the surface appears inappropriate or out of context amid poverty may cause anxiety. In such cases, it is down to the tour leaders to manage expectations and to help place actions in the context of the cultures so greater understanding can be achieved.

It is acknowledged by Quest that young people want to have fun, but part of the experience is about helping the volunteers understand the impact of their behaviour on communities and on the reputation of themselves and fellow travellers. Leaders can help to ensure that inappropriate behaviour is curbed and, in cases of problems, can try to resolve any issues before they escalate. One advantage of operating in so few regions is that the tour leaders know areas well and can recognize and limit problems early. If areas are prone to unrest then routes can be quickly changed and groups moved. The small number of tours operating at any one time allows the head office to maintain close contact with teams.

There has been increasing pressure on travel companies to be more socially and environmentally aware. Yet for Quest this has long been an underpinning part of their philosophies, embedded in their actions, so little has had to change to meet such expectations. Going back to the same places repeatedly highlights the changes that they are bringing to communities, and for them to be welcomed means they need to maintain their positive social and environmental impact.

Looking to the future for Quest Overseas

The gap-year market is being affected in the short term by uncertainly linked to the increase in tuition fees in England and Wales, with many students electing to go straight to university. The 2011/12 year has seen fewer trips planned in advance, but it may be that students unable to get a suitable place then plan trips for the year beyond. For Quest the introduction of the school and corporate trips (through Experience Quest) is a means of diversifying their reliance on the gap-year market.

There is a marked trend towards shorter planning times; rather than booking eight or nine months in advance, many gap-year travellers are choosing projects only three months or so in advance. There is also a trend towards cramming more into the year, with travellers 'wanting to do everything'. This raises a question as to whether a consequence of this may be that 'nothing is done that well'. One result of this changing demand has been a shift in the industry, as it becomes more commercially (and less community) focused. It seems that organizations have less opportunity to encourage gap-year travellers to think through the impacts of what they are doing and why.

Competition has expanded, and the involvement of mass tour operators has increased commercialization of this sector. For such companies, often the focus is now on the consumer experience, with any charity project becoming a conduit for attracting tourists, much as a pretty landscape might do. If that is all the consumer cares about, then these offer an often quite affordable option. However, with limited examination of the background behind the project and the negative impacts caused, few volunteers participating in such trips consider whether there is an ethical or moral dilemma in choosing such holidays over those provided by organizations such as Quest.

Future of educational gap-year travel

Historically, gap-year travel received a negative press, which argued that few gained worth-while experiences or that it contributed little of value to the communities visited. Clearly from this case we can see that some – though clearly not all – gap-year companies do consider the role they play and the impacts they bring to local communities. During 2011, a YouTube video called 'The Gap Yah' became widely reported. This comedy sketch depicted a student named Orlando discussing his gap-year travel experience, which largely involved describing his excessive drinking – and vomiting – escapades. One response was increased media coverage of the benefits of participating in well-thought-out projects that do benefit the local community as well as the volunteer. The outcome of this may be an increase in demand for projects which clearly display their community and environmental credentials.

Summary

There is evidence that the gap-year market is changing, with more countries accepting the benefits of travel as a form of educational development. Pressure on the cost of education may lead to the shortening of gap-year travel, with mini-gaps being preferred over summer vacations from university or during sabbaticals from work. There are more companies entering this sector, including the mainstream tour operators, such as TUI. There now appears to be increased expectation that gap-year travel will include involvement in projects and initiatives which benefit the local populations and destinations directly. The extent to which this currently occurs is still up for debate.

Questions and discussion points

1. Quest Overseas choose to interview all applicants wishing to participate in their projects. Many other companies do not choose to do this. What are the benefits and limitations of each approach?

2. Why has Quest made the effort to become BS8848 accredited? Are such standards and codes of practice important for all sectors of the gap-year travel industry?

3. What are your predictions for the future demand for gap-year travel? Looking beyond absolute numbers, do you think the type of activities and resources sought will change? What about the demographic and socio-economic characteristics of the gap-year traveller?

Bibliography

Anon (2011) Gap year travel to Australia increases in popularity as studies show benefits, *Canada Newswire*, 8 March.

Boffey, D. (2011) Students given tips to stop gap-year travel becoming a new colonialism for rich west, *The Observer*, 31 July.

Goodley, S. (2010) The 'grey gap year': a new breed of adventurers boost travel industry, *The Guardian*, 20 October.

O'Reilly, C. C. (2006) From drifter to gap year tourist, *Annals of Tourism Research*, **33** (4), 998–1017.

TRAM (2008) *Volunteer tourism: A global analysis*, Barcelona, Tourism Research and Marketing/ATLAS.

Urwin, R. (2011) Gap year kids still do more good than harm, *London Evening Standard*, 1 August.

Crisis management for tourism destinations: defusing disaster

Prepared by Tom Buncle, Managing Director: Yellow Railroad (www.yellowrailroad.com)

This is the end of Western civilization.

US Budget Director Lewis Douglas's response to President Franklin D. Roosevelt's announcement that the USA would abandon the gold standard in 1933

With hindsight, not all crises turn out to be as disastrous as they seem at the time. Preventing a crisis from turning into a disaster requires clear thinking, honest communication and a focus on emerging at the other end of the crisis as fit to face the future as possible. Much of the effort goes into communicating the facts before speculation results in damaging misperceptions.

This case study looks at the nature of crisis, how to ride it out and how to come out wiser and fitter. It also includes examples of recent crisis management in the world of tourism in the UK and references to the impact of different crises elsewhere in the world. Its main focus is on the impact of crises on tourism destinations and businesses.

Crisis – definition and impact

A crisis involves the occurrence of an unexpected event, which introduces uncertainty about the future; and it involves a threat to the status quo. If this threat is not addressed, then the crisis can turn into a disaster. In tourism, this can mean a damaged reputation and lost business for a destination and for its tourism businesses. Minimizing the impact of the crisis and recovering as quickly as possible are priorities for everyone involved in the tourism industry when a crisis hits.

Western business mythology – regularly perpetrated by self-help books that crowd the shelves of airport bookstores around the world – often refers to the Mandarin Chinese characters weiji, which mean 'crisis', by suggesting that these two characters separately signify the  words 'danger' and 'opportunity', thereby indicating that every danger carries an opportunity.

This is in fact incorrect. Although they mean 'crisis' when combined, these characters do not separately strictly mean 'danger' and 'opportunity'. Nevertheless, it's a good story and an interesting concept. If they did, this would be a useful way of thinking about a crisis: a danger in which there is an inherent opportunity – because, if the opportunity to recover as quickly as possible is not taken, then the threat (which must be inherent also in the danger) will materialize. So a 'glass half full' approach, which views a crisis as an opportunity, is essential if the disaster waiting to happen is not to materialize from the crisis.

Types of crisis

In *Weathering the Storm*, Mary Lynch (2004) defines three broad types of crisis that affect tourism, according to their impact on travellers' perceptions and on tourism businesses, as:

Table 1 Recovery time for various crises

Event scale	Classification	Recovery period
Low	Singular localized event: e.g. earthquake, tropical storms	Up to three months (country)
Medium	Multiple event: e.g. widespread virus (SARS), extreme natural disaster	3–12 months (regional)
High	Global event: e.g. global financial shocks, World Trade Center attacks	12–36 months (globally)

Source: Rob Shaw, OAG: World Crisis Analysis White Paper, 2011 (www.oagaviation.com/WorldCrisisAnalysis) Copyright Rob Shaw, OAG Aviation.

natural disasters; accidents, environmental or man-made disasters; and political events or terrorism. She breaks these down into the impact of the crisis and actions required to address it within three stages: the first three weeks, the next three months and the next three years, which roughly correspond to stemming the haemorrhage, stabilizing the patient and planning for recovery. Clearly every crisis is different and their impact on a destination and its tourism businesses will vary. But how the destination and its businesses respond will determine how quickly they will recover.

The impact of crisis on travel

Research on the recovery rate for destinations in relation to different types of crisis is variable. However, the OAG (2011) *World Crisis Analysis White Paper* attempted to assess various types of crisis at country, regional and global levels and their potential impact on air travel. Given the close link between demand for air travel and destinations – whether on holiday or business – this seems a reasonable proxy indicator for the rate of recovery for destinations as well as air travel. Their conclusions, in short, are that the bigger the scale of the event, the longer it took air travel – and arguably, by association, the destination – to recover (see Table 1).

On the whole, tourism is a surprisingly resilient industry and people tend to have short memories – or perhaps forgiving natures – when it comes to natural disasters, accidents, environmental or man-made disasters. There are, however, other isolated events such as kidnapping, violence and murder, which relate to personal safety and security, that can be much more damaging, and from which a destination and its tourism businesses will take much longer to recover.

This is because crime against tourists generally attracts disproportionate media coverage in both the destination and, more significantly particularly if it involves violence, in the visitor's home country. Apart from the impact on the victim, this can have a much greater impact on the destination than is warranted by the actual level of risk to visitors. The combination of media interest, which results in disproportionate coverage, and the consequent effect on the destination's reputation, can significantly damage tourism for at least a season. If measures are not seen to be in place and vigorously enforced against such threats, the damage may continue for several years. Once gained, negative impressions are notoriously hard to change.

When it comes to personal safety, there is generally a considerable time lag between the popular memory of a country's tarnished image and its new reality, even after it has taken significant steps to clean up its act; and a time lag between the incident, trial and sentencing can, unfortunately, resurrect memories of the incident, with a renewed negative impact on the destination's image, as happened in 2010/11 following the murder of a British honeymoon couple in Antigua. This is because it re-emerges as headline news in the source market at each stage.

Equally, if a destination is seen to be a terrorism target, this will clearly reduce demand because of fears over personal safety. How long this drop in demand lasts will depend on the political situation and people's perception of the destination's security competence. If an attack is considered to be a one-off or unusual occurrence where there is no specific long-term underlying grievance against that country, people will perceive the risk as being relatively low and more in line with their perception of the likelihood of a recurring accident; but the threat of personal violence can feel much less random and more direct, with devastating consequences, as evidenced by the significant drop in travel to Mexico, particularly from its major market the USA, at the end of the first decade of the twenty-first century and the beginning of the next. As long as the authorities in any country appear inactive, incompetent or unable to address such threats, the fear of personal violence will continue to dampen demand significantly. Importantly, unsolved murders in exotic destinations will perpetuate this fear. 'Murder in paradise' guarantees media headlines and taps into holiday-makers' deep-seated fears.

People's perceptions are influenced significantly by media coverage of the crisis. Traditional broadcast and printed media, and word-of-mouth, are important sources of information and powerful influencers of people's perceptions of a destination in crisis. However, it remains to be seen whether digital and social media will overtake traditional media in terms of influencing people's attitudes about a destination in crisis, as opposed to being mere sources of immediate information.

What kind of crisis is it?

People respond differently to different types of crisis. A survey of UK consumers undertaken by TNS-RI for *Travel Weekly* in February 2011, following the overthrow of the government in Tunisia and conducted while Egypt was in turmoil, found that more than half (55%) of adults said they would be deterred by a terrorist attack from booking a destination, 44% by civil unrest or riots, 37% by a natural disaster and 28% by government collapse. However, almost nine out of 10 (87%) of the more than 1600 people surveyed had never changed, postponed or cancelled a holiday because of concerns about safety or security. One in 20 had cancelled a holiday, one in 25 had changed a destination and the same proportion had postponed a trip.

Presented with a list of destinations and asked whether they would consider visiting in the next three months, 62% said they would avoid Egypt and 33% would avoid Tunisia. However, this was at the height of the protests in Cairo's Tahrir Square. At the same time, the survey found only 8% would avoid Thailand, where there was serious social unrest in May 2010, and 7% would avoid Mexico, which experienced an outbreak of swine flu in April 2009 and whose violence had perhaps not received as much coverage in the UK press as in the USA. Short memories indeed.

One person's crisis is another person's disaster

Different nations tend to vary in their level of willingness to accept risk in a destination in crisis. Another study by TNS-RI (2011) conducted in the immediate aftermath of the riots in England in August 2011 showed the French to be least concerned, with 52% still intending to visit, but 13% less likely to visit the UK, 5% no longer planning to visit and 13% saying they would postpone their visit until later in the year. Germans were slightly more likely to be affected: while 43% of those who had been intending to visit were still determined to do so, 14% ruled out a visit, 8% were less likely to visit and 23% said they would postpone their visit until later in the year. Americans, however, were most affected: only 33% of those who had been planning to visit claimed to be unaffected; 26% were no longer considering a visit and 14% were less likely to visit than before.

Handling a crisis successfully

Every little thing counts in a crisis.
Jawaharlal Nehru, first Prime Minister of India.

Making a molehill out of a mountain

'Crisis, what crisis?' is a ubiquitous comedy line that usually precedes some cataclysmic event that the speaker is entirely unaware of, but which the audience can see coming only too clearly. However, that's the attitude that should underline the response to a crisis. That is not to belittle the magnitude of the event or suggest a state of denial about the extent of the crisis. On the contrary, it means being prepared. The more prepared you are, the better you will be able to cope with the crisis, remain 'calm under fire' and make clear, rational decisions. On the other hand, the less prepared you are, the greater the risk of a knee-jerk response, which, at best, might not help solve the situation and, at worst, might exacerbate it.

No one can be totally prepared for a crisis – otherwise it wouldn't be a crisis. It is an extreme and unusual situation which you are unlikely to have encountered before. Even though you've never found yourself in such circumstances before, there are certain prin-ciples that you can apply to manage your way out of a crisis. Quite simply, this means under-standing what might constitute a crisis for your business or destination, identifying the risk level of potential threats, planning for a crisis and training to handle it. In other words, crisis management should be a relatively normal business process. The more you understand this, the less you will be fazed by a crisis when it hits. The more you plan and train for a crisis, even though you've never experienced one before, the better you will be able to man-age it and the quicker you will recover. After all, this is what the emergency services – fire, ambulance, coastguard, mountain rescue and others – do. So why should a tourism business or destination be any different?

Planning avoids panic. It's about staying focused and managing unforeseen circum-stances with a cool head – 'Keep Calm and Carry On', as the World War II slogan urges, which has become fashionably retro and adorns t-shirts, posters and mugs in shops the length and breadth of the UK. Clichéd perhaps, but nevertheless an appropriate sentiment. Otherwise all will be chaos, rational response, which is essential to manage the way out of a crisis, will be absent and recovery will be delayed.

The UK's Tourism Industry Emergency Response Group (TIER) is an example of good crisis planning. TIER is a small group comprising key tourism industry organizations and government. The group develops plans for crisis scenarios as well as managing the tourism industry's response to a specific crisis. TIER is facilitated by VisitBritain and comprises around ten industry representatives (VisitBritain, 2011). It has ensured that crisis planning is embedded in the UK's tourism sector. Members of the TIER group include the Association of British Travel Agents, UKinbound, British Hospitality Association, the UK's national tourist boards, BA and the Association of Leading Visitor Attractions. Other groups are called on depending on the location and nature of the crisis.

Honesty is the best policy

I am a firm believer in the people. If given the truth, they can be depended upon to meet any national crisis. The great point is to bring them the real facts.
Abraham Lincoln, 16th President of the United States

There are two main aims in any crisis situation:

- to minimize the impact on your business or destination
- to return to normal as soon as possible.

Minimizing the impact of a crisis requires honest and up-to-date communication with your audience. They are not fools. Any attempt to mask the severity of the situation or lapse into marketing mode rather than factual communication will soon be rumbled – by word-of-mouth, by Twitter and by the media, who will be watching how you handle things like a hawk. The media can add significant fuel to the fire of a crisis and both exacerbate the immediate damage to your business and delay the prospect of recovery through sensationalist reporting. Even if this only lasts for a few days or weeks, the drama is what people will remember. Some destinations try to manage the media through limited communication, censorship or a wall of silence. In the era of digital communication and social media, this is sheer folly and commercial suicide. The media need to know what is happening, what you are doing about it and what the prognosis looks like from your expert point of view – the facts and the way forward. If they don't hear them from you, they'll find a much less reliable source.

For instance, during the 2001 foot and mouth disease outbreak in the UK, the priority was to tell the domestic market how much of the countryside was still open for visitors, in order to counter the perception, encouraged by media coverage of closed areas, that the entire countryside was out of bounds. Similarly, in September 2011, after the tragic murder of a British tourist and abduction of his wife on the north Kenyan coast near the Somali border, the Ministry of Tourism quickly published a statement on the Kenyan Tourism Board website explaining the facts and what was being done, with some reassurance about the level of security elsewhere in the country. Clearly, the credibility of these messages will depend on the listener and his/her preconceptions about the place; but the important common thread is that both start from a factual and explanatory point of view. They state the facts honestly, and then address the issue from the visitor's point of view, with information (NB not marketing hype), which is honest and aimed at reassuring potential visitors about the true situation. To do anything else would not only be disrespectful to the victims, it would also be counter-productive by not being credible.

Clear, honest and up-to-date communication requires a spokesperson to be identified, someone who has credibility and can speak on behalf of the tourism industry. He/she should ideally be available 24/7. It also means clear and regular internal communication within the organization (e.g. NTO, DMO, tourism business) so that everyone knows what is happening and no one is tempted to indulge in speculation, which can be damaging. The tourism industry and the destination need to speak with one voice – clearly and authoritatively, and with the backing of evidence. Rumours are not only powerful because they can damage business; but, because they are intriguing, they can also often run faster than the truth.

An example of rumour gaining unwarranted 'legs' lay in the delayed response by Namibian tourism authorities to initial press coverage in Germany regarding repossession of some white-owned farms by the Namibian government in the mid-2000s. These were few in number, undertaken according to Namibian law and were, allegedly, warranted by circumstances that legally triggered this action, such as mistreatment of long-term farm workers. Unsurprisingly, Namibia's former colonial 'godmother' and major European source market for visitors, Germany, took a keen interest in this. An immediate parallel was drawn with Zimbabwe in the German media, even though neither the scale nor the motive was remotely similar. Forests of negative press coverage resulted over the next few days throughout Germany, erroneously implying that Namibia was going down the route of Zimbabwe in pursuit of national policy of wholesale repossession of white-owned farms, thereby raising unwarranted fears amongst potential German visitors that they might no longer be welcome or even subject to personal threat. This was seen as a diplomatic matter to which the government should respond. While much of this coverage could not have been averted, a swift message from the Namibian tourism authorities to German tour operators and travel media to emphasize the fact that Namibia was still open for business and as welcoming as ever might have helped put this in perspective amongst an influential group of travel professionals who had the ear of potential visitors to Namibia, thereby minimizing the potential damage to Namibia's tourism from Germany.

After the maelstrom

A third aim should be to learn lessons from how you handled the crisis and incorporate them in your crisis planning and training so you will be even better prepared in future.

But there's a chance that the new 'normal' will be different from the old 'normal'. Chances are that the crisis will have changed the environment in which you operate and you will need to change some business practices and develop new skills to maintain your business after the crisis is over. For instance, after a terrorist attack, personal attacks on visitors, a bus crash, an epidemic or illness caused by poor hygiene standards, potential visitors will want some reassurance on safety before they commit to booking. This will affect the type of destination marketing messages conveyed and the way in which they are communicated. It might mean a switch by the NTO/DMO from advertising – which might seem too crass and therefore wasteful and inappropriate – to PR over the short term. More importantly, it will require businesses to remedy the problem and convince potential visitors that it is unlikely to happen again. This might require individual businesses (e.g. hotels, coach operators and others) to put new safety systems in place, introduce stricter hygiene standards, or employ security guards, and to communicate these measures in order to reassure potential visitors. It might even mean that national standards have to be improved through tighter government regulation and official inspection. As an example of matching tactics to the audience and the situation, at the height of the troubles in Northern Ireland during the early 1980s the Northern Ireland Tourist Board (NITB) pursued a policy of attracting journalists to come and see the place for themselves through a very astute PR strategy, rather than advertising, which would not have been credible and therefore would not have worked.

After a terrorist attack, potential visitors will want reassurance about safety. The way you handle this will depend on the underlying political situation – whether this represents an ongoing threat from a disaffected group or whether it's a random, one-off incident. The answer to this will determine the messages you convey and how you communicate them. This requires a subtle, but honest approach.

The end of a crisis is just the beginning

For many businesses the worst impact often takes place after the crisis is over. For instance, in England many rural businesses were left facing potential bankruptcy in 2001 after the foot and mouth disease epidemic was over, having lost so many months of business and with an unsure future. £550m was lost to the local economy in the northwest of England (Cabinet Office, 2011), where the outbreak was most prevalent. This loss was not confined to tourism; but tourism, along with agriculture, was the main economic driver on which many other businesses depended. Such difficult circumstances require concerted action to maintain fragile SMEs in business. Emergency support measures can be put in place to support local businesses; but this can only be done if there is empirical evidence of damage or likely damage across the sector or region. Clear evidence is needed to convince the authorities to provide short-term emergency assistance. Local businesses, ideally led by a regional DMO, should pull together an economic impact assessment of the crisis and present this to local or national government, who may be in a position to assist with temporary emergency support measures, such as business rate relief, tax holidays and regeneration grants.

Examples

Two UK examples indicate the importance of swift action, honest communication, and coordination between tourism authorities, the tourism industry and government.

Recovering tourism to the UK after 9/11

Challenge

Global tourism appeared to be heading for freefall following the terrorist attacks in the USA on September 11th, 2001. This threatened the livelihoods of thousands in the UK and the destruction of many businesses in tourism and other sectors reliant on inbound tourism. Cooperation was required on a scale as never before by the UK inbound tourism industry.

Solution

- The solution was not so much about providing reassurance, but about stimulating people to start travelling again – and particularly to the UK – in the aftermath of an event to which the French newspaper *Le Monde* had responded in an expression of solidarity by saying 'Nous sommes tous Americains' (we are all Americans).

- UK tourism officials and businesses reacted swiftly to address the need for recovery with a 'Million Visitor Campaign' led by the former British Tourist Authority (BTA – now VisitBritain).

- A team of 12 people was established to recover a million visitors to the UK from seven key markets (USA, Canada, Germany, France, Holland, Belgium and Ireland).

- 31 partners were recruited to co-fund and work together on the recovery campaign along with BTA (including BA; P & O Ferries; BAA; Avis; BMI; Hilton, Intercontinental, Holiday Inn, Marriott, Accor, Best Western, De Vere, Millenium Copthorne, Travel Inn, Queens Moat House, Radisson Edwardian, Red Carnation, Thistle and Jarvis Hotels; the Savoy Group; British Hospitality Association; Passenger Shipping Association; Seafrance; DFDS Seaways; American Express; National Express; English Tourism Council; VisitScotland; Wales Tourist Board; Heart of England Tourist Board; and the London Tourist Board and Convention Bureau).

- A highly innovative marketing campaign was swiftly developed under the banner 'Only in Britain, Only in 2002'.

- A mix of TV advertising, PR, direct marketing and e-marketing highlighted the unique features of the UK in 2002 in seven countries.

- While the major funders were the 31 multinational partner companies along with the UK government via BTA, the importance of small businesses to the UK's tourism landscape was also recognized. A website was developed to give the UK's SMEs immediate access to international markets. Over 3000 holiday offers were distributed through this site in the campaign's first three months.

- A TV advertisement aired in the USA included a personal invitation from the then Prime Minister, Tony Blair, to visit the UK.

- Throughout the campaign period, BTA maintained close contact not only with the tourism industry, it also worked closely with government through the high-level COBRA (Cabinet Office Briefing Room A), a meeting of cross-government departments responsible for responding to national emergencies.

Result

The Million Visitor Campaign was a textbook example of the government, the tourist boards and the private sector working in partnership towards a common goal.... The campaign generated an additional 1.1 million visitors and additional revenue to Britain of £518m which was an extremely good investment for Britain plc.

(Tourism Alliance, 2004)

Tourism to the UK from the USA recovered at a rate 16% faster than to the rest of Europe in the year following the 9/11 attacks (2002). The UK was seen by its tourism industry and competitors to be both astute and innovative in its attempts to recover tourism, one of the country's most vital industries.

It was important to launch a campaign in designated target markets as quickly as possible to maximize the chance of recovering tourism in the imminent tourism season, which was already about to enter the main booking period. A critical factor in the success of this campaign, in such an internationally widespread organization as BTA with offices in all target countries and with such a wide range of partners, was the need to have a central point of authority (i.e. London – BTA head office). An 'access all areas' authority was delegated to the core team to negotiate with partners and make decisions, rather than include all BTA country managers in the decision-making process, which might have delayed implementation and risked commercial partners withdrawing in frustration if the pace had slackened. Achieving consensus among 31 senior partners, while maintaining the balance between fast central decision-making and keeping overseas BTA offices informed and involved, required continual communication, effective leadership and diplomatic skills.

The 'Million Visitor Campaign' has since been used by other destinations and academics as a model of good practice for tourism destinations in crisis.

Minimizing the impact of foot and mouth disease on English domestic tourism

Challenge

An outbreak of foot and mouth disease had effectively closed down large parts of rural Britain to visitors in 2001. However, media messages exaggerated the extent of the closures. Consequently, people were unsure as to what was open and where they could go. In fact, the UK was far more open than the impression gained from the media. Tourism businesses were beginning to suffer badly. It was therefore important to reduce this confusion and let people know how much of the countryside was open, so that they would start travelling again within the country. Domestic tourism in England – which included day visits, short breaks and longer holidays – was particularly badly affected.

Solution

- The former English Tourism Council established a team to manage the English tourism industry's response to the impact of foot and mouth disease on the tourism industry.

- This team maintained close contact with the tourism industry, but it also worked closely with government through the high-level COBRA meeting.

- A first step and core element of the campaign – in the pre-Internet days of 2001 – was to establish a dedicated telephone 'hotline', for people to obtain credible, up-to-the minute information on the situation and, in particular, on which areas were open and closed.

- A domestic marketing campaign was swiftly developed with partners to reassure people that England remained largely open and to encourage people to travel again within England. The information 'hotline' was included in all marketing activities, so that people could obtain the most up-to-date information. (Today, that role is much more easily and ubiquitously undertaken by websites and social media, such as Facebook and Twitter.)

Result

Domestic tourism in England gradually recovered, albeit at different rates in different areas. Clear up-to-date information about the situation was included with tourism marketing messages. This helped counter misleading messages in the media about the amount of countryside that was closed to visitors. It also helped to build public trust in the marketing messages, which stimulated travel – and particularly day trips – that people might not otherwise have taken as a result of misinformation and sensational media stories.

Summary

In summary, minimizing the immediate impact and maximizing the chances of returning to normal as soon as possible after a crisis requires: a clear understanding of the potential threats; preparation of a crisis plan; allocation of responsibility for key tasks; training staff and involving appropriate stakeholders; developing systems for managing unforeseen events; establishing a strong on-going relationship between the NTO/DMO, the tourism industry and government; communicating clearly, honestly and frequently; and appointing a spokesperson who is constantly available, in order to ensure that the media are up-to-date with every critical step or change in circumstances and have confidence in the organization's pronouncements so that they can report the facts accurately and thereby minimize harmful speculation.

After a crisis, it is important to identify the lessons learnt during the crisis and to ensure they are used to update your crisis plan. Good planning is the key to crisis response. Planning brings crisis management as close as possible to a normal business process. Embedding crisis planning in the organization is the best preparation for handling any crisis. This is summarized as ten critical steps in managing a crisis.

C   Clarify the potential threats facing your business or destination.

R   Review your crisis plan and procedures.

I   Involve your staff and make sure key people are properly trained.   **Pre-crisis**

S   Systems need to be developed for when a crisis hits (cf VisitBritain TIER group).

I   Identify your spokesperson and allocate responsibility for communicating the facts as they emerge. Identify your key stakeholder group, who need to be kept in the loop.

S   Speak with one voice, in order to minimize confusion, speculation and rumour.   **During crisis**

P   Plain-speaking – clear and honest communication is critical for the sake of credibility.

L   Live news is essential – it's a 24-hour news world. Your spokesperson needs to be available 24/7 during the height of the crisis.

A   Analyse what you've learnt from the crisis and incorporate it in your crisis plan.

N   No complacency – review and revise your crisis plan on a regular basis, so that it is up-to-date and you and your staff are all well-prepared for the next crisis, because you won't have the   **Post crisis** luxury of adhering to Henry Kissinger's dismissive declaration that 'There cannot be a crisis next week. My schedule is already full'.

Questions and discussion points

1. The case advocates planning and training for a crisis. What activities could be introduced to train staff to deal with a crisis? What are the benefits of using practice drills?

2. You are the manager of a small (10 bedroom) independent hotel based on the outskirts of a major city. How would you justify to the owner the monetary and time cost of developing a crisis management plan?

3. Why is it important to manage the media in the event of a crisis? What factors may make this difficult? Do the emerging social media tools help or hinder in times of crisis?

Bibliography

Cabinet Office (2011) *National Recovery Guidance – Economic Issues – Economy and business recovery*, available online at: http://www.cabinetoffice.gov.uk/content/national-recovery-guidance-economic-issues-economy-and-business-recovery (accessed November 2011).

Lynch, M. (2004) *Weathering the Storm – A Crisis Management Guide for Tourism Businesses*, Leicester, Matador.

OAG (2011) *World Crisis Analysis White Paper*, OAG Market Intelligence, available online at: http://www.platma.org/index.php/mod.publicaciones/mem.descargar/fichero.publicaciones_2011-World-Crisis-Analysis_776f6d38%232E%23pdf/chk.b75275f27bda47343b6a227577634552 (accessed November 2011).

TNS-RI (2011) *Will the Recent UK Riots Damage Foreign Tourism?*, available online at: http://www.tns-ri.co.uk/_assets/files/Riots_whitepaper.pdf (accessed November 2011).

Tourism Alliance (2004) Annual Report, available online at: http://www.tourismalliance.com/downloads/Annual%20Report.pdf (accessed November 2011).

VisitBritain (2011) *Industry Groups and Bodies*, available online at: http://www.visitbritain.org/britaintourismindustry/industrygroupsandbodies/index.aspx (accessed November 2011).

Dark tourism – the Holocaust Exhibition at the Imperial War Museum, London

Prepared by Claire Humphreys with the help of Emily Fuggle, Research Officer (Holocaust and Genocide History), Imperial War Museum, London

This case study explores the realm of dark tourism. This controversial form of tourism is discussed in Chapter 10 and here we explore some of the issues and challenges in the development and operation of a dark tourism attraction.

The case looks at the introduction of an exhibition related to the Holocaust, presented as part of the displays at the Imperial War Museum (IWM) in London. The case considers the challenges of developing an exhibition which focuses on a dark part of world history and highlights some of the issues encountered.

The concept of dark tourism

Attractions which have associations with death and the macabre are not new – visits to battlefield sites, catacombs and prisons have taken place for centuries. However, the past decade has seen the publication of academic research which explores this field in more critical depth. Examining the motivations for visiting, and the challenges of operating, dark tourism attractions provides a basis for debate of the moral and ethical dilemmas surrounding the use of sites of death or disaster as attractions for tourism. The term dark tourism provided the title of a seminal text on the subject by Lennon and Foley (2000) which encouraged discussion of the concept more widely in the press, as well as in academia.

One outcome of these discussions has been recognition that nuances fragment the dark tourism sector. Phillip Stone, Executive Director of the Institute for Dark Tourism Research, based at the University of Lancashire, proposed a dark tourism spectrum (2006). Drawing on earlier work by Miles (2002), he separated sites of death and suffering from those which are associated with death but where no loss of life was actually experienced. At the darkest end of the spectrum, he noted greater focus on an educational orientation, where a perceived authentic experience was achieved through a history-centric approach focused on conservation and commemoration. Conversely, the lightest attractions are oriented towards entertainment, commercially oriented and perhaps perceived as less authentic. Stone also distinguished the darkest attractions as having location authenticity, as well as the likelihood that the tragic events occurred more recently in time.

Such characteristics can thus separate sites such as the concentration camps of Europe from the museums around the globe dedicated to the Holocaust, and from the guided tours of film locations used in the Hollywood blockbuster *Schindler's List*. Thus we can infer that a museum exhibition, such as that which forms the basis of this case study, would fall at the mid-point of the dark tourism spectrum, where location authenticity is not present but where an education orientation and history-centric perspective is evident.

Background to the exhibition

The Holocaust Exhibition at the IWM was opened by the Queen in 2000, having taken four years to plan. The combined efforts of the IWM's project team of curators, researchers and historians, the exhibition designers (Steven Greenberg and Bob Baxter), film-makers and other specialists forming the advisory panel created an exhibition which has seen 3 million visitors pass though its doors in the decade since it first opened.

The project was funded through a £12.6 million heritage lottery fund grant and through the generous gifts of other donors. Press coverage of its opening was extensive – and generally encouraging – and, with more than 160 000 visitors in the first six months of opening in the UK (IWM, 2011), this exhibition proved immediately that it is a positive addition to the tourism attractions of London. When it first opened, there were few competitors dealing with this subject area and the exhibition was the only one in the UK and the biggest in Europe. Since then, other museums have developed their own provision, but visitors to the Holocaust Exhibition at the IWM remain high (see Figure 1).

Debates surrounding the development of a public display based on this topic were extensive. Concern was expressed that it would be difficult to do justice to such a vast and emotive subject while, at the same time, maintaining the interest of the visitor. These challenges were highlighted at the outset, and, throughout the design phase, consideration was given to balancing the expectations of the audience with the museum's demands to accurately recount facts and to conserve and preserve historical artifacts.

The development of the exhibition involved three key stages:

1. *Concept design.* This provided historical outlines forming the basis of a route through the exhibition space, and took approximately six months to plan.

2. *Scheme design.* The artifacts available were identified and integrated, along with film resources, into the overall design. This stage lasted four months.

3. *Detailed design.* One year was spent developing the fine detail for each section of the exhibition.

Once the detailed design was finished, the construction of the exhibition took only a matter of weeks. Space was allocated as part of a wider regeneration project of the museum site, consisting of 1200 square metres over two floors (see Figure 2). The principle behind the design was that the exhibition should be structured as a chronological narrative, with

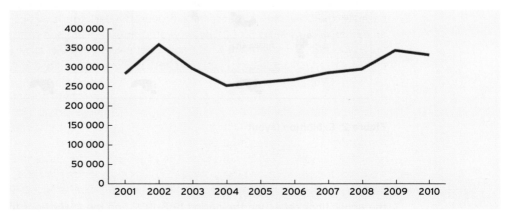

Figure 1 Annual visitor numbers to the Holocaust Exhibition
Source: Imperial War Museum – correspondence with author

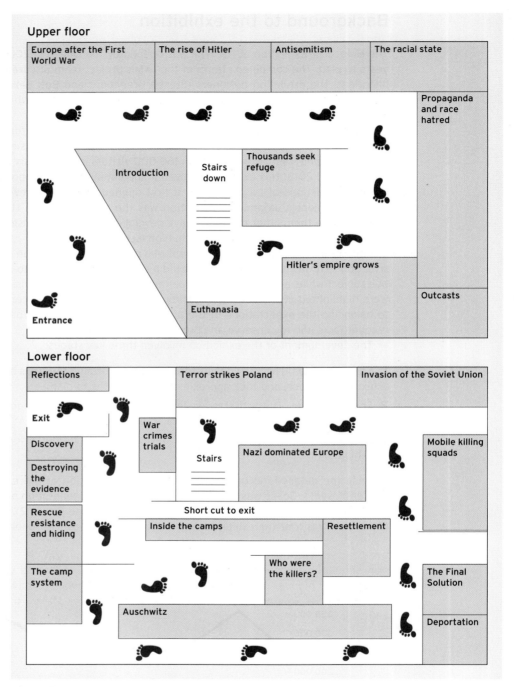

Figure 2 Exhibition layout

the upper floor reflecting the period 1918–1939 and the lower floor focusing on the period during the war (and the immediate aftermath of liberation). This physical space, set across two floors, allowed the designers the opportunity to play with ideas representing a literal descent into war.

Challenges

The challenges of designing and developing the Holocaust Exhibition really fell into two areas; one which focused on the ethical issues of dealing with such a sensitive project and how it might be portrayed, the second considering the logistical challenges of constructing displays which catered for the needs of the many different visitors. Clearly balancing these was vital.

In terms of the sensitivities associated with such a demanding history, the designers identified early in the process that creating an exhibition which encouraged visitors to reflect on the events – possibly even changing views and opinions on the causes, responses and impacts – could be achieved through a design which was both stimulating and thought-provoking. The advisory panel was critically important, helping the development team navigate many complex concerns relating to the exhibition content. This included guidance on interpretation, the historiographical debates about the events covered in the exhibition, the accuracy of the content and, crucially, ethical and sensitivity concerns regarding what should be displayed.

Logistically, there were obvious challenges in:

1. Finding materials and artifacts for the displays.

2. Recounting an accurate history of the events.

3. Designing a coherent series of displays which would engage and stimulate visitors.

The exhibition also had to fit within the wider context of the existing museum displays; in designing the Holocaust Exhibition, the designers recognized the need to manage the allocated space so that an ambience for reflection could be achieved, impervious to the visitors of other displays already in place at the museum.

Gathering artifacts for display highlighted another challenge, as the museum held few items relevant to the topic and thus required significant efforts, and funding, to develop the collection. A number of curators were each tasked with different aspects of the exhibition and set out to source and obtain relevant material to fill the exhibition.

One further complication lay in the decision to include the impact and response from a UK perspective. This recognized that parts of the exhibition may comment critically on the actions of the UK government, and response to this factor might have wider implications for the museum. The focus on the UK aspect was ultimately achieved through the use of four exhibition cases, located at different time stages of the exhibition, each revealing how the events of the time were portrayed, and responded to, in the UK.

It should be evident that creating an exhibition which informed visitors in a sensitive yet engaging manner of the dark, often distressing and hugely complicated issue that was the Holocaust required extensive planning of both the content to be included and its interpretation.

The content of the exhibition

The story of the Holocaust is complicated, and the many facets and beliefs which surround this event in history mean that portraying it is complex. Very early in the development phase of the project it was decided that a deliberately restrained approach would be employed, portraying the facts as a narrative which would drive the exhibition design, but avoiding sensationalizing the story or the events. The content of the exhibition would therefore rely on

● contextualized artifacts

● photographs

● archive film

● survivor testimony.

Figure 3 The model of Auschwitz–Birkenau
© Imperial War Museums (IWM 2008 002 007)

Key to gathering the artifacts was the decision that only items strictly 'of the time' would be shown in the exhibition (Bardgett, 2000). This attention to the authentic was vital, and ensuring it often added to the challenge. The sole exception to this principle was the incorporation of a large model of Auschwitz–Birkenau representing the camp as it was in May 1944, based on photographs, discovered in 1945, taken by a professional German SS photographer (see Figure 3). The model depicts the arrival by train of a convoy of deportees. The decision to reproduce this exhibit lay in the difficulty faced in representing the 'Final Solution' (Fuggle, 2011), and this provides visitors with a perspective of the huge numbers of people transported to Birkenau, as well as symbolizing the vast scale of the camp and its operations.

Gathering artifacts was a time-consuming process requiring detailed negotiations with other museums and individuals who held historical objects suitable for display. For example, the display of shoes taken from those killed in the concentration camps was provided by the Majdanek camp in Poland. Agreement by the IWM to repair and conserve the condition of the shoes ensures that this loan benefits both parties. Alongside loans and the purchases of artifacts, the IWM received several donations of display materials. The largest single donation was offered by Gianfranco Moscati, an Italian who escaped war-time persecution by fleeing to Switzerland. In accepting his collection of memorabilia, the IWM agreed to digitize this work (IWM, 2011) and provide access to the resources so that a wider audience could have access to this rich historic material – currently more than 1200 items from this collection can be viewed on the IWM website.

Within the exhibition, some areas have few historic objects to view. One reason is that few relevant artifacts exist today, perhaps due to the nature of the tragedy and the lack of survivors able to provide such materials. A further issue facing the curators of the exhibition is that of loaned artifacts. Over the decade since opening, some exhibits reached the end of their loan spell and had to be returned. Where possible, the museum sought to receive these items as gifts. Where this has not been possible, alternative resources have been included in the exhibition. This has meant that subtle shifts in content have occurred over time. Content has also changed as the museum has purchased or been gifted additional relevant artifacts.

The historical narratives from survivors provide many hours of footage and cover many different aspects of living through the Holocaust. Gathering video testimony was managed through a specialist independent film company, October Films, who, prior to their work on the exhibition, had been working on factual documentaries. October Films recorded and edited the testimony to provide short excerpts designed to add a human perspective to the event. In addition to the video testimony, the exhibition also uses audio testimony. The museum already held a large sound archive and searches of this provided many examples of survivor testimony in English – a requirement of much of the media used in the exhibition. The variety of experiences provided in the survivor narratives helps to reveal the complexity of the issues surrounding the events of the Holocaust.

The exhibition as an educational tool

Many school groups use the exhibition as a key educational resource – in 2009, more than 20 000 children visited (and more than 200 000 have visited since the exhibition opened) (IWM, 2011). From the beginning of the design process, the needs of such groups were considered, influencing the pre- and post-visit activities provided, the management of groups around the displays and the resources and teaching materials developed to enhance understanding of this complex event.

To ensure success, one of the many roles of the advisory panel was to guide the designers so that the requirements of school curricula could be embedded into the provision. This included ensuring that school sessions provided time for reflection and discussion of the materials viewed (Salmons, 2001). Prior to entering the exhibition area, students are shown a short video explaining the way of life prior to the outbreak of World War II, to aid contextual understanding. To further enhance the student experience, audio guides are provided – these assist by identifying areas of focus to aid reflection. To date, five different audio tours are provided by the museum. Three are based on level of education – year 9 (aged 14), GCSE and A-level – and two are for visually impaired visitors (one designed for GCSE students). For the visually impaired visitors, the exhibition includes a number of display cases which contain items which can be handled, the visitor being provided with a key to open the case. The exhibits chosen for such cases must be robust enough to withstand such attention as well as being meaningful to the visually impaired. Some, but not all, are replicas and selecting suitable items is clearly an on-going challenge.

The museum also hosts a seminar series for university students, primarily for postgraduate and PhD students studying the Holocaust or related themes.

Outside of school groups, there is an inherent expectation that visitors will develop their knowledge and understanding of the Holocaust. However, there remains a question as to whether the 'restrained historical' fact-based approach has meant that the visitor does not give sufficient consideration to the dilemmas facing many who lived through this period. There is a need to question whether judgements are made by the visitor without reflection on the diverse influences which led to the chain of events. Positively for the IWM, feedback suggests that some visitors, at least, do come to appreciate some of these complex issues.

Interpretation issues

Interpretative text is provided throughout the exhibition, with the expectation that no visitor is likely to engage with all the material provided, but that the detailed explanations can meet the needs and interests of different visitors. To date, no study relating to the dwell-time of visitors has been undertaken, but the museum recommends visitors should consider spending at least 90–120 minutes inside the exhibition.

It was recognized in the design phase that photographs and film have the capacity to overpower the story, overly dramatizing a situation or suggesting a greater significance than they actually represent. Therefore these aspects were developed with care, ensuring they did not sensationalize the story. Many hours of film were reviewed and edited to provide suitable clips. Logistically these could not be overly long as this had the potential to cause a bottleneck of visitors. Therefore, the layout of the exhibition required space for visitors to stand or sit as they were watching these clips, while still allowing others to circulate through the exhibition. The maximum clip time is seven minutes.

A second issue linked to the use of film is the need to manage the sound pollution this can cause to other areas of the exhibition; consequently, the design team sought out auditory systems specifically designed to reduce sound spillage into other sections of the exhibition.

Lighting has also proved an important aspect of the design. Much of the exhibition is dimly lit. This was determined because it is seen to be 'respectful' of the tragic events. It also serves to protect some of the exhibits, which are fragile and would be damaged under higher levels of lighting. The conservation role of the museum remains ever present in the minds of the curators, and one outcome of this has been the removal of some artifacts, being replaced by more durable alternatives, or, in the case of letters and photographs, with a facsimile of the original. This has meant that not every artifact could be called 'genuine', but, in such cases, the museum is either the owner of the original, or has identified its owner. While the authenticity of such material is subject to debate, it is important to highlight that facsimiles are copies of documents from originals in existence, not a theatrical creation designed only to embellish a story (Bardgett, 2000).

With a chronological approach structuring the exhibition, the use of survivor stories provided a vital dimension, acting as a human guide to events as they took place. The stories as they are recounted by survivors allow visitors to learn more about the experience of living through these troubled times – feedback from visitors has highlighted positively the educational but emotive aspect of these tales.

The material displayed is often evocative and can be distressing. From the outset, the museum established a recommended minimum age limit of 14 years, and this provided greater freedom in the choices made regarding materials incorporated. It is possible for parents to take children under this age into the exhibition, but the museum provides an advisory desk explaining the content included, to ensure parents make an informed choice.

Conclusions

Dealing with the past, especially a dark and tragic one, can be difficult. The IWM was clearly well-placed to take on the subject of the Holocaust. Although the museum held limited artifacts at the outset, one advantage has been the expertise within its existing departments, which ensured that many aspects were already in place, both in terms of scientific preservation and conservation and with respect to the tourist elements of visitor care and management, marketing, promotion and ticketing. Ensuring the protection of historical artifacts and the accurate representation of these has always been high on the agenda for the museum. Loans and donations were often confidently made, knowing that the IWM would ensure their protection as well as providing wider public access.

The existence of historic artifacts may be limited for some dark tourism attractions, since the very nature of the tragic events may have made it impossible for materials to be retained and protected over the years. The scarcity of such exhibits also means that conservation is ever more vital, making the display of such materials for a public audience impossible. Finally, the cost of obtaining such rarities may be beyond the budgets of some institutions. For the IWM, while funding remains a constant issue, their reputation generally and the positive response to the Holocaust Exhibition has encouraged donors to provide continued support.

Survivor testimony has proved to add significantly to the experience of the visitor, feedback highlighting its value to the experience. As a consequence, this has led to the introduction of similar approaches in other areas of the IWM. For tourism attractions at the darker end of the spectrum, it is perhaps beneficial to locate the narrative of the tragedy within a human perspective, to enhance visitor engagement in difficult subject matter.

Dealing with different audiences adds to the management issues; serving educational audiences, parents with children, visitors with disabilities and the general public requires that the design of the exhibition meets many different needs. Perhaps the success of this exhibition has been in recognizing these differing demands from the outset.

Finally, it is useful to say that both public awareness and academic scholarship of the Holocaust have moved on significantly over the past decade. As a consequence, minor adaptations to the exhibition have occurred. Remaining relevant to its audience is important for any tourist attraction, and this dark tourism exhibition is no different, successfully maintaining its appeal to large volumes of visitors.

Questions and discussion points

1. What are the sensitivities that may need to be considered when designing an exhibition which draws on the Holocaust as a subject?

2. How might this exhibition have differed if it had been a stand-alone attraction rather than part of an existing, internationally renowned museum?

3. Why might the educational element be so important for the Holocaust Exhibition?

Bibliography

Bardgett, S. (2000) Exhibiting Hatred, *History Today*, **50** (6), 18–20.

Fuggle, E. (2011) IWM Research Officer (Holocaust and Genocide History), personal interview with author.

IWM (2011) *The Holocaust Exhibition – Ten years on*, London, Imperial War Museum.

Lennon, J. J. and Foley, M. (2000) *Dark Tourism: the Attraction of Death and Disaster*, London, Cassell.

Miles, W. F. S. (2002) Auschwitz: Museum Interpretation and Darker Tourism, *Annals of Tourism Research*, **29** (4), 1175–1178.

Salmons, P. (2001) *Moral dilemmas: history-teaching and the Holocaust*, downloaded from http://london.iwm.org.uk/server/show/nav.1025 (accessed August 2011).

Stone, P. R. (2006) A dark tourism spectrum: towards a typology of death and macabre related tourist sites, attractions and exhibitions, *Tourism*, **54** (2), 145–160.

Understanding the use of social media for tourism organizations

Prepared by Claire Humphreys

Over the past decade, a range of technologies has developed for personal computers, smartphones and, more recently, for tablet computers such as the iPad, which lets the individual easily upload their views and comments onto the Internet. 'Apps' – small software programmes – have further eased this process, allowing blogs, images and other content to be conveniently shared.

This case study discusses how key social media tools can have an impact on the ways customers engage with the tourism industry and highlights the importance of having a presence in this realm. As you will appreciate, developments in this ever-growing sector are fast-paced so this case merely provides a brief snapshot to highlight the use of social media.

What are social media?

Lon Safko (2010) launched his discussion of the term by recognizing that it refers to the media we use in order to be sociable. While this may well be true, it adds little to our appreciation of what social media really is. Understanding the concept must come with an insight into the development of Web 2.0 – brought about both by a shift in technology and by a shift in the approach employed by developers – which meant that content was no longer driven by the website owners but by developing platforms which allowed content to be conveniently added and modified by a community of users. This user-generated content (UGC) 'can be seen as the sum of all ways in which people make use of Social Media' (Kaplan and Haenlein, 2010, 61). If we look to Wikipedia – itself a construction of UGC – we can see considerable discussion surrounding its definition of the term. This debate concluded that 'Social media take on many different forms, including Internet forums, weblogs, social blogs, microblogging, wikis, podcasts, photographs or pictures, video, rating and social bookmarking' (Wikipedia, 2011). These forms attract their own communities and modes of behaviour, and offer different advantages for tourism organizations.

New platforms are emerging constantly so, at this point, it is possible only to consider some of the popular types of social media tools used to engage with the tourism industry. We shall separate these into five groups:

1. blogging and microblogging (using platforms such as Wordpress, Typepad, Twitter)
2. content sharing (sites include YouTube, Flickr, Slideshare)
3. social networks (such as Facebook, Myspace, Bebo)
4. professional networks (these include LinkedIn, Xing, Ecademy)
5. others (including democratic voting for content on sites such as Digg and virtual game worlds, such as Second Life).

Companies may find that all of these offer opportunities for social interaction with their communities (who may be customers, stakeholders, fans and others), but, in this case, we will concentrate on the use of the first three of these forms – particularly focusing on Twitter,

Figure 1 The standard 'Like' image for Facebook

YouTube and Facebook. These three have large communities and are frequently used to comment on and engage with the tourism industry.

Why use social media?

Such platforms develop dialogues between users. As content is added, so conversations can surround this – with views and opinions offered which are related not just to the original content but also to additional opinions given by others in the community. For companies, these conversations can provide significant insight into the opinions of community members. A discussion about a newly launched product, the places to visit at a destination or a particular event can help the business appreciate the consumer (or potential consumer) view. It can reveal problems experienced by customers or the misinterpretation of information provided, creating an opportunity for these issues to be resolved.

Social media platforms also provide an opportunity for one-to-one dialogue with a customer, in an environment which feels less as if the customer is being 'marketed to'. Such conversations can create a closer relationship between company and stakeholder, with the potential to create an advocate for the company – 'liking' a company on Facebook (see Figure 1) is now an easy option as websites embed direct links from their home page. The development of a dialogue does, however, take time.

A comprehensive presence across many platforms will help communities find the company, understand more about its brand values and increase opportunities for interaction. It is important that any presence has a value or purpose. For example, it may be that a Facebook page provides a link to more information or exclusive offers while Twitter comments may provide latest news or quick responses to customer comments about service quality. Content posted on YouTube may include copies of a TV advertising campaign or coverage of an event or news story. Important to remember is the reality that UGC means that communities also post comments, videos and images, so negative experiences and problems also receive coverage. Responding to these is part of the dialogue; they cannot just be ignored. Such content should be seen as useful customer feedback, designed to improve business operations. This provides another clear justification for having a presence on these platforms – an opportunity to monitor comments and content and offer informed responses to the community.

Use of social media by tourism organizations

The tourism industry consists of many SMEs, often with limited financial and time resources. However, developing a social media presence can enhance customer relationships and improve awareness of the organization. It can also increase sales opportunities. The cost may be minimal (many accounts on these key platforms are free), but time investments to develop relevant content and maintain dialogues may be significant.

As technology develops, so new opportunities to enhance customer convenience are born. For example, Skyscanner, the flight comparison site, launched an innovative offering on a dedicated Facebook page (**www.facebook.com/skyscannerflightsearch**) (see Figure 2).

Figure 2 Skyscanner for Facebook

This provides the first 'free-text' search tool – a visitor could post on their wall a flight request as a simple sentence, for instance 'New York to Sydney 6 March to 25 April' and a reply would provide a quote offering the cheapest direct and indirect options, along with a link to the flight options. This reveals the potential for Facebook pages to be about more than just collecting friends and being liked.

External events may create a demand for information and an interest in your product or destination. The wedding of Prince William to Catherine Middleton in April 2011 stimulated a significant increase in the Internet profile of VisitBritain, with its Twitter feed entering the top 1% of influential users while retweeting meant that discussions and articles started by VisitBritain reached more than 2 million people. Furthermore, its 'Love UK' Facebook page became the 6th 'most explosive' page, gaining 127 000 new fans, with content viewed by over 1.3 million people (VisitBritain, 2011). The royal wedding also received coverage on YouTube, which offered a live video stream on the official 'Royal Channel'; to date, the edited video has been viewed over 900 000 times.

The power of 'sharing' can be easily seen when we consider the speed that links can be spread across media sites. A rather humorous passenger complaint letter, emailed to Richard Branson following a poor experience on a Virgin Airways flight, was posted on the Telegraph travel pages in 2009, and has since received more than 60 000 recommendations to view it placed on Facebook and 1600 tweet links created directly from this site. Almost three years later this story is still being retweeted. Answering, Virgin provide a brief statement of their response to the email.

One final example to consider is that of Tourism Australia, which launched a social media campaign entitled 'There's nothing like Australia' (see Figure 3). This used crowdsourcing to gather verbal and visual content from residents of Australia, which in turn was used to provide visitors to the site with a reason to visit the country. With more than 28 000 images

Figure 3 'There's nothing like Australia' smartphone app

uploaded, each with a brief explanation beginning 'There is nothing like . . .', the UGC formed the bulk of the materials on these webpages. This content was also conveniently accessible via a free smartphone app, which also offered links directly to the tourist board website to assist with the travel booking process. This campaign has not been without issues, however, as the tourist board failed to register all variations of the URL – by holding only the .com address and not the .net domain name, this soon allowed a spoof site to be set up.

It is clear that a variety of problematic issues can easily arise if social media interaction is not managed effectively. However, choosing not to have a presence does not mean that communities will ignore a company entirely, merely that the organization is unable to participate in such discussions and misses the opportunity for constructive dialogue.

Interestingly, more and more tourism industry groups are offering seminars and training in this topic area. The 2011 World Travel Market offered more than a dozen sessions linked to social media during its three-day event in London. In the preceding month, Scottish Enterprise promoted a 'Social Media for Tourism' event in Edinburgh and the Tourism Society, a UK-based professional body, offered a 'Tourism and Social Media' evening event in London.

Future issues

Choosing to have a social media presence is really no longer an option but a necessity for many tourism businesses; therefore, ensuring efforts are beneficial is perhaps key to justifying the investment of time. Responses to comments must be appropriate and timely.

Developing discussions and two-way communication will help to create positive relationships. Providing opportunities for users to generate content – for example, suggesting a hashtag (a short term preceded by a # sign) for Twitter users to follow at an event will encourage attendees to tweet as well as allowing them to conveniently follow the tweets of others present. With 80% of Twitter posts being sent from mobile devices, it is useful to realize that comments are often 'in the moment' and can help disseminate the experience to others. An alternative way to encourage UGC is to provide visual stimulus which can encourage photos or videos to be taken and uploaded to sharing websites.

One final aspect to consider is the smartphone apps which further encourage UGC. The Tripadviser app has employed the GPS technology embedded in the smartphone to provide the user with local travel resources, as well as allowing new reviews to be posted. This convenience means that customers post their views immediately, while the issue or experience is fresh in their mind.

Summary

Social media have provided some important opportunities, allowing the tourism industry opportunity to develop closer links with their customer base – making use of these tools is expected (rather than optional) when dealing with some markets, particularly the younger Y-generation. It is therefore vital to have a presence across a wide variety of social media platforms, monitoring and, importantly, responding to the positive and negative comments posted. It is also important to offer content, be it video, images or blogs, which add value to the community.

Questions and discussion points

1. You are the manager of a small tourist attraction in rural England. What might be the effect on your business if you fail to monitor the comments from your visitors placed on Facebook?

2. How might you encourage your customers to provide positive content about your organization? Are there ethical concerns about encouraging such activities?

3. What are the difficulties in developing a successful social media presence? How might these be overcome?

Bibliography

Kaplan, A. M. and Haenlein, M. (2010) Users of the world, unite! The challenges and opportunities of Social Media, *Business Horizons*, **53** (1), 59-68.

Safko, L. (2010) *The Social Media Bible: Tactics, Tools, and Strategies for Business Success*, Hoboken, NJ, Wiley.

VisitBritain (2011) *VisitBritain Royal Wedding activity*, available online at: http://www.visitbritain.org/mediaroom/pressreleases/vbrwwedding.aspx (accessed November 2011).

Wikipedia (2011) *Social Media*, available online at: http://en.wikipedia.org/wiki/Social_media (accessed November 2011).

The European Wind Energy Association Annual Event

Prepared by Rob Davidson

There are many events hosted to bring together individuals and company representatives with a common interest or agenda. Often these are members of an association. Chapter 11 has contrasted associations with corporate conferences, and this case focuses directly on an association conference and the procedure employed to select the location for its annual event.

European Wind Energy Association (EWEA)

The European Wind Energy Association (EWEA) is the voice of the wind energy industry, actively promoting the utilization of wind power in Europe and worldwide. It has over 600 members from nearly 60 countries, including manufacturers of wind turbines, component suppliers, research institutes, national wind and renewable energy associations, developers, contractors, electricity providers and consultants. Their combined strength makes the EWEA the world's largest and most powerful wind energy network.

Objectives of the EWEA Annual Event

Every year, generally between the end of February and the beginning of April, the EWEA runs its Annual Event – a conference at which major issues of importance to European and global wind energy markets are discussed, from resource assessment and innovative turbine design to market and policy developments. An exhibition is run in parallel with the conference.

The EWEA Annual Event positions itself as being the premier wind energy event in terms of quality of services, networking and high-level attendance. The overall objectives of EWEA Annual Events are closely aligned with the association's key strategy to promote the use of wind energy and its benefits, and to improve and disseminate knowledge of this sector. In addition, the Annual Events constitute the main source of income for the association; therefore, their potential to generate revenue is crucial for the on-going funding of the EWEA's operations.

Background to the event

Previously known as the European Wind Energy Conference & Exhibition (EWEC), the EWEA Annual Event was rebranded with this name in 2011. The first EWEC took place in July 2001 in Copenhagen, followed by June 2003 in Madrid and November 2004 in London. After that event, it was decided to move from a two-year/18-month cycle to a yearly basis as from Athens 2006, and to hold the event in spring each time.

Participants

Three types of participants attend EWEA Annual Events:

- *Conference delegates*:
  - paying/reduced/free passes depending on their status/organization
  - average fees of €700–800
  - access to conference and exhibition, and lunch.
- *Exhibitor staff – paying/free*:
  - employees of the exhibitors
  - passes cost €50/day
  - access to exhibition only, and lunch.
- *Exhibition visitors – paying*:
  - passes cost €45/day
  - access to exhibition only
  - options to buy lunch access or single conference session ticket.

Details of the countries of origin and profiles of attendees together with host locations and attendance are given in Tables 1–4.

Table 1 Participants at 2011 EWEA Annual Event

Geographical breakdown of all participants	% of total participants
EU	76.49
Non-EU	11.42
USA	3.19
Latin America	0.25
Middle East and Africa	0.41
Asia Pacific	4.69
No country	3.56
Total number of countries	83

Table 2 Top 10 countries of origin of participants

	Attendance numbers
Germany	1698
Belgium	1395
The Netherlands	965
France	885
Britain	835
Denmark	676
Spain	468
USA	265
Italy	229
Finland	183

Table 3 Profile of participants

	% of total participants
Senior management	26.59
PA/policy	1.50
Sales/marketing/business development	36.66
Technical/engineering	20.44
Research	10.12
Purchasing	1.66
Finance/administration	3.04

Table 4 Previous host locations for the event

Year, date	Destination	Venue	Approximate attendance
2006: 27 February–02 March	Athens, Greece	Megaron International Conference Centre	2800
2007: 07–10 May	Milan, Italy	Fiera Milano City	5000
2008: 31 March–03 April	Brussels, Belgium	Brussels Expo	6000
2009: 16–19 March	Marseille, France	Parc Chanot	7500
2010: 20–23 April	Warsaw, Poland	Expo XXI	3000
2011: 14–17 March	Brussels, Belgium	Brussels Expo	9000

As a European association, the choice of destination for the EWEA Annual Event is made according to the rotation principle, moving between European cities, particularly those in countries that have an active wind energy sector.

It can be seen from Table 4 that attendance at the Annual Event has increased each year, with the exception of 2010, when air traffic disruption caused by the eruption of the Eyjafjallajökull volcano in Iceland prevented many delegates from travelling to Poland. Since the size of the event has increased so much, there are very few places in Europe that can host the event effectively. Therefore, since 2009 the EWEA has adopted a rotation principle, which is geographically balanced and includes four major destinations including Copenhagen and Vienna. Accordingly, dependent on the success of Copenhagen 2012 and Vienna 2013, the EWEA reserves the option of returning to these cities four years later – i.e., Copenhagen in 2016 and Vienna in 2017. This system provides the EWEA with a better negotiating position and greater efficiencies in terms of cost and time, through knowing the destination and venue and through the destination and venue understanding the EWEA's specific requirements for their Annual Event.

The destination selection procedure

The procedure for the selection of the destination comprises two steps:

1. Initial proposal, or pre-selection

Formal expressions of interest to host an EWEA Annual Event can only be submitted by EWEA members (national associations) in tandem with the host country. Expressions of interest must be supported by the relevant local/national authorities such as the Ministry of Environment/Energy, the municipality and the local/national government. They should, in addition, include an indication of the potential financial support that the destination will offer the Annual Event.

2. Feasibility study

The feasibility study for the Annual Event is carried out by a project team chaired by a member of the EWEA Membership and Events Department and has to be submitted to the EWEA Board for approval. In addition to the elements included in the Initial Proposal, the following aspects must also be covered:

- Information on other competing non-EWEA events taking place in the destination during the proposed period.
- Proposed general programme for the Annual Event (including number of sessions, plenary and/or parallel sessions, technical visits and social programme).
- Details of the proposed destination (including accessibility, accommodation, weather conditions, pre- and post-conference tourism opportunities, local attractions, technical visits and social activities).
- Local conference and exhibition facilities (suitability, accessibility, technical equipment and itemized costing).
- Side events (committee meetings, press/media activities).
- Promotion and marketing programme (target audience and means, actions, tools and timings).

The feasibility study must be submitted to the EWEA Board at least two to three years before the actual date of the Annual Event being planned. This lead time is considered the minimum time necessary to ensure the successful organization of the conference and exhibition.

Once the destination has been selected, an EWEA Project Team is set up, to coordinate the planning of that Annual Event. The Project Team meets regularly to exchange information on the progress of the various tasks linked to the planning of the event and to make practical decisions. The tasks are undertaken by three distinct committees, responsible for:

- the elaboration of the scientific programme and the selection of speakers
- administration, logistics, finance, organization, the exhibition and the management of speakers
- promotion and marketing of the event.

The EWEA Annual Event General Programme

The General Programme of any EWEA Annual Event comprises the following elements:

- The conference programme (topics, speakers, etc.).
- The social programme (reception, dinner, etc.).
- The exhibition.

The conference programme

Duration	3.5-4 days, usually from Monday to Thursday
Languages	The official language is English. Other languages (i.e. the local language) are subject to special approval and financial restrictions.
Opening session	Welcome by EWEA and supporters/local authorities. Keynote introduction. Cultural entertainment.
Sessions	3 plenary sessions and approximately 40 parallel sessions of 90 minutes each. An average of 5 speakers per session. 1-2 session chairs per session. Time for discussions and conclusions by the chair.
Sessions layout	1 plenary session room, minimum 1000 seats. 3 parallel session rooms, minimum 500 seats each - the plenary room may be used as one of the parallel session rooms. All session rooms must be directly connected to the exhibition facilities.
Closing session	Presentation of general conclusions and follow-up actions. Announcement of the next Annual Event. Recognition of Supporters/Award winners.
Catering	Layouts which allow interaction between delegates and exhibitors. *Welcome coffee*: - Duration: 1 hour before conference opening - Number of attendees: 800-1000 per day - Location: poster area - Menu: coffee, tea, water, biscuits. *Lunch*: - Duration: 1.5 hours - Number of attendees: 2500-2800 per day - Location: exhibition halls/catering area - Menu: light menu when followed by an evening dinner; buffet with 2-3 starters, main dishes and desserts; drinks include water, soft drinks, coffee, wine, beer. *Coffee breaks, morning and afternoon*: - Duration: 30 minutes - Number of attendees: 2000-2500 per break - Location: exhibition halls/catering area - Menu: coffee, tea, water, juice, biscuits, cake. *Exhibition reception (second day of event)*: - Duration: 1.5 hours - Number of attendees: 2000 - Location: exhibition hall - Menu: finger food (4-5 hot and 4-5 cold items, drinks including sparkling wine, wine, beer, soft drinks).

→

Technical visits	These may be organized one morning or afternoon during a conference day.
	They are part of the total conference duration.
	They are organized by the local supporters or sponsor, at their own expense.

The social programme

Members-only reception	By invitation only.
	Sunday evening before the Board dinner.
	Time: 18:00–21:00.
	Number of participants: 300.
	Standing cocktail reception.
	Welcome speech by the President of the EWEA.
Board dinner	By invitation only.
	Sunday evening after the members-only reception, preferably within walking distance of the reception location.
	Time: 20:00–23:00.
	Number of participants: 40.
	Welcome cocktail and snacks, followed by an elegant seated dinner.
	Welcome speech by the President of the EWEA.
Conference reception	By invitation to all conference delegates only.
	Evening of the first conference day.
	Time: 19:00–21:00.
	Number of participants: 800–1000.
	Standing cocktail reception/networking evening.
	If not sponsored, participation is optional and subject to the payment of a separate fee.
	Cultural entertainment welcomed.
	Venue preferably close to public transport or within walking distance of the conference venue.
Conference dinner	If not sponsored, participation is optional and subject to the payment of a separate fee.
	Evening of the third conference day.
	Time: 19:30–23:00.
	Number of participants: 700.
	Representative venue of the location, not too far from the main conference hotels.
	Formal dinner style, round tables, head table(s).
	Short speeches by supporters, sponsors and EWEA representative.
	Cultural entertainment welcomed.
	Venue preferably close to public transport or within walking distance of the conference venue.

The exhibition

Timing	From Monday to Thursday, with a maximum of 6 days prior to the event for buildup, plus 1–3 days post-event for dismantling.
Venue specifications	Required area: minimum 20 000 square metres (ideally 30 000 square metres) gross space for exhibition and catering, ideally on one level and within easy reach of the conference facilities.
	Heavy-duty floor.
	Preferably pillar-free.
	Wide and adequate door access.
	Easy access for very heavy exhibits.

Changing trends in the EWEA Annual Event

Changes in how the event is organized

A growing share of the planning of the Annual Event is being in-sourced, to keep financial control and to increase revenue for the association, by reducing the number of intermediaries used. The inhouse planning team has built a network of core-suppliers and trusted partners with whom they collaborate on various aspects of the event's organization.

Growing challenge of attracting delegates

EWEA, in common with many other associations, is experiencing new challenges in maintaining attendance levels at their Annual Events. This is in part due to the increasing pressure on companies' budgets, as a result of the financial crisis. In part, it is also caused by the growth in the number of conferences and events on the theme of renewable energy that are competing for delegates' time and funds.

As a response to this challenge, those within the EWEA who are responsible for planning the event are increasingly involving stakeholders in the process, in order more closely to adapt the concept to their needs and thus be ahead of the growing competition for potential participants.

More use of technology

The EWEA is constantly considering how it can harness technology in order to add value to the events it organizes. At the 2011 conference in Brussels, the organizers experimented with a customized mobile app for smartphones that provided participants with easy access to the EWEA 2011 conference programme and exhibitor list as well as a floor plan of the exhibition. The app was provided, free of charge, to all EWEA 2011 participants to help them use their time in the most efficient way and get the greatest benefits out of the event.

Summary

As can be seen in this case, conferences are often planned many years in advance. Producing a feasibility study can be time-consuming and complex, requiring the support of many companies and individuals with no guarantee that the event will be held at their location. Alongside the main conference, there is usually a requirement to organize a social programme – this in itself can add to the appeal of the event and ensure that attendees leave satisfied with the overall experience.

In the case of the EWEA event, the project team dedicates significant effort to ensuring that the conference programme, social programme and exhibition run smoothly to ensure that the four-day event is a success.

Questions and discussion points

1. At the initial proposal stage there is a requirement that hosting the event is supported by the local government and the municipality. Why is it important for EWEA that the local community is keen to host their annual event?

2. Why is it useful to understand the profile of the participants?

3. The case highlights that the project team splits responsibility into three areas (the scientific programme, logistics and marketing). What are the advantages of managing the event organization in this way?

Consuming the cruise product? Factors influencing the decision to stay on board or to disembark during port visits

Prepared by Derek Robbins & Laura Bragg, School of Tourism, Bournemouth University

Chapter 14 highlighted the growth of the cruise industry into a genuine form of mass tourism over the last 30 years, with annual growth rates of 8.2% per annum between 1980 and 2005 (CLIA, 2006). Although growth rates have slowed since 2006, this is not uniform in all markets, with North America, the dominant traveller-generating region, experiencing a period of stagnation. The UK market (the world's second largest traveller-generating region) has continued to grow, but modestly, whilst the rest of Western Europe has demonstrated much more rapid growth.

Understanding the different markets for the cruise sector is key, and this case study presents research which has explored customer views related to the role of the destination in the appeal of cruising.

Background

This growth in passenger numbers has come from a combination of loyal customers making repeat cruises and passengers new to cruising. Between 1980 and 2009, over 176 million passengers have taken a deep-water cruise (2+ days), with 68% being new passengers that have been generated in the past 10 years (CLIA, 2010).

To accommodate growth rates of 7–8% per annum over the past 20–30 years, the cruise fleet has expanded dramatically. Occupancy levels of cruise ships are high, at around 96%, so there is a need for new vessels. Thirteen new cruise ships were delivered in 2010 alone, and, whilst some of these new vessels will replace older cruise ships that are withdrawn, there is also a net increase in the overall size of the fleet.

Continued expansion of the cruise fleet has had important impacts on the structure of the cruise industry. The industry has now developed into an oligopoly with three cruise companies (Carnival, Royal Caribbean and Star Alliance) providing almost 80% of all capacity. This increased concentration is partly a result of continued acquisition, but is also the result of organic growth. These three large companies have the financial resources to order new vessels, with a trend to larger vessels aiding capacity expansion.

Table 1 shows how ship sizes have been getting larger. In 1985, only one ship had over 70 000 gwt (gross tonnage) and there were no ships over 100 000 gwt. In 1996, *Carnival Destiny*, the first cruise ship with a tonnage of over 100 000 gwt, was introduced and the trend of increased ship size has continued; by 2006, there were 24 ships over 100 000 gwt.

Although there has been a small increase in the number of small cruise ships delivered in 2010 to serve specialized niche markets, most orders are for large or megaships. The

Table 1 The largest cruise ships

Year	Vessel	Size	Capacity (passengers)	Cruise line
1988	*Sovereign of the Seas*	73 000 gwt	2852	Royal Caribbean
1996	*Carnival Destiny*	101 353 gwt	2642	Carnival
1999	*Voyager of the Seas*	137 300 gwt	3114	Royal Caribbean
2004	*Queen Mary 2*	150 000 gwt	2620	Cunard (Carnival)
2005	*Freedom of the Seas*	158 000 gwt	3643	Royal Caribbean
2009	*Oasis of the Seas*	225 000 gwt	5400	Royal Caribbean

average capacity of new vessels delivered in 2010 was in excess of 3000 passengers, including a further megaship, *Allure of the Seas*, a Royal Caribbean ship holding 5400 passengers and the sister ship to *Oasis of the Seas*. The larger vessels (see, for example, Figure 1) bring about economies of scale, both in construction costs per bedspace and also some operational economies of scale; for example, fewer maritime crew are required per passenger. However, crew to passenger ratios, which tend to range between 1:2 and 1:3, are not significantly different for the largest vessels. Much of the crew is employed in service sector functions on the ship (ranging from waiter, housekeeping through to entertainments) and ratios vary more according to the quality of the ship rather than ship size; budget cruises employ fewer staff per passenger than luxury cruises. Nevertheless, the larger vessels have made a contribution to the falling cost of a cruise holiday.

The development of megaships has given cruise lines the opportunity to serve several different market segments on the same cruise ship as an alternative approach to using smaller ships to target a single market segment. The greater range of facilities offered by a single megaship increases the potential to include specialist facilities targeted at several different customer groups on a single vessel.

Figure 1 RCI *Brilliance of the Seas*
Photo by Chris Holloway

What is the cruise product, the ship or the destination ports?

Clearly, the attraction of a cruise holiday is a balance between the ports of call and the vessel itself; cruise passengers are able to visit a range of destinations without having to change accommodation.

When cruise travel began in the early twentieth century, the ports of call, rather than the cruise ships themselves, were the main attraction for the tourist. However, there has been considerable debate recently over the relative importance of the ship versus the port destinations as the main attraction of a cruise holiday. As the vessels get larger with more facilities on board, they become 'floating resorts', and it is argued that the ship has become a far more dominant component of the destination, a process some have called 'destinization' (Weaver, 2005). The debate proposes that megaships have become travel destinations in their own right, with many tourists deciding to spend most of their money and time on the ship. In essence, some commentators question whether the ship has become the trip as more tourists decide to remain on board when the ship is in port.

Clearly, the megaships have more space to accommodate a wider range of facilities designed to entertain the passenger. For example, the Voyager class of ships were the first to include ice skating rinks and climbing walls among their facilities, and such facilities may encourage tourists to stay on board when the ship is in port. Furthermore, some facilities have very limited capacity, such as the 'Flowrider' (a system designed to create a wave on which it is possible to surf). These facilities can be prebooked prior to the commencement of the cruise and are often fully booked even prior to boarding the vessel. Not surprisingly, repeat cruise passengers are more familiar with the booking systems and more aware of the heavy demand, and whatever limited availability remains during the cruise tends to be greater when the ship is in port.

There is also a relationship between ship size and the number of ports that can accommodate it. As ships get bigger, there are fewer ports at which they can berth. The length of the quayside is often more of a problem than the depth of water. Large vessels are more likely to have to anchor offshore and use tenders to ferry the passengers to and from the quayside. A number of authors believe tendering leads to a higher number of people opting to stay onboard. Archer (2008, 18) describes 'vivid memories of cruising in the Caribbean in a snake-like queue of sweaty passengers waiting for a tender back to the ship'. Certainly, wet and windy weather contributes to reduced use of tenders (Robbins, 2006).

There are a number of reasons why cruise passengers may choose to stay on board at a port of call. These can be summarized as follows:

- large number of more exciting facilities and activities on board cruise ship
- the need to use tenders to visit destination
- value for money – since all meals on board are invariably included in the price, some passengers may be inclined to take full advantage of them rather than spend time ashore and miss meals
- lack of interest towards onshore activities
- health restrictions
- previous visit to port
- lack of knowledge on what the port has to offer.

A final reason why some cruise passengers stay on board, or at least only venture ashore as part of an organized excursion, is that as the cruise market has become a mass market and mainstream, increasing numbers of tourists may lack the confidence to explore independently. In short, there may be more cruise passengers in the psychocentric category, using the typologies identified by Plog (1972) and discussed in detail in Chapter 4.

The precise numbers of cruise passengers who stay on board vessels in port is unknown. Such data are recorded both by the cruise lines and also the port authorities, not least for security purposes, but it does not appear in the literature and is regarded by most cruise lines as commercially sensitive information. Without doubt, it varies from one destination port to another, and industry sources suggest an average figure of 18% of passengers remaining on board.

There is an alternative view that puts forward the argument that it is still the ports of call that are the reasoning behind people booking a cruise. It is argued that the destinations visited by a cruise ship are an important component in the decision-making process of selecting which cruise holiday to take and 'most passengers prefer a day in port over a day at sea and would not take a cruise if there were no ports of call' (Klein, 2008, 4).

Cruise ships as mobile tourism enclaves

If the ports become a less important component of the destination, the cruise passengers will have less opportunity to sample local culture. The cruise ships create a tourist bubble, where the cruise ship is a place designed for tourists and those who serve them. It could be argued that a cruise ship is by nature a space of containment, as tourists on board are confined within a mobile enclave that is distant from shore and therefore encourages tourists to become 'captive consumers' (Weaver, 2005). This results in cruise companies using this encapsulation to create ways of earning additional revenue. Tourism enclaves have been studied for a number of years by numerous researchers, all of whom state that a tourism enclave relates to an environment that is in some ways separated from wider societies. Therefore, by creating environments which encourage passengers to remain on board, the cruise ships are beginning to discourage, rather than encourage, engagement with the local population. Wood (2004) also suggests that these megaships are mobile vacation compounds that are built by cruise shipping companies for the purpose of revenue capture.

There is a clear conflict between the interests of the destination and the interest of the cruise line, both of which are competing for cruise passenger spend.

Key benefits of the cruise industry for the destination: economic spend

It is extremely important to note the distinction between a port of call, usually termed a port visit, and a port of embarkation (also termed a turnaround port). The economic impact at the port of embarkation is generally higher.

There are two principal economic impacts from cruising. First, there are the direct earnings from ports in the shape of port fees, landing charges and any other port taxes. These are relatively low for most ports as the cruise industry is in a strong negotiating position, particularly for port visits. The oligopoly structure of the industry means that ports are negotiating with relatively few cruise line companies, and there are more ports seeking cruise calls in a destination area than there is demand. As a result, cruise lines can dictate prices, and, if the port declines to negotiate, the cruise lines can select an alternative destination. There are indeed a minority of ports where a call is essential for the cruise itinerary, such as St Petersburg for Baltic cruises, where the bargaining position of the port is much stronger, but these are rare. The cruise lines may even re-position away from a whole region if they regard it as too expensive, as happened in Alaska in 2009 with the introduction of a head tax (Peisley, 2010).

The second impact of cruising is the wider economic benefit to the region. 'The arrival of cruise ships carrying around 3,000 passengers into a small port in the Caribbean or any part of the world, would have a major economic impact' (Cartwright and Baird, 1999, 161). This economic impact is more limited than staying, land based visitors as accommodation is a main source of revenue. Cruise ships have half-day and whole-day stays, and the average stay is little more than five hours. The cruise tourists will spend on refreshments, souvenirs and shopping and possibly lunch, although that is available free on board.

Research studies show that the spend can vary considerably from port to port (Douglas and Douglas, 2004), although most studies assume a figure of between $50-80 per passenger per port of call. The most recent study of the economic contribution of cruise tourism to the economies of Europe quotes an average spend per passenger of €70 at embarkation ports and €60 on a port visit (Wild, 2010). There is direct competition between the cruise ship and the port for visitor spend; for example, the shops on the ship sell souvenirs similar to those available on shore. Moreover, the cruise lines try to retain much of the onshore spend. One of the three main sources of income from 'on board' spend is the sale of tours and excursions for the shore visit. Dowling (2006) established that many passengers undertake excursions rather than self-exploration with '50-80% of passengers buying an excursion as they are most convenient' (Dowling, 2006, 264). These are very profitable for the cruise companies, and, while they also benefit the local economy through the hire of coaches, local tour guides and other shore-based staff, the mark-up is high with significant passenger spend being retained by the cruise company as profit.

One potential and perhaps unexpected longer term economic benefit of cruising to a destination is the prospect of a return visit to a port. The cruise industry has the potential to showcase the area to thousands of cruise passengers who may then decide to return as independent travellers. The time spent in port during the one-day visit can have a positive effect on the likelihood of return. CLIA surveys claim that 40% of cruise passengers return to a destination first visited on a cruise for a land-based vacation (CLIA, 2010).

Historically, the economic benefits of cruising are believed to have been overstated as it is becoming increasingly clear that not all cruise passengers go ashore at all ports and that some cruise passengers go ashore quite rarely (Cruises.co.uk, 2011).

What factors influence whether passengers go ashore?

Clearly an area that warrants further more detailed research is cruise passenger behaviour at the ports of call. Quantitative surveys would add data on the percentage of cruise passengers who go ashore and whether they do so independently or as part of an organized excursion, and would be useful research for the future. However, qualitative research brings insight into the factors which most influence a cruise passenger's decision to go ashore.

We report here the findings of three focus group interviews with 24 British cruise passengers (Table 2). The sample was recruited to try to include a range of cruise passenger

Table 2 Sample of cruise passengers

Gender	Male	11
	Female	13
Age	16-25	4
	25-34	0
	35-44	1
	45-54	3
	55-64	14
	65+	2
Number of cruises	1-2	4
	3-10	12
	More than 10	8
Size of ship	There were a mixture of respondents who had been on small ships, large ships and some who had experienced both.	

types incorporating experienced repeat cruisers and those new to cruise holidays. The sample attempted to include a range of ages although it is dominated by the over 55s, which reflects the current UK market.

The evidence from these qualitative interviews challenges some of the conventional theories set out in the literature.

Destinization

The interviews did not support the theory that the ship was emerging as the destination. All respondents clearly revealed that the ports were very much still the destination and not the ship and only a small proportion of respondents said the onboard facilities available were important when booking a cruise. Some repeat passengers were loyal to specific cruise lines or specific ships, but they attributed this to familiarity with the product and the standard of service rather than specific onboard facilities, and this was not the decisive factor in their decision-making process.

The vast majority of respondents stated that they had disembarked at every port of call on their last cruise. Interestingly, the over 55s were even more inclined to get off at each port. As one couple put it 'as we will never go there again so got off to ensure that they had seen the place'.

Onboard lectures about the ports of call were attended by most of the inexperienced respondents, conflicting with literature which suggests that cruise companies tried to encapture all cruisers by providing little information about the ports of call.

The idea that experienced cruise passengers stayed on board because they had made previous visits to the port was also strongly disagreed with by all the experienced cruisers who said they would simply seek something different to see at previously visited ports.

Tenders

All but one of the respondents had used tendering facilities on prior cruises. Some respondents confirmed that queues for a tender were an issue, particularly for larger megaships. 'When you choose to get off the ship for an excursion the volume of people can sometimes be a problem with queues.' Nevertheless, most respondents confirmed that tendering would not influence their decision to go ashore and was actually something that they 'relatively enjoyed and looked upon as a chance to have a chat and catch up on recommendations from other passengers'.

Respondents who had young children had slightly varying opinions, as the experience became slightly more stressful with the extra luggage and waiting around, but these still agreed that if instructions are followed tendering was not an issue.

Size of ship

Several of the respondents commented that they would be very unlikely to book onto a megaship, partly due to the belief that they attracted a certain type of passenger; 'A lot more families tend to go on the larger ships, and we like it to be a bit quieter.' The general consensus amongst the experienced cruisers was that some ships were oversized and most concluded that large ships did not make it more likely that they would stay on board. If they did stay on board, it was simply to relax and sunbathe rather than undertake any activities that the megaship made available. Megaships were a more popular choice among new cruise passengers.

The visit - independent or organized tours

The vast majority of the experienced cruisers had significant knowledge before the cruise on destinations where they planned to get off the ship, compared to the inexperienced cruisers who got off at ports not really knowing what to expect. As expected, first-time cruise passengers were more interested in booking excursions than the more experienced passengers, as they felt this was the best option to overcome their unfamiliarity with the destinations.

Several of the repeat cruise passengers suggested that organized tours dramatically affect spending at port, as 'you get off and get onto a coach or bus for usually an hour so there is no spend there, then you just follow the guide around and don't venture to the town shops to buy anything'. This supports findings in the existing literature.

Cruise ships as mobile enclaves

The concept that part of the attractiveness of a cruise was for the emotionally reassuring, complexity-reducing 'cocoon' was counter to all responses from participants. All participants agreed that they wanted to be able to get away from the ship's environment. Cruise passengers, especially the experienced, tended to know exactly what they want from a cruise holiday.

Eating ashore

It became evident that the offering of the 24-hour food service on ships was not a factor when deciding to stay on board when at port, directly contradicting literature. Several respondents actually strongly felt that trying new cuisines and 'not queuing for buffet food' was one of their favourite parts of the port experience.

Distance

One theme that became apparent from conducting the focus groups was that some ports of call were not visited simply because the cruise passengers were too tired from a full and busy previous day in port. For example, experienced cruise passengers said a port they would not return to was Rome as 'it's such a long journey into Rome itself and also it's the day before the ship docks at Florence, which is another long trip to the city, so is a bit much to visit both'.

The weather

All of the participants in this study revealed the strong correlation between the weather and their decision to leave the ship at port. This concurs with literature suggesting the weather as being a main reason for influencing the passengers' decision to stay on board (Robbins, 2006), with agreement that 'if it was chucking it down with rain for example they certainly wouldn't make the effort to go ashore'. However, the conclusion was that if the weather continued for the duration of the cruise, it would become less of a problem as they would need to get off the ship.

Conclusions

The cruise ship industry has shown dramatic growth over the last 30 years, resulting in greater variety in the age and socio-economic profile of the type of people who take a cruise. To meet this growing market there have been significant changes in the product itself, which is now supplied by a decreasing number of cruise companies, resulting in an oligopoly. The most marked development is in the increasing size of the cruise ship.

There is a developing literature arguing that changes in the supply are influencing the cruise product itself and the attractions and motivations of cruise passengers. It is argued that more cruise passengers are spending more time on the cruise ship, even when it is in port, and that the ship itself has become the more dominant component of the overall holiday destination.

While qualitative data can never offer statistically valid results, this research exploring the UK market casts considerable doubt on the assertion that passengers are more likely to stay on board. The ports visited remained the most important component of the cruise holiday for the UK market. While cruise passengers did not go ashore at every port, the vast majority went ashore at most ports and the research seriously questioned some of the explanations offered for passengers not going ashore. In particular, cruise passengers did not find tender services as much of a disincentive as the literature implied, and taking meals ashore was seen as a positive rather than a negative feature.

There is clearly a need for more detailed and larger scale research. In particular, it would be interesting to compare the attitudes of British passengers with other source markets, particular the USA. However, interesting issues arise from this case study that meant further research.

Questions and discussion points

1. The cruise ship market has performed less well in the two largest markets since 2006; it has stagnated in the USA and growth has slowed down in the UK. Discuss the reasons for this.

2. What factors influence whether cruise passengers go ashore? Discuss what barriers, if any, discourage shore visits.

3. Megaships have emerged as floating resorts, and a major component of the cruise destination. Discuss the implications of this for European ports.

Bibliography

Archer, J. (2008) *Cruising can be a tender misery*, available online at: http://www.telegraph.co.uk/travel/cruises/typesofcruises/2041703/Cruising-can-be-tender-misery.html (accessed November 2011).

Cartwright, R. and Baird, C. (1999) *The Development and Growth of the Cruise Industry*, Oxford, Butterworth-Heinemann.

CLIA (2006) *Cruise Industry Overview: Marketing Edition*, New York, Cruise Line International Association.

CLIA (2010) *Cruise Industry Overview: Marketing Edition*, New York, Cruise Line International Association, available online at: http://www2.cruising.org/press/overview2010/ (accessed November 2011).

Cruises.co.uk (2011) http://www.cruises.co.uk/109-cruise_news/15716-shipbound_shock_one_fifth_cruisers_never_get_off.html?utm_source=040211&utm_medium=ship&utm_campaign=ship (accessed November 2011).

Douglas, N. and Douglas, N. (2004) Cruise ship passenger spending patterns in pacific island ports, *International Journal of Tourism Research*, **6** (3), 251–261.

Dowling, R. K. (2006) *Cruise Ship Tourism*, 2nd edn, Wallingford, CABI.

Klein, R. A. (2008) *Paradise Lost at Sea: Rethinking Cruise Vacations*, Halifax, NS, Fernwood.

Peisley, T. (2010) *Cruising at the Crossroads – A worldwide analysis to 2025*, Colchester, Seatrade Communications Ltd.

Plog, S. (1972) *Why destination areas rise and fall in popularity*, unpublished paper presented to the Southern Chapter of the Travel Research Association, Los Angeles.

Robbins, D. (2006) Cruise ships in the UK and North European market: development opportunity or illusion for UK ports? in Dowling, R. K., *Cruise Ship Tourism*, Wallingford, CABI, 363–376.

Weaver, A. (2005) Spaces of containment and revenue capture: 'super-sized' cruise ships as mobile tourism enclaves, *Tourism Geographies*, **7** (2), 165–184.

Wild, G. P. (2010) *The Cruise Industry – Contribution of Cruise Tourism to the Economies of Europe*, Brussels, European Cruise Council.

Wood, R. (2004) Cruise ships: deterritorialized destinations, in Lumsdon, L. and Page, S., *Tourism and Transport*, Oxford, Elsevier, 133–145.

Glossary

CLIA   Cruise Lines International Association. A US body representing the interests of cruise lines in North America. The largest trade body for cruise lines.

Gwt   Gross weight tonnage. Calculated on the volume of all enclosed spaces of the ship.

Tender   Smaller vessel used for transporting passengers between the cruise ship and the shore.

Mega-events, tourism and host resident opinions of the 2012 Olympic and Paralympic Games in Weymouth and Portland, UK

Dr Richard Shipway and Dr Holly Henderson, School of Tourism, Bournemouth University

Understanding the social dimension of hosting a mega sports event is crucial in order to develop local support for hosting such events (Fredline, 2005). Assessing the perceptions of residents toward mega-events is one potential indicator within the broader social impact assessment of mega-events and the subsequent implications for tourism development. The concept of social impacts, and, more broadly sustainability, highlights the importance of a long-term approach and integrating community interests into decision-making.

In preparation for the London 2012 Games, significant developments have taken place both centrally in London, and within the Borough of Weymouth and Portland in the South West of England, the host venue for the Olympic and Paralympic Sailing competitions. This case study investigates Weymouth and Portland residents' opinions towards Olympic-related development based on two surveys undertaken in 2007 and 2010. The emphasis here is to explore the impact on tourism development and mega-event planning issues. In order to assist Olympic policy-making, it is important to understand not only the level of support or opposition for events but also the reasons behind such support or opposition and ways to improve Olympic outcomes for both the 2012 event stakeholders and local host communities. More fundamentally, the results highlight the impact that tourism-driven events can have on the local residents.

Costs and benefits of hosting mega-events

It is widely known that mega-events have substantial economic impacts ranging from tax revenues, employment and sources of income before, during and after hosting a mega-event such as the Olympics (Kang and Perdue, 1994). They can also provide opportunities for increased publicity and enhanced awareness for host cities and nations (Ritchie et al., 2009), and can attract potential investment in new infrastructure and the creation of new facilities which locals and tourists alike can enjoy (Ritchie and Lyons, 1990). Many researchers believe that the social impacts and benefits of hosting mega sports events are just as important as the economic impacts. Positive social impacts can include increased community pride, improved quality of life, strengthening of cultural values and traditions and helping to build national identity (Waitt, 2003; Kim and Petrick, 2005). Sports mega-events, in particular, may also increase levels of sports participation or reduce social exclusion, although evidence for these impacts is not as widespread as that for the economic benefits and impacts. Whilst much of the rationale for bidding for these events is to leverage the tourism benefits, the impacts on the host community often proves to be significant and far-reaching.

As well as producing positive impacts and benefits to a host community, it is recognized that negative impacts and costs also occur in each of the impact areas (economic, social and environmental). The costs associated with hosting a mega sporting event such as the Olympics may outweigh the positive benefits for some residents, who may reduce or withdraw their support for the event. Residents who benefit from tourism, perhaps through employment or business turnover, may have more favourable perceptions than those who do not (Fredline, 2004), while those locals able to enjoy recreational facilities created from mega-events are found to be more supportive of the hosting of such events.

Impact on the host Borough of Weymouth and Portland: tourism and the 2012 Games

The sailing events for the 2012 Games will be held at the National Sailing Academy in Portland, host venue to over 2500 acres of sheltered waters in Portland Harbour, with easy access to Weymouth Bay. It is considered by many that the very benign tidal conditions and other climatic factors together form one of the best areas for small boat sailing in the world. Since the announcement on 6th July 2005 that the Borough would be a host venue for the 2012 Games, there has been much debate and discussion on how the Olympic and Paralympic events can best be leveraged to optimize tourism opportunities.

Sailing will form one of 26 Olympic sports and one of 20 Paralympic sports. The National Sailing Academy at Weymouth and Portland, the furthest venue for London at which a complete sport will be hosted, will be the venue for both the Olympic and Paralympic sailing events. It is anticipated that the events will attract 480 sailing athletes over 20 days of the competition and the ODA (Olympic Delivery Authority) estimated that the Borough could receive up to 60 000 visitors per day, which is an additional 30 000 compared with the average visitor levels for the time of year. The Olympics are estimated to attract a global audience in excess of 4 billion people, and Weymouth and Portland anticipated they would be able to maximize this global exposure to raise the profile of the Borough as a leading tourism destination and venue for hosting sailing events. In addition to a free venue for many spectators, LOCOG (London Organizing Committee of the Olympic and Paralympic Games) sold in excess of 64 000 ticketed seats. LOCOG also estimated the Borough would attract up to 10 000 non-accredited international and regional media representatives during the Games. In terms of opportunities for the Borough, various stakeholders viewed the

Figure 1 Elite athlete accommodation for the 2012 Games, situated adjacent to the sailing venue

Photo by Holly Henderson

Figure 2 A 2012 Games themed ice cream van

Photo by Holly Henderson

Games as an opportunity to use 2012 and the international stage to help re-profile the area, highlight the natural tourism assets, encourage business interests and inward investments and enhance the long-term stability of the local economy. This case study highlights the fact that the local community has a key role to play in achieving these objectives and provides a preview of the community opinions on some of these strategic objectives.

Prior to the Games, a series of existing benefits had already been identified by the Borough Council. These included improved transport links, expansion and use of the National Sailing Academy, enhanced publicity for the Borough across all media, a rise in marine-based development, cultural Olympiad events which are already inspiring community activity, potential 2012 sponsors' investment, marine and coastal access improvements and investment by Arts Council and English Heritage in Weymouth seafront regeneration. The results which now follow explore some of these developments, as perceived by local residents across the Borough of Weymouth and Portland.

The changes in host resident perceptions between 2007 and 2010

As previously outlined, the first stage of this longitudinal research study was undertaken in 2007 to establish baseline levels of support and perceptions of the 2012 Games throughout the Borough. The second stage, completed in 2010, enabled comparisons to take place on a range of areas that are perceived as being of importance and interest to residents, in the context of sports events and Olympic development. Many of these areas have significant impact on and implications for the tourism industry and tourism stakeholders. The primary research instrument used for collecting the data in this case study was a self-completion questionnaire to examine residents' perceptions about the hosting of the Olympic sailing events and the perceived impact on their community. Surveys were also distributed within selected areas of both Weymouth and Portland, which comprises 15 borough wards, using a street ward road index where streets were randomly selected after numbering, using a systematic sampling procedure. A high percentage of the impact statements incorporated have far reaching implications for tourism development.

Table 1 Comparisons between Impact Statements 2007 and 2010

	2007	2010	% change
Routes cope with emergency services	22	x	x
The 2012 Games will disrupt the lives of the locals in terms of peace and tranquillity	52	63	11
The sailing academy and 2012 Games will cause an increase in crime levels	30	32	2
Overall, I am in favour of the tourism industry in Weymouth and Portland (W&P)	85	82	−3
In future locals may avoid the town centre and beaches if they know there are too many tourists	69	70	1
Increased sailing events will lead to increased litter on the beaches, and in W&P	55	56	1
Prices of everyday products & sailing goods in shops will increase because of the 2012 Games and the sailing academy	63	63	0
The local area will become too crowded which will cause hostility between locals and tourists	37	37	0
Sailing events will lead to an increase in noise levels which will disturb residents	34	34	0
Traffic congestion and parking will become increasingly difficult	92	91	−1
Visitors to W&P are inconsiderate of residents	36	35	−1
It would be better to have fewer tourists and less money if it means freer access to the beaches and town centre	27	24	−3
Local transport routes will be sufficient to cope with increased congestion	19	13	−6
Sailing & water based events will encourage the wrong type of people to the area	17	11	−6
Sailing & water sports will spread tourism throughout the year which is positive	69	62	−7
The 2012 Games gives young people in both W&P new opportunities to play sport	55	48	−7
The sailing academy & the 2012 Games will further promote W&P as tourist destinations	85	77	−8
The sailing academy promotes British water sports	78	70	−8
Money spent on the feasibility of the sailing development was a good investment	68	59	−9
The sailing academy and the 2012 Games will give W&P an international identity	79	70	−9
The 2012 Games will bring new facilities that the borough will benefit from and be able to use	60	48	−12
The sailing academy and the 2012 Games will be a positive step for the economy of W&P	79	66	−13
Young people in both W&P will be inspired by the 2012 Games	65	52	−13
The 2012 Games will increase pride of local residents in their borough	57	44	−13
The 2012 Games will give residents an opportunity to meet new people	65	52	−13
The sailing academy and 2012 Games will increase trade for local businesses	80	65	−15
The 2012 Games will bring the community together	40	25	−15
The 2012 Games will make W&P a more interesting place to live and work	48	32	−16
The 2012 Games and sailing events will increase employment opportunities in W&P	69	53	−16
The 2012 Games may lead to higher levels of services offered by local businesses	56	39	−17
The 2012 Games will enhance local residents' spirit of hospitality	45	27	−18
The appearance of W&P will be improved by the changes between now and the 2012 Games	66	47	−19
The 2012 Games will lead to greater sporting participation in the borough	63	42	−21
The demand and price of property in W&P will increase due to the 2012 Games	82	52	−30

The results in Table 1 highlight the changes in resident opinions over a three-year period between 2007 and 2010. One of the main headline results, featured separately at the end of the questionnaire, asked residents if they were in favour of hosting the Olympic and Paralympic events. Despite a *13 point drop* from a figure of *89%* in 2007, *76%* of those residents surveyed indicated that they supported the 2012 developments in the Borough.

With regard to transport issues – of key importance for tourism policy and planning – in the 2010 findings, **92%** of residents indicated that they thought traffic congestion and parking would become increasingly difficult. Whilst it could be suggested that the timing of this survey might have influenced these results, given the extensive transport infrastructure development taking place within the Borough during the data collection period in the build up to the 2012 Games, it should be noted that **91%** of those residents responding in 2007 indicated similar concerns that traffic congestion and parking would become increasingly difficult. Therefore, these findings remained constant.

There was a change in perceptions that the 2012 Games would disrupt the lives of the locals in terms of peace and tranquillity, with an *11 point increase*; **63%** in 2010 perceived this as causing disruption as opposed to **52%** in 2007. Whilst Table 1 illustrates that some areas remain relatively constant (crime, litter, prices of everyday products, noise, traffic congestion), there were certain areas of potential event impact where opinion had changed significantly, both positively and negatively, in relation to the 2012 Games. There was a *12 point reduction* (from **60%** in 2007 to **48%** in 2010) in residents who thought the Games would bring new facilities which the Borough would benefit from and would be able to use; a *13 point reduction* (from **65%** in 2007 to **52%** in 2010) for those who thought young people in the Borough would be inspired by the Games; and also a 13 point reduction (from **57%** in 2007 to **44%** in 2010) among residents who thought the Games would increase the pride of local residents in the Borough. Previous studies of major sports events indicate that feelings of pride are generally enhanced during and after the hosting of the event, so it could be logically anticipated that this percentage might be positively reversed in 2012/13, assuming the Games are perceived to have been successfully delivered.

There were also quite significant shifts in residents who thought the 2012 Games would be positive for the economy (*13 point reduction*); increase trade for local businesses (*15 point reduction*); increase employment opportunities in Weymouth and Portland (*16 point reduction*); and a *17 point reduction* in residents who thought the 2012 Games would lead to higher levels of service offered by local businesses. Interestingly, the largest change related to perceptions regarding the demand for and price of property in the Borough. In 2007, **82%** of residents thought the Games would lead to significant increases in both the demand for and price of property in Weymouth and Portland; however, three years later, this figure had been *significantly reduced by 30 points*, with only just over half those respondents, **52%**, perceiving an increase. Finally, from a sports participation perspective (one of the primary national and regional objectives of the 2012 Games beyond the economic dimension), there was a significant reduction (*21 points*) in people who thought the 2012 Games would lead to greater sporting participation in the Borough (falling from **63%** in 2007 to only **42%** in 2010). The remainder of the comparative findings between 2007 and 2010 are identified in Table 1, illustrating changes in resident opinions toward the 2012 Olympic and Paralympic Games. Several of these social impacts can be closely linked to tourism development.

To conclude the survey, and taking into account the diverse range of resident opinions regarding the 2012 Games (clearly meaning different things to different people), residents were asked to provide answers to one final qualitative question; they were asked to provide the first one word which came to mind with regard to the 2012 Olympic and Paralympic Games (one word only). The most frequently cited words are detailed below in Table 2.

Table 2 Host residents keywords about the 2012 Games

Chaos	Cost	Weymouth
Exciting	Sailing	Money
Expensive	Waste	Interesting
Traffic	Disruption	Portland
Congestion	Fantastic	Competition
Great	Pride	Excitement
Good	Sport	Expense
Opportunity		

Conclusions

This Olympic case study highlights the need to undertake longitudinal research in order to monitor changes, and highlights the importance of investigating reasons for these changes before, during and after the hosting of mega-events. It is suggested that such information can be used in decision-making for event planning and communication strategies, and also to help alleviate negative impact. The findings emphasize the need to include local resident opinions in any attempt to measure the impacts of the 2012 Games in Weymouth and Portland. As with previous mega-event resident opinion studies, the second stage of the results indicates a relatively high level of support (76%) for hosting the Olympic sailing events to be held in the local area. However, there was still a 13 point reduction based on the high initial levels of support in 2007. Previous studies have also indicated some movement in resident support for mega sports events over time, and it clearly remains important for event stakeholders to understand these changes over time in order to assist in Olympic event planning and communication.

Figure 3 British Olympic Gold Medallist Ben Ainslie pictured with local volunteers and event organizers at one of the pre-2012 Games Test Events
Photo by Holly Henderson, courtesy of Ben Ainslie

As a direct result of this research, several changes have been implemented by the Borough Council. Residents expressed concerns specifically with regard to, firstly, the lack of information they were receiving about the 2012 Games, and, secondly, the perceived lack of consultation on Olympic-related developments. The council now regularly provides 'Olympic Updates' through different communication channels, including council newsletters, the borough council website and community presentations throughout Weymouth and Portland, in an attempt to provide information and to consult more proactively with residents. The research highlighted traffic congestion as being the primary area of concern. It is anticipated that many of these issues have now been resolved with the completion of a new 'relief road' to ease traffic congestion. One area which is proving difficult to resolve is linked to the organizers' claim that the 2012 Games will lead to increased resident participation in sport and physical activity.

Despite the construction of new Olympic facilities, there have been significant reductions in funding through national and regional sport development initiatives; this clearly remains a cause for concern amongst residents, and it is highly probable that the original 2012 legacy objective of increased sports participation is unlikely to be achieved among the host community. Researchers at Canterbury Christchurch University, UK, have extensively explored opportunities linked to both the *'demonstration effect'* (the extent to which the Olympic and Paralympic values inspire more participation within sport and most formal physical activities) and the *'festival effect'* (opportunities for general physical activity and very informal sport-related activities which build a sense of community involvement in the occasion to promote active celebration of the Olympic and Paralympic festival). Further investigations in this area of mega-event impacts within society are on-going.

In order to address resident concerns about the 2012 Games and its ability to increase pride in the borough and to bring the community together, several successful volunteering initiatives and programmes have been introduced. The *Weymouth and Portland Ambassadors* volunteer programme is one such example, providing residents with both the opportunity to be part of the 2012 'Olympic experience' and to meet Olympic athletes and medallists. These volunteering schemes were given high priority status by 2012 event organizers, as they strive both to provide a warm welcome to tourists during the Olympic events and to involve local residents in the event experience. In summary, the results of this research shed light on the complex relationships between the host community, event stakeholders and tourism policy-makers. Continual tracking over time will be crucial.

Acknowledgement

Financial assistance, support and general advice in connection with the data collection for this project were kindly provided by both Jacqui Gisborne and Simon Williams from Weymouth and Portland Borough Council.

Questions and discussion points

1. How would the social impacts of a mega-event, such as the Olympic Games, differ from the impacts of other local, regional, national or international events?

2. Pick a destination of your choice and then consider both the possible positive and negative impacts of hosting a mega-event on the immediate host community and the associated event stakeholders. Once you have undertaken this task, consider the long-term repercussions of failing to consider the social impacts on the local community from hosting events.

3. Rank the following potential economic and social impacts and legacies associated with sports events in terms of their importance to tourism, and then justify your choice:
   1. economic injection to cities, regions and national economies
   2. increased employment
   3. inter-cultural experiences
   4. community pride
   5. tourism development & marketing
   6. improved sporting and cultural infrastructure and facilities
   7. town and rural development
   8. increased sport participation through events
   9. positive and lasting memories
   10. human resources and skills development (including event volunteering).

4. Why is it important that we consider a range of effects of hosting events, rather than simply establishing the economic impacts?

Bibliography

Fredline, E. (2004) Host community reactions to motorsports events: The perception of impact on quality of life, in Ritchie B. and Adair D. (eds) *Sport Tourism: Interrelationships, Impacts and Issues*, Clevedon, Channel View, 155-173.

Fredline, E. (2005) Host and guest relations and sport tourism, *Sport in Society*, **8** (2), 263-279.

Kang, Y. S. and Perdue, R. (1994) Long-term impact of a mega-event on international tourism to the host country: A conceptual model and the case of the 1988 Seoul Olympics, *Journal of International Consumer Marketing*, **6** (3-4), 205-226.

Kim, S. and Petrick, J. (2005) Residents' perceptions on impacts of the FIFA2002 World Cup: The case of Seoul as a host city, *Tourism Management*, **26**, 25-38.

Ritchie, J. R. B. and Lyons, M. (1990) Olympulse VI: A post-event assessment of resident reaction to the XV Olympic Winter Games, *Journal of Travel Research*, **28** (3), 14-23.

Ritchie, B. W., Shipway, R. and Cleeve, B. (2009) Resident perceptions of mega-sporting events: a non-host city perspective of the 2012 London Olympic Games, *Journal of Sport & Tourism*, **14** (2-3), 143-167.

Waitt, G. (2003) Social impacts of the Sydney Olympics, *Annals of Tourism Research*, **30** (1), 194-215.

Websites

London 2012: **www.london2012.com**

Weymouth and Portland National Sailing Academy: **www.wpnsa.org.uk**

Further reading

The flow of books on tourism now appearing on the market is such that any attempt to offer a comprehensive listing of available and appropriate textbooks to aid the reader would be unnecessarily long and less than helpful. Instead, in this new edition, the list given here will, for the first time, include those books that will allow students to read around the topics covered in this book at a level appropriate for their courses. The books have been chosen for their suitability for those studying tourism at post-A level up to undergraduate level and are identified according to their principal topics, apart from those that, in the view of the authors, offer useful supplementary reading about the nature of tourism in general – these are included in the section for Chapter 1. Books which span topics covered in several chapters of this text are listed in the general reference section. Books earlier than 1980 are included only where they are classic and seminal books or throw light on some particular aspect of tourism that cannot be readily found in more recent books. Publications other than books are largely excluded – again, except where they are deemed vital to the contemporary study of the subject.

General reference

Beaver, A. (2005) *A Dictionary of Travel and Tourism Terminology*, 2nd edn, Wallingford, CABI.

Beech, J. and Chadwick, S. (eds) (2006) *The Business of Tourism Management*, Harlow, Pearson Education.

Buhalis, D. and Costa, C. (eds) (2006) *Tourism Business Frontiers*, Oxford, Butterworth-Heinemann.

Burles, D. and Quinn, B. (2006) *World Travel Atlas*, 10th edn, Swanley, Columbus Travel Publishing.

Cohen, E. (2005) *Contemporary Tourism: Diversity and Change*, Oxford, Elsevier.

Cooper, C., Fletcher, J., Fyall, A., Gilbert, D. and Wanhill, S. (2008) *Tourism Principles and Practice*, 4th edn, London, Longman.

Cooper, C. and Hall, C. (2008) *Contemporary Tourism*, Oxford, Butterworth-Heinemann.

Insight (2008) *Deluxe World Travel Atlas and CD-ROM*, Singapore, APA Publishers.

Jafari, J. (ed.) (2000) *Encyclopedia of Tourism*, London, Routledge.

Jones, I. and Mason, P. (2007) *Dictionary of Leisure and Tourism*, London, Routledge.

Medlik, S. (1996) *Dictionary of Travel, Tourism and Hospitality*, 2nd edn, Oxford, Butterworth-Heinemann.

Page, S. (2011) *Tourism Management: an introduction*, 4th edn, London, Oxford, Elsevier Butterworth-Heinemann.

Page, S. and Connell, J. (2009) *Tourism: A Modern Synthesis*, 3rd edn, Andover, Cengage Learning.

Weaver, D. and Lawton, L. (2010) *Tourism Management*, 4th edn, Milton, Wiley.

Chapter 1 An introduction to tourism

Alford, P. (2000) *E-Business in the Travel Industry*, London, Travel and Tourism Intelligence.

Biederman, P., Lai, J., Laitamaki, J., Messerli, H., Nyheni, P. and Plog, S. (2008) *Travel and Tourism: An industry primer*, Harlow, Prentice Hall.

Boniface, P. (2001) *Dynamic Tourism: Journeying with change*, Clevedon, Channel View.

Boniface, B. and Cooper, C. (2005) *Worldwide Destinations: The geography of travel and tourism*, 4th edn, Oxford, Elsevier Butterworth-Heinemann.

Boorstin, D. J. (1988) *The Image: A Guide To Pseudo-Events in America*, New York, Macmillan.

Brown, F. (1998) *Tourism Reassessed: Blight or blessing?*, Oxford, Butterworth-Heinemann.

Burkart, A. J. and Medlik, S. (1981) *Tourism: Past, present and future*, London, Heinemann.

Burns, P. and Holden, A. (1995) *Tourism: A new perspective*, Harlow, FT Prentice Hall.

Butcher, J. (2002) *The Moralisation of Tourism: Sun, sand . . . and saving the world?*, London, Routledge.

Cochrane, J. (ed.) (2008) *Asian Tourism: Growth and change*, Oxford, Elsevier.

Faulkner, B., Laws, E. and Moscardo, G. (eds) (2001) *Tourism in the 21st Century*, London, Continuum.

Goeldner, J. R. and Ritchie, J. R. Brent (2009) *Tourism: Principles, Practices, Philosophies*, 11th edn, Hoboken, NJ, Wiley.

Lanfant, M.-F., Allcock, J. B. and Bruner, E. M. (1993) *International Tourism: Identity and change*, London, Sage.

Lavery, P. and Van Doren, C. (1990) *Travel and Tourism: A North American–European perspective*, Huntingdon, Elm Publications.

Lickorish, L. J. and Jenkins, C. (1995) *An Introduction to Tourism*, Oxford, Butterworth-Heinemann.

Lockwood, A. and Medlik, S. (2002) *Tourism and Hospitality in the 21st Century*, Oxford, Elsevier Butterworth-Heinemann.

Lumsdon, L. and Swift, J. (2001) *Tourism in Latin America*, London, Continuum.

Medlik, S. (1999) *Understanding Tourism*, Oxford, Butterworth-Heinemann.

Mill, R. C. and Morrison, A. (1992) *The Tourism System: An introductory text*, 2nd edn, Harlow, Prentice Hall.

ONS (2010) *Measuring Tourism Locally. Guidance Note 1: Definitions of Tourism*, London, Office for National Statistics.

Pape, R. (1964) Touristry: a type of occupational mobility, *Social Problems*, **11** (4), 336–344.

Ryan, C. (1991) Tourism, Terrorism and Violence: the risks of wider world travel, *Conflict Studies*, No. 244, Research Institute for the Study of Conflict and Terrorism.

Seaton, A. V., Jenkins, C. L., Wood, R. C., Dieke, P. U. C., Bennett, M. M., MacLellan, L. R. and Smith, R. (eds) (1994) *Tourism: The state of the art*, Chichester, Wiley.

Sharpley, R. (ed.) (2002) *The Tourism Business: An introduction*, Sunderland, Business Education Publishers.

Sharpley, R. and Telfer, D. (2007) *Tourism and Development*, London, Routledge.

Theobald, W. (ed.) (2005) *Global Tourism: the Next Decade*, 3rd edn, Oxford, Butterworth-Heinemann.

Toffler, A. (1970) *Future Shock*, London, Bodley Head.

Tribe, J. (ed.) (2009) *Philosophical Issues in Tourism*, Clevedon, Channel View.

UNSD/OECD (2010) *International Recommendations for Tourism Statistics 2008*, New York, United Nations.

Vellas, F. and Bécherel, L. (1995) *International Tourism*, Houndsmill, Palgrave.

Vukonic, B. (1997) *Tourism and Religion*, Oxford, Elsevier Science.

Weiler, B. and Hall, C. M. (eds) (1992) *Special Interest Tourism*, London, Belhaven Press.

Youell, R. (1998) *Tourism: An introduction*, Harlow, Addison-Wesley Longman.

Chapter 2 The development and growth of tourism up to the mid-twentieth century

Adams, C. (2003) *Transport and Travel in the Roman World*, Stroud, Sutton.

Adamson, S. H. (1977) *Seaside Piers*, London, Batsford.

Addison, W. (1951) *English Spas*, London, Batsford.

Alderson, F. (1973) *The Inland Resorts and Spas of Britain*, Newton Abbot, David & Charles.

Bennett, T. (1995) *The Birth of the Museum: History, Theory, Politics*, London, Routledge.

Braggs, S. and Harris, D. (2000) *Sun, Fun and Crowds: Seaside holidays between the wars*, Stroud, Tempus.

Brendon, P. (2005) *Thomas Cook: 150 years of popular tourism*, London, Secker and Warburg.

Brodie, A., Sargent, A. and Winterby, G. (2005) *Seaside Holidays in the Past*, UK, English Heritage.

Burton, A. and Burton, P. (1978) *The Green Bag Travellers: Britain's first tourists*, London, Deutsch.

Buzzard, J. (1993) *The Beaten Track: European tourism, literature and the ways to culture, 1800–1918*, Oxford, Clarendon Press.

Casson, L. (1974) *Travel in the Ancient World*, London, George Allen and Unwin.

Chaney, E. (1998) *The Evolution of the Grand Tour*, London, Frank Cass.

Corbin, A. (1994) *The Lure of the Sea: The discovery of the seaside in the Western world, 1750–1840*, Cambridge, Polity Press.

Cormack, B. (1998) *A History of Holidays, 1812–1990*, London, Routledge.

Delgado, A. (1977) *The Annual Outing and Other Excursions*, London, George Allen & Unwin.

Drower, J. (1982) *Good Clean Fun: The story of Britain's first holiday camp*, London, Arcadia.

Feifer, M. (1985) *Going Places: The ways of the tourist from imperial Rome to the present day*, London, Macmillan.

Gordon, S. (1972) *Holidays*, London, Batsford.

Havins, P. J. N. (1976) *The Spas of England*, London, Robert Hale.

Hembry, P. (1990) *The English Spa, 1560–1815: A social history*, London, Athlone Press.

Hern, A. (1967) *The Seaside Holiday: The history of the English seaside resort*, London, Cresset Press.

Hibbert, C. (1969) *The Grand Tour*, London, Weidenfeld & Nicolson.

Hindley, G. (1983) *Tourists, Travellers and Pilgrims*, London, Hutchinson.

Jakle, J. A. (1985) *The Tourist: Travel in 20th-century North America*, Lincoln, NE, University of Nebraska Press.

Kapuscinski, R. (2008) *Travels with Herodotus*, London, Penguin.

Löfgren, O. (1999) *On Holiday: A History of Vacationing*, Berkeley CA, University of California Press.

Lloyd, M. (2003) *The Passport: The history of man's most travelled document*, Phoenix Mill, Sutton.

Mighall, R. (2008) *Sunshine: One Man's Search for Happiness*, London, John Murray.

Moir, E. (1964) *The Discovery of Britain: The English tourists, 1540–1840*, London, Routledge & Kegan Paul.

North, R. (1962) *The Butlin Story*, London, Jarrolds.

Ousby, I. (1990) *The Englishman's England: Taste, travel and the rise of tourism*, Cambridge, CUP.

Perrottet, T. (2003) *Route 66AD: Pagan holiday on the trail of ancient Roman tourists*, New York, Random House.

Pimlott, J. A. R. (1976) *The Englishman's Holiday*, Hassocks, Harvester.

Sillitoe, A. (1995) *Leading the Blind: A century of guide book travel, 1815–1914*, London, Macmillan.

Smith, P. (ed.) (1998) *The History of Tourism: Thomas Cook and the origins of leisure travel*, London, Routledge/Thoemmes Press.

Soane, J. V. N. (1993) *Fashionable Resort Regions: Their evolution and transformation*, Wallingford, CABI.

Somerville, C. (1990) *Britain Beside the Sea*, London, Grafton.

Stokes, H. G. (1947) *The Very First History of the English Seaside*, London, Sylvan Press.

Studd, R. G. (1948) *The Holiday Story*, London, Percival Marshall.

Swinglehurst, E. (1974) *The Romantic Journey: The Story of Thomas Cook and Victorian Travel*, London, Pica Editions.

Swinglehurst, E. (1982) *Cook's Tours: The story of popular travel*, Poole, Blandford Press.

Walton, J. K. (1983) *The English Seaside Resort: A social history 1750–1914*, Leicester, University of Leicester Press.

Walton, J. K. (2000) *The British Seaside: Holidays and resorts in the twentieth century*, Manchester, Manchester University Press.

Walton, J. K. and Walvin, J. (1983) *Leisure in Britain, 1780–1939*, Manchester, Manchester University Press.

Walvin, J. (1978) *Beside the Seaside: A social history of the popular seaside holiday*, London, Allen Lane.

Ward, C. and Hardy, D. (1986) *Goodnight Campers! The history of the British holiday camps*, London, Mansell.

Chapter 3 The era of popular tourism: 1950 to the twenty-first century

Akhtar, M. and Humphries, S. (2000) *Some Liked it Hot: The British on holiday at home and abroad*, London, Virgin Publishing.

Apostolopoulos, Y., Leontidou, L. and Loukissas, P. (eds) (2000) *Mediterranean Tourism*, London, Routledge.

Bray, R. and Raitz, V. (2000) *Flight to the Sun: The story of the holiday revolution*, London, Continuum.

Hodgson, G. (1995) *A New Grand Tour*, London, Viking.

Lencek, L. and Bosker, G. (1998) *The Beach: The history of paradise on Earth*, London, Secker and Warburg.

Middleton, V. and Lickorish, L. (2005) *British Tourism: The remarkable story of growth*, Oxford, Elsevier Butterworth-Heinemann.

Richardson, D. and Richards, B. (2000) *ABTA: The first 50 years*, London, ABTA.

Chapter 4 The demand for tourism

Apostolopoulos, Y., Leivadi, S. and Yiannakis, A. (eds) (1996) *The Sociology of Tourism*, London, Routledge.

Arit, W. (2006) *China's Outbound Tourism*, London, Routledge.

Clift, S. and Grabowski, P. (eds) (1997) *Tourism and Health: Risks, research and responses*, London, Cassell.

Clift, S., Luongo, M. and Callister, C. (2002) *Gay Tourism: Culture, identity and sex*, London, Continuum.

Clift, S. and Page, S. (1995) *Health and the International Tourist*, London, Routledge.

Decrop, A. (2006) *Vacation Decision-making*, Wallingford, CABI.

Gullahorn, J. E. and Gullahorn, J. T. (1963) An extension of the U-curve hypothesis, *Journal of Social Sciences*, **19**, 33–47.

Hall, C. M. and Ryan, C. (2001) *Sex Tourism: Marginal people and liminalities*, London, Routledge.

Hall, C. M., Timothy, D. J. and Duval, D. T. (eds) (2004) *Safety and Security in Tourism: Relationships, management and marketing*, New York, Haworth Hospitality Press.

Hughes, H. (2006) *Pink Tourism: Holidays of gay men and lesbians*, Wallingford, CABI.

Johnson, P. and Thomas, B. (eds) (1992) *Choice and Demand in Tourism*, London, Mansell.

Krippendorf, J. (1991) *The Holiday Makers: Understanding the impact of leisure and travel*, 2nd edn, Oxford, Heinemann.

MacCannell, D. (1992) *Empty Meeting Grounds: The tourist papers*, London, Routledge.

March, R. and Woodside, A. (2005) *Tourism Behaviour*, Wallingford, CABI.

Mayo, E. J. and Jarvis, L. P. (1981) *The Psychology of Leisure Travel: Effective marketing and selling of travel services*, Boston, MA, CBI.

Novelli, M. (ed.) (2005) *Niche Tourism: Contemporary issues, trends and cases*, Oxford, Elsevier.

Patterson, I. (2006) *Growing Older: Tourism and leisure behaviour of older adults*, Wallingford, CABI.

Pearce, P. L. (2011) *Tourist Behavior and the Contemporary World*, Clevedon, Channel View.

Pizam, A. and Mansfield, Y. (eds) (2005) *Consumer Behaviour in Travel and Tourism*, Mumbai, Jaico Publishing.

Plog, S. (1991) *Leisure Travel: Making it a growth market again!*, New York, Wiley.

Rapoport, R. and Rapoport, R. N. (1974) 'Four themes in the sociology of leisure', *British Journal of Sociology*, **15**, 215–229.

Rath, J. (ed.) (2006) *Tourism, Ethnic Diversity and the City*, London, Routledge.

Reader, I. and Walter, T. (eds) (1993) *Pilgrimage in Popular Culture*, Basingstoke, Macmillan.

Richards, G. (ed.) (2007) *Cultural Tourism: Global and local perspectives*, New York, Haworth Hospitality Press.

Robinson, M. and Boniface, P. (eds) (1998) *Tourism and Cultural Conflicts*, Wallingford, CABI.

Robinson, M., Evans, N. and Callaghan, P. (eds) (1996) *Culture as the Tourist Product*, Sunderland, Business Education Publishers.

Ross, G. F. (1998) *The Psychology of Tourism*, 2nd edn, Melbourne, Hospitality Press.

Ryan, C. (1995) *Researching Tourist Satisfaction: Issues, concepts, problems*, New York, Routledge.

Ryan, C. (ed.) (2002) *The Tourist Experience*, 2nd edn, London, Continuum.

Sheller, M. and Urry, J. (eds) (2004) *Tourism Mobilities: Places to play, places in play*, London, Routledge.

Swarbrooke, J., Beard, C., Leckie, S. and Pomfret, G. (2003) *Adventure Tourism: The new frontier*, Oxford, Butterworth-Heinemann.

Swarbrooke, J. and Horner, S. (1999) *Consumer Behaviour in Tourism*, Oxford, Butterworth-Heinemann.

Swarbrooke, J. and Horner, S. (2001) *Business Travel and Tourism*, Oxford, Butterworth-Heinemann.

Timothy, D. and Olsen, D. (eds) (2006) *Tourism, Religion and Spiritual Journeys*, London, Routledge.

Urry, J. (1995) *Consuming Places*, London, Routledge.

Urry, J. and Larsen, J. (2011) *The Tourist Gaze 3.0*, London, Sage.

Uysal, M. (ed.) (1994) *Global Tourist Behaviour*, New York, International Business Press.

Voase, R. (1995) *Tourism: The human perspective*, London, Hodder & Stoughton.

Waitt, G. and Markwell, K. (2006) *Gay Tourism: Culture and context*, New York, Haworth Hospitality Press.

Woodside, A., Crouch, G., Mazanek, J., Oppermann, M. and Sakai, M. (eds) (1999) *Consumer Psychology of Tourism, Hospitality and Leisure*, Wallingford, CABI.

Zurick, D. (1995) *Errant Journeys: Adventure travel in a modern age*, Austin, TX, University of Texas Press.

Chapter 5 The economic impacts of tourism

Ateljevic, I., Pritchard, A. and Morgan, N. (eds) (2007) *The Critical Turn in Tourism Studies: Innovative research methodologies*, Oxford, Elsevier.

Badger, A. (1996) *Trading Places: Tourism as trade*, London, Tourism Concern.

Buglear, J. (2000) *Stats to Go: A guide to statistics for hospitality, leisure and tourism studies*, Oxford, Butterworth-Heinemann.

Bull, A. (1995) *The Economics of Travel and Tourism*, 2nd edn, Harlow, Longman.

Clarke, M., Riley, M. and Wood, R. C. (1997) *Research Methods in Hospitality and Tourism*, London, International Thomson Business Press.

Coles, T. and Hall, C. M. (2008) *International Business and Tourism: Global issues, contemporary interactions*, London, Routledge.

Dwyer, L., Forsyth, P. and Dwyer, W. (2010) *Tourism Economics and Policy*, Clevedon, Channel View.

Frechtling, D. (2001) *Forecasting Tourism Demand: Methods and strategies*, Oxford, Butterworth-Heinemann.

Go, F. and Jenkins, C. (eds) (1998) *Tourism and Economic Development in Asia and Australia*, London, Pinter.

Goodson, L. and Phillimore, J. (eds) (2004) *Qualitative Research in Tourism: Ontologies, epistemologies and methodologies*, London, Routledge.

Harrison, D. (2001) *Tourism and the Less Developed Countries*, Wallingford, CABI.

Ioannides, D. and Debbage, K. G. (eds) (1998) *The Economic Geography of the Tourist Industry: A supply-side analysis*, London, Routledge.

de Kadt, E. (1979) *Tourism: Passport to Development?*, Oxford, OUP.

Knowles, T., Diamantis, D. and El-Mourhabi, J. (2004) *The Globalization of Tourism and Hospitality*, 2nd edn, London, Thomson Publishing.

Ladkin, A., Szivas, E. and Riley, M. (2002) *Tourism Employment: Analysis and planning*, Clevedon, Channel View.

Lennon, J. (ed.) (2003) *Tourism Statistics: International perspectives and current issues*, London, Continuum.

Lundberg, D., Stavenga, M. H. and Krishnamoorthy, M. (1995) *Tourism Economics*, New York, Wiley.

Pearce, D. G. and Butler, R. W. (eds) (1999) *Contemporary Issues in Tourism Development*, London, Routledge.

Preuss, H. (2007) *The Economics of Staging the Olympics*, Cheltenham, Edward Elgar.

Ritchie, B. W., Burns, P. and Palmer, C. (eds) (2005) *Tourism Research Methods: Integrating theory with practice*, Wallingford, CABI.

Sharpley, R. and Telfer, D. (eds) (2002) *Tourism and Development: Concepts and issues*, Clevedon, Channel View.

Smith, M. and Duffy, R. (2003) *The Ethics of Tourism Development*, London, Routledge.

Stabler, M., Papatheodorou, A. and Sinclair, M. T. (2009) *The Economics of Tourism*, London, Routledge.

Tribe, J. (2011) *The Economics of Recreation, Leisure and Tourism*, 4th edn, Oxford, Butterworth-Heinemann.

Vanhove, N. (2005) *The Economics of Tourism Destinations*, Oxford, Elsevier.

Veal, A. J. (1997) *Research Methods for Leisure and Tourism: A practical guide*, 2nd edn, Harlow, Longman.

Wall, G. and Mathieson, A. (2006) *Tourism: Change, impacts and opportunities*, 2nd edn, Harlow, Pearson Education.

Williams, A. and Shaw, G. (eds) (1991) *Tourism and Economic Development: Western European experiences*, 2nd edn, London, Wiley.

Wong, K. and Song, H. (eds) (2002) *Tourism Forecasting and Marketing*, New York, Haworth Hospitality Press.

Chapter 6 The socio-cultural impacts of tourism

Ashworth, G. J. and Larkham, P. J. (1994) *Building a New Heritage: Tourism, culture and identity in the new Europe*, London, Routledge.

Bauer, T. and McKercher, B. (eds) (2003) *Sex and Tourism: Journeys of romance, love and lust*, New York, Haworth Hospitality Press.

Boissevain, J. (ed.) (1992) *Revitalising European Rituals*, New York, Routledge.

Boissevain, J. (ed.) (1997) *Coping with Tourists: European reactions to mass tourism*, Oxford, Berghan.

Boniface, P. (1995) *Managing Quality Cultural Tourism*, London, Routledge.

Boniface, P. and Fowler, P. (1993) *Heritage and Tourism in the 'Global Village'*, London, Routledge.

Briguglio, L., Archer, B., Jafari, J. and Wall, G. (eds) (1996) *Sustainable Tourism in Islands and Small States: Issues and policies*, London, Pinter.

Butcher, J. (2002) *The Moralisation of Tourism: Sun, sand . . . and saving the world?* London, Routledge.

Butler, R. W. and Hinch, T. (eds) (1996) *Tourism and Indigenous Peoples*, London, International Thomson Business Press.

Clift, S. and Carter, S. (eds) (2000) *Tourism and Sex: Culture, Commerce and Coercion*, London, Cassell.

Dahles, H. and Keune, L. (eds) (2003) *Tourism Development and Local Participation: Latin American and Caribbean cases*, New York, Cognizant Communication.

Doxey, G. V. (1975) A causation theory of visitor-resident irritants: Methodology and research inferences, *The Impact of Tourism: Travel Research Association Sixth Annual Conference Proceedings*, San Diego, CA, Travel Research Association, 57–72.

Graburn, N. H. H. (ed.) (1976) *Ethnic and Tourist Arts: Cultural expressions from the Fourth World*, Berkeley, CA, University of California Press.

Hall, C. Michael and Lew, A. (2009) *Understanding and Managing Tourism Impacts: An integrated approach*, London, Routledge.

Harrison, L. and Husbands, W. (1996) *Practising Responsible Tourism: International case studies in tourism planning, policy and development*, New York, Wiley.

Hickman, L. (2007) *The Final Call: In search of the true cost of our holidays*, London, Eden Project Books.

Holden, A. (2005) *Tourism Studies and the Social Sciences*, London, Routledge.

MacCannell, D. (1999) *The Tourist: A new theory of the leisure class*, 3rd edn, London, University of California Press.

McCabe, S., Minnaert, L. and Dickmann, A. (2011) *Social Tourism in Europe*, Clevedon, Channel View.

Pattullo, P. (1996) *Last Resorts: The cost of tourism in the Caribbean*, London, Cassell.

Pearce, P. L., Moscardo, G. M. and Ross, G. F. (1996) *Tourism Community Relationships*, Oxford, Pergamon Press.

Price, M. (ed.) (1996) *People and Tourism in Fragile Environments*, Chichester, Wiley.

Reisinger, Y. and Turner, L. (2003) *Cross-Cultural Behaviour in Tourism: Concepts and analysis*, Oxford, Butterworth-Heinemann.

Richards, G. (ed.) (1996) *Cultural Tourism in Europe*, Wallingford, CABI.

Richards, G. and Hall, D. (eds) (2000) *Tourism and Sustainable Community Development*, London, Routledge.

Scheyvens, R. (2002) *Tourism for Development: Empowering communities*, Harlow, Pearson Education.

Singh, T. V. (2004) *New Horizons in Tourism: strange experiences and stranger practices*, Wallingford, CABI.

Smith, V. (ed.) (1992) *Hosts and Guests: An anthropology of tourism*, Oxford, Blackwell.

Smith, V. and Brent, M. (eds) (2001) *Hosts and Guests Revisited: Tourism issues in the 21st century*, New York, Cognizant Communication.

Stabler, M. J. (ed.) (1997) *Tourism and Sustainability: Principles to practice*, Wallingford, CABI.

Sutton, W. A. (1967) Travel and understanding: notes on the social structure of touring, *International Journal of Comparative Sociology*, **8** (2), 218–223.

Wall, G. and Mathieson, A. (2006) *Tourism: Change, impacts and opportunities*, 2nd edn, Harlow, Pearson Education.

Wood, K. and House, S. (1991) *The Good Tourist*, London, Mandarin.

Young, G. (1973) *Tourism: Blessing or blight?* London, Pelican.

Chapter 7 The environmental impacts of tourism

Aronsson, L. (2000) *The Development of Sustainable Tourism*, London, Continuum.

Boo, E. (1990) *Eco-tourism: The potentials and the pitfalls*, Washington, DC, World Wildlife Fund.

Bramwell, B. and Lane, B. (eds) (1993) *Rural Tourism and Sustainable Rural Development*, Clevedon, Channel View.

Bramwell, H., Henry, I., Jackson, G., Goytia Prat, A., Richards, G. and van der Straaten, J. (eds) (1996) *Sustainable Tourism Management: Principles and practice*, Tilburg, Tilburg University Press.

Buckley, R. (ed.) (2004) *Environmental Impacts of Ecotourism*, Wallingford, CABI.

Bushell, R. and Eagles, P. F. (eds) (2006) *Tourism and Protected Areas: Benefits beyond boundaries*, Wallingford, CABI.

Butcher, J. (2007) *Ecotourism, NGOs and Development: A critical analysis*, London, Routledge.

Cater, E. and Lowman, G. (1994) *Ecotourism: A sustainable option?*, Chichester, Wiley.

Croall, J. (1995) *Preserve or Destroy: Tourism and the environment*, London, Calouste Gulbenkian Foundation.

Eagles, P. F. and McCool, S. F. (2004) *Tourism in National Parks and Protected Areas: Planning and management*, Wallingford, CABI.

Eber, S. (ed.) (1992) *Beyond the Green Horizon: A discussion paper on principles for sustainable tourism*, London, Tourism Concern/World Wildlife Fund.

Elkington, J. and Hailes, J. (1992) *Holidays that Don't Cost the Earth*, London, Victor Gollancz.

Fennell, D. A. (2007) *Ecotourism*, 3rd edn, London, Routledge.

Font, X. and Tribe, J. (eds) (1999) *Forest Tourism and Recreation: Case studies in environmental management*, Wallingford, CABI.

Forsyth, T. (1996) *Sustainable Tourism: Moving from theory to practice*, London, Tourism Concern/ Worldwide Fund for Nature.

France, L. (ed.) (1997) *The Earthscan Reader in Sustainable Tourism*, London, Earthscan/Kogan Page.

Hall, C. M. (ed.) (1998) *Sustainable Tourism: A geographical perspective*, Harlow, Longman.

Hall, C. Michael and Lew, A. (2009) *Understanding and Managing Tourism Impacts: An integrated approach*, London, Routledge.

Harris, R., Griffin, T. and Williams, P. (eds) (2002) *Sustainable Tourism: A global perspective*, Oxford, Elsevier Butterworth-Heinemann.

Holden, A. (2007) *Environment and Tourism*, 2nd edn, London, Routledge.

Honey, M. (1999) *Ecotourism and Sustainable Development: Who owns paradise?*, Washington, DC, Island Press.

Hunter, C. and Green, H. (1995) *Tourism and the Environment: A sustainable relationship?*, London, Routledge.

Inskip, E. (1991) *Tourism Planning: An integrated and sustainable development*, New York, Van Nostrand Reinhold.

Ioannides, D., Apostolopoulos, Y. and Sonmez, S. (eds) (2001) *Mediterranean Islands and Sustainable Tourism Development: Practices, management and policies*, London, Continuum.

Middleton, V. with Hawkins, R. (1998) *Sustainable Tourism: A marketing perspective*, London, Butterworth-Heinemann.

Mowforth, M. and Munt, I. (2008) *Tourism and Sustainability: Development, globalization and new tourism in the Third World*, 3rd edn, London, Routledge.

Neale, G. (ed.) (1997) *The Green Travel Guide*, London, Kogan Page.

Newsome, D., Moore, S. and Dowling, R. (2002) *Natural Area Tourism: Ecology, impacts and management*, Clevedon, Channel View.

Priestley, G. K., Edwards, J. A. and Coccossis, H. (eds) (1996) *Sustainable Tourism?: European experiences*, Wallingford, CABI.

Stonehouse, B. and Snyder, J. (2010) *Polar tourism: an environmental perspective*, Clevedon, Channel View.

Tribe, J., Font, X., Griffiths, N., Vickery, R. and Yale, K. (2000) *Environmental Management for Rural Tourism and Recreation*, London, Continuum.

Wahab, S. and Pigram, J. (eds) (1997) *Tourism Development and Growth: The challenge of sustainability*, London, Routledge.

Wall, G. and Mathieson, A. (2006) *Tourism: Change, impacts and opportunities*, 2nd edn, Harlow, Pearson Education.

Wearing, S. (2009) *Ecotourism: Impacts, Potentials and Possibilities*, 2nd edn, Oxford, Butterworth-Heinemann.

Weaver, D. B. (1998) *Ecotourism in the Less Developed World*, Wallingford, CABI.

Weaver, D. B. (ed.) (2003) *The Encyclopaedia of Ecotourism*, Wallingford, CABI.

Chapter 8 The structure and organization of the travel and tourism industry

Buhalis, D. and Laws, E. (eds) (2001) *Tourism Distribution Channels: Practices, issues and transformations*, London, Continuum.

Gee, C. Y., Choy, D. J. L. and Makens, J. C. (1997) *The Travel Industry*, 3rd edn, London, van Nostrand Reinhold.

Hodgson, A. (ed.) (1987) *The Travel and Tourism Industry: Strategies for the future*, Oxford, Pergamon Press.

Horner, P. (1991) *The Travel Industry in Britain*, Cheltenham, Stanley Thornes.

Pearce, D. (1992) *Tourism Organisations*, Harlow, Longman.

Pender, L. (2001) *Travel Trade and Transport: An introduction*, London, Continuum.

Sinclair, M. T. and Stabler, M. (eds) (1991) *The Tourism Industry: An international analysis*, Wallingford, CABI.

Uysal, M. and Fesenmaier, D. (eds) (1993) *Communication and Channel Systems in Tourism Marketing*, New York, Haworth Hospitality Press.

Weiermair, K. and Mathies, C. (eds) (2004) *The Tourism and Leisure Industry: Shaping the future*, New York, Haworth Hospitality Press.

Chapter 9 Tourist destinations

Ashworth, G. J. and Goodall, B. (1990) *Marketing Tourism Places*, London, Routledge.

Ashworth, G. and Tunbridge, J. (1990) *The Tourist-Historic City*, London, Belhaven Press.

Ashworth, G. J. and Voogd, H. (1990) *Selling the City: The use of publicity and public relations to sell cities and regions*, London, Belhaven Press.

Bachmann, P. (1988) *Tourism in Kenya: A basic need for whom?*, Berne, Peter Lang.

Barke, M., Towner, J. and Newton, M. (1995) *Tourism in Spain*, Wallingford, CABI.

Beeton, S. (2005) *Film-induced Tourism*, Clevedon, Channel View.

Brodie, A. and Winter, G. (2007) *England's Seaside Resorts*, UK, English Heritage.

Brown, F. and Hall, D. (eds) (2000) *Tourism in Peripheral Areas*, Clevedon, Channel View.

Burton, R. (1994) *Travel Geography*, 2nd edn, London, Pitman.

Butler, R., Hall, C. M. and Jenkins, J. (1998) *Tourism and Recreation in Rural Areas*, Chichester, Wiley.

Cohen, M. (2006) *No Holiday: 80 places you don't want to visit*, New York, The Disinformation Company.

Cohen, M. and Bodeker, G. (2008) *Understanding the Global Spa Industry*, Oxford, Butterworth-Heinemann.

Conlin, M. V. and Baum, T. (1995) *Island Tourism: Management principles and practice*, Chichester, Wiley.

Davidson, R. and Maitland, R. (1997) *Tourism Destinations*, London, Hodder & Stoughton.

Frost, W. and Hall, C. M. (eds) (2008) *Tourism and National Parks: International perspectives on development, histories and change*, London, Routledge.

Gabler, K., Maier, G., Mazenac, J. and Wober, K. (1997) *International City Tourism: Analysis and strategy*, London, Pinter Cassell.

Getz, D. and Page, S. (1997) *Business of Rural Tourism*, London, International Thomson Business Press.

Goodall, B. and Ashworth, G. (1987) *Marketing in the Tourism Industry: The promotion of destination regions*, London, Routledge.

Hall, C. M. and Johnston, M. (1995) *Polar Tourism: Tourism in the Arctic and Antarctic regions*, Chichester, Wiley.

Hall, C. M. and Page, S. J. (eds) (1996) *Tourism in the Pacific: Issues and challenges*, London, International Thomson Business Press.

Hall, C. M. and Page, S. J. (2005) *The Geography of Tourism and Recreation*, 3rd edn, London, Routledge.

Hall, D., Marciszewska, B. and Smith, M. (eds) (2006) *Tourism in the New Europe: The challenges and opportunities of EU enlargement*, Wallingford, CABI.

Hancock, D. (2006) *The Complete Medical Tourist*, London, John Blake Publishing.

Higham, J. (ed.) (2005) *Sports Tourism Destinations: Issues, opportunities and analysis*, London, Elsevier.

Howie, F. (2001) *Managing the Tourist Destination: A practical interactive guide*, London, Continuum.

Huybers, T. (ed.) (2007) *Tourism in Developing Countries*, Cheltenham, Edward Elgar.

Jones, A. L. and Phillips, M. (2010) *Disappearing Destinations: climate change and future challenges for coastal tourism*, Wallingford, CABI.

Judd, D. R. and Fainstein, S. (eds) (1999) *The Tourist City*, New Haven, CT, Yale University Press.

Kearns, G. and Philo, C. (1993) *Selling Places: The city as cultural capital, past and present*, Oxford, Pergamon Press.

King, B. (1997) *Creating Island Resorts*, London, Routledge.

Kozak, M. (2004) *Destination Benchmarking: Concepts, practices and operations*, Wallingford, CABI.

Law, C. M. (ed.) (1996) *Tourism in Major Cities*, London, International Thomson Business Press.

Law, C. M. (2002) *Urban Tourism: The visitor economy and the growth of large cities*, 2nd edn, London, Continuum.

Laws, E. (1995) *Tourism Destination Management: Issues, analysis and policies*, London, International Thomson Business Press.

Lickorish, L. J., Bodlender, J., Jefferson, A. and Jenkins, C. L. (1991) *Developing Tourism Destinations: Policies and perspectives*, Harlow, Longman.

Lockhart, D. and Smith, D. (eds) (1996) *Island Tourism: Trends and prospects*, London, Cassell.

Maitland, R. and Newman, P. (eds) (2008) *World Tourism Cities: developing tourism off the beaten track*, London, Routledge.

Morgan, N., Pritchard, A. and Pride, R. (eds) (2001) *Destination Branding: Developing a destination proposition*, Oxford, Butterworth-Heinemann.

Müller, D. K. and Jansson, B. (2006) *Tourism in the Peripheries*, Wallingford, CABI.

Oppermann, M. and Chon, K.-S. (1997) *Tourism in Developing Countries*, London, International Thomson Business Press.

Page, S. J. (1995) *Urban Tourism*, London, Routledge.

Page, S. J. and Getz, D. (1997) *The Business of Rural Tourism: International perspectives*, London, International Thomson Business Press.

Papatheodorou, A. (ed.) (2006) *Managing Tourism Destinations*, Cheltenham, Edward Elgar.

Prideaux, B. (2009) *Resort Destinations: evolution, management and development*, Oxford, Butterworth-Heinemann.

Ringer, G. (ed.) (1998) *Destinations: Cultural landscapes of tourism*, London, Routledge.

Selby, M. (2004) *Understanding Urban Tourism: Image, culture, experience*, London, I. B. Tauris.

Shackley, M. (1996) *Wildlife Tourism*, London, International Thomson Business Press.

Sharpley, R. (1996) *Tourism and Leisure in the Countryside*, 2nd edn, Huntingdon, Elm Publications.

Sharpley, R. and Sharpley, J. (1997) *Rural Tourism: An introduction*, London, International Thomson Business Press.

Shaw, G. and Williams, A. M. (eds) (1996) *The Rise and Fall of British Coastal Tourism: Cultural and economic perspectives*, London, Mansell.

Shaw, G. and Williams, A. M. (2004) *Tourism and Tourism Spaces*, London, Sage.

Singh, S., Timothy, D. and Dowling, R. (eds) (2003) *Tourism in Destination Communities*, Wallingford, CABI.

Smith, M. K. (2006) *Tourism, Culture and Regeneration*, Wallingford, CABI.

Soane, J. V. N. (1993) *Fashionable Resort Regions: Their evolution and transformation*, Wallingford, CABI.

Tyler, D., Guerrier, Y. and Robertson, M. (eds) (1998) *Managing Tourism in Cities: Policy, process and practice*, Chichester, Wiley.

Tzanelli, R. (ed.) (2007) *The Cinematic Tourist: Explorations in globalization, culture and resistance*, London, Routledge.

Williams, S. (2009) *Tourism Geography: A new synthesis*, 2nd edn, London, Routledge.

Chapter 10 Tourist attractions

Ashworth, G. and Hartmann, R. (eds) (2004) *Horror and Human Tragedy Revisited: The management of sites of atrocities for tourism*, New York, Cognizant Communications.

Buckley, R. (2006) *Adventure Tourism*, Wallingford, CABI.

Crouch, D., Jackson, R. and Thomson, F. (eds) (2005) *The Media and the Tourist Imagination: Converging cultures*, London, Routledge.

Dann, G. and Seaton, A. (eds) (2002) *Slavery, Contested Heritage and Thanatourism*, New York, Haworth Hospitality Press.

Dallen, J. T. (2005) *Shopping Tourism, Retailing and Leisure*, Clevedon, Channel View.

Drummond, S. and Yeoman, I. (2000) *Quality Issues in Heritage Visitor Attractions*, Oxford, Butterworth-Heinemann.

Fjellman, S. (1992) *Vinyl Leaves: Walt Disney World and America*, Boulder, CO, Westview Press.

Fyall, A., Garrod, B. and Leask, A. (eds) (2003) *Managing Visitor Attractions: New directions*, Oxford, Butterworth-Heinemann.

Gammon, S. and Jones, I. (2001) *Sports Tourism: An introduction*, London, Continuum.

Getz, D. (1990) *Festivals, Special Events and Tourism*, New York, Van Nostrand Reinhold.

Getz, D. (1997) *Event Management and Event Tourism*, New York, Cognizant Communications.

Getz, D. (2001) *Explore Wine Tourism: Management, development and destinations*, New York, Cognizant Communications.

Gibson, H. J. (ed.) (2006) *Sport Tourism*, London, Routledge.

Goldblatt, J. J. (1990) *Special Events: The art and science of celebration*, New York, Van Nostrand Reinhold.

Hall, C. M. (1992) *Hallmark Tourist Events: Impacts, management and planning*, Chichester, Wiley.

Hall, C. M., Sharples, L., Cambourne, B. and Macionis, N. (2000) *Wine Tourism around the World: Development, management and markets*, Oxford, Butterworth-Heinemann.

Hall, C. M., Sharples, L., Mitchell, F., Macionis, N. and Camborne, B. (2003) *Food Tourism around the World*, Oxford, Butterworth-Heinemann.

Harrison, R. (1994) *Manual of Heritage Management*, Oxford, Butterworth-Heinemann.

Hewison, R. (1987) *The Heritage Industry: Britain in a climate of decline*, London, Methuen.

Higham, J. and Hinch, T. (2009) *Sport and Tourism. Globalization, Mobility and Identity*, Oxford, Elsevier.

Hinch, T. and Higham, J. (2004) *Sport Tourism Development*, Clevedon, Channel View.

Hjalager, A.-M. and Richards, G. (eds) (2002) *Tourism and Gastronomy*, London, Routledge.

Hudson, S. (2000) *Snow Business: A study of the international ski industry*, London, Cassell.

Hudson, S. (ed.) (2003) *Sport and Adventure Tourism*, New York, Haworth Hospitality Press.

Hughes, H. (2000) *Arts, Entertainment and Tourism*, Oxford, Butterworth-Heinemann.

Jencks, C. (2005) *The Iconic Building: The power of enigma*, London, Frances Lincoln.

Johnson, P. and Thomas, B. (1992) *Tourism, Museums and the Local Economy*, Cheltenham, Edward Elgar.

Klugman, K., Kuenz, J., Waldrep, S. and Willis, S. (1995) *Inside the Mouse: Work and play at Disneyworld*, Durham, NC, Duke University Press.

Kozak, M. (2008) *Managing and Marketing Tourist Destinations: Strategies to gain a competitive edge*, London, Routledge.

Leask, A. and Yeoman, I. (eds) (1999) *Heritage Visitor Attractions: An operations management perspective*, London, Cassell.

Lennon, J. and Foley, M. (2000) *Dark Tourism: The attraction of death and disaster*, London, Continuum.

Lovelock, B. (ed.) (2007) *Tourism and the Consumption of Wildlife: Hunting, shooting and sport fishing*, London, Routledge.

Murphy, L., Benckendorff, P., Moscardo, G. and Pearce, P. (2009) *Tourist Shopping Villages: Forms and functions*, London, Routledge.

Prentice, R. (1993) *Tourism and Heritage Attractions*, London, Routledge.

Preuss, H. (2006) *The Economics of Staging the Olympics*, Cheltenham, Edward Elgar.

Richards, B. (1992) *How to Market Tourism Attractions, Festivals and Special Events*, Harlow, Longman.

Richards, G. (ed.) (2001) *Cultural Attractions and European Tourism*, Wallingford, CABI.

Richards, G. and Wilson, J. (eds) (2007) *Tourism, Creativity and Development*, London, Routledge.

Ritchie, B. and Adair, D. (eds) (2004) *Sport Tourism: Interrelationships, impacts and issues*, Clevedon, Channel View.

Robertson, M. and Frew, E. (eds) (2008) *Events and Festivals: Current trends and issues*, London, Routledge.

Robinson, M., Evans, N. and Callaghan, P. (eds) (1996) *Tourism and Culture: Image, identity and marketing*, Sunderland, Business Education Publishers.

Robinson, T., Gammon, S. and Jones, I. (2000) *Sports Tourism: An introduction*, London, Continuum.

Rojek, C. (1993) *Ways of Escape: Modern transformations in leisure and travel*, Basingstoke, Macmillan.

Sharpley, R. and Stone, P. (2009) *The Darker Side of Travel*, Clevedon, Channel View.

Swarbrooke, J. (2002) *The Development and Management of Visitor Attractions*, 2nd edn, Oxford, Butterworth-Heinemann.

Syme, G. J. (1989) *The Planning and Evaluation of Hallmark Events*, Aldershot, Gower.

Timothy, D. and Boyd, S. (2003) *Heritage Tourism*, Harlow, Pearson Education.

Timothy, D. and Olsen, D. (eds) (2006) *Tourism, Religion and Spiritual Journeys*, London, Routledge.

Toohey, K. and Veal, A. J. (2007) *The Olympic Games: A social science perspective*, 2nd edn, Wallingford, CABI.

Uzzell, D. (ed.) (1989) *Heritage Interpretation: Vol. 1: The Natural and Built Environment, Vol. 2: The Visitor Experience*, London, Belhaven Press.

Watt, D. (1998) *Event Management in Leisure and Tourism*, Harlow, Addison-Wesley Longman.

Weed, M. (ed.) (2007) *Sport and Tourism: A reader*, London, Routledge.

Weed, M. (2008) *Olympic Tourism*, Amsterdam, Butterworth-Heinemann.

Weed, M. and Bull C. J. (2009) *Sports Tourism: Participants, Policy and Providers*, 2nd edn, Oxford, Elsevier Butterworth-Heinemann.

Yeoman, I., Robertson, M., Ali-Knoight, J., Drummond, S. and McMahon-Beattie, U. (2004) *Festival and Events Management: An international arts and culture perspective*, Oxford, Elsevier.

Chapter 11 Business tourism

Allen, J. (2000) *The Ultimate Guide to Successful Meetings, Corporate Events, Fundraising Galas, Conferences, Conventions, Incentives and Other Special Events*, Toronto, Wiley.

Allen, J. (2002) *The Business of Event Planning, Behind-the-scenes Secrets of Successful Special Events*, Toronto, Wiley.

Astroff, M. and Abbey, J. (2006) *Convention Sales and Services*, Las Vegas, NV, Waterbury Press.

Bowdin, G., McDonnell, I., Allen, J. and O'Toole, W. (2010) *Events Management*, 3rd edn, Oxford, Elsevier Butterworth-Heinemann.

Campbell, F., Robinson, A., Brown, S. and Race, P. (2003) *Essential Tips for Organising Conferences and Events*, London, Kogan Page.

Davidson, R. and Cope, B. (2003) *Business Travel: Conferences, incentive travel, exhibitions, corporate hospitality and corporate travel*, Harlow, Pearson Education.

Davidson, R. and Rogers, T. (2006) *Marketing Destinations and Venues for Conferences, Conventions and Business Events*, Oxford, Butterworth-Heinemann.

Goldblatt, J. (2010) *Special Events: A New Generation and the Next Frontier*, New York, Wiley.

Harrill, R. (ed.) (2005) *Fundamentals of Destination Management and Marketing*, Washington, DC, IACVB.

Krugman, C. and Wright, R. (2007) *Global Meetings and Exhibitions*, Hoboken, NJ, Wiley.

McCabe, V., Poole, B. and Leiper, N. (2000) *The Business and Management of Conventions*, Milton, Wiley.

Rogers, T. (2008) *Conferences and Conventions: A global industry*, Oxford, Butterworth-Heinemann.

Rutherford, D. (1990) *Introduction to the Conventions, Expositions and Meetings Industry*, New York, Van Nostrand Reinhold.

Shone, A. (1998) *The Business of Conferences*, Oxford, Butterworth-Heinemann.

Shone, A. and Parry, B. (2001) *Successful Event Management: A practical handbook*, London, Continuum.

Silvers, J. R. (2004) *Professional Event Coordination*, Hoboken, NJ, Wiley.

Swarbrooke, J. and Horner, S. (2001) *Business Travel and Tourism*, Oxford, Butterworth-Heinemann.

Weber, K. and Chon, K. (eds) (2002) *Convention Tourism: International research and industry perspectives*, New York, Haworth Hospitality Press.

Chapter 12 The hospitality sector: accommodation and catering services

Cunill, O. (2006) *The Growth Strategies of Hotel Chains: Best business practices by leading companies*, New York, Haworth Hospitality Press.

Go, F. and Pine, R. (1995) *Globalization Strategy in the Hotel Industry*, London, International Thomson Business Press.

Lawson, F. (1995) *Hotels and Resorts: Planning, design and refurbishment*, Oxford, Butterworth-Heinemann.

Lockwood, A. and Medlik, S. (2002) *Tourism and Hospitality in the 21st Century*, Oxford, Elsevier Butterworth-Heinemann.

Lynch, P., Morrison, A. and Lashley, C. (2006) *Hospitality*, London, Routledge.

Medlik, S. and Ingram, H. (2000) *The Business of Hotels*, 4th edn, Oxford, Elsevier.

Tesone, D.V. (2009) *Principles of Management for the Hospitality Industry*, London, Routledge.

Chapter 13 Tourist transport by air

Ashford, N., Martin Stanton, H. P. and Moore, C. A. (1991) *Airport Operations*, London, Pitman.

Barlay, S. (1994) *Cleared for Take-off: Behind the scenes of air travel*, London, Kyle Cathie.

Bell, G., Bowen, P. and Fawcett, P. (1984) *The Business of Transport*, Plymouth, Macdonald & Evans.

Benson, D. and Whitehead, G. (1985) *Transport and Distribution*, Harlow, Longman.

Blackshaw, C. (1991) *Aviation Law and Regulation*, London, Pitman.

Button, K. (ed.) (1990) *Airline Deregulation*, London, David Fulton.

Calder, S. (2003) *No Frills: The truth behind the low-cost revolution in the skies*, London, Virgin Books.

Committee of Inquiry into Civil Air Transport (1969) *British Air Transport in the Seventies*, London, HMSO.

Dobson, A. (1994) *Flying in the Face of Competition*, Aldershot, Avebury Aviation/Ashgate.

Doganis, R. (1992) *The Airport Business*, London, Routledge.

Doganis, R. (2002) *Flying Off Course – the Economics of International Airlines*, 3rd edn, London, Routledge.

Eaton, A. J. (1995) *The International Airline Business: Globalisation in action*, Aldershot, Avebury Aviation/Ashgate.

Graham, A. (2008) *Managing Airports: An international perspective*, 3rd edn, Oxford, Butterworth-Heinemann.

Graham, B. (1995) *Geography and Air Transport*, Chichester, Wiley.

Hanlon, J. P. (2007) *Global Airlines: Competition in a transnational industry*, 3rd edn, Oxford, Butterworth-Heinemann.

Holloway, S. (2003) *Straight and Level: Practical Airline Economics*, 2nd edn, Aldershot, Ashgate.

Lumsdon, L. and Page, S. J. (2004) *Tourism and Transport: Issues and agenda for the new millennium*, Oxford, Elsevier Butterworth-Heinemann.

Page, S. J. (2009) *Transport and Tourism: Global Perspectives*, 3rd edn, Harlow, Pearson Education.

Pender, L. (2001) *Travel Trade and Transport: An introduction*, London, Continuum.

Phipps, D. (1991) *The Management of Aviation Security*, London, Pitman.

Shaw, S. (1990) *Airline Marketing and Management*, 3rd edn, London, Pitman.

Wheatcroft, S. (1994) *Aviation and Tourism Policies*, London, Routledge.

Williams, G. (1994) *The Airline Industry and the Impact of Deregulation*, Aldershot, Avebury Aviation/Ashgate.

Chapter 14 Tourist transport by water

Berger, A. (2004) *Review of Ocean Travel and Cruising: A cultural analysis*, New York, Haworth Hospitality Press.

Cartwright, R. and Baird, C. (1999) *The Development and Growth of the Cruise Industry*, Oxford, Butterworth-Heinemann.

Chin, C. (2008) *Cruising in the Global Economy: Profits, pleasure and work at sea*, Aldershot, Ashgate.

Dickinson, R. H. and Vladimir, A. N. (1997) *Selling the Sea: An inside look at the cruise industry*, New York, Wiley.

Douglas, N. and Douglas, B. (2004) *The Cruise Ship Experience*, French's Forest, Pearson Hospitality Press.

Dowling, R. K. (ed.) (2006) *Cruise Ship Tourism*, Wallingford, CABI.

Jennings, G. (ed.) (2007) *Water-based Tourism, Sport, Leisure and Recreation Experiences*, Oxford, Elsevier.

Peisley, T. (2003) *Global Changes in the Cruise Industry 2003–2010*, Colchester, Seatrade Communications.

Prideaux, B. and Cooper, M. J. M. (2009) *River Tourism*, Wallingford, CABI.

Chapter 15 Tourist transport on land

Dickinson, J. and Lumsdon, L. (2010) *Slow Travel and Tourism*, London, Earthscan.

Page, S. J. (2009) *Transport and Tourism: Global Perspectives*, 3rd edn, Harlow, Pearson Education.

Prideaux, B. and Carsen, D. (eds) (2011) *Drive Tourism: trends and emerging markets*, Abingdon, Routledge.

Chapter 16 The management of visitors

Evans, N., Campbell, D. and Stonehouse, G. (2003) *Strategic Management for Travel and Tourism*, Oxford, Elsevier.

Fyall, A., Garrod, B. and Leask, A. (eds) (2003) *Managing Visitor Attractions: New directions*, Oxford, Butterworth-Heinemann.

Glaesser, D. (2003) *Crisis Management in the Tourism Industry*, Oxford, Butterworth-Heinemann.

Gunn, C., with Var, T. (2002) *Tourism Planning: Basics, concepts, cases*, 4th edn, London, Routledge.

Horner, S. and Swarbrooke, J. (2004) *International Cases in Tourism Management*, Oxford, Elsevier Butterworth-Heinemann.

Inskip, E. (1991) *Tourism Planning: An integrated and sustainable development*, New York, Van Nostrand Reinhold.

Inskip, E. (1994) *National and Regional Tourism Planning: Methodologies and case studies*, London, Routledge.

Leask, A. and Yeoman, I. (eds) (1999) *Heritage Visitor Attractions: An operations management perspective*, London, Cassell.

Leiper, N. (2004) *Tourism Management*, 3rd edn, Melbourne, Hospitality Press.

Pender, L. and Sharpley, R. (2005) *The Management of Tourism*, London, Sage.

Richardson, J. I. and Fluker, M. (2004) *Understanding and Managing Tourism*, French's Forest, Pearson Hospitality Press.

Ritchie, B. (2009) *Crisis and Disaster Management for Tourism*, Clevedon, Channel View.

Swarbrooke, J. (2002) *The Development and Management of Visitor Attractions*, 2nd edn, Oxford, Butterworth-Heinemann.

Chapter 17 The structure and role of the public sector in tourism

Allcock, J. B. (1990) *Tourism in Centrally Planned Economies*, Oxford, Pergamon.

Ashworth, G. J. (1991) *Heritage Planning*, Groningen, Geo Pers.

Ashworth, G. J. and Dietvorst, A. G. J. (1995) *Tourism and Spatial Transformations: Implications for policy and planning*, Wallingford, CABI.

Bosselman, F., Peterson, C. and McCarthy, C. (1999) *Managing Tourism Growth: Issues and applications*, Washington, DC, Island Press.

Bramwell, B. and Lane, B. (eds) (2000) *Tourism Collaboration and Partnership: Politics, practice and sustainability*, Clevedon, Channel View.

Deegan, J. and Dineen, D. (1997) *Tourism Policy and Performance*, London, International Thomson Business Press.

Edgell, D. (1990) *International Tourism Policy*, New York, Van Nostrand Reinhold.

Edgell, D., DelMastro Allen, M., Smith, G. and Swanson, J. (2007) *Tourism Policy and Planning: yesterday, today and tomorrow*, Oxford, Butterworth-Heinemann.

Elliott, J. (1997) *Tourism: Politics and public sector management*, London, Routledge.

Godde, P. M., Price, M. and Zimmermann, F. (2000) *Tourism Development in Mountain Regions*, Wallingford, CABI.

Godfrey, K. and Clarke, J. (2000) *The Tourism Development Handbook: A practical approach to planning and marketing*, London, Cassell.

Gunn, C. (1997) *Vacationscape: Designing Tourist Regions*, 4th edn, New York, Van Nostrand Reinhold.

Gunn, C. and Var, T. (2002) *Tourism Planning: Basics, concepts and cases*, 4th edn, London, Routledge.

Hall, C. M. (1994) *Tourism and Politics: Policy, power and place*, New York, Wiley.

Hall, C. M. (1994) *Tourism in the Pacific: Development, impacts and markets*, London, Pitman.

Hall, C. M. (2008) *Tourism Planning: Policies, processes and relationships*, 2nd edn, Harlow, Pearson Education.

Hall, C. M. and Jenkins, J. M. (1995) *Tourism and Public Policy*, London, Routledge.

Jeffries, D. (2001) *Governments and Tourism*, Oxford, Butterworth-Heinemann.

Johnson, P. and Thomas, B. (eds) (1992) *Perspectives on Tourism Policy*, London, Mansell.

Laws, E., Richins, H., Agrusa, J. F. and Scott, N. (2011) *Tourism Destination Governance: practice, theory and issues*, Wallingford, CABI.

Leslie, D. and Muir, F. (1997) *Local Agenda 21, Local Authorities and Tourism: A UK perspective*, Glasgow, Glasgow Caledonian University.

Morgan, N. and Pritchard, A. (1998) *Tourism Promotion and Power: Creating images, creating identities*, Chichester, Wiley.

Pompl, W. and Lavery, P. (1993) *Tourism in Europe: Structures and development*, Wallingford, CABI.

Reid, D. (2003) *Tourism Globalization and Development: Responsible tourism planning*, London, Pluto Press.

Singh, T. V. and Singh, S. (eds) (1999) *Tourism Development in Critical Environments*, New York, Cognizant.

Timothy, D. J. and Wall, G. (2000) *Tourism and Political Boundaries*, London, Routledge.

Chapter 18 Tour operating

Grant, D. and Mason, S. (1993) *The EC Directive on Package Travel, Package Holidays and Package Tours*, Newcastle, University of Northumbria.

Kärcher, K. (1997) *Reinventing the Package Holiday Business*, Wiesbaden, Deutscher Universitats Verlag.

Laws, E. (1997) *Managing Packaged Tourism*, London, International Thomson Business Press.

Poustie, M., Ross, J., Geddes, N. and Stewart, W. (1999) *Hospitality and Tourism Law*, London, International Thomson Business Press.

Poynter, J. (1989) *Foreign Independent Tours: Planning, pricing and processing*, Albany, Delmar.

Poynter, J. (1993) *Tour Design, Marketing and Management*, Harlow, Prentice Hall.

Yale, P. (1995) *The Business of Tour Operations*, Harlow, Longman.

Chapter 19 Selling and distributing travel and tourism

Bottomley Renshaw, M. (1997) *The Travel Agent*, 2nd edn, Sunderland, Business Education Publishers.

Burton, J. and Burton, L. (1994) *Interpersonal Skills for Travel and Tourism*, Harlow, Longman.

Coopers & Lybrand (1997) *Travel Agents' Benchmarking Survey*, London, Coopers & Lybrand.

Horner, P. (1996) *Travel Agency Practice*, Harlow, Longman.

Syratt, G. (1995) *Manual of Travel Agency Practice*, 2nd edn, Oxford, Butterworth-Heinemann.

Chapter 20 Ancillary tourism services

Ap, J. and Wong, K. K. F. (2001) Case study on tour guiding: professionalism, issues and problems, *Tourism Management*, **22** (5), 551–563.

Hallett, R. and Kaplan-Weinger, J. (2010) *Official Tourism Websites: a discourse analysis perspective*, Clevedon, Channel View.

Holloway, J. C. (2004) *Marketing for Tourism*, 4th edn, Harlow, Pearson Education.

Pond, K. L. (1993) *The Professional Guide: Dynamics of tour guiding*, New York, Van Nostrand Reinhold.

Reily Collins, V. (2000) *Becoming a Tour Guide: Principles of guiding and site interpretation*, London, Continuum.

Key trade, professional and academic magazines and journals

In addition to the growing number of international academic and professional publications listed below, readers are also directed to the many magazines and journals aimed at the general public, many of which are valuable sources of material for students and practitioners of travel and tourism. They include such periodicals as *Airline World*, *Flight International*, *Buses*, *Heritage*, and so on.

ABTA Magazine	monthly
Anatolia	3 per annum
Annals of Tourism Research	quarterly
ASEAN Journal on Hospitality and Tourism	bi-annually
Asia Pacific Journal of Tourism Research	6 per annum
Business Destinations	6 per annum
Business Travel	6 per annum
Business Traveller	monthly
Business Travel World	monthly
Current Issues in Tourism	8 per annum
Destination UK	bi-monthly
Event Management	quarterly
Executive Travel	monthly
Flight International	weekly
Group Travel & Coach World	Monthly
ICAO Journal	6 per annum
Information Technology and Tourism	3 per annum
International Journal of Culture, Tourism and Hospitality Research	quarterly
International Journal of Hospitality and Tourism Administration	quarterly
International Journal of Tourism Research	6 per annum
International Tourism Quarterly (EIU)	quarterly
Journal of Air Transport Management	8 per annum
Journal of China Tourism Research	quarterly
Journal of Convention and Event Tourism	quarterly

Journal of Ecotourism	3 per annum
Journal of Heritage Tourism	quarterly
Journal of Hospitality and Tourism Research	quarterly
Journal of Hospitality Marketing and Management	8 per annum
Journal of Human Resources in Hospitality and Tourism	quarterly
Journal of Leisure Research	quarterly
Journal of Policy Research in Tourism, Leisure & Events	3 per annum
Journal of Quality Assurance in Hospitality and Tourism	quarterly
Journal of Sport & Tourism	quarterly
Journal of Sustainable Tourism	8 per annum
Journal of Tourism and Cultural Change	3 per annum
Journal of Tourism History	3 per annum
Journal of Transport Economics and Policy	Jan/May/Sept
Journal of Travel and Tourism Marketing	8 per annum
Journal of Travel Research	quarterly
Journal of Vacation Marketing	quarterly
Leisure, Recreation and Tourism Abstracts (CABI)	quarterly
Leisure Studies (Leisure Studies Association)	quarterly
Scandinavian Journal of Hospitality and Tourism	quarterly
Service Industries Journal	16 per annum
Tourism (Bulletin of the Tourism Society)	quarterly
Tourism Analysis	6 per annum
Tourism and Hospitality Research	quarterly
Tourism, Culture and Communication	3 per annum
Tourism Economics	quarterly
Tourism Geographies	quarterly
Tourism in Focus (Tourism Concern)	quarterly
Tourism in Marine Environments	quarterly
Tourism Management	6 per annum
Tourism Planning and Development	quarterly
Tourism Recreation Research	3 per annum
Tourism Review International	quarterly
Tourist Studies	3 per annum
Transport Reviews	6 per annum
Travel Agent	bi-monthly
Travel and Tourism Analyst (EIU)	bi-monthly
Travel Business Analyst	monthly
Travel GBI	monthly
Travel Industry Monitor (EIU)	quarterly
Travel Trade Gazette	weekly
Travel Trade Gazette Europa (Continental edition)	weekly
Travel Weekly	weekly
Which? Travel (Consumers Association)	quarterly
World Leisure Journal	quarterly

Many of the articles from these journals are available online and some magazines and journals are now produced exclusively to access on the Internet. The following are useful sources of such information.

e-Review of Tourism Research, an electronic bulletin for tourism research, available at:
http://ertr.tamu.edu

Journal of Hospitality, Leisure, Sport and Tourism, bi-annual e-journal, available at:
www.heacademy.ac.uk/johlste.

Index